Lecture Notes in Artificial Intelligence 3070

Edited by J. G. Carbonell and J. Siekmann

Subseries of Lecture Notes in Computer Science

W0234418

Springer-Verlag Berlin Heidelberg GmbH

Leszek Rutkowski   Jörg Siekmann
Ryszard Tadeusiewicz   Lotfi A. Zadeh (Eds.)

Artificial Intelligence and Soft Computing - ICAISC 2004

7th International Conference
Zakopane, Poland, June 7-11, 2004
Proceedings

 Springer

Series Editors

Jaime G. Carbonell, Carnegie Mellon University, Pittsburgh, PA, USA
Jörg Siekmann, University of Saarland, Saarbrücken, Germany

Volume Editors

Leszek Rutkowski
Technical University of Czestochowa, Department of Computer Engineering
Al. Armii Krajowej 36, 42-200 Czestochowa, Poland
E-mail: lrutko@kik.pcz.czest.pl

Jörg Siekmann
German Research Center for Artificial Intelligence (DFKI)
Stuhlsatzenhausweg 3, 66123 Saarbrücken, Germany
E-mail: Joerg.Siekmann@dfki.de

Ryszard Tadeusiewicz
AGH University of Science and Technology, Institute of Automatics
Al. Mickiewicza 30, 30-059 Kraków, Poland
E-mail: rtad@agh.edu.pl

Lotfi A. Zadeh
University of California
Computer Science Division and the Electronics Research Laboratory
Department of EECs
Berkeley, CA 94720-1776, USA
E-mail: zadeh@cs.berkeley.edu

Library of Congress Control Number: 2004106909

CR Subject Classification (1998): I.2, F.4.1, F.1, F.2, I.4

ISSN 0302-9743
ISBN 978-3-540-22123-4   ISBN 978-3-540-24844-6 (eBook)
DOI 10.1007/978-3-540-24844-6

This work is subject to copyright. All rights are reserved, whether the whole or part of the material is
concerned, specifically the rights of translation, reprinting, re-use of illustrations, recitation, broadcasting,
reproduction on microfilms or in any other way, and storage in data banks. Duplication of this publication
or parts thereof is permitted only under the provisions of the German Copyright Law of September 9, 1965,
in its current version, and permission for use must always be obtained from Springer-Verlag. Violations are
liable to prosecution under the German Copyright Law.

springeronline.com

© Springer-Verlag Berlin Heidelberg 2004
Originally published by Springer-Verlag Berlin Heidelberg New York in 2004.

Typesetting: Camera-ready by author, data conversion by PTP-Berlin, Protago-TeX-Production GmbH
Printed on acid-free paper   SPIN: 11010999   06/3142   5 4 3 2 1 0

Preface

This volume constitutes the proceedings of the 7th Conference on Artificial Intelligence and Soft Computing, ICAISC 2004, held in Zakopane, Poland, June 7–11, 2004. The conference was organized by the Polish Neural Network Society in cooperation with the Department of Computer Engineering at the Technical University of Częstochowa, WSHE University in Łódź and IEEE Neural Networks Society. The previous conferences took place in Kule (1994), Szczyrk (1996), Kule (1997) and Zakopane (1999, 2000, 2002) and attracted a large number of papers and internationally recognized speakers: Prof. Lotfi A. Zadeh, Prof. Robert Marks, Prof. Enrique Ruspini, Prof. Zdzisław Bubnicki, Prof. Jacek Żurada, Prof. Shun-ichi Amari, Prof. Kaoru Hirota, Prof. Ryszard Tadeusiewicz, Prof. Shiro Usui, Prof. Włodzisław Duch, Prof. Erkki Oja, Prof. Syozo Yasui, Prof. Witold Pedrycz, Prof. Janusz Kacprzyk, Prof. Laszlo T. Koczy, Prof. Soo-Young Lee and Prof. Daniel Amit. The aim of this conference is to build a bridge between traditional artificial intelligence techniques and recently developed soft computing techniques. It was pointed out by Prof. Lotfi A. Zadeh that "Soft Computing (SC) is a coalition of methodologies which are oriented toward the conception and design of information/intelligent systems. The principal members of the coalition are: fuzzy logic (FL), neurocomputing (NC), evolutionary computing (EC), probabilistic computing (PC), chaotic computing (CC), and machine learning (ML). The constituent methodologies of SC are, for the most part, complementary and synergistic rather than competitive". This volume presents both traditional artificial intelligence methods and soft computing techniques presented in 14 parts:

1. Invited Papers
2. Neural Networks and Their Applications
3. Fuzzy Systems and Their Applications
4. Evolutionary Algorithms and Their Applications
5. Rough Sets and Their Applications
6. Soft Computing in Classification
7. Image Processing
8. Robotics
9. Multiagents Systems
10. Various Problems of Artificial Intelligence
11. Control, Modelling and System Identification
12. Medical Applications
13. Mechanical Applications
14. Various Applications

The conference attracted a total of 250 submissions from 35 countries and after the review process, 175 papers were accepted.

I would like to thank our participants, invited speakers and reviewers of the papers for their scientific and personal contribution to the conference. I also thank Alfred Hofmann editor-in-chief of Springer-Verlag's Lecture Notes in Computer Science/Artificial Intelligence series and Christine Günther from the LNCS Editorial for their cooperation in the preparation of this volume. Finally I thank my co-workers Jarosław Bilski, Marcin Gabryel, Marcin Korytkowski and Rafał Scherer, for their enormous efforts to make the conference a very successful event.

June 2004   Leszek Rutkowski
                              President of the Polish Neural Network Society

Organization

ICAISC 04 was organized by the Polish Neural Network Society and the Department of Computer Engineering at Częstochowa University of Technology in cooperation with WSHE University in Łódź and the IEEE Neural Network Society.

Chairpersons

Honorary chairmen	Lotfi Zadeh (USA)
	Zdzislaw Bubnicki (Poland)
	Zdzisław Pawlak (Poland)
	Jacek Żurada (USA)
General chairman	Leszek Rutkowski (Poland)
Co-chairmen	Włodzisław Duch (Poland)
	Janusz Kacprzyk (Poland)
	Józef Korbicz (Poland)
	Ryszard Tadeusiewicz (Poland)

Program Committee

S. Amari (Japan)
J. Arabas (Poland)
R. Babuska (The Netherlands)
A. Bargiela (UK)
I. Batyrshin (Russia)
E. Bayro-Corrochano (Mexico)
M. Białko (Poland)
L. Bobrowski (Poland)
L. Bolc (Poland)
P. Bonissone (USA)
B. Bouchon-Meunier (France)
J.J. Buckley (USA)
T. Burczyński (Poland)
A. Cader (Poland)
W. Cholewa (Poland)
B. De Baets (Belgium)
N. Derbel (Tunisia)
E. Dudek-Dyduch (Poland)
L. Dymowa (Poland)
J. Fodor (Hungary)
D. Fogel (USA)

R. Galar (Poland)
M. Gorzałczany (Poland)
J.W. Grzymała-Busse (USA)
P. Hajek (Czech Republic)
S. Halgamuge (Australia)
R. Hampel (Germany)
Z. Hasiewicz (Poland)
T. Hendtlass (Australia)
Y. Hayashi (Japan)
K. Hirota (Japan)
Z. Hippe (Japan)
J. Józefczyk (Poland)
T. Kacprzak (Poland)
T. Kaczorek (Poland)
W. Kamiński (Poland)
N. Kasabov (New Zealand)
O. Kaynak (Turkey)
V. Kecman (New Zealand)
J. Kluska (Poland)
M. Kłopotek (Poland)
L.T. Koczy (Hungary)

L. Kompanec (Poland)
R. Kosiński (Poland)
W. Kosiński (Poland)
J.M. Kościelny (Poland)
Z. Kowalczuk (Poland)
R. Kruse (Germany)
J.L. Kulikowski (Poland)
R. Kulikowski (Poland)
V. Kurkova (Czech Republic)
M. Kurzyński (Poland)
J. Kusiak (Poland)
H. Kwaśnicka (Poland)
S.Y. Lee (Korea)
A. Ligęza (Poland)
J. Łęski (Poland)
B. Macukow (Poland)
K. Madani (France)
W. Malina (Poland)
K. Malinowski (Poland)
J. Mańdziuk (Poland)
A. Materka (Poland)
R. Mesiar (Slovakia)
Z. Michalewicz (USA)
W. Moczulski (Poland)
W. Mitkowski (Poland)
D. Nauck (Germany)
E. Nawarecki (Poland)
A. Niederliński (Poland)
E. Oja (Finland)
S. Osowski (Poland)
M. Partyka (Poland)
W. Pedrycz (Canada)

A. Piegat (Poland)
E. Rafajłowicz (Poland)
S. Raudys (Lithuania)
R. Rojas (Germany)
I. Rudas (Hungary)
D. Rutkowska (Poland)
E.H. Ruspini (USA)
N. Sano (Japan)
R. Setiono (Singapore)
P. Sewastianow (Poland)
J. Siekmann (Germany)
P. Sincak (Slovakia)
A. Skowron (Poland)
E. Skubalska-Rafajłowicz (Poland)
R. Słowiński (Poland)
P. Szczepaniak (Poland)
P. Strumiłło (Poland)
M. Sugeno (Japan)
J. Świątek (Poland)
H. Takagi (Japan)
R. Takahashi (Japan)
B. Turksen (Canada)
S. Usui (Japan)
M. Wagenknecht (Germany)
Z. Waszczyszyn (Poland)
B.M. Wilamowski (USA)
M. Wygralak (Poland)
R. Wyrzykowski (Poland)
J. Yen (USA)
R. Yager (USA)
J. Zieliński (Poland)

Referees

R. Adamczak
R. Babuska
A. Bargiela
L. Bobrowski
J. Buckley
T. Burczyński
A. Cader
K. Cetnarowicz
W. Cholewa

R. Cierniak
B. De Baets
W. Duch
L. Dymowa
M. Flasiński
D.B. Fogel
R. Galar
A. Gawęda
M. Giergiel

M.B. Gorzałczany
W. Greblicki
M. Grzenda
J.W. Grzymala-Busse
K. Grąbczewski
Z. Hasiewicz
Y. Hayashi
T. Hendtlass
Z. Hendzel

K. Hirota
A. Janczak
N. Jankowski
J. Józefczyk
J. Kacprzyk
W. Kamiński
O. Kaynak
V. Kecman
J. Kluska
L. Kompanets
J. Korbicz
P. Korohoda
R. Kosiński
W. Kosiński
J.M. Kościelny
R. Kruse
V. Kurkova
M. Kurzyński
J. Kusiak
H. Kwaśnicka
M.A. Kłopotek
S.-Y. Lee
J. Lęski
A. Ligęza

B. Macukow
K. Madani
W. Malina
A. Materka
J. Mańdziuk
J.M. Mendel
R. Mesiar
Z. Michalewicz
Z. Mikrut
W. Mitkowski
W. Moczulski
M. Mrugalski
E. Nawarecki
R. Nowicki
A. Obuchowicz
E. Oja
S. Osowski
K. Patan
W. Pedrycz
A. Pieczyński
A. Piegat
V. Piuri
E. Rafajłowicz
S. Raudys

I.J. Rudas
R. Scherer
R. Setiono
P. Sevastjanov
A. Skowron
E. Skubalska-Rafajłowicz
P. Strumiłło
P.S. Szczepaniak
E. Szmidt
P. Śliwiński
J. Świątek
H. Takagi
B. Turksen
S. Usui
M. Wagenknecht
T. Walkowiak
B.M. Wilamowski
M. Witczak
M. Wygralak
R.R. Yager
S. Zadrożny
J.S. Zieliński

Table of Contents

Invited Papers

Evolutionary Design of Information Systems Architectures 1
  Danilo Ardagna, Chiara Francalanci, Vincenzo Piuri, Fabio Scotti

Clifford Support Vector Machines for Classification 9
  Eduardo Bayro-Corrochano, Nancy Arana-Daniel,
  J. Refugio Vallejo-Gutiérres

Uncertain Variables and Systems – New Problems and Results 17
  Zdzislaw Bubnicki

Blind Signal Separation and Extraction: Recent Trends, Future
Perspectives, and Applications 30
  Andrzej Cichocki, Jacek M. Zurada

Visualization of Hidden Node Activity in Neural Networks:
I. Visualization Methods 38
  Włodzisław Duch

Visualization of Hidden Node Activity in Neural Networks:
II. Application to RBF Networks 44
  Włodzisław Duch

Rough Set Approach to Incomplete Data 50
  Jerzy W. Grzymala-Busse

Neural Networks of Positive Systems 56
  Tadeusz Kaczorek

Support of Natural, by Artificial, Intelligence Using Utility
as Behavioral Goal 64
  Roman Kulikowski

Top-Down Selective Attention for Robust Perception
of Noisy and Confusing Patterns 73
  Soo-Young Lee

On ANN Based Solutions for Real-World Industrial Requirements 79
  Kurosh Madani

ACTIVEMATH: An Intelligent Tutoring System for Mathematics 91
  Erica Melis, Jörg Siekmann

Inference Rules and Decision Rules 102
  Zdzisław Pawlak

Survival of Intelligent Agents in Changing Environments 109
  Šarūnas Raudys

Inducing Robust Decision Rules from Rough Approximations
of a Preference Relation 118
  Roman Slowinski, Salvatore Greco

The New Concept in Computer Vision:
Automatic Understanding of the Images 133
  Ryszard Tadeusiewicz, Marek R. Ogiela

Neural Networks and Their Applications

Dynamic High Order Neural Networks: Application for Fault Diagnosis .. 145
  Eugen Arinton, Józef Korbicz

Momentum Modification of the RLS Algorithms 151
  Jarosław Bilski

Parallel Realisation of QR Algorithm for Neural Networks Learning 158
  Jarosław Bilski, Sławomir Litwiński, Jacek Smoląg

Rainfall-Runoff Modelling Using Three Neural Network Methods 166
  H. Kerem Cigizoglu, Murat Alp

Probability Distribution of Solution Time in ANN Training
Using Population Learning Algorithm 172
  Ireneusz Czarnowski, Piotr Jędrzejowicz

Parallelization of the SOM-Based Integrated Mapping 178
  Gintautas Dzemyda, Olga Kurasova

Training Radial Basis Functions by Gradient Descent 184
  Mercedes Fernández-Redondo, Carlos Hernández-Espinosa,
  Mamen Ortiz-Gómez, Joaquín Torres-Sospedra

Generalized Backpropagation through Time for Continuous Time
Neural Networks and Discrete Time Measurements 190
  Krzysztof Fujarewicz, Adam Galuszka

Experiments on Ensembles of Radial Basis Functions 197
  Carlos Hernández-Espinosa, Mercedes Fernández-Redondo,
  Joaquín Torres-Sospedra

Orthodoxy Basis Functions and Convergence Property in
Procedure Neural Networks 203
  Jiong Jia, Jiuzhen Liang

Confidence Estimation of GMDH Neural Networks 210
Józef Korbicz, Mihai F. Metenidis, Marcin Mrugalski,
Marcin Witczak

On Some Factors Influencing MLP Error Surface..................... 217
Mirosław Kordos, Włodzisław Duch

Discovery of Linguistic Rules by Means of RBF Network
for Fault Detection in Electronic Circuits 223
Jan Koszlaga, Pawel Strumillo

Combining Space-Filling Curves and Radial Basis Function Networks ... 229
Adam Krzyżak, Ewa Skubalska-Rafajłowicz

Chaotic Itinerancy for Patterns Separation 235
Pawel Matykiewicz

Dynamic Search Trajectory Methods for Neural Network Training 241
Y.G. Petalas, D.K. Tasoulis, M.N. Vrahatis

Visualizing and Analyzing Multidimensional Output
from MLP Networks via Barycentric Projections 247
Filip Piękniewski, Leszek Rybicki

Optimization of Centers' Positions for RBF Nets
with Generalized Kernels 253
E. Rafajłowicz, M. Pawlak

Fixed Non–linear Combining Rules versus Adaptive Ones 260
Sarunas Raudys, Zidrina Pabarskaite

Learning and System Modeling via Hamiltonian Neural Networks 266
Wieslaw Sienko, Wieslaw Citko, Dariusz Jakóbczak

Recurrent Network Structure for Computing Quasi-inverses
of the Sierpiński Space-Filling Curves............................... 272
Ewa Skubalska-Rafajłowicz

Fuzzy Systems and Their Applications

Comparison of Reasoning Methods for Fuzzy Control 278
Bohdan Butkiewicz

Fuzzy Modelling with a Compromise Fuzzy Reasoning 284
Krzysztof Cpalka, Leszek Rutkowski

A Self Tuning Fuzzy Inference System for Noise Reduction 290
Nevcihan Duru, Tarik Duru

Fuzzy-Neural Networks in the Diagnosis
of Motor-Car's Current Supply Circuit............................. 296
    Stanisław Gad, Mariusz Łaskawski, Grzegorz Słoń,
    Alexander Yastrebov, Andrzej Zawadzki

Fuzzy Number-Based Hierarchical Fuzzy System 302
    Adam E. Gaweda, Rafał Scherer

Stock Trend Prediction Using Neurofuzzy Predictors
Based on Brain Emotional Learning Algorithm 308
    Mahdi Jalili-Kharaajoo

Digital Implementation of Fuzzy Petri Net Based on Asynchronous
Fuzzy RS Flip-Flop 314
    Jacek Kluska, Zbigniew Hajduk

Fuzzy Calculator – Useful Tool for Programming with Fuzzy Algebra 320
    Roman Koleśnik, Piotr Prokopowicz, Witold Kosiński

On Defuzzyfication of Ordered Fuzzy Numbers 326
    Witold Kosiński

Information Criterions Applied to Neuro-Fuzzy Architectures Design 332
    Robert Nowicki, Agata Pokropińska

On Hesitation Degrees in IF-Set Theory 338
    Anna Pankowska, Maciej Wygralak

Fuzzy Cognitive Maps Learning through Swarm Intelligence 344
    E.I. Papageorgiou, K.E. Parsopoulos, P.P. Groumpos, M.N. Vrahatis

Application of the General Gaussian Membership Function
for the Fuzzy Model Parameters Tunning 350
    Andrzej Pieczyński, Andrzej Obuchowicz

Are Linguistic Evaluations Used by People
of Possibilistic or Probabilistic Nature? 356
    Andrzej Piegat

Fuzzy Linear Programming in Ship Trajectory Optimization
in a Restricted Area 364
    Zbigniew Pietrzykowski

Application of Fuzzy Weighted Feature Diagrams
to Model Variability in Software Families 370
    Silva Robak, Andrzej Pieczyński

Neuro-Fuzzy Relational Classifiers................................. 376
    Rafał Scherer, Leszek Rutkowski

What Differs Interval Type-2 FLS from Type-1 FLS? 381
  Janusz T. Starczewski

A Similarity Measure for Intuitionistic Fuzzy Sets
and Its Application in Supporting Medical Diagnostic Reasoning 388
  Eulalia Szmidt, Janusz Kacprzyk

Evolutionary Algorithms and Their Applications

Multi-criterion Evolutionary Algorithm with Model of the Immune
System to Handle Constraints for Task Assignments 394
  Jerzy Balicki

Parallel Genetic Algorithm for Minimizing Total Weighted
Completion Time 400
  Wojciech Bożejko, Mieczysław Wodecki

Adaptive Evolutionary Computation –
Application for Mixed Linear Programming 406
  Ewa Dudek-Dyduch, Dominik Jarczyk

Adaptive Evolutionary Computation
of the Parametric Optimization Problem 414
  Tadeusz Dyduch

Concentration of Population in Phenotypic Evolution 420
  Iwona Karcz-Dulęba

An Evolutionary Clustering Algorithm 426
  Marcin Korzeń

An Evolutionary Algorithm for Oblique Decision Tree Induction 432
  Marek Kretowski

Propagation of Building Blocks in SGA and MPGA 438
  Grzegorz Kusztelak, Marek Rudnicki, Sławomir Wiak

Selection Pressure and an Efficiency
of Neural Network Architecture Evolving 444
  Halina Kwaśnicka, Mariusz Paradowski

Rule Extraction from Neural Network by Genetic Algorithm
with Pareto Optimization 450
  Urszula Markowska-Kaczmar, Paweł Wnuk-Lipiński

Graph Transformations in Evolutionary Design 456
  Piotr Nikodem, Barbara Strug

A Genetic Algorithm for Probabilistic SAT Problem 462
  Zoran Ognjanović, Uroš Midić, Jozef Kratica

Design and Optimization of Combinational Digital Circuits
Using Modified Evolutionary Algorithm 468
 Adam Słowik, Michał Białko

Modified Version of Roulette Selection for Evolution Algorithms
– The Fan Selection 474
 Adam Słowik, Michał Białko

New Genetic Crossover Operator for the TSP 480
 Sang-Moon Soak, Byung-Ha Ahn

Rough Sets and Their Applications

Hybridization of Blind Source Separation and Rough Sets
for Proteomic Biomarker Indentification 486
 Grzegorz M. Boratyn, Tomasz G. Smolinski, Jacek M. Zurada,
 Mariofanna Milanova, Sudeepa Bhattacharyya, Larry J. Suva

Inducing Jury's Preferences in Terms of Acoustic Features
of Violin Sounds 492
 Jacek Jelonek, Ewa Łukasik, Aleksander Naganowski,
 Roman Słowiński

Fuzzy Implication Operators in Variable Precision Fuzzy Rough
Sets Model 498
 Alicja Mieszkowicz-Rolka, Leszek Rolka

Fuzzyfication of Indiscernibility Relation for Structurizing
Lists of Synonyms and Stop-Lists for Search Engines 504
 A. Niewiadomski, P. Kryger, P.S. Szczepaniak

Rough Sets in the Neuro-Fuzzy Architectures Based on Monotonic
Fuzzy Implications 510
 Robert Nowicki

Rough Sets in the Neuro-Fuzzy Architectures Based on
Non-monotonic Fuzzy Implications 518
 Robert Nowicki

On L–Fuzzy Rough Sets 526
 Anna Maria Radzikowska, Etienne E. Kerre

Application of Rough Sets Techniques to Induction Machine Broken
Bar Detection 532
 M.R. Rafimanzelat, B.N. Araabi

Application of Rough Sets and Neural Networks to Forecasting
University Facility and Administrative Cost Recovery................. 538
 Tomasz G. Smolinski, Darrel L. Chenoweth, Jacek M. Zurada

Soft Computing in Classification

Selection of the Linearly Separable Feature Subsets.................... 544
Leon Bobrowski, Tomasz Lukaszuk

Short-Time Signal Analysis Using Pattern Recognition Methods 550
Piotr Boguś, Katarzyna D. Lewandowska

Application of Genetic Algorithms and Kohonen Networks
to Cluster Analysis 556
Marian B. Gorzałczany, Filip Rudziński

Modified Kohonen Networks for Complex Cluster-Analysis Problems 562
Marian B. Gorzałczany, Filip Rudziński

Reducing the Computational Demands
for Nearest Centroid Neighborhood Classifiers 568
Szymon Grabowski

SSV Criterion Based Discretization for Naive Bayes Classifiers 574
Krzysztof Grąbczewski

Comparison of Instance Selection Algorithms II.
Results and Comments 580
Marek Grochowski, Norbert Jankowski

SBL-PM-M: A System for Partial Memory Learning 586
Karol Grudziński

Relevance LVQ versus SVM 592
Barbara Hammer, Marc Strickert, Thomas Villmann

Comparison of Instances Seletion Algorithms I. Algorithms Survey 598
Norbert Jankowski, Marek Grochowski

Towards Grammatical Inferencing of GDPLL(k) Grammars
for Applications in Syntactic Pattern Recognition-Based
Expert Systems 604
Janusz Jurek

Intelligent Layer of Two-Way Voice Communication
of the Technological Device with the Operator 610
Wojciech Kacalak, Maciej Majewski

A Neural Network Based Method for Classification
of Meteorological Data 616
K. Kaminski, W. Kaminski, P. Strumillo

An Empirical Test Suite for Message Authentication Evaluation
in Communications Based on Support Vector Machines 622
    D.A. Karras

Efficient Digital Fingerprint Production and Evaluation
for Secure Communication Systems Based on Genetic Algorithms 628
    D.A. Karras

On Chinese Web Page Classification 634
    Jiuzhen Liang

A New Fuzzy Clustering Method with Constraints in Time Domain 640
    Jacek Leski, Aleksander Owczarek

Special Cluster Analysis and Basic Feature Estimation
with a Modification of Self-Organizing Map 646
    Janusz Morajda

An Unsupervised Cluster Analysis and Information
about the Modelling System 652
    Izabela Rejer

Cursive-Character Script Recognition Using Toeplitz Model
and Neural Networks 658
    Khalid Saeed, Marek Tabedzki

Learning with an Embedded Reject Option 664
    Ramasubramanian Sundararajan, Asim K. Pal

Image Processing

Impulsive Noise Suppression from Highly Corrupted Images by Using
Resilient Neural Networks 670
    Erkan Beşdok, Pınar Çivicioğlu, Mustafa Alçı

A New Methodology for Synthetic Aperture Radar (SAR) Raw Data
Compression Based on Wavelet Transform and Neural Networks 676
    Giacomo Capizzi, Salvatore Coco, Antonio Laudani,
    Giuseppe Pappalardo

Fuzzy Processing Technique for Content-Based Image Retrieval 682
    Ryszard S. Choraś

Human Ear Identification Based on Image Analysis 688
    Michał Choraś

Automatic Change Detection Based on Codelength Differences
in Multi-temporal and Multi-spectral Images 694
    Joselíto J. Chua, Peter E. Tischer

Estimating Face Direction via Facial Triangle 700
  Min Gyo Chung, Jisook Park, Jiyoun Dong

An Image Compression Algorithm Based on Neural Networks 706
  Robert Cierniak

Fuzzy Nonparametric Measures for Image Matching 712
  Boguslaw Cyganek, Jan Borgosz

Neural Computation of the Fundamental Matrix 718
  Boguslaw Cyganek

Face Detection Using CMAC Neural Network 724
  H. Fashandi, M.S. Moin

A Biologically Inspired Active Stereo Vision System Using a
Bottom-Up Saliency Map Model 730
  Bum-Soo Jung, Sang-Bok Choi, Sang-Woo Ban, Minho Lee

Problems Connected with Application of Neural Networks
in Automatic Face Recognition 736
  Rafal Komanski, Bohdan Macukow

Czestochowa-Faces and Biometrics of Asymmetrical Face 742
  Leonid Kompanets, Mariusz Kubanek, Szymon Rydzek

Wafer Die Position Detection Using Hierarchical Gray Level
Corner Detector 748
  Jae Hyung Na, Hae Seok Oh

On Fuzzy Labelled Image Segmentation Based on
Perceptual Features 754
  Pilar Sobrevilla, Eduard Montseny

Generalized Multi-layer Kohonen Network and Its Application to
Texture Recognition 760
  A. Tomczyk, P.S. Szczepaniak, B. Lis

Robotics

Translation STRIPS Planning in Multi-robot Environment
to Linear Programming 768
  Adam Galuszka, Andrzej Swierniak

Fuzzy Combiner of Behaviors for Reactive Control
of Wheeled Mobile Robot 774
  Zenon Hendzel

Artificial Intelligence of the Decision Unit of a Mobile Robot 780
  Jan Kazimierczak

Finding Location Using a Particle Filter and Histogram Matching 786
    Bogdan Kwolek

Calculation of Model of the Robot by Neural Network
with Robot Joint Distinction 792
    J. Możaryn, J.E. Kurek

Multi-robot Coordination Based on Cooperative Game 798
    Krzysztof Skrzypczyk

Model Based Predictive Robotic Manipulator Control
with Sinusoidal Trajectory and Random Disturbances 804
    Hasan Temurtas, Fevzullah Temurtas, Nejat Yumusak

Multiagent Systems

Performance Evaluation of Multiagent Personalized
Information System 810
    Tomasz Babczyński, Zofia Kruczkiewicz, Jan Magott

A Neural-Based Agent for IP Traffic Scanning and Worm Detection 816
    Andrzej Bielecki, Paweł Hajto

Evolutionary Neural Networks in Collective Intelligent
Predicting System. 823
    Aleksander Byrski, Jerzy Bałamut

Development of a Personalized Digital Library System Based on the
New Mobile Multi Agent Platform 829
    Young Im Cho

FOOD: An Agent-Oriented Dataflow Model 835
    Nicolas Juillerat, Béat Hirsbrunner

Flock-Based Architecture for Distributed Evolutionary Algorithms 841
    Marek Kisiel-Dorohinicki

Quickprop Neural Network Short-Term Forecasting Framework
for a Database Intrusion Prediction System 847
    P. Ramasubramanian, A. Kannan

Various Problems of Artificial Intelligence

The New Concepts in Parallel Simulated Annealing Method 853
    Wojciech Bożejko, Mieczysław Wodecki

Simulated Annealing with Restart to Job Shop Scheduling Problem
Using Upper Bounds 860
    Marco Antonio Cruz-Chavez, Juan Frausto-Solis

Requirements and Solutions for Web-Based Expert System 866
  Maciej Grzenda, Marcin Niemczak

Information Structuring in Natural Language Communication:
Syntax versus Semantic 872
  Wladyslaw Homenda

Strategic Planning through Model Checking of ATL Formulae 879
  Wojciech Jamroga

On a Special Class of Dempster-Shafer Theories 885
  Mieczysław Alojzy Kłopotek

A Computer Based System Supporting Analysis
of Cooperative Strategies 891
  Lech Kruś

Application of Soft Computing Techniques to Rescue
Operation Planning 897
  Jiří Kubalík, Jiří Kléma, Miroslav Kulich

Reduction of Tabular Systems 903
  Antoni Ligęza, Marcin Szpyrka

Temporal Difference Approach to Playing Give-Away Checkers 909
  Jacek Mańdziuk, Daniel Osman

Artificial Neural Networks for Solving Double Dummy Bridge Problems.. 915
  Krzysztof Mossakowski, Jacek Mańdziuk

On Application of Ant Algorithms to Non-bifurcated Multicommodity
Flow Problem 922
  Krzysztof Walkowiak

A Parallel Clustering Algorithm for Categorical Data Set 928
  Yong-Xian Wang, Zheng-Hua Wang, Xiao-Mei Li

Intensive versus Non-intensive Actor-Critic Reinforcement
Learning Algorithms 934
  Pawel Wawrzynski, Andrzej Pacut

Virtual Modeling and Optimal Design of Intelligent
Micro-accelerometers 942
  Slawomir Wiak, Andrzej Cader, Pawel Drzymala, Henryk Welfle

Control, Modelling, and System Identification

Local Pattern-Based Interval Models 948
  Wojciech Cholewa

Implementation of Two-Stage Hopfield Model and Its Application in
Nonlinear Systems 954
   Ivan Nunes da Silva, Jose Alfredo C. Ulson, Andre Nunes de Souza

Genetic Algorithm Based Fuzzy Sliding Mode with Application
to Building Structures 960
   Kambiz Falsafian, Mahdi Jalili-Kharaajoo

Influence of the Training Set Selection on the Performance of the
Neural Network State Variables Estimators in the Induction Motor 966
   Jerzy Jelonkiewicz, Andrzej Przybył

LMI-Based Design of Optimal Controllers
for Takagi-Sugeno Fuzzy Systems 972
   J. Park, Y. Park, K. Kwak, J.H. Hong

Design of Multi-objective Evolutionary Technique Based
Intelligent Controller for Multivariable Nonlinear Systems 978
   Farzan Rashidi, Mehran Rashidi

Design of a Robust Sliding Mode Fuzzy Controller
for Nonlinear HVAC Systems 984
   Farzan Rashidi, Behzad Moshiri

Global Identification of Complex Systems with Cascade Structure 990
   Jerzy Swiatek

Medical Applications

Diagnosis of Melanoma Using IRIM, a Data Mining System 996
   Jerzy W. Grzymala-Busse, Jay Hamilton, Zdzislaw S. Hippe

Detection of Spiculated Masses in Mammograms Based on Fuzzy
Image Processing 1002
   Aboul Ella Hassanien, Jafar M. Ali, Hajime Nobuhara

Artificial Neural Networks in Identifying Areas
with Homogeneous Survival Time 1008
   Małgorzata Krętowska, Leon Bobrowski

Multistage Diagnosis of Myocardial Infraction Using a Fuzzy Relation ... 1014
   Marek Kurzynski

Application of SVM to Ovarian Cancer Classification Problem 1020
   Maciej Kusy

ROC Analysis for Fetal Hypoxia Problem by Artificial Neural Networks.. 1026
   Lale Özyılmaz, Tülay Yıldırım

The Challenge of Soft Computing Techniques
for Tumor Characterization 1031
    E.I. Papageorgiou, P.P. Spyridonos, C.D. Stylios, P. Ravazoula,
    G.C. Nikiforidis, P.P. Groumpos

A Multi-stage Classification Method in Application to Diagnosis
of Larynx Cancer 1037
    Danuta Rutkowska, Jacek K. Klimala

Multi-neural Network Approach for Classification of Brainstem
Evoked Response Auditory 1043
    Mariusz Rybnik, Saliou Diouf, Abdennasser Chebira,
    Veronique Amarger, Kurosh Madani

The Study of Hierarchy Importance of Descriptive Attributes in
Computer Assisted Classification of Melanocytic Skin Lesions 1050
    Aleksander Sokołowski, Alicja Dereń

Medical Knowledge Representation in Terms of IF-THEN Rules and
the Dempster-Shafer Theory 1056
    Ewa Straszecka

Online Neural Network Training for Automatic Ischemia
Episode Detection.. 1062
    D.K. Tasoulis, L. Vladutu, V.P. Plagianakos, A. Bezerianos,
    M.N. Vrahatis

Mechanical Applications

Sequential and Distributed Evolutionary Computations
in Structural Optimization 1069
    Tadeusz Burczyński, Wacław Kuś, Adam Długosz,
    Arkadiusz Poteralski, Mirosław Szczepanik

Neural Analysis of Concrete Fatigue Durability by the
Neuro-fuzzy FWNN 1075
    Magdalena Jakubek, Zenon Waszczyszyn

Neural and Finite Element Analysis of a Plane Steel Frame Reliability
by the Classical Monte Carlo Method.................................. 1081
    Ewa Pabisek, Joanna Kaliszuk, Zenon Waszczyszyn

The Solution of an Inverse Problem in Plates by Means of
Artificial Neural Networks 1087
    Grzegorz Piątkowski, Leonard Ziemiański

Filtering of Thermomagnetic Data Curve Using Artificial Neural
Network and Wavelet Analysis... 1093
    Łukasz Rauch, Jolanta Talar, Tomáš Žák, Jan Kusiak

Various Applications

Evolutionary Negotiation Strategies in Emerging Electricity Markets 1099
    Salem Al-Agtash

Evolutionary Algorithm for Scheduling of CHP Plant with Urban
Heat Distribution Network 1105
    Krzysztof Dziedzicki, Andrzej Augusiak, Roman Śmierzchalski

Semi-mechanistic Models for State-Estimation – Soft Sensor for
Polymer Melt Index Prediction 1111
    *Balazs Feil, Janos Abonyi, Peter Pach, Sandor Nemeth, Peter Arva,
    Miklos Nemeth, Gabor Nagy*

Neural Approach to Time-Frequency Signal Decomposition 1118
    Dariusz Grabowski, Janusz Walczak

ANN Based Modelling and Correction in Dynamic
Temperature Measurements 1124
    Lidia Jackowska-Strumiłło

One Day Prediction of NIKKEI Index Considering Information
from Other Stock Markets 1130
    Marcin Jaruszewicz, Jacek Mańdziuk

Application of Neural Network Topologies in the Intelligent Heat
Use Prediction System 1136
    Leszek Kiełtyka, Robert Kucęba, Adam Sokołowski

Genetic Algorithm for Database Indexing 1142
    Marcin Korytkowski, Marcin Gabryel, Robert Nowicki, Rafał Scherer

Application of Neural Networks and Two Representations of Color
Components for Recognition of Wheat Grains Infected by *Fusarium
Culmorum* Fungi 1148
    Aleksander Kubiak, Zbigniew Mikrut

Hybrid Neural Model of the Sea Bottom Surface 1154
    Jacek Lubczonek

Fuzzy Economic Analysis of Simulated Discrete Transport System....... 1161
    Jacek Mazurkiewicz, Tomasz Walkowiak

A Survey on US Economic Sanction Effects on Iranian High Tech
Industries: Fuzzy Logic Approach 1168
    *Mohammad R. Mehregan, Hossein Safari, Parviz Naseri,
    Farshid Hosseini, Kumars Sharifi*

Modeling of Optoelectronic Devices through Neuro-Fuzzy Architectures .. 1175
    Antonio Vanderlei Ortega, Ivan Nunes da Silva

Neural Network Based Simulation of the Sieve Plate Absorption
Column in Nitric Acid Industry 1181
    Edward Rój, Marcin Wilk

Artificial Neural Networks for Comparative Navigation 1187
    Andrzej Stateczny

Predicting Women's Apparel Sales by Soft Computing 1193
    Les M. Sztandera, Celia Frank, Balaji Vemulapali

Model Improvement by the Statistical Decomposition 1199
    Ryszard Szupiluk, Piotr Wojewnik, Tomasz Zabkowski

Author Index 1205

Evolutionary Design of Information Systems Architectures

Danilo Ardagna[1], Chiara Francalanci[1], Vincenzo Piuri[2], and Fabio Scotti[2]

[1] Politecnico di Milano,Department of Electronics and Information
piazza L. da Vinci 32, 20133 Milano (Mi), Italy
{ardagna,francala}@elet.polimi.it,
[2] University of Milan Department of Information Technologies,
via Bramante 65, 26013 Crema (Cr), Italy
{fscotti,piuri}@dti.unimi.it

Abstract. Information system design and optimum sizing is a very complex task. Theoretical research and practitioners often tackle the optimization problem by applying specific techniques for the optimization of individual design phases, usually leading to local optima. Conversely, this paper proposes the definition of a design methodology based on an evolutionary approach to the optimization of the client/server-farm distributed structure, which is typical of a distributed information technology (IT) architecture. The optimization problem consists of finding the minimum-cost physical systems that satisfy all architectural requirements given by the designer. The proposed methodology allows for the identification of the architectural solution that minimizes costs, against different information system requirements and multiple design alternatives, thorough a genetic-based exploration of the solution space. Experimental results show that costs can be significantly reduced with respect to conventional approaches adopted by IT designers and available in the professional literature.

1 Introduction

Information system design and sizing constitute a complex, top-down process that tailors the technology architecture to application requirements. Practitioners usually tackle this top-down process by focusing on individual design aspects, such as data or specific applications, and by relying on their previous experiences to compare alternative architectural solutions. Acquisition costs are usually accounted for, but related operating and maintenance costs are often neglected or underestimated. The complexity of optimizing individual design problems leads researchers to avoid a global optimization perspective and, thus, the IT architecture is usually a result of the juxtaposition of multiple local-optima. The historical cost-minimizing design principle was centralization, which was advocated to take advantage of hardware scale economies according to Grosch's law. A further attempt to formulate a general design principle has been made in the mid '80s, when Grosch's law has been revised as "It is most

L. Rutkowski et al. (Eds.): ICAISC 2004, LNAI 3070, pp. 1–8, 2004.
© Springer-Verlag Berlin Heidelberg 2004

cost effective to accomplish any task on the least powerful type of computer capable of performing it" [3]. Decentralization and its operating rule, referred to as downsizing, became the methodological imperative for cost-oriented infrastructural design. Although academic studies have challenged the generality of the decentralization principle ([4], [5]), the empirical recognition of the cost disadvantages of decentralization has only occurred in the '90s with the observation of client-server costs. Addressing this failure, empirical studies have showed that initial acquisition expenses represent at most 20% of the total cost of a computer over its life cycle and as a consequence, the minimization of acquisition costs does not deliver the most convenient infrastructural design solutions. The concept of "total cost of ownership" (TCO) has been introduced and defined as the summation of both investments and management costs of infrastructural components. It has been observed that while decentralization reduces investment costs, it increases management costs, due to a more cumbersome administration of a greater number of infrastructural components. Recentralization has been thereafter considered to reduce management costs and thin clients (TCs) are currently proposed as a less expensive alternative to personal computers that can be exploited through a recentralization initiative [8]. Thin clients have lower computing capacity than PCs, which is sufficient for the execution or the emulation of the presentation tier, but requires the recentralization of the application logic on a server and have management costs 20-35% lower than personal computers ([8],[9]). Furthermore, the Independent Computing Architecture (ICA) and Remote Desktop Protocol (RDP) standards allow remote access to the application logic by traditional PCs. This translates into hybrid configurations of PCs which execute only a subset of applications which will be referred to in the following as hybrid fat clients (HFCs) (see also Section 2). Thin client can be supported by multiple coordinated machines, known as server farm [7]. This load sharing allows downsizing and reduces acquisition costs. Furthermore, it has limited negative effects on management costs, since server farms are equipped with software tools that allow the remote management and simultaneous administration of all servers [10]. In previous works ([1], [2]), the problem of design of IT architecture has been represented as a single cost minimization problem. Optimization was accomplished by implementing a tabu-search algortihm. In this paper we consider the problem of design of the client architecture and the optimization of the server farm which supports thin client and HFC systems by implementing a genetic algorithm. A comparison of the two methods allow to verify the quality of the solution that can be obtained by a heuristic approach.

2   Client Technologies in Modern IT Architectures

In the '90s, two-tier client/server systems were classified by Gartner Group as Distributed Presentation, Remote Presentation, etc. [1]. From the hardware point of view, client systems can be classified as fat, i.e. traditional PCs, and thin. A thin client is a computing device that enables users to remotely perform computing tasks on a server. A thin client is diskless and cannot work without being connected to a server; the physical desktop unit only needs enough memory and computing power to recognize keystrokes and mouse events and to display pixel data received from the server. No computing is performed locally. Considering this latter characteristic, a thin client is very similar to the dumb terminal of host-based systems. Nowadays, thin clients allow access to graphical applications and traditional PC applications. The main advantage of thin-client architectures is the reduction of TCO. The physical device is virtually free of mechanical breakdowns and the absence of local files and applications means that the desktop does not have to be administered; users are administered centrally on the server. This implies that thin clients have management costs 20-35% lower than personal computers ([8], [9], [10], [11]). Furthermore, the ICA and RDP standards allow remote access to the application logic by traditional PCs as well as new hand-held devices. This translates into hybrid fat clients which execute only a subset of client and monolithic applications. Hybrid configuration are considered since thin client architecture are not suited to support the execution of CPU intensive applications while the TCO of applications executed remotely at the server and accessed by HFCs can be reduced by 20-35% [8]. 75% of the thin clients' market is constituted by Windows Based Terminals (WBT). WBTs are the result of a joint project between Microsoft and Citrix [10]. The computational model is based on two main components: a multi-user operating system and a remote presentation protocol (RDP or ICA). Nowadays the multi-user operating system adopted is Microsoft Windows 2000/2003 (the first implementation was on Windows NT in the late '90s). The operating system has to support the execution of multiple user sessions and thin/HFC clients access to the server. The remote presentation protocol implements the message delivery of thin client inputs and desktop devices screen updates. The remaining 25% of the thin-client market is shared among X-terminals, Linux terminals and Sun Ray systems. The latter is an evolution of the Network Computer project where the desktop device is also able to locally execute the browser and some Java applications. In this work, only WBT devices will be considered, since more widespread and suitable for the optimization of the IT architecture.

3 Optimization of the Client Architecture

In [1] and [2] a general framework for the design of IT architectures has been presented. User classes and applications used by user classes are the main requirement variables which define the solution domain for the IT architecture. Users are divided in user classes C_i characterized by the same set of applications. The percentage of concurrent users is also specified. Each user class can be assigned to multiple types of client architectures (thin, fat or hybrid). User classes assigned to thins or HFCs can also share the server farm in order to reduce cost. This is obtained formally by defining groups. Note that, if a group includes n user classes, then $2^n - 1$ configurations have to be analyzed (that is the power set of the group excluding the empty set). Furthermore, for HFCs some applications are assigned to the fat PC (for example if an application is CPU intensive) or to the server (for example a data entry client application) but some applications can be indifferently executed by the fat PC or by the server exploiting the cost trade-off that a remote execution implies. The remote execution reduces management costs while increases the computing capacity of the remote server and hence investment costs. If a class of users uses a set o n applications that can be executed indifferently by the HFC or by the remote server then $2^n - 1$ configurations have to be evaluated. The computing capacity of PCs is obtained as the maximum value of MIPS required by locally executed applications.

Similarly, computing capacity of thin/HFC servers (servers supporting thin and HFC clients) is evaluated as the maximum value of MIPS required by applications that are executed remotely, considering the number of concurrent users of the corresponding user class ([5], [1], [2]). RAM requirements are evaluated in the same way by considering the total memory required by applications. The problem of the design of the optimum configuration of server farms for thin/HFC users can be modeled as a set-partitioning problem ([2], [12]). Table 1 shows how the overall cost of the system can be evaluated. The system can be partitioned in two components: thin/HFC servers and clients. The cost of the two components can be evaluated by considering software costs, hardware costs and maintenance costs. Hardware costs include investment costs and installation costs ($Cost_{ServerFarmHW}$, $Cost_{SingleClientHW}$). Software costs include license and installation costs. Maintenance costs for hardware and software are calculated over a period of three years.

The genetic algorithm represents the system to be optimized as a chromosome. Different values of the genes of the chromosome represent different configurations of the system (solutions). The basic idea consists of maintaining and/or manipulating a family, or population, of solutions based on the so called *survival of the fittest* strategy in searching the best solution. It also gives the possibility to explore some sub-domains of the solution space at the same time [13] achieving an intrinsic parallelism.

Table 1. Evaluation of total system cost

$$
\begin{aligned}
Cost_{System} &= Cost_{Thin/HFCServers} + Cost_{Clients} \\
Cost_{Thin/HFCServers} &= ServerHWCost(MIPS, RAM) \\
Cost_{Clients} &= \sum_{j \in Classes} NumberOfUser(j)Cost_{SingleClient}(j) \\
Cost_{SingleClient}(j) &= Cost_{SingleClientHW} + Cost_{SingleClientSW} \\
Cost_{SingleClientHW}(j) &= ClientHWCost(MIPS, RAM) \\
Cost_{SingleClientSW}(j) &= \sum_{i \in Application(j)}(Cost_{SW}(i, Loc)) + (Cost_{Maint}(i, Loc))
\end{aligned}
$$
Loc = 1 : Application i is resident on the server
Loc = 0 : Application i is resident on the client

A genetically-optimized solution to the presented problem requires the definition of the following issues: the representation of the solution as a chromosome, the creation of the selection function for the population of the current solutions, the genetic operators used by the optimization process, the initialization, the termination and the function that drives the optimization. Figure 1 represents how it is possible to map the configuration of the clients-server system into a chromosome. In the chromosome (the integer array at the bottom of the figure) a set of integers is assigned to each user class. In each set, the first integer corresponds to the server farm SF_i that the user class has been allocated. This integer can typically range from 0 to the number of user classes. Zero means a class made of fat clients. The opposite situation is encountered when each group of applications has its server farm. Subsequent integers represent the locations of the applications. The applications have only two states: 1 if application is allocated on the server farm and 0 if it is allocated on the client. Hence, one integer is present for each application in the current user class. Each system configuration can be directly mapped into the chromosome by proper mutation of the integers.

Figure 2 shows the application of mutation and cross-over operators to the chromosome plotted in Figure 1. All applications of class C_2 are now allocated on a server (integers corresponding to A_5, A_6, A_7 are equal to 1). Hence, the genetic operators transformed the clients of C_2 from *HFC* into *thin* clients. For this reason a new server farm SF_3 for user class C_2 has been created.

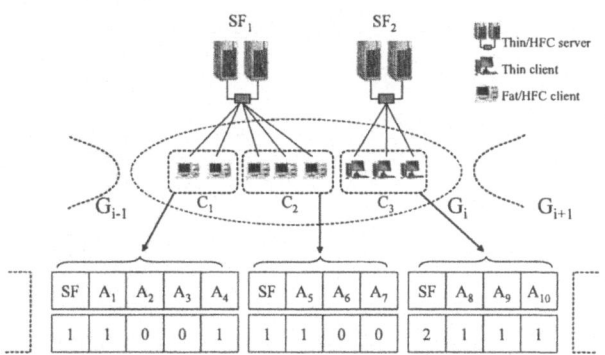

Fig. 1. Chromosome representation of the system

Fixed applications represent applications that have been assigned to clients or to server farms. In this case the mapping of the chromosome is different. Only applications declared as *Free* by the designer are coded into the chromosome since only they represent the *variables* of the problem (Figure 3). Such a kind of requirements change the permitted ranges for chromosome integers. If a class have fixed application to server farms, then the clients cannot become FAT, hence the integer value SF must start from 1, see class C_3 in Figure 3. Consequent, users of class C_3 will be always connected to a server farm. On the other hand, if some applications have been fixed by the designer on the client, then the

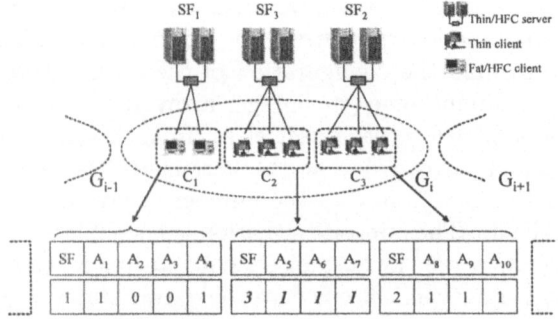

Fig. 2. Mutations and cross-over operator applied to the chromosome shown in Fig. 1

client cannot become *thin* (see class C_1 in Figure 3). It is important to note that *each* configuration of the chromosome (obtained by mutating the integers in their proper ranges) correspond to a systems which completely fulfills the requirements expressed by the designer, but with different costs.

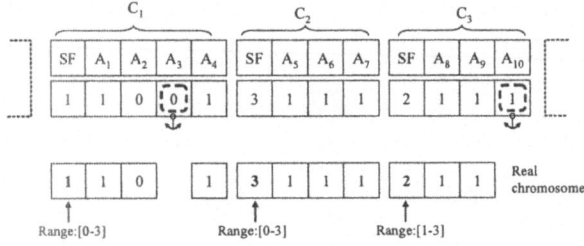

Fig. 3. Chromosome representation for fixed applications indicated by dashed boxes

Let us define the remaining elements of the genetic algorithm. The selection function is the *roulette wheel*, and the genetic operators we used are *simple cross-over*[1] and *binary mutation* [13]. Initial populations have been created by randomly initializing the chromosomes of individuals. The termination criterion chosen is the maximum number of generations. The evaluation function is the cost of the current system. Since the fitting function is a cost, the proposed problem is a minimization of the fitting of the individuals.

4 Experimental Results

Empirical verifications were performed in order to evaluate the effectiveness of our cost minimization approach. Analyses are based on a database of commercial

---

[1] The simple cross-over operator exchanges the genes of two chromosomes satisfying the admitted ranges of integers.

components and related cost data. Management costs of physical components have been estimated by means of information provider benchmarks ([8], [9]). Cost effectiveness is evaluated by comparing the optimization's output with the output that can be obtained by applying the following *professional guidelines*:

1. Thin clients and HFCs are adopted whenever possible to minimize the cost of clients.
2. Server farms are implemented whenever possible and designed by selecting the smallest server that can support applications, to reduce hardware acquisition costs.
3. Users classes in the same group are centralized on a single server/server farm, to reduce management costs.

The case study we propose considers two groups. The first group (Data-Entry workers) contains 4 classes which use Word, Excel, IE6 and Outlook. Data-Entry workers are associated with Fat/Thin/NFC clients and all applications can be allocated on the remote server or on the client. The second group (Power-User workers) contains 4 classes and is assigned to a Fat/HFC client architecture. Users use Word, Excel, IE6 and Outlook, which can be allocated on the server or on the client, and Matlab is allocated on the client.

Results are reported in Table 2. It is straightforward that if all the applications are free (the Data-Entry group), the thin philosophy gives better results. Note anyway that, over 2000 users, the genetic optimization found a minimum cost system by partitioning users in two server farms (last row of the first group). This contradicts the #3 rule of professional guidelines.

In the power user group, due to the fixed application on the client side (Matlab) and to its computational-intensive nature, the best systems are composed by fat clients. The genetic optimization proves that it does not exist an intermediate "hybrid" solution that is less expensive. Again the results seem to contradict classical guidelines which tend to propose hybrid solutions.

Results highlight that the design of a complex system should always consider an optimization of the hardware infrastructure. Evolutionary techniques properly face this computationally intensive optimization allowing for considerable overall cost reductions. Experiments performed by using a tabu-search engine confirm the results obtained by the proposed genetic engine and showed that the parameters' tuning of the genetic optimizer is not critical. A suitable large initial population (50 individuals) and a moderately large number of optimization epochs (500) tends to produce acceptable solutions.

5   Conclusions

Professional guidelines can lead to sub-optimal architectural choices. A methodological approach and evolutionary optimization can improve solutions and they should be always considered during the design phases by allowing considerable cost reductions.

Table 2. Comparison between designing strategies

Data-Entry Group
Freely allocable applications

Users	Optimization strategies				Saving	
	Guidelines	#SF	Optimized	#SF	Total	per User
12	31180 $	1	**31180 $**	1	0 $	0 $
100	248900 $	1	**248900 $**	1	0 $	0 $
500	1234790 $	1	**1234790 $**	1	0 $	0 $
2000	4985010 $	1	**4973560 $**	2	11450 $	5.72 $

Power-User Group
Freely allocable applications except Matlab

Users	Optimization strategies				Saving	
	Guidelines	#SF	Optimized	#SF	Total	per User
12	101928 $	1	**94704 $**	0	7224 $	602.00 $
100	618560 $	1	**5919000 $**	0	26660 $	266.60 $
500	3130270 $	1	**2959500 $**	0	170770 $	341.54 $
1000	6675966 $	1	**5919000 $**	0	756966 $	756.96 $

References

1. Ardagna, D., Francalanci, C., Piuri. V. Designing and Rightsizing the Information System Architecture. To appear on Information Systems Frontiers, Kluwer Academic Publishers.
2. Ardagna, D., Francalanci, C., Trubian, M. 2004. A Cost-oriented Approach for Inftrastructural Design. SAC 2004 Proceedings. Nicosia, Cyprus.
3. Ein-Dor, P. 1985. Grosch's Law Revisited: CPU Power and the Cost of Computing. Management Communication of the ACM. 28(2), 142-150.
4. Gavish, B., Pirkul, H. 1986. Computer and Database Location in Distributed Computer Systems. IEEE Transaction on Computers. 35(7), 583-590.
5. Jain, H. K. 1987. A comprehensive model for the design of distributed computer systems. IEEE Transactions on software engineering. 13(10), 1092-1104.
6. Dewire D. T. 1997. Second-generation Client/Server Computing. McGraw Hill.
7. Menasce, D. A., Alameida, V. A. F. 2000. Scaling for E-business. Technologies, models, performance and capacity planning. Prentice-Hall.
8. Molta, D. 1999. Thin Client computers come of age. Network Computing. www.networkcomputing.com/1009/1009buyers1.html.
9. The Tolly Group. 1999. Total Cost of Application Ownership. www.tolly.com.
10. Microsoft. 2003. Windows Server 2003 Terminal Server Capacity and Scaling. www.microsoft.com/windowsserver2003/ techinfo/overview/tsscaling.mspx.
11. Sun 2003. Sun Ray Overview. White Paper. http://wwws.sun.com/sunray/whitepapers/
12. Papadimitriou, C., Steiglitz K. 1982. Combinatorial Optimization. Prentice Hall.
13. Koza, J., R. 1998. Genetic programming Encyclopedia of Computer Science and Technology volume 39, James G. Williams and Allen Kent 29–43
14. Houck, C., Joines, J., Kay, M. 1996. A genetic algorithm for functionoptimization: A Matlab implementation, citeseer.nj.nec.com/houck96genetic.html

Clifford Support Vector Machines for Classification

Eduardo Bayro-Corrochano, Nancy Arana-Daniel, and
J. Refugio Vallejo-Gutiérres

Centro de Investigaciónes y Estudios Avanzados,
CINVESTAV, Unidad Guadalajara,
Computer Science Department, GEOVIS Laboratory,
Apartado Postal 31-438, Plaza la Luna,
Guadalajara, Jal. 44550, Mexico, edb@gdl.cinvestav.mx

Abstract. This paper introduces the Clifford Support Vector Machines
as a generalization of the real- and complex- valued Support Vector Machines. The major advantage of this approach is that one requires only
one CSVM which can admit multiple multivector inputs and it can carry
multi-class classification. In contrast one would need many real valued
SVMs for a multi-class problem which is time consuming.

1 Introduction

This paper presents the design of Support Multi-Vector Machines for Classification which from now on-wards they will be call Clifford Support Vector Machines.
In this paper we generalize the real- and complex-valued Support Multi-Vector
for classification. We show that the kernels involve the Clifford or geometric product and they can makes use of nonlinear mappings for nonlinear classification.
Due to limited length of the paper we were compelled not to give an introduction
to Clifford geometric algebra, the reader can find friendly introduction in [1,2,
3].

In this article we present the design of a SVM in the Clifford geometric
algebra. This approach will be called Clifford valued Support Vector Machine
(CSVM). A CSVM is a multivector (hypercomplex) generalization of the real
and complex valued Support Vector Machines [4,5].

2 Linear Clifford Support Vector Machines for Classification

For the case of the Clifford SVM for classification we represent the data set in
a certain Clifford Algebra G_n where $n = p + q + r$, where any multivector base
squares to 0, 1 or -1 depending if they belong to p, r, or s multivector bases respectively. Each data ith-vector has multivector entries $x_i = [x_{i1}, x_{i2}, ..., x_{iD}]^T$,
where $x_{ij} \in G_n$ and D is its dimension. Thus the ith-vector dimension is $D \times 2^n$.
Each data ith-vector $x_i \in \mathcal{G}_n^D$ of the N data vectors will be associated with
their labels as follows: $(x_{i1}, y_{i1}),(x_{i2}, y_{i2}),...,(x_{ij}, y_{ij}),...,(x_{iD}, y_{iD})$, where

L. Rutkowski et al. (Eds.): ICAISC 2004, LNAI 3070, pp. 9–16, 2004.
© Springer-Verlag Berlin Heidelberg 2004

each $\boldsymbol{y}_{ij} = y_{ij_s} + y_{ij_{\sigma_1}} + y_{ij_{\sigma_2}} + ... + y_{ij_I} \in \{\pm 1 \pm \sigma_1 \pm \sigma_2 ... \pm I\}$, where the first subindex s stands for scalar part. The 2^n classification problem is to separate these multivector-valued samples into 2^n groups by selecting a right function from the set of functions $\{f(\boldsymbol{x}) = \boldsymbol{w}^{*T}\boldsymbol{x} + \boldsymbol{b}, \ \boldsymbol{x}, \boldsymbol{w} \in \mathcal{G}_n^D, \ \boldsymbol{b} \in \mathcal{G}_n^D$. The optimal weight vector will be

$$\boldsymbol{w} = [\boldsymbol{w}_1, \boldsymbol{w}_2, ..., \boldsymbol{w}_D]^T \in \mathcal{G}_n^D. \tag{1}$$

Let us see in detail the last equation

$$f(\boldsymbol{x}) = \boldsymbol{w}^{*T}\boldsymbol{x} + \boldsymbol{b} = [\boldsymbol{w}_1^*, \boldsymbol{w}_2^*, ..., \boldsymbol{w}_D^*][(\boldsymbol{x}_1, \boldsymbol{x}_2, ..., \boldsymbol{x}_D]^T + \boldsymbol{b} = \sum_{i=1}^{D} \boldsymbol{w}_i^* \boldsymbol{x}_i + \boldsymbol{b}, \tag{2}$$

where $\boldsymbol{w}_i^* \boldsymbol{x}_i$ corresponds to the Clifford product of two multivectors and $\boldsymbol{w}_i^*$ is the conjugated of the multivector $\boldsymbol{w}$.

We introduce now a structural risk functional similar to the real valued one of the SVM and use loss function similar to the *function insensitive* ξ of Vapnik.

$$min \quad \frac{1}{2}\boldsymbol{w}^{*T}\boldsymbol{w} + C \cdot \sum_{j=1}^{l} \xi_i^2 \tag{3}$$

$$subject\,to \quad Coef_s(y_{ij})Coef_s(f(\boldsymbol{x}_{ij})) \geq 1 - Coef_s(\xi_{ij})$$
$$Coef_{\sigma_1}(y_{ij})Coef_{\sigma_1}(f(\boldsymbol{x}_{ij})) \geq 1 - Coef_{\sigma_1}(\xi_{ij})$$

$$...$$

$$Coef_I(y_{ij})Coef_I(f(\boldsymbol{x}_{ij})) \geq 1 - Coef_I(\xi_{ij})$$
$$Coef_s(\xi_{ij}) \geq 0, \ Coef_{\sigma_1}(\xi_{ij}) \geq 0, \ ..., \ Coef_I(\xi_{ij}) \geq 0, \ j = 1, ..., l,$$

where the subindex $i = 1, ..., D$.

The dual expression of this problem can be derived straightforwardly. Firstly let us consider the expression of the orientation of optimal hyperplane.

Since the $\boldsymbol{w}_i = [w_{i1}, w_{i2}, ..., w_{iD}]^T$, each of the $\boldsymbol{w}_{ij}$ is given by the multivector

$$\boldsymbol{w}_{ij} = w_{is} + w_{i\sigma_1}\sigma_1 + ... + w_{i\sigma_n}\sigma_n + w_{i\sigma_1\sigma_2}\sigma_1\sigma_2 + ... + w_{iI}I. \tag{4}$$

Each component of these weights are computed as follows:

$$w_{is} = \sum_{j=1}^{l} \left((\alpha_{is})_j (y_{is})_j\right)(x_{is})_j, \ w_{i\sigma_1} = \sum_{j=1}^{l} \left((\alpha_{i\sigma_1})_j (y_{i\sigma_1})_j\right)(x_{i\sigma_1})_j \ ...,$$

$$w_{iI} = \sum_{j=1}^{l} \left((\alpha_{iI})_j (y_{iI})_j\right)(x_{iI})_j. \tag{5}$$

According the Wolfe dual programing [4] the dual form reads

$$min \quad \frac{1}{2}(\boldsymbol{w}^{*T}\boldsymbol{w}) - \sum_{j=1}^{l} \left(\sum_{i=1}^{D} \left((\alpha_{is})_j + ... + (\alpha_{i\sigma_1\sigma_2})_j + ... + (\alpha_{iI})_j\right)\right) \tag{6}$$

subject to $\boldsymbol{a}^T \cdot \boldsymbol{1} = 0$, where the entries of the vector

$$a = [a_s, a_{\sigma_1}, a_{\sigma_2}, ..., a_{\sigma_1\sigma_2}, a_I] \tag{7}$$

are given by

$$a_s^T = \Big[[(\alpha_{1s1})(y_{1s1}), (\alpha_{2s1})(y_{2s1}), ..., (\alpha_{Ds1})(y_{Ds1})], ...,$$

$$[(\alpha_{1sl})(y_{1sl}), (\alpha_{2sl})(y_{2sl}), ..., (\alpha_{Dsl})(y_{Dsl})] \Big],$$

$$a_{\sigma_1}^T = \Big[[(\alpha_{1\sigma_11})(y_{1\sigma_11}), (\alpha_{2\sigma_11})(y_{2\sigma_11}), ..., (\alpha_{D\sigma_11})(y_{D\sigma_11})], ...,$$

$$[(\alpha_{1\sigma_1l})(y_{1\sigma_1l}), (\alpha_{2\sigma_1l})(y_{2\sigma_1l}), ..., (\alpha_{D\sigma_1l})(y_{D\sigma_1l})] \Big]$$

$$a_I^T = \Big[[(\alpha_{1I1})(y_{1I1}), (\alpha_{2I1})(y_{2I1}), ..., (\alpha_{DI1})(y_{DI1})], ...,$$

$$[(\alpha_{1Il})(y_{1Il}), (\alpha_{2Il})(y_{2Il}), ..., (\alpha_{DIl})(y_{DIl})] \Big], \tag{8}$$

note that each data ith-vector, $i = 1, ... N$, has D multivector entries and after the training we take into account not N but l ith-vectors which is the number of the found support vectors each one belonging to $\mathcal{G}_n^D$. Thus a^T has the dimension: $(D \times l) \times 2^n$, the latter multiplicand corresponds to the length of a multivector of $\mathcal{G}_n$.

In $a^T \cdot 1 = 0$, 1 denotes a vector of all ones, and all the Lagrange multipliers should fulfill $0 \leq (\alpha_{is})_j \leq C$, $0 \leq (\alpha_{i\sigma_1})_j \leq C$, ..., $0 \leq (\alpha_{i\sigma_1\sigma_2})_j \leq C$, ..., $0 \leq (i\alpha_I)_j \leq C$ for $i = 1, ..., D$ and $j = 1, ..., l$.

We require a compact an easy representation of the resultant *GRAM matrix* of the multi-components, this will help for the programing of the algorithm. For that let us first consider the Clifford product of $(w^{*T}w)$, this can be expressed as follows

$$w^*w = \langle w^*w \rangle_s + \langle w^*w \rangle_{\sigma_1} + \langle w^*w \rangle_{\sigma_2} + ... + \langle w^*w \rangle_I. \tag{9}$$

Since w has the components presented in equation (5), the equation (9) can be rewritten as follows

$$w^*w = a_s^{*T} \langle x^*x \rangle_s a_s + ... + a_s^{*T} \langle x^*x \rangle_{\sigma_1\sigma_2} a_{\sigma_1\sigma_2} + ... + a_s^{*T} \langle x^*x \rangle_I a_I +$$

$$a_{\sigma_1}^{*T} \langle x^*x \rangle_s a_s + ... + a_{\sigma_1}^{*T} \langle x^*x \rangle_{\sigma_1\sigma_2} a_{\sigma_1\sigma_2} + ... + a_{\sigma_1}^{*T} \langle x^*x \rangle_I a_I +$$

$$\tag{10}$$

$$a_I^{*T} \langle x^*x \rangle_s a_s + a_I^T \langle x^*x \rangle_{\sigma_1} a_{\sigma_1} + ... + a_I^{*T} \langle x^*x \rangle_{\sigma_1\sigma_2} a_{\sigma_1\sigma_2} + ... + a_I^{*T} \langle x^*x \rangle_I a_I.$$

Renaming the matrices of the t-grade parts of $\langle x^*x \rangle_t$, we rewrite previous equation as:

$$w^*w = a_s^{*T} H_s a_s + a_s^{*T} H_{\sigma_1} a_{\sigma_1} + ... + a_s^{*T} H_{\sigma_1\sigma_2} a_{\sigma_1\sigma_2} + ... + a_s^{*T} H_I a_I +$$

$$a_{\sigma_1}^{*T} H_s a_s + a_{\sigma_1}^{*T} H_{\sigma_1} a_{\sigma_1} + ... + a_{\sigma_1}^{*T} H_{\sigma_1\sigma_2} a_{\sigma_1\sigma_2} + ... + a_{\sigma_1}^{*T} H_I a_I +$$

$$a_I^{*T} H_s a_s + a_I^{*T} H_{\sigma_1} a_{\sigma_1} + ... + a_I^{*T} H_{\sigma_1\sigma_2} a_{\sigma_1\sigma_2} + ... + a_I^{*T} H_I a_I. \tag{11}$$

These results help us finally to rewrite equation (6) as a compact equation as follows

$$min \quad \frac{1}{2}\boldsymbol{w}^{*T}\boldsymbol{w} + C \cdot \sum_{j=1}^{l}\xi_i^2 = \frac{1}{2}\boldsymbol{a}^{*T}\boldsymbol{H}\boldsymbol{a} + C \cdot \sum_{j=1}^{l}\xi_i^2 \qquad (12)$$

$$subject\ to \quad Coef_s(y_{ij})Coef_s(f(\boldsymbol{x}_{ij})) \geq 1 - Coef_s(\xi_{ij}), \qquad (13)$$

where $\boldsymbol{a}$ is given by equation (7).

$\boldsymbol{H}$ is a positive semidefinite matrix which is the expected *Gramm* matrix. This matrix in terms of the matrices of the t-grade parts of $\langle \boldsymbol{x}^*\boldsymbol{x}\rangle_t$ is written as follows:

$$\boldsymbol{H} = \begin{bmatrix} \boldsymbol{H}_s\boldsymbol{H}_{\sigma_1}\boldsymbol{H}_{\sigma_2}\cdots\cdots\cdots\cdots\boldsymbol{H}_{\sigma_1\sigma_2}\cdots\boldsymbol{H}_I \\ \boldsymbol{H}_{\sigma_1}^T\boldsymbol{H}_s\cdots\boldsymbol{H}_{\sigma_4}\cdots\cdots\boldsymbol{H}_{\sigma_1\sigma_2}\cdots\boldsymbol{H}_I\boldsymbol{H}_s \\ \boldsymbol{H}_{\sigma_2}^T\boldsymbol{H}_{\sigma_1}^T\boldsymbol{H}_s\cdots\boldsymbol{H}_{\sigma_1\sigma_2}\cdots\boldsymbol{H}_I\boldsymbol{H}_s\boldsymbol{H}_{\sigma_1} \\ . \\ . \\ . \\ \boldsymbol{H}_I^T\cdots\boldsymbol{H}_{\sigma_1\sigma_2}^T\cdots\cdots\cdots\cdots\boldsymbol{H}_{\sigma_2}^T\boldsymbol{H}_{\sigma_1}^T\boldsymbol{H}_s \end{bmatrix}, \qquad (14)$$

note that the diagonal entries equal to $\boldsymbol{H}_s$ and since $\boldsymbol{H}$ is a symmetric matrix the lower matrices are transposed.

The optimal weight vector $\boldsymbol{w}$ is as given by equation 1.

The threshold $\boldsymbol{b} \in \mathcal{G}_n^D$ can be computed by using KKT conditions with the Clifford support vectors as follows

$$\boldsymbol{b} = \begin{bmatrix} \boldsymbol{b}_1\boldsymbol{b}_2\boldsymbol{b}_3\dots\boldsymbol{b}_D \end{bmatrix}$$
$$= \big[(b_{1s} + b_{1\sigma_1}\sigma_1 + \dots + b_{1\sigma_1\sigma_2}\sigma_1\sigma_2 + \dots + b_{1I}I)$$
$$(b_{2s} + b_{2\sigma_1}\sigma_1 + \dots + b_{2\sigma_1\sigma_2}\sigma_1\sigma_2 + \dots + b_{2I}I)\dots$$
$$(b_{Ds} + b_{D\sigma_1}\sigma_1 + \dots + b_{D\sigma_1\sigma_2}\sigma_1\sigma_2 + \dots + b_{DI}I)$$
$$= \sum_{j=1}^{l}(\boldsymbol{y}_j - \boldsymbol{w}^{*T}\boldsymbol{x}_j)/l. \qquad (15)$$

The decision function can be seen as sectors reserved for each involved class, i.e. in the case of complex numbers $(\mathcal{G}_{1,0,0})$ or quaternions $(\mathcal{G}_{0,2,0})$ we can see that the circle or the sphere are divide by means spherical vectors. Thus the decision function can be envisaged as

$$y = csign_m\Big[f(\boldsymbol{x})\Big] = csign_m\Big[\boldsymbol{w}^{*T}\boldsymbol{x} + \boldsymbol{b}\Big]$$
$$= csign_m\Big[\sum_{j=1}^{l}(\alpha_j \circ \boldsymbol{y}_j)(\boldsymbol{x}_j^{*T}\boldsymbol{x}) + \boldsymbol{b}\Big], \qquad (16)$$

where m stands for the state valency, e.g. bivalent, tetravalent and the operation "$\circ$" is defined as

$$(\alpha_j \circ \boldsymbol{y}_j) = <\alpha_j>_0<\boldsymbol{y}_j>_0 + <\alpha_j>_1<\boldsymbol{y}_j>_1\sigma_1 +$$

$$...+ <\alpha_j>_{2^n} <y_j>_{2^n} I, \tag{17}$$

simply one consider as coefficients of the multivector basis the multiplications between the coefficients of blades of same degree. For clarity we introduce this operation "o"which takes place implicitly in previous equation (5).

Note that the cases of 2-state and 4-state (Complex numbers) can be solved by the multi-class real valued SVM, however in case of higher representations like the 16-state using quaternions, it would be awkward to resort to the multi-class real valued SVMs.

The major advantage of this approach is that one requires only one CSVM which even can admit multiple multivector inputs. A naive and time consuming approach will be to use a real valued SVM. Let us see an example we want to use two quaternions as inputs and we have 16 classes. Using real valued machines you need to run the optimization procedure once for each Gramm matrix that means 16 SVMs with 8-D inputs. In contrast using a CSVM with multiple quaternion entries on need only one SCVM, see equation (13). This example and equation (13) is a incredible fact to be seriously taken into account. We manage with our method to be able to compute problems with multiple entries using multivectors (or hypercomplex numbers) by using only one machine instead of using the amount of $n \times m \times N_{classes}$ real valued machines, here n, m and $N_{classes}$ stand for n inputs of m-D real vectors for N classes. Other important comment is that the authors [5] with the complex valued SVM they can handle only for complex multiple entries a limited number of classes, in contras our method can use multiple hypercomplex entries and practically it has no limit in classes number.

3   Non Linear Clifford Valued Support Vector Machines for Classification

For the nonlinear Clifford valued classification problems we require a Clifford valued kernel k(x,y). In order to fulfill the Mercer theorem we resort to a component-wise Clifford-valued mapping

$$x \in G_n \xrightarrow{\phi} \Phi(x) = \Phi_s(x) + \Phi_{\sigma_1}\sigma_1 + \tag{18}$$
$$... + \Phi_{\sigma_1}\sigma_2(x)\sigma_2 + ... + I\Phi_I(x) \in G_n.$$

In general we build a Clifford kernel $k(x_m, x_j)$ by taking the Clifford product between the conjugated of x_m and x_j as follows

$$k(x_m, x_j) = \Phi(x)^* \Phi(x), \tag{19}$$

note that the kind of conjugation operation ()* of a multivector depends of the signature of the involved geometric algebra $\mathcal{G}_{p,q,r}$. Next as illustration we present kernels using different geometric algebras.

Complex-valued linear kernel function in $\mathcal{G}_{1,0,0}$ (the center of this geometric algebra is isomorph with $\mathbb{C}$):

$$k(\boldsymbol{x}_m, \boldsymbol{x}_n) = \boldsymbol{x}_m^* \boldsymbol{x}_n \qquad (20)$$
$$= (\boldsymbol{x}_{s_m}^T \boldsymbol{x}_{sn} + \boldsymbol{x}_{I_m}^T \boldsymbol{x}_{In}) + I(\boldsymbol{x}_{s_m}^T \boldsymbol{x}_{In} - \boldsymbol{x}_{I_m}^T \boldsymbol{x}_{sn}),$$
$$= (k(\boldsymbol{x}_m, \boldsymbol{x}_n)_{ss} + k(\boldsymbol{x}_m, \boldsymbol{x}_n)_{II}) + I(k(\boldsymbol{x}_m, \boldsymbol{x}_n)_{Is}) - k(\boldsymbol{x}_m, \boldsymbol{x}_n)_{sI})$$
$$= \boldsymbol{H}_r + I\boldsymbol{H}_i \qquad (21)$$

where $(\mathbf{x}_s)_m$, $(\mathbf{x}_s)_n$, $(\mathbf{x}_I)_m$, $(\mathbf{x}_I)_n$ are vectors of the individual components of the complex numbers $(x)_m = (\mathbf{x}_s)_m + I(\mathbf{x}_I)_n \in \mathcal{G}_{1,0,0}$ and $(x)_n = (\mathbf{x}_s)_n + I(\mathbf{x}_I)_n \in \mathcal{G}_{1,0,0}$ respectively.

Quaternion-valued Gaussian window Gabor kernel function (we use here $i = \sigma_2\sigma_3$, $j = -\sigma_3\sigma_1$, $k = \sigma_1\sigma_2$):

The Gaussian window Gabor kernel function reads

$$k(\boldsymbol{x}_m, \boldsymbol{x}_n) = g(\boldsymbol{x}_m, \boldsymbol{x}_n) exp^{-i\mathbf{w}_0^T(\boldsymbol{x}_m - \boldsymbol{x}_n)} \qquad (22)$$

where the normalized Gaussian window function is given by

$$g(\boldsymbol{x}_m, \boldsymbol{x}_n) = \frac{1}{\sqrt{2\pi}\rho} exp^{\frac{||\boldsymbol{x}_m - \boldsymbol{x}_n||^2}{2\pi^2}} \qquad (23)$$

and the variables $\boldsymbol{w}_0$ and $\boldsymbol{x}_m - \boldsymbol{x}_n$ stand for the frequency and space domains respectively.

As opposite as the Hartley transform or the 2D complex Fourier this kernel function separates nicely the even and odd components of the involved signal, i.e.

$$k(\boldsymbol{x}_m, \boldsymbol{x}_n) = k(\boldsymbol{x}_m, \boldsymbol{x}_n)_s + k(\boldsymbol{x}_m, \boldsymbol{x}_n)_{\sigma_2\sigma_3} + k(\boldsymbol{x}_m, \boldsymbol{x}_n)_{\sigma_3\sigma_1} + k(\boldsymbol{x}_m, \boldsymbol{x}_n)_{\sigma_1\sigma_2}$$
$$= g(\boldsymbol{x}_m, \boldsymbol{x}_n)cos(\mathbf{w}_0^T\boldsymbol{x}_m)cos(\mathbf{w}_0^T\boldsymbol{x}_m) +$$
$$g(\boldsymbol{x}_m, \boldsymbol{x}_n)cos(\mathbf{w}_0^T\boldsymbol{x}_m)sin(\mathbf{w}_0^T\boldsymbol{x}_m)\boldsymbol{i}$$
$$+g(\boldsymbol{x}_m, \boldsymbol{x}_n)sin(\mathbf{w}_0^T\boldsymbol{x}_m)cos(\mathbf{w}_0^T\boldsymbol{x}_m)\boldsymbol{j}$$
$$+g(\boldsymbol{x}_m, \boldsymbol{x}_n)sin(\mathbf{w}_0^T\boldsymbol{x}_m)sin(\mathbf{w}_0^T\boldsymbol{x}_m)\boldsymbol{k}.$$

Since $g(\boldsymbol{x}_m, \boldsymbol{x}_n)$ fulfills the Mercer's condition it is straightforward to prove that $k(\boldsymbol{x}_m, \boldsymbol{x}_n)_u$ in the above equations satisfy these conditions as well.

After we defined these kernels we can proceed in the formulation of the SVM conditions. We substitute the mapped data $\Phi(\boldsymbol{x}) = \sum_{u=1}^{2^n} < \Phi(\boldsymbol{x}) >_u$ into the linear function $f(\boldsymbol{x}) = \boldsymbol{w}^{*T}\boldsymbol{x} + b = \boldsymbol{w}^{*T}\Phi(\boldsymbol{x}) + b$. The problem can be stated similarly as equations (4-6). In fact we can replace the kernel function in equations 13 to accomplish the Wolfe dual programming and thereby to obtain the kernel function group for nonlinear classification

$$H_s = [k_s(\boldsymbol{x}_m, \boldsymbol{x}_j)]_{m,j=1,..,l} \qquad (24)$$
$$H_{\sigma_1} = [k_{\sigma_1}(\boldsymbol{x}_m, \boldsymbol{x}_j)]_{m,j=1,..,l}$$
$$...$$
$$H_{\sigma_n} = [k_{\sigma_n}(\boldsymbol{x}_m, \boldsymbol{x}_j)]_{m,j=1,..,l} .$$
$$H_I = [k_I(\boldsymbol{x}_m, \boldsymbol{x}_j)]_{m,j=1,..,l} .$$

In the same way we use the kernel functions to replace the the dot product of the input data in the equation (16). In general the output function of the nonlinear Clifford SVM reads

$$y = csign_m\Big[f(\boldsymbol{x})\Big] = csign_m\Big[\boldsymbol{w}^{*T}\varPhi(\boldsymbol{x}) + \boldsymbol{b}\Big]$$

$$= csign_m\Big[\sum_{j=1}^{l}(\alpha_j \circ \boldsymbol{y}_j)(k(\boldsymbol{x}_j, \boldsymbol{x}) + \boldsymbol{b}\Big]. \tag{25}$$

where m stands for the state valency.

4   Experimental Analysis

We extended the well known 2-D spiral problem to the 3-D space. This experiment should test whether the CSVM would be able to separate three 1-D manifolds embedded in $\mathbb{R}^3$. The functions were generated as follows:

$$f_1(t) = [x_1(t), y_1(t), z_1(t)] = [z_1 * cos(\theta) * sin(\theta), z_1 * sin(\theta) * sin(\theta), z_1 * cos(\theta)]$$
$$f_2(t) = [x_2(t), y_2(t), z_2(t)] = [z_2 * cos(\theta) * sin(\theta), z_2 * sin(\theta) * sin(\theta), z_2 * cos(\theta)]$$
$$f_3(t) = [x_3(t), y_3(t), z_3(t)] = [z_3 * cos(\theta) * sin(\theta), z_3 * sin(\theta) * sin(\theta), z_3 * cos(\theta)],$$

where in Mathlab code $\theta = linspace(0.2 * pi, 32)$, $z_1 = 4 * linspace(0, 10, 32) + 1$, $z_2 = 4 * linspace(0, 10, 32) + 10$ and $z_3 = 4 * linspace(0, 10, 32) + 20$. For the the depiction these vectors were normalized by 10. In Figure 1 on can see that the problem is nonlinear separable. The CSVM uses for training 32 input quaternions of each of the three functions, since these have three coordinates we use simply the bivector part of the quaternion, namely $\boldsymbol{x}_i = x_i(t)\sigma_2\sigma_3 + y_i(t)\sigma_3\sigma_1 + z_i(t)\sigma_1\sigma_2 \equiv [0, x_i(t), y_i(t), z_i(t)]$. The CSVM used the kernel given by the equation 24. The CSVM found 16 support vector for $f_1(t)$, 21 support vector for $f_2(t)$ (in the middle) and 16 support vector for $f_3(t)$. Note that the CSVM indeed manage to separate the three classes. If we think in a real valued SVM (naive approach), one will require to do the job three SVMs.

5   Conclusions

This paper generalizes the real valued SVM to Clifford valued SVM. Thus we can generate for example complex-, quaternion- and hypercomplex-valued SVMS.

The major advantage of this approach is that one requires only one CSVM which can admit multiple multivector inputs and it can carry multi-class classification. If we use a real valued SVM for multi-class classification one needs high memory capacity and for the training it will be necessary to run n times the optimization procedure and for the recall phase one requires to evaluate n times the decision function. In contrast the CSVM will require one optimization procedure and one evaluation of the multi-class decision function.

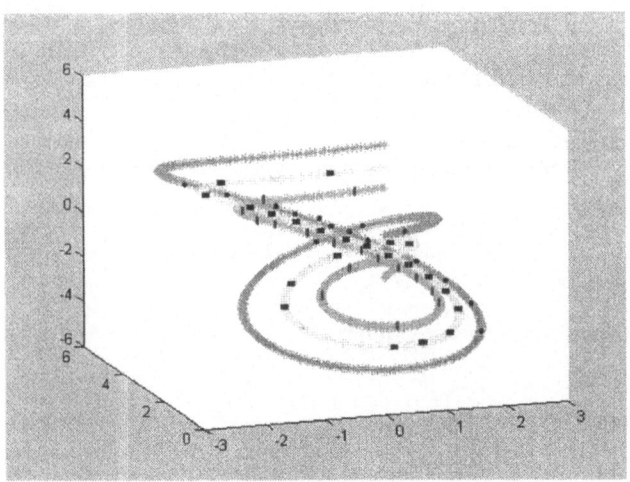

Fig. 1. 3D spiral with three classes. The marks represent the support vectors found by the CSVM.

References

1. Bayro-Corrochano E. *Geometric Computing for Perception Action Systems.* Springer Verlag, New York, 2001.
2. Bayro-Corrochano E., Arana-Daniel N. and Vallejo-Gutierrez R. *Design of kernels for support multivector machines involving the Clifford geometric product and the conformal geometric neuron.* In Proc. of the Int. Join Conference on Neural Networks'2003, Portland, Oregon, USA, July 20-24, pp. 2893-2898.
3. Li :, Hestenes D. and Rockwood A. Generalized homogeneous coordinates for computational geometry. In Geometric Computing with Clifford Algebra, G. Sommer (Ed.), Springer-Verlag, pp. 27-59, 2001.
4. Vapnik V. N. *Statistical Learning Theory.* Wiley, New York, 1998.
5. Zhang L., Zhou W. and Jiao L. Complex-valued support vector machine for classification. To appear in a special issue on learning of IEEE Trans. Signal Processing, 2004.

Uncertain Variables and Systems – New Problems and Results

Zdzislaw Bubnicki

Wroclaw University of Technology, Institute of Control and Systems Engineering,
Wyb. Wyspianskiego 27, 50-370 Wroclaw, Poland

Abstract. At the beginning, a short description of uncertain variables and a basic decision problem for a class of uncertain systems are presented. The main part of the paper is devoted to a review of new applications of the uncertain variables to: nonparametric decision problems, allocation and project management under uncertainty, systems with uncertain and random parameters, systems with distributed knowledge, pattern recognition and selected practical problems. The presentation is based on the author's book *Analysis and Decision Making in Uncertain Systems* (Springer, 2004).

1 Introduction

There exists a variety of definitions and formal models of uncertainties and uncertain systems, adequate for different types of the uncertainty and used for different problems concerning the systems. The idea of uncertain variables, introduced and developed in recent years, is specially oriented for decision problems in a class of uncertain systems described by traditional mathematical models and by relational knowledge representations (with number variables) which are treated as an extension of classical functional models [2,3,4,12]. The considerations are then directly related to respective problems and methods in traditional decision systems theory. The uncertain variable is described by a certainty distribution given by an expert and characterizing his/her knowledge concerning approximate values of the variable. The uncertain variables are related to random and fuzzy variables, but there are also essential differences discussed in the book cited above. The purpose of this paper is to present a brief review of new ideas, problems and results concerning the uncertain variables and their applications to uncertain systems: a new approach to nonparametric decision problems, allocation problems and project management under uncertainty, decision making in systems with uncertain and random parameters (Sects. 3, 4, 5), other problems and selected practical applications listed in Sect. 6. At the beginning, a short description of the uncertain variables and the basic decision problem are presented. Details and examples may be found in [2,3,4,12].

L. Rutkowski et al. (Eds.): ICAISC 2004, LNAI 3070, pp. 17–29, 2004.
© Springer-Verlag Berlin Heidelberg 2004

2   Uncertain Logics and Variables

Consider a universal set Ω, $\omega \in \Omega$, a set $\overline{X} \subseteq R^k$, a function $g : \Omega \to \overline{X}$, a crisp property (predicate) $P(\overline{x})$ and the crisp property $\Psi(\omega, P)$ generated by P and g: "For $\overline{x} = g(\omega) \triangleq \overline{x}(\omega)$ assigned to ω the property P is satisfied". Let us introduce the property $G_\omega(x) = $ "$\overline{x}(\omega) \cong x$" for $x \in X \subseteq \overline{X}$, which means: "$\overline{x}$ is approximately equal to x" or "x is the approximate value of $\overline{x}$". The properties P and G_ω generate the soft property $\overline{\Psi}(\omega, P)$ in Ω: "the approximate value of $\overline{x}(\omega)$ satisfies P", i.e.

$$\overline{\Psi}(\omega, P) = \text{"}\overline{x}(\omega) \widetilde{\in} D_x\text{"}, \qquad D_x = \{\overline{x} \in \overline{X} : P(\overline{x})\}, \qquad (1)$$

which means: "$\overline{x}$ approximately belongs to D_x". Denote by $h_\omega(x)$ the logic value of $G_\omega(x)$:

$$w[\overline{x}(\omega) \cong x] \triangleq h_\omega(x), \qquad \bigwedge_{x \in X} h_\omega(x) \geq 0, \qquad \max_{x \in X} h_\omega(x) = 1$$

Definition 1. *The uncertain logic L is definied by Ω, $\overline{X}, X$, crisp predicates $P(\overline{x})$, the properties $G_\omega(x)$ and the corresponding functions $h_\omega(x)$ for $\omega \in \Omega$. In this logic we consider soft properties (1) generated by P and G_ω. The logic value of $\overline{\Psi}$ is*

$$w[\overline{\Psi}(\omega, P)] \triangleq v[\overline{\Psi}(\omega, P)] = \begin{cases} \max_{x \in D_x} h_\omega(x) & \text{for } D_x \neq \varnothing \\ 0 & \text{for } D_x = \varnothing \end{cases}$$

and is called a certainty index. The operations are defined as follows:

$$v[\neg\overline{\Psi}(\omega, P)] = 1 - v[\overline{\Psi}(\omega, P)],$$

$$v[\Psi_1(\omega, P_1) \vee \Psi_2(\omega, P_2)] = \max\{v[\Psi_1(\omega, P_1)], v[\Psi_2(\omega, P_2)]\},$$

$$v[\Psi_1(\omega, P_1) \wedge \Psi_2(\omega, P_2)] = \begin{cases} 0 & \text{if for each } x \; w(P_1 \wedge P_2) = 0 \\ \min\{v[\Psi_1(\omega, P_1)], v[\Psi_2(\omega, P_2)]\} & \text{otherwise} \end{cases}$$

where Ψ_1 is $\overline{\Psi}$ or $\neg\overline{\Psi}$, and Ψ_2 is $\overline{\Psi}$ or $\neg\overline{\Psi}$ $\quad\Box$

For the logic L one can prove the following statements:

$$v[\overline{\Psi}(\omega, P_1 \vee P_2)] = v[\overline{\Psi}(\omega, P_1) \vee \overline{\Psi}(\omega, P_2)], \qquad (2)$$

$$v[\overline{\Psi}(\omega, P_1 \wedge P_2)] \leq \min\{v[\overline{\Psi}(\omega, P_1)], v[\overline{\Psi}(\omega, P_2)]\}, \qquad (3)$$

$$v\left[\overline{\Psi}(\omega, \neg P)\right] \geq v\left[\neg\overline{\Psi}(\omega, P)\right].$$ (4)

The interpretation (semantics) of the uncertain logic L is the following: The uncertain logic operates with crisp predicates P, but for the given ω it is not possible to state if P is true or false because the function g and consequently the value $\overline{x}$ is unknown. The function $h_\omega(x)$ is given by an expert, who "looking at" ω obtains some information concerning $\overline{x}$ and uses it to evaluate his opinion that $\overline{x} \cong x$.

Definition 2 (the *uncertain logic C*). *The first part is the same as in Def.1. The certainty index of $\overline{\Psi}$ and the operations are defined as follows:*

$$v_c\left[\overline{\Psi}(\omega, P)\right] = \frac{1}{2}\left\{v\left[\overline{\Psi}(\omega, P)\right] + 1 - v\left[\overline{\Psi}(\omega, \neg P)\right]\right\},$$

$$\neg\overline{\Psi}(\omega, P) = \overline{\Psi}(\omega, \neg P),$$ (5)

$$\overline{\Psi}(\omega, P_1) \vee \overline{\Psi}(\omega, P_2) = \overline{\Psi}(\omega, P_1 \vee P_2),$$

$$\overline{\Psi}(\omega, P_1) \wedge \overline{\Psi}(\omega, P_2) = \overline{\Psi}(\omega, P_1 \wedge P_2) \qquad \square$$

For the logic C one can prove the following statements:

$$v_c\left[\overline{\Psi}(\omega, P_1 \vee P_2)\right] \geq \max\left\{v_c\left[\overline{\Psi}(\omega, P_1)\right], v_c\left[\overline{\Psi}(\omega, P_2)\right]\right\},$$ (6)

$$v_c\left[\overline{\Psi}(\omega, P_1 \wedge P_2)\right] \leq \min\left\{v_c\left[\overline{\Psi}(\omega, P_1)\right], v_c\left[\overline{\Psi}(\omega, P_2)\right]\right\},$$ (7)

$$v_c\left[\neg\overline{\Psi}(\omega, P)\right] = 1 - v_c\left[\overline{\Psi}(\omega, P)\right].$$ (8)

The variable $\overline{x}$ for a fixed ω will be called an uncertain variable. Two versions of uncertain variables will be defined by: $h(x)$ given by an expert and the definitions of certainty indexes $w(\overline{x}\widetilde{\in} D_x)$, $w(\overline{x}\widetilde{\notin} D_x)$, $w(\overline{x}\widetilde{\in} D_1 \vee \overline{x}\widetilde{\in} D_2)$, $w(\overline{x}\widetilde{\in} D_1 \wedge \overline{x}\widetilde{\in} D_2)$.

Definition 3. *The uncertain variable $\overline{x}$ is defined by X, the function $h(x) = v(\overline{x} \cong x)$ given by an expert and the following definitions:*

$$v(\overline{x}\widetilde{\in} D_x) = \max_{x \in D_x} h(x) \quad for \quad D_x \neq \varnothing \quad and \quad 0 \quad for \quad D_x = \varnothing,$$

$$v(\overline{x}\widetilde{\notin} D_x) = 1 - v(\overline{x}\widetilde{\in} D_x),$$

$$v(\overline{x}\widetilde{\in} D_1 \vee \overline{x}\widetilde{\in} D_2) = \max\left\{v(\overline{x}\widetilde{\in} D_1), v(\overline{x}\widetilde{\in} D_2)\right\},$$

$$v(\overline{x}\widetilde{\in} D_1 \wedge \overline{x}\widetilde{\in} D_2) = \begin{cases} \min\left\{v(\overline{x}\widetilde{\in} D_1), v(\overline{x}\widetilde{\in} D_2)\right\} & for \ D_1 \cap D_2 \neq \varnothing \\ 0 & for \ D_1 \cap D_2 = \varnothing. \end{cases}$$

The function $h(x)$ will be called a certainty distribution $\qquad \square$

The definition of the uncertain variable is based on logic L. Then for (1) the properties (2), (3), (4) are satisfied. In particular, (4) becomes $v(\overline{x}\widetilde{\in}\overline{D}_x) \geq v(\overline{x}\widetilde{\notin}D_x) = 1 - v(\overline{x}\widetilde{\in}D_x)$ where $\overline{D}_x = X - D_x$.

Definition 4. *C-uncertain variable is defined by* X, $h(x) = v(\overline{x} \cong x)$ *given by an expert and the following definitions:*

$$v_c(\overline{x}\widetilde{\in}D_x) = \frac{1}{2}\left[\max_{x\in D_x} h(x) + 1 - \max_{x\in X-D_x} h(x)\right], \tag{9}$$

$$v_c(\overline{x}\widetilde{\notin}D_x) = 1 - v_c(\overline{x}\widetilde{\in}D_x),$$

$$v_c(\overline{x}\widetilde{\in}D_1 \vee \overline{x}\widetilde{\in}D_2) = v_c(\overline{x}\widetilde{\in}D_1 \cup D_2),$$

$$v_c(\overline{x}\widetilde{\in}D_1 \wedge \overline{x}\widetilde{\in}D_2) = v_c(\overline{x}\widetilde{\in}D_1 \cap D_2) \qquad \square$$

The definition of C-uncertain variable is based on logic C. Then for (1) the properties (6), (7), (8) are satisfied. According to (5) and (8) $v_c(\overline{x}\widetilde{\notin}D_x) = v_c(\overline{x} \widetilde{\in} X - D_x)$. The function $v_c(\overline{x} \cong x) \triangleq h_c(x)$ may be called *C-certainty distribution*. In the case of C-uncertain variable the expert's knowledge is used in a better way.

In a *continuous case* $h(x)$ is a continuous function in X and in a *discrete case* $X = \{x_1, x_2, \ldots, x_m\}$. The mean value of $\overline{x}$ is defined as follows:

$$M(\overline{x}) = \int_X xh(x)dx \cdot \left[\int_X h(x)dx\right]^{-1} \quad \text{or} \quad M(\overline{x}) = \sum_{i=1}^{m} x_ih(x_i) \cdot \left[\sum_{i=1}^{m} h(x_i)\right]^{-1}$$

in a continuous case or a discrete case, respectively. For a pair of variables $(\overline{x}, \overline{y})$ described by $h(x,y) = v\left[(\overline{x}, \overline{y}) \cong (x,y)\right]$ we may consider marginal and conditional distributions with the following relationships:

$$h_x(x) = v(\overline{x} \cong x) = \max_{y\in Y} h(x,y), \quad h_y(y) = v(\overline{y} \cong y) = \max_{x\in X} h(x,y),$$

$$h(x,y) = \min\{h_x(x), h_y(y|x)\} = \min\{h_y(y), h_x(x|y)\}$$

where $h_y(y|x) = v\left[\overline{x} = x \rightarrow \overline{y} \cong y\right]$, $h_x(x|y) = v\left[\overline{y} = y \rightarrow \overline{x} \cong x\right]$.

3   Decision Problems

Let us consider an uncertain plant described by a relation $R(u, y, z; x) \subset U \times Y \times Z$ (*a relational knowledge representation*) where $u \in U$, $y \in Y$ are the input and output vectors, respectively, $z \in Z$ is the vector of external disturbances, and $x \in X$ is an unknown vector parameter, which is assumed to be a value of an uncertain variable described by $h_x(x)$ given by an expert. For the property $y \in D_y \subset Y$ required by a user, we can formulate the following **decision problem**: For the given $R, z, h_x(x)$ and D_y one should find the decision u^* maximizing the certainty index of the property: "the set of all possible outputs approximately belongs to D_y"or "the set of all possible outputs belongs to D_y for an approximate value of $\bar{x}$". Then

$$u^* = \arg\max_{u \in U} v\left[D_y(u, z; \bar{x}) \widetilde{\subseteq} D_y\right] = \arg\max_{u \in U} \max_{x \in D_x(u,z)} h_x(x) \qquad (10)$$

where $D_y(u, z; x) = \{y \in Y : (u, y, z) \in R\}$ and $D_x(u, z) = \{x \in X : D_y(u, z; x) \subseteq D_y\}$. If u^* is the unique result of the maximization then $u^* = \Psi(z)$ denotes a deterministic decision algorithm in the open-loop decision system. If $\bar{x}$ is considered as C-uncertain variable, then one should determine u_c^* maximizing $v_c[\bar{x} \widetilde{\in} D_x(u, z)]$. In this case the calculations are more complicated.

The uncertain variables may be applied for a nonparametic description of the uncertain plant. Let us assume that (u, y, z) are values of uncertain variables $(\bar{u}, \bar{y}, \bar{z})$, and the knowledge of the plant (KP) has the form of the conditional certainty distribution $h_y(y|u, z)$ given by an expert. The decision problem may consist in finding a conditional distribution $h_u(u|z)$ for the given certainty distribution $h_y(y)$ required by a user. The **nonparametic decision problem** is then the following: For the given $h_y(y|u, z)$ and $h_y(y)$ one sholud determine $h_u(u|z)$. The determination of $h_u(u|z)$ may be decomposed into two steps. In the first step, one should find the distribution $h_{uz}(u, z)$ satisfying the equation

$$h_y(y) = \max_{u \in U, z \in Z} \min\{h_{uz}(u, z), h_y(y|u, z)\}, \qquad (11)$$

and in the second step, one should determine the distribution $h_u(u|z)$ satisfying the equation

$$h_{uz}(u, z) = \min\{h_z(z), h_u(u|z)\}. \qquad (12)$$

where

$$h_z(z) = \max_{u \in U} h_{uz}(u, z). \qquad (13)$$

The distribution $h_u(u|z)$ may be considered as a knowledge of the decision making (KD) or an *uncertain decision algorithm*. The deterministic decision algorithm Ψ may be obtained via a *determinization* of the uncertain algorithm, which may consist in using the mean value: $u_d = M(\bar{u}|z) = \Psi(z)$. It is worth noting that the anologous problem may be considered for the nonparametric descriptions of the uncertainty using random or fuzzy variables. If (u, y, z) are values of continuous random variables $(\tilde{u}, \tilde{y}, \tilde{z})$ then KP has the form of a conditional probability density $f_y(y|u, z)$ and the formulas analogous to (11), (12), (13) are as follows:

$$f_y(y) = \int_U \int_Z f_{uz}(u, z) f_y(y|u, z) du dz, \qquad (14)$$

$$f_u(u|z) = f_{uz}(u, z) \cdot \left[\int_U f_{uz}(u, z) du \right]^{-1}. \tag{15}$$

In this case, the *random decision algorithm* (KD) has the form of $f_u(u|z)$ and the determinization may consist in using the expected value: $u_d = E(\bar{u}|z) = \Psi(z)$. If (u, y, z) are values of fuzzy variables $(\hat{u}, \hat{y}, \hat{z})$, the nonparametric description of the uncertainty is formulated by introducing three soft properties concerning u, y, z: $\varphi_u(u), \varphi_y(y), \varphi_z(z)$. Then KP given by an expert has the form of a conditional membership function

$$w\left[\varphi_u \wedge \varphi_z \to \varphi_y\right] \triangleq \mu_y(y|u, z)$$

where $w \in [0, 1]$ denotes the logic value. The formulas analogous to (11), (12), (13) are now as follows:

$$\mu_y(y) = \max_{u \in U, z \in Z} \min\{\mu_{uz}(u, z), \mu_y(y|u, z)\},$$

$$\mu_{uz}(u, z) = \min\{\mu_z(z), \mu_u(u|z)\},$$

$$\mu_z(z) = \max_{u \in U} \mu_{uz}(u, z)$$

where $\mu_y(y) = w[\varphi_y]$, $\mu_z(z) = w[\varphi_z]$, $\mu_{uz}(u, z) = w[\varphi_u \wedge \varphi_z]$, $\mu_u(u|z) = w[\varphi_z \to \varphi_u]$. In this case, the *fuzzy decision algorithm* (KD) has the form of $\mu_u(u|z)$ and the deterministic decision algorithm $u_d = \Psi(z)$ may be obtained via the determinization (defuzzification) using the mean value. The formulas for the fuzzy variables, similar to those for the uncertain variables, have different practical interpretations caused by the fact that they do not concern directly the *values* of the variables but are concerned with the *properties* φ. The differences between the descriptions using uncertain and fuzzy variables are discussed in [12] where the generalization in the form of so called *soft variables* $\check{u}$ described by *evaluating functions* $g_u(u), g_y(y), g_z(z), g_y(y|u, z), g_u(u|z)$ is presented. The general approach to the nonparametric decision problem, common for the different descriptions presented above, is illustrated in Fig. 1.

In general, for a variable $\check{u}$ it is possible to formulate an uncertain (imprecise) knowledge on its value $x \in X$ in two ways: by introducing monotonic nonadditive measure $m(D_x)$ where the value m evaluates the property $x \in D_x$ for the given $D_x \subset X$, or directly by introducing a distribution $g(x)$ where the value g evaluates the given value x. In the second description of the uncertainty (used in the definition of the soft variable and sufficient for nonparametric problems), it is not necessary to define $m(D_x)$. The details concerning the definition of the soft variable and its application to nonparametric decision problems are presented in [12].

It is worth noting that for the uncertain variables $v(\bar{x}\tilde{\in}D_x) \triangleq m(D_x)$ is a possibility measure with a specific interpretation, and $v_c(\bar{x}\tilde{\in}D_x) \triangleq m_c(D_x)$ is neither a belief nor a plausibility measure.

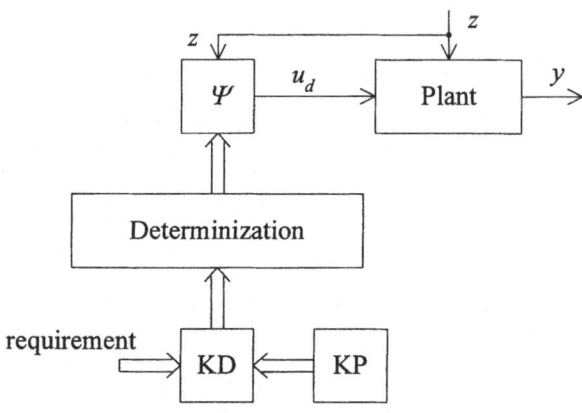

Fig. 1. Open-loop knowledge-based decision system

4   Allocation Problems and Project Management

The uncertain variables may be applied to allocation problems consisting in the proper task or resource distribution in a complex of operations described by a relational konwledge representation with unknown parameters [12]. The parts of the complex may denote manufacturing operations [5], computational operations in a computer system [11] or operations in a project to be managed [8]. Let us consider a complex of k parallel operations described by a set of inequalities

$$T_i \leq \varphi_i(u_i, x_i), \qquad i = 1, 2, ..., k \tag{16}$$

where T_i is the execution time of the i-th operation, u_i is the size of a task in the problem of task allocation or the amount of a resource in the problem of resource allocation, an unknown parameter $x_i \in R^1$ is a value of an uncertain variable $\bar{x}_i$ described by a certainty distribution $h_i(x_i)$ given by an expert, and $\bar{x}_1, \ldots, \bar{x}_k$ are independent variables. The complex may be considered as a decision plant described in Sect. 3 where y is the execution time of the whole complex $T = \max\{T_1, \ldots, T_k\}$, $x = (x_1, \ldots, x_k)$, $u = (u_1, \ldots, u_k) \in \overline{U}$. The set $\overline{U} \subset R^k$ is determined by the constraints: $u_i \geq 0$ for each i and $u_1 + \cdots + u_k = U$ where U is the total size of the task or the total amount of the resource to be distributed among the operations (Fig. 2).

According to the general formulation of the decision problem presented in Sect. 3, the allocation problem may be formulated as an optimization problem consisting in finding the optimal allocation u^* that maximizes the certainty index of the soft property: "the set of possible values T approximately belongs to $[0, \alpha]$" (i.e. belongs to $[0, \alpha]$ for an approximate value of $\bar{x}$). **Optimal allocation problem**: For the given φ_i, h_i ($i \in \overline{1, k}$), U and α find

$$u^* = \arg\max_{u \in \overline{U}} v(u)$$

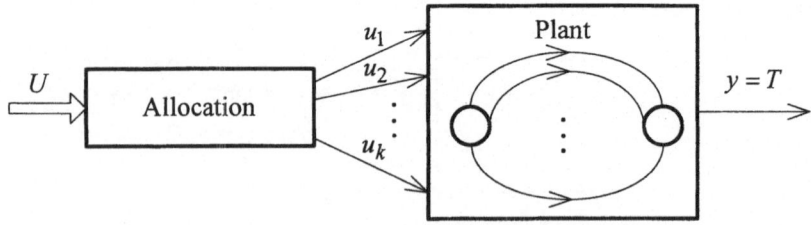

Fig. 2. Complex of parallel operations as a decision plant

where

$$v(u) \;=\; v\left\{ D_T(u; \overline{x}) \widetilde{\subseteq} [0, \alpha] \right\} \;=\; v\left(T(u, \overline{x}) \widetilde{\leq} \alpha \right).$$

The soft property "$D_T(u; \overline{x}) \widetilde{\subseteq} [0, \alpha]$" is denoted here by "$T(u, \overline{x}) \widetilde{\leq} \alpha$", and $D_T(u; x)$ denotes the set of possible values T for the fixed u, determined by the inequality

$$T \leq \max_i \varphi_i(u_i, x_i).$$

According to (16)

$$v(u) \;=\; v\left\{ \left[T_1(u_1, \overline{x}_1) \widetilde{\leq} \alpha \right] \wedge \left[T_2(u_2, \overline{x}_2) \widetilde{\leq} \alpha \right] \wedge \cdots \wedge \left[T_k(u_k, \overline{x}_k) \widetilde{\leq} \alpha \right] \right\}.$$

Then

$$u^* \;=\; \arg \max_{u \in \overline{U}} \min_i v_i(u_i)$$

where

$$v_i(u_i) \;=\; v\left[T_i(u_i, \overline{x}_i) \widetilde{\leq} \alpha \right] \;=\; v\left[\varphi_i(u_i, \overline{x}_i) \widetilde{\leq} \alpha \right] \;=\; v\left[\overline{x}_i \widetilde{\in} D_i(u_i) \right],$$

$$D_i(u_i) \;=\; \left\{ x_i \in R^1 \;:\; \varphi_i(u_i, x_i) \leq \alpha \right\}.$$

Finally

$$v_i(u_i) = \max_{x_i \in D_i(u_i)} h_i(x_i)$$

and

$$u^* = \arg \max_{u \in \overline{U}} \min_i \max_{x_i \in D_i(u_i)} h_i(x_i).$$

The presented approach may be applied to the allocation of computational tasks in a group of parallel processors with uncertain execution times. In this case (16) is reduced to $T_i \leq x_i n_i$ where n_i is a number of elementary tasks (programs or parts of programs) and x_i is the upper bound of the execution time for the elementary task, estimated by an expert. The considerations may be extended to more complicated structures of the complex of operations and applied to a knowledge-based project management with cascade-parallel structures [8].

5   Systems with Uncertain and Random Parameters

It is interesting and useful to consider a decision plant containing two kinds of unknown parameters in the relational knowledge representation: uncertain parameters described by certainty distributions and random parameters described by probability distributions. The different versions of problem formulations in this case are presented in [10,12]. Let us consider shortly selected versions. Assume that the plant is described by a relation $R(u, y, z; x, w)$ where x is a value of an uncertain variable described by $h(x)$ and $w \in W$ is a value of a random variable described by a probability density $f(w)$. Now the certainty index in (10) depends on w, i.e.

$$v \left[D_y(u, z; \overline{x}, w) \widetilde{\subseteq} D_y \right] \triangleq v(u, z, w)$$

and u^* may be obtained as a result of the maximization of the expected value of v. In another version (case a), the plant is described by $R(u, y, z; x)$ with the uncertain parameter described by $h(x; w)$ where w is a value of a random variable described by $f(w)$. Then $v(u, z, w)$ depends on w and the deterministic algorithm $u^* = u_d = \Psi(z)$ may be obtained by the maximization of the expected value of v, as in the first version. It is possible to invert the order of uncertain and random paramters (case b): The plant is described by $R(u, y, z; w)$, the random parameter w has the density $f(w; x)$ and x is a value of $\overline{x}$ with the distribution $h(x)$. Now $u_d = \Psi(z)$ may be obtained via the maximization of the mean value (with respect to $\overline{x}$) of the probability $P[D_y(u, z; w) \subseteq D_y] \triangleq p(u, z, x)$. The knowledge-based decision systems with three levels of uncertainty in cases a and b are illustrated in Figs. 3 and 4, respectively. The result of the determinization $G(u, z)$ denotes the expected value of $v(u, z, w)$ in case a and the mean value of $p(u, z, x)$ in case b.

6   Other Problems and Results

1. Stability and stabilization of uncertain systems. The uncertain variables have been applied to the estimation of the stability of dynamical systems with unknown parameters characterized by certainty distributions. For the known necessary and sufficient stability conditions, it is possible to determine the lower and upper bounds of the certainty index that the system is stable. New results have been obtained for the systems with uncertain and random parameters and for the stabilization problem [7].

2. Application of uncertain variables to learning process. For a class of uncertain decision systems described by a relational knowlege representation with unknown parameters, learning algorithms have been elaborated. The learning process consists here in *step by step* knowledge evaluation and updating [1, 5,14,12]. The combination with the approach based on the uncertain variables leads to the learning system based on the current expert's knowledge. In such a system, at each step of the learning process the expert's knowledge in the form

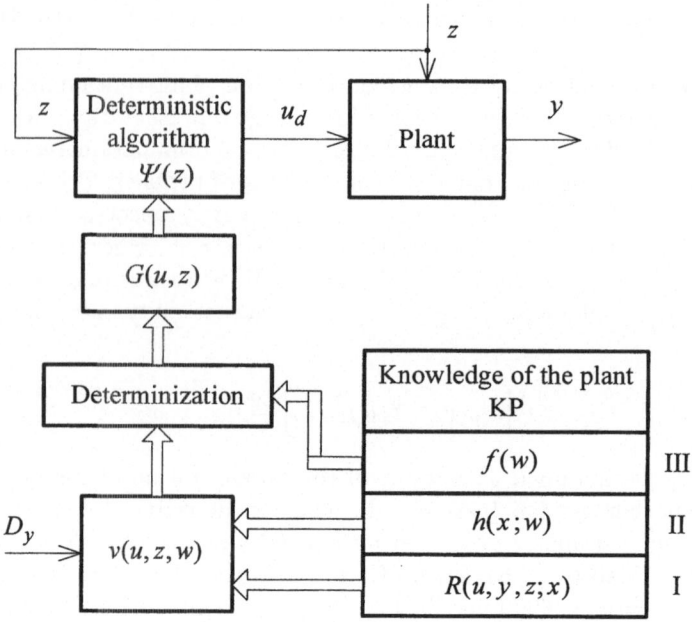

Fig. 3. Decision system with three-level uncertainty in case a; I - relational level, II - uncertain level, III - random level

of the certainty distribution is modified according to the current result of the learning [13,15].

3. Quality of decisions based on uncertain variables. For the known deterministic models of the decision plants, it is possible to evaluate the quality of the decisions based on the certainty distributions given by an expert. The quality index may be used to compare different values of parameters in the certainty distributions and consequently, to compare different experts. It may be also used in an adaptive system with *step by step* adjusting of the parameters in the certainty distributions, based on the current quality evaluation [12,17].

4. Application to pattern recognition. Let an object to be recognized or classified be characterized by a vector of features u and the index of a class j to which the object belongs. The set of the objects may be described by a relational knowledge representation $R(u, j; x)$ where the vector of unknown parameters x is assumed to be a value of an uncertain variable described by a certainty distribution. Optimal recognition problem may consist in the determination of a class j maximizing the certainty index that j belongs to the set of all possible classes for the known u. Different versions of this problem and the corresponding results are presented in [12,9].

5. Selected practical applications. It has been shown how to apply the description of the uncertainty based on the uncertain variables to:

a. Analysis and design of a congestion control system in computer networks [18].

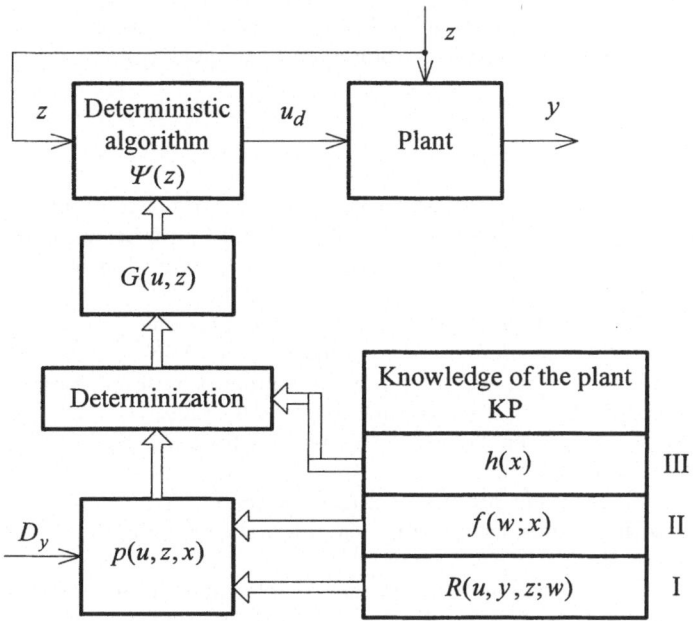

Fig. 4. Decision system with three-level uncertainty in case b; I - relational level, II - random level, III - uncertain level

b. Intelligent control of an uncertain assembly process and other manufacturing processes [12,5].

c. Design of an intelligent transportation system [16].

6. Complex systems with distributed knowledge. Interesting results in this area concern the complex structures of uncertain systems and the knowledge-based computer systems with the distributed knowledge. Each part of the complex system is described by a relational knowledge representation with unknown parameters characterized by an expert in the form of certainty distributions [1,6,15].

7   Conclusions

The uncertain variables have been proved to be a convenient tool for handling the decision problems based on an uncertain knowledge given by an expert in the form of certainty distributions. The problems and methods described in the paper for static (memoryless) systems have been extended to systems described by a dynamical knowledge representation. The formalism of the uncertain variables and its application in a wide spectrum of uncertain systems (complexes) of operations, systems with distributed knowledge, pattern recognition and various practical systems) has been used as a basis for a uniform description of analysis and decision making in uncertain systems, presented in the book [12], where one can find the indications of new problems and perspectives in this area.

References

1. Bubnicki, Z.: Knowledge validation and updating in a class of uncertain distributed knowledge systems. Proc. of 16th IFIP World Computer Congress. Intelligent Information Processing. Publishing House of Electronics Industry, Beijing (2000) pp 516–523
2. Bubnicki, Z.: Uncertain variables and their applications for a class of uncertain systems. International Journal of Systems Science **32** (2001) 651–659
3. Bubnicki, Z.: Uncertain variables and their application to decision making. IEEE Trans. on SMC, Part A: Systems and Humans **31** (2001) 587-596
4. Bubnicki, Z.: Uncertain Logics, Variables and Systems. Springer Verlag, Berlin London, N. York (2002)
5. Bubnicki, Z.: Learning process in a class of computer integrated manufacturing systems with parametric uncertainties. Journal of Intelligent Manufacturing **13** (2002) 409–415
6. Bubnicki, Z.: Application of uncertain variables to decision making in a class of distributed computer systems. Proc. of 17th IFIP World Computer Congress. Intelligent Information Processing. Kluwer Academic Publishers, Norwell, MA (2002) 261–264
7. Bubnicki, Z.: Stability and stabilization of discrete systems with random and uncertain parameters. Proc. of 15th IFAC World Congress. Pergamon, Oxford, vol E (2003) pp 193–198
8. Bubnicki, Z.: Application of uncertain variables to a project management under uncertainty. Systems Science, **29** (2003)
9. Bubnicki, Z., Szala, M.: Application of uncertain and random variables to knowledge-based pattern recognition. Proc. of 16th International Conference on Systems Engineering. Coventry University, Coventry, UK, vol 1 (2003) pp 100-105
10. Bubnicki, Z.: Application of uncertain variables in a class of control systems with uncertain and random parameters. Proc. of the European Control Conference. Cambridge, UK (2003)
11. Bubnicki, Z.: Application of uncertain variables to task and resource distribution in complex computer systems. Computer Aided Systems Theory. Lecture Notes in Computer Science. Springer Verlag, Berlin, Heidelberg (2003) 38–49
12. Bubnicki, Z.: Analysis and Decision Making in Uncertain Systems. Springer Verlag, Berlin, London, N. York (2004)
13. Bubnicki, Z.: Application of uncertain variables to learning process in knowledge-based decision systems. Proc. of 9th International Symposium on Artificial Life and Robotics. Oita, Japan, vol 2 (2004) 396–399
14. Bubnicki, Z.: Knowledge-based and learning control systems. Control Systems, Robotics and Automation, Encyclopedia of Life Support Systems (EOLSS), Developed under the auspices of the UNESCO. Eolss Publishers, Oxford, UK [http://www.eolss.net]
15. Bubnicki, Z.: Application of uncertain variables and learning algorithms in a class of distributed knowledge systems. Proc. of 18th IFIP World Computer Congress. Artificial Intelligence Applications and Innovations. Kluwer Academic Publishers, Norwell, MA (2004)

16. Bubnicki, Z.: Uncertain variables and learning process in an intelligent transportation system with production units. Proc. of 5th IFAC Symposium on Intelligent Autonomous Vehicles. Lisbon, Portugal (2004) (in press)
17. Orski, D.: Quality analysis and adaptation in control systems with a controller based on uncertain variables. Proc. of 16th International Conference on Systems Engineering. Coventry University, Coventry, UK, vol 2 (2003) pp 525-530
18. Turowska, M.: Application of uncertain variables to stability analysis and stabilization for ATM ABR congestion control systems. Proc. of the International Conference on Enterprise Information Systems. INSTICC Press, Porto, Portugal (2004)

Blind Signal Separation and Extraction: Recent Trends, Future Perspectives, and Applications

Andrzej Cichocki[1] and Jacek M. Zurada[2]

[1] Riken, Brain Science Institute, Wako, JAPAN,
cia@brain.riken.jp,
http://www.bsp.brain.riken.jp
[2] University of Louisville, USA
jmzura02@athena.louisville.edu,
http://ci.uofl.edu/zurada/

Abstract. Blind source separation (BSS) and related methods, e.g., ICA are generally based on a wide class of unsupervised learning algorithms and they found potential applications in many areas from engineering to psychology and neuroscience. The recent trends in BSS is to consider problems in the framework of probabilistic generative and tree structured graphical models and exploit a *priori* knowledge about true nature and structure of latent (hidden) variables or sources such as statistical independence, spatio-temporal decorrelation, sparseness, smoothness or linear predictability. The goal of BSS can be considered as estimation of sources and parameters of a mixing system or more generally as finding a new reduced or compressed representation for the observed (sensor) data that can be interpreted as physically meaningful coding or blind source extraction. The key issue is to find a such transformation or coding (linear or nonlinear) which has true physical meaning and interpretation. In this paper, we briefly review some promising linear models and approaches to blind source separation and extraction using various criteria and assumptions.

1 Introduction

A fairly general blind signal separation (BSS) problem often referred as blind signal decomposition or blind signal extraction can be formulated as follows (see Fig.1 (a)). We observe records of sensor signals $\mathbf{x}(t) = [x_1(t), \ldots, x_m(t)]^T$ from a MIMO (multiple-input/multiple-output) nonlinear dynamical system. The objective is to find an inverse system, termed a reconstruction system, neural network or an adaptive inverse system, if it exists and is stable, in order to estimate the primary source signals $\mathbf{s}(t) = [s_1(t), \ldots, s_n(t)]^T$. This estimation is performed on the basis of only the output signals $\mathbf{y}(t) = [y_1(t), \ldots, y_n(t)]^T$ and sensor signals. Preferably, the inverse system should be adaptive in such a way that it has some tracking capability in non-stationary environments. Instead of estimating the source signals directly, it is sometimes more convenient to identify

L. Rutkowski et al. (Eds.): ICAISC 2004, LNAI 3070, pp. 30–37, 2004.
© Springer-Verlag Berlin Heidelberg 2004

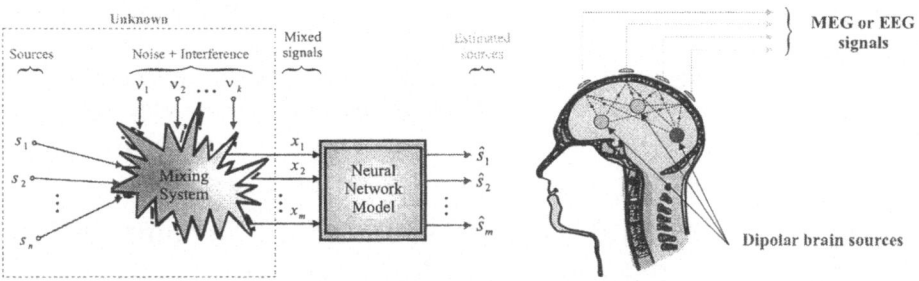

Fig. 1. (a)Block diagrams illustrating blind signal separation or blind identification problem, (b) Such model is exploited in non-invasive multi-sensor recording of brain activity using EEG or MEG.

an unknown mixing and filtering dynamical system first (e.g., when the inverse system does not exist or the number of observations is less than the number of source signals, i.e., $m < n$) and then estimate source signals implicitly by exploiting some *a priori* information about the system and applying a suitable optimization procedure. The problems of separating or extracting the original source waveforms from the sensor array, without knowing the transmission channel characteristics and the sources can be expressed briefly as a number of related BSS or blind signal decomposition problems such Independent Component Analysis (ICA) (and its extensions: Topographic ICA, Multidimensional ICA, Kernel ICA, Tree-dependent Component Analysis, Multiresolution Subband Decomposition -ICA), Sparse Component Analysis (SCA), Sparse PCA, Non-negative Matrix Factorization (NMF), Smooth Component Analysis (SmoCA), Parallel Factor Analysis (PARAFAC), Time-Frequency Component Analyzer (TFCA) and Multichannel Blind Deconvolution (MBD) [1]-[14].

The mixing and filtering processes of the unknown input sources $s_j(k)$ may have different mathematical or physical models, depending on the specific applications [1,2,3]. Most of linear BSS models in the simplest forms can be expressed algebraically as some specific problems of matrix factorization: Given observation (often called sensor or data) matrix $\mathbf{X} = [\mathbf{x}(1), \ldots, \mathbf{x}(N)] \in \mathbb{R}^{m \times N}$ perform the matrix factorization:

$$\mathbf{X} = \mathbf{AS} + \mathbf{E}, \tag{1}$$

or equivalently $\mathbf{x}(k) = \mathbf{As}(k)$, $(k = 1, 2, \ldots, N)$,where N is the number of available samples, m is the number of observations, n is the number of sources, $\mathbf{A} \in \mathbb{R}^{m \times n}$ represents the unknown basis data matrix or mixing matrix (depending on applications), $\mathbf{E} \in \mathbb{R}^{m \times N}$ is an unknown matrix representing errors or noise and matrix $\mathbf{S} = [\mathbf{s}(1), \ldots, \mathbf{s}(N)] \in \mathbb{R}^{n \times N}$ contains the corresponding hidden components that give the contribution of each basis vectors. Usually these components represent unknown source signals with specific temporal structures, or statistical properties. The matrices have usually clear physical meanings. For example, the rows of matrix $\mathbf{S}$ that represent of sources should be sparse as possible for SCA or statistically mutually independent as possible for ICA.

Often it is required that estimated components are smooth (SmoCA) or take only nonnegative values (NMF) or values with specific constraints [6,5].

In some applications the mixing matrix $\mathbf{A}$ is non-square or ill-conditioned or even singular. In such cases the special neural network models and algorithms should be applied [3].

2 Beyond ICA: Multiresolution Subband Decomposition – Independent Component Analysis

Independent component analysis (ICA) can be considered an extension of principal component analysis (PCA) or Factor Analysis (FA) [1,2]. In ICA, the aim is to process a number of measured signal vectors $\mathbf{X}$ and extract a set of statistically independent vectors $\mathbf{Y} = \mathbf{WX}$ which are estimates of some unknown source signals $\mathbf{S}$ (under strong assumption that they are mutually independent) which have been linearly mixed together via a mixing matrix $\mathbf{A}$ to form the observed input data. ICA seeks to ensure maximum independence, typically by minimizing or maximizing the higher order moments or cumulants of the outputs.

For example, for signals corrupted by additive Gaussian noise, as measure of statistical independence, we can use higher order matrix cumulants in the for of the following objective function [1]:

$$J(\mathbf{y}, \mathbf{W}) = -\frac{1}{2} \log | \det(\mathbf{WW}^T)| - \frac{1}{1+q} \sum_{i=1}^{n} |C_{1+q}(y_i)|, \qquad (2)$$

where $C_q(y_1)$ denotes the q-order cumulants of the signal y_i and $\mathbf{C}_{p,q}(\mathbf{y}, \mathbf{y})$ denotes the cross-cumulant matrix whose elements are $[\mathbf{C}_{pq}(\mathbf{y}, \mathbf{y})]_{ij} = Cum(\underbrace{y_i, y_i, \ldots, y_i}_{p}, \underbrace{y_j, y_j, \ldots, y_j}_{q})$. The first term in the objective function assures that the determinant of the global separating matrix will not approach zero. By including this term, we avoid the trivial solution $y_i = 0, \ \forall i$. The second terms force the output signals to be as far as possible from Gaussianity, since the higher order cumulants are a natural measure of non-Gaussianity and they will vanish for Gaussian signals. It can be shown that by minimizing the cost function using the natural gradient approach, we can derive the following equivariant iterative algorithm

$$\Delta\mathbf{W}(l) = \mathbf{W}(l+1) - \mathbf{W}(l) = \eta_l \left[\mathbf{I} - \mathbf{C}_{1,q}(\mathbf{y}, \mathbf{y})\, \mathbf{S}_{q+1}(\mathbf{y}) \right] \mathbf{W}(l),$$

where $\mathbf{S}_{q+1}(\mathbf{y}) = \text{sign}(\text{diag}(\mathbf{C}_{1,q}(\mathbf{y}, \mathbf{y})))$.

Despite the success of using standard ICA in many applications, the basic assumptions of ICA may not hold for some source signals hence some caution should be taken when using standard ICA to analyze real world problems, especially in biomedical signal processing. In fact, by definition, the standard ICA algorithms are not able to estimate statistically dependent original sources, that is, when the independence assumption is violated. In this section, we will discuss briefly one of powerful extension and generalization of ICA called Multiresolution Sub-band Decomposition ICA (MSD-ICA) which relaxes considerably the assumption regarding mutual independence of primarily sources [1,5]. The key idea in this approach is the assumption that the wide-band source signals can be dependent, however only some of their narrow band subcomponents are independent. In other words, we assume that each unknown source can be modelled or represented as a sum of narrow-band sub-signals (sub-components): $s_i(k) = s_{i1}(k) + s_{i2}(k) + \cdots + s_{iK}(k)$. Let us assume that only a certain set of sub-components are independent. Provided that for some of the frequency sub-bands (at least one, say j) all sub-components, say $\{s_{ij}(k)\}_{i=1}^n$, are mutually independent or temporally decorrelated, then we can easily estimate the mixing or separating system under condition that these sub-bands can be identified by some *a priori* knowledge or detected by some self-adaptive process. For this purpose, we simply apply any suitable standard ICA/BSS algorithm, however not for all available raw sensor data but only for suitably pre-processed (e.g., sub-band filtered) sensor signals. The basic concept in the MSD-ICA is to divide the sensor signal spectra into their subspectra or sub-bands, and then to treat those subspectra individually for the purpose at hand. The sub-band signals can be ranked and further processed independently. By applying any standard ICA/BSS algorithm for specific sub-bands and raw sensor data, we obtain sequence of separating matrices $\mathbf{W}_0, \mathbf{W}_1, \ldots, \mathbf{W}_K$, where $\mathbf{W}_0$ is the separation matrix from the original data $\mathbf{x}$ and $\mathbf{W}_j$ is the separating matrix from preprocessing sensor data $\mathbf{x}_j$ in j-th sub-band. In order to identify for which sub-bands corresponding source subcomponents are independent, we propose to compute the matrices $\mathbf{G}_{jq} = \mathbf{W}_j \mathbf{W}_q^{-1}$, $\forall j \neq q$, where $\mathbf{W}_q$ is estimating separating matrix for q-th sub-band. If subcomponents are mutually independent for at least two sub-bands, say for the sub-band j and sub-band q, then the global matrix $\mathbf{W}_j \mathbf{W}_q^{-1} = \mathbf{P}_{jq}$ will be generalized permutation matrix with only one nonzero (or dominated) element in each row and each column. This follows from the simple observation that in such case the both matrices $\mathbf{W}_j$ and $\mathbf{W}_q$ represent inverses (for $m = n$) of the same mixing matrix $\mathbf{A}$ (neglecting nonessential scaling and permutation ambiguities). In this way, we can blindly identify essential information for which frequency sub-bands the source subcomponents are independent and we can easily identify correctly the mixing matrix. Furthermore, the same concept can be used to estimate blindly the performance index and to compare performance of various ICA algorithms, especially for large scale problems. In the preprocessing stage we can use any linear transforms, especially, more sophisticated methods, such as block transforms, multirate sub-band filter bank or wavelet transforms, can be applied. We can extend and generalize further this concept by performing the decomposition of sensor signals in a composite time-frequency domain rather than in frequency sub-bands as such. This naturally leads to the concept of wavelets packets (sub-band hierarchical trees) and to block transform packets [1,10,11]. Such preprocessing techniques has been implemented in ICALAB [8].

3   Sparse Component Analysis and Sparse Signal Representations

Sparse Component Analysis (SCA) and sparse signals representations (SSR) arise in many scientific problems, especially, where we wish to represent signals of interest by using a small (or sparse) number of basis signals from a much larger set of signals, often called dictionary. Such problems arise also in many applications such as electro-magnetic and biomagnetic inverse problems (EEG/MEG), feature extraction, filtering, wavelet denoising, time-frequency representation, neural and speech coding, spectral estimation, direction of arrival estimation, failure diagnosis and speed-up processing [1,13].

In opposite to ICA where the mixing matrix and source signals are estimated simultaneously the SCA is usually a multi stage procedure. In first stage we need to find a suitable linear transformation which guarantee that sources in the transformed domain are sufficiently sparse. Typically, we represent the observed data in the time-frequency domain using wavelets package. In the next step, we estimate the columns a_i of the mixing matrix $\mathbf{A}$ using a sophisticated hierarchical clustering technique. This step is the most difficult and challenging task since it requires to identify precisely intersections of all hyperplanes on which observed data are located [13,12]. In the last step, we estimate sparse sources using for example a modified robust linear programming (LP), quadratic programming (QP) or semi-definite programming (SDP) optimization. The big advantage of SCA is its ability to reconstruct of original sources even if the number of observations (sensors) is smaller than number of sources under certain weak conditions [12].

We can state the subset selection sub-problem as follows: Find an optimal subset of $r << n$ columns from the matrix $\mathbf{A}$ which we denote by $\mathbf{A}_r \in \mathbb{R}^{m \times r}$ such that $\mathbf{A}_r \mathbf{s}_{r*} \cong \mathbf{x}$, or equivalently $\mathbf{A}\mathbf{s}_* + \mathbf{e}_r = \mathbf{x}$, where $\mathbf{e}_r$ represents some residual error vector which norm should below some threshold. The problem consists often not only in estimating the sparse vector $\mathbf{s}_*$ but also correct or optimal sparsity profile that is the sparsity index r, that is detection the number of sources.

Usually, we have interest in sparsest and unique representation, i.e., it is necessary to find solution having the smallest possible number of non-zero-components. The problem can be reformulated as the following robust optimization problem:

$$(P_\rho) \quad J_\rho(\mathbf{s}) = \|\mathbf{s}\|_\rho = \sum_{j=1}^{n} \rho(s_j) \quad \text{s. t.} \quad \mathbf{A}\mathbf{s} = \mathbf{x}, \tag{3}$$

where $\mathbf{A} \in \mathbb{R}^{m \times n}$, (usually with $n >> m$) and $\|\mathbf{s}\|_\rho$ suitably chosen function which measures the sparsity of the vector $\mathbf{s}$. It should be noted the sparsity measure does not need be necessary a norm, although we use such notation. For example, we can apply Shannon, Gauss or Renyi entropy or normalized kurtosis as measure of the (anti-)sparsity [1,7,10]. In the standard form, we use l_p-norm with $0 \le p \le 1$. Especially, l_0 quasi-norm attract a lot of attention since it ensures sparsest representation [13,10]. Unfortunately, such formulated problem

(3) for l_p-norm with $p < 1$ is rather very difficult, especially for $p = 0$ it is NP-hard, so for a large scale problem it is numerically untractable. For this reason, we often use Basis Pursuit (BP) or standard Linear Programming (LP) for $\|\dot{\mathbf{s}}\|_\rho = \|\mathbf{s}\|_1$, with $\rho = p = 1$.

In practice, due to noise and other uncertainty (e.g. measurement errors) the system of linear underdetermined equations should not be satisfied precisely but with some prescribed tolerance (i.e., $\mathbf{A}\,\mathbf{s} \cong \mathbf{x}$ in the sense that $\|\mathbf{x} - \mathbf{A}\,\mathbf{s}\|_q \le \varepsilon$). From the practical point of view as well as from a statistical point of view, it is convenient and quite natural to replace the exact constraints $\mathbf{x} = \mathbf{A}\,\mathbf{s}$ by the constraint $\|\mathbf{x} - \mathbf{A}\,\mathbf{s}\|_q \le \varepsilon$, where choice of l_q-norm depends on distribution of noise and specific applications. For noisy and uncertain data we should to use a more flexible and robust cost function (in comparison to the standard (P_ρ) problem) which will be referred as Extended Basis Pursuit Denoising $(EBPD)$:

$$(EBPD) \qquad J_{q,\rho}(\mathbf{s}) = \|\mathbf{x} - \mathbf{A}\,\mathbf{s}\|_q^q + \alpha\,\|\mathbf{s}\|_\rho, \qquad (4)$$

There are several possible basic choices for l_q and sparsity criteria ($\|\mathbf{s}\|_\rho = \|\mathbf{s}\|_p$) For example, for the uniform (Laplacian) distributed noise we should choose l_∞-Chebyshev norm (l_1-norm). Some basic choices of ρ (for $l_q = 2$) are $\rho = 0$ (minimum l_0 quasi norm or atomic decomposition related with the matching pursuit (MP) and FOCUSS algorithm), $\rho = 1$ (basis pursuit denoising) and $\rho = 2$ (ridge regression) [7,10]. The optimal choice of ρ norms depends on distribution of noise in sparse components. For example, for noisy components, we can use robust norms such as Huber function defined as $\|\mathbf{s}\|_{\rho_H} = \sum_i \rho_H(s_i)$, where $\rho_H(s_i) = s_i^2/2$ if $|s_i| \le \beta$ and $\rho_H(s_i) = \beta\,|s_i| - \beta^2/2$ if $|s_i| > \beta$, and/or epsilon norm defined as $\|\mathbf{s}\|_\varepsilon = \sum_j |s_j|_\varepsilon$ where $|s_j|_\varepsilon = \max\{0,\ (|s_j| - \varepsilon)\}$.

The practical importance of the $EBPD$ approach in comparison to the standard LP or BP approach is that the $EPBD$ allows for treating the presence of noise or errors due to mismodeling. Moreover, using the $EBPD$ approach, we have possibility to adjust the sparsity profile (i.e., adjust the number of non-zero components) by tuning the parameter α. In contrast, by using the LP approach we do not have such option. Furthermore, the method can be applied both for overcomplete and undercomplete models.

3.1 Applications and Future Perspectives

BSS and its related methods are promising in many application, especially data analysis and data mining including: redundancy reduction, denoising, feature extraction, preprocessing for various classification and recognition tasks. Furthermore, BSS approach is useful in modelling higher mechanisms of the brain, including modelling of olfactory bulb, auditory system, selective attention and sparse coding [1,9,14]. Moreover, the BSS methods may help to solve some fundamental problems in data analysis : What is valuable information in the observed multi-sensory, multi-modal data and what is only noise or interference? How can the observed (sensor) data be transformed into features characterizing the system in a reasonable way? What are the latent variables real properties and how can we get information about them?

For example, ICA approach has been applied successfully for the elimination of artifacts and noise from EEG/MEG and fMRI data including eye movements, eye-blinks, electrical activity of the heart, muscle artifacts and environmental noise efficiently. However, most of the methods require manual detection, classification of interference components and the estimation of the cross-correlation between independent components and the reference signals corresponding to specific artifacts [1,2]. One important problem is how to automatically detect, extract and eliminate noise and artifacts, especially for high density array EEG system for which the number of components is large.

Another relevant problem is how to extract and classify the true "brain sources". In fact, the BSS methods is a promising approach for the blind extraction of useful signals from the high density array of EEG/MEG data. The EEG/MEG data can be first decomposed into useful signal and noise subspaces using standard techniques like local and robust PCA or Factor Analysis (FA) and nonlinear adaptive filtering. Next, we apply BSS algorithms to decompose the observed signals (signal subspace) into specific components. The BSS approaches enable us to project each component (independent "brain source") onto an activation map at the skull level. For each activation map, we can apply an EEG/MEG source localization procedure, looking only for a single equivalent dipole (or brain source) per map. By localizing multiple sources independently, we can dramatically reduce the computational complexity and increase the likelihood of efficiently converging to the correct and reliable solution.

The decomposition is usually based on the underlying assumption of statistical independence between the activation of different cell assemblies involved. An alternative criterion for the decomposition is sparsity, temporal predictability or smoothness of estimated components. These approaches lead to interesting and promising new ways of investigating and analyzing brain data and develop new hypotheses how the neural assemblies communicate and process information. This is actually an extensive and potentially promising research area. However, these approaches still remain to be validated at least experimentally.

4   Discussion and Conclusions

The BSS algorithms, especially ICA, SCA, NMF techniques are relative simple optimization procedures, but may fail to find desirable signals if model or some assumptions are not precisely satisfied. The successful and efficient use of these techniques strongly depends on *a priori* knowledge, selection of appropriate model and criteria and common sense. Furthermore, the appropriate use of the preprocessing and postprocessing tools in many cases allows to reconstruct (recover) the original sources and to estimate basis or mixing matrices, even if the original sources are not completely independent or sparse. In fact, the preprocessing of data and postprocessing of models are very essential and they can improve considerably performance of the standard algorithms, especially ICA, NMF and SCA [1,8,12]. In this paper we have discussed several extensions and modifications of the standard algorithms for ICA and SCA, where various constraints or preprocessing are imposed in order to satisfy physical conditions. The optimization approach is quite flexible and general in the sense that can be applied for noisy data with various distributions of noise. The optimal solutions can be obtained by converting the optimization problems to the standard procedures: LP, QP, SDP (Semi-definite Program) or SOCP (Second Order Cone Program) and solved by powerful and efficient algorithms.

References

1. A. Cichocki and S. Amari, *Adaptive Blind Signal and Image Processing*, John Wiley, Chichester, May 2003 (Revised and corrected edition).
2. A. Hyvärinen, J. Karhunen, and E. Oja, *Independent Component Analysis*, John Wiley, New York, 2001.
3. Y. Li, J Wang, and J.M. Zurada, "Blind extraction of singularly mixed source signals", IEEE Transactions on Neural Networks, vol. 11, No. 6, November 2000, pp. 1413-1422.
4. Y. Tan, J. Wang, and J.M. Zurada, "Nonlinear blind source separation using a radial basis function network" , IEEE Transactions on Neural Networks, vol. 11, No. 1, January 2001, pp. 124-134.
5. A. Cichocki and P. Georgiev P, "Blind source separation algorithms with matrix constraints", IEICE Transactions on Information and Systems, vol. E86-A, No.3, March 2003, pp.522-531.
6. J. S. Lee, D. D. Lee, S. Choi, K. S. Park, and D. S. Lee. Non-negative matrix factorization of dynamic images in nuclear medicine. IEEE Medical Imaging Conference, San Diego, California, November 4-10, 2001.
7. K. Kreutz-Delgado, J.F. Murray, B.D. Rao, K. Engan, T.-W. Lee and T.J. Sejnowski, "Dictionary learning algorithms for sparse representation", Neural Computation, vol.15, No. 2, pp. 349-396, 2003.
8. A. Cichocki, S. Amari, K. Siwek, T. Tanaka et al. (2002) "ICALAB Toolboxes for Signal and Image Processing", *www.bsp.brain.riken.go.jp*
9. Hyung-Min Park, Soo-Young Lee, "Adaptive moise canceling based on independent component analysis", Electronics Letters, Vol. 38, No. 5, Vol. 7, pp. 832 - 833, 2002.
10. M. Zibulevsky, P. Kisilev, Y.Y. Zeevi, and B.A. Pearlmutter, "Blind source separation via multinode sparse representation", In Advances in Neural Information Processing Systems, (NIPS2001), Vol. 14. Morgan Kaufmann, pp. 185–191.
11. F. R. Bach, M. I. Jordan, "Beyond independent components: trees and clusters", Journal of Machine Learning Research, 4, 1205-1233, 2003.
12. P. Goergiev, F. Theis, A. Cichocki and H. Bakrdjian, "Sparse component nalysis: A new tool for data mining", Int Conf. on Data Mining in Biomedicine, Gainesville Fl. USA, Feb. 2004, (in print).
13. Y.Li, A. Cichocki and S. Amari, "Analysis of sparse representation and blind source separation", Neural Computation, vol.16, pp. 1-42, 2004.
14. M. Lysetskiy, A. Lozowski, and J.M. Zurada, J.M., "Temporal-to-spatial dynamic mapping, flexible recognition, and temporal correlations in an olfactory cortex model", Biological Cybernetics, vol. 87, Issue 1, 2002, pp. 58-67.

Visualization of Hidden Node Activity in Neural Networks: I. Visualization Methods

Włodzisław Duch

School of Computer Engineering, Nanyang Technological University, Singapore, and
Department of Informatics, Nicholaus Copernicus University, Grudziądzka 5, Toruń, Poland,
http://www.phys.uni.torun.pl/~duch

Abstract. Quality of neural network mappings may be evaluated by visual inspection of hidden and output node activities for the training dataset. This paper discusses how to visualize such multidimensional data, introducing a new projection on a lattice of hypercube nodes. It also discusses what type of information one may expect from visualization of the activity of hidden and output layers. Detailed analysis of the activity of RBF hidden nodes using this type of visualization is presented in the companion paper.

1 Introduction

Feedforward networks provide non-linear mappings $M(\mathbf{X}; \mathbf{W})$ that applied to complex feature space regions $\mathcal{X}$ convert them into localized (sometimes point-like) images of these regions, for $\mathbf{X} \in \mathcal{X}, M(\mathbf{X}; \mathbf{W}) = \mathbf{Y} \in \mathcal{Y}$. Although this is a common knowledge the mapping properties in classification tasks are almost never used, with focus being on network decisions or estimation of probabilities of decisions. Performance of a typical neural network is evaluated using such measures as the mean square error (MSE), or estimation of the overall classification accuracy. These measures are global averages over the whole feature space, estimated on the whole training or validation set. Detailed properties of multidimensional mappings learned by the hidden layers, and mappings from inputs to outputs that they provide, are regarded as inscrutable, possibly containing singularities and various kinks. Neural mappings may exhibit surprising behavior in novel situations and there is no simple way to find out what potential problems they may hide.

The state of the network, expressed by the values of the weights and biases, may be visualized using Hinton diagrams [1] displayed by some neural network simulators. These diagrams contain interesting information about the network and allow for identification of important connections and hidden nodes. They are not helpful to see what type of internal representations have developed for a given data set, or how well the network performs on some data. A few attempts to visualize the training process are restricted to network trajectories in the weight space ([2], Kordos and Duch, in print). The usefulness of visualization of network outputs has been shown recently [3]. The focus of this paper is on visualization of images created by the hidden layer of feedforward networks with localized functions.

L. Rutkowski et al. (Eds.): ICAISC 2004, LNAI 3070, pp. 38–43, 2004.
© Springer-Verlag Berlin Heidelberg 2004

For classification problems with K categories images of the training vectors may be displayed as a scatterogram in K-dimensional space. For $K > 3$ this cannot be displayed directly in one figure, but a linear projection, parallel coordinate representation or scatterograms for all pairs of outputs may be used. In the next section direct visualization methods are introduced, and a new projection on a lattice of hypercube nodes is described. This approach will be used to visualize patterns of activity of hidden neurons, displaying internal representations created during the learning process. In section three scatterograms of hidden node activities are advocated to reveal internal representations of networks. In the last section discussion and some remarks on the usefulness and further development of such visualization methods are given. Applications of these ideas to the visualization of the hidden layer activity, showing what type of information may be uncovered and how it can be used to improve the quality of neural solutions, are discussed in the companion paper. Because the use of color makes it easier to understand the figures the reader is advised to view the color PDF version of the figures available on-line [4].

2 How to Visualize?

Neural classifiers, committees and several other classification systems, map inputs first to at least one internal space $\mathcal{X} \to \mathcal{H}$, and from there to the output space, $\mathcal{H} \to \mathcal{Y}$. In case of feedforward neural networks with more than one hidden layer one internal space per layer $\mathcal{H}_k$ is defined. The training data set $\mathcal{T} = \{\mathbf{X}^{(i)}\}, i = 1 \ldots n$ is defined in N-dimensional input space, $\mathbf{X}_i \in \mathcal{X}, i = 1..N$. In this paper only vector mappings $H(\mathbf{X})$ between the input space $\mathcal{X}$, and N_H-dimensional internal (or hidden) space $\mathcal{H}$ are considered (see [3] for the total network mappings).

For two hidden nodes scatterograms showing for all vectors $\mathbf{X} \in \mathcal{T}$ their images $\mathbf{H}(\mathbf{X}) = [H_1(\mathbf{X}), H_2(\mathbf{X})]$ give full details of the internal representation of the training data. For three dimensions scatterograms are still useful, especially with the ability to rotate the point of view that is easy to implement. The $\mathbf{H}(\mathbf{X})$ values lie inside a unit cube; projecting this cube on a plane perpendicular to the $(1, 1, 1)$ diagonal shows vectors near the $(0, 0, 0)$ vertex (no activation of outputs) as overlapping with those near the $(1, 1, 1)$ vertex (all outputs fully active). This information may be added by scaling the size of the markers, depending on the distance of the point to the $(1, 1, 1)$ vertex [3]. Linear projections on any 3 independent planes preserves full 3D information. In particular 3 pairs of scatterograms (H_1, H_2), (H_1, H_3) and (H_2, H_3) may be used.

For $N_H > 3$ dimensions multiple scatterograms to view various 2D projections may show all information, but $N_H(N_H - 1)/2$ pairs of scatterograms are needed. First two PCA components calculated for the hypercube vertices (2^{n-1} points if $(0, 0, ...0)$ point is removed) define an interesting projection, but for more than 3 dimensions it hides important relations among hypercube vertices. For example, in 4 dimensions all points on the diagonal $a[1, 1, 1, 1]$ are mapped on the $(0, 0)$ point. This diagonal provides an interesting first direction $\mathbf{W}^{(1)}$ because projections of hypercube vertices $\mathbf{P}^{(i)}$ on this direction give the number of "1" bits, $Y_1 = \mathbf{W}^{(1)} \cdot \mathbf{P}^{(i)}$, thus clearly separating the vertices with different number of non-zero bits (incidentally, this provides a general solution to the n-bit parity problem if $\cos(\omega Y_1)$ is taken as the output function, where

ω is a single adaptive parameter). Projecting the vertices on the space orthogonal to the main diagonal $(1 - \mathbf{W}^{(1)}\mathbf{W}^{(1)T})\mathbf{P}^{(i)}$ and selecting the first PCA component for this data gives for some N_H an interesting second direction that maximizes variance.

For $N_H = 3$ this is not a good projections because pairs of vertices (1,0,0), (0,1,0), and (1,0,1), (0,1,1), overlap, but rotating the 3D plot is easy. For $N_H = 4$ the second direction is $\mathbf{W}^{(2)}$ =(−0.211, 0.789, -0.577, 0), and all vertices are clearly separated. Connecting vertices that differ on one bit leads to a lattice (Fig. 1), a non-planar graph representing the 4-dimensional hypercube. For $N_H = 5$ the hypercube has already 32 vertices. Using the same approach to generate the second direction results in several vertices that lie very close after the projection. Optimization of the average spacing leads to $\mathbf{W}^{(2)} = (−0.1, 0.2, −0.5, −0.33, 0.75)$, with all vertices clearly separated (Fig. 1). Lattice projection for 6 dimensions could also be used but with 64 vertices it is hardly legible. One solution could be to show only those parts of the lattice where data points are found, but it is clear that lattice projection is useful only for relatively small number of dimensions.

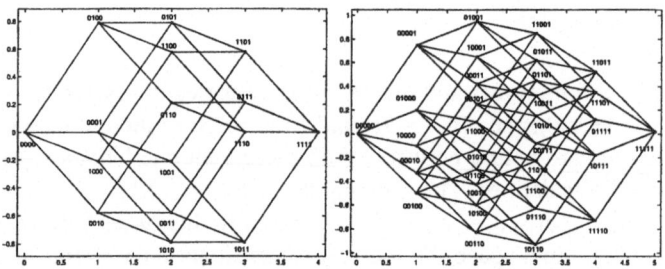

Fig. 1. Lattices corresponding to the vertices of 4 and 5-dimensional hypercubes, obtained by linear projection of their vertices.

Other interesting projection directions may be found, for example mapping the unit vectors of the hypercube axis into polygon vertices. For $N_H = 4$ projection directions $\mathbf{W}^{(1)} = 1/2(−1, 1, 1, −1)$; $\mathbf{W}^{(2)} = (−0.4, −0.6, 1, 1)$ give the mapping of hypercube from a different perspective, shown in Fig. 2. For $N_H = 5$ dimensions the first direction goes along the main diagonal $\mathbf{W}^{(1)} = (1, 1, 1, 1, 1)$, and $\mathbf{W}^{(2)} = 3/2(1.1, −1, 2/3, −2/3, 0.1)$, creating a view that shows all vertices at approximately the same distance from each other (Fig. 2).

Because many neural networks use small number of nodes specialized visualization methods are of considerable interest. If $N_H \leq 6$, scatterograms of the training data in hidden or the output space may be displayed using lattice or polygon projections. It is much easier to derive information from such images than from the analysis of numerical output. For more than 6 dimensions parallel coordinates, popular in bioinformatics, are frequently used, but in such visualization some loss of information is inevitable.

Other unsupervised visualization methods that may be used to create images of training data in the hidden and output space include ICA projections, multidimensional scaling (see [5, 6] and the references therein), and barycentric mappings using Gaussian

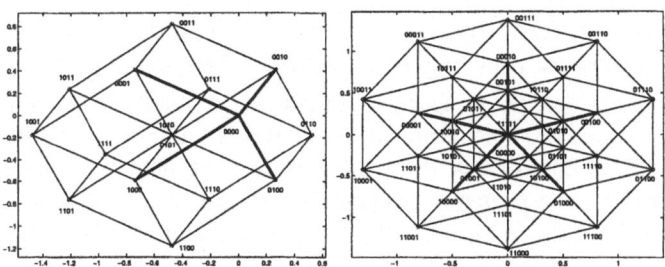

Fig. 2. Linear projection of hypercube vertices in 4 and 5-dimensions; the thick lines are the coordinate axes, ending in vertices that are on a square (left) and pentagon (right).

functions centered at the hypercube corners (Duch and Orlowski, unpublished; Pieknie-wski and Rybicki, in print).

3 What to Visualize?

Visualization of network outputs has been used recently [3] to understand the dynamics of the learning process and expose its pathologies, show under- and over-fitting effects, compare quality of different networks, display border vectors and outliers identifying input space regions where potential problems may arise, show differences in network solutions due to the regularization, early stopping and various optimization procedures, investigate stability of network classification under perturbation of original vectors, place new data samples in relation to the known data to estimate confidence in classification of a given sample. Here the main goal is to understand different internal representations created by the learning process.

In classification problems the training data is divided into labeled subsets $\mathcal{T}_k, k = 1 \ldots K$ corresponding to classes. Neural networks and other classification systems usually try to map each of the training subsets $\mathcal{T}_k$ into one of the K vertices that lie on the hypercube $[0, 0, .., 1, 0, ..0]$ coordinate axes. Hidden layer should map subsets $\mathcal{T}_k, k = 1 \ldots K$ of the training vectors from the feature (input) space creating images, or internal representations $\mathcal{H}_k$ of these subsets, in such a way that would make it easy to separate these images by the hyperplanes, based either on linear nodes or on perceptron nodes provided by the output layer. Without any loss of generality one may assume that all mappings are between hypercubes, with input data rescaled to N-dimensional hypercube, hidden data to N_H dimensional (for a single layer), and output data to the K-dimensional hypercube.

Networks with localized functions may map input $\mathbf{X} \in \mathcal{T}_k$ clusters into subsets $\mathcal{H}_k$ in the hidden space, allowing for reliable classification by inspection of the $H(\mathbf{X})$ images even in cases when linear separability cannot be achieved. Class-dependent distributions may of course overlap and then images $\mathcal{H}_k$ created by hidden layer will not make separable clusters. Visualization of these overlapping areas will identify the border vectors and the input space regions where only low confidence predictions are possible. Mappings provided by networks of different type may differ in many respects.

Neural networks may achieve the same classification in various ways; this is clearly seen visualizing the structure of internal representations of the training data $\mathcal{T}$.

For two-dimensional output space if the network outputs Y_i are independent (i.e. they are not forced to sum to 1) the desired answers may fall into $(1, 0)$ and $(0, 1)$ corners of a square in (Y_1, Y_2) coordinates. If the values of two outputs of the mapping are forced to sum to 1 to estimate posterior probabilities $p(C_i|\mathbf{X}; M) = \mathbf{Y}_i(\mathbf{X})$, images of all vectors will fall on a single line $Y_1 + Y_2 = 1$ connecting these two corners. For 2 or 3-dimensional feature spaces one may create a regular mesh of input points and look at their hidden and the output images to see the properties of the mapping. In higher number of dimensions this will be prohibitively expensive due to the exponentially growing number of points. High dimensional feature spaces are always almost empty, therefore such mapping should concentrate on the areas in the vicinity of the data. Scatterogram images of all training vectors, sometimes extended by adding noise to the training data, will show the character of mappings in the most important parts of the feature space, where the training vectors are concentrated.

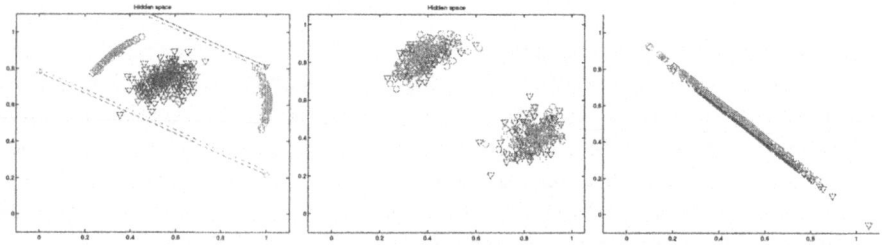

Fig. 3. Activity of two hidden Gaussian neurons for fuzzy XOR problem: good (left) and bad (middle) internal representations, give the same output image (right). Left plot shows lines based on the RBF output weights and biases.

In Fig. 3 a simple example of analysis based on scatterograms is shown for the noisy XOR problem (4 non-overlapping Gaussian clusters, 50 points each). RBF network [7] with two Gaussian nodes is not able to solve XOR problem, but in some runs perfect clusterization is observed in the hidden space. In other runs centers of the Gaussians are placed in a symmetrical way, leading to a complete overlap of the clusters from the two different classes in the internal space. In both cases RBF classification accuracy is close to the default 50% because the clusters are not linearly separable. The training algorithms aimed at reducing output errors is not able to improve internal representations – from the point of view of mean error it is as good as many other representations. The output weights calculated by the RBF program are shown as lines in the left subfigure. They are parallel, indicating that only biases are different and the output (Y_1, Y_2) values fall on the $Y_1 + Y_2 = 1$ line.

4   Discussion

Concentration on numbers makes evaluation of many aspects of neural network mappings rather difficult. In this paper lattice projection techniques have been introduced and the need for visualization of internal representations stressed. There is no reason why scatterogram images of the known data should not be displayed as a part of the neural network output. Such visualization may elucidate many aspects of neural network functions [3]. Visualization of internal representations may suggest different network architectures and training algorithms. Looking at Fig. 3 it is evident that paying more attention to the improvement of internal representations will increase accuracy of a network with the same architecture (2 hidden nodes) to 100%, instead of the default 50% that standard RBF training algorithm achieves [7].

Neural networks are used in various ways for data visualization. Self-Organized-Maps and other competitive learning algorithms, neural Principal and Independent Component Analysis algorithms, autoassociative feedforward networks and Neuroscale algorithms are all aimed at using neural algorithms to reduce dimensionality of the data or to display the data (for a summary of such visualization methods see [6]). All these methods may be used to visualize neural mappings, creating images of the hidden or output neuron activity for presentation of all training data, although in many cases linear projection techniques discussed here will be sufficient. More applications of visualization of the activity of hidden layers are presented in the companion paper.

References

1. Hinton, G.E., McClelland, J.L., Rumelhart, D.E. (1986): In: Parallel Distributed Processing, Vol. 1: Foundations, eds. D.E. Rumelhart, J.L. McClelland, MIT Press, Cambridge, pp. 77-109.
2. Gallagher, M., Downs, T. (2003): Visualization of Learning in Multi-layer Perceptron Networks using PCA. IEEE Transactions on Systems, Man and Cybernetics-Part B: Cybernetics, vol. 33, pp. 28-34.
3. Duch, W. (2003): Coloring black boxes: visualization of neural network decisions. Int. Joint Conference on Neural Networks, Portland, Oregon, 2003, Vol. 1, pp. 1735-1740.
4. PDF version of the color figures and the Matlab programs used in experiments are available at: http://www.phys.uni.torun.pl/kmk/publications.html
5. M. Jambu, *Exploratory and Multivariate Data Analysis*. Boston, MA: Academic Press, 1991.
6. A. Naud, *Neural and statistical methods for the visualization of multidimensional data.* PhD thesis, Dept of Informatics, Nicholaus Copernicus University, 2001; available at http://www.phys.uni.torun.pl/kmk/publications.html
7. C. Bishop, *Neural networks for pattern recognition*. Oxford: Clarendon Press, 1994.

Visualization of Hidden Node Activity in Neural Networks: II. Application to RBF Networks

Włodzisław Duch

School of Computer Engineering, Nanyang Technological University, Singapore, and
Department of Informatics, Nicholaus Copernicus University, Grudziądzka 5, Toruń, Poland,
http://www.phys.uni.torun.pl/~duch

Abstract. Scatterograms of images of training vectors in the hidden space help to evaluate the quality of neural network mappings and understand internal representations created by the hidden layers. Visualization of these representations leads to interesting conclusions about optimal architectures and training of such networks. The usefulness of visualization techniques is illustrated on parity problems solved with RBF networks.

1 Introduction

Understanding multidimensional mappings learned by neural networks is of primary importance. Visualization of network outputs has proved to be very useful in this respect [1]. In part I of this paper [2] visualization methods based on lattice projections have been introduced and the motivation for this work outlined. This paper is focused on understanding internal representations created by the hidden layer of RBF networks [3]. Two networks with the same mean square error and identical number of classification errors may create very different internal mappings of the data, and it has a strong influence on their generalization capabilities. Understanding what neural networks really do requires analysis of internal mappings, and visualization is the easiest way to achieve it.

Several examples using parity problems are presented to gain insight into internal representations that are created by RBF networks with Gaussian nodes. All results were generated using the Netlab package [4], that trains RBF networks using the maximum likelihood approach [3]. Since the use of color makes it easier to understand the figures the reader is advised to view the color PDF version of the figures available on-line [5]. Data is always scaled to unit hypercubes. Input, hidden and output hypercubes thus refer to the normalized feature space, space of hidden neuron activities, and the space of output nodes activities. In the next section the concept of admissible spaces is introduced, covering points in the hypercube representing internal activations that can be reached by network mappings. Section three shows some internal representations for parity problems. The last section contains short discussion.

2 Admissible Spaces

Setting the dispersion and other parameters determining localization of the RBF hidden nodes is very important. Network with two inputs, four hidden nodes, and two output

L. Rutkowski et al. (Eds.): ICAISC 2004, LNAI 3070, pp. 44–49, 2004.
© Springer-Verlag Berlin Heidelberg 2004

nodes has been trained on noisy XOR data (a Gaussian distribution with 0.1 variance centered at each of the 4 points is used to generate 99 additional points). For all input vectors **X** activity of the hidden nodes **H(X)** is mapped using 4-dimensional lattice projection [2] (Fig. 1, left column). The middle columns show the same information using parallel coordinate plots (each of the four **H(X)**$_i$ components is marked on the vertical axis and connected). The right column shows the values of two network outputs; they are on the line showing perfect correlation (see [2] for explanation).

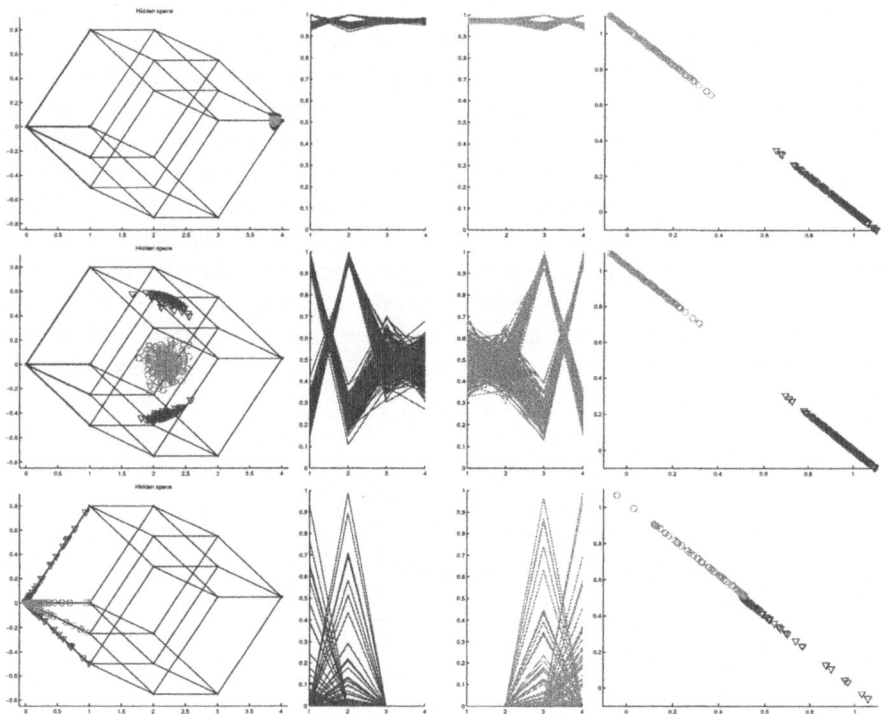

Fig. 1. RBF solution of the noisy XOR problem, using 4 Gaussians; for dispersion $\sigma = 7$ the map is clustered in the (1,1,1,1) corner of the hypercube (top row) for $\sigma = 1$ optimum separation is achieved (middle row), and for $\sigma = 1/7$ all activities are very small (bottom row). See text for description.

For very large dispersions of Gaussian nodes all input vectors always excite the four hidden nodes strongly and all images are near the (1,1,1,1) corner. Surprisingly though, it is still possible to achieve quite good separation (note large gap in the output plot); magnification of the area around the (1,1,1,1) corner reveals four well separated clusters. Additional experiments with more noisy data confirmed that degradation of accuracy even for very large node dispersions is rather small. Moderate node dispersions (middle row) creates images closer to the center of the lattice (middle row in Fig. 1) achieving largest separation. Parallel plots show in this case quite clear "signatures" of each cluster;

for the first class they may be roughly labeled as (1/3,1,1/2,1/2), and (1,1/3,1/2,1/2), and for the second class (1/2, 1/2, 1, 1/3) and (1/2, 1/2, 1/3, 1). For very small dispersions only those input vectors that are quite close to the centers of RBF nodes may excite one of these nodes in a stronger way, while other nodes show zero activity. As a result images of most vectors are very near to the hidden hypercube origin, and images of a few are along the coordinate axes.

It is intuitively obvious that the ability to learn is limited for too large or too small dispersions. With localized network nodes taking all $\mathbf{X}$ from the input space hypercube $\mathcal{X}$ the mapping $H(\mathbf{X})$ does not reach all points in the hidden space hypercube. For all $\mathbf{X} \in \mathcal{X}$ vectors mapped by $H(\mathbf{X}) \in \mathcal{A}_H \subset \mathcal{X}$ comprise a subspace that will be called here H-admissible subspace. The volume of the admissible spaces is always < 1. In low dimensional cases the RBF-admissible subspace of the hidden space may be visualized by generating the input points on a regular mesh and propagating such inputs through the trained network. Examples of $\mathcal{A}_H$ are shown in Fig. 2 for the Iris data and the XOR data. If functions are well localized the probability of finding an image of a randomly selected vector from high-dimensional input space will be the highest around the $(0..0)$ vertex. The shapes of the envelopes of $\mathcal{A}_H$ subspaces are difficult to determine even for the maps that are sums of Gaussian functions. Although topological considerations are very interesting they cannot be pursued here. Networks with largest volume of admissible spaces have largest capacity for learning, therefore maximization of this volume could be used to optimize dispersions or other parameters of localized functions.

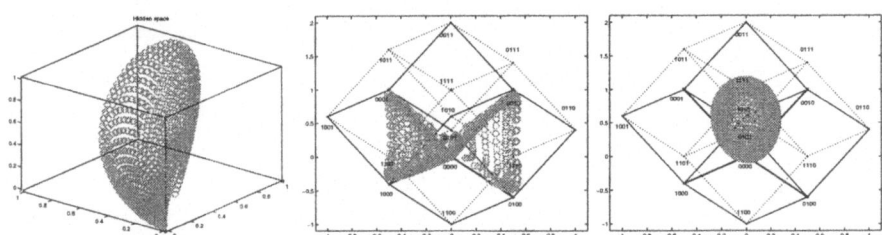

Fig. 2. A mesh spanning all possible input values mapped using RBF network with 3 hidden nodes trained on the Iris data (left) and with 4 nodes trained on the noisy XOR data with $\sigma = 0.25$ and $\sigma = 1.5$ shows the admissible subspace of hidden node activations.

3   Internal Representations in RBF Networks

RBF networks with localized response "cover" the input data regions where vectors from a single class dominate. The output layer provides a single reference hyperplane for each class. Non-linear perceptrons in MLPs define separating hyperplanes passing between clusters, but the role of linear outputs used in RBF networks is different. A strong output activation is achieved for vectors at a large distance from the hyperplane, therefore it is usually placed far from the data.

Parity problems have been studied in great details and are well suited for a discussion of internal representations. RBF solution to the noisy XOR problem is rather easy if 4 hidden nodes are used. In the low noise situation (variance 0.1) clusters are well localized and separated, and in the high noise situation (variance 0.25) some overlap between 4 clusters occurs. RBF network may create many different internal representations of this data. It is important to distinguish between representations that are permutationally equivalent and those that are really different. N_H hidden nodes may be assigned to the same number of clusters in $N_H!$ ways. To display only those plots that really differ the vector that leads to a maximum response of each hidden node is identified, and its class is determined. The nodes are then re-grouped according to the classes, and within each class according to their maximum response. Thus on the parallel plots usually the first dimension corresponds to the hidden node that responded in a strongest way to some vector from the first class. For the 4-node solution to the XOR problem 7 types of internal representations have been noticed, the most frequent solution corresponding to zero errors, and less common solutions with 8-75 errors.

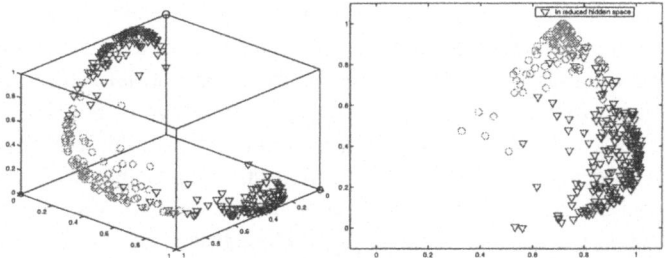

Fig. 3. Left: 3 hidden Gaussian nodes trained on the XOR data; right: reduced representation.

If 3 hidden nodes are used, activity of these nodes is mixed and simple correlation between the class labels and hidden node activity is lost (Fig. 3). Five different arrangements of clusters appear in different runs; they may be classified looking at the shapes of parallel plots. Two of them are rare, but the remaining three appear equally often. They are equivalent because the XOR problem has high symmetry. The training data images in the hidden space are not separable any more, and the classification error is at the default level (40-50%). This is a clear indication that the complexity of the model is too low to achieve separability.

The number of dimensions may be reduced from the number of clusters in the data to the number of classes $K = 2$ by summing the outputs from nodes that belong to each class (Fig. 3, right). This reduced hidden space still shows overlapping areas and well separated regions, although detailed information about the number and structure of clusters is lost. Mapping a new vector of unknown class will show how typical it is, how close to decision border or how far from the training data. This internal mapping is useful even if the number of nodes is too small to achieve output separability, showing the cluster structure and allowing for correct classification by visual inspection both at the level of hidden space images and the reduced hidden space images (Fig. 3).

3-bit parity problem is quite difficult to solve for RBF network. Visualization of the hidden space may help to understand why it is difficult to converge to an optimal solution. For training 10 vectors were generated around each corner of a cube (Gaussian noise

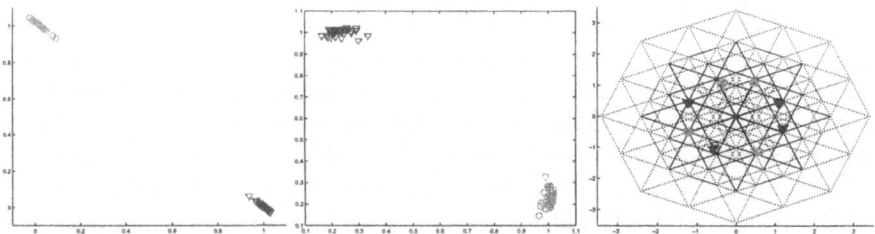

Fig. 4. 3 bit fuzzy parity problem solved with RBF network with 8 Gaussian nodes. Left: outputs show perfect separation; middle: reduced internal space shows perfect clustering; right: lattice projection show clusters around coordinate axes.

with σ =0.1), labeled with the parity of the corresponding binary string, and for test 20 vectors were generated, with σ =0.2. With 8 hidden nodes and optimal dispersion (about $\sigma = 0.5$) perfect solution may be easily found if each of the 8 clusters is mapped on one of the hypercube coordinate axis vertex in 8 dimensions. A good initialization procedure will easily find the corners of the cube and place a center of a Gaussian there, but many RBF programs (including Netalb [4]) rarely find the best initial configuration, and as a result give suboptimal solutions with accuracy in the range of 50-75%. Images in the hidden space are almost always well clustered but not separable, so a single hyperplane is usually not sufficient to find a solution. It may still be possible to obtain good results if more outputs are added and new output codes are defined. Visualization may help to design error-correcting output codes [6]. Reduced two-dimensional projections also show well-clustered images, and a number of methods, such as the nearest neighbor rule or linear classifiers, will give perfect classification.

RBF based on maximum likelihood training does not find a good solution for the 3-bit parity problem with less than 8 hidden nodes, but even with 2 or 3 hidden nodes perfect clusterization is observed in the hidden space. Images (Fig. 5) show one cluster per group of input nodes with the same number of "1" bits. They are not separable, and the accuracy in the output space is at the 50% level. These solutions are found in less than 10% of the runs and correspond to 38 or 40 errors (out of 80), while the most common solutions has 39 errors and creates two mixed clusters in the hidden space. Of course the training algorithm is designed to reduce the errors at the output level and not to find compact and well separated clusters in the hidden space. As a result even if the number of hidden nodes is sufficient to find an optimal, large margin solution, many inferior solutions may be generated. Visual inspection allows for comparison of these solutions. Positions of Gaussian functions may be correlated with the signatures of clusters displayed using parallel coordinates – in case of parity data it is easy (clusters are in hypercube's vertices), and in case of arbitrary data clusterization methods may be used first.

4   Discussion and Conclusions

RBF network may solve classification problems either by providing sufficient number of localized basis functions – but then generalization of the network will be poor – or by analyzing the image of the training data in the hidden space with something more

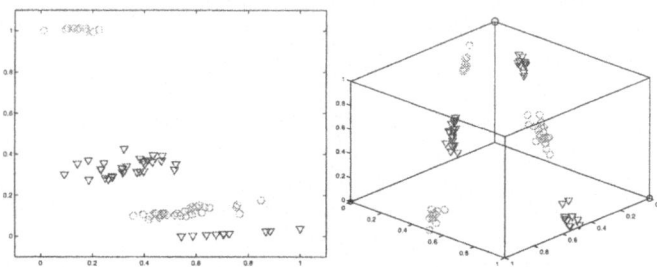

Fig. 5. 3 bit fuzzy parity problem solved with RBF network with 2 and 3 Gaussian nodes. Although errors are at the base rate level images in the internal space are well clustered.

sophisticated than a single hyperplane per class. Images of the training data in the hidden space, and in the reduced hidden space, carry important information which may be used to evaluate new data vectors placing them in known clusters and informing the user how typical these cases are, how close to cases from other classes, or perhaps give "don't know" answer. Most of this information is removed by the output layer that leaves just one information: how close to the decision hyperplane in the hidden space is the new case.

The need for modifications of the RBF algorithm that should improve convergence and retain more information is rather obvious, but there was no space to discuss it here. The main purpose of this article was to show visualization techniques that help to understand internal representations of networks. Representations in MLP networks are more complex and will be discussed in subsequent articles. As shown in [1] visualization of outputs is also very useful. There is no reason why neural networks users should restrict themselves to numerical outputs only.

References

1. Duch, W.: Coloring black boxes: visualization of neural network decisions. Int. Joint Conference on Neural Networks, Portland, Oregon, 2003, vol. I, pp. 1735-1740
2. Duch, W.: Visualization of hidden node activity in neural networks: I. Visualization methods. This volume (ICAISC 2004, Zakopane, Poland), in print.
3. Bishop, C.: *Neural networks for pattern recognition.* Oxford: Clarendon Press, 1994
4. Nabnay, I., Bishop, C.: NETLAB software, Aston University, Birmingham, UK, 1997 http://www.ncrg.aston.ac.uk/netlab/
5. Color figures are available at: http://www.phys.uni.torun.pl/kmk/publications.html
6. Dietterich, T.G., Bakiri, G.: Solving Multiclass Learning Problems via Error-Correcting Output Codes. J. of Artificial Intelligence Research, **2** (1995) 263–286

Rough Set Approach to Incomplete Data

Jerzy W. Grzymala-Busse

Department of Electrical Engineering and Computer Science, University of Kansas,
Lawrence, KS 66045, USA
and
Institute of Computer Science, Polish Academy of Sciences, 01-237 Warsaw, Poland
Jerzy@ku.edu
http://lightning.eecs.ku.edu/index.html

Abstract. In this paper incomplete data are assumed to be decision tables with missing attribute values. We discuss two main cases of missing attribute values: lost values (a value was recorded but it is unavailable) and "do not care" conditions (the original values were irrelevant). Through the entire paper the same calculus, based on computations of blocks of attribute-value pairs, is used. Complete data are characterized by the indiscernibility relations, a basic idea of rough set theory. Incomplete data are characterized by characteristic relations. Using characteristic relations, lower and upper approximations are generalized for incomplete data. Finally, from three definitions of such approximations certain and possible rule sets may be induced.

1 Introduction

Real-life data are frequently imperfect: data may be affected by uncertainty, vagueness, and incompleteness. In this paper we will concentrate on incomplete data. We will assume that data are presented in a decision table. In such a table, cases (entries, examples) are characterized by attribute values. Additionally, each case is labeled by a decision value, i.e., it was classified by an expert as being in a specific concept (class). Decision tables are usually considered a starting point for many data mining techniques, e.g., rule induction, tree generation, etc. One of the imperfections of decision tables is occurrence of conflicting cases, i.e., cases for which all attribute values are identical yet they belong to different concepts. Decision tables with conflicting cases are called inconsistent. Rough set theory offers one of the best approaches to inconsistent data sets, in which concepts are represented by pairs of lower and upper approximations. Typical rule induction algorithms for consistent decision tables, such as LEM2 [2], [3], may be applied to concept lower approximations, inducing thus certain rule sets, and to concept upper approximations, inducing possible rule sets.

Though computing concept lower and upper approximations for complete decision tables (in which all attribute values are given) is quite simple, it is more complicated for incomplete decision tables, i.e., tables with some missing attribute values.

L. Rutkowski et al. (Eds.): ICAISC 2004, LNAI 3070, pp. 50–55, 2004.
© Springer-Verlag Berlin Heidelberg 2004

Incompleteness of decision tables is caused by two main reasons. In the first an attribute value is lost, meaning that in the past it was given but currently it is unavailable. The second possibility is based on assumption that the original value was irrelevant, i.e., the case was classified on the basis of remaining, existing attribute values. Such missing attribute values will be called do not care conditions. We will assume that an incomplete decision table may be affected by both kinds of missing attribute values: lost values and do not care conditions. For incomplete decision tables there exist three definitions of lower and upper approximations.

Initially, decision tables with all missing attribute values that are lost were studied, within rough set theory, in [5], where two algorithms for rule induction from such data were presented. This approach was studied later, see, e.g., [9],[10] where the indiscernibility relation was generalized to describe such incompletely specified decision tables.

The first attempt to study "do not care" conditions using rough set theory was presented in [1], where a method for rule induction was introduced in which missing attribute values were replaced by all values from the domain of the attribute. "Do not care" conditions were also studied later, see, e.g., [6], [7], where the indiscernibility relation was again generalized, this time to describe incomplete decision tables with "do not care" conditions.

Through the entire paper we will use the same methodology based on computing blocks of attribute-value pairs. This methodology is not only very simple but also universal, it may be used for the entire analysis of a data set.

2   Complete and Incomplete Data

An example of a decision table is presented in Table 1. Rows of the decision table represent *cases*, while columns represent *variables*. The set of all cases is denoted by U. In Table 1, $U = \{1, 2, ..., 7\}$. Independent variables are called *attributes* and a dependent variable is called a *decision* and is denoted by d. The set of all attributes will be denoted by A. In Table 1, $A = \{Diameter, Color, Border\}$. Any decision table defines a function ρ that maps the direct product of U and A into the set of all values. For example, in Table 1, $\rho(1, Diameter) = large$. A decision table with completely specified function ρ will be called *completely specified*, or, simpler, *complete*. A decision table with an incompletely specified (partial) function ρ will be called *incompletely specified*, or *incomplete*.

For the rest of the paper we will assume that all decision values are specified, i.e., they are not missing. Also, we will assume that all missing attribute values are denoted either by "?" or by "*", lost values will be denoted by "?", "do not care" conditions will be denoted by "*". Additionally, we will assume that for each case at least one attribute value is specified.

An important tool to analyze decision tables is a block of the attribute-value pair. Let a be an attribute, i.e., $a \in A$ and let v be a value of a for some case. For complete decision tables if $t = (a, v)$ is an attribute-value pair then a *block* of t, denoted $[t]$, is a set of all cases from U that for attribute a have value v.

Table 1. An incomplete decision table

		Attributes		Decision
Case	Diameter	Color	Border	Disease
1	large	red	*	no
2	small	black	sharp	no
3	?	black	fuzzy	yes
4	large	*	fuzzy	yes
5	small	brown	sharp	no
6	small	brown	?	yes
7	large	red	sharp	no

For incomplete decision tables the definition of a block of an attribute-value pair must be modified. If for an attribute a there exists a case x such that $\rho(x, a) =?$, i.e., the corresponding value is lost, then the case x should not be included in any block $[(a, v)]$ for all values v of attribute a. If for an attribute a there exists a case x such that the corresponding value is a "do not care" condition, i.e., $\rho(x, a) = *$, then the corresponding case x should be included in all blocks $[(a, v)]$ for every possible value v of attribute a. This modification of the definition of the block of attribute-value pair is consistent with the interpretation of missing attribute values, lost and "do not care" condition. Thus, for Table 1

[(Diameter, large)] = {1, 4, 7},
[(Diameter, small)] = {2, 5, 6},
[(Color, red)] = {1, 4, 7},
[(Color, black)] = {2, 3, 4},
[(Color, brown)] = {4, 5, 6},
[(Border, fuzzy)] = {1, 3, 4}, and
[(Border, sharp)] = {1, 2, 5, 7}.

We define a *characteristic set* $KB(x)$ as the intersection of blocks of attribute-value pairs (a, v) for all attributes a from B for which $\rho(x, a)$ is specified and $\rho(x, a) = v$. For Table 1 and $B = A$,

$K_A(1) = \{1, 4, 7\} \cap \{1, 4, 7\} = \{1, 4, 7\}$,
$K_A(2) = \{2, 5, 6\} \cap \{2, 3, 4\} \cap \{1, 2, 5, 7\} = \{2\}$,
$K_A(3) = \{2, 3, 4\} \cap \{1, 3, 4\} = \{3, 4\}$,
$K_A(4) = \{1, 4, 7\} \cap \{1, 3, 4\} = \{1, 4\}$,
$K_A(5) = \{2, 5, 6\} \cap \{4, 5, 6\} \cap \{1, 2, 5, 7\} = \{5\}$,
$K_A(6) = \{2, 5, 6\} \cap \{4, 5, 6\} = \{5, 6\}$, and
$K_A(7) = \{1, 4, 7\} \cap \{1, 4, 7\} \cap \{1, 2, 5, 7\} = \{1, 7\}$.

The characteristic set $KB(x)$ may be interpreted as the smallest set of cases that are indistinguishable from x using all attributes from B and using a given interpretation of missing attribute values. Thus, $K_A(x)$ is the set of all cases that cannot be distinguished from x using all attributes. The *characteristic relation* $R(B)$ is a relation on U defined for $x, y \in U$ as follows:

$(x, y) \in R(B)$ *if and only if* $y \in K_B(x)$.

We say that $R(B)$ is *implied* by its characteristic sets $K_B(x)$, $x \in U$. The characteristic relation $R(B)$ is reflexive but—in general—does not need to be symmetric or transitive. Also, the characteristic relation $R(B)$ is known if we know characteristic sets $K(x)$ for all $x \in U$. In our example, R(A) = {(1, 1), (1, 4), (1, 7), (2, 2), (3, 3), (3, 4), (4, 1), (4, 4), (5, 5), (6, 5), (6, 6), (7, 1), (7, 7)}.

3   Lower and Upper Approximations

In this paper we suggest three different definitions of lower and upper approximations, following [4]. Let $R(B)$ be the characteristic relation of the incomplete decision table with characteristic sets $K(x)$, where $x \in U$. Lower and upper approximations may be defined by constructing both sets from singletons. We will call these definitions *singleton*. A singleton B-lower approximation of X is defined as follows:

$$\underline{B}X = \{x \in U | K_B(x) \subseteq X\}.$$

A singleton B-upper approximation of X is

$$\overline{B}X = \{x \in U | K_B(x) \cap X \neq \emptyset\}.$$

In our example of the decision table presented in Table 1 let us say that $B = A$. Then the singleton A-lower and A-upper approximations of the two concepts: {1, 2, 5, 7} and {3, 4, 6} are:

$\underline{A}\{1, 2, 5, 7\} = \{2, 5, 7\}$,
$\underline{A}\{3, 4, 6\} = \{3\}$,
$\overline{A}\{1, 2, 5, 7\} = \{1, 2, 4, 5, 6, 7\}$,
$\overline{A}\{3, 4, 6\} = \{1, 3, 4, 6\}$.

Any finite union of characteristic sets of B is called a *B-definable* set. Note that the sets {3} and {1, 3, 4, 6} are not A-definable. Therefore singleton approximations are not useful. The second method of defining lower and upper approximations for complete decision tables uses another idea: lower and upper approximations are unions of characteristic sets. There are two ways to do this. Using the first way, a *subset* B-lower approximation of X is defined as follows:

$$\underline{B}X = \cup\{K_B(x) | x \in U, K_B(x) \subseteq X\}.$$

A *subset* B-upper approximation of X is

$$\overline{B}X = \cup\{K_B(x) | x \in U, KB(x) \cap X \neq \emptyset\}.$$

Since any characteristic relation $R(B)$ is reflexive, for any concept X, singleton B-lower and B-upper approximations of X are subsets of the subset B-lower and B-upper approximations of X, respectively. For the same decision table, presented in Table 1, the subset A-lower and A-upper approximations are

$\underline{A}\{1, 2, 5, 7\} = \{1, 2, 5, 7\},$
$\underline{A}\{3, 4, 6\} = \{3, 4\},$
$\overline{A}\{1, 2, 5, 7\} = \{1, 2, 4, 5, 6, 7\},$
$\overline{A}\{3, 4, 6\} = \{1, 3, 4, 5, 6, 7\}.$

The second possibility is to modify the subset definition of lower and upper approximation by replacing the universe U from the subset definition by a concept X. A *concept* B-lower approximation of the concept X is defined as follows:

$$\underline{B}X = \cup\{K_B(x)|x \in X, K_B(x) \subseteq X\}.$$

Obviously, the subset B-lower approximation of X is the same set as the concept B-lower approximation of X. A concept B-upper approximation of the concept X is defined as follows:

$$\overline{B}X = \cup\{K_B(x)|x \in X, KB(x) \cap X \neq \emptyset\} = \cup\{K_B(x)|x \in X\}.$$

The concept B-upper approximation of X is a subset of the subset B-upper approximation of X. Besides, the concept B-upper approximations are truly the smallest B-definable sets containing X. For the decision presented in Table 1, the concept A-lower and A-upper approximations are

$\underline{A}\{1, 2, 5, 7\} = \{1, 2, 5, 7\}$
$\underline{A}\{3, 4, 6\} = \{3, 4\},$
$\overline{A}\{1, 2, 5, 7\} = \{1, 2, 4, 5, 7\},$
$\overline{A}\{3, 4, 6\} = \{1, 3, 4, 5, 6\}.$

Note that for complete decision tables, all three definitions of lower approximations, singleton, subset and concept, coalesce to the same definition. Also, for complete decision tables, all three definitions of upper approximations coalesce to the same definition. This is not true for incomplete decision tables, as our example shows. Similar three definitions of lower and upper approximations (for complete decision tables) were also studied in [11].

4 Conclusions

The paper shows a rough-set approach to incomplete data. Through the entire process, from the very beginning to the very end, the same methodology based on computing blocks of attribute-value pairs is utilized. In particular, a characteristic relation for incomplete decision tables, a generalization of the indiscernibility relation for a complete decision table, may be computed using attribute-value blocks. All three definitions of lower and upper approximations of concepts for incomplete decision tables are based on computation with attribute-value pair blocks. Finally, the LEM2 rule induction algorithm utilizes the same idea of attribute-value pair blocks. For complete decision tables all three characteristic relations are reduced to the indiscernibility relation. Note that the presented rough-set approach to incomplete data sets may be used not only for symbolic incomplete data but also for numerical attributes and definitions of missing attribute values different than lost values and do not care conditions. Preliminary experimental results on real-life data sets using the rough set approach to incomplete data show usefulness of this approach. Further experiments are currently conducted.

References

1. Grzymala-Busse, J.W.: On the unknown attribute values in learning from examples. Proc. of the ISMIS-91, 6th International Symposium on Methodologies for Intelligent Systems, Charlotte, North Carolina, October 16–19, 1991. Lecture Notes in Artificial Intelligence, vol. 542, Springer-Verlag, Berlin, Heidelberg, New York (1991) 368–377.
2. Grzymala-Busse, J.W.: LERS—A system for learning from examples based on rough sets. In Intelligent Decision Support. Handbook of Applications and Advances of the Rough Sets Theory, ed. by R. Slowinski, Kluwer Academic Publishers, Dordrecht, Boston, London (1992) 3–18.
3. Grzymala-Busse, J.W.: MLEM2: A new algorithm for rule induction from imperfect data. Proceedings of the 9th International Conference on Information Processing and Management of Uncertainty in Knowledge-Based Systems, IPMU 2002, Annecy, France, July 1-5, 2002, 243–250.
4. Grzymala-Busse, J.W.: Rough set strategies to data with missing attribute values. Workshop Notes, Foundations and New Directions of Data Mining, the 3-rd International Conference on Data Mining, Melbourne, FL, USA, November 19–22, 2003, 56–63.
5. Grzymala-Busse, J.W. and Wang, A.Y.: Modified algorithms LEM1 and LEM2 for rule induction from data with missing attribute values. Proc. of the Fifth International Workshop on Rough Sets and Soft Computing (RSSC'97) at the Third Joint Conference on Information Sciences (JCIS'97), Research Triangle Park, NC, March 2–5, 1997, 69–72.
6. Kryszkiewicz, M.: Rough set approach to incomplete information systems. Proceedings of the Second Annual Joint Conference on Information Sciences, Wrightsville Beach, NC, September 28–October 1, 1995, 194–197.
7. Kryszkiewicz,M.: Rules in incomplete information systems. *Information Sciences* **113** (1999) 271–292.
8. Pawlak, Z.: Rough Sets. Theoretical Aspects of Reasoning about Data. Kluwer Academic Publishers, Dordrecht, Boston, London (1991).
9. Stefanowski, J. and Tsoukias, A.: On the extension of rough sets under incomplete information. Proceedings of the 7th International Workshop on New Directions in Rough Sets, Data Mining, and Granular-Soft Computing, RSFDGrC'1999, Ube, Yamaguchi, Japan, November 8–10, 1999, 73–81.
10. Stefanowski, J. and Tsoukias, A.: Incomplete information tables and rough classification. *Computational Intelligence* **17** (2001) 545–566.
11. Yao, Y.Y.: Two views of the theory of rough sets in finite universes. *International J. of Approximate Reasoning* **15** (1996) 291–317.

Neural Networks of Positive Systems

Tadeusz Kaczorek

Warsaw University of Technology
Institute of Control and Industrial Electronics
00-662 Warszawa, Koszykowa 75, Poland
kaczorek@isep.pw.edu.pl

Abstract. Some definitions and theorems concerning positive continuous-time and discrete-time linear systems are presented. The notion of a positive estimator maping a positive cone into a positive cone is introduced. A multi-layer perceptron and a radial neural network approximating the nonlinear estimator are proposed.
A neural network modeling the dynamics of a positive nonlinear dynamical system is also proposed. The new neural networks are verified and illustrated by an example.

1 Introduction

In the last decade a dynamic development in positive systems has been observed. Positive systems are systems whose inputs, state variables and outputs take only nonnegative values. Examples of positive systems are industrial processes involving chemical reactors, heat exchangers and distillation columns, storage systems, compartmental systems, water and atmospheric pollution models. A variety of models having positive linear system behaviour can be found in engineering, management science, economics, social sciences, biology and medicine, etc. Positive linear systems are defined on cones and not on linear spaces. This is why the theory of positive systems is more complicated and less advanced. The theory of positive systems has some elements in common with theories of linear and non-linear systems [5]. Positive linear systems, for example, satisfy the superposition principle. Limiting the consideration of positive linear systems only to R_+^n (the first quarter of R^n) shows that the theory of positive linear systems has some elements in common with the theory of non-linear systems. An overview of the neural networks theory can be found in [1,2,6-9]. Fukushima in [3,4] has suggested neural networks with all nonnegative weights and all nonnegative inputs and outputs. In this paper a notion of a positive nonlinear estimator maping a given positive cone into a given positive cone will be introduced. A multi-layer perceptron and a radial neural network that approximate the nonlinear estimator will be proposed. A neural network modeling the dynamics of a positive nonlinear dynamical system will be also proposed. To the best authors knowledge the neural networks of positive systems have not been considered yet.

L. Rutkowski et al. (Eds.): ICAISC 2004, LNAI 3070, pp. 56–63, 2004.
© Springer-Verlag Berlin Heidelberg 2004

2   Positive Systems

2.1   Continuous-Time Positive Systems

Let $R_+^{m \times n}$ be the set of $m \times n$ matrices with nonnegative entries and $R_+^n := R_+^{n \times 1}$. Consider the linear continuous-time system

$$\dot{x} = Ax + Bu, \quad x(0) = x_0$$
$$y = Cx + Du \tag{1}$$

where $x = x(t) \in R^n$ is the state vector at the instant t, $u = u(t) \in R^m$ is the input vector, $y = y(t) \in R^p$ is the output vector and $A \in R^{n \times n}$, $B \in R^{n \times m}$, $C \in R^{p \times n}$, $D \in R^{p \times m}$.

Definition 1. [5] The system (1) is called externally positive if and only if for every input $u \in R_+^m$ and $x_0 = 0$, the output $y \in R_+^p$ for all $t \geq 0$.

Theorem 1. [5] The system (1) is externally positive if and only if its matrix of impulse responses is nonnegative, i.e.

$$g(t) \in R_+^{p \times m} \text{ for all } t \geq 0. \tag{2}$$

Definition 2. [5] The system (1) is called internally positive (shortly positive) if and only if for any $x_0 \in R_+^n$ and every $u \in R_+^m$ we have $x \in R_+^n$ and $y \in R_+^p$ for all $t \geq 0$. A matrix $A = [a_{ij}] \in R^{n \times n}$ is called the Metzler matrix if and only if $a_{ij} \geq 0$ all $i \neq j$. It is well-known [5] that $e^{At} \in R_+^{n \times n}$ for $t \geq 0$ if and only if A is the Metzler matrix.

Theorem 2. [5] The system (1) is internally positive if and only if the matrix A is a Metzler matrix and $B \in R_+^{n \times m}$, $C \in R_+^{p \times n}$, $D \in R_+^{p \times m}$.

Every continuous-time internally positive system is always externally positive.

Definition 3. [5] The positive system

$$\dot{x} = Ax, x(0) = x_0 \ (A \in R^{n \times n} \text{ is the Metzler matrix}) \tag{3}$$

is called asymptotically stable if and only if its solution $x(t) = e^{At}x_0$ satisfies the condition

$$\lim_{t \to \infty} x(t) = 0 \text{ for every } x_0 \in R_+^n \tag{4}$$

Theorem 3. [5] The internally positive system (3) is asymptotically stable if and only if all coefficients $a_i (i = 0, 1, ..., n-1)$ of the characteristic polynomial

$$p_A(s) = \det[Is - A] = s^n + a_{n-1}s^{n-1} + \cdots + a_1 s + a_0 \tag{5}$$

are positive, i.e. $a_i > 0$ for $i = 0, 1, ..., n-1$ or equivalently, if and only if all principal minors of the matrix $-A$ are positive, i.e.

$$|-a_{11}| > 0, \begin{vmatrix} -a_{11} & -a_{12} \\ -a_{21} & -a_{22} \end{vmatrix} > 0, ..., \det[-A] > 0 \tag{6}$$

2.2 Discrete-Time Positive Systems

Consider the linear discrete-time system

$$x_{i+1} = Ax_i + Bu_i, \ i \in Z_+ = \{0, 1, ...\}$$
$$y_i = Cx_i + Du_i \tag{7}$$

where $x_i \in R^n$ is the state vector at the discrete instant $i \in Z_+$, $u_i \in R^m$ is the input vector, $y_i \in R^p$ is the output vector and $A \in R^{n \times n}, B \in R^{n \times m}, C \in R^{p \times n}, D \in R^{p \times m}$.

Definition 4. [5] The system (7) is called externally positive if and only if for every input $u_i \in R_+^m, i \in Z_+$ and $x_0 = 0$ the output $y_i \in R^p$ for all $i \in Z_+$.

Theorem 4. [5] The system (7) is externally positive if and only if its matrix of impulse responses is nonnegative, i.e.

$$g_i \in R_+^{p \times m} \text{ for all } i \in Z_+ \tag{8}$$

Definition 5. [5] The system (7) is called internally positive (shortly positive) if and only if for every $x_0 \in R_+^n$ and any input sequence $u_i \in R_+^m, i \in Z_+$ we have $x_i \in R_+^n$ and $y_i \in R_+^p$ for all $i \in Z_+$.

Theorem 5. [5] The system (7) is internally positive if and only if

$$A \in R_+^{n \times n}, \ B \in R_+^{n \times m}, \ C \in R_+^{p \times n}, \ D \in R_+^{p \times m} \tag{9}$$

Every discrete-time internally positive system is always externally positive.

Definition 6. [5] The internally positive system

$$x_{i+1} = Ax_i, \ A \in R_+^{n \times n} \tag{10}$$

is called asymptotically stable if and only if its solution $x_i = A^i x_0$ satisfies the condition

$$\lim_{t \to \infty} x_i(t) = 0 \text{ for every } x_0 \in R_+^n \tag{11}$$

The internally positive system (10) is asymptotically stable if and only if all eigenvalues $z_1, z_2, ..., z_n$ of the matrix $A \in R_+^{n \times n}$ have moduli less 1, i.e. $|z_k| < 1$ for $i = 1, ..., n$.

Theorem 6. [5] The internally positive system (10) is asymptotically stable if and only if all coefficients $\bar{a}_i (i = 0, 1, ..., n-1)$ of the characteristic polynomial

$$p_{A-I}(s) = \det[Iz - A + I] = z^n + \bar{a}_{n-1} z^{n-1} + \cdots + \bar{a}_1 z + \bar{a}_0 \tag{12}$$

are positive, i.e. $\bar{a}_i > 0$ for $i = 0, 1, ..., n-1$ or equivalently, if and only if all principal minors of the matrix $\bar{A} = [\bar{a}_{ij}] := I - A$ are positive, i.e.

$$|-\bar{a}_{11}| > 0, \ \begin{vmatrix} -\bar{a}_{11} & -\bar{a}_{12} \\ -\bar{a}_{21} & -\bar{a}_{22} \end{vmatrix} > 0, ..., \det \bar{A} > 0 \tag{13}$$

3   Neural Networks as Positive Estimators

Let V_+ and W_+ be positive cones of R_+^n, i.e. $V_+ \subset R_+^n$ and $W_+ \subset R_+^n$

Definition 7. A nonlinear vector function $f : R^n \to R^n$ is called the positive estimator if and only if it maps a positive cone $V_+ \subset R_+^n$ into a positive cone $W_+ \subset R_+^n$. The positive estimator will be denoted by $A_{V_+ \to W_+}$.

Let us consider the following problem.

Problem 1. Given positive cones $V_+ \subset R_+^n$ and $W_+ \subset R_+^n$, find a neural network that is the estimator $A_{V_+ \to W_+}$. One of the simplest neural network solving the

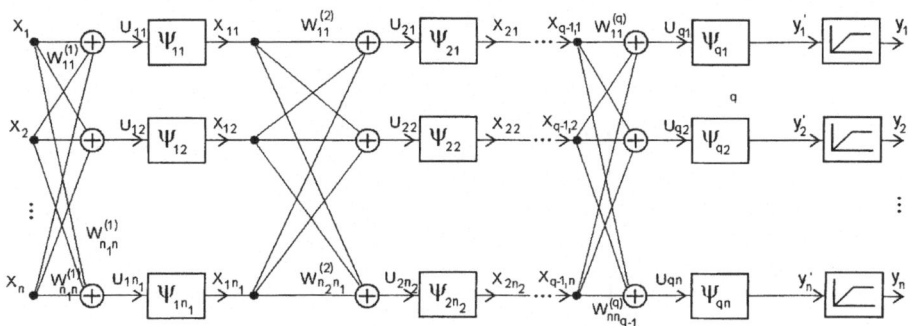

Fig. 1.

Problem 1 is a multi-layer perceptron (Fig. 1) satisfying the following conditions:

1. the input vector $x = [x_1, x_2, ..., x_n]^T$ (T denotes the transpose) has only nonnegative components $x_k \geq 0$, $k = 1, ..., n$,

2. the weighted sum $u_{ji} = \sum_{t=1}^{n_i} w_{jt}^{(i)} x_{jt}$ is nonnegative for $j = 1, ..., q$; $i = 1, ..., q$,

3. the activation functions $\Psi_{ij}(u_{kl})$ of the neurons are unipolar (Fig. 2),

4. for every bounded output y_i, $i \in \{1, ..., n\}$ a limiter with characteristic shown in Fig. 3 is added.

The input-output mapping of the q-layer perceptron can be represented by the nonlinear vector function [1,2,6-9]

$$y = f(x), \tag{14}$$

where $x_i \in R_+^n, y_i \in R_+^p$ and f is determined by the activation functions $f_{ij}(u_{kl})$. To adjust the $w_{jt}^{(i)}$ of the multi-layer perceptron so that (14) is the desired estimator $A_{V_+ \to W_+}$ any of the well-known [1,2,6-9] techniques can be used. The desired estimator can be also modelled by a radial neural network shown in Fig. 4. The output y_i ($i = 1, ..., p$) of the radial neural network is given by

$$y_i = \sum_{j=1}^{k} w_{ij} \varphi_j (\|x - c_j\|) \quad i = 1, ..., n, \tag{15}$$

where $\varphi_j (\|x - c_j\|)$ is a radial function, for example of the Gaussian form

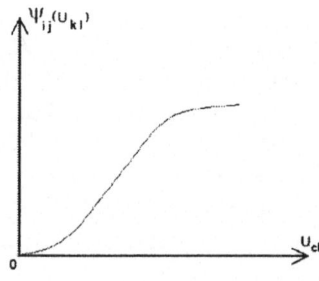

Fig. 2.

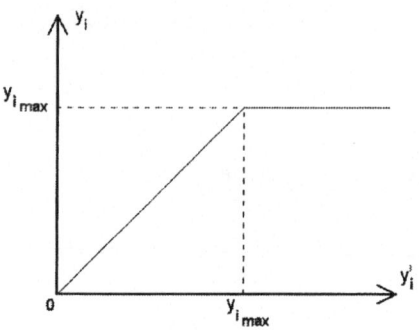

Fig. 3.

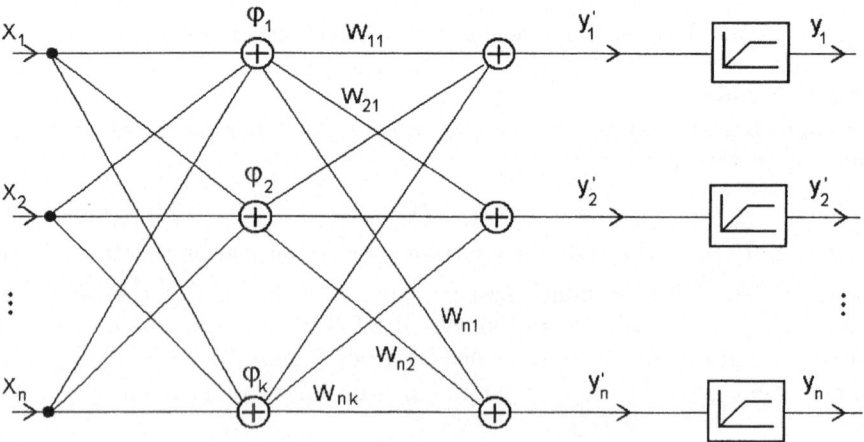

Fig. 4.

$$\varphi_j\left(\|x - c_j\|\right) = \exp\left(-\frac{\|x - c_j\|}{2\delta_j}\right), \quad j = 1, ..., k \tag{16}$$

Using the well-known procedures we can adjust the weights w_{ij} ($i = 1, ..., n; j = 1, ..., k$) and the parameters c_j and δ_j.

Example.

Let

$$V_+ = \left\{ x = \begin{bmatrix} x_1 \\ x_2 \end{bmatrix} : 0 \le x_1 \le 3, \ 0 \le x_2 \le 2 \right\}$$

and

$$W_+ = \left\{ y = \begin{bmatrix} y_1 \\ y_2 \end{bmatrix} : 0 \le y_1 \le 13, \ 0 \le y_2 \le 6 \right\} \tag{17}$$

Find a neural estimate $A_{V_+ \to W_+}$ for (17). Two cases of the neural estimator shown in Fig. 5 with the activation functions of the form

$$\Psi_i(u_i) = u_i\left(1 - e^{-\alpha_i u_i}\right) \quad i = 1, 2, \tag{18}$$

has been considered. To adjust the weights w_{ij} and the parameters α_i of the neural estimator the following data have been used

x_1	0	0	1	3	2	2	3
x_2	0	2	1	0	1	2	2
y_1	0	4	2	9	5	8	13
y_2	0	0	1	0	2	4	6

Using the MICROSOFT EXCEL 2002 the following values of the parameters α_i and the weights w_{ij} have been obtained:

Case 1: $\alpha_1 = 483.77208, ; \alpha_2 = 0.00319; w_{11} = 2.751196; w_{21} = 10.93466; w_{22} = 2.751196$ and

Case 2: $\alpha_1 = 10.57921; \alpha_2 = 0.000135; \alpha_3 = 10.95721; \alpha_4 = 0.025; w_{11}^{(1)} = 2.495357; w_{12}^{(1)} = -0.123103; w_{21}^{(1)} = 3.201556; w_{22}^{(1)} = -0.1516028; w_{11}^{(2)} = 2,65198; w_{12}^{(2)} = 3.486359; w_{21}^{(2)} = 31.48747; w_{22}^{(2)} = 58.30414$. The trained neural networks has been tested for $x_1 = 3$, $x_2 = 1$ and the following has been got $y_1 = 9.77$, $y_2 = 2.91$ (case 1) and $y_1 = 9.75$; $y_2 = 3.12$ (case 2) that are quite good approximation of the exact values $y_1 = 10$ and $y_2 = 3$ ($y_1 = x_1^2 + x_2^2$, $y_2 = x_1 x_2$).

4   Positive Dynamical Neural Networks

In this section the following problem will be considered.

Problem 2. Given a positive dynamical system described by the equations

$$\begin{aligned} \dot{x} &= f(x, u, t) , \quad x_0 \in R_+^n \\ y &= g(x, u, t) \end{aligned}, \tag{19}$$

where $x = x(t) \in R_+^n$, $u = u(t) \in R_+^m$, $y = y(t) \in R_+^p$ are the state, input and output vectors and $f : R^{n+m+1} \to R^n$, $g : R^{n+m+1} \to R^p$ are smooth vector

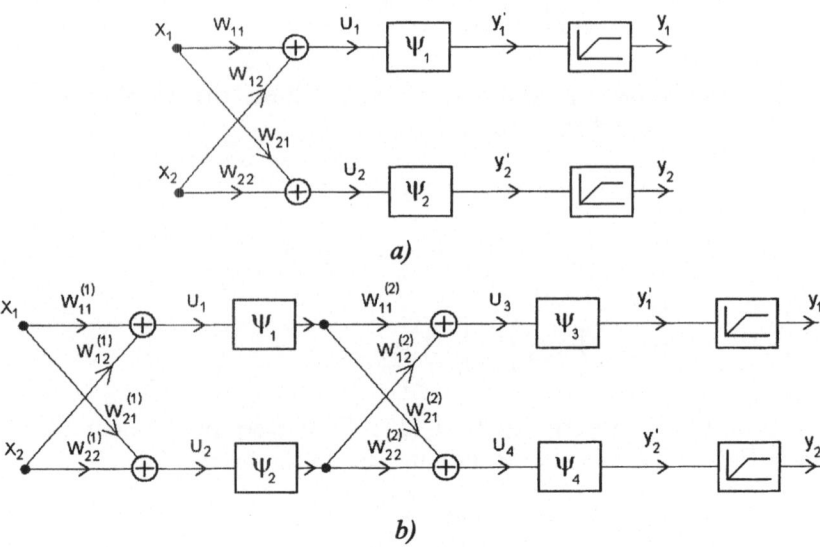

Fig. 5.

functions. Find a neural network that approximates the dynamics described by
(18) for any initial conditions $x_0 \in R_+^n$ and $u(t) \in R_+^m$, $t \geq 0$.

A neural network solving the Problem 2 is shown in Fig. 6. The three first conditions assumed for the multi-layer perceptron should be also satisfied. Knowing the activation functions $\Psi_{ij}(i, j = 1, ..., n)$ and using the known techniques [1,2,6] we can adjust weights w_{ij}, $w_{ij}^{(l)}$ of the neural network.

5   Concluding Remarks

An overview of main definitions and theorems on positive continuous-time and discrete-time linear systems has been presented. The notion of a positive estimator mapping a given positive cone into a given positive cone has been introduced. It has been shown that: a multi-layer perceptron and a radial neural network satisfying some additional conditions approximate the nonlinear estimator. A neural network modelling the dynamics of a given positive nonlinear dynamical system has been proposed. The new neural networks have been verified and illustrated by a simple example. This is a very beginning of the research on neural networks of positive systems. A lot of open problems arises in this new field. For example, an open problem is an extension of these considerations for two-dimensional positive systems [5].

Acknowledgement. I wish to thank very much Professor B. Beliczyński and his Ph.D student R. Gąsowski for valuable discussion and the training of the neural networks in the example.

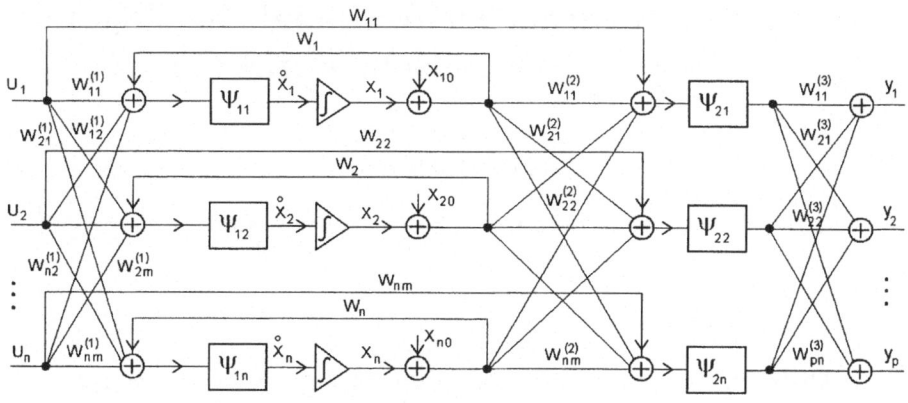

Fig. 6.

References

1. A. Cichocki and R. Unbehauen, Neural Networks for Optimization and Signal Processing, J. Wiley, Chichester (1993)
2. W. Duch, J. Korbicz, L. Rutkowski and R. Tadeusiewicz, Neural Networks, Biocybernetyka i Inżynieria Biomedyczna, Warszawa (2000), Akad. Ofic. Wyd. (in Polish)
3. K. Fukushima, Cognition a self organizing multilayered neural network, Biolog. Cybernetics, vol. 20 (1975) 121–136
4. K. Fukushima, Neocognition a self organizing neural network model for a mechanism of pattern recognition uniffected by shift in position, Biolog. Cybernetics, vol. 36 (1980) 193–202
5. T. Kaczorek, Positive 1D and 2D Systems, Springer-Verlag (2003)
6. J. Korbicz, A. Obuchowicz and D. Uciński, Artifical Neural Networks, Fundamentals and Applications, Akad. Ofic. Wyd. Warszawa (1994) (in Polish)
7. S. Osowski, Neural Networks for Processing of Information, Ofic. Wyd. PW Warszawa (2000) (in Polish)
8. D. Rutkowska, M. Piliński and L. Rutkowski, Neural Networks, Genetic Algorithms and Fuzzy Systems, PWN Warszawa (1997) (in Polish)
9. R. Tadeusiewicz, Neural Networks, Akadem. Ofic. Wyd., Warszawa (1993) (in Polish)

Support of Natural, by Artificial, Intelligence Using Utility as Behavioral Goal

Roman Kulikowski

Systems Research Institute, Polish Academy of Sciences,
Newelska 6, 01-447 Warsaw, Poland

Abstract. The paper deals with support of natural intelligence employing the concept of two factors utility which characterizes the sustainable development. The first factor represents the long-term expected profit of generalized capital investment.
The second factor represents the worse case profit necessary for survival of crises. Using that concept it is possible to support the individual decisions connected with choosing the best alternative. It enables also to support the cooperation strategies connected with exploitation of innovations and new technologies.

1   Introduction

The natural intrlligence can be defined as the, based on knowledge, human behaviour, which enables one to foresee the future state of the world (resulting also from an action undertaken) assess its value (called utility) and choose the best (with maximum utility) action from a set of possible alternatives. The intelligent behavior enables people to implement the development process, which can be characterized as any welfare improving change in the set of opportunities open to the society. The welfare state can broadly be represented in multidimensional context as composed of: natural capital (e.g. land, forest), built capital (e.g. buildings, machinery), social capital (i.e. human, intelectual, cultural), institutional capital (i.e. institutions that the society has at disposal), and the safety (related to security, self and social esteem and opposite to risk) etc.

According to the modern views development process should be sustainable, i.e. besides achieving the long term (strategic)objectives one is also concerned with survival of short term crises, avoiding bankruptcy, natural and other disasters. It is also suggested (e.g. to the countries accessing the U.E.) that in order to achieve the sustainable development the existing policies and planning techniques should be improved, i.e. they should be based on knowledge. These suggestions require that the systems supporting inferences and decisions, made by natural intelligence, are constructed what creates a new challenge for system and computer sciences. In order to develop such systems it is necessary, first of all, to construct the behavioral goal function, which will be called ntility of sustainable development (U.S.D.)

L. Rutkowski et al. (Eds.): ICAISC 2004, LNAI 3070, pp. 64–72, 2004.
© Springer-Verlag Berlin Heidelberg 2004

It should be noticed that the first, axiomatically justified, concept of utility for evaluation of games and economic behavior was developed in 1947 by J. Von Neumann and O.Morgenstern. Then, to avoid some criticism L.Savage, in 1954, has introduced a new system of axioms and the notion of subjective probability, which was investigated experimentally by A. Tversky (for details see Ref [2]).

One of some deficiences of the early theoretical concespts of utility was the lack of methods enabling the valuation of subjective psychological factors (such as risk and subjective probability) and representing utility in numerical form, which is necessary when computers are applied in support systems. For that reason in 1998 the concept of two-factors utility [4] was introduced and developed in papers [5,6,7,8,9]. That concept rests on the basic psychological assumption that behavior is a function of two factors: drives (challenges) and defences (restraining people from undertaking risky actions). Such an approach is also in agreement with neurophysiological findings, [3] which explain the mechanisms of emotion rising and quelling processes accompanying the risky actions.

In the present paper the basic concept of U.S.D. evaluation and some applications are described.

2   Utility of Sustainable Development Concept

The USD function (F), which is a measure of welfare increments resulting from the investment of generalized capital (I), being a part $x = I/P$ of the investors liquid capital P, is assumed in the form

$$U(x) = F[Zx, Y]$$

where

a. Z is the long term (strategic)expected profit equal PR, $R = (P_m - I) : I$ is the expected rate of return (i.e. $R = E\{\tilde{R}\}$, where the variance of random variable $\tilde{R} : V\{\tilde{R}\} = \sigma^2$), $P_m = E\{\tilde{P}_m\}$ = expected market return value;
b. $Y = Z - \kappa\sigma P$ is the short term "worse case profit", where κ is a subjective parameter characterizing the fear of failure. The value $VAR = \kappa\sigma P$ is called "Value at Risk".

Since Z, Y, are expressed in monetary terms and U should not change when one changes monetary units, it is assumed that F is "constant return to scale" and can be approximated by Cobb-Douglas function, i.e.

$$U(x) = F[Zx, ZS] \cong PRS^{1-\beta}x^\beta, \quad \beta \in [0,1], \tag{1}$$

where

$S = 1 - \kappa\frac{\sigma}{R}$ is called the safety index, $0 < S \leq 1$

$\beta \cong \dfrac{\Delta U}{U} : \dfrac{\Delta x}{x}$ is a subjective parameter characterizing the investor's entrepreneurship (when $\beta = 1$ the value of $S^{1-\beta} = 1$ so the investor ignores the risk and for $\Delta x/x = const$ his $\Delta U/U$ attains maximum value).

In order to evaluate R and S one can use the simple success-failure model, where the maximum return R_u (reward) is attained with probablity p and the failure ($\tilde{R} = R_d = 0$) with probability $1 - p$. Using that model one gets $R = pR_u$ and

$$S = 1 - \kappa \frac{\sqrt{p(1-p)}}{p} = 1 - \kappa \sqrt{\frac{1-p}{p}}. \tag{2}$$

The subiective parameter κ can be evaluated using the following scaling procedure.

a. Find the lower admissible value of success probability $\bar{p}(p \geq \bar{p})$ such that during the worse interval the expected return $PR_u\bar{p}$ will cover the expected, minimal liabilities (costs)minus the level of liquid capital reserves (workind capital) A, i.e.

$$PR_u\bar{p} = L_m - A, \ or$$

$$\bar{p} = \lambda/R_u, \quad \lambda = \frac{L_m - A}{P} \tag{3}$$

b. Find the lower bound of S and $U(x)$ for the worse interval when $U(x)$ drops to the minimal value $U_o(x) = PR_u\bar{p}S_0^{1-\beta}x^\beta$.

Assuming that the lowest utility is also attained for fisk-free investment (e.g. in government bonds) with utility $U_F(x) = PR_Fx^\beta$ one can write $U_0(x) = U_F(x)$ and find

$$S_0 = (R_F/\lambda)^\gamma, \quad \gamma = \frac{1}{1-\beta} \tag{4}$$

Since, on the other hand, $S_0 = 1 - \kappa\sqrt{\frac{1-\bar{p}}{\bar{p}}}$, one gets

$$\kappa(\lambda) = (1 - S_0)\sqrt{\frac{\bar{p}}{1-\bar{p}}} = [1 - (R_F/\lambda)^\gamma]\sqrt{\frac{\lambda}{R_u - \lambda}} \tag{5}$$

and

$$S = 1 - [1 - (R_F/\lambda)^\gamma]\sqrt{\frac{\lambda}{R_u - \lambda} \cdot \frac{1-p}{p}}. \tag{6}$$

The condition (3) can be also interpreted in terms of statistical estimation theory. Using e.g. Tchebyshev inequality one can estimate the confidence interval for expected value R employing the spot estimator $R_n = \frac{1}{n}\sum_{t=1}^{n}\tilde{R}_t$:

$$Pr(R_n - \varepsilon < R < R_n + \varepsilon) \geq 1 - \frac{\sigma^2}{n\varepsilon^2} \triangleq \alpha, \tag{7}$$

Since, according to (3) the lower bound of R is $\bar{p} R_u = \lambda$, $(\bar{p} \leq p)$ so assuming $R_n - \varepsilon = \lambda$ one can write (7) in an equivalent from

$$P_r(\lambda < R < 2R_n - \lambda) \geq 1 - \frac{1}{n}\left(\frac{\sigma}{R_n - \lambda}\right)^2 \triangleq \alpha(\lambda). \tag{8}$$

It is possible to observe that when the historic data sample n decreases and λ is growing the confidence level of worse time survival $\alpha(\lambda)$ as well as S (according to (6)) decline. It should be also noted that the condition $b.$ of the scaling procedure enables one to compare the welfare increment in worse case $U_o(x)$ with risk free idling activity which proceduces welfare increment $U_F(x)$.

Expressing USD (1) in the equivalent form

$$U(x) = s(p)PR_u x^\beta, \tag{9}$$

where $s(p) = pS^{1-\beta}$ can be called the subjective success probability, one can see that $s(p) < p$ (where p is the objective probability of success). As shown in [6] for small λ (but large R_u and small p)$s(p) > p$. In such a situation the gamblers participation in the lotteries is rational despite the fact that the expected value of the lottery is negative.

In order to analyse the impact of the long and short term strategies on the USD consider the binominal success-failure model with k successes in n trials. Each trial (such as a service of one client or production of one unit) requires the given time interval ΔT. When the production or service capacity is π the number of trials per 1 year is $n = \pi \Delta T$. If, for example, one is analysing the production project with $\pi = 3$ unit/day and 1 year planning horizon (with 12 x 26 = 312 working days) $n = 3 \cdot 312 = 936$.

Suppose that the estimated (by historical data) probability of success is $p = k/n$. The planned rate of return $R_u = P_m/P - 1$ where P_m-market price of the unit of production, P- production cost per unit. When k units are sold (i.e. k elementary successes achieved) the expected rate of return becomes $R_u p$. Assume the binominal probability distribution function of successes in the form

$$P_r\{x = k\} = \binom{n}{k}p^k(1-p)^{n-k}, \quad k = 1, 2, ..., n. \tag{10}$$

Since $E\{x\} = np$, $V\{x\} = np(1-p)$ one can finld

$$\sigma/R = \frac{\sqrt{np(1-p)}}{np} = \sqrt{\frac{1-p}{np}}$$

and

$$S = 1 - \kappa(\lambda)\sqrt{\frac{1-p}{np}} \tag{11}$$

The $\kappa(\lambda)$ can be derived using the scaling procedure for 1 month worse-case subinterval, characterized by $\bar{n} = n/12$.

Then

$$\kappa(\lambda) = (1 - S_0)\sqrt{\frac{\overline{np}}{1-\bar{p}}}, \quad S = 1 - (1 - S_0)\sqrt{\frac{\overline{np}}{1-\bar{p}} \cdot \frac{1-p}{np}} \tag{12}$$

Using the maximum likelihood estimators for $p = k/n$ and $\bar{p} = \bar{k}/\bar{n}$ one gets

$$S = 1 - [1 - (R_F/\lambda)^\gamma]\sqrt{\frac{1/k - 1/n}{1/\bar{k} - 1/\bar{n}}}, \tag{13}$$

$$VaR = P[1 - (R_F/\lambda)^\gamma]\sqrt{\frac{1/k - 1/n}{1/\bar{k} - 1/\bar{n}}}, \tag{14}$$

It is possible to observe that the growing $\bar{n}/n$ ratio increases VaR and decreases S and USD.

When $n \to \infty$, according to the Moivre-Laplace theorem the binomial distribution tends to the normal p.d.f. with the central point $np = R$ and $np(1 - p) = \sigma^2$.

Besides market activity where the reward $\tilde{P}_m$ is random, one should also consider the contracts, where the given reward $P_m = P^*$ is paid at fixed time $T = T^*$. In such a situation the external (market) risk should be replaced by the internal (operational) risk, connected with random cost outlays $I(\tilde{T}) = C_c + C_v\tilde{T}$, where C_c = constant cost, C_v = variable cost , $\tilde{T}$ =random time of contract accomplishment. As a result the contract rate of return $\tilde{R} = P^*/I(\tilde{T}) - 1$ is random with success $R_u = P^*/I(T^*) - 1 > 0$ attained with probability p and failure $R_d = P^*/I(T_u) - 1 = 0$, $T_u = \dfrac{P^* - C_c}{C_v}$ attained with probability $1 - p$.

The contract expected rate of return $\tilde{R} = pR_u$ and the USD becomes

$$U = IRS^{1-\beta}x^\beta = [P^* - I(\tau)]S^{1-\beta}x^\beta \tag{15}$$

where τ =expected time of contract accomplishment.

Denoting by $\bar{T}$ the minimum admissible accomplishment time and by $Z(\bar{T})$ the worse case profit one can use the following scaling procedure:

a.

$$Z(\bar{T}) = I(\bar{T})R(\bar{T})p(\bar{T}) = L_m - A, \tag{16}$$

b.

$$U_0 = Z(\bar{T})S_0^{1-\beta} = I(\bar{T})R_F\bar{T} \tag{17}$$

which yields

$$S = R\bar{T}/\lambda, \quad \lambda = \frac{L_m - A}{I(\bar{T})} \tag{18}$$

Assuming the exponential p.d.f. for $\tilde{T}$:

$$f(\tilde{T}) = 1/\tau C^{-\tilde{T}/\tau} \text{ for } \tilde{T} > 0$$
$$= 0 \qquad\qquad \text{for } \tilde{T} \leq 0$$

one gets $E\{\tilde{T}\} = \tau$, $Var\{\tilde{T}\} = \tau^2$ and

$$p(\overline{T}) = \int_0^{\overline{T}} f(t)dt = 1 - e^{-\overline{T}/\tau} \tag{19}$$

Since $\sigma/R = 1$, S does not depend on p and is equal S_o. The numerical value of $\overline{T}$ one can derive, introducing the variable $\overline{T}/\tau \triangleq y$ and solving the eq (16) i.e.

$$(1 - \frac{\tau}{T_u}y)(1 - e^{-y}) = \frac{L_m - A}{P^* - C_c} = l \tag{20}$$

If. e.g. $\tau/T_u = 0.5$, $l = 0,2$, one gets $y = 1,48$ so $\overline{T} = 1,48\tau$. The contract can be accepted when $T^* \geq \overline{T}$. The expected time of contract accomplishment τ depends on the experience gained by n similar contracts performed in past. According to the so called "learning curve" $\tau = \tau_0 n^{-b}$, where $\tau_0 = $ the time of the first contract accomplishment, b =coefficient derived by using regression technique.

Summarizing the U.S.D. concept one should note that it depends on two behavioral (subjective) parameters: $\beta-$representing the driving, and $\kappa-$ the restraining (defense) forces. According to the neurophysiological theories (see e.g. [3]) the brain controls the behavior and emotions by changing drivers and defenses. When e.g. the life is endangered, and it is necessary to switch from the defending to offensive position, the fear of risk (κ) should be depressed (ignored), what can be achieved by incveasing β. In an alert (defence position) people should be sensitive to the risky situations, monitored by sensual system, and β should be set small. In the normal situation, when the risk (fear of bankruptcy) helps people to survive the short time crises, β should be kept at moderate, e.g. $\beta = 0.5$, level.

3 Support of Decisions

At the planning stage the decision maker evaluates his past activities and decides which of them should be continued. He decides also whether the new (innovative) activities should be undertaken. To support his decision assume that the set of m alternative decisions is characterized by the known R_i, S_i, $i = 1...m$, parameters. It can be assumed that i-th activity is accepted by the decision maker when the U.S.D.

$$U_i(x_i) = PR_i S_i^{1-\beta} x_i^{\beta} \quad \geq U_F(x_i), \quad x_i = P_i/P, \quad \forall_i$$

where $U_F(x_i) = PR_F x_i^{\beta} = $ is the U.S.D. risk free activity,
$P_i =$ capital invested in i-th activity, $P =$total capital invested.
The acceptance condition boils down to $R_i \geq R_F : S_i^{1-\beta}, \forall_i$. The next problem facing the decision marker is to find the strategy $\hat{x}_i \equiv \{\hat{x}_1, ...\hat{x}_m\}$, $\sum_{i=1}^m \hat{x}_i = 1$, such that the U.S.D. of independent concatenated activities $U(x)$ attains maximum i.e.

$$U(\hat{x}) = \frac{max}{x_i \in \Omega} \sum_{i=1}^n U_i(x_i) \qquad \Omega = \{x_i | \sum_{i=1}^n = 1, \forall_i\}$$

As shown in Ref [6] the optimum strategy becomes

$$\hat{x}_i = \frac{a_i^r}{\sum_{j=1}^n a_j^r}, \quad r = \frac{1}{1-\beta}, \quad a_i = R_i S_i^{1-\beta}, \quad \forall_i \tag{21}$$

For $\beta = 1/2$ one gets $U(\hat{x}) = P\left[\sum_{j=1}^n R_j^2 S_j\right]^{1/2}$,

when $\beta = 0$

$$\hat{\kappa}_i = \frac{R_i S_i}{\sum_{j=1}^n R_j S_j} \quad \forall i$$

while for $\beta \to 1$, $\beta \to \infty$ and the total capital is allocated to the activity with maximum R_i (i.e. $R_i = max_j\{R_j\}$) Such a policy characterizes the enterpreneurs who ignore the risk involved in the activities.

Deriving the support strategy (21) based on expectations of returns one can employ the maksimum likelihood estimators (MLE) of R_i, p_i using the historical (ex post) data. In order to improre the estimation accuracy one can use also the econometric models with r explanatory variables x_j, $j = 1, 2, ...r_j$,

$$R_t = \mu_0 + \mu_1 x_1 + \cdots + \mu_r x_r + e_t, \quad t = 1, 2, ...n,$$

where the residuals e_t of n observations are independent, normally distributed with constance variance σ^2. It is possible to show that the least squares estimators of μ_j are idenfical to MLE estimators while MLE and LS estimators of σ^2 differ by the factor $n/[n-(r+1)]$. In order to find the best model fit for inference purpose one can derive the Akaike information criterion $AIC = n log \hat{\sigma} + 2K$, where $\hat{\sigma}^2 = \frac{1}{n}\sum_t \hat{e}_t^2$, $\hat{e}_t$ = estimated residuals for a particular candidate model with $K = r + 2$.

According to the "principle of parsimony" [1] the best number of explanatory variables r can be determined by finding minimal value of AIC. In Ref [7] the econometric models for evaluation of expected returns (for alternative technologies)enabling computation of U.S.D., have been described.

One should also notice that in some cases (e.g. when the student choses a study at an university) the return (in the form of wages paid after completing the education) is delayed with respect to the investment outlays (i.e. tuition paid during the study). To evaluate the U.S.D. of different specializations it is necessary to derive the expected returns $R_i = P_{wi}/P_i^{-1}$, where P_{wi} is the present (discounted) value of expected wages and P_i the present value of tuition in the i-th specialization area [8].

The application of U.S.D. methodology for allocation of resources among different research and education units was described in Ref [7]. That metodology can be also used for supporting cooperation among given number of partners.

Suppose that n partners (research institutes, producers, investors etc.) consider the cooperation aimed at exploitation of an innovation or a new technology which will result in the expected market profit P_m. Denote the profit division strategy by y_i, $i = 1, 2, ..., n$, $\sum_{i=1}^n y_i = 1$. In the case when cooperation creates a company the y_i strategy can be used to divide the shares among the partners (share holders). The i-th partner, who engages I_i/P_i part of his capital P_i in the joint venture gets $P_m y_i$ of reward. The USD of i−th partner becomes

$$U_i(y_i) = \bar{I}_i R_i(y_i) S_i^{1-\beta_i}, \quad \bar{I}_i = P x_i^{\beta_i} = P_i\left(\frac{I_i}{P_i}\right)^{\beta_i} \tag{22}$$

where

$$R_i(y_i) = P_m y_i / I_i - 1, \quad \forall i$$

Denote also, by U_{iT} the utility of traditional activity (status quo) of i-th partner

$$U_{iT} = \bar{I}_i R_{iT} S_{iT}^{1-\beta_i}, \quad \forall i \tag{23}$$

It is assumed that cooperationm will hold when the utility increments, resulting from switching from the traditional to the innovative technology are positive i.e.

$$\Delta U_i(y_i) = U_i(y_i) - U_{iT} = M_i(y_i - E_i) > 0, \quad \forall i \tag{24}$$

where

$M_i = P_m(\frac{I_i}{P_i})^{\beta_i} S^{1-\beta_i}$ - cooperation motivation (driving factor),
$E_i = \frac{I_i}{P_m}[1 + R_{iT}(S_{iT}/S_i)^{1-\beta_i}]$- cooperation expense (restraining factor),

Using Nash principle the fair division of common benefits strategy $y_i = \hat{y}_i$, $\forall i$ can be derived by solving the problem $max_{y \in \Omega} \phi(y) = \phi(\hat{y})$, where

$$\phi(y) = \prod_{i=1}^{n} \Delta U_i(y_i), \quad \Omega = \left\{ y_i | \sum_{i=1}^{n} y_i = 1, \quad y_i > 0, \quad \forall i \right\} \tag{25}$$

The optimum strategy $y_i = \hat{y}_i$, $\forall i$ can be derived in an explicit form using the following theorem (on fair division of benefits), which was proved in Ref [9].

Theorem. There exists an unique fair (in the Nash sense) strategy $y_i = \hat{y}_i$, $i = 1, 2, ..., n$, of benefits division $(y_i P_m)$ among the n cooperating parties, characterized by positive USD increments $\Delta U_i(y_i) = M_i(y_i - E_i) > 0$, such that $\Delta U_i(\hat{y}_i) = M_i \delta$, $\forall i$, where

$$\hat{y}_i = \frac{1}{n}\left[1 + (n-1)E_i - \sum_{k \neq i}^{n} E_k \right], \tag{26}$$

$$\delta = \frac{1}{n}\left[1 - \sum_{k=i}^{n} E_k \right], \quad \forall i \tag{27}$$

The δ parameter, called cooperation benefit indicator (CBI) expresses the cummulative benefit resulting from cooperation. The E_i coefficients characterize the individual expense level (I_i/P_m), an increase of safety ratio $\left[\left(\dfrac{S_{iT}}{S_i}\right)^{1-\beta_i}\right]$ and the profits forgone (R_{iT}), resulting from swithing (from traditional status quo) to the innovative technology. The proposed methodology can be used for searching, choosing and matching of prospective partners, who are characterized by small E_i (expenses) producing large δ and ΔU_i and are able to exploit the innovations and new technologies.

Summarizing the above arguments one can conclude that the U.S.D. concept can help to construct the support systems of natural intelligence and, as well - the knowledge management systems.

References

1. Burnham, K.P., Anderson, D.R.: *Model selection and multimodel Inference,* Springer Verlag, (1998).
2. Coombs, C.H., Daves, R.M., Trersky, A.: *Mathematical Psychology,* Prentice Hall, Inc. (1970).
3. Le Doux, J.E.: *Emotion, memory and the brain,* Scietific American, June (1994).
4. Kulikowski, R.: Portfolio Optimization: Two factors-utility approach, Control and Cybernetics, **3** Warszawa (1998).
5. Kulikowski, R.: URS metodology - a tool for stimulation of economic growth by innovations. Bulletin of Polish Academy of Sciences, Ser.Techn. 50, **1**, Warszawa (2002).
6. Kulikowski, R.: On general theory of risk management and decision support systems, Bulletin of Polish Academy of Sciences, Ser.Techn. 51, **3**, Warszawa (2003).
7. Kulikowski, R.: Acceleration of economic growth by technological change and knowledge management, ibid. 51, **3**, (2003).
8. Kulikowski, R., Kruś, L.: Support of education decisions in Group Decisions and Voting. Ed. J.Kacprzyk, D.Wagner. Akademicka Oficyna Wydawnicza EXIT, Warszawa (2003).
9. Kulikowski, R.: Risk and Utility of Sustainable Development,(im press).

Top-Down Selective Attention for Robust Perception of Noisy and Confusing Patterns

Soo-Young Lee

Brain Science Research Center and Department of BioSystems
Korea Advanced Institute of Science and Technology, Daejeon 305-701, Korea
sylee@kaist.ac.kr

Abstract. A neural network model is developed for the top-down selective attention (TDSA), which estimates the most probable sensory input signal based on previous knowledge and filters out irrelevant sensory signals for high-confidence perception of noisy and confusing signals. The TDSA is modeled as an adaptation process to minimize the attention error, which is implemented by the error backpropagation algorithm for the multilayer Perceptron classifiers. Sequential recognition of superimposed patterns one by one is also possible. The developed TDSA model is applied to the recognition tasks of two-pattern images, superimposed handwritten characters, and noise-corrupted speeches.

1 Introduction

In the real-world applications sensory signals are almost always distorted by noise or spatio-temporally overlapped, which greatly degrade perception performance. Therefore, many efforts have been made for accurate recognition of noisy and superimposed patterns. In this paper, we present an approach that is based on the top-down selective attention (TDSA) process in our brain.

The TDSA starts from higher brain, which consists of acquired knowledge on sensory signals. When a confusing pattern comes as a sensory signal, the human brain estimates the most probable sensory signal and filters out irrelevant signals. Therefore, a virtual image of the sensory signal, which matches well in the personal experience and knowledge, is created in our brain and results in high-confidence perception.

Although the mechanism of the human selective attention has been investigated extensively in the cognitive science ([1] - [3]), only a few attempt has been made to utilize this concept into engineering applications, i.e., robust pattern classification in noisy and superimposed patterns.

Fukushima is the first to apply the human selective attention mechanism in pattern classification. [4] In his Neocognitron model Fukushima introduced backward paths for the TDSA. Rao also introduced a selective attention model based on Kalman filter, of which performance is limited due to the linear filtering and the nonlinear extension is not straightforward. [5]

In this paper we present a simple and efficient TDSA algorithm, which results in much improved recognition performance in noisy and superimposed sensory signals.

L. Rutkowski et al. (Eds.): ICAISC 2004, LNAI 3070, pp. 73–78, 2004.
© Springer-Verlag Berlin Heidelberg 2004

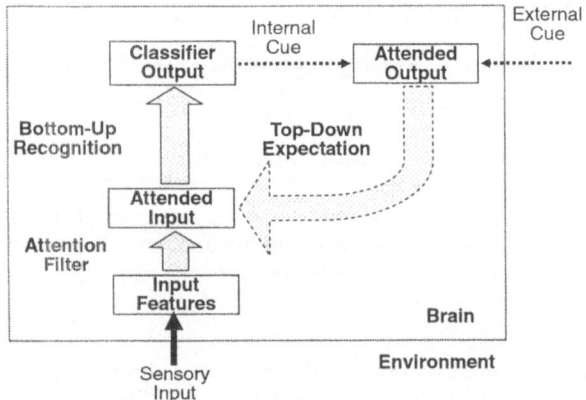

Fig. 1. Basic concept of top-down selective attention

2   Top-Down Selective Attention with MLP

Boradbent proposed that the human brain briefly stores incoming stimuli, but the stimulus information fades and is neither admitted to the conscious mind nor encoded in a way that would permit later recollection unless the attention is directed toward it. [6] Treisman modified the theory and proposed that the filter merely attenuates rather than totally preventing it for further analysis. [7]

According to the Broadbent's early selection theory, we put a selection filter be-tween the sensory input signal and the working memory. As shown in Figure 1, the output of the attention filter is the expected input to an attended class, which may be given internally or externally. The attention gain with one-to-one connectivity models the filter, and the multilayer Perceptron (MLP) classifier plays the role of the higher brain with the previously-acquired knowledge. [8]-[10]

The TDSA is applied into test (or recognition) stage only, and the MLP classifier is trained without the attention layer. At the recognition stage, the attention gains, or the expected input signals, are adjusted to minimize the attention error at the output with an attended output class. The attention gains work as either to suppress the irrelevant and noisy features in the sensory input or to enhance the relevant features in the sen-sory input. In this process, the previous knowledge stored in the pre-trained MLP is the driving force of the adjustment.

In adjusting the expected input signals, the gradient descent rule is used and the error backpropagation algorithm is still applicable. The target output vector $t = [t_1\ t_2 \ldots t_M]^T$ is defined. $t_i = 1$ for the attention class and -1 for the rest of the classes. Then, the expected signal $x = [x_1\ x_2 \ldots x_N]^T$ is initially set to the test sensory input signal $x^0 = [x_1{}^0\ x_2{}^0 \ldots x_N{}^0]^T$. Then, the expected signal x is adjusted to minimize the output error $E = \frac{1}{2}\sum_i [t_i - y_i(\mathbf{x},\mathbf{W})]^2$ with a given $\mathbf{W}$. Here, the i-th output of the MLP classifier with the synaptic weights $\mathbf{W}$ and an input $\mathbf{x}$. At the $(n+1)$-th adaptation epoch, the k-th component of the expected signal $\mathbf{x}$ is updated as

$$x_k[n+1] = x_k[n] - \eta(\partial E / x_k)[n] = x_k[n] + \eta \sum_j W_{jk}^{(1)} \delta_j^{(1)}[n] \qquad (1)$$

$$\delta_k^{(0)} = \sum_j W_{jk}^{(1)} \delta_j^{(1)} \qquad (2)$$

where $\delta^{(1)}$ is the backpropagated error at the first hidden-layer, $\mathbf{W}^{(1)}$ is the synaptic weight between the expected input and the first hidden layer, and η is the learning rate.

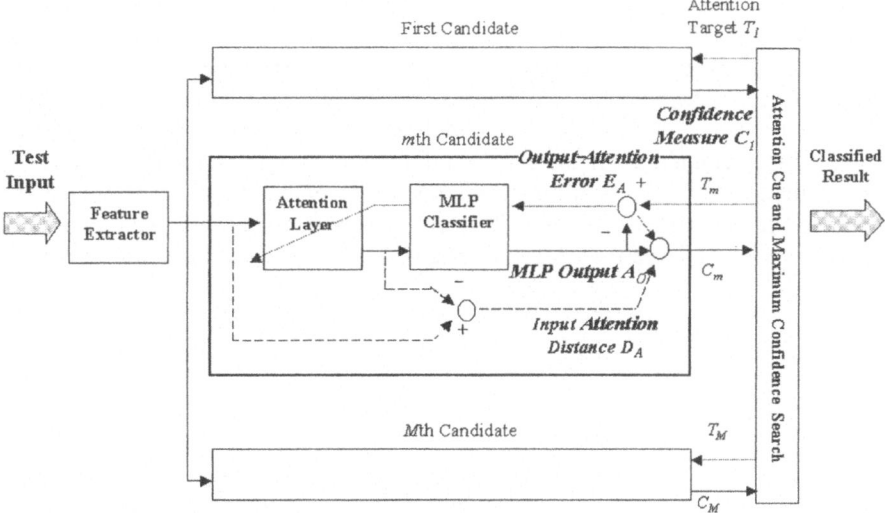

Fig. 2. Basic concept of robust recognition with top-down selective attention

3   Robust Recognition with Top-Down Selective Attention

The procedure of robust signal recognition with the TDSA is summarized in Figure 2. We repeat the estimation of the most probable sensory signals for each of the output class candidates, and calculate a confidence measure C. Then, the class with the highest confidence is chosen as the recognized class.

The confidence measure is defined as

$$C \equiv 1/D_I E_O{}^\alpha, \quad D \equiv \frac{1}{2N} \sum_{k=1}^{N} (\hat{x}_k - x_k^0)^2, \quad E_O \equiv \frac{1}{2M} \sum_{i=1}^{M} [t_i - y_i(\hat{\mathbf{x}})]^2 \qquad (3)$$

where $\hat{\mathbf{x}}$ is the converged expected signal, D_I is the square of Euclidean distance between the sensory signal $\mathbf{x}^o$ and the expected signal $\hat{\mathbf{x}}$, and E_O is the output error with the expected signal $\hat{\mathbf{x}}$. Here, we normalized D_I and E_O with the number of input pixels and output pixels, respectively. In equation (3), α is a parameter to emphasize on either of D_I or E_O above. When α is 0, the confidence measure C is only determined by D_I. When α is 1, D_I and E_O are equally important to determine the confidence measure C.

In Fig. ??, starting from the actual sensory signal at P, the TDSA estimates the most probable sensory signals at P_A, P_B, or P_C for attended class $A(\bullet)$, $B(+)$, and $C(o)$. D_I is the square distance between 2 points, P and $P_{A/B/C}$. Therefore, D_I is the minimal deformation of the sensory signal to belong to the attended class, and is a good measure for classification. However, for some attended classes quite far from P, the TDSA algorithm may stop at a local minimum with a large E_O. Therefore, both D_I and E_O need be considered for the confidence measure.

The developed TDSA algorithm is also applicable to recognize superimposed patterns in sequence. Our strategy for recognizing superimposed patterns consists of three steps as follows. First, one pattern of a superimposed pattern is recognized through the TDSA algorithm. Second, the attention is shifted from the recognized pattern to the remaining pixels by removing the attended pixels. During this attention shifting, the pixels of which value is larger than the sensory input value are removed from the attention. Finally, the recognition process is performed again with remaining pixels to recognize the second pattern.

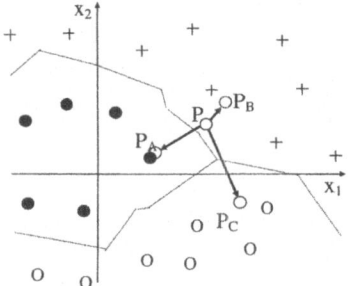

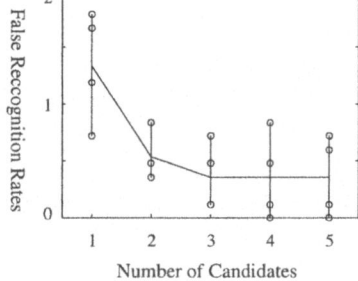

Fig. 3. Graphical view of the TDSA and the squared input distance D_I

Fig. 4. False recognition rates of noisy handwritten numerals

4   Recognition Results

The developed robust recognition algorithm is tested for several real-world applications. The algorithm was tested on the recognition of noisy numeral patterns. The numeral database consists of samples of the handwritten digits (0 through 9) collected from 48 people, for a total of 480 samples. Each digit is encoded as a 16x16 binary pixels. An one hidden-layer MLP was trained by back propagation. The numbers of input, hidden, and output neurons were 256, 30, and 10, respectively.

In Fig. 4, the false recognition rate is plotted as a function of the number of candidates considered for test patterns generated by random inversion of pixel values with a probability Pf =0.05. [8] Considering the average 16% of black pixels in the data, the noisy input patterns with $P_f = 0.05$ are severely distorted from the training patterns. The results with NIST OCR database also show much better performance with the TDSA algorithm. [9]

The proposed selective attention and attention switching algorithm was tested for recognition of 2 superimposed numeral data. As shown in Fig. 5, the superimposed patterns are recognizable one by one. With the small handwritten numeral database the recognition rate of the first and second patterns increase from 91.3% and 62.7% to 95.9% and 77.4%, respectively.[8] For the bigger NIST OCR database the recognition rates are worse, but the performance improvement with the TDSA is eminent in Table 1. [9] The TDSA algorithm also performs sequential recognition of well-known confusing patterns in Fig. 6. Again, the first, second, and third patterns from the left show the sensory input pattern, the first attended pattern, and the remaining pattern, respectively. [10]

(a)   (b)

Fig. 5. Selective attention and attention shifting for superimposed numerals. From the left, the superimposed patterns, the first attended patterns, and the remaining patterns after attention shifting. (a) 6/3; (b) 9/0

Table 1. Error rate of superimposed patterns for NIST OCR database

	First pattern	Second pattern
Standard MLP	33.7%	60.9%
MLP with TDSA	24.9%	34.3%

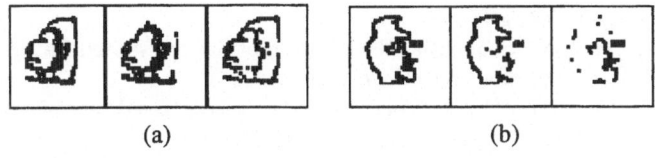

(a)   (b)

Fig. 6. Selective attention and attention shifting for confusing patterns. From the left, the superimposed patterns, the first attended patterns, and the remaining patterns after attention shifting. (a) Eskimo and lady face; (b) Trumpet player and lady face

The developed TDSA algorithm also demonstrated excellent performance for noisy speech recognition. [11] Also, it was applied to improve performance of blind signal separation based on independent component analysis (ICA). [?] In this case the ICA-based unsupervised learning is regarded as a bottom-up attention, which combines with the top-down attention for much better performance.

5   Conclusion

The TDSA algorithm demonstrates excellent recognition performance for real-world noisy and confusing patterns, and also allows sequential recognition of superimposed patterns. In the future the TDSA will be combined with bottom-up attention for better performance.

Acknowledgment. The author acknowledges technical contributions of his former students and staffs, especially Ki-Young Park, Su-In Lee, and Byung-Taek Kim, and financial supports from Korean Ministry of Science and Technology as a Brain Neuroinformatics Research Program.

References

1. Cowan, N.: *Attention and Memory: An Integrated Framework*, Oxford Univ. Press (1997)
2. Pashler, H.E: *The Psychology of Attention*, MIT Press (1997)
3. Parasuraman, R. (ed.) : *The Attentive Brain*, MIT Press(1998)
4. Fukushima, K.: Neural network model for selective attention in visual pattern recognition and associative recall, *Applied Optics* 26 (1987) 4985-4992
5. Rao, R.P.N.: Correlates of attention in a model of dynamic visual recognition. In *Neural Information Processing Systems 10*, MIT Press (1998)
6. Broadbent, D.E.: *Perception and Communication*. Pergamon Press (1958)
7. Treisman, A.: Contextual cues in selective listening, *Quarterly Journal of Experimental Psychology* 12 (1960) 242-248.
8. Lee, S.Y., Mozer, M.C.: Robust Recognition of Noisy and Superimposed Patterns via Selec-tive Attention, *Neural Information Processing Systems 12*, MIT Press (1999)
9. Lee, S.I., Lee, S.Y.: Robust Visual Pattern Recognition based on SOFFA Neural Network Model and Selective Attention, *LNCS Biologically-Motivated Machine Vision*, Springer-Verlag (1999)
10. Kim, B.T., Lee, S.Y.: Sequential Recognition of Superimposed Patterns with Top-Down Selective Attention, *Neurocomputing* (2004)
11. Park, K.Y., Lee, S.Y.: Out-of-Vocabulary Rejection based on Selective Attention Model, *Neural Processing Letters 12*, 41 - 48 (2000)
12. Bae, U.M., Park, H.M., Lee, S.Y.: Top-Down Attention to Complement Independent Component Analysis for Blind Signal Separation, *Neurocomputing* 49, 315 - 327 (2002)

On ANN Based Solutions for Real-World Industrial Requirements

Kurosh Madani

Intelligence in Instrumentation and Systems Lab. (I²S / JE 2353) – SENART
Institute of Technology - University PARIS XII, Avenue Pierre POINT, F-77127
Lieusaint, France
madani@univ-paris12.fr
http://li2S.free.fr

Abstract. The main goal of this paper is to present, through some of main ANN models and based techniques, their capability in real world industrial dilemmas solution. Several examples of real world applications and especially industrial ones have been presented and discussed.

1 Introduction

Real world dilemmas, and especially industry related ones, are set apart from academic ones from several basic points of views. The difference appears since definition of the "problem's solution" notion. In fact, academic (called also sometime theoretical) approach to solve a given problem often begins by problem's constraints simplification in order to obtain a "solvable" model (here, solvable model means a set of mathematically solvable relations or equations describing a behavior, phenomena, etc. . . .). If the theoretical consideration is an indispensable step to study a given problem's solvability, in the case of a very large number of real world dilemmas, it doesn't lead to a solvable or realistic solution. A significant example is the modeling of complex behavior, where conventional theoretical approaches show very soon their limitations. Difficulty could be related to several issues among which:
- large number of parameters to be taken into account (influencing the behavior) making conventional mathematical tools inefficient,
- strong nonlinearity of the system (or behavior), leading to unsolvable equations,
- partial or total inaccessibility of system's relevant features, making the model insignificant,
- subjective nature of relevant features, parameters or data, making the processing of such data or parameters difficult in the frame of conventional quantification,
- necessity of expert's knowledge, or heuristic information consideration,
- imprecise information or data leakage.

Examples illustrating the above-mentioned difficulties are numerous and may concern various areas of real world or industrial applications. As first example, one can emphasize difficulties related to economical and financial modeling and

L. Rutkowski et al. (Eds.): ICAISC 2004, LNAI 3070, pp. 79–90, 2004.
© Springer-Verlag Berlin Heidelberg 2004

prediction, where the large number of parameters, on the one hand, and human related factors, on the other hand, make related real world problems among the most difficult to solve. Another example could be given in the frame of the industrial processes and manufacturing where strong nonlinearities related to complex nature of manufactured products affect controllability and stability of production plants and processes. Finally, one can note the difficult dilemma of complex pattern and signal recognition and analysis, especially when processed patterns or signals are strongly noisy or deal with incomplete data.

Over the past decades, Artificial Neural Networks (ANN) and issued approaches have allowed the elaboration of many original techniques (covering a large field of applications) overcoming some of mentioned difficulties ([1] to [3]). Their learning and generalization capabilities offer make them potentially promising for industrial applications for which conventional approaches show their failure.

The main goal of this paper is to present, through main ANN models and based techniques, the effectiveness of such approaches in real world industrial problems solution. Several examples through real world industrial applications have been shown and discussed.

The paper has been organized as follows: the next section will present the general principle of Artificial Neural Networks relating it to biological considerations. In the same section two classes of neural models will be introduced and discussed: Multi-layer Perceptron and Kernel Functions based Neural Networks. The section 3 and related sub-sections will illustrate real world examples of application of such techniques. Finally, the last section will conclude the paper.

2 Industrial Application's Specificities

Several specificities distinguish the industrial world and related constraints from the others. In the context of the present paper, the word "specificity" intends characteristic or criterion channelling industrial preference for a strategy, option or solution as an alternative to the others. Of course, here the goal is not to analyse all those specificities but to overview briefly the most pertinent ones. As a first specificity one could mention the "reproducibility". That means that an industrial solution (process, product, etc...) should be reproducible. This property is also called solution stability. A second industrial specificity is "viability", which means implementation (realization) possibility. That signifies that an industrial solution should be adequate to available technology and achievable in reasonable delay (designable, realizable). Another industrial specificity is "saleability", which means that an industrial solution should recover a well identified field of needs. Finally, an important specificity is "marketability" making a proposed industrial solution attractive and concurrent (from the point of view of cost, price-quality ratio, etc...) to other available products (or solutions) concerning the same area.

Another key point to emphasize is related to the real world constraints consideration. In fact, dealing with real world environment and related realities, it is not always possible to put away the lower degree phenomena's influence or to neglect secondary parameters. That's why a well known solved academic problem could appear as an unachieved (unbearable) solution in the case of an industry related dilemma. In the same way a viable and marketable industrial solution may appear as primitive.

3   A Brief Overview of Some of Usual ANN Models

The goal of this section is to give a very brief overview of two ANN models: "Back-Propagation" (BP), known also as "Multi-Layer Perceptron" (MLP) and "Kernel Functions" based neural networks trough one of their particular cases which are "Restricted Coulomb Energy/Radial Basis Functions" (RCE/RBF). Of course the purpose is not to remind two well known models but to underline some of their attractive features regarding industrial specificity.

MLP ANN model is a multi-layer neural network. A neuron in this kind of neural network operates conformably to the general ANN's operation frame described in [4]. The principle of the BP learning rule is based on adjusting synaptic weights proportionally to the neural network's output error. For each of learning patterns, the neural network's output is compared to the desired one and an "error vector" is evaluated. Then all synaptic weights are corrected (adjusted) proportionally to the evaluated output error (generally a quadratic error criterion is used). Synaptic weights are modified according to relation (1).

$$dW_{i,j}^{h} = -\eta \bullet \mathbf{grad}_W\left(\varepsilon\right) \tag{1}$$

where S_i – i-th output vector's component, S_i^d – desired value of this component, $dW_{i,j}^{h}$ – synaptic variation of the synaptic weight connecting the j-th neurone and i-th neuron between two adjacent layers, and η – real coefficient called also "learning rate". This coefficient is decreased progressively during the learning process. The learning process stops when the output error reaches some acceptable value.

RCE/RBF neural models belong to the class of "evolutionary" learning strategy based ANN ([5], [6], [7]): neural network's structure is completed during the learning process. Generally, such kind of ANNs includes three layers: an input layer, a hidden layer and an output layer. It is the hidden layer which is modified during the learning phase. A neuron from hidden layer is characterized by its "centre" representing a point in an N dimensional space (if the input vector is an N-D vector) and some decision function, called also neuron's "Region Of Influence" (ROI). ROI is a kernel function, defining some "action shape" for neurons in treated problem's feature space.

The neural network's response is obtained from relation (2) where $P^j = \left[p_1^j \, p_2^j \ldots p_N^j\right]^T$ and C_j represent the j-th learned "prototype" and associated "category", $V = \left[V_1 \, V_2 \ldots V_N\right]^T$ is the input vector, , F(.) is the neuron's activation (decision) kernel like function and λ_j is the associated ROI boundary.

$$\begin{array}{llll} C_j = F\left(dist\left(V, P^j\right)\right) & If & dist\left(V, P^j\right) \leq \lambda_j \\ C_j = 0 & If & dist\left(V, P^j\right) > \lambda_j \end{array} \tag{2}$$

The IBM ZISC-036 [8] is a parallel neural processor implementing RCE/RBF. Each chip is capable of performing up to 250 000 recognitions per second. Each ZISC-036 like neuron implements two kinds of distance metrics called L1 and LSUP respectively (relation (3)). ZISC-036 is composed of 36 neurons.

$$\text{L1: } dist = \sum_{i=0}^{n} |V_i - P_i| \text{ and } \text{ LSUP: } dist = \max_{i=0...n} |V_i - P_i| \tag{3}$$

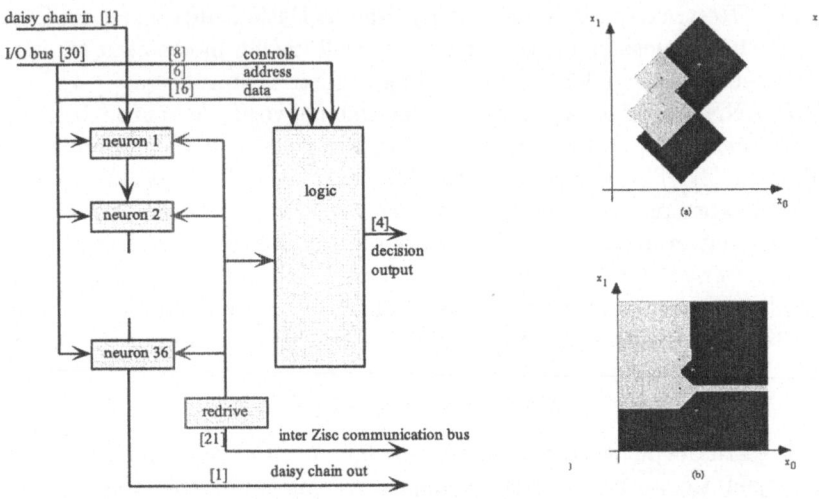

Fig. 1. IBM ZISC-036 chip's bloc diagram (left). Example of a 2-D input feature space mapping using ROI and 1-NN modes, using norm (right)

Figures 1 gives the ZISC-036 chip's bloc diagram and an example of input feature space mapping in a 2-D space. A 16 bit data bus handles input vectors as well as other data transfers (category, distance and chip controls). Within the chip, controlled access to various data in the network is performed through a 6-bit address bus.

4   ANN Based Real-World Industrial Applications

As it has been prompted in introduction section, learning and generalization capabilities of ANN are their most attractive features for industrial applications. But, progress accomplished over the lasts decades concerning electrical engineering, especially in the microprocessors area, is another key point offering new perspectives for real time execution capabilities enlarging the field in implementation ability and thus, in issued solution viability.

4.1 MLP Based Intelligent Adaptive Controller

Let us consider a neural network approximating (learning) a given system (process or plant). Let Y be the system's output, U be the system's command (U becomes also the neural network's output), W_{ij} be synaptic weights of the ANN andg εge the output error resulting from some perturbation occurring on output. The part of output perturbation (output error) due to the variation of a given synaptic weight (W_{ij}) noted as $\frac{\partial s}{\partial W_{ij}}$ could be written conformably to relation (4). One can remark that $\frac{\partial y}{\partial u}$ is the system's Jacobean element and $\frac{\partial u}{\partial W_{ij}}$ could be interpreted as the "neural network's Jacobean" element. As the output error is related to the system's controller characteristics (represented by system's Jacobean), so the modification of synaptic weights with respect to the measured error (e.g. the neural network appropriated training) will lead to the correction of the command (dU) minimizing the output error.

$$\frac{\partial \varepsilon}{\partial W_{ij}} = \frac{\partial \varepsilon}{\partial y}\frac{\partial y}{\partial u}\frac{\partial u}{\partial W_{ij}} \tag{4}$$

Several Neural Network based adaptive control architectures have still been proposed. However, the most effective scheme is the hybrid neuro-controller. This solution operates according to the Neural Network based correction of a conventional controller. The left picture of figure 2 shows the bloc diagram of such approach. As one can see in our ANN based control strategy, the command U(t) is corrected thanks to the additional correction dU, generated by neural device and added to the conventional command component. Several advantages

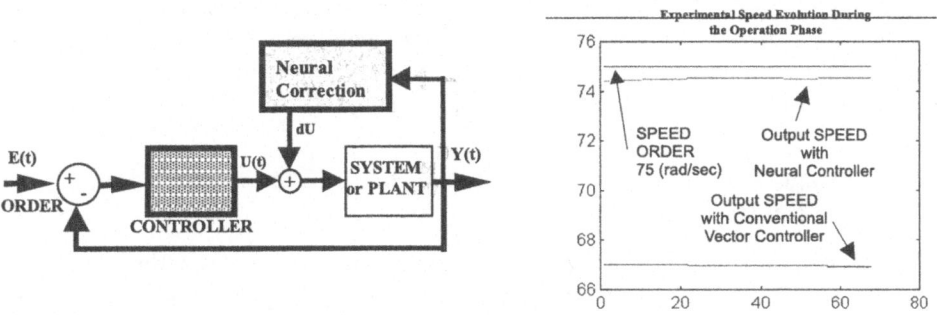

Fig. 2. IBM ZISC-036 chip's bloc diagram (left). Example of a 2-D input feature space mapping using ROI and 1-NN modes, using norm (right)

characterize the proposed strategy making it conform to the above-mentioned required industrial specificities. The first one is related to the control system stability. En fact, in the worst case the controlled plant will operate according to the conventional control loop performances and so, will ensure the control system's stability. The second advantage of such strategy is related to the fact that the proposed architecture acts as a hybrid control system where usual tasks are performed by a conventional operator and unusual operations (such as highly non linear operations or those which are difficult to be modelled by conventional approaches) are realized by neural network based component. This second advantage leads to another main welfare which is the implementation facility and so, the real-time execution capability. Finally, the presented solution takes into account industrial environment reality where most of control problems are related to existent plant dealing with an available (still implemented) conventional controller. This last advantage of the proposed solution makes it a viable option in industrial environment.

We have applied the above-exposed neural based adaptive controller to enhance the conventional vector-control driving a synchronous 3-phased alternative motor. The goal of a vector control or field-oriented control is to drive a 3-phased alternative motor like an independent excitation D.C motor. This consists to control the field excitation current and the torque generating current separately [9]. In synchronous machine, the main parameters are Ld (inductance of d-phase), Lq (inductance of q-phase), and Rs (statoric resistor), which vary in relation with currents (Id and Iq), voltages (Vd and Vq), mechanical torque and speed (of such machine). The relations between voltages or currents depend non linearly on these three parameters defining the motor's model. On the other hand, these parameters are not easily available because of their strongly nonlinear dependence to the environment conditions and high number of influent conditions. The neural network is able to identify these parameters and to correct the machine's reference model, feeding back their real values through the control loop. In a first step, the command is computed using nominal theoretical plant parameters. The neural network learns the plant's behaviour comparing outputs parameters (Vd ,Vq), with measured voltages (Vdm,Vqm). In the second step (after the system's learning operation), the neural network gives the estimated plant's parameters to the controller [9].

4.2   Image Enhancement and Coloration in Media and Movie Production Industry

The first class of application concerns image enhancement in order to: restore old movies (noise reduction, focus correction, etc.), improve digital television, or handle images which require adaptive processing (medical images, spatial images, special effects, etc.). The used principle is based on an image's physics phenomenon which states that when looking at an image through a small window, there exist several kinds of shapes that no one can ever see due to their proximity and high gradient (because, the number of existing shapes that can be seen with the human eye is limited).

Due to a large number of computational operations, a ZISC-036 based implementation has been achieved. The issued system learns as many shapes as possible that could exist in an image, and then to replace inconsistent points by the value of the closest memorized example. The training phase consists of learning small blocks of an image (as an example 5x5) and associating to each the middle pixel's value as a category. These blocks must be chosen in such a way that they represent the maximum number of possible configurations in an image. To determine them, the proposed solution consists of computing the distances between all the blocks and keeping only the most different. The learning algorithm used here incorporates a threshold and learning criteria (Learn_Crit (V)). The learning criteria is the criteria given by relation (5) where V_l^k represents the l-th component of the input vector V^k, P_l^j represents the l-th component of the j-th memorized prototype, C^k represents the category value associated to the input vector V^k, C^j is the category value associated to the memorized prototype P^j and, α and β are real coefficients adjusted empirically.

$$Learn\_Crit\left(V^k\right) = \alpha \sum_l \left|V_l^k - P_l^j\right| + \beta \left|C^k - C^j\right| \tag{5}$$

The image enhancement or noise reduction principles are the same as described above. The main difference lies in the pixel value associated to each memorized example. In noise reduction, the learned input of the neural network is a noisy form of the original image associated with the correct value (or form). For example, in the figure 3, for each memorized example (a block of 5x5) from the input image (degraded one), the middle pixel of the corresponding block from the output image (correct one) is used as the "corrected pixel value" and is memorized as the associated category. After having learned about one thousand five hundred examples, the ZISC-036 based system is able to enhance an unlearned image. In the case of image restoration and coloration, implemented for

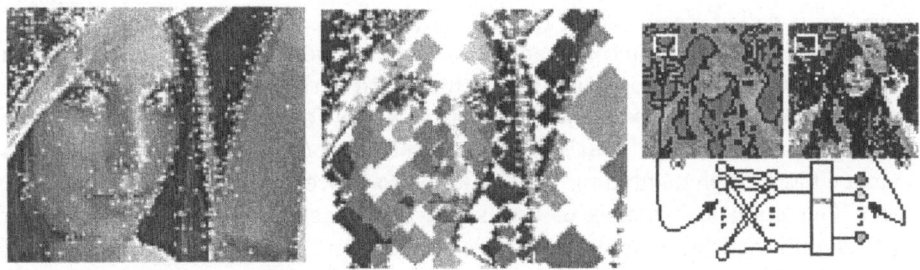

Fig. 3. Learning process examples showing learned pixels (left) and associated shapes (middle). Example of degraded image restoration showing input and output images (right)

old movies restoration and coloration, it has been shown in [10] that the same neural concept could perform different tasks which are necessary to restore a degraded movie: noise reduction as well as image enhancement or image coloration. Quantitative comparative studies established and analysed in above-mentioned references show pertinence of such techniques. Figure 4 gives a quantitative com-

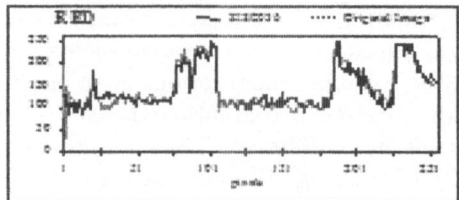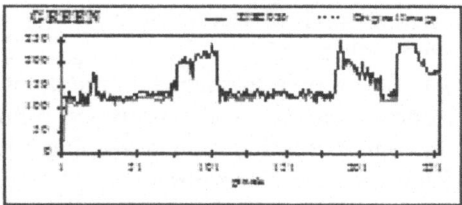

Fig. 4. Quantitative comparison of the colored (reconstructed) image with the original image in generalization phase

parison between colours in reconstructed images and those in the original image (which has been used as learning reference).

4.3   Intelligent Probe Mark Inspection in VLSI Production Industry

One of the main steps in VLSI circuit production is the testing step. This step verifies if the final product (VLSI circuit) operates correctly or not. The verification is performed thank to a set of characteristic input signals (stimulus) and associated responses obtained from the circuit under test. Stimulus are delivered to the circuit and the circuit's responses are catch through Input-Output pads (I/O pads) called also "vias". The test task is performed by units, which are called "probers" including a set of probes performing the communication with the circuit. The left picture of figure 5 shows a photograph of probes relative to such probers. The problem is related to the fact that the probes of the prober may damage the circuit under test. So, an additional step consists of inspecting the circuit's area to verify vias (I/O pads) status after circuit's testing: this operation is called Probe Mark Inspection (PMI).

Many prober constructors had already developed PMI software based on conventional pattern recognition algorithms with little success]. The difficulty is related to the compromise between real time execution (production constraints) and methods reliability. That's why a neural network based solution has been developed and implemented on ZISC-036 neuro-processor, for the IBM Essonnes plant. The main advantages of developed solutions are real-time control and high reliability in fault detection and classification tasks. Our automatic PMI, presented in [8] and [10], consists of software and a PC equipped with ZISC-036 neural board, a video acquisition board connected to a camera and a GPIB control board connected to a wafer prober system. Figure 5 represents the bloc diagram of the implemented system.

The process of analyzing a probe mark can be described as following: the PC controls the prober to move the chuck so that the via to inspect is precisely located under the camera; an image of the via is taken through the video acquisition board, then, the ZISC-036 based PMI:
- finds the via on the image.
- checks the integrity of the border (for damage) of via.
- locates the impact in the via and estimates its surface for statistics.

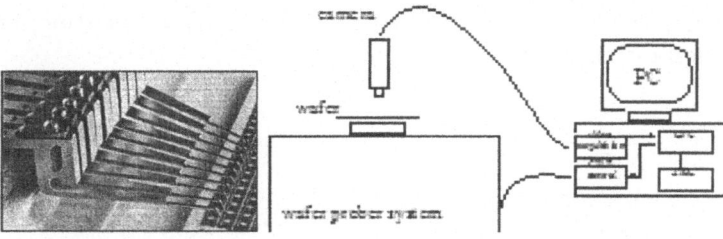

Fig. 5. Photograph giving an example of probes in industrial prober (left). Bloc-diagram of developed kernel neural networks based industrial PMI solution (right)

Figure 6 shows profile-to-fault association example. Experiments on different kinds of chips and on various probe defects have proven the efficiency of the neural approach to this kind of perception problem. The developed intelligent PMI system outperformed the best solutions offered by competitors by 30%: the best response time per via obtained using other wafer probers was about 600 ms and our neural based system analyzes one via every 400 ms, 300 of which were taken for the mechanical movements. Measures showed that the defect recognition neural module's execution time was negligible compared to the time spent for mechanical movements, as well as for the image acquisition (a ratio of 12 to 1 on any via). This application is presently inserted on a high throughput production line.

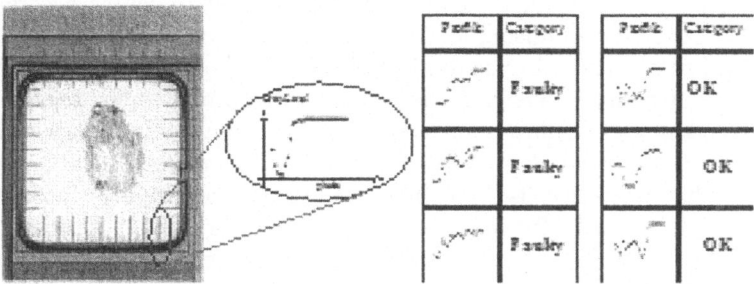

Fig. 6. Example of profiles extraction after via centring process

4.4 Non Linear Process Identification Using a Multiple Neural Network Based Models Generator

The identification task involves two essential steps: structure selection and parameter estimation. These two steps are linked and generally have to be realized in order to achieve the best compromise between error minimization and the total number of parameters in the final global model. In real world applications (situations), strong linearity, large number of related parameters and data nature complexity make the realization of those steps challenging, and so, the identification task difficult.

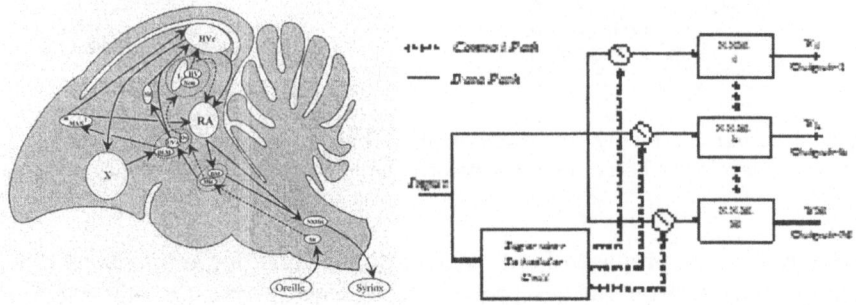

Fig. 7. Schematic representation of a lateral view of the left side of the bird's brain showing the auditory and motor pathways involved in the recognition and the production of song. (left). Bloc diagram of T-DTS Operation phase (right)

To overcome mentioned difficulties, one of the key points on which one can act is the complexity reduction. It concerns not only the problem solution level but also appears at processing procedure level. An issue could be model complexity reduction by splitting of a complex problem into a set of simpler problems: multi-modeling where a set of simple models is used to sculpt a complex behavior [11]. Another promising approach to reduce complexity takes advantage from hybridization [12]. On this basis and inspired from animal brain structure (left picture of figure 7, showing the left side of a bird's brain scheme and it's auditory and motor pathways involved in the recognition and the production of song), we have designed an ANN based data driven treelike Multiple Model generator, that we called T-DTS (Treelike Divide To Simplify), a data driven neural networks based Multiple Processing (multiple model) structure that is able to reduce complexity on both data and processing chain levels [13] (see right picture of figure 7). T-DTS and associated algorithm construct a treelike evolutionary neural architecture automatically where nodes (SU) are decision units and leafs correspond to neural based processing units (NNM).

We have applied T-DTS based Identifier to a real world industrial process identification and control problem. The process is a drilling rubber process used in plastic manufacturing industry. Several non-linear parameters influence the manufacturing process. To perform an efficient control of the manufacturing quality (process quality), one should identify the global process [14]. A Kohonen SOM based Supervisor/Scheduler Unit (SU) with a 4x3 grid generates and supervises 12 Neural Network based Models (NNM) trained from learning database. Figure 8 shows the bloc diagram of industrial processing loop and the identification result in the generalization phase. One can conclude that estimated output is in accord with the measured one.

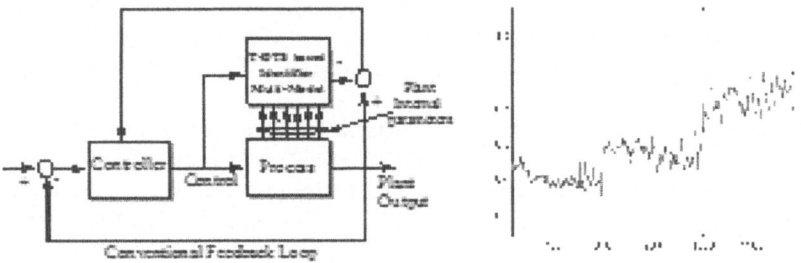

Fig. 8. Implemented industrial processing loop using a Kohonen SSU based T-DTS identifier (left). Identification of an unlearned sequence of drilling rubber plant's output (right)

5   Conclusion

The main goal of the present paper was focused on ANN based techniques and their application to solve real-world and industrial problems. The present paper show that today, conjunction of ANN's learnind and generalization ability with recent computational technologies offers attractive potential for designing and implementation of real-time intelligent industrial solutions. If this paper doesn't pretend to give an exhaustive state of art concerning huge potential offered by such approaches, it reports, through above-presented ANN based industrial applications, a plenty idea of promising capabilities of ANN based solutions to solve difficult future industrial changes.

Acknowledgements. Reported works were sponsored and supported by several research projects and industrial partners among which, French Ministry of Research and IBM-France Company. Author whish thank especially Dr. P. Tanhoff, and Dr. G. DeTremiolles from IBM-France for their partnership and joint collaboration. I would also acknowledge all members of my lab. as well as Dr. G. Mercier from PARIS XII University, who worked several years with me on intelligent adaptive control.

References

1. Faller W., Schreck S., Real-Time Prediction Of Unsteady Aerodynamics : Application for Aircraft Control and Maneuverability Enhancement, *IEEE Transactions on Neural Networks, Vol. 6, N¡ 6, Nov. 1995.*
2. Anderson C.W., Devulapalli, S.V., Stolz E.A., Determining Mental State from EEG Signals Using Parallel Implementations of Neural Networks, *Scientific Programming, Special Issue on Applications Analysis, 4, 3, Fall, pp 171-183, 1995.*
3. Sachenko A., Kochan V., Turchenko V., Golovko V., Savitsky J., Dunets A., Laopoulos T., Sensor errors prediction using neural networks, *Proceedings IJCNN'2000, Jul 24-Jul 27 2000, Como, Italy, pp. 441-446.*

4. Rumelhart D., Hinton G., Williams R., Learning Internal Representations by Error Propagation", *Rumelhart D., McClelland J., "Parallel Distributed Processing: Explorations in the Microstructure of Cognition", I & II, MIT Press, Cambridge MA, 1986.*
5. Kohonen T., Self-Organization and Associative Memory, *Springer-Verlag, 1984.*
6. Reyneri L.M., Weighted Radial Basis Functions for Improved Pattern Recognition and Signal Processing, *Neural Processing Letters, Vol. 2, No. 3, pp 2-6, May 1995.*
7. DeTrémiolles G., Madani K., Tannhof P., A New Approach to Radial Basis Function's like Artificial Neural Networks , *NeuroFuzzy'96, IEEE European Workshop, Vol. 6 N ° 2, pp 735-745, April 16 to 18, Prague, Czech Republic, 1996..*
8. DeTrémiolles G., Tannhof P., Plougonven B., Demarigny C., Madani K., Visual Probe Mark Inspection, using Hardware Implementation of Artificial Neural Networks, in VLSI Production, *LNCS - Biological and Artificial Computation : From Neuroscience to Technology, Ed. J. Mira, R. M. Diaz and J. Cabestany - Springer Verlag, pp 1374-1383, 1997.*
9. Madani K., Mercier G., Dinarvand M., Depecker J.C., A Neuro-Vector based electrical machines driver combining a neural plant identifier and a conventional vector controller, *SPIE International Symposium AeroSense'99, Orlando, Florida, USA, April 1999.*
10. Madani K., DeTremiolles G., Tanhoff P., Image processing using RBF like neural networks: A ZISC-036 based fully parallel implementation solving real world and real complexity industrial problems, *J. of Applied Intelligence N ° 18, 2003, Kluwer, pp. 195-231.*
11. Multiple Model Approaches to Modeling and Control, edited by R. Murray-Smith and T.A. Johansen, Taylor & Francis Publishers, 1997, ISBN 0-7484-0595-X.
12. Goonatilake S. and Khebbal S.: Issues, Classification and Future Directions. In Intelligent Hybrid Systems. John Wiley & Sons, pp 1-20, ISBN 0 471 94242 1.
13. Madani K., Chebira A., Rybnik M., Data Driven Multiple Neural Network Models Generator Based on a Tree-like Scheduler, LNC "Computational Methods in Neural Modeling", Ed. Jose Mira, Jose R. Alvarez - Springer Verlag 2003, ISBN 3-540-40210-1, pp. 382-389.
14. Chebira A., Madani K., Rybnik M., Non Linear Process Identification Using a Neural Network Based Multiple Models Generator, LLNCS "Artificial Neural Nets Problem Solving Methods", Ed. J. Mira, J. R. Alvarez - Springer Verlag 2003, ISBN 3-540-40211-X, pp. 647-654.

ACTIVEMATH: An Intelligent Tutoring System for Mathematics

Erica Melis and Jörg Siekmann

German Research Institute for Artificial Intelligence (DFKI)
Stuhlsatzenhausweg, 66123 Saarbrücken, Germany
phone: +49 681 302 4629, fax: +49 681 302 2235

Abstract. ACTIVEMATH is a web-based intelligent tutoring system for mathematics. This article presents the technical and pedagogical goals of ACTIVEMATH, its principles of design and architecture, its knowledge representation, and its adaptive behavior. In particular, we concentrate on those features that rely on AI-techniques.

1 Introduction

Intelligent tutoring systems (ITSs) have been researched in AI now for several decades. With the enormous development and increasing availability of the Internet, the application of web-based learning systems becomes more likely and realistic and research for intelligent features receives more attention than before. As a result, a number of new ITS have been developed over the last five years, among them ACTIVEMATH, a web-based, adaptive learning environment for mathematics.

These systems strive for improving long-distance learning, for complementing traditional classroom teaching, and for supporting individual and life-long learning. Web-based systems are available on central servers and allow a user to learn in her own environment and whenever it is appropriate for her.

Intelligent tutoring systems are a great field of application for AI-techniques. In a nutshell, our research for ACTIVEMATH has used and further developed results in

- problem solving
- rule-based systems
- knowledge representation
- user modeling ?
- adaptive systems and adaptive hyper-media
- diagnosis.

Learning environments have to meet realistic and complex needs rather than being a specific research system for specific demonstrations such as the famous blocksworld. Therefore, we point out important pedagogical and technical goals that our research for ACTIVEMATH had to satisfy.

L. Rutkowski et al. (Eds.): ICAISC 2004, LNAI 3070, pp. 91–101, 2004.
© Springer-Verlag Berlin Heidelberg 2004

Pedagogical Goals

ACTIVEMATH' design aims at supporting truly interactive, exploratory learning and assumes the student to be responsible for her learning to some extent. Therefore, a relative freedom for navigating through a course and for learning choices is given and by default, the student model is scrutable, i.e., inspectable and modifiable. Moreover, dependencies of learning objects can be inspected in a dictionary to help the student to learn the overall picture of a domain (e.g., analysis) and also the dependencies of concepts.

Several dimensions of adaptivity to the student and her learning context improve the learner's motivation and performance. Most previous intelligent tutor systems did not rely on an adaptive choice of content. A reason might be that the envisioned use was mostly in schools, where traditionally every student learns the same concepts for the same use. In colleges and universities, however, the same subject is already taught differently for different groups of users and in different contexts, e.g., statistics has to be taught differently for students of mathematics, for economics, or medicine. Therefore, the adaptive choice of content to be presented as well as examples and exercises is pivotal. In addition, an adaptation of examples and exercises to the student's capabilities is highly desirable in order to keep the learner in the zone of proximal development [13] rather than overtax or undertax her.

Moreover, web-based systems can be used in several learning contexts, e.g., long-distance learning, homework, and teacher-assisted learning. Personalization is required in all of them because even for teacher-assisted learning in a computer-free classroom with, say, 30 students and one teacher individualized learning is impossible. ACTIVEMATH's current version provides adaptive content, adaptive presentation features, and adaptive appearance.

Technical Goals

Building quality hyper-media content is a time-consuming and costly process, hence the content should be *reusable* in different contexts. However, most of today's interactive textbooks consist of a collection of predefined documents, typically canned HTML pages and multimedia animations. This situation makes a reuse in other contexts and a re-combination of the encoded knowledge impossible and inhibits a radical adaptation of course presentation and content to the user's needs.

ACTIVEMATH' knowledge representation contributes to re-usability and interoperability. In particular, it is compliant with the emerging knowledge representation and communication standards such as Dublin Core, OpenMath, MathML, and LOM[1]. Some of the buzzwords here are metadata, ontological XML, (OMDoc [8], and standardized content packaging. Such features of knowledge representations will ensure a long-term employment of the new technologies in browsers and other devices. In order to use the potential power of existing web-based technology e-Learning systems need an open architecture to integrate and connect

---

[1] http://ltsc.ieee.org/wg12/

to new components including student management systems such as WebCT, assessment tools, collaboration tools, and problem solving tools.

Organization of the Article. This article provides an overview of the current ACTIVEMATH system. It describes some main features in more detail, in particular, the architecture and its components, the knowledge representation, the student model and the adaptation based on the information from the student model.

2   Architecture

The architecture of ACTIVEMATH, as sketched in Figure 1, strictly realizes the principle of separation of (declarative) knowledge and functionalities as well as the separation of different kinds of knowledge. For instance, pedagogical knowledge is stored in a pedagogical rule base, the educational content is stored in MBase, and the knowledge about the user is stored in the student model. This principle has proved valuable in many AI-applications and eases modifications as well as configurability and reuse of the system.

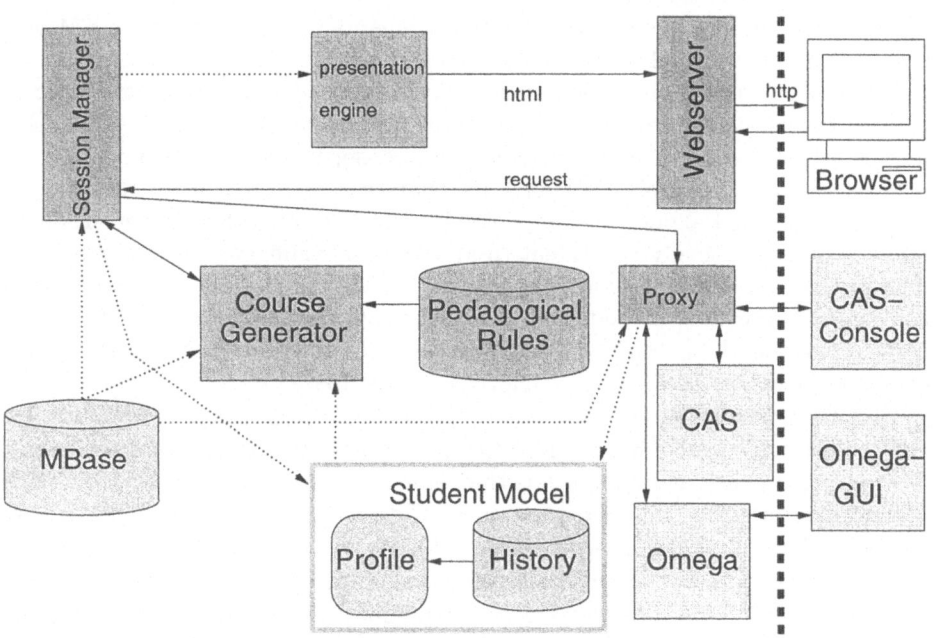

Fig. 1. Architecture of ACTIVEMATH

ACTIVEMATH has a client-server architecture whose client can be restricted to a browser. This architecture serves not only the openness but also the *platform independence.* On the client side, a browser – netscape higher than 6, Mozilla, or IE with MathPlayer – is sufficient to work with ACTIVEMATH. On the server-side components of ACTIVEMATH have been deliberately designed in a *modular* way in order to guarantee exchangeability and robustness.

When the user has chosen her goal concepts and learning scenario, the session manager sends a request to the *course generator*. The course generator is responsible for choosing and arranging the content to be learned. The course generator contacts the *mathematical knowledge base* in order to fetch the identifiers (IDs) of the mathematical concepts that are required for understanding the goal concepts, queries the student model in order to find out about the user's prior knowledge and preferences, and uses *pedagogical rules* to select, annotate, and arrange the content – including examples and exercises – in a way that is suitable for the learner. The resulting instructional graph, a list of IDs, is sent to the *presentation engine* that retrieves the actual mathematical content corresponding to the IDs and that transforms the XML-data to output-pages which are then presented via the user's browser.

The *course* generator and the suggestion mechanism [10] work with the rule-based system Jess [6] that evaluates the (pedagogical) rules in order to decide which particular adaptation and content to select and which actions to suggest. Jess uses the Rete algorithm [5] for optimization.

External systems such as the computer algebra systems Maple and MuPad and the proof planner Multi are integrated with ACTIVEMATH. They serve as cognitive tools [9] and support the learner in performing complex interactive exercises and they assist in producing feedback by evaluating the learner's input.Also, a diagnosis is passed to the student model in order to update the model.

In these exercises, ACTIVEMATH does not necessarily guide the user strictly along a predefined expert solution. It may only evaluate whether the student's input is mathematically equivalent to an admissible subgoal, i.e., maybe irrelevant but not outside the solution space (see [3]). Moreover, the external systems can support the user by automated problem solving, i.e., they can take over certain parts in the problem solving process and thereby help the user to focus on certain learning tasks and to delegate routine tasks.

Actually, most diagnoses are known to be AI-hard problems. Most ITSs encode the possible problem solving steps and the most typical misconceptions into their solution space or into systems that execute them. From this encoding, the system diagnoses the misconception of a student. This is, however, (1) infeasible in realistic applications with large solution spaces and (2) it is in general impossible to represent all potential misconceptions of a student [17].

The *presentation engine* generates personalized web pages based on two frameworks: Maverick and Velocity. Maverick[2] is a minimalist MVC framework for web publishing using Java and J2EE, focusing solely on MVC logic. It provides a wiring between URLs, Java controller classes and view templates.

The presentation engine is a reusable component that takes a structure of OMDocs and transforms them into a presentation output that can be PDF

---

[2] Maverick: http://mav.sourceforge.net/

(print format) or HTML with different maths-presentations – Unicode or MathML – (screen format) [7]. Basically, the presentation pipeline comprises two stages: stage 1 encompasses Fetching, Pre-Processing and Transformation, while stage 2 consists of Assembly, Personalization and optional Compilation. Stage 1 deals with individual content fragments or items, which are written in OMDoc and stored in a knowledge base. At this stage, content items do not depend on the user who is to view them. They have unique identifiers and can be handled separately. It is only in stage 2 that items are composed to user-specific pages.

3   Adaptivity

ACTIVEMATH adapts its course generation (and presentation) to the student's

- technical equipment (customization)
- environment variables, e.g., curriculum, language, field of study (contextualization) and
- her cognitive and educational needs and preferences such as learning goals, and prerequisite knowledge (personalization).

As for personalization, individual preferences (such as the style of presentation), goal-competencies, and mastery-level are considered by the course generator. On the one hand, the goal-competencies are characterized by concepts that are to be learned and on the other hand, by the competency-level to be achieved: knowledge (k), comprehension (c), or application (a). The learner can initialize her student model by self-assessment of her mastery-level of concepts and choose her learning goals and learning scenario, for instance, the preparation for an exam or learning from scratch for k-competency level. The course generator processes this information and updates the student model and generates pages/sessions as depicted in the screenshots of Figure 2 and 3. These two screenshots differ in the underlying scenarios as the captions indicate.

Adaptation to the capabilities of the learner occurs in course generation as well as in the suggestion mechanism. The course generation checks whether the mastery-level of prerequisite concepts is sufficient for the goal competency. If not, it presents the missing concepts and/or explanations, examples, exercises for these concepts to the learner when a new session is requested. The suggestion mechanism acts dynamically in response to the student's activities. Essentially, this mechanism works with two blackboards, a diagnosis blackboard and a suggestion blackboard on which particular knowledge sources operate.

We also investigated special scenarios that support a student's meta-cognitive activities, such as those proposed in the seminal book 'How to Solve it' by Polya [15]. A Polya-scenario structures the problem solutions by introducing headlines such as "understand the problem", "make a plan", "execute the plan", and "look back at the solution". It augments and structures exercises with additional prompts similar to the above headlines [12].

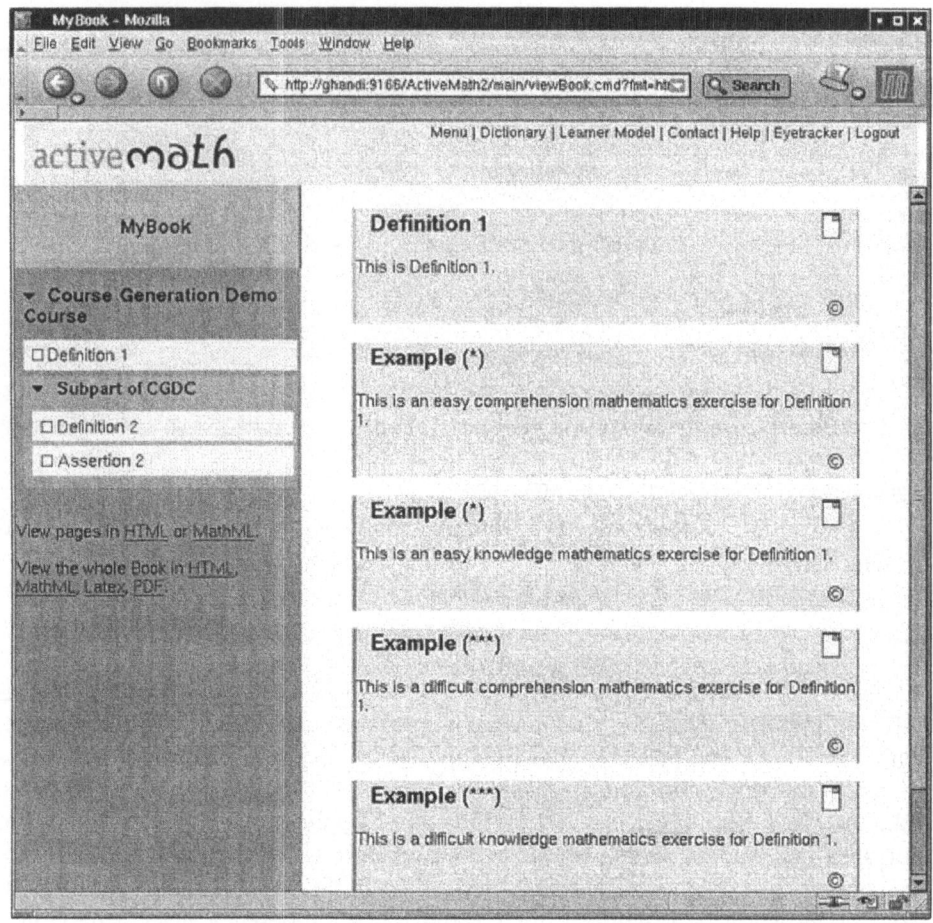

Fig. 2. A screen shot of an ACTIVEMATH session for exam preparation

4   Student Modeling

User modeling has been a research area in AI for a long time. Actually, it started with early student modeling and still continues with the investigation of representational issues as well as diagnostic and updating techniques.

As ACTIVEMATH' presentation is user-adaptive, it needs to incorporate persistent information about the user as well as a representation of the user's learning progress. Therefore, 'static' (wrt. the current session) properties such as field, scenario, goal concepts, and preferences as well as the 'dynamic' properties such as the mastery values for concepts and the student's actual behavior, are stored in the student model. These different types of information are stored separately in the *history* and the static and dynamic *profiles*.

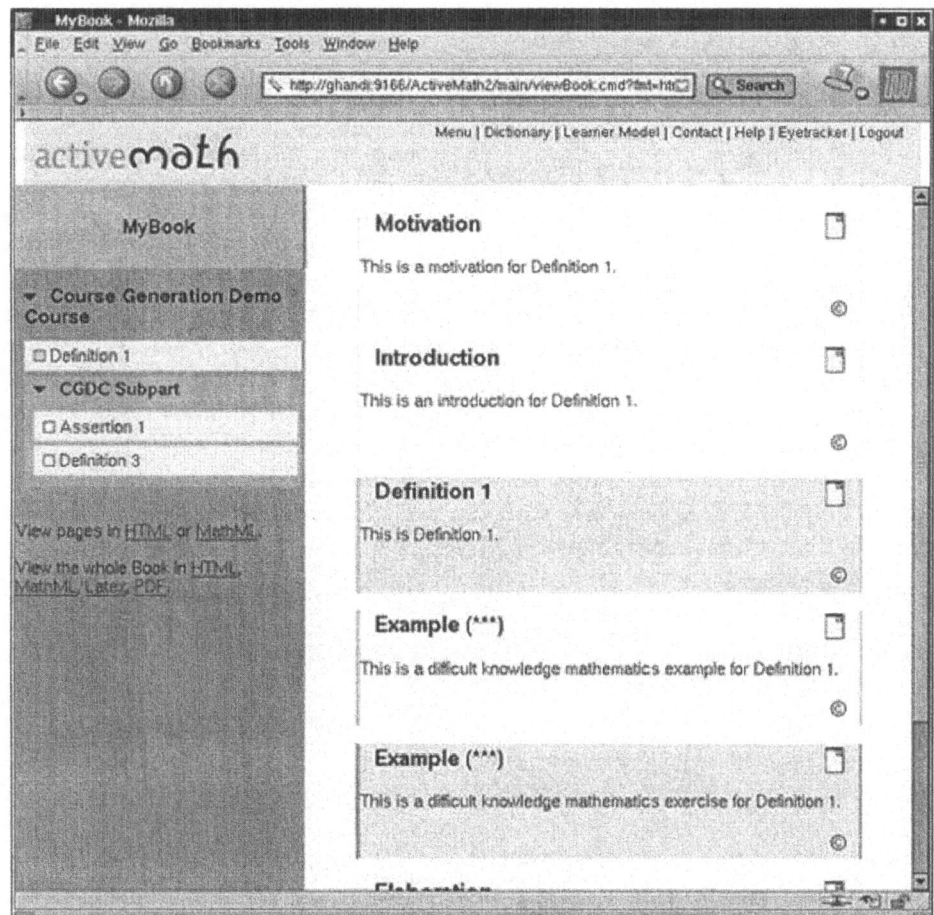

Fig. 3. k-level session of ACTIVEMATH

The profile is initialized with the learner's entries submitted to ACTIVE-MATH' registration page which describe the preferences (static), scenario, goals (static for the current session), and self-assessment values for knowledge, comprehension, and application of concepts (dynamic).

The history component stores the information about the learner's actions. Its elements contain information such as the IDs of the content of a read page or the ID of an exercise, the reading time, and the success rate of the exercise. Meanwhile, we developed a "poor man's eye-tracker" which allows to trace the student's attention and reading time in detail.

To represent the concept mastery assessment, the current (dynamic) profile contains values for a subset of the competences of Bloom's mastery taxonomy [2]:

- Knowledge
- Comprehension
- Application.

Finishing an exercise or going to another page triggers an updating process of the student model. Since different types of learner actions can exhibit different competencies, reading a concept mainly updates 'knowledge' values, following examples mainly updates 'comprehension', and solving exercises mainly updates 'application'. When the student model receives the notification that a student has finished reading a page, an evaluator fetches the list of its items and their types (concept, example, ...) and delivers an update of the values of those items. When the learner finishes an exercise, an appropriate evaluator delivers an update of the values of the involved concepts that depends on the difficulty and on the rating of how successful the solution was.

The student model is inspectable and modifiable by the student as shown in Figure 4. Our experience is that students tend to inspect their student model in order to plan what to learn next.

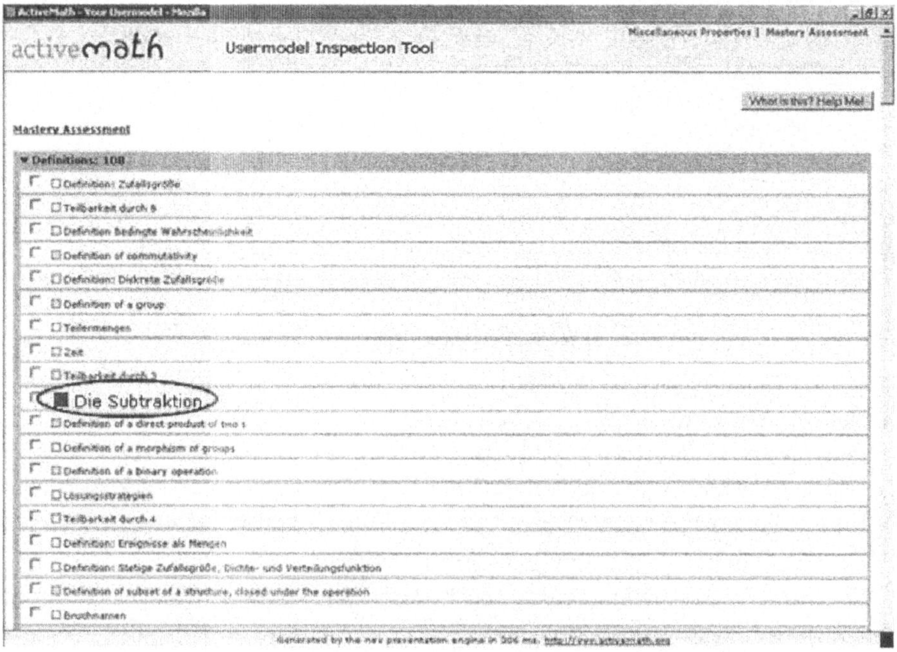

Fig. 4. Inspection of the student model (mastery-level)

5 Knowledge Representation

As opposed to the purely syntactic representation formats for mathematical knowledge such as LaTex or HTML, the knowledge representation used by ACTIVE-MATH is the *semantic* XML-language OMDoc which is an extension of OpenMath [4]. OpenMath provides a collection of OpenMath objects together with a grammar for the representation of mathematical objects and sets of standardized symbols (the content-dictionaries). That is, OpenMath talks about objects rather than syntax.

Since OpenMath does not have any means to represent the content of a mathematical *document* nor its structure, OMDoc defines logical units such as "definition", "theorem", and "proof". In addition, the purely mathematical OMDoc is augmented by educational metadata such as difficulty of a learning object or type of an exercise.

This representation has several advantages, among them

- it is human and machine understandable
- the presentation of mathematical objects can in principle be copied and pasted
- the presentations can automatically and dynamically be linked to concepts and learning objects and thus, found by ACTIVEMATH's dictionary when clicking on a concept or formula in the course.

For more details, see [11].

6 Conclusion, Related and Future Work

The intelligent tutoring systems group – at the DFKI Saarbrücken and at the University of Saarland – has been developing the web-based ITS ACTIVEMATH now for several years. A demo (and demo guide) is available at http://www.activemath.org.

This system is configurable with pedagogical strategies, content, and presentational style sheets as well as with external problem solving systems. It employs a number of AI-techniques to realize adaptive course generation, student modeling, feedback, interactive exercises, and a knowledge representation that is expedient for the semantic Web.

Related Work. Most web-based learning systems (particularly commercial ones) offer fixed multimedia web pages and facilities for user management and communication and most of them lack support for truly interactive problem solving and user-adaptivity. Moreover, they use proprietary knowledge representation formats rather than a standardized knowledge representation which is exchangeable between systems. Some user-adaptivity is offered by systems such as ELM-ART [18] and Metalink [14].

During the last decades research on pedagogy in the mathematics recognized that students learn mathematics more effectively, if the traditional rote learning of formulas and procedures is supplemented with the possibility to explore a broad range of problems and problem situations [16]. In particular, the international comparative study of mathematics teaching, TIMSS [1], has shown (1) that teaching with an orientation towards active problem solving yields better learning results in the sense that the acquired knowledge is more readily available and applicable especially in new contexts and (2) that a reflection about the problem solving activities and methods yields a deeper understanding and better performance.

Future Work. We are now working on cognitively motivated extensions of AC-TIVEMATH by new types of examples and exercises that have shown their merit for learning. In particular, the student model will be enhanced by information about the learner's motivation such that the system can properly react to excitement, boredom and other motivational states.

Other extensions are being realized in the EU-project LeActiveMath that investigates natural language facilitiesfor a tutorial dialogue in interactive exercises and dialogues about the student model.

Acknowledgment. The system reported in this article is the result of work of the ACTIVEMATH-Group and we thank its members Eric Andres, Michael Dietrich, Adrian Frischauf, Alberto Gonzales Palomo, Paul Libbrecht, Carsten Ullrich, and Stefan Winterstein.

References

1. J. Baumert, R. Lehmann, M. Lehrke, B. Schmitz, M. Clausen, I. Hosenfeld, O. Köller, and J. Neubrand. *Mathematisch-naturwissenschaftlicher Unterricht im internationalen Vergleich.* Leske und Budrich, 1997.
2. B.S. Bloom, editor. *Taxonomy of educational objectives: The classification of educational goals: Handbook I, cognitive domain.* Longmans, Green, New York, Toronto, 1956.
3. J. Buedenbender, E. Andres, A. Frischauf, G. Goguadze, P. Libbrecht, E. Melis, and C. Ullrich. Using computer algebra systems as cognitive tools. In S.A. Cerri, G. Gouarderes, and F. Paraguacu, editors, *6th International Conference on Intelligent Tutor Systems (ITS-2002)*, number 2363 in Lecture Notes in Computer Science, pages 802–810. Springer-Verlag, 2002.
4. O. Caprotti and A. M. Cohen. Draft of the open math standard. Open Math Consortium, http://www.nag.co.uk/projects/OpenMath/omstd/, 1998.
5. C.L. Forgy. Rete: a fast algorithm for the many pattern/many object pattern match problem. *Artificial Intelligence*, pages 17–37, 1982.
6. E. Friedman-Hill. Jess, the java expert system shell. Technical Report SAND98-8206, Sandia National Laboratories, 1997.
7. A. Gonzalez-Palomo, P. Libbrecht, and C. Ullrich. A presentation architecture for individualized content. In *The Twelfth International World Wide Web Conference*, 2003. submitted.
8. M. Kohlhase. OMDoc: Towards an internet standard for the administration, distribution and teaching of mathematical knowledge. In *Proceedings Artificial Intelligence and Symbolic Computation AISC'2000*, 2000.

9. S. Lajoie and S. Derry, editors. *Computers as Cognitive Tools*. Erlbaum, Hillsdale, NJ, 1993.

10. E. Melis and E. Andres. Global feedback in ACTIVEMATH. In *Proceedings of the World Conference on E-Learning in Corporate, Government, Healthcare, and Higher Education (eLearn-2003)*, pages 1719–1724. AACE, 2003.

11. E. Melis, J. Buedenbender E. Andres, A. Frischauf, G. Goguadse, P. Libbrecht, M. Pollet, and C. Ullrich. Knowledge representation and management in ACTIVE-MATH. *International Journal on Artificial Intelligence and Mathematics, Special Issue on Management of Mathematical Knowledge*, 38(1-3):47–64, 2003.

12. E. Melis and C. Ullrich. How to teach it – Polya-scenarios in ACTIVEMATH. In U. Hoppe, F. Verdejo, and J. Kay, editors, *AI in Education, AIED-2003*, pages 141–147. IOS Press, 2003.

13. T. Murray and I. Arroyo. Towards measuring and maintaining the zone of proximal development in adaptive instructional systems. In S.A. Cerri, G. Gouarderes, and F.Paraguacu, editors, *Intelligent Tutoring Systems, 6th International Conference, ITS 2002*, volume 2363 of *LNCS*, pages 749–758. Springer-Verlag, 2002.

14. T. Murray, C. Condit, T. Shen, J. Piemonte, and S. Khan. Metalinks - a framework and authoring tool for adaptive hypermedia. In S.P. Lajoie and M. Vivet, editors, *Proceedings of the International Conference on Artificial Intelligence and Education*, pages 744–746. IOS Press, 1999.

15. G. Polya. *How to Solve it*. Princeton University Press, Princeton, 1945.

16. A.H. Schoenfeld, editor. *A Source Book for College Mathematics Teaching*. Mathematical Association of America, Washington, DC, 1990.

17. K. VanLehn, C. Lynch, L. Taylor, A. Weinstein, R. Shelby, K. Schulze, D. Treacy, and M. Wintersgill. Minimally invasive tutoring of complex physics problem solving. In S.A. Cerri, G. Gouarderes, and F. Paraguacu, editors, *Intelligent Tutoring Systems, 6th International Conference, ITS 2002*, number 2363 in LNCS, pages 367–376. Springer-Verlag, 2002.

18. G. Weber and P. Brusilovsky. ELM-ART an adaptive versatile system for web-based instruction. *Artificial Intelligence and Education*, 2001.

Inference Rules and Decision Rules

Zdzisław Pawlak

Institute for Theoretical and Applied Informatics
Polish Academy of Sciences
ul. Bałtycka 5, 44-100 Gliwice, Poland
and
University of Information Technology and Management
ul. Newelska 6, 01-447 Warsaw, Poland
zpw@ii.pw.edu.pl

Abstract. Basic rules of inference used in classical logic are *Modus Ponens* (MP) and *Modus Tollens* (MT). These two reasoning patterns start from some general knowledge about reality, expressed by true implication, "*if Φ then Ψ*". Then basing on true *premise Φ* we arrive at true *conclusion Ψ* (MP), or from negation of true conclusion Ψ we get negation of true premise Φ (MT).

In reasoning from data (data mining) we also use rules "*if Φ then Ψ*", called *decision rules*, to express our knowledge about reality, but in this case the meaning of the expression is different. It does not express general knowledge but refers to partial facts. Therefore decision rules are not true or false but probable (possible) only.

In this paper we compare inference rules and decision rules in the context of decision networks, proposed by the author as a new approach to analyze reasoning patterns in data.

Keywords: *Modus Ponenes, Modus Tollens*, decision rules

1   Introduction

Basic rules of inference used in classical logic are *Modus Ponens* (MP) and *Modus Tollens* (MT). These two reasoning patterns start from some general knowledge about reality, expressed by true implication, "*if Φ then Ψ*". Then basing on true *premise Φ* we arrive at true *conclusion Ψ* (MP), or if negation of conclusion Ψ is true we infer that negation of premise Φ is true (MT).

In reasoning from data (data mining) we also use rules "*if Φ then Ψ*", called *decision rules*, to express our knowledge about reality, but the meaning of decision rules is different. It does not express general knowledge but refers to partial facts. Therefore decision rules are not true or false but probable (possible) only.

In this paper we compare inference rules and decision rules in the context of decision networks, proposed by the author as a new approach to analyze reasoning patterns in data.

Decision network is a set of logical formulas $\mathcal{F}$ together with a binary relation over the set $\mathcal{R} \subseteq \mathcal{F} \times \mathcal{F}$ of formulas, called a *consequence relation*. Elements of

L. Rutkowski et al. (Eds.): ICAISC 2004, LNAI 3070, pp. 102–108, 2004.
© Springer-Verlag Berlin Heidelberg 2004

the relation are called *decision rules*. The decision network can be perceived as a directed graph, nodes of which are formulas and branches – are decision rules. Thus the decision network can be seen as a knowledge representation system, revealing data structure of a data base.

Discovering patterns in the database represented by a decision network boils down to discovering some patterns in the network. Analogy to the *modus ponens* and *modus tollens* inference rules will be shown and discussed.

2   Decision Networks

In this section we give after [3] basic notations of decision networks.

Let U be a non empty finite set, called the *universe* and let Φ , Ψ be logical formulas. The meaning of Φ in U, denoted by $|\Phi|$, is the set of all elements of U, that satisfies Φ in U. The truth value of Φ denoted $val(\Phi)$ is defined as $card|\Phi|/card(U)$, where $cardX$ denotes cardinality of X and can be interpreted as probability that Φ is true [1].

By *decision network* over $S = (U, \mathcal{F})$ we mean a pair $N = (\mathcal{F}, \mathcal{R})$, where $\mathcal{R} \subseteq \mathcal{F} \times \mathcal{F}$ is a binary relation, called a *consequence relation*.

Any pair $(\Phi, \Psi) \in \mathcal{R}, \Phi \neq \Psi$ is referred to as a *decision rule* (in N).

We assume that S is known and we will not refer to it in what follows.

A decision rule (Φ, Ψ) will be also presented as an expression $\Phi \to \Psi$, read if Φ *then* Ψ, where Φ and Ψ are referred to as *premise* (*conditions*) and *conclusion* (*decisions*) of the rule, respectively.

If $\Phi \to \Psi$ is a decision rule, then $\Psi \to \Phi$ will be called an *inversed* decision rule. If we invert all decision rules in a decision network, than the resulting decision network will be called *inverted*.

The number $supp(\Phi, \Psi) = card(|\Phi \wedge \Psi|)$ will be called a *support* of the rule $\Phi \to \Psi$. We will consider nonvoid decision rules only, i.e., rules such that $supp(\Phi, \Psi) \neq 0$.

With every decision rule $\Phi \to \Psi$ we associate its *strength* defined as

$$str(\Phi, \Psi) = \frac{supp(\Phi, \Psi)}{card(U)}. \tag{1}$$

Moreover, with every decision rule $\Phi \to \Psi$ we associate the *certainty factor* defined as

$$cer(\Phi, \Psi) = \frac{str(\Phi, \Psi)}{val(\Phi)} \tag{2}$$

and the *coverage factor* of $\Phi \to \Psi$

$$cov(\Phi, \Psi) = \frac{str(\Phi, \Psi)}{val(\Psi)}, \tag{3}$$

where $val(\Phi) \neq 0$ and $val(\Psi) \neq 0$.

We assume that

$$val(\Phi) = \sum_{\Psi \in Con(\Phi)} str(\Phi, \Psi) \tag{4}$$

and

$$val(\Psi) = \sum_{\Phi \in Pre(\Psi)} str(\Phi, \Psi), \tag{5}$$

where $Con(\Phi)$ and $Pre(\Psi)$ are sets of all conclusions and premises of the corresponding formulas respectively.

Consequently we have

$$\sum_{Con(\Phi)} car(\phi, \Psi) = \sum_{Pre(\Psi)} cov(\Phi, \Psi) = 1 \tag{6}$$

If a decision rule $\Phi \to \Psi$ uniquely determines decisions in terms of conditions, i.e., if $cer(\Phi, \Psi) = 1$, then the rule is *certain*, otherwise the rule is *uncertain*.

If a decision rule $\Phi \to \Psi$ covers all decisions, i.e., if $cov(\Phi, \Psi) = 1$ then the decision rule is *total*, otherwise the decision rule is *partial*.

Immediate consequences of (2) and (3) are:

$$cer(\Phi, \Psi) = \frac{cov(\Phi, \Psi)val(\Psi)}{val(\Psi)}, \tag{7}$$

$$cov(\Phi, \Psi) = \frac{cer(\Phi, \Psi)val(\Phi)}{val(\Psi)}. \tag{8}$$

Note, that (7) and (8) are Bayes' formulas. This relationship first was observed by Łukasiewicz [1].

Any sequence of formulas $\Phi_1 \ldots \Phi_n$, $\Phi_i \in \mathcal{F}$ and for every i, $1 \le i \le n - 1$, $(\Phi_i, \Phi_{i+1}) \in \mathcal{R}$ will be called a *path* from Φ_1 to Φ_n and will be denoted by $[\Phi_1 \ldots \Phi_n]$.

We define

$$cer[\Phi_1 \ldots \Phi_n] = \prod_{i=1}^{n-1} cer[\Phi_i, \Phi_{i+1}], \tag{9}$$

$$cov[\Phi_1 \ldots \Phi_n] = \prod_{i=1}^{n-1} cov[\Phi_i, \Phi_{i+1}], \tag{10}$$

and

$$str[\Phi_1 \ldots \Phi_n] = val(\Phi_1)cer[\Phi_1 \ldots \Phi_n] = val(\Phi_n)cov[\Phi_1 \ldots \Phi_n]. \tag{11}$$

The set of all paths form Φ to Ψ, detoted $< \Phi, \Psi >$, will be called a *connection* form Φ to Ψ.

For connection we have

$$cer < \Phi, \Psi >= \sum_{[\Phi \ldots \Psi] \in <\Phi, \Psi>} cer[\Phi \ldots \Psi], \tag{12}$$

$$cov < \Phi, \Psi >= \sum_{[\Phi \ldots \Psi] \in <\Phi, \Psi>} cov[\Phi \ldots \Psi], \tag{13}$$

$$str < \Phi, \Psi > = \sum_{[\Phi...\Psi]\in<\Phi,\Psi>} str[\Phi...\Psi] =$$
$$= val(\Phi)cer < \Phi, \Psi >= val(\Psi)cov < \Phi, \Psi > . \qquad (14)$$

With every decision network we can associate a flow graph [2, 3]. Formulas of the network are interpreted as nodes of the graph, and decision rules – as directed branches of the flow graph, whereas strength of a decision rule is interpreted as flow of the corresponding branch.

3   Rough *Modus Ponens* and Rough *Modus Tollens*

Classical rules of inference used in logic are *Modus Ponens* and *Modus Tollens*, which have the form

if $\Phi \rightarrow \Psi$ *is true*
and Φ *is true*
then Ψ *is true*

and

if $\Phi \rightarrow \Psi$ *is true*
and $\sim \Psi$ *is true*
then $\sim \Phi$ *is true*

respectively.

Modus Ponens allows us to obtain true consequences from true premises, whereas *Modus Tollens* yields true negation of premise from true negation of conclusion.

In reasoning about data (data analysis) the situation is different. Instead of true propositions we consider propositional functions, which are true to a "degree", i.e., they assume truth values which lie between 0 and 1, in other words, they are probable, not true.

Besides, instead of true inference rules we have now decision rules, which are neither true nor false. They are characterized by three coefficients, *strength, certainty* and *coverage factors*. Strength of a decision rule can be understood as a counterpart of truth value of the inference rule, and it represents frequency of the decision rule in a database.

Thus employing decision rules to discovering patterns in data boils down to computation probability of conclusion in terms of probability of the premise and strength of the decision rule, or – the probability of the premise from the probability of the conclusion and strength of the decision rule.

Hence, the role of decision rules in data analysis is somehow similar to classical inference patterns, as shown by the schemes below.

Two basic rules of inference for data analysis are as follows:

if	$\Phi \to \Psi$	has $cer(\Phi, \Psi)$ and $cov(\Phi, \Psi)$
and	Φ	is true with the probability $val(\Phi)$
then	Ψ	is true with the probability $val(\Psi) = \alpha val(\Phi)$.

Similarly

if	$\Phi \to \Psi$	has $cer(\Phi, \Psi)$ and $cov(\Phi, \Psi)$
and	Ψ	is true with the probability $val(\Psi)$
then	Φ	is true with the probability $val(\Phi) = \alpha^{-1} val(\Phi)$.

The above inference rules can be considered as counterparts of *Modus Ponens* and *Modus Tollens* for data analysis and will be called Rough *Modus Ponens* (RMP) and Rough *Modus Tollens* (RMT), respectively.

There are however essential differences between MP (MT) and RMP (RMT).

First, instead of truth values associated with inference rules we consider certainly and coverage factors (conditional probabilities) assigned to decision rules.

Second, in the case of decision rules, in contrast to inference rules, truth value of a conclusion (RMP) depends not only on a single premise but in fact depends on truth values of premises of all decision rules having the same conclusions. Similarly, for RMT.

Let us also notice that inference rules are transitive, i.e., *if* $\Phi \to \Psi$ *and* $\Psi \to \Theta$ *then* $\Phi \to \Theta$ and decision rules are not. *If* $\Phi \to \Psi$ *and* $\Psi \to \Theta$, then we have to compute the certainty, coverage and strength of the rule $\Phi \to \Theta$, employing formulas (9), (10), (12) and (13).

This shows clearly the difference between reasoning patterns using classical inference rules in logical reasoning and using decision rules in reasoning about data.

4   An Example

Suppose that three models of cars Φ_1, Φ_2 and Φ_3 are sold to three disjoint groups of customers Θ_1, Θ_2 and Θ_3 through four dealers Ψ_1, Ψ_2, Ψ_3 and Ψ_4.

Moreover, let us assume that car models and dealers are distributed as shown in Fig. 1.

Applying RMP to data shown in Fig. 1 we get results shown in Fig. 2. In order to find how car models are distributed among customer groups we have to compute all connections among cars models and consumers groups, i.e., to apply RMP to data given in Fig. 2. The results are shown in Fig. 3.

For example, we can see from the decision network that consumer group Θ_2 bought 21% of car model Φ_1, 35% of car model Φ_2 and 44% of car model Φ_3. Conversely, for example, car model Φ_1 is distributed among customer groups as follows: 31% cars bought group Θ_1, 57% group Θ_2 and 12% group Θ_3.

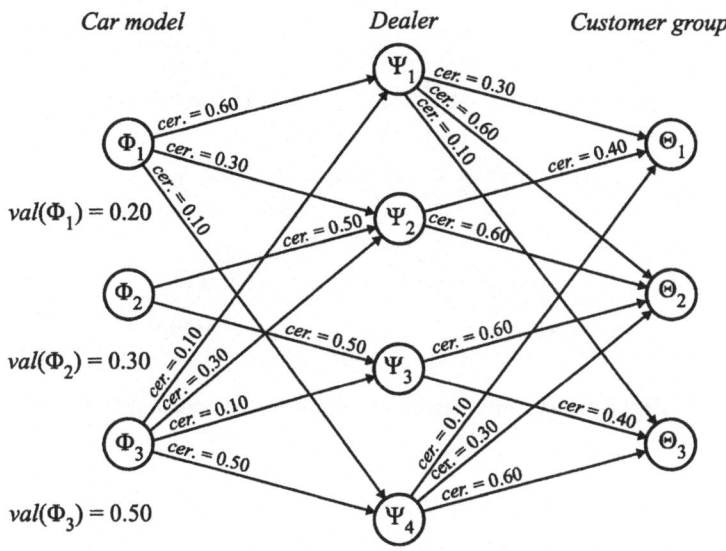

Fig. 1. Car and dealear distribution

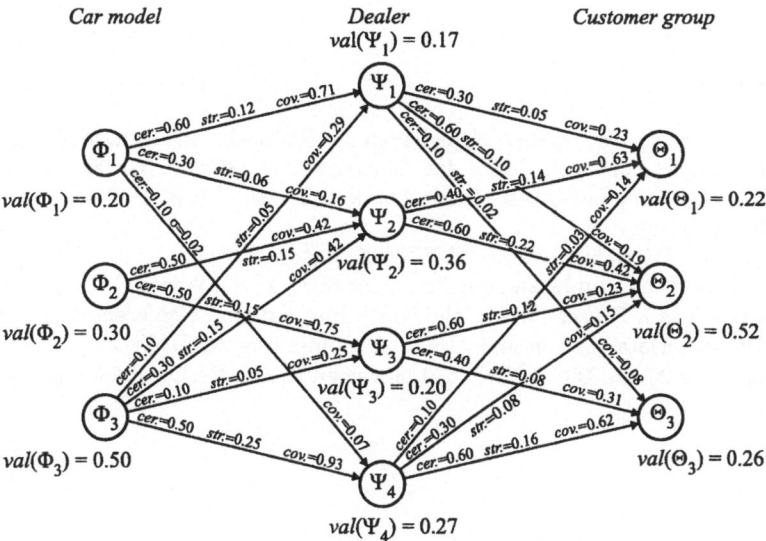

Fig. 2. Strength, certainty and coverage factors

108   Z. Pawlak

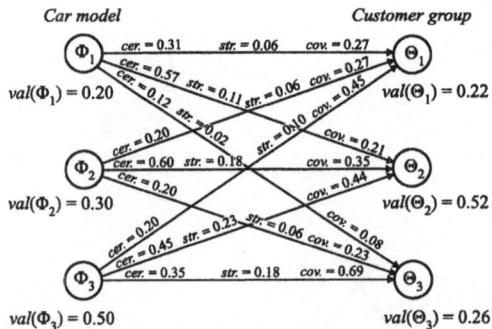

Fig. 3. Relation between car models and consumer groups

5 Conclusion

In this paper we compare inference rules and decision rules. Both are expressions in form "*if Φ then Ψ*" but the meaning of these rules in different. We study the differences and show how they work in logical inference and data analysis, respectively.

References

1. Łukasiewicz, J.: Die logishen Grundlagen der Wahrscheinilchkeitsrechnung. Kraków (1913), in: L. Borkowski (ed.), Jan Łukasiewicz – Selected Works, North Holland Publishing Company, Amsterdam, London, Polish Scientific Publishers, Warsaw (1970) 16-63
2. Pawlak, Z.: Decision networks, RSCTC2004 (to appear)
3. Pawlak, Z.: Flow graphs and decision algorithms, in: G. Wang, Q. Liu, Y. Y. Yao, A. Skowron (eds.), Proceedings of the Ninth International Conference on Rough Sets, Fuzzy Sets, Data Mining and Granular Computing RSFDGrC'2003), Chongqing, China, May 26-29, 2003, LNAI 2639, Springer-Verlag, Berlin, Heidelberg, New York, 1-11

Survival of Intelligent Agents in Changing Environments

Šarūnas Raudys

Vilnius Gediminas TU and Institute of Mathematics and Informatics
Akademijos 4, Vilnius 2600, Lithuania
raudys@ktl.mii.lt

Abstract. To analyze adaptation capabilities of individuals and agents in constantly changing environments, we suggested using of connectionist methodology and the solution of sequences of different pattern recognition tasks. Each time after the task change, we start training from previous perceptron weight vector. We found that large values of components of the weight vector decrease the gradient and learning speed. A noise injected into the desired outputs of the perceptron is used as a "natural" method to control the weight growth and adaptation to new environment. To help artificial population to withstand lengthy sequences of strong catastrophes, populations with offspring and "genetic" inheritance of the noise intensity parameter have to be created. It was found that the optimal interval for the noise intensity follows power of environmental changes. To improve the survivability of synthetic populations, we suggest "mother's training", and partial protection of offspring from artificially corrupted training signals. New simulation methodology could help explain known technical, biological, psychological and social phenomena and behaviors in quantitative way.

1 Introduction

A characteristic feature of current research for the development of intelligent machines is the requirement for robots and intelligent agents to operate in a new, unknown environment, to adapt to sudden situational changes, to compete with other agents and to survive [16]. In future applications, one would like the agents to be able to work in situations that would be unknown even to the designer. In order to foresee possible ways to tackle adaptation processes during sudden and severe environmental changes, consanguineous collaborative research efforts independent of any particular agent's structure and applications have to be carried out.

A possible ways to create adaptive, evolvable intelligent machines is to use the symbolicism approach [1, 7], and evolving artificial neural networks [2, 3, 5, 6, 8, 17]. In designing mobile robots, it was noticed that when the system is applied in a real environment, performance deteriorated. Miglino and his collaborators [9] have shown that the performance gap between the responses in simulated and real environments may be significantly reduced by introducing a "conservative"

L. Rutkowski et al. (Eds.): ICAISC 2004, LNAI 3070, pp. 109–117, 2004.
© Springer-Verlag Berlin Heidelberg 2004

form of noise. The positive effect of artificial noise added to training signals was also observed when analyzing stimulation, maturation and aging phenomena of artificial agents [12, 14].

Broad-spectrum type investigations of agents designed for concrete appli-cations require enormous computational resources. To obtain a general under-standing of the agents' behavior in changing environments we investigate rather universal model of adaptive agents. The nonlinear single layer perceptron (SLP) and a gradient descent training algorithm are applied to solve pattern recogni-tion task. Our main concern is to investigate the survivability of population of artificial agents in situations where environments are changing unexpectedly and dramatically.

2   Two Different Classification Task Model

Standard single-layer perceptron (SLP) calculates the weighted sum of inputs, *wsum*, and has a nonlinear activation function, like sigmoid $O = f(wsum) = 1/(1+\exp(-wsum))$. [4, 11, 15]. This function is bounded from below and above: it is equal or close to zero if the weighted sum is strongly negative, and is close to 1 if the sum is large positive. The slope (derivative) of function $f(wsum)$ is the largest when absolute value, *wsum*, is small. The slope tends to zero with an increase in *wsum*. *Saturation* of the activation function is *a basic feature* in our analysis.

In our investigations, SLP is utilized as a classifier. Here the input feature vector characterizes an unknown object, process, a situation. This vector has to be allocated to one of the pattern classes. In Fig. 1 we have two pairs of two-dimensional normally (Gaussian) distributed pattern classes. Training vectors of Class 1 are depicted as squares and that of Class 2 are depicted as circles.

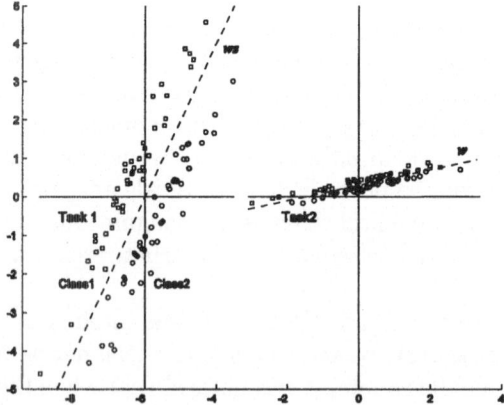

Fig. 1. Scatter diagrams of data in two classification problems, Task 1 and Task 2, and decision boundaries, *ws* and *w*, obtained after training with data Task 1 and Task 2.

Finding of the weights is formulated as an optimization problem. We consider standard sum-of-square-errors cost function as an optimization criterion which characterizes a mean difference between actual outputs, O, and desired ones, $t_{1j} = 0$ for Class 1, $t_{2j} = 1$ for Class 2. To find the weights, we exploit iterative *gradient descent training*. New weight vector is equal to the previous one, plus a correction term which depends on a gradient of cost function and parameter η, called a learning step. In our experiments, all training vectors are shown at a time. Mean values of the gradient are calculated. Then a correction is made. Such weight correction is called a learning epoch.

In neural network training, we start training the perceptron with small *initial weights*. After minimization of the cost, the magnitude of the weights depends on the training set error, $\hat{P}_{empirical}[10-12]$. If we have no error while classifying training vectors, the outputs turn out to be close either to 0 (for Class 1) or 1 (for Class 2). In order to decrease the cost, the training algorithm begins increasing the weights. When the weights are large, the gradient becomes small. A small gradient results in small changes in the weight vector, i.e. in slow training. *Vice versa*, if the components are small, the weighted sum, *wsum*, is also small. Consequently, training is fast.

If one starts training from small weights, at the beginning we have fast training. Later the weights are increasing and training slows down. Therefore, if the classification task changes abruptly, large weights begin reducing the speed of additional learning.

To investigate the behaviors of intelligent agents in changing environments, we shall use the adaptation model for simulation of the aging process, suggested in [12]. The model is based on two different pattern recognition tasks, Task 1 and Task 2. Initially, the perceptron is trained with data of Task 1. The weight vector **ws** is obtained. At some instance, the task changes abruptly. At this point, the perceptron is trained with the data Task 2, starting from weight vector, **ws**,. If the first training was successful, the components of the weight vector **ws** became large. However, large starting weights, **ws**, may be deleterious for efficient training with data Task 2. If the training time is limited, the perceptron may fail while attempting to learn to solve the second task.

In order to ensure fast training with data Task 2, one needs to control the growth of the weights while training with the previous data, Task 1. We were studying two different pattern recognition tasks, similar to those depicted in the scatter diagrams in Fig. 1 ab. To determine whether the second training was successful, the probability of misclassification of the SLP classifier was compared with an *a priori* given threshold, P_{goal}. Both classification tasks considered were two-class two-dimensional Gaussian data with different means, μ_1, μ_2, and a common covariance matrix, Σ . To achieve variability in distinct tasks learned by the perceptron, components of the means, μ_1, μ_2, and matrix Σ were random variables. To have representative results populations of SLP based agents were investigated. Preliminary simulation studies demonstrated that target values as well as random zero-mean noise injected to inputs or desired outputs (targets), t_{ij}, can be utilized for controlling the weights' growth [12, 14]. In experiments described below each single agent possessed its specific regularization, a noise injection parameter, γ_n, a fraction of training vectors with target values interchanged purposefully.

3   Genetic Search to Find the Best Training Parameters

Simulation experiments show that for each experimental conditions there exist optimal values of the weight control parameters. Nevertheless, for high point requirements to re-training performance (small P_{goal}) a large fraction of artificial agents fails to learn to solve sufficiently well the second recognition task. Suppose that a population of agents is acting in a situation where environmental conditions are changing abruptly and repeatedly. Below we consider sequences of 160 *data changes, called "catastrophes"*, occurring at regular time instances (after every 200 training epoch). The classification tasks to be learned by the agents were the two-category, two-dimensional Gaussian, with parameters described in the previous section. For the first 40 catastrophes, the data rotation parameter (we mark it by α) was changing in the sequence 4, $\frac{1}{4}$, 4, $\frac{1}{4}$, 4, $\frac{1}{4}$, etc. For the subsequent 40 catastrophes the values of the α, $\frac{1}{\alpha}$, pair varied according to the sinus law (Fig. 3b). For the 60-th and 61-th catastrophes, the parameter α fluctuated the most widely: 6, $\frac{1}{6}$. In the interval between catastrophes 81 and 120, the parameter α again fluctuated in the sequence 4, $\frac{1}{4}$, 4, $\frac{1}{4}$, 4, $\frac{1}{4}$, etc. In the interval between catastrophes 121 and 160, α fluctuated in the sequence 2, $\frac{1}{2}$, 2, $\frac{1}{2}$, 2, $\frac{1}{2}$ (Fig. 3b).

We had found that there is no the noise injection level parameter that helps the population composed of identical agents to withstand sufficiently long sequences of strong catastrophes. Simulation experiments with populations composed of a large number of agents having dissimilar values of γ_n confirmed this conclusion too. To withstand sequences of large and small catastrophes Nature has invented a way: if within a short time after a new catastrophe occurred, an individual does not adapt to the new situation, it dies. Nevertheless, the *population* of individuals does not die since it can produce offspring. The Lamarckian approach, with a combined local and evolutionary search was already utilized in neural network training (see [2, 5, 6, 8, 17] and references therein). In the papers mentioned, the task to be solved was fixed and did not change in time. In our analysis, however, the tasks are changing continuously; the magnitudes of the weight vector are playing a crucial role in determining the perceptron's retraining speed.

In an attempt to model Nature's behavior, we considered populations of intelligent agents with a priori fixed number of members M_{max}. The agent dies if after $t_{max} = 120$ training epochs it does not achieve the goal, P_{goal}. In this catastrophes and survival model, the best agents that survived were allowed to produce offspring with the same "genetic code", i.e., a noise level γ_n. The necessary condition to produce the offspring was that the parent agent's classification error satisfy $P_{agent} \leq \theta_{birth} \times P_{goal}(\theta_{birth} = 0.4)$. If at any one time instance several agents satisfy this condition, the agents with smallest P_{agent} were allowed to transmit their genetic code. In experiments, the noise strength, γ_n, was inherited by a newborn. During birth, a small deformation (mutation) of the parameter γ_n was introduced. The newborn receives a zero initial weight vector. It is given $t_{max}^{newborn} = 50 + 120$ iterations before the survival test ($P_{agent} \leq P_{goal}$) is applied for the first time. At the beginning of the experiments, the noise levels γ_n of all $M_{max} = 100$ agents in the population were selected as nonrandom scalar values distributed regularly in the interval $[\gamma_{min}, \gamma_{max}]$.

In the experiments with regularly occurring strong catastrophes, most of them were withstood with losses. In case of a moderate size catastrophe, there exist a certain number of agents that withstand the data change and satisfy the obligatory condition: $P_{agent} \leq P_{goal}$. The other agents die. The population, however, recovers quickly (see graph in Fig. 2a). In the lower part of the graph, we have depicted the dynamics of the fraction of agents that survived. In the upper part, we show the number of offspring.

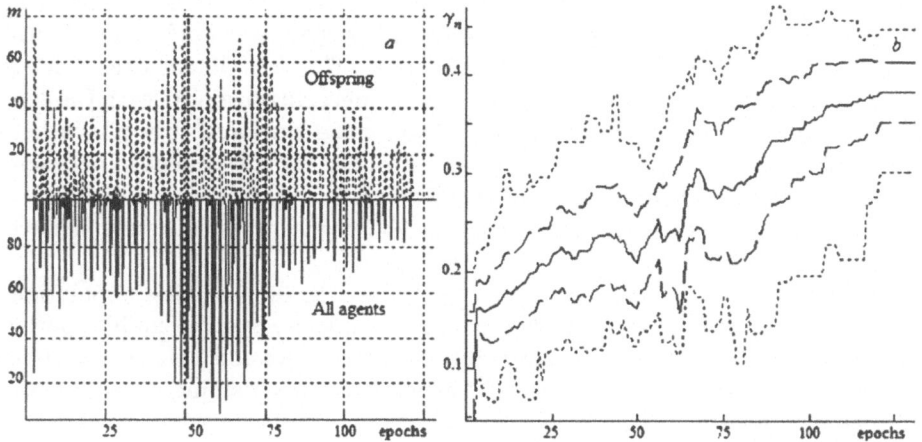

Fig. 2. Dynamics of the population's size $m(a)$ and distribution of genetic code $\gamma_n(b)$, when the catastrophes were occurring at regular time intervals. The strengths of the catastrophes (parameter α) were different and varied in time (see Fig. 3b).

Our principal concern in this paper was to investigate the survival of a synthetic population when very strong catastrophes occur. Therefore, by trial and error we selected $P_{goal} = 0.08$, a situation where only 7 agents survive the strongest catastrophe (the change of the parameter $\alpha = 6$ to $1/6$ or vice versa). In this experiment, initially $\gamma_{min} = 0$, $\gamma_{max} = 0.2$. In Fig. 2b we see the dynamics of the mean value $\bar{\gamma}_n$ of the noise injection parameter γ_n during a sequence of 130 catastrophes. In this figure, we also depicted the dynamics of $\bar{\gamma}_n \pm$ *stand. deviation* (dashdots) and the lowest and highest values of γ_n(dotted). We see that the agents' genetic code, *the parameter values γ_n, gradually adapt to the strengths of the catastrophes*: the mean value $\bar{\gamma}_n$ increases from 0.1 up to 0.38. In this experiment, the time required for the parameter γ_n to adapt to a rapidly increasing level of catastrophes was insufficient. Thus, the parameter values γ_n continue to increase even when the strengths of the catastrophes started to decrease. When the catastrophes become small (after 120th catastrophe), no agents die and there are no changes in parameter γ_n.

4   Means to Improve the Survival of Synthetic Populations

To withstand very strong catastrophes, a comparatively large noise level is required. Our experiments have shown that almost 40% (!) of desired targets should be interchanged. Therefore, many offspring are dying rapidly. In Fig. 3a we see very many offspring, especially when the catastrophes become very strong. On the scale of this figure, some delay in the number of offspring and of the agents that survived the catastrophes is noticeable. For severe environmental changes, a significant part ($\sim 50\%$) of the population is frequently composed of offspring. "Nature" suggests a possible way to tackle the problem with offspring: the targets used to train the offspring have to be selected by the parent agent, not by "Nature". Only if the parent agent dies, will the offspring begin to learn the same way as the other agents. In an attempt to increase the capability of synthetic populations to withstand very strong catastrophes, in subsequent experiments the targets for the offspring training we determined by the parent agents. Such training process was accomplished until newborn generalization error achieved the parents' level.

We found that *"mother's training"* helped to increase the population's resistance to the strongest catastrophes. In Fig. 3a we see the middle part of survival curves presented in the interval between the 40th and 87th catastrophes. Under identical conditions, instead of 7 agents, parent's training helped at least 37 agents to survive.

In an attempt to increase the populations' resistance to strong catastrophes we performed a number of simulations with $M_{max} = 50, 100, 250, 500$ and different artificial noise fractions (i.e., $\gamma_n/r, r = 1, 2, \ldots, 100$) assigned to offspring training, different time instances at which the parent stopped training its offspring, and initial noise level interval, $[\gamma_{min}\gamma_{max}]$. We found that increasing the size of population considerably increases its robustness. For the other parameters no obvious dependencies were observed. In each single simulation experiment, the minimal number of agents surviving the strongest catastrophes is a random variable, whose value depends crucially on minor changes in the model parameters that describe the experiments. It was noticed, however, that a moderate decrease in the noise level used to train the offspring increases the resistance of the population to the strongest catastrophes. This observation is common both for the Mother's and Nature's training and agrees fairly well with observations in real life where the parent and/or the population are protecting their offspring for a long time.

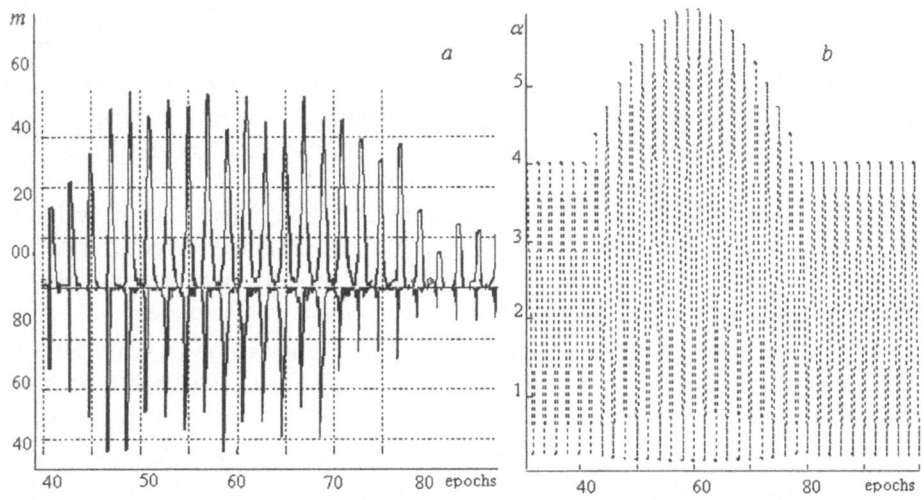

Fig. 3. Dynamics of the population's size (*a*) and magnitude of the catastrophes (*b*).

5   Concluding Remarks

Distinctive aspects of our analysis includes: (1) the examination of situations where environmental conditions are changing in time and (2) analysis of the influence of the magnitudes of the weights on the retraining speed of adaptive agent. To obtain general recommendations regarding the training of the agents, we model the agent by SLP designed to solve different pattern recognition tasks. In order to survive, the agents must learn new pattern recognition tasks promptly. We found that:

1. The sizes of the connection weights of the perceptron play a crucial role in retraining speed. If the pattern recognition task to be learned changes abruptly, large weights hamper the perceptrons' retraining process. If the agent must learn to solve a new task in a short period of time, it may fail to do so, since its newly established starting weights are already large.

2. In order to facilitate the retraining process, the designer has to use a special regularization methodology that resists the growth of the perceptron's weights. This can be accomplished by: controlling the target values, injecting noise into the inputs and/or the desired targets, using a weight decay term, etc. The regularization parameters control the growth of the weights and determine the "training style".

3. If the retraining performance criterion is fixed *a priori*, there exist optimal values for regularization parameters that are used to prevent weight growth. Optimal values depend on the difficulty of the pattern recognition tasks (in particular, the classification error), on the differences between the original and the altered pattern recognition tasks, and on the joint utilization of other regularization methods.

4. The experiments indicate that a priori fixed values of regularization parameters are inadequate to "save" a population of agents from extinction if the duration of the sequence of "powerful" data changes (catastrophes) is extensive. To enable a synthetic population to survive lengthy sequences of rather strong catastrophes, populations with offspring and inheritance of regularization parameters have to be created. The single agents in the population must possess diverse values of the regularization parameters. "Young" (with small weights), "mature" (with medium size weights) and "old" (with large weights) individuals ought to be present at any time. An interval of variation of regularization parameter is following the changes in strengths of the catastrophes.

5. The continued existence of synthetic populations can be enhanced if after birth, young offspring are protected from artificial noise and the disastrous effects of the catastrophes. An increase in the population's size is also advantageous.

The above analysis suggests that *a very simple model of adaptive agent is sufficient* to reproduce the behavior of the agent populations in changing environments. In spite of the simplicity of the model, rather general conclusions can be arrived at. Possible directions for future research include the replacement of Gaussian data with nonlinearly separable data, and the consideration of more complex adaptive classifiers. It seems a worthwhile generalization of the model to require that each agent solve a set of different pattern recognition problems, to imitate the agents by multilayer perceptrons, and to investigate the usefulness of good starting weights to train offspring [13]. The number of regularization parameters inherited by the offspring should be enlarged; inertia could be introduced into the genetic code, etc., etc.

The above conclusions characterize the agents' and populations' behavior qualitatively. In order to obtain quantitative predictions, methods will have to be developed to choose data type and data parameters (the classification tasks to be solved), the strengths and periodicity of the environmental changes, and the training and inheritance mechanisms.

Like other verbal and computerized models our explanations that retraining speed is aggravated by large connection strengths is only a rough abstraction of real world problems. In spite of simplicity of the model, the conclusions of our research agree with numerous observations in ongoing life. Striking resemblances between the simulation results and changes in various biological, psychological, relations in families and social phenomena could help explain them in quantitative way. One may assume that new methodology could describe some of human and social adaptation processes such as social and economic changes in post communist East European countries. Our conclusion that a noise injection intensity acting as the regularization is following the power of environmental changes suggests that nowadays crimes, corruption and other negative factors are caused by enormous alterations in economics and social life. Looking from a perspective of several centuries, our times we have especially great changes in technologies and human life style followed by unexpected increase in terrorism and birth of new maladies. The population survival and a noise injection analysis in the sequence of pattern recognition tasks possibly could be a constructive model helpful in understanding and controlling these phenomena. Both the genetic inheritance and a legacy of survivors' traditions and moral norms should be considered.

References

1 Anderson J. R. & Lebiere C. (1998). *The Atomic Components of Thought.* Mahwah, NJ, London: Lawrence Erlbaum Associates.

2 Cortez P., Rocha M. & Neves J. (2002). A Lamarckian approach for neural network training. *Neural Processing Letters,* 15: 105–116.

3 French V.A., Anderson E., Putman G. & Alvager T. (1999). The Yerkes-Dodson law simulated with an artificial neural network, *Complex Systems,* 5(2): 136–147.

4 Haykin S. (1999). *Neural Networks: A comprehensive foundation.* 2nd edition. Prentice-Hall, Englewood Cliffs, NJ.

5 Hinton G.E. & Nowlan, S.J. (1987). How learning guides evolution. *Complex Systems,* 1: 497–502.

6 Ku K.W.C., Mak M.W. & Sin W.C. (2000). A study of the Lamarckian evolution of recurrent neural networks. *IEEE Trans. on Evolutionary Computation,* 4(1): 31–42.

7 Newell A. & Simon H.A. (1976). Computer science as empirical enquiry: symbols and search. *Communications of the Association for Computing Machinery,* 19: 113–126.

8 Nolfi S. & Floreano D. (1999). Learning and evolution, *Autonomous Robots,* 7: 89–113.

9 Miglino O., Lund H.H. & Nolfi S. (1995). Evolving mobile robots in simulated and real environments, *Artificial Life,* 2: 417–434.

10 Raudys S. (1998). Evolution and generalization of a single neurone. I. SLP as seven statistical classifiers. *Neural Networks,* 11(2): 283–296.

11 Raudys S. (2001). *Statistical and Neural Classifiers: An integrated approach to design.* Springer-Verlag, NY.

12 Raudys S. (2002). An adaptation model for simulation of aging process. *Int. J. Modern Physics C,* 13(8): 1075–1086.

13 Raudys S. & Amari S. (1998). Effect of initial values in simple perception. *Proc. IEEE World Congress on Computational Intelligence,* IEEE Press, IJCNN'98: 1530–1535.

14 Raudys S. & Justickis V. (2003). Yerkes-Dodson law in agents' training. *Lecture Notes in Artificial Intelligence,* Springer-Verlag, 2902: 54–58.

15 Rumelhart D.E., Hinton G.E. & Williams R.J. (1986). Learning internal representations by error propagation. In: D.E. Rumelhart, J.L. McClelland (editors), *Parallel Distributed Processing: Explorations in the microstructure of cognition,* Bradford Books, Cambridge, MA. I: 318–62.

16 Weng J., McClelland J., Pentland A., Sporns O., Stockman I., Sur M. & Thelen E. (2001). Autonomous mental development by robots and animals. *Science,* 291(5504): 599–600.

17 Yao X. (1999). Evolving artificial neural networks. *Proceedings IEEE,* 87: 1423–1447.

Inducing Robust Decision Rules from Rough Approximations of a Preference Relation

Roman Slowinski[1] and Salvatore Greco[2]

[1] Institute of Computing Science, Poznan University of Technology, 60-965 Poznan, Institute for Systems Research, Polish Academy of Sciences, 01-447 Warsaw, Poland; Roman.Slowinski@cs.put.poznan.pl

[2] Faculty of Economics, University of Catania, Corso Italia, 55, 95129 Catania, Italy; salgreco@mbox.unict.it

Abstract. Given a data set describing a number of pairwise comparisons of reference objects made by a decision maker (DM), we wish to find a set of robust decision rules constituting a preference model of the DM. To accomplish this, we are constructing rough approximations of the comprehensive preference relation, called outranking, known from these pairwise comparisons. The rough approximations of the outranking relation are constructed using the Lorenz dominance relation on degrees of preference on particular criteria for pairs of reference objects being compared. The Lorenz dominance is used for its ability of drawing more robust conclusions from preference ordered data than the Pareto dominance. The rough approximations become a starting point for mining "*if . . .* , *then . . .* " decision rules constituting a logical preference model. Application of the set of decision rules to a new set of objects gives a fuzzy outranking graph. Positive and negative flows are calculated for each object in the graph, giving arguments about its strength and weakness. Aggregation of both arguments by the Net Flow Score procedure leads to a final ranking. The approach can be applied to support multicriteria choice and ranking of objects when the input information is a set of pairwise comparisons of some reference objects.

Keywords: Multicriteria decision, Knowledge discovery, Rough sets, Decision rules, Lorenz dominance

1 Introduction

We present a knowledge discovery paradigm for multicriteria decision making, based on the concept of rough sets. Rough set theory introduced by Pawlak (1991) has often proved to be an excellent mathematical tool for the analysis of a vague description of objects. The adjective vague – referring to the quality of information – means inconsistency or ambiguity which follows from information granulation. The rough set philosophy is based on the assumption that with every object of the universe U there is associated a certain amount of information (data, knowledge), expressed by means of some *attributes* (called also properties, features, characteristics) used for object description. Objects having the same

L. Rutkowski et al. (Eds.): ICAISC 2004, LNAI 3070, pp. 118–132, 2004.
© Springer-Verlag Berlin Heidelberg 2004

description are indiscernible (similar) with respect to the available information. The *indiscernibility relation* thus generated constitutes a mathematical basis of rough set theory; it induces a partition of the universe into blocks of indiscernible objects, called elementary sets, which can be used to build knowledge about a real or abstract world. The use of the indiscernibility relation results in information granulation.

Any subset X of the universe may be expressed in terms of these blocks either precisely (as a union of elementary sets) or approximately only. In the latter case, the subset X may be characterized by two ordinary sets, called *lower* and *upper approximations*. A rough set is defined by means of these two approximations, which coincide in the case of an ordinary set. The lower approximation of X is composed of all the elementary sets included in X (whose elements, therefore, certainly belong to X), while the upper approximation of X consists of all the elementary sets which have a non-empty intersection with X (whose elements, therefore, may belong to X). Obviously, the difference between the upper and lower approximation constitutes the boundary region of the rough set, whose elements cannot be characterized with certainty as belonging or not to X, using the available information. The information about objects from the boundary region is, therefore, inconsistent or ambiguous. The cardinality of the boundary region states, moreover, to what extent it is possible to express X in exact terms, on the basis of the available information. For this reason, this cardinality may be used as a measure of vagueness of the information about X. Moreover, the lower and upper approximations of a partition of U into decision classes, prepare the ground for induction of, respectively, certain and possible *classification patterns* in the form of "*if ... then ... *" *decision rules*, which are useful for decision support.

Several attempts have already been made to use rough set theory to decision support (Pawlak and Slowinski 1994, Pawlak *et al.* 1995, Slowinski 1993). The Classical Rough Set Approach (CRSA) is not able, however, to deal with preference-ordered attribute domains and preference-ordered decision classes. In decision analysis, an attribute with a preference-ordered domain (scale) is called *criterion*.

In late 90's, adapting CRSA to knowledge discovery from preference-ordered data became a challenging problem in the field of *multicriteria decision analysis* (MCDA). The importance of this problem follows from the nature of the input preferential information available in MCDA and of the output of the analysis. As to the input, the rough set approach requires a set of decision examples which is also convenient for acquisition of preferential information from *decision makers* (DMs). Very often in MCDA, this information has to be given in terms of *preference model* parameters, like importance weights, substitution rates and various thresholds. Giving such information requires a great cognitive effort of the DM. It is generally acknowledged that people prefer to make exemplary decisions than to explain them in terms of specific parameters. For this reason, the idea of inferring preference models from exemplary decisions provided by the DM is very attractive. Furthermore, the exemplary decisions may be inconsistent because of limited discriminatory power of criteria and because of hesitation of the DM (see, e.g., Roy 1996). These inconsistencies cannot be considered as a simple error or noise. They can convey important information that should be taken into account in the construction of the DM's preference model. The rough set approach is intended to deal with inconsistency and this is another argument for its application to MCDA. Finally, the output of the analysis, i.e. the *model of preferences in terms of decision rules* seems very convenient for decision support because it is intelligible and speaks the same language as the DM.

The extension of CRSA enabling analysis of preference-ordered data has been proposed by Greco, Matarazzo and Slowinski (1999, 2000, 2001, 2002a). This extension, called Dominance-based Rough Set Approach (DRSA) is mainly based on substitution of the indiscernibility relation by a *dominance* relation in the rough approximation of preference-ordered decision classes. An important consequence of this fact is a possibility of inferring from exemplary decisions the preference model in terms of decision rules being logical statements of the type "*if* ... , *then* ... ". The separation of certain and doubtful knowledge about the DM's preferences is done by distinction of different kinds of decision rules, depending whether they are induced from lower approximations of decision classes or from the difference between upper and lower approximations composed of inconsistent examples. Such a preference model is more general than the classical functional models considered within MAUT (Multi-Attribute Utility Theory) or relational models considered, for example, in outranking methods (Slowinski, Greco, Matarazzo 2002b; Greco, Matarazzo, Slowinski 2002b, 2003).

In this paper, we propose a new variant of DRSA, adapted to deal with *multicriteria choice and ranking* problems in such a way that the inconsistency in the input preferential information is detected using the *Lorenz dominance relation*, instead of the usual Pareto dominance relation. The use of the Lorenz dominance is intended to get more robust decision rules at the output of the analysis.

The paper is organized as follows. In section 2, we characterize the input data, concerning comparisons of some reference objects and presented in the Pairwise Comparison Table (PCT), and we define the Lorenz dominance relation in the set of these pairwise comparisons. In section 3, we briefly present the new variant of DRSA for the analysis of PCT. Section 4 is devoted to induction of decision rules and section 5 shows how to apply the set of rules for recommendation of the best choice or ranking on a new set of objects. The last section includes conclusions.

2   Main Steps, Input Data, Pairwise Comparison Table, and Lorenz Dominance Relation

2.1   Main Steps of Multicriteria Decision Support

Let A be a finite set of objects corresponding to all potential objects of the decision problem at hand. The objects are evaluated by a family C of n criteria

$g_i : A \to \boldsymbol{R}$, $i = 1, 2, \ldots, n$, such that, for each object $x \in A$, $g_i(x)$ represents the evaluation of x with respect to criterion g_i. We assume, without loss of generality, that the greater the value of $g_i(x)$, the better the evaluation of x. For the future use of the Lorenz dominance, we also assume that the scale of each criterion $g_i(x)$ is cardinal in the sense of utility, i.e. it is either an interval or a ratio scale. In consequence, one can specify intensity of preference for a given difference of evaluations.

While multicriteria classification is based on absolute evaluation of objects, multicriteria choice and ranking refer to relative evaluation, by means of pairwise comparisons of objects.

Solving a multicriteria choice or ranking problem defined for given sets A and C, consists of the following steps:

1) Collect some preferential information from the DM.
2) Construct a preference model of the DM.
3) Approve the preference model by the DM and then apply this model on set A.
4) Exploit the preference structure induced by the preference model on set A, so as to work-out a recommendation in terms of the best choice of an object from A or in terms of the ranking of objects from A from the best to the worst.

In our approach, the preferential information collected in step 1) has the form of pairwise comparisons of objects from a subset $A' \subseteq A$, called *reference objects*. These are objects relatively well known to the DM that (s)he is able to compare, at least in some part. Thus, for a given pair of objects $(x,y) \in A' \times A'$, the DM is asked to specify if object x is comprehensively at least as good as object y (i.e., x *outranks* y, denoted by xSy) or not (i.e., x *does not outrank* y, denoted by xS^cy). Each answer constitutes a pairwise comparison and the whole set of these comparisons is denoted by B. Remark that the outranking relation S in set $A' \times A'$ is neither necessarily transitive nor complete. It is also possible that instead of particular pairwise comparisons of objects from A', the DM specifies a ranking of these objects, called *reference ranking*; such a ranking (complete or partial) is then easily transformed to the set of pairwise comparisons B.

The preference model constructed in step 2) has the form of decision rules induced from rough approximations of the outranking and non-outranking relations. This step will be explained in the next section, and in the following section, application of this model on set A (step 3) will be presented together with the exploitation step.

Let us represent the input preferential information in the form of the Pairwise Comparison Table (PCT).

2.2 Pairwise Comparison Table (PCT)

Given set B of m pairwise comparisons, stating for any $(x,y) \in B$ either xSy or xS^cy, an $m \times (n+1)$ Pairwise Comparison Table (PCT) is created. The m rows are pairs from B. Its first n columns correspond to criteria from set C. In the last, $(n+1)$-th column of PCT, the comprehensive binary preference relation S or S^c is specified.

For each pair $(x,y) \in B$, a difference on criterion g_i is calculated as $\Delta_i(x,y) = g_i(x) - g_i(y), i = 1, \ldots, n$. This difference is translated to a *degree of intensity of preference* of x over y. We assume a common scale of the intensity of preference for all the criteria, coded by a subset of natural numbers from 1 to z, where z is odd and $\lceil z/2 \rceil$ is a rounded-up integer corresponding to the neutral point of the intensity scale. For example, z may be set equal to 7 and then the neutral point $\lceil z/2 \rceil$ of the scale is 4, corresponding to "asymmetric indifference", 5 corresponds to "weak preference", 6 to " strong preference" and 7 to "very strong preference", while 1 to "inverse very strong preference", 2 to "inverse strong preference" and 3 to "inverse weak preference".

Thus, each difference $\Delta_i(x, y) = g_i(x) - g_i(y)$ is converted to the degree $h_i \in \{1, \ldots, z\}$ and put in the intersection of row (x,y) and column i of PCT; it represents the *graded preference relation* $x P_i^{h_i} y$, for all $(x, y) \in B$ and $i = 1, \ldots, n$. Summing up, the graded preference relations $x P_i^{h_i} y$ are read as follows:

- $x P_i^{h_i} y, h_i \in \{ \lceil z/2 \rceil + 1, \ldots, z\}$, means that x is preferred to y by degree h_i with respect to criterion g_i,
- $x P_i^{h_i} y, h_i \in \{1, \ldots, \lceil z/2 \rceil - 1\}$, means that x is *not* preferred to y, by degree h_i with respect to criterion g_i,
- $x P_i^{\lceil z/2 \rceil} y$ means that x is similar (asymmetrically indifferent) to y with respect to criterion g_i.

To simplify the notation, we will use h_i instead of $P_i^{h_i}$, thus $x P_i^{h_i} y \equiv x h_i y$. Of course, for each $g_i \in C$ and for every $(x, y) \in B$,

$$[x h_i y, \ h_i \in \{\lceil z/2 \rceil + 1, \ldots, z\}] \Rightarrow [y k_i x, \ k_i \in \{1, \ldots, \lceil z/2 \rceil \}],$$

$$[x h_i y, \ h_i \in \{1, \ldots, \lceil z/2 \rceil - 1\} \Rightarrow [y k_i x, \ k_i \in \{ \lceil z/2 \rceil, \ldots, z\}].$$

In the last column of PCT there is the comprehensive preference relation for each pair $(x,y) \in B$, specified by the DM; thus, there is either outranking relation S or non-outranking relation S^c (N.B. the presented approach can handle multi-graded comprehensive preference relations, however, for the sake of simplicity, we confine our presentation to single-graded relations S and S^c).

Example. Consider the reference objects presented in Table 1. The objects are evaluated on two criteria with an increasing interval scale from 1 to 100. The differences of evaluations $\Delta_i(x, y) = g_i(x) - g_i(y)$ are converted to the degree $h_i \in \{1, \ldots, 7\}$, for $i = 1, 2$, according to Table 2. A hypothetical comparison of 7 pairs of reference objects is shown in PCT in Table 3.

2.3   Lorenz Dominance on Pairs of Objects

In (Greco, Matarazzo, Slowinski 1999, 2001), the Dominance-based Rough Set Approach (DRSA) was applied to the PCT in order to express lower and upper

Table 1. Reference objects

Object	g_1	g_2
p	22	18
q	32	90
r	28	100
s	79	67
t	27	41
u	40	60
v	35	50
w	5	65
x	80	40
y	77	90
z	66	85

Table 2. Conversion of $\Delta_i(x,y)$ to $h_i \in \{1, \dots, 7\}$, $i=1,2$

$\Delta_i(x,y)$	h_i
[-100, -60]	1
(-60, -35]	2
(-35, -5]	3
(-5, 5)	4
[5, 35)	5
[35, 60)	6
[60, 100]	7

Table 3. Pairwise comparison table

Pair	h_1	h_2	Preference relation
(p,q)	3	7	S
(u,x)	2	5	S
(r,q)	4	5	S
(s,t)	6	5	S
(w,z)	1	3	S^c
(x,y)	4	2	S^c
(v,w)	5	3	S^c

approximations of preference relations S and S^c in terms of degrees of intensities of preference (h_i) on particular criteria. The dominance relation used in these approximations was the usual Pareto dominance relation defined as follows: given $P \subseteq C$ ($P \neq \emptyset$), $(x,y),(w,z) \in A \times A$, the pair of objects (x,y) is said to P-dominate (w,z) with respect to criteria from P (denoted by $(x, y) D_P(w, z)$), if x is preferred to y at least as strongly as w is preferred to z with respect to each $g_i \in P$; precisely, "at least as strongly as" means "by at least the same degree", i.e. $h_i \geq k_i$, where $h_i, k_i \in \{1, \dots, z\}$, $x\, h_i\, y$ and $w\, k_i\, z$, for each $g_i \in P$. Coming back to our example from p. 2.2, according to the above definition, for $P = \{g_1, g_2\}$, $(s,t) D_P (r, q)$ and not $(r, q) D_P (s,t)$, however, not $(u, x) D_P (v, w)$ and not $(v, w) D_P (u, x)$, for instance; this means that (s, t) is preferred to (r, q), while (u, x) and (v, w) are incomparable with the Pareto dominance.

Let us remark that the Pareto dominance, as defined above, leaves many pairs of objects in PCT incomparable with respect to intensity degrees on $P \subseteq C$. For two pairs, it is sufficient that the difference of the corresponding vectors of intensity degrees on $P \subseteq C$ has one element of different sign than other elements, to conclude that the pairs are incomparable. For instance, this is the case of vectors (u, x), (v, w) and (r, q), (p, q) above: $(u, x) - (v, w) = (2, 5) - (5, 3) = (-3, 2)$ and $(r, q) - (p, q) = (4, 5) - (3, 7) = (1, -2)$.

To reduce the number of incomparabilities among the pairs of reference objects, we could use a bit richer preference relation than Pareto dominance. As the intensity of preference on all criteria from C is expressed in the same scale, it could be interesting to use a dominance relation *comparing the distributions of the intensity degrees*. A possible relation of this type is the *Lorenz dominance* used for comparing income distributions within the utilitarian framework (Marshall, Olkin 1979). It is related to the *Pigou-Dalton principle* and to the welferist approach to inequality in the social choice theory. This principle says: for vector $h \in \mathbf{R}_+^n$, if $h_i > h_j$, then a slight improvement of h_j at the expense of h_i, while keeping the same average, improves the distribution of h. In our context, $\mathbf{R}_+^n$ boils down to $\mathbf{H}^n = \prod_{i=1}^n H_i$, where $H_i = \{1, \dots, z\}$, $i = 1, \dots, n$.

For each vector of intensity degrees $h \in H^q$, $0 < q \leq n$, the Lorenz vector associated with h is:

$$L(h) = (h_{[1]}, h_{[1]} + h_{[2]}, h_{[1]} + h_{[2]} + h_{[3]}, \ldots, h_{[1]} + \cdots + h_{[q]})$$

where $h_{[1]} \leq h_{[2]} \leq \ldots \leq h_{[q]}$ represent the components of vector h ordered increasingly; the k-th component of $L(h)$ is equal to $L_k(h) = \sum_{i=1}^{k} h_{[i]}$. Thus, according to this definition, the original space of evaluations H^q is transformed to the *Lorenz space* L^q. For $P \subseteq C$, $|P| = q$, the *P-Lorenz dominance* on H^q (denoted by $\hat{D}_P$ to distinguish from the Pareto dominance D_P) is defined as follows:

for every $h, t \in H^q$, $h \hat{D}_P t$ if an only if $L(h) D_P L(t)$, i.e.
$L_k(h) = \sum_{i=1}^{k} h_{[i]} \geq \sum_{i=1}^{k} t_{[i]} = L_k(t)$ for all $k \in \{1, \ldots, q\}$.

Let us comment shortly the Lorenz dominance from the viewpoint of multicriteria decision analysis. It has been introduced on the ground of MCDA in order to make equitable aggregations (Kostreva, Ogryczak, Wierzbicki 2003) and to find robust solutions in search problems with multiple scenarios (Perny, Spanjaard 2003). Indeed, the Lorenz dominance represents a decision attitude that gives priority to a more equitable (smooth) distribution of the degrees of intensity of preference on the considered criteria. For example if $P = \{g_1, g_2, g_3\}$ and $h_1 = 0.3$, $h_2 = 0.3$, $h_3 = 0.3$ while $t_1 = 0$, $t_2 = 0$, $t_3 = 0.9$, then $h \hat{D}_P t$ even if $h_1 + h_2 + h_3 = t_1 + t_2 + t_3$. The dominance of h over t is due to more equitable distribution of degrees of preferences for h comparing to t. An important implicit assumption behind the Lorenz dominance is the equal importance of all the considered criteria. This can be easily observed from the fact that for any $P \subseteq C$, $|P| = q$, for each permutation π of P and for each $h, t \in H^q$, such that $t_{\pi(i)}) = h_i$ for all $g_i \in P$, vectors h and t are equivalent from the viewpoint of the Lorenz dominance.

Thus, given $P \subseteq C$ ($P \neq \emptyset$), $(x, y), (w, z) \in A \times A$, the pair of objects (x, y) is said to *P-Lorenz dominate* (w, z) with respect to criteria from P (denoted by $(x, y)\hat{D}_P(w, z)$), if vector h of intensities of preference for (x, y) P-Lorenz dominates vector t of intensities of preference for (w, z) or, in other words, if the Lorenz vector $L(h)$ P-Pareto dominates Lorenz vector $L(t)$. Moreover, Pareto dominance $(x, y) D_P(w, z)$ implies Lorenz dominance $(x, y) \hat{D}_P(w, z)$ but the converse is not true, in general.

Coming back to our example from p. 2.2, in Fig. 1 and Fig.2, we represent graphically the P-Lorenz dominance in the original space of evaluations H^2 and the equivalent P-Pareto dominance in the Lorenz space L^2, respectively, for the pair $(x,y) = (4, 2)$.

Remark that the Lorenz dominance can make comparable some pairs of of reference objects that were incomparable with the Pareto dominance. Increasing the comparability of the pairs of reference objects in H^n may increase the number of *inconsistencies* observed in PCT; let us remind that two pairs, $(x, y), (w, z) \in B$, are inconsistent in PCT if (x,y) dominates (w,z) in H^n while, according to the DM, $xS^c y$ and wSz. In consequence of the increase of comparability

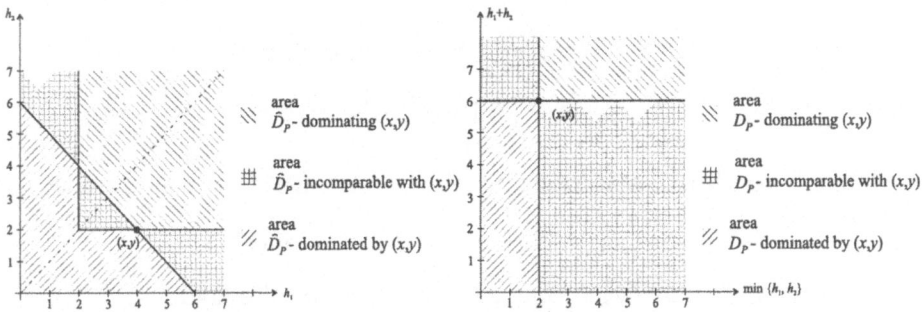

Fig. 1. Lorenz dominance for (x,y) in H^2 **Fig. 2.** Pareto dominance for (x,y) in L^2

and inconsistency, the difference between lower and upper approximations of preference relations S and S^c may also increase, however, those pairs which will remain in the lower approximations of S and S^c will constitute a *more robust support* for decision rules induced from these approximations. This is our motivation for using the Lorenz dominance instead of the Pareto dominance.

3   Rough Approximation of Preference Relations S and S^c Specified in PCT

Let us remark that the P-Lorenz dominance relation $\hat{D}_P$ is reflexive (i.e. for each $h \in H^q$, $q = |P|$, $h\,\hat{D}_P\,h$), and transitive (i.e. for each $h, t, v \in H^q$, $h\,\hat{D}_P\,t$ and $t\,\hat{D}_P\,v$ implies $h\,\hat{D}_P\,v$). Therefore, the P-Lorenz dominance relation $\hat{D}_P$ is a partial preorder on $A \times A$.

Let $R \subseteq P \subseteq C$ and $(x,y),(u,v) \in A \times A$; then the following implication holds: $(x,y)\,\hat{D}_P\,(u,v) \Rightarrow (x,y)\,\hat{D}_R\,(u,v)$.

Given $P \subseteq C$ and $(x,y) \in B$, we define:

- a set of pairs of objects dominating (x,y), called P-*Lorenz dominating set*, $\hat{D}_P^+(x,y) = \{(w,z) \in B : (w,z)\,\hat{D}_P\,(x,y)\}$,

- a set of pairs of objects dominated by (x,y), called P-*Lorenz dominated set*, $\hat{D}_P^-(x,y) = \{(w,z) \in B : (x,y)\,\hat{D}_P\,(w,z)\}$.

The P-Lorenz dominating sets and the P-Lorenz dominated sets defined on all pairs of reference objects from B are *"granules of knowledge"* that can be used to express P-lower and P-upper Lorenz approximations of comprehensive preference relations S and S^c, respectively:

$$\underline{P}(S) = \{(x,y) \in B : \hat{D}_P^+(x,y) \subseteq S\},$$

$$\overline{P}(S) = \bigcup_{(x,y)\in S} \hat{D}_P^+(x,y) = \{(x,y) \in B : \hat{D}_P^-(x,y) \cap S \neq \emptyset\}.$$

$$\underline{P}(S^c) = \{(x,y) \in B : \hat{D}_P^-(x,y) \subseteq S^c\},$$

$$\overline{P}(S^c) = \bigcup_{(x,y) \in S^c} \hat{D}_P^-(x,y) = \{(x,y) \in B : \hat{D}_P^+(x,y) \cap S^c \neq \emptyset\}.$$

Similarly to (Greco, Matarazzo, Slowinski 1999, 2001), we can prove that

$$\underline{P}(S) \subseteq S \subseteq \overline{P}(S), \ \underline{P}(S^c) \subseteq S^c \subseteq \overline{P}(S^c).$$

Furthermore, the following complementarity properties hold:

$$\underline{P}(S) = B - \overline{P}(S^c), \ \overline{P}(S) = B - \underline{P}(S^c), \ \underline{P}(S^c) = B - \overline{P}(S), \ \overline{P}(S^c) = B - \underline{P}(S).$$

Finally, for each $R \subseteq P \subseteq C$ the following monotonicity property holds:

$$\underline{R}(S) \subseteq \underline{P}(S), \ \overline{R}(S) \supseteq \overline{P}(S), \ \underline{R}(S^c) \subseteq \underline{P}(S^c), \ \overline{R}(S^c) \supseteq \overline{P}(S^c).$$

The P-boundaries (P-doubtful regions in the sense of Lorenz) of S and S^c are defined as

$$Bn_P(S) = \overline{P}(S) - \underline{P}(S), \ Bn_P(S^c) = \overline{P}(S^c) - \underline{P}(S^c).$$

From the above it follows that $Bn_P(S) = Bn_P(S^c)$.

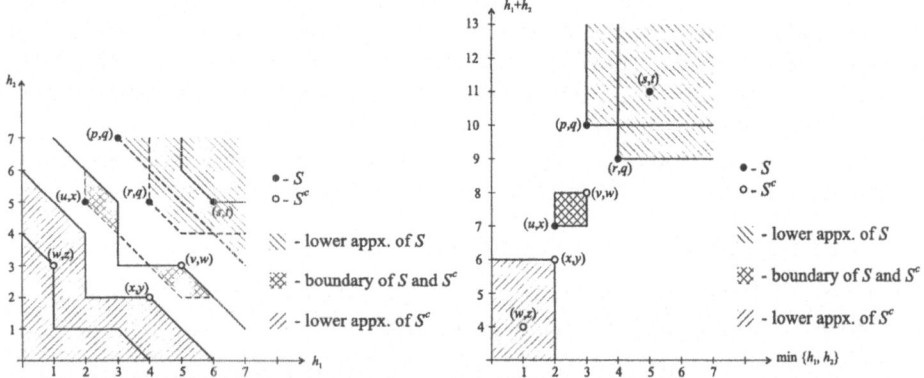

Fig. 3. Lorenz rough approximations of S & S^c in $\mathbf{H}^2$

Fig. 4. Pareto rough approximations of S & S^c in $\mathbf{L}^2$

The concepts of the quality of approximation, reducts and core can be extended also to the approximation of the outranking relation by the Lorenz dominance relation.

In particular, the coefficient $\gamma_P = |\underline{P}(S) \cup \underline{P}(S^c)|/|B|$ defines the *quality of approximation* of S and S^c by $P \subseteq C$. It expresses the ratio of all pairs of reference objects $(x,y) \in B$ consistently assigned to S and S^c by the set P of criteria to all the pairs of objects contained in B. Each minimal subset $P \subseteq C$, such that $\gamma_P = \gamma_C$, is called a *reduct* of C (denoted by RED_{PCT}). Let us remark that a PCT can have more than one reduct. The intersection of all B-reducts is called the *core* (denoted by $CORE_{PCT}$).

The P-lower and the P-upper Lorenz approximations of S and S^c for the PCT from Table 3 are shown graphically in space H^2 in Fig. 3. The equivalent Pareto rough approximations in space L^2 are shown in Fig. 4. The pairs (u,x), (v,w) being Lorenz inconsistent enter the boundary of S and S^c. Remark, for comparison, that these pairs are not Pareto inconsistent in H^2, as shown in Fig.5. Thus, in this example, the quality of Lorenz approximation is equal to $5/7$, while the quality of Pareto approximation is equal to 1.

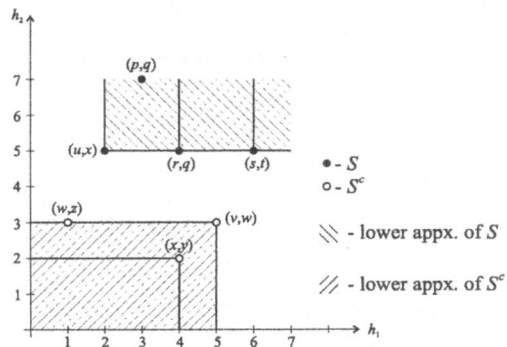

Fig. 5. Pareto rough approximations of S & S^c in H^2

In practice, it is worth using the Variable Consistency Model of rough approximations of S and S^c (Slowinski, Greco, Matarazzo 2002a), allowing that some of the pairs in dominating or dominated sets belong to the opposite relation. Here we propose the following interpretation of the Variable Consistency Model for Lorenz rough approximations of S and S^c.

Let $l \in [0,1]$ be the required consistency level (1 = full consistency, 0 = no consistency required). Let also $\delta_P^S(x,y) = \left|\hat{D}_P^+(x,y) \cap S\right| / \left|\hat{D}_P^+(x,y)\right|$ and $\delta_P^{S^c}(x,y) = \left|\hat{D}_P^-(x,y) \cap S^c\right| / \left|\hat{D}_P^-(x,y)\right|$. We will also need $\varepsilon_P^S(x,y) = \underset{(w,z)\in\hat{D}_P^-(x,y)}{Max} \left\{\delta_P^S(w,z)\right\}$ and $\varepsilon_P^{S^c}(x,y) = \underset{(w,z)\in\hat{D}_P^+(x,y)}{Max} \left\{\delta_P^{S^c}(w,z)\right\}$. Then the definition of P-lower Lorenz approximations of S and S^c at consistency level l, is:

$$\underline{P}^l(S) = \left\{(x,y) \in S : \varepsilon_P^S(x,y) \geq l\right\}, \ \underline{P}^l(S^c) = \left\{(x,y) \in S^c : \varepsilon_P^{S^c}(x,y) \geq l\right\}.$$

The P-upper Lorenz approximations of S and S^c at consistency level l are defined by complementarity:

$$\overline{P}^l(S) = B - \underline{P}^l(S^c), \ \overline{P}^l(S^c) = B - \underline{P}^l(S).$$

4   Induction of Decision Rules from Lorenz Rough Approximations of S and $\mathbf{S^c}$

Using the P-Lorenz rough approximations of S and S^c defined in section 3, it is then possible to induce a generalized description of the preferential information contained in the PCT in terms of suitable decision rules (Greco, Matarazzo, Slowinski, Stefanowski 2001). The syntax of these rules is based on the concept of *upward cumulated preferences* and *downward cumulated preferences* in each dimension k of the Lorenz space $\boldsymbol{L^n}$, denoted by $L_{\overline{k}}^{\geq}(h)$ and $L_{\overline{k}}^{\leq}(h)$, respectively. Remembering that $L_k(h) = \sum_{i=1}^{k} h_{[i]}$, the cumulated preferences have the following interpretation:

- $x L_{\overline{k}}^{\geq}(h)\, y$ means "x is preferred to y with respect to the k-th dimension in $\boldsymbol{L^n}$ by <u>at least</u> degree $L_k(h)$",

- $x L_{\overline{k}}^{\leq}(h)\, y$ means "x is preferred to y with respect to the k-th dimension in $\boldsymbol{L^n}$ by <u>at most</u> degree $L_k(h)$",

where $k=1, \ldots, n$ and $h = [h_1, \ldots, h_n]$ is a vector of degrees of intensity of preference of x over y in $\boldsymbol{H^n}$.

Exact definition of the cumulated preferences, for each $(x,y) \in A \times A$, $g_i \in C$ and $h_i \in \{1, \ldots, z\}$, is the following:

- $x L_{\overline{k}}^{\geq}(h)\, y$ if $x\, f_k\, y$, where $f_k \in \{1, \ldots, k \times z\}$ and $f_k \geq L_k(h)$,

- $x L_{\overline{k}}^{\leq}(h)\, y$ if $x\, f_k\, y$, where $f_k \in \{1, \ldots, k \times z\}$ and $f_k \leq L_k(h)$.

The decision rules have then the following syntax:

1) *certain* $\mathbf{D_{\geq}}$-*decision rules*:

$$\textit{if } x\, L_{\overline{k1}}^{\geq}(h)\, y \textit{ and} \ldots \quad x\, L_{\overline{kp}}^{\geq}(h)\, y, \quad \textit{then } x\, S\, y,$$

where $\{k1, \ldots, kp\} \subseteq \{1, \ldots, q\}$, $q = |P|, P \subseteq C$
and $(L_{k1}(h), \ldots, L_{kp}(h)) \in \{1, \ldots, k1 \times z\} \times \ldots \times \{1, \ldots, kp \times z\}$; these rules are supported by pairs of reference objects from the P-lower Lorenz approximation of S only;

2) *certain* $\mathbf{D_{\leq}}$-*decision rules*:

$$\textit{if } x\, L_{\overline{k1}}^{\leq}(h)\, y \textit{ and} \ldots \quad x\, L_{\overline{kp}}^{\leq}(h)\, y, \quad \textit{then } x\, S^c\, y,$$

where $\{k1, \ldots, kp\} \subseteq \{1, \ldots, q\}$, $q = |P|, P \subseteq C$
and $(L_{k1}(h), \ldots, L_{kp}(h)) \in \{1, \ldots, k1 \times z\} \times \ldots \times \{1, \ldots, kp \times z\}$; these rules are supported by pairs of reference objects from the P-lower Lorenz approximation of S^c only;

3) *approximate* $\mathbf{D}_{\geq \leq}$*-decision rules*:

$$\text{if } x\,L_{k1}^{\geq}(h)\,y \text{ and } \dots \quad x\,L_{kr}^{\geq}(h)\,y \text{ and } x\,L_{k(r+1)}^{\leq}(h)\,y \text{ and } \dots \quad x\,L_{kp}^{\leq}(h)\,y,$$
$$\text{then } x\,S\,y \text{ or } x\,S^c\,y,$$

where $O' = \{k1,\dots,kr\} \subseteq \{1,\dots,q\}$, $O'' = \{k(r+1),\dots,kp\} \subseteq \{1,\dots,q\}$, $q = |P|, P \subseteq C$, $P = O' \cup O''$, O' and O'' not necessarily disjoint, and $(L_{k(r+1)}(h),\dots,L_{kp}(h)) \in \{1,\dots,k1 \times z\} \times \dots \times \{1,\dots,kr \times z\}$, $(L_{k1}(h),\dots,L_{kr}(h)) \in \{1,\dots,k(r+1) \times z\} \times \dots \times \{1,\dots,kp \times z\}$; these rules are supported by pairs of objects from the P-boundary of S and S^c only.

A shorter notation of the above rules is the following:

- $D_{\geq}$-*decision rules*:   if $f_{k1} \geq L_k(h)$ and $\dots$ $f_{kp} \geq L_{kp}(h)$, then $x\,S\,y$,

- $D_{\leq}$-*decision rules*:   if $f_{k1} \leq L_k(h)$ and $\dots$ $f_{kp} \leq L_{kp}(h)$, then $x\,S^c\,y$,

- $D_{\geq \leq}$-*decision rules*:   if $f_{k1} \geq L_k(h)$ and $\dots$ $f_{kr} \geq L_{kr}(h)$ and $f_{k(r+1)} \leq L_k(h)$ and $\dots$ $f_{kp} \leq L_{kp}(h)$, then $x\,S\,y$ or $x\,S^c\,y$,

In our example, it is possible to induce the following decision rules from Lorenz rough approximations of S and S^c (supporting pairs are within braces, see Fig. 4):

#1 *if* $f_2 \geq 9$, *then* $x\,S\,y$ $\{(p,q),(r,q),(s,t)\}$,

#2 *if* $f_1 \geq 4$, *then* $x\,S\,y$ $\{(r,q),(s,t)\}$,

#3 *if* $f_2 \leq 4$, *then* $x\,S^c\,y$ $\{(x,y),(w,z)\}$,

#4 *if* $7 \leq f_2 \leq 8$, *then* $x\,S\,y$ *or* $x\,S^c\,y$ $\{(u,x),(v,w)\}$.

The same rules in the original space $\boldsymbol{H}^2$ have the form (see Fig. 3):

#1' *if* $h_1 + h_2 \geq 9$, *then* $x\,S\,y$,

#2' *if* $\min\{h_1,h_2\} \geq 4$, *then* $x\,S\,y$,

#3' *if* $h_1 + h_2 \leq 4$, *then* $x\,S^c\,y$,

#4' *if* $7 \leq h_1 + h_2 \leq 8$, *then* $x\,S\,y$ *or* $x\,S^c\,y$.

Remark that using Pareto rough approximations of S and S^c in $\boldsymbol{H}^2$, we get two certain rules (see Fig. 5):

#1^P *if* $h_2 \geq 5$, *then* $x\,S\,y$ $\{(p,q),(r,q),(s,t),(u,x)\}$,

#2^P *if* $h_2 \leq 3$, *then* $x\,S^c\,y$ $\{(x,y),(w,z),(v,w)\}$.

These rules are less robust than Lorenz certain rules #1, #2, #3 because #1^P, #2^P are supported by pairs (u,x), (v,w) which were found inconsistent with the Lorenz dominance principle.

5   Application of Decision Rules for Decision Support

The decision rules induced from a given PCT describe the comprehensive preference relations S and S^c either exactly ($D_\geq$- and $D_\leq$-decision rules) or approximately ($D_{\geq\leq}$-decision rules). A set of these rules covering all pairs of PCT represent a preference model of the DM who gave the pairwise comparisons of reference objects. Application of these decision rules on a new subset $M \subseteq A$ of objects induces a specific preference structure on M.

In fact, any pair of objects $(u,v) \in M \times M$ can match the decision rules in one of four ways:

- at least one $D_\geq$-decision rule and neither $D_\leq$- nor $D_{\geq\leq}$-decision rules,
- at least one $D_\leq$-decision rule and neither $D_\geq$- nor $D_{\geq\leq}$-decision rules,
- at least one $D_\geq$-decision rule and at least one $D_\leq$-decision rule, or at least one $D_{\geq\leq}$-decision rule, or at least one $D_{\geq\leq}$-decision rule and at least one $D_\geq$- and/or at least one $D_\leq$-decision rule,
- no decision rule.

These four ways correspond to the following four situations of outranking, respectively:

- $u\,S\,v$ and *not* $u\,S^c\,v$, that is *true* outranking (denoted by $u\,S^T v$),
- $u\,S^c\,v$ and *not* $u\,S\,v$, that is *false* outranking (denoted by $u\,S^F v$),
- $u\,S\,v$ and $u\,S^c\,v$, that is *contradictory* outranking (denoted by $u\,S^K v$),
- *not* $u\,S\,v$ and *not* $u\,S^c\,v$, that is *unknown* outranking (denoted by $u\,S^U v$).

The four above situations, which together constitute the so-called *four-valued outranking* (Greco, Matarazzo, Slowinski, Tsoukias 1998), have been introduced to underline the presence and absence of *positive* and *negative* reasons for the outranking. Moreover, they make it possible to distinguish contradictory situations from unknown ones.

A final *recommendation* (choice or ranking) can be obtained upon a suitable exploitation of this structure, i.e. of the presence and the absence of outranking S and S^c on M. A possible exploitation procedure consists in calculating a specific score, called Net Flow Score, for each object $x \in M$:

$$S_{nf}(x) = S^{++}(x) - S^{+-}(x) + S^{-+}(x) - S^{--}(x), \text{ where}$$

$$S^{++}(x) = |\{y \in M: \text{there is at least one decision rule which affirms } x\,S\,y \}|,$$

$$S^{+-}(x) = |\{y \in M: \text{there is at least one decision rule which affirms } y\,S\,x\}|,$$

$$S^{-+}(x) = |\{y \in M: \text{there is at least one decision rule which affirms } y\,S^c\,x \}|,$$

$$S^{--}(x) = |\{y \in M: \text{there is at least one decision rule which affirms } x\,S^c\,y\}|.$$

The recommendation in ranking problems consists of the total preorder determined by $S_{nf}(x)$ on M; in choice problems, it consists of the object(s) $x^* \in M$ such that $S_{nf}(x^*) = \underset{x \in M}{Max}\{S_{nf}(x)\}$.

The above procedure has been characterized with reference to a number of desirable properties in (Greco, Matarazzo, Slowinski, Tsoukias 1998). Let us remark that instead of the above cardinalities, the Net Flow Score procedure can take into account some finer characteristics of rules which affirm the presence or absence of the outranking relation for a pair of objects – these can be relative strength or confirmation factors of the rules.

6 Conclusions

We proposed a new variant of Dominance-based Rough Set Approach, adapted to deal with *multicriteria choice and ranking* problems in such a way that the inconsistency in the input preferential information is detected using the *Lorenz dominance relation*, instead of the usual Pareto dominance relation. Let us point out the main features of the described methodology:

- preference information necessary to deal with a multicriteria choice or ranking problem is asked to the DM in terms of pairwise comparisons of some reference objects,
- the preference model induced from the rough Lorenz approximations of S and S^c is expressed in a natural and comprehensible language of "*if* ... , *then* ... " decision rules; the decision rules concern pairs of objects and conclude either presence or absence of a comprehensive outranking relation; conditions for the presence are expressed in "at least" terms, and for the absence in "at most" terms, on a subset of n dimensions of an evaluation space transformed to the Lorenz space L^n,
- the use of Lorenz dominance instead of Pareto dominance results in more robust certain decision rules because lower approximations of S and S^c by Lorenz dominance do not include the pairs of reference objects that were found incomparable by Pareto dominance, while being compared inconsistently in the sense of Lorenz dominance principle.

Acknowledgement. The first author wishes to acknowledge financial support from the State Committee for Scientific Research (KBN) and from the Foundation for Polish Science, (FNP). The research of the second author has been supported by Italian Ministry of Education, University and Scientific Research (MIUR).

References

Greco, S., Matarazzo, B., Slowinski, R.: The use of rough sets and fuzzy sets in MCDM. [In]: T.Gal, T.Stewart, T.Hanne (eds.), *Advances in Multiple Criteria Decision Making*. Kluwer, Boston, 1999, pp. 14.1-14.59
Greco, S., Matarazzo, B., Slowinski, R.: Extension of the rough set approach to multicriteria decision support. *INFOR* 38 (2000) 161-196

Greco, S., Matarazzo, B., Slowinski, R.: Rough sets theory for multicriteria decision analysis. *European J. of Operational Research* 129 (2001) 1-47

Greco, S., Matarazzo, B., Slowinski, R.: Multicriteria classification. [In]: W. Kloesgen, J. Zytkow (eds.), *Handbook of Data Mining and Knowledge Discovery*. Oxford University Press, New York, 2002a, chapter 16.1.9, pp. 318-328

Greco, S., Matarazzo, B., Slowinski, R.: Preference representation by means of conjoint measurement and decision rule model. [In]: D.Bouyssou, E.Jacquet-Lagrèze, P.Perny, R.Slowinski, D.Vanderpooten, Ph.Vincke (eds.), *Aiding Decisions with Multiple Criteria – Essays in Honor of Bernard Roy*. Kluwer, Boston, 2002b, pp. 263-313

Greco, S., Matarazzo, B., Slowinski, R.: Axiomatic characterization of a general utility function and its particular cases in terms of conjoint measurement and rough-set decision rules. *European J. of Operational Research* (2003) to appear

Greco, S., Matarazzo, B., Slowinski, R., Stefanowski, J.: An algorithm for induction of decision rules consistent with dominance principle. [In]: W.Ziarko, Y.Yao (eds.): *Rough Sets and Current Trends in Computing*. LNAI 2005, Springer-Verlag, Berlin, 2001, pp. 304-313

Greco, S., Matarazzo, B., Slowinski, R., Tsoukias, A.: Exploitation of a rough approximation of the outranking relation in multicriteria choice and ranking. [In]: T.J.Stewart, R.C. van den Honert (eds.), *Trends in Multicriteria Decision Making*. LNEMS 465, Springer-Verlag, Berlin, 1998, pp. 45-60

Kostreva, M.M., Ogryczak, W., Wierzbicki, A.: Equitable aggregations in multiple criteria analysis. *European J. of Operational Research* (2003), to appear

Marshall, A.,W., Olkin, I.: *Inequalities – Theory of Majorization and its Applications*, Academic Press, New York, 1979

Pawlak, Z.: *Rough Sets. Theoretical Aspects of Reasoning about Data*. Kluwer, Dordrecht, 1991

Pawlak, Z., Grzymala-Busse, J.W., Slowinski, R., Ziarko, W.: Rough sets. *Communications of the ACM* 38 (1995) 89-95

Pawlak, Z., Slowinski, R.: Rough set approach to multi-attribute decision analysis. *European J. of Operational Research* 72 (1994) 443-459

Perny, P., Spanjaard, O.: An axiomatic approach to robustness in search problems with multiple scenarios. [In]: *Proc. 19th Conference on Uncertainty in Artificial Intelligence*, Acapulco, Mexico, 2003, pp. 469-476

Roy, B.: *Multicriteria Methodology for Decision Aiding*. Kluwer, Dordrecht, 1996

Slowinski, R.: Rough set learning of preferential attitude in multi-criteria decision making. [In]: J. Komorowski, Z.W. Ras (eds.), *Methodologies for Intelligent Systems*. LNAI, vol. 689, Springer-Verlag, Berlin, 1993, pp. 642-651

Slowinski, R., Greco, S., Matarazzo, B.: Mining decision-rule preference model from rough approximation of preference relation. [In]: Proc. 26th IEEE Annual Int. Conference on *Computer Software & Applications (COMPSAC 2002)*. Oxford, England, 2002a, pp. 1129-1134

Slowinski, R., Greco, S., Matarazzo, B.: Axiomatization of utility, outranking and decision-rule preference models for multiple-criteria classification problems under partial inconsistency with the dominance principle. *Control and Cybernetics* 31 (2002b) 1005-1035

The New Concept in Computer Vision: Automatic Understanding of the Images

Ryszard Tadeusiewicz and Marek R. Ogiela

Biocybernetic Department of the AGH University of Science and Technology,
Kraków, POLAND

Abstract. Paper presents absolutely new ideas about needs and possibilities of automatic understanding of the image semantic content. The idea under consideration can be found as next step on the way starting from capturing of the images in digital form as two–dimensional data structures, next going throw images processing as a tool for enhancement of the images visibility and readability, applying images analysis algorithms for extracting selected features of the images (or parts of images e.g. objects), and ending on the algorithms devoted to images classification and recognition. In the paper we try to explain, why all procedures mentioned above can not give us full satisfaction, when we do need understand image semantic sense, not only describe the image in terms of selected features and/or classes. The general idea of automatic images understanding is presented as well as some remarks about the successful applications of such ides for increasing potential possibilities and performance of computer vision systems dedicated to advanced medical images analysis.

1 Introduction

Almost everybody know nowadays about computer vision. Popular scanners and digital cameras, multimedial websites in Internet, many technical devices giving digital images as the output (e.g. ultrasonography or computer tomography scanners, electron microscopes, robot vision systems, astronomical instruments, and many, many other) make us familiar with the digital images. Everybody find also digital images as the very important sources of useful or pleasant information, because human eye (powered with brain) is very convenient source of information for men. Using image as a two–dimensional digital data structure (Fig. 1) we can not only store it in computer memory and send it throw many communication channels, but also we can process the image in many ways, obtaining more and more useful information.

At the present stage computer vision enables three kinds of computer elaboration of the images [1], [2] (Fig. 2):

- *image processing* – aimed **to improve the quality** of the image (enhancement, sharping and contrasting) and to separate and highlight only those **objects** which are vital from the merit point of view (segmentation)

L. Rutkowski et al. (Eds.): ICAISC 2004, LNAI 3070, pp. 133–144, 2004.
© Springer-Verlag Berlin Heidelberg 2004

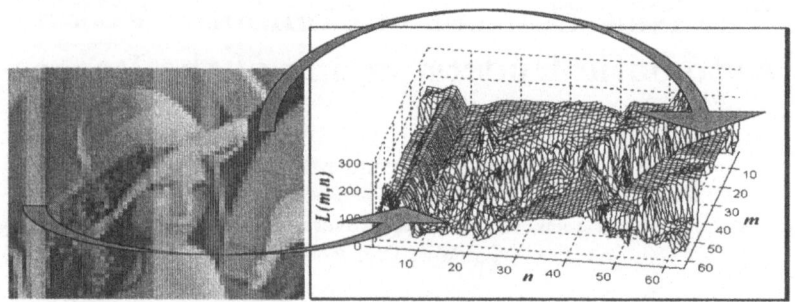

Fig. 1. Digital image as two–dimensional data structure

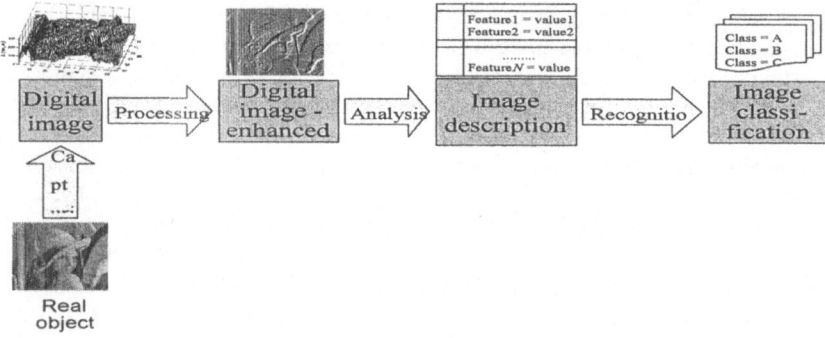

Fig. 2. Steps of information processing in classical computer vision system

– *image analysis* – aimed to determine the features of the whole image or specified objects, to count the objects and compute the value of quantitative parameters **or names of categories** assigned to quality features
– *image recognition (or pattern recognition)* – aimed to identify and classify the highlighted elements or areas through indexing them as objects belonging to certain categories determined a priori– mainly on the basis of their shape, dimensions and texture.

The classical computer vision techniques mentioned above will be described in this paper very briefly, because there are numerous books and other publications on the subject. Nevertheless we do stress, that all modern techniques of image processing, analysis and recognition can not answer for much more fundamental questions:

– What follows the visualized details?
– What is the meaning of the features extracted from the image?
– What are the results of the fact, that some objects belong to particular classes?

The answer for such question is connected with **new** technology: **automatic image understanding** instead of its automatic processing, analysis, and recognition.

2   Why We Do Need Automatic Understanding of the Images?

Before we can go to the details we must show, that in fact **exists** fundamental difference between formal description of the image (typically achieved by means of the variety of computer vision methods) and merit sense of the image, which can be discovered by the intelligent subject who can understood the profound merit **sense** of the image. Although the problem under consideration is rather serious one, we do use at this moment a joke for showing, how week can be in fact traditional computer vision technology in applications, in which understanding of the images is the "bottleneck" of the proper solution.

A joke goes as follows: Imagine, that we have big multimedial database with many images different types. Let assume we try to find picture "telling the same story", as pictures given as the examples. The example images are presented on the Fig. 3. Let us think together, how to describe criteria for intelligent selection

Fig. 3. Exemplary images

of next pictures similar (in sense of semantic content) to the shown on the Fig. 3 from a multimedial database?

For solving of selected problem using classical image analysis one needs following operations:

– Segmentation of all pictures and selection of important objects on all images
– Extraction and calculation of the main features of the selected objects
– Objects classification and recognition
– Selection of features and classes of recognised objects which are the same on all images under consideration
– Searching in database for images having the same objects with the same features.

After performing pointed out steps for the first given image we can find elements shown on Fig. 4. Similar analysis can be done for next example images

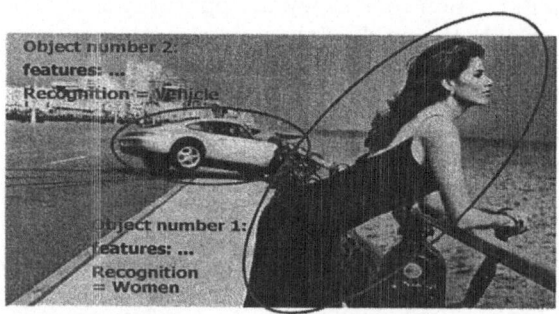

Fig. 4. Results of the formal analysis and classification applied to thefirst image under consideration

(we skip here the figures, but reader can easily imagine the results). After this analysis, summarizing all information we can do such induction:

– On all images we can find two objects: *Women* and *Vehicle*
– On some images there are also object *Man*, but not on all – so Men can be automatically considered as not important in searching criteria.

Result: computer finds and presents as desired answer all images with *Women* and *Vehicle*, for example images given on Fig. 5.

(For people form non–communistic countries it is necessary the comment at this point of the joke: selected images are very known allegories given on the Soviet posters named "all young girls ought to work on tractors").

It is very easy to find out, that the method of the image selection discovered by the automate is wrong in such situation, because example of proper image from the database is shown on Fig. 6. It is proper solution although Fig. 6 does not contain *Vehicle* at all, because in fact general meaning of all presented images is covered by the sentence: *Now we can see, why* (**and because of who**) *the men's life can be so often shortened!*

Fig. 5. Wrong images selected from the database

Fig. 6. Proper result of the **semantic** searching process

It was off course only joke (we apologize...), the matter although is quite serious because very often images apparently very different in fact can hide the semantically identical content – and vice versa: apparently very similar images can have dramatically different meaning.

3 General Structural Approach to Image Understanding

The joke presented in previous chapter shows, that sometimes we really need a method of extraction of some kind of semantic content, which is **present** in the image, but is not simply **visible** on it. This job can be difficult, because the matter of things is often hidden and needs precisely **understanding** of the image instead of its simple analysis, segmentation and even recognition. On the base of analysis of many definitely serious examples (of the medical images) we try formulate such three assumptions:

- Problem of proper interpretation of many images can not be solved by means of traditional image processing, picture analysis and pattern recognition.
- Only way is formulating of new paradigm of images interpretation and development of new method of its full automatisation based on application of advanced tools of artificial intelligence.

- Automatic reasoning about images semantic content, performed on the base of picture analysis is called by us automatic **understanding of the image**. The name can be of course different, but the meaning of images elaboration we need will be the same.

Fundamental features of the automatic understanding of the images (according to the our proposition) can be listed as follows:

- We try to simulate natural method of thinking of the man, who needs to understand "the story" presented on the image. The man can be – for example – physician, who must understand symptoms of the illness visible on the image before formal diagnosis and selection of treatment.
- First we must make **linguistic description** of the of the merit content of the image using special kind of image description language (we elaborate many such kind languages see [10], [9], [6]). Thanks to that idea we can describe every image without pointing to any limited number of a priori selected or described classes.
- The linguistic description of the image content can not be readable for men. In fact it is only formal (symbolic) description, which must serve as the base for understanding of the image. For expressing this feature of our linguistic description we do use Greek letters as elements of linguistic description.
- During automatic understanding process we must use knowledge base, in which most important **expected** features of the images are listed according to many kinds of semantic interpretations of images under consideration. In previous papers we presented examples how it can be achieved for diagnosis based on medical images or for indexing of multimedial database (see [7], [8]).

Very important difference between all traditional ways of automatic image processing (or recognition) and the new paradigm of images understanding includes one directional scheme of the data flow in traditional methods and definitely two–directional interaction between signals (features) extracted from the image analysis and demands taken from the merit knowledge about the images, given by experts (e.g. physicians).

Let us see once more to the Fig. 2, on which we can follow up traditional scheme of the image processing. It is evident feed-forward process with one source of information (input image) and one stream of processed data. When we try apply new methodology of automatic images understanding – we must introduce to our scheme additional source of information, which is knowledge (acquired form experts e.g. men who have such knowledge). Than the scheme of total system consist of two interfering streams of information (Fig. 7) and all process of image understanding will be based on two–directional flow of data. The source of first data stream is very known: it is digital image and selected results of its processing, analysis and linguistic description. The second data stream is more complex and is knowledge based. We try to describe very shortly our concept of very specific using of the merit knowledge in automatic understanding of the images (for more detail information please refer to [4], [5]).

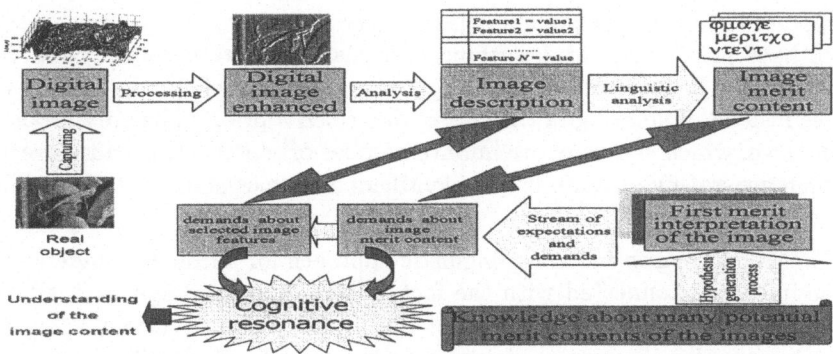

Fig. 7. General structure of the image understanding process

Nevertheless we know many knowledge–based systems the application of knowledge in proposed methodology is very different as in typical expert systems. In typical expert system the knowledge is treated only as a static formation of data, serving as a material for processing and discovering of answer and/or explanation we need by special "inference engine". In contrast to this static model in our image understanding systems we try to apply knowledge in its dynamical form. Knowledge works in our technology as a source of many hypothesis about merit sense of the images. From every hypothesis can be taken many suppositions, expectations, and demands about image under consideration. Of course not every supposition must be proven and not every expectation can be satisfied also if our image includes interesting merit content. But we can build the process named cognitive resonance. Short description of this process can be given as follows.

4   Linguistic Description of the Image – Key to Its Understanding

According to general description of the system of automatic understanding of the image, given in previous chapter, very important role in such methodology plays linguistic description of the image. Possibility of using special kind of languages for describing of many kind of images is known from years, but until now linguistic description of the image was applied to special purposes in CAD/CAM technologies (Computer Aided Design or Computer Aided Manufacturing of selected things – e.g. parts of machines, cars, airplanes or for architectural visualizations). Sometimes image description languages was used also for pictures calcification (mainly as part of so called syntactic methods for pattern recognition). In our methodology there are two important reasons for the selection of linguistic (syntactic) methods of image description as the fundamental tool for images understanding.

First takes from the fact, that (as we mentioned above) in case of understanding we have not any a priori known classes or templates, because in fact the potential number of possible classes goes to infinity. So we must use tool, which have possibilities of describing potentially infinite number of categories. It means, that it necessary to have tool for **generation** of the description of the classes instead of pointing of the classes described a priori. The only proper tool is language, which can generate infinite number of sentences, because every mechanism generating of finite list of identifiers or names is absolutely insufficient in such case.

The second reason for using linguistic approach for automatic understanding of the images is connected with the fact, that in linguistic approach after processing we do obtain a description of the image content without using any a priori known classification, because even the criteria of classification are constructed and developed during the automatic reasoning process. This is possible because of very strong mechanism of generalization included (or build in) into grammar parsing process. Thanks formal and powerful technologies of automatic parsing of all linguistic formulas (describing concrete images), we can recommended mathematical linguistic technology as the most powerful technology for any generalization.

In fact every grammar is always tool for generalization. When we write in natural language "dog", "cat", "tree", "car" – we describing concrete objects. But after this we can use the grammar and obtain much more general category "noun", which is much more useful for understanding of roles of al thinks under consideration and its mutual relationships.

Only problem is connected with proper adaptation of terms and methods of formal grammars and artificial languages to the applications in the domain of images (instead of strings of symbols, like in natural languages and even most artificial languages e.g. languages for computer programming). The problem is very known for specialist, but for the completeness of our presentation let us explain some fundamental ideas. Readers familiar with syntactic approaches in image processing please skip rest o this chapter.

When we try to build language for the description of the images we must started with the fundamental definitions of the element of the proper graph grammar. Let assume we must build the grammar for description of the class of landscapes like images presented on Fig. 8. Analysis of the scenes under consideration shows, that we have some classes of graphical objects ("primitives"), which can be build in into the grammar as the substantives (nouns). We have also some classes of relations between objects, which can be treated as verbs of our grammar. So the vocabulary of grammar for the images under consideration can be shown as on Fig. 9.

Using proposed vocabulary we can replace every landscape image to the equivalent scheme for the grammar, as it is shown on Fig. 10 (please compare this figure with Fig. 8 for analysis of source images and with Fig. 9 for considering grammar rules).

On the base of such symbolic description of the image under consideration we can use also symbolic notations for the elements of the vocabulary obtaining

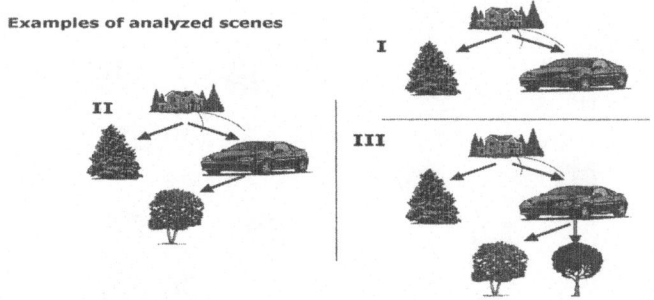

Fig. 8. Images selected as examples for syntactic description

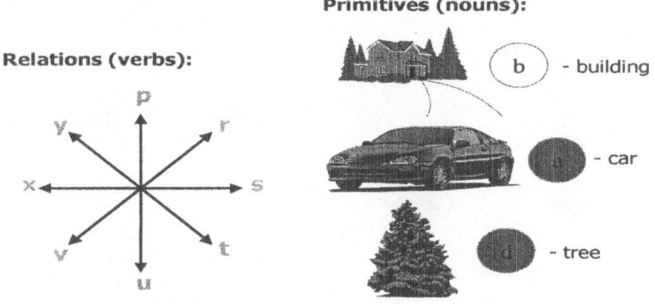

Fig. 9. Elements of the vocabulary

for every image its representation in terms of terminal symbols belongings to the definition of the used grammar (see Fig. 11).

5   Cognitive Resonance as the Main Element of Proposed Concept

After final description of the image by means of elements of selected (or most often – build for this purpose) image description language (for details refer to the chapter 4) we must realize cognitive resonance concept. It is of course most difficult point of the all work. During cognitive resonance we must generate hypothesis about semantic meaning of the image under consideration and we must have effective algorithm for its on–line verification. Both mentioned activities are performed by the parser of the used grammar. Hypothesis generation is connected with the use of selected production (mappings included into formal description of the grammar). The hypothesis generation process depends very much on the problem under consideration – Fig. 12.

Verification of the hypothesis is performed by permanent comparing of the selected features of the image with the expectations taken from the source of knowledge (mostly it is physicians experience based on his or her previous visual experience).

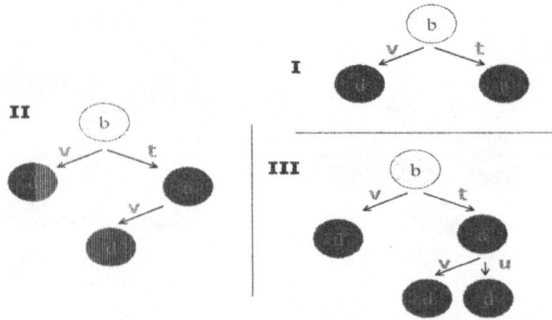

Fig. 10. Symbolic representation of the scene before describing its in terms of graph–grammar

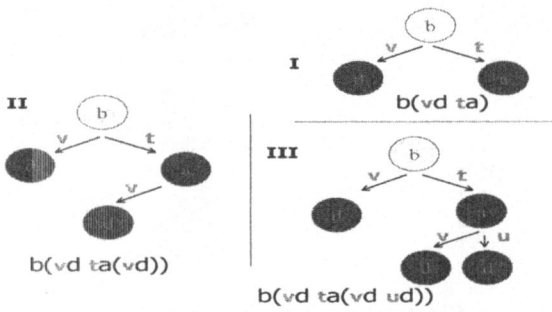

Fig. 11. Conversion of graph diagram of the image into its symbolic description

The main idea of cognitive resonance is based on iterative performing of following steps. Let us assume semantic linguistic description of some image is done in usual form of the string of terminal symbols:

$$\sigma\epsilon\mu\alpha\nu\tau\psi\chi\zeta\nu\psi o\pi\iota\sigma\alpha\nu\alpha\lambda\iota\zeta o\omega\alpha\nu\epsilon\gamma oo\beta\rho\alpha\zeta\upsilon\mu\alpha$$

We do use the Greek symbols according to the tradition of mathematical linguistic and as a signal informing, that man not needs understand symbols produced by the linguistic processor–it is enough if the parser can manage it.

Now starts parsing process. Let assume, that **working hypothesis no.1** about meaning of this image leads to the assumption, that image must include at least one pattern:

$$o\chi\zeta\epsilon\kappa$$

Parser starts the searching process throw all string of terminal symbols describing (in terms of used language) important semantic features of the analysed image.

The searching process fails, what means, that strength of the working hypothesis no. 1 is decreasing. Another working hypothesis leads to the assumption, that image must include at least one pattern:

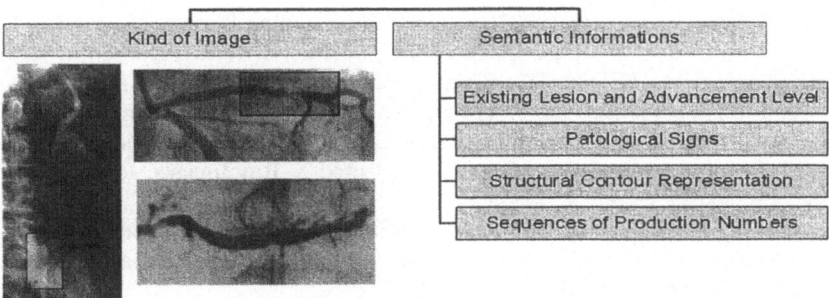

Fig. 12. Hypothesis generation process depends on the kind of medical image

$$\chi\varsigma\nu\psi$$

This pattern can be found in the string:

$$\sigma\epsilon\mu\alpha\nu\tau\psi\boxed{\chi\varsigma\nu\psi}o\pi\iota\sigma\alpha\nu\alpha\lambda\iota\varsigma o\omega\alpha\nu\epsilon\gamma oo\beta\rho\alpha\varsigma\upsilon\mu\alpha$$

what means that the **working hypothesis no.2** can be now find as a more probable, but we still are not exactly sure, is the hypothesis true or not, because for its full validation it is necessary to test also another assumptions taken from this hypothesis and from all other hypothesis.

All the validation process is in fact very similar to physical processes named interference phenomena. Validation is also based on the specific interference between two "waves". First is "reality wave" coming from digital image and all its algorithmically extracted properties. Second is "expectations wave" coming form knowledge base and controlled by the linguistic rules represented by graph–grammar parser. By means of generation of several hypothesis and consecutive increasing or decreasing of its plausibility during special kind of cognitive interference with "reality wave", we can eventually obtain "understanding" of the image content in form of **one** hypothesis with evident highest (peak) plausibility. Like in interference of every physical wave its amplitude can increase up to very big values in some regions of wave propagation environment because of resonance processes, we can also expect big values of plausibility of some hypothesis after above described process, named for this reason "cognitive resonance".

The description of the cognitive resonance presented here is of course the most simplified one. In fact the set of methods and formulas used by real parser designed by us especially for this works is much, much more complicated! But it can be analysed only on the base of practical examples presented in papers listed in bibliography (below).

References

1. Kurgan, L.A., Cios K.J., Tadeusiewicz, R., Ogiela, M., Goodenday L.S. (2001) Knowledge Discovery Approach to Automated Cardiac SPECT Diagnosis, *Artificial Intelligence in Medicine*, **23**(2), 149–189

2. Leś, Z., Tadeusiewicz, R. (2000) Shape Understanding System–Generating Exemplars of the Polygon Class. Hamza M.H., Sarfraz E. (eds.): Computer Graphics and Imaging, IASTED/ACTA Press, Anaheim, Calgary, Zurich, 139–144

3. Ogiela, M.R., Tadeusiewicz, R. (1999) Syntactic Analysis and Languages of Shape Feature Description in Computer Aided Diagnosis and Recognition of Cancerous and Inflammatory Lesions of Organs in Selected X–Ray Images. Journal of Digital Imaging, 12(2), Suppl. 1, 24–27

4. Ogiela, M., Tadeusiewicz, R. (2000) Artificial Intelligence Methods in Shape Feature Analysis of Selected Organs in Medical Images. Image Processing & Communications, 6, No 1-2, 3–11

5. Ogiela, M. and Tadeusiewicz, R. (2000) Syntactic pattern recognition for X–ray diagnosis of pancreatic cancer – Algorithms for Analysing the Morphologic Shape of Pancreatic Ducts for Early Diagnosis of Changes in the Pancreas. IEEE Engineering In Medicine and Biology Magazine, 19(6), 94–105

6. Ogiela, M. R., Tadeusiewicz, R. (2001) Image Understanding Methods in Biomedical Informatics and Digital Imaging. Journal of Biomedical Informatics, 34, No. 6, 377–386

7. Ogiela, M. R., Tadeusiewicz, R. (2001) Advances in syntactic imaging techniques for perception of medical images. The Imaging Science Journal, 49, Issue: 2, 113–120

8. Ogiela, M. R., Tadeusiewicz, R. (2001) New Aspects of Using the Structural Graph–Grammar Based Techniques for Recognition of Selected Medical Images. Journal of Digital Imaging, 14, No 2, Suppl. 1, 231–232

9. Ogiela, M. R., Tadeusiewicz, R. (2002) Syntactic reasoning and pattern recognition for analysis of coronary artery images. Artificial Intelligence in Medicine, 26, 145–159

10. Ogiela, M.R., Tadeusiewicz, R. (2003) Artificial Intelligence Structural Imaging Techniques in Visual Pattern Analysis and Medical Data Understanding. Pattern Recognition, Elsevier 2003, 36(10) 2441–2452.

Dynamic High Order Neural Networks: Application for Fault Diagnosis

Eugen Arinton and Józef Korbicz

University of Zielona Góra,
Institute of Control and Computation Engineering,
65-246 Zielona Góra, Poland
{E.Arinton, J.Korbicz}@issi.uz.zgora.pl

Abstract. The paper discusses the application of a multi layered high order neural network in modelling and fault diagnosis of dynamic processes. Dynamic properties can be obtained by adding a finite impulse response filter to the neuron. A combinatorial algorithm is used for selecting the network structure. If a linear activation function is used, the universal approximation capabilities of these networks are easy to prove. To show the applicability of such networks, the modelling and fault detection results for the two-tank-system are presented in the last part.

1 Introduction

Artificial Neural Networks (ANN) can be used to solve practical problems in engineering, e.g. to build models especially when dealing with non-linear processes. The importance of models in many disciplines has lead to a strong demand for advanced modelling and identification schemes. Models are useful for system analysis, prediction or simulation of system behaviour, design of controllers, optimisation, supervision and also for fault detection and diagnosis [5,7]. If sufficient data is available, than there is enough information to build and train an ANN. In such case the problem and its solution is described giving examples and the ANN is mapping these examples and tries to learn and to generalize the phenomena connected with the presented problem.

The High Order Neural Network (HONN) has better approximation properties comparing to the Multi Layer Perceptron (MLP) network. HONNs are capable of dealing with pattern classification problems by capturing the nonlinear properties of the input pattern space, e.g. solving the XOR problem only with one neuron. Such networks with a single hidden layer have been successfully used in engineering applications for non-linear system identification [6] or nonlinear surface fitting [9]. In the case of multi layered HONN the number of weights increases exponentially with the number of inputs. Such problem can be tackled using a second or third order neuron with a combinatorial algorithm to select the structure of the network. There are many ways to introduce dynamics in neural networks [4]. Adding a filter module to the neuron, the Dynamic High Order Neural Network (DHONN) obtained can be used to deal with dynamic processes.

L. Rutkowski et al. (Eds.): ICAISC 2004, LNAI 3070, pp. 145–150, 2004.
© Springer-Verlag Berlin Heidelberg 2004

The paper is organized as follows. At first, in Section 2, the structure of Dynamic High Order Neural Unit (DHONU) is presented. Section 3 describes the combinatorial algorithm used in selecting the network structure. The approximation properties of HONN are discussed in Section 4. In Section 5, the DHONN are applied for modelling and fault diagnosis of a two-tank-system. Last Section presents the conclusions.

2   Dynamic High Order Neural Unit

The structure of a n order DHONU is presented in Fig. 1. These neurons are used for the construction of the hidden layers of the DHONN. Such neuron can be interpreted as a combination between the so-called N-Adaline [8] (Adaptive linear element with a non-linear preprocessor) neuron and a perceptron with internal dynamics and non-linear activation function.

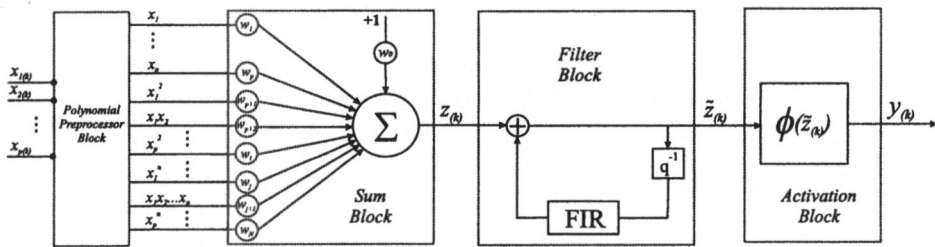

Fig. 1. DHONU structure

The main feature of the HONU is that the neuron's inputs are non-linearly preprocessed. The outputs of the polynomial preprocessor block are weighted and summed in the sum block. Assuming that the neuron has p inputs $\mathbf{x} = [x_1, x_2, \ldots, x_p]$, the output of this block is described by the relation:

$$z = w_0 + \sum_{i_1=1}^{p} w_{i_1} x_{i_1} + \sum_{i_1,i_2=1}^{p} w_{i_1 i_2} x_{i_1} x_{i_2} + \ldots + \sum_{i_1,i_2,\ldots i_n=1}^{p} w_{i_1 i_2 \ldots i_n} x_{i_1} x_{i_2} \ldots x_{i_n}$$

(1)

where w_0, w_{i_1}, $w_{i_1 i_2}, \ldots, w_{i_1 i_2 \ldots i_n}$ are the neuron weights. Dynamics properties are introduced to the neuron by adding a filter Finite Impulse Response (FIR) module before the activation module. For the first and second order dynamic, this module can be described by one of the following equations:

$$\tilde{z}_{(k)} = z_{(k)} + w_{F_1^1} \tilde{z}_{(k-1)}$$

(2)

$$\tilde{z}_{(k)} = z_{(k)} + w_{F_1^2} \tilde{z}_{(k-1)} + w_{F_2^2} \tilde{z}_{(k-2)}$$

(3)

where $z_{(k)}$ and $\tilde{z}_{(k)}$ are input and output of the filter module respectively, k is the discrete time and $w_{F_1^1}, w_{F_1^2}$, $w_{F_2^2}$ are feedback weights. To ensure stability of the neuron dynamics, these parameters must satisfy the following conditions derived from the Jury criterion:

- for the first order of filter: $-1 < w_{F_1^1} < 1$;
- for the second order of filter: $-1 < w_{F_2^2} < 1$, $1 + w_{F_2^1} - w_{F_2^2} > 0$ and $1 - w_{F_2^1} - w_{F_2^2} > 0$.

The activation function $\phi(\tilde{z}_{(k)})$ (the last module) can be linear, sigmoid or tangent hyperbolic function. The neuron output is given by: $y_{(k)} = \phi(\tilde{z}_{(k)})$.

3   HONN Development Structure

Since the number of weights in a HONN increase exponentially with the number of inputs it is necessary to keep an acceptable number of weights in the network. For this an algorithm for reducing and selecting the structure of the network is employed. The combinatorial algorithm used is based on the multilayered iterative Group Method of Data Handling (GMDH) algorithm [3]:

1. Add a hidden layer of neurons to the network. Each neuron has a fixed number of p inputs, (where $p < m$ or $p < m_i$) from the total m network inputs or m_i neurons outputs from the ith layer respectively. The number of neurons with p inputs created is $s = m!/(p!(m-p)!)$.
2. Estimate the weights of each neuron by a parameter estimation technique. Each neuron is trained separately to model the system's output before incorporating in the network by means of least square method when the linear activation function is applied or of a non-linear least square method for a hyperbolic tangent or sigmoid type of activation function.
3. Compute quality measures of neurons according to an evaluation criterion which can be the mean squared error.
4. Choose the N_i best neurons based on the value of quality measures of neurons. The others neurons are removed.
5. Create a new layer. The neurons outputs from the previous layer become inputs for the new formed layer, and the process is repeated from Step 1.
6. After a number of N_L layers, feed the outputs of the selected neurons to the output layer. The output layer is built based on neuron models known for the standard perceptron networks. The number of such neurons is equal to the number of system outputs.
7. Retrain the network. For stopping the learning process a cross validation technique can be used to obtain better generalization properties.

The presented algorithm used for structure selection gives possibility to choose and select only the relevant inputs and neurons. The neurons that model the searched input-output dependence most accurately are included in corresponding layers, and the elements that introduce too big processing error are removed.

4   HONN as Universal Approximator

The universal approximation properties of feedforward neural networks can be proven using the Stone-Weierstrass theorem, as a basis theorem of functional analysis and approximation theory [4]. A HONN can be treated as a feedforward neural network with non-linearly preprocessed inputs. With a linear activation function such networks become regular polynomial networks and is simple to verify that the network satisfies the conditions given in the Stone-Weierstrass theorem. Using a squashing activation function like the hyperbolic tangent or sigmoid functions, the network converges to the desired solution due to the properties of the squashing function [2], which divides the output space between the neurons. In this way each division can be modelled by a different polynomial.

The main advantage of the HONN over the classic MLP networks is that these networks have faster convergence properties and can give a solution which has less parameters in comparison with MLP. A good example in this sense is the solution given by HONN for the XOR problem. A second order HONU used to realize the XOR logic function can be: $y = \phi(x_2^2 + 1.25x_1^2 - 2x_1x_2 - 1)$, with the Heaviside function as activation function ϕ.

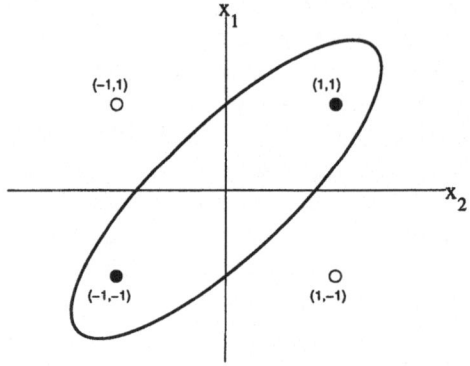

Fig. 2. Geometric representation of input space

In Fig. 2 a geometrical representation of the input domain is given. It can be seen that the HONU can separate the points $(-1, 1)$, $(1, -1)$ from $(-1, 1)$, $(1, 1)$ in the input space.

5   Experiments and Results

To illustrate the application effectiveness of the DHONN for modelling and fault diagnosis, a laboratory two-tank-system is considered. The process is depicted in Fig. 3. The notation used is the following: Q_i is the input flow command in

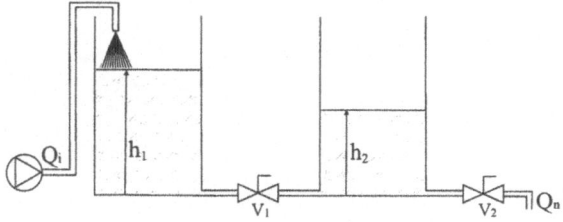

Fig. 3. Two-tank-system

tank 1 supplied by the pump, h_1 and h_2 are the water levels in tank 1 and 2. The two tanks are connected by valve V_1. The nominal outflow Q_n is from tank 2 and is given by valve V_2. The aim of the system control is to keep a constant level in the second tank.

Based on DHONN the level h_2 in the second tank was modelled using experimental data from the real process $\hat{h}_2^{(k)} = \text{DHONN}(h_1^{(k)}, h_1^{(k-1)}, Q_i^{(k)}, Q_i^{(k-1)})$, where k is the discrete time. The constructed network has one layer with 5 second order DHONU.

The constructed model was used in a model based fault detection scheme. Different faults were considered and simulated, e.g. leak in tank or pump external leakage. A residual is computed as the difference between the system and the model outputs and a constant threshold was used to determine if a fault appeared or not in the system. The threshold value was established based on the size of the modelling error for the training data. When the magnitude of this residual exceeds the threshold, it is likely the system is faulty. To eliminate false alarms the detection decision signal DD is computed based on the residual using two time windows as described in [1].

As can be seen in Fig. 4, in the no fault cases, the DHONN is able to model with good accuracy the water level h_2. The detection decision signal DD is made robust with respect to the variations of the residual below the threshold in the presence of fault. This is accomplished in the decision making stage by analyzing the residual in a window time before taking the decision.

6   Conclusions

A HONN has superior storage capacity in comparison with MLP. The main drawback of large number of multi layered HONN weights can be handled by using the combinatorial algorithm described. Adding a filter to the neuron, the obtained network can model with good accuracy dynamic systems. The success of model-based fault detection depends on the residual. As a consequence, it depends on the model used to generate this residual, which makes the DHONN a useful tool for fault diagnosis of non linear dynamic processes.

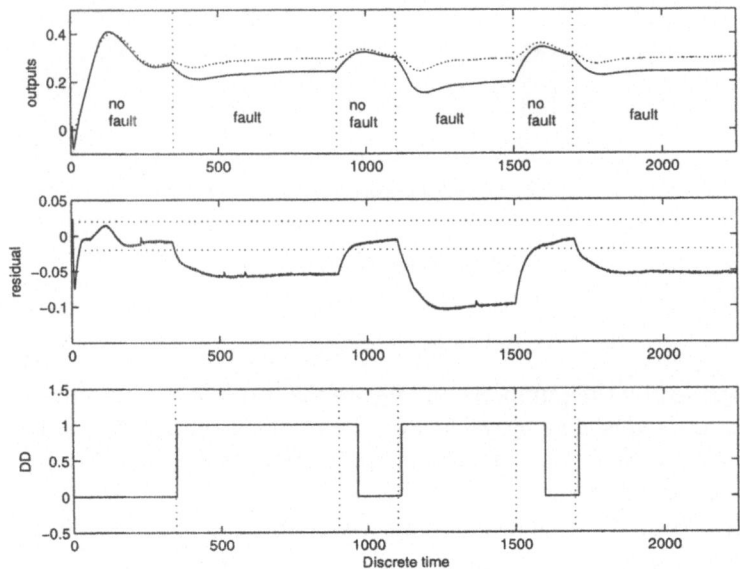

Fig. 4. The system (dotted) and model (solid) outputs for level h_2, the residual and the detection decision signal DD

References

1. Arinton, E. and Korbicz, J.: Model-Based Fault Detection Using Adaptive Threshold. Proc. 6th Nat. Conf. Diagnostics of Industrial Processes, Władysławowo, Poland, (2003) 121–126
2. Castro, J.L., Mantas, C.J. and Benitez, J.M.: Neural Networks with a Continuous Squashing Function in the Output are Universal Approximators. Neural Networks **6** (2000) 561–563
3. Farlow, S.J. (Ed.): Self-organizing Methods in Modelling: GMDH-type Algorithms. Marcel Dekker Inc., New York (1984)
4. Gupta, M.M., Jin, L. and Homma, N.: Static and Dynamic Neural Networks: From Fundamentals to Advanced Theory. Wiley-IEEE Press (2003)
5. Korbicz, J., Kościelny, J.M., Kowalczuk, Z. and Cholewa, W.: Fault Diagnosis. Models, Artificial Intelligence, Applications. Springer-Verlag, Berlin Heidelberg (2003)
6. Kosmatopoulos, E.B., Polycarpou, M.M., Christodoulou M.A. and Ioannou, P.A.: High-Order Neural Network Structures for Identification of Dynamical Systems. IEEE Trans. on Neural Networks **6** (1995) 422–431
7. Nelles, O.: Nonlinear System Identification: From Classical Approaches to Neural Networks and Fuzzy Models. Springer-Verlag, Berlin (2000)
8. Pham, D.T. and Xing, L.: Neural Networks for Identification, Prediction and Control, Springer-Verlag, London (1995)
9. Taylor, J.G. and Coombes, S.: Learning higher order correlations. Neural Networks **3** (1993) 423–428

Momentum Modification of the RLS Algorithms

Jarosław Bilski

Department of Computer Engineering, Technical University of Częstochowa,
Al. Armii Krajowej 36, 42-200 Częstochowa, Poland
bilski@kik.pcz.czest.pl

Abstract. This paper presents a momentum modification of two RLS
algoritms: momentum RLS and UD momentum RLS, each in classical
and linear version. All methods are tested on two standart benchmarks.
The results are discussed.

1 Introduction

In the last years various methods have been developed for the feed-forward neural
network training [1], [5], [6] and [7]. In this paper the momentum scheme is
applied to recursive least square algorithms [2], [3] and [8]. The RLS methods
update weight vectors in the following way

$$\mathbf{w}_i^{(k)}(n) = \mathbf{w}_i^{(k)}(n-1) + \mathbf{g}_i^{(k)}(n)\,\varepsilon_i^{(k)}(n). \tag{1}$$

Now equation (1) is replaced by

$$\mathbf{w}_i^{(k)}(n) = \mathbf{w}_i^{(k)}(n-1) + \mu\mathbf{g}_i^{(k)}(n)\,\varepsilon_i^{(k)}(n) + \alpha\varDelta\mathbf{w}_i^{(k)}(n-1) \tag{2}$$

where

$$\varDelta\mathbf{w}_i^{(k)}(n-1) = \mathbf{w}_i^{(k)}(n-1) - \mathbf{w}_i^{(k)}(n-2). \tag{3}$$

This leads to new momentum RLS algorithms.

2 Momentum RLS Algorithms

The RLS algorithms minimize one of the performance measures:

$$J_\varepsilon(n) = \sum_{t=1}^{n} \lambda^{n-t} \sum_{j=1}^{N_L} \varepsilon_j^{(L)^2}(t) = \sum_{t=1}^{n} \lambda^{n-t} \sum_{j=1}^{N_L} [d_j^{(L)}(t) - f(x^{(L)^T}(t)w_j^{(L)}(n))]^2, \tag{4}$$

$$J_e(n) = \sum_{t=1}^{n} \lambda^{n-t} \sum_{j=1}^{N_L} e_j^{(L)^2}(t) = \sum_{t=1}^{n} \lambda^{n-t} \sum_{j=1}^{N_L} \left[b_j^{(L)}(t) - \mathbf{x}^{(L)^T}(t)\,\mathbf{w}_j^{(L)}(n)\right]^2. \tag{5}$$

Criterion (4) is the classical RLS performance measure while (5) is used when error is transferred back (ETB) throught inverse to activation function. All depicted algorithms could be applied to the classical neural networks as well as to
completely connected (CC) neural networks [4]. For terminology we refer to [3].

L. Rutkowski et al. (Eds.): ICAISC 2004, LNAI 3070, pp. 151–157, 2004.
© Springer-Verlag Berlin Heidelberg 2004

2.1   Classical Momentum RLS Algorithms

This section shows new RLS algorithms minimizing performance measure (4) and (5). All equations are presented for the k-th layer.

Classical Momentum RLS Algorithm (MRLS)

$$\varepsilon_i^{(k)}(n) = d_i^{(k)}(n) - \mathbf{x}^{(k)^T}(n)\,\mathbf{w}_i^{(k)}(n-1) \tag{6}$$
$$= d_i^{(k)}(n) - y_i^{(k)}(n)$$

$$\mathbf{g}_i^{(k)}(n) = \frac{\mathbf{P}_i^{(k)}(n-1)\,\mathbf{x}^{(k)}(n)}{\lambda + \mathbf{x}^{(k)^T}(n)\,\mathbf{P}_i^{(k)}(n-1)\,\mathbf{x}^{(k)}(n)} \tag{7}$$

$$\mathbf{P}_i^{(k)}(n) = \lambda^{-1}\left[\mathbf{I} - \mathbf{g_i}^{(k)}(n)\,\mathbf{x}^{(k)^T}(n)\right]\mathbf{P}_i^{(k)}(n-1) \tag{8}$$

$$\mathbf{w}_i^{(k)}(n) = \mathbf{w}_i^{(k)}(n-1) + \mu\mathbf{g}_i^{(k)}(n)\,\varepsilon_i^{(k)}(n) + \alpha\Delta\mathbf{w}_i^{(k)}(n-1) \tag{9}$$

where $i = 1, ..., N_k$, $k = 1, ..., L$. The initial conditions are given by:

$$\mathbf{P}_i^{(k)}(0) = \delta\mathbf{I}, \delta > 0. \tag{10}$$

ETB Momentum RLS Algorithm (ETB MRLS)

$$e_i^{(k)}(n) = b_i^{(k)}(n) - \mathbf{x}^{(k)^T}(n)\,\mathbf{w}_i^{(k)}(n-1) \tag{11}$$
$$= b_i^{(k)}(n) - s_i^{(k)}(n)$$

$$b_i^{(k)}(n) = \begin{cases} b_i^{(L)}(n) \text{ for } k = L \\ s_i^{(k)}(n) + e_i^{(k)}(n) \quad \text{ for } k = 1, ..., L-1 \end{cases} \tag{12}$$

$$e_i^{(k)}(n) = \begin{cases} b_i^{(L)}(n) - s_i^{(L)}(n) \text{ for } k = L \\ f'\left(s_i^{(k)}(n)\right) \sum_{l=k+1}^{L} \sum_{m=1}^{N_l} e_m^{(l)}(n)\,w_{mi}^{(lk)}(n) \\ \text{for } k = 1, ..., L-1 \end{cases} \tag{13}$$

$$\mathbf{g}^{(k)}(n) = \frac{\mathbf{P}^{(k)}(n-1)\,\mathbf{x}^{(k)}(n)}{\lambda + \mathbf{x}^{(k)^T}(n)\,\mathbf{P}^{(k)}(n-1)\,\mathbf{x}^{(k)}(n)} \tag{14}$$

$$\mathbf{P}^{(k)}(n) = \lambda^{-1}\left[\mathbf{I} - \mathbf{g}^{(k)}(n)\,\mathbf{x}^{(k)^T}(n)\right]\mathbf{P}^{(k)}(n-1) \tag{15}$$

$$\mathbf{w}_i^{(k)}(n) = \mathbf{w}_i^{(k)}(n-1) + \mu\mathbf{g}^{(k)}(n)\,e_i^{(k)}(n) + \alpha\Delta\mathbf{w}_i^{(k)}(n-1) \tag{16}$$

The initial conditions are given by:

$$\mathbf{P}^{(k)}(0) = \delta\mathbf{I}, \delta > 0. \tag{17}$$

2.2   UD Momentum RLS Algorithms

In this section the UD modification of the RLS algorithms are presented [2]. The UD modification is based on the following transformation of matrix $\mathbf{P}$:

$$\mathbf{P}(n) = \mathbf{U}(n)\mathbf{D}(n)\mathbf{U}^T(n) \tag{18}$$

where $\mathbf{U}$ is an upper triangular matrix and $\mathbf{D}$ is a diagonal matrix.

Classical UD Momentum RLS Algorithm
Step 1

$$\varepsilon_i^{(k)}(n) = f'\left(s_i^{(k)}(n)\right)\left[b_i^{(k)}(n) - \mathbf{x}^{(k)^T}(n)\mathbf{w}_i^{(k)}(n-1)\right] \approx d_i^{(k)}(n) - y_i^{(k)}(n) \tag{19}$$

$$\mathbf{f}_i^{(k)} = \mathbf{U}_i^{(k)^T}(n-1)\mathbf{x}^{(k)}(n) \tag{20}$$

$$\mathbf{h}_i^{(k)} = \mathbf{D}_i^{(k)}(n-1)\mathbf{f}_i^{(k)} \tag{21}$$

$$\beta_{i,-1}^{(k)} = \lambda \tag{22}$$

Step 2
For $j = 0$ to N_{k-1}

$$\beta_{ij}^{(k)} = \beta_{i,j-1}^{(k)} = +f'^2\left(s_i^{(k)}(n)\right)f_{ij}^{(k)}h_{ij}^{(k)} \tag{23}$$

$$c_{ij}^{(k)}(n) = c_{ij}^{(k)}(n-1)\frac{\beta_{i,j-1}^{(k)}}{\beta_{ij}^{(k)}\lambda} \tag{24}$$

$$k_{ij}^{(k)} = h_{ij}^{(k)} \tag{25}$$

$$\mu_{ij}^{(k)} = -f'^2\left(s_i^{(k)}(n)\right)\frac{f_{ij}^{(k)}}{\beta_{i,j-1}^{(k)}} \tag{26}$$

Step 2.1
For $m = 0$ to $j - 1(j > 0)$

$$u_{imj}^{(k)}(n) = u_{imj}^{(k)}(n-1) + \mu_{ij}^{(k)}k_{im}^{(k)} \tag{27}$$

$$k_{im}^{(k)} = k_{im}^{(k)} + u_{imj}^{(k)}(n-1)k_{ij}^{(k)} \tag{28}$$

Step 3

$$\mathbf{g}_i^{(k)}(n) = \frac{\left[k_{i0}^{(k)}, ..., k_{iN_{k-1}}^{(k)}\right]^T}{\beta_{iN_{k-1}}} \tag{29}$$

$$\mathbf{w}_i^{(k)}(n) = \mathbf{w}_i^{(k)}(n-1) + \mu\mathbf{g}_i^{(k)}(n)\varepsilon_i^{(k)}(n) + \alpha\Delta\mathbf{w}_i^{(k)}(n-1) \tag{30}$$

The initial conditions are given by

$$\mathbf{D}_i^{(k)}(0) = \delta\mathbf{I}, \delta > 0. \tag{31}$$

ETB UD Momentum RLS Algorithm
Step 1

$$e_i^{(k)}(n) = b_i^{(k)}(n) - \mathbf{x}^{(k)^T}(n)\,\mathbf{w}_i^{(k)}(n-1) \tag{32}$$
$$= b_i^{(k)}(n) - s_i^{(k)}(n)$$

$$\mathbf{f} = \mathbf{U}^{(k)^T}(n-1)\,\mathbf{x}^{(k)}(n) \tag{33}$$

$$\mathbf{h} = \mathbf{D}^{(k)}(n-1)\,\mathbf{f} \tag{34}$$

$$\beta_{-1} = \lambda \tag{35}$$

Step 2
For $j = 0$ to N_{k-1}

$$\beta_j = \beta_{j-1} + f_j h_j \tag{36}$$

$$c_j^{(k)}(n) = c_j^{(k)}(n-1)\frac{\beta_{j-1}}{\beta_j \lambda} \tag{37}$$

$$k_j = h_j \tag{38}$$

$$\mu_j = \frac{-f_j}{\beta_{j-1}} \tag{39}$$

Step 2.1
For $m = 0$ to $j - 1 (j > 0)$

$$u_{mj}^{(k)}(n) = u_{mj}^{(k)}(n-1) + \mu_j k_m \tag{40}$$

$$k_m = k_m + u_{mj}^{(k)}(n-1)\,k_j \tag{41}$$

Step 3

$$\mathbf{g}^{(k)}(n) = \frac{\left[k_0, ..., k_{N_{k-1}}\right]^T}{\beta_{N_{k-1}}} \tag{42}$$

$$\mathbf{w}_i^{(k)}(n) = \mathbf{w}_i^{(k)}(n-1) + \mu\mathbf{g}^{(k)}(n)\,e_i^{(k)}(n) + \alpha\Delta\mathbf{w}_i^{(k)}(n-1) \tag{43}$$

The initial conditions are given by:

$$\mathbf{D}^{(k)}(0) = \delta\mathbf{I}, \delta > 0. \tag{44}$$

3   Simulation Results

The two following typical problems are simulated: the logistic function and the circle in the square problem. In all simulations the learning algorithms run one hundred times. The results will be depicted in tables with entries showing both the average number of epochs requied to meet a stopping criterion and the percentage of successful runs. The boldface font is used for momentum algorithms while the normal font for classical ones. In a case of unsuccessful runs a dash sign is shown.

Table 1. The number of epochs and percent successfull trainings for classical neural networks in logistic function problem

Structure / Algorithm	131		151		171	
RLS	20,93 100	$\lambda = 0,91$ $\delta = 1$	11,17 100	$\lambda = 0,95$ $\delta = 100$	8,86 100	$\lambda = 0,93$ $\delta = 100$
MRLS	*26,46* *99*	$\mu=0,7$ $\alpha=0,15$	*12,5* *100*	$\mu= 1$ $\alpha=0,05$	*9,24* *100*	$\mu= 0,9$ $\alpha=0$
ETB RLS	181,78 87	$\lambda = 0,99$ $\delta = 100$	70,06 100	$\lambda = 0,99$ $\delta = 100$	30,82 100	$\lambda = 0,95$ $\delta = 1000$
ETB MRLS	*70,49* *94*	$\mu= 0,4$ $\alpha=0$	*39,15* *99*	$\mu= 0,9$ $\alpha=0$	*16,99* *99*	$\mu= 0,1$ $\alpha=0,15$
UD-RLS	697 7	$\lambda = 0,99$ $\delta = 100$	837,89 9	$\lambda = 0,99$ $\delta = 10$	543,8 10	$\lambda = 0,99$ $\delta = 10$
UD-MRLS	*273,75* *16*	$\mu= 0,6$ $\alpha=0,15$	*167,33* *27*	$\mu= 0,4$ $\alpha=0$	*285,11* *36*	$\mu= 0,2$ $\alpha=0,15$
ETB UD-RLS	182,28 90	$\lambda = 0,99$ $\delta = 1$	81,97 100	$\lambda = 0,95$ $\delta = 100$	24,23 100	$\lambda = 0,95$ $\delta = 100$
ETB UD-MRLS	*70,01* *99*	$\mu= 0,3$ $\alpha=0,95$	*16,06* *100*	$\mu=0,9$ $\alpha=0,25$	*9,24* *100*	$\mu=1$ $\alpha=0,15$

Table 2. The number of epochs and percent successfull trainings for completely connected neural networks in logistic function problem

Structure / Algorithm	131CC		151CC		171CC	
RLS	9,63 100	$\lambda = 0,92$ $\delta = 100$	7,12 100	$\lambda = 0,96$ $\delta = 100$	6,47 100	$\lambda = 0,91$ $\delta = 100$
MRLS	*3,27* *100*	$\mu= 1,2$ $\alpha=0,05$	*7,2* *99*	$\mu= 0,9$ $\alpha=0$	*6,98* *100*	$\mu= 0,7$ $\alpha=0,35$
ETB RLS	15,2 100	$\lambda = 0,91$ $\delta = 100$	2,93 100	$\lambda = 0,92$ $\delta = 1000$	4,77 100	$\lambda = 0,91$ $\delta = 1000$
ETB MRLS	*1* *100*	$\mu= 0,2$ $\alpha=0$	*1* *100*	$\mu= 0,2$ $\alpha=0,05$	*1* *100*	$\mu= 0,2$ $\alpha=0,05$
UD-RLS	27,86 100	$\lambda = 0,91$ $\delta = 1000$	403,61 100	$\lambda = 0,91$ $\delta = 10$	270,99 98	$\lambda = 0,9$ $\delta = 1$
UD-MRLS	*21,92* *100*	$\mu=0,8$ $\alpha=0,55$	*368,42* *99*	$\mu= 0,7$ $\alpha=0,5$	*216,19* *97*	$\mu= 1,3$ $\alpha=0,05$
ETB UD-RLS	69,08 100	$\lambda = 0,9$ $\delta = 10$	9,15 100	$\lambda = 0,9$ $\delta = 100$	4,85 100	$\lambda = 0,93$ $\delta = 1000$
ETB UD-MRLS	*18,89* *100*	$\mu= 0,9$ $\alpha=0$	*9,15* *100*	$\mu= 1,1$ $\alpha=0$	*5,25* *100*	$\mu= 0,9$ $\alpha=0,05$

Table 3. The number of epochs and percent successfull trainings for normal neural networks in round in the square problem

Structure / Algorithm	2221		2331		2441	
RLS	219,4	λ = 0,984	86,05	λ = 0,998	26,82	λ = 0,988
	90	δ = 10	100	δ = 1000	100	δ = 1000
MRLS	51,55	μ=3,6	77,39	μ= 0,6	14,01	μ= 2
	91	α=0	100	α=0,15	100	α=0,35
ETB RLS	346,9	λ = 0,994	155,86	λ = 0,998	55,84	λ = 0,98
	91	δ = 100	96	δ = 100	99	δ = 100
ETB MRLS	208,65	μ= 0,1	107,46	μ= 0,9	28,93	μ= 0,8
	88	α=0	96	α=0	96	α=0,2
UD-RLS	–	λ = 0,99	–	λ = 0,99	574,63	λ = 0,996
		δ = 100		δ = 100	51	δ = 10
UD-MRLS	741,05	μ= 0,1	317,74	μ= 0,1	235,85	μ= 0,1
	21	α=0,05	35	α=0,05	55	α=0,05
ETB UD-RLS	301,69	λ = 0,998	107,68	λ = 0,986	22,1	λ = 0,994
	91	δ = 100	95	δ = 100	99	δ = 100
ETB UD-MRLS	184,61	μ= 0,9	23,77	μ=0,9	13,42	μ= 0,9
	90	α=0	97	α=0,15	100	α=0,15

Table 4. The number of epochs and percent successfull trainings for completely connected neural networks in round in the square problem

Structure / Algorithm	2221CC		2331CC		2441CC	
RLS	9,88	λ = 0,98	5,25	λ = 0,98	4,65	λ = 0,98
	100	δ = 1000	100	δ = 1000	100	δ = 1000
MRLS	5,74	μ= 2,3	4,54	μ= 2,6	4,72	μ= 0,6
	100	α=0,15	100	α=0	100	α=0,25
ETB RLS	39,7	λ = 0,986	11,75	λ = 0,986	3,31	λ = 0,986
	100	δ = 10	100	δ = 10	100	δ = 100
ETB MRLS	12,52	μ= 0,3	10,81	μ= 0,1	6,48	μ= 0,2
	100	α=0,56	100	α=0,85	100	α=0,65
UD-RLS	–	λ = 0,99	–	λ = 0,99	365,34	λ = 0,998
		δ = 100		δ = 100	94	δ = 10
UD-MRLS	89,51	μ= 0,1	264,48	μ= 0,2	37,01	μ= 0,1
	87	α=0,05	87	α=0,05	100	α=0,25
ETB UD-RLS	34,01	λ = 0,98	20,07	λ = 0,992	3,84	λ = 0,984
	100	δ = 100	100	δ = 1	100	δ = 100
ETB UD-MRLS	4,9	μ= 0,6	8,3	μ= 2,2	2,43	μ= 0,7
	100	α=0,15	100	α=0,15	100	α=0,25

The logistic function problem. For this problem 1-3-1, 1-5-1 and 1-7-1 classical and completely connected (CC) networks, with a sigmoidal hidden layer and a linear output layer was trained to approximate the logistic function $y = 4x(1-x)$. The training set consisted of 11 input-output pairs. The network was trained until sum of squares of the errors was less than 0.01. The results for the classical and CC architectures are given in Table 1 and Table 2, respectively.

The circle in the square problem. In this simulation, a neural network structure has to decide if a point of coordinate (x, y) varying from -0.5 to +0.5 is in the circle of radius equals to 0.35. The input coordinates are selected evenly. If the training point is inside the circle to the desired output is assigned the value 0.9, othewise the desired output becomes 0.1. In one epoch is 100 input-output patterns. The results for both the classical and CC 2-2-2-1, 2-3-3-1 and 2-4-4-1 architectures are given in Tables 3 and 4. The network was trained until sum of squares of the errors was less than 0.1.

4   Summary

In this paper the momentum modification of the RLS algorithms was presented. They seem to be an interesting alternative to the classical RLS algorithms. In both cases the computational load for one iteration is nearly the same but the momentum algorithms need significantly less iterations to train the network. In most cases the performance ratio (number of epochs of the classical RLS to number of epochs of the momentum RLS) ranges from 1 up to 10 depending on the problem and network structure.

References

1. Azimi-Sadjadi, M.R., Liou, R.J.,: Fast learning process of multi-layer neural network using recursive least squares method. IEEE Transactions on Signal Processing, Vol. 40, No. 2.(1992)
2. Bilski, J.,: New algorithms for learning of the feedforward neural networks. II KS-NiIZ, Szczyrk (1996) 39–45
3. Bilski, J., Rutkowski, L.,: A fast training algorithm for neural networks. IEEE Trans. on Circuits and Systems II, June (1998) 749–753
4. Bilski, J.,: The extended RLS algorithm with weight decrease for neural networks learning. IV KSNiIZ, Zakopane (1999) 41–46
5. Hagan, M., Menhaj, M.B.,: Training feed forward networks with the Marquardt algorithm. IEEE Trans. on Neural Networks, Vol. 5, (1994) 989–993
6. Karras, D., Perantonis, S.,: An efficient constrained training algorithm for feedforward networks. IEEE Transaction on Neural Networks, Vol. 6, (1995) 1420–1434
7. Riedmiller, M., Braun, H.,: A direct method for faster backpropagation learning: The RPROP Algorithm. IEEE International Conference on Neural Networks (ICNN93), San Francisco, (1993) 586–591
8. Strobach, P.,: Linear Prediction Theory - A Mathematical Basis for Adaptive Systems. Springer-Verlag, New York 1990.

Parallel Realisation of QR Algorithm for Neural Networks Learning

Jarosław Bilski, Sławomir Litwiński, and Jacek Smoląg

Department of Computer Engineering, Technical University of Częstochowa,
Al. Armii Krajowej 36, 42-200 Częstochowa, Poland
{bilski,slawlit,jsmolag}@kik.pcz.czest.pl

Abstract. In this paper we present a parallel realization of QR learning algorithm. We use the Householder reflection method to transform matrices to QR form. Parallel structures and performance discusion are included.

1 Introduction

Possibility of using QR algorithm for learning neural networks is well known [1]. Classical implementations of QR alghorithm require high computational load. The paper describes a new idea of the parallel realization of QR algorithm for neural network learning. The performance of this new architecture is very interesting and usefull for neural networks. In our aproach we use Householder reflection method [5] to transform matrices to QR form. The single iteration of a parallel architecture requires less computation cycles then a serial implementation. The final part of this work explains efficiency of the proposed architecture.

In our implementations of the method we introduce a performance measure

$$J(n) = \sum_{t=1}^{n} \lambda^{n-t} \sum_{j=1}^{N_L} e_j^{(L)^2}(t) = \sum_{t=1}^{n} \lambda^{n-t} \sum_{j=1}^{N_L} \left[b_j^{(L)}(t) - \mathbf{x}^{(L)^T}(t) \mathbf{w}_j^{(L)}(n) \right]^2 \quad (1)$$

where λ is a positive constant, called forgetting factor, close to but less then 1. For the terminology and a model of the i-th neuron in the k-th layer consult [1]. To learn the neural network we solve the following equation

$$\mathbf{h}_i^{(k)}(n) = \mathbf{A}^{(k)}(n) \mathbf{w}_i^{(k)}(n) \quad (2)$$

where

$$\mathbf{A}^{(k)}(n) = \sum_{t=1}^{n} \lambda^{n-t} \mathbf{x}^{(k)}(t) \mathbf{x}^{(k)^T}(t) \quad (3)$$

$$\mathbf{h}_i^{(k)}(n) = \sum_{t=1}^{n} \lambda^{n-t} b_i^{(k)}(t) \mathbf{x}^{(k)}(t) \quad (4)$$

recursively using the QR decomposition algorithm:

L. Rutkowski et al. (Eds.): ICAISC 2004, LNAI 3070, pp. 158–165, 2004.
© Springer-Verlag Berlin Heidelberg 2004

$$e_i^{(k)}(n) = \begin{cases} b_i^{(L)}(n) - s_i^{(L)}(n) = f^{-1}\left(d_i^{(L)}(n)\right) - s_i^{(L)}(n) \; for \; k = L \\ f'\left(s_i^{(k)}(n)\right) \sum\limits_{m=1}^{N_{k+1}} w_{mi}^{(k+1)}(n)\, e_m^{(k+1)}(n) \qquad\quad for \; k < L \end{cases} \tag{5}$$

$$b_i^{(k)}(n) = \begin{cases} b_i^{(L)}(n) = f^{-1}\left(d_i^{(L)}(n)\right) \; for \; k = L \\ s_i^{(k)}(n) + e_i^{(k)}(n) \qquad\quad for \; k = 1\ldots L-1 \end{cases} \tag{6}$$

$$\hat{\mathbf{w}}_i^{(k)}(n) = \mathbf{R}^{(k)^{-1}}(n)\, \mathbf{Q}^{(k)^T}(n)\, \mathbf{h}_i^{(k)}(n) \tag{7}$$

$$\mathbf{w}_i^{(k)}(n) = (1-\eta)\, \mathbf{w}_i^{(k)}(n-1) + \eta \hat{\mathbf{w}}_i^{(k)}(n) \tag{8}$$

where $\mathbf{Q}^{(k)}(n)$, $\mathbf{R}^{(k)}(n)$ and $\mathbf{A}^{(k)}(n)$ are related by

$$\mathbf{A}^{(k)}(n) = \mathbf{Q}^{(k)}(n)\, \mathbf{R}^{(k)}(n) \tag{9}$$

and vector $\hat{\mathbf{w}}_i^{(k)}(n)$ is a temporary solution while η is a learning factor.

The initial values of the weight vector $\mathbf{w}_i^{(k)}(n)$ can be chosen as small random numbers.

2   Parallel Realization

The main idea of the parallel realization of QR learning algorithm is using the Hauseholder reflection to transform matrix A to form $Q^T R$ where Q is ortoghonal matrix and R is upper triangular matrix. The Householder method lies in conversion of matrix A as it is shown in Fig. 1. The r and ρ elements create the matrix R, and v elements (in the same column) are vector coordinates. These vectors describe the hyperplanes of Householder reflection. The first step of the algorithm is calculation of matrices $\mathbf{A}$ and $\mathbf{H}$ (Eqn. 3 - 4). This step is shown in Fig. 2. Structure in Fig. 2 is applied to both matrices $\mathbf{A}$ and $\mathbf{H}$.

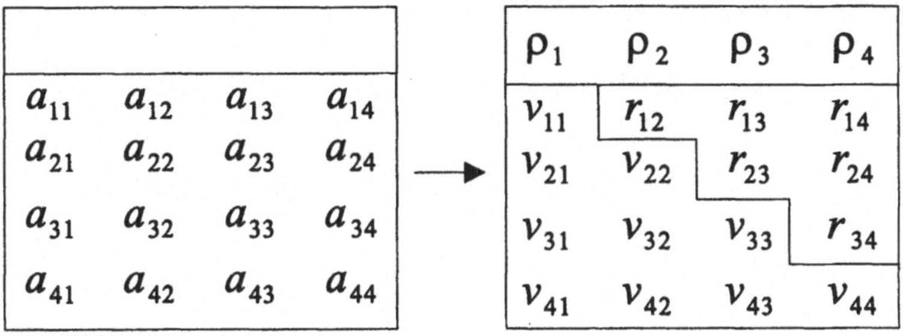

Fig. 1. Idea of Householder tranformation of matrix $\mathbf{A}$ *in situ*

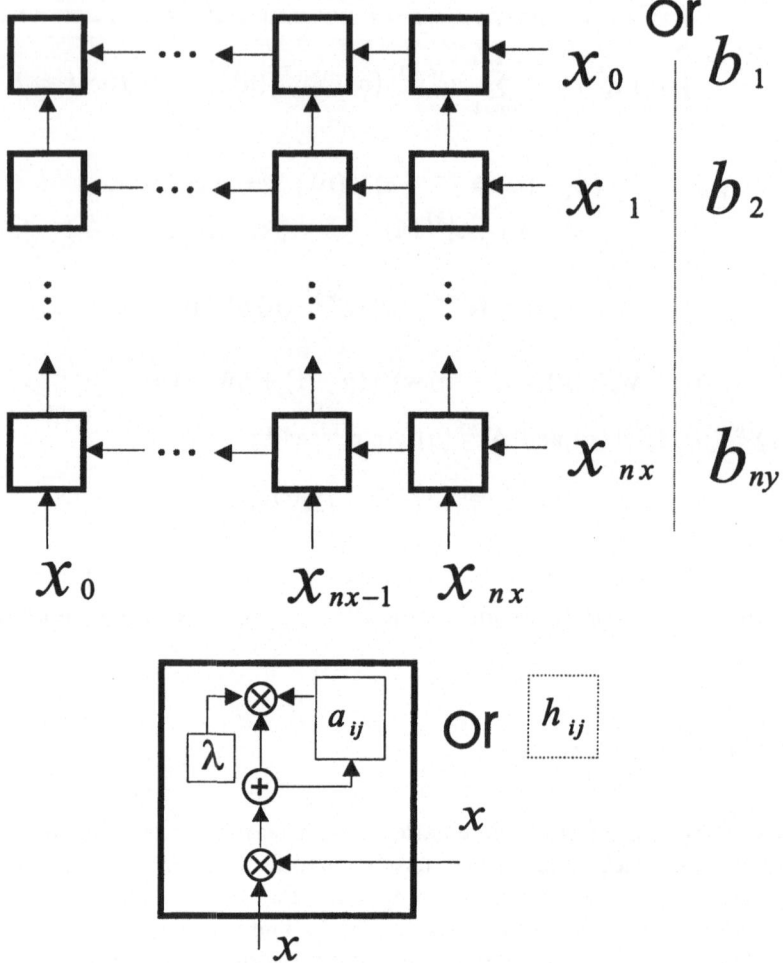

Fig. 2. Parallel realisation of two vectors multiplication (Eqn. 3 and 4)

Figures 3 and 4 present in turn first steps of transformation of matrix **A**. Here vector $\rho_\mathbf{k}$ and vectors $\mathbf{v}_k$ are computed according to the following equations:

$$\rho_k = \begin{cases} \left\| [a_{kk}, \ldots, a_{nx,k}]^T \right\|_2 & for\ a_{kk} \leq 0 \\[2mm] -\left\| [a_{kk}, \ldots, a_{nx,k}]^T \right\|_2 & for\ a_{kk} > 0 \end{cases} \tag{10}$$

$$v_{kk} = 1 - a_{kk}/\rho_k; \quad v_{ik} = -a_{ik}/\rho_k \quad for\ i = k+1, \ldots, nx \tag{11}$$

Figure 5 shows the final transformation of matrix **A**. In each iteration next vector **v** is obtained and it is sent to structure shown in Fig. 6.

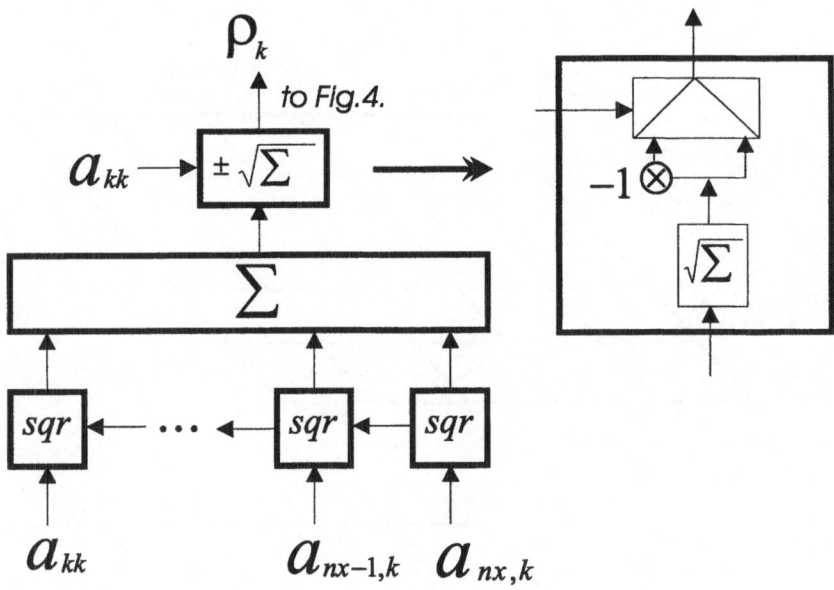

Fig. 3. Calculation of column vector lenght

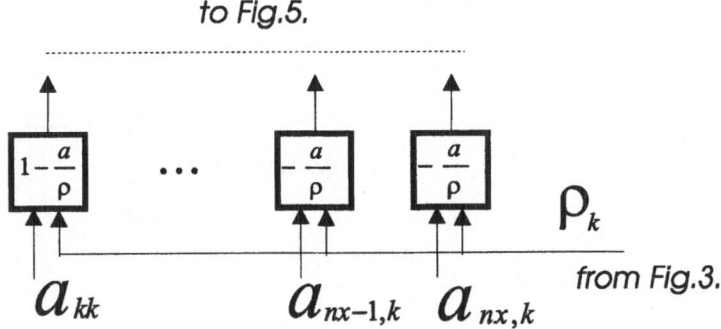

Fig. 4. First step of transforming matrix **A**

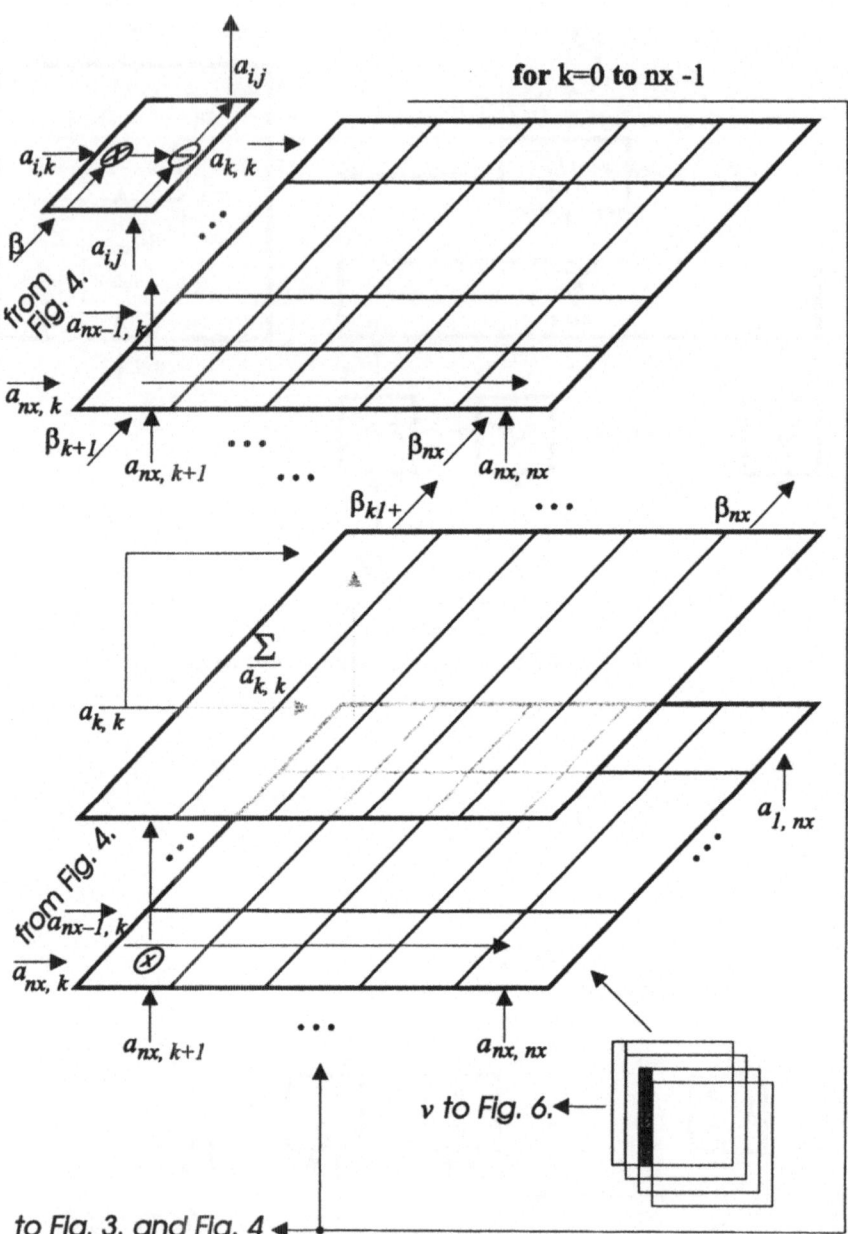

Fig. 5. Final step of transforming matrix **A**

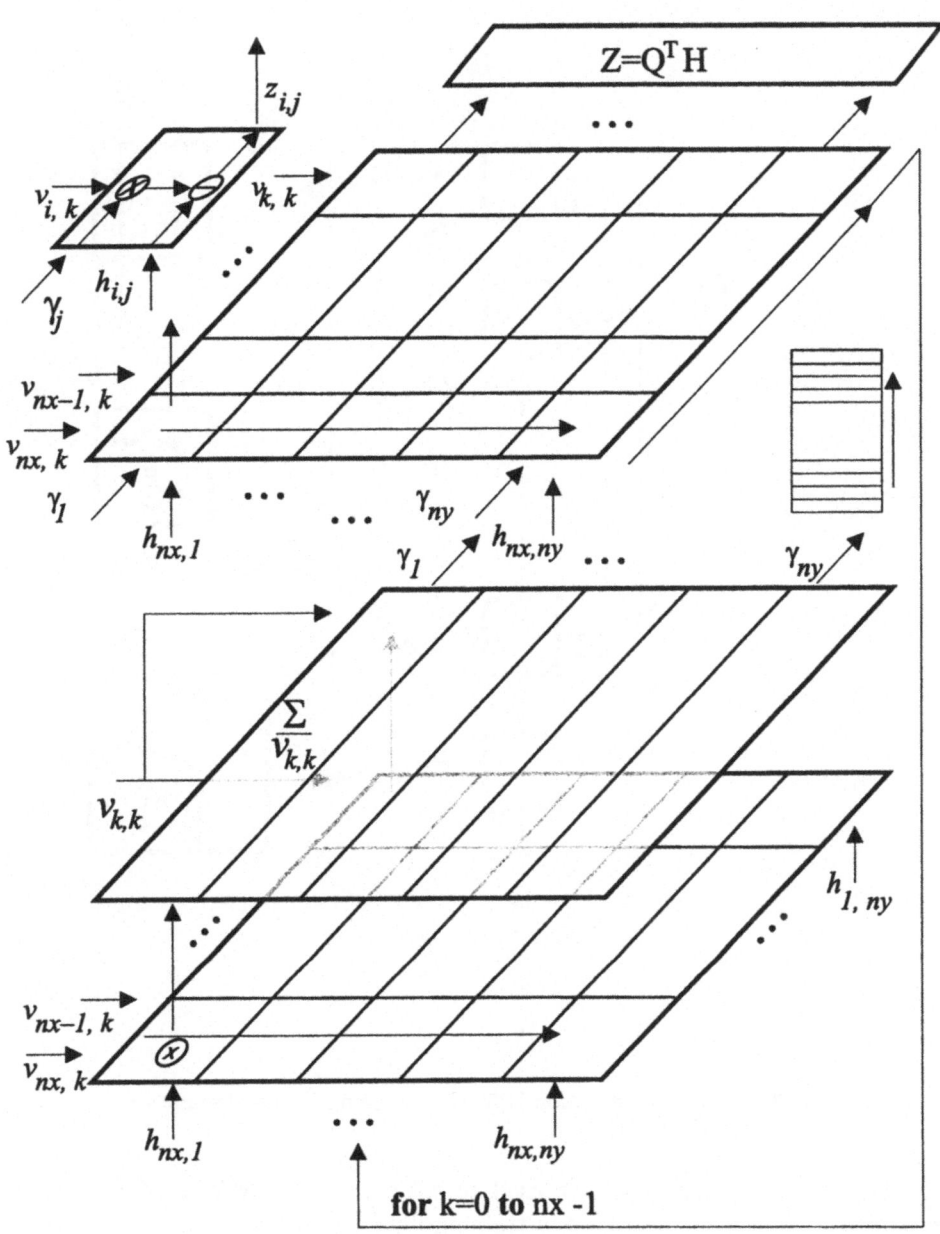

Fig. 6. Parallel computation of equation $\mathbf{Z} = \mathbf{Q^T H}$

In Fig. 6 the structure which computes $\mathbf{Z} = \mathbf{Q^T H}$ is proposed. The matrix $\mathbf{Q}^T$ is a product of the Householder matrices obtained from vectors $\mathbf{v}_i$. Note that in each iteration one row of matrix $\mathbf{Z}$ is obtained from shifted matrix $\mathbf{H}$ and vector $\mathbf{v}$.

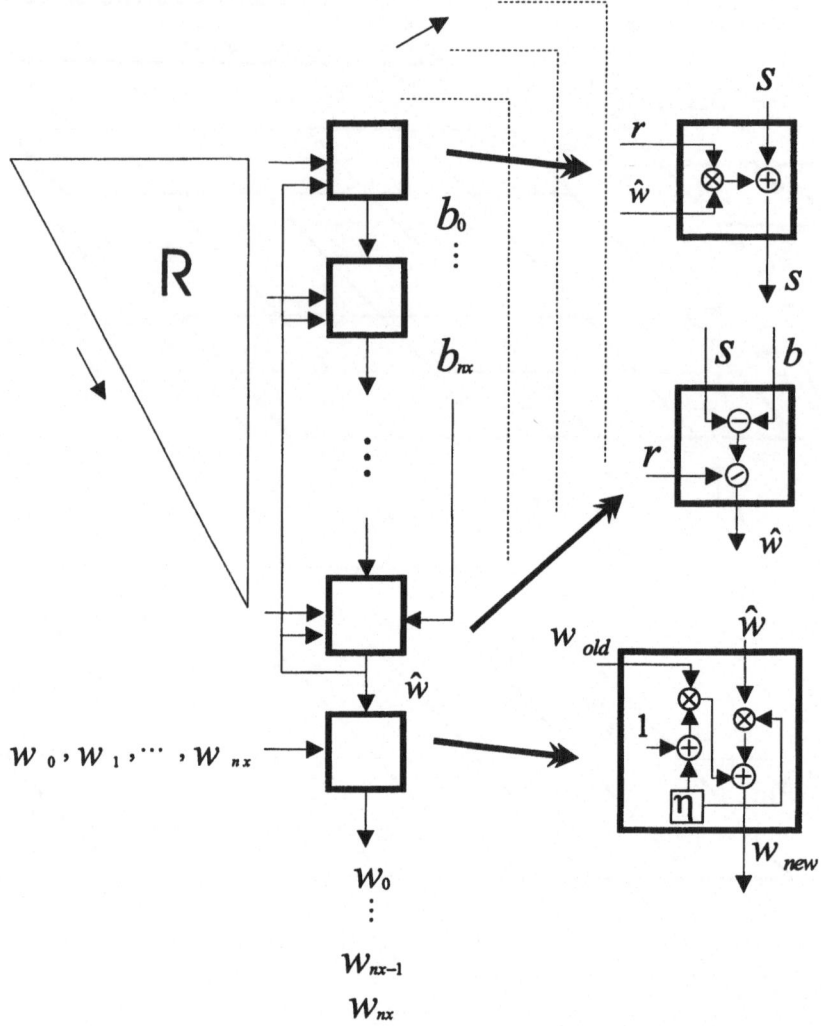

Fig. 7. Solution of equation $\mathbf{RW} = \mathbf{Z}$ by using Gauss elimination

The structure from Fig. 7 is used to solve equation $\mathbf{RW} = \mathbf{Z}$ by Gauss elimination. This is the last step in training iteration and it updates the weight matrix in one layer.

The above procedure should be repeated until the satisfied level of error measure is achieved.

3   Conclusion

In this paper the parallel realization for single layered neural networks was proposed. Suppose that all multiplication and additions operations take the same

time unit. We compare computational performance of the QR parallel imple-
mantation with sequential architectures up to 10 inputs and 10 outputs neural
network layer.

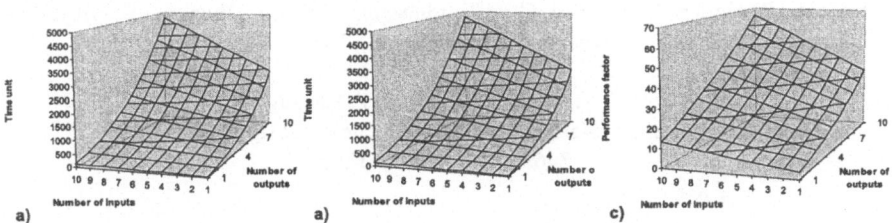

Fig. 8. Number of time cycles in a)classical, b)parallel implementations; c)performance
factor

Performance factor of parallel realization of QR algorithm achieves 65 for 10
inputs and 10 outputs neural network layer, and it grows fast when the number of
layer inputs or outputs grows (see Fig. 8). We observe a remarkable performance
of the proposed solution.

References

1. Bilski, J., Rutkowski, L.: Numerically Robust Learning Algorithms for Feed Forward Neural Networks In: Advances in Soft Computing - Neural Networks and Soft
   Computing Physica-Verlag Heidelberg New York (2002) 149–154
2. Kung, S. Y.: Digital Neural Networks Prentice Hall (1993)
3. Smoląg, J., Rutkowski, L., Bilski, J.: Systolic array for neural networks IV KSNiIZ,
   Zakopane (1999) 487–497
4. Smoląg, J., Bilski, J.: A systolic array for fast learning of neural networks VNNSC
   Zakopane (2000) 754–758
5. Kiełbasiński, A., Schwetlick, H.: Numerical linear algebry (in Polish) WNT Warszawa (1992)

Rainfall-Runoff Modelling Using Three Neural Network Methods

H. Kerem Cigizoglu[1] and Murat Alp[2]

[1] Istanbul Technical University, Civil Engineering Faculty, Division of Hydraulics,
Maslak 34469 Istanbul, Turkey
cigiz@itu.edu.tr
http://cv.ins.itu.edu.tr/abeteng.asp
[2] State Hydraulic Works, 14. Regional Directorate, Kucukcamlica,
34696 Istanbul, Turkey

Abstract. Three neural network methods, feed forward back propagation (FFBP), radial basis function (RBF) and generalized regression neural network (GRNN) were employed for rainfall-runoff modelling of Turkish hydrometeorologic data. It was seen that all three different ANN algorithms compared well with conventional multi linear regression (MLR) technique. It was seen that only GRNN technique did not provide negative flow estimations for some observations. The rainfall-runoff correlogram was successfully used in determination of the input layer node number.

1 Introduction

The rainfall-runoff relationship is one of the most complex hydrologic phenomena to comprehend due to the tremendous spatial and tremendous spatial and temporal variability of watershed characteristics and precipitation patterns, and the number of variables involved in the modelling of the physical processes. Conceptual models provide daily, monthly, or seasonal estimates of streamflow for long-term forecasting on a continuous basis. The entire physical process in the hydrologic cycle is mathematically formulated in conceptual models that are composed of a large number of parameters. The accuracy of model predictions is very subjective and highly dependent on the user's ability, knowledge, and understanding of the model and of the watershed characteristics.

The artificial neural network (ANN) approach is extensively used in the water resources literature([1][2][3][4] [5] [6]). In these studies either the conventional feed forward error back propagation method (FFBP) or the radial basis function was employed to train the neural networks. As well known the FFBP algorithm has some drawbacks. It is very sensitive to the selected initial weight values and may provide performances differing from each other significantly. Another problem faced during the application of FFBP is the local minima issue. The performance of another ANN algorithm, Generalized Regression Neural Network (GRNN) is not extensively analyzed in water resources problems. [7] found GRNN quite successfull in daily intermittent flow forecasting. In this study the

L. Rutkowski et al. (Eds.): ICAISC 2004, LNAI 3070, pp. 166–171, 2004.
© Springer-Verlag Berlin Heidelberg 2004

employment of GRNN in rainfall-runof modelling is compared with the FFBP and RBF performances. The hydrometeorologic data employed in the whole study belonged to a Turkish river basin.

2   Neural Network Methods in the Study

2.1   The Feed Forward Back Propagation (FFBP)

A FFBP distinguishes itself by the presence of one or more hidden layers, whose computation nodes are correspondingly called hidden neurons of hidden units. In this study the FFBP were trained using Levenberg-Marquardt optimization technique. This optimization technique is more powerful than the conventional gradient descent techniques [8].

2.2   The Radial Basis Function-Based Neural Networks (RBF)

RBF networks were introduced into the neural network literature by [9]. The RBF network model is motivated by the locally tuned response observed in biological neurons. The theoretical basis of the RBF approach lies in the field of interpolation of multivariate functions. The solution of the exact interpolating RBF mapping passes through every data point. Different number of hidden layer neurons and spread constants were tried in the study.

2.3   The Generalized Regression Neural Networks (GRNN)

The GRNN consists of four layers: input layer, pattern layer, summation layer and output layer. The number of input units in the first layer is equal to the total number of parameters, including from one to six previous daily flows [10]. The first layer is fully connected to the second, pattern layer, where each unit represents a training pattern and its output is a measure of the distance of the input from the stored patterns. Each pattern layer unit is connected to the two neurons in the summation layer: S-summation neuron and D-summation neuron. The optimal value of spread parameter (s) is often determined experimentally. The larger that spread is the smoother the function approximation will be. In this study the optimum spreads were found between 0.0015 and 0.019 for this investigation.

3   Data Analysis

The rainfall and river flow data belongs to Bykmenderes basin in Aegean region (Western part of Turkey). The daily mean flow data of a measurement station (stations 701) are provided by Turkish general directorate of electrical power resources survey and development administration (EE). The data covers a period of 10496 days. Rainfall data for this region was provided by Turkish State Meteorological Service (DM). Several rainfall measurement stations were subjected to correlation analysis. The rainfall stations having highest correlations with the

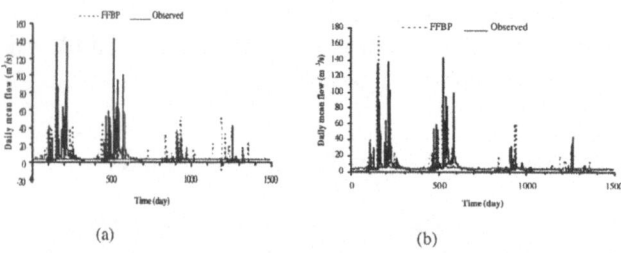

Fig. 1. Flow estimations for station 701 by FFBP (a) based only rainfall values and (b) based both rainfall and flow values for the testing period.

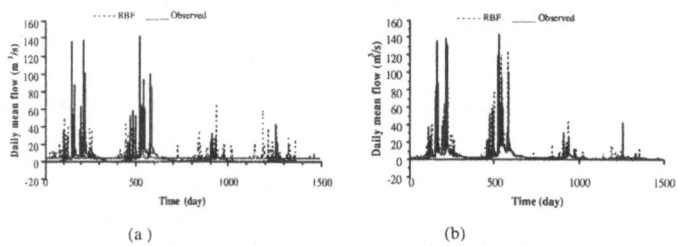

Fig. 2. Flow estimations for station 701 by RBF (a) based only rainfall values and (b) based both rainfall and flow values for the testing period.

flow station were selected. Final selection was made by considering the location coordinates of the rainfall and runoff stations with respect to each other. At the end the rainfall station 17886 was paired with runoff station 701.

4   Method Applications

3 MATLAB codes were written for three different ANN methods (FFBP, RBF and GRNN) as explained before. The data was divided into two parts for training and testing. The flow estimation simulations were carried out in two steps. First, only rainfall data was employed for the input layer. Then previous daily flow value was also incorporated into the input data group. The improvement with adding flow value was discussed for all ANN method applications. Mean square error (MSE) value for the testing period was considered for performance evaluation and all testing stage estimates were plotted in the form of hydrograph.

The ANN training data covered the first 9000 daily total rainfall and daily mean flow values of the record. However because of the computer memory limitation only first 5000 and 4500 daily values could be used for RBF and GRNN training stages, respectively. The following 1490 daily values were kept for testing purpose (Table 1). The initial training simulations have shown that one hidden layer was sufficient. The number of hidden layer nodes were found by trial and error. The number of nodes in the input layer were determined using the rainfall-runof correlograms as suggested by [6]. The correlogram for the station pair 701

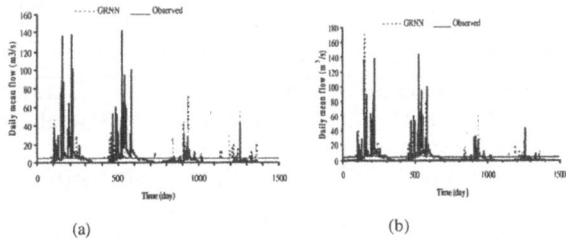

(a)   (b)

Fig. 3. Flow estimations for station 701 by GRNN (a) based only rainfall values and (b) based both rainfall and flow values for the testing period.

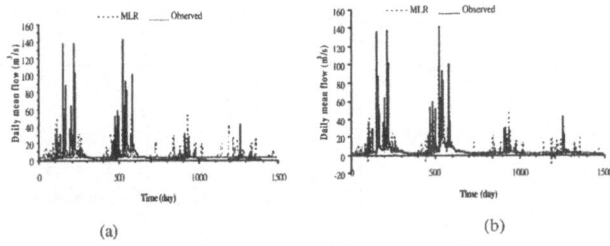

(a)   (b)

Fig. 4. Flow estimations for station 701 by MLR (a) based only rainfall values and (b) based both rainfall and flow values for the testing period.

(flow)-17886 (rainfall) shows that the correlation values do not decrease noticeably after lag 4. The highest correlation corresponds for lag 0 meaning that the concentration time of the basin is shorter than one day. The simulation results for three ANN methods are presented in Figs. 1a-3a. For the purpose of comparison multi linear regression (MLR) was employed. Accordingly the independent variables of MLR were the input nodes of ANNs and the calibration period was the ANN training duration (Table 1). The MLR estimations are depicted in Fig.4a. The most convenient ANN configuration for each method is given in Table 1. An ANN structure FFBP(5,4,1) consists of 5, 4 and 1 nodes in input, hidden and output layers, respectively. RBF(5,x,1) with s=0.5 has 5 and 1 nodes in input and output layers, respectively, and a spread parameter equal to 0.5. Similarly GRNN (5,x,1) with s=0.10 represents a structure with 5 input- and 1 output nodes and a spread equal to 0.10. The spread parameters are found simply by trial and error. Generally the ANN and MLR estimates showed deviations from the observations. For station 701, FFBP, RBF and MLR provided MSE values close to each other for the testing period. The MSE obtained by GRNN is slightly higher compared with other methods. Then the flow at the precedent day (Q_{t-1}) was also added to the input layer in order to increase the estimation performance. The estimation results are presented in Figs.1b-3b and Table 1. It is clear that a noticeable improvement in estimation performance was obtained with the incorporation of flow value into the input layer.

Table 1. Estimation results for the flow station 701 using different methods for the testing period.

	Method Training Period	Method Testing Period	Variables in the input layer	ANN Structure	MSE (m^6/s^2)
FFBP	05.01.1973-	27.08.1996-	$R_{t-4}, R_{t-3},$ R_{t-2}, R_{t-1}, R_t	FFBP(5,4,1)	96.13
	26.08.1996	30.09.2001	$R_{t-4}, R_{t-3}, R_{t-2},$ $R_{t-1}, R_t, Q_{(t-1)}$	FFBP(6,4,1)	68.00
RBF	05.01.1973-	27.08.1996-	$R_{t-4}, R_{t-3},$ R_{t-2}, R_{t-1}, R_t	RBF(5,x,1) $s = 0.5$	95.06
	14.09.1985	30.09.2001	$R_{t-4}, R_{t-3}, R_{t-2},$ $R_{t-1}, R_t, Q_{(t-1)}$	RBF (6,x,1) $s = 0.5$	**40.02**
GRNN	05.01.1973-	27.08.1996-	$R_{t-4}, R_{t-3}, R_{t-2},$ R_{t-1}, R_t	GRNN (5,x,1) $s = 0.10$	105.45
	01.05.1984	30.09.2001	$R_{t-4}, R_{t-3}, R_{t-2},$ $R_{t-1}, R_t, Q_{(t-1)}$	GRNN(6,x,1) $s = 0.10$	67.99
MLR	05.01.1973-	27.08.1996-	$R_{t-4}, R_{t-3},$ R_{t-2}, R_{t-1}, R_t	-	**94.92**
	26.08.1996	30.09.2001		-	53.22

It was seen that RBF and MLR simulations resulted in negative flow estimations for some low flows. This problem, however, was not faced in GRNN simulations and this approach does not require an iterative training procedure as in back propagation method as explained by [10]. The forecast of GRNN is bounded by the minimum and maximum of the observed series preventing the network to provide forecasts physically not possible. The GRNN forecast can not converge to poor solutions corresponding to local minima of the error criterion which is one of the drawbacks of FFBP algorithm. It was shown that FFBP method performance is very sensitive to the randomly assigned initial weight values. Several simulations are needed in order to obtain the best FFBP performances and only these superior FFBP results are presented in the study. RBF and GRNN, however, provide estimations with a unique simulation.

5   Conclusions

In this study three different ANN methods, FFBP, RBF and GRNN, were successfully applied to rainfall-runoff modelling study. It was seen that GRNN flow estimation performances were close to those of the FFBP, RBF and MLR. During the simulations GRNN did not provide physically non plausible estimations (negative values). The training time of a single FFBP application is relatively shorter than GRNN. This handicap can be easily overcome with GRNN algorithms by including clustering, which was not employed in this study [11]. Besides, it was seen that multiple FFBP simulations were required until obtaining a satisfactory performance criteria. This total duration for FFBP simulations was longer than the unique GRNN application. Another important result of the study is the positive contribution of the utilization of initial statistical analysis results in determining the ANN input layer node number. The rainfall-runoff correlograms point to the number of rainfall values significant in flow estimations. This can be a time saving feature since the input layer nodes are found by trial and error in general.

Acknowledgement. This work has been supported by the Scientific and Technical Research Council of Turkey (TUBITAK) under grant ICTAG I841. The data is provided by General Directorate of Electrical Power Resources Survey and Development Administration of Turkey (EIE) and Turkish State Meteorological Service (DMI).

References

1. Cigizoglu, H.K. (2003a) Estimation, forecasting and extrapolation of river flows by artificial neural networks, Hydrological Sciences Journal, 48(3), 349-361.
2. Cigizoglu, H.K. (2003b) Incorporation of ARMA models into flow forecasting by artificial neural networks, Environmetrics, 14(4), 417-427.
3. Cigizoglu, H.K., and Kisi, O. (2005) Flow Prediction by two Back Propagation Techniques Using k-fold Partitioning of Neural Network Training Data, Nordic Hydrology, (in press).
4. Cigizoglu, H.K. (2004) Estimation and forecasting of daily suspended sediment data by multi layer perceptrons, Advances in Water Resources, 27, 185-195.
5. Maier, H.R., and Dandy, G.C. (2000) Neural network for the prediction and forecasting of water resources variables: a review of modeling issues and applications, Environmental Modeling and Software, 15, 101-124.
6. Sudheer, K.P, Gosain, A.K., and Ramasastri, K.S. (2002) A data-driven algorithm for constructing artificial neural network rainfall-runoff models, Hydrological Processes, 16, 1325-1330.
7. Cigizoglu, H.K, (in press) Application of Generalized Regression Neural Networks to Intermittent Flow Forecasting and Estimation, ASCE Journal of Hydrologic Engineering.
8. Hagan, M.T., and M.B.Menhaj, (1994) Training feedforward techniques with the Marquardt algorithm, IEEE Transactions on Neural Networks, 5 (6), 989-993.
9. Broomhead, D. and Lowe, D. (1988) Multivariable functional interpolation and adaptive networks, Complex Syst. 2, 321-355.
10. Specht, D.F. (1991) A general regression neural network, IEEE Transactions on Neural Networks, 2(6), 568-576.
11. Parzen, E. (1962) On estimation of a probability density function and mode, Ann.Math.Statist., 33, 1065- 1076.

Probability Distribution of Solution Time in ANN Training Using Population Learning Algorithm

Ireneusz Czarnowski and Piotr Jędrzejowicz

Department of Information Systems, Gdynia Maritime University
Morska 83, 81-225 Gdynia, Poland
{irek, pj}@am.gdynia.pl

Abstract. Population based methods, and among them, the population learning algorithm (PLA), can be used to train artificial neural networks. The paper studies the probability distribution of solution time to a sub-optimal target in the example implementation of the PLA-trained artificial neural network. The distribution is estimated by means of the computational experiment. Graphical analysis technique is used to compare the theoretical and empirical distributions and estimate parameters of the distributions. It has been observed that the solution time to a sub-optimal target value fits a two parameter exponential distribution.

1 Introduction

Population-based methods handle a population of individuals that evolves with a help of the information exchange and self-improvement procedures. It should be noted that many different algorithms could be described within a population-based framework. Well known population-based algorithms include genetic algorithms, evolution strategies, evolution programming, scatter search, adaptive memory algorithms, and ant systems.

Population learning algorithm, originally proposed in [6], is a population-based method inspired by analogies to the phenomenon of social education processes in which a diminishing number of individuals enter more and more advanced learning stages. In PLA an individual represents a coded solution of the considered problem. Initially, an initial population is generated (possibly randomly). Controlling the initial population size serves as a mean for diversification, helping to escape from the local optima.

Once the initial population has been generated, individuals enter the first learning stage. It involves applying some improvement schemes or conducting simple learning sessions. These can be based on local search procedures. Improved individuals are then evaluated and better ones pass to the subsequent stages. A strategy of selecting better or more promising individuals must be defined and duly applied. At the following stages the whole cycle is repeated. Individuals are subject to improvement and learning, either individually or through information exchange, and the selected ones are again promoted to a higher stage with the

L. Rutkowski et al. (Eds.): ICAISC 2004, LNAI 3070, pp. 172–177, 2004.
© Springer-Verlag Berlin Heidelberg 2004

remaining ones dropped-out from the process. At the final stage the remaining individuals are reviewed and the best represents a solution to the problem at hand.

At different stages of the process, different improvement schemes and learning procedures are applied. These gradually become more and more sophisticated and, possibly, time consuming as there are less and less individuals to be taught.

Possibility of applying the PLA to training ANN has been investigated in earlier papers of the authors [3, 4, 5]. Several versions of the PLA have been designed, implemented and applied to solving variety of benchmark problems. Initial results were promising, showing a good or a very good performance of the PLA as a tool for ANN training [3]. In order to increase efficiency of the approach it has been decided to design a parallel PLA and to run it using the parallel computing environment based on PVM (Parallel Virtual Machine). This has allowed for running parallel learning processes or groups of such processes and thus speeding up ANN training [3].

The paper studies the probability distribution of solution time to a suboptimal target in the example implementation of the PLA-trained artificial neural network. The distribution is estimated experimentally. Graphical analysis is used to compare the theoretical and empirical distributions and estimate parameters of the distributions. In this paper we follow the methodology proposed by Aiex in [1], which in turn a standard approach in case of the two-parameter exponential distribution [8].

The exponential distribution behavior of solutions times is a feature of a number of metaheuristics, including simulated annealing, iterated local search, tabu search and GRASP. For the last approach, several experiments and the methodology for analyzing and comparing the empirical and theoretical distribution of solution time are described in [1, 2]. The experiments have confirmed that the probability distribution of solution times for GRASP fit a two parameter exponential distribution. The objective of this paper is to determine that the solution times in ANN training using population learning algorithm also fit a two parameter exponential distribution. This would imply that parallelization of PLA implementation will result in the linear speedup of the computations.

The paper is organized as follows. Section 2 contains a description of PLA implementation to training ANN designed for solving a popular benchmarking classification problem - Cleveland heart disease. Section 3 describes the layout and results of the experiments carried and analysis of the solution times. The last section presents a set of conclusions.

2   PLA Implementation

This section contains a brief overview of PLA implementation aimed at training of the ANN used in the reported experiment. The implementation in question is based on the following assumptions: an individual is a vector of real numbers from the predefined interval, each representing a value of the weight of the respective link between neurons in the considered ANN; the initial population of individuals is generated randomly; there are five learning/improvement procedures - standard mutation, local search, non-uniform mutation, gradient mutation and application of the gradient adjustment operator; the fitness of an individual is defined as a mean squared error of training results (MSE); there is a common selection criterion for all stages; at each stage individuals with fitness below the current average are rejected.

The proposed approach involves the following steps executed sequentially: generation of the initial population, application of the respective learning (improvement) procedure, selection of individuals, entering the next stage with different learning/improvement procedure and continuation until all stages have been completed. The above scheme implemented as a sequential algorithm can be run in a single processor environment.

The improvement procedures require some additional comments. The first procedure - standard mutation, modifies an individual by generating new values of two randomly selected elements within an individual. The second learning/improvement procedure involves mutual exchange of values between two randomly selected elements within an individual. The third learning/improvement procedure - non-uniform mutation, involves modifying an individual by repeatedly adjusting value of the randomly selected element (in this case a real number) until the fitness function value has improved or until a number of consecutive improvements have been attempted unsuccessfully. The fourth improvement procedure - gradient mutation changes two randomly selected elements within an individual by incrementing or decrementing their values. Direction of change (increment/decrement) is random and has identical probabilities equal to 0.5. The value of change is proportional to the gradient of an individual. The fifth learning/improvement procedure adjusts the value of each element of the individual by a constant value Δ proportional to its current gradient. Δ is calculated as $\Delta = \alpha\xi$, where α is the factor determining a size of the step in direction of ξ known as a momentum; α takes values from (0, 1]. In the proposed algorithm its value iterates starting from 1 with the step equal to 0.02. ξ is a vector determining a direction of search and is equal to the gradient of an individual. Generally, in each of the above described procedures, each move improving value of the fitness function of an individual is accepted. Number of iterations for procedures number 1,2 and 4 has to be set by a user at the fine-tuning phase.

The described implementation of the PLA algorithm has been used to training neural networks designed to solve a popular benchmarking classification problem - Cleveland heart disease (13 attributes, 303 instances, 2 classes) [7]. To evaluate the performance of the PLA-trained neural network MSE was calculated using 10-*fold cross validation test* - 10*CVtest*.

3   Computational Experiment Layout and Results

It has been decided to design the experiment to verify the initial hypothesis that the probability distribution of solution time in ANN training using population learning algorithm fits a two parameter exponential distribution. The experiment involved measuring the CPU time to find an objective function value at least as good as given target value for the selected test classification problem. Computations were carried for two different target values including one easily reachable by the PLA-trained ANN, and the other close to the best value produced by PLA. The ANN was trained n=200 times for all target combinations in each of the subsets in 10-*fold cross validation test*. To compare the empirical and the theoretical distributions a standard methodology for data analysis [8] was followed.

For each target, the training times were sorted in increasing order. With the ith sorted running time t_i a probability $p_i = (1 - \frac{1}{2})/n$ was associated. Next all the points $z_i = (t_i, p_i)$ for $t_i = 1, \ldots, 200$ were plotted. The approach is based on assumptions given in [1].

Fig. 1 shows empirical and theoretical probability distributions for the PLA implementation for training ANN in the heart classification problem. It shows distribution plots only for the three example subsets from 10-*fold cross validation test* and for target solution set to 0.1 (The smallest solution error obtained by a PLA-trained ANN and calculated as a mean of results in 10*CV test* was equal to 0.075). Estimated probabilities of finding the solution with MSE at least as good as the MSE target solution are shown in Table 1. These probabilities cover the PLA implementation for training ANN used in the heart classification problem and are shown for different numbers of subsets in the validation test.

Table 1. Probability estimation of finding a solution at least as good as the target solution (here 0.1) in 10*CV test* and the estimated parameter values of the two-parameter exponential distribution

Number of subset in *CV test*	Time (sec.) 10	20	30	50	60	Estimated parameters μ	λ
1	0.623	0.768	0.808	0.848	0.868	-10.94	32.246
2	0.568	0.773	0.808	0.863	0.898	-8.9037	26.69
3	0.453	0.578	0.628	0.753	0.813	-0.0572	28.577
4	0.368	0.453	0.698	0.833	0.918	2.4075	22.111
5	0.463	0.753	0.858	0.983	0.983	0.0799	15.262
6	0.933	0.983	0.998	0.998	0.998	-0.3226	3.9394
7	0.968	0.998	0.998	0.998	0.998	0.5967	2.5777
8	0.663	0.858	0.933	0.948	0.953	-3.7856	15.523
9	0.368	0.453	0.698	0.833	0.918	-5.9158	19.74
10	0.853	0.933	0.953	0.968	0.978	-4.7984	11.704

To estimate the parameters of the two-parameter exponential distribution we used methodology proposed in [8], where theoretical quantile-quantile plot (Q-Q plots) for data to estimate the parameters of exponential distribution is first obtained. To obtain Q-Q plots we used the cumulative distribution function for the two-parameter exponential distribution given by $F(t) = 1 - e^{-(t-\mu)/\lambda}$, where λ and μ are the parameters of the distribution.

In the next step, basing on the Q-Q plots, the theoretical probability distribution of solution time is estimated (for details see [1]). Fig. 1 (right column) shows the respective Q-Q plots. For each plotted point we also show variability information obtained as plus and minus one standard deviation in the vertical direction from line fitted to the plot. This information confirms the straightness of the Q-Q plots, which suggests that the theoretical distribution is a close approximation of the empirical one. The estimated parameters for the analysed case are shown in Table 1. Hence, it is shown that the initial hypothesis holds.

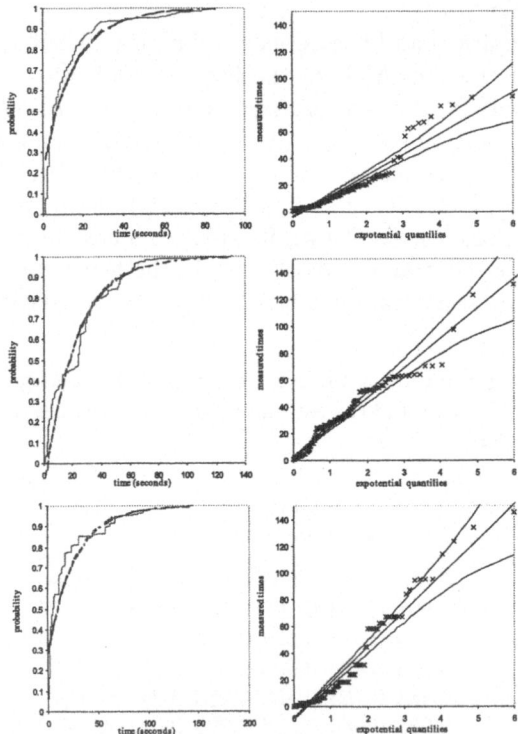

Fig. 1. Empirical and theoretical probability distribution of time to target (left column) and Q-Q plots (right column) for the PLA-based ANN training in the heart classification problem with target set to 0.1

Further experiments, which details could not have been reported in this paper because of the length constraint, have been additionally carried. This experiments involved more restriction target solution set to 0.09 and two others classification problems - Wisconsin breast cancer (9 attributes, 699 instances, 2 classes) and credit approval (15 attributes, 690 instances, 2 classes). In each case the time to target for PLA-based training of the respective ANN fits a two-parameter exponential distribution.

The experiments were conducted on a PC computer with Pentium IV processor with 256 MB of memory. The PLA used for training was set to 100 individuals in the initial population and each learning/improvement process was run for 1000 iterations.

4 Conclusions

Results of the computational experiment carried allows to conclude that the initial hypothesis holds. Ours study was limited only to three PLA implementations (although in the paper we show results only of one) but basing on this results it could be expected that the observed property would characterize different implementations of the PLA.

Following the reasoning presented in [2], it can be claimed that time to target value in the process of ANN training using PLA fits well a two-parameter exponential distribution. If time to target solution fits a two-parameter exponential distribution then the probability of finding a solution of a given value in time, say at with a sequential process is equal to the probability of finding a solution at least as good as that given value in time t using a independent parallel processes. Hence, using a parallel PLA scheme would result in the linear speedup.

References

1. Aiex R.M., Resende M., Ribeiro C. (2000), Probability distribution of solution time in GRASP: an experiment investigation. Technical Report, AT&T Labs Research, Folorham Park, NJ07733
2. Aiex R.M., Binato S., Resende M.G.C. (2003), Parallel GRASP with path-relinking for job shop scheduling. Parallel Computing 29, p. 393-430
3. Czarnowski I., Jędrzejowicz P. (2002), Application of the Parallel Population Learning Algorithm to Training Feed-forward ANN. Proceedings of the Euro-International Symposium on Computational Intelligence (E-ISCI), Kosice
4. Czarnowski I., Jędrzejowicz P. (2002), Population Learning Metaheuristic for Neural Network Training. In: Rutkowski, L., Kacprzyk, J. (eds.). Neural Networks and Soft Computing. Advances in Soft Computing, Springer Verlag, p. 161-166
5. Czarnowski I., Jędrzejowicz P., Ratajczak E. (2001), Population Learning Algorithm - Example Implementations and Experiments. Proceedings of the Fourth Metaheuristics International Conference, Porto, p. 607-612
6. Jędrzejowicz P. (1999), Social Learning Algorithm as a Tool for Solving Some Difficult Scheduling Problems, Foundation of Computing and Decision Sciences, 24, p. 51-66
7. Merz C.J., Murphy P.M. (1998), UCI Repository of machine learning databases [http://www.ics.uci.edu/~mlearn/MLRepository.html]. Irvine, CA: University of California, Department of Information and Computer Science.
8. Chambers J.M., Cleveland W.S., Kleiner B., Tukey P.A. (1983), Graphical Methods for Data Analisys, Chapman & Hall

Parallelization of the SOM-Based Integrated Mapping

Gintautas Dzemyda and Olga Kurasova

Institute of Mathematics and Informatics
Akademijos St. 4, Vilnius, Lithuania
{Dzemyda, Kurasova}@ktl.mii.lt

Abstract. In this paper, we have developed a parallel approach for minimizing the projection error in Sammon's mapping applied in combination with the self-organizing map (SOM). In the so-called integrated mapping, Sammon's algorithm takes into account the learning flow of the self-organizing neural network. As a final result in the integrated mapping, we need to visualize the neurons-winners of the SOM. The criterion of visualization quality is the projection error of Sammon's mapping.

1 Introduction

There exist a lot of methods that can be used for reducing the dimensionality of data, and, particularly, for visualizing the n-dimensional vectors: (a) traditional methods (Sammon's projection, multidimensional scaling, principal components, direct methods, and others), (b) neural networks (self-organizing maps, feedforward networks), (c) combinations of traditional methods and neural networks. Most of references to these methods may be found e.g. in [4]. However there is no universal method. The self-organizing map (SOM) [4] and Sammon's algorithm (mapping, projection) [6] are the methods often used for the visualization of multidimensional data, i.e. for projection of data points from a high-dimensional space onto a space of lower dimensionality. Two combinations of these methods are considered in [2,3]: (1) a consecutive application of the SOM and Sammon's mapping, and (2) Sammon's mapping taking into account the learning flow of the self-organizing neural network (so-called integrated mapping). The goal of both combinations is to obtain lower projection errors and lower their dependence on the so-called "magic factor" in Sammon's mapping. It is experimentally shown in [2] that a combination of the SOM and Sammon's mapping is an effective method of visualization. The vectors-winners, obtained after neural network training, are analysed and visualized here by using Sammon's algorithm. However, the results of Sammon's algorithm are very dependent on the so-called "magic factor" and on the initial values of the projected points. The experiments showed that the integrated mapping [3] leads to the lower dependence of the results on the "magic factor" and other parameters.

In this paper, we have developed and examined a parallel realization of the integrated mapping. Parallel computations were managed using the Message Passing Interface (MPI) [5].

L. Rutkowski et al. (Eds.): ICAISC 2004, LNAI 3070, pp. 178–183, 2004.
© Springer-Verlag Berlin Heidelberg 2004

2   Basic Algorithms

The self-organizing map (SOM) [4] is a class of neural networks that are trained in an unsupervised manner using competitive learning. It is a well-known method for mapping a high-dimensional space onto a low-dimensional one. We consider here the mapping onto a two-dimensional grid of neurons. Let $X_1, ..., X_s \in R^n$ be a set of n-dimensional vectors for mapping. Usually, the neurons are connected to each other via a rectangular or hexagonal topology. The rectangular SOM is a two-dimensional array of neurons $M = \{m_{ij}, i = 1, ..., k_x, j = 1, ..., k_y\}$. Here k_x is the number of rows, and k_y is the number of columns. Each component of the input vector is connected to every individual neuron. Any neuron is entirely defined by its location on the grid (the number of row i and column j) and by the codebook vector, i.e., we can consider a neuron as an n-dimensional vector $m_{ij} = (m_{ij}^1, m_{ij}^2, ..., m_{ij}^n) \in R^n$.

After a large number of training steps, the network has been organized and n-dimensional input vectors $X_1, ..., X_s$ have been mapped – each input vector is related to the nearest neuron, i.e. the vectors are distributed among the elements of the map during training. Some elements of the map may remain unrelated with any vector of the set $\{X_1, ..., X_s\}$, but there may occur elements related with some input vectors. The neurons related with the input vectors are called by neurons-winners.

Sammon's projection [6] is a nonlinear projection method to map a high-dimensional space onto a space of lower dimensionality. In our case, the initial dimensionality is n, and the resulting one is 2. Let us have vectors $X_1, ..., X_s \in R^n$. The pending problem is to get a projection of these vectors X_i, $i = 1, ..., s$ onto the plane R^2. Two-dimensional vectors $Y_1, Y_2, ..., Y_s \in R^2$ correspond to them. Sammon's algorithm tries to minimize the distortion of projection E [4,6].

Combining the SOM and Sammon's mapping. Using the SOM-based approach above we can draw a table with cells corresponding to the neurons. The cells corresponding to the neurons-winners are filled with the numbers of vectors $X_1, X_2, ..., X_s$. Some cells remain empty. One can decide visually on the distribution of vectors in the n-dimensional space according to their distribution among the cells of the table. However, the table does not answer the question, how much the vectors of the neighboring cells are close in the n-dimensional space. A natural idea arises to apply the distance-preserving projection method to additional mapping of the neurons-winners in the SOM. Sammon's mapping may be used for such purposes.

Two combined methods are developed: (1) consecutive combination, (2) integrated mapping, where Sammon's mapping takes into account the learning flow of the self-organizing neural network.

The neural network is trained using e training epochs. The epoch consists of s learning steps: the input vectors from X_1 to X_s are passed to the neural network once. All the e epochs are divided into equal training parts – blocks. γ is the total number of training blocks. In the consecutive combination, Sammon's mapping follows the SOM training. In the integrated mapping, the vectors-winners obtained after each training block are analysed by using Sammon's algorithm, and the results (two-dimensional vectors correspondent to the neurons-winners) are passed to the next Sammon's mapping (see [3] for more details).

Table 1 grounds the efficiency of integrated mapping compared with the consecutive combinations of the methods. The ratios between the projection errors obtained by the consecutive and integrated combination are always greater than one. Cases with various parameters of the algorithms and their constituent parts have been analysed (size of the SOM, number of training epochs e, number of training blocks γ; various values of the "magic factor"). The results have been averaged over 200 experiments with different (random) initial values of the neurons-vectors m_{ij}.

Table 1. The ratio between the projection errors

e	100					200					300				
e/γ	50	25	20	10	5	50	40	25	20	10	5	50	25	20	10	5
γ	2	4	5	10	20	4	5	8	10	20	40	6	12	15	30	60
2x2	2.30	2.85	2.84	2.85	2.86	3.07	3.09	3.12	3.11	3.10	3.15	3.25	3.30	3.29	3.23	3.34
3x3	1.11	1.14	1.14	1.20	1.26	1.12	1.14	1.18	1.20	1.25	1.31	1.15	1.20	1.22	1.27	1.30
4x4	1.49	1.66	1.67	1.75	1.79	2.85	2.96	3.06	3.10	3.18	3.23	4.60	4.83	4.92	4.95	5.05
5x5	1.03	1.04	1.05	1.06	1.06	1.04	1.05	1.06	1.06	1.07	1.07	1.06	1.07	1.07	1.07	1.08
6x6	1.07	1.08	1.11	1.13	1.13	1.11	1.20	1.20	1.22	1.23	1.24	1.23	1.24	1.25	1.26	1.27

3   Parallelization of the Integrated Combination

Table 1 indicates that namely the integrated combination of the SOM and Sammon's mapping is good for a more precise projection of multidimensional vectors in the sense of criterion E. A larger number of training blocks γ decreases the projection error. However, it requires much more computing time. The way to speed up the time-consuming computing is a parallelization of the integrated mapping. We disclose the advantages of the parallelization below.

The integrated mapping may be separated into two independent processes: the first processor executes the SOM training and regularly, after each training block, prepares data for another processor; the second processor executes Sammon's mapping (a task for Sammon's mapping of neurons-winners of the SOM). The scheme of two-processor parallel algorithm is as follows:

1. The first processor starts executing the first training block and sends the obtained vectors-winners to the second processor; the second processor waits.
2. When the second processor gets the data, it begins Sammon's mapping. Meanwhile, the first processor executes the next training block.
3. After completing the current training block, the first processor
   - takes the two-dimensional vectors, obtained by Sammon's mapping, from the second processor,
   - prepares the initial values of coordinates of two-dimensional vectors for the next Sammon's mapping and sends them to the second processor,

- sends vectors-winners obtained after current training block to the second processor,
- continues the SOM training.

4. The second processor performs Sammon's mapping as soon as it gets all necessary data (see item 3) from the first processor.
5. The sequence of operations 3 and 4 continues until the SOM training finishes.
6. The second processor gets the final data from the first one and executes Sammon's mapping the last time.

The integrated combination of the algorithms is rather sophisticated, therefore it is necessary to evaluate its several peculiarities with a view to ensure the optimal performance. A larger number of training blocks decreases the projection error but requires much more computing time. The computing time of one SOM training block decreases with an increase in the order number q of the block, while the computing time of Sammon's algorithm increases. This is grounded below.

The number of neurons, recalculated in an epoch, decreases with growing the order number of epoch (and block, because one training block consists of e/γ epochs) due to a specific of the SOM training – see [2,4]). Therefore, the SOM training needs less computing time when the order number of epoch increases. The dependence of the computing time on the order number of epoch has a staircase form. Fig. 1 illustrates the average dependence of computing time (in seconds) on the order number of epoch. 1000 20-dimensional vectors have been analyzed in the experiments. The values of coordinates are generated at random in the interval $[-1; 1]$. The 10x10 SOM have been analyzed. The experiments have been repeated for 100 times with different (random) initial values of the components of neurons.

Figures 2a and 2b show the dependence of the mean number of the neurons-winners on the order number q of the training block ($e=300$, $\gamma = 30$). 100 experiments were carried out for both cases: (a) different (random) initial values of the components of the neurons were used; (b) the SOM was trained by different sets of 1000 vectors whose dimensionality is 20. When the order number q of training block increases, the number of the neurons-winners increases, too. Therefore, more n-dimensional vectors are analyzed by Sammon's mapping after training blocks with a higher order number.

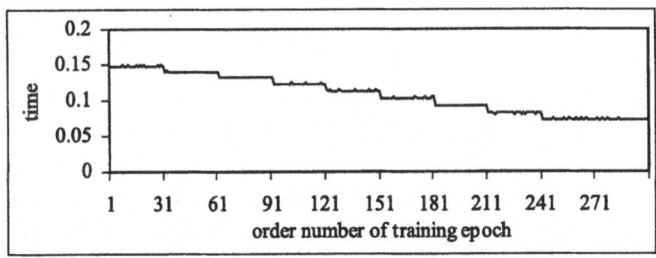

Fig. 1. Average dependence of computing time on the order number of training epoch

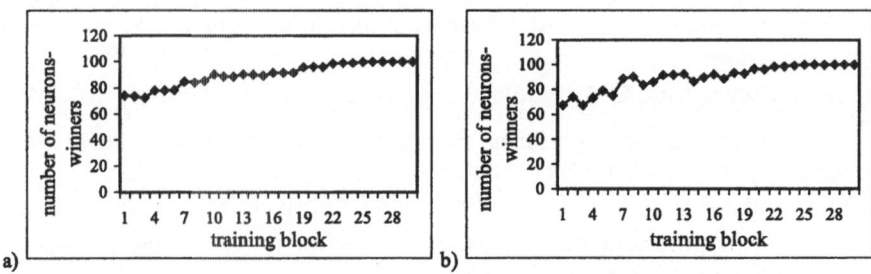

Fig. 2. Dependence of the neurons-winners on the order number q of the training block

Therefore, the problem arises to select the optimal number of epochs e and training blocks γ for the SOM, and iterations of Sammon's mapping Sam_it.

One of the criteria for a balanced processor workload is the makespan (maximum completion time) [1]. It tends to minimize the workload of the mostly loaded processor. The peculiarity of the integrated mapping is that it is impossible to estimate the duration of separate tasks in advance. Therefore, the way for optimizing the computing time is as follows: for a fixed number of the SOM training epochs e and the number of training blocks γ, choose the number of iterations of Sammon's mapping Sam_it such that the computing time of one training block be as similar to that of Sammon's mapping as possible. In this case, the tasks would be distributed between both the processors more evenly. However, in order to keep a high projection quality, we cannot decrease the number of iterations of Sammon's mapping too much. The inequality should hold: $Sam\_it \geq 100$.

Denote the computing time of the qth training block of the SOM by $t^1(e, \gamma, q)$ and that of Sammon's mapping of the results of the qth block by $t^2(Sam\_it, q)$. In order to get a lower value of the maximum completion time, it is necessary to choose the number of iterations of Sammon's mapping Sam_it such that

$$\text{a) } \frac{1}{\gamma - 1} \sum_{q=2}^{\gamma} t^1(e, \gamma, q) \approx \frac{1}{\gamma - 1} \sum_{q=2}^{\gamma} t^2(Sam\_it, q - 1), \quad \text{b) } Sam\_it \geq 100.$$

With a view to distribute the tasks between both the processors more evenly, we have derived experimentally such a formula for iterations of Sammon's mapping:

$$Sam\_it \approx 35e/\gamma \tag{1}$$

Speedup and efficiency are two important measures of the quality of parallel algorithms. The speedup $S_p = T_0/T_p$ estimates an acceleration that we obtain when the tasks are solved using p processors. Here T_p is the computing time (in seconds) to complete an algorithm with p processors; T_0 is the computing time to complete the same algorithm with one processor. In our case, the number of processors is $p = 2$. The efficiency $E_p = S_p/p$ indicates a part of processors capacity used by a parallel algorithm. The results indicate that the efficiency is $E_p \geq 0.8$,

Table 2. Speedup and efficiency of parallel algorithm

Number of training epochs e	Number of training blocks γ	Size of training block e/γ	Number of iterations of Sammon's mapping Sam_it	T_0	T_p	S_p	E_p
300	30	10	350	67	41	1.63	0.82
300	15	20	700	66	41	1.61	0.81
300	25	12	400	66	40	1.65	0.83
300	25	12	420	67	40	1.68	0.84
400	20	20	700	86	53	1.62	0.81
400	40	10	350	88	54	1.63	0.82
400	80	5	175	91	54	1.67	0.84
300	10	30	100	37	34	1.09	0.54
300	50	6	600	128	93	1.38	0.69
400	20	20	200	57	46	1.24	0.62
400	10	40	300	54	46	1.17	0.59

if the parameters are chosen by the proposed formula (1) (see the top of Table 2), otherwise the processors are used inefficiently (see the bottom of Table 2).

4   Conclusions

Visualization of multidimensional data is a complicated problem. Parallel methods and aggregation of methods for their joint use are the directions of extensive researches in this field. A parallel approach for integrated mapping that combines the SOM and Sammon's mapping has been developed. Its efficiency depends on the number of epochs and training blocks for the SOM, and iterations of Sammon's mapping. The derived experimental formula allows distributing the tasks between both the processors more evenly. This ensures a good quality of mapping and a balanced processor workload.

The parallel integrated mapping discussed in this paper, is oriented to the two-processor case. Further research would lead to the extension of the integrated mapping for a larger number of processors.

References

1. Dzemyda, G.: Mean squared load criteria for scheduling independent tasks. International Journal of Applied Mathematics and Computer Science **9(4)** (1999) 939–954
2. Dzemyda, G.: Visualization of a set of parameters characterized by their correlation matrix. Computational Statistics and Data Analysis **36(10)** (2001) 15–30
3. Dzemyda, G., Kurasova, O.: Visualization of multidimensional data taking into account the learning flow of the self-organizing neural network. Journal of WSCG **11(1)** (2003) 117–124
4. Kohonen, T.: Self-Organizing Maps. 3nd ed. Springer Series in Information Sciences, Springer–Verlag, Vol. 30 (2001)
5. The Message Passing Interface (MPI) Standard. http://www-unix.mcs.anl.gov/mpi/
6. Sammon, J.W.: A nonlinear mapping for data structure analysis. IEEE Transactions on Computers **18** (1969) 401–409

Training Radial Basis Functions by Gradient Descent[*]

Mercedes Fernández-Redondo, Carlos Hernández-Espinosa,
Mamen Ortiz-Gómez, and Joaquín Torres-Sospedra

Universidad Jaume I, D. de Ingeniería y Ciencia de los Computadores, Avda. Vicente
Sos Baynat s/n, 12071 Castellón, Spain. espinosa@icc.uji.es

Abstract. In this paper we present experiments comparing different
training algorithms for Radial Basis Functions (RBF) neural networks.
In particular we compare the classical training which consist of a unsupervised training of centers followed by a supervised training of the
weights at the output, with the full supervised training by gradient descent proposed recently in same papers. We conclude that a fully supervised training performs generally better. We also compare *Batch training*
with *Online training* and we conclude that *Online training* suppose a
reduction in the number of iterations.

1 Introduction

A RBF has two layer of neurons. The first one, in its usual form, is composed of
neurons with Gaussian transfer functions (GF) and the second has neurons with
linear transfer functions. The output of a RBF can be calculated with (1), (2).

$$\hat{y}_{i,k} = \mathbf{w}_i^T \cdot \mathbf{h}_k = \sum_{j=1}^{c} w_{ij} \cdot h_{j,k} \tag{1}$$

$$h_{j,k} = \exp\left(-\frac{\|\mathbf{x}_k - \mathbf{v}_j\|^2}{\sigma^2}\right) \tag{2}$$

Where v_j are the center of the GF, σ control the width of the GF and w_i
are the weights among the Gaussian units (GU) and the output units.

As (1) and (2) show, there are three elements to design in the neural network:
centers and widths of the GU and the weights among the GU and output units.

There are two procedures to design the network. One is to train the networks
in two steps. First we find the centers and widths by using same unsupervised
clustering algorithm and after that we train the weights among hidden and
output units by a supervised algorithm. This process is usually fast [1-4].

The second procedure is to train the centers and weights in a full supervised
fashion, similar to the algorithm Backpropagation (BP) for Multilayer Feedforward. This procedure has the same drawbacks of BP, long training time and
high computational cost. However, it has received quite attention recently [5-6].

[*] This research was supported by project MAPACI TIC2002-02273 of CICYT in Spain.

L. Rutkowski et al. (Eds.): ICAISC 2004, LNAI 3070, pp. 184–189, 2004.
© Springer-Verlag Berlin Heidelberg 2004

In [5-6] it is used a sensitivity analysis to show that the traditional GU (called "exponential generator function") of the RBF network has low sensitivity for gradient descent training for a wide range of values of the widths. As an alternative two different transfer functions are proposed, called in the papers "lineal generator function" and "cosine generator function". Unfortunately, the experiments shown in the papers are performed with only two databases and the RBF networks are compared with equal number of GU. In contrast, in this paper we present more complete experiments with nine databases, and include in the experiments four traditional unsupervised training algorithms and a fully gradient descent training with the three transfer functions analysed in papers [5-6]. Furthermore, we also presents experiments with *Batch* and *Online learning*, in the original references the training was performed in *Batch* mode.

2 Theory

2.1 Training by Gradient Descent

"Exponential (EXP) Generator" Function. This RBF has the usual Gaussian transfer function described in (1) and (2). The equation for adapting the weights is:

$$\Delta \mathbf{w}_p = \eta \cdot \sum_{k=1}^{M} \varepsilon_{p,k}^0 \cdot \mathbf{h}_k \tag{3}$$

Where η is the learning rate, M the number of training patterns and $\varepsilon_{p,k}^0$ is the output error, the difference between target and output.

The equation for adapting the centers is the following:

$$\Delta v_q = \eta \cdot \sum_{k=1}^{M} \varepsilon_{p,k}^h \cdot (\mathbf{x}_k - \mathbf{v}_q) \tag{4}$$

Where η is the learning rate and $\varepsilon_{p,k}^h$ is the hidden error given by (5).

$$\varepsilon_{p,k}^h = \alpha_{q,k} \cdot \sum_{i=1}^{n_o} \varepsilon_{i,k}^0 \cdot w_{iq} \quad \alpha_{q,k} = \frac{2}{\sigma^2} \cdot \exp\left(-\frac{\|\mathbf{x}_k - \mathbf{v}_q\|^2}{\sigma^2}\right) \tag{5}$$

In the above equations n_o is the number of outputs and these equation are for *Batch training*, the equations for *Online training* are evident.

"Lineal (LIN) Generator" Function. In this case the transfer function of the hidden units is the following:

$$h_{j,k} = \left(\frac{1}{\|\mathbf{x}_k - \mathbf{v}_j\|^2 + \gamma^2}\right)^{\frac{1}{m-1}} \tag{6}$$

Where we have used $m = 3$ in our experiments and γ is a parameter that should be determined by trial and error and cross-validation.

The above equations (3), (4) and (5) are the same, but in this case $\alpha_{q,k}$ is different and is given in (7).

$$\alpha_{q,k} = \frac{2}{m-1} \cdot \left(\|\mathbf{x}_k - \mathbf{v}_q\|^2 + \gamma^2 \right)^{\frac{m}{1-m}} \tag{7}$$

"Cosine (COS) Generator" Function. In this case the transfer function is the following:

$$h_{j,k} = \frac{a_j}{\left(\|\mathbf{x}_k - \mathbf{v}_j\|^2 + a_j^2 \right)^{1/2}} \tag{8}$$

Equations 3 and 4 are the same, but in this case the hidden error is different:

$$\varepsilon_{p,k}^h = \left(\frac{h_{j,k}^3}{a_j^2} \right) \cdot \sum_{i=1}^{no} \varepsilon_{i,k}^0 \cdot w_{iq} \tag{9}$$

The parameter a_j is also adapted during training, the equation is (10).

$$\Delta a_j = \left(\frac{\eta}{a_j} \right) \cdot \sum_{i=1}^{no} h_{j,k} \cdot (1 - h_{j,k}^2) \cdot \varepsilon_{p,k}^h \tag{10}$$

2.2   Training by Unsupervised Clustering

Algorithm 1. This training algorithm is the simplest one. It was proposed in [1]. It uses adaptive k-means clustering to find the centers of the GU. After finding the centers, we should calculate the widths. For that, we calculate the mean distance between one center and one of the closets neighbors, P, for example, the first $(P = 1)$, second $(P = 2)$, etc. closest neighbor.

Algorithm 2. It is proposed in reference [2]. The GU are generated incrementally, in stages. A stage is characterized by a parameter δ that specifies the maximum radius for the hypersphere that includes the random cluster of points that is to define the GU. The GU at any stage are randomly selected, by choosing an input vector x_i from the training set and search for all other training vectors within the δ_k neighborhood of x_i. The training vector are used to define the GU. The algorithm is complex and the full description can be found in the reference.

Algorithm 3. It is proposed in [3]. They use a one pass algorithm called *APC-III*, clustering the patterns class by class. The *APC-III* algorithm uses a constant radius to create the clusters, in the reference this radius is calculated as the mean minimum distance between training patterns multiplied by a constant α.

Algorithm 4. It is proposed in reference [4]. The GU are generated class by class. In a similar way to algorithm 2 the GU are generated in stages. A stage is characterized by its majority criterion, a majority criterion of 60% implies that the cluster of the GU must have at least 60% of the patterns belonging to its class. The method will have a maximum of six stages, we begin with a majority criterion of 50% and end with 100%. The GU at any stage h are randomly selected, by picking a pattern vector x_i of class k from the training set and expand the radius of the cluster until the percentage of patterns belonging to the class falls below the majority criterion. The algorithm is complex and the full description is in the reference.

3   Experimental Results

We have applied the training algorithms to nine different classification problems from the UCI repository of machine learning databases. They are Balance Scale (Balance), Cylinders Bands (Bands), Liver Disorders (Bupa), Credit Approval (Credit), Glass Identification (Glass), Heart Disease (Heart), the Monk's Problems (Monk1, Monk2) and Voting Records (Vote). The complete data and a full description can be found in the repository (http:// www.ics.uci.edu/ ~mlearn/ MLRepository.html).

The first step was to determine the appropriate parameters of the algorithms by trial and error and cross-validation. We have used an extensive trial procedure.

After that, with the final parameters we trained ten networks with different partition of data in training, cross-validation and test set, also with different random initialization of parameters. With this procedure we can obtain a mean performance in the database (the mean of the ten networks) and an error.

These results are in Table 1, 2 and 3. We have for each database the mean percentage in the test and the mean number of units in the network (Nunit).

Comparing the results of the same algorithm trained by gradient descent in the case of *Batch training* and *Online training*, we can see that the differences in performance are not significant. The fundamental difference between both training procedures is in the number of iterations and the value of the learning step. For example, 8000 iterations, $\eta=0.001$ in *EXP* Batch for Balance and 6000 iterations, $\eta=0.005$ in *EXP* Online.

Comparing *EXP*, *LIN* and *COS* generator functions, we can see that the general performance is quite similar except in the case Monk1 where the performance of *EXP* is clearly better. In other aspect, *EXP* and *LIN* functions need a higher number of trials for the process of trial and error to design the network, because cosine generator functions adapt all parameters. But in contrast, the number of iterations needed to converge by *COS* functions is usually superior (*EXP*, Band= 10000 iterations; *LIN*, Band= 15.000; *COS*, Band= 75000), so globally speaking the computational cost can be considered similar.

Comparing unsupervised training algorithms among them, it seems clear that the classical algorithm 1, k-means clustering shows the better performance.

Table 1. Performance of the different algorithms, Radial Basis Functions.

	TRAINING ALGORITHM							
	Exp Batch		Exp Online		Lineal Batch		Lineal Online	
DATABASE	Perc.	Nunit	Perc.	Nunit	Perc.	Nunit	Perc.	Nunit
Balance	90.2±0.5	45	90.2±0.5	60	90.1±0.5	45	90.6±0.5	50
Band	74.1±1.1	110	74.0±1.1	40	74.5±1.1	30	73.4±1.0	35
Bupa	69.8±1.1	35	70.1±1.1	40	71.2±0.9	10	69.7±1.3	15
Credit	86.1±0.7	40	86.0±0.8	30	86.2±0.7	10	85.8±0.8	10
Glass	92.9±0.7	125	93.0±0.6	110	91.4±0.8	35	92.4±0.7	30
Heart	82.0±1.0	155	82.0±1.0	20	82.1±1.1	15	81.8±1.1	10
Monk1	94.7±1.0	60	98.5±0.5	30	93.2±0.7	15	94.5±0.7	15
Monk2	92.1±0.7	80	91.3±0.7	45	82.8±1.2	25	89.6±1.2	50
Vote	95.6±0.4	35	95.4±0.5	5	95.6±0.4	25	95.6±0.4	10

Table 2. Performance of the different algorithms, Radial Basis Functions.

	TRAINING ALGORITHM							
	Cosine Batch		Cosine Online		UC Alg. 1		UC Alg. 2	
DATABASE	Perc.	Nunit	Perc.	Nunit	Perc.	Nunit	Perc.	Nunit
Balance	89.9±0.5	25	90.0±0.7	40	88.5±0.8	30	87.6±0.9	88.5±1.6
Band	75.0±1.1	120	74.9±1.1	125	74.0±1.5	60	67±2	18.7±1.0
Bupa	69.9±1.1	15	70.2±1.1	40	59.1±1.7	10	57.6±1.9	10.3±1.5
Credit	86.1±0.8	10	86.1±0.8	25	87.3±0.7	20	87.5±0.6	95±14
Glass	93.5±0.8	105	92.6±0.9	15	89.6±1.9	100	79±2	30±2
Heart	82.1±1.0	25	81.9±1.1	15	80.8±1.5	100	80.2±1.5	26±4
Monk1	89.8±0.8	100	90.2±1.0	145	76.9±1.3	90	72±2	93±8
Monk2	87.9±0.8	125	86.6±1.1	45	71.0±1.5	90	66.4±1.7	26±4
Vote	95.6±0.4	20	95.4±0.4	10	95.1±0.6	40	93.6±0.9	53±5

Table 3. Performance of the different algorithms, Radial Basis Functions.

	TRAINING ALGORITHM			
	UC Alg. 3		UC Alg. 4	
DATABASE	Perc.	Nunit	Perc.	Nunit
Balance	88.0±0.9	94.7±0.5	87.4±0.9	45±7
Band	67±4	97.2±0.3	65.8±1.4	4.5±1.3
Bupa	60±4	106.2±0.3	47±3	11±5
Credit	87.9±0.6	161.10±0.17	86.4±0.9	32±4
Glass	82.8±1.5	59.9±0.7	81.2±1.8	22±2
Heart	72±4	71.8±0.6	78±3	10±2
Monk1	68±3	97.4±0.6	64±2	23±6
Monk2	66.5±0.8	143±0	71.6±1.5	20±2
Vote	94.1±0.8	120.30±0.15	76±5	5.0±1.1

Finally, comparing unsupervised training with gradient descent we can see that the best alternative (under the performance point of view) is supervised training by gradient descent, it achieves a better performance in 6 of 9 databases.

In order to perform a further comparison, we include the results of Multilayer Feedforward with Backpropagaion in Table 4. We can see that the results of RBF are better. This is the case in all databases except Credit, Heart and Voting.

Table 4. Performance of Multilayer Feedforward with Backpropagation.

DATABASE	N. Hidden	Percentage
Balance	20	87.6±0.6
Bands	23	72.4±1.0
Bupa	11	58.3±0.6
Credit	15	85.6±0.5
Glass	3	78.5±0.9
Heart	2	82.0±0.9
Monk1	6	74.3±1.1
Monk2	20	65.9±0.5
Vote	1	95.0±0.4

4 Conclusions

In this paper we have presented a comparison of unsupervised and fully supervised training algorithms for RBF networks. The algorithms are compared using nine databases. Our results show that the fully supervised training by gradient descent may be the best alternative under the point of view of performance. The results of RBF are also compared with Multilayer Feedforward with Backpropagation and the performance of a RBF network is better.

References

1. Moody, J., Darken, C.J.: Fast Learning in Networks of Locally-Tuned Procesing Units. Neural Computation. **1** (1989) 281–294
2. Roy, A., Govil, S., et alt: A Neural-Network Learning Theory and Polynomial Time RBF Algorithm. IEEE Trans. on Neural Networks. **8** no. 6 (1997) 1301–1313
3. Hwang, Y., Bang, S.: An Efficient Method to Construct a Radial Basis Function Neural Network Classifier. Neural Network. **10** no. 8, (1997) 1495–1503
4. Roy, A., Govil, S., et alt.: An Algorithm to Generate Radial Basis Function (RBF)-Like Nets for Classification Problems. Neural Networks. **8** no. 2 (1995) 179–201
5. Krayiannis, N.: Reformulated Radial Basis Neural Networks Trained by Gradient Descent. IEEE Trans. on Neural Networks. **10** no. 3 (1999) 657–671
6. Krayiannis, N., Randolph-Gips, M.: On the Construction and Training of Reformulated Radial Basis Functions. IEEE Trans. Neural Networks. **14** no. 4 (2003) 835–846

Generalized Backpropagation through Time for Continuous Time Neural Networks and Discrete Time Measurements

Krzysztof Fujarewicz and Adam Galuszka

Silesian University of Technology, Institute of Automatic Control
Akademicka 16, 44-100 Gliwice, Poland
kfujarewicz@ia.polsl.gliwice.pl

Abstract. This paper deals with the problem of identification of continuous time dynamic neural networks when the measurements are given only at discrete time moments, not necessarily uniformly distributed. It is shown that the modified adjoint system, generating the gradient of the performance index, is a continuous-time system with jumps of state variables at moments corresponding to moments of measurements.

1 Introduction

There are many learning algorithms of recurrent (dynamic) neural networks (see for example surveys [2],[11]). They can be divided into two groups – algorithms working on-line (Real Time Recurrent Learning [14], Dynamic Back Propagation [10]) and algorithms working off-line (Back Propagation Through Time [13] and similar algorithms). All these methods are formulated only for discrete time (recurrent) networks.

The following question appears: is it worth to learn continuous time dynamic neural networks? To answer this question let us analyze a continuous time system described by k state equations which are all linear except one equation containing simply nonlinearity having analytical form. Let us assume that the system is sampled with given sampling period. As a result we obtain k discrete time state equations which are created by integration of continuous time state equations between sampling moments. Carefully analysis of the form of these equations leads to conclusion that obtained discrete time model may be more complicated. In general, all discrete time state equations may be nonlinear. Moreover, these equations usually do not have analytical form. Therefore, the conclusion is that discrete time model is, in general, much more complicated, and this is the main reason why it is worth to use continuous time neural networks instead of discrete time neural networks when the identified plant is continuous time. Continuous time neural network may have simpler structure, less layers and neurons, because the mapping that is approximated is not so complicated. Another reason for using continuous time neural networks is the situation when sampling moments are not uniformly distributed.

GBPTT method [3] is similar to other structural approaches to gradient calculation, for example [1], [12]. However, it is more universal: different types of

L. Rutkowski et al. (Eds.): ICAISC 2004, LNAI 3070, pp. 190–196, 2004.
© Springer-Verlag Berlin Heidelberg 2004

tasks may be solved using this method (for example: identification, optimization of signals and/or parameters for control systems) for both continuous and discrete time nonlinear dynamical systems. In this method so called *input-output sensitivity function* is searched. This function denotes the sensitivity of the output signal of the system at particular time moment on output signal at previous moment. The GBPTT method has been successfully used for identification and optimization of different plants [5], [6], [7].

In this paper in order to solve the problem of learning of continuous time neural network an extension of GBPTT method will be used. This extension can be applied for hybrid continuous-discrete time systems and has been presented in [8] where the method has been utilized for optimization of discrete time control signal.

2   Problem Formulation

Let us consider the dynamic neural network presented in Fig.1.

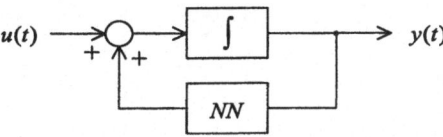

Fig. 1. The continuous time dynamical neural network

It is composed of feedforward neural network denoted by *NN* and the integrator. All signals acting in this system have the same dimension. Now we will formulate a problem of learning of this dynamical neural network such that the output $y(t)$ fits the output of an identified plant $d(t)$ at time moments t_n; $n = 0, 1, 2, \ldots, N$. The continuous time horizon, for which the identification experiment is done is T. To simplify the notation we will use symbols $y(n)$ instead of $y(t_n)$ for discrete time signals.

The performance index to be minimized is as follows

$$J = \frac{1}{2} \sum_{n=0}^{N} e^T(n)e(n) \tag{1}$$

where $e(n)$ is the identification error $e(n) = y(n) - d(n)$. The main task is to find the partial derivatives of the performance index (1) with respect to all weights of the feedforward neural network NN.

In next section the GBPTT method for sampled data systems will be presented and then it will be used to solve stated above problem.

3   Generalized Backpropagation through Time for Sampled Data Systems

The extension of GBPTT for sampled data systems has been derived in [8]. Here it will be shortly presented.

It is well known fact that any continuous-discrete system can be composed of typical continuous and discrete in time elements which are supplemented by two additional elements: ideal pulser and a sampler. Such a set of elements is listed in first column of Table 1. An ideal pulser situated between discrete and

Table 1. Rules for construction of the sensitivity model and the modified adjoint system

continuous systems, in sampling time moments generate on its output Dirac pulses with surface proportional to a value of discrete input signal. A set of sampling times $t_1, t_2, \ldots, t_N$ is denoted by $\{t_n\}$. These sampling times may be freely chosen from a time interval $\langle 0, T \rangle$, particularly they may be non-uniformly distributed and may be different for each pulser. The same remark goes for samplers, situated between continuous and discrete systems, which generates appropriate Kronecker's pulses. A construction of a sensitivity model depends on replacement of elements from first column of Table 1 by their equivalents from second column. The only difference appears in case of nonlinear elements. A modified adjoint system [9] may be created using equivalent elements from a column 2 on the base of the sensitivity model or immediately on the base of original system. Directions of all signals in adjoint model should be reversed. The key idea of the approach is an observation that all ideal pulsers should be replaced by samplers and all samplers should be replaced by pulsers. Furthermore, all sampling times should be reversed. It means the expression $\{T - t_n\}$ in the Table 1 describe a set of time moments $\{T - t_1, T - t_2, \ldots, T - t_N\}$

4   Problem Solution

In this Section we will solve the problem stated in Section 2 under the assumption that the feedforward neural network NN consists of one layer. It will clarify presented approach without loss of generality. There is not bias and W denotes the matrix of weights of the layer.

The main idea of GBPTT method is, at first, to bring the original problem into the problem of finding input-output sensitivity function [3], [5], [6]. In order to perform this step let us transform the dynamic neural network from the Fig.1 into the form presented in Fig.2. In Fig.2 several additional elements and signals

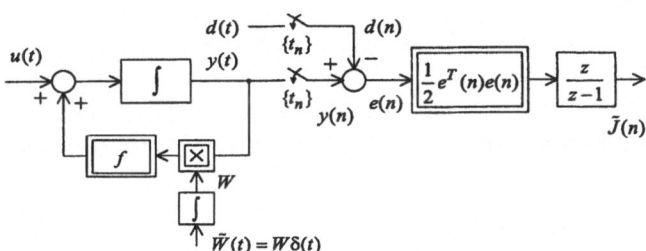

Fig. 2. The continuous time dynamical neural network with additional elements and signals

appeared. Firstly on the output of the system we can see the signal $\tilde{J}(n)$. Careful analysis of the diagram leads to the conclusion that at final discrete time moment N this signal is simply equal to the value of the performance index (1) J. In Fig.2 there is also an additional input signal $\tilde{W}(t)$ which is equal to matrix W multiplied by a Dirac pulse. Such a signal after passing the integrator gives constant "signal" W. Hence the system behavior is the same as before. All these modification are done in order to bring the problem of finding partial derivatives of the performance index with respect to weights into the problem of finding the input-output sensitivity function

$$S_{\tilde{W}(0)}^{\tilde{J}(N)} \tag{2}$$

Now let us construct the modified adjoint system. It can be easily done by using rules presented in Table 1. The result of this fully mnemonic step is presented in Fig.3.

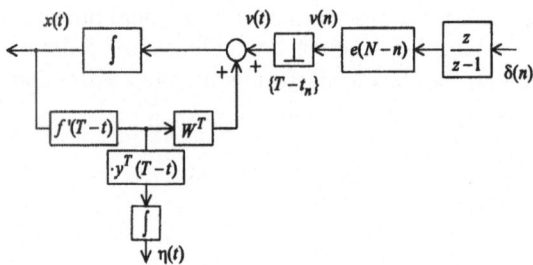

Fig. 3. The modified adjoint system generating the gradient of the performance index

To calculate the value of the input-output sensitivity function the modified adjoint system should be stimulated at discrete time moment $n = 0$ (corresponding to time moment $n = N$ in original system) by a Kronecker's pulse. Then the output signal $\eta(t)$ at time moment $t = T$ (corresponding to time moment $t = 0$ in original system) gives searched sensitivity function (2)

$$S_{\tilde{W}(0)}^{\tilde{J}(N)} = \eta^T(T) \tag{3}$$

The result (3) is a matrix which elements are equal to patrial derivatives of the performance index with respect to elements of the weights matrix W:

$$\frac{\partial J}{\partial w_{ij}} = \eta_{ji}(T) \tag{4}$$

and may be used for gradient descent learning of the dynamic neural network.

The result may be easily derived for dynamic nets where the feedforward neural network NN is multilayered. Moreover, it can be done for different structure than presented in Fig.1 or even for any other hybrid system containing neural network(s).

Now, let us focus on signals acting in the adjoint system (Fig.3). The signal $v(n)$ is simply equal to reversed in time signal of identification error $e(N - n)$, hence the signal $v(t)$ is a series of Dirac pulses $v(t) = \sum_{n=0}^{N} e(T - t_n)\delta(T - t_n)$ which leads to jumps of the state vector $x(t)$ in the adjoint system

$$x\left((T - t_n)^+\right) = x(T - t_n) + e(T - t_n) \tag{5}$$

Therefore it is not necessary to simulate Dirac pulses which could be difficult to realize.

5   Conclusions

In this paper the method for learning of sampled continuous time dynamic neural networks has been presented. The modified adjoint system, generating the gradient of the performance index, has been obtained using GBPTT method extended on sampled data systems. It was shown that the adjoint system, is a continuous-time system with jumps of state variables at moments corresponding to moments of measurements. Is was indicated that such neural networks may have better modeling/identification ability when the plant is continuous time. This property should be examined in the future work.

Acknowledgements. This work has been supported by KBN (Polish State Committee for Scientific Research) under grant No. 4 T11A 012 23 in the year 2004.

References

1. Ahmed M. S.: Block partial derivative and its application to neural-net-based direct-model-reference adaptive control, IEE Proc.-Control Theory Appl., vol. 141, pp. 305-314, 1994.
2. Baldi P.: Gradient descent learning algorithm overview: A general dynamical systems perspective, IEEE Trans. Neural Networks, vol. 6, pp. 182-195, 1995.
3. Fujarewicz K.: Optimal control of nonlinear systems using generalized back propagation through time, Proc. Eighteenth IASTED Conference Modelling, Identification and Control, Innsbruck, Austria, February 1999.
4. Fujarewicz K.: Systems transposed in time and their application to gradient calculation in dynamical systems containing neural nets, Proc. Fourth Conference - Neural Networks and Their Applications, Zakopane, Poland, May 1999.
5. Fujarewicz K.: Identification of heat exchanger using generalized back propagation through time, Proc. Nineteenth IASTED Conference Modelling, Identification and Control, pp. 267–273, Innsbruck, Austria, February 2000.
6. Fujarewicz K.: Identification and suboptimal control of heat exchanger using generalized back propagation through time, Archives of Control Sciences, vol.10(XLVI), No. 3–4. pp. 167–183.
7. Fujarewicz K.: Evaluation of a helicopter model using generalized back propagation through, in: L. Rutkowski, J. Kacprzyk (Eds.), Advances in Soft Computing – Neural Networks and Soft Computing, Physica-Verlag, 2002.
8. Fujarewicz K.: On construction of an adjoint system for continuous-discrete systems, Proc. of Seminar on Electrical Engineering, pp. 56–61, Istebna, Poland, 2003.
9. Kailath T. (1980): Linear Systems, Prentice-Hall, Inc., Engelwood Cliffs, N.J.
10. Narendra S. N., Parthasarathy K.: Gradient methods for the optimization of dynamical systems containing neural networks, IEEE Trans. Neural Networks, vol. 2, pp. 252-262, 1991.
11. Pearlmutter B. A. (1995): Gradient calculations for dynamic recurrent neural networks: A survey, IEEE Trans. Neural Networks, vol. 6, pp. 1212-1228.
12. Wan E., Beaufays F.: Diagrammatic derivation of gradient algorithms for neural networks, Neural Computation, vol. 8, no. 1, January 1996, pp. 182-201.

13. Werbos P. J. (1990): Backpropagation through time: what it does and how to do it, Proc. IEEE, vol. 78, pp. 1550-1560.
14. Williams R., Zipser D.: Learning algorithm for continually running fully recurrent neural networks, Neural Computation, vol. 1, pp. 270-280, 1989.

Experiments on Ensembles of Radial Basis Functions*

Carlos Hernández-Espinosa, Mercedes Fernández-Redondo, and
Joaquín Torres-Sospedra

Universidad Jaume I. Dept. de Ingeniería y Ciencia de los Computadores. Avda
Vicente Sos Baynat s/n. 12071 Castellon. Spain. espinosa@icc.uji.es

Abstract. Building an ensemble of classifiers is an useful way to improve
the performance. In the case of neural networks the bibliography has
centered on the use of Multilayer Feedforward (MF). However, there
are other interesting networks like Radial Basis Functions (RBF) that
can be used as elements of the ensemble. Furthermore, as pointed out
recently, the network RBF can also be trained by gradient descent, so
all the methods of constructing the ensemble designed for MF are also
applicable to RBF. In this paper we present the results of using eleven
methods to construct a ensemble of RBF networks. The results show
that the best method is in general the *Simple Ensemble*.

1 Introduction

Probably the most important property of a neural network (NN) is the generalization capability. One method to increase this capability with respect to a
single NN consist on training an ensemble of NNs, i.e., to train a set of NNs with
different properties and combine the outputs in a suitable manner.

In the field of ensemble design, the two key factors to design an ensemble are
how to train the individual networks and how to combine the different outputs.

It seems clear from the bibliography that this procedure generally increases
the generalization capability in the case of the NN Multilayer Feedforward (MF)
[1,2].

However, in the field of NNs there are other networks besides MF, and traditionally the use of ensembles of NNs has restricted to the use of MF.

Another useful network which is quite used in applications is Radial Basis
Functions (RBF). This network can also be trained by gradient descent [3]. So
with a fully supervised training, it can be also an element of an ensemble, and
all methods of constructing the ensemble which are applicable to MF can now
be also used with RBF networks.

2 Theory

In this section, first we review the basic concepts of RBF networks and after the
different method of constructing the ensemble.

* This research was supported by project MAPACI TIC2002-02273 of CICYT in Spain

L. Rutkowski et al. (Eds.): ICAISC 2004, LNAI 3070, pp. 197–202, 2004.
© Springer-Verlag Berlin Heidelberg 2004

2.1   RBF Networks with Gradient Descent Training

A RBF has two layer of networks. The first layer is composed of neurons with a Gaussian transfer function and the second layer has neurons with a linear transfer function. The output of a RBF network can be calculated with (1).

$$F_k(x) = \sum_{q=1}^{Q} w_q^k \cdot \exp\left(-\sum_{n=1}^{N}\left(C_{q,n}^k - X_n\right)^2 \Big/ (\sigma_q^k)^2\right) \tag{1}$$

Where $C_{q,n}^k$ and σ_q^k are the centers and widths of the Gaussian units and w_q^k are the weights among the Gaussian and output units.

The parameters which are changed during the training process [3] are $C_{q,n}^k$ and w_q^k, the width is the same for all Gaussian units and fixed before training. The equations for the adaptation of the weights is the following:

$$\Delta w_q^k = \eta \cdot \varepsilon_k \cdot \exp\left(-\sum_{n=1}^{N}\left(C_{q,n}^k - X_n\right)^2 \Big/ (\sigma)^2\right) \tag{2}$$

Where η is the step size and ε_k is the difference between the target and the output. And the equation for the adaptation of the centers is (3).

$$\Delta C_q = \eta \cdot (X_k - C_q) \cdot \frac{2}{\sigma} \cdot \exp\left(-\sum_{n=1}^{N}\left(C_{q,n}^k - X_n\right)^2 \Big/ (\sigma)^2\right) \cdot \sum_{k=1}^{n_o} \varepsilon_k \cdot w_q^k \tag{3}$$

2.2   Ensemble Design Methods

Simple Ensemble. A simple ensemble can be constructed by training different networks with the same training set, but with different random initialization.

Bagging. This method is described in [4]. It consists on generating different datasets drawn at random with replacement from the original training set. After that, we train the different networks in the ensemble with these different datasets.

Bagging with Noise (BagNoise). It was proposed in [2]. It is a modification of Bagging, we use in this case datasets generated like Bagging, but we also we introduce a random noise in every selected training point.

Boosting. It is reviewed in [4]. It is conceived for a ensemble of 3 networks. The first network is trained with the whole training set. For the second network, we pass all patterns through the first network and we use a subset of them with 50% of patterns incorrectly classified and 50% correctly classified. Finally, the patterns are presented to both networks. If the two networks disagree in the classification, we add the pattern to the third training set.

CVC. It is reviewed in [1]. The training set is divided into k subsets and k-1 subsets are used to train the network. By changing the subset that is left out we can train k networks, with different training sets.

Adaboost. We have implemented the algorithm *"Adaboost.M1"* in [5]. The successive networks are trained with a training set selected randomly, but the probability of selecting a pattern changes dinamically.

Decorrelated (Deco). This ensemble method was proposed in [6]. It consists on introducing a penalty added to the error function. The penalty for net j is:

$$Penalty = \lambda \cdot d(i,j)(y - f_i) \cdot (y - f_j) \tag{4}$$

Where λ is a parameter, y is the target and f_i and f_j are the outputs of networks i and j in the ensemble. The term $d(i,j)$ is 1 for $i = j - 1$ and 0 otherwise.

Decorrelated2 (Deco2). It was proposed in [6]. It is basically the same method of *"Deco"* but with a different term $d(i,j)$, is 1 when $i = j - 1$ and i is even.

Evol. This method was proposed in [7]. In each iteration (presentation of a training pattern), it is calculated the output of the ensemble by voting. If the output is correct we continue with the next iteration and pattern. Otherwise, the network with an erroneous output and lower MSE is trained until the output is correct. This procedure is repeated for several networks until the vote is correct.

Cels. It was proposed in [8]. This method also uses a penalty term added to error function. In this case the penalty term for network number i is in (5).

$$Penalty = \lambda \cdot (f_i - y) \cdot \sum_{j \neq i} (f_j - y) \tag{5}$$

Ola. It was proposed in [9]. First, several datasets are generated by using Bagging. Each network is trained with one of this datasets and with "virtual data". The virtual data is generated by selecting samples for the original training set and adding a random noise. The target of virtual data is calculated by the output of the ensemble.

3   Experimental Results

We have applied the eleven ensemble methods to nine problems from the UCI repository. Their names are Balance Scale (Balance), Cylinders Bands (Bands), Liver Disorders (Bupa), Credit Approval (Credit), Glass Identification (Glass), Heart Disease (Heart), the Monk's Problems (Monk1, Monk2) and

Voting Records (Vote). A full description can be found in the UCI repository (http://www.ics.uci .edu/~mlearn/MLRepository.html).

We trained ensembles of 3 and 9 networks. We repeated this process of training an ensemble ten times for different partitions of data in training, cross-validation and test sets. In this way, we can obtain a mean performance of the ensemble for each database (the mean of the ten ensembles) and an error in the performance. The results are in table 1 for the case of ensembles of 3 networks and in table 2 for 9 networks. We have omitted the results of databases Monk1, Monk2 y Vote in Tables 1 and 2 because of the lack of space. We have also included in table 1 the mean performance of a single network for comparison.

Table 1. Results for the ensemble of three networks.

	Balance	Band	Bupa	Credit	Glas	Heart
Single Net.	90.2 ± 0.5	74.0 ± 1.1	70.1 ± 1.1	86.0 ± 0.8	93.0 ± 0.6	82.0 ± 1.0
Adaboost	88.0 ± 1.2	73 ± 2	68.4 ± 0.5	84.7 ± 0.6	91.3 ± 1.3	82.0 ± 1.4
Bagging	89.7 ± 0.8	73 ± 2	70.1 ± 1.6	$87.4 \pm 05.$	93.8 ± 1.2	83.6 ± 1.8
Bag_Noise	89.8 ± 0.8	73.1 ± 1.3	64 ± 2	87.1 ± 0.7	92.2 ± 0.9	83.2 ± 1.5
Boosting	88.2 ± 0.8	70.7 ± 1.8	70.6 ± 1.6	86.6 ± 0.7	92.2 ± 0.9	82.4 ± 1.2
Cels	89.5 ± 0.8	75.3 ± 1.4	69.3 ± 1.4	86.9 ± 0.5	93.0 ± 1.0	82.7 ± 1.7
CVC	90 ± 0.7	75.1 ± 1.4	69.9 ± 1.5	87.5 ± 0.5	92.4 ± 1.1	83.9 ± 1.6
Decorrelated	89.8 ± 0.8	73.3 ± 1.7	71.9 ± 1.6	87.1 ± 0.5	93.2 ± 1.0	84.1 ± 1.4
Decorrelated2	89.8 ± 0.8	73.8 ± 1.4	71.3 ± 1.4	87.2 ± 0.5	93.4 ± 1.0	83.3 ± 1.4
Evol	89.5 ± 0.9	67.6 ± 1.3	63 ± 2	84.6 ± 1.1	88 ± 2	79 ± 2
Ola	88.2 ± 0.9	73.1 ± 1.3	68.1 ± 1.5	86.1 ± 0.7	89.4 ± 1.8	81.5 ± 1.2
Simple Ense	89.7 ± 0.7	73.8 ± 1.2	71.9 ± 1.1	87.1 ± 0.5	93.2 ± 1.0	84.6 ± 1.5

By comparing the results of tables 1 and 2 with the results of a single network we can see that the improvement of the ensemble is database and method dependent. Sometimes, the performance of an ensemble (as in case of Balance) is worse than the single network, the reason may be the combination method (*output averaging*) which does not exploit the performance of the individual networks. Besides that, there is one method which clearly perform worse than the single network which is *Evol*, but we obtained the same result for ensembles of Multilayer Feedforward.

To see the results more clearly, we have also calculated the percentage of error reduction of the ensemble with respect to a single network as (6).

$$PorError_{reduction} = 100 \cdot \frac{PorError_{\sin gle\ network} - PorError_{ensemble}}{PorError_{\sin gle\ network}} \quad (6)$$

In this last equation, $PorError_{singlenetwork}$ is the error percentage of a single network (for example, 100-90.2=9.8% in the case of Balance, see table 1) and $PorError_{ensemble}$ is the error percentage in the ensemble with a particular method.

Table 2. Results for the ensemble of nine networks.

	Balance	Band	Bupa	Credit	Glas	Heart
Single Net.	90.2 ± 0.5	74.0 ± 1.1	70.1 ± 1.1	86.0 ± 0.8	93.0 ± 0.6	82.0 ± 1.0
Adaboost	91.8 ± 0.8	71.5 ± 1.2	69.6 ± 1.1	84.8 ± 0.8	93.1 ± 1.3	81.0 ± 1.5
Bagging	90 ± 0.8	74.3 ± 1.4	71.0 ± 1.5	87.5 ± 0.5	93.6 ± 1.2	84.9 ± 1.2
Bag_Noise	90 ± 0.8	73.1 ± 1.1	64.1 ± 1.9	87.1 ± 0.5	91.4 ± 0.9	83.6 ± 1.6
Cels	89.7 ± 0.8	74.0 ± 1.2	69.4 ± 1.9	87.1 ± 0.5	92.4 ± 1.1	82.5 ± 1.4
CVC	89.8 ± 0.8	73.6 ± 1.3	70 ± 2	87.6 ± 0.5	93.0 ± 1.1	84.1 ± 1.3
Decorrelated	89.8 ± 0.8	73.5 ± 1.8	71.4 ± 1.4	87.2 ± 0.6	93.0 ± 1.0	84.1 ± 1.3
Decorrelated2	89.8 ± 0.8	73.8 ± 1.8	71.6 ± 1.2	87.2 ± 0.5	93.2 ± 1.0	84.7 ± 1.4
Evol	88.1 ± 1.1	67.6 ± 1.3	63 ± 2	83.4 ± 1.3	82.6 ± 1.8	78 ± 2
Ola	88.5 ± 0.7	74.5 ± 1.2	69.6 ± 1.4	81.8 ± 1.1	90.6 ± 1.2	78 ± 2
Simple Ense	89.7 ± 0.7	73.3 ± 1.4	72.4 ± 1.2	87.2 ± 0.5	93.0 ± 1.0	83.9 ± 1.5

The value of this percentage ranges from 0%, where there is no improvement by the use of a ensemble method with respect to a *single network*, to 100% where the error of the ensemble is 0%. There can also be negative values, which means that the performance of the ensemble is worse than the performance of the *single network*.

This new measurement is relative and can be used to compare clearly the methods. In table 3 we have the results for the ensemble of 9 networks. Furthermore we have calculated the mean of the percentage of error reduction across all databases and is in the last column with header "Mean".

According to this mean measurement there are five methods which perform worse than the *single network*, they are *Adaboost*, *BagNoise*, *Cels*, *Evol* and *Ola*. The performance of *Evol* is clear, in all databases is worse. *Ola*, *Adabbost*, *BagNoise* and *Cels* are in general problem dependent (unstable).

The best and most regular method across all databases is the *Simple Ensemble*.

Table 3. Percentage of error reduction for the ensemble of 9 networks.

	Bala	Band	Bupa	Cred	Glas	Heart	Mok1	Mok2	Vote	Mean
Adaboost	16.33	-9.62	-1.67	-8.57	1.43	-5.56	-493.33	-49.43	10.87	-59-95
Bagging	-2.04	1.15	3.01	10.71	8.57	16.11	60	-22.99	10.87	9.49
BagNoise	-2.04	-3.46	-20.07	7.86	-22.86	8.89	-200	-13.79	13.04	-25.82
Cels	-5.10	0	-2.34	7.86	-8.57	2.78	-346.67	-43.68	-10.87	-45-18
CVC	-4.08	-1.54	-0.33	11.43	0	11.67	60	-9.20	15.22	9.24
Deco	-4.08	-1.92	4.35	8.57	0	11.67	60	-11.49	15.22	9.14
Deco2	-4.08	-0.77	5.02	8.57	2.86	15	73.33	-2.30	15.22	12.53
Evol	-21.42	-24.62	-23.75	-18.57	-148.57	-22.22	-1580	-306.9	-67.39	-245.94
Ola	-17.35	1.92	-1.67	-30	-34.29	-22.22	-1826.67	-106.9	15.22	-224.66
Simp.Ens	-5.10	-2.69	7.69	8.57	0	10.56	73.33	1.15	19.57	12.56

Finally, to see the influence of the number of networks in the ensemble we have obtained the results of the mean percentage of error reduction for ensembles of 3 and 9 networks, from the results is clear that in general there is an improvement in performance from the ensemble of three to the ensemble of nine networks.

4 Conclusions

In this paper we have presented results of eleven different methods to construct an ensemble of RBF networks, using nine different databases. The results showed that in general the performance is method and problem dependent, sometimes the performance of the ensemble is even worse than the *single network*, the reason can be that the combination method (*output averaging*) is not appropriate. The best and most regular performing method across all databases was the simple ensemble, i.e., the rest of methods proposed to increase the performance of MF seems not to be useful in RBF networks. Perhaps, another reason of this result in the combination method which may not be very appropriate as commented before, the future research will go in the direction of trying other combination methods with ensembles of RBF networks.

References

1. Tumer, K., Ghosh, J.: Error correlation and error reduction in ensemble classifiers. Connection Science. **8** nos. 3 & 4, (1996) 385–404
2. Raviv, Y., Intrator, N.: Bootstrapping with Noise: An Effective Regularization Technique. Connection Science. **8** no. 3 & 4, (1996) 355–372, .
3. Karayiannis, N.B., Randolph-Gips, M.M.: On the Construction and Training of Reformulated Radial Basis Function Neural Networks. IEEE Trans. On Neural Networks. **14** no. 4 (2003) 835–846
4. Drucker, H., Cortes, C., Jackel, D., et alt.: Boosting and Other Ensemble Methods. Neural Computation. **6** (1994) 1289–1301
5. Freund, Y., Schapire, R.: Experiments with a New Boosting Algorithm. Proc. of the Thirteenth Inter. Conf. on Machine Learning. (1996) 148–156
6. Rosen, B.: Ensemble Learning Using Decorrelated Neural Networks. Connection Science. **8** no. 3 & 4 (1996) 373–383
7. Auda, G., Kamel, M.: EVOL: Ensembles Voting On-Line. Proc. of the World Congress on Computational Intelligence. (1998) 1356–1360
8. Liu, Y., Yao, X.: A Cooperative Ensemble Learning System. Proc. of the World Congress on Computational Intelligence. (1998) 2202–2207
9. Jang, M., Cho, S.: Ensemble Learning Using Observational Learning Theory. Proc. of the Int. Joint Conf. on Neural Networks. **2** (1999) 1281–1286

Orthodoxy Basis Functions and Convergence Property in Procedure Neural Networks

Jiong Jia and Jiu-zhen Liang

Institute of Computer Science, Zhejiang Normal University, Jinhua, China, 321004
jia@mail.zjnu.net.cn, liangjiuzhen@yahoo.com

Abstract. This paper deals with some theoretic and numerical issues in the learning algorithm for Procedure Neural Networks (PNNs). In PNNs the weights are time functions and can be expended by some basis functions. The properties of PNNs vary with the choice of weights functions. Orthodoxy basis functions have many advances in expending the weight functions and save training time in PNNs learning. In this paper several kinds of orthodoxy functions are proposed. Also the algorithm convergence of PNNs training is discussed.

1 Introduction

In 2000 the authors proposed a novel neural network named Procedure Neural Networks (PNNs)[1]. In PNNs it is considered the input-output vary with time, which describe a continuous procedure or a time sequence. PNNs also can be regarded as neural networks expanded in time domain. In a traditional neural network (NNs) a neuron is supposed to be static and has no various sate vs. time. Like NNs, PNNs have many good properties, such as continuous mapping, identical approximation to continuous function, computational capability equality to Turing machine, etc. These properties have been discussed in reference[2]. Also learning algorithm for PNNs takes the same role as in NNs, and [3] shows an example of PNNs training . Feedback PNNs models and learning algorithms also were discussed in [4]. Different from NNs, PNNs have more training data in learning for the reason of considering time factor. Therefore, PNNs training usually show more difficult than NNs and take long time in learning.

This paper includes six parts and is arranged as following. The second part introduces PNNs. Discusses its structure, mathematical expression, and some notations about PNNs. The third part mainly studies the choice of weight functions of PNNs. Orthodoxy basis function is the first alternative basis function. The fourth part surveys learning algorithm for PNNs. Describes supervised learning algorithm in training PNNs and deduces formulas of weight updating. The fifths part focus on the convergence property of supervised learning algorithm. The last part, section six, concludes the whole paper.

2 Procedure Neural Networks

Procedure neural networks are generalized models of traditional neural networks. In this kind of networks, the inputs are a serial of values varying with a procedure,

L. Rutkowski et al. (Eds.): ICAISC 2004, LNAI 3070, pp. 203–209, 2004.
© Springer-Verlag Berlin Heidelberg 2004

while the output is a static state vector. In reference [1], the concept of procedure neuron is presented. A PNN is composed of a number of procedure neurons. Owned the similar taxonomy with traditional neural networks, procedure neural networks can be generally classified into feedforward procedure neural networks and backward procedure neural networks. Considering the procedure neural network expanded on certain basis functions. For simplicity, suppose the number of the output neuron $m = 1$ and the basis function $B(t, u) = B(t)$, which is a multi-input and single output system. It is easy to generalize the discussion to the case $m > 1$.

In this paper, we only investigate the case that has finite dimensional continuous basis with dimension L. Topology structure for procedure neural network expanded on certain basis functions can be showed as Fig.2 in reference[3] . In which the first layer is for input functions, the second is for the products of weight functions and input functions, the third layer is for the operation of time cumulating and the fourth layer is for output of space aggregation. Restrict $w_i(t) \in C[0, T]$, and $b_k(t), (k = 1, 2, , L)$ is a group of orthodoxy basis functions. Operations in each layer are given as following.

$$w_i(t) = \sum_{k=1}^{L} w_{ik} b_k(t) \tag{1}$$

$$c_i = \int_0^T w_i(t) x_i(t) \mathrm{d}t \tag{2}$$

$$y = f(\sum_{i=1}^{n} c_i) \tag{3}$$

where θ is neuron threshold in the fourth layer and f is transfer function for the fourth layer. Combining formulation (1), (2) and (3), the relationship between inputs and outputs can be written as (4).

$$y = f(\int_0^T [\sum_{i=1}^{n} \sum_{k=1}^{L} w_{ik} x_i(t) b_k(t)] \mathrm{d}t) \tag{4}$$

3   Orthodoxy Basis Function

In this paper we choose orthodoxy function as basis function. An example is Chebshov orthodoxy polynomial.

$$b_k(t) = \frac{sin((k+1) \arccos(2t/T - 1))}{\sqrt{1 - (2t/T - 1)^2}} \tag{5}$$

where $t \in [0, T]$. For simple of computing, the basis function has finite dimension. Suppose $x(t) \in C[0, T], b_k(t), (k = 1, 2, , L)$ is the same as in (1). The following lemma refers to [2].

Lemma 1. Suppose $\{b_k(t)\}$ is a group of orthodoxy polynomial basis funcctions. Then there exists a series of weights u_i for each $i = 1, 2, \cdots, n$, such that

$$x_i(t) = \sum_{l=1}^{L_i} u_{il} b_l(t) + \xi_i(t) \tag{6}$$

Where L_i is an large enough integer number and $\|\xi_i(t)\| < \varepsilon_i$, while ε_i is any positive number. Denote $L = \max_i \{L_i\}$, $\xi(t) = \arg\max_i \{\|\xi_i(t)\|\}$ and $\varepsilon = \max_i \{\varepsilon_i\}$ in the following content and neglecting the error of $\xi(t)$, equation (4) can be rewritten as

$$y = f\left(\int_0^T \left[\sum_{i=1}^n \sum_{k=1}^L \sum_{l=1}^L w_{ik} u_{il} b_k(t) b_l(t)\right] dt\right) \tag{7}$$

Due to the hypothesis mentioned in the former, orthodoxy basis functions $\{b_k(t)\}$ satisfy

$$\int_0^T b_k(t) b_l(t) dt = \begin{cases} 0 & , k \neq l \\ B_l & , k = l \end{cases} \tag{8}$$

Where B_l is constant scale for all $l = 1, 2, ..., L$. In fact, if the basis functions are chosen as

$$\tilde{b}_k(t) = \frac{b_k(t)}{\sqrt{B_l}} \tag{9}$$

Then $\tilde{b}_k(t)$ are standard orthodoxy basis functions and satisfy

$$\int_0^T \tilde{b}_k(t) \tilde{b}_l(t) dt = \begin{cases} 0 & , k \neq l \\ 1 & , k = l \end{cases} \tag{10}$$

In this way formula (7) can be rewritten as

$$y = f\left(\sum_{i=1}^n \sum_{l=1}^L w_{il} \tilde{u}_{il}\right) \tag{11}$$

Where

$$\tilde{u}_{il} = \frac{u_{il}}{\sqrt{B_l}} \tag{12}$$

Practically, standard orthodoxy basis functions can be formed to the optimal approximation to a family of functions stated as the following lemma [5].

Lemma 2. Suppose $\{\tilde{b}_k(t)\}$ are standard orthodoxy basis functions as in (10), and $x(t) \in L^2[0, T]$ is any Lebesgue integrabel function. Then the optimal approximation to $x(t)$ is given by

$$\tilde{b}(t) = \sum_{l=1}^{L} \tilde{u}_l \tilde{b}_l(t) \tag{13}$$

Here

$$\tilde{u}_l = \int_0^T \tilde{b}_l(t) x(t) \mathrm{d}t \tag{14}$$

4   Supervised Learning for PNNs

To construct learning algorithm of PNN we focus on supervised technique on the labelled training data set:

$(x_{11}(t), \cdots, x_{1n}(t); d_1), (x_{21}(t), \cdots, x_{2n}(t); d_2), \cdots (x_{K1}(t), \cdots, x_{Kn}(t); d_K).$

Here d_i denotes the i-th desired output. Define the error function as following normalization form

$$\begin{aligned}
E &= \tfrac{1}{2}[\sum_{k=1}^{K}(y_k - d_k)^2 + \lambda \|w\|^2] \\
&= \tfrac{1}{2}[\sum_{k=1}^{K}(f(\sum_{l=1}^{L}\sum_{i=1}^{n} w_{il}\tilde{u}_{il}^k) - d_k)^2 + \lambda \sum_{l=1}^{L}\sum_{i=1}^{n} w_{il}^2]
\end{aligned} \tag{15}$$

Where λ is a Lagrange scale of normalization and $\tilde{u}_{il}^k$ are coefficients corresponding to the k-th sample input function, giving by

$$\tilde{u}_{il}^k = \int_0^T \tilde{b}_l(t) x_{ki}(t) \mathrm{d}t \tag{16}$$

Calculation of (16) can be recurred to the Trapezoid formula as

$$\tilde{u}_{il}^k = \frac{1}{2} \sum_{j=1}^{N-1} (\tilde{b}_l(t_{j+1}) x_{ki}(t_{j+1}) + \tilde{b}_l(t_j) x_{ki}(t_j))(t_{j+1} - t_j) \tag{17}$$

Here $0 = t_0 < t_1 < \cdots < t_N = T$. Updating of weights $\{w_{il}\}$ submits to gradient descent rule as following

$$w_{il}(s+1) = w_{il}(s) + \Delta w_{il}(s) \tag{18}$$

Where $i = 1, 2, \cdots, n; l = 1, 2, \cdots, L$; s is the learning loop number; and

$$\begin{aligned}
\Delta w_{il}(s) &= -\eta(s)\frac{\partial E}{\partial w_{il}(s)} \\
&= \eta(s)[\sum_{k=1}^{K}(f(\sum_{l=1}^{L}\sum_{i=1}^{n} w_{il}(s)\tilde{u}_{il}^k) - d_k)f'(\sum_{l=1}^{L}\sum_{i=1}^{n} w_{il}(s)\tilde{u}_{il}^k) + \lambda w_{il}]
\end{aligned} \tag{19}$$

Here $\eta(s)$ is the learning speed, usually $\eta(s) \in (0,1)$. Now the question is to compute $\tilde{u}_{il}^k$. Certainly, $\tilde{u}_{il}^k$ can be calculated according to (17). As in common case, $x(t)$ is given only in some discrete points, therefore the computing error is usually very large. In a sense, (17) proposes a rough method to calculate $\tilde{u}_{il}^k$ for training sets instead of analysis form of input functions. So we present another numerical method to compute $\tilde{u}_{il}^k$ by iteration strategy. As to (15), define the error function F_i as following

$$F_i = \frac{1}{2}[\sum_{k=1}^{K}\int_0^T (x_i^k(t) - \sum_{l=1}^{L}\tilde{u}_{il}^k b_l(t))^2 \mathrm{d}t + \lambda \sum_{l=1}^{L}\sum_{l=1}^{L}(\tilde{u}_{il}^k)^2] \tag{20}$$

We can compute the approximate solution of $\tilde{u}_{il}^k$ by iteration strategy, i.e.

$$\Delta\tilde{u}_{il}^k(s+1) = \tilde{u}_{il}^k(s) + \Delta\tilde{u}_{il}^k(s) \tag{21}$$

Where $i = 1, 2, \cdots, n; l = 1, 2, \cdots, L; k = 1, 2, \cdots, K; s$ is the learning loop number; and

$$\Delta\tilde{u}_{il}^k(s) = -\eta(s)\frac{\partial F_i}{\partial\tilde{u}_{il}^k(s)} \tag{22}$$

Clearly, learning algorithm for PNN can be departed into two parts. The first part is to compute the coefficients $\{\tilde{u}_{il}^k\}$ for input function of each sample. The second part is to find the weights $\{\tilde{w}_{il}\}$.

5 Convergence Property of Algorithm

Now, considering the first issue, it is expected to find the condition, under which for any positive $\varepsilon \geq \delta > 0$ the following limitation holds

$$\lim_{s\to\infty}\sum_{k=1}^{K}\int_0^T (x_i^k(t) - \sum_{l=1}^{L}\tilde{u}_{il}^k(s)b_l(t))^2 \mathrm{d}t = \delta \leq \varepsilon \tag{23}$$

Subject to

$$\sum_{i=1}^{n}\sum_{l=1}^{L}(\tilde{u}_{il}^k(s))^2 \leq 1 \tag{24}$$

This problem can also be stated as another typical form. That is whether there exists a convergent sequence $\{\tilde{u}_{il}^k(s)\}$ for every sample input function $x_i^k(t)$, such that

$$\lim_{s\to\infty}\tilde{u}_{il}^k(s) = \tilde{u}_{il}^k \tag{25}$$

and

$$\sum_{k=1}^{K}\int_0^T (x_i^k(t) - \sum_{l=1}^{L}\tilde{u}_{il}^k b_l(t))^2 \mathrm{d}t = \delta \leq \varepsilon \tag{26}$$

According to Lemma 1 inequality (23) is satisfied, i.e. for every sample input function $x_i^k(t)$, there is a series of $\tilde{u}_{il}^k$ that satisfy (26). Thus the focus problem is limitation (25), for detail, we will search the sufficient conditions that guarantee (25) is correct subjecting to the following inequality.

$$\sum_{i=1}^{n}\sum_{l=1}^{L}(\tilde{u}_{il}^{k})^2 \leq 1 \tag{27}$$

Considering a finite sampling value of $x(t)$ in time domain, $x(t_1), x(t_2)$, $\cdots, x(t_N)$, for gradient iteration stated as in (21) and (22) then the following convergence theorem is proved [6].

Theorem 1. Sequence $\{\tilde{u}_{il}^{k}(s)\}$ converges to one of minimum of F_i in (20), if $\Delta\tilde{u}_{il}^{k}(s)$ is bounded and the learning speed coefficient $\eta(s)$ satisfy

$$\sum_{s=1}^{\infty}\eta(s) = \infty, \sum_{s=1}^{\infty}\eta^2(s) < \infty \tag{28}$$

Corollary 1. Sequence $\{w_{il}(s)\}$ converges to one of minimum of E in (15) if $\Delta w_{il}(s)$ is bounded and the learning speed coefficient $\eta(s)$ satisfy (28).

Theorem 2. Sequence $\{w_{il}(s)\}$ converges to $\{w_{il}\}$ which is one of minimum of E with error $\delta > 0$ satisfying

$$E = \frac{1}{2}[\sum_{k=1}^{K}(f(\sum_{l=1}^{L}\sum_{i=1}^{n}w_{il}\tilde{u}_{il}^{k}) - d_k)^2 + \lambda\sum_{l=1}^{L}\sum_{i=1}^{n}w_{il}^2] \leq \delta \tag{29}$$

6   Conclusions

Procedure neural networks can be structured as many kinds of form. But it is difficult to give a strategy to determine what kinds of hidden neurons is the optimal choice, how many hidden layers and how many hidden nodes should be arranged. In this paper the basis function is corresponding to the hidden layer. However, there are many other choices of hidden layer types, such as Radial Basis Functions [7], SV basis functions [6], etc.

References

1. X. G. He and J. Z. Liang, Procedure neural networks, Proceedings of conference on intelligent information proceeding, 16th World Computer Congress 2000, pp. 143-146, August 21-25, 2000, Beijing, China, Publishing House of Electronic Industry.
2. X. G. He and J. Z. Liang, Some theoretic issues in Procedure Neural Networks, Engineering Science in China, Vol.2 (12): 40-44, 2000 (In Chinese)
3. Liang Jiuzhen, Zhou Jiaqing, He Xingui, Procedure Neural Networks With Supervised Learning, 9th International Conference on Neural Information Processing (ICONIP'02), 2002.11, Singapore, 523 527
4. J. Z. Liang, Feedback Procedure Neural Networks and Its Training. Proceedings of 2002 International Conference on Machine Learning and Cybernetics, November 4-5, 2002 Beijing, China.

5. Rudin W. Principles of mathematical analysis. Third Edition, New York: McGraw-Hill Press, 1976
6. V. N. Vapnik, Statistical Learning Theory, J. Wiley, New York, 1998.
7. S. Haykin, Neural Networks: A Comprehension Foundation, Second Edition, Prentice Hall, 2001

Confidence Estimation of GMDH Neural Networks

Józef Korbicz, Mihai F. Metenidis, Marcin Mrugalski, and Marcin Witczak
In memory of Mihai F. Metenidis, 1977-2004

University of Zielona Góra, Institute of Control and Computation Engineering,
ul. Podgórna 50, 65–246 Zielona Góra, Poland, fax: +48 68 3254615,
{J.Korbicz,M.Mrugalski,M.Witczak}@issi.uz.zgora.pl

Abstract. This paper presents a new parameter and confidence estimation techniques for static GMDH neural networks. The main objective is to show how to employ the outer-bounding ellipsoid algorithm to solve such a challenging task that occurs in many practical situations. In particular, the proposed approach can be relatively easy applied in robust fault diagnosis schemes.

1 Introduction

The complexity and reliability demands of contemporary industrial systems and technological processes requires the development of reliable fault diagnosis approaches. Undoubtedly, techniques employing the so-called analytical redundancy can provide means to tackle such a challenging problem [6]. Whilst the analytical redundancy is equivalent with the application of models (instead of hardware) one way to settle such a design task is to use Artificial Neural Networks (ANNs) [2,6]. Irrespective of the type of the neural network used, there is always the problem of model (ANN) uncertainty, i.e. the model-reality mismatch. Thus, the better model used to represent a system behavior, the better chance of improving the reliability and performance in diagnosing faults. Unfortunately, disturbances as well as model uncertainty are inevitable in industrial systems, and hence there exists a pressure creating the need for robustness in fault diagnosis systems. Bearing all these difficulties in mind, the paper focuses on the problem of designing GMDH neural networks [3] as well as describing their uncertainty. Knowing the model structure and possessing the knowledge regarding its uncertainty it is possible to design a robust fault detection scheme. Indeed, since we know the bounds of the admissible changes of the system behaviour in the normal operating mode, violating these bounds by the system means that it is in a faulty mode. The paper is organized as follows. Section 2 presents the structure of the GMDH neural network. Section 3 formulates the problem of parameter estimation and outlines some elementary information regarding the so-called bounded-error approach for parameter estimation [4]. While Section 4 shows how to use this approach to obtain model output uncertainty. The final part of this work contains an illustrative example, which confirms the effectiveness of the proposed approach.

L. Rutkowski et al. (Eds.): ICAISC 2004, LNAI 3070, pp. 210–216, 2004.
© Springer-Verlag Berlin Heidelberg 2004

2   The GMDH Neural Network

The GMDH neural network is constructed through the connection of a given number of elementary models (neurons) [2,3]:

$$y_n^{(l)}(k) = \left(r_n^{(l)}(k)\right)^T p_n^{(l)}, \tag{1}$$

where $y_n^{(l)}(k)$ stands for the elementary models output (l is the layer number, n is the neuron number in the l layer), corresponding the k-th measurement of the input $u(k) \in \mathbb{R}^{n_u}$ and output $y' \in \mathbb{R}$ of the system. $r_n^{(l)}(k) = [(u_i^{(l)}(k)),(u_j^{(l)}(k))]^T$, $p_n^{(l)} \in \mathbb{R}^{n_p}$, are the regressor and the parameter vectors, respectively. The parameter vectors of the elementary models are estimated separately [6]. The outline of the GMDH algorithm can be as follows:

Step 1 : Determine all elementary models whose inputs consist of all the possible couples of input variables, i.e. $(n_u - 1)n_u/2$ couples (elementary models).

Step 2 : Using a new data set (not employed during the model parameters estimation phase), select several elementary-models which are best-fitted in terms of the criterion chosen.

Step 3 : If the termination condition is reached (one of the models fits the data with a desired accuracy, or the introduction of new elementary models did not cause a significant increase in the approximation abilities of the whole model in terms of the criterion chosen), then STOP, otherwise use the outputs of the best-fitted elementary models (selected in *Step 2*) to form the input vector, and then go to *Step 1*.

3   Elementary Model Parameters Estimation Problem

While applying the least-square method (LSM) to parameter estimation of elementary models (1) a set of restrictive assumptions has to be satisfied (e.g. the structure of the model is the same as that of the system). For the structure (1), the LSM requires the system output to be described in the following way:

$$y_n'^{(l)}(k) = \left(r_n^{(l)}(k)\right)^T p_n^{(l)} + \varepsilon_n^{(l)}(k), \tag{2}$$

where

$$\mathcal{E}\left[\varepsilon_n^{(l)}\right] = 0, \tag{3}$$

$$\mathrm{cov}\left[\varepsilon_n^{(l)}\right] = \left(\sigma_n^{(l)}\right)^2 I, \tag{4}$$

and $\varepsilon_n^{(l)}(k)$ consists of a structural deterministic error caused by the model-reality mismatch, and the stochastic error caused by the measurement noise.

The problem is to estimate the parameter vector $\boldsymbol{p}_n^{(l)}(k)$, i.e. to obtain $\hat{\boldsymbol{p}}_n^{(l)}(k)$, as well as an associated parameter uncertainty. In order to simplify the notation the index $\overset{(l)}{n}$ is omitted. The knowledge regarding the set of admissible parameter values allows to obtain the confidence region of the model output which satisfies

$$y^m(k) \leq y(k) \leq y^M(k), \tag{5}$$

where $y^m(k)$ and $y^M(k)$ are the minimum and maximum admissible values of the model output. Under such assumptions the uncertainty of the ANNs can be obtained according to [5]. In this paper, it is assumed that $\varepsilon(k)$ is bounded as follows

$$\varepsilon^m(k) \leq \varepsilon(k) \leq \varepsilon^M(k), \tag{6}$$

where the bounds $\varepsilon^m(k)$ and $\varepsilon^M(k)$ $(\varepsilon^m(k) \neq \varepsilon^M(k))$ are known *a priori*. In this case the system output can be bounded as

$$\boldsymbol{r}^T(k)\boldsymbol{p}^m(k) + \varepsilon^m(k) \leq y'(k) \leq \boldsymbol{r}^T(k)\boldsymbol{p}^M(k) + \varepsilon^M(k). \tag{7}$$

The idea underlying the bounded-error approach is to obtain the feasible parameter set [4]. This set can be defined as

$$\mathbb{P} = \left\{ \boldsymbol{p} \in \mathbb{R}^{n_p} \mid y'(k) - \varepsilon^M(k) \leq \boldsymbol{r}^T(k)\boldsymbol{p} \leq y'(k) - \varepsilon^m(k) , k = 1, \ldots, n_u \right\}, \tag{8}$$

where n_u is the number of input-output measurements. It can be perceived as a region of parameter space that is determined by n_u pairs of hyperplanes where each pair defines the parameter strip

$$\mathbb{S}(k) = \left\{ \boldsymbol{p} \in \mathbb{R}^{n_p} \mid y'(k) - \varepsilon^M(k) \leq \boldsymbol{r}^T(k)\boldsymbol{p} \leq y'(k) - \varepsilon^m(k) \right\}, \tag{9}$$

and hence

$$\mathbb{P} = \bigcap_k^{n_u} \mathbb{S}(k). \tag{10}$$

Any parameter vector $\hat{\boldsymbol{p}}$ contained in $\mathbb{P}$ is a valid estimate of $\boldsymbol{p}$. In practice, the centre (in some geometrical sense) of $\mathbb{P}$ is chosen as the parameter estimate $\hat{\boldsymbol{p}}$:

$$\hat{p}_i = \frac{p_i^{\min} + p_i^{\max}}{2}, \quad i = 1, \ldots, n_p, \tag{11}$$

where

$$p_i^{\min} = \arg \min_{\boldsymbol{p} \in \mathbb{P}} p_i, \quad p_i^{\max} = \arg \max_{\boldsymbol{p} \in \mathbb{P}} p_i. \tag{12}$$

The problems (12) can be solved with well-known linear programming techniques, but when the n_u and/or n_p are large these tasks may be very time consuming. In order to overcome these difficulties an exact feasible parameter set can be approximated by an ellipsoid [4]. In a recursive outer-bounding ellipsoid (OBE) algorithm, the data are taken into account one after the other to construct a succession of ellipsoids containing all values of p consistent with all previous measurements. After the first k observations the set of feasible parameters is characterized by the ellipsoid

$$\mathbb{E}(\hat{p}(k), P(k)) = \left\{ p \in \mathbb{R}^{n_p} : (p - \hat{p}(k))^T P^{-1}(k)(p - \hat{p}(k)) \leq 1 \right\}, \qquad (13)$$

where $\hat{p}(k)$ is the center of the ellipsoid constituting k-th parameter estimate, and $P(k)$ is a positive-definite matrix which specifies its size and orientation. By means of an intersection of the strip (8) and the ellipsoid (13), a region of possible parameter estimates is obtained. This region is outerbouned, by a new ellipsoid. The OBE algorithm provides rules for computing $p(k)$ and $P(k)$ in such a way that ensuring that the volume of $\mathbb{E}(\hat{p}(k+1), P(k+1))$ is minimized.

$$\mathbb{E}(\hat{p}(k+1), P(k+1)) \supseteq \mathbb{E}(\hat{p}(k), P(k)) \cap \mathbb{S}(k). \qquad (14)$$

The center of the $n_{\mathcal{U}}$-th, ellipsoid constitutes the resulting parameter estimate while the ellipsoid itself represents the feasible parameter set.

4 Model Output Uncertainty

The methodology described in Section 3 makes it possible to obtain the parameter estimate $\hat{p}$ and the associated feasible parameter set $\mathbb{P}$. But from the point of view of practical applications it is more important to obtain the model output uncertainty, i.e. the interval in which the "true" output $y'(k)$ can be find. In the case of OBE algorithm it can be assume, that the errors lie between bounds:

$$-\varepsilon(k) \leq y'(k) - r^T(k)p \leq \varepsilon(k). \qquad (15)$$

Taking the size of the ellipsoid into consideration (cf. Fig.1) it is possible to determine the model output uncertainty:

$$r^T(k)\hat{p} - \sqrt{r^T(k)Pr(k)} \leq r^T(k)p \leq r^T(k)\hat{p} + \sqrt{r^T(k)Pr(k)}. \qquad (16)$$

The elementary models in the next layers are created based on outputs incoming from the previous layer. Since (16) describes the model output uncertainty, parameters of the elementary models in the next layers has to be obtained with an approach that solves the problem of an uncertain regressor [4]. Let $r(k)$ denote an known measured value of the regressor, while $r_n(k)$ is an unknown "true" value

$$r(k) = r_n(k) + e(k), \qquad (17)$$

where the regressor error $e(k)$ is bounded as follows:

$$-\epsilon_i \leq e_i(k) \leq \epsilon_i, \quad i = 1, \dots, n_p. \qquad (18)$$

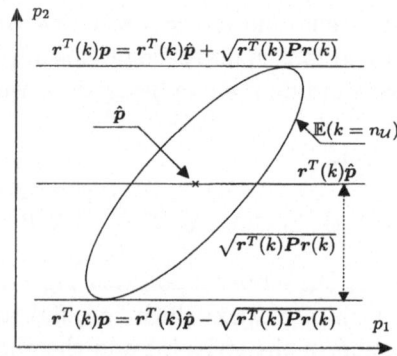

Fig. 1. Relation between the model output uncertainty and the ellipsoid

Substituting (17) into (16) and then using (18) it can be show that the elementary models output uncertainty have following form:

$$y^m(k)(\hat{p}) \leq r^T(k)p \leq y^M(k)(\hat{p}), \qquad (19)$$

where

$$y^m(k)(\hat{p}) = r_n^T(k)\hat{p} + \sum_{i=1}^{n_p} \mathrm{sgn}(\hat{p}_i)\hat{p}_i\epsilon_i - \sqrt{\bar{r}_n^T(k)P\bar{r}_n(k)}, \qquad (20)$$

$$y^M(k)(\hat{p}) = r_n^T(k)\hat{p} + \sum_{i=1}^{n_p} \mathrm{sgn}(\hat{p}_i)\hat{p}_i\epsilon_i + \sqrt{\bar{r}_n^T(k)P\bar{r}_n(k)}, \qquad (21)$$

$$\bar{r}_{n,i}(k) = r_{n,i}(k) + \mathrm{sgn}\left(r_{n,i}(k)\right)\epsilon_i. \qquad (22)$$

5   An Illustrative Example

Let us consider the following static system

$$y'(k) = p_1 \sin(u_1^2(k)) + p_2 u_2^2(k) + \varepsilon(k), \qquad (23)$$

where the nominal values of parameters are $p = [0.9, -0.3]^T$, the input data $u(k)$ and the noise $\varepsilon(k)$, $k = 1, \ldots, n_T$ are generated according to the uniform distribution, i.e. $u(k) \in \mathcal{U}(0,2)$ and $\varepsilon(k) \in \mathcal{U}(-0.05, 0.1)$. Note that the noise does not satisfy (3). The problem is to obtain the parameter estimate $\hat{p}$ and the elementary model output uncertainty using the set of input-output measurements $\{(u(k), y(k))\}_{k=1}^{n_T=200}$. To tackle this task, two methods were employed, i.e. the approach described in Section 4 and the LSM. In order to obtain the feasible parameter set for the LSM, the F-test [1] was employed and a 99% confidence region was obtained. Whilst in the case of the OBE it was assumed that $\varepsilon_k^m = -0.4$, $\varepsilon_k^M = 0.8$. The results are shown in Tab. 1 and Fig. 2.

Table 1. A comparative study - OBE vs. LSM

p	OBE $\hat{p}$	OBE $[p^{min}, p^{max}]$	LSM $\hat{p}$	LSM $[p^{min}, p^{max}]$
p_1	0.903	[0.714,1.092]	1.139	[1.102,1.176]
p_2	-0.309	[-0.362,-0.257]	-0.508	[-0.556,-0.460]

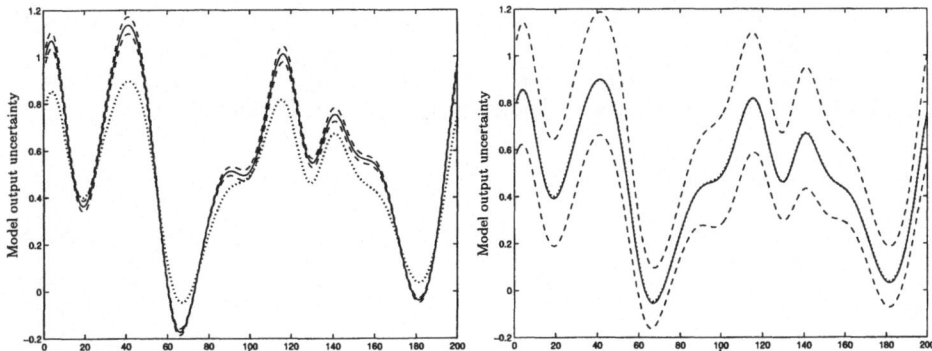

Fig. 2. True output $(\cdots)$, model output $(—)$ and its uncertainty (- -) for LSM (left) and OBE (right)

From the above results it is clear that the OBE is superior to the LSM. Indeed, as can be seen the parameter confidence interval for the LSM does not even contain the nominal parameter values. Whilst in the case of the OBE the parameter estimate is close to the nominal parameter values and they are, of course, contained in the parameter confidence interval.

6   Conclusions

The objective of this paper was concerned with obtaining models and calculating their uncertainty directly from the observed data. It was shown how to estimate parameters and the corresponding uncertainty of an individual elementary model and the whole GMDH neural network. The proposed solution is based on the OBE algorithm which is superior to the celebrated LSM in many practical applications. The presented methodology can by useful while using the quantitative model-based fault diagnosis techniques. The further research direction is oriented towards the design of robust fault detection systems based on the proposed approach.

References

1. Atkinson, A.C., Donev, A.N.: Optimum Experimental Designs. Oxford University Press New York (1992)

2. Duch, W., Korbicz, J., Rutkowski, L., Tadeusiewicz, R. (Eds.): Biocybernetics and Biomedical Engineering 2000. Neural Networks. Akademicka Oficyna Wydawnicza, Exit, Warsaw (2000) (in Polish)
3. Farlow, S. J.: Self-organizing Methods in Modelling. GMDH-type Algorithms. Marcel Dekker Inc. New York (1995)
4. Milanese, M., Norton, J., Piet-Lahanier, H., Walter, E. (Eds.): Bounding Approaches to System Identification. Plenum Press. New York (1996)
5. Papadopoulos, G., Edawrds, P.J., Murray, A. F.: Confidence estimation methods for neural networks: A practical comparison. IEEE Trans. Neural Networks **12** (2001) 1279-1287
6. Korbicz, J., Kościelny, J.M., Kowalczuk, Z., Cholewa, W. (Eds.): Fault Diagnosis. Models, Artificial Intelligence, Applications. Springer. Berlin (2004)

On Some Factors Influencing MLP Error Surface

Mirosław Kordos[1] and Włodzisław Duch[2,3]

[1] Faculty of Automatic Control, Electronics and Computer Science, The Silesian University of Technology, Gliwice, Poland.
[2] Department of Informatics, Nicholas Copernicus University, Toruń, Poland,
http://www.phys.uni.torun.pl/kmk
[3] School of Computer Engineering, Nanyang Technological University, Singapore.

Abstract. Visualization of MLP error surfaces helps to understand the influence of network structure and training data on neural learning dynamics. PCA is used to determine two orthogonal directions that capture almost all variance in the weight space. 3-dimensional plots show many aspects of the original error surfaces.

1   Introduction

Multi-layer perceptron (MLP) error surface (ES) $E(\mathbf{W}) = \sum_{\mathbf{X}} \|\mathbf{Y} - M(\mathbf{X}; \mathbf{W})\|$ is defined in the weight space $\mathbf{W}$ (including biases as W_0 weights) for a given training data $\mathbf{X}$, desired output vector $\mathbf{Y}$ and structure of network mapping $M(\mathbf{X}; \mathbf{W})$. Only mean-square error functions are considered here, so $\| \cdot \|$ is Euclidean norm and $E(\mathbf{W}) = \sum_{\mathbf{X}} \|\mathbf{Y} - M(\mathbf{X}; \mathbf{W})\|^2$. Learning processes are trajectories that lie on the hyper-surface $E(\mathbf{W})$ in the weight space $\mathbf{W}$. To understand learning dynamics error surface can be visualized using projections of the original space onto a three-dimensional subspace. In all plots presented here we use sigmoidal transfer functions, but ES projections obtained with hyperbolic tangent do not differ significantly.

It is beneficial to choose the projection directions which preserve most information about the original surface character. PCA (Principal Component Analysis) proved a good method of determining the directions. The network was trained using several algorithms, but the results were algorithm independent. The used algorithms included standard backpropagation (BP) [3], numerical gradient (NG) [1] and search-based methods (SM) [2]. Weight vectors $W(t)$ after each training epoch t were collected into the weight matrix. The training was stopped when the error begun decreasing very slowly (close to convergence). Singular Value Decomposition (SVD) was performed either on the weight matrix, or on the weight covariance matrix to determine principal components (all results here are for covariance matrices).

Typically the first and second PCA directions contain together about 95% of the total variance and therefore the plots reflect ES properties very well. The ES character is determined by the dataset and network structure but not by the training method and starting point. Several training methods (various versions of NG, SM and BP) have been used for the same network structure and training set. The training has been repeated several times for a given method with various random initial weights. Neither the random weight distribution, nor the training method, nor the number of training cycles for which PCA is calculated has significant influence on the ES presented in the space of two

L. Rutkowski et al. (Eds.): ICAISC 2004, LNAI 3070, pp. 217–222, 2004.
© Springer-Verlag Berlin Heidelberg 2004

main PCA components. The plots may differ slightly, especially those obtained with BP, because BP depends more on initialization and produces ES projections that are not so uniform. The surface may rotate from one plot to another, its fragments may be a bit higher or lower, but the overall structure is well preserved. Experiments with over 20 datasets, most of them from the UCI dataset repository [4], have been made. Due to the limited space only a few ES are shown here. The name of a dataset in figure labels is followed by numbers of neurons in the successive layers; for example, in Fig. 1 Iris 4-4-3 means that the network trained on Iris data had 4 input, 4 hidden and 3 output neurons.

At the final stage of the training weights of output neurons tend to grow quicker then those of hidden neurons, but since the training is stopped before convergence weights of each layer have comparable contributions in determining PCA directions. Vertical axis in the plots shows relative error $E_r(\mathbf{W}) = E(\mathbf{W})/N_v N_c$, where N_v is the number of vectors and N_c is the number of classes in the training set. For all error functions based on Minkovsky's metric $|| \cdot ||_\alpha$ the error function is bounded from above by $N_v N_c$, thus the relative error is bounded by 1. Horizontal axes show distances in the weight space in c_1 and c_2 PCA directions corresponding to the first and second eigenvector of the weight covariance matrix.

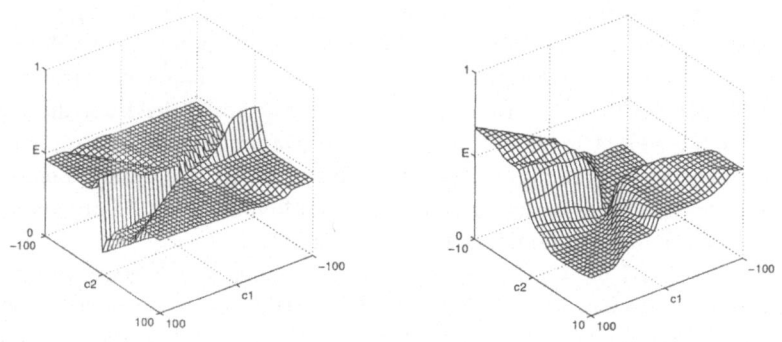

Fig. 1. The same error surface of a 3-layer network (Iris 4-4-3). Left: in original proportions, right: the scale of c2 axis multiplied by e_2/e_1 (this scaling is used for all drawings)

Usually the first PCA eigenvalue e_1 is an order of magnitude larger than the second one e_2. For that reason the plots are easier to interpret if unequal scales are used on horizontal exes (Fig. 1, right). For this purpose projections on c_2 are rescaled by the ratio e_2/e_1 of the second to the first eigenvalue of the weight covariance matrix. But it should be taken into consideration that in the rescaled plots the ill-conditioning and narrowness of the ravines are not so well visible as in pictures made in original proportions (Fig. 1, left).

2   Network Structure Influence on Error Surface

A network without a hidden layer has a very simple ES consisting only of two or four horizontal or slightly inclined half-planes, situated on various heights, with slopes connecting them (Fig. 2, left). ES of networks with hidden layers has a "starfish" structure. A
vivid depiction of such ES was given by Denker et. al [5] "$E(\mathbf{W})$ surface resembles a
sombrero or a phono record that has been warped in certain symmetric ways: near the
middle ($\mathbf{W}=0$) all configurations have moderately bad E values. Radiating out from the
center are a great number of ridges and valleys. The valleys get deeper as they go out, but
asymptotically level out. In the best valleys, E is exactly or asymptotically zero, other
valleys have higher floors". The pictures presented in this paper confirm that global minima rarely create craters but frequently ravines reaching their minimum in infinity. This
corresponds to the infinite growth of (usually output layer) weights when the training is
continued for a sufficiently long time.

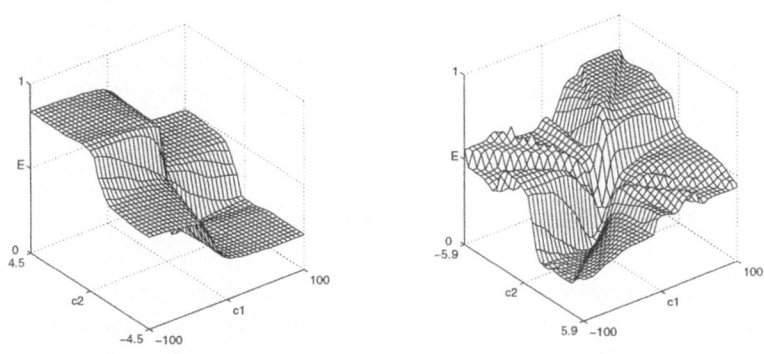

Fig. 2. Left: ES of 2-layer network (Iris 4-3); right: ES of 4-layer network (Iris 4-4-4-3)

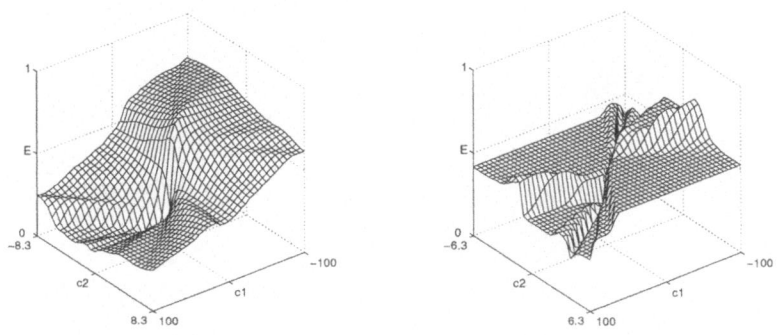

Fig. 3. Left: ES of 3-layer network with crossover connections (Iris 4-4-3); right: ES of 3-layer
network with too many hidden neurons (Iris 4-100-3)

Each of h hidden neurons may be labeled by an arbitrary and unique number from 1 to h. Renumerating the network parameters does not change the mapping implemented by the network thus giving $h!$ permutational symmetries. A neural activation function for which $f(-x) = -f(x) + const$ gives further 2^h sign-flip symmetries [6]. This gives together $2^h h!$ equivalent global minima. A training algorithm converges to that minimum, which is easiest to reach from the starting point. Only some of the minima are clearly visible in the PCA projections. Their number originally grows with the increase of hidden neurons number, but with too many hidden neurons big horizontal planes begin to appear Fig. 3, right). This effect caused by the weight redundancy is better perceptible in a two-weight coordinate system, where the projected ES is almost flat since many weights must be changed at the same time to change the error.

In 3-layer networks with crossover connections the output layer is connected directly to both; the input (as in 2-layer networks) and the hidden layer (as in 3-layer networks). Consequently their ES display features of 2-layer networks (asymmetry of ES) and 3-layers networks (complexity of ES) (Fig. 3, left). A network with too few neurons in any hidden layer cannot map all required information and as a result is unable to learn the task. Its ES consists of several horizontal planes, all placed relatively high, with some rough areas between them, but it does not show characteristic ravines leading to global minima (not shown here). Four-layer networks have more complex ES than the three-layer ones, even with fewer neurons. Thus they can map more complex data (Fig. 2, right).

3   Training Data Influence on Error Surface

In all the experiments presented in this section a similar network structure x-4-2 has been used for various datasets. More complex training data produces more complex ES, especially if the data is not linearly separable, as in the case of n-bit parity.

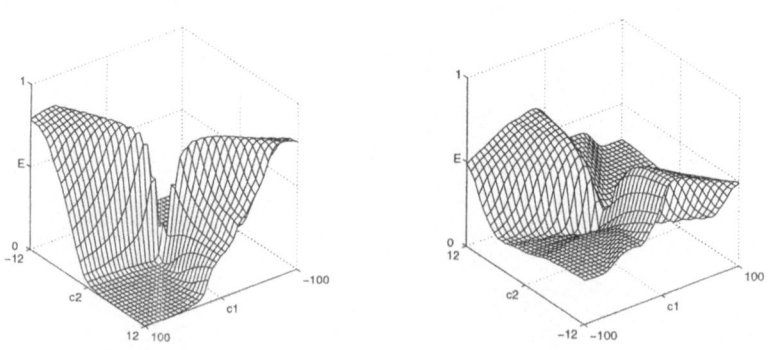

Fig. 4. Left: ES of Breast (10-4-3). Right: ES of Ionosphere (43-4-2)

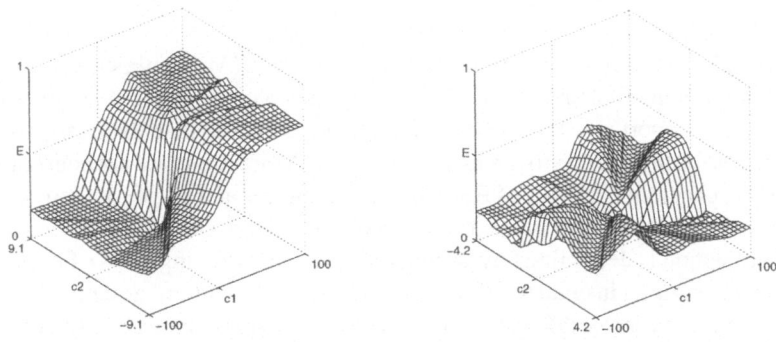

Fig. 5. Left: ES of entire Appendicitis dataset (12-4-3). Right: ES of Appendicitis dataset (12-4-3) with only 44 vectors - all 22 vectors of class 1 and randomly chosen 22 vectors of class 2

Equal distribution of examples among classes leads to a more symmetric ES [7]. Appendicitis (21 vectors of class 0 and 85 of class 1) gives a highly non-symmetric ES (Fig. 5, left). Selecting 42 vectors from the dataset, all of class 0 and 21 vectors randomly chosen from class 1, produces a quite symmetric error surface. Other datasets have approximately equal number of vectors in each class thus their ES are more symmetric. Breast dataset has two classes with a few overlapping vectors, and therefore its ES is quite simple (Fig. 4, left). Iris (Fig. 1, right) has 3 classes with little overlap, and ionosphere (Fig. 4, right) two classes with some more overlap, and they both give similar ES. XOR data is linearly non-separable and therefore has a complex ES (Fig. 6, left). 6-bit parity (Fig. 6, right) is linearly non-separable and has 32 clusters per class (XOR has only 2). ES for even-bit parity problems is highly intricate, however it is symmetric because of equal class distribution.

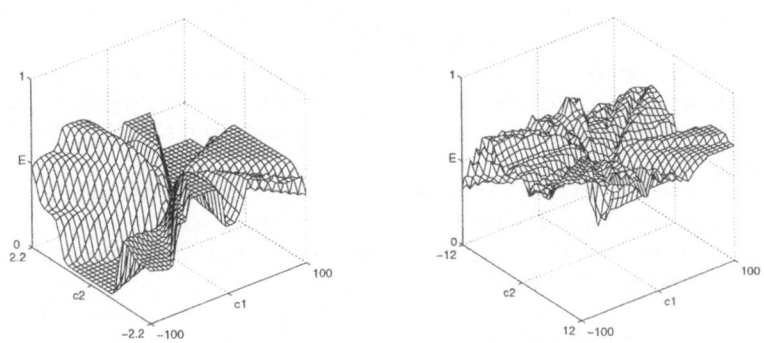

Fig. 6. Left: ES of xor (4-4-3). Right: ES of 6-bit parity (12-8-2)

4   Conclusions

Although it is impossible to see the error surface $E(\mathbf{W})$ without any distortions, displaying it in the first and second PCA component coordinate system gives good insight into many important ES properties (incomparably better than using any two weight system). Nevertheless due to the fact that local PCA directions are not constant in the entire weight space, such aspects of ES as ravine curvatures and slopes of their bottoms are not especially well reflected in the projections which use global PCA directions (the shape of ES projection is determined by weight changes in all training steps). For real-world data sets local minima in craters are very rare for networks with monotone transfer functions. Large plateaus accessible via narrow ravines, or ravines that lead to plateaus with larger error (due to poor network initialization) may cause many difficulties in neural training algorithms. The bigger is the difference between the first and the second eigenvalue, the more difficult and slower is the training procedure, because the training algorithm has to find proper direction very precisely. When the difference exceeds two orders of magnitude the training effectiveness may be severely affected.

ES depends on network structure, training data, transfer and error functions, but not on training methods. ES has greatest diversity close to its center. Far from the center flat horizontal planes occupy large areas. If the range of random initial weights is too broad then it is likely that the starting point lies somewhere on the flat area, and as a result the network cannot be trained with gradient-based or local search method. On the contrary, if all initial weights are zero the network can be successfully trained with search-based techniques [2]. Backpropagation methods cannot start from zero weights [3], but this is only due to the limitations of the algorithms, and not of the properties of the zero point on the error surface.

Perhaps an interesting suggestions from this study will be also to use PCA to re-duce the effective number of training parameters to a few.

References

1. M. Kordos, W. Duch, "Multilayer Perceptron Trained with Numerical Gradient." Int. Conf. on Artificial Neural Networks, Istanbul, June 2003, pp. 106-109
2. M. Kordos, W. Duch, "Search-based Training for Logical Rule Extraction by Multilayer Perceptron." Int. Conf. on Artificial Neural Networks, Istanbul, June 2003, pp. 86-89
3. S. Haykin, *Neural networks: a comprehensive foundations*. New York: MacMillian Publishing, 1994.
4. C.J. Mertz, P.M. Murphy, UCI repository of machine learning databases, http://www.ics.uci.edu/pub/machine-learning-data-bases
5. J. Denker et. al. "Large automatic learning, rule extraction and generalization". Complex Systems, 1, pp. 887-922, 1987.
6. H.J. Sussmann, "Uniqueness of the weights for minimal feedforward nets with a given input-output map", Neural Networks, 5, pp. 589-593, 1992.
7. M.R. Gallagher, "Multi-layer Perceptron Error Surfaces: Visualization, Structure and Modeling", PhD Thesis, University of Queensland, 2000

Discovery of Linguistic Rules by Means of RBF Network for Fault Detection in Electronic Circuits

Jan Koszlaga and Pawel Strumillo

Institute of Electronics, Technical University of Łódź, 223 Wólczańska, 90-924 Łódź, Poland, {koszlaga,pstrumil}@p.lodz.pl

Abstract. A neural network based knowledge discovery method for single fault detection in electronics circuits is presented. A functional equivalence of Radial Basis Function (RBF) neural network and Takagi-Sugeno (TS) fuzzy system is used in this process. A specially modified incremental RBF network training scheme suitable for rule discovery is used. Next, the RBF neural network is converted into the TS fuzzy system. A set of linguistic rules for detection of circuit catastrophic faults are obtained (100% detection accuracy was achieved for the tested electronic circuit).

1   Introduction

In recent years there has been an increased research interest in the development of new testing methods of analogue electronic circuits. Detection of two major faults of electronic circuits are of interest: catastrophic (hard) and soft (the so called deviation) faults. Catastrophic faults occur due to faulty element, either short or open circuit. Deviation faults occur when circuit parameter value is out of its predefined tolerance range [1]. Detection of faults in electronic circuits is based on a limited number of circuit inputs, outputs and types of testing signals [2]. Construction of analytical models of circuit faults is difficult due to complex nonlinear dependence between fault types and characteristics of the testing signals [3].

In this study a method for discovering linguistic rules between characteristics of the observed testing signals and catastrophic faults in electronic circuits is proposed. The method employs artificial neural network for knowledge acquisition. Network equivalence to fuzzy systems is exploited for working out the rules.

2   RBF Network Training for Rule Discovery

A limited a priori knowledge is available about faults in electronic circuits and their manifestations in the testing signals. An experienced engineer, however, works outs its own database of typical cases and rules leading to fault detection.

L. Rutkowski et al. (Eds.): ICAISC 2004, LNAI 3070, pp. 223–228, 2004.
© Springer-Verlag Berlin Heidelberg 2004

Collection of a large number of testing data (fault cases and signal characteristics) indicates concentrated clusters in a space spanned by variables representing different faults. Such a cluster like statistical distribution of data can be appropriately modelled by means of kernel-based density estimation. In fact a Radial Basis Function (RBF) neural network can be viewed as a special case of the density estimation approach [4]. This type of network is used it this study for modelling data representing faults in electronic circuits.

RBF network is a feedforward network with one hidden layer of radial transfer functions (kernels):

$$\varphi_j = \varphi\left(\| x - c_j \|\right), j = 1, \ldots, M \tag{1}$$

where: $x \in X$ is the network input vector, c_j identifies position of a radial function in the input space $X \in R^N$ and $\| . \|$ is the Euclidean norm. Typically, Gaussian function $\varphi(x) = \exp \frac{-(x-c)^2}{2\sigma^2}$ is used as the RBF network transfer function. Network output F, is the result of weighted linear superposition of radial functions outputs:

$$F(x) = \sum_{j=1}^{M} w_j \varphi_j \tag{2}$$

where: w_j - weight associated with j-th basis function.

Certain modifications have been introduced for the presented standard RBF network that make this network more suitable for data discovery applications.

2.1   Dimension Selective Perceptive Field of the RBF Network

RBF network layer plays the role of a receptive field sensing each of the input dimensions. For Gaussian basis functions one gets:

$$\varphi(x; c_j; \sigma_j) = \exp\left[-\left(\frac{(x_{i1} - c_{j1})^2}{2\sigma_{j1}^2} + \frac{(x_{i2} - c_{j2})^2}{2\sigma_{j2}^2} + \ldots + \frac{(x_{iN} - c_{jN})^2}{2\sigma_{jN}^2}\right)\right] =$$

$$= \exp\left[-\left(a_{j1} + a_{j2} + \ldots + a_{jN}\right)\right] \tag{3}$$

As shown in next sections, for data discovery applications an additional flexibility in which each basis function could sense a pre-selected subset of all N-dimensional space is of hand. Namely, a binary matrix is introduced:

$$L = \begin{bmatrix} l_{11} & l_{12} & \cdots & l_{1N} \\ l_{21} & l_{22} & \cdots & l_{2N} \\ \vdots & \vdots & \ddots & \vdots \\ l_{M1} & l_{M2} & \cdots & l_{MN} \end{bmatrix} \tag{4}$$

in which each element l_{ji} of L is either zero or one. Equation (3) thus can be modified to the following form:

$$\varphi\left(x; c_j; \sigma_j\right) = \varphi\left(\|\ x - c_j\ \|; \sigma_j\right) = \exp\left[-\left(a_{j1}l_{j1} + a_{j2}l_{j2} + \ldots + a_{jN}l_{jN}\right)\right] \quad (5)$$

Zero value of l_{ji} element in L indicates that j-th basis function neglects i-th dimension in N-dimensional input data space.

2.2 Network Training

An evolutionary algorithm for constructive optimisation of RBF network kernels [5,6] was used in which the optimised parameters were augmented by elements of matrix L i.e. for each m-th kernel matrix elements $L^m = \{l_1^m, l_2^m, \ldots, l_N^m\}$ were included into the optimization procedure. Steps of the network training algorithm are the following:

1. Generate initial population of random individuals.
2. Use genetic operators on the current population (crossover and mutation).
3. Select a new population.
4. Check network performance by using the values of matrix L.

This evolutionary procedure for constructive training of RBF network employs as many kernels as the extracted rules [7]. Each such rule is equally important in generating a rule base. Hence, output training of RBF network has been omitted and all weights in (2) are set to unity.

3 RBF Network to Fuzzy System Conversion

A functional equivalence between RBF network and the Takagi-Sugeno (TS) fuzzy system was shown in [8]. This equivalence is exploited in the reported application for building a knowledge discovery system. By converting a trained RBF neural network into a fuzzy system (with kernel membership functions) one can get a linguistic rule base for the modelled problem.

Takagi-Sugeno fuzzy system transfer function is given by:

$$y = \sum_{j=1}^{M} y_j\left(x\right) h_j\left(x\right) \quad (6)$$

where h_j - is the value associated with j-th rule derived from a product of membership functions, y_j - is a function of an action part of j-th rule in a fuzzy system. By using equations (2), (6) and the substitutions:

$$W_j\left(x\right) = y_j\left(x\right) \quad (7)$$

$$\Phi_j\left(x\right) = h_j\left(x\right) \quad (8)$$

the noted functional equivalence between RBF network and the TS fuzzy system can be established [8]. There are as many rules in a fuzzy system as the number of kernels in an RBF network.

4   Computing Results

The proposed method for rule extraction was tested on the problem of catastrophic fault detection in an electronic circuit [9]. The circuit under test (CUT) is a low-pass active filter as shown in Fig. 1a. In-system functional tests limit CUT measurements to input and output test points only. Hence, stimulation-response testing scheme was applied. The CUT SPICE model was stimulated with sinusoidal waves of constant amplitudes and different frequencies and the output voltage was measured. This testing scheme was carried out for all single catastrophic faults of CUT discrete components (resistors and capacitors). Frequency characteristics of the filter for such different circuit faults are shown in Fig. 1b.

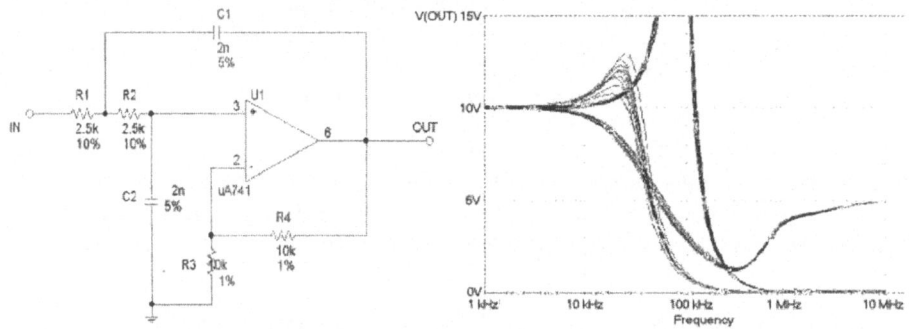

Fig. 1. Schematic of the CUT (an active low-pass filter $f_{3dB} = 60kHz$ (a), filter frequency transfer characteristics for different catastrophic single faults of CUT passive components (b)

For each of the fault case (Table. 1) and one non-fault case, ten Monte-Carlo simulations using PSCPICE software package (including elements' tolerances) were run. For each of the simulations four sinusoidal waves (1 kHz, 10 kHz, 0.1 MHz, 1 MHz) with 5V peak-to-peak amplitude were used as the input test signal. As a result of this simulation procedure, 90 four-element vectors of circuit output voltages were obtained. This data set was randomly partitioned into the training set (63 vectors) and the testing set (27 vectors).

Table 1. Faults in the tested circuit

Fault No	A kind of fault	Fault No	A kind of fault
1	Capacitor C1 short	5	Resistor R1 short
2	Capacitor C1 open	6	Resistor R1 open
3	Capacitor C2 short	7	Resistor R2 short
4	Capacitor C2 open	8	Resistor R2 open

Genetically driven RBF network training procedure as outlined in section 2.2 has generated eight basis functions defined in a four-dimensional inputs space. Network inputs correspond to voltage values of four frequencies of the signals obtained at the circuit output. Due to constructive network training procedure each kernel function is tuned to respond with logical high value to a different single fault occurrence only. The generated RBF network can be converted into the TS fuzzy system (see section 3). The set of fuzzy membership functions (given in Table 2) allows for detection of all circuit catastrophic faults with 100% accuracy.

Table 2. Parameters of kernel functions (coordinates of the centres and widths $(2\sigma^2)$ in the parenthesis). An empty field in the table informs that the kernel function is not sensitive to the indicated input space dimension.

| | Testing frequencies | | | |
	f=1 kHz	f=10 kHz	f=0.1 MHz	f=1 MHz
Kernel 1		0.0025 (0.0011)		0.0025 (0.0037)
Kernel 2		8.3915 (0.7975)	1.4543 (0.5102)	
Kernel 3	0.0000 (0.0480)			0.0603 (0.0186)
Kernel 4			3.3506 (0.7742)	0.2012 (0.0393)
Kernel 5				3.2671 (0.9192)
Kernel 6			0.0000 (0.0020)	
Kernel 7				0.2631 (0.0291)
Kernel 8		0.0000 (0.0002)		0.0020 (0.0004)

Example: for detection of short-circuited capacitor C1 if suffices to measure output voltage for f=10kHz and f=1MHz. If U_{10kHz} is close to 2.5mV (small) and (U_{1MHz} is close to 2.5mV (see kernel 1 parameters in Table 2) then fault type 1 (short-circuited C1) is detected.

A complete set of extracted linguistic rules for detecting single catastrophic faults in the CUT are the following:

R1: if (U_{10kHz} is "small") and (U_{1MHz} is "very small")   **then** C1 short
R2: if (U_{10kHz} is "large") and ($U_{0.1MHz}$ is "medium")   **then** C1 open
R3: if (U_{1kHz} is "small") and (U_{1MHz} is "small")   **then** C2 short
R4: if ($U_{0.1MHz}$ is "large") and (U_{1MHz} is "medium")   **then** C2 open
R5: if (U_{1MHz} is "very large")   **then** R1 short
R6: if ($U_{0.1MHz}$ is "small")   **then** R1 open
R7: if (U_{1MHz} is "large")   **then** R2 short
R8: if (U_{10kHz} is "small") and (U_{1MHz} is "very very small")   **then** R2 open

5   Conclusion

It was demonstrated that an artificial neural network can be a valid tool for discovering linguistic rules identifying faults in analog electronic systems. A specially designed RBF network training procedure allows for obtaining a compact size network for knowledge acquisition. A functional equivalence between RBF network and the TS fuzzy system was exploited for building a linguistic description of the acquired knowledge. This description is given in a form of optimised (due to constructive RBF network training scheme) set of simple linguistic rules.

The proposed method for knowledge discovery was validated on frequency-domain tests of an electronic circuit (low-pass active filter). The knowledge extraction system was trained to detect single catastrophic faults of circuit passive components. These types of faults were detected by the developed system with 100% accuracy.

Further work is under way for developing automatic testing procedures for location of soft and catastrophic faults in increasingly complex electronic circuits.

References

[1] Bandler J. W., Salama A. E.: Fault diagnosis of analog circuits. Proceedings of the IEEE, vol. 73, no. 8, 1985, pp. 1279-1325.
[2] Rutkowski J. Dictionary diagnostic methods for testing analog electronic cirucits. (in Polish) WKŁ, Warszawa 2003.
[3] Korbicz J.: Process diagnostics. (in Polish) WNT Warszawa 2002.
[4] Strumillo P., Kaminski W.: Radial Basis Function Neural Networks: Theory and Applicatiuons. Neural Networks and Soft Computing, Physica-Verlag, Heidelberg, (Eds. L. Rutkowski, J. Kacprzyk), 2003, pp. 107-119.
[5] Michalewicz Z. Genetic algorithms + data structures = evolution programs (in Polish). WNT, Warszawa 1996.
[6] Koszlaga J., Strumillo P.: Evolutionary algorithm vs. other methods for constructive optimisation of RBF network kernels. Neural Networks and Soft Computing (Eds. L. Rutkowski, J. Kacprzyk), Physica Verlag, Heidelberg, 2003, pp. 212-217.
[7] Koszlaga J., Strumillo P.: Rule Extraction from Trained Radial Basis Function Neural Networks. Colloquia in Artificial Intelligence £ód"Y, Poland, October 2000, pp. 97-106.
[8] Hunt K.J., Hass R., Murray-Smith R.: Extending the Functional Equivalence of Radial Basis Function Networks and Fuzzy Inference Systems. IEEE Trans. Neural Networks. vol. 7, no. 3, 1996, pp. 776-781.
[9] Catelani M., Fort A., Alippi C.: A fuzzy approach for soft fault detection in analog circuits. Measurement 32, 2002, pp. 73-83.

Combining Space-Filling Curves and Radial Basis Function Networks

Adam Krzyżak[1] and Ewa Skubalska-Rafajłowicz[2]

[1] Department of Computer Science, Concordia University, Montreal, Canada.
krzyzak@cs.concordia.ca
[2] Institute of Engineering Cybernetics, Wrocław University of Technology,
Wybrzeże Wyspiańskiego 27, 50 370 Wrocław, Poland.
raf@ldhpux.immt.pwr.wroc.pl

Abstract. We propose here to use a space-filling curve (SFC) as a tool to introduce a new metric in I_d defined as a distance along the space-filling curve. This metric is to be used inside radial functions instead of the Euclidean or the Mahalanobis distance. This approach is equivalent to using SFC to pre-process the input data before training the RBF net. All the network tuning operations are performed in one dimension. Furthermore, we introduce a new method of computing the weights of linear output neuron, which is based on connection between RBF net and Nadaraya-Watson kernel regression estimators.

1 Introduction

The radial basis function networks have been extensively applied to pattern recognition, function approximation or regression function estimation. Radial bases functions were introduced in the solution of the multivariate interpolation problem [15]. We refer the reader to [3], [4], [5], [9], [10], [21], [22], [8] and [6] for basic facts and some recent results concerning RBF nets.

A basic radial-basis function (RBF) network consists of three layers having entirely different roles: an input layer, a hidden layer, which applies a nonlinear transformation from the input space to the hidden space and a linear output layer (it could also be normalized so that outputs sum to one). We discuss RBF nets with one output only, since the generalization to multi-output nets is immediate. Thus, RBF net can be described in the following form

$$f_N(x) = \sum_{i=1}^{N} w_i G(||x - c_i||) + w_0, \qquad (1)$$

where $x \in R^d$, $c_i \in R^d$, are tunable vectors, w_i are tunable weights, and N is a number of neurons. Usually $||x||$ is the Euclidean norm, however also generalized weighted norm $||x||_{Q_i}$, defined by the quadratic form $||x||_{Q_i}^2 = x^T Q_i^T Q_i x$ can be used, where Q_i are (usually tunable) $d \times d$ matrices.

L. Rutkowski et al. (Eds.): ICAISC 2004, LNAI 3070, pp. 229–234, 2004.
© Springer-Verlag Berlin Heidelberg 2004

There exists a broad selection of radial functions $G(r)$ which are often used in RBF networks. Gausssian RBF nets i.e. the nets with

$$G(r) = \exp\left(-\frac{r^2}{2\sigma^2}\right) \text{ for some } \sigma > 0 \text{ and } r \in \mathcal{R}$$

seem to be the most popular in the neural networks literature.

The second type of RBF nets uses the normalized RBF activation functions, so the activations of all hidden neurons sum to one [11].

$$g_N(x) = \frac{\sum_{i=1}^{N} w_i G(||x - c_i||)}{\sum_{i=1}^{N} G(||x - c_i||)} \tag{2}$$

The parameters of the networks (1) or (2) can be learned from an n-sample observation data set (learning sequence) $L_n = ((X_1, Y_1), \ldots, (X_n, Y_n))$.

There are three groups of parameters in the RBF networks which may be learned or arbitrary chosen: the weights w_i, the centers c_i and some parameters of radial basis functions, for example σ or Q_i matrices.

RBF networks can be trained in many different ways [1], [18]. Especially, there exists a broad selection of papers on selecting the number and positions of the radial basis functions (see for example [7] for the review). It should be mentioned in the context of the space-filling curve, that Whitehead and Chaote [23] applied some kind of space-filling curves, namely, the devotail mapping, to uniformly distribute initial positions of the RBF's centers. In their approach the parameters of the devotail mappings (known also as "zig-zag" curves) are evolved genetically. Another method of selecting RBF centers is based on placing prototypes of the centers initially at equidistributed (EQD) points generated by an algorithm based on space-filling curves [16].

In general, the complexity of the RBF network increases when the dimension of the net's input grows. In this paper we propose to apply a space-filling curve (SFC) based metric in I_d defined as distance along the space-filling curve. This metric is to be used inside radial functions instead of the Euclidean or Mahalanobice distance. This approach is equivalent to using the SFC to pre-process the input data before training the RBF net.

2 Radial Bases Functions Network with Reduced Input Dimension Based on Space-Filling Curve

A space-filling curve is a continuous mapping from unit interval $I = [0, 1]$ onto the multi-dimensional cube $I_d = [0, 1] \times [0, 1] \times \ldots [0, 1]$. The examples of such curves have been given by Peano, Hilbert, Sierpiński among others [17].

The useful definition and properties of the space-filling curve are summarized in the Appendix (see also [20], [19] for other details and extended bibliography on the topic). The space-filling curve can serve as mathematical vehicle to organize multidimensional data along a line.

2.1 Metric Introduced by a Space-Filling Curve

Let $F(t) : I_1 \to I_d$ be a chosen space-filling curve. According to the invariance of domain theorem a space-filling curve cannot be one-to-one. Thus, its inverse does not exists, but it suffices to construct a quasi-inverse, which is defined almost everywhere and such that for each $x \in I_d$ we can quickly compute a $t \in I_1$ such that $F(t) = x$. Let $\Psi(x) : I_d \to I_1$ stands for the quasi-inverse of F_d.

One can define a new metric in I_d introduced by space-filling curve $F_d(t)$ (and its quasi-inverse $\Psi(x)$) as:

$$d_{SFC}(X, X') = |\Psi(X) - \Psi(X')|, \quad X, X' \in I_d \tag{3}$$

Note, that

1. $d_{SFC}(X, X') \geq 0$ for every $X, X' \in I_d$.

2. $d_{SFC}(X, X') = 0$ if and only if $X = X'$

3. (triangle inequality): If $X, X', X'' \in I_d$,
   then $d_{SFC}(X, X') \leq d_{SFC}(X, X'') + d_{SFC}(X'', X')$

A radial bases function based on the distance along SFC is of the form

$$G(\|x - c\|_{SFC}) = G(|\Psi(x) - \Psi(c)|),$$

where G is any chosen radial function. Thus, one obtains a new (one-dimensional) RBF net:

$$f_{SFC,N}(t) = \sum_{i=1}^{N} v_i G(|t - c_{SFC,i}|), \quad t = \Psi(x) \in [0, 1], \tag{4}$$

where $c_{SFC,i}$ and v_i, $i = 1, \ldots, N$ are tunable parameters of the net.

2.2 Preprocessing of Learning Sequence

Let $L_n = ((X_1, Y_1), \ldots, (X_n, Y_n))$ be a given learning sequence, where $X_i \in R^d$. For simplicity, it is assumed that all observations lie within a region which is hyper-cubic with unit volume, i.e. $X_i \in I_d$.

The RBF net with metric d_{SFC} can be effectively tuned (learned) by means of a new one-dimensional learning sequence obtained as follow:

1. For each sample (X_i, Y_i) compute $t_i \in [0, 1]$ such that $F_d(t_i) = X_i$, i.e., compute $\Psi(X_i)$.
2. Sort the new learning sequence according to their corresponding t_i's.

The new learning sequence is of the form

$$(t_{(1)}, Y_{(1)}), (t_{(2)}, Y_{(2)}), \ldots (t_{(N)}, Y_{(n)}),$$

where $(t_{(1)} \leq t_{(2)} \leq \ldots t_{(n)}$. The position of a point along the space-filling curve can be computed iteratively in time $O(d)$, linearly depending on dimension of the space I_d [20], [2], [12].

3   Learning RBF Networks with Reduced Data Dimension

RBF networks can be related to Parzen window estimators of a probability density or to Nadaraya-Watson regression estimators [6], [22], [1]. Similarities between the RBF network structure and kernel regression estimators lead to RBF networks with the centers chosen to be a subset of the training input vectors and associated weights which directly correspond to Y_i's [22].

The advantage of this approach is in the lack of the net training phase. On the other hand, the smaller is the number of the RBF functions the greater is the amount of learning data which are not used.

Assume that the centers of the net $c_{SFC,j}$ are already chosen, for example, using self-organizing map data quantization method [18].

Here, we propose to compute the weights of the net (4) as the kernel regression estimator [10] of the underling function in the center point $F(c_{SFC,j})$ based on the data closest to this center:

$$
v_j = \sum_{i \in P_j} Y_i \cdot \frac{K\left(\frac{\|t_i - c_{SFC,j}\|}{h}\right)}{\sum_{i \in P_j} K\left(\frac{\|t_i - c_{SFC,j}\|}{h}\right)} , \tag{5}
$$

where P_j is the subset of the learning data which is closest to the center $c_{SFC,j}$, i.e.

$$
P_j = \{i : |t_i - c_{SFC,j}| \leq |t_i - c_{SFC,l}|, \ l = 1, 2, \ldots, N, 1 \leq i \leq n\},
$$

$n_j = |P_j|$ and K is some kernel function and h is its smoothing parameters.

4   Concluding Remarks

Our aim was to introduce a new approach to the RBF networks design based on data transformation to one dimension. This approach is equivalent to using a new distance measure defined as a distance along space-filling curve as an argument of the radial functions, instead of the Euclidean or the Mahalanobis distance. Thus, the network learning process can be executed in one dimension which results in faster and easier performance.

The method of computing the weights of linear output neuron based on on the Nadaraya-Watson kernel regression estimators can be used also in multidimensional RBF (1) network and depends only on Y_i's values.

Acknowledgments. This paper was partially supported by the Council for Scientific Research of the Polish Government Grant 2002-2005.

References

1. Bishop C.M.: Neural Networks for Pattern Recognition (1995) Oxford University Press Oxford

2. Butz A.R.: Alternative algorithm for Hilbert's space-filling curve. IEEE Trans. Comput. **C-20** (1971) 424–426.
3. Girosi F.: Regularization theory, radial basis functions and networks. In V. Cherkassky, J. H. Friedman, and H. Wechsler, editors From Statistics to Neural Networks. Theory and Pattern recognition Applications (1992) 166–187 Springer-Verlag Berlin.
4. Girosi F. and Anzellotti G.: Rates of convergence for radial basis functions and neural networks. In R. J. Mammone edt. Artificial Neural Networks for Speech and Vision (1993) 97–113 Chapman & Hall London.
5. Girosi F., Jones M. and Poggio T.: Regularization theory and neural network architectures. Neural Computation **7** (1995) 219–267.
6. Györfi L., Kohler M., Krzyżak A., Walk H.: A Distribution-free Theory of Nonparametric Regression. (2002) Springer-Verlag Berlin New York.
7. Karayaiannis N.B. and Behnke S.: New radial basis neural networks and their application in a large-scale handwritten digit recognition problem. In Jain L. and Fanelli A.M., editors, Recent Advances in Artificial Neural Networks Design and Applications(2000) CRC Press London New York.
8. Krzyżak A., Niemann T.: Convergence and rates of convergence of radial basis function networks in function learning. Nonlinear Analysis **47** (2001) 281–292.
9. Krzyżak A., Linder T. and Lugosi G.: Nonparametric estimation and classification using radial basis function nets and empirical risk minimization. IEEE Transactions on Neural Networks **7** (1996) 475–487.
10. Krzyżak A., Linder T.: Radial basis function networks and complexity regularyzation in function learning. IEEE Transactions on Neural Networks **9** (1998) 247–256.
11. Krzyżak A., Schäfer D.: Nonparametric Regression Estimation by Normalized Radial Basis Function Networks, to appear in IEEE Transactions on Information Theory, 2004.
12. Milne S. C.: Peano Curves and Smoothness of Functions. Advances in Mathematics **35** (1980) 129–157.
13. Moody Moody J., Darken J.: Fast learning in networks of locally-tuned processing units. Neural Computation **1** (1989) 281–294.
14. Poggio T. and Girosi F.: Regularization algorithms for learning that are equivalent to multilayer networks. Science **247** (1990) 978–982.
15. Powell M. : Radial basis functions for multivariable interpolation: a review. Algorithms for Approximation(1987) Claredon Press Oxford.
16. Rafajłowicz E., Skubalska- Rafajłowicz E.: RBF nets based on equidistributed points. in Proc. of 9th IEEE International Conf. Methods and Models in Automation and Robotics MMAR 2003 **2** (2003) 921–926 .
17. Sagan H.: Space-Filling Curves. Springer-Verlag Berlin Heidelberg New York 1994.
18. Schwenker F., Kestler H., Palm G.: Unsupervised and supervised learning in radial-basis-function networks. in U. Seiffert and C. Jain Eds. Self-Organizing Neural Networks: Recent Advances and Applications (2002) 217–243 Physica Verlag Heidelberg.
19. Skubalska-Rafajłowicz E. : Pattern recognition algorithm based on space-filling curves and orthogonal expansion. IEEE Trans. on Information Theory **47** (2001) 1915–1927.
20. Skubalska-Rafajłowicz E.: Space-filling Curves in Multivariate Decision Problems (in Polish) (2001) Wrocław University of Technology Press Wrocław.

21. Xu L., Krzyżak A. and Oja E.: Rival penalized competitive learning for clustering analysis RBF net and curve detection. IEEE Transactions on Neural Networks **4** (1993) 636–649.
22. Xu L., Krzyżak A. and Yuille A.: On Radial Basis Function Nets and Kernel Regression: Statistical Consistency, Convergence Rates, and Receptive Field Size. Neural Networks **7** (1994) 609–628.
23. Whitehead B.A. and Chaote T.D.: Evolving space-filling curves to distribute radial basis functions over an input space. IEEE Transactions on Neural Networks **5** (1994) 15–23.

Appendix. Space-Filling Curves

A space-filling curve is a continuous mapping from unit interval $I = [0, 1]$ onto the multi-dimensional cube $I_d = [0, 1] \times [0, 1] \times \ldots [0, 1]$. Space-filling curves is a surjective mapping, let say $F : I_1 \to I_d$ such that for each $x \in I_d$ one can quickly compute a $t \in I_1$ satisfying $F(t) = x$. It is not possible to define $\Phi(t)$ in a analytical form. The mapping is regarded as the limit of a sequence of continuous functions [17] which fill the space more and more densely. For algorithms see [2], [20], [12].

From the formal point of view any space-filling curve, for which the conditions (C1 – C2) given below hold, is suitable for our purposes.

C1 F is a continuous mapping and satisfies the Hölder condition, i.e., $\|F(t_1) - F(t_2)\| \leq L_d |t_1 - t_2|^{1/d}$, $t_1, t_2 \in I_1$. $\|.\|$ is usually the Euclidean norm in I_d, and $L_d > 0$ is a certain constant, which depends on d.

We write $F^{-1}(B) = \{t \in I_1 : F(t) \in B\}$ for $B \subseteq I_d$. Let μ_d denote the Lebesgue measure in I_d, which is treated here as dimensionless quantity.

C2 F preserves the Lebesgue measure, i.e., for every Borel set $B \subseteq I_d$ we have

$$\mu_d(B) = \mu_1 \left(F^{-1}(B) \right). \tag{6}$$

Lemma 1. *There exists measurable mapping $\Psi : I_d \to I_1$, such that $\Psi(x) \in \Phi^{-1}(x)$, $x \in I_d$, which is a.e. inverse of F, i.e., $\Psi(x) \in F^{-1}(x)$ and $\Psi(x) \neq F^{-1}(x)$ on a set with zero Lebesgue measure.*

Lemma 2. *For every measurable function $f : I_d \to R$, $f \in L(I_d)$ the following Lebesgue integrals in I_d and I_1 are equal*

$$\int_{I_d} f(x)dx = \int_{I_1} f(F(t))dt. \tag{7}$$

Lemma 3. *Let $X_1, X_2, \ldots, X_n$ be a sequence of statistically independent, identically distributed points in I_d having an absolutely continuous probability measure (w.r.t. the Lebesgue measure) with density $f(x)$. The random variables $t_i = \Psi(X_i)$, $i = 1, \ldots, n$ are also i.i.d. with density $f(F(t))$.*

Chaotic Itinerancy for Patterns Separation

Paweł Matykiewicz*

Department of Informatics, Nicholaus Copernicus University,
ul. Grudziądzka 5, 87-100 Toruń, Poland
pawelm@phys.uni.torun.pl
http://www.neuron.m4u.pl

Abstract. Chaotic neural network with external inputs has been used as a mixed input pattern separator. In contrast to previous work on the subject, highly chaotic dynamical system (LLE $\approx$ 0.6) is applied here. The network is based on a "dynamical mapping" scheme as an effective framework for cortical mapping. This feature allows for a more effective pattern retrieval and separation by the network.

1   Introduction

A chaotic neuron model was proposed by Aihara et. al [1]. Such neurons have been used to construct chaotic associative memory model [2]. External inputs corresponding to one of the embedded patterns force the network to show this pattern with higher frequency rate than other patterns. Nearly zero largest Lyapunov exponents were found. This kind of network is also able to separate mixed input patterns [3]. The network state wonders between the patterns present in the mixed input, occasionally retrieving other patterns. In this case largest Lyapunov exponents was negative.

In [4] a basic framework for the distributed coding scheme called *dynamical map* has been presented. It is realized by itinerancy among dynamical attractors of the network. This framework, which is still being developed, is used for simulating various associative memory phenomena [5], [6]. The main concept is based on the fact that external input corresponding to one of the stored patterns should drive the network from global chaotic attractor to nearly periodic local attractor lying in the basin of attraction of this stored pattern.

This paper is based on a combination of these two approaches. A novel chaotic associative memory is introduced in order to obtain Lyapunov exponents that are higher then those already reported [3], [1], [2]. A slight modification of the chaotic neural network developed previously has better retrieval and separation abilities. To prove this numerical simulations are presented.

---

* Author would like to thank Prof. Włodzisław Duch, Prof. Masaharu Adachi and Prof. Osamu Hoshino for their valuable suggestions.

L. Rutkowski et al. (Eds.): ICAISC 2004, LNAI 3070, pp. 235–240, 2004.
© Springer-Verlag Berlin Heidelberg 2004

2   Network Model and Analysis Methods

In 1990 ([1]), the following chaotic neuron model in a n-neurons network was presented: $x_i(t+1) = f\left[\sum_{j=1}^{n} w_{ij} \sum_{d=0}^{t} k_f^d x_j(t-d) - \alpha \sum_{d=0}^{t} k_r^d g\{x_i(t-d)\} - \vartheta_i\right]$, where $x_i(t+1)$ denotes output of the ith neuron and f stands for a continuous output function. This equation, used also in [3], [2], is simplified and modified here to the following equations:

$$\eta_i(t+1) = k_a \eta_i(t) + \sum_{w_{ij} \in W_i^E} w_{ij} x_j(t) + e_i, \tag{1}$$

$$\zeta_i(t+1) = k_r \zeta_i(t) - \alpha x_i(t) + \sum_{w_{ij} \in W_i^I} w_{ij} x_j(t) + \theta, \tag{2}$$

$$\theta \equiv \vartheta_i(1 - k_r) \quad \text{for all} \quad i, \tag{3}$$

$$x_i(t+1) = f\{\eta_i(t+1) + \zeta_i(t+1)\}. \tag{4}$$

$$f(u) = \frac{1}{1 + \exp(\frac{-u}{\varepsilon})}. \tag{5}$$

Here, $\eta_i(t)$ denotes all positive post-synaptical potentials and $\zeta_i(t)$ all negative potentials. This makes $\zeta_i(t)$ a resting potential, $\eta_i(t)$ a *pseudo*-action potential and $\eta_i(t) + \zeta_i(t)$ an action potential. Constants k_r and k_a are decay parameters for resting and *pseudo*-action potentials, respectively. The remaining parameters are: e_i - strength of the external input applied to the ith neuron, α - a refractory scaling parameter, ϑ_i - a threshold value of a chaotic neuron model, whereas θ - a threshold value of a simplified neuron model independent of the serial number i of a neuron, and finally ε - a steepness parameter of the continuous output function f. When action potential is positive, f function generates an output signal $x(t+1)$. The sets W_i^E and W_i^I consist of excitatory and inhibitory weights, respectively. They have been obtained from the Hebbian learning rule:

$$w_{ij} = \frac{1}{n} \sum_{p=1}^{m} (2x_i^p - 1)(2x_j^p - 1), \tag{6}$$

where x^p are the memorized patterns, for example the m=4 patterns shown in Fig. 1. The number of synchronously updated neurons in the simulations is set at $n = 100$, as in the previous work. Therefore equations 4-5 define a 200-dimensional discrete dynamical system.

Moreover, in the case of mixed patterns, the same technique as in [3] was used: for any two stored patterns logical OR (+) operation is performed. Mixed pattern composed of these two patterns is obtained. There are six possibilities of mixing the pairs of four patterns: 1+2, 1+3, 1+4, 2+3, 2+4, 3+4.

In order to evaluate retrieval characteristics of the network, the Hamming distance is used. This measures difference between spatio-temporal output and

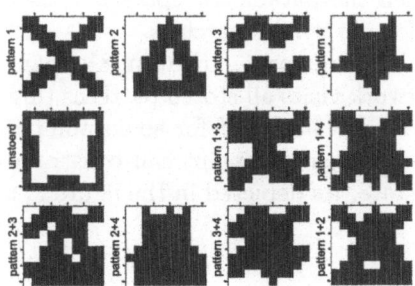

Fig. 1. Four stored patterns (1, 2, 3, 4), one additional pattern and six mixed patterns (1+3, 1+4, 2+3, 2+4, 3+4, 1+2) used in simulations of the associative chaotic neural network. 100-dimensional vectors are displayed in the form of a 10×10 matrix; white means 0 and black 1.

the stored patterns:

$$\mathrm{Ham}_p(x(t)) = \frac{1}{n} \sum_{i=1}^{n} |h(x_i(t)) - x_i^p|, \qquad (7)$$

where p ($p = 1 - 4$) is a p-th pattern and h is the threshold function: $h(x) = \Theta(x - 0.5)$

During the simulation, it is possible to evaluate *conditional* retrieval characteristic r_p for every p-th pattern, that is the number of $\mathrm{Ham}_p(x(t)) \le 0.5$ events. This condition helps to count every trajectory that is in the neighborhood of one of the stored patterns. With chaotic itinerancy the trajectory does not stay in the equilibrium, but wonders around the desired embedded patterns. To evaluate efficiency of the network the number of $\mathrm{Ham}_p(x(t)) = 0$ events are calculated. The number of these events is called an *exact* retrieval characteristic. The largest Lyapunov exponent is also used for evaluating dynamical properties of the network. It is evaluated from a Jacobian matrix and the Gram-Schmidt orthonormalization.

3   Parametric Space Search and Network Responses

First, 3-dimensional parametric space (k_r, α, θ) is searched in order to find network chaotically exploring all state space. A statistical function r is introduced:

$$r(r_p) = \frac{average(r_p)^{\frac{3}{2}}}{deviation(r_p)}, \qquad (8)$$

where r_p is a set consisting of r_1, r_2, r_3, r_4. For every point in the (k_r, α, θ) space every r_p value is assembled during 3000 iterations. Initial conditions of the neural network, which are near the pattern 1, and all r_p values are reset each time the next point from the parametric space is chosen. Other parameters of the network are fixed for the whole search: $k_a = k_r - 0.1$, $\varepsilon = 0.015$ and $e_i = 0$ for all i. High value of the function r (equation 8) means that in the case of no external inputs, the network visits all stored patterns (high average) with almost the same frequency (low deviation). If for some point $[k_r, \alpha, \theta]$ $average(r_p) > deviation(r_p)$ and $r > 50$ then this point can constrain the neural network to the chaotic itinerancy state. As depicted in the figure 2, the best result $(r(r_p) =$

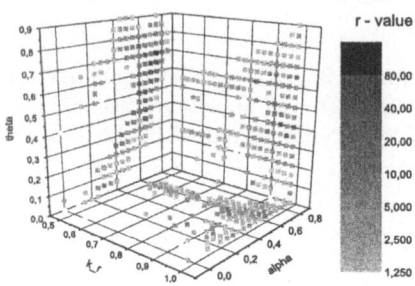

Fig. 2. Projections on the planes XY, YZ, XZ of the result of searching the parametric space (k_r, α, θ) for the best value of r. The $average(r_p)$ and $deviation(r_p)$ values are obtained during 3000 iterations.

86.26) is at the point $k_r = 0.975$, $\alpha = 0.75$, $\theta = 0.7$ and $k_a = 0.875$. These parameters are used for further search.

The next step is to find optimal e_i value. In order to establish this value, conditional retrieval characteristic r_1 for pattern 1 and r_2 for pattern 2 are evaluated for every 3000 iterations with changing parameter e_i, where i is a serial number of a neuron with an external input embedded corresponding to the pattern 2. The figure 3 shows that it is best to set $e_i = 0.6$ for neurons with external stimulus and $e_i = 0$ with no external input. Higher values of e_i can prevent chaos and pattern separation and lower values let the network visit other embedded pattern's basins.

With the set of all parameters fixed at optimal values after the searching phase responses of the network are investigated for presentations of single (table 1) and mixed (table 2) input patterns. The external input corresponds to one of the 100-pixel binary patterns or the logical OR mixture of these patterns shown in the figure 1. Table 1 shows the retrieval abilities of the network. The chaotic itinerancy among all embedded patterns and reverse patterns can be seen in the case of no input. When a single pattern is applied as an external stimulus the network stays in local chaotic attractor embedded near the desired pattern (see Fig. 4). For pattern that has not been stored nothing is retrieved, only occasionally reverse pattern 1 and 4 is retrieved because this pattern is slightly similar to them. Values of largest Lyapunov exponents are also given.

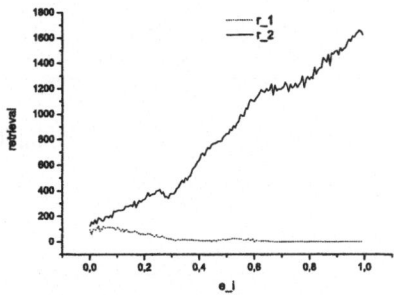

Fig. 3. Dependence of conditional retrieval characteristics for pattern 1 and 2 from on the changed parameter e_i.

Table 1. Retrieval ability: exact retrieval characteristics during 4000 iterations for every pattern and its reverse (in brackets). The largest Lyapunov exponents are also given.

Input	pattern 1	pattern 2	pattern 3	pattern 4	LLE
no input	63 (67)	73 (115)	20 (22)	47 (119)	≈ 0.475
pattern 1	334 (0)	0 (0)	0 (0)	0 (0)	≈ 0.593
pattern 2	2 (0)	324	0 (0)	2 (4)	≈ 0.570
pattern 3	0 (0)	0 (0)	222 (0)	0 (0)	≈ 0.612
pattern 4	0 (0)	0 (0)	0 (0)	139 (0)	≈ 0.635
unstored	0 (15)	0 (0)	0 (0)	0 (21)	≈ 0.592

Table 2 shows the separation ability of the chaotic network. No patterns other than components of the mixed pattern are retrieved. Conditional and exact retrieval characteristics prove that the trajectory of investigated system wonders chaotically around these components. Presented network visits other patterns only at the transition phase, which is the first several dozen iterations (see figure 4). High (but rather similar) values of largest Lyapunov exponents should be noted.

4 Conclusions

The novel associative chaotic neural network introduced in this paper has been used to separate mixed binary input patterns into components of the stored patterns. The retrieval properties of the network are more efficient than found in the previous reports [3], [2]. Although large Lyapunov exponents are present chaotic neural network can obtain high exact and conditional retrieval characteristics in the case of mixed external inputs.

Further investigation should focus on learning capabilities of the network. The significant difference between retrieval characteristics of the network in the

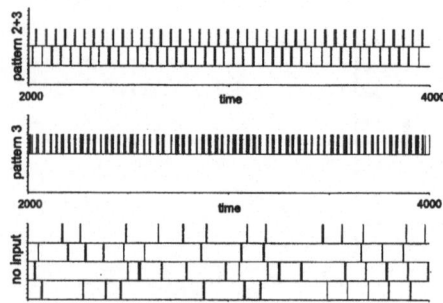

Fig. 4. Dynamical behavior of the network in the case of mixed, single and no pattern input. Temporal variation of the Hamming distances $\text{Ham}_p(t)$ $(p = 1 - 4)$. When $\text{Ham}_p \leq 0.5$, a vertical bar is drawn on pth row.

Table 2. Separation ability: retrieval characteristics during 4000 iterations for every pattern: the exact value and conditional value (in brackets). The largest Lyapunov exponents are also given.

Input	pattern 1	pattern 2	pattern 3	pattern 4	LLE
pattern 1+2	28 (168)	43 (345)	0 (0)	0 (0)	≈ 0.563
pattern 1+3	76 (400)	0 (0)	47 (344)	0 (0)	≈ 0.562
pattern 1+4	88 (394)	0 (0)	0 (6)	7 (60)	≈ 0.562
pattern 2+3	0 (2)	100 (366)	76 (375)	0 (0)	≈ 0.574
pattern 2+4	0 (0)	20 (268)	0 (0)	36 (220)	≈ 0.562
pattern 3+4	0 (3)	0 (0)	50 (410)	12 (105)	≈ 0.572

case of stored and unknown patterns can be used for effective learning. Another issue that should be discussed is the separation of mixtures of more than two patterns.

References

1. Aihara, K., Takabe, T., Toyoda, M.: Chaotic neural networks. Physics Letters A **144** (1990) 333–340
2. Adachi, M., Aihara, K.: Associative dynamics in a chaotic neural networks. Neural Networks **10** (1997) 83–98
3. Adachi, M., Aihara, K., Cichocki, A.: Separation of mixed patterns by chaotic neural network. In: International Symposium on Nonlinear Theory and its Application (NOLTA), Katsurahama-so, Kochi, Japan (1996) 93–96
4. Hoshino, O., Usuba, N., Kashimori, Y., Kambara, T.: Role of itinerancy as dynamical map in distributed coding scheme. Neural Networks **10** (1997) 1375–1390
5. Tsuda, I.: Dynamical link of memory - chaotic memory map in nonequilibrium neural networks. Neural Networks **5** (1992) 313–326
6. Nara, S., Davis, P., Toksuji, H.: Memory search using complex dynamics in reccurent neural network model. Neural Networks **6** (1993) 963–973

Dynamic Search Trajectory Methods for Neural Network Training*

Y.G. Petalas[1,2], D.K. Tasoulis[1,2], and M.N. Vrahatis[1,2]

[1] Department of Mathematics, University of Patras, GR–26110 Patras, Greece
{petalas,dtas,vrahatis}@math.upatras.gr
[2] University of Patras Artificial Intelligence Research Center (UPAIRC),
University of Patras, GR–26110 Patras, Greece

Abstract. Training multilayer feedforward neural networks corresponds to the global minimization of the network error function. To address this problem we utilize the Snyman and Fatti [1] approach by considering a system of second order differential equations of the form, $\ddot{x} = -\nabla E(x)$, where x is the vector of network weights and ∇E is the gradient of the network error function E. Equilibrium points of the above system of differential equations correspond to optimizers of the network error function. The proposed approach is described and experimental results are discussed.

Keywords: Trajectory Methods, Neural Networks Training, Ordinary Differential Equations

1 Introduction

Training multilayer feedforward neural networks is equivalent to the global minimization of the network error function with respect to the weights of the network. *Trajectory* methods constitute a class of global optimization methods [2]. An important property of these methods is that the generated trajectory passes through the neighborhood of many of the stationary points of the objective function. The simplest trajectory method is described by means of the following initial value problem:

$$\dot{x} = -\nabla E(x), \quad x(0) = x_0. \tag{1}$$

Trajectory methods can also be viewed, through a mechanical analogy, as an assignment of mass to a particle moving in a field of forces [3,4,5]. Let the mass of the particle be $m(t)$. Further, assume that the particle is moving in a field of forces defined by the potential E, subject to the dissipative force $-n(t)\dot{x}(t)$. Then the trajectory generated by the motion of the particle can be described by the following system of differential equations:

$$m(t)\,\ddot{x}(t) - n(t)\,\dot{x}(t) = -\nabla E(x(t)), \tag{2}$$

---

* This work is partially supported by the "Pythagoras" research grant awarded by the Greek Ministry of Education and Religious Affairs and the European Union.

L. Rutkowski et al. (Eds.): ICAISC 2004, LNAI 3070, pp. 241–246, 2004.
© Springer-Verlag Berlin Heidelberg 2004

where $m(t) \geqslant 0$ and $n(t) \leqslant 0$. Under certain conditions, the trajectory can determine a local minimum of the objective function E. A similar approach has been proposed in [6], where the motion of a particle with unit mass is described in a field with potential E without friction. We would like to note at this point that since the system is autonomous an interesting theorem due to Poincaré, which states that the trajectory passes through the neighborhood of all the stationary points of E, is applicable [6].

The efficient global optimization methods of Griewank [7] and Snyman and Fatti [1] can be derived from (2). The method due to Griewank [7] assumes $m(t) = (E(x(t)) - c)/e$ and $n(t) = -\nabla E(x(t))\dot{x}(t)$, where c is the target level, to be set somewhat higher than the global minimum of the the the objective function. Snyman and Fatti's method [1] considers the case where $m(t) = 1$ and $n(t) = 0$, i.e. the trajectory is determined by,

$$\ddot{x}(t) = -\nabla E(x(t)), \quad x(0) = x_0, \quad \dot{x}(0) = 0.$$

The paper is organized as follows: Section 2 presents the proposed class of neural network training methods; Section 3 is devoted to the presentation of the experimental results; the paper ends with concluding remarks and ideas for future research in Section 4.

2   The Proposed Method

Through this study each method for the numerical solution of ordinary differential equations corresponds to a Neural Network training algorithm. In previous work [8] we investigated the effectiveness of numerical methods for the solution of first order differential equations (1) on the task of neural network training. Here we consider the effectiveness of both the formulation and the local minimizer procedure proposed in [1]. Moreover, we propose a simple modification of this local minimizer algorithm which seems to be more efficient in Neural Network training applications. Our modification operates as follows. Following a trajectory, if the value of the error function decreases, the step of integration is increased by a factor ζ to speed–up convergence; while, if the ratio of the current function value to the previous function value exceeds a pre–specified factor, $\beta > 1$, the previously visited point is retained and a new trajectory starts from it. At the beginning of a new trajectory, the local minimizer procedure requires a reduction in the function value to render a step–size acceptable; otherwise the step–size is halved. Our experience indicates that when it holds that,

$$\frac{E(x_{t+1})}{E(x_t)} > \beta,$$

$\|x_t\|$ is small. Thus, in practice, the condition imposed by the local minimization procedure operates similar to the Armijo line search algorithm [9]. The modified local minimization procedure of [1] is presented below in pseudocode. The proposed modifications are indicated with the comment *Additional Step* in parentheses.

Modified Snyman–Fatti Algorithm (MSF)

1. Initial values for parameters $\alpha, \gamma, \epsilon, k_m, \Delta t, x_0$ are given. Δt is the time step of integration method and x_0 is the starting point.

2. Set $j \leftarrow 0$, $k \leftarrow 0$, $F_t \leftarrow \infty$.

3. Set $x_m \leftarrow x_k$, $x_s \leftarrow x_k$, $x_b \leftarrow x_k$ and
$\dot{x}_k \leftarrow -\nabla F_k \Delta t / \gamma$, $x_{k+1} \leftarrow x_k + \dot{x}_k \Delta t$
if $F_{k+1} < F_k$ set $F_b \leftarrow F_{k+1}$, $x_b \leftarrow x_{k+1}$ and **goto 4**
else set $\Delta t \leftarrow \Delta t/2$ and **goto 3**.

4. Set $F_s \leftarrow F_k$, $F_m \leftarrow F_k$.

5. Set $xprev_k \leftarrow x_k$, (**Additional Step**)
$$x_{k+1} \leftarrow x_k + \dot{x}_k \Delta t, \quad t_1 \leftarrow -\dot{x}_k^T \nabla F_{k+1}, \quad T = 0.5\|\dot{x}_k\|^2,$$
$$\dot{x}_{k+1} \leftarrow \dot{x}_k - \nabla F_{k+1} \Delta t, \quad k \leftarrow k+1.$$

if $F_k \leqslant Es$ **goto 16**. (**Additional Step**)(Es stopping error)
if $\|\nabla F_k\| \geqslant \epsilon$ **goto 6** else if $F_k < F_b$ and $F_k \leqslant F_m$ **goto 16**.
else if $F_m < F_b$ set $x_b \leftarrow x_m$, $x_k \leftarrow x_m$ and **goto 3**
else set $x_k \leftarrow x_b$ and **goto 3**.

6. if $k > k_m$ **goto 16**.
if $F_k/F_m > \beta$ set $x_k \leftarrow xprev_k$ and **goto 3**. (**Additional Step**)
if $F_k \leqslant F_m$ set $F_m \leftarrow F_k$, $x_m \leftarrow x_k$, $\dot{x}_m \leftarrow \dot{x}_k$
$\Delta t = \Delta t * \zeta$ (**Additional Step**)

7. if $t_1 < 0$ **goto 8** else set $j \leftarrow 0$ and **goto 5**.

8. if $F_T > F_m$ set $F_T \leftarrow F_m$.
if $(F_k - F_T) > \alpha(F_s - F_T)$ **goto 9**
else if $T < (1-a)(F_s - F_T)$ **goto 9**
else set $j \leftarrow 0$ and **goto 5**.

9. if $F_m < F_b$ set $x_b \leftarrow x_m$, $F_b \leftarrow F_m$ and **goto 10**.
else set $x_b \leftarrow x_m$ and continue

10. Set $x_k \leftarrow \frac{1}{2}(x_m + x_s)$, $x_s \leftarrow x_k$, $x_m \leftarrow x_k$, $\dot{x}_k \leftarrow \frac{1}{2}\dot{x}_m$.

11. if $j \leftarrow 0$ **goto 14**.

12. Set $t_2 \leftarrow -\dot{x}_k^T \nabla F_k$.

13. if $t_2 < 0$ set $j \leftarrow 0$ and **goto 3** else $\dot{x}_k \leftarrow \dot{x}_k/2^j$.

14. $j \leftarrow j+1$.

15. if $F_b \neq F_m$ **goto 4** else set $\dot{x}_m \leftarrow \frac{1}{2}\dot{x}_m$ and **goto 4**

16. Set $x_f \leftarrow x_k$, $F_f \leftarrow F(x_f)$ and terminate.

3   Experimental Results

The performance of the proposed method has been compared with that of well–known and widely used variations of the Backpropagation (BP) method, namely: Backpropagation with Momentum (MBP) [10,11], Second Order Momentum (SMBP) and Adaptive Backpropagation (ABP), using the adaptive scheme suggested by Vogl [10,12], Parallel Tangents method (PARTAN) [13], Scaled

Conjugated Gradient(SCG), Resilient Back Propagation [14] (RPROP) and Improved Resilient Back Propagation [15] (iRPROP).

3.1   Description of the Problems

The problems we used were Cancer1, Diabetes1, and Heart1. All three are classification problems from the proben1 [16] dataset with fixed training and test sets. A brief description of each problem follows.

Cancer1: The architecture used was 9–4–2–2. The stopping error criterion for training was an error goal of 0.05 within 1000 function (including gradient) evaluations. In the experiments the best results for the methods were given with the following parameters: For BP the step–size was set to 0.9, for PARTAN it was 0.9, for MBP and SMBP the step–size was 0.9 and the momentum term was 0.7. For ABP, the error ratio factor was 1.04, the stepsize increment factor was equal to 1.05, while the stepsize decrease factor was 0.7.

Diabetes1: The architecture used was an 8–2–2–2 feedforward neural network. The stopping error criterion for training was an error goal of 0.15 within 1000 function (also counting gradient) evaluations. In the experiments the best results for the methods were given with the following parameters: For BP the step–size was 0.6, for PARTAN it was 0.9, for MBP the step–size was 0.9 and the momentum term 0.4, for SMBP the stepsize was 0.9 while the momentum was 0.6. For ABP, the error ratio factor was 1.04, the step–size increment factor was equal to 1.05 while the step–size decrease factor was 0.7.

Heart1: The architecture used was 35–8–2. The stopping error criterion for training was an error goal of 0.1 within 1000 function (also counting gradient) evaluations. The parameter configuration for the previous two problems was also applied in this case. In the experiments the best results for the methods were given with the following parameters: For BP the step–size was 0.9, for PARTAN it was 0.9. For MBP the step–size was 0.9 and the momentum term was 0.6. For SMBP the step–size was 0.9 and the momentum term was 0.7. For ABP, the error ratio factor was 1.04, the step–size increment factor was equal to 1.05 while the step–size decrease factor was 0.7.

3.2   Presentation of the Results

The parameter setup for the proposed method was the default setup suggested in [1]: $\alpha = 0.95$, $\gamma = 2$, $\Delta t = 2$, $\epsilon = 10^{-4}$, $k_m = 1000$. The values of ζ and β, required for the modification of the algorithm, were set to 1.05 and 1.04, respectively. We performed 100 simulations for each problem. The evaluation measures we used are, the number of successes(suc), the mean, the standard deviation (stdev), the minimum (min), and the maximum (max), number of function evaluations (also counting gradient evaluations). In addition to the above measures we computed these statistics for the percentage of misclassification on the test set. Regarding the Cancer1 problem as it is shown in Table 1 the less computationally demanding method is iRPROP. MSF ranked third after iRPROP and RPROP. In the test set MSF exhibited the second best classification error after

Table 1. Cancer1 problem

Algorithm	Training Set					Test Set			
	Mean	Stdev	Max	Min	Suc.	Mean	Stdev	Max	Min
BP	583.25	154.72	1001	347	98	2.2	0.57	3.44	0.57
MBP	300.79	95.59	664	158	100	2.01	0.63	3.65	0.57
SMBP	323.98	102.93	773	157	100	2.02	0.60	3.44	0.57
ABP	74.26	8.87	95	63	100	1.93	0.83	3.44	0.57
PARTAN	159.12	39.99	273	87	100	2.15	0.48	3.45	1.15
SCG	259.36	807.77	1001	16	92	4.51	9.76	37.36	0.57
RPROP	16.26	2.93	24	9	100	**1.74**	0.67	4.02	0.00
iRPROP	**15.25**	4.66	38	9	100	1.89	0.78	3.44	0.57
MSF	52.25	14.05	109	33	100	1.82	0.55	2.87	0.57

Table 2. Diabetes1 problem

Algorithm	Training Set					Test Set			
	Mean	Stdev	Max	Min	Suc.	Mean	Stdev	Max	Min
BP	1001.00	0.00	1001	1000	0	36.45	36.45	36.45	36.45
MBP	863.75	186.39	1001	354	46	28.71	4.80	36.45	23.43
SMBP	865.45	190.57	1001	256	46	28.70	5.12	36.45	21.88
ABP	664.85	153.80	965	385	100	**24.54**	0.94	29.17	22.92
PARTAN	796.35	145.54	1001	549	81	26.44	3.01	36.45	23.96
SCG	499.69	973.11	1001	64	87	26.48	3.98	36.45	21.87
RPROP	90.11	31.62	206	47	100	25.94	1.54	30.20	21.87
iRPROP	**59.27**	20.91	159	35	100	25.00	1.56	28.12	20.31
MSF	112.87	92.80	1002	73	99	25.35	1.43	36.45	23.44

Table 3. Heart1 problem

Algorithm	Training Set					Test Set			
	Mean	Stdev	Max	Min	Suc.	Mean	Stdev	Max	Min
BP	1001.00	0.00	1001	1001	0	20.75	0.81	23.04	18.70
MBP	631.09	136.06	984	367	100	20.62	1.10	22.60	17.82
SMBP	638.17	161.63	1001	303	98	20.93	1.18	24.35	17.82
ABP	159.13	26.77	217	95	100	20.76	1.01	22.60	17.82
PARTAN	327.69	47.95	427	213	100	20.64	0.66	22.60	19.13
SCG	339.37	841.67	1001	46	91	21.60	4.76	47.82	17.82
RPROP	20.49	3.18	30	14	100	20.69	0.99	23.47	18.26
iRPROP	**16.89**	2.47	24	12	100	**20.34**	1.00	22.17	17.39
MSF	42.55	8.22	73	30	100	20.59	1.30	24.34	16.95

RPROP. The results for the problem Diabetes1 are reported in Table 2. Again RPROP and iRPROP performed less function evaluations than the other methods, while MSF ranked third. Concerning test set performance, ABP obtained the best classification error while MSF was the third best method. On the Heart1 problem, as shown in Table 3, iRPROP required the least function evaluations and produced the minimum classification error in the test set. MSF had the second best classification error and the third place with respect to function evaluations.

4 Conclusions

This paper presents a new scheme for feedforward multilayer neural networks training. We utilize the trajectory that results from the solution of the second–order ordinary differential equation $\ddot{x} = -\nabla E(x)$, using a modification of the method proposed in [1] to obtain minima of the network's error function. The proposed method clearly outperforms the well known and widely used family of BP and conjugate gradient methods. It is less efficient in terms of function evaluations than RPROP and iRPROP but with respect to generalization it exhibits almost the same performance. In a future correspondence we intend to apply our approach on the general second order differential equation (2). We will also study the implications that arise from the application of the Theorem due to Poincaré in the present setting.

References

1. Snyman, J., Fatti, L.: A multi–start global minimization algorithm with dynamic search trajectories. JOTA **54** (1987) 121–141
2. Törn, A., Žilinskas, A.: Global optimization. In Goos, G., Hartmans, J., eds.: Lecture Notes in computer Science. Volume 350. Springer Verlag (1987)
3. Incerti, S., Parisi, V., Zirilli, F.: A new method for solving nonlinear simultaneous equations. SIAM J.Num.Anal **16** (1979) 779–789
4. Inomata, S., Cumada, M.: On the golf method. Bulletin of the Electronical Laboratory **25** (1964) 495–512
5. Zhidkov, N., Shchdrin, B.: On the search of minimum of a function of several variables. Computing methods and Programming **10** (1978) 203–210
6. Pshenichnyi, B., Marchenko, D.: On one approach to the search for the global minimum. Optimal Decision theory **2** (1967) 3–12
7. Griewank, A.: Generalized descnet for global optimization. JOTA **34** (1981) 11–39
8. Petalas, Y.G., Tasoulis, D.K., Vrahatis, M.N.: Trajectory methods for neural network training. In: Proceedings of the IASTED International Conference on Artificial Intelligence and Applications (AIA'04), vol. 1, ACTA press (2004) 400–408.
9. Armijo, L.: Minimization of function having lipschitz continuous first partial derivatives. Pac J. Math. **16** (1966) 1–3
10. Magoulas, G., Vrahatis, M.N., Androulakis, G.: Effective backpropagation training with variable stepsize. Neural Networks **10** (1997) 69–82
11. Magoulas, G., Vrahatis, M.N., Androulakis, G.: Increasing the convergence rate of the error backpropagation algorithm by learning rate adaptation methods. Neural Computation **11** (1999) 1769–1796
12. Vogl, T., Mangis, J., Rigler, A., Zink, W., Alkon, D.: Accelerating the convergence of the back-propagation method. Biol. Cybern. **59** (1988) 257–263
13. Rao, S.: Optimization theory and Applications. Wiley Eastern Limited (1992)
14. Riedmiller, M., Braun, H.: A direct adaptive method for faster backpropagation learning: The rprop algorithm. In: Proceedings of the IEEE International Conference on Neural Networks, San Francisco, CA. (1993) 586–591
15. Igel, C., Hüsken, M.: Improving the Rprop learning algorithm. In Bothe, H., Rojas, R., eds.: Proceedings of the Second International ICSC Symposium on Neural Computation (NC 2000), ICSC Academic Press (2000) 115–121
16. Prechelt, L.: Proben1: A set of neural network benchmark problems and benchmarking rules. Technical Report 21/94 (1994)

Visualizing and Analyzing Multidimensional Output from MLP Networks via Barycentric Projections

Filip Piękniewski and Leszek Rybicki

Departament of Mathematics and Computer Science, Nicholaus Copernicus University, Toruń, Poland, http://www.mat.uni.torun.pl

Abstract. Barycentric plotting, achieved by placing gaussian kernels in distant corners of the feature space and projecting multidimensional output of neural network on a plane, provides information about the process of training and certain features of the network. Additional visual guides added to the plot show tendencies and irregularities in the training process.

1 Introduction

One of the important problems of modern neural network theory is to find a good measure, or a method for determining if the network is well trained and ready to solve "real life" problems, or if there are singularities that could render the network useless. The backprop algorithm (and other learning algorithms) minimizes a well defined error function, usually the Mean Square Error (MSE). One might ask, since the the value of the error function is so well defined and easy to calculate, what more can one need? In fact, mean square error (and other error functions) provides just a piece of statistical information about the learning process, while many important issues are lost. Neither the MSE nor any other real-valued measure is sufficient to tackle all relevant issues.

To get more information about the learning process, it would be necessary to analyze the whole output data, find out which vectors are problematic, which of them separate well and which don't. Obviously, analyzing thousands of numbers by hand is not a good idea. Economy, biology and physics know a common solution to that - plotting.

2 Visualization

From now on, we will focus on MLP networks, used for classification. The problem can be defined as follows:

- Input consists of n vectors $E^{(i)} \in \mathbb{R}^s$, each of them is assigned to one of k categories. Vector $E^{(i)}$ is assigned to category $Cat(i)$
- Network consists of two layers. There are s inputs, some number h of hidden neurons, and k output neurons.
- If the input vector $E^{(i)}$ is assigned to category t, then the network is trained to activate the t-th output neuron, while others should not be activated. The desired output vector corresponding to the i-th category will be denoted by $\overrightarrow{Cat(i)}$ as opposed to the actual network output $O^{(i)}$.

L. Rutkowski et al. (Eds.): ICAISC 2004, LNAI 3070, pp. 247–252, 2004.
© Springer-Verlag Berlin Heidelberg 2004

For example, if there are two categories then the output is two dimensional, and the categories are mapped onto vertices $(1,0)$ and $(0,1)$ of the unit square, which coincides in this case with the whole activation space. The activation space in general is a k-dimensional unit hypercube I_k, with $\overrightarrow{Cat(i)}$ concentrated on the bisecting hyperplane H_k of the main diagonal $[\overrightarrow{0}, \overrightarrow{1}]$ of I_k.

First of all, let's review the problem, pointing out important issues:

- We have n vector outputs in I_k which lay inside a k-dimensional hypercube.
- We map the categories onto corresponding vertices.
- The training process should result in most of the data clustering around these vertices.

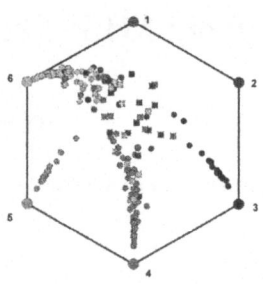

Fig. 1. A plot with six categories and 214 patterns of data. It visualizes the output of a sigmoidal MLP network with a MSE of 0.214. The plot was scaled by $\sigma = 0.35$.

Therefore the most effective method of visualization seems to be some kind of a projection. Now, what interests us the most about each vector $O^{(i)}$ is:

- Is it well classified (in other words, is the distance between $O^{(i)}$ and $\overrightarrow{Cat(i)}$ minimized among the categories)?
- Is it far from or close to its assigned category; does it tend to move towards another category?
- Is it an outlier or are there any other vectors in its vicinity?

Let's consider a mapping system, as follows. Each of the categories is a center of a Gaussian radial function

$$G(x; a, \sigma) = e^{-\frac{(x-a)^2}{2\sigma^2}}$$

which will be used for scaling. Categories will be mapped, one-to-one, onto the corners of a polygon. Assume there are k categories. Inside a k-gon, each output vector $O^{(i)}$ is projected as follows:

$$O_x^{(i)} = \frac{1}{\delta} \sum_{l=1}^{k} G\left(\left(\left\|O^{(i)} - \overrightarrow{Cat(l)}\right\|\right); 0, \sigma\right) \cdot \overrightarrow{Cat(l)}_x$$

$$O_y^{(i)} = \frac{1}{\delta} \sum_{l=1}^{k} G\left(\left(\left\|O^{(i)} - \overrightarrow{Cat(l)}\right\|\right); 0, \sigma\right) \cdot \overrightarrow{Cat(l)}_y,$$

(1)

where $\delta = \sum_{l=1}^{k} G\left(\left(\left\|O^{(i)} - \overrightarrow{Cat(l)}\right\|\right); 0, \sigma\right)$ is a normalizing factor, $(O_x^{(i)}, O_y^{(i)})$ are coordinates of the i-th output's projection, $(\overrightarrow{Cat(l)}_x, \overrightarrow{Cat(l)}_y)$ are coordinates of the l-th category projection (l-th vertex of k-gon), $\|\ \|$ is the Euclidean norm in a k-dimensional space.

A sample plot can be seen in Fig. 1. To make the plot more useful, some extra information coded as color has been added, defining where the sample belongs, and how it was classified. Further in the paper there will be some other add-ons like network dynamics, and convex hull around each data cluster.

Since the plot mechanism described above is just a projection, some information is lost. Two dots displayed as close to each other can be quite distant in the activation space. If dots from different categories tend to mix up in the plot, it doesn't always mean they mix in the activation space. These are obvious faults of plotting multidimensional data into two dimensions. One way to compensate for these faults is to look at different plots, and choose the one that gives the best view. This can be done by permuting the vertices of the polygon (which correspond to category centers). Unfortunately it's rather difficult to numerically choose an optimal (most suitable for a human) permutation, so the problem of choosing the best permutation is left to the plot reviewer (user).

Permuting categories is just one of many methods to make such plots more useful. We introduced some other self-adapting optimizations, that might make the plot just a bit better. The parameter σ, responsible for dispersion, is constant for all categories and data samples. What if σ is made dependent upon some parameters specific for a category? Put:

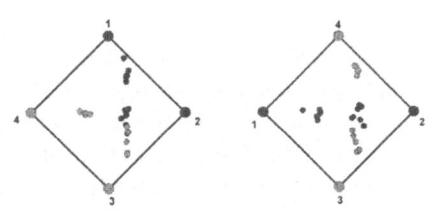

Fig. 2. Two plots, showing exactly the same data (sigmoidal MPL output, MSE 0.1, scaled by a factor $\sigma = 0.7$), but with different permutations of category vertices. Please notice that category 2 and 3 don't mix.

Fig. 3. Three plots created using MLP network on iris data (MSE=0.086), with different scaling options. Left: $\sigma = 2.0$, constant for all categories (1), middle: scaled using the maximum formula (2) with σ_0 set to 2.0, right: scaled using the average formula (3) again with $\sigma_0 = 2.0$.

$$\sigma_{(l)} = \sigma_0 \max_{i \in N, Cat(i)=l} \left\| O^{(i)} - \overrightarrow{Cat(l)} \right\| \tag{2}$$

In this case, the dispersion of the Gaussian kernel depends on the maximal distance between the center of a category l, and vectors assigned to l. If the vectors of category l are spread widely all over the activation space, the corresponding Gaussian function will have a big dispersion. A big dispersion means that the category will attract other vectors stronger. What consequences does it have for our plot? Since a "wide" category is a stronger attractor, this scaling will reveal the border regions in activation space, while most vectors from the l-th category will be projected close to the polygon corners.

This kind of projection is good for analyzing border regions of networks that are already trained, and is rather useless for fresh networks.

Another variant of adaptive, category dependent scaling is done by making σ depend on the average distance of vectors from their assigned category. This can be done as follows:

$$\sigma_{(l)} = \sigma_0 \left(\frac{1}{M} \sum_{Cat(i)=l} \left\| O^{(i)} - \overrightarrow{Cat(l)} \right\| \right) \tag{3}$$

As opposed to the previous method, suppose that most vectors are properly classified around their common category, and a few are not. The average distance between sample vectors and the category center is small, and so the σ parameter is small. It's as if those wrongly classified vectors were treated as data errors rather than network errors. This gives a slightly different projection that displays badly classified samples.

3   Additional Visual Guides

Adaptive scaling methods and vertex permutations are helpful when it comes to enhancing the informational value of the plot. We suggest several further enhancements.

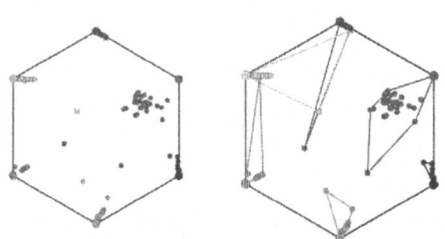

Fig. 4. The 5 categories are well separated... or are they? Convex hulls reval the problem.

It's not uncommon for a single data sample to float away from its category. The network would keep the MSE low by keeping the remaining samples close to their proper categories. While this might be satisfactory from a statistical point of view, the consequences might be catastrophical in real life applications. Imagine a patient with a very uncommon symptoms (due to genetic reasons for example) being categorized to (and treated for) a different disease.

An outlier sample could be unnoticed as its corresponding dot could be covered by other dots on the plot. To resolve this, as well as to provide a certain per-category measure of data similarity, the plot can be complemented with convex hulls marking the borders of each category. If a data sample happens to stand out, the hull will expand to contain it, making it clear that the category does mix up with another one.

From a non-overtrained, well generalizing neural net, it is expected that the convex hull of a given category should remain within a vicinity of the category's vertex. If two convex hulls overlap, it suggests that their categories might have been confused by the network, although not necessarily. If the convex hull is stretched away from the category vertex, but the samples remain tucked tight, it means that the net has trouble separating the category and its architecture and/or training process has to be reviewed.

To provide an extra information about the overlapping of categories, simple Voronoi border capability can be added to the plot. The borders separate only the category centers, yet they give a good view of relations between categories. One thing has to be put straight though. The fact that a sample is not in its assigned Voronoi cell, doesn't mean that it is not properly classified. The position of a sample in the plot depends on multiple factors, including relative weights of the output connections and adaptive scaling (σ parameters). Therefore the badly classified samples have been represented by an X symbol. The X mark is coloured with the color of the category it was (mis)assigned to. This gives extra information about misleading data or patterns misassigned in the process of data preparation. The X mark is independent of scaling, because its color coincides with the color of the vertex the dot approaches when σ approaches zero.

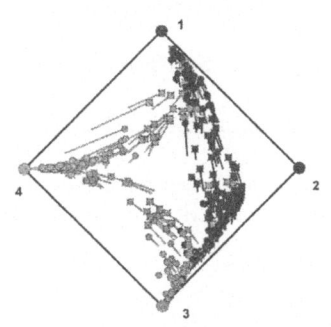

Fig. 5. The dynamics of a network's output in early stages of the training process (backprop algorithm with momentum), MSE=0.3, scaled adaptively (average) $\sigma_0 = 0.5$.

All the enhancements and visual guides described so far are meant to emphasize certain qualities of trained networks or to compensate for the limitations of dimension-reducing projection. To view the dynamic aspects of the training process, the user has either to watch the changing plot during training, or look at multiple plots representing the states of the network in subsequent stages of the process. Displaying multiple plots requires additional space and doesn't provide any visual clue on how far a given dot has moved (or if it has moved at all).

The solution to that is rather simple. The movement of a dot during a certain (user-defined) number of training epochs can be marked as a segment ending at this dot. This might not say much about an individual dot, but the whole plot seems to be enriched by another dimension: time. Extra information given by such a plot is useful in many ways. We know that the training process is going well if the dots are moving towards their assigned categories, but that is a pretty optimistic situation and doesn't really happen throughout most of the process.

The network separates the data well if a group of dots belonging to the same category is moving simultaneously. Any dot described as an outlier before, or a dot that is to become an outlier, would most certainly move in a different direction. In some situations one might observe that all categories move towards one that is rather stable. That means that the network has trouble separating that category and tends to decrease the MSE by warping the whole output in that direction. A situation like that suggests that maybe crossvalidation or data pre-separation might be required. The network might be too small or a committee of networks may be needed to solve the problem.

Acknowledgements. We thank our mentor, prof. W lodzis law Duch, who had suggested to take on this project. Great thanks go to dr Norbert Jankowski, who provided us with practical information about the implementation of the visualization module. Dr Tomasz Schreiber gained our gratitude by helping with various theoretical issues and helping us to solve optimalization problems. Last, but not least, we want to thank Paolo Marrone, the author of the JOONE engine.

References

1. W. Duch *Uncertainty of data, fuzzy membership functions, and multi-layer perceptrons (2003, subm. to IEEE Transactions on Neural Networks)*
2. W. Duch *Coloring black boxes: visualization of neural network decisions*. Int. Joint Conf. on Neural Networks, Portland, Oregon, 2003, Vol. I, pp. 1735-1740
3. Paolo Marrone *Java object oriented neural engine* www.joone.org
4. Stanis law Osowski *Neural Networks for Information Processing*. Warsaw University of Technology, Warsaw 2000 (in Polish)
5. J. Korbicz, A. Obuchowicz, D. Uciński *Artificial Neural Networks, Basics and Applications*. Academic Publishing House PLJ, Warsaw 1994 (in Polish)
6. Robert A. Kosiński *Artificial Neural Networks, Nonlinear Dynamics and Chaos*. Scientific-Technical Publishing, Warsaw 2002 (in Polish)
7. Stanis law Osowski *Neural Networks in Algorithmic Approach*. Scientific-Technical Publishing, Warsaw 1996 (in Polish)
8. W. Duch, J. Korbicz, L. Rutkowski, R. Tadeusiewicz *Biocybernetics and Biomedical Engineering 2000 - vol 6 Neural Networks* Academic Publishing House Exit, Warsaw 2000 (in Polish).

Optimization of Centers' Positions for RBF Nets with Generalized Kernels

E. Rafajłowicz and M. Pawlak

[1] Institute of Engineering Cybernetis, Wrocław University of Technology, Wybrzeże
Wyspiańskiego 27, 50 370 Wrocław, Poland. raf@ldhpux.immt.pwr.wroc.pl
[2] M. Pawlak is with Department of Electrical and Computer Engineering University
of Manitoba, Winnipeg, Canada

Abstract. The problem of locating centers for radial basis functions in
neural networks is discussed. The proposed approach allows us to apply
the results from the theory of optimum experimental designs. In typical
cases we are able to compose optimal centers' locations from the known
univariate experiment designs.

1 Introduction and Assumptions

Universal approximation property [7] and universal consistency [11] of radial
basis functions (RBF) artificial neural nets made their popularity still growing
in recent years. The importance of selecting centers of RBF's has been early
recognized (see [1] and the bibliography cited there in). We refer the reader to
[6], [4] for recent contributions to this topic. Our aim is to discuss a new approach
to the problem of locating RBF centers, which is based on the results from the
theory of optimal experiment design. The resulting optimal locations mainly
provide reduction of the variance in tuning the weights of RBF nets. However,
the resulting centers positions are spread sufficiently fairly in the input space in
order to provide small bias.

Let $\mathcal{X}_J^*$ denotes the sequence of centers x_j^*, $j = 1, 2, \ldots, J$. Then, generalized
RBF nets are of the form

$$y(x) = \sum_{j=1}^{J} a_j K\left(x, x_j^*\right), \tag{1}$$

where $K(x, x')$ is a generalized kernel being defined on $X \times X$, $x, x' \in X \subset \mathbf{R}^d$.
The kernel K is required to be continuous in $X \times X$, symmetric and positive
definite. For a given kernel $K(x, x')$, it is easy to verify its continuity and symmetry. It is, however, more difficult to check that $K(x, x')$ is positive definite.
The results due to Schoenberg [9] gives a helpful mean of proving the positivity
of a certain class of kernels. Clearly, one can select kernel in the classical way,
i.e., $K(x, x') = \mathcal{K}\left(\|x - x_j^*\| / h\right)$, where $\mathcal{K}$ is a univariate kernel (e.g., Gaussian),
$\|.\|$ is a norm in $\mathbf{R}^d$, while $h > 0$ is the smoothing parameter

Assume that for a certain unknown vector of weights $a \overset{def}{=} [a_1, a_2, \ldots, a_J]^T$
and for the learning sequence $\{(x_i, y_i), i = 1, 2, \ldots, n\}$ the following relationship
holds

L. Rutkowski et al. (Eds.): ICAISC 2004, LNAI 3070, pp. 253–259, 2004.
© Springer-Verlag Berlin Heidelberg 2004

$$y_i = a^T \bar{K}(x_i, \mathcal{X}_j^*) + \varepsilon_i, \quad i = 1, 2, \ldots, n, \tag{2}$$

where $\bar{K}(x, \mathcal{X}_j^*) \overset{def}{=} [K(x, x_1^*), K(x, x_2^*), \ldots, K(x, x_j^*)]^T$, while ε_i, $i = 1, 2, \ldots, n$ is a sequence of random errors, which are uncorrelated with $E(\varepsilon_i) = 0$, $var(\varepsilon_i) = \sigma^2 < \infty$, and where σ^2 is unknown. One can relax the assumption that the variances of all ε_i's are the same and that the errors are correlated at the expense of more complicated formulas. In (2) the observation points $\{x_i\}$ are assumed to be random vectors, which are independent and have the same probability distribution.

Suppose for a while that x_j^*'s are fixed. Then, one can estimate the weights a from the learning sequence using the classical MSE solution. Denote such a solution by $\hat{a}$. It is well known that $\hat{a} = M_n^{-1}(\mathcal{X}_j^*) \cdot \sum_{i=1}^n y_i \bar{K}(x_i, \mathcal{X}_j^*)$, provided that the information matrix $M_n(\mathcal{X}_j^*) \overset{def}{=} \sum_{i=1}^n \bar{K}(x_i, \mathcal{X}_j^*) \cdot \bar{K}^T(x_i, \mathcal{X}_j^*)$ is nonsingular. Clearly, $M_n(\mathcal{X}_j^*)$ depends also on observation points $\{x_i\}$ but we suppress this dependence for the simplicity of notation.

It is also well known that assuming correctness of the model in (2) we have $E(\hat{a}) = a$ and the covariance matrix of $\hat{a}$ has the form $cov(\hat{a}) = \sigma^2 M_n^{-1}(\mathcal{X}_j^*)$. One would like to increase the accuracy $\hat{a}$ by reducing $M_n^{-1}(\mathcal{X}_j^*)$ by a proper choice of $\mathcal{X}_j^*$. The difficulty is in that for two sequences of centers $\mathcal{X}_J$ and $\mathcal{X}_J'$ the matrices $M_n^{-1}(\mathcal{X}_J)$ and $M_n^{-1}(\mathcal{X}_J')$ are not always comparable in the sense of the Loewner ordering. In the optimum experiment design theory the standard way of circumventing this difficulty is to select a functional of $M_n^{-1}(\mathcal{X}_J)$, which is compatible with the Loewner ordering. Such a functional usually has a statistical interpretation and it is called the design optimality criterion. For further considerations we shall select the most popular D-optimality criterion, which is the determinant of $M_n^{-1}(\mathcal{X}_J)$. As it is known, $\det[M_n^{-1}(\mathcal{X}_J)]$ is proportional to volume of uncertainty ellipsoid and it is desirable to minimize it. Thus, we arrive to the following optimization problem: find a sequence of centers $\mathcal{X}_j^*$ such that

$$P1) \qquad \min_{\mathcal{X}_J} \det[M_n^{-1}(\mathcal{X}_J)] = \det[M_n^{-1}(\mathcal{X}_j^*)]. \tag{3}$$

The optimal sequence of centers depends both on the kernel K and on the positions of the observations $\{x_i\}$. It is however not easy to solve (3), since we are faced with a nonlinear optimization problem in $J \cdot d$ variables and constraints, since each element $x_j^* \in \mathcal{X}_J$ can be selected only from X. For example, for $d = 10$ and $J = 50$ we have rather intractable optimization problem involving 500 decision variables.

In the rest of the paper we discuss possible simplifications of this problem, which are based on asymptotic considerations and approximations. Let K be symmetric, continuous and positive definite kernel on compact set X. Consider the problem of finding eigenfunctions and eigenvalues of the integral operator with kernel K

$$\int_X K(x, x') \phi(x')dx' = \lambda \phi(x), \quad x \in X. \tag{4}$$

According to the Mercer theorem (see [10], Section 3-12) the above integral operator has a finite or countable sequence of real and positive eigenvalues $0 <$

$\lambda_1 \leq \lambda_2 \leq \ldots \leq \lambda_L \leq \ldots$. To each eigenvalue λ_k there is a corresponding nonzero eigenfunction ϕ_k, $k = 1, 2, \ldots$. This sequence of eigenfunctions can be orthonormalized so that they fulfill the following conditions

$$\int_X \phi_k^2(x)dx = 1, \quad \int_X \phi_k(x)\phi_l(x)dx = 0, \text{ if } k \neq l, \; k,l = 1,2,\ldots \quad (5)$$

Furthermore, $\{\phi_k, k = 1, 2, \ldots\}$ is a complete system in the space $L_2(X)$. Additionally, kernel K can be expressed either as

$$K(x,x') = \sum_{k=1}^{\infty} \lambda_k \phi_k(x)\,\phi_k(x'), \quad (x,x') \in X \times X, \quad (6)$$

where the series is uniformly and absolutely convergent, or as

$$K(x,x') = \sum_{k=1}^{L} \lambda_k \phi_k(x)\,\phi_k(x'), \quad (x,x') \in X \times X, \quad (7)$$

if K is the so called degenerate kernel with a finite number of eigenvalues.

Note that even if K has an infinite number of eigenvalues, one can approximate it by a degenerate kernel of the form (7), provided that L is sufficiently large. Later on we shall assume that for the kernel of a considered RBF net the representation in (7) is sufficiently accurate.

On the other hand, (7) provides a tool defining kernels for generalized RBF nets, which have some advantages, but they are not in common use. It suffices to select positive numbers $\{\lambda_k\}$ and a subsequence $\{\phi_k\}$ of an orthonormal and complete system of functions and to define a new kernel using (7). The examples of degenerate kernels, which were obtained in this way are shown in Fig. 1. We have set $\lambda_k = 1/k$, $k = 1, 2, \ldots, L$ and ϕ_k's were chosen to be: the Chebyshev polynomials of the first kind, the Legendre polynomials, the trigonometric system. As one can notice, a qualitative behavior of degenerate kernels is similar to that of the Gausssian kernel. Sign changing fluctuations of degenerate kernels can be reduced by selecting L larger (here $L = 20$ was used). For compactness of further

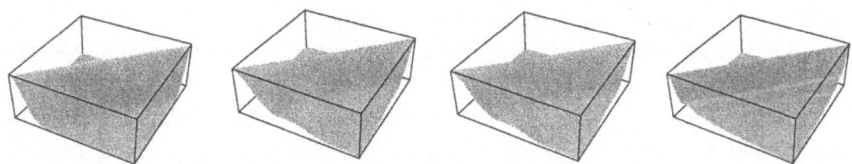

Fig. 1. Degenerate kernels generated by orthonormal systems and the Gaussian kernel for comparison (the most left). The most right figure was generated by the trigonometric system, while the middle left and middle right kernels are based on the Chebyschev and the Legendre polynomials, respectively.

formulas it is convenient to write approximating degenerate kernels as follows $K(x,x') = \sum_{l=1}^{L} v_l(x)v_l(x') = v^T(x) \cdot v(x')$, where $v_l(x) \overset{def}{=} \sqrt{\lambda_l}\,\phi_l(x)$, $v(x) \overset{def}{=} [v_1(x), v_2(x), \ldots, v_L(x)]^T$. Using this equation one can express $\bar{K}(x, \mathcal{X}_J^*)$ as follows $\bar{K}(x, \mathcal{X}_J^*) = V^T(\mathcal{X}_J^*) \cdot v(x)$, where $L \times J$ matrix $V(\mathcal{X}_J^*)$ is stacked from column vectors $v(x_j^*)$'s, i.e., $V(\mathcal{X}_J^*) = [v(x_1^*), v(x_2^*), \ldots, v(x_J^*)]$.

2   Asymptotics and Optimal Allocation of Centers

One can rewrite the information matrix in the form which splits the observation points and centers

$$M_n(\mathcal{X}_J^*) = V^T(\mathcal{X}_J^*) \left[\sum_{i=1}^n v(x_i) v^T(x_i) \right] V(\mathcal{X}_J^*). \tag{8}$$

Let us assume that $\{x_i\}$ are mutually independent random vectors with the same distribution function and such that the expectations in the following matrix $E[v(x_1)v^T(x_1)]$ exists and they are all finite. We postulate also the existence and finiteness of all the higher moments $E[v_k(x_1)v_p(x_1)v_m(x_1)v_l(x_1)]$. Define $\Omega = E[v(x_1)v^T(x_1)]$. Under the above assumptions the law of large numbers applies to the matrix in the brackets in (8) and we obtain

$$n^{-1} \sum_{i=1}^n v(x_i)v^T(x_i) \longrightarrow \Omega, \quad \text{as} \quad n \longrightarrow \infty \tag{9}$$

almost surely. Thus, for n sufficiently large we can approximate the information matrix as follows

$$M_n(\mathcal{X}_J^*) \approx n V^T(\mathcal{X}_J^*) \Omega V(\mathcal{X}_J^*). \tag{10}$$

Omitting the constant multiplier n, instead of (3) we can consider the following optimization problem: find $\mathcal{X}_J^*$ such that

$$\text{P2)} \qquad \max_{\mathcal{X}_J} \det[V^T(\mathcal{X}_J) \Omega V(\mathcal{X}_J)] = \det[V^T(\mathcal{X}_J^*) \Omega V(\mathcal{X}_J^*)]. \tag{11}$$

Note that in passing from (3) to (11) we have changed the min convention to max one, since for a nonsingular matrix, A say, we have $det[A^{-1}] = 1/det[A]$.

We have obtained somewhat simpler optimization problem, since the solution does not depend directly on $\{x_i\}$, but on the matrix Ω (which depends on the probability distribution of x's). Thus, one may expect that the solution of the P2) problem is less erratic than that of P1). Nevertheless, from the computational point of view P2) is of the same degree of complexity as P1).

The next step is to assume $L = J$, i.e., to consider the case when the number of RBF centers is the same as the number of terms used for generating (or approximating) kernel K in (7). This assumption looks artificially, but in fact we need both L and J to be of moderate size and we have much freedom in selecting these numbers.

Selecting $J = L$ we get

$$\det[V^T(\mathcal{X}_J) \Omega V(\mathcal{X}_J)] = \left(\det[V^T(\mathcal{X}_J)] \right)^2 \det[\Omega] \tag{12}$$

or in the mathematically equivalent form

$$\det[V^T(\mathcal{X}_J) \Omega V(\mathcal{X}_J)] = \det[\Omega] \det[V(\mathcal{X}_J)V^T(\mathcal{X}_J)]. \tag{13}$$

Comparison (12) and (13) with (11) yields.

Corollary 1 *If approximate equality (10) is sufficiently accurate and we have that $J = L$, then the D-optimal location of RBF centers does not depend on the probability distribution of observations $\{x_i\}$.*

Note, however, that the estimation quality, as measured by D-criterion, depends on $\det[\Omega]$.

Expression (12) is convenient for numerical search of $\mathcal{X}_J^*$ using DETMAX algorithm of Mitchell [5] or its later more enhanced versions. One should take into account that algorithms of this type usually finds a suboptimal solution, which can be very far from optimum when $J \cdot d$ is large. Therefore, it is expedient to impose more assumptions on components of vector v in order to get more explicit characterization of the best sequence of centers. Even if these assumptions are difficult to verify for typical kernels, we always can generate degenerate kernels with required properties with the aid of (7).

To simplify further formulas we present the idea for $d = 2$. We shall write $(x^{(1)}, x^{(2)})$ for generic components of x_j^*'s. Recall that $v(x) = [v_1(x), \ldots, v_L(x)]^T$ and, by assumption, $J = L$. Let us suppose that components $v(x)$ have the following form:

$$\psi_l(x^{(1)}) \cdot \varphi_m(x^{(2)}), \quad l = 1, 2, \ldots, L_1, \ m = 1, 2, \ldots, L_2, \tag{14}$$

where φ_m's and ψ_l's are selected from univariate orthonormal and complete sequences. We must also select L_1 and L_2 in such a way that $L = L_1 \cdot L_2$. If components of $v(x)$ have the form as in (14), then it can be expressed as follows

$$v(x) = \bar{\psi}(x^{(1)}) \otimes \bar{\phi}(x^{(2)}), \quad \bar{\psi}(t) \overset{def}{=} [\psi_1(t), \psi_2(t), \ldots, \psi_{L_1}(t)]^T, \tag{15}$$

where $\otimes$ denotes the Kronecker product of matrices, while $\bar{\phi}(t)$ is defined analogously to $\bar{\psi}(t)$.

We shall search for centers x_j^*, $j = 1, 2, \ldots J$, which are linearly ordered pairs of the form

$$(x_i^{*(1)}, x_k^{*(2)}), \quad i = 1, 2, \ldots J_1, \quad k = 1, 2, \ldots, J_2, \tag{16}$$

where J_1 and J_2 are selected in such a way that $J = J_1 \cdot J_2$.

Corollary 2 *If all the assumptions of Corollary 1 hold, $v(x)$ is of the form (15) and we search for D-optimal allocation of centers of the form (16), then the solution of the problem P2) is the tensor product of the solutions of the following optimization problems*

$$\max_{t_1, \ldots t_{J_1}} \det \left[\sum_{i=1}^{J_1} \bar{\psi}(t_i) \bar{\psi}^T(t_i) \right], \quad \max_{t_1, \ldots t_{J_2}} \det \left[\sum_{k=1}^{J_2} \bar{\phi}(t_k) \bar{\phi}^T(t_k) \right] \tag{17}$$

Proof follows from the algebraic properties of the Kronecker product (see, e.g., [3]). It can also be shown that the above allocation of centers is optimal also in a wider class of admissible allocations, which are not a priori restricted to grid points. This statement can be proved by modifying the proof from [8]. In multivariate case $(d > 2)$, the optimal allocation of centers is the Cartesian product of the solutions of optimization problems analogous to (17).

From practical point of view it is important that the optimal solutions of (17) problems are known for many important orthonormal systems of functions

$\bar{\psi}(t)$ generating the kernel of our RBF net. A valuable source of the solutions can be found in [2], where, e.g., it was proved that if $\bar{\psi}(t)$ is defined in terms of the Legendre polynomials, then the centers t_i^* derived from (17) are zeros of the polynomial $(1 - t^2) \cdot dL_{J_1-1}(t)/dt$, where $L_k(t)$ denotes the Legendre polynomial of kth degree.

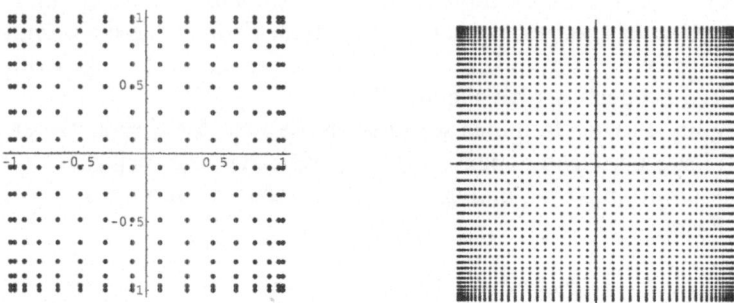

Fig. 2. Optimal centers positions for RBF with kernels generated by the Legendre polynomials.

Acknowledgements. The work of E. Rafajłowicz was supported by the grant of Polish Council for Scientific Research under grant ranging from 2002 to 2005.

References

1. Bishop, C. M. *Neural Networks for Pattern Recognition.* Oxford, England: Oxford University Press, 1995.
2. Karlin S. and Studden W.J. *Tchebycheff Systems, with Applications in Analysis and Statistics.* Interscience, New York, 1972.
3. Lankaster P. *Theory of Matrices.* Academic Press, London, 1969.
4. Mao K. Z. RBF neural network center selection based on Fisher ratio class separability measure. *IEEE Transactions on Neural Networks*, vol. 13, pp.1211-1217, 2002.
5. Mitchell T.J. An algorithm for the construction of "D-optimal" experimental designs. *Technometrics*, vol.16, pp.203–210, 1974.
6. Panchapakesan Ch., Palaniswami M., Ralph D., and Manzie Ch. Effects of moving the centers in an RBF network. *IEEE Transactions on Neural Networks*, vol. 13, pp.1299-1307, 2002.
7. Park J. and Sandberg I. Universal approximation using radial basis function networks, *Neural Computation*, vol. 3, pp. 246-257, 1991.
8. Rafajłowicz E. and Myszka W. Optimum experimental design for a regression on a hypercube – generalization of Hoel's result. *Ann. Inst. Statist. Math.*, vol. 40, pp.821–827, 1988.

9. Schoenberg I.J. Metric spaces and completely monotone functions. *Ann. of Math.* vol.39, pp.811-841, 1938.
10. Tricomi F.G. *Integral Equations.* Dover, New York 1985.
11. Xu L., Krzyzak A. and Yuille A. On radial basis function nets and kernel regression: Statistical consistency, convergence rates, and receptive field size, *Neural Networks*, vol. 4, , pp. 609-628, 1994.

Fixed Non–linear Combining Rules versus Adaptive Ones

Sarunas Raudys and Zidrina Pabarskaite

Institute of Mathematics and Informatics,
Akademijos 4, Vilnius LT-2021, Lithuania
raudys@das.mii.lt, zidrina@pabarska.com

Abstract. We consider fixed non–linear combining rules as a strategy for information fusion in neural network based machine learning problems and compare them with adaptive ones. In this strategy, essential part of the work is overloaded to examiner–operator who ought to split the data "reliably". In small sample size situations, non–trainable combination rules allow creating committee with performance comparable or even lower with that obtained with more sophisticated information fusion methods. Fixed rule's solutions are easier interpreted by end users.

1 Introduction

Combining individual decisions is becoming more popular approach while solving complex pattern classification and artificial neural networks problems in economics, web log data mining and machine diagnostics applications. In pattern recognition task, a number of "experts classify" input vector firstly. Afterwards, a combiner utilizes solutions of the experts and makes the final classification [1]. In this approach, the task is decomposed into simpler ones and allows designing decision making rules even in cases where data size is relatively small. Experts usually are adaptive classifiers in committee machines while combiners could be adaptive or fixed *a priori*.

Theoretical analysis shows that *committee machines with adaptive combiners suffer from small sample effects:* 1) generalization errors of expert classifiers as well as adaptive combiner increase in comparison to the ideal case, 2) complex experts trained on learning sets of insufficient size begin to "boast" themselves to the combiner. Consequently, there is a need to adjust complexity of trainable combiner to the size of the learning set. Fixed non–trainable combining rules do not require training data. Obviously fixed rules do not suffer from small sample problems. Majority voting and sum of continuous experts' outputs are the simplest non–adaptive combining rules where all experts are considered to be equally important. Popular maximum rule can be considered as the sum or the majority voting combining rules where only one (the best) expert is selected. Time and again experts differ in their "qualifications" measured as a classification error. A conventional approach to distinguish experts is to assign to them different weights in adaptive combination rule. Unfortunately, fixed linear combination rule cannot solve this task. Hence, a necessity to utilize non–linear information

L. Rutkowski et al. (Eds.): ICAISC 2004, LNAI 3070, pp. 260–265, 2004.
© Springer-Verlag Berlin Heidelberg 2004

fusion rules appears such as Bayesian combining rules (belief functions), standard Kernel classifiers or their modifications, the single layer perceptron. Well known non–linear rules, such as behavior–knowledge–space method, k–nearest neighbour, kernel based classifiers, multilayer perceptrons (MLP), bagging, mixture of local experts are adaptive ones [2], [3]. Unfortunately, we lack of fixed *non–trainable* combination rules that make *non–linear* decisions. Simple, almost trivial strategy is to design such multiple classifiers systems where the designer inspects the training data and distributes it among the local experts purposefully. In the recognition phase, for each test vector, the combining rule finds responsible local expert and allocates the final solution to it. In this approach, training of the combining rule is not performed. *Instead of training the combining (gating) rule regions of experts competence are defined a priori.* Essential part of the work is overloaded to examiner–operator who ought to split the data "reliably". Such combining rule is named as fixed *non–linear* one.

To split input data to experts and rely on their decisions is not a new approach in committee design. To find regions where distinct experts are the most competent authors in [4] suggested a sample based oracle. Its decisions were based on kernel function classifier. Our main concern, however, is to consider fixed rules where the experts' competence regions are defined *a priori*. In this paper, we consider ways to decompose the data by means of criteria weakly related with classification error as *a principle to design non–linear fixed combiners*. We will try to define situations were this principle performs well and where not.

2 Splitting Training Data to Local Experts

Training sample size is a very important factor while choosing a proper expert and combining rules. Let $N_1, \ldots, N_K$ be p-variate training vectors belonging to K classes and let P_B be the Bayes error. Suppose the designer splits input feature space Ω into L non–intersecting regions $\Omega_1, \ldots, \Omega_L$ corresponding to each of L local experts. In order to have committee machine with classification error equal to P_B, experts ought to utilize optimal Bayes classification rules in their own regions. It is well known that sample based classifier's generalization error EP_N depends on Bayes error, complexity of the classification rule and training set size (see e.g. [5], [6], [7]). An increase in generalization error due to the finite training set size is directly proportional to complexity and inversely proportional to the training set size. After input space division into L regions, we have smaller amount of training vectors in each of them. Therefore, in order to have maximal success, division of input space should allow utilizing simple classifiers in each of the regions. It is the main requirement. Classifiers for uni–modal pattern classes should be considered simpler in comparison with classifiers designed to discriminate multimodal ones. Consequently, while dividing the input space into sub–regions $\Omega_1, \Omega_2, \ldots, \Omega_L$ the designer should try to have uni–modal densities in each of them. Universal learning curves' theory [8] claims that asymptotically as the training set size N increases, an increase in generalization error $EP_N - P_B$ is proportional to $1/N$, i.e. $EP_N - P_B = c\, 1/N$. Here c is a term which characterizes the data and complexity of the training algorithm. Detailed analysis of numerical results indicates that in different classification algorithms, we have different terms of theoretical dependence $EP_N - P_B = constant \times (1/N)^\alpha$. For statistical classifiers, such as standard linear Fisher discriminant function, we have $= 2$, if sample size N is close to dimensionality of the input feature space. The universal constant approaches to 1 when $N \to \infty$. For non-parametric local classifiers such as Kernel discriminant analysis, k-NN rule and Multinomial classifier $a < 1$ [7].

Consider an example with $p = 50$, where the Bayes classification error in region Ω_h is $P_B \approx 0.03$, and N the number of training vectors from each pattern class in this region is 100. Theory shows that generalization error of standard quadratic discriminant function Q exceeds asymptotical error almost seven times. Thus, classifier Q cannot be used as the expert in such situation. An alternative is to use standard linear Fisher classifier F. It is less sensitive to the training set size. For $p = 50$, $N = 100$, and $P_B \approx 0.03$, the generalization error increases 2 times. If we succeed to select 10 informative features ($p = 10$), relative increase in generalization error of classifier Q is 2 times and that of classifier F is only 1.15 times (Table 1 in [6]). We see that theoretical estimates are extremely important while choosing a way to split training data among the expert classifiers and for choosing their complexity.

Task decomposition. Due to computational difficulties, criteria used to determine competence areas of each local expert are weakly related to classification error. Accuracy of competence estimators is diminished by insufficiency of training set size. Thus, as a rule we have inaccurate estimates. In fixed non–adaptive combiners, the researcher–operator refuses using "exact" criteria. In particular, we suggest exploiting linear projection of the multivariate data into 2D space and dividing it to experts either manually in interactive modus operandi or by some simple cluster analysis algorithm, a technique that is unrelated to classification error directly. Methods like shallow decision trees can be utilized too. There is a great number of methods for linear mapping of multivariate vectors x into r–variate space y $= (y_1, y_2, \ldots, y_r) = [t_1, t_2, \ldots, t_r]$x $=$ Tx ([5], [3]). The most popular are principal component (PC) and auto associative neural networks (AANN). The PC and AANN algorithms, however, do not use classification error as a minimization criterion. The Foley–Sammon's optimal discriminant plane is supervised linear data mapping tool aimed to apply if data is uni–modal. Intermediate way between supervised and unsupervised feature extraction methods is utilization of weighted sums $y_j = t_j$x $(j = 1, 2, \ldots, r)$ calculated in r hidden layer of MLP trained in supervised mode [9]. Using MLP, *feature extraction is linear* operation, however, the *minimization criterion is non–linear*. Degree of nonlinearity depends on the number of new extracted features r. If data is mapped into 2D space, the designer can inspect two–dimensional displays of the data and evaluate visually diverse hypothesis concerning structure and resolution of the pattern classes and split 2D space into L non–intersecting regions. In comparison with formal data splitting methods the operator exploits non–formalized human ability to assess the 2D display of the data. Actually it is *a new non–formalized information*. In the recognition (test) phase, the combiner utilizes exactly the same data transformation rule $(y_1, y_2) = [t_1, t_2]$x to map multivariate data into a new 2D feature space and allocates each vector to be classified to one of L experts. To divide data into L parts automatic splitting (cluster analysis) can

be used too. While splitting the data we deliberately stay away from joint utilization of training set and classification error criteria. It seems intuitively that
margins between diverse groups have to be obtained while division the feature
space among the experts. We acknowledge, however, that certain slips are unavoidable in this space partition. Experiments confirmed that while distributing
data for training L experts, the artificially introduced intersections of regions
$\Omega_1, \ldots, \Omega_L$ are useful.

3   Simulation Experiments

Artificial 15–dimensional "palm data"[9], 8–dim. satellite, 6–dim. debit card
transaction and 23–dim. stock exchange real world data sets were investigated.
Multilayer perceptrons trained by Levenberg–Marquardt method in multistart
mode were used as expert classifiers. Like in [10] to find an optimal complexity of expert rules and stopping moments artificial pseudo–validation sets were
constructed, which were obtained from the training data by means of colored
noise injection [11]. In experiments with the palm data (4000 vectors), decision
boundary is highly non–linear (palm–shaped). If the number of hidden units h
is not high (e.g. $h = 9$), it was impossible to avoid local minima problem and
to get a proper data separation. The MLP based classifier with 10 hidden units
resulted 3.8% error on average and in 0.8% error if the "best" MLP was selected
out of 10 ones and trained in 10 multistart sessions. Fixed non–adaptive sum
rule and majority voting gave much worse results. To distribute the data among
four experts (MLP with 6 hidden units), we used PC method and performed
training data clustering in 2D space. Non–linear fixed combining rule gave the
best result: 0.65% error rate while classifying test data. In experiments with Satellite data (15,000 vectors), MLP with two hidden units was used to map data
into 2D space and split it into 3 regions by the operator (Fig.1); only 25% of training vectors are displayed). Separate data subsets were used to train 3 first local
experts. In addition 7 global MLP experts (with 5 and 15 hidden units) were designed. The experts' classification errors are presented in Table 1. Crisp (binary)
outputs of the experts were used to design various combination rules. We investigated 12 experts groups composed of 3, 5 or 7 MLP based classifiers. The fixed
non–linear combination rule resulted in 3.9% error for $h = 5$ and in 3.77% error
for $h = 15$. For comparison we used adaptive weighted linear voting realized by
the single layer perceptron (SLP) and non–linear Behaviour–Knowledge Space
(BKS) method.

   We remind, that in BKS method we investigate all $m = 2^L$ combinations
(cells) of binary crisp outputs of L expert classifiers. Allocation of unknown L-
variate binary valued vector falling into k-th cell ($k = 1, 2, \ldots, m$) is performed
according to a minimal number of training vectors in this particular cell. If the
number of experts L is too high for a given training set size, we have many empty
cells. The BKS combination rule has to be simplified. In order to control the
BKS rule's complexity and to reduce generalization error, we utilized artificial
validation set considered above. The artificial validation set was exploited to
train the BKS combination rule (to estimate frequencies of $2(m-1)$ cells). Error
rates of the various competing combination schemes are presented in Table 2.

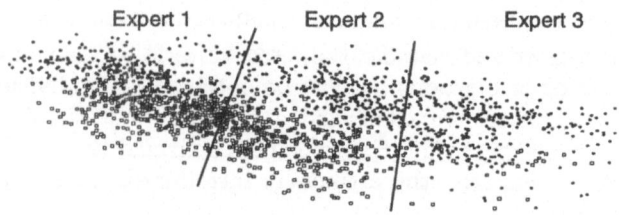

Fig. 1. A central part of Satellite training data in 2D space

Table 1. Classification error (in percents) of 10 experts in experiments with Satellite data

	Local Experts			Global Experts						
$h\backslash expert$ 1	2	3	4	5	6	7	8	9	10
5	28.2	15.4	41.8	5.1	5.1	5.1	5.4	6.1	7.0	7.8
15	28.3	3.8	15.1	3.0	3.0	4.0	4.0	4.6	4.7	4.9

Upper 6 rows correspond to experts with $h = 5$ hidden units and the lower 6 ones relate to experts with $h = 15$. Experiments indicate that *if experts are rather simple* (MLP with $h = 5$ hidden units), more sophisticated combination methods loses against fixed non-linear combiner ($P_{Fixed} = 3.9.\%$) If experts are more complex ($h = 15$), fixed non–linear information fusion rule can be outperformed by more sophisticated methods. *Joint utilization* of 3 local experts together with generic ones was beneficial if BKS or weighted voting rules were applied. Experiments with debit card transactions (89,000 vectors; see [12]) showed a bit higher efficiency of fixed non–linear combination rule in comparison with the adaptive rules. In example with "Stock" data (1383 records) we obtained practically the same classification accuracy, however, committee solution with fixed non–linear combiner was easier to interpret by end users.

4   Conclusions

In small sample size situations, human ability to interpret 2D displays of the data and/or simplified data clustering methods in 2D space assist in creating fixed non–linear combination rules that can result classification accuracy comparable or even lower as fusion with more sophisticated adaptive information fusion rules. Fixed combiner's solutions are easier to interpret by users.

Acknowledgment. The authors thank Dr. Krystyna Stankiewicz from Institute of Geodesy and Cartography, Warszawa, for providing real-world Satellite data.

Table 2. The generalization errors (in percent) of different MCS (Satellite data)

h	Groups of experts	BKS $P_{asympt.}$	Standard BKS	BKS(with NI)	SLP(with NI)
5	1, 2, 3	**4.60**	**4.60**	4.60	5.12
	4, 5, 6	5.11	5.11	5.11	5.11
	1, 2, 3, 4, 5	4.22	4.50	4.50	4.27
	4, 5, 6, 7, 8	4.37	4.52	**4.46**	4.82
	1, 2, 3, 4, 5, 6, 7	3.75	4.04	4.15	4.08
	4, 5, 6, 7, 8, 9, 10	4.08	4.66	**4.49**	4.56
15	1, 2, 3	5.11	**5.21**	**5.21**	**5.21**
	4, 5, 6	3.57	3.57	3.57	3.57
	1, 2, 3, 4, 5	3.31	3.50	**3.41**	3.47
	4, 5, 6, 7, 8	3.40	3.66	3.57	3.57
	1, 2, 3, 4, 5, 6, 7	2.79	3.45	**3.17**	3.27
	4, 5, 6, 7, 8, 9,10	2.79	3.81	3.44	3.49

References

1. Rahman, A. F. R., Fairhurst, M. C.: Multiple classifier decision combination strategies for character recognition. Int. J. Document Analysis and Recognition. **5(4)** (2003) 166–194
2. Jordan, M. I., Jacobs, R. A.: Hierarchical mixture of experts and the EM algorithm, Neural Computation **6** (1994) 181–214
3. Haykin, S.: Neural Networks: A comprehensive foundation, 2nd edition, Prentice-Hall, Englewood Cliffs, NJ (1999)
4. Rastrigin, L. A., Erenstein, R. Ch.: Method of Collective Recognition, Energoizdat, Moscow (in Russian) (1981)
5. Fukunaga, K.: Introduc. to Statistical Pattern Recognition. Academic Press, NY (1990)
6. Raudys, S., Pikelis, V.: On dimensionality, sample size, classification error and complexity of classification algorithm in pattern recognition. IEEE Trans. on Pattern Analysis and Machine Intelligence, PAMI-2 **3** (1980) 242–252
7. Raudys, S.: Statistical and Neural Classifiers. Springer, London (2001)
8. Amari, S.: A universal theorem on learning. Neural Net. **6**(1993) 161–166
9. Raudys, A., Long, J. A.: MLP based linear feature extraction for nonlinearly separable data. Pattern Analysis and Applications. **4(4)**(2001) 227–234
10. Raudys, S.: Experts' boosting in trainable fusion rules. IEEE Trans. on Pattern Analysis and Machine Intelligence. PAMI 25 (9): (2001)
11. Skurichina M., Raudys, S., Duin, R.P.W.: K–nearest neighbours directed noise injection in multilayer perceptron training, IEEE Trans. on Neural Networks **11** (2000) 504–511
12. Pabarskaite, Z., Long, J.A.: Detecting fraud transactions in large–scale databases. Proc. 22nd Conf. Information systems architecture and technology, Wroclaw (2000) 224–231

Learning and System Modeling via Hamiltonian Neural Networks

Wieslaw Sienko[1], Wieslaw Citko[1], and Dariusz Jakóbczak[2]

[1] Maritime Academy, Dept. Electrical Engineering, Morska 83, 81-455 Gdynia, Poland.
wcitko@am.gdynia.pl
[2] Technical University of Koszalin, Dept. Electrical Engineering, 75-411 Koszalin, Poland

Abstract. Hamiltonian Neural Networks based orthogonal filters are universal signal processors. The structure of such processors rely on family of Hurwitz-Radon matrices. To illustrate, we propose in this paper a procedure of nonlinear mapping synthesis. Hence, we propose here system modeling and learning architectures which are suitable for very large scale implementations.

1 Introduction

Even competent mathematicians (T. Poggio and S. Smale) have recently stated [1] that the problem of learning represents a gateway to understanding intelligence in brains and machines. They believe that supervision learning will become a key technology to extract information from the flood of data around us. The supervised learning techniques, ie. learning from examples, are similar to implementation of the mapping $y = F(u)$ relying on the fitting of experimental data pairs $\{u_k, y_k\}$. The key point is that the fitting should be predictive and uncover the underlying physical law, which is then used in a predictive or anticipatory way. A great number of models implementing the supervised learning techniques has been proposed in literature. Neural networks, RBF and fuzzy logic based models should be here mentioned. In article [1] a new learning algorithm named Regularized Least Squares Classification (RLSC) has been described and compared with Support Vector Machines (SVM). A central question in the learning theory is how well the learning models or machines generalize, i.e. how well they approximate the outputs for previously unseen inputs. Hence, the property of generalization should be the objective for further study. Inspired by results known from classical and quantum mechanics we showed that very large scale artificial neural networks could be implemented as Hamiltonian systems, i.e. as so called Hamiltonian Neural Networks (HNN) [2,3]. Moreover, we showed that the unique feature of HNN is the fact that they can exist as algorithms or physical devices performing the Haar-Walsh analysis in real-time. Since the structures of HNN can be based on family of Hurwitz-Radon matrices, we present in this paper how to design large scale nonlinear mappings by using HNN with weight

L. Rutkowski et al. (Eds.): ICAISC 2004, LNAI 3070, pp. 266–271, 2004.
© Springer-Verlag Berlin Heidelberg 2004

matrices determined by Hurwitz-Radon matrices. Thus, described here implementation of nonlinear mappings can be seen as a model of supervised learning. Due to passivity of used HNN, this implementation is well-posed.

2   Hamiltonian Neural Networks

A lossless neural network composed of $N/2$ lossless neuron pairs and described by the following state-space equation:

$$\dot{x} = W\Theta(x) + d \tag{1}$$

where:

$W - (N \times N)$ skew-symmetric, orthogonal weight matrix i.e. $W = -W^T$, $W^2 = -1$

$\Theta(x)$ – vector of activation functions, where: $\mu_1 \leq \frac{\Theta(x)}{x} \leq \mu_2$; $\mu_1, \mu_2 \in [0, \infty]$

d – input data

has been named Hamiltonian Neural Network (HNN).

On the other hand, set of orthogonal, skew-symmetric matrices A_k with following properties:

$$A_j A_k + A_k A_j = 0; \; A_j^2 = -1; \quad \text{for } j \neq k, k = 1, \ldots, s \tag{2}$$

are known as a family of Hurwitz-Radon matrices [4].

Any family of Hurwitz-Radon matrices $(N \times N)$ consists of s_{max} matrices, where $s_{max} = \rho(N) - 1$ and Radon number $\rho(N) \leq N$.

For our purposes, the following statements on family of Hurwitz-Radon matrices could be interesting:

1. The maximum number of continuous orthogonal tangent vector fields on sphere $S^{N-1} \subset R^N$ is $\rho(N) - 1$.
2. Let $W_1, \ldots, W_s$ be a set of orthogonal Hurwitz-Radon matrices and $W_0 = 1$. Let $w_0, \ldots, w_s$ be real numbers with:

$$\sum_{i=0}^{s} w_i = 1 \; . \tag{3}$$

Hence, matrix: $W(w) = \sum_{i=0}^{s} w_i W_i$ is orthogonal.

Since $w = (w_0, w_1, \ldots, w_s)^T \in S^s \subset R^{s+1}$, then (3) can be seen as a map of sphere S^s into the orthogonal group $O(N)$. Moreover, the (2) can be treated as a problem of finding the maximum number of orthogonal tangent vector fields on S^{N-1}.

It is worth noting that Hurwitz-Radon matrices can be used for creating the weight matrices of HNN and to formulate some essential issues in signal processing, namely:

1. Finding the best-adapted basis for a given signal.
2. Decomposition of a given signal into orthogonal components.

Equation (3) can be seen as a formula for finding a best-adapted basis, namely:

1. Find such a vector of parameters w that the weight matrix $W(w)$ of HNN sets up the best-adapted basis.
2. Use this weight matrix for implementation of mapping $y = F(u)$ given by a set of training points: $u_k \mapsto y_k$, $k = 1, \ldots, n$, where u_k and y_k belong to input and output vector spaces, respectively.

Matrix $W(w)$ can be implemented as weight matrix of HNN in structure of an orthogonal filter shown in Fig.1 It can be seen that such a filter performs the

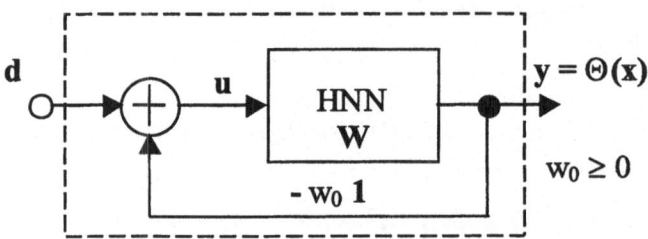

Fig. 1. Structure of an orthogonal filter

following decomposition:

$$d = u + w_0 y \tag{4}$$

where: u and y are orthogonal i.e. $y = Wu$, $(u, y) = 0$.

At the same time (4) sets up the following orthogonal mapping:

$$y = \frac{1}{1 + w_0^2}(W + w_0 1)d = \frac{1}{1 + w_0^2}W(w)d . \tag{5}$$

According to (5) the input signal d is decomposed into a Haar or Walsh basis, and the output signal y constitutes the Haar or Walsh spectrum, respectively. Moreover, matrix $W(w)$ constitutes the best adapted basis, if (5) is fulfilled for given vector pair d and y i.e. if input vector d is mapped into given output vector y.

As mentioned above, Radon number fulfills $\rho(N) = N$ only for $N = 2, 4, 8$. Hence, for example, matrix $W(w)$ for $N = 8$ can be composed as follows:

$$W(w) = w_0 1 + \sum_{i=1}^{7} w_i W_i \tag{6}$$

where: $\boldsymbol{W}_i$; $i = 1, \ldots, 7$ – Hurwitz-Radon integer $\{-1, 0, 1\}$ matrices. Thus, one obtains the weight matrix of filter from Fig. 1 as follows:

$$
\boldsymbol{W}(\boldsymbol{w}) =
\begin{bmatrix}
-w_0 & w_1 & w_2 & w_3 & w_4 & w_5 & w_6 & w_7 \\
-w_1 & -w_0 & w_3 & -w_2 & w_5 & -w_4 & -w_7 & w_6 \\
-w_2 & -w_3 & -w_0 & w_1 & w_6 & w_7 & -w_4 & -w_5 \\
-w_3 & w_2 & -w_1 & -w_0 & w_7 & -w_6 & w_5 & -w_4 \\
-w_4 & -w_5 & -w_6 & -w_7 & -w_0 & w_1 & w_2 & w_3 \\
-w_5 & w_4 & -w_7 & w_6 & -w_1 & -w_0 & -w_3 & w_2 \\
-w_6 & w_7 & w_4 & -w_5 & -w_2 & w_3 & -w_0 & -w_1 \\
-w_7 & -w_6 & w_5 & w_4 & -w_3 & -w_2 & w_1 & -w_0
\end{bmatrix}
\tag{7}
$$

and solution of (5) for given $\boldsymbol{d}$ and $\boldsymbol{y}$:

$$
\begin{bmatrix}
w_0 \\ w_1 \\ w_2 \\ w_3 \\ w_4 \\ w_5 \\ w_6 \\ w_7
\end{bmatrix}
=
\frac{1}{\sum\limits_{i=1}^{8} y_i^2}
\begin{bmatrix}
y_1 & y_2 & y_3 & y_4 & y_5 & y_6 & y_7 & y_8 \\
-y_2 & y_1 & -y_4 & y_3 & -y_6 & y_5 & y_8 & -y_7 \\
-y_3 & y_4 & y_1 & -y_2 & -y_7 & -y_8 & y_5 & y_6 \\
-y_4 & -y_3 & y_2 & y_1 & -y_8 & y_7 & -y_6 & y_5 \\
-y_5 & y_6 & y_7 & y_8 & y_1 & -y_2 & -y_3 & -y_4 \\
-y_6 & -y_5 & y_8 & -y_7 & y_2 & y_1 & y_4 & -y_3 \\
-y_7 & -y_8 & -y_5 & y_6 & y_3 & -y_4 & y_1 & y_2 \\
-y_8 & y_7 & -y_6 & -y_5 & y_4 & y_3 & -y_2 & y_1
\end{bmatrix}
\begin{bmatrix}
d_1 \\ d_2 \\ d_3 \\ d_4 \\ d_5 \\ d_6 \\ d_7 \\ d_8
\end{bmatrix}
. \tag{8}
$$

Note 1. It is easy to see that the above problem of the best adapted basis synthesis is linear for $N = 8$ (eight neuron HNN). The only constraint is: $w_0 \geq 0$ (due to stability). Moreover, it can be pointed out that for high dimensionality $(N > 8)$ this problem is simply solvable but quasi-nonlinear (one needs to tune the shape of activation functions).

3   Design of HNN Based Mappings

The purpose of this consideration is to show how a mapping can be implemented in the form of composition of HNN based orthogonal filters (Fig. 1). A design of such a mapping is based on the following procedure:

Let a mapping $\boldsymbol{y} = \boldsymbol{F}(\boldsymbol{d})$ be generally given by the following training points:

$$
\boldsymbol{d}_k \mapsto \boldsymbol{y}_k \equiv \boldsymbol{\Theta}_k(\boldsymbol{x}_k) \tag{9}
$$

where: $\boldsymbol{d}_k$ and $\boldsymbol{y}_k$ belong to input and output vector spaces, respectively.

In this paper we limit our considerations to the linear case $(N = 8)$ i.e.:

$$
\boldsymbol{d}_k = [d_1, d_2, \ldots, d_8]_k^T \text{ and } \boldsymbol{y}_k = y_k \text{ (scalar)} . \tag{10}
$$

One of the possible architectures, implementing the mapping (10), is presented in Fig 2.

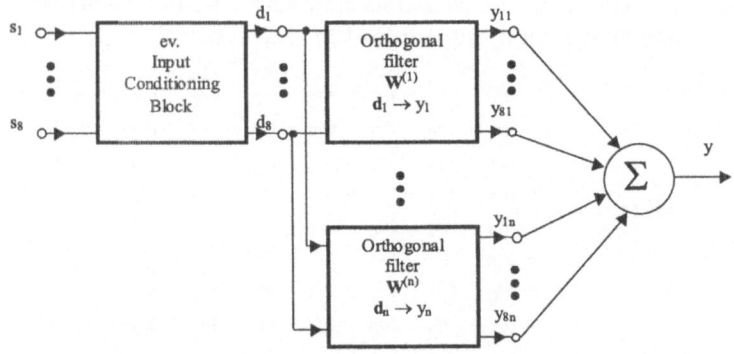

Fig. 2. An architecture implementing a given mapping.

Note 2. The structure from Fig. 2 can be seen as a superposition of n orthogonal filters with weight matrices $\boldsymbol{W}^{(n)}$ given by (7). It means that approximation points (10) are implemented by these filters and following equations are fulfilled:

$$d_k \mapsto y_k \text{ and } y_{ik} = (c_k/8)\, y_k;\ i = 1, 2, \ldots, 8 \tag{11}$$

where: $c_k = \text{const } (\approx 1)$.

It is assumed that for $\boldsymbol{d} = \boldsymbol{d}_k;\ k \in [1, 2, \ldots, n]$ this input vector is spread to zero mean value random vector through all $\boldsymbol{W}^{(i)}$, $i \neq k$ orthogonal filters. Hence for $\boldsymbol{d} = \boldsymbol{d}_k$; one obtains $y = y_k$, $k = 1, 2, \ldots, n$. This assumption has been justified by the random experiments performed on orthogonal filters.

As an example one obtains:

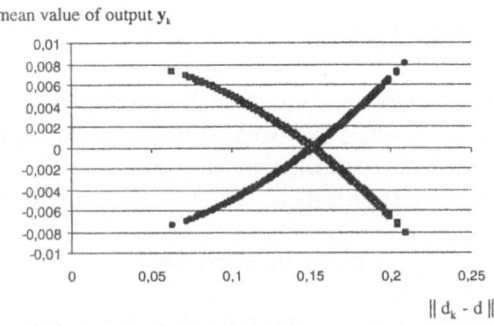

Fig. 3. Characteristics of orthogonal filter outputs

where:
$\boldsymbol{d}_1 = [\ 0.0192\ \ 0.0244\ \text{-}0.0567\ 0.0456\ 0.0345\ 0.0673\ 0.0129\ \text{-}0.02456\ ]^T \mapsto 0.01$
$\boldsymbol{d}_2 = [\ \text{-}0.0192\ \text{-}0.0244\ \text{-}0.0567\ 0.0456\ 0.0345\ 0.0673\ 0.0129\ \text{-}0.02456\ ]^T \mapsto \text{-}0.01$

Presented in Fig. 2 Input Conditioning Block can be used as

- transformation of an input space into vector space.
- Haar-Walsh spectrum analysis.
- Selective orthogonal filtering etc.

Finally, it is worth noting that the structure from Fig. 2 is similar to known architectures which are based on weighted superposition of algebraic, nonlinear kernels, e.g. Gaussian distributions. Moreover, it should be stressed that more advanced structures than considered in this paper can be conceived through, for example, symplectic i.e. preserving the skew-symmetry, coupling of the orthogonal filters.

4   Conclusion

In this paper, we have presented how to find an architecture for implementation of mappings, given through input-output pairs of data. This architecture, based on composition of orthogonal filters is robust and well-posed (due to the passivity). Comparative study on the quality and features (e.g. generalization) of HNN based systems [5] versus other known learning machines and algorithm is being prepared.

References

1. Poggio T., Smale S.: The Mathematics of Learning: Dealing with Data. Notices of the AMS 5 (2003) 537–544
2. Sienko W., Citko W.: On Very Large Scale Hamiltonian Neural Nets. In: Rutkowski, L., Kacprzyk, (eds.): Neural Networks and Soft Computing. Springer Physica-Verlag, Heidelberg, New York (2003)
3. Sienko W., Citko W., Wilamowski B.: Hamiltonian Neural Nets as a Universal Signal Processor. The 28th Annual Conference of the IEEE Industrial Electronics Society. Seville, SF-007388, (2002)
4. Eckmann B.: Topology, Algebra, Analysis-Relations and Missing Links. Notices of the AMS 5 (1999) 520–527
5. Sienko W., Citko W.: Quantum Signal Processing via Hamiltonian Neural Networks. To be published in International Journal of Computing Anticipatory Systems Ed. by D. M. Dubois, Publ. by CHAOS, Liege, Belgium, Vol. 14-16, (2004)

Recurrent Network Structure for Computing Quasi-inverses of the Sierpiński Space-Filling Curves

Ewa Skubalska-Rafajłowicz

Institute of Engineering Cybernetics, Wrocław University of Technology,
Wybrzeże Wyspiańskiego 27, 50 370 Wrocław, Poland.
raf@ldhpux.immt.pwr.wroc.pl

Abstract. This paper deals with the design of the recurrent neural network structure approximating the quasi-inverses of the multi-dimensional Sierpiński space-filling curves. The network consists of two subsequent recurrent layers. The network structure shows that computing the quasi-inverse of the Sierpiński space-filling curve can be performed massively parallel.

1 Introduction

A space-filling curve (SFC) is a continuous mapping from unit interval onto the multi-dimensional cube. SFC is a continuous surjection from unit interval onto n-dimensional unit cube (I_n, $n \leq \infty$), that is, a curve going through each point of I_n. The examples of such curves have been given by Peano, Hilbert, Sierpiński among others [17]. Space-filling curves were at first described by Peano [10], Hilbert [4], and Sierpiński [18] as an evidence that a lower dimensional space can be mapped continuously onto a space of higher dimension.

In many application one is interested in reducing dimension of the input space, i.e. in mappings from a space of higher dimension to a lower dimensional, possibly one-dimensional space.

The SFCs and theirs quasi-inverses have been applied in image processing [9], [30], [13], [5], [6], [7], [12], [16], pattern recognition [27], [21], and combinatorial optimization [1], [11], [29], [28].

We propose here a recurrent network structure for computing quasi-inverses of the Sierpiński SFCs. This network can be used as an input dimension reducing layer for the neural networks analyzed in [26], [24], [23], [22], [20].

SFC can also be exploited for neural network design. For example, Whitehead and Chaote [31] applied some kind of SFC, namely, the devotail mapping, to uniformly distribute initial positions of the RBF's centers. In their approach the parameters of the devotail mappings (known also as "zig-zag" curves) are evolved genetically. Another method of selecting RBF centers is based on placing prototypes of the centers initially at equidistributed (EQD) points generated by an algorithm based on space-filling curves [15].

L. Rutkowski et al. (Eds.): ICAISC 2004, LNAI 3070, pp. 272–277, 2004.
© Springer-Verlag Berlin Heidelberg 2004

We restrict here to the multi-dimensional versions of the Sierpiński space-filling curve. Nevertheless, similar network structures based on functional equation given in [20] can be also design for the Peano or Hilbert space-filling curves.

2   The Sierpiński Multi-dimensional Space-Filling Curves and Their Quasi-inverses

Space-filling curve (SFC) is a continuous, surjective mapping, let say $\Phi : [0,1] \to I_n$, $I_n = [0,1] \times [0,1] \times \ldots [0,1]$.

The SFC is regarded as the limit of a sequence of continuous functions [17] which fill the space (mostly I_n) more and more densely. However, any SFC cannot be one-to-one because, in general, I_n and I_1 are not homeomorphic whenever $n \neq 1$ (by invariance of dimension number theorem [29]). Thus, the inverse of a SFC does not exist. Fortunately, one can easily obtain a quasi-inverse of the SFC which in many cases (the Peano, Hilbert or Sierpiński SFCs) is almost everywhere inverse of the SFC.

The quasi-inverse of the SFC is the measurable mapping $\Psi : I_n \to I_1$, such that $\Psi(x) \in \Phi^{-1}(x)$, $x \in I_n$. Ψ is an almost everywhere inverse of Φ, i.e., $\Psi(x) \neq \Phi^{-1}(x)$ on a set with zero Lebesgue measure. For algorithms see [1], [2], [8], [11], [20].

The space-filling curve performs a transformation between an interval and a multi-dimensional bounded space resulting in substantial compression of the information and retaining some of the spatially associative properties of the space. The quasi-inverse mapping acts as the Lebesgue measure preserving transformation from multi-dimensional cube into unit interval. The transformation has the property that the points which are close to each other in the unit interval are mapped onto points close together in the hyperspace. Thus, from a general point of view, the multidimensional SFC leads to linear ordering of data in higher-dimensional problems.

The original Sierpiński curve was defined in 1912 as a two-dimensional curve which fills a square. Two different generalizations of the Sierpiński square-filling curve to the multi-dimensional case are known [20]. The first one was proposed in [1]. Unfortunately, in two dimensions this space-filling curve differs from the original one. Further this version of the multi-dimensional Sierpiński curve will be refer as the modified Sierpiński curve. Another generalization is given in details in [20]. This generalization is valid only for even dimension n, but in two dimension it produces the original Sierpiński curve. Let $\Phi_{Sn}(x)$ stands for the multi-dimensional generalization of the Sierpiński SFC and $\Phi_{Mn}(x)$ – for the modified Sierpiński SFC.

The mapping $\Psi_{Sd} : I_n \to I_1$, where n is an even number is the quasi-inverse of the multidimensional Sierpiński SFC Φ_{Sn} if it satisfy [20]:

$$\Psi_{Sn}(x) = (-c_n/2^{2n} + \Psi_{Sn}(\hat{x})/2^n) \, mod(1),$$
$$\hat{x} = (1 - 2x_1, \ldots, 1 - 2x_n), \quad x = (x_1, \ldots, x_n), \quad x_i \in [0, 1/2], \tag{1}$$

$$\Psi_{Sn}(x) = (2^n + b_n)/2^{2n} - \Psi_{Sn}(\hat{x})/2^n,$$
$$\hat{x} = (2x_1 - 1, 1 - 2x_2, \ldots, 1 - 2x_n), \quad x = (x_1, \ldots, x_n), \tag{2}$$
$$x_1 \in (1/2, 1], \quad x_2, \ldots, x_n \in [0, 1/2],$$

$$\Psi_{Sn}(x) = 2t_1 - \Psi_{Sn}(\hat{x}),$$
$$\hat{x} = (x_1, 1 - x_2, x_3, \ldots, x_n), \quad x = (x_1, \ldots, x_n), \tag{3}$$
$$x_1 \in [0, 1], \quad x_2 \in (1/2, 1], \quad x_3, \ldots, x_n \in [0, 1/2],$$

$$\ldots$$

$$\Psi_{Sn}(x) = 2t_{n-2} - \Psi_{Sn}(\hat{x}),$$
$$\hat{x} = (x_1, \ldots, x_{n-2}, 1 - x_{n-1}, x_d), \quad x = (x_1, \ldots, x_n), \tag{4}$$
$$x_1, \ldots, x_{n-2} \in [0, 1], \quad x_{n-1} \in (1/2, 1], \quad x_n \in [0, 1/2],$$

$$\Psi_{Sn}(x) = 2t_{n-1} - \Psi_{Sn}(\hat{x}),$$
$$\hat{x} = (x_1, x_2, \ldots, x_{n-1}, 1 - x_n), \quad x = (x_1, \ldots, x_n), \tag{5}$$
$$x_1, \ldots, x_{n-1} \in [0, 1], \quad x_n \in (1/2, 1],$$

where $t_{n-1} = 1 - c_n/2^{2n} - 1/2$, $t_l = t_{l+1} - 1/2^{n-l}$, $l = 1 \ldots, n - 2$ and $b_n/2^n = 1 - c_n/2^n$ and $c_{2n} = 2/3 \cdot (1 - 2^{-2n}) 2^{2n}$, $c_{2n-1} = c_{2n}/2$, $n = 1, 2, \ldots$.

The quasi-inverse of the modified Sierpiński SFC $\Psi_{Mn}(x)$ differs from Ψ_{Sn} in such a way that functional equation (2) should be replaced by the equation

$$\Psi_{Mn}(x) = b_n/2^{2n} + \Psi_{Mn}(\hat{x})/2^n,$$
$$\hat{x} = (2x_1 - 1, 1 - 2x_2, \ldots, 1 - 2x_n), \quad x = (x_1, \ldots, x_n), \tag{6}$$
$$x_1 \in (1/2, 1], \quad x_2, \ldots, x_n \in [0, 1/2].$$

3 Recurrent Network for Computing the Quasi-inverse of the Multi-dimensional Sierpiński Space-Filling Curves

Here we propose the recurrent network structure for computing the quasi-inverse of the multi-dimensional Sierpiński SFC. The network consists of two subsequent layers. The inputs to the network is vector $x = (x_1, \ldots, x_n)$. The output signal approximates $\Psi_{Sn}(x)$ or after small modification of the network weights – the quasi-inverse of the modified Sierpiński curve $\Psi_{Mn}(x)$. The topology of the networks is described in Figures 1 and 2. In the first network's layer each input vector coordinate is processed independently from others. The second layer consists of $2n$ nodes followed by multiplication nodes. The consecutive multiplication nodes produce the recurrence signal. Assume that $x_i(0) = x_i$, $i = 1, \ldots, n$. Then for $k = 1, 2, \ldots$ one obtains

$$x_1(k + 1) = G(x_1(k)),$$
$$x_i(k + 1) = G(F(x_i(k))), \quad i = n, \ldots, 2, \tag{7}$$

where

$$G(s) = \begin{cases} 1 - 2s, & \text{if } s \in [0, 1/2] \\ 2s - 1, & \text{if } s \in (1/2, 1] \end{cases}, \quad F(s) = \begin{cases} s, & \text{if } s \in [0, 1/2] \\ 1 - s, & \text{if } s \in (1/2, 1]. \end{cases}$$

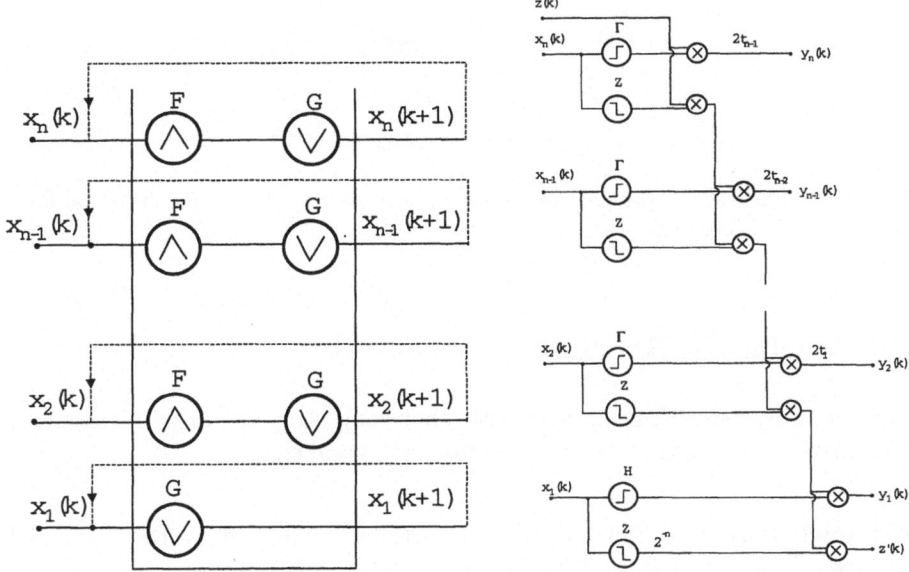

Fig. 1. Left panel – the first layer of the recurrent network for computing the quasi-inverse of the Sierpiński SFC. Right panel– the second layer of the recurrent network for computing the quasi-inverse of the Sierpiński SFC.

Define the following functions restricted to the unit interval:

$$\Gamma(s) = \begin{cases} 0, & \text{if } s \in [0, 1/2] \\ 1, & \text{if } s \in (1/2, 1]. \end{cases}, \quad Z(s) = \begin{cases} 1, & \text{if } s \in [0, 1/2] \\ -1, & \text{if } s \in (1/2, 1]. \end{cases}$$

$$H(s) = \begin{cases} -c_n 2^{-d}, & s \in [0, 1/2] \\ 2^{-2n}(2^n + b_n), & s \in (1/2, 1]. \end{cases}$$

Furthermore,

$$\begin{aligned} y_j(k) &= z_j(k)\Gamma(x_j(k)), \\ z_{j-1}(k) &= z_j(k)Z(x_j(k)), \quad j = n, \ldots, 2, \end{aligned} \tag{8}$$

where $z_n(k) = z(k)$ and

$$\begin{aligned} y_1(k) &= z_1(k)H(x_1(k)), \\ z(k+1) &= z'(k) = z_1(k)Z(x_1(k))2^{-n}. \end{aligned} \tag{9}$$

We assume that the starting point (input to the network) is $z(0) = 1$.

$$\Psi(x) = \sum_{k=1}^{\infty}\sum_{j=1}^{n} y_j(k) \, mod(1). \tag{10}$$

We stop recurrence when $x_i(k) = x_i(k+1) = 0$, $i = 1, \ldots, n$ or after given K re-iterations. Since $y_j(K) \leq 2^n 2^{-nK}$, thus after K iterations $\Psi(x)$ is approximated with the accuracy $O(2^{-nK})$.

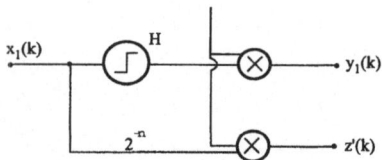

Fig. 2. Modification of the part of recurrent network for computing the quasi-inverse of the modified Sierpiński SFC

4   Concluding Remarks

The proposed network structure shows that computing the quasi-inverse of the Sierpiński space-filling curve can be massively parallel.

Acknowledgments. This paper was partially supported by the Council for Scientific Research of the Polish Government Grant 2002-2005.

References

1. Bartholdi J.J., Platzman L.K.: Heuristics based on space-filling curves for combinatorial problems in Euclidean space.Management Science **34** (1988) 291–305
2. Butz A.R.: Alternative algorithm for Hilbert's space-filling curve. IEEE Trans. Comput. **C-20** (1971) 424–426
3. Cole A.J.:, Halftoning without dither or edge enhancement, Visual Computer **7** (1991) 232–246
4. Hilbert D.: Ueber die stetige abbildung einer linie auf ein flaechenschtueck. Mathematische Annalen **38** (1891) 459–469
5. Kamata S., Niimi M., Kawaguchi E.: A gray image compression using a Hilbert scan. in Proc. of the 13th ICPR Vienna 1996 **2** (1996) 905–909
6. Krzyżak A., E.Rafajłowicz E., Skubalska–Rafajłowicz E.:Clipped median and space-filling curves in image filtering. Nonlinear Analysis **47**(2001) 303–314
7. Lamarque C.H., Robert F.: Image analysis using space-filling curves and 1D wavelet basis, Pattern Recognition **29** (1996) 1309–1322
8. Milne S. C.: Peano Curves and Smoothness of Functions. Advances in Mathematics **35** (1980) 129–157.
9. Patrick E.D., Anderson D.R., Bechtel F.K.: Mapping multidimensional space to one dimension for computer output display. IEEE Trans. on Comput. **17** (1968) 949–953
10. G. Peano Sur une courbe qui remplit toute une aire plane Math. Ann. **36** (1890) 157–160.
11. Platzman L. K. and Bartholdi J.J.: Space-filling curves and the planar traveling salesman problem., Journal of ACM **36** (1989) 719–737
12. Phuvan S., Oh T.K., Cavris N.,Li Y., and Szu H.H.: Texture analysis by space-filling curves and one-dimensional Haar Wavelets. Optical Eng. **31** (1992) 1899–1906

13. Quweider M.K. and Salari E.: Peano scanning partial distance search for vector quantization.IEEE Signal Processing Letters **2** (1995) 170–171
14. E.Rafajłowicz E., Skubalska- Rafajłowicz E.:, Nonparametric regression estimation by Bernstein-Durmayer polynomials.Tatra Mountains Mathematical Publications **17** (1999) 227–239
15. Rafajłowicz E., Skubalska–Rafajłowicz E.: RBF nets based on equidistributed points. in Proc. of 9th IEEE International Conf. Methods and Models in Automation and Robotics MMAR 2003 **2** (2003) 921–926
16. Regazzoni C.S. and Teschioni A.: A new approach to vector median filtering based on space filling curves.IEEE Transactions on Image Processing **6** (1997) 1025–1037
17. Sagan H.: Space-Filling Curves. Springer-Verlag Berlin Heidelberg New York 1994.
18. Sierpiński W.: Sur une nouvelle courbe continue qui remplit toute une aire plane. Bulletin de l'Acad. des Sciences de Cracovie A. (1912) 463–478.
19. Skubalska-Rafajłowicz E.: Neural networks with orthogonal activation functions approximating space-filling curves.in Proc. of 9th IEEE International Conf. Methods and Models in Automation and Robotics MMAR 2003 **2** (2003) 927–934
20. Skubalska-Rafajłowicz E.: Space-filling Curves in Multivariate Decision Problems (in Polish) (2001) Wrocław University of Technology Press Wrocław.
21. Skubalska-Rafajłowicz E. : Pattern recognition algorithm based on space-filling curves and orthogonal expansion. IEEE Trans. on Information Theory **47** (2001) 1915–1927
22. Skubalska-Rafajłowicz E.:, Data compression for pattern recognition based on space-filling curve pseudo-inverse mapping. Nonlinear Analysis **47** (2001) 315–326
23. Skubalska-Rafajłowicz E.: One-dimensional Kohonen LVQ nets for multidimensional pattern recognition. Int. J. Appl. Math. and Computer Sci. **10** (2000) 767–778
24. Skubalska-Rafajłowicz E.: On using space-filling curves and vector quantization for constructing multidimensional control charts. Proc. of the 5–th Conf. Neural Networks and Soft Computing, Zakopane 2000, 162–167
25. Skubalska-Rafajłowicz E.: Applications of the space-filling curves with data driven measure preserving property. Nonlinear Analysis **30** (1997) 1305–1310
26. Skubalska-Rafajłowicz E., Space-filling curves and Kohonen's 1-D SOM as a method of a vector quantization with known asymptotic level density. Proc. of the 3rd Conf. Neural Networks and Their Applications Kule (1997) 161–166
27. Skubalska–Rafajłowicz E. and Krzyżak A.: Fast k-NN classification rule using metric on space-filling curves. Proc. of the 13th ICPR, Vienna, Austria, August 25- 29, 1996 **2** (1996) 221–225
28. Skubalska–Rafajłowicz E. and Rafajłowicz E.:, Serching for optimal experimental designs using space-filling curves. Int. J. Appl. Math. and Computer Sci. **8** (1998) 647–656
29. Steele J.M.: Efficacy of space-filling heuristics in Euclidean combinatorial optimization.Operations Reserch Letters **8** (1989) 237–239
30. Stevens R.J., Lehar A.F., and Preston F.H.: Manipulation and presentation of multidimensional image data using the Peano scan. IEEE Trans. PAMI **5** (1983) 520–525
31. Whitehead B.A. and Chaote T.D.: Evolving space-filling curves to distribute radial basis functions over an input space. IEEE Trans. on Neural Networks **5** (1994) 15–23.

Comparison of Reasoning Methods for Fuzzy Control

Bohdan Butkiewicz

Warsaw University of Technology, Institute of Electronic Systems,
Nowowiejska 15/19,
00-665 Warsaw, Poland
bb@ise.pw.edu.pl
http://www.ise.pw.edu.pl/~bb/index.html

Abstract. Many of the reasoning methods are suitable neither for fuzzy control nor for fuzzy modeling. In the paper some possible reasoning methods are compared from this point of view. The author proposes new methods for fuzzy control, better than Mamdani, Larsen, Tsukamoto. Fuzzy systems are described by a set of rules using connectives "and", "or", "also". Different aggregation operators, as triangular norms and mean operations, are used for interpretation of these connectives. In the paper are discussed possible interpretations for if ... then rules, as different implications and other operations, in combination with defuzzification methods. Examples of the systems with PID fuzzy controllers are presented using different reasoning methods, aggregation operations, and linear and nonlinear plants. Some best methods are proposed.

1 Introduction

There are many methods of approximate reasoning. More popular approach is based on if ... then rules. Using this approach four general problems must be solved:

(1) what mathematical interpretations of sentence connectives "and" "or" and negation "not" may be used for antecedent (*if*) part

(2) what implication or operation may be used for conclusion (*then*) part

(3) what interpretation to use for rule aggregator "also"

(4) what defuzzification procedure can be applied.

The widely applied reasoning in fuzzy control as Mamdani, Larsen [11] Tsukamoto (see ex. [12]), Takagi-Sugeno [16] uses triangular norms [10] for "and", "or", "also". However, it is possible to use more general $\mathcal{B}$-operations [2] or generalized mean operations [7]. The implication methods: Kleene-Dienes, early Zadeh, Willmott, standard sharp, standard strict, standard star, Łukasiewicz, Gaines, Mamdani, and some combination of them can be found in the literature [12]. Mamdani method is called min-max method because minimum is used for interpretation of "and" and maximum for "or". Other triangular norms give also good results. In Larsen reasoning membership function of conclusion set is multiplied by the weight of rule. Mizumoto [14] introduced product-sum-gravity

L. Rutkowski et al. (Eds.): ICAISC 2004, LNAI 3070, pp. 278–283, 2004.
© Springer-Verlag Berlin Heidelberg 2004

and some other methods mixing different kinds of operations. He compared also a few reasoning methods using one practical example of fuzzy control system. Many researchers proposed different kinds of reasoning, but no many who try to compare them in practice. Schwartz [15], Butnariu et al [4], Li [13], Gupta [9] compared the reasoning methods from theoretical point of view. Practical comparison can be found in Mizumoto [14], Czogała and Łeski [6], Cao and Kandel [5]. The author of the paper proofed [1]–[3] for large class of fuzzy MIMO systems that if steady-state exists then output signal of fuzzy system tends in steady-state to the same value independent on the mathematical interpretations of sentence connectives "and" "or". The property is true for all triangular norms and B-operations, more general class than triangular norms, introduced by the author [2] used as mathematical interpretations of "and" "or" when generalized Mamdani reasoning is applied. It was shown that dynamics of fuzzy control system are very similar for different reasoning. This paper presents some comparison of the best reasoning methods for fuzzy control choused by the author from large set of methods.

2   General Remarks

Conventional approach gives many solutions for controller's structures and optimal control strategies. Here, fuzzy versions of the most popular PD and PID controllers are considered. Three solutions are used in practice: Mamdani, Larsen, and Tsukamoto controllers. These solutions use logic operations (minimum for "and", maximum for "or") to interpretation of the if part of the rule. Mamdani use minimum for then part, Larsen use product. Tsukamoto proposed other solution, using as conclusion the linear functions, similarly as in the Takagi-Sugeno approach. Many previous experience of the author of the paper showed that Tsukamoto method are not very good and gives worse results then other methods. Thus, here it will be omitted in comparison. The most popular defuzzification methods (see ex. [14]) are:
- height (HM), area (AM) and gravity (GM) - all use weighted mean procedure
- center of area (COA), center of gravity (COG) - use union of the conclusions.
Here, only HM, AM, and GM are taken in consideration. Fuzzy controller must produce an optimal control signal using input values. Thus, it can be described by a multidimensional function. The fuzzy controller must to approximate this function. There are many theorems about approximation by fuzzy Mamdani, Larsen and Takagi-Sugeno systems, see for example [18] [19] [17] [20]. The necessary and sometimes sufficient conditions were established for such approximation. For example, Wang showed that infinite fuzzy system with gaussian membership functions is universal approximator and might to approximate exactly any continuous function. Thus, theoretically many reasoning methods can be used for fuzzy control. Moreover, the author experience shows that the control results obtained are very often similar. However, it is interesting what kind of reasoning is better if only a few fuzzy sets are used for approximation. The second important remark concerns the steady-state value of a fuzzy system. As

it was mentioned above, the author proofed that under some general conditions the output of the fuzzy system tends in the steady-state to the same value, which is independent on the pair of the triangular norms used for interpretation of the connectives "and" "or". Such a situation is true for example for PD and PID controllers.

3   Comparison of Reasoning

Mathematicians, specialists on fuzzy logic, developed many kinds of reasoning. Generally, the methods are based on triangular norms, but there are also another ideas using mean operations, as arithmetic, geometric, harmonic mean, generalized mean operations, and some others as simple sum. The author of the paper, using three examples of fuzzy control systems, performed a comparison of the results of control. The examples are simple, but can be considered as representative: the system 1 with PID controller and linear plant of first order with large delay, the system 2 with PD controller and linear plant of third order with small delay, and the system 3 with PID controller with nonlinear plant. The membership functions are presented in the Fig. 1. In both cases the universe of discourse for error e, derivative d, and integral of error i is the same (-10,10). In the paper, by fuzzy reasoning is understand an ordered sequence of operations

Reasoning = [operation 1, operation 2, operation 3, defuzzification]

where operation 1 is generally a triangular norm, operation 2 is generally s-norm (triangular co-norm, not necessary dual), operation 3 serves as implication (but may not fulfilled the axioms for implication). Sometimes are used means or other operations, for example sum, not normalized to 1. Structure of the systems contains controller, plant, and feedback loop. Below are explained some abbreviations used in the tables: prod, sum – arithmetic product and sum; b.prod, b.sum – bounded t-norm and s-norm (Łukaszewicz triangular norms); d.prod, d.sum, e.prod, e.sum, h.prod, h.sum, y.prod, y.sum – drastic, Einstein, Hamacher, Yager (p=2) triangular norms; arith.m, geom.m, harm.m, d.geom., d.harm – arithmetic, geometric, harmonic means and dual means; height, area, grav – defuzzification methods: HM, AM, GM; force – force implication $a \rightarrow b = a(1- \mid a-b \mid)$ $a, b \in [0, 1]$ introduced in [8].

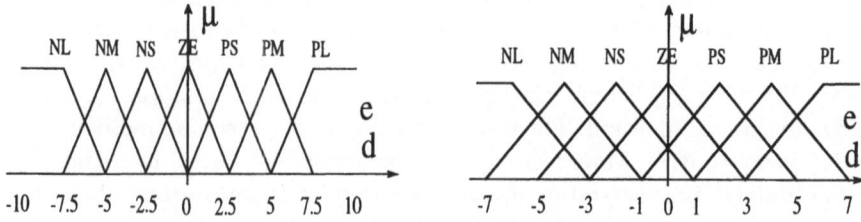

Fig. 1. The membership function for the System 1(right), System 2 and 3 (left)

System 1
Mizumoto [14] firstly proposed this system for comparison of reasoning. Hear the memberships functions were slightly modified to obtain more realistic shapes in practice. The PID controller has input scale factors: g_e=10, g_d=100, g_i=0.02. The output scaling g_u was choused to obtain the same overshoot equal 15% for each of the 40 types of reasoning. Plant is described by transfer function $H(s) = e^{-2s}/(1 + 20s)$. The step signal is applied to the system. Table 1 shows parameters of some best responses.

Table 1. The response for different reasoning. System 1.

Reasoning t.n.-s.n.-oper.-defuz.	Rise time	y_{1min}	Sqr error	y_{Tmax} abs. err.	Osc. amp. $\Delta \cdot 10^{-3}$	Rank
prod-sum-force-grav	11.92	.9887	276	0.000	0.000	1
dr.prod-dr.sum-force-grav	8.70	-	223	0.334	0.000	2
b.prod-b.sum-prod-grav	12.01	.9843	281	0.002	0.000	3
dr.prod-dr.sum-prod-grav	8.10	-	217	0.001	0.000	4
b.prod-b.sum-prod-area	12.20	.9948	284	0.007	0.000	5
m.dr.prod-m.dr.sum-prod-grav	10.80	.9880	267	0.241	0.590	6
b.prod-b.sum-b.prod-grav	12.89	.9811	291	0.001	0.000	7
prod-sum-prod-grav	12.76	.9815	291	0.008	0.000	8
b.prod-b.sum-force-grav	12.94	.9979	291	0.000	0.000	9
b.prod-b.sum-b.prod-area	13.03	.9815	293	0.001	0.000	10
geom.m-d.geom.m-prod-grav	12.99	.9670	297	0.308	0.795	13
prod-b.sum-prod-grav	13.64	.9759	302	2.033	2.974	16
e.prod-e.sum-prod-grav	13.28	.9752	299	2.322	3.922	17
b.prod-b.sum-b.prod-height	13.71	.9793	308	1.969	3.330	18
h.prod-h.sum-prod-grav	14.31	.9677	311	1.042	1.698	20
min-max-min-grav	15.87	.9640	330	1.174	1.866	33

System 2
The controller is fuzzy PD type with parameters: g_e=20, g_d=100. Transfer function of the plant: $H(s) = 1/(1 + 10s)(1 + 5s)(1 + s)$. Table 2 shows some results.
System 3
Controller fuzzy PID: g_e=2, g_d=2, g_i=0.02. Plant: $\ddot{y}+2\zeta\omega_n\dot{y}+\omega_n^2 y=\alpha_1 x(t-t_0)+\alpha_2 x(t-t_0) \mid x(t-t_0) \mid$ with ζ=1.5, ω_n=100, α_1=1, α_2=−0.1, t_0=0.2ms.

4 Conclusions

Traditional methods: Mamdani, Larsen, Tsukamoto are not good for all the cases (rank 25–33). The best results was obtained for product-sum-force-gravity method. The sum is not normalized to 1. The drastic norms take second place but it gives sometimes strange nonliner effects and cannot be recommended for all cases. Good results give bounded (Łukaszewicz) norms. Generally, gravity defuzzification is better then area and height method.

Table 2. The response for different reasoning. System 2.

Reasoning t.n.-s.n.-oper.-defuz.	Rise time [s]	y_{1min}	Square error	y_{Tmax}	Osc. amp. $\Delta \cdot 10^{-3}$	Rank
y.prod-y.sum-prod-grav	9.079	.7567	202.5	.8891	0.951	1
prod-sum-prod-area	8.948	.7537	203.4	.8801	1.031	2
prod-sum-prod-grav	9.031	.7750	204.3	.8812	1.102	3
prod-sum-force-grav	8.954	.7509	203.9	.8810	0.235	4
alg.prod-alg.sum-min-height	8.884	.7493	204.4	.8783	1.010	5
b.prod-b.sum-prod-height	9.032	.7504	203.7	.8826	1.867	6
b.prod-b.sum-b.prod-height	-"-	-"-	-"-	-"-	-"-	7
dr.prod-dr.sum-prod-grav	9.366	.7484	189.2	.9383	1.053	8
dr.prod-dr.sum-force-grav	9.216	.7441	203.3	.8876	0.492	9
arith-arith-b.prod-area	9.251	.7692	205.6	.8827	1.661	10
harm.m-d.harm.m-prod-grav	9.969	.7581	205.0	.8829	1.509	11
b.prod-b.sum-prod-area	9.155	.7539	204.9	.8832	2.050	12
b.prod-b.sum-prod-grav	9.185	.7553	204.9	.8834	2.136	13
min-max-force-grav	9.079	.7491	205.6	.8814	0.609	14
arith-arith-b.prod-grav	9.273	.7700	206.6	.8814	1.651	15
geom.m-d.geom.m-prod-grav	9.191	.7623	205.5	.8810	1.884	16
alg.prod-alg.sum-min-grav	9.054	.7530	207.3	.8779	1.233	17
e.prod-e.sum-prod-grav	9.089	.7540	206.7	.8790	1.341	18

Table 3. The comparison of different reasoning.

Reasoning t.n.-s.n.-oper.-defuz.	Rank System 1	Rank System 2	Rank System 3	Total score	Rank
prod-sum-force-grav	1	4	1/2	98	1
dr.prod-dr.sum-prod-grav	4	7	7	135.5	2
prod-sum-prod-grav	8	3	13/14	143.5	3
prod-sum-prod-area	10/11	2	13/14	144.5	4
dr.prod-dr.sum-force-grav	2	10	15	159.5	5
b.prod-b.sum-prod-grav	3	12/13	10/11	160	6
b.prod-b.sum-b.prod-grav	7	21	3/4	161	7
b.prod-b.sum-prod-area	5	11	10/11	161.5	8/9
b.prod-b.sum-force-grav	9	17	5/6	161.5	8/9
m.dr.prod-m.dr.sum-prod-grav	6	23	8	178	10

References

1. Butkiewicz B. S.: Steady-State Error of a System with Fuzzy Controller. IEEE Transactions on System, Man, and Cybernetics —Part B: Cybernetics, **6**, (1998) 855–860
2. Butkiewicz B. S.: Fuzzy Control System with B-operations. In: R. John, R. Birkenhead (eds.): Advances in Soft Computing, Developments in Soft Computing. Physica-Verlag, Heidelberg, New York (2001), 48–55

3. Butkiewicz   B. S.: About Robustness of Fuzzy Logic PD and PID Controller under Changes of Reasoning Methods. In: H-J. Zimmermann, G. Tselentis, M. van Someren, G. Dounias (eds.): Advances in Computational Intelligence and Learning Methods and Applications. Kluwer Academic Publishers (2001), 307–318
4. Butnariu D., Klement E. P., Zafrany S.: On triangular norm-based propositional fuzzy logics. Fuzzy Sets and Systems, **69**, (1995) 241–255
5. Cao Z., Kandel A.: Applicability of Some Fuzzy Implications Oprators. Fuzzy Sets and Systems, **31**, (1989) 151–186
6. Czogała E., Leski J.: On equivalence of approximate reasoning results using different interpretations of fuzzy if-then rules. Fuzzy Sets and Systems, **117**, (2001) 279–296
7. Dyckhoff H., Pedrycz W.: Generalized means as model of compensative connectives. Fuzzy sets and Systems, **14**, (1984) 143–154
8. Dujet Ch., VincentN.: Force implication: A new approach to human reasoning. Fuzzy Sets and Systems, **69**, (1995) 53–63
9. Gupta M. M., Qi J.: Theory of t-norms and fuzzy inference methods. Fuzzy Sets and Systems, **40**, No. 3, (1991) 431–450
10. Klement E. P., Mesiar R., Pap E.: Triangular norms. Kluwer Academic Publishers, Dordrecht (2000)
11. Larsen P. M.: Industrial Applications of Fuzzy Logic Control. Int. J. Man Machine Studies, **12**, 1980, No. 1, 3–10
12. Lee E. S., Zhu Q.: Fuzzy and Evidence Reasoning. Physica-Verlag, Heidelberg, 1995.
13. Li Z.: Suitabilityof fuzzy reasoning methods. Fuzzy Sets and Systems, **108**, (1999) 299–311.
14. Mizumoto M.: Improvement of Fuzzy Control Method. In: Li H. Gupta M. (ed.): Fuzzy Logic and Intelligent Systems, Kluwer Acad. Publishers, Dordrecht (1995) 1–16
15. Schwartz D. G.: Fuzzy inference in a formal theory of semantic equivalence. Fuzzy Sets and Systems, **31**, (1989) 205–216
16. Takagi T., Sugeno M.: Fuzzy Identification of Systems and its Application to Modeling and Control. IEEE Trans. on Systems, Man, and Cybernetics, **15**, (1985), No.1, 116–132
17. Ying H.: Sufficient condition on uniform approximation of multivariate functions by general Takagi-Sugeno systems. IEEE Trans. on Systems, Man, and Cybernetics, Part A: Systems and Humans, **28**,(1998) 515–520
18. Wang X. L.: Fuzzy systems are universal approximators. Proc IEEE Int. Conf. on Fuzzy systems. San Diego (CA) (1992) 1163–1169
19. Wang X. L., Mendel J. M.: Fuzzy basis functions, universal approximation, and orthogonal least-square learning. IEEE Trans. on Neural Network, **3**, (1992) No. 5, 807–814
20. Ying H., Ding Y., Li S., Shao S.: Comparison of necessary conditions for typical Takagi-Sugeno and Mamdani fuzzy system as universal approximators. IEEE Trans. on Systems, Man, and Cybernetics, Part A: Systems and Humans, **29**, (1999) No. 5, 508–514

Fuzzy Modelling with a Compromise Fuzzy Reasoning

Krzysztof Cpalka[1,2] and Leszek Rutkowski[1,2]

[1] Technical University of Czestochowa, Poland,
Department of Computer Engineering
[2] WSHE University in Lodz, Poland,
Department of Artificial Intelligence
lrutko@kik.pcz.czest.pl

Abstract. In the paper we study flexible neuro-fuzzy systems based on a compromise fuzzy implication. The appropriate neuro-fuzzy structures are developed and the influence of a compromise parameter on their performance is investigated. The results are illustrated on typical benchmarks.

1 Introduction

In the literature several architectures of neuro-fuzzy systems have been developed [1]-[4]. Most of them are based on the Mamdani-type reasoning described by a t-norm, e.g. product or min, applied to connect antecedents and consequences in the individual rules. Another approach is based on the logical method, e.g. an S-implication used to connect antecedents and consequences in the rule base. The third alternative is the Takagi-Sugeno scheme which involves a functional dependence between consequents and inputs. Another approach to designing neuro-fuzzy systems has been proposed by the authors in [5]-[8]. The main idea is based on the incorporation of various parameters into construction of such systems leading to high accuracy in problems of modelling and classification. In this paper we connect antecedents and consequences in the individual rules by a compromise fuzzy implication given by:

$$I(a, b) = (1 - \lambda) T \{a, b\} + \lambda S \{1 - a, b\} \tag{1}$$

where $\lambda \in [0, 1]$. We will develop the appropriate neuro-fuzzy structures based on formula (1) and investigate the influence of parameter λ on their performance. The results will be illustrated on typical benchmarks.

2 Flexible Neuro-fuzzy System

In this paper, we consider multi-input, single-output flexible neuro-fuzzy system mapping $\mathbf{X} \rightarrow \mathbf{Y}$, where $\mathbf{X} \subset \mathbf{R}^n$ and $\mathbf{Y} \subset \mathbf{R}$. The fuzzifier performs a mapping from the observed crisp input space $\mathbf{X} \subset \mathbf{R}^n$ to the fuzzy sets defined in $A' \subseteq \mathbf{X}$.

L. Rutkowski et al. (Eds.): ICAISC 2004, LNAI 3070, pp. 284–289, 2004.
© Springer-Verlag Berlin Heidelberg 2004

The most commonly used fuzzifier is the singleton fuzzifier which maps $\bar{\mathbf{x}} = [\bar{x}_1, \ldots, \bar{x}_n] \in \mathbf{X}$ into a fuzzy set $A' \subseteq \mathbf{X}$ characterized by the membership function:

$$\mu_{A'}(\mathbf{x}) = \begin{cases} 1 \; if \; \mathbf{x} = \bar{\mathbf{x}} \\ 0 \; if \; \mathbf{x} \neq \bar{\mathbf{x}} \end{cases} \tag{2}$$

The fuzzy rule base consists of a collection of N fuzzy IF-THEN rules in the form:

$$R^{(k)}: \text{IF} \mathbf{x} \text{ is} A^k \text{ THEN} y \text{ is} B^k \tag{3}$$

where $\mathbf{x} = [x_1, \ldots, x_n] \in \mathbf{X}$, $y \in \mathbf{Y}$, $A_1^k, A_2^k, \ldots, A_n^k$ are fuzzy sets characterized by membership functions $\mu_{A_i^k}(x_i)$, whereas B^k are fuzzy sets characterized by membership functions $\mu_{B^k}(y)$, respectively, $k = 1, \ldots, N$.

The fuzzy inference determines a mapping from the fuzzy sets in the input space $\mathbf{X}$ to the fuzzy sets in the output space $\mathbf{Y}$. Each of N rules (3) determines a fuzzy set $\bar{B}^k \subseteq \mathbf{Y}$ given by the compositional rule of inference:

$$\bar{B}^k = A' \circ \left(A^k \to B^k \right) \tag{4}$$

where $A^k = A_1^k \times A_2^k \times \ldots \times A_n^k$. Fuzzy sets $\bar{B}^k$, according to the formula (4), are characterized by membership functions expressed by the sup-star composition:

$$\mu_{\bar{B}^k}(y) = \sup_{\mathbf{x} \in \mathbf{X}} \left\{ \mu_{A'}(\mathbf{x}) * \mu_{A_1^k \times \ldots \times A_n^k \to B^k}(\mathbf{x}, y) \right\} \tag{5}$$

where $*$ can be any operator in the class of t-norms. It is easily seen that for a crisp input $\bar{\mathbf{x}} \in \mathbf{X}$, i.e. a singleton fuzzifier (2), formula (5) becomes:

$$\mu_{\bar{B}^k}(y) = \mu_{A_1^k \times \ldots \times A_n^k \to B^k}(\bar{\mathbf{x}}, y) = \mu_{A^k \to B^k}(\bar{\mathbf{x}}, y) = I\left(\mu_{A^k}(\bar{\mathbf{x}}), \mu_{B^k}(y)\right) \tag{6}$$

where $I(\cdot)$ is an "engineering implication" or fuzzy implication. The aggregation operator, applied in order to obtain the fuzzy set B' based on fuzzy sets $\bar{B}^k$, is the t-norm or s-norm operator, depending on the type of fuzzy implication. The defuzzifier performs a mapping from a fuzzy set B' to a crisp point $\bar{y}$ in $\mathbf{Y} \subset \mathbf{R}$. The COA (centre of area) method is defined by following formula:

$$\bar{y} = \frac{\int_{\mathbf{Y}} y \mu_{B'}(y) dy}{\int_{\mathbf{Y}} \mu_{B'}(y) dy} \; or \, by \; \bar{y} = \frac{\sum_{r=1}^{N} \bar{y}^r \mu_{B'}(\bar{y}^r)}{\sum_{r=1}^{N} \mu_{B'}(\bar{y}^r)} \tag{7}$$

in the discrete form, where $\bar{y}^r$ denotes centres of the membership functions $\mu_{B^r}(y)$, i.e. for $r = 1, \ldots, N$:

$$\mu_{B^r}(\bar{y}^r) = \max_{y \in \mathbf{Y}} \left\{ \mu_{B^r}(y) \right\} \tag{8}$$

Following ideas in [7], [8] we introduce the following flexibility parameters:

- soft strength of firing controlled by parameter α^τ, soft implication controlled by parameter α^I and soft aggregation of the rules controlled by parameter α^{agr},
- weights in antecedents of the rules $w^\tau_{i,k} \in [0,1]$, $i = 1,\ldots,n$, $k = 1,\ldots,N$, and weights in aggregation of the rules $w^{agr}_k \in [0,1]$, $k = 1,\ldots,N$.

The triangular norms in connection of antecedents, implication and aggregation are parameterised by parameters p^τ, p^I, p^{agr} respectively. The flexible neuro-fuzzy system based on parameterised triangular norms is given by (we use the same notation as that in [5], [7]):

$$\tau_k\left(\bar{\mathbf{x}}\right) = \begin{pmatrix} (1-\alpha^\tau)\,\mathrm{avg}\left(\mu_{A^k_1}\left(\bar{x}_1\right),\ldots,\mu_{A^k_n}\left(\bar{x}_n\right)\right) + \\ \alpha^\tau \overset{\leftrightarrow}{T}{}^* \left\{\begin{matrix} \mu_{A^k_1}\left(\bar{x}_1\right),\ldots,\mu_{A^k_n}\left(\bar{x}_n\right); \\ w^\tau_{1,k},\ldots,w^\tau_{n,k},p^\tau \end{matrix}\right\} \end{pmatrix} \tag{9}$$

$$I_{k,r}\left(\bar{\mathbf{x}},\bar{y}^r\right) = \begin{pmatrix} (1-\alpha^I)\,\mathrm{avg}\left(\tilde{N}_{1-\lambda}\left(\tau_k\left(\bar{\mathbf{x}}\right)\right),\mu_{B^k}\left(\bar{y}^r\right)\right) + \\ \alpha^I \begin{pmatrix} (1-\lambda)\overset{\leftrightarrow}{T}\left\{\tau_k\left(\bar{\mathbf{x}}\right),\mu_{B^k}\left(\bar{y}^r\right);p^I\right\} \\ +\lambda\overset{\leftrightarrow}{S}\left\{1-\tau_k\left(\bar{\mathbf{x}}\right),\mu_{B^k}\left(\bar{y}^r\right);p^I\right\} \end{pmatrix} \end{pmatrix} \tag{10}$$

$$agr_r\left(\bar{\mathbf{x}},\bar{y}^r\right) = \begin{pmatrix} (1-\alpha^{agr})\,\mathrm{avg}\left(I_{1,r}\left(\bar{\mathbf{x}},\bar{y}^r\right),\ldots,I_{N,r}\left(\bar{\mathbf{x}},\bar{y}^r\right)\right) + \\ \alpha^{agr} \begin{pmatrix} (1-\lambda)\overset{\leftrightarrow}{S}{}^* \left\{\begin{matrix} I_{1,r}\left(\bar{\mathbf{x}},\bar{y}^r\right),\ldots,I_{N,r}\left(\bar{\mathbf{x}},\bar{y}^r\right); \\ w^{agr}_1,\ldots,w^{agr}_N,p^{agr} \end{matrix}\right\} \\ +\lambda\overset{\leftrightarrow}{T}{}^* \left\{\begin{matrix} I_{1,r}\left(\bar{\mathbf{x}},\bar{y}^r\right),\ldots,I_{N,r}\left(\bar{\mathbf{x}},\bar{y}^r\right); \\ w^{agr}_1,\ldots,w^{agr}_N,p^{agr} \end{matrix}\right\} \end{pmatrix} \end{pmatrix} \tag{11}$$

$$\bar{y} = \left(\sum_{r=1}^N \bar{y}^r agr_r\left(\bar{\mathbf{x}},\bar{y}^r\right)\right) \Big/ \left(\sum_{r=1}^N agr_r\left(\bar{\mathbf{x}},\bar{y}^r\right)\right) \tag{12}$$

Compromise operator in formula (10) is defined as follows:

$$\tilde{N}_\nu\left(a\right) = (1-\nu)\,N\left(a\right) + \nu N\left(N\left(a\right)\right) = (1-\nu)\,N\left(a\right) + \nu a \tag{13}$$

where $\nu \in [0,1]$, for details see [5].

3   Simulation Results

The flexible neuro-fuzzy system, described by formulas (9)-(12), is simulated on Chemical Plant problem [9] and Wine Recognition problem [10].

3.1   Chemical Plant Problem

We deal with a model of an operator's control of a chemical plant. The plant produces polymers by polymerising some monomers. Since the start-up of the plant is very complicated, men have to perform the manual operations at the plant. Three continuous inputs are chosen for controlling the system: monomer concentration, change of monomer concentration and monomer flow rate. The output is the set point for the monomer flow rate. The experimental results for the Chemical Plant problem are shown in Fig. 1 and Table 1, for not-parameterised (Zadeh and algebraic) and parameterised (Dombi and Yager) triangular norms.

3.2   Wine Recognition Problem

The Wine data contains a chemical analysis of 178 wines grown in the same region of Italy but derived from three different vineyards. The 13 continuous attributes available for classification are: alcohol, malic acid, ash, alkalinity of ash, magnesium, total phenols, flavanoids, nonflavanoid phenols, proanthocyanins, colour intensity, hue, OD280/OD315 of diluted wines and proline. In our experiments all sets are divided into a learning sequence (125 sets) and a testing sequence (53 sets). The problem is to classify wine samples based on the learning sequence. The experimental results for the Wine Recognition problem are shown in Fig. 2 and Table 2, for not-parameterised (Zadeh and algebraic) and parameterised (Dombi and Yager) triangular norms.

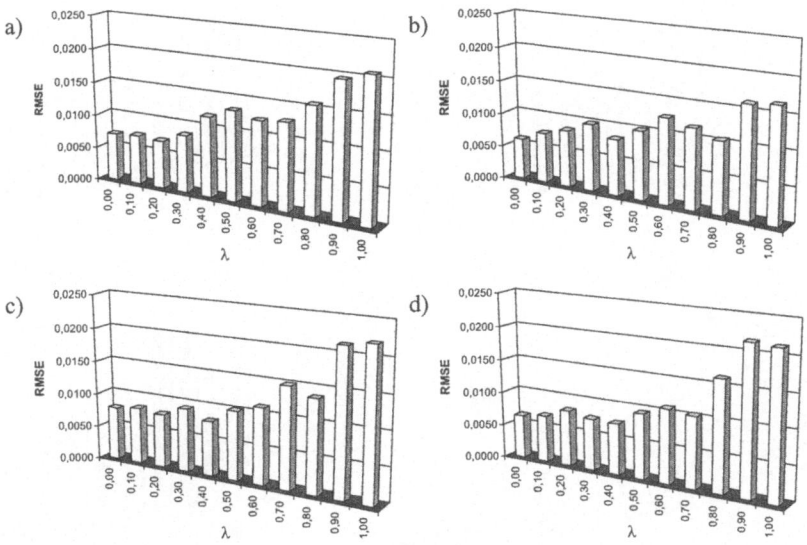

Fig. 1. Training RMSE for various values of the compromise parameter λ in the Chemical Plant problem for system (9)-(12) and a) Zadeh tr. norms, b) algebraic tr. norms, c) Dombi tr. norms, d) Yager tr. norms

Table 1. Experimental results

λ	Training RMSE			
	Zadeh tr.norms	Algebraic tr.norms	Dombi tr.norms	Yager tr.norms
0.0	0.0071	0.0061	0.0079	0.0064
0.1	0.0074	0.0075	0.0084	0.0069
0.2	0.0071	0.0085	0.0079	0.0083
0.3	0.0086	0.0100	0.0094	0.0077
0.4	0.0120	0.0084	0.0081	0.0076
0.5	0.0134	0.0102	0.0102	0.0097
0.6	0.0125	0.0127	0.0113	0.0109
0.7	0.0128	0.0117	0.0150	0.0105
0.8	0.0157	0.0106	0.0138	0.0163
0.9	0.0197	0.0162	0.0214	0.0217
1.0	0.0208	0.0166	0.0221	0.0214

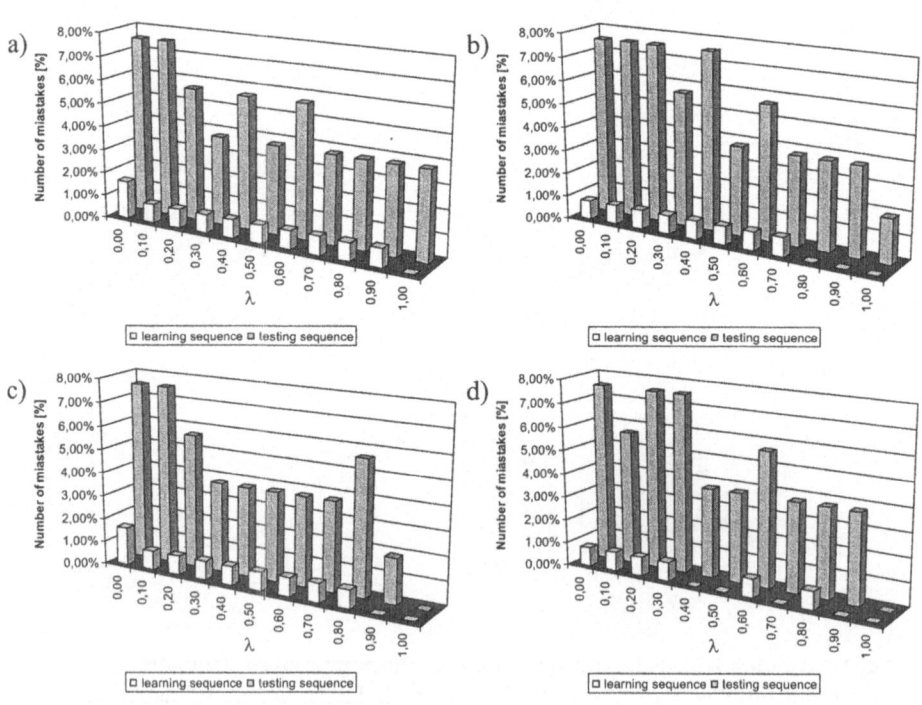

Fig. 2. Training and testing accuracy [%] for various values of the compromise parameter λ in the Wine Recognition problem for system (9)-(12) and a) Zadeh tr. norms, b) algebraic tr. norms, c) Dombi tr. norms, d) Yager tr. norms

Table 2. Experimental results

λ	Zadeh tr. norms		Algebraic tr. norms		Dombi tr. norms		Yager tr. norms	
	Train. Acc.[%]	Test. Acc.[%]	Train. Acc.[%]	Test. Acc.[%]	Train. Acc.[%]	Test. Acc.[%]	Train. Acc.[%]	Test. Acc.[%]
0.0	1.60	7.55	0.80	7.55	1.60	7.55	0.80	7.55
0.1	0.80	7.55	0.80	7.55	0.80	7.55	0.80	5.66
0.2	0.80	5.66	0.80	7.55	0.80	5.66	0.80	7.55
0.3	0.80	3.77	0.80	5.66	0.80	3.77	0.80	7.55
0.4	0.80	5.66	0.80	7.55	0.80	3.77	0.00	3.77
0.5	0.80	3.77	0.80	3.77	0.80	3.77	0.00	3.77
0.6	0.80	5.66	0.80	5.66	0.80	3.77	0.80	5.66
0.7	0.80	3.77	0.80	3.77	0.80	3.77	0.00	3.77
0.8	0.80	3.77	0.00	3.77	0.80	5.66	0.80	3.77
0.9	0.80	3.77	0.00	3.77	0.00	1.89	0.00	3.77
1.0	0.00	3.77	0.00	1.89	0.00	0.00	0.00	0.00

4 Final Remarks

In the paper we studied the influence of parameter λ in model (1) on performance of neuro-fuzzy structures. It has been shown that boundary values of λ, i.e. $\lambda = 0$ or $\lambda = 1$, give the best results. We have obtained the same conclusion in our previous works [5], [7].

References

1. E. Czogala and J. Leski. Fuzzy and Neuro-Fuzzy Intelligent Systems, Physica-Verlag Company, Heidelberg, New York, 2000.
2. M. B. Gorzalczany. Computational Intelligence Systems and Applications, Neuro-Fuzzy and Fuzzy Neural Synergisms, Springer-Verlag, New York, 2002.
3. J. M. Mendel. Uncertain Rule-Based Fuzzy Logic Systems: Introduction and New Directions, Prentice Hall PTR, Upper Saddle River, NJ, 2001.
4. D. Rutkowska. Neuro-Fuzzy Architectures and Hybrid Learning, Springer 2002.
5. L. Rutkowski. Flexible Neuro-Fuzzy Systems, Kluwer Academic Publishers, 2004.
6. L. Rutkowski and K. Cpalka. A general approach to neuro-fuzzy systems, The 10th IEEE Intern. Conference on Fuzzy Systems, Melbourne 2001.
7. L. Rutkowski and K. Cpalka. Flexible neuro-fuzzy systems, IEEE Trans. Neural Networks, vol. 14, pp. 554-574, May 2003.
8. L. Rutkowski and K. Cpalka. Designing and learning of adjustable quasi-triangular norms with applications to neuro-fuzzy systems, IEEE Trans. on Fuzzy Systems, vol. 14, 2004.
9. M. Sugeno and T. Yasukawa. A fuzzy-logic based approach to qualitative modeling, IEEE Trans. on Fuzzy Systems, vol. 1, pp. 7-31, February 1993.
10. UCI respository of machine learning databases, C. J. Mertz, P. M. Murphy. Available online: http://www.ics.uci.edu/pub/machine-learning-databases.
11. R. R. Yager and D. P. Filev. Essentials of Fuzzy Modeling and Control. John Wiley & Sons, 1994.

A Self Tuning Fuzzy Inference System for Noise Reduction

Nevcihan Duru[1] and Tarik Duru[2]

[1] Department of Computer Eng., University of Kocaeli
41440 Kocaeli, Turkey
[2] Department of Electrical Eng., University of Kocaeli
41440 Kocaeli, Turkey
{nduru,tduru}@kou.edu.tr

Abstract. In this paper, a method for the reduction of noise in a speech signal is introduced. In the implementing of the method, firstly a high resolution frequency map of the signal is obtained. Each frequency band component of the signal is then segmented. Fuzzy inference system (FIS) is used for the determination of the noise contents of the segments. The output of the FIS is the suppression level of the segment. If the FIS decides that the segment contains only noise, then the segment is deleted or if the FIS decides that the segment is noise free, it is allowed to be passed without suppression. Since the signal to noise ratio (SNR) varies from case to case, the limits of the membership functions are tuned accordingly. This self tuning capability gives flexibility and robustness of the system.

1 Introduction

In many cases, received speech signal is corrupted by noise [1]-[4]. Depending on the signal to noise ratio, noise may cause unwanted results In applications such as speech recognition, noise may result in partial lost of information and improper operation. Therefore noise reduction and denoising continue to be the important issues of the signal processing. Beside the classical methods such as adaptive filtering and spectral subtraction, modern methods based on wavelet denoising and soft computing techniques such as neural networks and fuzzy logic are increasingly used in noise reduction systems. In the spectral subtraction approach, the amplitude spectrum of a noisy signal is obtained by STFT (Short time Fourier transform). The estimated noise level is then subtracted from the each frequency components. "denoised" frequency domain components of the signal are transformed into the time domain by IDFT (Inverse Discrete Fourier Transformation). The hereby introduced process has some similarities to the wavelet approach in the time frequency modeling of the signal. In order to get rid of time and frequency resolution interaction of Fast Fourier Transformation (FFT), a Band Pass Filter Bank (BPFB) is used to model signal in time-frequency plane. In this approach, signal is passed trough band pass filters. The number o filters depend on the desired frequency resolution. The frequency resolved components

L. Rutkowski et al. (Eds.): ICAISC 2004, LNAI 3070, pp. 290–295, 2004.
© Springer-Verlag Berlin Heidelberg 2004

of signal is then absolute valued and segmented. The number of segments can be freely chosen depending on the desired time resolution on each frequency band. This approach, gives chance to select time and frequency resolutions independent of each other. Different time resolutions are also possible for each channel, which is impossible in the FFT approach. In speech signal, this possibility has a practical importance. In a speech signal, it is common that, low frequency components have higher energy and lasts longer than higher frequency components, while higher frequency components have low energy and consist of short pulses. In order to track the speech more precisely, segments should be chosen as short as to allow instant variations of high frequency pulses. However, these short segments distort the lower frequency components since a long sound is segmented into small parts. The superiority of the possibility of applying short segments to high frequency range and rather long segments to the low frequency range is clear. The segmented data samples are then processed to have amplitude computation, which gives an amplitude spectrum-like view of the signal. This is simply implemented as averaging of each segment. The average value of the segments is used as the amplitudes (levels). Beside of the amplitude, the rate of change of the amplitude values is also computed from the differences of segment levels. These two parameters are then used as the inputs of a fuzzy inference system to decide to which segments will be allowed to pass and which segments should be reduced by multiplication a factor.

The limits of the membership functions and partitioning of spaces are automatically constructed from the maximum and minimum values of levels and the estimated noise level. Noise level is rather coarsely estimated from the highest frequency band pass filter output. This assumption comes from the analysis of numbers of different speech signal corrupted by white noise with different SNR values. In normal speech sampled at about 10 kHz, the highest frequency filter bank is empty of signal in the most of the words, but, if presented, it has only band-limited portion of noise. In case of white noise, it can be assumed that, all the filter banks has the same level of noise on their outputs. Note that, the nature of the language and sound types of typical words can affect this assumption.

2 Band-Pass Filter Approach for Time-Frequency Modeling of the Speech Signal

As stated above, time-frequency model of a signal can be obtained by either FFT or a bank of band pass filters. The second method is used in this study because of the flexibility in choosing time and frequency resolutions independently and allowing the use of different data segments in each frequency bands. The basic scheme of BPFB approach is given in Fig. 1. The level of any segment is obtained simply summing all the values and averaging them. The number of filters in the particular sample studies are between 50 -150. However, higher numbers are also possible. Data segments in the range of 50-250 seem to be suitable for normal speech samples.

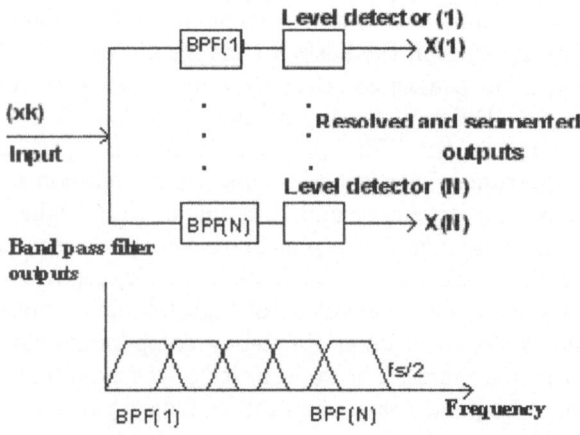

Fig. 1. Band pass filter bank and level detection

In Figure 2, an example of a female voice, who says the word "connection", is shown as its amplitude normalized to unity. In the computer environment, the signals of 8-bit resolution, which has been sampled at 11025 Hz are used. Due to the sampling theorem, the highest frequency component in such speech signal is 5501.25 Hz. Band pass filters are designed to have equally spaced pass bands, 4th order IIR filters are used. In Fig. 3a and 3b) , time-frequency map

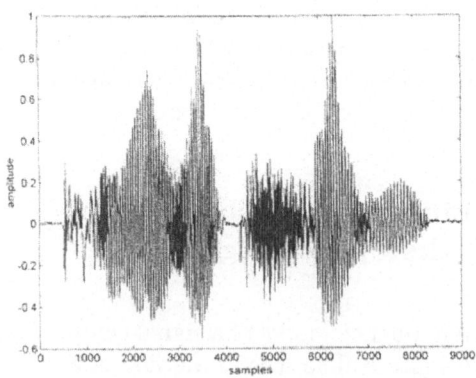

Fig. 2. Sample speech signal

of the sample signal is shown. As assumed, in case of original signal, the highest frequency bank's output has nearly zero average level. However, in Figure 3b), 50th filter output has an average level which is due to the white noise.

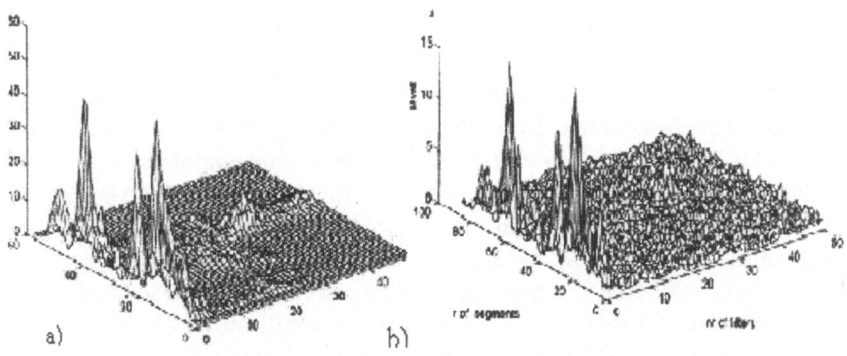

Fig. 3. a)The original and b) The noisy signal in time-frequency map. (50 filters and segments of 150 samples are used.)

3   The Implementation of Self-Tuning Fuzzy Inference System

A fuzzy inference system produces an output depending on the inputs, membership functions and the rules. In many applications, the fuzzy inference system is used to get a deduction from the variables, rules and membership functions. In the particular noise reduction process, the fuzzy inference system is used for this purpose either. Here the inputs are the average level of a segment and the rate of the change of level, which are abbreviated as LEV and DLEV respectively. The output is the factor of suppression, called as FACT. Three membership variables and functions for the each of the input - output variables are used. The membership functions for LEV, DLEV and FACT are given in Figure 4. The rule base is given in Table 1.

Table 1. The rules in compact form

DLEV

L	FACT	NBIG	NMED	ZERO	PMED	PBIG
E	ZERO	MED	MED	ZERO	MED	MED
V	MED	HIGH	MED	MED	MED	HIGH
	HIGH	HIGH	HIGH	HIGH	HIGH	HIGH

Since ZERO, MEDIUM and HIGH degree of the level and the rate of change of the level all depend on the signal and the SNR, no certain values of limits are available. In the determination of best-suited values, some characteristic quantities of the signal itself, is used. In Fig. 4, the considered parameters are also shown. Related parameters of the limits of membership functions are determined as follows.

XLZERO: Since the highest frequency band is assumed to be free of signal, the ZERO level is determined from the maximum value of all the segments in this band. This choice provides elimination of only-noise segments.

XLHIGH2: This value is obtained from the highest level of all the segments of all of the bands. This choice guarantees avoiding of overflows. XLMEDIUM2: The upper limit of MEDIUM level is obtained from the highest average level of all of the bands XDZERO: According the assumption mentioned above, the highest frequency band rate of change is taken as the limit of ZERO.

XDHIGH2: Similar to XLHIGH2, this value is obtained from the highest value of the segments of all of the bands.

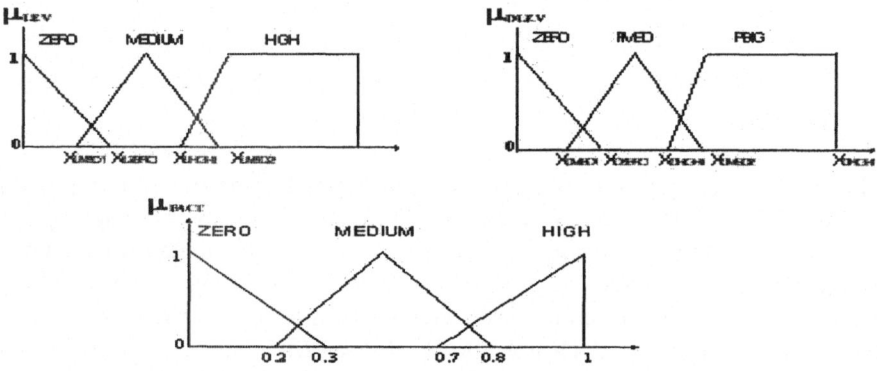

Fig. 4. Membership functions and limits a) for the variable LEV, b) for the variable DLEV c) for the variable FACT

The other values for XL's and XD's are geometrically determined by means of above limits. Allowing small overlap (about 20-30 percent of XLMEDIUM2) between XLMEDIUM2 and XLHIGH1, XLHIGH1 is obtained. The same overlap is used for determining XlZERO. The similar method is applied for the determination of the unknown limits of XD's. By the definition of this partitioning of the values between HIGH and ZERO, the system gains a self tuning feature against the variation of the SNR. Therefore, if the signal is free of noise, it passes through the bands nearly unchanged. Otherwise, some of the segments are either eliminated or suppressed. In Fig. 5, noisy and denoised signal are shown.

In Fig. 6, determined membership function limits of the variable "LEV" are shown for the same signal with two different SNR. Since noise level higher in the 10 dB case, the limit of the "ZERO" level is clearly shifted towards right which means the average level of the deleted segments are automatically increased.

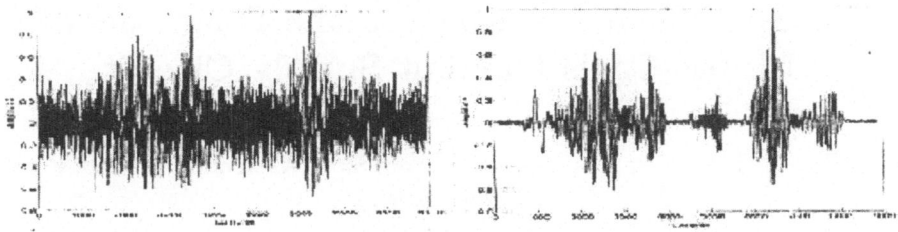

Fig. 5. Noisy and denoised speech signal in time domain. (SNR=5 dB for input)

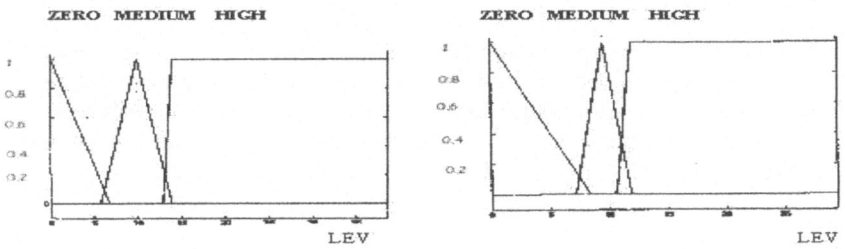

Fig. 6. Variation of membership function limits of LEV variable according to SNR. a)SNR=10 dB and b)SNR=0 dB

4 Conclusions

A simple method of noise reduction of digitally recorded speech signal is introduced. The results are acceptable by clarity and understandability means, when compared to the noise-corrupted signal. The presented method is easy to implement off line with the help of popular signal processing software packages. Self-tuning feature of the proposed method provides robustness for the process. Properly increasing the number of rules and membership functions may give better results. The real time application of the method will be a significant task for the future.

References

1. Ephraim, Y., Statistical-Model-Based Speech Enhancement Systems: Proc. Of the IEEE, Vol 80 No. 10, Oct. (1992).
2. Hellendoorn, H., Reinfrank, M., Driankov D.:An Introduction to Fuzzy Control, Springer (1996).
3. Stearns, S. D.: Adaptive Signal Processing, Bernard Widrow, Prentice Hall (1985).
4. Vashegi, S. V.:Advanced Signal Processing and Digital Noise Reduction, , Willey-Teubner (1996).
5. Duru, N., Fuzzy Logic Based Noise Reduction System (in Turkish), Ph. D. Thesis, KOU Inst. of Science, (1998).

Fuzzy-Neural Networks in the Diagnosis of Motor-Car's Current Supply Circuit

Stanisław Gad, Mariusz Łaskawski, Grzegorz Słoń, Alexander Yastrebov, and
Andrzej Zawadzki

Kielce University of Technology, Al. Tysiaclecia P. P. 7, 25-314 Kielce, POLAND
enegs@tu.kielce.pl

Abstract. In this paper general diagnostic model of cars' current supply circuit is presented. The set of defects with appropriate symptom signals is described. Binary diagnostic matrix is built. Fuzzy-neural models bank is presented. Some results of computer analysis of experimental research are described.

1 Introduction

Diagnostic task consists of the following elements: detection, localization and identification of faults [1]. Regarding this, the problem of diagnostic in the complex technical system is difficult to solve, considering nonlinearity and very often unknown dependences between some faults and selected symptom signals. During consideration of that kind of problem, various diagnostic methods are adapted; choice depending on selection of the model of a diagnostic object as well on solving the method of the diagnostic problems [1]. We notice that specification of the electric vehicle equipment diagnostic consists of short-lived processes (e.g. ignition system) and limitation when obtaining diagnostic signals from the sensing elements, which should be taken into consideration in creating the process of a suitable diagnostic system. In the papers [2,3,4] were presented a scheme of the intelligent computer diagnostic system, which is composed of the fixed symptom signals, neural detector and the possible adaptation of the different type of the faults localization models. In this paper a diagnostic symptom model of current supply circuit is built in the shape of an equivalent binary table, which connects the symptom signals and the faults [1]. In addition, we present computer methods of the detection and localization of the faults, for which in particular case one can relate to fuzzy neural algorithms. Chosen results of research, are also quoted.

2 The Symptom Models of Diagnosis of Vehicle's Current Supply Circuit

In Table 1 possible faults of motor-car electrical equipment and the corresponding symptom signals are described.

L. Rutkowski et al. (Eds.): ICAISC 2004, LNAI 3070, pp. 296–301, 2004.
© Springer-Verlag Berlin Heidelberg 2004

Table 1. The faults and the corresponding symptom signals.

SYMPTOMS	FAULTS
S1 – voltage supply; S2 – adjusted voltage – charging voltage of the accumulator – output from the alternator; S3 – driving torque of the combustion engine; S4 – input signal of the adjusted voltage into regulator; S5 – exciting current of the alternator; S6 – output signal from the ignition switch; S7 – command signal for the ignition coil; S8 – output from the ignition coil into ignition distributor; S9 – output from the ignition distributor; S10 – ignition spark; S11 – command signal for the ignition distributor; S12 – command signal of the impulse of the electronic ignition system; S13 – signal of the sub atmospheric pressure of the engine suction manifold; S14 – driving torque of the roller of the timer distributor; S15 – command impulse of the ignition moment; S16 – output signal from the ignition switch, command signal for the electromagnetic circuit breaker; S17 – signal of the switching on the contacts of the electromagnetic circuit breaker; S18 – current signal of the power supply of the starter winding; S19 – torque of the starter rotor; S20 – break away torque of the starter; S21 – power supply of the relay of the fuel pump; S22 – power supply of the fuel pump; S23 – fueling jet.	F0 – correct work; F1 – fault of the combustion engine; F3 – fault of the voltage regulator; F4 – fault of the accumulator; F5 – fault of the ignition switch; F6 – fault of the electronic ignition system; F7 – fault of the ignition coil; F8 – fault of the timer distributor; F9 – fault of the ignition distributor; F10 – fault of the system of the command impulse of ignition; F11 – fault of the electromagnetic circuit breaker; F12 – fault of the starter; F13 – fault of the join mechanism; F14 – fault of the relay of the fuel pump; F15 – fault of the fuel pump; F16 – fault of the ignition plug;

Besides general symptom models for the whole electric vehicle equipment, similar models are developed for individual circuit and devices.

In Fig. 1 the general scheme of the power supply circuit is presented.

In Table 2 possible faults in the object from Fig. 1 and the corresponding symptom signals are described.

The diagnostic analysis of the binary matrix gives the fallowing results of the faults distinction:

– faults {F2, F3} have the same fault signatures (the same values in the binary matrix columns) and in connection with that, these are not distinct,
– remaining faults are distinct.

3 The Fuzzy-Neural Algorithm of the Faults Diagnosis and Localization

Below the system for the fault localization realized by the bank of fuzzy – neural models is presented.

In Figs. 2–4 TSK models, which realize fuzzy inference by the fuzzy – neural model are presented. Presented structure consists of six layers, the premises are

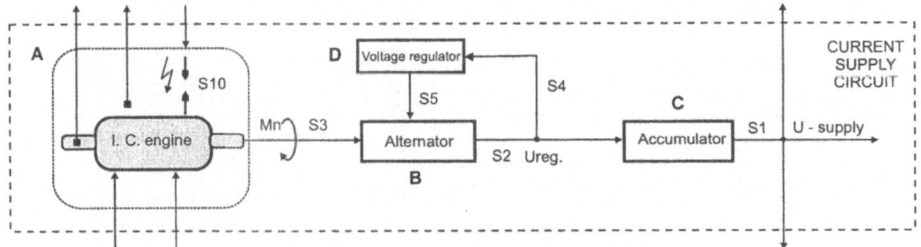

Fig. 1. The general scheme of the motor-car's current supply circuit

Table 2. The binary matrix of the faults and the corresponding symptom signals for vehicle's power supply circuit.

SF	F0	F1	F2	F3	F4
S1	1				1
S2	1	1	1	1	1
S3	1	1			
S4	1	1	1	1	1
S2	1	1	1	1	1

realized via layers L1 and L2, the concluding block contains the layers L3 and L4, the defuzzyfication block is realized via L5 and L6 [4].

In Fig. 4 a block scheme of the bank of fuzzy logic models for $M=4$, for 4 faults is presented (particular models for single faults are presented in Fig. 3).

For every fault F_i diagnostic is realized via fuzzy-neural network $\hat{S}_i$, where every i-network is completed from i-base of rules, i-fuzzification block, i-concluding block, i-defuzzification block, $i = 1, \ldots, M$. The number of fuzzy rules for each network can be, but it does not have to be identical. It is likewise is with fuzzy sets and with membership function.

4   Some Experimental Results

The computer analysis is performed using *NeuroSolutions 4* packet [4]. For every network is used gaussian or bell membership function and momentum learning rule. The fuzzy logic models is learned and tested for different data obtained during measurement process on the one real model. In the paper are presented simulations with the minimum value of the mean square error. Below are presented some selected results of the experimental fault diagnostic for elements described in scheme 1. The fuzzy – neural networks of TSK type are used. There were learning, verifying and testing signals. Testing results are presented below.

In Fig. 5 some results of the computer analysis of the fault localization for current supply circuit using the bank of the fuzzy logic models of TSK type are presented.

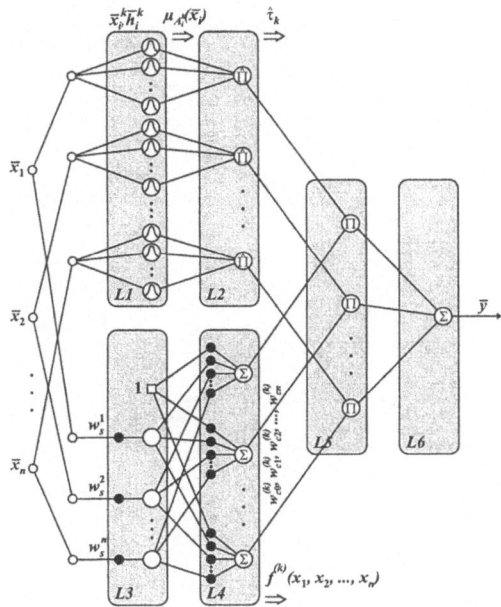

Fig. 2. The structure of the fuzzy-neural model of the diagnostic of TSK type, where:$(\bar{x}_1, \ldots, \bar{x}_n)$ – numerical input data, $\bar{x}_i^k, \bar{h}_i^k$ – parameters of the shape of the membership function, $(w_{c0}^{(k)}, \ldots, w_{cn}^k)$ – weights corresponding parameters $(c_0^{(k)}, \ldots, c_n^{(k)}), (w_s^1, \ldots, w_s^n)$ – weights of the connection in $L3$ layers

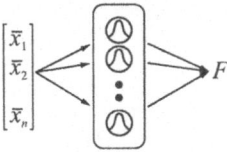

Fig. 3. The universal diagram of the fuzzy-neural model of diagnostic presented on Fig. 2, where $\bar{y}$ is transported to F

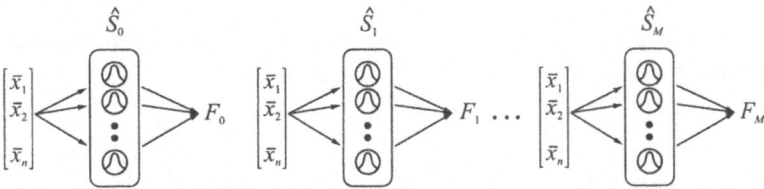

Fig. 4. The bank of the fuzzy-neural models of diagnostic for many outputs ($M{=}4$ – possible number of the faults for the object, $\hat{S}_0, \ldots, \hat{S}_M$ – particular single network in the bank of networks, corresponding faults $F_0, \ldots, F_M$)

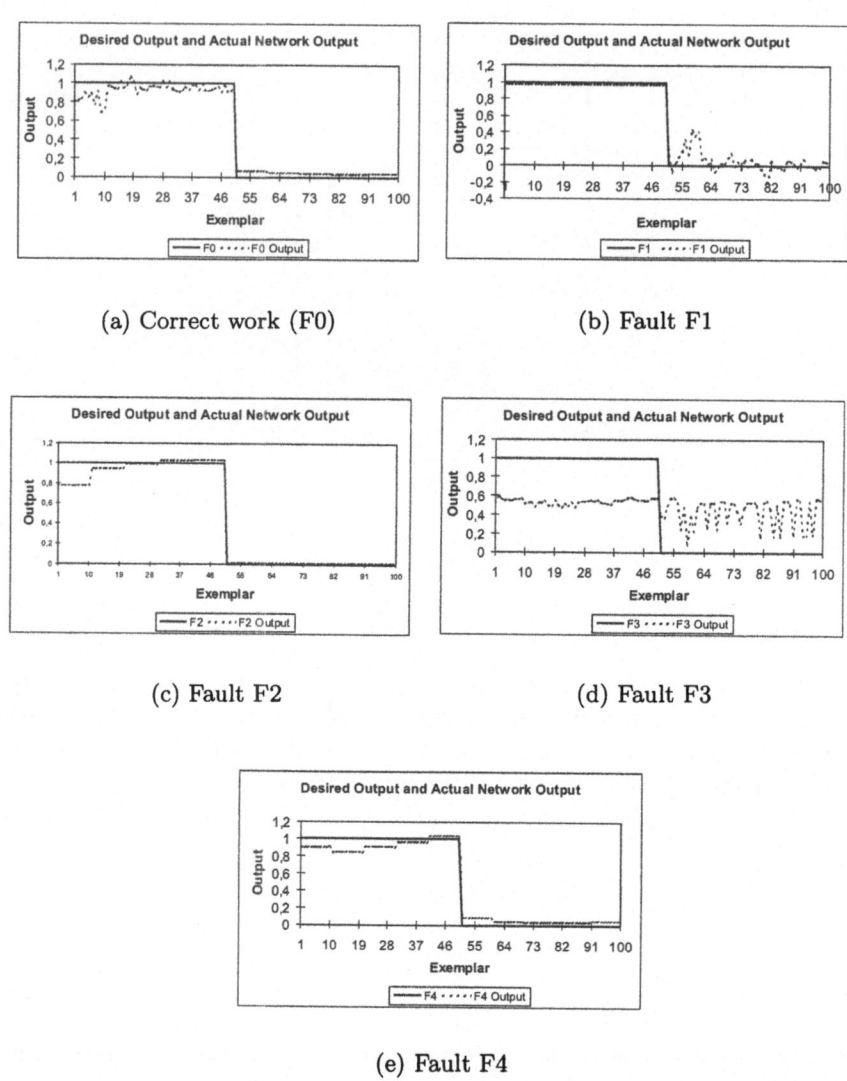

(a) Correct work (F0)   (b) Fault F1

(c) Fault F2   (d) Fault F3

(e) Fault F4

Fig. 5. The fault diagrams and their approximations by fuzzy logic models of TSK type for current supply circuit

Results of experiments shows that fault F3 is not diagnosable. It is also confirmed by analysis of binary matrix (Table 2), where it's shown that faults F2 and F3 are not distinct.

5   Conclusions

In this paper a scheme of the diagnostic model of the vehicle's current supply circuit is presented. Possible faults together with corresponding diagnostic signals are described. A diagnostic matrix for faults and corresponding symptom signals is built. For fault localization are applied fuzzy logic models (in the shape of a bank of TSK networks). Selected results of experimental research of diagnostic for vehicle's current supply circuit are presented. The research follow that correct diagnosing by fuzzy–neural networks is possible for defects which are distinguishable.

References

1. Korbicz J., Kościelny J.M., Kowalczuk Z., Cholewa W. (2002), The process diagnostic. Models, methods of the artificial intelligence. Adaptations. WNT, Warszawa, Poland.
2. Gad S., Słoń G., Yastrebov A. (2001). Computer diagnosis and identification of selected systems of electrical equipment of cars. In: Proc. of XIV International Conference On Systems Science, SYSTEMS SCIENCE XIV, Wrocław, Poland, pp. 150–157.
3. Yastrebov A., Gad S., Slon G. (2001) Computer diagnosis of the electrical vehicle equipment (in Polish). In: Proc. of IX National Congress on Exploitation of Technical Equipment, Krynica Górska, Poland, pp. 203–214.
4. Yastrebov A., Gad S., Slon G., Laskawski M. (2003) Computer analysis of electrical vehicle equipment diagnosing with artificial neural networks. – In: Proc. of International Conference SICPRO'03, Moscov, Russia, pp. 1331–1348.

Fuzzy Number-Based Hierarchical Fuzzy System

Adam E. Gaweda[1] and Rafał Scherer[2,3]

[1] Kidney Disease Program, School of Medicine
University of Louisville
Louisville, KY 40202, USA
agaweda@kdp.louisville.edu
[2] Dept. of Computer Engineering, Czestochowa Univ. of Technology
Al. Armii Krajowej 36, 42-200 Czestochowa, Poland
rafal@ieee.org
http://kik.pcz.pl
[3] Department of Artificial Intelligence, WSHE University in Łódź
ul. Rewolucji 1905 nr 64, Łódź, Poland
http://www.wshe.lodz.pl

Abstract. Hierarchical fuzzy systems allow for reducing number of rules and for prioritization of rules. To retain fuzziness, intermediate signals should be fuzzy. Transferring fuzzy signal is computationally demanding. Special form of hierarchical fuzzy system is proposed to reduce computational burden.

1 Introduction

Fuzzy systems have established their place in scientific and engineering world for good. Most of them utilize the single stage reasoning, i.e. there are only input variables, fed to the input of the system, and the output variables as an outcome of a reasoning process. Expert knowledge in the form of fuzzy rules with linguistic terms is comprehensible and easily interpretable. The most popular of them are Mamdani and TSK systems, which served as the basis of numerous network structures, developed so far. Such fuzzy-neural networks have ability to learn, thanks to their connectionist architecture. The rules, the shapes of membership functions and their positions can be adjusted through supervised or unsupervised training. But when the number of input variables is very high, the resultant fuzzy system is extremely complex. When the whole input space has to be covered by the fuzzy rules, each combination of input linguistic terms constitutes a fuzzy rule. Having given n inputs and m linguistic terms for every input, we have m^n possible rules. It shows that the number of fuzzy rules increases exponentially with the number of inputs. This phenomenon is called the curse of dimensionality. It causes multidimensional systems to have enormous number of adjustable parameters. Learning of such systems is inconvenient because of great number of local minima, computational complexity and memory requirements.

L. Rutkowski et al. (Eds.): ICAISC 2004, LNAI 3070, pp. 302–307, 2004.
© Springer-Verlag Berlin Heidelberg 2004

2 Hierarchical Fuzzy Systems

Hierarchical fuzzy systems use multi-stage fuzzy logic inference, and hence three kinds of linguistic variable are involved, namely: input, intermediate and output variables. This kind of reasoning is similar to human thinking [6]. We would choose the most important input variables to be placed in the first stage and the next important ones in the consecutive stages. Hierarchical fuzzy systems have been first introduced by Raju et al. in 1994 [9], as a solution to the curse of dimensionality. The system was composed of several low-dimensional fuzzy systems, connected in hierarchical way. There was only one system in each stage. It was proved that the overall number of fuzzy rules is minimal when each stage has only two inputs.

From the structural point of view, hierarchical systems can be divided into three groups [1][2][3] (Fig.1). In aggregated hierarchical fuzzy systems, the lowest level serves as an input of the entire structure. Outputs of this first level are connected to the second stage inputs and so on, until the highest level whose outputs become the outputs of the whole structure. Because this structure is a combination of several single stage fuzzy systems, the number of rules is smaller than in single stage systems.

In incremental hierarchical fuzzy system, outputs of subsystems from previous stage are also fed to the one of the next stage subsystem input, but in every stage there is only one subsystem. The subsystems have one of their inputs connected to previous stage output and the next input (or inputs) serves as one of the inputs of the whole structure. Thus, every stage has one or more input variables connected, until all input variables are used. The intermediate variables

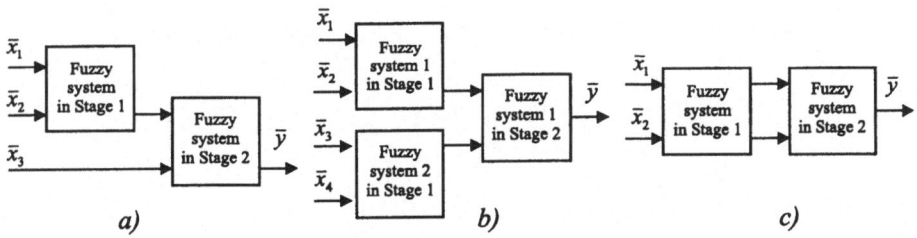

Fig. 1. Examples of hierarchical fuzzy systems: a) aggregated, b) incremental, c) cascaded.

can be fuzzy or crisp. Using fuzzy numbers seems intuitive and straightforward but may be computationally demanding. We must determine an intersection of the input fuzzy set and fuzzy set in IF-part of a rule. Then, we have to find maximum of this resultant fuzzy set. Crisp numbers are easier to handle, but they require defuzzyfication and fuzzyfication, and we miss the information carried by fuzzy signals. In this paper, we propose a computationally efficient way of dealing with fuzzy numbers as intermediate variables.

3   Computing with Fuzzy Numbers

Fuzzy rule antecedents contain propositions "x is A". When "x" is a crisp number ($x = a$), the degree of matching between a and A can be computed using singleton fuzzification. When "x" is a fuzzy number (x is A'), one of the possible ways of computing the matching degree is based on mutual subsethood [5]

$$E(A, A') = \frac{c(A \cap A')}{c(A) + c(A') - c(A \cap A')} \,, \tag{1}$$

where $c()$ represents set count. Mutual subsethood is a similarity measure based on the degree of inclusion A' in A and and at the same time on the degree of inclusion of A in A'. It has been applied to perform processing of fuzzy signals in Neuro-Fuzzy systems [8].

Let us assume, that the fuzzy sets A and A' are described by the following membership functions:

$$\mu(x) = e^{-2(x-m)^2 / ((1-\mathrm{sgn}(x-m))s_l^2 + (1+\mathrm{sgn}(x-m))s_r^2)} \,, \tag{2}$$

where the parameters m represent the center, and s_l and s_r represent the left and right spread of the membership function. Assuming that $m_A < m_{A'}$, the expressions for $c(A)$, $c(B)$, and $c(A \cap B)$ can be computed as follows:

$$c(A) = \frac{\sqrt{\pi}}{2} (s_{lA} + s_{rA}), \tag{3}$$

$$c(B) = \frac{\sqrt{\pi}}{2} (s_{lA'} + s_{rA'}), \tag{4}$$

$$c(A \cap A') = \frac{\sqrt{\pi}}{2} \left(\tilde{s}_1 e^{-\frac{(m_A - m_{A'})^2}{s_{lA}^2 + s_{lA'}^2}} \left[erf \left(\frac{m_A - \tilde{m}_1}{\tilde{s}_1} \right) + 1 \right] + \right.$$

$$\tilde{s}_2 e^{-\frac{(m_A - m_{A'})^2}{s_{rA}^2 + s_{lA'}^2}} \left[erf \left(\frac{m_{A'} - \tilde{m}_2}{\tilde{s}_2} \right) - erf \left(\frac{m_A - \tilde{m}_2}{\tilde{s}_2} \right) \right] +$$

$$\left. \tilde{s}_3 e^{-\frac{(m_A - m_{A'})^2}{s_{rA}^2 + s_{rA'}^2}} \left[1 - erf \left(\frac{m_{A'} - \tilde{m}_3}{\tilde{s}_3} \right) \right] \right) \,, \tag{5}$$

where:

$\tilde{m}_1 = (m_A s_{lA'}^2 + m_{A'} s_{lA}^2)/(s_{lA}^2 + s_{lA'}^2), \quad \tilde{s}_1 = s_{lA} s_{lA'}/\sqrt{s_{lA}^2 + s_{lA'}^2}$,

$\tilde{m}_2 = (m_A s_{lA'}^2 + m_{A'} s_{rA}^2)/(s_{rA}^2 + s_{lA'}^2), \quad \tilde{s}_2 = s_{rA} s_{lA'}/\sqrt{s_{rA}^2 + s_{lA'}^2}$,

$\tilde{m}_3 = (m_A s_{rA'}^2 + m_{A'} s_{rA}^2)/(s_{rA}^2 + s_{rA'}^2), \quad \tilde{s}_3 = s_{rA} s_{rA'}/\sqrt{s_{rA}^2 + s_{rA'}^2}$.

Having obtained degree of fulfillment for each rule premise, the activation levels of the rules $\tau_k(x)$ are computed using arithmetic product. The consequent fuzzy sets B have the same form as (2). It is further assumed that the aggregated output fuzzy set B^{out} is convex and can be described by an asymmetric Gaussian in the same manner. The center of the output fuzzy set is computed as a weighted average of the centers of the consequent fuzzy sets and its left and right spreads are computed as the weighted averages of the left and right spreads of the consequent fuzzy sets, respectively

$$m_{Bout} = \sum_{k=1}^{K} \hat{\tau}_k(x) \, m_{B_k} \, , \tag{6}$$

$$s_{l,r\,Bout} = \sum_{k=1}^{K} \hat{\tau}_k(x) \, s_{l,r\,B_k} \, , \tag{7}$$

where $\hat{\tau}_k$ are normalized rule activation levels.

4   Hierarchical Fuzzy System with Fuzzy Numbers as Intermediate Variables

For simplicity we assume we have only one system in each stage l of a system consisting of L stages. Each system has a set of rules

$$R^{kl} : \text{IF } \mathbf{x} \text{ is } A^{kl} \text{ THEN } y \text{ is } B^{kl} \tag{8}$$

or

$$R^{kl} : \text{IF } x_1 \text{ is } A_1^{kl} \text{ AND} \ldots \text{AND } x_N \text{ is } A_N^{kl} \text{ THEN } y \text{ is } B^{kl} \, , \tag{9}$$

where k is a rule number in the l-th layer, $l = 1 \ldots L$, and $k = 1 \ldots K^l$. $\mathbf{x} = [x_1, x_2, \ldots, x_N]^T \in \mathbf{X} = \mathbf{X}_1 \times \mathbf{X}_2 \times \ldots \times \mathbf{X}_N$ is a vector of input linguistic values (e.g. features of state or object being classified), y is an output linguistic variable. We use also the following notation for rule antecedents and consequents: $A^{kl} = A_1^{kl} \times A_2^{kl} \times \ldots \times A_N^{kl}$ and B^{kl}. Input data is depicted as a premise in the form

$$\mathbf{x} \text{ is } A' \, , \tag{10}$$

or

$$x_1 \text{ is } A_1' \, , \ldots , \, x_N \text{ is } A_N' \, . \tag{11}$$

The outcome of the reasoning process from a rule R^{kl} for a given premise is the following conclusion

$$y \text{ is } B'^{kl} \, , \tag{12}$$

where a fuzzy set B'^{kl}, in case of modus ponens reasoning, is defined as a composition

$$B'^{kl} = A' \circ \left(A^{kl} \to B^{kl} \right) \, . \tag{13}$$

If we use sup-T composition, the membership function of B'^{kl} is defined

$$\mu_{B'^{kl}}(y) = \sup_{\mathbf{x} \in \mathbf{X}} \left\{ \mu_{A'}(\mathbf{x}) \overset{T}{*} \mu_{A^{kl} \to B^{kl}}(\mathbf{x}, y) \right\} \, , \tag{14}$$

where $\overset{T}{*}$ denotes a T-norm, and $A^{kl} \to B^{kl}$ denotes an implication. In this case, so called "engineering (Larsen) implication" is used:

$$\mu_{A^{kl} \to B^{kl}}(\mathbf{x}, y) = \mu_{A^{kl}}(\mathbf{x}) \cdot \mu_{B^{kl}}(y) . \tag{15}$$

In our case we compute activation level of the k-th rule by

$$\tau_k = \prod_{n=1}^{N} E_n , \tag{16}$$

where E_n is the mutual subsethood between n-th input fuzzy set and premise set A_n^{kl}. Then consequent fuzzy set is computed by weighted average of all sets B^{kl} using (6)-(7).

5   Illustrative Example

We built an incremental 3-stage hierarchical fuzzy system to demonstrate and evaluate the proposed approach. The auto-mpg data set is widely used as a benchmark for testing performance of fuzzy systems. The system in this example is organized as follows. The inputs to Stage 1 system are *weight* and *year*, while Stage 2 receives *horsepower* and *displacement*. Stages 1 and 2 work in parallel and compute first estimates of the gas mileage, denoted as MPG_1 and MPG_2, respectively. These estimates are the intermediate variables. Stage 3 performs fusion of the intermediate variables and computes the actual MPG as output. In this example, the systems in each stage were obtained by fuzzy c-means clustering. The whole data set was divided into equally sized training and testing subsets. Stage 1 and 2 were obtained first and the data was passed through them in order to produce the training vectors for Stage 3. The membership functions are depicted in Fig. 2. The whole system was tested using the testing subset. We first evaluated the approximation performance of each Stages 1 and 2 using the RMSE error and obtaining values 5.0 for Stage 1 and 4.7 for Stage 2, respectively. With crisp numbers as intermediate variables, the error of Stage 3 was 5.1. When fuzzy numbers were used as intermediate variables, the error dropped to 4.4. This example indicates that retaining fuzziness of the intermediate variables may improve the approximation accuracy. A further improvement of the approximation performance could be achieved by tuning the system using gradient-descent techniques.

6   Conclusions

Our new system has fuzzy intermediate variables, so we retain fuzzy form of the signals through the whole structure. The system is not computationally demanding thanks to the new way of computing fuzzy inputs and simplified fuzzy inference. Such fuzzy systems can be chained and fuzzy signal is retained during bypassing through consecutive stages. The feasibility of the proposed approach and its potential benefits have been demonstrated with a simple application example.

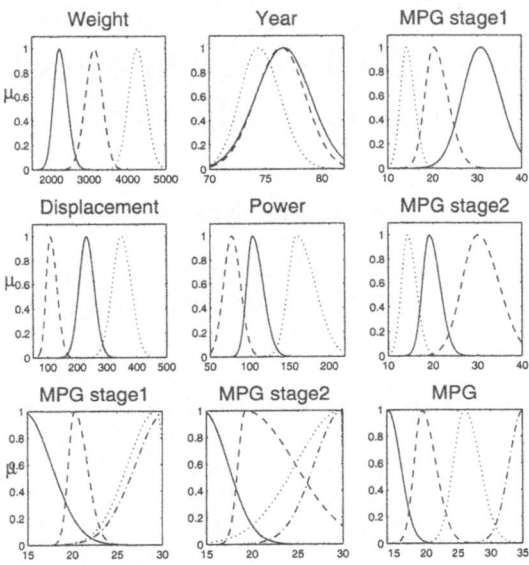

Fig. 2. Fuzzy membership functions for Stage 1 (top), Stage 2 (middle), and Stage 3 (bottom) systems

References

1. Chung F.-L., Duan J.-C., Deriving Multistage FNN Models From Takagi and Sugeno's Fuzzy Systems, Proceedings of 1998 IEEE World Congress on Computational Intelligence, FUZZ-IEEE, 1259–1264
2. Chung F.-L., Duan J.-C., On Multistage Fuzzy Neural Network Modeling, IEEE Transactions On Fuzzy Systems, Vol. 8, No. 2, April (2000)
3. Duan J.-C., Chung F.-L., A Mamdani Type Multistage Fuzzy Neural Network Model, Proceedings of 1998 IEEE World Congress on Computational Intelligence, FUZZ-IEEE, 1253–1258
4. Fukuda T., Hasegawa Y., Shimojima K., Structure Organization of Hierarchical Fuzzy Model using Genetic Algorithm, Japanese Journal of Fuzzy Theory and Systems, Volume 7, Number 5, 631–643
5. Kosko B., Neural Networks and Fuzzy Systems, Prentice Hall (1991)
6. Nowicki R., Scherer R., A Hierarchical Fuzzy System With Fuzzy Intermediate Variables, Proceedings of The 9th Zittau Fuzzy Colloquium, Germany (2001) 88–93
7. Nowicki R., Scherer R., Rutkowski L., A Hierarchical Neuro-Fuzzy System Based on S-Implications, 2003 International Joint Conference on Neural Networks, June 17-27, 2003, Portland, Oregon, USA (CD-ROM)(2003)
8. Paul S., Kumar S., Subsethood-product fuzzy neural inference system (SuPFuNIS), IEEE Transactions on Neural Networks, Vol. 13, No. 3, May (2002) 578–599
9. Raju G.V.S., Zhou J., Kisner R.A.: Hierarchical fuzzy control, in: Advances in Intelligent Control, Taylor & Francis Ltd, (1994) 243–258

Stock Trend Prediction Using Neurofuzzy Predictors Based on Brain Emotional Learning Algorithm

Mahdi Jalili-Kharaajoo

Young Researchers Club, Islamic Azad University, Tehran, Iran
mahdijalili@ece.ut.ac.ir

Abstract. Short term trends, particularly attractive for neural network analysis, can be used profitably in scenarios such as option trading, but only with significant risk. To predict stock trends, we exploit Emotional Learning Based Fuzzy Inference System (ELFIS). ELFIS has the advantage of low computational complexity in comparison with other multi-objective optimization methods. The performance of ELFIS in the prediction of stock prices will be compared with that of Adaptive Network Based Fuzzy Inference System (ANFIS). Simulations show better performance for ELFIS.

1 Introduction

Predicting the future has been an interesting important problem in human mind. Alongside great achievements in this endeavor there remain many natural phenomena the successful predictions of which have so far eluded researchers. Some have been proven unpredictable due to the nature of their stochasticity. Others have been shown to be chaotic: with continuous and bounded frequency spectrum resembling white noise and sensitivity to initial conditions attested via positive Lyapunov exponents resulting in long term unpredictability of the time series. There are several developed methods to distinguish chaotic systems from the others, however model-free nonlinear predictors can be used in most cases without changes.

Following the directions of biologically motivated intelligent computing, the emotional learning method has been introduced as a kind of reinforcement learning [1-3]. This approach is based on an emotional signal which shows the emotions of a critic about the overall performance of the system. In [4] Emotional Learning Based Fuzzy Inference System (ELFIS) has been introduced. The emotional learning algorithm is a model-free method which has three distinctive properties in comparison with other neurofuzzy learning algorithms. For one thing, one can use very complicated definitions for emotional signal without increasing the computational complexity of algorithm or worrying about differentiability or renderability into recursive formulation problems. For another, the parameters can be adjusted in a simple intuitive way to obtain the best performance. Besides, the training is very fast and efficient.

L. Rutkowski et al. (Eds.): ICAISC 2004, LNAI 3070, pp. 308–313, 2004.
© Springer-Verlag Berlin Heidelberg 2004

Our approach to market forecasting capitalizes on two observations: that predictions over a relatively short time are easier to do reliably, and that attempts to profit on short term moves need this reliability to compensate for risks, taxes, and transaction costs [5-7]. We arbitrarily select a 2

2 Neurofuzzy Prediction Based on Emotional Learning Algorithm

The Takagi-Sugeno fuzzy inference system is based on fuzzy rules of the following type

$$Rule_i = if u_1 = A_{i1} and u_p = A_{ip},$$
$$then \hat{y} = f_i(u_1, u_2, ..., u_p) \tag{1}$$

where $i = 1, ..., M$ and M is the number of fuzzy rules. $u_1, ..., u_p$ are the inputs of network, each A_{ij} denotes the fuzzy set for input u_j in rule i and $f_i(\cdot)$ is a crisp function which is defined as a linear combination of inputs in most applications

$$\hat{y} = \omega_{i0} + \omega_{i1}u_1 + ... + \omega_{ip}u_p \tag{2}$$

Thus, the output of this model can be calculated by

$$\hat{y} = \frac{\sum f_i(u)\mu_i(u)}{\sum \mu_i(u)}, \mu_i(u) = \prod \mu_{ij}(u_j) \tag{3}$$

where $\mu_{ij}(u_j)$ is the membership function of jth input in the ith rule and $\mu_i(u)$ is the degree of validity of the ith rule.

This system can be formulated in the basis function realization which leads to relation between Takagi-Sugeno fuzzy model and normalized RBF network. The basis function will be

$$\phi_i(u) = \frac{\mu_i(u)}{\sum \mu_j(u)} \tag{4}$$

as a result

$$\sum \phi_j(u) = 1 \tag{5}$$

This neurofuzzy model has two sets of adjustable parameters; first the antecedent parameters, which belong to the input membership functions such as centers and deviations of Gaussians; second the rule consequent parameters such as the linear weights of output in equation (2). Gradient based learning algorithms can be used in the optimization of consequent linear parameters. Supervised learning is aimed to minimize the following loss function (mean square error of estimation)

$$J = \frac{1}{N} \sum (y(i) - \hat{y}(i))^2 \tag{6}$$

where N is the number of data samples.

According to the matrix form of (2) this loss function can be expanded in the quadratic form

$$J = W^T R W - 2W^T P + \frac{Y^T Y}{N} \tag{7}$$

where $R = \frac{1}{N} A^T A$ is the autocorrelation matrix, A is the $N \times p$ solution matrix whose ith row is $a(u_i(i))$ and $P = \frac{1}{N} A^T Y$ is the p dimensional cross correlation vector.

From

$$\frac{\partial J}{\partial W} = 2RW - 2P = 0 \tag{8}$$

the following linear equations are obtained to minimize J

$$RW = P \tag{9}$$

and W is simply defined by pseudo inverse calculation.

One of the simplest local nonlinear optimization techniques is the steepest descent. In this method the direction of changes in parameters will be opposite to the gradient of cost function

$$\triangle W(i) = -\frac{\partial J}{\partial W(i)} = 2P - 2RW(i) \tag{10}$$

and

$$W(i+1) = W(i) + \eta \triangle W(i) \tag{11}$$

where η is the learning rate.

Some of the advanced learning algorithms that have been proposed for the optimization of parameters in Takagi-Sugeno fuzzy inference system include AS-MOD (Adaptive Spline Modeling of Observation Data) [8], ANFIS (Adaptive Network Based Fuzzy Inference System) [9]. ANFIS is one of the most popular algorithms used for different purposes, such as system identification, control, prediction and signal processing. It is a hybrid learning method based on gradient descent and least square estimation.

The Emotional learning method is a psychologically motivated algorithm which is developed to reduce the complexity of computations in prediction problems [3,4], which is based on an emotional signal. The definition of emotional signal is absolutely problem dependent. It can be a function of error, rate of error change and many other features. Then a loss function is defined based on the emotional signal. A simple form can be

$$J = \frac{1}{2} K \sum es(i)^2 \tag{12}$$

where es is the emotional signal. Learning is adjusting the weights of model by means of a nonlinear optimization method, e.g. the steepest descent or conjugate gradient.

With steepest descent method the weights will be adjusted by the following variations

$$\triangle \omega = -\eta \frac{\partial J}{\partial \omega} \tag{13}$$

where η is the learning rate of the corresponding neurofuzzy controller and the right hand side can be calculated by chain rule

$$\frac{\partial J}{\partial \omega} = \frac{\partial J}{\partial es} \frac{\partial es}{\partial y} \frac{\partial y}{\partial \omega} \tag{14}$$

According to (12)

$$\frac{\partial J}{\partial \omega} = Kes \tag{15}$$

and $\frac{\partial y}{\partial \omega}$ is accessible from (3) where $f_i(\cdot)$ is a linear function of weights.

Calculating the remaining part, $\frac{\partial es}{\partial y}$, is not straightforward in most cases. This is the price to be paid for the freedom to choose any desired emotional cue as well as not having to impose presuppose any predefined model. However, it can be approximated via simplifying assumptions. If, for example error is defined by

$$e = y_r - y \tag{16}$$

where y_r is the output to be estimated, then

$$\frac{\partial es}{\partial y} = -\frac{\partial es}{\partial e} \tag{17}$$

can be replaced by its sign (-1) in (14). The algorithm is after all, supposed to be satisfying rather than optimizing.

Finally, the weights will be updated by the following formula

$$\triangle \omega = -K\eta es \frac{\partial y}{\partial \omega} = -K\eta es \frac{\sum u_i \mu_i(u)}{\sum \mu_i(u)} \tag{18}$$

3   Stock Trend Prediction Using ELFIS

Forecasting tests have been run on a variety of stocks and on different data sets, where some are more recent than the others. Generally the later tests confirm the earlier ones. The tests run in or before June 2002 include only Apple and Motorola. The most recent tests run in 2003 include the following stocks, which cover a larger variety of categories: Apple (AAPL) and Motorola (MOT) represent the technology group which generally has high volatility. American Express (AXP) and Wells Fargo (WFC) represent the banks. Walt Disney Co. (DIS) and McDonald (MCD) represent the consumer stocks.

For simulations, we have considered the closed price for this stock in each day. Simulation results have been summarized in Table I and Figs. 1 and 2. In Table 1, the performance of predictions price for different stocks using ELFIS and ANFIS are compared with together. According to this table, learning in ELFIS is at least three times faster than ANFIS. Also, ELFIS is more accurate, i.e., the prediction using ELFIS results a response with less Normalized Mean Square Error (NMSE) than that of ANFIS. It is remarkable that using a functional description of emotional signal rather than the fuzzy description will generate faster algorithm, but finding such a suitable function is not easy. Figs. 1 and 2 show the actual and predicted prices using ELFIS for AAPL and AXP, respectively. As it can be seen, the prices can be predicted with acceptable accuracy.

Table 1. Comparison of predictions using ANFIS and ELFIS for different stocks

Stock	CT of ANFIS	CT of ELFIS	NMSE of ANFIS	NMSE of ELFIS
AAPL	24.35s	8.31s	0.08421	0.08103
MOT	28.42s	9.98s	0.06194	0.05422
AXP	31.12s	12.45s	0.06671	0.06229
WFC	21.78s	7.35s	0.07138	0.07011
DIS	19.48s	7.19s	0.07355	0.06839
MCD	37.71s	14.77s	0.05471	0.53040

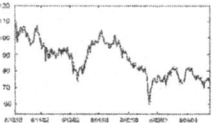

Fig. 1. Actual (*solid line*) and predicted (*dotted line*) prices for AAPL using ELFIS

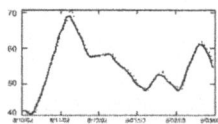

Fig. 2. Actual (*solid line*) and predicted (*dotted line*) prices for AXP using ELFIS

4   Conclusion

Predicting short term stock trends based on history of daily closing prices is possible using any kind of neural network based computation. In this paper we used ELFIS for prediction of stock prices in some instants, which resulted in good prediction. In fact the use of a combination of error and rate of error change led to late overtraining of neurofuzzy model and thus more accurate predictions have been obtained. The definition of emotional signal is an important aid in emotional learning algorithms, which provides high degrees of freedom. Better performance can be obtained through the use of variables in addition to the lagged values of the process to be predicted (e.g. fundamentalist as well as chartist data).

References

1. Balkenius, C., J. Moren, A Computational Model Of Emotional Conditioning In The Brain, Proc. Grounding Emotions in Adaptive Systems, Zurich, 1998.
2. Moren, J., C. Balkenius, A Computational Model of Emotional Learning in The Amygdala, Proc. 6th Int. conf. Sim. Adaptive Behavior, MIT Press, 2000.
3. Lucas, C., D. Shahmirzadi, N. Sheikholeslami, Introducing BELBIC: Brain Emotional Learning Based Intelligent Controller, to appear in International Journal of Intelligent Automation and Soft Computing (Autosoft), 2004.
4. Lucas, C., A. Abbaspour, A. Gholipour, B.N. Araabi, M. Fatourechi, Enhancing the Performance of Neurofuzzy Predictors by Emotional Learning Algorithm, informatica, October, 2003.
5. Tan, H., D. Prokhorov, and D. Wunsch, Probabilistic and time-delay neural-network techniques for conservative short-term stock trend prediction, Proc. World Congr. N.N., Washington D.C., July 1995.
6. Kreesuradej, W., D. Wunsch, and M. Lane, Time-delay neural network for small time series data sets, Proc. World Congr. N.N., CA, 1994.
7. Saad, E., D. Prokhorov, and D. Wunsch, Advanced neural-network training methods for low false alarm stock trend prediction, Proc. IEEE Int. Conf. N.N., Washington D.C., pp. 2021-2026, 1996.
8. Kavli T., ASMOD: An algorithm for adaptive spline modeling of observation data, Int. Journal of Control, 58(4), pp. 947-967, 1993.
9. Jang J.R., ANFIS: Adaptive network based fuzzy inference system, IEEE Tran. On Systems, Man and Cybernetics, 23(3), pp. 665-685, 1993.

Digital Implementation of Fuzzy Petri Net Based on Asynchronous Fuzzy RS Flip-Flop

Jacek Kluska[1] and Zbigniew Hajduk[2]

[1] Faculty of Electrical and Computer Engineering, Rzeszow University of Technology,
35-959 Rzeszow, W. Pola 2, Poland
jacklu@prz.rzeszow.pl
[2] Faculty of Electrical and Computer Engineering, Rzeszow University of Technology,
35-959 Rzeszow, W. Pola 2, Poland
zhajduk@prz-rzeszow.pl

Abstract. The paper presents a method of digital implementation of a fuzzy Petri net (FPN) based on asynchronous fuzzy RS flip-flop. The FPN can be viewed as a formal description of a control algorithm of a plant. The idea of FPN and its dynamics were characterized. A digital architecture of the asynchronous fuzzy RS flip-flop was given. A conception of the hardware implementation of the FPN was described.

1   Introduction

A lot of industrial processes can be modelled using Petri nets [20], [16]. If all the process variables or events are assumed to be two-valued signals, then it is possible to obtain a hardware or software control device, which works according to the algorithm described by conventional Petri net. As a result of the use of Petri nets and design methods based on Boolean logic, a number of procedures have been developed for the synthesis of the so called parallel controllers, which are able to control complex processes [5], and reconfigurable logic controllers [18]. The constructed models using Petri nets and traditional logic can be directly applied for implementing control system hardware or software [3], [15], [1].

The method of hardware implementation of the Petri net, which is based on Boolean logic and described in [15], was extended to the fuzzy domain [23] in a very natural way in [13], [7]. The observation that the values of real signals are contained in some bounded intervals seems to be crucial to this extension; the signals can be interpreted as events which are true in some degree. Such a natural interpretation concerns sensor outputs, control signals, time expiration, etc. It leads to the idea of fuzzy Petri net (FPN) as a controller, which is able to process both analog, and binary signals of a multi-input-multi-output (MIMO) plant. The FPN in [13] and [7] differs from the other nets described in the literature [17], [21], [2] or [19]. Such a net can be implemented as a software module designed for programmable logic controllers [13] or a hardware device [14]. In the second case, the fuzzy JK flip-flops [6] can be directly applied, or

L. Rutkowski et al. (Eds.): ICAISC 2004, LNAI 3070, pp. 314–319, 2004.
© Springer-Verlag Berlin Heidelberg 2004

the other fuzzy hardware components, e.g. described in [12], [9] or [4]. Hardware implementation of the FPN based on VLSI digital circuits is very attractive from the engineering point of view, because as result we obtain a low cost and fast hardware controller. In [14] a synchronous digital version of the FPN has been described. However, the asynchronous circuits have a number of advantages over synchronous ones, but they are not easy to design and testing [10], [8], [22]. The main goal of this paper is to describe a new architecture of an asynchronous fuzzy RS flip-flop, and to give a method of a digital implementation of the fuzzy Petri net based on such flip-flops.

2   The Fuzzy Petri Net Dynamics

Formally, our fuzzy Petri net is a system $FPN = \langle P, T, D, G, R, \Delta, \Gamma, \Theta, m_0 \rangle$, where P, T, D, G, are nonempty finite sets of places, transitions, statements, and conditions, correspondingly, and any two of the sets P, T, D, G have no common elements. $R \subseteq (P \times T) \cup (T \times P)$ is the incidence relation, $\Delta : P \to D$ - the function assigning the statement for any place, $\Gamma : T \to G$ - the function assigning the condition for any transition, $\Theta : T \to [0, 1]$ - the function defining the degree to which the conditions corresponding to the transitions are satisfied, and $M_0 : P \to [0, 1]$ - the initial marking function.

Let us denote by $°t = \{p \mid (p, t) \in R\}$ - the set of input places for the transition t, and by $t° = \{p \mid (t, p) \in R\}$ - the set of output places for the transition t. The considered Petri net is assumed to be clean and all capacities of the places, and all weights of the arcs are assumed to be 1.

The Petri net dynamics defines how new marking is computed from the current marking when the transitions are fired. Only enabled transitions can be fired.

Definition 1. *The transition t_1 in T is enabled from the moment at which all input places of t_1 have markers equal to 1 and all output places of t_1 have null markers, to the moment at which all input places of the transition t_1 have null markers, and all output places of t_1 have markers equal to 1.*

Definition 2. *Let M be the marking in FPN, for which the transition $t \in T$ is enabled, and $\Theta(t) = \vartheta \in [0, 1]$ denotes the degree to which the condition corresponding to the enabled transition t is satisfied. A new marking M' of the net is computed according to the following rule:*

$$
M'(p) = \begin{cases}
M(p) \wedge (1 - \vartheta) & \Leftrightarrow & p \in °t \setminus t° \\
M(p) \vee \vartheta & \Leftrightarrow & p \in t° \setminus °t \\
M(p) & \Leftrightarrow & \text{otherwise}
\end{cases}
$$

where $\wedge = \min$, $\vee = \max$.

The features of FPN are described in [7].

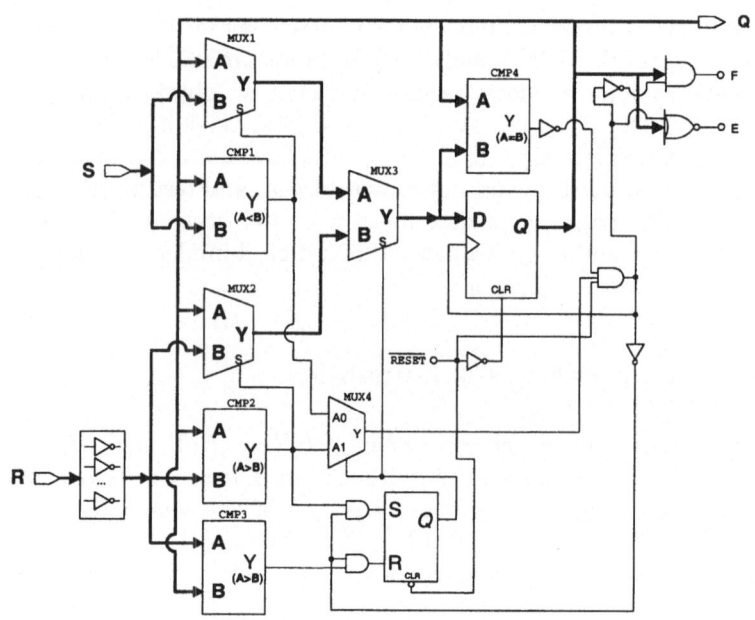

Fig. 1. Asynchronous fuzzy RS flip-flop architecture.

3   Asynchronous Fuzzy RS Flip-Flop

According to our idea, the asynchronous fuzzy RS flip-flops will be used as the main components of digital hardware implementation of the FPN.

Definition 3. *The fuzzy RS flip-flop is a digital circuit that uses n-bit data bus, i.e. it has the output* $\mathbf{Q} = Q_{n-1} \ldots Q_1 Q_0$, *the set input* $\mathbf{S} = S_{n-1} \ldots S_1 S_0$, *and the reset input* $\mathbf{R} = R_{n-1} \ldots R_1 R_0$, *where* $Q_i, S_i, R_i \in \{0, 1\}$, $i = 0, 1, \ldots, n-1$. *Its behaviour describes the following recursive equation:*

$$\mathbf{Q}' = \overline{\mathbf{R}} \wedge (\mathbf{S} \vee \mathbf{Q}), \qquad \mathbf{R}, \mathbf{S}, \mathbf{Q}, \mathbf{Q}' \in Z_n = \{0, 1, 2, \ldots, 2^n - 1\} \qquad (1)$$

where $\mathbf{Q}'$ *is the next state of* $\mathbf{Q}$ *in the sense of asynchronous circuits dynamics description, and* $\overline{\mathbf{R}}$ *is the negation of* $\mathbf{R}$, $(\overline{\mathbf{X}} = 2^n - 1 - \mathbf{X}$ *for* $\mathbf{X} \in Z_n)$.

The equation (1) generalizes the recursive equation describing the binary RS flip-flop. Formally, instead of a finite subset of the unit interval $[0, 1]$, we use the set $Z_n = \{0, 1, 2, \ldots, 2^n - 1\}$.

Digital implementation of the asynchronous fuzzy RS flip-flop described by (1) and developed by the authors is shown in Fig. 1. The subsystem containing the CMP1 comparator and the MUX1 multiplexer performs the function $\max(\mathbf{S}, \mathbf{Q})$, whereas the CMP2 comparator and the MUX2 multiplexer perform $\min(\overline{\mathbf{R}}, \mathbf{Q})$. Taking additionally into account the multiplexer MUX3 we obtain

$$\mathbf{Q}' = \left(\overline{Q_{RS}} \wedge (\mathbf{S} \vee \mathbf{Q})\right) \vee \left(Q_{RS} \wedge (\overline{\mathbf{R}} \wedge \mathbf{Q})\right)$$

where $\overline{Q_{RS}} = 1 - Q_{RS}$, and $Q_{RS} \in \{0,1\}$ is the output of the auxiliary conventional RS flip-flop. If $Y_{CMP3} = 1$, or equivalently $\overline{R} > Q$, then $Q_{RS} = 0$ and $Q' = S \vee Q$. If $\overline{R} < Q$, then $Y_{CMP2} = 1$ and $Q_{RS} = 1$, thus, $Q' = \overline{R} \wedge Q$. The last function is performed to the moment at which $\overline{R} \leq Q$, $(Y_{CMP3} = 1 \Rightarrow R_{RS} = 1)$. Hence, we obtain the output of the fuzzy flip-flop shown in Fig. 1:

$$Q' = \begin{cases} S \vee Q & \Leftrightarrow & \overline{R} > Q \\ \overline{R} \wedge Q & \Leftrightarrow & \overline{R} \leq Q \end{cases} \tag{2}$$

The output Q can be unstable during a very short period of time. This phenomenon, known as *noncritical race* [8], [10], we are able to predict and examine in our system. It was proved theoretically and checked experimentally, that the system described by (2) and shown in Fig. 1, works according to the recurrent equation (1), so that the output Q of the fuzzy RS flip-flop is stable after one or two consecutive steps.

4   Conception of Hardware Implementation of the FPN

One can prove that the FPN defined in Section 2 can be decomposed into the fragments containing a transition t_m with j input and k output places, $(1 \leq j, k < \infty)$ as shown in Fig. 2. According to our design procedure we propose to transform such a fragment of the net to the digital logic circuit using asynchronous fuzzy RS flip-flops, as shown in Fig. 3.

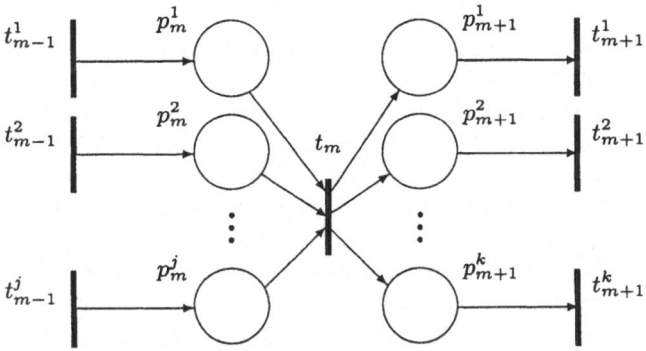

Fig. 2. Transition t_m with j input places and k output places.

In this way any FPN can be completely assembled by making the appropriate connections between blocks shown in Fig. 3. Finally, it should be noted that the net from Fig. 3 is race-free circuit.

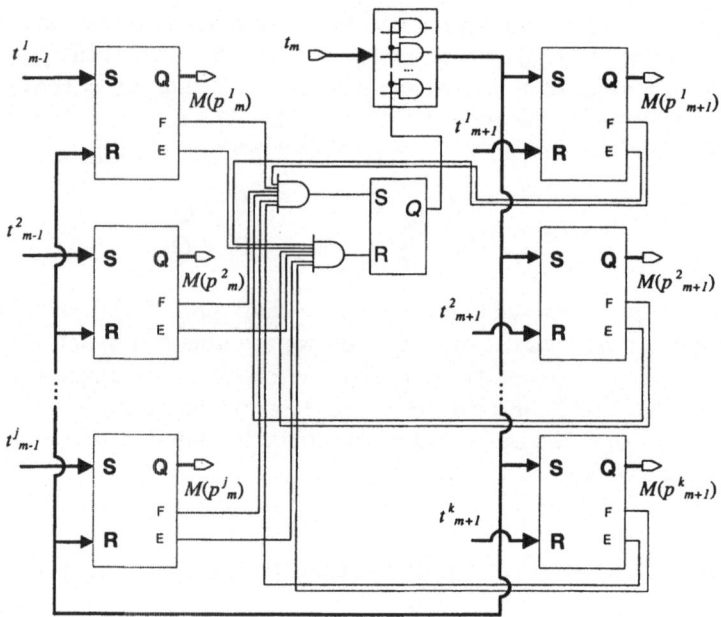

Fig. 3. Hardware implementation of FPN shown in Fig. 2 based on asynchronous RS flip-flops.

5   Conclusions

A new digital architecture of an asynchronous fuzzy RS flip-flop was described. The correctness of the developed circuit was proved mathematically and checked experimentally during a full (i.e. exhaustive) functional testing, which took $2^{3n} = 4096$ test vectors for $n = 4$-bit implementation. The noncritical race was observed in the real system corresponding to the architecture shown in Fig. 1, where the distortion impulse was of the length 8.5 ns. It should be noted that the influence of the noncritical race for the asynchronous fuzzy RS flip-flop results only in slightly longer propagation time (ca. 27 ns for the whole circuit), but the whole circuit works correctly.

The fuzzy Petri nets as digital circuits, which use the asynchronous fuzzy RS flip-flops, are very high speed devices. They have been built and tested on FPGA structures of Xilinx (XC2S100-5TQ144), and used as control devices for several laboratory plants (a concrete production process, a technological line, and a system of vehicles).

References

1. Andreu, D., Pascal, J.C., Valette, R.: Fuzzy Petri Net-Based Programmable Logic Controller. IEEE Trans. Syst., Man, Cybern. Vol. 27 (1997) 952–961

2. Cardoso, J., Camargo, H. (eds.): Fuzziness in Petrii Nets. Studies in Fuzziness and Soft Computing, Vol. 22. Springer-Verlag, Berlin Heidelberg New York (1999)
3. David, R., Alla, H.: Petri Nets and Grafcet: Tools for Modelling Discrete Event Systems. Prentice Hall, London (1992)
4. Diamond, J., Pedrycz, W., McLeod, D.: Fuzzy J-K Flip-Flops as Computational Structures: Design and Implementation. IEEE Trans. Circuit a. Systems-II: Analog and Digital Signal Processing. Vol. 41, No. 3 (1994) 215–226
5. Fernandes, J.M., Adamski, M., Proença, A.J.: VHDL Generation from Hierarchical Petri Net Specifications of Parallel Controllers. IEE Proc.-Comput. Digit. Tech.. Vol. 144, No. 2 (1997) 127–137
6. Gniewek, L., Kluska, J.: Family of Fuzzy J-K Flip-Flops Based on Bounded Product, Bounded Sum and Complementation. IEEE Trans. Syst., Man, Cybern. Vol. 28, No. 6 (1998) 861–868
7. Gniewek, L., Kluska, J.: Hardware implementation of fuzzy Petri net as a controller. IEEE Trans. Syst., Man, Cybern. (to appear)
8. Hauck, S.: Asynchronous Design Methodologies: An Overview. Proceedings of the IEEE. Vol. 83, No. 1 (1995) 69–93
9. Hirota, K., Ozawa, K.: The concept of fuzzy flip-flop. IEEE Trans. Syst., Man, Cybern. No. 19 (1989) 980–987
10. Hulgaard, H., Burns, S.M., Borriello, G.: Testing Asynchronous Circuits: A Survey. Tech. Rep. 94-03-06, University of Washington, Seattle (1994)
11. Jensen, K.: Coloured Petri nets. Vol. 1–3. Springer-Verlag, Berlin Heidelberg New York (1997)
12. Kandel, A., Langholtz, G. (eds.): Fuzzy Hardware: Architectures and Applications. Kluwer, Norwell, MA (1998)
13. Kluska, J., Gniewek, L.: A New Method of Fuzzy Petri Net Synthesis and its Application for Control Systems Design. In: Hampel, R., Wagenknecht, M., Chaker, N. (eds.): Fuzzy Control. Advances in Soft Computing. Physica-Verlag, Heidelberg New York (2000) 222–227
14. Kluska, J., Hajduk, Z.: Hardware implementation of a fuzzy Petri net based on VLSI digital circuits. Proc. of Third EUSFLAT Conf. Zittau (2003) 789–793
15. Misiurewicz, P.: Lectures on real-time microprocessor control systems. Lecture Notes. University of Minnesota (1976)
16. Murata, T.: Petri Nets: Properties, Analysis and Applications. Proc. IEEE. Vol. 77, No. 4, (1989) 541–580
17. Pedrycz, W., Gomide, F.: A Generalized Fuzzy Petri Net Model. IEEE Trans. Fuzzy Syst. Vol. 2, No. 4 (1994) 295–301
18. Park, E., Tilbury, D.M., Khargonekar, P.P.: A Modeling and Analysis Methodology for Modular Logic Controllers of Machining Systems Using Petri Net Formalism. IEEE Trans. Syst., Man, Cybern.-Part C. Vol. 31, No. 2 (2001) 168–188
19. Pedrycz, W., Camargo, H.: Fuzzy timed Petri nets. Fuzzy Sets and Systems. Vol. 140 (2003) 301–330
20. Peterson, J.L.: Petri Net Theory and the Modelling of Systems. Prentice Hall. Englewood Cliffs, NJ (1981)
21. Scarpelli, H., Gomide, F., Yager, R.R.: A Reasoning Algorithm for High-Level Fuzzy Petri Nets. IEEE Trans. Fuzzy Syst. Vol. 4, No. 3 (1996) 282–294
22. Wakerly, J.F.: Digital Design Principles and Practices (third edition). Prentice Hall International, Inc. (2000)
23. Zadeh L.A.: Fuzzy sets. Information and Control. No. 8 (1965) 338–353

Fuzzy Calculator – Useful Tool for Programming with Fuzzy Algebra

Roman Koleśnik[1], Piotr Prokopowicz[2], and Witold Kosiński[1]

[1] Polish-Japanese Institute of Information Technology
ul. Koszykowa 86, 02-008 Warszawa, Poland
rkolesnik@wp.pl, wkos@pjwstk.edu.pl
[2] University of Bydgoszcz Institute of Environmental Mechanics
and Applied Computer Science
ul. Chodkiewicza 30, 85-064 Bydgoszcz, Poland
reiden10@wp.pl

Abstract. Process of implementing operations'algorithms for ordered fuzzy numbers (OFN's)are presented. First version of the program in the Delphi environment is created that uses algorithms dedicated to trapezoidal-type membership relations (functions). More useful implementation is a Fuzzy Calculator which allows counting with OFN's of general type membership relations and is equipped with a graphical shell.

1 Introduction

Few years ago the present authors (W.K., P.P.) founded an extended model of fuzzy numbers and algebraic operations on them where real numbers with their operations are a part of the model [10]- [12]. One of the aims was to get results of algebraic operations on real numbers equal to results of the same operations but performed in the standard algebra of reals. The next aim was to have the operations' algorithms as simple as possible to be able to implement the algorithms in some programmers' environment.

The new model of fuzzy numbers,called ordered fuzzy numbers (OFN's),already presented in [10],[11],[12],[13], has the following properties: subtracting is a consequent of adding opposite number so $A - B = A + (-B)$ where $(-1) \cdot B = -B$, result of many operations on fuzzy number must not always be "more fuzzy", $A - A = 0$ – crisp zero, so it is neutral element of addition, operations are enough simply to program without very complicated methods.

As a consequent the new model has extra properties: it is a linear space and even more, Banach algebra with unity. It should be added at this stage that in the literature a number of different models of fuzzy numbers and their generalization exist ([2,3,4,6,7,8]). Moreover, the particular case of the known set of the so-called convex fuzzy numbers can be obtained as a particular subset of our space of ordered fuzzy numbers; for the members of this set the arithmetic operations are compatible, to some extent, with the interval arithmetics.

The idea of the ordered fuzzy numbers is quite original and the present authors have planned to implement it as a new project without using existing popular tools for fuzzy logic (numbers) calculation like MATLab, for example.

L. Rutkowski et al. (Eds.): ICAISC 2004, LNAI 3070, pp. 320–325, 2004.
© Springer-Verlag Berlin Heidelberg 2004

2   Ordered Fuzzy Numbers

Definition 1. *By an ordered fuzzy number A we mean an ordered pair of function*

$$A = (f, g) \tag{1}$$

where elements of the pair are continuous functions $f, g : [0, 1] \to \mathbf{R}$.

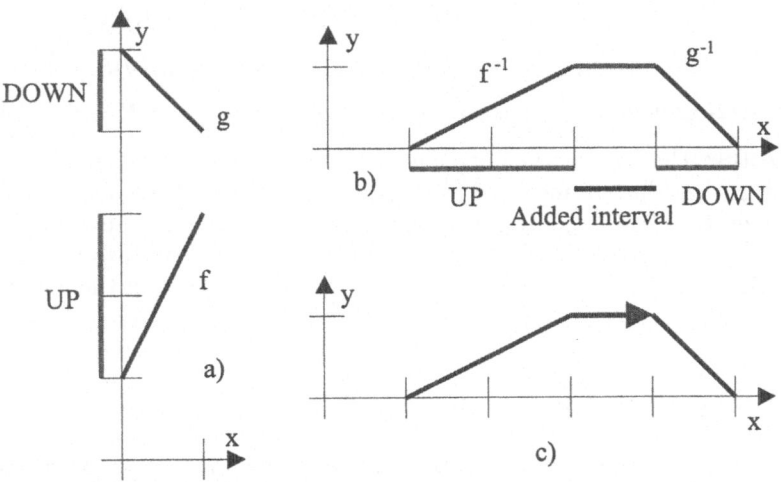

Fig. 1. a) The example of ordered fuzzy number, b) Ordered fuzzy number presented as fuzzy number in classical meaning, c) Simplified mark denotes the order of inverted functions

We call the corresponding elements: f – an **up-part** and g – the **down-part** of the fuzzy number A. The continuity of both parts implies their images are bounded intervals, say UP and $DOWN$, respectively (Fig. 1a). Let us use symbols to mark boundaries for $UP = (l_A, 1_A^+)$ and for $DOWN = (1_A^-, p_A)$.

   In general neither of both functions needs to be invertible, only continuity is required. However, if both functions (parts of ordered fuzzy number) are monotonic then they are invertible and possess corresponding inverse functions defined on $\mathbf{R}$ with values in $[0, 1]$. The inverse functions are defined on the bounded intervals UP and $DOWN$, respectively. Now, if we add a function on the interval $[1_A^+, 1_A^-]$ with constant value equal to 1, we may define a kind of membership function (sometimes it is a relation) of a fuzzy sets on real axis (Fig. 1b). Notice that in the above case when $f \le g$ and both invertible functions are such that f is increasing and g is decreasing we get a mathematical object which presents a convex fuzzy numbers in the classical sense [6,7,8].

   We can appoint here an extra feature, named an **orientation** (marked in graphs by arrow - Fig 1c), to underline the fact that we are dealing with an ordered pair of functions, since in general the pairs (f, g) and (g, f) represent two different

OFN's. In consequence the intervals $UP \cup [1_A^+, 1_A^-] \cup DOWN$ form the support of the fuzzy number A.

Let $A = (f_A, g_A), B = (f_B, g_B)$ and $C = (f_C, g_C)$ are mathematical objects called ordered fuzzy numbers.

Definition 2. *The sum $C = A + B$, the product $C = A \cdot B$ and the division $C = A/B$ are defined by*

$$f_A(y) + f_B(y) = f_C(y) \wedge g_A(y) + g_B(y) = g_C(y). \tag{2}$$

$$f_A(y) \cdot f_B(y) = f_C(y) \wedge g_A(y) \cdot g_B(y) = g_C(y), \tag{3}$$

$$f_A(y)/f_B(y) = f_C(y) \wedge g_A(y)/g_B(y) = g_C(y), \tag{4}$$

where A/B is defined iff zero does not belong to intervals UP and DOWN of B.

Notice that the subtraction of B is the same o as the addition of the opposite of B, i.e. the number $(-1) \cdot B$. Moreover, if for $A = (f, g)$ we define its complementary $\bar{A} = (-g, -f)$ then the sum $A + \bar{A}$ gives in general a fuzzy zero $0 = (f - g, -(f - g))$. It is the complementary of the given fuzzy number which plays the role of the opposite number, in the Zadeh sense in the classical fuzzy number calculus.

3   Fuzzy Calculator

First application was "nowaalgebra" (ang. newalgebra), created with use of Delphi environment for programming. That program has been evolving with the development of new ideas in modelling fuzzy numbers: it has changed from arithmetic operations on selected elements from equivalence classes [5] to all operations on inverted functions, i.e. on ordered fuzzy numbers. The main purpose for that program was the graphical presentation of the operations' algorithm while dealing with a working model of fuzzy numbers. The main limitations of that first application of the program was its validity for functions with piecewise linear parts (quasi-trapezoidal representations), only. The application was used to present our ideas on some conferences which are listed in Bibliography. It was obvious that one needs a new program, more useful in examining and using ideas of the new look of fuzzy numbers. In consequence "Fuzzy Calculator" (worked name zCalc) has been created with a graphical shell named zWinCalc (the author R.K.).

To create the main zCalc program the following components were used: Visual Studio 6.0 - environment for programming in language C++, Bison-Flex - generator of language - useful tool to build syntax analyzer.

The tool zCalc was written as a component of operating system – Windows (9x/XP). To this a console interface which allows to use the main module as a kind of the interpreter of a specifical simply language is added. It has instructions which can declare mathematical objects (cf. Sec.2) and basic operations on them. The language gives a possibility to work with scripts which are text files with lists of proper commands. Other important feature is a group of instructions which allow to export results to the file formats with text and graphic (i.e. formats of XML, ps, svg). That files can be read by other applications. One can use an extra group of commands to prepare proper parameters of graphs, and then to adapt some part of the results to individual wishes.

The Fuzzy Calculator was created to let an easy use in future open projects all mathematical objects described as ordered fuzzy numbers. The basic functional field of module zCalc are: algebraic operations (sum, subtract, multiplication and division) with ordered fuzzy numbers identified by a set of special (with view to figure of functions) points, algebraic operations with the ordered fuzzy numbers identified and marked as some polynomial functions, exchanging both representations: set of points and polynomials.

Author has given the user a possibility of two kinds descriptions of component functions (parts up and down). The first is by giving formula, the other by a list of characteristic points. Functions for use can have forms of polynomials: simply linear functions as well as functions with complicated graphs with many parameters. In the case of piecewise linear functions they can be defined by a list of the characteristic points. Then the list of points is transformed into a piecewise linear functions. In a more general (curved–shape functions) case the list is transformed into a polynomial representation. To make this transform the Lagrange interpolation is used. Independently of the used interpolation (linear or curved), one should also have a possibility to transform any polynomial form to a list of points. Moreover, actual calculations is made on the functional representation of both parts of the ordered fuzzy number.

The transformation of polynomial object $A = (f_A, g_A)$ is realized by using the following algorithm:

1. determine (graphs of) two simply linear functions, such that first connects two points $(l_A, 0)$ and $(1_A^+, 1)$ (this is for the part f_A), and the second which connects two points $(1_A^-, 1)$ and $(p_A, 0)$ (for the part g_A);
2. for each point of graphs of functions f_A, g_A determine (with 0.01 step) its distance to the linear functions founded in step 1;
3. choose point which is most distanced to the functions from step 1;
4. the last chosen point is added to the list (of characteristic points) if it is true that the distance between the curve (at this point) and the linear function is not smaller that a given threshold (or 0.2, if the threshold was not fixed by the user);
5. repeating steps 1,2,3 and 4. but in steps 1 exchange one of limiting points on the list with that added to the list founded in steps 4.

The algorithm ends if all segments, which are created by each pair of the neighbor points, are analyzed and no new point is founded. We can see that the precision of describing the functions can be controlled by the threshold parameter (in step 2). Although the list of points is simply and gives the description of the function, we can also adapt the precision by an appropriate choice of the threshold parameter.

The Fuzzy Calculator has graphical shell – worked name zWinCalc. It is windows'type interface which makes easy and direct calculation with the module zCalc. Programmer which will use the main module as component in further works does not need zWinCalc. So this program will be used generally by people who need to make calculations on fuzzy numbers directly on Fuzzy Calculator

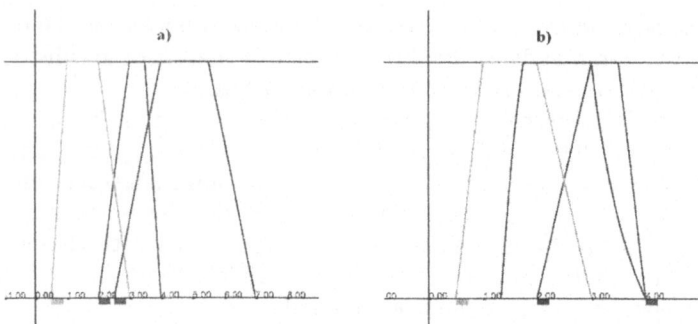

Fig. 2. Fig. a) Sum $C = A + B$, b) Division $C = A/B$

and/or will write scripts and watch results as graphs. Application zWinCalc makes easier: editing commands, watching objects which have been already defined, watching and editing properties of defined objects, carrying properties of objects to other tools (in text form), watching figures of objects as graphs (installation of free plug-in Adobe's SVG is necessary).

The module zWinCalc is only a graphical shell and no algorithms of operations on any presentations of the fuzzy numbers are implemented here. Proper module which makes all calculations, definitions and transforms is zCalc. Integration of the program zWinCalc with zCalc gives a chance to use the graphical shell without any changes even a new version of the main module appear.

To work only with the console interface (zCalc), no any other program in the system is necessary, but if one plans to use a graphical support in the form of zWinCalc then it is necessary to install the list of the programs: MSXML2 in version 4.0, SVG viewer, MathPlayer and optional GhostView. Figures Fig 2. and Fig 3. present graphs generated by program zCalc and consist of the example results of the algebraic operations on the ordered fuzzy numbers A and B described by the lists of points: $A = (2, 3, 3.5, 4)$ (blue colour) and $B = (0.5, 1, 2, 3)$ (green colour). The actual order (orientation) on the graph is matched by a small rectangular, which has the meaning of the initial point of the list.

4   Conclusions

Thanks to the opened structure of the Fuzzy Calculator it is a very useful tool in future studies of the ordered fuzzy numbers (and fuzzy numbers, as well). Main practical advantage of the Fuzzy Calculator is that the operations can be used by programmers in different programming environments. This allows the use of the algebra of OFN's in different programs, as a ready module, and then the implementation of all needed operations is possible. We are planning as a next step of our investigation of OFN's to use the Fuzzy Calculator for a fuzzy controller.

Acknowledgement. The research work on the paper was partially done in the framework of the KBN Project (State Committee for Scientific Research) No. 4 T11C 038 25.

References

1. Dubois D., Prade H., (1978) , Operations on fuzzy numbers, *Int. J. System Science*, **9**, 576-578.
2. Czogała E., Pedrycz W., (1985), Elements and methods of fuzzy set theory (in Polish), (Elementy i metody teorii zbiorów rozmytych) PWN, Warszawa.
3. Nguyen H.T., (1978), A note on the extension principle for fuzzy sets, *J. Math. Anal. Appl.* **64**, 369-380.
4. Sanchez E., (1984), Solutions of fuzzy equations with extended operations, *Fuzzy Sets and Systems*, **12**, 237-248.
5. Goetschel R. Jr., Voxman W., (1986), Elementary fuzzy calculus, *Fuzzy Sets and Systems*, **18**, 31-43.
6. Klir G.J., (1997) , Fuzzy arithmetic with requisite constraints, *Fuzzy Sets and Systems*, **91**, 165-175.
7. Drewniak J., (2001), Fuzzy numbers (in Polish), in: *Zbiory rozmyte i ich zastosowania*, Fuzzy sets and their applications, J. Chojcan, J. Lęski (eds.), Wydawnictwo Politechniki Śląskiej, Gliwice, pp. 103-129.
8. Wagenknecht M., (2001), On the approximate treatment of fuzzy arithmetics by inclusion, linear regression and information content estimation, in: *Zbiory rozmyte i ich zastosowania, Fuzzy sets and their applications*, J. Chojcan, J. Lęski (eds.), Wydawnictwo Politechniki Śląskiej, Gliwice, 291-310.
9. Kosiński W., Piechór K., Prokopowicz P., Tyburek K., On algorithmic approach to operations on fuzzy reals, in: *Methods of Artificial Intelligence in Mechanics and Mechanical Engineering*, Gliwice, October, 2001, T. Burczyński and W. Cholewa (Eds.), PACM, Gliwice, 2001, pp. 95-98.
10. Kosiński W., P. Prokopowicz P., Ślezak D.: Fuzzy numbers with algebraic operations: algorithmic approach, in: *Intelligent Information Systems 2002*, M. Klopotek, S.T. Wierzchoń, M. Michalewicz(eds.) Proc.IIS'2002, Sopot, June 3-6, 2002, Poland, Physica Verlag, 2002, pp. 311-320.
11. Kosiński W., Prokopowicz P., Ślezak D.: Drawback of fuzzy arthmetics - new intutions and propositions, in: *Proc. Methods of Aritificial Intelligence*, T. Burczyński, W. Cholewa, W. Moczulski(eds), PACM,Gliwice, Poland (2002), pp. 231-237.
12. Kosiński W., P. Prokopowicz P., Ślezak D.: On algebraic operations on fuzzy numbers,in *Intelligent Information Processing and Web Mining*, Proc. of the International IIS: IIPWM,03 Conference held in Zakopane, Poland, June 2-5,2003, M. Klopotek, S.T. Wierzchoń, K. Trojanowski(eds.), Physica Verlag, 2003, pp. 353-362.
13. Kosiński W., P. Prokopowicz P., Ślezak D.: Ordered fuzzy number, *Bulletin of the Polish Academy of Sciences*, Ser. Sci. Math., **51** (3), 2003, 327-338.
14. Kosiński W., Koleśnik R., Prokopowicz P., Frischmuth K.: On Algebra of Ordered Fuzzy Numbers, in: *Proc. Warsaw, International Seminar on Soft Computing - WISSC 2003*, in print.

On Defuzzyfication of Ordered Fuzzy Numbers

Witold Kosiński

Polish-Japanese Institute of Information Technology
Research Center
ul. Koszykowa 86, 02-008 Warszawa, Poland
wkos@pjwstk.edu.pl

Abstract. Ordered fuzzy number is an ordered pair of continuous real functions defined on the interval $[0, 1]$. Such numbers have been introduced by the author and his co-workers as an enlargement of classical fuzzy numbers by requiring a *membership relation*. It was done in order to define four algebraic operations between them, i.e. addition, subtraction, multiplication and division, in a way that renders them an algebra. Further, a normed topology is introduced which makes them a Banach space, and even more, a Banach algebra with unity. General form of linear functional on this space is presented which makes possible to define a large family of defuzzification methods of that class of numbers.

1 Introduction

A number of attempts to introduce non-standard operations on fuzzy numbers have been made recently proposed [8,7,10,11,12], in order to eliminate some drawbacks of fuzzy number calculation. They were observed mainly in the case of the so-called (L, R) - numbers' representation. For example approximations of fuzzy functions and operations are needed, if one wants to stay within this representation while following the Zadeh's extension principle [2]. It was noticed that in order to construct more suitable for their algorithmisation operations on fuzzy numbers a kind of invertibility of their membership functions is required. In [4,14] the idea of modelling fuzzy numbers by means of convex or quasi-convex functions (cf. [13]) is discussed. We continue this work by defining quasi-convex functions related to fuzzy numbers in a more general fashion, enabling modelling both dynamics of changes of fuzzy membership levels and the domain of fuzzy real itself. Even starting from the most popular trapezoidal membership functions, algebraic operations can lead outside this family, towards such generalized quasi-convex functions.

The goal of the authors of the previous papers [14,16,17] was to overcome the above some drawbacks by constructing a revised concept of the fuzzy number and at the same time to have the algebra of crisp (non-fuzzy) numbers inside the concept. The new concept makes possible a simple utilizing the fuzzy arithmetic and construct an algebra.

L. Rutkowski et al. (Eds.): ICAISC 2004, LNAI 3070, pp. 326–331, 2004.
© Springer-Verlag Berlin Heidelberg 2004

2   Membership Function and Membership Relation

Classically [1] in the definition of a fuzzy set A on $\mathbf{R}$ we relate to A the so-called membership function with values between 1 and 0. Doing their development the authors of [16,17] have referred to one of the very first representations of a fuzzy set defined on a universe X (the real axis $\mathbf{R}$, say) of discourse. In that representation (cf. [1,5]) a fuzzy set (read here: a fuzzy number) A is defined as a set of ordered pairs $\{(x, \mu_x)\}$, where $x \in X$ and $\mu_x \in [0,1]$ has been called the grade (or level) of membership of x in A. At that stage, no other assumptions concerning μ_x have been made. Later on, Zadeh assumed that μ_x is (or must be) a function of x. However, originally, A was just a relation in a product space $X \times [0,1]$.

That more general definition enables to cope with the main drawback of other approaches, namely with finding a unique solution X to the fuzzy equation $A + X = B$. Moreover, it seems to provide a solution for other problems, like, e.g., the problem of defining partial ordering over fuzzy numbers (cf. [17]). We should mention that Klir was the first, who in [10] has revised fuzzy arithmetic to take relevant requisite constraint (the equality constraint, exactly) into account and obtained $A - A = 0$ as well as the existence of inverse fuzzy numbers for the arithmetic operations. Some partial results of the same type were obtained by Sanchez in [7] by introducing an extended operation of a very complex structure. Our approach, however, is much simpler, since it does not use the extension principle but refers to the functional representation of fuzzy numbers in a more direct way.

3   Ordered Fuzzy Numbers

In the classical approach for numerical handling of the so-called convex fuzzy numbers (cf. [11] the arithmetic operations are algoritmized with the help of the so-called α-sections of membership functions. The local invertibility of quasi-concave membership functions, on the other hand, enables to define operations in terms of the inverses of the corresponding monotonic parts, as was pointed out in our previous papers [15,16,17]. In our last paper [19] we went further and have defined a more general class of fuzzy number, called ordered fuzzy number, just as a pair of continuous functions defined on the interval [0,1]. Those pairs are counterparts of the mentioned inverses.

Definition 1 *An ordered fuzzy number* $x \in \mathcal{R}$ *is an ordered pair of two con-tinuous functions*, $x = (x_{up}, x_{down})$, *called the up-branch and the down-branch*, respectively, both defined on the closed interval $[0,1]$.

Usually, the up-branch comes first, i.e. left, which means that the values of x_{up} are pointwise smaller or equal to those of x_{down}. However, as it was pointed out in [16], to make the set of ordered fuzzy numbers closed under arithmetic operations, this assumption has to be dropped. Graphically the curves (x_{up}, x_{down}) and (x_{down}, x_{up}) do not differ, if drawn on the coordinate system in which x-axis proceeds y axis. However, the corresponding curves determine two different ordered fuzzy numbers: they differ by the orientation: if the first curve has the positive orientation, then the second one has negative. It will be seen in the figure below.

According to the definition introduced in our previous papers (cf. [19] for the arithmetic operations and [18] for all algebraic operations)we perform arithmetic operations componentwise. In the present notation they will be:

$$
\begin{array}{ll}
(x+y)_{up} = x_{up} + y_{up} & (x+y)_{down} = x_{down} + y_{down} \\
(x-y)_{up} = x_{up} - y_{up} & (x-y)_{down} = x_{down} - y_{down} \\
(x \cdot y)_{up} = x_{up} \cdot y_{up} & (x \cdot y)_{down} = x_{down} \cdot y_{down} \\
(x/y)_{up} = x_{up}/y_{up} & (x/y)_{down} = x_{down}/y_{down}
\end{array}
\tag{1}
$$

where the division is only defined when 0 does not belong to the values of y_{up}, y_{down}. To avoid confusion at this stage of development, let us stress that any fuzzy number, classical (crisp or convex fuzzy) or ordered (new type), has its *opposite number* (only one), which is obtained from the given number by multiplication with minus one. For the new type of fuzzy numbers, multiplication by a negative real not only affects the support, but also the orientation swaps. Now, to an ordered fuzzy number one can as well relate (additionally to its opposite) its *complementary number* which can play the role of the opposite number in the sense of Zadeh's model, since the sum of both – the (ordered fuzzy) number and its complementary number – gives a fuzzy zero, which is non-crisp in general. However, the sum of any new type fuzzy number and its opposite number gives the crisp zero

4   Banach Algebra

Let us notice that all operations defined are suitable for pairs of functions. The pointwise multiplication has a neutral element – the pair of two constant functions equal to one, i.e. the crisp one.

Linear structure of $\mathcal{R}$ is obvious: the set of all pairs of continuous functions $\mathcal{R}$ is isomorphic to the linear space of real 2D vector-valued functions defined on the unit interval $I = [0, 1]$. *Normed structure* of $\mathcal{R}$ is introduced by the norm:

$$
||x|| = \max(\sup_{s \in I} |x_{up}(s)|, \sup_{s \in I} |x_{down}(s)|).
$$

Hence $\mathcal{R}$ can be identified with $C([0,1]) \times C([0,1])$.

The space $\mathcal{R}$ is an Abelian group under addition, its neutral element is a pair of constant function equal to zero, the space $\mathcal{R}$ is topologically a Banach space. Moreover, $\mathcal{R}$ is a **Banach algebra** with the unity $(1,1)$ - a pair of constant functions equal to one.

It should be added at this point that a partial order in the set $\mathcal{R}$ can be introduced by defining the subset of those ordered fuzzy numbers which are bigger or equal to zero. We say the fuzzy number pair $A = (x_{up}, x_{down})$ is not less than zero, and write

$$
A \geq 0 \quad \text{if} \quad (x_{up} + x_{down}) \geq 0,
\tag{2}
$$

where the plus is taken pointwise . We should notice, that Goetschel and Voxman, authors of [9], in which a Banach structure of an extension of convex fuzzy numbers was introduced. However, the authors of [9] were only interested in the linear structure of this extension.

5   Defuzzyfication of Ordered Fuzzy Numbers

Defuzzyfication is a main operation in fuzzy controllers and fuzzy inference systems [8,6] where fuzzy inference rules appear. If the consequent part of a fuzzy rule is fuzzy, i.e. represents a fuzzy set, then a defuzzyfication process is needed, in the course of which to the membership function representing the fuzzy set a real number is attached.We know a number of defuzzyfication procedures from the literature cf. [6]. Since fuzzy numbers are particular case of fuzzy sets the same problem appears when the rule consequent part is a fuzzy number. Then the problem arises what can be done when a generalization of classical fuzzy number in the form of an ordered fuzzy number follows? Are the same defuzzyfication procedures applicable? The answer is partial positive: if the ordered fuzzy number is *proper* one, i.e. its membership relation is functional (the relation is a function), then the same procedure can be applied. What to do, however, when the number is non-proper, i.e. the relation is by no means of functional type.

In the case of fuzzy rules in which ordered fuzzy numbers appear as their consequent part we need to introduce a new defuzzyfication procedure. In this case the concept of functional, even linear, which maps element of a Banach space into reals, will be useful.

The Banach space $\mathcal{R}$ with its Tichonov product topology of $C^0([0,1]) \times C^0([0,1])$ may lead to a general representation of linear and continuous functional on $\mathcal{R}$. According to the Banach-Kakutami-Riesz representation theorem [20,21] any linear and continuous functional ϕ on a Banach space $C(S)$ of continuous functions defined on a compact topological space S is uniquely determined by a Radon measure μ on S such that

$$\phi(f) = \int_S f(s)\mu(ds) \quad \text{where } f \in C(S). \tag{3}$$

It is useful to remind that a Radon measure is a regular signed Borel measure (or differently: a difference of two positive Borel measures). A Boreal measure is a measure defined on σ-additive family of subsets of S which contains all open subsets.

In the case when the space S is an interval $[0,1]$ each Radon measure is represented by a Stieltjes integral with respect to a function of a bounded variation, i.e. for any continuous functional ϕ on $C([0,1])$ there is a function of bounded variation g such that

$$\phi(f) = \int_0^1 f(s)dg(s) \quad \text{where } f \in C([0,1]). \tag{4}$$

It is rather obvious that in the case of the product space $\mathcal{R}$ each bounded linear functional is given by a sum of two bounded, linear functionals defined on the factor space $C([0,1])$, i.e.

$$\phi(x_{up}, x_{down}) = \int_0^1 x_{up}(s)\mu_1(ds) + \int_0^1 x_{down}(s)\mu_2(ds) \tag{5}$$

where the pair of continuous functions $(x_{up}, x_{down}) \in \mathcal{R}$ represents an ordered fuzzy number and μ_1, μ_2 are two Radon measures on $[0,1]$.

From this formula an infinite number of defuzzyfication methods can be defined. The standard defuzzyfication procedure given in terms of the area under membership function can be defined; it is realized by the pair of linear combinations of the Lebesgue measure of $[0,1]$. In the present case, however, the area has to be calculated in the so-called y-variable, since the ordered fuzzy number is represented by a pair of continuous functions in y variable. Moreover to each point (a, b) of the strip $\mathbf{R} \times [0, 1]$ a 'delta' (an atom) measure can be related, and such a measure represents a linear and bounded functional which realizes corresponding defuzzyfication procedure. Such a functional to a pair of functions (x_{up}, x_{down}) a sum (or in a more general case - a linear combination) of their values at this point, i.e. $x_{up}(a) + x_{down}(b)$ attaches. Discussion of other linear functional as well as their non-linear generalizations will be done in the next paper.

6   Conclusions

We want to point out to the new notion introduced in [17], called a *fuzzy observation* f, which can help us in understanding the concept of the orientation of a graph of the membership relation, the main concept of ordered fuzzy number. The problem is that the application of the new type of fuzzy algebra requires more information about the meaning of the operands in the model at hand. Without such additional knowledge we cannot expect the benefits of the new calculus and are thus restricted to the classical concept.

Acknowledgement. The research work on the paper was partially done in the framework of the KBN Project (State Committee for Scientific Research) No. 4 T11C 038 25.

References

1. Zadeh L.A., (1965), Fuzzy sets, *Information and Control*, **8** 338-353.
2. Zadeh L.A., (1975), The concept of a linguistic variable and its application to approximate reasoning, Part I, *Information Sciences*, **8**, 199-249.
3. Dubois D., Prade H., (1978) , Operations on fuzzy numbers, *Int. J. System Science*, **9**, 576-578.
4. Nguyen H.T., (1978), A note on the extension principle for fuzzy sets, *J. Math. Anal. Appl.* **64**, 369-380.
5. Kacprzyk J. (1986), *Fuzzy Sets in System Analysis* (in Polish), PWN, Warszawa, Poland .
6. Piegat A., *M*odelling and fuzzy control (Modelowanie i sterowanie rozmyte (in Polish)). Akademicka Oficyna Wydawnicza PLJ, Warszawa, 1999.a

7. Sanchez E., (1984), Solutions of fuzzy equations with extended operations, *Fuzzy Sets and Systems*, **12**, 237-248.
8. Czogała E., Pedrycz W., (1985), *E*lements and Methods of Fuzzy Set Theory (in Polish), PWN, Warszawa.
9. Goetschel R. Jr., Voxman W., (1986), Elementary fuzzy calculus, *Fuzzy Sets and Systems*, **18**, 31-43.
10. Klir G.J., (1997) , Fuzzy arithmetic with requisite constraints, *Fuzzy Sets and Systems*, **91**, 165-175.
11. Drewniak J., (2001), Fuzzy numbers (in Polish), in: *Zbiory rozmyte i ich zastosowania, Fuzzy sets and their applications*, J. Chojcan, J. Łęski (eds.), Wydawnictwo Politechniki Śląskiej, Gliwice, pp. 103-129.
12. Wagenknecht M., (2001), On the approximate treatment of fuzzy arithmetics by inclusion, linear regression and information content estimation, in: *Zbiory rozmyte i ich zastosowania, Fuzzy sets and their applications*, J. Chojcan, J. Łęski (eds.), Wydawnictwo Politechniki Śląskiej, Gliwice, 291-310.
13. Martos B., (1983), *Nonlinear Programming - Theory and methods*, (Polish translation of the English original published by Akadémiai Kiadó, Budapest, 1975), PWN, Warszawa .
14. Kosiński W., Słysz P., (1993) , Fuzzy reals and their quotient space with algebraic operations, *Bull. Pol. Acad. Sci., Sér. Techn. Scien.*, **41** (30), 285-295.
15. Kosiński W., Prokopowicz P., Ślęzak D., (2002), Fuzzy numbers with algebraic operations: algorithmic approach, in: *Intelligent Information Systems 2002*, M. Kłopotek, S.T. Wierzchoń, M. Michalewicz (eds.), Proc. IIS'2002, Sopot, June 3-6, 2002, Poland, Physica Verlag, pp. 311-320.
16. Kosiński W., Prokopowicz P., Ślęzak D., (2002),On algebraic operations on fuzzy reals, in: *Advances in Soft Computing*, Proc. of the Sixth Int. Conference on Neural Network and Soft Computing, Zakopane, Poland, June 11-15, 2002, Physica-Verlag, Rutkowski L., Kacprzyk J., (eds.), 2003, pp. 54-61.
17. Kosiński W., P. Prokopowicz P., Ślęzak D., (2002), On algebraic operations on fuzzy numbers, in *Intelligent Information Processing and Web Mining, Proc. of the International IIS: IIPWM'03*, Conference held in Zakopane, Poland, June 2-5,2003, M. Kłopotek, S.T. Wierzchoń, K. Trojanowski (eds.), 2003, pp. 353-362.
18. Kosiński W., Prokopowicz P., Ślęzak D., (2002), Drawback of fuzzy arthmetics - new intuitions and propositions, in: *Proc. AI METH, Methods of Aritificial Intelligence*, T. Burczyński, W. Cholewa, W. Moczulski, (eds), Gliwice, Poland (2002), pp. 231-237.
19. Kosiński W., Prokopowicz P., Ślęzak D., (2003), Ordered fuzzy numbers, *Bull. Pol. Acad . Sci. , Sér. Sci. Math.*, **51** (3), 327-339.
20. Alexiewicz A., (1969),*A*naliza funkcjonalna (in Polish), PWN, Warszawa.
21. Yosida K.,(1980), *F*unctional Analysis, Springer-Verlag, Berlin Heidelberg New York.

Information Criterions Applied to Neuro-Fuzzy Architectures Design

Robert Nowicki[1,2] and Agata Pokropińska[1]

[1] Department of Computer Engineering, Częstochowa University of Technology,
Al. Armii Krajowej 36, 42-200 Częstochowa, POLAND,
{rnowicki,agatap}@kik.pcz.czest.pl,
WWW home page: http://kik.pcz.czest.pl
[2] Department of Artificial Inteligence
The Academy of Humanities and Economics in Łódź,
ul. Rewolucji 1905r. 64, 90-222 Łódź, POLAND

Abstract. In this paper we present results of application of information cirterions to neuro-fuzzy systems (NFS) design. The criterions come from autoregression estimation theory and are employed to describe the level of NFS quality. Based on this method the preferred size of systems is determined. Various criterions are compared and discussed.

1 Introduction

In the last decade various neuro-fuzzy systems (NFS) have been developed. They include Mamdani systems [3], [7], [9], [11], logical systems [10], relational systems [14] type-2 systems [15], hierarchical systems [13] and others [12]. They are characterized by learning properties and natural language description. The neuro-fuzzy systems have been applied to pattern classification, system identification, approximation, prediction and control. The main problem is to design neuro-fuzzy systems which are transparent and give good performance in terms of accuracy (mean square error or percentage of mistakes). The knowledge necessary to carry out the inference process in fuzzy systems is stored in rule base. The size of this base, i.e. number of rules is not a trivial problem. The most desirable are systems with small rule base. They are fast, low-cost and usually have a better generalization ability. On the other hand the neuro-fuzzy systems with large rule base are characterized by low inaccuracy measure. Designers have to find an optimal solution. In this paper we present the concept of adaptation of information criterions taken from autoregression estimation theory to assessment of neuro-fuzzy systems. The proposed methodology is adequate for both classification and approximation problems. The results are illustrated on approximation problems using the simplest NFS.

L. Rutkowski et al. (Eds.): ICAISC 2004, LNAI 3070, pp. 332–337, 2004.
© Springer-Verlag Berlin Heidelberg 2004

2   The Simplest Neuro-Fuzzy Structures

The neuro-fuzzy architectures [4], [5], [6], [16] comprise the fuzzifier, fuzzy inference engine, fuzzy rule base and defuzzifier in one structure. In most solutions the fuzzifier uses the singleton fuzzification

$$\mu_{A'}(\mathbf{v}) = \begin{cases} 1 & \text{if } \mathbf{v} = \overline{\mathbf{v}} \\ 0 & \text{if } \mathbf{v} \neq \overline{\mathbf{v}} \end{cases}, \tag{1}$$

where $\mathbf{v} = [v_1, v_2, ..., v_n]$ is the input linguistic variable, $\overline{\mathbf{v}} = [\overline{v}_1, \overline{v}_2, ..., \overline{v}_n]$ is the input, i.e. crisp value of $\mathbf{v}$ and A' is the input fuzzy set used in a premise

$$\mathbf{v} \text{ is } A'. \tag{2}$$

The fuzzy rule base includes rules in the form

$$\begin{aligned} R^k\colon \text{IF } v_1 \text{ is } A_1^k \text{ AND } v_2 \text{ is } A_2^k \text{ AND...} \\ \text{... AND } v_n \text{ is } A_n^k \text{ THEN } y \text{ is } B^k \end{aligned}, \tag{3}$$

and in case of classification task in the form

$$\begin{aligned} R^k\colon \text{IF } v_1 \text{ is } A_1^k \text{ AND } v_2 \text{ is } A_2^k \text{ AND...} \\ \text{... AND } v_n \text{ is } A_n^k \text{ THEN } x \in \omega_1(\overline{z}_1^k), x \in \omega_2(\overline{z}_2^k), ..., \\ ...x \in \omega_m(\overline{z}_m^k) \end{aligned} \tag{4}$$

where $\overline{z}_j^k$ is the membership degree of the object x to the j–th class.

In case of Mamdani approach, we get

$$\overline{z}_j = \frac{\sum\limits_{r=1}^{N} \overline{z}_j^r \cdot \mu_{A^r}(\overline{\mathbf{v}})}{\sum\limits_{r=1}^{N} \mu_{A^r}(\overline{\mathbf{v}})}. \tag{5}$$

Note, that in classification problems we can write down

$$\mu_{\omega_j}(x) = \overline{z}_j. \tag{6}$$

3   The Methods of Autoregresion Process Order Estimation

In autoregression estimation problems [8], when order p of proces is unknown, we can estimate it by minimization special criterions. The Final Prediction Error (FPE) is expressed as

$$FPE(p) = \frac{M+p}{M-p}\widehat{Q}_p^f. \tag{7}$$

The Akaike Information Criterion (AIC) is defined as follows

$$AIC(p) = M \log \widehat{Q}_p^f + 2p. \tag{8}$$

The Schwarz criterion has got a form

$$S(p) = M \log \widehat{Q}_p^f + p \log M. \tag{9}$$

The Criterion Autoregressive Transfer Function (CAT) is defined by equation

$$CAT(p) = \frac{1}{M} \sum_{i=1}^{p} \frac{1}{\overline{Q}_i^f} - \frac{1}{\overline{Q}_p^f}, \tag{10}$$

where

$$\overline{Q}_i^f = \frac{m}{M-i} \widehat{Q}_i^f. \tag{11}$$

In equations (7)-(10) p is the estimated order of autoregression, M is a size of problem under consideration, $\widehat{Q}_p^f$ is an estimation of average square error of prediction.

The idea presented in the paper is to employ these criterions to determine the size (number of rules) of neuro-fuzzy structures.

Looking for analogy between autoregression and neuro-fuzzy systems, we decide that parameters p, M and $\widehat{Q}_p^f$ with regard to NFS, will be treated as number of parameters, size of learning epoche and average square error for the epoch, respectively. Note that number of parameters p in NFS depends on membership functions used for antecedent fuzzy sets in the following way

$$p = \begin{cases} N(2n+m) & \text{for Gaussian membership function} \\ N(3n+m) & \text{for triangular membership function} \\ N(4n+m) & \text{for trapezoidal membership function} \end{cases} \tag{12}$$

4   Experimental Result

The experiment was realized for the Rice Taste database, which contains 105 instances. Each instance is described by five attributes: flavour, appearance, taste, stickiness, toughness and overall evaluation ($n = 5$ and $m = 1$). In simulations the input-output pairs of the rice taste data were normalized in the interval [0,1]. The database was randomly divided into two part: learning contains 75 instances and testing contains 30 instances. We tested architectures with 10 rules then gradually reduced it to two. The number of learned parameters is 110, 99, 88, 77, 66, 55, 44, 33 and 22 respectively (Gauusian membership functions). Fig. 1 shows the error level for each final NFS. The values of quoted criterions were calculated for each case and are presented in Fig. 2- Fig. 5. Looking at the charts, we see that the AIC and Schwarz criterions suggest the solution with 4 rules, CAT - with 3 rules and FPE - with 7 rules. When we compare this result with a graph in Fig. 1, we note that the obtained solution is proper. The different result in case of FPE criterion comes from local extreme depicted in Fig. 1.

5   Conclusion

In the paper four information criterions were adopted to neuro-fuzzy systems design. The idea was tested on approximation problem (Rise Taste). The AIC, Schwarz and CAT criterions gives similar results and the FPE criterion is sensitive to local minimums in error course. It should be noted that our approach differs from that given in [17].

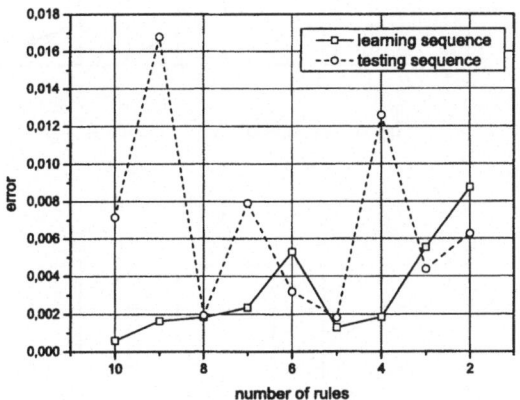

Fig. 1. Average square error

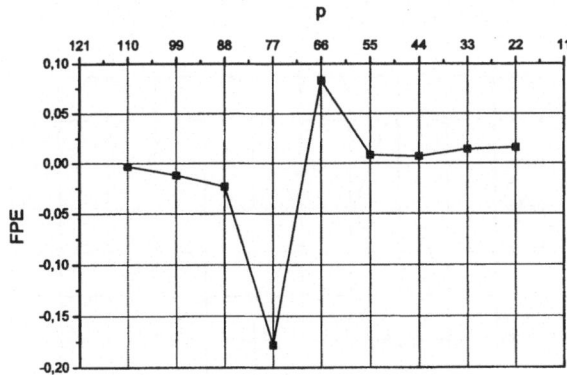

Fig. 2. Values of FPE criterion

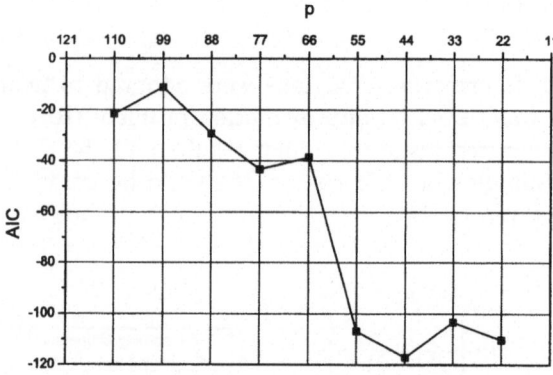

Fig. 3. Values of AIC criterion

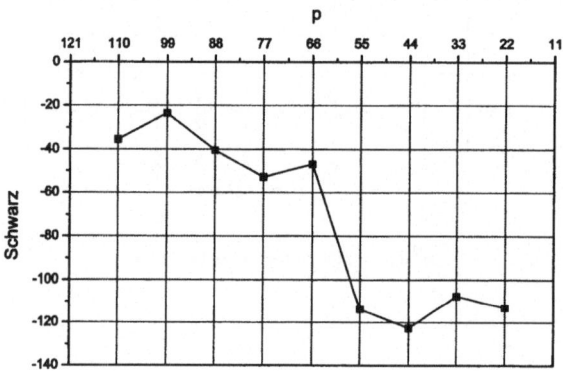

Fig. 4. Values of Schwarz criterion

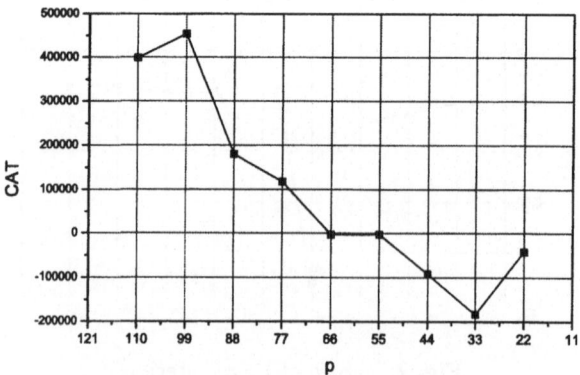

Fig. 5. Values of CAT criterion

References

1. Czogała E., Łęski J.: Fuzzy and Neuro-Fuzzy Intelligent Systems, Physica-Verlag, A Springer-Verlag Company, Heidelberg, New York (2000)
2. Fodor J. C.: On fuzzy implication, Fuzzy Sets and Systems, vol. 42 (1991) 293-300
3. Gorzałczany M. B.: Computational Inteligence Systems and Applications, Neuro-Fuzzy and Fuzzy Neural Synergisms, Studies in Fuzziness and Soft Computing, Physica-Verlag, A Springer-Verlag Company, Heidelberg (2002)
4. Nauck D., Klawonn F., Kruse R.: Foundations of Neuro-Fuzzy Systems, Wiley (997)
5. Rutkowska D., Nowicki R.: New neuro-fuzzy architectures, Proc. Int. Conf. on Artificial and Computational Intelligence for Decision, Control and Automation in Engineering and Industrial Applications, ACIDCA'2000, Intelligent Methods, Monastir, Tunisia, March (2000) 82-87
6. Rutkowska D., Nowicki R.: Implication - based neuro-fuzzy architectures, International Journal of Applied Mathematics and Computer Science, No.4 (2000) 675-701
7. Rutkowska D. and Rutkowski L.: Neural-Fuzzy-Genetic Parallel Computing System as a Tool for Various Applications, Proceedings of the Third International Conference on Parallel Processing & Applied Mathematics (PPAM'99), Kazimierz Dolny (1999) 489-498
8. Rutkowski L.: Adaptive filters and adaptive signal processing: Thory and Applications, WNT, Warszawa (1994) (in Polish)
9. Rutkowski L.: Flexible Neuro-Fuzzy Systems: Structures, Learning and Performance Evaluation, Kluwer (2004)
10. Rutkowski L. and Cpałka K.: Flexible Structures of Neuro - Fuzzy Systems, Quo Vadis Computational Intelligence, Studies in Fuzziness and Soft Computing, Vol. 54, Springer (2000) 479-484
11. Rutkowski L., Cpałka K.: Flexible Neuro-Fuzzy Systems, IEEE Trans. Neural Networks, vol. 14 (2003) 554-574
12. Scherer R. and Rutkowski L.: Survey of selected fuzzy rule pruning methods, Proceedings of the Fourth Conference Neural Networks and Their Applications (1999) 308-313
13. Scherer R. and Rutkowski L.: A survey of hierarchical fuzzy systems, Proceedings of the Fifth Conference Neural Networks and Soft Computing, June 6-10, Zakopane (2000) 374-379
14. Scherer R. and Rutkowski L.: A fuzzy relational system with linguistic antecedent certainty factors, in: Rutkowski L., Kacprzyk J. (Eds.), Neural Networks and Soft Computing, Physica-Verlag, A Springer-Verlag Company, Heidelberg , New York (2003) 563-569
15. Starczewski J. and Rutkowski L.: Interval type 2 neuro-fuzzy systems based on interval consequents, in: Rutkowski L., Kacprzyk J. (Eds.), Neural Networks and Soft Computing, Physica-Verlag, A Springer-Verlag Company, Heidelberg , New York (2003) 570-577
16. Wang L. X.: Adaptive Fuzzy Systems and Control, PTR Prentice Hall, Englewood Cliffs (1994)
17. Wang L., Yen J.: Application of statistical information criteria for optimal fuzzy model construction, IEEE Transactions on Fuzzy Systems, vol. 6, August (1998) 353-362

On Hesitation Degrees in IF-Set Theory

Anna Pankowska and Maciej Wygralak

Faculty of Mathematics and Computer Science
Adam Mickiewicz University
Umultowska 87, 61-614 Poznań, Poland
wygralak@math.amu.edu.pl

Abstract. In this paper, we propose a generalization of the definition of an IF-set, an intuitionistic fuzzy set, and related hesitation degrees. We flexibilize the original method of computing these values by the use of triangular norms. Next, we present its application to group decision making problems.

1 Introduction

In some practical problems, we encounter with a need of hesitation modeling. A good example could be questions of decision making. The decision maker is not always certain of his/her preferences as to given options. So, we have to be able to formally model his/her hesitation if we want to construct adequate models of decision making problems.

A convenient tool for hesitation modeling is the IF-set theory, the theory of so-called intuitionistic fuzzy sets by Atanassov, equipped with triangular norm-based operations introduced by Deschrijver and Kerre (see [1,2,3]). However, an intrinsic feature of the classical IF-set theory, which will be recollected in Section 2, is that hesitation degrees are therein always computed by means of the same method of aggregation of membership and nonmembership degrees. Consequently, in Section 2 we also propose a generalization of the notion of an IF-set, and we define hesitation degrees in a flexible way involving triangular norms. In Section 3 we concisely present how this general theory can be applied to group decision making problems with individual fuzzy preference relations.

2 A General Concept of IF-Sets and Hesitation Degrees

An IF-set is a pair $\mathcal{E} = (A, A^d)$ of functions $A, A^d : M \to [0,1]$, where M is a given universal set. These functions are interpreted as a *membership* and a *nonmembership* function, respectively. $A(x)$ and $A^d(x)$ are a membership and a nonmembership degree of x in $\mathcal{E}$. According to [1,2,3], the relationship between A and A^d, being fundamental in the classical IF-set theory, is

$$A^d \subset A' \tag{1}$$

with the standard complementation $A'(x) = 1 - A(x)$. Hence

L. Rutkowski et al. (Eds.): ICAISC 2004, LNAI 3070, pp. 338–343, 2004.
© Springer-Verlag Berlin Heidelberg 2004

$$\forall x \in M : A(x) + A^d(x) \leq 1. \tag{2}$$

The difference

$$\chi_{\mathcal{E}}(x) = 1 - A(x) - A^d(x) \tag{3}$$

is called a *degree of hesitation* whether or not x is in $\mathcal{E}$. Trivially,

$$\forall x \in M : A(x) + A^d(x) + \chi_{\mathcal{E}}(x) = 1. \tag{4}$$

According to [3], the sum $\mathcal{E} \cup_{t,s} \mathcal{F}$ and the intersection $\mathcal{E} \cap_{t,s} \mathcal{F}$ of IF-sets $\mathcal{E} = (A, A^d)$ and $\mathcal{F} = (B, B^d)$ satisfying (1) are defined as

$$\mathcal{E} \cup_{t,s} \mathcal{F} = (A \cup_s B, A^d \cap_t B^d) \quad \text{and} \quad \mathcal{E} \cap_{t,s} \mathcal{F} = (A \cap_t B, A^d \cup_s B^d), \tag{5}$$

where t and s denote a t-norm and a t-conorm, respectively, and $(A \cup_s B)(x) = A(x)sB(x)$ and $(A \cap_t B)(x) = A(x)tB(x)$.

Looking at (1) and (5), we notice an inconsistency lying in that $\chi_{\mathcal{E}}(x)$ is always computed in the same way, no matter which t-norm t one uses. Therefore we propose a general concept of IF-sets with the operations (5) in which the relationship between A and A^d is more flexible and $\chi_{\mathcal{E}}(x)$'s are t-dependent (see also [5,6,7]). Namely, assume that

$$A^d \subset A^\nu, \tag{6}$$

where ν is an arbitrary strong negation, not necessarily the Lukasiewicz negation $\nu_L(a) = 1 - a$. Since $A^\nu(x) = \nu(A(x))$, (6) could be rewritten as

$$\forall x \in M : A^d(x) \leq \nu(A(x)). \tag{7}$$

An IF-set representing a fuzzy set F is (F, F^ν). Sums and intersections from (5) are still IF-sets satisfying (6) whenever $s \leq t^\nu$, where t^ν denotes the $\nu - dual$ t-conorm, i.e. $a \ t^\nu \ b = \nu(\nu(a) \ t \ \nu(b))$.

If t is nonstrict Archimedean and we use the negation $\nu = \nu_t$ induced by t $(\nu_t(a) = \bigvee \{c : atc = 0\})$, then (6) is equivalent to the equality

$$A \cap_t A^d = 1_\emptyset. \tag{8}$$

For $t = t_L$, one has $\nu_t = \nu_L$ and, then, (6) - (8) collapse to the classical condition (1) (t_L denotes the Lukasiewicz t-norm with $at_Lb = 0 \vee (a + b - 1)$).

Generally speaking, hesitation is inability of a categorical declaration of being for or against. In particular, for a given object x, it means that we cannot say that it belongs to an IF-set and, simultaneously, we cannot say it does not belong. Basing on this intuition, we define a degree of hesitation as

$$\chi_{\mathcal{E}}(x) = \nu(A(x) \ t^\nu \ A^d(x)) = \nu(A(x)) \ t \ \nu(A^d(x)). \tag{9}$$

Again, for $t = t_L$, (9) collapses to (3). We thus generally have

$$\forall x \in M : \phi(A(x) \ t^\nu \ A^d(x)) + \phi(\chi_{\mathcal{E}}(x)) = 1, \tag{10}$$

which forms a generalization of the equality (4), where $\phi : [0,1] \rightarrow [0,1]$ is an automorphism generating ν, i.e. $\nu(a) = \phi^{-1}(1 - \phi(a))$.

It is obvious that $\chi_{\mathcal{E}}(x) \in [0,1]$. Let us ask when the extreme values 0 and 1 are attained. By virtue of (9),

$$\chi_{\mathcal{E}}(x) = 1 \Leftrightarrow A(x) = A^d(x) = 0.$$

If t is nonstrict Archimedean and $\nu = \nu_t$, then (see Fig.1 c))

$$\chi_{\mathcal{E}}(x) = 0 \Leftrightarrow A^d(x) = \nu(A(x)).$$

If t has no zero divisors, e.g. t is strict or $t = \wedge$, we get instead

$$\chi_{\mathcal{E}}(x) = 0 \Leftrightarrow (A(x), A^d(x)) \in \{(1,0),(0,1)\}.$$

The very occurrence of positive values $A(x)$ and $A^d(x)$ is in this case identical with a positive hesitation and $\chi_{\mathcal{E}}(x)$ behaves in a way which is similar to fuzziness measures. To see this more clearly, notice that if $\nu = \nu_L$ and t is strict or $t = \wedge$, (9) and (10) are of the form

$$\chi_{\mathcal{E}}(x) = 1 - A(x) \, t^* A^d(x)$$

and

$$\forall x \in M : A(x) \, t^* A^d(x) + \chi_{\mathcal{E}}(x) = 1,$$

where $t^* = t^{\nu_L}$ is the t-conorm associated with t. Thus,

$$\chi_{\mathcal{E}}(x) = A(x) \, t \, (1 - A(x)) \quad \text{whenever} \quad A^d(x) = 1 - A(x),$$

i.e. $\chi_{\mathcal{E}}(x)$ becomes a t-based fuzziness degree of x. For instance, different hesitation (fuzziness) degrees are then assigned to elements x and y with $(A(x), A^d(x)) = (0.5, 0.5)$ and $(A(y), A^d(y)) = (0.1, 0.9)$. Using, say, the algebraic t-norm, those degrees are equal to 0.25 and 0.09, respectively (see also Fig. 1 b)). In classical IF-set theory, we get $\chi_{\mathcal{E}}(x) = \chi_{\mathcal{E}}(y) = 0$ (see Fig. 1 a)). Concluding, hesitation appears to be a generalization of fuzziness.

Finally, for a nonstrict Archimedean t and $\nu = \nu_t$, we get

$$\chi_{\mathcal{E}}(x) = \nu_t(A(x)t^\circ A^d(x)) = \nu_t(A(x))t\nu_t(A^d(x))$$

and

$$\forall x \in M : A(x)t^\circ A^d(x)t^\circ \chi_{\mathcal{E}}(x) = 1$$

with $t^\circ = t^{\nu_t}$ being the t-conorm complementary to t.

3   Application to Group Decision Making

In this section, we would like to present a generalization of the algorithms of group decision making first proposed by Kacprzyk in [4] and developed by Szmidt

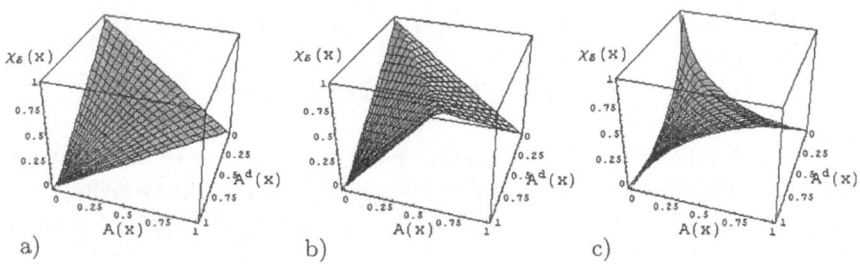

Fig. 1. 3D plot of χ_ε for a) $t = t_L$, b) $t = \wedge$ and c) $t = t_{Y,2}$ with a $t_{Y,p}$ $b = 0 \vee (1 - ((1-a)^p + (1-b)^p)^{1/p})$ (Yager t-norm)

and Kacprzyk ([8]). By the use of relative scalar cardinalities together with the general hesitation formula (9), we obtain a more flexible method unifying specific variants considered in [8].

By a *generalized sigma count* of A we mean the number (see [9])

$$\sigma_f(A) = \sum_{x \in supp(A)} f(A(x))$$

with a *cardinality pattern* f, where $f : [0,1] \to [0,1]$ is nondecreasing, $f(0) = 0$ and $f(1) = 1$. Generalized sigma counts can be applied to define in a flexible way relative scalar cardinalities as

$$\sigma_f(A|B) = \frac{\sigma_f(A \cap_t B)}{\sigma_f(B)}.$$

In particular, we thus have

$$\sigma_f(A|1_M) = \frac{1}{|M|} \sum_{x \in supp(A)} f(A(x)).$$

Let $P = \{p_1, ..., p_m\}$ be a set of $m \geq 1$ *individuals*, and $S = \{s_1, ..., s_n\}$ with $n \geq 2$ be a set of *options*. Each individual p_k formulates his preferences over S by means of a fuzzy relation $R_k : S \times S \to [0,1]$ that can be represented as an $n \times n$ matrix $R_k = [r_{ij}^k]$ with $i, j = 1, 2, ..., n$. The number $r_{ij}^k \in [0,1]$ is a *degree to which* p_k *prefers* s_i *to* s_j; for each i we put $r_{ii}^k = 0$. Moreover, we assume that

$$r_{ij}^k \leq \nu(r_{ji}^k)$$

with a strong negation ν having a unique fixed point $a^* \in (0,1)$. Finally, Q denotes a relative linguistic quantifier of "most"-type (see [10]). Our task is to find a solution understood as a fuzzy set S_Q of options such that a soft majority, Q individuals, is not against them. For the sake of notational convenience, put $P = 1_P$, $S_j = S \setminus \{s_j\}$ and $S_j = 1_{S_j}$.

Let us present a general algorithm of group decision making with fuzzy individual preference relations, including hesitation factor. t denotes a nonstrict Archimedean t-norm and $\nu = \nu_t$. f, f^*, g and g^* are cardinality patterns.

Step 1. Construct hesitation matrices $H_k = [h_{ij}^k]$ such that (see (9))

$$h_{ij}^k = \nu(r_{ij}^k)\, t\, \nu(r_{ji}^k) \text{ whenever } i \neq j$$

and $h_{ii}^k = 0$. Notice that all H_k's are zero matrices whenever $r_{ij}^k = \nu(r_{ji}^k)$ for each k and $i \neq j$. Then Steps 1, 4, 5 should be skipped, and we take $Q(d_i t^\circ e_i) = Q(d_i)$ in Step 6 - Step 7. Further, put $r_{ij}^k = r_{ji}^k = 1$ whenever $r_{ij}^k, r_{ji}^k < \alpha$ for $i \neq j$ with a given threshold $\alpha \leq a^*$.

Step 2. Construct fuzzy sets $R_{k,j} : S_j \to [0,1]$ of options which p_k prefers to s_j. So, $R_{k,j}(s_i) = r_{ij}^k$. A degree to which p_k is not against s_j is equal to

$$r_{*j}^k = \nu(\sigma_f(R_{k,j}|S_j)) = \nu\left(\frac{1}{n-1}\sum_{\substack{i=1\\i\neq j}}^{n} f(r_{ij}^k)\right).$$

Step 3. Construct fuzzy sets $I_j : P \to [0,1]$ of individuals being not against an option s_j with $I_j(p_k) = r_{*j}^k$. Let

$$d_j = \sigma_{f^*}(I_j|P) = \frac{1}{m}\sum_{k=1}^{m} f^*(r_{*j}^k).$$

Step 4. Construct fuzzy sets $H_{k,j} : S_j \to [0,1]$ of options such that p_k is hesitant as to his/her preference between them and s_j. So, $H_{k,j}(s_i) = h_{ij}^k$. Put

$$h_{*j}^k = \sigma_g(H_{k,j}|S_j) = \frac{1}{n-1}\sum_{\substack{i=1\\i\neq j}}^{n} g(h_{ij}^k).$$

Step 5. Construct fuzzy sets $L_j : P \to [0,1]$ of individuals who hesitate as to their preferences between s_j and other options, i.e. $L_j(p_k) = h_{*j}^k$. Let

$$e_j = \sigma_{g^*}(L_j|P) = \frac{1}{m}\sum_{k=1}^{m} g^*(h_{*j}^k).$$

Step 6. Compute a degree to which Q individuals are not against s_j taking into account a possible change of their mind due to their hesitation, i.e. compute $Q(d_j)$ and $Q(d_j t^\circ e_j)$ for $j = 1, ..., n$.

Step 7. Finally, the solution is an interval-valued fuzzy set

$$S_Q = [Q(d_1), Q(d_1 t^\circ e_1)]/s_1 + ... + [Q(d_n), Q(d_n t^\circ e_n)]/s_n.$$

Example. Consider the example of fuzzy preference relations and linguistic quantifier used in [8]: $Q(x) = [1$ if $x \geq 0.8, 2x - 0.6$ if $x \in (0.3, 0.8), 0$ if $x \leq 0.3]$ and

$$
R_1 = \begin{bmatrix} 0 & 0.3 & 0.7 & 0.4 \\ 0.7 & 0 & 0.6 & 0.9 \\ 0.3 & 0.4 & 0 & 0.5 \\ 0.4 & 0 & 0.3 & 0 \end{bmatrix} \quad
R_2 = \begin{bmatrix} 0 & 0.4 & 0.6 & 0.5 \\ 0.6 & 0 & 0.7 & 0.7 \\ 0.4 & 0.3 & 0 & 0.4 \\ 0.3 & 0.1 & 0.3 & 0 \end{bmatrix} \quad
R_3 = \begin{bmatrix} 0 & 0.5 & 0.7 & 0.3 \\ 0.5 & 0 & 0.8 & 0.7 \\ 0.3 & 0.2 & 0 & 0.5 \\ 0.4 & 0.1 & 0.2 & 0 \end{bmatrix} \quad
R_4 = \begin{bmatrix} 0 & 0.4 & 0.7 & 0.6 \\ 0.6 & 0 & 0.4 & 0.6 \\ 0.3 & 0.6 & 0 & 0.4 \\ 0.1 & 0.1 & 0.1 & 0 \end{bmatrix}.
$$

Applying $t = t_L$ with $\nu = \nu_t = \nu_L$, $f(a) = (1$ if $a \geq a^*$, else $0)$ and $f^* = g = g^* = id$, one obtains a solution identical to that from [8] ($a^* = 0.5$): $S_Q = [0.4, 0.57]/s_1 + [1, 1]/s_2 + [0, 0.12]/s_3$.

If, say, t is the Schweizer t-norm $t_{S,p}$ with $p = 2$, i.e. $atb = (0 \vee (a^2 + b^2 - 1))^{1/2}$, then $h_{ij}^k = (1 - (r_{ij}^k)^2 - (r_{ji}^k)^2)^{1/2}$ and

$$
H_1 = \begin{bmatrix} 0 & 0.65 & 0.65 & 0.82 \\ 0.65 & 0 & 0.69 & 0.44 \\ 0.65 & 0.69 & 0 & 0.81 \\ 0.82 & 0.44 & 0.81 & 0 \end{bmatrix}, \quad
H_2 = \begin{bmatrix} 0 & 0.69 & 0.69 & 0.81 \\ 0.69 & 0 & 0.65 & 0.71 \\ 0.69 & 0.65 & 0 & 0.87 \\ 0.81 & 0.71 & 0.87 & 0 \end{bmatrix},
$$

$$
H_3 = \begin{bmatrix} 0 & 0.71 & 0.65 & 0.87 \\ 0.71 & 0 & 0.57 & 0.71 \\ 0.65 & 0.57 & 0 & 0.84 \\ 0.87 & 0.71 & 0.84 & 0 \end{bmatrix}, \quad
H_4 = \begin{bmatrix} 0 & 0.69 & 0.65 & 0.79 \\ 0.69 & 0 & 0.69 & 0.79 \\ 0.65 & 0.69 & 0 & 0.91 \\ 0.79 & 0.79 & 0.91 & 0 \end{bmatrix}.
$$

Consequently, $S_Q = [1, 1]/s_1 + [1, 1]/s_2 + [0.52, 1]/s_3 + [0, 0.96]/s_4$. The solution is now less "selective" as $a^* = 0.71$ and, thus, the preferences in the R_k's become "small" in comparison with a^*, which leads to hesitation degrees being much greater than for $t = t_L$.

References

1. Atanassov K. (1999) *Intuitionistic Fuzzy Sets. Theory and Application*, Physica-Verlag, Heidelberg New York.
2. Atanassov K. and Stoeva S. (1983), *Intuitionistic fuzzy sets*, in: *Proc. Polish Symp. Interval and Fuzzy Mathematics*, Poznań, 23-26.
3. Deschrijver G. and Kerre E. E. (2002), *A generalisation of operators on intuitionistic fuzzy sets using triangular norms and conorms*, Notes on IFS **8**, 19-27.
4. Kacprzyk J. (1986), *Group decision making with a fuzzy linguistic majority*, Fuzzy Sets and Systems **18**, 105-118.
5. Pankowska A. and Wygralak M. (2003), *Intuitionistic fuzzy sets - An alternative look*, in: *Proc. 3rd EUSFLAT Conf.*, Zittau, 135-140.
6. Pankowska A. and Wygralak M. (2004), *A General Concept of IF-Sets with Triangular Norms*, submitted.
7. Pankowska A. and Wygralak M. (200x), *On triangular norm-based IF-sets and their application to group decision making*, Fuzzy Sets and Systems, submitted.
8. Szmidt E. and Kacprzyk J. (1998), *Group decision making under intuitionistic fuzzy preference relations*, in: *Proc. 7th IPMU Conf.*, Paris, 172-178.
9. Wygralak M. (2003) *Cardinalities of Fuzzy Sets*, Springer-Verlag, Berlin Heidelberg.
10. Zadeh L. A. (1983), *A computational approach to fuzzy quantifiers in natural languages*, Comput. and Math. with Appl. **9**, 149-184.

Fuzzy Cognitive Maps Learning through Swarm Intelligence

E.I. Papageorgiou[1,3], K.E. Parsopoulos[2,3], P.P. Groumpos[1,3], and M.N. Vrahatis[2,3]*

[1] Department of Electrical and Computer Engineering, University of Patras,
GR–26500 Patras, Greece, {epapageo, groumpos}@ee.upatras.gr
[2] Department of Mathematics, University of Patras, GR–26110 Patras, Greece,
{kostasp, vrahatis}@math.upatras.gr
[3] University of Patras Artificial Intelligence Research Center (UPAIRC),
University of Patras, GR–26110 Patras, Greece

Abstract. A technique for Fuzzy Cognitive Maps learning, which is based on the minimization of a properly defined objective function using the Particle Swarm Optimization algorithm, is presented. The workings of the technique are illustrated on an industrial process control problem. The obtained results support the claim that swarm intelligence algorithms can be a valuable tool for Fuzzy Cognitive Maps learning, alleviating deficiencies of Fuzzy Cognitive Maps, and controlling the system's convergence.

1 Introduction

Fuzzy Cognitive Maps (FCMs) constitute a promising modeling methodology that provides flexibility on the simulated system's design, modeling and control. They were introduced by Kosko for the representation of causal relationships among concepts as well as for the analysis of inference patterns [1,2]. Up–to–date, FCMs have been applied in various scientific fields, including bioinformatics, manufacturing, organization behavior, political science, and decision making. Although FCMs constitute a promising modeling methodology, they have some deficiencies regarding the robustness of their inference mechanism and their ability to adapt the experts' knowledge through optimization and learning [1, 2]. These properties are crucial in several applications. Therefore, FCMs need further enhancement, stronger mathematical justification, and improvement of their operation. This can be attained through the development of new learning algorithms that alleviate the deficiencies and improve the performance of FCMs.

In this paper, an approach for FCMs learning, based on a swarm intelligence algorithm, is presented. In particular, the Particle Swarm Optimization (PSO) method is applied to determine an appropriate configuration of the FCM's weights, through the minimization of a properly defined objective function [3]. The technique is applied on a process control problem, with promising results.

---

* Partially supported by the "Pythagoras" research grant awarded by the Greek Ministry of Education and Religious Affairs as well as the European Union.

L. Rutkowski et al. (Eds.): ICAISC 2004, LNAI 3070, pp. 344–349, 2004.
© Springer-Verlag Berlin Heidelberg 2004

The paper is organized as follows: the PSO algorithm is briefly presented in Section 2, while the basic principles of FCMs as well as the learning procedure are described in Section 3. In Section 4 the process control problem is described and the experimental results are reported and discussed. The paper concludes in Section 5.

2   The Particle Swarm Optimization Algorithm

Particle Swarm Optimization (PSO) is a population–based stochastic optimization algorithm. It belongs to the class of *swarm intelligence* algorithms, which are inspired from and based on the social dynamics and emergent behavior that arise in socially organized colonies [4,5]. In the context of PSO, the population is called a *swarm* and the individuals (search points) are called *particles*.

Assume a D–dimensional search space, $S \subset \mathbb{R}^D$, and a swarm consisting of N particles. The i–th particle is in effect a D–dimensional vector, $X_i = (x_{i1}, x_{i2}, \ldots, x_{iD})^\top \in S$. The velocity of this particle is also a D–dimensional vector, $V_i = (v_{i1}, v_{i2}, \ldots, v_{iD})^\top \in S$. The best previous position encountered by the i–th particle is a point in S, denoted by $P_i = (p_{i1}, p_{i2}, \ldots, p_{iD})^\top$. Assume g_i to be the index of the particle that attained either the best position of the whole swarm (global version) or the best position in the neighborhood of the i–th particle (local version). Then, the swarm is manipulated by the equations [6]:

$$V_i(t+1) = \chi \left[V_i(t) + c_1\, r_1 \big(P_i(t) - X_i(t) \big) + c_2\, r_2 \big(P_{g_i}(t) - X_i(t) \big) \right], \quad (1)$$

$$X_i(t+1) = X_i(t) + V_i(t+1), \quad (2)$$

where $i = 1, \ldots, N$; χ is a parameter called *constriction factor*; c_1 and c_2 are two parameters called *cognitive* and *social* parameters respectively; and r_1, r_2, are random numbers uniformly distributed within $[0,1]$. The value of the constriction factor can be derived analytically [6]. The initialization of the swarm and the velocities, is usually performed randomly and uniformly in the search space.

3   Fuzzy Cognitive Maps Learning

FCMs combine properties of fuzzy logic and neural networks. An FCM models the behavior of a system by using concepts, C_i, $i = 1, ..., N$, that represent the states, variables or characteristics of the system. The system is then represented by a fuzzy signed directed graph with feedback, which contains nodes–concepts and weighted edges that connect the nodes and represent the cause and effect relations among them. The values, A_i, of the concepts lie within $[0,1]$ and they are susceptible to change over time. The weights, W_{ij}, of the edges assume values in $[-1, 1]$, and represent the extent of the impact of the interconnected concepts on each other. The design of an FCM is a process that heavily relies on the input from a group of experts [7] and results in an initial weight matrix, $W^{\text{initial}} = [W_{ij}]$, with $W_{ii} = 0$, $i, j = 1, \ldots, N$. After the determination of its structure, the FCM is let to converge to a steady state by applying the rule,

$A_i(t+1) = f\left(A_i(t) + \sum_{\substack{j=1 \\ j \neq i}}^{n} W_{ji}A_j(t)\right)$, with arbitrary initial values of A_i [2], where t stands for the time counter. The function f is the threshold function, $f(x) = 1/(1 + e^{-\lambda x})$, where $\lambda > 0$ is a parameter that determines its steepness. In the present study the value of λ was set to 1. A steady state of the FCM is characterized by concept values that are not further modified through the application of the aforementioned rule. After this stage, the FCM can simulate the system accurately. The heavy dependence on the experts' opinion regarding the FCM's design; the convergence to undesired steady states starting from the experts recommendations; as well as the need for specific initial values of the concepts, are significant weaknesses of FCMs, which can be addressed through learning procedures. Up–to–date, a few learning algorithms have been proposed [8,9], and they are mostly based on ideas coming from the field of neural network training. Recently, a new technique for FCMs learning, which is based on the minimization of a properly defined objective function using the Particle Swarm Optimization algorithm, has been developed [3]. For completeness purposes, this technique is outlined in the rest of this section.

The main goal of learning in FCMs is to determine the values of the weights of the FCM that produce a desired behavior of the system. The desired behavior of the system is characterized by values of the output concepts that lie within prespecified bounds, determined by the experts. These bounds are in general problem dependent. Let $C_{\mathrm{out}_1}, \ldots, C_{\mathrm{out}_m}$, $m \in \{1, 2, \ldots, N\}$, be the output concepts of the FCM, while the remaining concepts are considered input or interior concepts. The user is interested in restricting the values of these output concepts in strict bounds, $A_{\mathrm{out}_i}^{\min} \leqslant A_{\mathrm{out}_i} \leqslant A_{\mathrm{out}_i}^{\max}$, $i = 1, \ldots, m$, which are crucial for the proper operation of the modeled system. Thus, the main goal is to detect a weight matrix, $W = [W_{ij}]$, $i, j = 1, \ldots, N$, that leads the FCM to a steady state at which, the output concepts lie in their corresponding bounds, while the weights retain their physical meaning. The latter is attained by imposing constraints on the potential values assumed by weights. To do this, the following objective function is considered [3]:

$$F(W) = \sum_{i=1}^{m} H\left(Q_{\mathrm{out}_i}^{\min}\right) \left|Q_{\mathrm{out}_i}^{\min}\right| + \sum_{i=1}^{m} H\left(Q_{\mathrm{out}_i}^{\max}\right) \left|Q_{\mathrm{out}_i}^{\max}\right|, \tag{3}$$

where $Q_{\mathrm{out}_i}^{\min} = A_{\mathrm{out}_i}^{\min} - A_{\mathrm{out}_i}$; $Q_{\mathrm{out}_i}^{\max} = A_{\mathrm{out}_i} - A_{\mathrm{out}_i}^{\max}$; H is the well–known Heaviside function, i.e. $H(x) = 0$, if $x < 0$, and $H(x) = 1$ otherwise; and A_{out_i}, $i = 1, \ldots, m$, are the steady state values of the output concepts that are obtained using the weight matrix W. Obviously, the global minimizers of the objective function F are weight matrices that lead the FCM to a desired steady state. An FCM with N fully interconnected concepts, corresponds to an $N(N-1)$–dimensional minimization problem [3].

The application of PSO for the minimization of the objective function F, starts with an initialization phase, where a swarm of weight matrices is generated randomly, and it is evaluated using F. Then, (1) and (2) are used to evolve the swarm. When a weight configuration that globally minimizes F is reached, the algorithm stops. There is, in general, a plethora of weight matrices for which the FCM converges to the desired regions of the output concepts. PSO is a stochastic

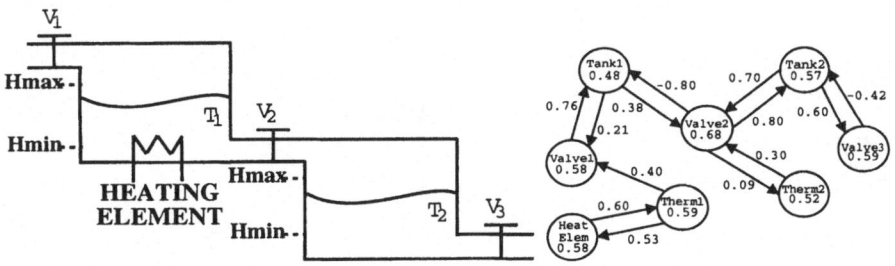

Fig. 1. The process control problem (left) and the corresponding FCM (right).

algorithm, and, thus, it is quite natural to obtain such suboptimal matrices that differ in subsequent experiments. The approach has proved to be very efficient in practice [3]. In the following section, its operation on an industrial process control problem, is discussed.

4 An Application to a Process Control Problem

The learning algorithm previously described, is applied on a complex industrial process control problem [7]. This problem consists of two tanks, three valves, one heating element and two thermometers for each tank, as depicted in Fig. 1. Each tank has an inlet valve and an outlet valve. The outlet valve of the first tank is the inlet valve of the second. The objective of the control system is to keep the height as well as the temperature of the liquid in both tanks, within prespecified bounds. The temperature, T^1, of the liquid in tank 1, is regulated by a heating element. The temperature, T^2, of the liquid in tank 2, is measured using a thermometer; if T^2 is decreased, then valve V^2 opens, and hot liquid from tank 1 is pured into tank 2. Thus, the main objective is to ensure that the relations $H^1_{\min} \leqslant H^1 \leqslant H^1_{\max}$, $T^1_{\min} \leqslant T^1 \leqslant T^1_{\max}$, $H^2_{\min} \leqslant H^2 \leqslant H^2_{\max}$, $T^2_{\min} \leqslant T^2 \leqslant T^2_{\max}$, hold, where H^1 and H^2 denote the height of the liquid in tank 1 and tank 2, respectively. An FCM that models this system has been developed in [7] and depicted in Fig. 1. The output concepts are C_1, C_2, C_6 and C_7. The sign and the weight of each interconnection have been determined by three experts [7]. All the experts agreed regarding the direction of the interconnections among the concepts, and they determined the overall linguistic variable and the corresponding fuzzy set for each weight. The final ranges for the weights, as implied by the fuzzy regions, are: $0.00 \leqslant W_{13} \leqslant 0.50$, $0.00 \leqslant W_{14} \leqslant 0.75$, $0.00 \leqslant W_{24} \leqslant 0.90$, $0.00 \leqslant W_{25} \leqslant 1.00$, $0.50 \leqslant W_{31} \leqslant 1.00$, $-1.0 \leqslant W_{41} \leqslant -0.25$, $0.25 \leqslant W_{42} \leqslant 1.00$, $-0.50 \leqslant W_{47} \leqslant 0.50$, $-0.75 \leqslant W_{52} \leqslant 0.75$, $0.00 \leqslant W_{63} \leqslant 0.75$, $0.25 \leqslant W_{68} \leqslant 0.75$, $0.00 \leqslant W_{74} \leqslant 0.60$, $0.00 \leqslant W_{86} \leqslant 0.90$, and the initial weights, derived through the CoA defuzzification method, are $W^{\text{initial}} = [0.21, 0.38, 0.70, 0.6, 0.76, -0.80, 0.80, 0.09, -0.42, 0.4, 0.53, 0.30, 0.60]$.

Two different scenarios have been considered to investigate the performance of our approach on the process control problem. For each scenario, 100 independent experiments have been performed using the global variant of a constriction

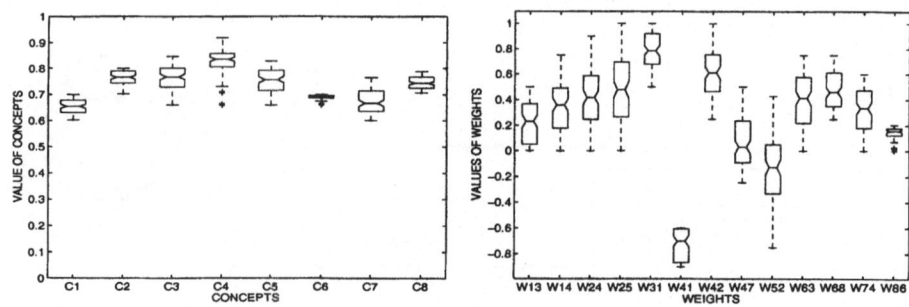

Fig. 2. Boxplots for the first scenario.

factor PSO. The swarm size was set to 5. The constriction factor as well as the cognitive and the social parameter have been set to their default values, $\chi = 0.729$, $c_1 = c_2 = 2.05$ [6].

The first scenario considers the constrained weights, and the following desired values for the four output concepts: $0.5 \leqslant C_1 \leqslant 0.7$, $0.7 \leqslant C_2 \leqslant 0.8$, $0.6 \leqslant C_6 \leqslant 0.7$, $0.6 \leqslant C_7 \leqslant 0.8$. The convergence regions of the concepts and weights are depicted in the boxplots of Fig. 2. A suboptimal weight vector is $W = [0.01, 0.36, 0.41, 0.82, 0.50, -0.60, 0.29, 0.39, 0.42, 0.22, 0.36, 0.11, 0.18]$, and the corresponding values of the output concepts are $C_1 = 0.62$, $C_2 = 0.79$, $C_6 = 0.69$, $C_7 = 0.74$. Comparing the derived convergence regions of the weights with the bounds provided by the experts, it can be observed that three weights, namely W_{47}, W_{52}, and W_{86} take values in ranges significantly smaller than their bounds. This can serve as an indication that the experts determined relatively wide initial bounds. The values of the remaining weights lie in their bounding regions. The mean number of required function evaluations was 32.85.

In the second scenario, the desired values for the output concepts are different: $0.5 \leqslant C_1 \leqslant 0.7$, $0.7 \leqslant C_2 \leqslant 0.8$, $0.73 \leqslant C_6 \leqslant 0.81$, $0.65 \leqslant C_7 \leqslant 0.75$. The convergence regions of the concepts and weights are depicted in the boxplots of Fig. 3. A suboptimal weight vector is $W = [0.21, 0.49, 0.01, 0.04, 0.51, -0.89, 0.61, 0.09, -0.40, 0.09, 0.29, 0.01, 0.84]$, and the corresponding values of the output concepts are $C_1 = 0.56$, $C_2 = 0.71$, $C_6 = 0.80$, $C_7 = 0.67$. Again, the weights W_{47}, W_{52}, and W_{86} assume values in ranges significantly smaller than their bounds, while the values of the remaining weights lie in their bounding regions. The mean number of required function evaluations was 15.35.

It is clear that the learning algorithm is capable of providing proper weight matrices for the FCM, efficiently and effectively. Moreover, the statistical analysis through the boxplots provides indications regarding the quality of the weights' bounds determined by the experts, which can be used in the future as a mechanism for the evaluation of the experts by taking into consideration the deviation of their suggestions from the obtained values.

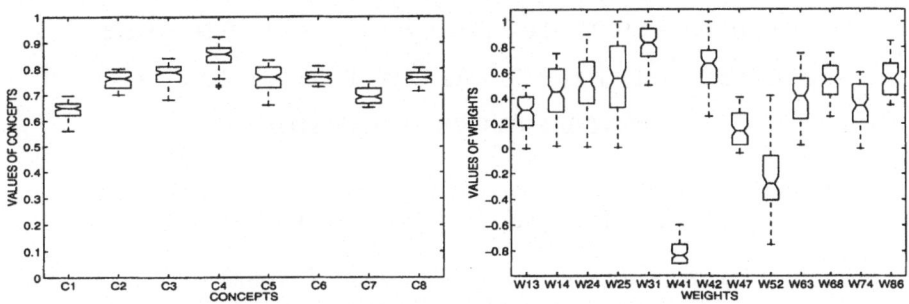

Fig. 3. Boxplots for the second scenario.

5 Conclusions

A methodology for determining the cause–effect relationships (weights) among the concepts of Fuzzy Cognitive Maps, has been presented. This approach is based on the minimization of a properly defined objective function through the Particle Swarm Optimization algorithm. A complex process control problem has been used to illustrate the algorithm. The results are very promising, verifying the effectiveness of the learning procedure. Moreover, the physical meaning of the obtained results is retained. This approach can provide a robust solution in the case of divergent opinions of the experts, and it will be considered, in a future work, as means for the evaluation of the experts.

References

1. Kosko, B.: Fuzzy cognitive maps. Int. J. Man–Machine Studies **24** (1986) 65–75
2. Kosko, B.: Fuzzy Engineering. Prentice Hall, New York (1997)
3. Parsopoulos, K.E., Papageorgiou, E.I., Groumpos, P.P., Vrahatis, M.N.: A first study of fuzzy cognitive maps learning using particle swarm optimization. In: Proc. IEEE 2003 Cong. Evol. Comput., (2003) 1440–1447
4. Parsopoulos, K.E., Vrahatis, M.N.: Recent approaches to global optimization problems through particle swarm optimization. Natural Computing **1** (2002) 235–306
5. Kennedy, J., Eberhart, R.C.: Swarm Intelligence. Morgan Kaufmann (2001)
6. Clerc, M., Kennedy, J.: The particle swarm–explosion, stability, and convergence in a multidimensional complex space. IEEE Trans. Evol. Comput. **6** (2002) 58–73
7. Stylios, C.D., Georgopoulos, V., Groumpos, P.P.: Fuzzy cognitive map approach to process control systems. J. Adv. Comp. Intell. **3** (1999) 409–417
8. Aguilar, J.: Adaptive random fuzzy cognitive maps. Lecture Notes in Computer Science., Vol. 2527, Springer (2002) 402–410
9. Papageorgiou, E.I., Stylios, C.D., Groumpos, P.P.: Active hebbian learning algorithm to train FCMs. Int. J. Approx. Reas. (2004) accepted for publication.

Application of the General Gaussian Membership Function for the Fuzzy Model Parameters Tunning*

Andrzej Pieczyński and Andrzej Obuchowicz

Institute of Control and Computation Engineering, University of Zielona Góra,
Podgórna 50 Str., 65-246 Zielona Góra, Poland
{A.Pieczynski, A.Obuchowicz}@issi.uz.zgora.pl
http://www.issi.uz.zgora.pl

Abstract. A system input-output response is modeled using a knowledge-based method of signal processing known as neuro-fuzzy logic. The paper presents a new method of the fuzzy model parameters tunning. Fuzzy model tuning procedures based on an evolutionary algorithm are also given. As an example, the analysis of the membership function kind is carried out for the fuzzy modeling of parameters, which are necessary to describe the state of a pressure vessel with water-steam mixture during accidental depressurizations.

1 Introduction

Fuzzy logic as a modern method of signal processing can be used not only for control purposes but also for the modeling of non-linear processes [3]. Using a data base and a knowledge base, fuzzy logic makes it possible to obtain a rule-based description of the system input-output response. The advantage of this solution, in contrast to the application of neural networks, is a low number of data sets which are necessary for the reproduction of non-linear process behavior [9].

The fuzzy neural network (FNN) is an approach combining two artificial intelligence techniques. The fuzzy knowledge representation facilitates the use of unprecise and uncertainty knowledge. The neural network represents a learnable, parallel and distributed platform for the implementation of different fuzzy models [11]. There are various types of FNNs described in the literature [1]. The best known are the Mamdani-type and the Takagi-Sugeno-Kanga (TSK) type FNNs [11]. The Mamdani fuzzy reasoning implementation using a layered feed-forward neural network has been first developed by Lin and Lee [5]. Jang [4] has introduced TSK fuzzy reasoning implementation, known as the ANFIS model based on a layered neural network.

Most of FNNs can be trained using the well-known learning algorithms used in a conventional neural network, e.g., competitive learning, least square estimation (LSE), backpropagation error and evolutionary algorithms. The learning

* This work was supported by the EU FP5 project DAMADICS and in part by the State Committee for Scientific Research in Poland (KBN)

L. Rutkowski et al. (Eds.): ICAISC 2004, LNAI 3070, pp. 350–355, 2004.
© Springer-Verlag Berlin Heidelberg 2004

process consists of two phases. The first one, structural, concerns several degrees of freedom such as: the number of fuzzy sets, the kind of membership function and the kinds of the aggregation and implication operators. The other one, parametric, includes very important parameters describing the shapes and distribution of the membership functions [10].

1.1 Motivation of the New Approach

Industrial processes are often described by families of nonlinear characteristics. For the reproduction of the input-output behavior, different of fuzzy model structures can be used [9]. The input fuzzification process may be perform by the different kind of the membership function shape. In most cases the triangular, Gaussian or trapezoidal function are used [8]. The selecting task of the membership function often is made by expert or after a few experiments. There are the method based on a trial-and-error approach.

For this task authors have proposed apply the general Gaussian function as a membership function and the evolutionary algorithm for the others fuzzy model parameters tuning.

The paper is organized as follows. In Section 2, the general Gaussian function will be reviewed. The fuzzy model structure and the tuning algorithm is described in Section 3. The applied industrial example is discussed in Section 4. Based on an industrial example, the influence of characteristic Gaussian function factor β on fuzzy modeling quality are described in Section 5. In this section simulation results are shown, too. Section 6 concludes the paper, and contains a comparison of the modeling quality for different value of the factor β.

2 The General Gaussian Function

The general Gaussian function is described as following:

$$\mu_F(x) = \exp\left(-\left(\frac{x-b}{a}\right)^{\beta}\right) \tag{1}$$

where: b is a modal value, a is a range factor and β is a characteristic factor.

The factor β is used to change of the Gaussian function shape (Fig.1). For $\beta = 2$ is obtained the classical shape of Gaussian function. The closely triangular or trapezoidal shapes are obtained for suitable factors $\beta_1 = 0.5$ or $\beta_2 = 5$.

3 The Fuzzy Model Structure and Tuning Procedures

The apply fuzzy model is constructed on Mamdani structure. Input signal (*pressure*) preliminary is fuzzified using 14 fuzzy sets [9] and symmetric distribution. Fuzzy sets are represented by general Gauss functions. The singleton functions are used as output membership functions. The defuzzification process is made by means of the COA method.

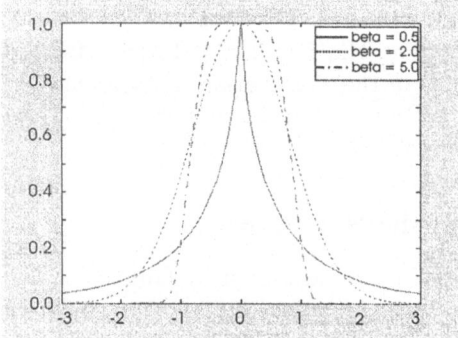

Fig. 1. Influence of β factor on general Gaussian function shape

Many approaches to the tuning of the majority fuzzy model parameters are based on expert knowledge, gradient methods [10] and evolutionary algorithm. Authors propose using evolutionary algorithm to allocate fuzzy model parameters.

The proposed approach is based on the evolutionary search with soft selection algorithm [2,7]. This is probably the simplest selection-mutation model of Darwinian evolution. The n-dimensional real space is the search process domain. At the beginning, the population of points is selected from the domain, and next it is iteratively transformed by selection and mutation operations. As a selection operator the well-known proportional selection (roulette method) is chosen. The coordinates of selected parents are mutated by adding normally-distributed random values. In the proposed approach, an individual $x \in \mathbb{R}^{56}$ contains information of 28 fuzzy sets (14 for input and 14 for output) described by two parameters a and b (1). The population consist of 30 individuals, the standard deviation of normally-distributed mutation decreases according to the plan shown in Table 1.

Table 1. The changing plane of the mutation range factor

Amount of iteration	1000	1000	1000	1000	1000	1000
Mutation range factor	0.2	0.1	0.05	0.025	0.01	0.005

4   The Process Example Description

The presented example describes strong nonlinear thermodynamic and thermohydraulic effects within a pressure vessel during accidental depressurizations [9]. The thermohydraulic and thermodynamic processes in pressure vessels with water-steam mixture are characterized by nonlinearities.

The global aim is the calculation of the collapsed level hc (representing the water inventory) within the defined zones of the pressure vessel during negative pressure gradients $(dp/dt < 0)$ which occur as a result of leaks [9]. To solve this task, a hybrid observer that combines a classical linear observer with a fuzzy-based adaptation of observer model matrices A and B was proposed [9].

For the process analysis, a number of blow down experiments have been carried out which are characterized by different values of the initial pressure p_0 and the initial collapsed level hc_0 at the beginning of depressurization (Fig.2).

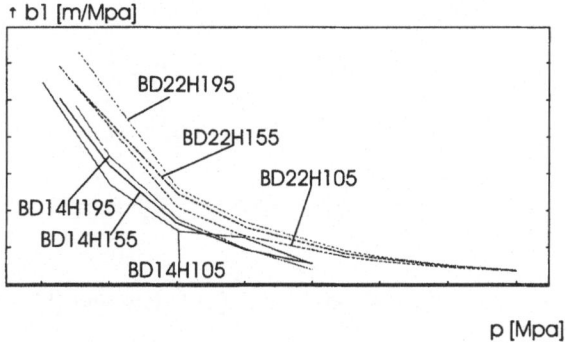

Fig. 2. Dependence of the input matrix element $b1$ on the actual pressure $p(t)$ for blow down (BD) experiments with the initial pressures $p_0 = 14$ bar, $p_0 = 22$ bar and the initial collapsed levels $hc_0 = 105; 155; 195$ cm

5   Experiments and Simulation Results

The experiments schedule consist of two phases. In the first phase, the value of factor β is defined. The other phase comprises the learning process of the remaining parameters of the fuzzy model. Let $\beta = 0.5$ is used in the first experiment. The fuzzification of the input signal before and after tuning procedure is shown in figure 3. Applied tuning procedure is based on evolutionary algorithm (see section 3). After the tuning procedure the fuzzy model is obtained, which represents a reference nonlinear characteristics (Fig.2) with satisfactory accuracy $(SSE = 4.46)$. The tuning procedure at $\beta = 0.5$ improves a convergence of learning task (see Fig.5a). In figure 4, fuzzification of input signal before and after completing of the tuning procedure at $\beta = 5$ is shown. The results of similar experiments at $\beta = 5$, shown in figure 5b, are worse, $(SEE = 5.12)$. The results of others experiments with different values of β are given in Table 2.

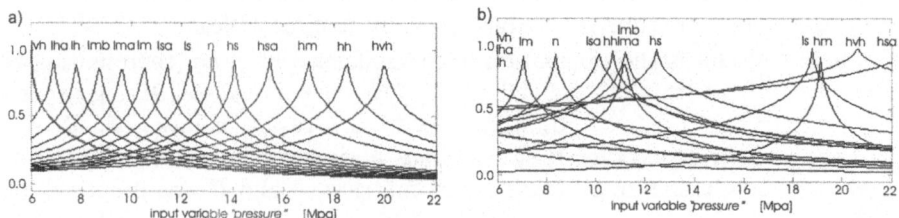

Fig. 3. Fuzzification of input signal pressure p: (a) before and (b) after tuning procedures at $\beta = 0.5$

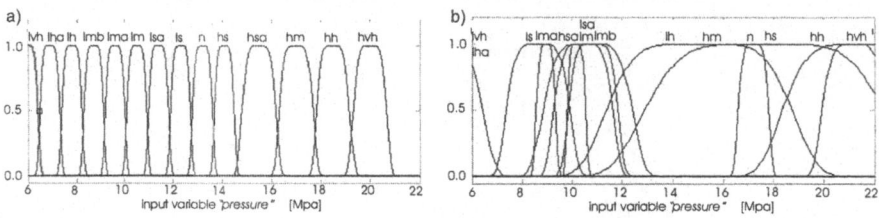

Fig. 4. Fuzzification of input signal pressure p: (a) before and (b) after tuning procedures at $\beta = 5$

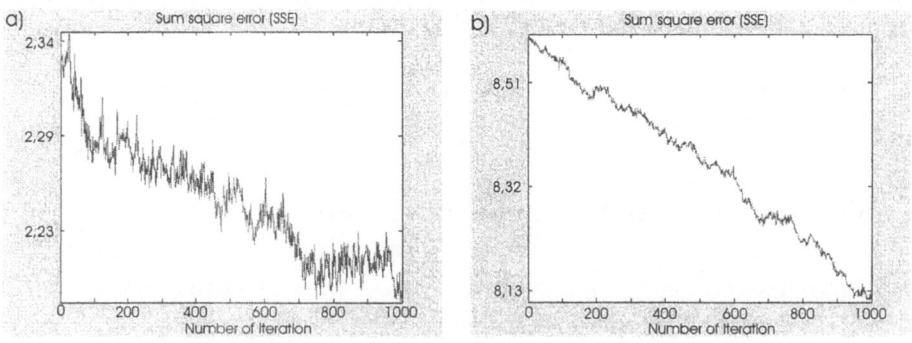

Fig. 5. Passes of the modeling error for: (a) $\beta = 0.5$, (b) $\beta = 5$

Table 2. Results of accuracy of fuzzy model for different value of factor β

Value of β	0.5	0.9	1.3	1.7	2.1	2.5	3.1	5.0
SSE	4.46	4.01	2.96	2.81	2.81	2.76	6.40	5.12

6 Conclusion

The better fuzzy model for a chosen benchmark example, have been obtained at $\beta = 2.5$ (see Table 2).

The main conclusion is that the factor β strongly influences the fuzzy model accuracy. The application of general Gaussian membership functions to neuro-fuzzy modeling process seems to be very attractive approach. A problem of the membership function selection reduces to problem of β allocation. The automatic procedure of β selection focuses our interest in the future research.

References

1. Chung F.L. and Duan J.C.: On Multistage Fuzzy Neural Network Modeling. IEEE Trans. on Fuzzy Systems. Vol 8, No 2, April 2000, pp. 125-142.
2. Galar R.: Evolutionary search with soft selection. Biological Cybernetics, Vol. 60, 1989, pp 357-364.
3. Georgescu C., Afshari A., Bornard G.: A comparison between fuzzy logic neural networks and conventional approaches to system modeling and identification. EU-FIT'93 Proc. First European Congress on Fuzzy Intelligent Technologies, Aachen, Sep. 7-10, 1993, pp. 1632-1640.
4. Jang J.S.: ANFIS: Adaptive network based fuzzy inference system. IEEE Trans. Sys. Man. Cybern., Vol. 23, May/June 1993, pp 665-684.
5. Lin C.T. and Lee C.S.G.: Neural network based fuzzy logic control and decision system. IEEE Trans. Comput., Vol. 40, Dec. 1991, pp 1320-1336.
6. Lęski J.: Improving the generalization ability of neuro-fuzzy systems by ε-intensitive learning. Int. Journal of Applied Mathematics and Computer Science, University of Zielona Góra Press, 2002, Vol. 12, No. 3, pp. 437-447.
7. Obuchowicz A.: Evolutionary Algorithms for Global Optimization and Dynamic System Diagnosis. Lubusky Scientific Society Press, Zielona Gra, 2003.
8. Pieczyński A.: Fuzzy modeling of multidimensional non-linear process – influence of membership function shape. Proc. 8th East West Zittau Fuzzy Colloquium, Zittau, Germany, Sept. 6-8, 2000,pp. 125-133.
9. Pieczyński A. and Kästner W.: Fuzzy modeling of multidimensional non-linear process – design and analysis of structures. In: Hampel R., Wagenknecht M. and Chaker N. (Eds.): Advances in Soft Computing – Fuzzy Control, Theory and Practice – Heidelberg New York: Physica – Verlag, 2000, pp. 376-386.
10. Pieczyński A.: Fuzzy modeling of multidimensional nonlinear processes – tuning procedures. Proc. 8th IEEE Int. Conf., Methods and Models in Automation and Robotics, MMAR 2002, Szczecin, Poland, Sept. 2002, Vol. 1, pp. 667-672.
11. Rutkowska D.: Intelligent Computation Systems. Akademicka Oficyna Wydawnicza, Warszawa, 1997 (in Polish)

Are Linguistic Evaluations Used by People of Possibilistic or Probabilistic Nature?

Andrzej Piegat

Faculty of Computer Science and Information Systems
Technical University of Szczecin
Faculty of Economic Sciences and Management
University of Szczecin
Andrzej.Piegat@wi.ps.pl

Abstract. Defining linguistic fuzzy evaluations of various quantities e.g. very *small, average, approximately 5, a little more than 10*, we usually assume that membership functions qualifying for these evaluations are of possibilistic character. The paper presents a comparison of a measurement realization by a technical instrument and of evaluation by man (uncertainty of the measurement realized by technical instrument is mainly of probabilistic character) to determine their common features. Next, the question is analyzed: what is the character of human evaluations. It is of great importance for the way in which operations of fuzzy arithmetic have to be realized and for *Computing with Words*.

1   Introduction

The idea of *Computing with Words* has been popularized from years by Professor Zadeh [6]. It is a fascinating idea because it enables constructing computers programmable with words which would understand human language and would process information in the way similar as people do. Unfortunately *Computing with Words* develops rather slowly. The probable reason is that it bases on possibilistic fuzzy arithmetic in which linguistic fuzzy evaluations as e.g. *large, about 7* are supposed to be of possibilistic character. The possibilistic character of a membership function $\mu_F(x)$ of element x of universe X was suggested in [5] where Profesor Zadeh placed the following statement: "... *the possibility distribution function associated with X ... is denoted by π_X and is defined to be numerically equal to the membership function of F, i.e. $\pi_X = \mu_F$*". Since that time membership functions have been treated in literature on Fuzzy Set Theory as possibility distributions and operations of fuzzy arithmetic are only realized in the possibilistic way based on extension principle of Zadeh. This realization way of arithmetic operations leads to a very great fuzziness of results of fuzzy arithmetic making it in many cases completely uselessness for solution of practical tasks, e.g. tasks from area of *Computing with Words*. Also certain paradoxes occur in fuzzy calculations. One of them is described in [2]. Therefore some scientists try to formulate new methods of fuzzy arithmetic or to revise it.

One can give following questions concerning fuzzy arithmetic:

L. Rutkowski et al. (Eds.): ICAISC 2004, LNAI 3070, pp. 356–363, 2004.
© Springer-Verlag Berlin Heidelberg 2004

What is the character of membership functions ? Are they always of possibilistic character or can they also be e.g. of probabilistic or of deterministic character?, If certain membership functions are non-possibilistic ones then how should operations of fuzzy arithmetic be realized?.

All the above questions require an explanation. In this paper, in Chapter 2 one of the above questions will be analyzed.

2　Comparison of Measurements Realized by Technical Instruments and Evaluations Made by People

It seems that in many cases there exists a great similarity of the measurement way of physical quantities realized by measuring instruments and of the way in which people make linguistic evaluations of these quantities. To examine this problem let us consider the measurement and the evaluation of height in Example 1.

Example 1

Let us assume the measuring instrument has an indicator that indicates height of the measured object with dispersion of 0.1 cm. It can indicate only such heights as e.g. 169.9, 170.0, 170.1 etc. We have 7 lots of height standards consisting of 100 standard per lot (together 700 standards) of height 169.7, 169.8, 169.9, 170.0, 170.1, 170.2, 170.3 cm correspondingly. All standards have been mixed randomly so that successive measured standards would possibly be of different height and we measure their heights with the aid of the possessed instrument. Our aim is to determine the number of standards from each lot for which the instrument will indicate the height 170.0 cm. Table 1 shows exemplary results of these measurements.

In the case of the lot of 100 standards of the real height 170.0 cm, the measuring instrument indicated for 34 standards the correct height 170.0 cm and for remaining 66 standards other heights as e.g.: 169.9 cm, 170.1 cm and so on. Reason of this fact was its inaccuracy that is an inherent feature of each measuring instrument. This inaccuracy is mainly of probabilistic character [3,4] and it can be caused by e.g. changes of electric supply parameters, moisture, temperature etc. If the number of indications of 170.0 cm for each height lot is divided by the total number of standards in the lot (100) then the probability is achieved

Table 1. Results of measurements of 700 standards – 7 lots, 100 standards of equal height in each lot

Real height h_r [cm] of the standard	169.7	169.8	169.9	170.0	170.1	170.2	170.3
Number of standards from the lot of 100 standards for which the measuring instrument indicated h_{mi} = 170.0 [cm]	0	7	26	34	26	7	0

that a standard of the real height h_r [cm] can be recognized by the measuring instrument as a standard of the 170.0 cm-height, or with other words that the standard can be qualified for this height. Fig. 1 graphically presents measurement results from Table 1 in form of dispersion of the qualification probability for the 170.0 cm-height.

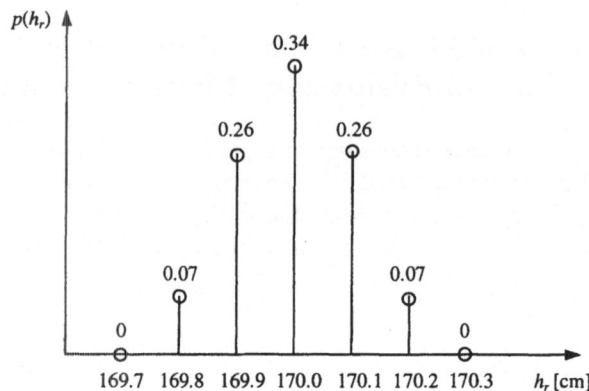

Fig. 1. Dispersion of probability that the measuring instrument will qualify the standard of the real height h_r [cm] as the height 170.0 cm

The probability function from Fig. 1 can be called *about 170.0 cm*, because the indication $h_{mi} = 170.0$ cm does not mean that the measured standard really has this height. The probability dispersion function informs us which other heights can the standard be of and how high are probabilities of particular heights h_r [cm]. This function can be called *qualification function* because it informs us about the qualifying probability of a measured height for the indication 170.0 cm of the measuring instrument. Similar qualifying functions can experimentally be identified for other indications of the instrument as e.g.: 169.9 cm, 170.1 cm, and so on (Fig. 2).

It should be noticed that qualification functions from Fig. 2 fulfill condition of the unity partition ($\sum \mu_i(h_r) = 1$). The functions from Fig. 2 can be normalized to interval $[0, 1]$. Then they will represent **relative probability** $rp(h_r)$ of qualifying the standard of the h_r [cm]-height for particular indications h_{mi} [cm] of a measuring instrument and they will become **membership functions** of the corresponding indication sets *about 169.9 cm*, *about 170.0 cm*, etc, Fig. 3.

Let us now analyze an example of the visual height evaluation by man.

Example 2

Let us assume that Mr. John Stachursky visually can recognize people of height *about 160 cm*, *about 170 cm*, *about 180 cm*, etc. He calls the particular heights *short-*, *medium-*, *tall-height*, etc. We want to identify the real (not the declarative) membership function to the height about 170 cm (*medium* height) used

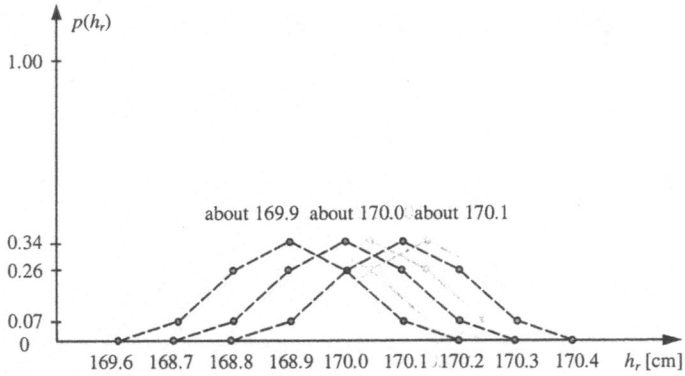

Fig. 2. Dispersions $p(h_r)$ of probability that the real height h_r [cm] will be qualified (recognized by the measuring instrument) as the height 169.9 cm, 170.0 cm, or 170.1 cm (qualifying functions)

by Stachursky. To this aim we organize 7 groups (with 100 persons a group) of height 160 cm, 163 cm, 167 cm, 170 cm, 173 cm, 177 cm, 180 cm. Persons from all groups are mixed randomly and presented to John Stachursky, who qualifies each person for the *short* or *medium* or *tall* height without knowing his/her numerical height. Results of the qualification to the *medium* height are shown in Table 2.

Table 2. Results of qualification of persons of various heights for the *medium* (*about 170 cm*) height

Real height h_r [cm] of the person	160	163	167	170	173	177	180
Number of persons from particular height groups qualified for medium height (about 170 cm)	0	20	80	100	80	20	0

Because particular persons had various body proportions, corpulence, head-dress, clothes, etc, not all persons of the height e.g. 167 cm (close to 170 cm) were recognized and qualified by Stachursky for the *medium* height (*about 170 cm*). A part of them were qualified for the *short* height. However, all persons of the height 170 cm were qualified by him for the *medium* height, although the qualification can have been not so ideal (a part of persons from the 170 cm-group with very slim body, who make impression of high persons can have been qualified for the class of *tall* persons). If the number of persons from each height-group, which were qualified for the *medium* height is divided by 100 (number of all

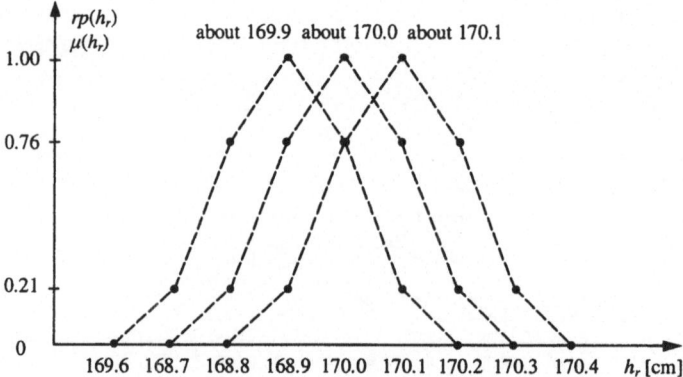

Fig. 3. Dispersions of relative probability that the real height h_r [cm] will be qualified as the height 169.9 cm, 170.0 cm, or 170.1 cm, which are numerically equal to membership functions $\mu(h_r)$ of the corresponding indication sets

persons in each group) the probability $p_m(h_r)$ of qualifying the given numerical height h_r [cm] for the *medium* height is achieved, Fig. 4.

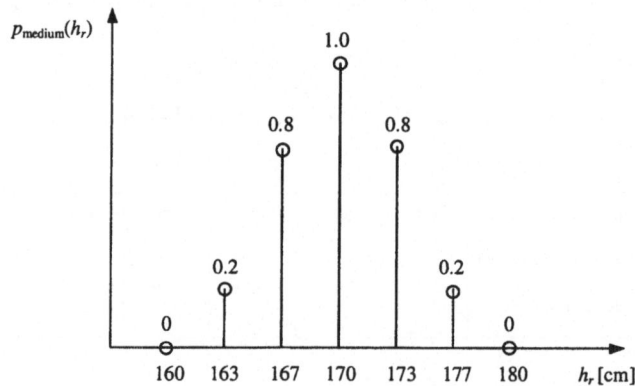

Fig. 4. Probability distribution $p_m(h_r)$ that person of h_r [cm] – height will be qualified for the *medium* height (*about 170 cm*)

In Fig. 5 functions qualifying the height h_r [cm] for particular classes *short, medium, tall* height are shown.

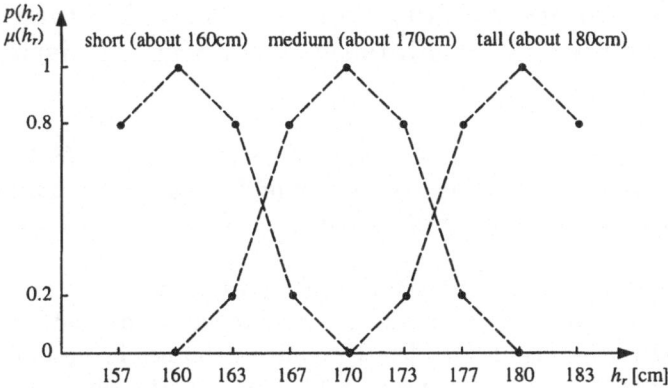

Fig. 5. Distributions $p(h_r)$ of qualification probability of persons of the h_r [cm] – height for the classes *short*, *medium*, and *tall* height, which are numerically equal to membership functions $\mu(h_r)$ of the particular indication sets (classes)

3   Conclusions from Comparison of the Measurement Way Realized by Technical Instrument and of the Evaluation Realized by People

1. Both the measurement of a quantity realized by technical instruments and the evaluation of the quantity realized by man consists in qualification of the measured real value x_r of the quantity for the fuzzy set *about x_{mi}*, where x_{mi} is the value assigned by measuring instrument or by man to the given real value x_r. E.g. the height 170.1 cm can be indicated by the instrument as 170.0 cm and by man as *medium* height.
2. Both technical instruments and people qualify real values x_r of measured quantities for their possible indications x_m according to probability distributions $p_{xm}(x_r)$, which after normalization become membership functions $\mu_{xm}(h_r)$ for possible indications of the measuring instrument or of the person.
3. The number of possible indications of a measuring instrument usually is much higher that that of man. E.g. the instrument can indicate height every 0.1 cm (169.9 cm, 170.0 cm, 170.1 cm, etc) and man visually can measure the height with considerably lower resolution e.g. *short (about 160 cm)*, *medium (about 170 cm)*, and *tall (about 180 cm)* etc.

Recapitulating the conclusions 1, 2, 3 one can state that the difference between measurements realized by technical instrument and by man often is only quantitative and not qualitative one. Therefore **human evaluations frequently can be treated as measurements.**

4   Are Membership Functions of Fuzzy Linguistic Evaluations of Possibilistic or of Probabilistic Character?

As Example 1 and Example 2 have shown the membership $\mu_A(x_r)$ of the measured value x_r to fuzzy set A has character of probability or of relative probability that the value x_r will be qualified for the set A. What practical consequence has this fact?

Let us assume that John Stachursky, who uses the membership function from Fig. 6a for qualification of persons for the *medium* height has only visually (without knowing the precise height [cm]) evaluated the height of a certain person as *medium* one. Then, if the membership grade to the set is of probabilistic character **can we on the basis of the membership function answer the question what is the probable height of the man?** It is the inverse task to the task of qualifying the precise numerical height [cm] for linguistic evaluations. It is the task to determine the numerical height on the basis of its linguistic evaluation under **assumption** that **this evaluation is our only information** we have at disposal to solve the problem (a very important assumption!).

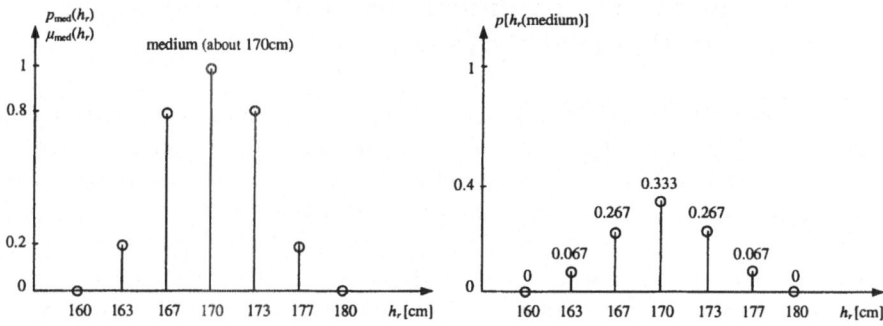

Fig. 6. (a) – Membership function $\mu_{\text{medium}}(h_r)$ and simultaneously probability $p_{\text{medium}}(h_r)$ that a man of height h_r [cm] will be qualified for the *medium* height class, (b) – probability distribution $p[h_r(medium)]$ that a man qualified for the *medium* height has numerical height h_r [cm].

Determination of the dispersion function $p[h_r(medium)]$ of the probable height of the man can be achieved on the basis of the reasoning presented in the sequel.

On the basis of the membership function from Fig. 6a one can state that probability of qualifying a person of the 170 cm-height for the *medium* height equals 1 and is 5 times higher than the probability 0.2 of qualifying a person of the 163 cm-height (and of 177 cm-height) and is 1.25 times higher than that of persons of 167 cm- and 173 cm-height. The same relation must exist between probabilities $p[h_r(medium)]$ that the corresponding person, which was classified as *medium* one has the numerical height h_r [cm]. Hence the probability $p[h_r(medium)]$ can be calculated from formula (1) resulting from the condition that the sum of all probabilities must be equal to 1.

$$p[h_r(medium)] = \frac{p_{med}h_r}{\sum\limits_i p_{med}h_r} \tag{1}$$

where: i – number of a possible numerical, discrete height-value (in the considered example $i = 1, 2, \ldots, 7$). Calculation results of the probability $p[h_r(medium)]$ for particular heights are shown in Fig. 6b.

5   Conclusions

Uncertainty of human linguistic evaluations is in many cases of probabilistic character. It is of great importance for fuzzy arithmetic because it means that arithmetic operations on fuzzy numbers should be realized in a different way for possibilistic and for probabilistic membership functions. If a membership function is possibilistic one then the possibilistic extension principle [1] should be used. If a membership function is probabilistic one then the probabilistic extension principle [2] should be used or the problem should be solved in the framework of probability theory. This subject matter will be analyzed in next publications of the author.

References

1. Klir G.L.: Fuzzy arithmetic with requisite constraints. Fuzzy Sets and Systems **91**, pp. 165–175 (1997)
2. Piegat A.: Informative value of the possibilistic extension principle. Proceedings of 10th International Conference Advanced Computer Systems ACS'2003, Międzyzdroje, Poland (2003)
3. Sowiński A.: Digital measurement technics. Publishing House of Communication, Warsaw (In Polish) (1975)
4. Sydenham P.H.(Ed): Handbook of measurement science. Theoretical fundamentals. A Wiley-Interscience Publication (1982)
5. Zadeh L.A.: Fuzzy sets as a basis for a theory of possibility. Fuzzy Sets and Systems **1**, vol. 3, pp. 165–175 (1978)
6. Zadeh L.A.: From computing with numbers to computing with words – From manipulation of measurements to manipulation of perceptions. Applied mathematics and computer science, vol. **12**, No. 3, pp. 307–324 (2002)

Fuzzy Linear Programming in Ship Trajectory Optimization in a Restricted Area

Zbigniew Pietrzykowski

Szczecin Maritime University, ul. Waly Chrobrego 1-2, 70-500 Szczecin
zbip@wsm.szczecin.pl

Abstract. The problem of determining a safe trajectory of a ship moving in a restricted area is presented. Goals and constraints are formulated for the optimal trajectory of ship movement in a fairway. The problem is presented as an optimization problem in a fuzzy environment. To solve it, the method of fuzzy linear programming is proposed. The results for a ship passing manoeuvre are given and conclusions are drawn.

1 Introduction

Equipment and systems of ship control are constantly improved in order to enhance navigational safety and prevent accidents. Much attention is put on decision support systems used in sea-going vessel movement control. They are supposed to identify dangerous situations and work out manoeuvres for accident prevention. These systems enable further automation of ship control processes. Solutions determined by the systems should take into consideration relevant regulations in force, assure safe manoeuvres and be rational. This means, inter alia, the application of criteria used and accepted by the human being. This refers to both open and restricted areas. New information technologies and methods and tools of artificial intelligence allow to utilize the knowledge of navigator experts for overcoming dangerous situations and working out decisions appropriate for the current navigational conditions.

2 A Restricted Area

A restricted area is an area of waters in which the wave system generated by a ship moving full ahead is disturbed. The area can be restricted due to insufficient depth or width.

The navigator's task while handling a ship is to avoid dangerous situations. Such situations are, among others, ship encounter situations (passing, overtaking, crossing, following another ship, passing a ship moored or anchored. Besides, there are hydrographic dangers (shape of the area, different shapes of seabed, engineering structures, wrecks, etc.). The navigator aims at safe passing of a ship or another object at the same satisfying the constraints due to regulations in force, specific character of the area and present traffic situation. For instance, a manoeuvre of two ships passing each other (meeting on opposite courses) in a fairway requires the target ship to be passed in a safe distance (goal),

L. Rutkowski et al. (Eds.): ICAISC 2004, LNAI 3070, pp. 364–369, 2004.
© Springer-Verlag Berlin Heidelberg 2004

while maintaining a safe distance to the starboard side of the fairway limit (constraint) (Fig. 1). Similarly, an overtaking manoeuvre requires safe distances to be maintained between the ships as well as to the fairway limit. Consequently, the navigators on the ships involved have to coordinate their manoeuvres.

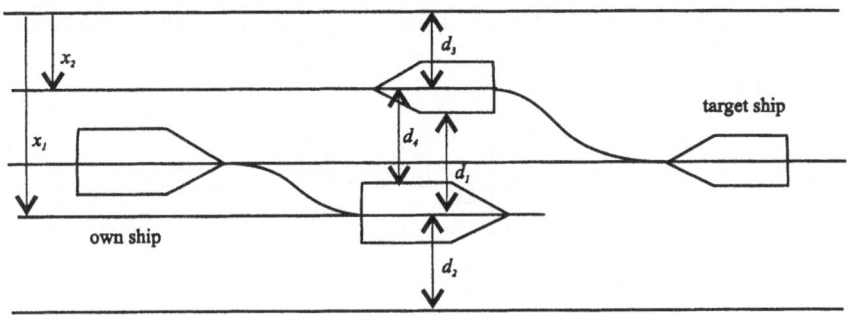

Fig. 1. A manoeuvre of ship's passing (meeting on opposite courses

For the manoeuvre of passing a ship moored at the fairway, the goal also consists in maintaining a safe distance to that ship such as not to cause damage, e.g. breaking the mooring lines, or damage to a moored ship or its cargo due to generated waves. At the same time a safe distance to the opposite side of the fairway limit has to be kept. This also refers to other manoeuvres: overtaking, crossing other ship's course, or passing a hydrographic danger.

In each of the above cases goals and constraints can be considered in terms of fuzziness. That is why ship movement trajectory optimization can be presented as an optimization task in a fuzzy environment.

In the case of fuzzy goals and fuzzy constraints described by membership functions which at sections are linear, the problem can be formulated as a fuzzy linear programming problem and one can apply the method proposed by Zimmermann, [1], [4], [5].

3   Zimmermann's Model

Zimmermann's model is defined as follows:

$$
\begin{aligned}
c^T x &\overset{\sim}{\leq} z \\
A &\overset{\sim}{\leq} b \\
x &\geq 0
\end{aligned}
\tag{1}
$$

where:

$x \in R$ – vector of variables,

$c \in R$ – vector of the objective function,

z − a level of aspiration of the objective function chosen by the
             decision maker,
$A \in R$ − constraint coefficient matrix,
$b \in R$ − vector of constraint right-hand sides.

This means that the value of the objective function should be, if possible, smaller than the chosen level of aspiration z of the objective function. Constraints, too, should be possibly well satisfied.

Denoting:

$$B = \begin{bmatrix} c \\ A \end{bmatrix} \text{ and } d = \begin{bmatrix} z \\ b \end{bmatrix} \tag{2}$$

the problem has this form:

$$\begin{bmatrix} Bx \widetilde{\leq} d \\ x \geq 0 \end{bmatrix} \tag{3}$$

The membership function is introduced in this form:

$$\mu_i(x) = \left\{ \begin{array}{ll} 1 & for\ (Bx)_i \leq d_i \\ 1 - \frac{(Bx)_i - d_i}{p_i} & for\ d_i \leq (Bx)_i \leq d_i + p_i \\ 0 & for\ (Bx)_i > d_i + p_i \end{array} \right\} \tag{4}$$

where $i = 1, ..., m + 1$.

The interpretation of the fuzzy constraint is as follows: the satisfaction of the constraint (d_i) is complete; the constraint may not be satisfied to some extent $(d_i + p_i)$; going beyond the constraint is unacceptable $(d_i + p_i)$.

It is assumed that a fuzzy decision is a conjunction (operator of the minimum type) of fuzzy constraints:

$$\mu_D(x) = \min_{x \in R^n} \left(\mu_1(x), \mu_2(x), ..., \mu_{m+1}(x) \right) \tag{5}$$

and an optimal decision is defined as:

$$\mu_D(x^*) = \max_{x \geq 0} \left(\min_{x \in R^n} \left(\mu_1(x), \mu_2(x), ..., \mu_{m+1}(x) \right) \right) \tag{6}$$

By introducing a new variable l the optimization problem (3) can be rewritten in a non-fuzzy, i.e. crisp form:

$$\begin{array}{l} \max \lambda \\ d_i \leq (Bx)_i \leq d_i + (1 - \lambda) p_i\ i = 1, ..., m + 1 \\ x \geq 0 \\ \lambda \in [0, 1] \end{array} \tag{7}$$

The solution to the problem (7) is a vector (λ^*, x^*) such that

$$
\begin{aligned}
&\lambda^* = \max_{\lambda \in [0,1]} \lambda \\
&\lambda p_i + (Bx)_i \leq d_i + p_i \ i = 1, ..., m+1 \\
&x \geq 0
\end{aligned}
\tag{8}
$$

The vector x^* is at the same time an optimal solution to the task (6).

4   Optimization of a Safe Trajectory of Ship Movement

A ship passing manoeuvre has been considered. Two cases are possible here:

1. Own ship's safe trajectory is to be determined for a preset distance of the target ship to the port fairway limit at the moment of passing
2. Safe trajectories for both ships have to be determined.

The safe distance (d_1) of passing an object (target ship) was assumed as a goal (compare Fig 1.). The constraints, were, respectively: for case 1– safe distance of own ship to starboard limit of the fairway (d_2), for case 2 – additionally, safe distance of target ship from the port fairway limit (d_3) and safe passing distance between own and target ships (d_4).

The optimization problem consists in the determination of distance:

case 1 – safe trajectory of own ship from the port fairway limit (x_1),

case 2 – safe trajectories of both ships from the port fairway limit (x_1, x_2).

The case 2 was considered. Zimmerman's model was used for the determination of safe trajectories of both passing ships. It was assumed that safe distances for port and starboard sides of own ship are described by membership functions μ_{OP} and μ_{OS} , while those of the target ship by functions μ_{TP} and μ_{TS} and that they are linear at some sections (compare (4)). The goal and constraints have this form then:

$$
\begin{aligned}
&x_1 \leq d_w - d_{\min \ OS} - \lambda \left(d_{\max \ OS} - d_{\min \ OS}\right) \\
&x_2 - x_1 - \tfrac{1}{2}s_T \geq d_{\min \ OP} - \lambda \left(d_{\max \ OP} - d_{\min \ OP}\right) \\
&x_2 \geq d_{\min \ TS} + \lambda \left(d_{\max \ TS} - d_{\min \ TS}\right) \\
&x_2 - x_1 - \tfrac{1}{2}s_O \geq d_{\min \ TP} + \lambda \left(d_{\max \ TP} - d_{\min \ TP}\right)
\end{aligned}
\tag{9}
$$

where:

$d_{\min \ OP}, d_{\max \ OP}$ -   minimum and maximum values of passing distance for the port side of own ship,

$d_{\min \ OS}, d_{\max \ OS}$ -   minimum and maximum values of passing distance for the starboard side of own ship,

$d_{\min \ TP}, d_{\max \ TP}$ -   minimum and maximum values of passing distance for the port side of target ship,

$d_{\min \ TS}, d_{\max \ TS}$, -   minimum and maximum values of passing distance for the starboard side of target ship,

d_w -   fairway width,

s_O, s_T -   own and target ships breadths.

The above problem can be transformed to this form:

$$\max \lambda$$
$$\lambda \left(d_{\max\ OS} - d_{\min\ OS}\right) + x_1 \leq d_w - d_{\min\ OS}$$
$$\lambda \left(d_{\max\ OP} - d_{\min\ OP}\right) - x_1 + x_2 \leq -d_{\min\ OP} - \tfrac{1}{2}s_T$$
$$\lambda \left(d_{\max\ TS} - d_{\min\ TS}\right) - x_2 \leq -d_{\min\ TS} \qquad (10)$$
$$\lambda \left(d_{\max\ TP} - d_{\min\ TP}\right) - x_1 + x_2 \leq -d_{\min\ TP} - \tfrac{1}{2}s_O$$
$$x_1, x_2 \geq 0$$
$$\lambda \in [0, 1]$$

The solution to problem (10) is the vector (λ^*, x^*), which maximizes the passing distance to the target ship, where the vector $x = [x_1, x_2]^T$ represents distances of own and target ships to the port fairway limit.

Thus formulated problem may also refer to other types of ship encounters, the necessity of keeping clear of hydrographic dangers, or situations when more than one object have to be passed. What has to be done here is the determination of membership functions describing fuzzy sets of goals and constraints.

5   Research

Expert research with the participation of navigators was conducted in order to determine membership functions of fuzzy sets of safe distances for various ship encounter situations and situations of passing navigational dangers in a restricted area. The research, which covered a straight section of the fairway, was of two kinds; questionnaires and simulations, both performed by expert navigators. Various ship sizes and fairway widths were taken into consideration. Examples of the membership functions of safe distance for port and starboard side of two different ships (goal and constraints) for an area 200 metres wide are presented in Fig. 2.

The membership functions were approximated by linear section functions. They were used for the determination of a safe trajectory of a ship proceeding along the fairway with the application of Zimmermann's model. The solution to the optimization problem (10) is the vector (λ^*, x^*). The following solution has been obtained:

$\lambda^* = 0,4909$, $x_1^* = 132$ m, $x_2^* = 59$ m,

where x_1 and x_2 represent distances of own and target ships to the port fairway limit.

The process of ship control can be implemented by the navigator or by using systems of trajectory tracking.

The data on parameters of the area and objects being passed are essential in the process of determining a safe trajectory of a ship moving in a restricted area. These data can be obtained with the use of existing VTS systems (Vessel Traffic Service) operated in port approach areas and areas where vessel traffic is heavy. Necessary data can also be obtained with the use of on-board systems

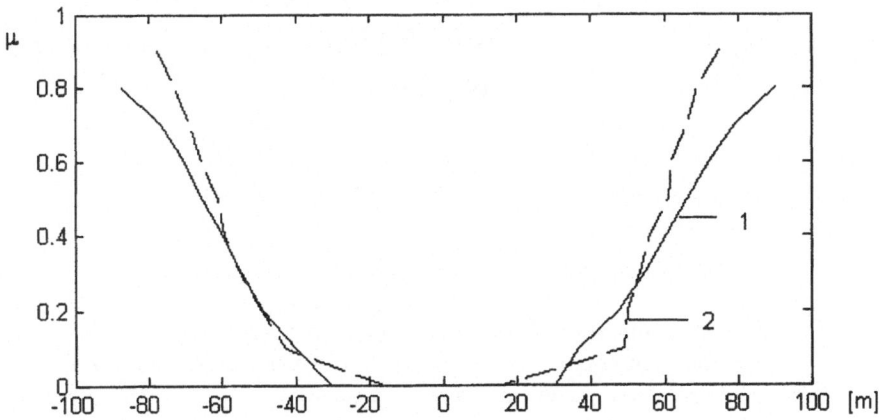

Fig. 2. Membership functions of the fuzzy sets safe distances for port (-) and starboard side (+) of two different ships (goal and constraints): 1) own ship – length 95,5 [m], breadth 18,2 [m]; 2) target ship – length 60,3 [m], breadth 10,5 [m]

ECDIS (Electronic Chart Display and Information System) and AIS (Automatic Identification System).

Notes and conclusions. The presented method for determining a safe trajectory of a ship sailing in a restricted area takes into consideration criteria used and accepted by the human being and ensures performance of safe manoeuvres within such areas. The existing shipboard and shore-based navigational systems make it possible to obtain the data for the determination of a safe trajectory with the use of this method. A major difficulty is to define membership functions describing fuzzy sets of goals and constraints of the optimization problem. One solution to this problem can be knowledge bases created for particular navigational areas. The presented solutions can also find applications in navigator decision support systems used both on board ships and in VTS centres.

References

1. Kacprzyk J., Fuzzy sets in systems analysis, PWN, Warszawa 1986, (in Polish)
2. Pietrzykowski, Z.: Ship fuzzy domain in assessment of navigational safety in restricted areas, III. Navigational Symposium, Gdynia 1999, Vol. I (in Polish)
3. Pietrzykowski Z., The analysis of a ship fuzzy domain in a restricted area, IFAC Conference Computer Applications in Marine Systems CAMS'2001, Elsevier Science Ltd 2001
4. Rommelfanger H., Fuzzy Decision Support Systems, Springer Verlag, Berlin 1994 (in German)
5. Slowinski R., Fuzzy sets in decision analysis, operations research and statistics, Kluwer Academic Publishers, Boston, Dordrecht, London 1998

Application of Fuzzy Weighted Feature Diagrams to Model Variability in Software Families

Silva Robak[1] and Andrzej Pieczyński[2]

[1] Chair of Computer Science and Management,
[2] Institute of Control and Computation Engineering,
University of Zielona Góra,
Podgórna 50 Str., 65-246 Zielona Góra, Poland
A.Pieczynski@issi.uz.zgora.pl, S.Robak@kpim.uz.zgora.pl
http://www.uz.zgora.pl

Abstract. In the paper the employment of fuzzy logic in feature models for software system families is presented. The fuzzy weights of some variable features are introduced. The approach is demonstrated on the example of the feature model describing car properties. The formulas resulting from the description of the feature tree and its constraints can be used as input for an expert system validating possible feature combinations.

1   Introduction

Software program families [7], have to deal with problems of maintaining variability included in software artifacts, which is necessary to support the needs of different users or to enable arrangements to diverse environments and constraints [2]. Possible features of a software product family vary according to the needs of particular market segments and purposes. In the paper describing of software variability with means of feature modeling [4,1] is applied, and enhanced.

Variable features can be annotated with priorities within the implementation scoping, determining which features will be implemented first [1]. The assigned priorities may perhaps change and the usage of fuzzy description of the feature priorities (captured as weights) can be helpful for the updating of feature models for different purposes.

The basic elements of the generative domain model for software families are defined in [1] as: problem space, configuration knowledge and the solution space. The problem space contains the terminology that specifies the family members, i.e. the domain specific concepts and features. The configuration knowledge embraces the default settings and dependencies, possible illegal combinations, optimizations and construction rules. The solution space specifies the elementary components with their possible configuration. The feature models with fuzzy weights of features as presented in the paper can be advisable used within the configuration knowledge of the generative domain model.

L. Rutkowski et al. (Eds.): ICAISC 2004, LNAI 3070, pp. 370–375, 2004.
© Springer-Verlag Berlin Heidelberg 2004

2   Fuzzy Set Theory – Basic Notions

The concept of fuzzy sets as a collection of objects which might belong to it to a certain degree - from full belongingness (1) to full nonbelongingness (0) through all intermediate values was introduced by Zadeh [11]. The *intensity of belongingness* assigning to each element a number from the unit interval was done by the *membership function*.

Suppose that $X = \{x\}$ is a universe of discourse i.e., the set of all possible elements with respect to a fuzzy property. Then *a fuzzy set A* in X is defined as set of ordered pairs $\{x, \mu_A(x)\}$, where $x \in X$ and $\mu_A : X \to [0,1]$ is *a membership function* of A.

The crisp output value of the fuzzy output representation, can be obtained using a defuzzifier. The defuzzifier specifies a point in the universe of discourse of output, which best represents the fuzzy set at the output of the fuzzy system. The well-known defuzzification method COA [10] (Center of area) is used in our system.

Fuzzy logic as a method of signal processing is applied, e.g., to the control and modeling of non-linear processes [10]. In this work it will be used for the description of a system's features. Based on a database and a knowledge base the fuzzy logic will be applied to a rule-based description of the feature diagram and the composition rules for the features.

3   Application of Weighted Features with Partially Fuzzy Representation

The modified version of a simple car description with a feature diagram is depicted in Figure 1. The example is based on the example given in [1], but on Figure 1 the variable features are additionally annotated with weights. In the example of the simple car the mandatory features are: *Car Body, Transmission, Engine Power* and *Engine*. Two possible kinds of *Transmission* (i.e., *Automatic* and *Manual*) are represented as its alternative sub-features; the possible types of *Engine* (i.e., *Fuel, Gasoline*) are represented as the or-features group. The car's options are those features that do not come as standard with a certain model. Two of the car's features in the example are optional (*Pulls Trailer* and *Air Conditioning*).

The weights which are applied to a few variable features: *Air Conditioning, Pulls Trailer, Automatic, Manual, Fuel* and *Gasoline* (see Figure 1) will be considered below in fuzzy representation. The fuzzyfication of the weight allows capturing the importance of the feature according to the specific customer profile. The customers can also denote it in the descriptive way, how important the feature is (*less important, important,* or *very important*). The linguistic values will be then interpreted by the expert system using the values for defuziffication. The values will be interpreted according to the chosen values for the sets represented as *Low, Medium* and *High* (see Figure 2). The adjustment of the sets on the X-axis represents the importance of the described feature. The adjustment in the right direction (towards positive values) results in the higher

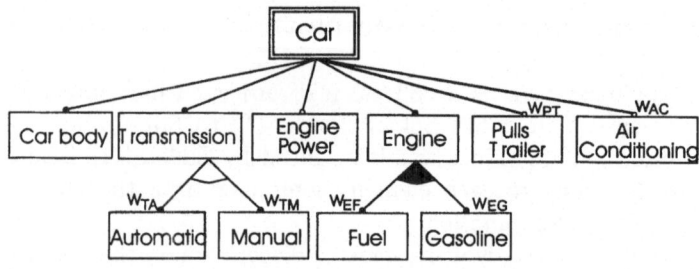

Fig. 1. The feature diagram of a simple car (variable features are annotated with weights)

importance of the feature i.e. the greater weights denoting it. The additional external information in the simple car example is:

- Composition rule "Air Conditioning requires horsepower ≥ 100";
- Rationale: "Manual (transmission) is more fuel efficient".

In the example of a simple car the feature weights may be interpreted as priorities based on choice frequency for a "typical user of a family car". For such a user's profile the features, such as, "leather-wrapped steering wheel" will not be taken into consideration and so are not part of the car's feature diagram.

Fuzzification operation maps a crisp point into a fuzzy set. To design a representation system for fuzzy features, two basic assumptions are to be made. The first is the type of membership functions [5]; the other is the number and kind of distribution of fuzzy sets [6] that are necessary to perform the representation effectively. The selection of membership functions plays an important role in any fuzzy inference system. The triangular, trapezoidal, sigmoidal, generalized bell, and Gaussian membership functions are few examples of membership functions that are frequently used [10]. If we want to apply them in a fuzzy inference system, then we have further to state, how many fuzzy rules and what kind of distribution is necessary to describe the behavior of some car features.

The fuzzy representation of the weights used in our system uses one triangular and two half trapezoidal membership functions, as shown in Figure 2. The remaining features of the car are represented on crisp base. Let:

$$\forall_{w_j \in W} \sum_{i=L}^{H} \mu_i(w_j) = 1 \tag{1}$$

Where: w_j = feature weight with index j; W set of applied features weights; μ = membership function; L,N,H = *Low, Normal, Hight* are linguistic value. The formula (1) defines a condition of the complete fuzzification of the weights w_j.

The associations between the car's features may be described on the basis of the following conditions:

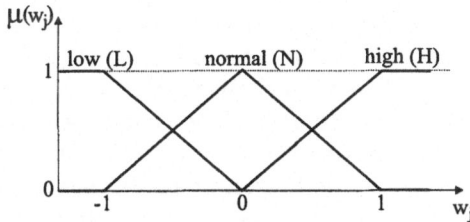

Fig. 2. Membership function used for representation of two optional features of a simple car

Car **requires** *Car body* **and** *Transmission* **and** *Engine* **or** *Pulls Trailer with* $CF = w_{PT}$ **or** *Air Conditioning with* $CF = w_{AC}$;

Transmission **requires** *Manual with* $CF = w_{TM}$ **or** *Automatic with* $CF = w_{TA}$;

Engine **requires** *Fuel with* $CF = w_{EF}$ **and-or** *Gasoline with* $CF = w_{EG}$;

Air Conditioning **requires** *Engine Power* $\geq$ 100 HP;

Car **requires** *Engine Power* $\geq$ 100 HP **and** $\Psi(w_{AC}, w_{PT}, w_{TM}) \geq \delta_1$ **and** $w_{EF} \geq \delta_2$ **and** $w_{EG} \leq \delta_3$;

Car **requires** *Engine Power* $\geq$ 120 HP **and** $\Psi(w_{AC}, w_{PT}, w_{TM}) \geq \delta_1$ **and** $w_{EG} \geq \delta_4$ **and** $w_{EF} \leq \delta_5$;

Where: $\delta_1, \delta_2, \delta_3, \delta_4, \delta_5$ are the thresholds assumed by the experts; CF represents the certainty factor (weight), which is to be defined using defuzzification procedures; *and-or* represents an *n-of-many* choice (any nonempty subset).

The importance function $\Psi(w_{AC}, w_{PT}, w_{TM})$ is described in the following way:

$$\Psi(w_{AC}, w_{PT}, w_{TM}) = \max\{w_{AC}, w_{PT}, w_{TM}\}, \qquad (2)$$

The feature diagram can also be described using IF-THEN rules for representation of knowledge. The rule-based knowledge representation of the features of a simple car, as shown in Figure 1 (i.e., the feature diagram and the external composition rules, as well as the rationale) is as following:

IF *Car body* **and** *Transmission* **and** *Engine* **or** *Pulls Trailer with* $CF = w_{PT}$ **or** *Air Conditioning with* $CF = w_{AC}$ **Then** *Car* ;

IF *Manual with* $CF = w_{TM}$ **or** *Automatic with* $CF = w_{TA}$ **Then** *Transmission*;

IF *Fuel with* $CF = w_{EF}$ **and-or** *Gasoline with* $CF = w_{EG}$ **Then** *Engine*;

IF *Engine Power* $\geq$ 100 HP **Then** *Air Conditioning*;

IF *Engine Power* $\geq$ 100 HP **and** $\Psi(w_{AC}, w_{PT}, w_{TM}) \geq \delta_1$ **and** $w_{EF} \geq \delta_2$ **and** $w_{EG} \leq \delta_3$ **Then** *Car*;

IF *Engine Power* $\geq$ 120 HP **and** $\Psi(w_{AC}, w_{PT}, w_{TM}) \geq \delta_1$ **and** $w_{EG} \geq \delta_4$ **and** $w_{EF} \leq \delta_5$ **Then** *Car*;

In the simple car feature diagram there may be some additional features included - such as price or other parameters suggested by experts. The weight thresholds $(\delta_1, \delta_2, \delta_3, \delta_4, \delta_5)$ may be changed and customized to the specific customer profiles. For instance, there will be other preferences for a low-priced family car and others for a sport or luxury version of the car.

The described system may be further employed in the expert systems advertising, e.g., the choice of features for a product family member. The feature diagram description is suitable for inclusion in the general knowledge base, as well as the representation for the inference mechanisms. The case-specific variable data may be obtained from experts preparing the predicted customer profiles. The results gained from customers initially expressed with linguistic representation (e.g., weights for *Air Conditioning*: low importance, important, high importance) are then described with fuzzy logic, which allows an easy transformation of the customers' needs into suitable representation for a computer.

The advantage of the presented approach is the integration of the external constraints (attending the cross-tree dependencies in a feature diagram) directly into the homogenous description of a software family member. For instance: the external composition rule:

$$\text{Air conditioning requires horsepower} \geq 100;$$

is directly included. The rationale: Manual is more fuel efficient may also be described with an appropriate weight for the manual transmission from the point of view of the user for whom the car's economics would be the decisive factor. In the given example (a simple car), e.g., the choice of the "Pulls Trailer"-feature results in higher values of engine power needed, and it causes an increase of the car's price and, further, the insurance policy costs, etc. The further constraints (facts) may be easily attached as additional rules.

The simple car description has been used only to show the principle of modeling variable features with weights and to describe some of the variant weighted features described with fuzzy representation. The description of such cases is also possible with the given approach using the "requires" relationship ("mandatory with") for the mutually dependent features, i.e., using the **and**-operator.

4   Conclusion and Related Work

The similar approach was presented in [8] and [9]. The proposed use of fuzzy logic was there limited to the fuzzy description of the variable features; the feature weights were given a priori from experts. In this paper the approach is enhanced with the application of the fuzzy weights of the features. The usage of the introduced fuzzy weights of some variable features is demonstrated on an example of the choice of the car properties.

References

1. Czarnecki K. and Eisenecker U.: Generative Programming: Methods, Tools and Applications. Addison-Wesley , New York, 2000.

2. Clements P. and Northrop L.M.: A Framework for Software Product Line Practice" - Version 3.0 [online]. Pittsburgh, PA: Software Engineering Institute, Carnegie Mellon University. March 2002. Available: http://www.sei.cmu.edu/plp/framework.html.
3. Dubois D., Hüllermeister F. and Prade H.: Fuzzy Set-Based Methods in Instance-Based Reasoning, IEEE Trans. on Fuzzy Systems, Vol.10, No. 3, June 2002, pp. 322-332.
4. Kang K., Cohen S., Hess J., Nowak W. and Peterson S.:, Feature-Oriented Domain Analysis (FODA) Feasibility Study. Technical Report No. CMU/SEI-90-TR-21, Software Engineering Institute, Carnegie Mellon University, Pittsburgh, 1990. Pennsylvania.
5. Pieczyński A.: Fuzzy modeling of multidimensional non-linear process – influence of membership function shape. Proc. 8th East West Zittau Fuzzy Colloquium, Zittau, Germany, Sept. 6-8, 2000,pp. 125-133.
6. Pieczyński A.: Fuzzy modeling of multidimensional nonlinear processes – tuning procedures. Proc. 8th IEEE Int. Conf., Methods and Models in Automation and Robotics, MMAR 2002, Szczecin, Poland, Sept. 2002, Vol. 1, pp. 667-672.
7. Robak S.: Developing Software Families, Proceedings Promise 2002, Potsdam. Lecture Notes on Informatics, GI-Edition, Vol. P-21, Gesellschaft fuer Informatik, Bonn 2002, pp.138-149.
8. Robak S. and Pieczyński A.: Employment of fuzzy logic in feature diagrams to model variability in software families. Journal of Integrated Design and Process Science, USA, 2003, Vol. 7, no 3, pp. 79-94.
9. Robak S. and Pieczyński A.: Employing fuzzy logic in feature diagrams to model variability in software product-lines. 10th IEEE Int. Conf. and Workshop - Engineering of Computer-Based Systems - ECBS 2003. Huntsville, USA, 2003, pp. 305-311.
10. Yager F. and Filev D.: Essentials of fuzzy modeling and control. WNT Warszawa 1995 (in polish).
11. Zadeh L.A.: Fuzzy Sets. Information and Control 8, 1965, pp.338-353.

Neuro-Fuzzy Relational Classifiers

Rafał Scherer[1,2] and Leszek Rutkowski[1,2]

[1] Department of Computer Engineering
Częstochowa University of Technology
Al. Armii Krajowej 36, 42-200 Częstochowa, Poland
rafal@ieee.org, lrutko@kik.pcz.czest.pl
http://kik.pcz.pl
[2] Department of Artificial Intelligence, WSHE University in Łódź
ul. Rewolucji 1905 nr 64, Łódź, Poland
http://www.wshe.lodz.pl

Abstract. In the paper, we present a new fuzzy relational system with multiple outputs for classification purposes. Rules in the system are more flexible than the rules in linguistic fuzzy systems because of the additional weights in rule consequents. The weights comes from an additional binary relation. Thanks to this, input and output fuzzy sets are related to each other with a certain degree. The size of the relations is determined by the number of input fuzzy sets and the number of output fuzzy sets for a given class. Simulation results confirmed the system ability to classify data.

1 Introduction

There are many various fuzzy systems developed so far [1][3][5][7][10][15]. They are usually based on intelligible fuzzy rules. These fuzzy rules are obtained through expert knowledge or some heuristic methods, but they lacked the ability to learn from data as e.g. neural networks. Neuro-fuzzy systems emerged some time ago as a solution to the problem. They have the ability to learn from numerical data, using so called data-driven learning. The structure of these systems looks like a neural network but its units reflect fuzzy sets and operations performed on fuzzy sets like T-norms or T-conorms. Thanks to this, it is easy to see the construction of the fuzzy system and to learn the system by a gradient algorithm. A learning algorithm can be used to approximate any n-dimensional function. And yet the structure consists of fuzzy rules which are easy to extract unlike in the case of neural networks. In traditional fuzzy systems the input-output mapping is defined by the relation built from fuzzy rules and input and output fuzzy sets. Usually, output fuzzy sets are singleton sets in neuro-fuzzy systems. Neuro-fuzzy systems are used for various tasks, as they are able to approximate any function [14]. In case of classification, a fuzzy system has to approximate discriminant functions. Fuzzy classifiers [6][7][13] are developed as an alternative approach to traditional classifiers [11]. One kind of fuzzy systems are relational fuzzy systems [2][9][12][13], where there is an addinal relation binding input

L. Rutkowski et al. (Eds.): ICAISC 2004, LNAI 3070, pp. 376–380, 2004.
© Springer-Verlag Berlin Heidelberg 2004

and output fuzzy sets. In this case we obtain fuzzy rules with additional weights that can be regarded as a kind of rule weights [8]. In the paper we propose a relational fuzzy system for classification. In Section 2 we describe relational fuzzy systems, and in the next section we propose a relational neuro-fuzzy classifier. Finally, we test the system on the Iris dataset.

2   Fuzzy Relational Systems for Classification

Fuzzy relational models can be regarded as a generalization of linguistic fuzzy systems, where each rule has more than one linguistic value defined on the same output variable, in its consequent. Fuzzy rules in a MIMO relational model have the following form

$$R^k : \text{IF } \mathbf{x} \text{ is } A^k \text{ THEN}$$
$$y_c \text{ is } B_c^1 (r_{k1}), y_c \text{ is } B_c^m (r_{km}), \dots, y_c \text{ is } B_c^M (r_{kM}) , \tag{1}$$

where r_{km} is a weight, responsible for the strength of connection between input and output fuzzy sets, c is the output number. Relational fuzzy systems store associations between the input and the output linguistic values in the form of a discrete fuzzy relation

$$\mathbf{R}_c (A, B) \in [0, 1] . \tag{2}$$

In case of a multi-input multi-output system (MIMO), the relation $\mathbf{R}_c$ is a matrix containing degree of connection for every possible combination of input and output fuzzy sets for a class c. We consider a fuzzy system with multidimensional input linguistic values, where input fuzzy sets are common for all classes. Thus, we have only one set A of fuzzy linguistic values

$$A = \left\{ A^1, A^2, ..., A^K \right\} , \tag{3}$$

thus the relational matrix $\mathbf{R}_c$ is only two-dimensional, because every output has its own relation $\mathbf{R}_c$. Output variable y_c has a set of M_c linguistic values B_c^m with membership functions $\mu_{B_c^m} (y)$, for $m_c = 1, ..., M_c$

$$B_c = \left\{ B_c^1, B_c^2, ..., B_c^M \right\} . \tag{4}$$

Sets A and B_c are related to each other with a certain degree by the $K \times M_c$ relation matrix

$$\mathbf{R}_c = \begin{bmatrix} r_{11} & r_{11} & \cdots & r_{1M_c} \\ r_{21} & r_{22} & \cdots & r_{2M_c} \\ \vdots & \vdots & r_{km} & \vdots \\ r_{K1} & r_{K2} & \cdots & r_{KM_c} \end{bmatrix} . \tag{5}$$

3   Neuro-Fuzzy Relational Classifiers

In this section we present neuro-fuzzy systems for classification. Let $\mathbf{x}$ is a vector of features of an object ν, and $\Omega = \{\omega_1, ..., \omega_C\}$ is a set of classes. The classifier knowledge is represented by a set of K rules in the form

$$\mathrm{R}^k : \mathrm{IF}\ \mathbf{x}\ \mathrm{is}\ A^k\ \mathrm{THEN}\ \nu \in \omega_1(z_1^k),\ \ \nu \in \omega_2(z_2^k), \ldots,\ \nu \in \omega_C(z_C^k)\,, \qquad (6)$$

where z_c^k, $c = 1, ..., C$, $k = 1, ..., K$, are interpreted as a "support" for a class ω_c given by a rule R^k. Farther we redefine a description of the fuzzy relational system using this idea. Let us introduce a vector $\mathbf{z} = [z_1, ..., z_C]$, where z_c, $c = 1, ..., C$, is the "support" for a class ω_c given by all C rules. We can scale the support values to the interval $[0, 1]$, so that z_c is the membership degree of an object ν to class ω_c according to all K rules. Now a k-th rule for a class c has the form

$$\mathrm{R}^{kc} : \mathrm{IF}\ \mathbf{x}\ \mathrm{is}\ A^k\ \mathrm{THEN}\ y_c\ \mathrm{is}\ B_c^1\,(r_{km})\,,\ y_c\ \mathrm{is}\ B_c^2\,(r_{km})\,,\ldots,y_c\ \mathrm{is}\ B_c^M\,(r_{km}) \tag{7}$$

and this form will be used to design our relational classifier. Having given vector $\bar{A}$ of K membership values $\mu_{A^k}(\bar{\mathbf{x}})$ for a crisp observed feature values $\bar{\mathbf{x}}$, vector $\bar{B}_c$ of M_c crisp memberships μ_{mc} is obtained through a fuzzy relational composition

$$\bar{B}_c = \bar{A} \circ \mathbf{R}_c\,, \tag{8}$$

implemented element-wise by a generalized form of sup-min composition [1], i.e. s-t composition

$$\mu_{mc} = \mathop{\mathrm{S}}_{k=1}^{K} \left[\mathrm{T}\left(\mu_{A^k}(\bar{\mathbf{x}}), r_{km}^c\right) \right]\,. \tag{9}$$

The crisp output of the relational system is computed by the weighted mean

$$\bar{y}_c = \frac{\sum_{m=1}^{M_c}\left\{\bar{y}_c^m\, \mathrm{S}_{k=1}^{K}\left[\mathrm{T}\left(\mu_{A^k}(\bar{\mathbf{x}}), r_{km}^c\right)\right]\right\}}{\sum_{m=1}^{M}\mathrm{S}_{k=1}^{K}\left[\mathrm{T}\left(\mu_{A^k}(\bar{\mathbf{x}}), r_{km}^c\right)\right]}\,, \tag{10}$$

where $\bar{y}_c^m$ is a centre of gravity (centroid) of the fuzzy set B_c^m.

4   Numerical Simulations

Numerical simulations were carried out on the Iris dataset. The set consists of 3 classes, with 150 instances (50 in each of three classes). The instances are described by four features: sepal length and width and petal length and width. Our system had three outputs, according to the number of classes. Each input had three fuzzy sets and each output subsystem had 3×3 relational matrix. The dataset was divided into 100 training instances and 50 testing ones. Classification result was 95.3%.

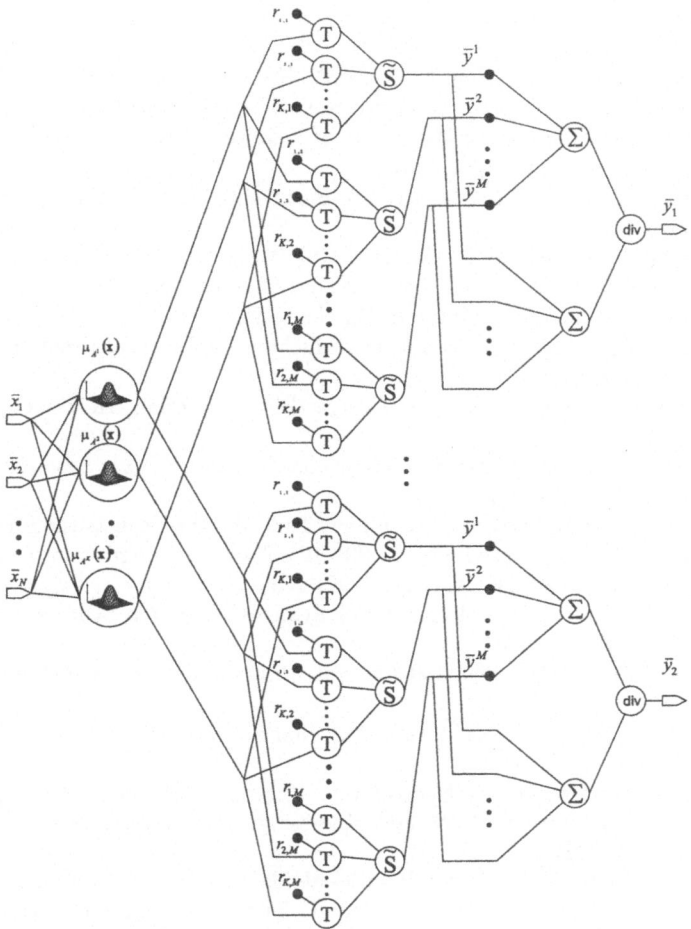

Fig. 1. Neuro-fuzzy relational system with two outputs

5   Conclusions

Fuzzy classifiers are developed simultaneously with other classifiers. In fuzzy classifiers we can use vague knowledge, and rules are intelligible and easier to define than in purely data-driven classifiers. In the paper, we presented a new fuzzy relational system with multiple outputs for classification purposes. Rules in the system are more flexible because of the additional weights in rule consequents. The weights comes from binary relations $\mathbf{R_c}$, one for each class. The size of the relations is determined by the number of input fuzzy sets and the number of output fuzzy sets for a given class. Simulation results confirmed the system ability to classify data.

References

1. Babuska R.: Fuzzy Modeling For Control, Kluwer Academic Press, Boston (1998)
2. Branco P.J.C., Dente J.A., A Fuzzy Relational identification Algorithm and its Application to Predict the Behaviour of a Motor Drive System, Fuzzy Sets and Systems, vol. 109, (2000) 343-354
3. Czogała E., Łęski J., Fuzzy and Neuro-Fuzzy Intelligent Systems, Physica-Verlag, Heidelberg (1999)
4. Ischibuchi H., Nakashima T., Effect of Rule Weights in Fuzzy Rule-Based Classification Systems, IEEE Transactions on Fuzzy Systems, vol. 9, no. 4 (2001) 506-515
5. Jang R. J.-S., Sun C.-T., Mizutani E., Neuro-Fuzzy and Soft Computing, A Computational Approach to Learning and Machine Intelligence, Prentice Hall, Upper Saddle River (1997)
6. Kuncheva L. I., Fuzzy Classifier Design, Physica Verlag, Heidelberg, New York (2000)
7. Nauck D., Klawon F., Kruse R., Foundations of Neuro - Fuzzy Systems, Chichester, U.K., John Wiley (1997)
8. Nauck D., Kruse R., How the Learning of Rule Weights Affects the Interpretability of Fuzzy Systems, Proceedings of 1998 IEEE World Congress on Computational Intelligence, FUZZ-IEEE, Alaska, (1998) 1235-1240
9. Pedrycz W., Fuzzy Control and Fuzzy Systems, Research Studies Press, London (1989)
10. Piegat A., Fuzzy Modeling and Control, Physica Verlag, Heidelberg, New York (2001)
11. Ripley B.D., Pattern Recognition and Neural Networks, Cambridge University Press (1996)
12. Scherer R., Rutkowski L., Neuro-Fuzzy Relational Systems, 2002 International Conference on Fuzzy Systems and Knowledge Discovery, November 18-22, Singapore (CD-ROM)(2002)
13. Setness M., Babuska R., Fuzzy Relational Classifier Trained by Fuzzy Clustering, IEEE Transactions on Systems, Man and Cybernetics - Part B: Cybernetics, Vol. 29, No. 5, October (1999) 619-625
14. Wang L.-X., Adaptive Fuzzy Systems And Control, PTR Prentice Hall, Englewood Cliffs, New Jersey, (1994)
15. Yager R.R., Filev D.P., Essentials of Fuzzy Modeling and Control, John Wiley & Sons, Inc. (1994)
16. Yager R.R., Filev D.P., On a Flexible Structure for Fuzzy Systems Models, in Fuzzy Sets, Neural Networks, and Soft Computing, R.R. Yager, L.A. Zadeh, Eds.,Van Nostrand Reinhold, New York (1994) 1-28

What Differs Interval Type-2 FLS from Type-1 FLS?

Janusz T. Starczewski[1,2]

[1] Department of Computer Engineering, Częstochowa University of Technology,
ul. Armii Krajowej 36, 42-200 Częstochowa, Poland,
jasio@kik.pcz.czest.pl
[2] Department of Artificial Intelligence,
Academy of Humanities and Economics in Łódź,
ul. Rewolucji 1905 r. nr 64, 90 - 222 Łódź, Poland

Abstract. In this study both classical type-1 and interval type-2 fuzzy systems have been compared with the perspective on overall output of both systems. Some analytical aspects have been examined for the case of two and three activated rules.

1 Introduction to Type-2 FLS

The idea of incorporating type-2 fuzzy sets into a fuzzy logic system (FLS) framework stems from the ability of modelling uncertainty in the description of antecedents and consequents in the system rule base. The type-2 fuzzy set is equipped with a fuzzy membership function, which is a fuzzy subset of the truth interval $[0, 1]$. More formally the fuzzy set of type-2 $\tilde{A}$ in the real line R, is a set of ordered pairs $\{x, \mu_{\tilde{A}}(x)\}$, which is denoted by $\tilde{A} = \int_{x \in R} \mu_{\tilde{A}}(x)/x$, where x is an element of the fuzzy set associated with the fuzzy membership grade (MG) $\mu_{\tilde{A}}(x)$ being a classical fuzzy subset of the unit interval $[0, 1]$, i.e.,

$$\mu_{\tilde{A}}(x) = \int_{u \in [0,1]} f_x(u)/u ,$$

where $f_x \colon [0, 1] \to [0, 1]$. Making the use of type-2 fuzzy sets, the rule base reflects uncertainties as to the memberships of antecedents and consequents and can be described by K rules of the form

$$\tilde{R}^k : \text{IF } x_1 \text{ is } \tilde{A}_1^k \text{ and } x_2 \text{ is } \tilde{A}_2^k \text{ and } \cdots \text{ and } x_N \text{ is } \tilde{A}_N^k \text{ THEN } y \text{ is } \tilde{B}^k ,$$

where $\tilde{A}_n$ is the n-th antecedent fuzzy set of type-2, $n = 1, \dots, N$, $\tilde{B}$ is the consequent type-2 fuzzy set, x_n is the n-th input variable; $k = 1, \dots, K$.

Memberships of intersection of two type-2 fuzzy sets $\tilde{A}$ and $\tilde{B}$, with their membership functions $\mu_{\tilde{A}}(x) = \int_{u \in [0,1]} f_x(u)/u$ and $\mu_{\tilde{B}}(x) = \int_{v \in [0,1]} g_x(v)/v$

L. Rutkowski et al. (Eds.): ICAISC 2004, LNAI 3070, pp. 381–387, 2004.
© Springer-Verlag Berlin Heidelberg 2004

may be computed according to the generalized extension principle. Thus for any arbitrary t-norms T and T_*, an extended operation T based on T_* is as follows

$$\tilde{T}_{T_*}\left(\mu_{\tilde{A}}\left(x\right),\mu_{\tilde{B}}\left(x\right)\right) = \int_{w\in[0,1]} \sup_{T(u,v)=w} T_*\left(f_x\left(u\right),g_x\left(v\right)\right)/w \ . \tag{1}$$

Note that operations T and T_* are not required to be necessarily the same. This result is however difficult in computing, because the resultant MG is the maximal value for all equivalent pairs $\{u,v\}$, i.e., such that they produce the same element w. Basing on the extended t-norm and other extended operations of the defuzzification process (called the type reduction) several type-2 FLS have been constructed (e.g., [1], [2], [3], [4], [5]). In the general inference scheme with the assumption that fuzzy premises $\tilde{A}_n$ are singleton in the domain of x with singleton MG, i.e., $\tilde{A}_n = (1/1)/x'_n$, the k-th conclusion is presented as follows

$$\mu_{\tilde{B}'^k}\left(y\right) = \mu_{\tilde{A}'\circ\left(\tilde{A}^k\cap\tilde{B}^k\right)}\left(y\right) = \tilde{T}_{infer}\left(\mu_{\tilde{A}^k}\left(\mathbf{x}'\right),\mu_{\tilde{B}^k}\left(y\right)\right)$$

$$= \tilde{T}_{infer}\left(\tilde{T}\left(\mu_{\tilde{A}_1^k}\left(x'_1\right),\mu_{\tilde{A}_2^k}\left(x'_2\right),\ldots,\mu_{\tilde{A}_N^k}\left(x'_N\right)\right),\mu_{\tilde{B}^k}\left(y\right)\right) \ .$$

Throughout this study only interval memberships of type-2 FLS will be considered. Henceforth, any type-2 fuzzy set $\tilde{A}$ will be described by a fuzzy MG of the form $\mu_{\tilde{A}}\left(x\right) = 1/(u \in [\hat{\mu}_A\left(x\right),\check{\mu}_A\left(x\right)])$, where $\hat{\mu}_A\left(x\right)$ is called a lower MG and $\check{\mu}_A\left(x\right)$ is called an upper MG. Furthermore, in Eq. (1) the formula of T_* is not important for interval type-2 fuzzy arguments since for each t-norm $T_*\left(1,1\right) = 1$ and $T_*\left(0,1\right) = 0$. Therefore, the upper MG can be calculated according to traditional t-norms independently from the same calculation of the lower MG.

2   Comparison between Type-2 and Type-1 FLS

It would be trivial to show that in the case of only one active rule (consequents are singleton in the output domain) both type-2 and type-1 FLS give the same output value. However the distance between type-2 and type-1 FLS may be significant due to the computational complexity of the type-2 FLS. On the other hand, certain circumstances when both type-2 and type-1 FLS produce similar or identical outputs, with the use of interval fuzzy MG, will be shown. Hereby, the question arises: is it worth making use of type-2 FLS instead of type-1 FLS at the cost of the complexity? From this point the study will focus on singleton and interval function forms in the domain of an output variable, retaining their interval fuzzy truth values.

2.1   Singleton Conclusions with Interval MG

Suppose that only two singleton (in the output domain) consequents have been activated in a type-2 FLS (see Fig. 1 a). Then their type-2 intermediate outputs

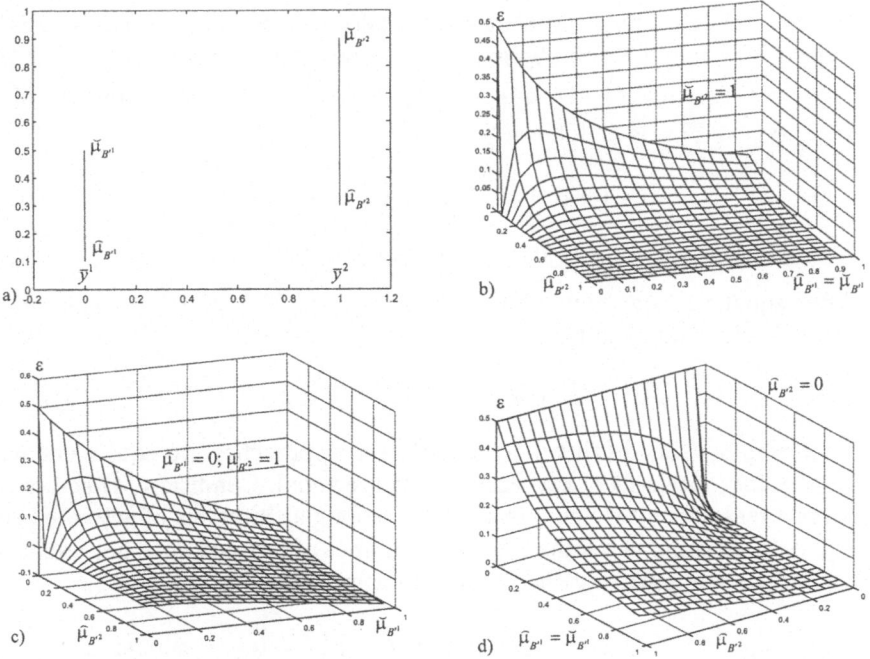

Fig. 1. Singleton conclusions of interval type-2 FLS; a) conclusions; b,c,d) output difference between type-1 and type-2 FLS

are centroids of outputs weighted by memberships chosen in such a way from intervals $\mu_{A^1} \in [\widehat{\mu}_{A^1}, \widecheck{\mu}_{A^1}]$, $\mu_{A^2} \in [\widehat{\mu}_{A^2}, \widecheck{\mu}_{A^2}]$ that the centroids reach maximal and minimal values:

$$y'_{\max} = \frac{\widecheck{\mu}_{A^1}\bar{y}_1 + \widehat{\mu}_{A^2}\bar{y}_2}{\widehat{\mu}_{A^1} + \widecheck{\mu}_{A^2}}, \quad y'_{\min} = \frac{\widecheck{\mu}_{A^1}\bar{y}_1 + \widehat{\mu}_{A^2}\bar{y}_2}{\widecheck{\mu}_{A^1} + \widehat{\mu}_{A^2}},$$

where $\widecheck{\mu}_{A^1}, \widecheck{\mu}_{A^2}$ are called upper membership grades and $\widehat{\mu}_{A^1}, \widehat{\mu}_{A^2}$ are called lower MG.

The crisp (type-0) output value is simply an average of intermediate outputs

$$y'_{II} = \frac{y'_{\max} + y'_{\min}}{2} = \frac{\widecheck{\mu}_{A^1}\bar{y}_1 + \widehat{\mu}_{A^2}\bar{y}_2}{2\left(\widehat{\mu}_{A^1} + \widecheck{\mu}_{A^2}\right)} + \frac{\widecheck{\mu}_{A^1}\bar{y}_1 + \widehat{\mu}_{A^2}\bar{y}_2}{2\left(\widecheck{\mu}_{A^1} + \widehat{\mu}_{A^2}\right)} . \tag{2}$$

In the case of two conclusions, the output of a type-1 FLS can be written as

$$y'_I = \frac{\mu_{A^1}\bar{y}_1 + \mu_{A^2}\bar{y}_2}{\mu_{A^1} + \mu_{A^2}},$$

where μ_{A^1}, μ_{A^2} act as activation membership grades (MG). Without the loss of generality it can be supposed that the transformation from the type-2 FLS to the type-1 FLS may be done by applying average MG of upper and lower MG, i.e., $\mu_{A^1} = \left(\widehat{\mu}_{A^1} + \widecheck{\mu}_{A^1}\right)/2$, $\mu_{A^2} = \left(\widehat{\mu}_{A^2} + \widecheck{\mu}_{A^2}\right)/2$. The crisp output of the referring type-1 FLS is as follows

$$y'_I = \frac{\left(\widehat{\mu}_{A^1} + \widecheck{\mu}_{A^1}\right)\bar{y}_1 + \left(\widehat{\mu}_{A^2} + \widecheck{\mu}_{A^2}\right)\bar{y}_2}{\widehat{\mu}_{A^1} + \widecheck{\mu}_{A^1} + \widehat{\mu}_{A^2} + \widecheck{\mu}_{A^2}}. \tag{3}$$

After equating right hand sides of Eqs. (2) and (3) trivial transformations lead to the following condition

$$\widecheck{\mu}_{A^1} - \widehat{\mu}_{A^1} = \widecheck{\mu}_{A^2} - \widehat{\mu}_{A^2}. \tag{4}$$

This explains that both type-2 and type-1 approaches are equivalent when the uncertainty intervals of two active rules are equal. Condition (4) shows that there is no reason to use type-2 computing as long as intervals of activated rules are equal. In all other cases the relative difference of outputs does not equal zero and it may be computed by the following formula

$$\varepsilon = \frac{y'_I - y'_{II}}{\bar{y}_2 - \bar{y}_1} = \frac{\left(\widecheck{\mu}_{A^2} - \widehat{\mu}_{A^2} - \widecheck{\mu}_{A^1} + \widehat{\mu}_{A^1}\right)\left(\widecheck{\mu}_{A^1}\widecheck{\mu}_{A^2} - \widehat{\mu}_{A^1}\widehat{\mu}_{A^2}\right)}{2\left(\widehat{\mu}_{A^1} + \widecheck{\mu}_{A^1} + \widehat{\mu}_{A^2} + \widecheck{\mu}_{A^2}\right)\left(\widehat{\mu}_{A^1} + \widecheck{\mu}_{A^2}\right)\left(\widecheck{\mu}_{A^1} + \widehat{\mu}_{A^2}\right)}.$$

This difference is the biggest when one fuzzy set has the widest interval of its membership grades, i.e. $\widehat{\mu}_{A^2} = 0$, $\widecheck{\mu}_{A^2} = 1$, and the second fuzzy set has a small positive crisp membership grade, i.e. $0 < \widehat{\mu}_{A^1} = \widecheck{\mu}_{A^1} \to 0$,

$$\varepsilon_{\max} = \lim_{0 < \widecheck{\mu}_{A^1} \to 0} \frac{1}{2\left(2\widecheck{\mu}_{A^1} + 1\right)\left(\widecheck{\mu}_{A^1} + 1\right)} = \frac{1}{2}.$$

In many papers (e.g., [1], [2], [3]) type-2 FLS have constrained membership intervals. Usually the constraint is such that all intervals of antecedent and consequent MG are equal to $\alpha \in [0, 1]$ and frequently $\widetilde{\min}$ (extended t-norm) is chosen as both the antecedent Cartesian product and the inferencing rule operator. If only two rules are activated, i.e. $\widecheck{\mu}_{A^1} > 0$ and $\widecheck{\mu}_{A^2} > 0$, then $\widehat{\mu}_{A^1} = /\widecheck{\mu}_{A^1} - \alpha/$, $\widehat{\mu}_{A^2} = /\widecheck{\mu}_{A^2} - \alpha/$, where the bounding operator is defined as $/x/ = \max(x, 0)$. As long as $\widecheck{\mu}_{A^1} > \alpha$ and $\widecheck{\mu}_{A^2} > \alpha$ condition (4) holds. But when $\widehat{\mu}_{A^1} = 0$ and $\widehat{\mu}_{A^2} > 0$ the relative difference is as follows

$$\varepsilon = \frac{\left(\alpha - \widecheck{\mu}_{A^1}\right)\widecheck{\mu}_{A^1}}{2\left(\widecheck{\mu}_{A^1} + 2\widecheck{\mu}_{A^2} - \alpha\right)\left(\widecheck{\mu}_{A^1} + \widecheck{\mu}_{A^2} - \alpha\right)}$$

and the maximal difference is obtained for $\widecheck{\mu}_{A^2} = 1$, $0 < \widecheck{\mu}_{A^1} \to 0$, $\widehat{\mu}_{A^2} = 0$.

The second common case is when the memberships of antecedents and consequents have constraints of the form $\widehat{\mu}_{A^1i} = \beta_1\widetilde{\mu}_{A^1i}$ and $\widehat{\mu}_{A^2i} = \beta_1\widetilde{\mu}_{A^2i}$, $i = 1, 2, \ldots, N; b_1 \in [0, 1]$, the consequents may have crisp MG $\widehat{\mu}_{B^1} = \widetilde{\mu}_{B^1} = 1$, and both the Cartesian product and the rule type are extended product t-norms (e.g., [4], [5]). In the case of two rules activation $\widetilde{\mu}_{A^k} = \widetilde{\mu}_{A_1^k}\widetilde{\mu}_{A_2^k} \cdots \cdot \widetilde{\mu}_{A_N^k}$ and $\widehat{\mu}_{A^k} = \beta_1^N\widetilde{\mu}_{A^k} = \beta\widetilde{\mu}_{A^k}$, $k = 1, 2$, then the difference is expressed as follows

$$\varepsilon = \frac{(1-\beta)^2 \left(\widetilde{\mu}_{A^2} - \widetilde{\mu}_{A^1}\right)\widetilde{\mu}_{A^1}\widetilde{\mu}_{A^2}}{2\left(\widetilde{\mu}_{A^1} + \widetilde{\mu}_{A^2}\right)\left(\beta\widetilde{\mu}_{A^1} + \widetilde{\mu}_{A^2}\right)\left(\widetilde{\mu}_{A^1} + \beta\widetilde{\mu}_{A^2}\right)} \, . \tag{5}$$

Eq. (5) equals zero if $\widetilde{\mu}_{A^2} = \widetilde{\mu}_{A^1}$ and reaches its maximum $\varepsilon_{max} = 0.5$ when $\beta = 0$, $\widetilde{\mu}_{A^2} = 1$ and $0 < \widetilde{\mu}_{A^1} \to 0$, which has also been described in the previous case. More details can be seen on the difference surfaces in Fig. 1.

However the case of three fired rules seems less likely to occur, it may be important to study this case as well. Therefore,

$$y'_{max} = \max\left(\frac{\widetilde{\mu}_{A^1}\bar{y}_1 + \widetilde{\mu}_{A^2}\bar{y}_2 + \widetilde{\mu}_{A^3}\bar{y}_3}{\widetilde{\mu}_{A^1} + \widetilde{\mu}_{A^2} + \widetilde{\mu}_{A^3}}, \frac{\widehat{\mu}_{A^1}\bar{y}_1 + \widehat{\mu}_{A^2}\bar{y}_2 + \widehat{\mu}_{A^3}\bar{y}_3}{\widehat{\mu}_{A^1} + \widehat{\mu}_{A^2} + \widehat{\mu}_{A^3}}\right) \, ,$$

$$y'_{min} = \min\left(\frac{\widetilde{\mu}_{A^1}\bar{y}_1 + \widehat{\mu}_{A^2}\bar{y}_2 + \widehat{\mu}_{A^3}\bar{y}_3}{\widetilde{\mu}_{A^1} + \widehat{\mu}_{A^2} + \widehat{\mu}_{A^3}}, \frac{\widehat{\mu}_{A^1}\bar{y}_1 + \widetilde{\mu}_{A^2}\bar{y}_2 + \widetilde{\mu}_{A^3}\bar{y}_3}{\widehat{\mu}_{A^1} + \widetilde{\mu}_{A^2} + \widetilde{\mu}_{A^3}}\right) \, .$$

Because of max and min functions, this case is difficult to differentiate in order to obtain an extremum ε. Henceforth, only equidistant conclusions are assumed, i.e. $\bar{y}_2 = \bar{y}_1 + \zeta = \bar{y}_3 - \zeta$, $\zeta > 0$. In case of fixed intervals α for $\widetilde{\mu}_{A^1} > \alpha$, $\widetilde{\mu}_{A^2} > \alpha$, $\widetilde{\mu}_{A^3} > \alpha$ and with condition $\widetilde{\mu}_{A^3} > \widetilde{\mu}_{A^1} + \alpha$ the overall output of the type-2 FLS is given by

$$y'_{II} = \bar{y}_2 + \frac{\zeta}{2}\left(\frac{\widetilde{\mu}_{A^3} - \widetilde{\mu}_{A^1} + \alpha}{\widetilde{\mu}_{A^1} + \widetilde{\mu}_{A^2} + \widetilde{\mu}_{A^3} - 2\alpha} - \frac{\widetilde{\mu}_{A^1} - \widetilde{\mu}_{A^3} + \alpha}{\widetilde{\mu}_{A^1} + \widetilde{\mu}_{A^2} + \widetilde{\mu}_{A^3} - \alpha}\right) \, .$$

while under conditions $\mu_{A^1} = \left(\widehat{\mu}_{A^1} + \widetilde{\mu}_{A^1}\right)/2 = \widetilde{\mu}_{A^1} - \alpha/2$ and $\mu_{A^2} = \widetilde{\mu}_{A^2} - \alpha/2$ the output of the corresponding type-1 FLS is given by

$$y'_I = \bar{y}_2 + \frac{(\mu_{A^3} - \mu_{A^1})\zeta}{\mu_{A^1} + \mu_{A^2} + \mu_{A^3}} = \bar{y}_2 + \frac{2\left(\widetilde{\mu}_{A^3} - \widetilde{\mu}_{A^1}\right)\zeta}{2\widetilde{\mu}_{A^1} + 2\widetilde{\mu}_{A^2} + 2\widetilde{\mu}_{A^3} - 3\alpha} \, .$$

The difference formula $\varepsilon = \frac{y'_I - y'_{II}}{2\zeta}$ does not equal zero for $1 \geq \widetilde{\mu}_{A^3} > \widetilde{\mu}_{A^1} > \alpha > 0$, $\widetilde{\mu}_{A^2} \in [0, 1]$, but if $\widetilde{\mu}_{A^1} = \widetilde{\mu}_{A^3}$ then obviously $\varepsilon = 0$.

In case of the proportional constraint, i.e., when $\widetilde{\mu}_{A^3} > \beta\widetilde{\mu}_{A^3} > \widetilde{\mu}_{A^1} > \beta\widetilde{\mu}_{A^1}$

$$y'_{max} = \bar{y}_2 + \frac{\left(\widetilde{\mu}_{A^3} - \beta\widetilde{\mu}_{A^1}\right)\zeta}{\beta\widetilde{\mu}_{A^1} + \beta\widetilde{\mu}_{A^2} + \widetilde{\mu}_{A^3}}, \qquad y'_{min} = \bar{y}_2 - \frac{\left(\widetilde{\mu}_{A^1} - \beta\widetilde{\mu}_{A^3}\right)\zeta}{\widetilde{\mu}_{A^1} + \widetilde{\mu}_{A^2} + \beta\widetilde{\mu}_{A^3}} \, .$$

The overall output of the type-2 FLS is given by

$$y'_{II} = \bar{y}_2 + \frac{\zeta}{2}\left(\frac{\bar{\mu}_{A^3} - \beta\bar{\mu}_{A^1}}{\beta\bar{\mu}_{A^1} + \beta\bar{\mu}_{A^2} + \bar{\mu}_{A^3}} - \frac{\bar{\mu}_{A^1} - \beta\bar{\mu}_{A^3}}{\bar{\mu}_{A^1} + \bar{\mu}_{A^2} + \beta\bar{\mu}_{A^3}}\right),$$

and under condition that $\mu_{A^1} = \left(\widehat{\mu}_{A^1} + \breve{\mu}_{A^1}\right)/2 = \breve{\mu}_{A^1}\left(\beta + 1\right)/2$ and $\mu_{A^2} = \breve{\mu}_{A^2}\left(\beta + 1\right)/2$ the output of the corresponding type-1 FLS is given by

$$y'_I = \bar{y}_2 + \frac{\left(\breve{\mu}_{A^3} - \breve{\mu}_{A^1}\right)\zeta}{\breve{\mu}_{A^1} + \breve{\mu}_{A^2} + \breve{\mu}_{A^3}}.$$

With an additional assumption that $\breve{\mu}_{A^3} > \beta\breve{\mu}_{A^1}; \breve{\mu}_{A^1} > \beta\breve{\mu}_{A^3}$ the difference is as follows

$$\varepsilon = \frac{1}{2}\frac{\breve{\mu}_{A^3} - \breve{\mu}_{A^1}}{\breve{\mu}_{A^1} + \breve{\mu}_{A^2} + \breve{\mu}_{A^3}} - \frac{1}{4}\left(\frac{\breve{\mu}_{A^3} - \beta\breve{\mu}_{A^1}}{\beta\breve{\mu}_{A^1} + \beta\breve{\mu}_{A^2} + \breve{\mu}_{A^3}} - \frac{\breve{\mu}_{A^1} - \beta\breve{\mu}_{A^3}}{\breve{\mu}_{A^1} + \beta\breve{\mu}_{A^2} + \beta\breve{\mu}_{A^3}}\right),$$

which equals zero only in the trivial case of $\breve{\mu}_{A^1} = \breve{\mu}_{A^3}$. In the both mentioned cases the difference ε has its extremum $|\varepsilon_{\max}| = \frac{1}{2}$ at $\breve{\mu}_{A^3} = 1$, $0 < \breve{\mu}_{A^2} \to 0$ and $0 < \breve{\mu}_{A^1} \to 0$, while $\alpha = 1$ or $\beta = 0$.

2.2 Interval Conclusions with Interval MG

In order to compute the centroid of interval conclusions with interval MG a special type reduction procedure, described in [1], [3], should be used. Fig. 2 presents the case of two activated rules. Since two interval-output (and interval-membership) conclusions may be treated as an infinite collection of singleton-output (and interval-membership) type-2 fuzzy sets, it could have been expected that the difference surface has a similar shape to the surface of the singleton conclusion case, but the maximal difference value is no longer as high as 0.5 in the singleton conclusion case.

3 Concluding Remarks

If the dominant rule is characterized by a wide interval of its membership uncertainty then less activated rules (but with upper MG greater than lower MG of the dominant rule) significantly mark its presence in the crisp output of the type-2 FLS. Otherwise, if the dominant rule has precise MG then the crisp output of the type-2 FLS is close to the corresponding type-1 FLS, which invalidates the type-2 approach in the majority of real application tasks. It seems to be "logical" that if a conclusion is significant but not certain and there is no alternative then

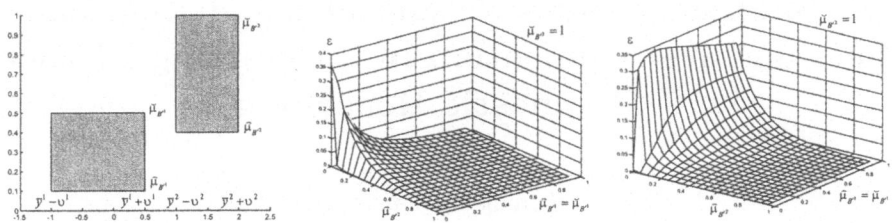

Fig. 2. Interval-output conclusions of interval-membership type-2 FLS: a) conclusions, b,c) output difference between type-1 and type-2 FLS; b) $\bar{y}^1 = 0$, $v = 1$, $\bar{y}^2 = 2.25$, $v = 0.25$, c) $\bar{y}^1 = -1.25$, $v = 0.25$, $\bar{y}^2 = 1$, $v = 1$

this conclusion is a reliable answer of the system, on the contrary if apart from the uncertain

significant conclusion there is an other less significant but certain conclusion then the latter has comparable influence on the output.

Nevertheless, the rules of the working type-2 system have to be diversified in their memberships. By reason of that, it is still hard to encounter a real problem when some of the fuzzy rules are much more precise than others. Usually some inputs of the system are more or less certain, but that kind of uncertainty does not diversify the uncertainty of rules since the uncertainty of inputs influences all rules proportionally. Unfortunately in cases when all antecedents and consequents of type-2 FLS are characterized with the same uncertainties, the system of type-2 reduces accurately to the system of type-1, when not more than two rules are activated.

References

1. Karnik, N. N., Mendel, J. M.: An Introduction to Type-2 Fuzzy Logic Systems, Univ. Southern California Rep., October (1998)
2. Karnik, N. N., Mendel, J. M., Liang, Q.: Type-2 Fuzzy Logic Systems, IEEE Trans. on Fuzzy Systems 7 (6) (1999) 643–658
3. Mendel, J. M.: Uncertain Rule-Based Fuzzy Logic Systems: Introduction and New Directions, Prentice Hall PTR, Upper Saddle River, NJ (2001)
4. Starczewski, J., Rutkowski, L.: Neuro-Fuzzy Systems of Type 2, 1st Int'l Conf. on Fuzzy Systems and Knowledge Discovery **2**, Singapore, November (2002) 458–462
5. Starczewski, J., Rutkowski, L.: Interval Type 2 Neuro-Fuzzy Systems Based on Interval Consequents, in: L. Rutkowski and J. Kacprzyk (Eds.) Neural Networks and Soft Computing, 6th Int'l Conf. on Neural Networks & Soft Computing, Zakopane, June 2002, Advances in Computing, Springer (2003) 570–577

A Similarity Measure for Intuitionistic Fuzzy Sets and Its Application in Supporting Medical Diagnostic Reasoning

Eulalia Szmidt and Janusz Kacprzyk

Systems Research Institute, Polish Academy of Sciences
ul. Newelska 6, 01–447 Warsaw, Poland
{szmidt,kacprzyk}@ibspan.waw.pl

Abstract. We propose a new similarity measure for intuitionistic fuzzy sets and show its usefulness in medical diagnostic reasoning. We point out advantages of this new concept over the most commonly used similarity measures being just the counterparts of distances. The measure we propose involves both similarity and dissimilarity.

1 Introduction

Intuitionistic fuzzy sets (Atanassov [1], [2]) can be viewed as a generalization of fuzzy sets (Zadeh [13]) that may better model imperfect information which is omnipresent in any conscious decision making. We present here intuitionistic fuzzy sets as a tool for a more human consistent reasoning under imperfectly defined facts and imprecise knowledge, with an application in supporting medical diagnosis. More specifically, we have set of data, i.e. a description of a set of symptoms S, and a set of diagnoses D. We describe a state of a patient knowing results of his/her medical tests. We use the concept of an intuitionistic fuzzy set that makes it possible to express many new aspects of imperfect information. For instance, in many cases information obtained cannot be classified due to lack of knowldge, discriminating power of measureing tools, etc. In such a case the use of a degree of membership and nonmebership can be an adequate knowledge representation solution.

The proposed method of diagnosis involves a new measure of similarity for intuitionistic fuzzy sets. For each patient the similarity measures for his or her particular set of symptoms and a set of symptoms that are characteristic for each diagnosis are calculated. The highest similarity points out a proper diagnosis.

In Section 2 we briefly overview intuitionistic fuzzy sets. In Section 3 we propose a new measure of similarity for intuitionistic fuzzy sets. In Section 4 we use the proposed similarity measure to single out a diagnosis for considered patients. We compare the solution obtained with a final diagnosis pointed out by looking for the smallest distance between symptoms characteristic for a patient and symptoms decsribing the illnesses (see Szmidt and Kacprzyk [11]). We give some conclusions in Section 5.

L. Rutkowski et al. (Eds.): ICAISC 2004, LNAI 3070, pp. 388–393, 2004.
© Springer-Verlag Berlin Heidelberg 2004

2   Brief Introduction to Intuitionistic Fuzzy Sets

As opposed to a fuzzy set in X(Zadeh [13]), given by

$$A' = \{< x, \mu_{A'}(x) > | x \in X\} \tag{1}$$

where $\mu_{A'}(x) \in [0,1]$ is the membership function of the fuzzy set A', an intuitionistic fuzzy set (Atanassov [1], [2]) A is given by

$$A = \{< x, \mu_A(x), \nu_A(x) > | x \in X\} \tag{2}$$

where: $\mu_A : X \to [0,1]$ and $\nu_A : X \to [0,1]$ such that

$$0 \leq \mu_A(x) + \nu_A(x) \leq 1 \tag{3}$$

and $\mu_A(x)$, $\nu_A(x) \in [0,1]$ denote a degree of membership and a degree of non-membership of $x \in A$, respectively.

Obviously, each fuzzy set may be represented by the following intuitionistic fuzzy set

$$A = \{< x, \mu_{A'}(x), 1 - \mu_{A'}(x) > | x \in X\} \tag{4}$$

For each intuitionistic fuzzy set in X, we call

$$\pi_A(x) = 1 - \mu_A(x) - \nu_A(x) \tag{5}$$

an *intuitionistic fuzzy index* (or a *hesitation margin*) of $x \in A$ and, it expresses a lack of knowledge of whether x belongs to A or not (cf. Atanassov [2]).

A complement of an intuitionistic fuzzy set A, A^C, is

$$A^C = \{< x, \nu_A(x), \mu_A(x) > | x \in X\} \tag{6}$$

Applications of intiutionistic fuzzy sets to group decisions, negotiations and other situations are given in Szmidt [3], Szmidt and Kacprzyk [5], [6], [8], [10], [11].

3   A New Similarity Measure

We propose here a new similarity measure for intuitionistic fuzzy sets using a geometrical interpretation of intuitionistic fuzzy sets given in Szmidt [3], Szmidt and Baldwin [4], Szmidt and Kacprzyk [7],[9] which implies that any combination of the parameters characteristic for elements belonging to an intuitionistic fuzzy set can be represented inside triangle ABD (Figure 1).

In the simplest situations we assess a similarity of any two elements X and F belonging to an intuitionistic fuzzy set (or sets). The proposed measure indicates if X is more similar to F or to F^C, where F^C is a complement of F, i.e. if X is more similar or more dissimilar to F (Figure 1).

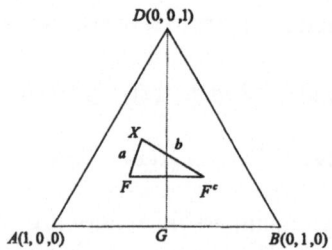

Fig. 1. Triangle ABD explaining a ratio-based measure of similarity

Definition 1.

$$Sim(X, F) = \frac{l_{IFS}(X, F)}{l_{IFS}(X, F^C)} = \frac{a}{b} \tag{7}$$

where: a is a distance(X, F) *from* $X(\mu_X, \nu_X, \pi_X)$ *to* $F(\mu_F, \nu_F, \pi_F)$,
b is the distance(X, F^C) *from* $X(\mu_X, \nu_X, \pi_X)$ *to* $F^C(\nu_F, \mu_F, \pi_F)$,
F^C *is a complement of* F.

For (7) we have $0 \leq Sim(X, F) \leq \infty$ and $Sim(X, F) = Sim(F, X)$.

Note that: (1) $Sim(X, F) = 0$ means the identity of X and F, (2) $Sim(X, F) = 1$ means that X is to the same extent similar to F and F^C (i.e., values bigger than 1 mean in fact a closer similarity of X and F^C to X and F), (3) when $X = F^C$ (or $X^C = F$), i.e. $l_{IFS}(X, F^C) = l_{IFS}(X^C, F) = 0$ means the complete dissimilarity of X and F (or the identity of X and F^C), and then $Sim(X, F) \to \infty$, (4) when $X = F = F^C$ means the highest entropy (see [9]) for both elements F and X i.e. the highest "fuzziness" – not too constructive a case when looking for compatibility (both similarity and dissimilarity). So, when applying the measure (7) to analyse the similarity of two objects, the values $0 \leq Sim(X, F) < 1$ are of interest.

The proposed measure (7) was constructed for selecting objects which are more similar than dissimilar, cf. Szmidt and Kacprzyk [12].

Now we show that a measure of similarity (7) between $X(\mu_X, \nu_X, \pi_X)$ and $F(\mu_F, \nu_F, \pi_F)$ is more powerful then a simple distance, giving an example of medical diagnostic reasoning.

4   Medical Diagnostic Reasoning via Distances for Intuitionistic Fuzzy Sets

To make a proper diagnosis D for a patient with given values of symptoms S, a medical knowledge base is necessary that involves elements described in terms of intuitionistic fuzzy sets. We consider the same data as in Szmidt and Kacprzyk [11]: the set of diagnoses is $D = \{$ *Viral fever, Malaria, Typhoid, Stomach problem, Chest problem*$\}$, and the set of symptoms is $S = \{$ *temperature, headache, stomach pain, cough, chest-pain*$\}$. The data are given in Table 1 – each symptom

Table 1. Symptoms characteristic for the diagnoses considered

	Viral fever	Malaria	Typhoid	Stomach problem	Chest problem
Temperature	(0.4, 0.0, 0.6)	(0.7, 0.0, 0.3)	(0.3, 0.3, 0.4)	(0.1, 0.7, 0.2)	(0.1, 0.8, 0.1)
Headache	(0.3, 0.5, 0.2)	(0.2, 0.6, 0.2)	(0.6, 0.1, 0.3)	(0.2, 0.4, 0.4)	(0.0, 0.8, 0.2)
Stomach pain	(0.1, 0.7, 0.2)	(0.0, 0.9, 0.1)	(0.2, 0.7, 0.1)	(0.8, 0.0, 0.2)	(0.2, 0.8, 0.0)
Cough	(0.4, 0.3, 0.3)	(0.7, 0.0, 0.3)	(0.2, 0.6, 0.2)	(0.2, 0.7, 0.1)	(0.2, 0.8, 0.0)
Chest pain	(0.1, 0.7, 0.2)	(0.1, 0.8, 0.1)	(0.1, 0.9, 0.0)	(0.2, 0.7, 0.1)	(0.8, 0.1, 0.1)

Table 2. Symptoms characteristic for the patients considered

	Temperature	Headache	Stomach pain	Cough	Chest pain
Al	(0.8, 0.1, 0.1)	(0.6, 0.1, 0.3)	(0.2, 0.8, 0.0)	(0.6, 0.1, 0.3)	(0.1, 0.6, 0.3)
Bob	(0.0, 0.8, 0.2)	(0.4, 0.4, 0.2)	(0.6, 0.1, 0.3)	(0.1, 0.7, 0.2)	(0.1, 0.8, 0.1)
Joe	(0.8, 0.1, 0.1)	(0.8, 0.1, 0.1)	(0.0, 0.6, 0.4)	(0.2, 0.7, 0.1)	(0.0, 0.5, 0.5)
Ted	(0.6, 0.1, 0.3)	(0.5, 0.4, 0.1)	(0.3, 0.4, 0.3)	(0.7, 0.2, 0.1)	(0.3, 0.4, 0.3)

is described by: membership μ, non-membership ν, hesition margin π. For example, for malaria the temperature is high ($\mu = 0.7$, $\nu = 0$, $\pi = 0.3$), for a chest problem the temperature is low ($\mu = 0.1$, $\nu = 0.8$, $\pi = 0.1$), etc. The set of patients is $P = \{Al, Bob, Joe, Ted\}$. The symptoms are given in Table 2 – as before, we need all three parameters (μ, ν, π) to describe each symptom (see Szmidt and Kacprzyk [11]). We seek a diagnosis for each patient p_i, $i = 1, \ldots, 4$. In Szmidt and Kacprzyk [11] we proposed to solve the problem in the following way: (1) to calculate for each patient p_i a distance (we used the normalised Hamming distance) of his symptoms (Table 2) from a set of symptoms s_j, $j = 1, \ldots, 5$ characteristic for each diagnosis d_k, $k = 1, \ldots, 5$ (Table 1), (2) to determine the lowest distance which points out to a proper diagnosis.

The normalised Hamming distance for all symptoms of patient i-th from diagnosis k is

$$l(s(p_i), d_k) = \frac{1}{10} \sum_{j=1}^{5} (|\mu_j(p_i) - \mu_j(d_k)| + |\nu_j(p_i) - \nu_j(d_k)| +$$
$$+ |\pi_j(p_i) - \pi_j(d_k)|) \tag{8}$$

The distances (8) for each patient from the set of possible diagnoses are given in Table 3. The lowest distance points out a proper diagnosis: Al suffers from malaria, Bob from a stomach problem, Joe from typhoid, whereas Ted from fever.

Now we derive a diagnosis for each patient p_i, $i = 1, \ldots, 4$ using the proposed similarity measure (7). We propose: (1) to calculate for each patient p_i a similarity measure (7) between his or her symptoms (Table 2) and symptoms s_j, $j = 1, \ldots, 5$ characteristic for each diagnosis d_k, $k = 1, \ldots, 5$ (Table 1), (2) to single out the lowest numerical value from the obtained similarity measures

Table 3. The normalized Hamming distances for each patient from the considered set of possible diagnoses

	Viral fever	Malaria	Typhoid	Stomach problem	Chest problem
Al	0.28	0.24	0.28	0.54	0.56
Bob	0.40	0.50	0.31	0.14	0.42
Joe	0.38	0.44	0.32	0.50	0.55
Ted	0.28	0.30	0.38	0.44	0.54

Table 4. Similarities of symptoms for each patient to the considered set of possible diagnoses

R	Viral fever	Malaria	Typhoid	Stomach problem	Chest problem
Al	0.75	1.19	1.31	3.27	∞
Bob	2.1	3.73	1.1	0.35	∞
Joe	0.87	1.52	0.46	2.61	∞
Ted	0.95	0.77	1.67	∞	2.56

which points out a proper diagnosis (for (7 the lower obtained number the bigger similarity).

From Definition 1, similarity measure (7) for patient p_i - between his or her symptoms and the symptoms characterisctic for diagnosis d_k, is

$$Sim(s(p_i), d_k) = \frac{1}{5} \sum_{j=1}^{5} [(|\mu_j(p_i) - \mu_j(d_k)| + |\nu_j(p_i) - \nu_j(d_k)| +$$
$$+ |\pi_j(p_i) - \pi_j(d_k)|)] / [(|\mu_j(p_i) - \nu_j(d_k)| +$$
$$+ |\nu_j(p_i) - \mu_j(d_k)| + |\pi_j(p_i) - \pi_j(d_k)|)] \qquad (9)$$

For example, for Al, the similarity measures for his temperature and the temperature characteristic for the chest problem Ch is

$$Sim_T(Al, Ch) = [|0.8 - 0.1| + |0.1 - 0.8| + |0.1 - 0.1|]/$$
$$/ [|0.8 - 0.8| + |0.1 - 0.1| + |0.1 - 0.1|] \to \infty \qquad (10)$$

i.e. Al's temperature is the complementary temperature [see (6)] to the one characteristic for Chest problem.

Similarly, for all five symptoms, from (9) we get the similarity measure indicating how close are Al's symptoms to symptoms for a chest problem, and obtain ∞ [because of (10)], i.e. that at least one of symptoms is opposite to that for a chest problem. This indication cannot be obtained while considering just distances between symptoms.

All the results for the considered patients are in Table 4. These results (Table 4) are different than those when we just considered the distances (Table 3). As previously, Bob suffers from stomach problems, Joe from typhoid, but Al from fever (not from malaria), and Ted suffers from malaria (not from fever). These differences are because the similarity measure (8) can be small but at the same time the distance between the symptom of the patient and the complementary symptom characteristic for the examined illness can be smaller (even equal to 0 as it was for (10)). See also Szmidt and Kacprzyk [12].

5 Conclusions

The method proposed, performing diagnosis on the basis of the calculation of a new similarity measure for intuitionistic fuzzy sets, makes it possible to avoid drawing conclusions about strong similarity between intuitionistic fuzzy sets on the basis of the small distances between these sets.

References

1. Atanassov K. (1986) Intuitionistic fuzzy sets, Fuzzy Sets and Syst., 20, 87–96.
2. Atanassov K. (1999) Intuitionistic Fuzzy Sets: Theory and Applications. Physica-Verlag, Heidelberg and New York.
3. Szmidt E. (2000): Applications of Intuitionistic Fuzzy sets in Decision Making. (D.Sc. dissertation) Techn. Univ., Sofia, 2000.
4. Szmidt E. and Baldwin J. (2003) New Similarity Measure for Intuitionistic Fuzzy Set Theory and Mass Assignment Theory. Notes on IFSs, 9, pp. 60–76.
5. Szmidt E. and Kacprzyk J. (1996b) Remarks on some applications of intuitionistic fuzzy sets in decision making, *Notes on IFS*, 2, pp. 22–31.
6. Szmidt E. and Kacprzyk J. (1998a) Group Decision Making under Intuitionistic Fuzzy Preference Relations. Proc. IPMU'98, pp. 172-178.
7. Szmidt E. and J. Kacprzyk J. (2000) Distances between intuitionistic fuzzy sets, Fuzzy Sets and Syst., 114, pp.505–518.
8. Szmidt E. and Kacprzyk J. (2000) On Measures on Consensus Under Intuitionistic Fuzzy Relations. proc. IPMU'2000, pp. 1454–1461.
9. Szmidt E., Kacprzyk J. (2001) Entropy for intuitionistic fuzzy sets. Fuzzy Sets and Syst., 118, pp. 467–477.
10. Szmidt E. and Kacprzyk J. (2002) Analysis of Agreement in a Group of Experts via Distances Between Intuitionistic Fuzzy Preferences. Proc. IPMU'2002, pp. 1859–1865.
11. Szmidt E. and Kacprzyk J. (2002) An Intuitionistic Fuzzy Set Based Approach to Intelligent Data Analysis: An application to medical diagnosis. In: A. Abraham, L.Jain, J. Kacprzyk (Eds.): Recent Advances in Intelligent Paradigms and and Applications. Springer-Verlag, pp. 57–70.
12. Szmidt E. and Kacprzyk J. Similarity of Intuitionistic Fuzzy Sets and Jaccard Coefficient. (accepted for IPMU'04)
13. Zadeh L.A. (1965) Fuzzy sets. Information and Control, 8, pp. 338 - 353.

Multi-criterion Evolutionary Algorithm with Model of the Immune System to Handle Constraints for Task Assignments

Jerzy Balicki

Computer Science Department, The Naval University of Gdynia
ul. Śmidowicza 69, 81-103 Gdynia, Poland
jbalicki@amw.gdynia.pl

Abstract. In this paper, an evolutionary algorithm based on an immune system activity to handle constraints is discussed for three-criteria optimisation problem of finding a set of Pareto-suboptimal task assignments in parallel systems. This approach deals with a modified genetic algorithm cooperating with a main evolutionary algorithm. An immune system activity is emulated by a modified genetic algorithm to handle constraints. Some numerical results are submitted.

1 Introduction

Evolutionary algorithms (EAs) are an unconstrained search technique and, subsequently, have to exploit a supplementary procedure to incorporate constraints into fitness function in order to conduct the search correctly. The penalty technique is frequently used to handle constraints in multi-criteria evolutionary algorithms to find the Pareto-suboptimal outcomes [1]. However, penalty functions have some familiar limitations, from which the most noteworthy is the complicatedness to identify appropriate penalty coefficients [11].

Koziel and Michalewicz have proposed the homomorphous mappings as the constraint-handling technique of EA to deal with parameter optimisation problems in order to avoid some impenetrability related to the penalty function [11]. Then, Coello Coello and Cortes have designed a constrained-handling scheme based on a model of the immune system to optimisation problems with one criterion [2].

In this paper, we propose an improved model of the immune system to handle constraints in multi-criteria optimisation problems. The problem that is of interest to us is the new task assignment problem for a distributed computer system. Both a workload of a bottleneck computer and the cost of machines are minimized; in contrast, a reliability of the system is maximized. Moreover, constraints related to memory limits, task assignment and computer locations are imposed on the feasible task assignment. Finally, an evolutionary algorithm based on tabu search procedure and the immune system model is proposed to provide solutions to the distributed systems.

L. Rutkowski et al. (Eds.): ICAISC 2004, LNAI 3070, pp. 394–399, 2004.
© Springer-Verlag Berlin Heidelberg 2004

2   Immune Systems

The immune system can be seen, from the information processing perspectives, as a parallel and distributed adaptive system [2]. Capabilities of learning, using memory, associative retrieval of information in recognition, and many local interactions supply, in consequence, fault tolerance, dynamism and adaptability [5]. Some conceptual and mathematical models of these properties of the immune system were constructed with the purpose of understanding its nature [10,14]. A model of primary reaction in the attendance of a trespasser was examined by Forrest et al. [7]. Furthermore, the model of secondary response related to memory was assembled by Smith [12]. Both detectors and antigens were represented as strings of symbols in a small alphabet in the first computer model of the immune system by Farmer et al. [6]. In addition, molecular bonds were represented by interactions among these strings.

Most of the current models are based on the model of immune network and the negative selection algorithm [8]. Additionally, there are others used to imitate ability of the immune system to discover patterns in a noise environment, capability to determine and preserve diverse classes of patterns and ability to learn efficiently, even when not all the potential sorts of assailants had been formerly presented to the immune system [12].

Differential equations to simulate the dynamics of the lymphocytes by computation the changes of the concentration of lymphocytes' clones has been applied by Jerne [9]. Lymphocytes do not act in an isolated mode, but they work as an interconnected group. On the other hand, the negative selection algorithm (NSA) for recognition of changes has been developed by Forrest at el. [7]. This algorithm is based on the discrimination rule that is used to identify what is a fraction of the immune system and what is not [8]. Detectors are randomly generated to exterminate those detectors that are not capable to identify themselves. Consequently, a detector capable to recognize trespassers is kept. A change recognition is performed probabilistically by the NSA. It is also robust because it looks for any indefinite action instead of just looking for certain explicit sample of changes.

In this paper, the NSA is used to handle constraints by dividing the contemporary population in two groups [2]. Feasible solutions called "antigens" produce the first assembly, and the second collection of individuals consists of "antibodies" – infeasible solutions. Consequently, the NSA is applied to create a set of detectors that establish the state of constraints. We assume the fitness for antibodies is equal to zero. After that, a randomly chosen antigen G^- is compared against the σ antibodies that were selected without replacement. Subsequently, the distance S between the antigen G^- and the antibody B^- is calculated due to the quantity of similarity at the genotype level [2]:

$$S(G^-, B^-) \sum_{m=1}^{M} s_m(G^-, B^-), \tag{1}$$

where:

- M - the length of the sequence representing the antigen G^- (the length of the antibody B^- is the same),
- $s_m = \begin{cases} 1 \ if \ G_m^- \ is \ a \ matching \ to \ B_m^- \ at \ position \ m, \\ 0 \ in \ the \ other \ case. \end{cases} m = \overline{1, M}$;

The fitness of the antibody with the highest magnitude S is increased by adding its amount of resemblance. The antibodies are returned to the existing population and the procedure of increasing the fitness of the conqueror is repeated usually tree times the number of antibodies. Each time, a randomly selected antigen is compared against the same division of antibodies.

Afterwards, a new population is constructed by reproduction, crossover and mutation without calculations of fitness. Above process is repeated until a convergence of population or until a maximal number of iterations is exceeded. Then, the final population of the NSA is returned to the external evolutionary algorithm.

The negative selection algorithm is a modified genetic algorithm in which infeasible solutions that are similar to feasible ones are preferred in the current population. Although, almost all random selections are based on the uniform distribution, the force is directed to develop the fitness of appropriate infeasible solutions.

The assess of genotype similarity between antigen and antibody depends on the representation. The measure of similarity for the binary representation can be re-defined for integer representation:

$$S'(G^-, B^-) = \sum_{m=1}^{M} |G_m^- - S_m^-|. \tag{2}$$

3   Advanced Negative Selection Algorithm

The fact that the fitness of the winner is increased by adding the magnitude of the similarity measure to the current value of fitness may pass over a non-feasible solution with the relatively small value of this total measure. However, some constraints may be satisfied by this alternative. What is more, if one constraint is exceeded and the others are performed, the value of the likeness evaluate may be low for some cases. That is, the first of two similar solutions, in genotype sense, may not satisfy this constraint and the second one may satisfy it.

To avoid this limitation of the NSA, we suggest introducing some distance measures from the state of an antibody to the state of the selected antigen, according to the constraints. The constraints that are of interest to us are, as follows:

$$g_k(x) \leq 0, \quad k = \overline{1, K}, \tag{3}$$

$$h_l(x) = 0, \quad l = \overline{1, L}. \tag{4}$$

The distance measures from the state of an antibody B^- to the state of the selected antigen G^- are defined, as follows:

$$f_n(B^-, G^-) = \begin{cases} g_k(B^-) - g_k(G^-), & k = \overline{1, K}, \ n = k, \\ |h_l(B^-)|, l = \overline{1, L}, n = K + l, \end{cases} \quad n = \overline{1, N}, \ N = K + L.$$

(5)

We suggest introducing a ranking procedure to calculate fitness of antibodies and then to select the winners. A ranking idea for non-dominated individuals has been introduced to avoid the prejudice of the interior Pareto alternatives. We adjust this procedure to the negative selection algorithm and a subset of antibodies. Firstly, distances between antigen and antibodies are calculated. Then, the nondominated antibodies are determined according to their distances, and after that, they get the rank 1. Subsequently, they are temporary eliminated from the population. Next, the new nondominated antibodies are found from the reduced population and they get the rank 2. In this procedure, the level is increased and it is repeated until the subset of antibodies is exhausted. All non-dominated antibodies have the same reproduction fitness because of the equivalent rank.

If B^- is the antibody with the rank r B^- and $1 \le r(B^-) \le r_{\max}$, then the increment of the fitness function value is estimated, as below:

$$\Delta f(B^-) = r_{\max} - r(B^-) + 1.$$

(6)

Afterwards, the fitness of the all chosen antibodies are increased by adding their increments. The antibodies are returned to the current population and the process of increasing the fitness of antibodies is repeated typically tree times the number of antibodies as it was in the previous version of the NSA. Each time, a randomly chosen antigen is compared against the same subset of antibodies. Next, the same procedure as for the NSA is carried out. Afterwards, a new population is constructed by reproduction, crossover and mutation without calculations of fitness. Above process is repeated until a convergence of population emerges or until a maximal number of iterations is exceeded. Then, the final population of the negative selection algorithm is returned to the external evolutionary algorithm.

4   Developed Tabu-Based Adaptive Evolutionary Algorithm

Let the negative selection algorithm with the ranking procedure be called NSA+. To exam its ability to handle constraints, we consider a multicriteria optimisation problem of task assignment in a distributed computer system [1]. Finding allocations of program modules may reduce the total time of a program execution by taking a advantage of the particular properties of some workstations or a benefit of the computer load. An adaptive evolutionary algorithm and an adaptive evolution strategy have been considered for solving multiobjective optimisation problems related to task assignment that minimize Z_{max} – a workload of a bottleneck computer and F_2 – the cost of machines [1]. The total numerical performance of workstations is another measure for assessment of task assignment and it has been involved to multicriteria task assignment problem in [1]. Furthermore, a reliability R of the system is an supplementary criterion that is significant to assess the quality of a task assignment.

In the considered problem, both a workload of a bottleneck computer and the cost of machines are minimized; in contrast, a reliability of the system is maximized. Moreover, constraints related to memory limits, task assignment and computer locations are imposed on the feasible task assignment. Above problem has been formulated in [1].

An overview of evolutionary algorithms for multiobjective optimisation problems is submitted in [3,4]. Zitzler, Deb, and Thiele have tested an elitist multicriterion evolutionary algorithm with the concept of non-domination in their strength Pareto evolutionary algorithm SPEA [15]. An analysis of the task assignments has been carried out for two evolutionary algorithms. The first one was an adaptive evolutionary algorithm with tabu mutation AMEA+ [1]. Tabu search algorithm [12] was applied as an additional mutation operator to decrease the workload of the bottleneck computer.

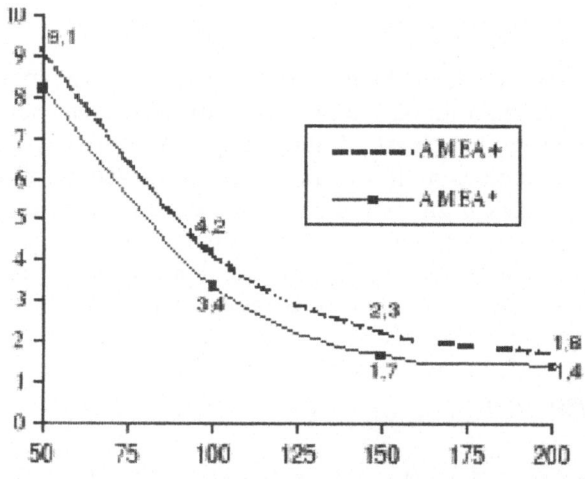

Fig. 1. Outcome convergence for the AMEA* and the AMEA+.

Better outcomes from the NSA are transformed into improving of solution quality obtained by the adaptive multicriteria evolutionary algorithm with tabu mutation AMEA*. This adaptive evolutionary algorithm with the NSA (AMEA*) gives better results than the AMEA+ (Fig. 1). After 200 generations, an average level of Pareto set obtaining is 1.4% for the AMEA*, 1.8% for the AMEA+. 30 test preliminary populations were prepared, and each algorithm starts 30 times from these populations.

5 Concluding Remarks

The tabu-based adaptive evolutionary algorithm with the negative selection algorithm can be used for finding Pareto-optimal task allocations. In a three-objective optimisation problem, the system reliability is maximised. Furthermore, the workload of the bottleneck computer and the cost of computers are minimized. Our upcoming works will centre of attention on a development the NSA and evolutionary algorithms for finding Pareto-optimal alternatives of the other multiobjective optimisation problems.

References

1. Balicki, J., Kitowski, Z.: Multicriteria Evolutionary Algorithm with Tabu Search for Task Assignment, Lectures Notes in Computer Science, Vol. 1993 (2001) 373-384
2. Coello Coello, C. A., Cortes, N.C.: Use of Emulations of the Immune System to Handle Constraints in Evolutionary Algorithms, Knowledge and Information Systems. An International Journal, Vol. 1 (2001) 1-12
3. Coello Coello, C. A., Van Veldhuizen, D. A., Lamont, G.B.: Evolutionary Algorithms for Solving Multi-Objective Problems, Kluwer Academic Publishers, New York (2002)
4. Deb, K.: Multi-Objective Optimization using Evolutionary Algorithms, John Wiley & Sons, Chichester (2001)
5. D'haeseleer, P., et al.: An Immunological Approach to Change Detection. In Proc. of IEEE Symposium on Research in Security and Privacy, Oakland (1996)
6. Farmer, J.D., Packard, N.H., Perelson, A.S.: The Immune System, Adaptation, and Machine Learning. Physica D, Vol. 22 (1986) 187-204
7. Forrest, S., Perelson, A.S.: Genetic Algorithms and the Immune System. Lecture Notes in Computer Science (1991) 320-325
8. Helman, P. and Forrest, S.: An Efficient Algorithm for Generating Random Antibody Strings. Technical Report CS-94-07, The University of New Mexico, Albuquerque (1994)
9. Jerne, N.K.: The Immune System. Scientific American, Vol. 229, No. 1 (1973) 52-60
10. Kim, J. and Bentley, P. J.: Immune Memory in the Dynamic Clonal Selection Algorithm. Proc. of the First Int. Conf. on Artificial Immune Systems, Canterbury, (2002) 57-65
11. Koziel, S., Michalewicz, Z.: Evolutionary Algorithms, Homomorphous mapping, and Constrained Parameter Optimisation. Evolutionary Computation, Vol. 7 (1999) 19-44
12. Smith, D.: Towards a Model of Associative Recall in Immunological Memory. Technical Report 94-9, University of New Mexico, Albuquerque (1994)
13. Weglarz, J. (ed.): Recent Advances in Project Scheduling. Kluwer Academic Publishers, Dordrecht (1998)
14. Wierzchon, S. T.: Generating Optimal Repertoire of Antibody Strings in an Artificial Immune System. In M. Klopotek, M. Michalewicz and S. T. Wierzchon (eds.) Intelligent Information Systems. Springer Verlag, Heidelberg/New York (2000) 119-133
15. Zitzler, E., Deb, K., and Thiele, L.: Comparison of Multiobjective Evolutionary Algorithms: Empirical Results. Evolutionary Computation, Vol. 8, No. 2 (2000) 173-195

Parallel Genetic Algorithm for Minimizing Total Weighted Completion Time

Wojciech Bożejko[1] and Mieczysław Wodecki[2]

[1] Institute of Engineering, Wrocław University of Technology
Janiszewskiego 11-17, 50-372 Wrocław, Poland
wbo@ict.pwr.wroc.pl
[2] Institute of Computer Science, University of Wrocław
Przesmyckiego 20, 51-151 Wrocław, Poland
mwd@ii.uni.wroc.pl

Abstract. We have considered the problem of job scheduling on a single machine with deadlines. The objective is to find a feasible job sequence (satisfying the deadlines) to minimize the sum of weighted completion times. Since the problem is NP-hard, heuristics have to be used. Methods of artificial intelligence: simulated annealing, neural networks and genetic algorithms, are some of the recent approaches. We propose a very effective parallel genetic algorithm PGA and methods of determining lower and upper bounds of the objective function. Since there are difficulties with determining the initial population of PGA for this scheduling problem, therefore the algorithm also adds random generated unfeasible solutions to the population. We announce a method of elimination of these kind of solutions. The examined algorithms are implemented in Ada95 and MPI. Results of computational experiments are reported for a set of randomly generated test problems.*

1 Introduction

Nowadays artificial intelligence methods: neural networks, simulated annealing and genetic algorithms, are successfully used to solve the most difficult (strongly *NP*-hard) problems of combinatorial optimization. Implementation of such an algorithm in multiprocessor environment, if cleverly done, considerably accelerates calculations and makes it possible to solve large instances of the problem relatively fast.

Many scheduling problems are an important part of short-term production planning. We present a problem of sequencing set of jobs on a single machine. Each job has to be done before its deadline. The objective is to find a schedule of jobs that minimizes the sum of weighted completion times.

This problem was defined by Smith [8] and is denoted as $1|d_i| \sum w_i C_i$ in literature. Lenstra et al. [4] shows, that it is strongly *NP*-hard which indicates that the existence of a polynomial bounded algorithm is unlikely.

---

* The work was supported by KBN Poland, within the grant No. T11A01624

L. Rutkowski et al. (Eds.): ICAISC 2004, LNAI 3070, pp. 400–405, 2004.
© Springer-Verlag Berlin Heidelberg 2004

An optimal branch and bound algorithm was proposed by Bensal [1], Posner [6] and Yupeng Pan [5]. The algorithm of Posner solve all instances of up to 40 jobs and most instances of 50-60 jobs, see [5]. In the paper [5], Yupeng Pan presents a branch and bound algorithm (based on an idea by Posner) that extensively utilizes the principle of optimality to reduce the size of the search tree. This algorithm can solve instances of up to 90 jobs. In this paper we announce a parallel genetic algorithm based on the island model of migration with a new crossover operator (modified PMX) and deadline flowing technique. Through lack of reference instances, we compare the obtained solutions (for random instances) with calculated upper bound. This work is a continuation of [9].

2   Problem Definition

The single machine total weighted completion time problem (SWCT) may be stated as follows. In a given instance, each job i has a due date (deadline) d_i, a processing time p_i and weight w_i. For a given schedule, if a job is completed before its due date, its feasible. The schedule is called feasible if any job in this schedule is feasible. Our goal is to find a feasible schedule that minimizes the total weighted completion time $\sum_{i=1}^{n} w_i C_i$, where C_i is the completion time of job i.

Let $N = \{1, 2, \ldots, n\}$ be a set of n jobs. By Φ_n we mean a set of all permutations of elements of the set N. The permutation $\pi \in \Phi_n$ is feasible, if

$$\forall i \in N, \ d_{\pi(i)} \geq C_{\pi(i)} \text{ where } C_{\pi(i)} = \sum_{j=1}^{i} p_{\pi(j)}.$$

The SWCT problem consist in determining optimal element π^* such, that

$$F(\pi^*) = \min\{F(\pi): \ \pi \in \Pi\},$$

where $\Pi \subseteq \Phi_n$ is a set of feasible solutions and the goal function is

$$F(\pi) = \sum_{i=1}^{n} w_{\pi(i)} * C_{\pi(i)}, \quad \pi \in \Pi.$$

For a sequence of jobs $\pi = (\pi(1), \pi(2), \ldots, \pi(n))$, if $d_{\pi(1)} \leq d_{\pi(2)} \leq, \ldots, \leq d_{\pi(n)}$, then such a schedule (permutation) is called Earliest Due Date (EDD).

Property 1. If for a certain instance of SWCT problem, EDD jobs' schedule is feasible, then the set of solutions $\Pi \neq \emptyset$, otherwise $\Pi = \emptyset$.

Using this property we can easily check if an instance has any feasible solution.

3   Genetic Algorithm

Genetic algorithms are inspired by natural selection and evolution. Search strategy based on a theme borrowed from genetics was introduced by Holland [3]. Goldberg [2] described this method as a search algorithm for optimization. He used concepts from population genetics and the evolution theory to construct algorithms that try to optimize the fitness of a population of elements through recombination and mutation of their genes. Key components of a genetic algorithm are: a mechanism to generate an initial population, a measure of solution fitness, and genetic operators that combine and alter current solutions to new solution forms.

We have applied a partially mapped crossover (PMX), and cycle crossover (CX) operators in our algorithm. The generated descendant (permutation) is modified in such a way that the distance between it and one of the parents is minimal. The distance between permutations $\alpha, \beta \in \Phi_n$ is denoted as a minimal number of transpositions of adjacent elements that should be performed to obtain β from α.

4   Parallel Genetic Algorithm

There are three basic types of parallelization strategies which can be applied to the genetic algorithm: global, diffusion model and island (migration) model.

Algorithms based on the island model divide the population into a few subpopulations. Each of them is assigned to a different processor which performs a sequential genetic algorithm based on its own subpopulation. The crossover involves only individuals within the same population. Occasionally, the processor exchanges individuals through a migration operator. The main determinants of this model are: (1) size of the subpopulations, (2) topology of the connection network, (3) number of individuals to be exchanged, (4) frequency of exchanging.

The island model is characterized by a significant reduction of the communication time, compared to previous models. Shared memory is not required, so this model is more flexible too.

Below, a parallel genetic algorithm is proposed. The algorithm is based on the island model of parallelizm. Let P be a population, P' a set of parents and P'' a set of offspring of the random parents from P'.

Algorithm 1. Parallel genetic algorithm
    <u>parfor</u> $j = 1, 2, ..., p$ { p *is number of processors* }
        $i \leftarrow 0$; $P_j \leftarrow$ random subpopulation connected with processor j;
        $p_j \leftarrow$ number of individuals in subpopulation j;
        <u>repeat</u>
            Selection(P_j, P'_j);   Crossover(P'_j, P''_j);   Mutation(P''_j);
            <u>if</u> $(k \mod S = 0)$ <u>then</u> {*Migration*}
                $r := random(1, p)$;
                Remove $\beta = 25$ percentage of individuals in subpopulation P_j;
                Replenish P_j by the best individuals from subpopulation P_r
                taken from processor r;
            <u>end if</u>;
        <u>until</u> *Stop_Condition*;
    <u>end parfor</u>

The frequency of communication between processors (migration) is very important for the parallel algorithm performance. It must not be too frequent because of the long time of communication between processors. In this implementation the processor gets new individuals quite rarely, every $S = 20$ iterations.

5   Lower Bound and Upper Bound

For each instance the lower bound (LB) and upper bound (UB) of the optimal goal function value is calculated.

A Lower Bound from the Assignment Problem.

Let us suppose that we have found that there exists an optimal schedule whereby, for the job $i \in N$, the set of jobs $\Gamma_i^- \subseteq N$ precedes i and the set of jobs $\Gamma_i^+ \subseteq N$ follows i. If in any established relation job i precedes j, than $i \in \Gamma_j^-$ and $j \in \Gamma_i^+$.

Theorem 1. *(Elimination rule). If at least one of the following conditions holds*

$$p_i < p_j, \ w_i \geq w_j, \ d_i \leq P(\Gamma_j^-) + p_j \ \ or \ w_i \geq w_j, \ d_j \geq d_i, \ d_j \geq P(N \backslash \Gamma_i^+) - p_j.$$

then job i precedes j, $(i, j \in N)$.

Proof. The proof is based on the more general results of Rinnoy Kan et al. [7].

For any $Q \subseteq N, \quad P(Q) = \sum\limits_{\pi(i) \in Q} p_{\pi(i)}.$

Let $T_i(q) = \min\{P(Q) : Q \subset N \backslash \{\Gamma_i^- \cup \Gamma_i^+ \cup \{i\}\}\}$, where $q = |Q|$.

Next $t_{ij} = P(\Gamma_j^-) + p_i + T_i\left(j - |\Gamma_j^-| + 1\right), \quad |\Gamma_i^-| \leq j \leq |N \backslash \Gamma_i^+|,$

and

$$c_{ij} = \begin{cases} w_i t_{ij} & \text{for } |\Gamma_i^-| \leq j \leq |N \backslash \Gamma_i^+|, \\ \infty & \text{for } 1 \leq j < |\Gamma_i^-| \text{ and } |N \backslash \Gamma_i^+| < j \leq n. \end{cases}$$

The lower bound is equal to the optimal solution of the following assignment problem: Minimize $\sum\limits_{i=1}^{n} \sum\limits_{j=1}^{n} c_{ij} x_{ij}$, for

$$\sum\limits_{i=1}^{n} x_{ij} = 1, \ j = 1, 2, \ldots, n, \ \sum\limits_{j=1}^{n} x_{ij} = 1, \ i = 1, 2, \ldots, n \text{ and } x_{ij} \in \{0, 1\}$$

In the paper of Rinnoy Kan et al. [7] the lower bound for TWTS problem is calculated similarly.

The Upper bound.

The upper bound is the value of a solution calculated by the heuristic algorithm WBH:

Step 1: Order n jobs by decreasing of due date d_i (EDD schedule);

Step 2: Take the first two jobs and schedule them in order to minimize the partial goal function as if there were only these two jobs;

Step 3: For k=3 to n **do**

insert the k-th job in the place, among k possible ones, which minimizes (for k jobs) the partial goal function.

The complexity of algorithm is $O(n^2 m)$.

6   Computer Simulations

We have tested the proposed algorithm on a set of randomly generated problems on a Sun Enterprise 8x400MHz using Ada95 language and MPI library. For each job i, an integer processing time p_i was generated from the uniform distribution $[1, 100]$ and an integer weight w_i was generated from the uniform distribution $[1, 10]$. Let $P = \sum_{i=1}^{n} p_i$. The deadlines d_i distribution depends on P and two additional parameters L and R, where L takes on values from 0.2 to 1.0 in increments of 0.1, and R takes on values from 0.2 to 1.6 in increments of 0.2. An integer deadline d_i was generated from the uniform distribution $[P(L - R/2), P(L + R/2)]$. Ten instances of the problem were generated for each of the 40 pairs of R and L values, creating 400 problems for each value of n. Number of jobs was n=20, 40, 60, 80, 100, 120. Many of the generated instances have no feasible sequence. This fact can be quickly determined using the EDD rule.

There are computational results for two heuristics EDD and WBH in Table 1.

Table 1. Heuristic algorithms.

	n=20		n=40		n=60		n=80		n=100		n=120	
	δ_{avg}^1	δ_{max}^2	δ_{avg}	δ_{max}	δ_{avg}	δ_{max}	δ_{avg}	δ_{max}	δ_{avg}	δ_{max}	δ_{avg}	δ_{max}
EDD	36.2	49.6	43.5	55.1	49.7	61.7	48.6	68.6	53.7	72.4	56.9	93.7
WBH	18.9	26.6	21.4	32.7	25.8	35.4	27.1	39.7	26.2	33.6	31.4	41.8

[1]average percentage deviation to the lower bound.
[2]maximal percentage deviation to the lower bound.

Initial population:

Property 1 follows if in permutation $\pi \in \Phi_n$ all jobs are feasible ($C_{\pi(i)} \leq d_{\pi(i)}$, $i \in N$), then π is also a feasible solution, $\pi \in \Pi$. In a classical genetic algorithm the initial population P_0 is a randomly generated subset of a feasible set of solutions, ($P_0 \subset \Phi_n$). For many instances of the SWCT problem it is very hard to determine this kind of subset. Therefore, we generate the initial population, which also includes unfeasible solutions. In further iterations of the algorithm unfeasible solutions are eliminated using the decreasing deadline technique.

For each of the test instances of the problem, we compute the following values: F^{UB} – upper bound and F^* – the value of objective function found by the genetic algorithm. Having these values, we define a relative measure for the algorithm quality: $PRD^{UB} = ((F^{UB} - F^*)/F^*) \cdot 100\%$ – the mean value of the percentage relative deviation of the objective function F^{UB} with respect to F^*.

The computational results can be found in Table 2. The number of iterations was counted as a sum of iterations on processors, and was permanently set to 3,200. For example, 4-processor implementations make 800 iterations on each of the 4 processors, 8-processor implementation – 400 iterations on every processor.

As we can see in Table 2, results of the algorithms are the best for the 8-processor implementation of parallel genetic algorithm. The improvement of the relative distance to reference solutions was at the level of 22.6%, compared to solutions of the sequential algorithm, with the same number of iterations equal to 3,200 for the sequential and parallel algorithm. The time of the computing amount of a few seconds up to a few dozen seconds, depends on the size n of the problem instance.

Table 2. Percentage relative deviation of PGA solutions compared to the solutions of WBH constructive algorithm. NFI – number of feasible instances.

n	NFI	processors		
		1	4	8
20	229	-4.796%	-6.020%	-6.110%
40	245	-5.685%	-5.615%	-7.902%
60	249	-5.700%	-6.010%	-8.474%
80	251	-6.901%	-7.903%	-9.025%
100	250	-10.103%	-10.496%	-11.595%
120	251	-9.816%	-10.004%	-9.608%
average		-7.167%	-7.675%	-8.786%

7   Conclusions

We have discussed a new approach to the single machine total weighted completion time problem based on the parallel asynchronous genetic algorithm. The advantage is especially visible for large problems. As compared to the sequential algorithm, parallelization increases the quality of the solutions obtained. The idea of dynamic floating deadlines and the best individual migration was used. Computer experiments show, that the parallel algorithm is considerably more efficient with relation to the sequential algorithm.

References

1. Bensal S.: Schingle machine scheduling to minimize weighted sum of completion times with secondary criterion – a branch and bound approach. European J. Oper. Res. **5** (1980) 177–181
2. Goldberg D.: Genetic Algorithms in Search, Optimization, and Machine Learning. Addison-Wesley Publishing Company, Inc., Massachusetts (1989)
3. Holland J.H.: Adaptation in natural and artificial systems: An introductory analysis with applications to biology, control, and artificial intelligence. University of Michigan Press (1975)
4. Lenstra J.J., Rinnoy Kan A.H.G., Brucker P.: Complexity of machine scheduling problems. Ann. Discrete Math. (1979) 287–326
5. Pan Y.: An improved branch and bound algorithm for single machine scheduling with deadlines to minimize total weighted completion time, Operation Research Letters **31** (2003) 492–496
6. Posner M.: Minimizing weighted completion times with deadlines, Oper. Res. **33** (1985) 562–574
7. Rinnoy Kan A.G.H, Lageweg B.J., Lenstra J.K.: Minimizing total cost one-machine scheduling. Operations Research **26** (1975) 908–972
8. Smith W.E.: Various optimizers for single-stage production, Naval Res. Logist. Quart. **3** (1956) 59–66
9. Wodecki M., Bożejko W., Solving the flow shop problem by parallel simulated annealing, LNCS No. **2328**, Springer Verlag (2002) 236–247

Adaptive Evolutionary Computation – Application for Mixed Linear Programming

Ewa Dudek-Dyduch and Dominik Jarczyk

AGH University of Science and Technology
Mickiewicza Av. 30, 30-059 Cracow, Poland
{edd,dominik}@ia.agh.edu.pl

Abstract. This paper deals with the two-level, partially stochastic optimization method named Two Level Adaptive Evolutionary Computation (TLAEC). New adaptation mechanism is embedded in the method. The aim of the paper is to present an algorithm based on TLAEC method, solving so-called development problem. A mathematical model of this problem assumes the form of mixed discrete-continuous programming. A concept of the algorithm is described in the paper and the proposed, new adaptation mechanism that is introduced in the algorithm is described in detail. The results of computation experiments as well as their analysis are also given.

1 Introduction

At present it is necessary to solve tasks for which no analytic algorithms exist or the existing ones are not effective. The large-scale discrete programming, scheduling and some nonanalytic problems belong to the class of such tasks.

The paper deals with a method, which can be applied to solve some of the above mentioned problems. The method is named Two Level Adaptive Evolutionary Computation (TLAEC). The formal description of the method is given in [3]. Novelty of the method consists in a new adaptation mechanism that is embedded in it.

The aim of the paper is to present an algorithm based on TLAEC method, solving so-called development problem. A mathematical model of this problem assumes the form of mixed discrete-continuous programming. A concept of the algorithm is described in the paper and the proposed, new adaptation mechanism that is introduced is described in detail. The results of computation experiments and their analysis are given.

2 Two-Level Adaptive Evolutionary Computation

TLAEC method [3] can be applied to optimization tasks, which have been transformed to the form suitable for two-level algorithms [5].

Thus, the task: to find $\hat{x} \in X$ minimizing function f:

$$f(\hat{x}) = \min_{x \in X} f(x)$$

L. Rutkowski et al. (Eds.): ICAISC 2004, LNAI 3070, pp. 406–413, 2004.
© Springer-Verlag Berlin Heidelberg 2004

where X is a subset of linear space X' can be replaced by: to find the pair $(\hat{u}, \hat{v}) \in U \times V$ such that

$$f(\hat{u}, \hat{v}) = \min_{(u,v) \in U \times V} f(u, v) = \min_{u \in U} \left[\min_{v \in V} f(u, v) \right]$$

where $V(u) \subset V$ is a set of feasible vectors v determined by means of a fixed vector u. Fig.1 shows a simplified scheme of TLAEC method. According to the

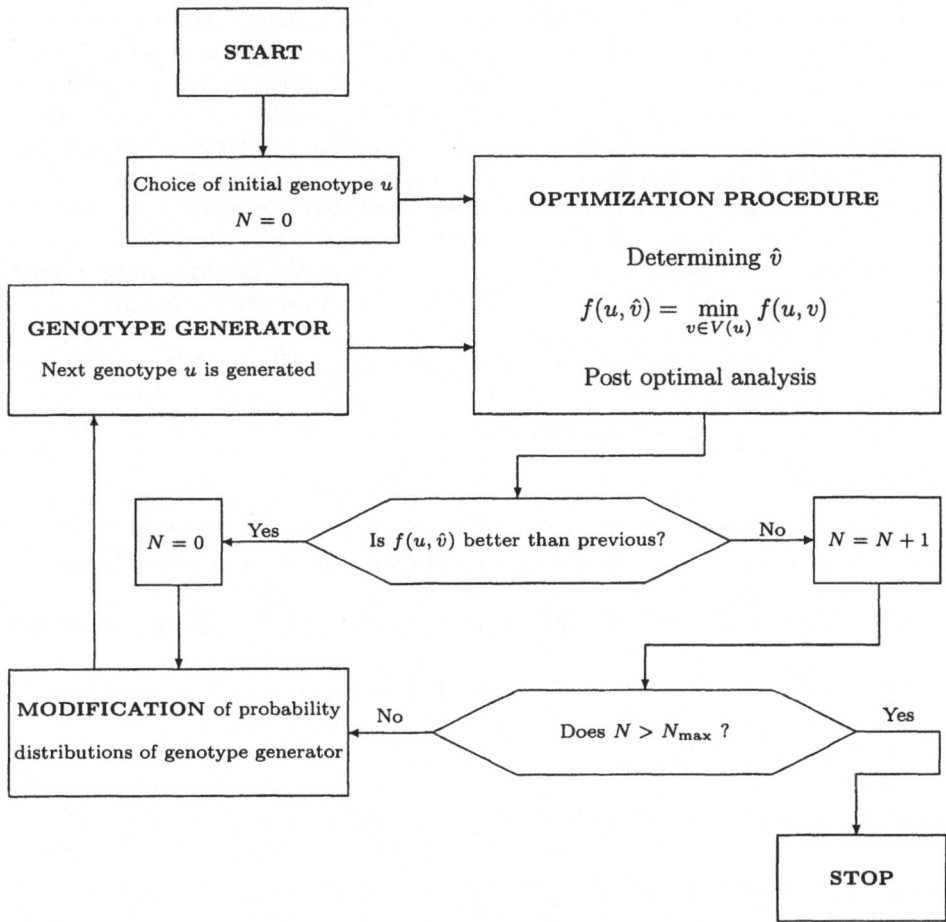

Fig. 1. The simplified flow diagram of TLAEC method

method vector u is a genotype and its gene values are generated by random procedure on the higher level. Then vector v is computed on a lower level as a result of solving some optimization task, where u constitutes parameters. Vector v corresponds to a phenotype and is evaluated on this level. Parameters of probability distributions are modified after any iteration on the basis of information obtained during post optimal analysis.

3   Optimization of Development Problem

Let us consider the problem of best investments choice, named here development problem. Planning the development of its economic status in market, an economic organization intends to predominate in a defined section of market. This necessitates a delivery of basic and auxiliary products in quantities strictly predefined by forecasts and expansion plans. The sale of own products is a target here. However, the investment plans, conditioning the development of production capacities, should be realized in time. Therefore, supplementary import or export of a given type of products to other markets should be also considered. The organization has a prognosis of demand for the market section group of products. The organization possessed production lines of different types. Maximum production level is determined for the each type of line. There are several production lines of the same type. In order to meet the demand, the organization considers purchase of new production lines. Obviously the investment outlay is limited. The organization should optimize the numbers of production lines of particular types, that are to be purchased, as well as the production level both the possessed production line and production lines that can be purchased. Let there are given:

n - total number of types of products that are to be delivered to the market,

$b_{[n]}$ - vector of domestic demand for each product in the fixed period of time,

m - number of various types of production lines,

$u^0_{[m]}$ - vector of existing production lines of particular types; k-th co-ordinate u^0_k denotes the number of existing production lines of the k-th type,

$h_{[m]}$ - vector of maximum production levels of particular production line types,

$g_{[m]}$ - vector of investment costs of particular production line types,

c_1, c_2 - vector of export and import prices, respectively,

c_3 - vector of unit cost of production for each type of production line,

G - maximum value of investment outlay,

$A_{[n \times m]}$ - matrix where a_{ij} is coefficient of utilization or production for the i-th product in the j-th production line type, matrix represents all production line types, existing and those that can be built.

Let z denotes the vector of production level of particular type of production lines. We assume a linear relation between vector z and vector d determining production of each product: $Az = d$.

Let u denotes the vector representing numbers of production lines of particular types; k-th co-ordinate u_k denotes the number of production lines of the k-th type both existing and considered to be purchased. Obviously u^0, u are integer vectors,

$$u \geq u^0 \geq 0 .$$

One should compute: the optimal arrangement of investments $(u - u^0)$, vector of production level z, export and import vectors y, x, which assure fulfilling the forecasted demand in terms of minimal cost. The role of export and import is auxiliary in this task, i.e. we assume that it is possible to sell or buy all products, the production of which is greater or less then domestic demand.

The arrangement of investments $(u - u^0)$ must fulfil the following constraint

$$(u - u^0)g \le G .$$

Therefore, the development problem can be formally described as a mixed discrete-continuous linear optimization task: to find z, x, y, u that minimize function f

$$f = c_2 x - c_1 y + c_3 z, \qquad c_1 < c_2 \tag{1}$$

and satisfy constraints:

$$Az + x - y = b \tag{2}$$
$$z_k \le u_k h_k, \quad k = 1, 2, \ldots, m \tag{3}$$
$$(u - u^0)g \le G \tag{4}$$
$$x, y, z, u \ge 0 \tag{5}$$
$$u \in \mathbb{N} \cup \{0\} \tag{6}$$

where $\mathbb{N}$ stands for the set of natural numbers. The relation $c_1 < c_2$ causes that a unique and limited solution exists.

4 TLAEC Algorithm

It is easy to notice that when u is fixed, the rest of the searched variables x, y, z can be computed by means of linear programming procedure. Because of that the vector u is assumed to be a genotype. Thus, on the upper level the vector u that satisfies (4) is randomly generated. Let

$$u = u^i \tag{7}$$

where u^i is the value of u generated in i-th iteration. The rest of variables constitute a phenotype. The phenotype is computed on the lower level as a result of solving the following linear programming task (8)÷ (11): to minimize

$$c_2 x - c_1 y + c_3 z + \lambda(u^i - u) \tag{8}$$

under constraints:

$$Az + x - y = b \tag{9}$$
$$\frac{z_k}{h_k} \le u_k, \quad k = 1, 2, \ldots, m \tag{10}$$
$$x, y, z, u \ge 0 . \tag{11}$$

The optimization task (8)÷(11) is a Lagrangian relaxation of the primary optimization task (1)÷(6), in which the constraints (4), (6) are replaced by (7).

Which information obtained from this task solution can be utilized and how to determine the direction of u changes?

Let us notice that after solving a linear programming task also the Lagrange multipliers λ for equalities (7) are known. This information is a basis for the adaptation mechanism applied on the upper level evolutionary algorithm. In order to modify probability distributions for generation of new vectors u, two vectors e and d are defined. Both are used to approximate the most promising direction of vector u changes.

Let e_k, $k = 1, \ldots, m$ be defined by (12)

$$e_k = \lambda_k \frac{h_k}{g_k} \, . \tag{12}$$

If the value of coordinate e_k is big, then this indicates that the k-th type of production line has big influence on the value of performance index f and it suggests that the number of this type lines should increase in a new arrangement of investment. Thus, u_k value should increase for a new vector u.

Let d_k, $k = 1, \ldots, m$ be defined by (13)

$$d_k = \left(1 - \frac{z_k}{h_k u_k}\right) \frac{g_k}{h_k} \, . \tag{13}$$

If the value of indicator d_k is big, then this indicates that the k-th type of production line has low utilization rate and it suggests that the number of this type lines should decrease in a new arrangement of investment. Thus, u_k value should decrease for a new vector u.

Because of the discrete set of admissible vectors u and discrete set of vectors g, the introduced adaptation mechanism has a heuristic character. The new vector u^{i+1} is generated as follows:

1. Probabilistic choice of types of production lines, numbers of which are to be reduced in the new arrangement u^{i+1}. The probability p_k that the number of production lines of k-th type will decrease is proportional to $q_k(u^i)$ where vector q is defined:

$$q(u^i) = \begin{cases} rd(u^i), & \text{if } i = 1 \\ (1-r)d(u^{i-1}) + rd(u^i), & \text{if } i \geq 2 \end{cases}, \quad r \in (0,1) \,, \tag{14}$$

$$p_k^i = \frac{q_k(u_k^i)}{\sum\limits_{k=1}^{m} q_k(u_k^i)} \, . \tag{15}$$

2. Probabilistic choice of new investments. The probability p_k that the number of production lines of k-th type will increase is proportional to $s_k(u^i)$. Vector u^{i+1} must belong to the neighborhood of u^i.

$$s(u^i) = \begin{cases} re(u^i), & \text{if } i = 1 \\ (1-r)e(u^{i-1}) + re(u^i), & \text{if } i \geq 2 \end{cases}, \quad r \in (0,1) \,, \tag{16}$$

$$p_k^i = \frac{s_k(u_k^i)}{\displaystyle\sum_{k=1}^{m} s_k(u_k^i)} \ . \qquad (17)$$

When the new vector u^{i+1} is generated then the new linear programming task is solved and value of function f, which plays a role of evaluation function in evolutionary algorithm, is calculated. Let this value is denoted as $f(u^{i+1})$.

If $f(u^{i+1})$ is better than the previous ones, then vector u^{i+1} replaces u^i. If value of evaluation function is not improved, the sampling is repeated.

Computing stops after a fixed number of iterations, when the best value of performance index does not change.

The vectors $s(u)$, $q(u)$ and parameter r are used to improve the stability of the procedure.

5   Results of Experiments

To verify the correctness of the algorithm, the evSiMpLe program has been implemented in Matlab® 5.3.1 environment. The program uses a ready procedure *linprog(..)* implemented in Matlab®, that solves linear programming tasks.

Procedure *linprog(..)* returns the value of the Lagrange multipliers.

For purpose of experiments vectors c_1, c_2, c_3, were assumed such that

$$\bar{c}_3 = 1.5\bar{c}_1, \ \bar{c}_2 = 2\bar{c}_1 \Longrightarrow \bar{c}_1 < \bar{c}_3 < \bar{c}_2 \ .$$

Thus, the condition for a unique solution is fulfilled.

The first stage in the experiment was to find the best values of r and $N_{\max}$. The tests were carried out for some matrixes differing both in structure and size. The parameter r was changed in a range $[0.1, 1]$ with step 0.1. For each value of r, 40 tests were carried out while $N_{\max} = 25$. The obtained at a fixed value of r solutions were compared with the known, optimal solutions. As a measure of accuracy, a number of optimal solutions obtained by means of TLAEC algorithm was taken. The results turned out to be very interesting. The influence of parameter r on the course of optimization turned out to be similar for all matrices and the best results were obtained for $r = 0.4$. An exemplary course of influence of coefficient r on the course of optimization has been shown in Fig.2.

At the next stage influence of coefficient $N_{\max}$ was tested. Due to limited length of the paper, detailed analysis of it is omitted. When parameters r and $N_{\max}$ were fixed, a convergence of algorithm was tested for matrixes of various size (vector u from 7 to 20 elements) and various elements values, e.g. for great differences between elements of the matrix.

Regardless the size and value of the matrixes elements, the algorithm converged to the solution. After the first few steps, the values of the evaluation function significantly improved. Experiments conducted with the use of the proposed algorithm shown its high efficiency in searching for a global minimum of a discrete-continuous programming task. Therefore, it is worth considering its use instead of traditional algorithms, which do not employ information from Lagrange multipliers

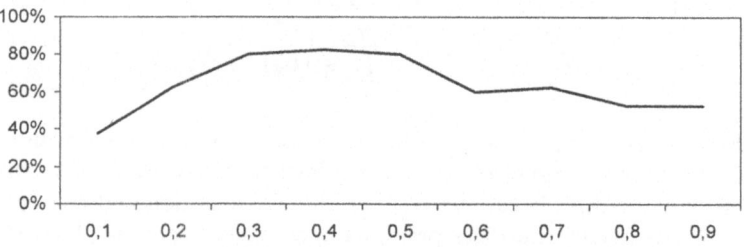

Fig. 2. Influence of parameter r on algorithm efficiency

For the sake of brevity, only results of computations obtained for two selected tasks are presented. The first task is small in size (vector u consists of 7 elements) and a considerable spread of matrix elements (from -0.00001 to 690). The other example shows how the algorithm operates for a bigger task (vector u consists of 20 elements). Fig.3 shows the evaluation function values in the successive

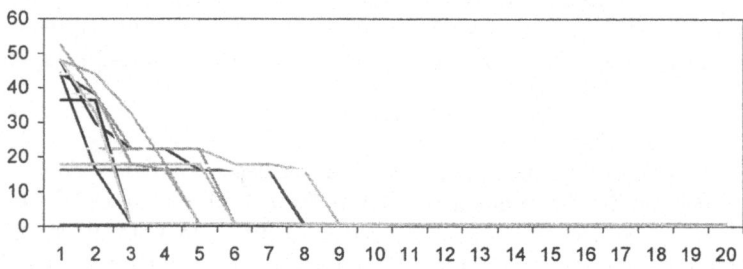

Fig. 3. Course of optimization, where vector u consists of 7 elements

iterations. Parameters of the algorithm were assumed as follows: $r = 0.4$, $N_{max} = 10$. To determine a precise solution, $2^7 = 128$ linear optimizations had to be carried out. However, the algorithm ended after maximum 20 optimizations, reaching the solution in 13 out of 15 cases. In the remaining 2 cases the result was also satisfactory. The result can be improved by increasing the value of parameter N_{max}. The precise solution has been marked on the bottom of the figure with a horizontal line. Fig.4 illustrates values of the evaluation function in the successive steps (generation) of an algorithm for a bigger task (vector u consists of 20 elements). The following values of algorithm parameters were assumed: $r = 0.4$, $N_{max} = 30$. The Figure 4 shows 65 steps of the algorithm and the result, which is very good. The minimum solution was obtained in 6 out of 15 trials. In the remaining cases the result was also close to minimum. This result can be improved by increasing the value of N_{max}.

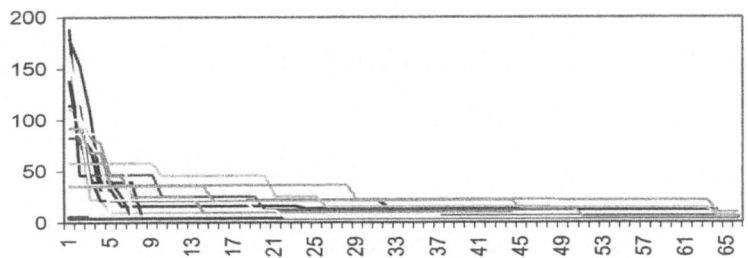

Fig. 4. Course of optimization, where vector u consists of 20 elements

6   Conclusion

The paper presents an application of Two Level Adaptive Evolutionary Computation (TLAEC) method for solving very complicated, large scale investment problem, so-called development problem. A mathematical model of this problem assumes the form of mixed discrete-continuous programming. A concept of the proposed TLAEC algorithm and a first stage of computer experiments are described in the paper. The results of experiments confirmed a high efficiency of proposed algorithm.

It should be stressed that the adaptation mechanism devised for TLAEC method essentially differs from the ones applied in evolutionary strategy [4], [6]. Because of that the emphasis was put just on presenting the introduced new, adaptation mechanism.

References

1. E. Dudek-Dyduch, Evolutionary method in discrete programming. Lecture Notes In Control and Information Sciences, Springer-Verlag, Berlin 1984, pp.220-225
2. E. Dudek-Dyduch, On Evolutionary Algorithm. Proc.1st IASTED Symp. on Applied Informatics vol.III p.37, Lille France 1983
3. T. Dyduch, Adaptive Evolutionary Computation (AEC) of the parametric optimization problem. ICAISC, Zakopane Poland 2004
4. A.E. Eiben, R. Hinterding and Z. Michalewicz, Parameter Control in Evolutionary Algorithms, IEEE Trans. On Evolutionary Computation, vol.3, No 2, 1999, pp. 124-141
5. W. Findeisen, Multi-level control systems. (in Polish) PWN Warszawa 1974
6. Z. Michalewicz, Genetic Algorithms + Data Structures = Evolution Programs. Springer-Verlag, Berlin 1996.

Adaptive Evolutionary Computation of the Parametric Optimization Problem

Tadeusz Dyduch

AGH University of Science and Technology
Mickiewicza Av. 30, 30-059 Cracow, Poland
tdyduch@uci.agh.edu.pl

Abstract. The aim of the paper is to present a special type of adaptive evolutionary method, named here Two-Level Adaptive Evolutionary Computation (TLAEC). The method consists in combination of evolutionary computation with deterministic optimization algorithms in a hierarchy system. Novelty of the method consists also in a new type of adaptation mechanism. Post optimal analysis of the lower level optimization task is utilized in order to modify probability distribution for new genotype generations. The formal description of the method is presented in the paper. The application of this method to a mixed, discrete-continuous linear optimization task is given as an example.

1 Introduction

Evolutionary Computation (EC) is very popular among artificial intelligence methods in soft computing. Numerous scientific works, conferences, commercial software offers and academic handbooks were devoted to this method. Evolutionary computations can be classified as iterative optimization methods based on a partially stochastic search through an optimization domain. In order to improve convergence of evolutionary computation, evolutionary strategies have been devised, where the adaptation mechanism have been introduced [3], [5].

The aim of the paper is to present a special type of adaptive evolutionary method, named here two-level adaptive evolutionary computation (TLAEC). Although the adaptation mechanism is embedded in the method, the adaptation differs from the classical evolutionary strategy. The presented method consists of the following stages.

1. The primary optimization task is transformed to the form suitable for hierarchical two-level algorithms. Thus, the set of searched variables are divided into two disjoint subsets. Similarly, the constraints are divided into two disjoint subsets.

   The first subset of variables corresponds to a genotype. Values of the variables are computed on the higher level by means of random procedures using mutations and/or crossover operators. Only the first subset of constraints is taken into account here. These constraints refer only to the genotype. The value of the genotype constitutes parameters for the lower level optimization task.

L. Rutkowski et al. (Eds.): ICAISC 2004, LNAI 3070, pp. 414–419, 2004.
© Springer-Verlag Berlin Heidelberg 2004

The remained variables (second subset) are computed on the lower level as a result of deterministic optimization procedure. Only the second subset of constraints is taken into account here. Because the variables can be calculated when the genotype is known, they correspond to a phenotype (or part of a phenotype). The individual is evaluated on this level too.

2. After each iteration a post optimal analysis is done. Its aim is to gather information about the lower level solution (or solutions computed in the earlier iterations). The gather information is utilized to modify probability distributions for genetic operators on the upper level.

Let us point out two features of the presented method. Firstly, a phenotype (or some part of it) is calculated as a result of solving some optimization task where a value of genotype constitutes parameters of the task. Secondly, a modification of probability distributions for generation new genotypes (adaptation) in each iteration is based on information about the solution of the lower level task. The modification is not based only on the evolutionary algorithm course. Thus the adaptation mechanism differs from the adaptation mechanism of evolutionary strategies $(1+1)$, $(\mu + \lambda)$, (μ, λ) [5].

The adaptation of parameters for the mutation and recombination, based on the post optimal analysis of the lower level optimization task, made for each iteration is a very important element here. Because of limited length of the paper only the main idea of the TLAEC will be presented. Details of particular stages of evolutionary computation will be omitted.

2   Formal Description of the Method

The primary optimization task is of the form: to find $\hat{x} \in X$ minimizing function f

$$f(\hat{x}) = \min_{x \in X} f(x) \text{ where } X \text{ is a subset of linear space } X' . \tag{1}$$

In order to apply TLAEC method, the task should be transformed to the form suitable for two level parametric optimization algorithms [4]. Thus the task (1) should be replaced by: to find the pair $(\hat{u}, \hat{v}) \in U \times V = X$ such that

$$f(\hat{u}, \hat{v}) = \min_{(u,v) \in U \times V} f(u, v) = \min_{u \in U} [\min_{v \in V(u)} f(u, v)] \tag{2}$$

where $V(u)$ denotes a set of admissible vectors v determined at a fixed value of vector u. This task does not generally have an analytical solution unless it is trivial. Because of that it must be solved iteratively. Let u^i, v^i denote the value of vectors u, v computed in i-th iteration. Vector u^i is determined on a higher level while vector v^i on a lower level. Let's present the searched variables in the evolutionary computation terms.

Individual: pair of vectors (u^i, v^i), representing a temporary point in the optimization domain (solution in the i-th iteration),

Genotype: vector u^i representing a temporary point in the subspace of optimization domain, searched at random with an evolutionary algorithm.

Phenotype: vector v^i representing a temporary point in the subspace of optimization domain, here computed by a deterministic, lower level optimization algorithm. In some cases a pair of vectors (u^i, v^i) may be a phenotype. When the genotype u^i is established on the higher level then the lower level optimization task is of the form : to find v^i such that

$$Q^i = f(u^i, v^i) = \min_{v \in V(u^i)} f(u^i, v) \tag{3}$$

where Q^i denotes value of evaluation function of individual (u^i, v^i). The task should be effectively computable.

The solution of problem (2), or point of its vicinity $(\hat{u}, \hat{v})$ can be reached with an iterative procedure (4)

$$f(\hat{u}, \hat{v}) = \min_{(u,v) \in U \times V} f(u, v) = \lim_{i \to \infty} (\min_{v \in V(u^i)} f(u^i, v)) \tag{4}$$

$$\text{where } u^i = \text{rnd}(u^{i-1}, u^{i-2}, ...)$$

The function ,,rnd" is a random function, the probability distributions of which can be changed in the successive iterations.

There is a number of ways for presenting an optimization task (1) as a parameter two level optimization task. The variables should be so divided that the lower level optimization task could be solved by an efficient (polynomial) algorithm what enables multiple solving the task. Moreover, the internal optimization task should be constructed in such a way that information, gathered as a result of its post optimal analysis, be useful for the modification probability distributions on the higher level. Variables under complex restrictions should be rather selected for the upper level task.

3 Data Flow Diagram

A Data Flow Diagram (DFD) presented in Fig.1 will describe the proposed computation method. There are 6 processes and Data Storage ST denoted as no.7. Continuous lines linking processes denote transmission of data and control; broken lines denote only control transmission. Two arrows pointing to a process denote that this process can be initiated only when control has been transmitted from two preceding processes. The broken line, linking processes 6 and 1 represents a several times realized loop aimed at creating an initial population consisting of a few individuals.

INI process generates start points for TLAEC. Depending on the number of individuals in the initial population, it may be one or more genotypes. Also the operator should have a possibility to introduce the start point. In the case of a multimode optimization and need to restart the optimization process at different start points, the INI process should provide a diversification of these points. The OPT process has two aims. Firstly, it solves the lower layer optimization task (3), i.e. computes v^i values and value of the evaluation function Q^i. Secondly,

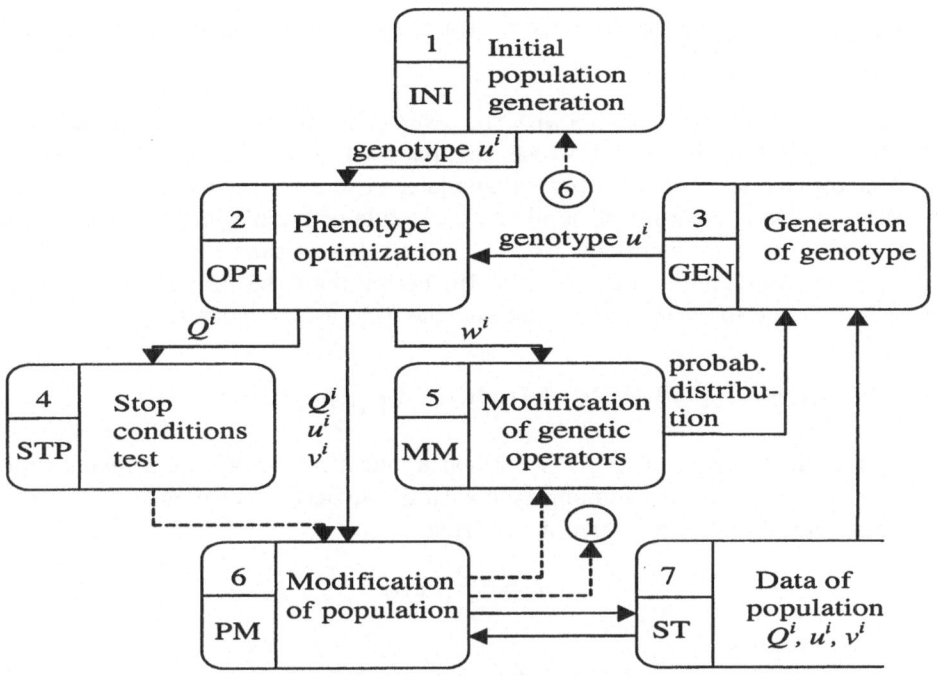

Fig. 1. A Data Flow Diagram of the system

the process also realizes a post-optimal analysis, gathering information for modification of probability distributions in the MM process. This information is synthetically represented by an index w^i, which may assume a form of a vector. If possible, index w^i constitutes assessed coefficients that characterize genotype influence on the quality index Q^i at point (u^i, v^i) , $w^i \approx \left.\dfrac{\delta Q}{\delta u}\right|_{u=u^i}$.

GEN process generates new genotypes by mutation or crossover operator. The applied probability distributions undergo modification in the MM process. The parent genotypes are taken from the population storage ST. This process should enable ,,taboo search" strategy, i.e. eliminate those generated in the last n steps genotypes.

STP process tests the stop conditions. These can be some of the below: reaching a required number of computations at different start points, reaching a required number of generated individuals, reaching a required number of generation changes, generation of a required number of individuals without changing a generation, i.e. without correcting the solution. If none of the stop conditions holds, control is transmitted to the PM process.

MM process modifies parameters of probability distributions employed by the GEN process when generating new genotypes. Modifications are based on the course of an earlier optimization process and/or assumed strategy and/or

index w^i that characterizes influence of particular genes on the quality index f
at (u^i, v^i), $w^i \approx \left. \dfrac{\delta f}{\delta u} \right|_{u=u^i}$.

PM process controls, in line with the assumed strategy, the number and quality of population, the data of which are preserved in the ST storage. Moreover, it controls the list of last 'n' individuals (stored in ST), needed for the ,,taboo search" analyses. Bearing in mind the basic rule of population updating, each new individual that evaluation function value is better than the worst one, substitutes the worst individual. If it is still better than the best individual in a population, the solution is improved and the generation changes.

4   Example of TLAEC Method Application

Let's give an example of TLAEC method application for solving a mixed-type discrete-continuous programming task with linear performance index.

One should find vectors u, v minimizing

$$f = c_1 u + c_2 v \tag{5}$$

under restrictions

$$Au + Bv \leq b, \quad u, v \geq 0 \tag{6}$$

where v is a vector of real numbers and u is a vector of integers, c_1, c_2, b are given vectors of real numbers and A, B are given matrixes of real numbers.

The pair of vectors (u, v) corresponds to an individual. The vector u corresponds to genotype and is generated on the upper level by means of mutation operator. Let's assume that value of vector u in i-th iteration is equal to u^i. We add equation (7) to the problem (5), (6).

$$u = u^i \tag{7}$$

and obtain the relaxed problem of continuous only variables: to minimize

$$f = c_1 u + c_2 v + \lambda(u^i - u) \tag{8}$$

under restrictions

$$Au + Bv \leq b, \quad u, v \geq 0 . \tag{9}$$

The resulting task (8), (9) is solved with a simplex algorithm. As a result we may obtain values not only vectors v^i, u^i, but also Lagrange coefficients λ^i, corresponding to limitations (7). It well fits the formula

$$w^i \approx \left. \frac{\delta f}{\delta u} \right|_{u=u^i} = c_1 - \lambda^i \, ,$$

used by TLAEC method. In the case of the simplest adaptation strategy, a probability of change of any integer coordinate of vector u is proportional to value of the corresponding to it coordinate of vector w.

Therefore, standard software for solving linear programming tasks by means of simplex algorithm can be used. It provides efficient optimization procedure for the lower level task as well as post optimal analysis.

In [2] TLAEC algorithm for more complex, mixed discrete-continuous programming task is described as well as the results of computer experiments are discussed.

5   Conclusions

In the paper a special type of adaptive evolutionary method, named here Two-Level Adaptive Evolutionary Computation (TLAEC), has been proposed. This method is applicable for solving a large class of complex optimization problems. The method consists in combination of evolutionary computation with deterministic optimization algorithms in a hierarchy system. In order to apply the method, the primary optimization task must be transformed to the form suitable for hierarchical, two level algorithms. Novelty of the method consists also in a new type of adaptation mechanism. Post optimal analysis of the lower level optimization task is utilized in order to modify probability distribution for new genotype generations.

The formal description of the method has been presented in the paper. Then, as an example, the application of this method to a mixed, discrete-continuous linear optimization task is described

References

1. Dudek-Dyduch, E. Evolutionary method in discret programming. Proc.12-th IFIP Conference on System Modeling and Optimization p. 220, Budapest Hungary 1984
2. Dudek-Dyduch E., Jarczyk D. Adaptive Evolutionary Computation – Application for Mixed Linear Programming, ICAISC, Zakopane Poland 2004
3. Eiben A.E., Hinterding R., Michalewicz Z. Parameter Control in Evolutionary Algorithms, IEEE Trans. On Evolutionary Computation, vol. 3, No 2, 1999, pp. 124-141
4. Findeisen W. Multi-level control systems. (in polish) PWN Warszawa 1974
5. Michalewicz Z. Genetic Algorithms + Data Structures = Evolution Programs. Springer-Verlag, Berlin 1996
6. Smith S. The simplex method and evolutionary algorithms. 5th Int. Conference on Evolutionary Computation ICEC'98, IEEE Press 1998

Concentration of Population in Phenotypic Evolution

Iwona Karcz-Dulęba

Wrocław University of Technology
Institute of Engineering Cybernetics
Wybrzeże Wyspiańskiego 27, 50-370 Wrocław, Poland
kdiwona@ict.pwr.wroc.pl

Abstract. An effect of the loss of diversity and the rapid concentration of an initially broadly spread population is analyzed for models of phenotypic evolution. The impact of the population size, different selection schemes, and dimensionality of the search space on population diversity is studied. Obtained results confirm common opinions that in large populations the diversity is greater and that the stronger selection pressure causes the faster concentration. High dimensional search spaces do not restrain the concentration of a population. In this case, populations cluster even faster than in one-dimensional search space.

1   Introduction

The phenomenon of premature convergence bothers evolutionary algorithms community for years [8]. The loss of variety in population may cause either to stop the search process in an evolutionary trap or to deteriorate penetration abilities of the algorithms. Various methods have been developed to overcome the trouble-making phenomenon. The methods used to apply hybrid algorithms, to vary individuals' life time, to limit the selection range, and to maximize diversity of the initial population. Our past experience [2,3,5,6,7] prompts that the loss of diversity could be considered as the important property of evolutionary processes. The concentration of initially fairly diversified population is caused by selection mechanism whereas mutation maintains the diversity. Simulations shown [2,3,5,7] that a population quickly concentrates and, further on, it evolves as a compact "cloud" of individuals. Those observations were also theoretically confirmed by the analysis of evolution of small populations in the space of population states [5,6].

This contribution deals with Darwinian, phenotypic asexual evolution. A proportional selection and normally distributed mutation form a framework for the evolution. Other selection schemes are also reported and compared with each other. The influence of the population size, dimensionality of fitness functions and selection schemes applied on the diversity of population was analyzed. In Section 2 basic definitions and assumptions are presented. Models of phenotypic selection, different selection schemes and definitions of population diversities are described. Section 3 presents simulation results. Section 4 concludes the report.

L. Rutkowski et al. (Eds.): ICAISC 2004, LNAI 3070, pp. 420–425, 2004.
© Springer-Verlag Berlin Heidelberg 2004

2   Model of Phenotypic Evolution and Selection Schemes

Phenotypic asexual evolution in unlimited space of real traits R^n is considered [4]. The population consists of m individuals, each described by the n-
dimensional vector of traits - its type, and a non-negative quality value - its
fitness. The successive generation is based on the current generation. It is created with the use of two operators only: selection and mutation. The parents of
new individuals are determined according to a selected selection strategy. Des-
cendants inherit parental traits mutated with an independent random variable.
In this study normally distributed Gaussian mutation with the standard deviation of mutation σ is assumed. Six selection schemes are examined. They follow:

Proportional selection (also called soft or roulette-wheel selection). The probability $P(x_k)$ of choosing the k-th individual x_k as a parent is proportional
to its fitness $q(x_k)$:

$$P(x_k) = \frac{q(x_k)}{\sum_{j=1}^{m} q(x_j)},$$

where m denotes the number of individuals in the population.

Hard selection. Only the best so far individual is reproduced. The type of the
best individual is modified until new offspring with higher fitness is found.

Tournament selection (binary). Two parents are chosen randomly with the
same uniform probability distribution (with replacement) and the better
individual from the pair locates an offspring in the next generation.

Truncation selection. Parents are selected, with the same selection probability, from the fraction of T best individuals.

Proportional selection with best individual. The best individual from the
current population is always reproduced. The other $m-1$ individuals produce
offspring according to the proportional selection rule.

Random selection. The randomly chosen individual (with equal probability)
becomes the parent to a new individual.

Diversity of population

In genetic algorithms the loss of diversity has been defined by Blickle and Thiele
[1] as a proportion of individuals in a population that are not chosen during
the selection. In the paper, the diversity of population is described as a measure
of individuals' deviation from the mean of population, which can be a measure
of population "compactness". For one-dimensional search spaces, the standard
deviation is a natural measure of diversity. For high dimensional search spaces a
function should be defined on a vector composed of variaties of each coordinate of
traits to project the vector onto one dimensional "variety" space. Chorążyczewski
and Galar proposed to take the Euclidean distance ($r = 2$) as a resulting measure
of diversity [3]:

$$\text{diversity} = (\sum_{j=1}^{n} D_j^r)^{1/r} \text{ where } \bar{x}_j = \frac{1}{m} \sum_{k=1}^{m} x_{k,j}, \text{ and } D_j^2 = \frac{1}{m} \cdot \sum_{k=1}^{m} (x_{k,j} - \bar{x}_j)^2$$

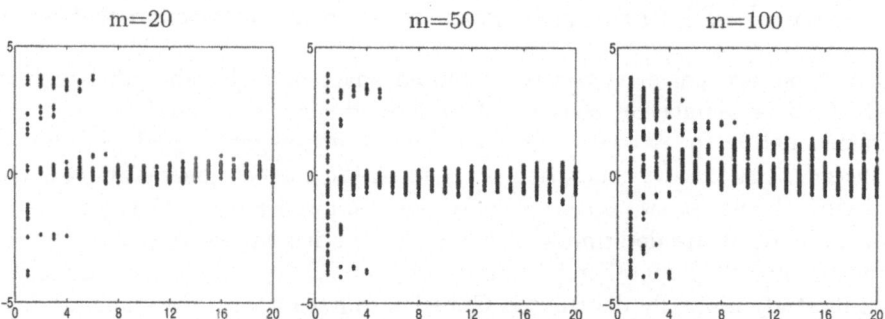

Fig. 1. Locations of the population through 20 generations ($\sigma = 0.1$, $n = 1$).

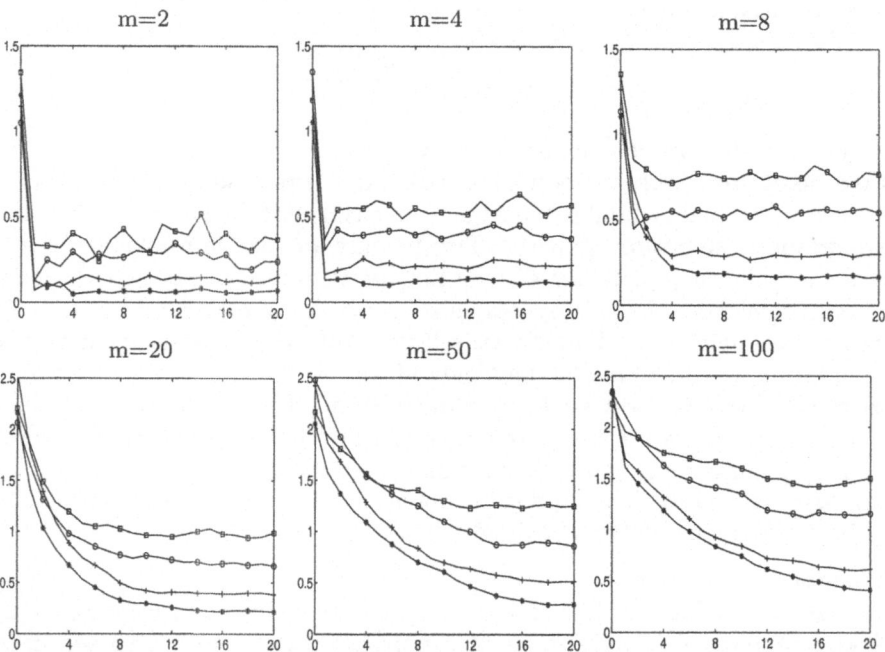

Fig. 2. Mean diversity of the population (100 runs, 20 generations) for the standard deviation of mutation varied. Lines marked with $*, +, \circ, \Box$ symbols correspond to $\sigma = 0.1, 0.2, 0.4, 0.6$ respectively ($n = 1$).

Also other distances can be exploited, parameter r varied. The diversity increase should reduce the risk of premature convergence as various phenotypes are preserved for the next generation.

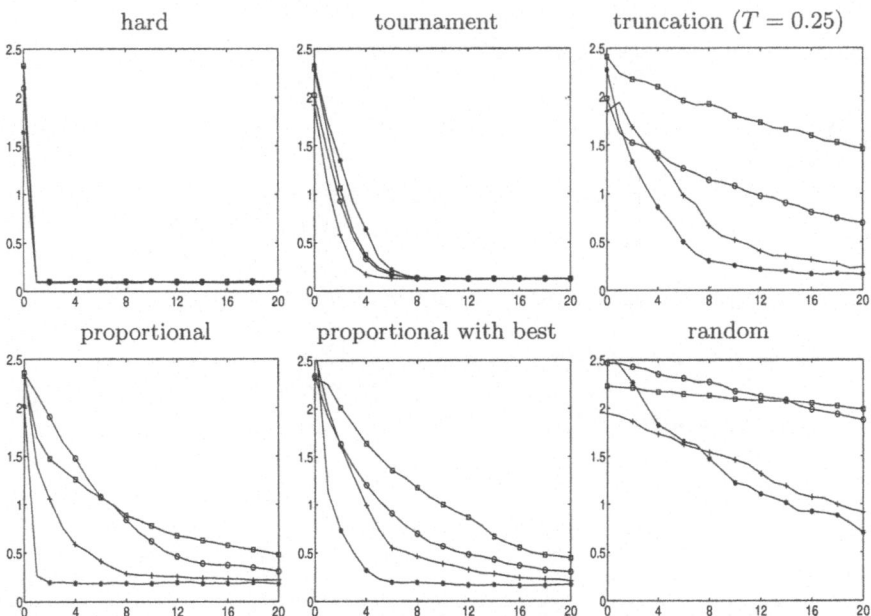

Fig. 3. Impact of selection on population diversity. Mean diversity of population (100 runs, 20 generation) for various population sizes. Lines marked with $*, +, \circ, \square$ symbols correspond to $m = 10, 20, 50, 100$ respectively ($n=1$, $\sigma=0.1$).

3   Simulation Results

Evolution of population was studied in the landscape of unimodal Gaussian fitness function with optimum placed at zero, $q(x) = \exp(-a\,x^2)$, $a = 5$. Simulations were run with a widely distributed initial population, uniformly sampled. The proportional selection was assumed in simulations as a basic scheme [7]. Locations of large populations ($m = 20, 50, 100$) evolving in one-dimensional search space ($n = 1$) in consecutive 20 generations are presented in Fig. 1. Populations, initially randomly split on the range $[-4, 4]$, lost their diversity very fast, just after a few generations. Individuals of similar types form a compact cloud around the fitness function optimum. The unification process is faster for relatively small populations.

The dependence of dispersion on the standard deviation of mutation and the population size is presented in Fig 2. 100 runs of evolution were averaged. Initial populations were randomly chosen from the range $[-2, 2]$ for $m = 2, 4, 8$ and the range $[-4, 4]$ for $m = 20, 50, 100$. Originally dispersed populations concentrate quickly and their average dispersion is about σ for small populations and two or three σ for big ones.

An impact of the selection type, used in evolution process, on population diversity is illustrated in Fig. 3. Initial populations were randomly chosen from the range $[-4, 4]$. The stronger selection intensity (pressure), the faster unification

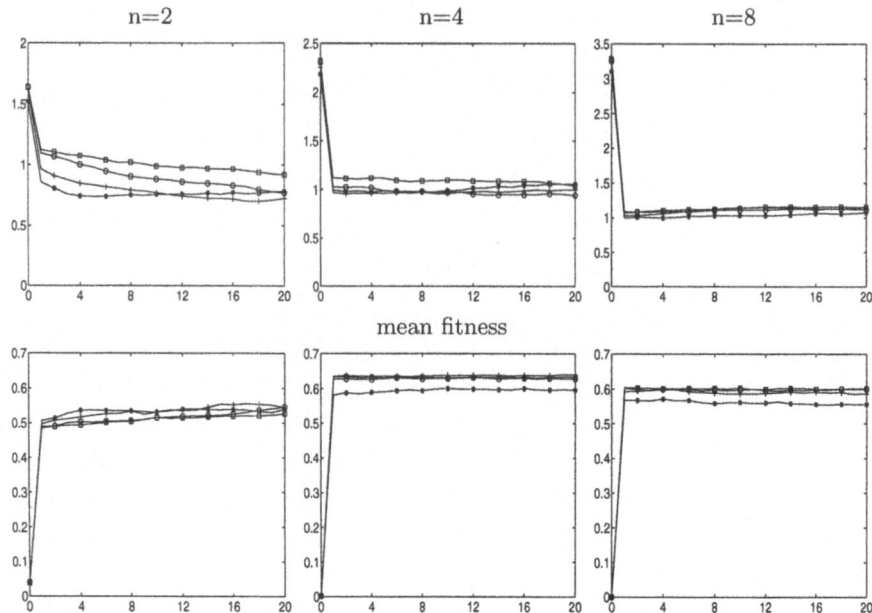

Fig. 4. Diversity of populations and mean fitness in multidimensional search spaces. Mean diversity (100 runs, 20 generation) for different population sizes. Lines marked with $*, +, \circ, \square$ symbols correspond to $m = 10, 20, 50, 100$ respectively ($\sigma=0.1$).

of population progresses. Hard selection, it reproduces only the best individuals, caused the rapid concentration of population around the best individual. The only source of diversity is mutation and individuals differs about the standard deviation of mutation σ. Tournament selection maintains diversity in population only through a few generations. Variety in population under the truncation selection is rather high. Although only a quarter of population is involved during selection, the diversity is preserved, especially for large populations. The proportional and proportional with best selections result in fast concentration of population, with a speed inversely proportional to the population size. Even in the random selection the loss of diversity was observed for small populations. It could be caused by random drawing with replacement, so not all individuals were chosen during the selection.

For proportional selection, the impact of dimensionality of the search space on population diversity and on mean fitness of the population is presented in Fig. 4. Initial populations were randomly chosen from the range $[-2, 2]$ for each coordinate. Populations in multidimensional search spaces concentrate even faster than in one-dimensional ones. With the dimensionality increase, the influence of population size on the variety is smaller. Populations of different sizes cluster in clouds of similar radius located near the optimum. The mean fitness is higher for larger n and it may effect from the bigger concentration of population.

4   Conclusions

Reported results confirm earlier observations that the phenomenon of quick concentration of population seems to be the immanent feature of evolutionary processes. The unification of a population results from selection. Simulations comparing different selection schemes confirm common statement, that the stronger selection pressure, the faster concentration. The compactness of the population depends on its size and, in large populations, could exceed the mutation standard deviation. The fast concentration of population was observed when the dimensionality of a search space increases. The simulations shown that, in search spaces of unimodal fitness functions, populations concentrate in the neighborhood of the optimum what confirm optimization abilities of evolution. In global optimization, the idea of finding optima very precisely (i.e. using selection with strong pressure or mutation with a small probability and a small range) may restrict exploration of the search space. Therefore, the choice of parameters of evolutionary algorithms should strongly depend on the optimization aim and attain a thin balance between exploration and exploitation.

References

1. Blickle, T., Thiele, L. (1996), A comparison of selection schemes used in evolutionary algorithms. Evolutionary Computation, 4(4) 361–395
2. Chorążyczewski, A., Galar, R., Karcz-Dulęba, I. (2000), Considering phenotypic Evolution in the Space of Population States. In: L. Rutkowski, R. Tadeusiewicz (ed) Proc. 5th Conf. on Neural Networks and Soft Computing, Zakopane, 615–620
3. Chorążyczewski, A., Galar, R. (2001), Evolutionary Dynamics of Population States. Proc. Congress on Evolutionary Computation, Seoul, Korea 1366-1373
4. Galar, R. (1985), Handicapped individua in evolutionary processes. Biol. Cyberern. **51**(1), 1–9.
5. Karcz-Dulęba, I. (2000), Dynamics of evolution of population of two in the space of population states. The case of symmetrical fitness functions. Proc. 4th Nat. Conf. on Evol. Algorithms and Global Opt., Lądek Zdrój, Poland 115-122 (in Polish)
6. Karcz-Dulęba, I. (2002), Evolution of Two-element Population in the Space of Population States: Equilibrium States for Asymmetrical Fitness Functions. In: Evolutionary Algorithms and Global Optimization (J. Arabas Ed.). Warsaw, Univ. of Technology Press, 35–46.
7. Karcz-Dulęba, I. (2003), Analysis of population concentration in phenotypic evolution. Workshop on Evolutionary Computation, Wdzydze (in Polish).
8. Michalewicz, Z. (1993), Genetic Algorithms +Data Structures=Evolution Programs. Springer-Verlag.

An Evolutionary Clustering Algorithm

Marcin Korzeń

Faculty of Computer Science and Information Systems
Technical University of Szczecin,
Zolnierska Street 49,Pl-71210 Szczecin, Poland
mkorzen@wi.ps.pl

Abstract. There are many heuristic algorithms for clustering, from which the most important are the hierarchical methods of agglomeration, especially the Ward's method. Among the iterative methods the most universally used is the C–means method and it's generalizations. These methods have many advantages, but they are more or less dependent on the distribution of points in space and the shape of clusters. In this paper the problem of clustering is treated as a problem of optimization of a certain quality index. For that problem the author proposes two solutions: a hierarchical partitioning algorithm and an evolutionary algorithm.

1 Introduction

The problem of clustering is the division of a finite set of points X in a metric space into a given number m of classes, such that $X = \bigcup_{i=1}^{m} A_i, \quad A_i \cap A_j = \emptyset$, if $i \neq j$. In practice we are particularly interested in clusterings, which are the most compatible with the structure of given set of samples and also with the metric of considered space. There are many known methods, which divide a given set of data into clusters. These methods often produce different clusterings. Some methods work properly only in the case of existence of clear clusters. Other methods work well when data is uniformly distributed and work properly in the case of convex clusters. Some methods are based on the assumption, that the classes have elliptic distribution (e.g. normal distribution). We distinguish many methods in dependence of the method of joining. One of the best from them is the Ward's method (see [8], [4]). On a different approach the C–means method and it's fuzzy variant are based. (see [2], [5]).

2 Heuristic Partitioning Algorithm

The hierarchical algorithms of agglomeration create the classes from the bottom up (directed by inclusion relation). The top-down approach is also possible. It treats the whole set as a single class, and after that it divides the set into two parts. In each step the largest of the obtained classes is divided into two parts, and so on. The process terminates when all the classes become single data

L. Rutkowski et al. (Eds.): ICAISC 2004, LNAI 3070, pp. 426–431, 2004.
© Springer-Verlag Berlin Heidelberg 2004

points, or when the number of classes becomes equal to some given number. Such a method depends on the way of dividing the set into two parts. The proposed algorithm is based on the concept of the minimum spanning tree of the set of points. For that problem there exists a simple algorithm. (Prim's algorithm [6], see also [7, pp. 407–417]). The tree has such a property, that it is the shortest (of minimal sum of edge lengths) tree connecting all the points of set X.

Let's adopt the following notation: $k(x_i, x_j)$ - the edge connecting the vertices (x_i, x_j), A - adjacency matrix, of the minimal spanning tree, and $n = \#X$. Before we define the division criterion division we define the following concepts:

A vertex of the 1-st degree (or a leaf) is a point x_i, which has exactly one neighbor. In the average case leaves are the outermost points of the cluster. In order to check whether a given vertex x_i is a leaf, it is enough to check whether there is only one 1 in the i-th row and in the i-th column of the matrix that represents the tree.

A vertex of $n - th$ **degree** is a point which becomes a point of 1-st degree after deleting all the vertices of degree up to (and including) $n - 1$. In the average case the higher the degree of a point is, the closer to the middle of the X set the point is situated. The degree of the point (the leaf) is denoted by $r(x_i)$, $x_i \in X$. In order to determine the degrees of successive vertices we remove the leaves one after another from the tree obtaining a new subtree.

The degree of the edge $k(x_i, x_j)$ we call the lower degree of the points it connects: $r(k(x_i, x_j)) = \min(r(x_i), r(x_j))$. The degree of the edge determines in which step the edge will be removed, when we are removing points of successive degrees.

The proposed way of cutting the tree into two parts consists in removing the edge $k(x_i, x_j)$, for which the product of the edge length and the degree of the edge is the highest one, which means that the relationship $\max_{1 \le i < j \le n} (d(x_i, x_j) \cdot r(k(x_i, x_j)))$ is true.

3   The Application of the Evolutionary Algorithm

An overview of the basic techniques of genetic and evolutionary algorithms can be found e.g. in [1]. The motivation for using an evolutionary algorithm for clustering was the fact, that the basic heuristic algorithms, such as classical hierarchical algorithms and C–means method, were not always giving expected results. The easy estimation of the quality of dividing the set into clusters is possible only in two or three dimensional case. It is enough then to visualize the analyzed set and estimate visually obtained classes. When we use the quantitative index of the clustering quality, the problem of choosing the classes can be transformed to the problem of optimization of the chosen index. In the case of genetic algorithms, different kinds of indexes of class quality have been tested – both those, which consist of minimization of the inside-class distances and also those, which consist of maximization of the between-class distances. These experiments have shown, that each of the tested quality indexes was more or less sensitive to different variants of the testing data sets. The relatively good results were obtained when the weighted sum of distances from the center of gravity was used as the measure of quality. This index for clustering $A = \{A_i\}_{i=1}^k$ is defined as: $IQ(A_i) = \sum_{i=1}^k \left(\frac{1}{\#A_i} \sum_{x_j \in A_i} d(x_c, x_j) \right)$

It is worth noting, that such a task consists of finding the optimal element in a finite set Ω of all the possible k-element clusterings of the set X. The number of all the clusterings of the n-element set, containing k classes, is equal $\frac{1}{k!} \sum_{j=0}^k (-1)^j \binom{k}{j} (k-j)^n$, what by condition $k \ll n$ is in approximation equal to k^{n-1} (see [4, p. 149]). Thus the 'naive' algorithm, searching all the possible results is very impractical.

Behind the evolutionary algorithm there is heuristic algorithm of division (myHeur), which was described in the previous section. But to make it more effective and to fully use the advantages of genetic algorithms, we added two mutation operators and a class joining operator. The structure of the evolutionary algorithm used is compatible with the basic structure proposed by J. Holland [1, p. 66]. Each individual represents a fixed k-element clustering. The algorithm has been implemented in Matlab.

The genetic operators used:

The operation of joining consists in joining of two random chosen classes, and next in partition in two. That operation is realized by the *clJoin* function.

The operation of division consists in choosing a random class, next in dividing it into few smaller classes and in joining the created parts either together or attaching to remaining classes. The probability of random choice of a bigger class is higher, the number of division parts is also chosen randomly. That operation is realized by the *clDivide* function.

The operation of external mutation consists in ordering the points from outside the chosen class in the increasing order, depending on the distance from class (from the best to the worst). Next we choose randomly the point depending on the distance and join it to chosen class. That operation is realized by the *clSmoothE* function.

The operation of the internal mutation consists in ordering the points of chosen class in decreasing order (from the worst to the best), depending on the order of belonging to the class. Next we randomly choose the point from the class with probability depending on the order of belonging to the class and join it to the nearest neighbor class. That operation is realized by the *clSmoothI* function.

The parameters of the algorithm are: the number of classes k, the size of population sPop, the number of generations of evolutionary algorithm nEp, the probabilities of executing particular genetical operations (pMe, pMi, pD, pJ).

Table 1. Comparison of results of clustering.

Mathod	set#1 /IQ/	set#2 /IQ/
evolAlg	4.686e4	1.247e3
myHeur	4.818e4	1.352e3
Ward	6.012e4	1.285e3
fcm	4.894e4	1.266e3

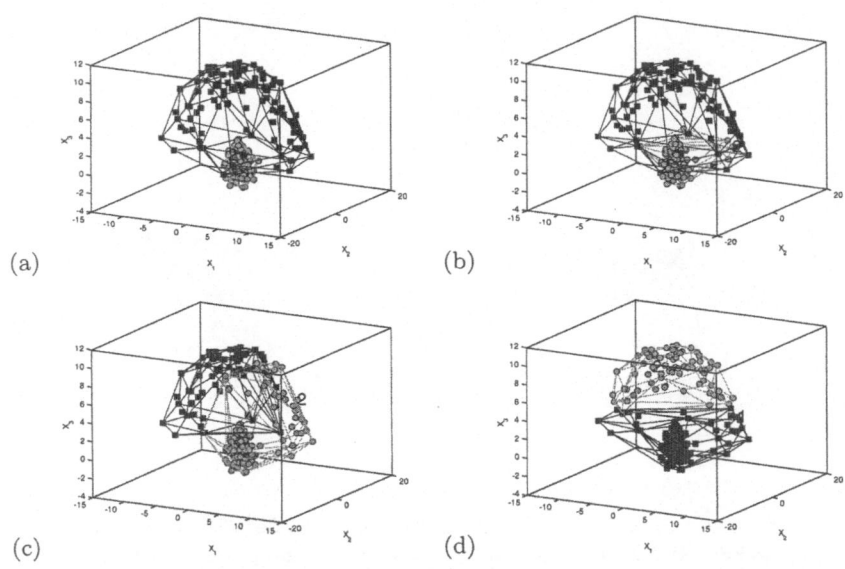

Fig. 1. Comparison of results with the first test set (Set#1) use: (a) evolAlg, (b) myHeur, (c) Ward, (d) fcm.

4   Experimental Results

The proposed evolutionary algorithm (evolAlg) has been compared with classical methods of clustering: the fuzzy C–means method (fcm) and agglomeration methods, from which the best is the Ward's method (Ward). The action of algorithm was presented on two example tests sets: Set#1 – random generated semi-sphere with a cluster in the middle; Set#2 – the real set of data concerning the economic situation of communities in West-Pomeranian province; each of communes was characterized by 7 economic factors (X_1 – the percent of population in before-productive age [%], X_2 – the percent of population in after-productive age [%], X_3 – the unemployment rate [%], X_4 – birth rate [%], X_5 – the density of gaseous mains [km/km^2], X_6 – the number of flats for 1 person, X_7 – the budget deficit in proportion to commune income.

As it results from the experimentation, the evolutionary algorithm in both cases found better solution than the other. As it is shown on the figures (fig. 1,

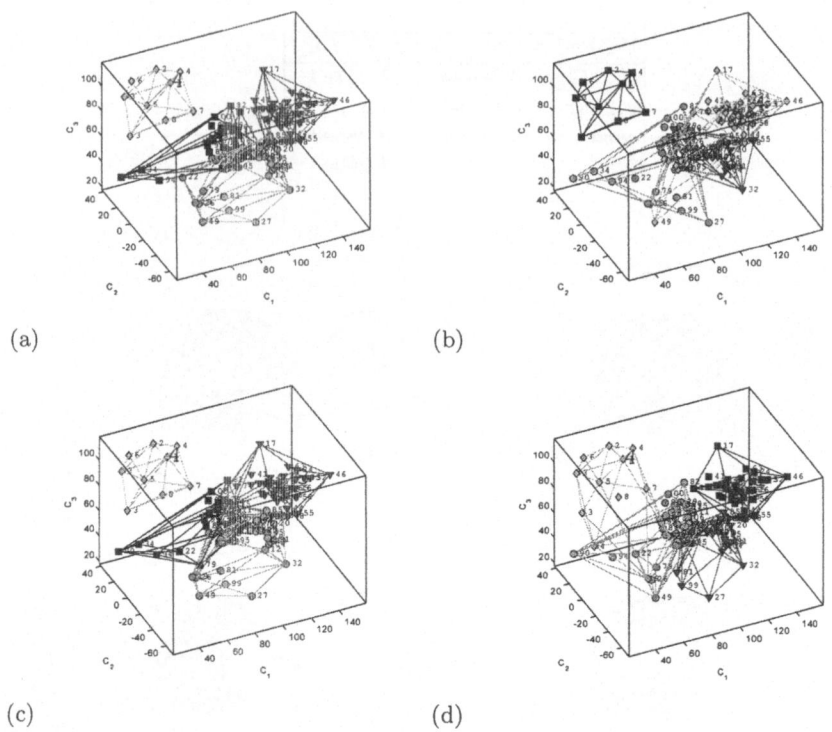

(a)

(b)

(c)

(d)

Fig. 2. Comparison of results with the second test set (**Set#2**) use. (a) **evolAlg**, (b) **myHeur**, (c) **Ward**, (d) **fcm**. In this case we have shown the projection form of the first three principal component.

2) the C–means method gives weak results in case of not convex clusters, in the other cases it works relatively well and above all fast.

5   Conclusions

The analysis of the evolutionary algorithm work should concern both the quality of achieved clustering and the speed of working. As far as the quality is concerned, examples show that the evolutionary algorithm has always found better solution then other methods (see tab. 1), no matter which index was chosen. As far as the quality and usefulness of used genetic operator is concerned, the algorithm, which used only the operator of mutation converged to the same optimum as all the operators. But the algorithm, that used only the division and joining operators, did not have that property. The time of working was of course better (shorter) in the case of the algorithm, which used all the operators. In this case operators of division and joining, that were used, directed given individual to near the optimum relatively fast. It is necessary to note, that the cost (time) of working of the division and joining operators are longer, than in the case of operators of mutation.

The selection of the initial population can be done randomly. That means, that initial classes can be chosen randomly and that fact do not influence the convergence of the algorithm. It only influences the time of converging. If there is an individual having the value near the optimal in the initial population, the time of working the evolutionary algorithm can be much shorten. That algorithm can be used to smoothing the solutions, that are found by heuristic methods.

Interesting is the fact, that algorithm converged to the optimal solution using only the operators of mutation or even one of the operators of mutation. Experiments also showed, that the size of population did not influence the convergence, the algorithm with only one individual worked well and relatively fast. That behaving can be partly caused by the lack of the crossing operator or another operator, which enable the exchange of information between the individuals.

First of all, the lack of the cross-over operator was caused by our unability of finding a sensible way of joining two clusterings. Such way is supported by some scientists, who claim that cross-over is an unnecessary (or redundant) operator and the mutation is the only operator of searching [1, p. 166]. Besides, from the point of convergence, there is a necessity of existence of at least one operator, that would guarantee the cohesion of the genotype space.

References

1. J. Arabas, *Lectures of evolutionary algorithms (in polish)*, WNT Warszawa, 2001.
2. J. C. Bezdek, *Pattern Recognition with Fuzzy Objective Function Algorithms*, Plenum Press, New York, 1981
3. P. J. F. Groenen, K. Jajuga, Fuzzy clastering with squared Minkowski distances, *Fuzzy Sets and Systems*, **120**, pp. 227–237, 2001.
4. K. Jajuga, *Multivariate statistical analysis (in polish)*, PWN Warszawa, 1993.
5. A. Piegat, *Fuzzy modeling and control*, Springer-Verlag Company, Heidelberg-New York, 2001.
6. R. C. Prim, Shortest connection networks and some generalizations, *Bell System Technical Journal*, **36**, pp. 1389–1401, 1957.
7. R. Sedgewick, *Algorithms*, Addison-Weseley Co., 1983.
8. P. Sneath, R. R. Sokal, *Numerical Taxonomy*, W. Freeman & Co, San Fracisco, 1973.
9. J. H. Ward, Hierarchical grouping to optimize an objective function, *Journal of the American Statistical Association*, **58**, pp. 236–244, 1963.

An Evolutionary Algorithm for Oblique Decision Tree Induction

Marek Krętowski

Faculty of Computer Science, Białystok Technical University
Wiejska 45a, 15-351 Białystok, Poland
e-mail: mkret@ii.pb.bialystok.pl

Abstract. In the paper, a new evolutionary approach to induction of oblique decision trees is described. In each non-terminal node, the specialized evolutionary algorithm is applied to search for a splitting hyperplane. The feature selection is embedded into the algorithm, which allows to eliminate redundant and noisy features at each node. The experimental evaluation of the proposed approach is presented on both synthetic and real datasets.

1 Introduction

Decision trees (DT) have been extensively investigated in statistics, machine learning and pattern recognition (see [11] for a very good multi-disciplinary survey) and now they are one of the most popular classification tools. Clones of the most renowned induction algorithms e.g. CART [4] or C4.5 [12] are included in virtually every data mining system. Advantages of the DT-based approach include natural representation, fast induction (especially in case of univariate splits) and ease of interpretation of obtained predictions.

The simplest variant of a decision tree is so called *univariate* tree. In each non-terminal node, it exploits a test, which is based on a single attribute. Such a split is equivalent to partitioning the set of objects with an axis-parallel hyperplane. The use of univariate tests may lead to very complicated classifier if decision borders are not axis-parallel. *Oblique* decision trees allow to avoid the aforementioned problem by using more flexible test based on a linear combination of attributes. It should be noted however that finding the optimal oblique split is generally much more difficult.

Several algorithms for oblique trees induction have been introduced so far. One of the first trials is done in CART [4]. The system is able to search for linear combinations of the continuous-valued attributes and also to simplify them by feature elimination procedure. Generally CART prefers univariate tests and chooses oblique one very rare. Murthy *et al.* [10] introduce OC1 (*Oblique Classifier 1*), the algorithm that combines deterministic (hill-climbing) and randomized procedures to search for a good tree. The method was applied to classify a set of patients with breast cancer and showed excellent accuracy. Another interesting approach was proposed by Gama *et al.* [8]. Their *Linear tree* system combines an

L. Rutkowski et al. (Eds.): ICAISC 2004, LNAI 3070, pp. 432–437, 2004.
© Springer-Verlag Berlin Heidelberg 2004

univariate tree with a linear discrimination by means of constructive induction. At each node a new instance space is defined by insertion of new attributes that are projections over the hyper-planes given by a linear discrimination function and new attributes are propagated downward. A system proposed by Bobrowski et al. [2] is based on the dipolar criterion functions and exploits the basis exchange algorithm as an optimization procedure. The system can be treated as a predecessor of the approach proposed in the paper.

Evolutionary algorithms (EA) [9] are stochastic search techniques, which have been successfully applied to many optimization problems. The success of EAs is attributed to their ability to avoid local optima, which is their main advantage over greedy search methods. One of the first applications of evolutionary approach to induction of oblique tree is presented in Binary Tree-Genetic Algorithm (BTGA) system [6]. In this approach, a linear decision function at each non-terminal node is searched by standard genetic algorithm with binary representation. The maximum impurity reduction is adopted as the optimality criterion. Recently, Cantu-Paz et al. [5] present two extensions of the OC1 algorithm by using two standard algorithms: (1+1) evolution strategy and simple genetic algorithm. The empirical results show that their system is able to find competitive classifiers quickly and that EA-based systems scale better than traditional methods to size of the training dataset.

In the paper, a new specialized evolutionary algorithm for searching the hyper-plane in non-terminal modes of the oblique decision tree is proposed. The most important innovations concern the fitness function and genetic operators.

2 Oblique Tree Induction

Lets assume that a learning set is composed of M objects belonging to one of K classes. Each object is described by a feature vector $\mathbf{x}^j = [x_1^j, ..., x_N^j]^T$ $(j = 1, ..., M)(\mathbf{x}^j \in R^N)$. The feature space could be divided into two regions by the hyper-plane $H(\mathbf{w}, \theta) = \{\mathbf{x} : \langle \mathbf{w}, \mathbf{x} \rangle = \theta\}$, where $\mathbf{w} = [w_1, ..., w_N]$ $(\mathbf{w} \in R^N)$ is the weight vector, θ is the threshold and $\langle \mathbf{w}, \mathbf{x} \rangle$ is the inner product.

A dipole [3] is a pair $(\mathbf{x}^i, \mathbf{x}^j)$ of the feature vectors. The dipole is called mixed if and only if the objects constituting it belong to two different classes and a pair of the vectors from the same class constitutes the pure dipole. Hyper-plane $H(\mathbf{w}, \theta)$ splits the dipole $(\mathbf{x}^i, \mathbf{x}^j)$ if and only if:

$$(\langle \mathbf{w}, \mathbf{x}^i \rangle - \theta) \cdot (\langle \mathbf{w}, \mathbf{x}^j \rangle - \theta) < 0 \tag{1}$$

It means that the input vectors $\mathbf{x}^i$ and $\mathbf{x}^j$ are situated on the opposite sides of the dividing hyper-plane.

Like most of the existing tree induction algorithm the presented system proceeds in a greedy, top-down fashion. At each non-terminal node, starting from the root, the best split is learned by using the evolutionary algorithm described below. The main components (e.g. fitness function, specific genetic operator) of the algorithm are based on the concept of dipoles. The learned hyper-plane divides the training subset into two subsets generating child nodes. The process is repeated at each newly created child node until the stop condition (the number of objects is lower than the fixed value or all objects are from the same class) is satisfied and the node is declared as terminal one.

It is well known fact, that the data over-fitting can decrease the classifier's performance in a significant way, especially in a noisy domain. Post-pruning procedure allows to avoid the problem and to improve the generalization power. In the system, a modified Quinlan's pessimistic pruning is utilized.

2.1   Evolutionary Algorithm for Hyper-plane Searching

Representation, initialization and termination condition. The searched hyper-plane $H(\mathbf{w}, \theta)$ is represented in chromosomes as $N+1$ real numbers corresponding to weight vector $\mathbf{w}$ and threshold θ. Initial population is created based on simple algorithm: for each chromosome one mixed dipole $(\mathbf{x}^i, \mathbf{x}^j)$ is randomly drawn and $H_{ij}(\mathbf{w}, \theta)$ is placed to split it:

$$\mathbf{w} = \mathbf{x}^i - \mathbf{x}^j \quad \text{and} \quad \theta = \frac{1}{2}[\langle \mathbf{w}, \mathbf{x}^i \rangle + \langle \mathbf{w}, \mathbf{x}^j \rangle]. \tag{2}$$

$H_{ij}(\mathbf{w}, \theta)$ is perpendicular to the segment connecting the opposite ends of the dipole (placed in halfway).

The algorithm terminates if the fitness of the best individual in population does not improve during the fixed number of generations (default value is equal to 200) or the maximum number of generations is reached (default value: 1000).

Fitness function. From the dipolar point of view the optimal hyper-plane should divide as many as possible mixed dipoles and try not to split pure dipoles. This leads to the following criterion function:

$$F(\mathbf{w}, \theta) = f_{mixed} + \alpha \cdot (1 - f_{pure}), \tag{3}$$

where f_x is the fraction of divided dipoles (concerning only mixed or pure dipoles) and α is user supplied coefficient, which allows to control the importance of pure dipoles. It should be noted that α should be less than 1.0 (default value: 0.01). Otherwise, this can lead to such a situation, where none of dipoles is divided, which is obviously useless.

It is commonly accepted that the dividing hyper-plane should be as simple as possible. Embedding the feature selection mechanism into fitness function enables to eliminate noisy (or/and irrelevant) features. It results in increased understandability of the test and what is even more important, it can improve the overall performance of the classifier. The final form of the fitness function is as follows:

$$Fitness(\mathbf{w}, \theta) = F(\mathbf{w}, \theta) \cdot [(1 - \beta) + \beta \frac{n}{N}], \tag{4}$$

where n is the number of non-zero weights in hyper-plane (i.e. number of features used in the test) and β ($\beta \in 0..1$) is the user supplied parameter destined for controlling the complexity of the test (default value: 0.2).

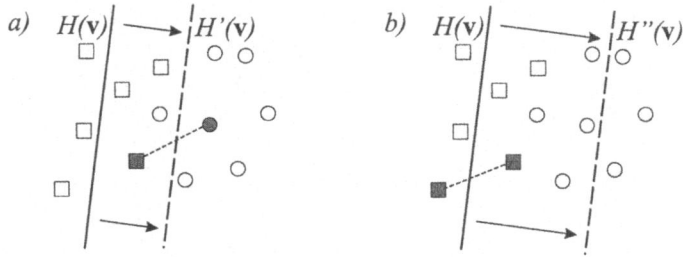

Fig. 1. Examples of dipolar operator in action: (a) splitting the mixed dipole, and (b) avoiding to split the pure dipole.

The problem which is directly connected with feature selection is "underfitting" the training data [7], which often occurs near the leaves of the tree. The number of objects used to search for a split has to be significantly greater than the number of features used. In the presented system, the maximal number of features in test is restricted based on the number of available training objects.

Genetic operators. The standard real number representation of the hyperplane in the chromosome is not especially suited for the feature selection. There is no special mechanism for representing the elimination of features (zero weight corresponding to an excluded feature is not very likely). It means that at least one genetic operator (*i.e.* mutation in the proposed solution) has to be modified to significantly increase the probability of the feature drop. The modified mutation operator has a strong preference in assigning zero value to weights.

Apart from the slightly modified mutation and the standard two-point crossover, a new specialized dipolar operator is proposed. The dipolar operator works as follows: first, the dipole type is drawn (mixed or pure). If the mixed type is chosen, one dipole is drawn from the set of not divided mixed dipoles and the hyper-plane is shifted to separate the pair of feature vectors. The new position is obtained by modifying only one randomly chosen feature. In case of the pure type, one dipole is drawn from the set of divided pure dipoles. The hyper-plane is shifted to avoid of separation of objects from the same class and similarly like in the mixed case only one randomly chosen weight is modified. In figure 1, two examples of dipolar operator behaviour are presented.

As a selection mechanism the proportional selection with linear scaling is applied. Additionally, the chromosome with the highest value of the fitness function in each iteration is copied to the next population (elitist strategy).

3   Experimental Results

Two types of experiments were performed. In the first series 4 datasets with analytically defined classes were analyzed. For these datasets the optimal solution

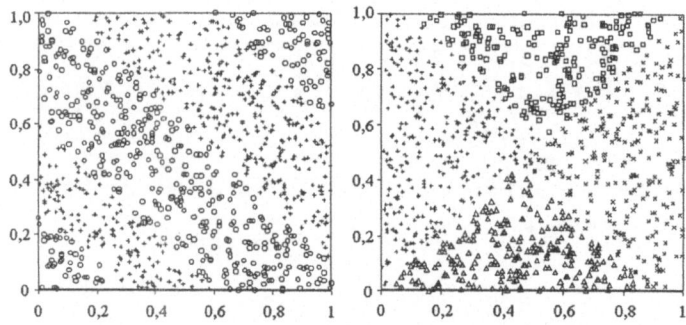

Fig. 2. Synthetic datasets: "zebra" and rotated "chessboard".

is known. Analogous tests are described in [10], but original datasets are not publicly available, hence direct comparison is not possible. In the second series, a few well-known real-life datasets taken from UCI repository [1] were analyzed.

All results were obtained by using 5-times repeated 10-fold stratified cross-validation. Number of leaves (terminal nodes) is given as a complexity measure of the obtained classifier. The induction times were measured on PC (PII 350MHz).

All synthetical datasets have 2000 of feature vectors belonging to 2 or 4 classes. First two datasets (LS2 and LS10, where the final number denotes dimension) represent simple 2-class Linearly Separable problems. The optimal hyperplanes are defined as follows: $x_1 - x_2 = 0$ and $x_1 + x_2 + x_3 + x_4 + x_5 - x_6 - x_7 - x_8 - x_9 - x_{10} = 0$. Two remaining synthetic datasets are depicted in figure 2. The results of the experiments (the quality of classification, the complexity of the tree and time needed to induce the classifier) are presented in table 1.

Table 1. The results of the experiments

Dataset	Quality[%]	Complexity[#leaves]	Time[s]
LS2	99.9	2	10
LS10	98.3	8	20
Zebra	99.4	6	23
Chessboard	99.6	6	17
Breast	95.2	11	28
Heart	78.2	20	29
Segmentation	95.1	51	453
Waveform	77.5	39	98

For all synthetical domains the proposed system based on EA performed well, especially in the classification accuracy. LS10 dataset was the most difficult artificial domain in the study [10], where OC1 system obtained 97.2% with 14 leaves. The extended OC1 (GA) described in [5] gave more compact tree (9 leaves), but the classification quality was decreased (95.4%). The proposed system obtained slightly better results for this dataset: 98.3% with 8 nodes.

Concerning real datasets the classification quality of the system is equivalent to obtained by OC1 and its variants, however it seems that number of leaves is higher in the proposed system. This could be associated with different pruning algorithms utilized by systems.

4 Conclusion

In the paper, the search for optimal hyper-plane in each non-terminal node of the oblique decision tree is performed by a specialized evolutionary algorithm with embedded feature selection. Proposed fitness function and key genetic operator are based on dipole concept. Results of the experimental validation are promising and furthermore there are still many places for possible improvements (e.g. local fitting the hyper-plane position to enlarge the margin between the feature vectors from different classes).

Acknowledgments. The author is grateful to Prof. Leon Bobrowski for his support and useful comments. This work was supported by the grant W/WI/1/02 from Białystok Technical University.

References

1. Blake, C., Keogh, E., Merz, C.: *UCI repository of machine learning databases*,[http://www.ics.uci.edu/~mlearn/MLRepository.html]. Irvine, CA: University of California, Dept. of Computer Science (1998).
2. Bobrowski, L., Krętowski, M.: Induction of multivariate decision trees by using dipolar criteria. In *Principles of Data Mining and Knowledge Discovery, PKDD'00*. Springer LNCS 1910, (2000)
3. Bobrowski, L.: Piecewise-linear classifiers, formal neurons and separability of the learning sets, In: *Proc. of 13th Int. Conf. on Pattern Recognition* (1996) 224–228
4. Breiman, L., Friedman, J., Olshen, R., Stone C.: *Classification and Regression Trees*. Wadsworth Int. Group (1984)
5. Cantu-Paz, E., Kamath, C.: Inducing oblique decision trees with evolutionary algorithms. *IEEE Transcations on Evolutionary Computation* **7**(1) (2003) 54–68.
6. Chai, B., Huang, T., Zhuang, X., Zhao, Y., Sklansky, J.: Piecewise-linear classifiers using binary tree structure and genetic algorithm. *Pattern Recognition* **29**(11) (1996) 1905–1917.
7. Duda, O., Heart, P., Stork, D.: *Pattern Classification.* 2nd edn. J. Wiley (2001).
8. Gama, J., Brazdil, P.: Linear tree. *Inteligent Data Analysis* **3**(1) (1999) 1–22.
9. Michalewicz, Z.: *Genetic Algorithms + Data Structures = Evolution Programs.* 3rd edn. Springer (1996).
10. Murthy, S., Kasif, S., Salzberg, S.: A system for induction of oblique decision trees. *Journal of Artificial Intelligence Research* 2 (1994) 1–33.
11. Murthy, S.: Automatic construction of decision trees from data: A multi-disciplinary survey. *Data Mining and Knowledge Discovery* 2 (1998) 345–389.
12. Quinlan, J.: *C4.5: Programs for Machine Learning.* Morgan Kaufmann (1993).

Propagation of Building Blocks in SGA and MPGA

Grzegorz Kusztelak[1], Marek Rudnicki[2], and Slawomir Wiak[3]

[1] Institute of Mathematics, Technical University of Lodz,
Al. Politechniki 11, 90-924 Lodz, Poland
`gkusztelak@p.lodz.pl`
[2] Institute of Computer Science, Technical University of Lodz,
Wolczanska 215, 93-005 Lodz, Poland
and Academy of Humanities and Economics, Rewolucji 1905 r. 64, Lodz, Poland
`rudnicki@ics.p.lodz.pl`
[3] Institute of Mechatronics and Information Systems, Technical University of Lodz,
90-537 Lodz, ul. Stefanowskiego 18/22
and Academy of Humanities and Economics, Rewolucji 1905 r. 64, Lodz, Poland
`wiakslaw@p.lodz.pl`

Abstract. The goal of this paper is to demonstrate the rate at which building blocks evolve in time during run of GA. We compare the building block propagation rate for the simple genetic algorithm (SGA) with the building block propagation rate for the migration (island) genetic algorithm (MPGA). The results are checked against the lower bound given by Holland's schema theorem. Using genetic programming, we made symbolic regression on the number of individuals matching given schema versus generation number. As a result, a new expression describing the propagation rate was found, and its correctness was confirmed in all cases considered in the paper.

1 Introduction

Theoretically, the computational power of genetic algorithms lies in their ability to process schemata simultaneously in every generation. Schemata are subsets of bit strings that form sub-partitions of the search space. A schema is denoted by a concatenation of bits of L values drawn from the ternary alphabet 0,1,*. Each schema describes a subset of the 2^L possible bit strings of length L in the search space. The asterisk (*) indicates a wildcard symbol, meaning either 0 or 1. The order of the schema is the number of bits occurring in the string concatenation. Genetic algorithms process schemata by using the population to hold competitions between schemata implicitly and in parallel. The result of the competitions is that the low order schemata of higher fitness (based on the population) will be allocated exponentially larger numbers of trials over time. Regardless of their specific form, genetic algorithms tend to perform a large amount of exploration, in the first few generations. This exploration can be viewed as a global sampling of the search space. Thus it is reasonable to

L. Rutkowski et al. (Eds.): ICAISC 2004, LNAI 3070, pp. 438–443, 2004.
© Springer-Verlag Berlin Heidelberg 2004

associate low order schemata with the genetic algorithm behaviour. Low order schema relationships are considered the driving force behind genetic algorithms, assuming that they exist in the optimization problem itself [5]. The schema theorem provides a lower bound on the change in the sampling rate of a single schema from generation t to $t + 1$. The bound is as follows [6]:

$$P(H, t+1) \geq P(H, t)\frac{f(H, t)}{\bar{f}}\left[1 - p_c\frac{\Delta(H)}{L-1}\left(1 - P(H, t)\frac{f(H, t)}{\bar{f}}\right)\right](1 - p_m)^{o(H)}$$

(1)

A simpler (if less accurate) bound was earlier generated by Holland, who approximates the mutation loss factor as $1 - o(H)p_m$, assuming $p_m \ll 1$.

$$P(H, t+1) \geq P(H, t)\frac{f(H, t)}{\bar{f}}\left[1 - p_c\frac{\Delta(H)}{L-1} - o(H)p_m\right]$$

(2)

Typically, the building block hypothesis is based on the premise that a GA works by combining short, low-order schemata of the-above average fitness (building blocks) to form higher-order ones over and over again, until it converges to an optimum or near-optimum solution. Therefore, one cannot preclude the possibility that the building block hypothesis might be a good first approximation of the behaviour of GA with a single-point crossover. The main criticism levelled against schema theorems is that they cannot be used easily to predict the behaviour of a GA over multiple generations [1], [3]. One reason for this is that schema theorems give only the lower bound for the expected value of the number of instances of a schema H at the next generation given the number of instances of it at the previous generation. Therefore, unless one assumes the population is infinite, it is impossible to use the schema theorem recursively to predict the behaviour of a genetic algorithm over multiple generations. In addition, since the schema theorem provides only a lower bound, it is sometimes argued that the predictions of the schema theorem are not very useful even for a single generation ahead [2]. The goal of this paper is to demonstrate the rate at which building blocks evolve in time. For this purpose a simple genetic algorithm (SGA) and a migration (island) genetic algorithm (MPGA) are used. Partially inspired by parallel/clustered systems, MPGAs are well suited for the analysis of the propagation rate of building blocks over time. As is known, MPGAs are less prone to premature convergence and preserve genetic diversity. MPGA evolves each sub-population in time and, occasionally, individuals migrate from one island to another [4]. The amount of migration of individuals and the pattern of that migration determine how much genetic diversity can occur. The complete net topology (cf. Fig. 1) will be applied.

2   Analysis of Schemata Propagation in Genetic Algorithms

Our task was to evaluate the growth rate of chromosomes corresponding to a given building block when running SGA and MPGA, respectively. To this end,

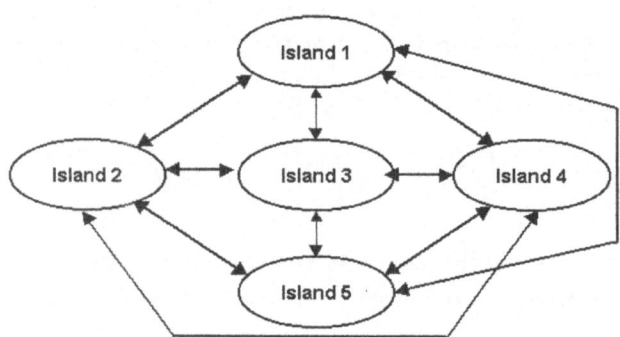

Fig. 1. Unrestricted migration topology

for the purpose of producing and analysing corresponding numerical data, a Matlab toolbox, based on [4], was developed.

The toolbox is made of 3 functional blocks:

- test function suite to optimize (e.g. De Jong's, Easom's, Rosenbrock's, Schwefel's) by a MPGA or SGA;
- adjustable GA parameters (population size / number of islands, number of generations, crossover operator [1-point, 2-point, uniform, etc.]);
- analysis of growth rate of chromosomes that sample a given schema.

For the MPGA, the following assumptions are adopted:

- all sub-populations are of the same size;
- the migration rate of individuals between sub-populations equals 0.2 (20
- the number of generations between migration (migration gap) equals 20;
- migration selection method - fitness-based migration.

Fitness-based migration selects individuals according to their fitness level, the fit-test individuals being the ones selected for migration, and replaces individuals in a sub-population uniformly at random. The structure of the sub-populations for migration is assumed to be a complete net structure (unrestricted migration). It means that individuals may migrate from any sub-population to any other. For each sub-population, a pool of potential immigrants is constructed from the other sub-populations. The individual migrants are then determined according to the fitness-based strategy.

The number of chromosomes that sample a particular schema in a given generation is difficult to estimate as it is necessary to know the number of chromosomes sampling the particular schema in the previous generation. Therefore, another approach, based on a direct analysis of the expected number of individuals sampling a given schema as a function of the generation number, has been chosen. The function may, of course, depend on some extra parameters.

For the above analysis the symbolic regression by genetic programming has been applied, and a number of formulae have been produced. The relationship is best ex-pressed by the following formula:

$$E\left[P\left(H,t\right)\right] \approx a_1 \sinh\left(a_2 \exp\left(a_3 \arctan\left(a_4 t + a_5\right)\right)\right) \qquad (3)$$

where E stands for expected value. The unknown coefficients a_1, a_2, a_3, a_4, a_5 can be found with the use of the least squares approach. In most cases considered, formula (3) has been found to be extremely precise in estimation of the investigated growth rate. The formula is considered an approximation of the expected number of chromosomes sampling a particular building block.

3   Numerical Experiments: Verification of Bounds on Growth Rate

All numerical simulations, performed to compare the number of chromosomes that fit a particular schema with that of lower bound given by Holland's schema theorem, have been carried out in Matlab 6.5 environment employing a developed toolbox. In the present paper, a focus of interest is the analysis of building blocks propagation with respect to crossover effects.

Regression parameters a_1, a_2, a_3, a_4, a_5 reflect variation in a number of chromosomes sampling a particular schema in all numerical experiments. Moreover, they preserve a certain common feature of the relationship, at a certain level of the genetic algorithm they all reach the "saturation point" (Figs. 2, 3, 4, 5). Since the nature of the test functions is known, it is possible to select a building block for the analysis as a short-length, well above an average fitness schema matching a global solution.

The numerical experiment consisted of the following four typical steps:

1. finding the number of chromosomes matching the building block introduced above in subsequent generations of genetic algorithms (circles);
2. calculating, for each generation, the lower bound given by Holland's schema theorem (triangles);
3. in each experiment, symbolic regression based on genetic programming is applied in order to discover a functional relationship investigated in step 1 (solid line);
4. finding unknown coefficients a_1, a_2, a_3, a_4, a_5 in a derived, general purpose formula (8) using the least squares method (squares).

Following the above steps for a relatively simple, unimodal De Jong's function, we have demonstrated Holland's lower bound to be quite rough (Fig. 2). Moreover, this fact holds for the whole class of such functions.

For difficult multimodal functions (e.g. Schwefel function), Holland's estimate proves significantly better (Fig. 3).

To investigate Holland's theorem further, the migration (multi-population) genetic algorithm (MPGA) has been applied. The results of numerical experiments are shown in Figures 4 and 5.

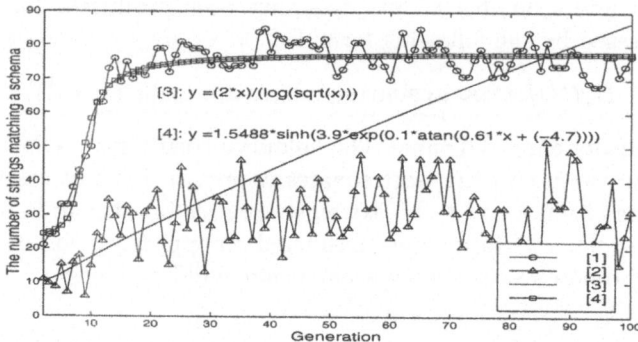

Fig. 2. Experimental results for De Jong's function using SGA, single crossover and 100 chromosomes

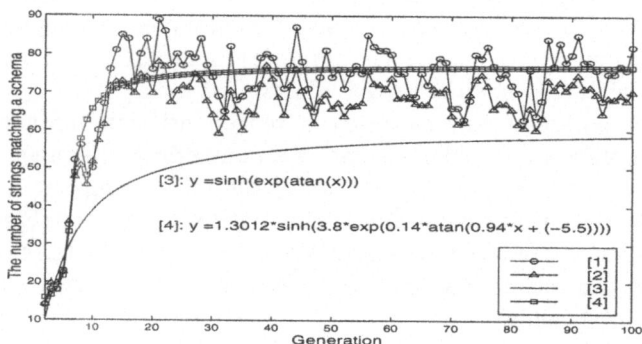

Fig. 3. Experimental results for Schwefel's function using SGA, single crossover and 100 chromosomes

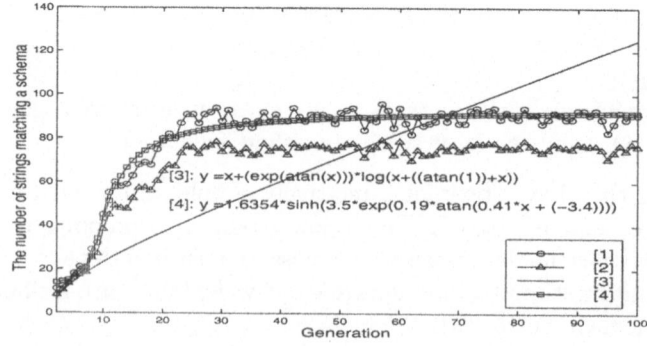

Fig. 4. Experimental results for Schwefel's function using MPGA, single crossover and 100 chromosomes

MPGA shows similar features, regardless whether a single or a multi-point crossover is used. There is, however, an interesting issue related to the uniform crossover. On occasion it results in an over-estimated Holland's bound (Fig. 5).

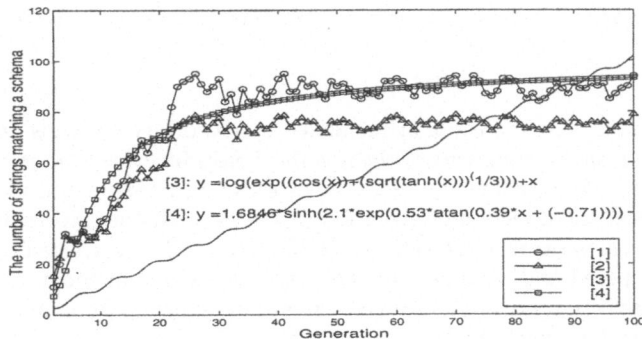

Fig. 5. Experimental results for Schwefel's function using MPGA, uniform crossover and 100 chromosomes

4 Final Conclusion

The main result of the paper is formula (3), which has been proven numerically against all test cases. The formula can be considered an extension of the classical Holland's bound. Further research will be focused on investigating the relationship between regression parameters a_i , the kind of genetic algorithm and its adjustable parameters.

References

1. Culberson, J. C.: On the Futility of Blind Search, Technical Report TR 96-18, The Univer-sity of Alberta (1996)
2. Poli, R.: Hyperschema Theory for GP with One-Point Crossover, Building Blocks, and Some New Results in GA Theory, Proceedings of EuroGP'2000 (2000) 163–180
3. Radcliffe, N. J., Surry P. D.: Fundamental Limitations on Search Algorithms: Evolutionary Computing in Perspective. Lecture Notes in Computer Science (1995) 275–291
4. Chipperfield A., Fleming P., Pohlheim H., Fonseca C.: Genetic Algorithm Toolbox for Use with MATLAB, Version 1.2, User's Guide, University of Sheffield (1994)
5. Michalewicz, Z.: Genetic Algorithms + Data Structures = Evolution Programs. 3rd edn. Springer-Verlag, Berlin Heidelberg New York (1996)
6. Goldberg, D. E.: Genetic Algorithms in Search, Optimisation, and Machine Learning, Addison-Wesley (1989)

Selection Pressure and an Efficiency of Neural Network Architecture Evolving

Halina Kwaśnicka and Mariusz Paradowski

Department of Computer Science, Wroclaw University of Technology

Abstract. The success of artificial neural network evolution is determined by many factors. One of them is the fitness function used in genetic algorithm. Fitness function determines selection pressure and therefore influences the direction of evolution. It decides, whether received artificial neural network will be able to fulfill its tasks. Three fitness functions are proposed and examined in the paper, every one of them gives different selection pressure. Comparison and discussion of obtained results for every function is made.

1 Introduction

GAs and NNs are proposed as the imitation of natural process, biological evolution and real neural systems respectively. The papers describing attempts to combine the two above mentioned techniques started to appear in the late 1980's [7,6,10]. GAs can be used to NNs optimization in different ways [11]: to optimize a number of layers, number of neurons or connections [10]; to settle connection weights instead of use a training algorithm [7]; to select the optimal values of adjustable parameters associated with a model of NNs [8]; to design whole structures of NN [3,5]. It is worth to mention that designing of NNs architecture is still rather a matter of art, not the routinized task. A designer of NN must rely on his experience and on the informal heuristics arising from the works of others researchers [10]. We can distinguish two types of non-evolutionary approaches of designing NNs architecture – *constructive* and *destructive*. Constructive methods start from a neural network made of small number of nodes and add new nodes until expected effect is achieved. Destructive methods do the opposite. They start from a large network and remove existing nodes.

The smaller the network is, the larger capability to generalize it has, because large networks have enough capacity to memorize all presented examples during training process. Developing a NN for a given task we try to reduce the network size as much as possible, taking into account learning and generalizing possibilities. Genetic Algorithm (GA) is a global optimum search heuristic that does not require any additional information about the optimized function. It can be used as a tool for searching 'good' architecture of designed network.

Presented paper is focused on the examination of selection pressure on effectiveness of developing NN's architectures able to solve classification problems. We use Backpropagation training method; it is a gradient method and tends

L. Rutkowski et al. (Eds.): ICAISC 2004, LNAI 3070, pp. 444–449, 2004.
© Springer-Verlag Berlin Heidelberg 2004

to find only local minima. It is crucial for success to pick proper training parameters. The evolution of artificial NN architectures is based on the algorithm schema used in GA [4]. The additional element it uses is the training and testing mechanism used during fitness function evaluation [11]. The separation between architecture evolution and neural network training is the advantage of this solution. Very large computation time makes the separation very important. From the technical point of view it allows to distribute training process on many independent computers.

2   Genotype and Genetic Operators

We use a genotype with direct encoding [1,2]. Genotype contains two elements: vector V and matrix E. Vector V is used to store information about nodes, E – information about edges. Both V and E contain only binary information.

$$V = \begin{bmatrix} v_1 & v_2 & \cdots & v_n \end{bmatrix} \quad , \quad E = \begin{bmatrix} e_{11} & e_{12} & \cdots & e_{1n} \\ e_{21} & \ddots & & \vdots \\ \vdots & & \ddots & \vdots \\ e_{n1} & \cdots & \cdots & e_{nn} \end{bmatrix} \tag{1}$$

where n – denotes maximum number of nodes (including input and output neurons); $v_i = 1$ denotes that i-th node is active and $v_i = 0$ – i-th node is inactive; $e_{ij} = 1$ denotes that output of i-th node is connected to input of j-th node and $e_{ij} = 0$ – a lack of such connection.

For feedforward artificial NNs only a half of matrix E is used. The lower-left part of the matrix is irrelevant but the genotype is designed to handle recurrent network as well, in which every cell of the matrix is used. From the algorithmic point of view vector V and matrix E can represent a directional graph, in which edges and vertices can be added and removed. The biggest advantage of direct encoding is its ability to evolve a large class of neural network architectures. This makes direct encoding suitable for such tasks as: artificial neural network pruning or elimination of unnecessary inputs. The biggest disadvantage of direct encoding is its memory complexity. For k genotypes and maximum number of nodes set to n, memory complexity equals $O(kn^2)$.

We use two types of mutation (*Node* and *Edge mutation*) and one type of single-point crossover. Let us denote: n – maximum number of nodes; p_{va} – probability of adding a node; p_{vr} – probability of removing a node; p_{ea} – probability of adding an edge; p_{er} – probability of removing an edge; x – split point used in V and E; y – secondary split point used in E; upper indices [1] and [2] – the first and the second parent genotype, respectively.

Node mutation

```
For every node v[i] in V:
    r := random number in range <0; 1>, uniform distribution;
    if r <= pva then v[i] := 1;
    if pva < r <= pva + pnr then v[i] := 0;
```

Edge mutation

```
For every edge e[i,j] in E:
  r := random number in range <0; 1>, uniform distribution;
  if r <= pea then e[i,j] := 1;
  if pea < r <= pea + per then e[i,j] := 0;
```

Single-point crossover

$$v_i = \begin{cases} v_i^1 & if \quad i \leq x \\ v_i^2 & otherwise \end{cases} \quad , \quad e_{ij} = \begin{cases} e_{ij}^1 & if \quad (i < x) \vee ((i = x) \wedge (j \leq y)) \\ e_{ij}^2 & otherwise \end{cases}$$

All nodes with indices lower than x and all their input edges are taken from the first parent. For node with index x all input edges from nodes lower or equal to y are taken from the first parent. Otherwise all edges are taken from the second parent.

Let us notice that setting one v_i to 1 can increase the number of edges in coded NN in range $[0, n]$, similarly, setting to zero decreases the number of edges.

3   Evaluation Functions

Three fitness functions with different selection pressure are proposed and examined, each is a combination of simpler fitness functions: training fitness function f_t, and two size fitness functions f_s^1, f_s^2.

Functions f_s^1 and f_s^2 are based only on the number of edges in phenotype. Number of nodes is not used directly but it has a very strong indirect influence on these fitness functions. As we remember a number of nodes has strong direct influence on number of edges.

3.1   Training Fitness Function

We use the following denotations: n_o – number of output nodes; k – number of test examples used in evaluation; m – number of training-testing processes; e_i – error for i-th test example; e – error for all test examples; f_t^{ij} – training fitness function for j-th process of training-testing, for i-th division of the problem set; f_t^i – training fitness function for i-th division of the problem set.

$$e_i = 0.5 \sum_{y=1}^{n_o} (o_y - t_y)^2, \quad e = \sum_{i=1}^{k} e_i$$

$$f_t^{ji} = \left(\frac{max(2n_o k - e, 0)}{2n_o k} \right)^4, \quad f_t^i = max(f_t^{1i}, f_t^{2i}, \ldots, f_t^{mi}), \quad f_t = \frac{1}{s} \sum_{i=1}^{s} f_t^i$$

Training and testing process is repeated m times for every problem set division and the maximum training fitness function from all m testing processes is taken. This allows to test whether the NN is able to provide correct answers. For

$m = 1$ the noise in results, caused by Backpropagation method and it's tendency to stuck in local minima, is too strong. For higher values of m (e.g. $m = 3$) computation time increases m times but the results are much more satisfying. All fitness function f_t^{ji} values are in range $[0, 1]$. The higher the fitness function is, the lower is the penalty for the current phenotype. Maximum acceptable error is defined. Its value is set to 0.01 – maximum acceptable error e equals 1% of the maximum possible error. Term to pass training test is used in this paper. An artificial neural network passes training test when it has $f_t > 0.99^4$. Value 0.99^4 is referred as f_t^{min} in next sections of the paper.

3.2   Size Fitness Functions

Following denotations are used: s – size of the population; r_i – number of edges in i-th phenotype; s_p – number of phenotypes that passed training test; r_i^p – number of edges in i-th phenotype that passed training test; x_i and x_i^p – scaled values of r_i and r_i^p respectively.

$$x_i = max(0, 1 + \frac{\sum_{i=1}^{s} r_i}{s} - r_i), \quad x_i^p = max(0, 1 + \frac{\sum_{i=1}^{s_p} r_i^p}{s_p} - r_i^p)$$

$$f_s^1 = \frac{x_i}{max(x_1, x_2, \dots, x_s)}, \quad f_s^2 = \frac{x_i^p}{max(x_1^p, x_2^p, \dots, x_{s_p}^p)}$$

Size fitness functions f_s^1 and f_s^2 cause selection pressure dependent only on the size of NNs in current generation. Function f_s^1 evaluates fitness of all phenotypes larger than the average size of the whole population as equal to 0, the smallest phenotype is given the fitness function equal to 1. In function f_s^2 the average value is taken from phenotypes that have passed training test. This makes selection pressure for finding smaller solutions higher than in f_s^1.

3.3   Fitness Functions

The three final fitness functions are given by following equations:

$$f_1 = \begin{cases} f_t(1 + f_s^1) & if \quad f_t > f_t^{min} \\ f_t & if \quad f_t \le f_t^{min} \end{cases} \tag{2}$$

NNs with architecture capable of solving stated problems are preferred. The main purpose is to evolve ANNs that answers to test examples correctly; the secondary purpose is to minimize the size of artificial neural network.

$$f_2 = \begin{cases} f_t(1 + f_s^2) & if \quad f_t > f_t^{min} \\ f_t & if \quad f_t \le f_t^{min} \end{cases} \tag{3}$$

Usage of f_s^2 size fitness function causes higher than in f_1 selection pressure to minimize phenotypes that passes training test. Artificial neural networks that have not passed training test have smaller than in f_1 chance to reproduce.

$$f_3 = f_t(1 + f_s^1) \tag{4}$$

Every phenotype is rewarded for its size. Selection pressure on phenotypes that have very good results during testing is reduced. Both purposes – to minimize size and error – have similar priorities.

4   Results and Short Summary

Presented approach was tested on 6 benchmark problems: *Exclusive-OR, Thermometer, Parity of a number, ZOO*[9], *IRIS*[9], *HOUSING*[9]. The importance of the maximum acceptable error has been shown. This factor is responsible for two behaviors:

1. finding an acceptable solution at the beginning of evolution
2. disallowing to find too small networks which are unable to learn properly

In case of Exclusive-OR and Parity of a number the f_3 function gives better results much quicker than functions f_1 and f_2. Testing larger problems, function f_3 almost in every case minimizes the network too strong, and in result, finds unacceptable solutions. There is no selection pressure to find good solutions, significantly better than average during testing. Functions f_1 and f_2 force evolution to find neural networks that pass the training test at the very beginning. There is no room for minimalization of size until an acceptable solution is found. This causes the GA to sweep the domain for optimal solutions for only one criterion. When proper networks are found the second criterion introduces the minimalization process, which is slower than in f_3 and forces the minimalization process to abort when created networks are unable to learn due its too small size. The efficiency and importance of mentioned behaviors is shown by evolution with use of function f_2, in which minimalization criterion is much stronger than in f_1. Despite the strength of minimalization criterion in f_2 evolution is able to stop it when generating smaller networks would result in receiving networks with smaller abilities to solve stated problem.

Figures 1 and 2 show exemplary results of NN evolution for two data sets: *ZOO* and *IRIS*. We can see a training fitness function and a number of edges during evolution. For both datasets we can see that f_3 produces very quickly small NNs that are not able to learn assumed task. Functions f_1 and f_2 find NNs that can learn stated problem, and next they try to minimize the size of developed network. Function f_1 also works properly for *IRIS* data set. It is able to find NNs with correct answers and then, it starts to minimize their size. Function f_2 is able to find NNs with correct answers but it is not able to minimize the size of NNs.

Summarizing we can say that using GA as a tool for designing NNs for a given classification task we should evolve architectures of NNs in two phases: the first phase is focused on finding the NNs able to solve stated problem, and next – minimalization of a size of neural networks. Further research will be focused on the two problems: (1) finding the best adjusted fitness function, taking into account the two phases of evolution, and (2) including evolutionary learning of developed NN, it means that Backpropagation method will be used as a tuning method of evolved NNs.

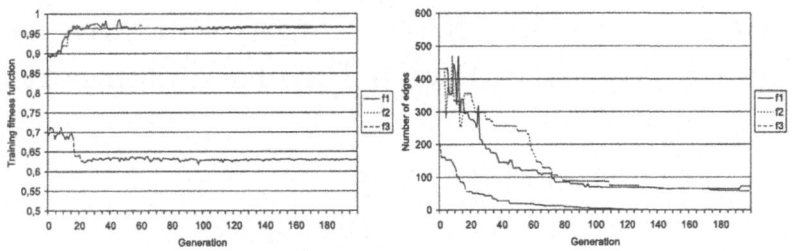

Fig. 1. *ZOO* – Training fitness function and number of edges

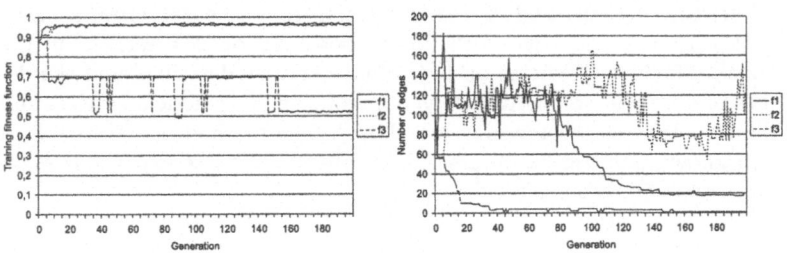

Fig. 2. *IRIS* – Training fitness function and number of edges

References

1. BALAKRISHNAN K., HONAVAR V.: Evolutionary Design of Neural Architectures - A Preliminary Taxonomy and Guide to Literature, 1995.
2. BALAKRISHNAN K., HONAVAR V.: Properties of Genetic Representations of Neural Architectures, Department of Computer Science, Iowa State University.
3. BORNHOLDT S., GRAUDENZ D.: General Asymmetric Neural Networks and Structure Design by Genetic Algorithms, Neural Networks, Vol.5, pp. 327-334, 1992.
4. GOLDBERG D.E.: Genetic Algorithms in Search, Optimization, and Machine Learning, Addison-Wesley Publishing Company, Inc.1989.
5. HARP S.A., SAMAD T., GUHA A.: Towards the genetic synthesis of Neural Networks, Proceeding of the third ICGA, Morgan Kaufmann, Inc., San Mateo, 1989.
6. MEDSKER L. R.: Hybrid Intelligent Systems, Kluver Academic Publishers, Boston/Dordrecht/London, 1995.
7. MONTANA J.D., DAVIS L.: Training Feedforward Neural Networks Using Genetic Algorithms, BBN Systems and Technologies Corp., Cambridge, 1989.
8. MURRAY D.: Tuning Neural Networks with Genetic Algorithms, AI Expert 1994.
9. PERCHELT L.: Proben1 - A Set of Neural Network Benchmark Problems and Benchmarking Rules, Technical Report 21/94.
10. SCHAFER J.D., WHITLEY D., ESHELMAN L.J.Combinations of Genetic Algorithms and Neural Networks: A Survey of the State International Workshop on CGA&NN, Baltimore, Maryland, 1992.
11. YAO X.: Evolving Artificial Neural Networks, School of Computer Science, The University of Birmingham, 1999.

Rule Extraction from Neural Network by Genetic Algorithm with Pareto Optimization

Urszula Markowska-Kaczmar and Paweł Wnuk-Lipiński

Wroclaw University of Technology, Poland
kaczmar@ci.pwr.wroc.pl

Abstract. The method of rule extraction from a neural network based on the genetic approach with Pareto optimization is presented in the paper. The idea of Pareto optimization is shortly described and the details of developed method such as fitness function, genetic operators and the structure of chromosome are shown. The method was tested with well known benchmark data sets. The results of these experiments are presented and discussed.

1 Introduction

In some application of neural networks (NN) the fundamental obstacle is the trouble with understanding the method, in which the solution is produced by NN. This is the reason to develop methods extracting knowledge from NN in the comprehensible way [3], [2], [4]. Often it has the form of propositional rules. In the last few years many rule extraction methods were developed. The expressive power of extracted rules varies depending on the method. Many of them are dedicated to problems with binary attributes [6] or they need special training rule [5], so the need for developing an efficient method of rule extraction still exists.

In the paper we describe new rule extraction method based on evolutionary algorithm and Pareto optimization, called $GenPar$[1]. Genetic algorithm (GA) is the well known technique for searching single optimal solution in a huge space of possible solutions. In the case of rule extraction we are interested in acquiring the set of rules and satisfying different criteria. This possibility offers multiobjective optimization in Pareto sense [7].

2 Multiobjective Optimization in Pareto Sense

A a lot of problems require to make allowances for different objectives $f_i (i = 1, .., k)$. Sometimes they are mutually exclusive. In most cases there may exist several comparable solutions representing different trade-offs between objectives. In the Pareto approach each individual is evaluated for each single objective f_i. The quality of the specific solution is expressed by the objective vector. The

---

[1] This work was supported by Polish Committee for Scientific Research under grant number 4 T11 E 02323

© Springer-Verlag Berlin Heidelberg 2004

solutions can be categorized as *dominated* or *nondominated*. The solution **a** is *dominated* if there exists other solution **b** and the following is satisfied: $f_i(\mathbf{a}) \leq f_i(\mathbf{b})$ for each $1 \leq i \leq k$. If the solution is not dominated by other solution it is called *nondominated* or Pareto-optimal [7]. It represents the solution, which is the best for all objectives. The problem is how to find *nondominated* vectors. One of the possible approach is its calculation as a product of components f_i of the objective vector, which is implemented in *GenPar*.

3   Basic Concepts of the *GenPar* Method

GenPar is the method of a NN description in classification problems by means of genetic algorithm. For that reason NN produces the training examples for developed method. In other word, it is used as an oracle for the proposed rule extraction method. General idea of *GenPar* in pseudocode is presented in Table 1. It can be easily noticed that the evaluation of one individual (set of rules) needs a cycle, which is composed of some steps. At the beginning, the chromosome is decoded to a rule set. Afterwards, the set of training patterns are applied to the rule set and NN. Each individual is evaluated on the base of accuracy (interpreted as fidelity decreased by the number of misclassified examples) and comprehensibility (expressed by the number of rules and the number of premises). Then, the algorithm searches for nondominated individuals and calculates the global adaptation value for each of them. In the last step individuals are drawn to the reproduction and finally by applying genetic operators the new population is produced.

3.1   The Form of Chromosome

Each rule has IF – THEN form. The body of the rule is a conjunction of premises. Each premise imposes a constraint on the values of attribute given on the neural network input. After THEN stands a class label (code) and it forms the conclusion part of the rule. For the real type of attribute a_i the premise shows the range of values $[a_{imin}; a_{imax}]$, for which the rule is active. For attribute b_j of enumerative type premise contains the subset B_j of values, for which rule can fire.

In the *GenPar* the hierarchic way of coding is applied. On the first level there is a list of genes, which codes the set rules (Fig.1). The second level is created by genes representing single rules. That form of an individual produces the solution directly by decoding a chromosome but it increases the complexity of the chromosome. Even so, we implemented the chromosome in that form because GA is very fast searching wide spaces of solutions and the perspective to obtain the set of rules directly from one chromosome seems very promising. On the second level a code of a single rule is composed of genes representing premises (constraints set upon attributes) and one gene of conclusion. Before each gene representing real type attribute stands flag (A). It can take two values 0 or 1. Only when it is set to value 1 the premise is active. The flag is followed by two limits of a range $[a_{imin}; a_{imax}]$. Enumerate parameters are coded in the bit sequence form, where

Table 1. Pseudocode of the *Genpar* method

For every individual in the population **do**
    Decode genotype in the rule set
    For every pattern **do**
        Calculate the neural network response
        Calculate the rule set response
        Compare both responses
    End {For}
    Calculate the *accuracy* part of the fitness function
    Calculate the *comprehensibility* part of fitness function
End {For}
While in the base population exist individuals **do**
    Find nondominated individuals in the base population
    Set nondominated individual's fitness as:
                1/(number of nondominated individuals +
                     number of earlier evaluated individuals)
    move evaluated individuals to the temporary population
End {While}
base population := temporary population
While size of the offspring population is less than size of parent's population **do**
    Draw two parents from parent's population
    Make offspring from the drawn parents
    Add that offspring to the offspring population
End {while}
the offspring population becomes the base population

---

for every possible value of the attribute stands one bit. If a bit is set to 1, rule is active for that value of attribute. Binary attribute is treated as enumerative one.

3.2   Genetic Operators

In the *GenPar* two genetic operations are implemented. That is crossover and mutation. Because the individual is a list of genes with variable length, the operators differ from their standard form. Individuals are selected by applying roulette wheel method. Because of individuals have different genotype length, we have to assure that both parents have equal gene contribution in the offspring chromosome. During the crossover, the offspring chromosome is created by a

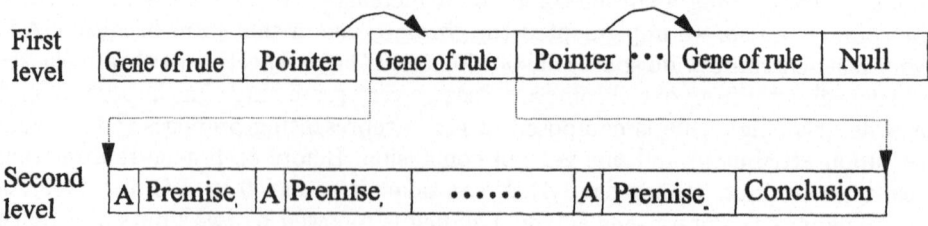

Fig. 1. The form of chromosome in the *GenPar*

random choice of a gene from one of parents according to (1), till to the length of shorter parent.

$$Y_i = \begin{cases} X_i^1 & \text{when} \quad \mu < 1 - \frac{r_2}{r_1 + r_2} \\ X_i^2 & \text{in other case} \end{cases} \qquad (1)$$

In (1) X_i^1 is i-th gene of the first parent; X_i^2 is i-th gene of the second parent; Y_i is i-th gene of offspring; r_1 is the number of genes coding rules of the first parent; r_2 is the number of genes coding rules of the second parent; μ is a random number between 0 and 1. Genes of longer parent that do not posses their counterparts at the second parent are copied to the offspring chromosomes with the probability p given in (2), where the meaning of symbols is defined by (1).

$$p = 1 - \frac{r_2}{r_1 + r_2} \qquad (2)$$

There are two forms of mutation. The first one, on the higher level, adds or deletes a gene representing a single rule. On the second level it is realized as a random change of binary values like: flag or a bit in the binary sequence for enumerative parameters. Limit values of real attributes, which are implemented as 32 bits numbers, are mutated in the same way.

3.3   Fitness Function

Individuals are evaluated because of two objectives: *accuracy* and *comprehensibility*. Because of Pareto optimization, for both objectives single evaluation function is created. The first one called *accuracy* expresses the *fidelity* between classification based on the set of rules and that one made by NN for every pattern, which is decreased by the number misclassified patterns (3).

$$accuracy = fidelity - misclassified \qquad (3)$$

In other words, *fidelity* in (3) is the number of properly classified patterns by the set of rules, while *misclassified* is the number of misclassified patterns by the set of rules (in the sense of classification made by NN). *Comprehensibility* of the set of rules is described by (4). It depends on the rule number (*nrules*) in the individual and the number of premises (*npremises*) in rules.

$$comprehensibility = \frac{x}{x + (nrules + npremises)} \qquad (4)$$

Parameter x enables the user to determine, which criterion is more important. For large value of x, the number of rules and premises is not significant, so the *comprehensibility* is not important in the final fitness value. For a small value of x, *comprehensibility* is near to $x/(rulenumber + premisenumber)$ and that objective will dominate. In the Pareto optimization in order to calculate the global fitness value nondominated individuals have to be found. In *GenPar* it is implemented by means of product of the *accuracy* and *comprehensibility* adaptation values. Next, nondominated individuals get the highest global fitness value and they are moved to the temporary population. After that, from remaining individuals nondominated individuals have to be found in the new base population. They get a little bit smaller value of the global fitness value than the former nondominated individuals. That cycle is repeated until the base population will be empty. In the next step, the temporary population becomes the new base population.

4 Experiments

The experimental study has the aim to test whether the proposed method works effectively independently on the type of attributes. All presented further experiments were performed with multilayered feedforward neural network, with one hidden layer, trained by backpropagation. In experiments we use *Iris*, *Monk*, LED and *Quadruped Mammals* benchmark data sets included in [1]. The characteristics of these data sets and the classification level of neural network are shown in Table 2. In all presented experiments population consists of 30 individuals. Each individual in the initial population is created by the choice of 20 rules in random. On the base of initial experiments the probability of mutation was set to 5 %. The results of experiments are shown in Table 3, where for different values of x the results are the round averages from 5 runs of program.

It is easy to notice that for the small value of the parameter x (*Iris* data set), *GenPar* found the most general rule, which properly classified all 50 examples from one class. With the increase of the value x, grew the number of properly classified examples (*fidelity*). These observation in experimental way confirm the appropriate influence of the parameter x. The *fidelity* of *GenPar* is about 96 %, what is comparable with the results of other methods (for example 97 % for FullRe [6]), but it offers the user the easy way to decide which objective is the most important one. *Monk Problems* were chosen in order to test efficiency of the method for enumerative type of attributes. The results are not included in Table 3, but for *Monk-1* and *Monk-3*, the method easily found the set of appropriate rules (respectively 6 and 2 rules). The most difficult problem was *Monk-2*. It is because of the training examples were created on the base of the relationship between two input attributes what was not detracted in the form of rule assumed in the *GenPar*. The data set *Mammals* was used in order to test scalability of the method. In this experiment population consists of 50 individuals. Each of them initially contained 30 rules. Finally, only 4 rules were found that have fidelity equal to 90 %. In the last experiment LED problem was used. LED-7-1000 in Table 3 is the abbreviation for 7 input attributes and 1000 noisy examples. Thanks of the NN ability to remove noise it was much easer to find rules for this difficult LED problem than directly from data.

5 Conclusion

Even the *GenPar* was tested with the feedforward NN it is independent on the NN architecture. There is no need for special learning rule during rule extraction,

Table 2. Characteristic of data sets used in experiments

problem	attributes	classes	examples	NN classification in %
Iris	4	3	150	98
Monk	5	2	124	100
LED-7-100	7	10	100	89
LED-7-1000	7	10	1000	67
LED-24-1000	24	10	1000	69
Mammals	72	4	500	97

Table 3. Results of experiments for *GenPar*

Iris			LED- 7-1000			Mammals		
x	n. of rules	fidelity	x	n. of rules	fidelity	x	n. of rules	fidelity
100	1	50	100	1	87	1000	2	182
500	2	94	500	4	324	5000	4	468
1000	2	94	1000	5	473	10000	4	471
2000	4	137	2000	13	918			
5000	5	144	5000	13	928			

as well. Experimental study has shown that it works efficiently for both continuous and enumerate attributes. Thanks to Pareto optimization it easy for the user to indicate, which criterion is more important for him. Developed method treats the neural network as a black box. It means that it uses NN to produce training example for the rule extraction method. *GenPar* can be easily used for extracting set of rules directly from data. However because of the good ability of NN to remove noise its using is recommended.

References

1. Blake C. C., Merz C.: UCI Repository of Machine Learning Databases, University of California, Irvine, Dept. of Information and Computer Sciences (1998)
2. Darbari A.: Rule Extraction from Trained ANN:A survey, Technical report Institut of Artificial intelligence, Dep. of Comp. Science, TU Dresden (2000)
3. Mitra S., Hayashi Y.: Neuro-fuzzy rule generation: Survey in soft computing framework, IEEE Transaction on Neural Networks, (2000).
4. Santos R., Nievola J., Freitas A.: Extracting Comprehensible Rules from Neural Networks via Genetic Algorithm, Proc.2000 IEEE Symp. On Combination of Evolutionary Algorithm and Neural Network (2000) pp. 130-139, S. Antonio, RX, USA
5. Setiono R.: Extracting rules from pruned neural networks for breast cancer diagnosis, Artificial Intelligence in Medicine, Vol: 8, Issue: 1, Feb. (1996) pp. 37-51
6. Taha I., Ghosh J.: Symbolic Interpretation of Artificial Neural Networks, Technical Rep. TR-97-01-106, University of Texas, Austin (1996)
7. Zitzler E, Thoele L.: An Evolutionary Algorithm for Multiobjective Optimization: The Strength Pareto Approach http://citeseer.nj.nec.com/225338.html

Graph Transformations in Evolutionary Design

Piotr Nikodem and Barbara Strug

Institute of Computer Science, Jagiellonian University,
Nawojki 11, Cracow, Poland
{nikodem,strug}@softlab.ii.uj.edu.pl

Abstract. This paper deals with the problems of hierarchical representation of skeletal structures and their optimization by means of an evolutionary algorithm. We describe the main advantages of using hierarchical
graph structures to represent the designed objects as well as specialized
genetic operators able to work on these graphs A top-down algorithm
allowing for optimization of structures at different levels of hierarchy is
also introduced. We illustrate the proposed method with examples of its
application to the problem of designing optimal transmission towers.

1   Introduction

The research project described in this paper [1] deals with developing a tool that
can be used for the optimum design of skeletal structures.

As any structure may be seen as a number of interconnected components the
design of such an object may be dealt with at different levels. These levels may
be generally described as topological, geometrical and component ones.

At the topological level the problem of how the components should be connected to form an optimal structure must be solved. The choice of the appropriate
types of components is also expected to be addressed at this level.

Having found an optimal layout a geometrical optimization is carried out.
At this level a positioning of components in space is done. In case of skeletal
structures it means that geometrical coordinates of its nodes are to be optimized.

At the lowest level, i.e. the component level, the parameters of individual
elements of the structure (such as cross-sectional areas of bars or material properties) are optimized.

The optimization of skeletal structures has been widely researched but majority of papers deal with parametrical optimization i.e. searching for optimal
parameters of bars with topology and geometry given a priori [12],

In this paper we will deal mainly with the topological optimization as it can
bring high cost reduction in terms of material used [10]. This type of optimization
was researched by Kirsch and Rozvany [8],[10]. There are two main approaches
to layout optimization. One of them is based on the theory of homogenization
[1].The second approach uses the adaptation of randomly placed cavities [4].

---

[1] The work reported in this paper was partially supported by State Committee for
Scientific Research grant 8T07A01621.

L. Rutkowski et al. (Eds.): ICAISC 2004, LNAI 3070, pp. 456–461, 2004.
© Springer-Verlag Berlin Heidelberg 2004

Many authors have also applied evolutionary methods to the design of trusses [3] [6].There was also an attempt to combine formal languages with genetic optimization [11]

Neither of this approaches takes into account the fact that the connections between different components usually form complicated structures. So we think it is natural to represent such objects by means of graphs. In this paper an extension of traditional graphs to hierarchical ones is presented. We use graph grammars to generate such graphs and a modified genetic algorithm to search for the optimal solutions.

The proposed system will generate objects automatically or with a minimal user input rather then only optimize some parameters of a structure with other ones given a priori.

2 Structure Representation and Generation

We consider objects to be designed as consisting of a number of interconnected components as it was mentioned above.Thus it seems reasonable and natural to represent them by graphs. In our approach we use a representation based on a composition graph (CP-graph) [5].

The CP-graphs are able to represent a wide range of object for design purposes but as the relations between components may be not only spatial but also they may form a hierarchy plain graphs are usually not sufficient for structural description. Hence we will use hierarchical CP-graphs (hCP-graphs). They allow the designer to look at the object being designed at different levels of abstraction i.e. to have a detailed view of all sub-components and relation between them or only the highest level of the structure without too much details. Moreover such representation allows an optimization of topology to be carried out hierarchically starting from the optimization of the highest level of the structure and then optimizing its internal components. The most important fact is that whatever the level of abstraction is considered at a given moment of the designing process the same representation can be used.

Nodes of hierarchical CP-graphs (hCP-graphs) can contain internal nodes, called children. Each node can be connected to other nodes except its ancestors. There may exist edges connecting children of different nodes, i.e. not having the same ancestor. This property is very useful in design applications. Nodes and edges can be labeled and attributed.

Such graphs define only structures of designs so the interpretation must be defined for a given design problem. An interpretation assigns geometrical objects to nodes' labels and establishes a correspondence between edges' labels and sets of relations between objects (components of a design). Geometrical objects used depend on the domain of application. Attributes in turn represent different properties :geometrical (like size or position),the strength parameters or materials.

Figure 1 shows an example of a hCP-graph. Nodes labeled T, P, B are hierarchical nodes and they contain children nodes labeled x and K. Its interpretation for the design of transmission towers is also depicted. It shows only the top-level structure of a tower. More formal definitions of CP-graphs can be found in [5] and of their extension to hierarchical graphs in [2].

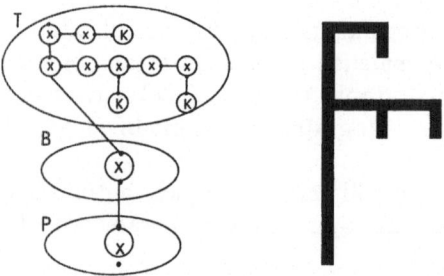

Fig. 1. A hCP-graph (left) and one of its possible interpretations (right)

To generate hCP-graphs a mechanism of graph grammars is used [5] [2]. A graph grammar is designed in such a way that it generates graphs belonging to a required class. Thus such a grammar is able to produce all solutions that are formally correct.

Having layouts represented in the form of hCP-graph and generated by a graph grammar we are only able to generate objects belonging to a certain class of structures declared as correct or proper. The only way to overcome this restriction is to allow for modification of these structures. The natural candidate for such a modification mechanism is the genetic search.

3   Evolutionary Optimization

The main difficulty in applying evolutionary methods to optimize objects represented by graphs consists in the non-applicability of the standard genetic operators (crossover and mutation) which were originally defined for the binary string representation [7] [9]. Graphs have much more complicated internal structure. While it is advantageous in terms of their ability to represent wide range of objects, it is necessary to introduce different operators in order to obtain correct graphs after genetic operations were applied to their ancestors.

To ensure that the crossover operator will produce correct graphs we introduced a similarity-like relation called homology. This relation is responsible for establishing sub-graphs of selected graphs that are homologous - or similar in some way- and thus can be exchanged in the crossover process.

The definition of this relation is based upon the assumption that both graphs selected for crossover represent designs consisting of parts having similar or even identical functions (even if these parts have different internal structure, material or/and geometrical properties). In other words, both graphs are assumed to belong to the same class what is rather weak assumption in context of design.

The homology relation is defined on three levels that differ in terms of requirements put on graphs to be in the relation. The weakest of these relations is called context free homology and it only requires two sub-graphs to have the same number of top-level nodes of identical labels (without taking into account the number and labels of their children-nodes or ancestors). The second one, a strongly context dependent homology requires that all top-level nodes of both sub-graphs have not only identical labels but also have identically labeled ancestors up to the top level of the hierarchy. The internal structure of a node and its attributes are not taken into account. Finally, a weakly context dependent homology takes into consideration direct ancestors of a given node but not any ancestors of higher level in graph hierarchy. The homology relation was used to define the generalized crossover operators.

The generalized mutation operator for graphs is easier to define. We assume that random variation can affect attributes stored in nodes and labels attached to edges of the graph. These variations are restricted by constrains corresponding to the domains of particular attributes and sets of labels. These constrains ensure that the resulting elements are formally correct.

The fitness value for a structure is calculated as a sum of elements' values. An element value is a function of the its weight and forces affecting it. The value assigned to each structure by the fitness functions is used in establishing the probability of selecting a structure as a parent for the crossover. The elitism is also used to preserve the best solutions during the evolution.

4   Results

We applied the proposed methodology to the design of transmission towers. The prototype software includes the graph grammar editor, the graph generator, the optimization module and the visualization tool.

The use of a representation based on hierarchical graphs allows the topology of the transmission tower to be optimized in two levels corresponding to the level of details considered at a given step.

In the first step of optimization we find a layout of a transmission tower; i.e positions where the cables should be placed. At this level we consider parts of tower to be uniform bars. We restricted our optimization to towers with three places for power cables. The evolution is started with a population generated by a graph grammar. The population is then evolved for a predefined number of generations and it produces a number of layouts (one of them is depicted in fig. 1). This algorithm generated all structures used in engineering practice among others. At the end of the first level of optimization a single topology is selected to form the basis for the second level. This selection is done by the user but it may also be based on fitness value (and thus be automatic).

We allow the user to make the final selection at this stage because in practice not always the best structure in terms of weight is used. In our experiments the Y-shaped layout with all three cables positioned in one line was found to be the best. It is actually used very often but it has a disadvantage of being very wide what excludes it use in certain situations.

In the second step we optimize structure of parts of the tower i.e. a topology of the truss it consists of. It starts with a population of randomly generated elements based on the one selected in the previous step. Figure 2 shows the element selected and one of the elements from the first population in the second step.

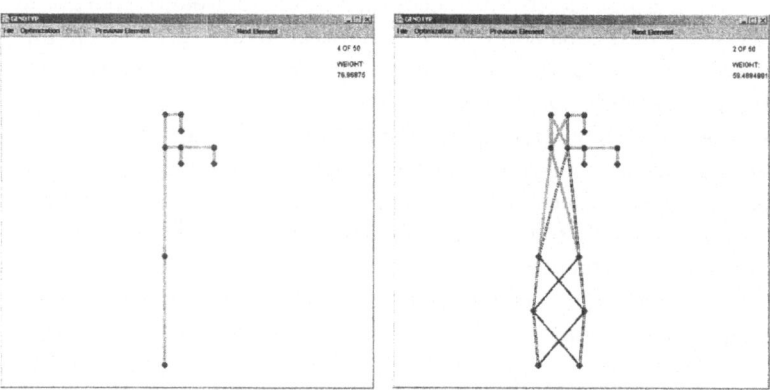

Fig. 2. The topology selected for the second level of optimization and one of the elements from the first generation of the second level of optimization.

This randomly generated population is then evolved. Figure 3 shows the best (in terms of the fitness value) structures received after 20 steps of evolution and a poor one.

Having found optimal topology of a transmission tower the geometry of the bar structure and component properties has to be optimized. This stages were presented in details in [2]. We used a relatively small populations of 50 elements run for 50 generations at each level of hierarchy.

5 Conclusions

It should be noted here that the topological optimization is not absolutely independent from other levels (geometrical and component). The best topology depends partially on geometrical information and geometry in turn is related to components. It seems, however, possible to neglect, at least partially, these interdependence as the algorithm that would try to solve this optimization problem at one step would have too high computational complexity to be of practical use. Thus solutions obtained this way should be regarded as sub-optimal but it does not exclude their usefulness.

Hierarchical graphs seem to be a promising tool for of structural layouts. To generate a class of layouts a graph grammar may be used and in turn they may be modified by the specialized genetic operators we introduced. We think that the combination of the generative power of graph grammars and searching

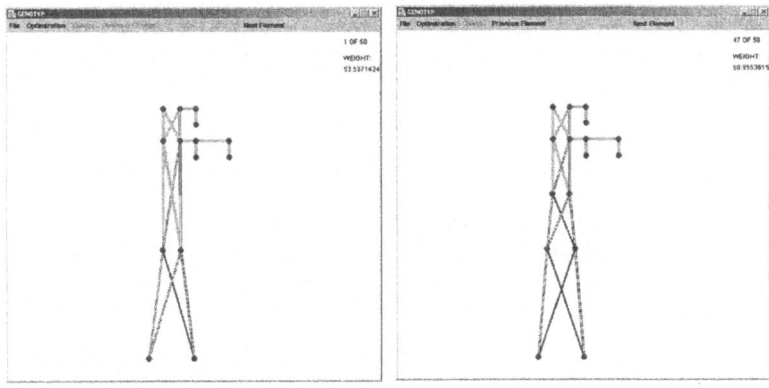

Fig. 3. The resulting towers after 20 steps of evolution.

by evolutionary methods can produce innovative designs yielding gains in.terms of weight of structures and other cost factors that were not researched in this project.

We are going to develop further our software to include more classes of objects. The tool for automatic generation of grammars on the basis of provided structures is also planned.

References

1. Bendsoe, M. Methods for the Optimization of Structural Topology, Shape and Material. Berlin: Springer-Verlag, (1995)
2. Borkowski A., Grabska E., Nikodem P, and Strug B., Searching for Innovative Structural Layouts by Means of Graph Grammars and Evolutionary Optimization,, Proc. 2nd Int. Structural Eng. and Constr. Conf, Rome (2003)
3. De Jong K, Arciszewski T, and Vyas H, An Overview of Evolutionary Computation and its Applications, in. Artificial Intelligence in Engineerig,9-22, Warsaw (1999)
4. Eschenauer, H. and Schumacher, A. Bubble method for topology and shape optimization of structures. Journal of Structural Optimization, 8: 42-51, (1994).
5. Grabska, E.. Graphs and designing. Lecture Notes in Computer Science, 776 (1994).
6. Hajela P. and Lee, J, genetic Algorith in Truss Topological OpJournal of Solids and Structures vol.32, no 22 , 3341-3357, (1995)
7. Holland, J. H. Adaptation in Natural and Artificial Systems, Ann Arbor,(1975)
8. Kirsch, U., Optimal Topologies of Structures, App.Mech.Rev. 42, 223-239, (1989)
9. Michalewicz, Z.: Genetic Algorithms + Data Structures = Evolution Programs.. Springer-Verlag, Berlin Heidelberg New York (1996)
10. Rozvany, G., Bendsoe, M. and Kirsch, U. Layout optimization of structures, Appl. Mech. Rev., 48: 41-119, (1995).
11. Rudolph, S and Noser H., On Engineering Design Genaration with XML-Based Knowledge Enhanced Grammars, Proc. IFIP WG5.2, Parma, (2000)
12. Save, M,and Prager W.,Structural Optimization, Plenum Press New York, (1990)

A Genetic Algorithm for Probabilistic SAT Problem

Zoran Ognjanović, Uroš Midić, and Jozef Kratica

Mathematical Institute
Kneza Mihaila 35, 11000 Belgrade, Serbia and Montenegro
{zorano,uros.m,jkratica}@mi.sanu.ac.yu

Abstract. We describe new results in developing of a satisfiability checker for probabilistic logic based on the genetic algorithm approach combined with a local search procedure. Computational experiences show that problems with 200 propositional letters can be solved. They are, to the best of our knowledge, the largest PSAT-problems reported in the literature.

1 Introduction

Most of the formalisms for representing and reasoning with uncertain knowledge are based on probability theory. In this paper we focus our interest on probabilistic logic [3,10]. In that logic classical propositional language is expanded by expressions that speak about probability, while formulas remain true or false. The problem of satisfiability of a probabilistic formula (PSAT, for short) is NP-complete [3]. PSAT can be reduced to the linear programming problem. However, the number of variables in the linear system corresponding to a formula is exponential in the number of propositional letters from the formula. It makes any standard linear system solving procedure (Fourier-Motzkin elimination, for example) not suitable in practice when scaling up to larger formulas. In [4,5,6] the powerful column generation technique of linear programming were applied to PSAT.

Genetic algorithms (GA, for short) are general problem solving methods inspired by processes of natural evolution [2]. GA's are used to solve SAT, the satisfiability problem for classical propositional logic [1,9] which is an NP-complete problem. In our previous paper [11] the first steps in building of a GA-based satisfiability checker for probabilistic logic were described. The preliminary results were encouraging and we continued with developing and improving of the checker. In this paper we report new results obtained since [11] was published. The results show that the checker is able to solve PSAT-instances with 200 propositional letters which is, to the best of our knowledge, the largest PSAT-problems reported in the literature.

The rest of the paper is organized as follows. In Section 2 we give a brief description of probabilistic logic and PSAT. In Section 3 we summarize how the general GA-approach is adapted to PSAT. Section 4 contains some experimental results. Section 5 contains a conclusion.

L. Rutkowski et al. (Eds.): ICAISC 2004, LNAI 3070, pp. 462–467, 2004.
© Springer-Verlag Berlin Heidelberg 2004

2   Probabilistic Logic and PSAT

Let $Var = \{p, q, r, \ldots\}$ be the set of propositional letters. A weight term is an expression of the form $a_1 w(\alpha_1) + \ldots + a_n w(\alpha_n)$, where a_i's are rational numbers, and α_i's are classical propositional formulas containing propositional letters from Var. The intended meaning of $w(\alpha)$ is probability of α. A basic weight formula has the form $t \geq c$, where t is a weight term, and c is a rational number. $(t < c)$ denotes $\neg(t \geq c)$. A weight literal is an expression of the form $t \geq c$ or $t < c$. The set of all weight formulas contains all basic weight formulas, and it is closed under Boolean operations. Let α be a classical propositional formula and $\{p_1, \ldots, p_k\}$ be the set of all propositional letters that appear in α. An atom of α is defined as a formula $at = \pm p_1 \wedge \ldots \wedge \pm p_k$ where $\pm p_i \in \{p_i, \neg p_i\}$. There are 2^k different atoms of a formula containing k primitive propositions. Let $At(\alpha)$ denote the set $\{at_1, \ldots, at_{2^k}\}$ of all atoms of α. Every classical propositional formula α is equivalent to formulas $DNF(\alpha)$ and $CDNF(\alpha) = \vee_{i=1}^{m} at_i$, called disjunctive normal form and complete disjunctive normal form of α, respectively. We use $at \in CDNF(\alpha)$ to denote that the atom at appears in $CDNF(\alpha)$. A formula f is in the weight conjunctive form (wfc-form) if it is a conjunction of weight literals. Every weight formula f is equivalent to a disjunctive normal form $DNF(f) = \vee_{i=1}^{m} \wedge_{j=1}^{k_i} (a_1^{i,j} w(\alpha_1^{i,j}) + \ldots + a_{n_{i,j}}^{i,j} w(\alpha_{n_{i,j}}^{i,j}) \, \rho_i \, c_{i,j})$, where disjuncts are wfc-formulas, i.e., ρ_i is either $\geq$ or $<$. Since a disjunction is satisfiable if at least one disjunct is satisfiable, we will consider formulas in wfc-form only.

PSAT is the following problem: given a formula f in the wfc-form, is there any probability function defined on $At(f)$ such that f is satisfiable? Note that a wfc-formula f is satisfiable iff the following linear system is satisfiable:

$$\sum_{at \in At(f)} \mu(at) = 1$$
$$\mu(at) \geq 0, \text{ for every } at \in At(f),$$
$$(a_1 \sum_{at \in CDNF(\alpha_1)} \mu(at) + \ldots + a_n \sum_{at \in CDNF(\alpha_n)} \mu(at)) \, \rho \, c$$
(for every weight literal $a_1 w(\alpha_1) + \ldots + a_n w(\alpha_n) \, \rho \, c$ in f)

For example, $w(p \to q) \wedge w(p) \geq 1.7 \wedge w(q) \geq 0.6$ is satisfiable formula since the same holds for the linear system $\mu(p \wedge q) + \mu(p \wedge \neg q) + \mu(\neg p \wedge q) + \mu(\neg p \wedge \neg q) = 1$, $\mu(p \wedge q) \geq 0$, $\mu(p \wedge \neg q) \geq 0$, $\mu(\neg p \wedge q) \geq 0$, $\mu(\neg p \wedge \neg q) \geq 0$, $\mu(p \wedge \neg q) + \mu(\neg p \wedge q) + \mu(\neg p \wedge \neg q) + 2\mu(p \wedge q) \geq 1.7$, $\mu(p \wedge q) + \mu(\neg p \wedge q) \geq 0.6$.

NP-completeness of PSAT follows from the statement that a system of L linear (in)equalities has a nonnegative solution if it has a nonnegative solution with at most L entries positive such that the sizes of entries are bounded by a polynomial function of the size of the longest coefficient from the system.

3   A Genetic Algorithm for PSAT

Our GA for PSAT was implemented on the top of a general GA's simulator [7]. The input of the program is a weight formula f in the wfc-form with L weight literals. Without loss of generality, we demand that classical formulas appearing in weight terms are in disjunctive normal form. Let $Var(f) = \{p_1, \ldots, p_N\}$ denote the set of all propositional letters from f, and $|Var(f)| = N$.

An individual M consists of L pairs of the form (atom, probability) that describe a probabilistic model. The first coordinate is given as a bit string of length N, where 0 at the position i denotes $\neg p_i$, while 1 denotes p_i. Probabilities are represented by floating point numbers.

There are two evaluation functions that rank individuals: $t(M)$ gives the total number of weight literals in f that are true for an individual M, while $d(M)$ measures a degree of unsatisfiability of an individual M. If $t(M) = L$, the individual M is a solution. $d(M)$ is defined as the distance between left and right side values of the weight literals not satisfied in the model described by M:

$$d(M) = \sqrt{\sum_{M \not\models t_i\, \rho_i\, c_i} (a_1^i \sum_{at \in \text{CDNF}(\alpha_1^i)} \mu(at) + \ldots + a_{n_i}^i \sum_{at \in \text{CDNF}(\alpha_{n_i}^i)} \mu(at) - c_i)^2}.$$

The main features of our GA are as follows: the population consists of 10 individuals, selection is performed using the rank-based operator (with the rank from 2.5 for the best individual to 1.6 for the worst individual - the step is 0.1), the crossover operator is one-point (with the probability 0.85), the elitist strategy with one elite individual is used in the generation replacement scheme, multiple occurrences of an individual is removed from the population, as an additional finishing criterion a measure of population homogenity is used (when that measure exceeds, the trial is finished), and the least recently used GA-caching strategy is used to avoid permanent attempts to compute objective values of the same individuals [7]. Since there were no previous attempts to solve PSAT using the GA approach, the choice of the mentioned parameters was based on our previous experiences with applications of GA to other fields [7,8].

Beside the simple mutation operator, we propose a new *two-parts* mutation operator with two different probabilities of mutation for the parts (atom, probability) of individuals. The reason is as follows. Since the probability part of an individual represents a real number, and the first part denotes an integer, it is naturally that those parts have different mutation probabilities.

The local search procedure used in our algorithm consists of the following steps. For an individual M all the weight literals are divided into two sets: the first set (B) contains all satisfied weight literals, while the second one (W) contains all the remained literals. The formula $t_B\, \rho_B\, c_B \in B$ (called the best one) with the biggest difference $|\mu(t_B) - c_B|$ between the left and the right side, and the formula $t_W\, \rho_W\, c_W \in W$ (the worst one) with the biggest difference $|\mu(t_W) - c_W|$ are found. Then, two sets of atoms are determined: the first set $B_{At(f)}$ contains all the atoms from M satisfying at least one classical formula α_i^B from $t_B = a_1^B w(\alpha_1^B) + \ldots + a_n^B w(\alpha_k^B)$, while the second one $W_{At(f)}$ contains all the atoms from M satisfying at least one classical formula α_i^W from $t_W = a_1^W w(\alpha_1^W) + \ldots + a_n^W w(\alpha_k^W)$. The probabilities of atoms from $B_{At(f)} \setminus W_{At(f)}$ are changed such that $t_B\, \rho_B\, c_B$ remains satisfied, although the distance $|\mu(t_B) - c_B|$ is decreased, while the probabilities of atoms from $W_{At(f)} \setminus B_{At(f)}$ are changed trying to satisfy $t_W\, \rho_W\, c_W$.

Table 1. Results of tests with various simple mutation rates

N, L, instance no.	max. num. of generations	1	2	4	8	16
50, 50, 1	10000	5/16	5/13	5/6	5/6	5/8
50, 50, 2	10000	5/13	5/8	5/8	5/3	5/4
50, 50, 3	10000	5/10	5/5	5/5	5/3	5/6
50, 100, 1	10000	3/1565	5/1520	5/1057	5/996	5/1602
50, 100, 2	10000	5/622	5/286	5/302	5/228	5/229
50, 100, 3	10000	3/1853	5/1536	5/1130	5/990	5/1521
50, 250, 1	10000	5/997	5/696	5/574	5/336	5/497
50, 250, 2	10000	5/3802	5/2627	5/2352	5/2011	5/2812
50, 250, 3	10000	5/1451	5/735	5/659	5/466	5/775
100, 100, 1	7000	5/58	5/17	5/9	5/12	5/9
100, 100, 2	7000	5/54	5/89	5/49	5/25	5/20
100, 100, 3	7000	5/348	5/193	5/168	5/123	5/109
100, 200, 1	7000	2/553	5/571	5/320	5/383	5/266
100, 200, 2	7000	0	5/1919	5/1896	5/1707	5/1407
100, 200, 3	7000	0	5/2030	5/1505	5/1312	5/1218
100, 500, 1	7000	1/3519	5/2751	5/1906	5/1797	5/1626
100, 500, 2	7000	0	4/4978	5/4051	5/4158	5/2994
100, 500, 3	7000	0	1/4801	3/6208	5/5154	3/6480
200, 200, 1	5000	0	0	0	0	0
200, 200, 2	5000	2/237	5/125	5/67	5/70	5/102
200, 200, 3	5000	3/77	5/11	5/32	5/17	5/5
200, 400, 1	5000	3/299	5/92	5/42	5/55	5/40
200, 400, 2	5000	0	2/3460	4/3071	5/2255	5/1834
200, 400, 3	5000	0	0	5/3153	5/2132	5/1897
200, 1000, 1	5000	0	3/1891	5/1635	5/805	5/668
200, 1000, 2	5000	0	0	0	0	0
200, 1000, 3	5000	0	1/1257	5/2092	5/1125	5/542

4   Experimental Results

The considered set of test problems contains 27 satisfiable formulas in wfc-form
(with classical formulas in disjunctive normal form). For every instance the maximal number of summands in weight terms, and the maximal number of disjuncts
in DNF's of classical formulas are 5. Three PSAT-instances were generated for
each pair N, L. All of our experiments were done under Linux operating system
running on an 800MHz Pentium III computer. The variants of the algorithm
differ in the type of the mutation operator, the mutation probability and the
type of local search procedure. All the presented results represent data average
over 5 independent trials for each problem instance. These parameters were chosen having in mind the number of problem instances, as well as relatively low
performances of our computer. We decided that it would be better to test more
problem instances of different sizes (even very large scale instances) rather than
making more trials on a smaller set of instances (of smaller or average size).

Table 2. Results of tests with various two-parts mutation rates

N, L, instance no.	max. num. of generations	(4,12)	(8,8)	(12,4)	(12,4) lsp
50, 50, 1	10000	5/6	5/6	5/6	5/3
50, 50, 2	10000	5/5	5/4	5/6	5/2
50, 50, 3	10000	5/7	5/4	5/6	5/2
50, 100, 1	10000	5/1339	5/1684	5/1754	5/498
50, 100, 2	10000	5/275	5/277	5/279	5/104
50, 100, 3	10000	5/1494	5/1454	5/1599	5/353
50, 250, 1	10000	5/443	5/308	5/370	5/347
50, 250, 2	10000	5/2246	5/2490	5/2676	5/4216
50, 250, 3	10000	5/656	5/644	5/562	5/429
100, 100, 1	7000	5/9	5/11	5/16	5/1
100, 100, 2	7000	5/13	5/19	5/15	5/1
100, 100, 3	7000	5/111	5/82	5/75	5/13
100, 200, 1	7000	5/2317	5/798	5/314	5/149
100, 200, 2	7000	0	4/2871	5/1712	5/1156
100, 200, 3	7000	1/6557	4/2940	5/1704	5/1768
100, 500, 1	7000	5/1151	5/1441	5/1379	5/1149
100, 500, 2	7000	5/3517	5/4023	5/3636	5/3866
100, 500, 3	7000	0	1/6914	1/5192	2/4537
200, 200, 1	5000	0	0	0	0
200, 200, 2	5000	5/352	5/201	5/151	5/11
200, 200, 3	5000	5/46	5/19	5/15	5/3
200, 400, 1	5000	5/14	5/14	5/20	5/4
200, 400, 2	5000	0	0	2/4384	4/2162
200, 400, 3	5000	0	0	5/4167	5/573
200, 1000, 1	5000	0	5/2405	5/1403	5/340
200, 1000, 2	5000	0	0	0	0
200, 1000, 3	5000	1/4581	5/2825	5/1404	5/466

The results are summarized in the tables 1 and 2. They correspond to experiments in which we use the simple and the two-parts mutations, respectively. Each table entry contains the number of successful trials (out of 5) and the average number of generations in successful trials. Columns of Table 1 are denoted by the expected numbers of bit mutations per an individual. In Table 2 the columns are denoted by pairs of parameters representing expected numbers of bit mutations in both parts of individuals. The last column in Table 2 corresponds to tests involving the local search procedure. Table 1 shows that success rate increases with the increase of mutation probability. However, tests on small problem instances show that at a certain point, the success rate starts to decrease, as the algorithm tends to behave as a random search procedure. The results given in Table 2 can be compared with the last test of simple mutation (using parameter 16) which is a special case of the two-parts mutation. The results show that (except for some of the smaller instances) the mutation of the atom part of the individual is more important than the mutation of the probability part. Finally, we repeated the last test (the two-parts mutation $(12, 4)$) enriched with local search procedure. Although the local search procedure increases evaluation costs (per a generation cycle), it significantly increases the success rates and decreases the number of generation cycles needed to find the solution.

5   Conclusion

It is natural to develop heuristic based algorithms for NP-complete problems such as PSAT trying to make a trade-off between completeness and computation time. Even if the underline procedure is semi decidable, it may still be preferable to a slow decision procedure which guarantees to find a solution if one exists.

To the best of our knowledge, [11] and this paper are the first papers which study PSAT using the GA-approach. Problems described in preliminary testing in [11] had the dimensions at most $N = 60$ and $L = 60$. It means that our current set of problem instances contains significantly larger problems which we are able to solve thanks to the improvements of the algorithm (the two-parts mutation, for example). We are not aware of any larger PSAT-instances reported in the literature. For example, in [5] N and L were at most 140, and 300, respectively.

Although it is clear that far more tests and an exhaustive study should be done, our results indicates that the genetic approach for PSAT works well.

References

1. T. Baeck, A. E. Eiben, and M. E. Vink. A superior evolutionary algorithm for 3-SAT. LNCS vol. 1744, 125 – 136, 1998.
2. Evolutionary computation, Vol. I, II, T. Baeck, D. B. Fogel, and T. Michalewicz edts., Institute of Physics Publishing, Bristol and Philadelphia, 2000.
3. R. Fagin, J. Halpern, and N. Megiddo. A logic for reasoning about probabilities.Information and Computation, 87:78–128, 1990.
4. G. Georgakopoulos, D. Kavvadias, and C. Papadimitriou. Probabilistic satisfiability. Journal of Complexity, 4(1):1–11, 1988.
5. P. Hansen, B. Jaumard, G.-B. D. Nguetse, and M. P. de Aragao. Models and algorithms for probabilistic and Bayesian logic. IJCAI-95, 1862–1868, 1995.
6. B. Jaumard, P. Hansen, and M. P. de Aragao. Column generation methods for probabilistic logic. ORSA Journal on Computing, 3:135–147, 1991.
7. J. Kratica. Improving Performances of the Genetic Algorithm by Caching. Computers and Artificial Intelligence, Vol. 18, No. 3, pp. 271–283, 1999.
8. J. Kratica, I. Ljubić, D. Tošić. A genetic algorithm for the index selection problem. LNCS vol. 2611, 281–291, 2003.
9. E. Marchiori, and C. Rossi. A flipping genetic algorithm for hard 3-SAT problems. In Proc. of the GECCO-99, 393–400, 1999.
10. Z. Ognjanović and M. Rašković. Some first-order probability logics. Theoretical Computer Science, 247(1-2):191-212, 2000.
11. Z. Ognjanović, J. Kratica, M. Milovanović. A genetic algorithm for satisfiability problem in a probabilistic logic: A first report. LNCS 2143, 805 - 816, 2001. 23.

Design and Optimization of Combinational Digital Circuits Using Modified Evolutionary Algorithm

Adam Słowik and Michał Białko

Department of Electronic, Technical University of Koszalin,
ul. Śniadeckich 2, 75-453 Koszalin, Poland
adamslowik@go2.pl

Abstract. In this paper posibility of design and optimization of combinational digital circuits using modified evolutionary algorithm is presented. Modification of evolutionary algorithm depends on introduction of multilayer chromosomes and genetic operators operating on them. Design results for four combinational circuits obtained using this method are compared with described in literature methods: Karnaugh Maps, Quine-McCluskey and NGA and MGA genetic algorithms. Described evolutionary algorithm leads in many cases to better results.

1 Introduction

Among design methods of combinational circuits, two of them are most popular: Karnaugh Maps [1] and Quine-McCluskey method [2][3]. Design of combinational digital circuits based on these methods uses usually only gates NOT, AND, OR. Also many different methods useful for evolutionary design of digital circuits were created. Among them we can enumerate Miller [4], Kalganova [5] and Coello [6][9] works where NGA algorithm (*Genetic Algorithm with N-cardinality representation*) was described. In his work [7] Coello has proposed multiobjective version of algorithm useful for digital circuits design. The main idea of MGA algorithm (*Multiobjective Genetic Algorithm*) is a utilisation of multiobjective optimization (similarly as in VEGA [8] system) to solve optimization problem consisting of k equality constraints. In this paper evolutionary algorithm useful for design and optimization (with regard to gate number) of combinational digital circuits is presented. In presented algorithm a new representation of multilayer chromosomes is introduced. Compared to existing algorithms, multilayer chromosomes with p+1 layers (p - number of gate inputs) and m genes in each layer are introduced. This algorithm is named MLCEA (*Multi-Layer Chromosome Evolutionary Algorithm*). For multilayer structure of chromosome specially designed crossover and mutation operators with suitable repair procedures are introduced. Results obtained using the proposed MLCEA algorithm are compared with those obtained by: Karnaugh Maps (KM), Quine-McCluskey method (QM) and NGA and MGA algorithms.

L. Rutkowski et al. (Eds.): ICAISC 2004, LNAI 3070, pp. 468–473, 2004.
© Springer-Verlag Berlin Heidelberg 2004

2   Evolutionary MLCEA Algorithm

2.1   Representation of Individuals (Potential Solutions)

In order to create an initial population, we create a pattern (template) of designed circuit, shown in Fig. 1a, which structure is similar to the pattern used in
work [7].

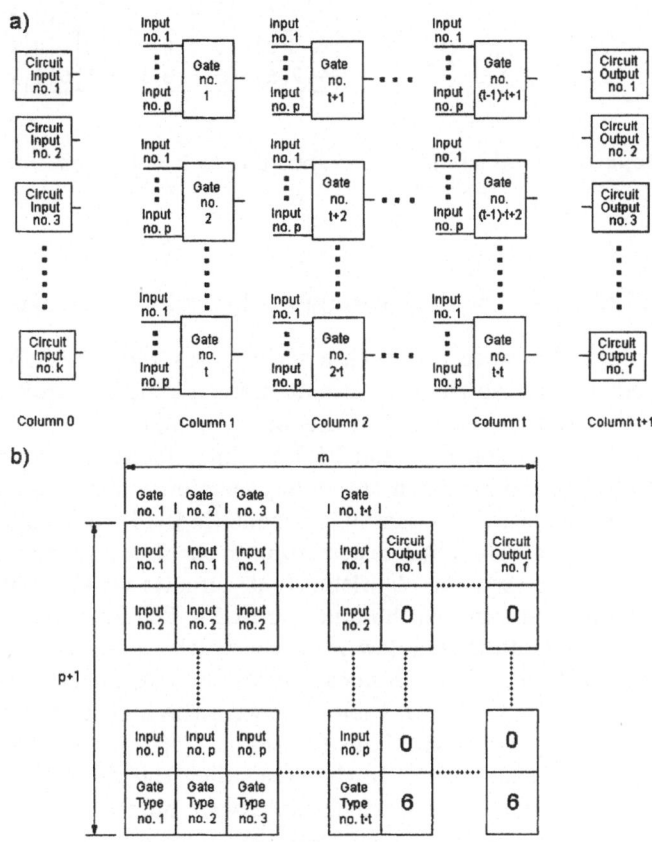

Fig. 1. The structure of circuit coding: a-pattern, b-chromosome

The structure and coding of chromosomes is shown in Fig. 1b. In the place
marked as "Input no. x" in chromosome we put the number of the circuit input
or the gate number from the pattern, which output is to be connected to this
input; in the place "Gate Type no. x" we put one of the five digits, which
represent respectively: 1-NOT gate, 2-AND gate, 3-XOR gate, 4-OR gate, 5-
direct connection (DC) of this gate input with its output. Digit "0" represents
lack of connection of this gate input in the pattern, and digit "6" represents the

circuit output. In the place "Output no. x" we put the pattern gate number, which output is to be connected to this circuit output. All circuit inputs are represent by negative numbers, that is the first input is represent by the number "-1", etc. In Fig. 2 an example circuit (a) and corresponding to it chromosome (b) are presented; in this case pattern consists of 4·4=16 gates.

a)

b)

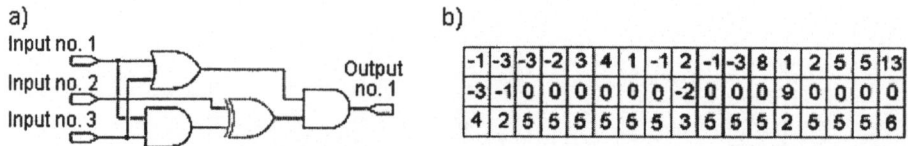

-1	-3	-3	-2	3	4	1	-1	2	-1	-3	8	1	2	5	5	13
-3	-1	0	0	0	0	0	0	-2	0	0	0	9	0	0	0	0
4	2	5	5	5	5	5	5	3	5	5	5	2	5	5	5	6

Fig. 2. Example of digital circuit-a, corresponding to it multilayer chromosome-b

2.2   General Concept of Evolutionary Algorithm Operation

A goal of the algorithm is to find such a set of gates and connections between them in created pattern, so that the circuit fulfils all the constraints described by the truth table and is composed of the lowest number of gates. In the algorithm two objective function FC1 and FC2 are introduced. At the begining we create an initial circuit population (randomly) avoiding feedback occurence in the circuits, which consists of potential solutions (individuals - multilayer chromosomes). Then we evaluate a fitness according to the first objective function for each individual; in this step the algorithm finds circuits which fulfil a specified truth table (algorithm minimizes the function FC1). The function FC1 specifies the number of constraints that follow from the truth table, which are not fulfilled by a particular individual. Besides, we are looking for circuits that fulfil the constraints posed by the truth table, but with the highest number of gates allowed by the circuit pattern size. This treatment increases the search space in the second phase of the algorithm. In the case, when the value of FC1≠ 0 then modified roulette selection is used, which increases a number of the best solutions in a new created population. Then, crossover and simple mutation operators described in section 2.3 are used. In the case when the value of FC1=0 then we compute the value of the objective function FC2, which determines the number of gates in the circuit (algorithm minimizes FC2 function value). Then, we check whether the algorithm converged (lack of changes of the best solution).

2.3   Genetic Operators and Repair Mechanism

In this work novel crossover and mutation operators operating on p+1 layer chromosomes are introduced. One point crossover depends on cutting all p+1 layers in one randomly chosen point. Thanks to this created new chromosome includes the gates with unchanged input structure. Simple mutation depends on choosing of one gene of the chromosome to mutation with equal probability. In the case when to mutation a gene from the last p+1 layer of chromosome is chosen, where the gate type number is written down, then an integer value from the range [1, 5] is randomly chosen, what corresponds to gate type changing. The genes of the p+1 layer of the chromosome, but corresponding to the columns associated with circuit outputs are not used for mutation (they always have the value "6"). In the case when to mutation the gene from other layers is chosen, then one of connections between the gates in the pattern is changed. After mutation it is necessary to repair mutated chromosome. The repair mechanism depends on looking through all genes which are palced in the last p+1 layer of chromosome, where the gate type is written down. If the gate type is AND, XOR, or OR, then we check if any input (from 1 to p) of the gate is not connected (chosen gene belonging to this gate has value 0). In the case of its disconnection a new connection is randomly chosen. If the gate type is NOT, DC or represents particular circuit output, then we check if the first input of the gate is connected. In the case of its disconnection also a new connection is chosen and other inputs of these gates (from 2 to p) are disconnected by writing down a digit "0".

3   Description of Experiments

During performed experiments the parameters of evolutionary algorithm were: population size=100, crossover probability=0.5, mutation probability=0.05. For digital circuit realization two-input gates were chosen (comparative results based on such gates were available). In all experiments pattern size was chosen experimentaly. In Table 1 the truth tables for each designed circuit are presented. Symbol "In" represent inputs, and symbol "O" corresponds to circuit outputs.

Table 1. Truth tables of designed circuits

Circuit no. 1				Circuit no. 2					Circuit no. 3					Circuit no. 4						
In			O	In				O	In				O	In				O		
X	Y	Z	F	Z	W	X	Y	F	A	B	C	D	F	A_1	A_0	B_1	B_0	X_2	X_1	X_0
0	0	0	0	0	0	0	0	1	0	0	0	0	1	0	0	0	0	0	0	0
0	0	1	0	0	0	0	1	1	0	0	0	1	0	0	0	0	1	0	0	1
0	1	0	0	0	0	1	0	0	0	0	1	0	0	0	0	1	0	0	1	0
0	1	1	1	0	0	1	1	1	0	0	1	1	0	0	0	1	1	0	1	1
1	0	0	0	0	1	0	0	0	0	1	0	0	1	0	1	0	0	0	0	1
1	0	1	1	0	1	0	1	0	0	1	0	1	1	0	1	0	1	0	1	0
1	1	0	1	0	1	1	0	1	0	1	1	0	1	0	1	1	0	0	1	1
1	1	1	0	0	1	1	1	1	0	1	1	1	1	0	1	1	1	1	0	0
				1	0	0	0	1	1	0	0	0	1	1	0	0	0	0	1	0
				1	0	0	1	0	1	0	0	1	1	1	0	0	1	0	1	1
				1	0	1	0	1	1	0	1	0	1	1	0	1	0	1	0	0
				1	0	1	1	1	1	0	1	1	0	1	0	1	1	1	0	1
				1	1	0	0	0	1	1	0	0	0	1	1	0	0	0	1	1

Table 1. Continuation

	1	1	0	1	1	1	1	0	1	1	1	1	0	1	1	0	0
	1	1	1	0	0	1	1	1	0	0	1	1	1	0	1	0	1
	1	1	1	1	0	1	1	1	1	1	1	1	1	1	1	1	0

To design circuits with numbers 1, 2, 3 patterns having 25 gates (5·5) were chosen, and for the circuit number 4, the pattern possessed 16 gates (4·4). Comparative results of design using traditional methods and using methods based on genetic algorithms NGA, and MGA are taken from [7]. Results obtained by those methods and by MLCEA method for circuits fulfilling the truth tables from Table 1 are presented in Table 2 (sign "~" in function description represents negation).

Table 2. Comparison results for designed circuits

Method	Obtained function - circuit number 1	Number of gates
KM	$F=Z\cdot(X\oplus Y)+Y\cdot(X\oplus Z)$	5
QM	$F=\sim X\cdot Y\cdot Z+X\cdot(Y\oplus Z)$	6
NGA	$F=(Z+Y)\cdot\sim(Y\oplus(X\oplus Z))$	5
MGA	$F=(X+Y)\cdot Z\oplus(X\cdot Y)$	4
MLCEA	$F=(X\cdot Z)\oplus(Y\cdot(X+Z))$	4
Method	Obtained function - circuit number 2	Number of gates
KM	$F=((\sim Z\cdot X)\oplus(\sim Y\cdot\sim W))+((\sim X\cdot Y)\cdot(Z\oplus\sim W))$	11
NGA	$F=\sim((W\cdot Y\cdot\sim X)\oplus((W+Y)\oplus Z\oplus(X+Y+Z)))$	10
MGA	$F=\sim(((W\oplus Y)+(W\cdot X))\oplus((Z+X+Y)\oplus Z))$	8
MLCEA	$F=((X+Y)\cdot Z)\oplus(((Y\cdot X)+W)\oplus\sim X)$	7
Method	Obtained function - circuit number 3	Number of gates
KM	$F=((A\oplus B)\oplus((A\cdot D)(B+C)))+\sim((A+C)+D)$	9
QM	$F=\sim(\sim B\cdot(\sim A\cdot(D+C)+C\cdot D)+(A\cdot B\cdot\sim D))$	12
NGA	$F=((B\oplus A)\oplus(A\cdot D))+\sim(C+(D\oplus A))$	7
MGA	$F=((A\oplus B)\oplus(A\cdot D))+\sim(C+(A\oplus D))$	7
MLCEA	$F=((\sim D\cdot A)\oplus B)+((\sim D\oplus A)\cdot\sim C)$	7
Method	Obtained function - circuit number 4	Number of gates
KM	$X_0=A_0\oplus B_0$; $X_1=(A_1\oplus B_1)\cdot\sim B_0+((A_1\oplus B_1)\oplus A_0)\cdot B_0$; $X_2=A_1\cdot B_1+A_0\cdot B_0\cdot(A_1+B_1)$	12
NGA	$X_0=A_0\oplus B_0$; $X_1=A_0\cdot B_0\oplus(A_1\oplus B_1)$; $X_2=(A_0\cdot B_0)\cdot(A_1\oplus B_1)+(A_1\cdot B_1)$	7
MGA	$X_0=A_0\oplus B_0$; $X_1=A_0\cdot B_0\oplus(A_1\oplus B_1)$; $X_2=(A_1\cdot B_1)+A_0\cdot B_0\cdot(A_1\oplus B_1)$	7
MLCEA	$X_0=A_0\oplus B_0$; $X_1=(A_1\oplus B_1)\oplus(A_0\cdot B_0)$; $X_2=(A_1\oplus B_1)\cdot(A_0\cdot B_0)+(A_1\cdot B_1)$	7

4   Conclusions

Circuits designed by MLCEA method consist of lower number of gates, than circuits designed using Karnaugh Maps and Quine-McCluskey methods. Compared to NGA and MGA systems, the circuits designed using MLCEA were in 3 cases better and in 5 cases (on 8 possible) comparable. No one solution obtained using MLCEA method was worse than solutions obtained by other methods.

References

1. M. Karnaugh, "A Map Method for Synthesis of Combinational Logic Circuits", Transaction of the AIEE, Communications and Electronic, 72(I):593-599, November, 1953
2. W. V. Quine, "A Way to Simplify Truth Function", American Mathematical Monthly, 62(9):627-631, 1955
3. E. J. McCluskey, "Minimization of Boolean Function", Bell Systems Technical Journal, 35 (5):1417-1444, November 1956
4. J. Miller, T. Kalganova, N. Lipnitskaya, D. Job, "The Genetic Algorithm as a Discovery Engine: Strange Circuits and New Principles", In Proceedings of the AISB Symposium on Creative Evolutionary Systems (CES'99), Edinburgh, UK, 1999
5. T. Kalganova and J. Miller, "Evolving more efficient digital circuits by allowing circuit layout and multi-objective fitness", Proceedings of the First NASA/DoD Workshop on Evolvable Hardware, pages 54-63, Los Alamitos, California, 1999
6. C. A. Coello, A. D. Christiansen, and A. H. Aguirre, "Automated Design of Combinational Logic Circuits using Genetic Algorithms", Proceedings of the International Conference on Artificial Neural Nets and Genetic Algorithms, pages 335-338, April, 1997
7. C. A. Coello, A. H. Aguirre, and B. P. Buckles, "Evolutionary Multiobjective Design of Combinational Logic Circuits", Proceedings of the Second NASA/DoD Workshop on Evolvable Hardware, pages 161-170, Los Alamitos, California, July 2000
8. J. D. Schaffer, "Multiple Objective Optimization with Vector Evaluated Genetic Algorithms", In Genetic Algorithms and their Applications: Proceedings of the First International Conference on Genetic Algorithms, pages 93-100, Lawrence Erlbaum, 1985
9. C. A. Coello, A. D. Christiansen, A. H. Aguirre, "Use of Evolutionary Techniques to Automate the Design of Combinational Circuits", International Journal of Smart Engineering System Design, 2000

Modified Version of Roulette Selection for Evolution Algorithms – The Fan Selection

Adam Słowik and Michał Białko

Department of Electronic, Technical University of Koszalin,
ul. Śniadeckich 2, 75-453 Koszalin, Poland
adamslowik@go2.pl

Abstract. In this paper modified version of roulette selection for evolution algorithms - the fan selection, is presented. This method depends on increase of survive probability of better individuals at the expense of worse individuals. Test functions chosen from literature are used for determination of quality of proposed method. Results obtained for fan selection are compared with results obtained using roulette selection and elitist selection.

1 Introduction

In literature we can find different methods of selection used in genetic algorithms. These are: roulette method, elitist method, deterministic methods, random choise method according to rest (with repetition and without repetition), randomly tournament method. But the most common selection methods used in practice are roulette and elitist methods. However in the roulette selection the best chromosome (solution) can be destroyed and schemata coded in it can be stopped to spread out. To avoid this situation the elitist selection is used, in which the best individual found is remembered and replaces an individual with the worst fitness in the next generation (when the best individual did not survive). With such an approach we know for sure that the best solution found will not be destroyed. However we can make a modification of the roulette method and increase survive probability for the best individual (survive schemata existing in it) without guarantee that the best individual will be in the next population for sure (thus, we assure a certain random factor during selection). Such a modification described in this paper is called the fan selection.

2 The Fan Selection

In the fan selection a selection probability of the best individual (potential solution) is increased with a decrease of selection chances for other individuals, at the same time. Relative fitness values for particular individuals (that is probability values of selection to the next generation) are modified in suitable way using formulae (1) and (2):

L. Rutkowski et al. (Eds.): ICAISC 2004, LNAI 3070, pp. 474–479, 2004.
© Springer-Verlag Berlin Heidelberg 2004

- For the best individual

$$rfitness'_{max} = rfitness_{max} + (1 - rfitness_{max}) \cdot a \qquad (1)$$

- For other individuals

$$rfitness' = (1 - rfitness'_{max}) \cdot \left(rfitness + \frac{rfitness_{max}}{popsize - 1}\right) \qquad (2)$$

where:

$rfitness'_{max}$-new relative fitness of the best individual; $rfitness_{max}$-relative fitness of the best individual; a-parameter causing the "fan expansion" $a \in [0, 1]$; $rfitness'$-new relative fitness of chosen individual; $rfitness$-relative fitness of chosen individual; $popsize$-population size

Depending on value of parameter a, the value of selection probability for given individual (potential solution) changes as is show in Fig. 1.

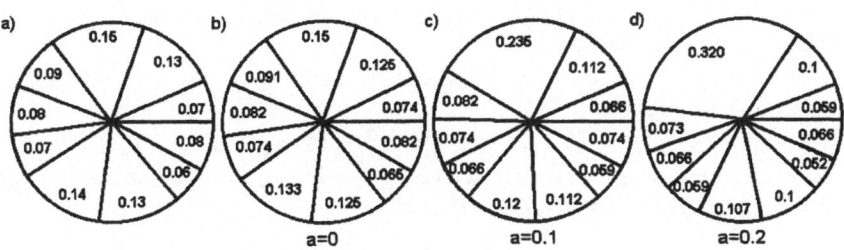

Fig. 1. Roulette wheel: roulette selection(a), fan selection for different a (b, c, d)

3   Experiments with "Fan Selection"

Experiments were performed using evolutionary algorithm with individual representations in the form of lists of real numbers (each gene was represented by a real number from a given range). One point crossover (simple) and uniformly distributed mutation are used. Several test functions (from literature) are chosen for verification and comparison of different selection methods (abbreviation GM stands for global minimal value):

- De Jong function F1
   $\sum_{i=1}^{3} x_i^2$; -5.12$\leq x_i \leq$ 5.12; GM=0 in (x_1, x_2, x_3)=(0, 0, 0)

- De Jong function F2
   $100 \cdot (x_1^2 - x_2)^2 + (1 - x_1)^2$; -2.048$\leq x_i \leq$ 2.048; GM=0 in (x_1, x_2)=(1, 1)

- De Jong function F3

  $\sum_{i=1}^{5}$integer(x_i); -5.12$\leq x_i \leq$ 5.12; GM=-25 for all -5.12$\leq x_i \leq$ -5.0

- De Jong function F4

  $\sum_{i=1}^{30}$i$\cdot x_i^4$; -1.28$\leq x_i \leq$ 1.28; GM=0 in $(x_1, x_2, ..., x_{30})$=(0, 0, ..., 0)

- De Jong function F5

  $\frac{1}{1/K+\sum_{j=1}^{25} f_j^{-1}(x_1,x_2)}$; $f_j(x_1,x_2)$=c_j+$\sum_{i=1}^{2}(x_i - a_{ij})^6$; -65.536$\leq x_i \leq$ 65.536,

  K=500, $c_j = j$, and $[a_{ij}] = \begin{bmatrix} -32 & -16 & 0 & 16 & 32 & -32 & -16 & ... & 0 & 16 & 32 \\ -32 & -32 & -32 & -32 & -32 & -16 & -16 & ... & 32 & 32 & 32 \end{bmatrix}$

  GM=0.998 in (x_1, x_2)=(-32, -32)

- Schaffer function F6

  $0.5+\frac{\sin^2 \sqrt{x_1^2+x_2^2}-0.5}{[1.0+0.001\cdot(x_1^2+x_2^2)]^2}$; -100$\leq x_i \leq$ 100; GM=0 in (x_1, x_2)=(0, 0)

- Schaffer function F7

  $(x_1^2 + x_2^2)^{0.25} \cdot [\sin^2(50 \cdot (x_1^2 + x_2^2)^{0.1}) + 1.0]$; -100$\leq x_i \leq$ 100;
  GM=0 in (x_1, x_2)=(0, 0)

- Goldstein-Price function F8

  $[1 + (x_1 + x_2 + 1)^2 \cdot (19 - 14 \cdot x_1 + 3 \cdot x_1^2 - 14 \cdot x_2 + 6 \cdot x_1 \cdot x_2 + 3 \cdot x_2^2)]\cdot$
  $[30+(2 \cdot x_1-3 \cdot x_2)^2 \cdot (18-32 \cdot x_1+12 \cdot x_1^2+48 \cdot x_2-36 \cdot x_1 \cdot x_2 + 27 \cdot x_2^2)]$;
  -2$\leq x_i \leq$ 2; GM=3 in (x_1, x_2)=(0, -1)

- Six-humps camel back function F9

  $\left[4 - 2.1 \cdot x_1^2 + \frac{x_1^4}{3}\right] \cdot x_1^2+x_1 \cdot x_2+(-4+4\cdot x_2^2)\cdot x_2^2$; -3$\leq x_1 \leq$ 3 and -2$\leq x_2 \leq$ 2;
  GM=-1.0316 in (x_1, x_2)=(-0.0898, 0.7126) and (0.0898, -0.7126)

- Coldville function F10

  $100 \cdot (x_2 - x_1^2)^2 + (1 - x_1)^2 + 90 \cdot (x_4 - x_3^2)^2 + (1 - x_3)^2+$
  $+10.1 \cdot ((x_2 - 1)^2 + (x_4 - 1)^2) + 19.8 \cdot (x_2 - 1) \cdot (x_4 - 1)$;
  -10$\leq x_i \leq$ 10; GM=0 in $(x_1, x_2, x_3, x_4) = (1,1,1,1)$

Evolutionary algorithms were searching for test function minima with different selection methods (roulette, elitist, fan). Evolutionary algorithm parameters were as follows: probability of crossover 0.7, probability of mutation 0.1, population size 50, fan "expansion" parameter a 0.3, number of generations 100; computations were repeated 10 times. The best obtained values of minima are shown in Table 1, and in Table 2 average values of minima after 10-fold evolutionary algorithm (EA) running are presented.

Table 1. The best minimal function values after 10-fold EA repetition

Test function	GM	Roulette	Elitist	Fan
F1	0	0.0418242379	0.0042113859	0.0000541613
F2	0	0.0832227970	0.0178523657	0.0004724523
F3	-25	-23	-23	-25
F4	0	24.9520119980	8.9775226397	0.8073591386
F5	0.998	0.9980038468	0.9983851080	0.9980046406
F6	0	0.0222164039	0.0116290217	0.0100615968
F7	0	0.5523068587	0.7287314706	0.2766703935
F8	3	11.8576124230	4.53552008698	3.00122213608
F9	-1.0316	-1.0107767187	-1.0011167311	-1.0316258036
F10	0	788.6252691000	34.1297397950	0.8440666100

Table 2. Average values of function minima after 10-fold EA repetition

Test function	GM	Roulette	Elitist	Fan
F1	0	0.1841809694	0.1599502473	0.0023664491
F2	0	0.6953592685	0.5983826940	0.0677531789
F3	-25	-21.8	-22.3	-24.9
F4	0	41.3072482397	24.3159325593	4.5070213132
F5	0.998	5.0637858363	3.0972643133	1.0068605951
F6	0	0.0630875070	0.0527291985	0.0237162355
F7	0	2.0273245243	1.4804677983	0.9439756637
F8	3	144.5219502725	31.2145634872	3.0448517040
F9	-1.0316	-0.8008051940	-0.8829070527	-1.0300083243
F10	0	1724.2734558910	363.4354645230	11.7094948051

It follows from Table 1, that the solutions found using the fan selection (after 100 generations) are much better than solutions found in the same run-time using roulette selection, and are better (or comparable) than solutions found using elitist selection. Also, average values after 10 repetitions (Table 2) show that the fan selection (for selected parameter a) is the most stable, that is it gives the least deviation from the best solutions. It is understandable, because higher part of the best individuals have a chance to enter to the next population. The highest differences we can find for De Jong function F4, Goldstein-Price function F8, and Coldvill function F10. Those differences apply to both the best solutions found after 100 generations and average values of solutions found in 10 subsequent tests. In the case of De Jong function F4 it is probably caused by fact, that this function has 30 variables, what with mutation probability of order of 0.1, and population size of order of 50 causes that during one generation, approximately 150 genes can be mutated. That means that each individual in the population will undergo mutation, that is the searching will have more random character. It is possible to conclude from this, that the fan selection behaves much better, in the case of existence of large number of mutated genes in population, than remaining selection methods.

In the second experiment it was examined how fan "expanding" parameter a influences the solution quality found by evolutionary algorithm. Here only parameter a was changed and has values selected from the range [0.1; 0.5], and other algorithm parameters were constant. Two function were chosen to this experiment: F6, because it has the lowest variations of average value (after 100 generations), and function F4 for which the highest variations of average value were observed (after 100 generations). The best values of function minima and their average values after 10 repetitions of evolutionary algorithm are shown in Table 3.

Table 3. Influence of parameter a on function minimum values

Param. a	Function F6		Function F4	
	$F_{thebest}$	$F_{average}$	$F_{thebest}$	$F_{average}$
0.10	0.00973789	0.02911110	11.66665770	17.66929815
0.15	0.00971622	0.03286266	6.82471561	14.25474764
0.20	0.00971812	0.01906702	5.03260339	9.58437152
0.30	0.00978173	0.02835693	2.33821870	4.21488056
0.50	0.01006137	0.03371673	0.31903844	1.03942541

It follows from Table 3, that in the case of Schaffer F6 function, increasing of value of the parameter a does not cause considerable improvement in obtained results. We can conclude from this, that in the case when the computed function values are slightly spread around the minimum value (it may happen when algorithm converges to the best solution or local extremum), the increase of the fan expanding parameter a does not improve significantly the results. In the case of De Jong F4 function the increase of parameter a value causes considerable improvement of obtained minima and improve algorithm convergence (during the same run-time better and better solutions are found).

In the subsequent experiment performed, an algorithm convergence with the fan selection (for different a values) was checked and compared with roulette and elitist selections. Evolutionary algorithm parameters were the same as before. Computations were repeated 10 times after each change of parameter a. Evolutionary algorithm with fan selection has shown the same or better convergence for all test functions. In Fig. 2 average values of function F4 minima for different selection methods are presented (signs represent: □-roulette, ○-elitist, △-fan); global extremum has value 0; X axis represents generation number, and Y axis represent average values of function minima for 10 repetitions of evolutionary algorithm.

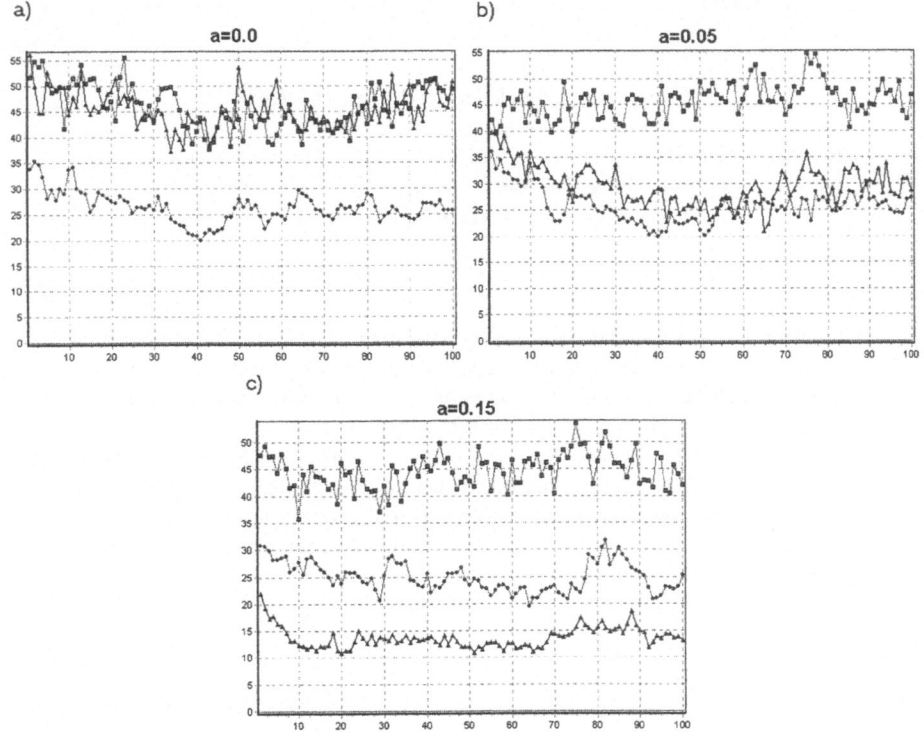

Fig. 2. Average values of minima: a=0.00 (a), a=0.05 (b), a=0.15 (c)

From graphs of Fig. 2 we can see, that in case when parameter a is equal to 0.0 then fan selection is similar to roulette selection. When value of parameter a is equal to 0.05 then results for fan selection are placed between results for roulette selection and results for elitist selection. For parameter value a=0.15 obtained results using fan selection are better than two remaining selections. From graphs of Fig. 2 is also visible, that together with increase of parameter a value a random dispersion of generated results by the fan selection becomes smaller.

Summing up, we can observe, that a new selection method called the "fan selection" is better or not worse than roulette and elitist selections.

References

1. Z. Michalewicz, "Genetic Algorithms + Data Structures = Evolution Programs" (in polish), WNT, Warsaw, 1999
2. D. Goldberg, "Genetic Algorithms in Search, Optimization, and Machine Learning" (in polish), WNT, Warsaw, 1998
3. J. Arabas, "Lectures of evolutionary algorithms" (in polish), WNT, Warsaw, 2001

New Genetic Crossover Operator for the TSP

Sang-Moon Soak[1] and Byung-Ha Ahn[1]

Kwang-Ju Institute of Science and Technology, Dept. of Mechatronics,
1 Oryong-dong, Buk-gu, Gwangju, Republic of Korea
{soakbong,bayhay}@kjist.ac.kr

Abstract. Genetic algorithm is very useful method for global search of large search space and has been applied to various problems. It has two kinds of important search mechanisms, crossover and mutation. Especially many researchers have more interested in crossover operator than mutation operator because crossover operator has charge of the responsibility of local search. In this paper we introduce a new crossover operator avoiding the drawback of conventional crossovers. We compare it to several crossover operators for travelling salesman problem (TSP) for showing the performance of proposed crossover.

1 Introduction

Since Holland introduced the Genetic Algorithm (GA) in the early of 1970's, many researchers have become interested in it as a new method for solving large and difficult problems in search and optimization [1]. And for a long time, a large number of operators have been developed for improving the performance of GA because the performance of algorithm depends on an ability of these operators. Especially many researchers have more interest in crossover operator than mutation operator. Because it is the important element that performs the exchange of information between individuals during the generation and global optimal solution is generally known as existing near sub-optimal solution [9], more crossover operators have been developed.

In this paper, we deal with only crossover operators, especially for solving travelling salesman problem (TSP). The TSP is a classical NP-complete problem, which has extremely large search spaces and is very difficult to solve. Since in the early of using GA for solving TSP, just many kinds of permutation crossover operators were introduced such as Cycle crossover (CX), Order Crossover (OX), Position-Based Crossover (PBX), Order-Based Crossover (OBX), Partial-Mapped Crossover (PMX) and so on. Recently, researcher's interest has been changed more and more in direction of using information of parents such as subtour [3], [4], [7], edge [3], [5], [10] or edge and distance [2], [6], [8] information of parents. In this paper we propose new subtour-based crossover operator to show that adjacency information of parents may be important and should be preserved and it can be more performed than other operators, and compare with both some permutation crossovers and edge or subtour-based crossovers.

L. Rutkowski et al. (Eds.): ICAISC 2004, LNAI 3070, pp. 480–485, 2004.
© Springer-Verlag Berlin Heidelberg 2004

2   Subtour Preservation Crossover (SPX)

The proposed crossover, Subtour Preservation Crossover (SPX), is motivated by various features of edge-based crossover and subtour-based crossover. SPX uses a similar subtour enumeration method to other subtour-based crossovers but it has an amount of difference in method that generates a valid tour. Subtour Exchange Crossover (SXX) [7] and Complete Subtour Exchange Crossover (CSEX) [4] generate simply several offsprings through a process that exchanges and inverts each other common subours in parents and then choose two tours producing the shortest distance in offspring pool as offspring and Distance Preserving Crossover (DPX) [12] uses a greedy reconnection procedure which reconnects the nearest available neighbor among the endpoints of subtours. Otherwise, SPX generates offsprings using common subtour which parents share and edges included in each parents. That is, the method uses maximum information involved in parents.

All the subtour-based crossovers have a severe drawback. If the same parents are selected for crossover, any subtour-based crossovers do not generate offsprings different with parents, so they cannot improve the performance of current solution and should depend on mutation operator for improvement of solution. It is the reason that offsprings are exactly identical with their parents because the subtour itself is offspring. However, as generation increases more and more, the number of same solution in population will be exponentially increased by a selection strategy. So the improvement of solutions will be very difficult by degrees. But in case of SPX, we can solve this problem as introducing new predominant solutions instead of parents. We will explain more detail later. And if SXX and CSEX find a subtour of cities with the same order such as $Subtour_1(1, 2, 3, 4)$ and $Subtour_2(1, 2, 3, 4)$, they generate the same offsprings as current parents. So a supplementary method for solving this problem is very needed. But, although SPX finds the same subtour, it can generate different offsprings provided that selects different starting points at each process reconnecting subtours and isolated cities. Also, subtour-based crossover operators use only subtour among an amount of information of parents augmented over thousands of generations. That is, they are only different from permutation-based crossover operators in that point. The remaining process is very similar to permutation process. So other parental information besides subtour is never considered. But, as mentioned above, proposed method is a crossover operator using amount of parental information, not only common subtour but edges involved in each parent.

2.1   Subtour Analysis

First, we investigate how many identical parents will be selected over generation to generation. It is very important measure because if so, subtour-based crossover operators will be for nothing in the performance. Fig. 1 shows the average number of times selected two identical parents. After 200 generations, the average number of times selected two identical parents is over 20. That is, it shows the identical parents are selected about over 30% for total crossover process (Pc = 0.6). So if we do not consider a supplementary method for avoiding this problem, the improvement of solutions will be more and more difficult.

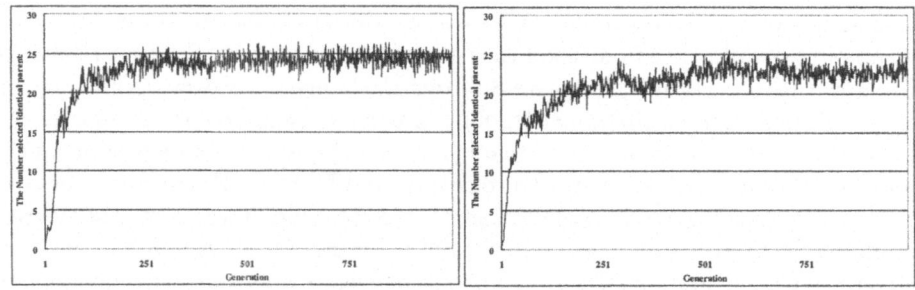

Fig. 1. The average number of times selected identical parents : (a) Instance (left) = kroA100, (b) Instance (right) = kroB200 (*pop_size* = 200, *Pc* = 0.6, *Tournament selection*, *Total generation* = 1000, *Iteration* = 30)

2.2   New Offspring

If the identical parents are selected for crossover, SPX generates new offsprings using a local search method. If offsprings produced by simple permutation would be introduced in population, they cannot survive in population filled with solutions holding already good fitness values. So if identical parents are selected in SPX, it first generates two solutions randomly and then apply 2-opt algorithm to each solution for competing with good solution existing already in population. The solutions generated by 2-opt algorithm are local minimum solution. So it will be able to compete with solutions in population.

2.3   Outline of SPX

The procedure of SPX is divided into two steps. The first step is to enumerate common subtours and next is to reconnect each subtour. We will explain more detail using an example. Fig. 2 shows an example of SPX. (a) and (b) is two parents selected respectively, (c) is an overlapped tour of parent tours and (d) shows a common subtours. And (e) shows three offsprings generated by various random selection of starting point and the process of connecting subtours and isolated points. At (d), total 15 points (the end points (8) of each subtours and isolated nodes (7)) can be selected as starting points. In here, note the end points of each subtours and isolated nodes have two possible edges derived from parent. So, if a point is selected as a starting point, shorter edge between two possible edges is selected. If shorter edge was already selected, another edge is selected. And if both edges were already selected at previous step, random selection is performed among endpoints not selected at previous step. If the edge selected has the length of subtour more than 1 (not an isolated node), all elements within the subtour are connected in turn. This process is continued until a tour is formed. As shown in this figure, SPX can generate various offsprings with preserving common dominant features of parent generation.

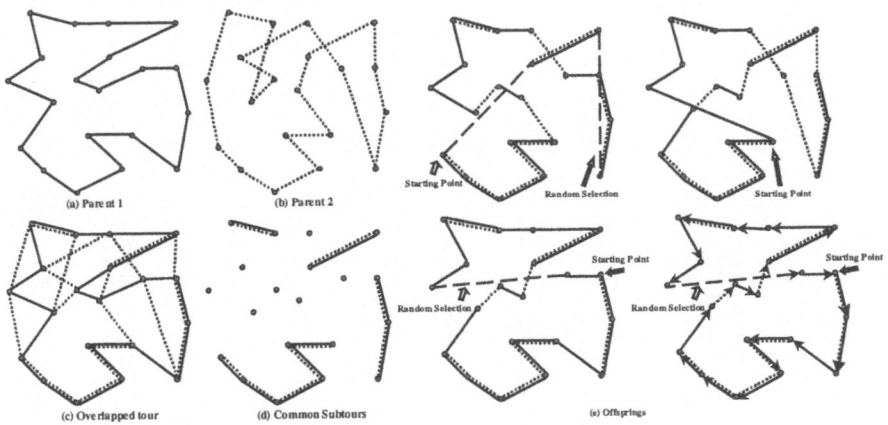

Fig. 2. Example of Subtour Preservation Crossover

3   Experimental Results

We performed an experiment for comparing proposed crossover operator with several crossover operators and all algorithms are implemented in Visual C++ and tested on Pentium IV 1.6Ghz personal computer. All the test problems was obtained from TSPLIB [13]. In order to demonstrate the superiority of SPX, we compared SPX's performance with those of the most outstanding crossover. With regards to compare each crossover operator in justice, we used simple GA. And initial individuals are randomly generated and used tournament strategy and elitist selection rule for the selection. The number of preserved best tour is 3. The mutation operator used in this experiment is inversion operator. The population size (pop_size), crossover probability (P_c) and mutation probability (P_m) are 200, 0.6 and 0.4 respectively. The termination condition is satisfied either when the optimal solution is found or when the best solution of the population remains unchanged for 1000 generations. The experiment was carried out 30 runs on each operator by changing the seed of the random number. The number of offspring generated by SPX sets 5. In this experiment, the quality is defined as $quality = \frac{Fitness - Optimal}{Optimal} \times 100(\%)$, i.e. the quality indicates the percentage over the optimal value.

Table. 1 shows the simulation results of each operator. * indicates the case of $pop\_size = 100$. SPX was needed much computation time in comparison to

Table 1. Experiment Results

		eil51(426)						rat99(1211)			
	Min	Avg.(Quality)	Max	Gen.	Time(sec.)	Min	Avg.(Quality)	Max	Gen.	Time(sec.)
MPX	432	440.2(3.3)	450	2019.2	22.7	1286	1334.6(10.2)	1382	2396.1	85.6
SCH.	430	448.8(5.4)	464	1520.5	6.6	1260	1337.3(10.4)	1431	1947	20.6
ROX	427	437.9(2.8)	451	1734.8	5.7	1249	1289.6(6.5)	1332	2631	19.3
HX	426	439.2(3.1)	453	1743.3	8.3	1240	1300.0(7.4)	1382	2135.4	24.7
GX	431	443.9(4.2)	466	1414.4	6.7	1264	1333.7(10.1)	1430	1643.2	19.2
ER	430	443(3.9)	459	1794.3	12.6	1285	1329.9(9.8)	1394	2172.9	38.4
EER	433	448.3(5.2)	464	1506.6	9.7	1282	1339.8(10.6)	1432	1744.2	28.9
SXX	438	449.4(5.5)	470	1638.5	15.5	1280	1341.1(10.7)	1403	1863.1	41.8
CSEX	433	447.8(5.1)	471	1500.5	15.3	1286	1340.1(10.6)	1412	1930.9	45.7
DPX	428	433.8(1.8)	443	1225.2	8.9	1213	1250.9(3.3)	1287	1384.0	47.6
SPX	426	429.0(0.7)	435	1321.9	35.1	1212	1227.4(1.3)	1283	1518.7	142.9
*	426	430(0.9)	437	1546.5	23.1	1212	1228.1(1.4)	1283	1798.3	94.1

		kroA(21282)						rat195(2323)			
	Min	Avg.(Quality)	Max	Gen.	Time(sec.)	Min	Avg.(Quality)	Max	Gen.	Time(sec.)
MPX	21552	22683.0(6.6)	23779	2482.5	90.1	2551	2623.0(12.9)	2697	4089	528.5
SCH.	22026	23073.9(8.4)	25262	1766.6	18.7	2577	2638.7(13.6)	2761	3474.6	106.8
ROX	21315	22528.2(5.8)	23947	2525.6	18.5	2466	2532.7(9.0)	2617	5315.5	106.7
HX	21391	22258.9(4.6)	23285	1837	21.6	2483	2593.7(11.6)	2707	3064.7	105.9
GX	21668	22755.2(6.9)	24865	1685.1	19.7	2524	2627.4(13.1)	2725	3051	104.6
ER	21785	22939.4(7.8)	24355	1815.8	32.5	2548	2625(13.0)	2727	3371.6	175
EER	21638	23115.0(8.6)	24837	1686.3	28.1	2526	2633.9(13.4)	2737	3218.6	159.2
SXX	21807	22775.7(7.0)	23954	1989.8	44.3	2522	2635.3(13.4)	2715	3618.3	409
CSEX	21721	22919.5(7.7)	24945	1998.4	47.3	2558	2642.9(13.8)	2717	4142.9	490
DPX	21292	21940.5(3.1)	23059	1292.6	48.1	2370	2400.9(3.4)	2471	1818.5	357.8
SPX	21282	21445.1(0.8)	21841	1412.5	140.1	2334	2378.2(2.4)	2466	2746.5	1120.0
*	21282	21418.3(0.6)	21841	1632.5	91.7	2345	2385.3(2.7)	2465	3401.3	701

Note: () : optimal solution; Gen. : Average Generation; Time : Average CPU Time; * : pop_size = 100

other operators but the performance was much superior to the others in all the cases. At the instance eil51 and kroA100, SPX found optimal solution, on the other hand other operators could not find. The proposed operators generated the quality not to excess 3% from optimal solution in all the case. The reason much computation time is needed is for selection of identical parents and this case is increased more and more. So for decreasing computation time, we cut down population size as 100 but the performance was not changed nearly. Especially, SPX indicates better results than DPX, which is known as one of the most effective and predominant operators. It is very encouraging fact.

4   Conclusion

In this paper, we proposed a highly efficient subtour-based crossover, subtour preservation crossover (SPX) for TSP, and experimented the features and performance of SPX. and pointed out the necessity of a supplementary method in subtour-based crossovers. By means of several computational experiments, it has been confirmed that SPX can get better results than permutation based crossovers and other operators using parental information. Although the proposed new crossover operators needed more computation time than others, performance is superior to them. As future work we plan to investigate more powerful local search algorithms such as Lin-Kernighan algorithm (LN) and develop a predominant hybrid genetic algorithm. Because the objective of this paper is to show that the more parental information is used, the better performance can be obtained, we use small size instances. But, for the effectiveness of the SPX, we will apply it to more large problems.

References

1. D. Goldberg : Genetic Algorithms in Search, Optimization, and Machine Learning. Addison Wesley, Reading, MA (1989).
2. J. Grefenstette, R. Gopal, B. Rosmaita, D. Gucht : Genetic Algorithms for the Traveling Salesman Problem. First Int. Conf. on GA & App's, (1985) 160-168.
3. K. Maekawa, N. Mori, H. Tamaki, H. Kita, Y. Nishikawa : A Genetic Solution for the Traveling Salesman Problem by Means of a Thermodynamical Selection Rule. Proc. of IEEE Int. Conf. on EC, (1996) 529-534.
4. K. Katayama, H. Hirabayashi, H. Narihisa : Performance Analysis of a New Genetic Cross-over for the Traveling Salesman Problem. IEICE TRANS. FUNDAMENTALS, VOL. E81-A, NO. 5 (1998) 738-750.
5. K. Mathias, D. Whitley : Genetic operators, the fitness landscape and the traveling salesman problem. Proc. Parallel Problem Solving from Nature II, (1992) 219-228.
6. R. Yang : Solving Large Traveling Salesman Problems with Small Populations. Genetic Algorithms in Engineering Systems: Innov's and App's, (1997) 157-162.
7. M. Yamamura, I. Ono, S. Kobayashi : Character-preserving genetic algorithms for traveling salesman problem. Jour. of Japan Society for AI, vol. 6, (1992) 1049-1059.
8. L. Yang, D.A. Stacey : Solving the Traveling Salesman Problem Using the Enhanced Ge-netic Algorithm. LNCS, Vol.2056, Springer-Verlag, 307-316.
9. K.D. Boese : Cost Versus Distance In the Traveling Salesman Problem. Tech. Rep. TR-950018, UCLA CS Department, (1995).
10. D. Whitley, T. Starkweather, D. Fuquay : Scheduling problems and traveling salesman: the genetic edge recombination and operator. Proc. 3rd Int. Conf. GA and their Applications, (1989) 133-140. 441-456.
11. P. Moscato : On Genetic Crossover Operators for Relative Order Preservation. Caltech Concurrent Computation Program, C3P Report 778, (1989).
12. B. Freisleben, P. Merz : A Genetic Local Search Algorithm for Solving Symmetric and Asymmetric Traveling Salesmen Problems. IEEE Int. Conf. on EC, (1996) 616-621.
13. TSPLIB. Web Site, http://www.iwr.uni-heidelberg.de/iwr/comopt/ soft/ TSPLIB95/TSPLIB.html

Hybridization of Blind Source Separation and Rough Sets for Proteomic Biomarker Identification

Grzegorz M. Boratyn[1], Tomasz G. Smolinski[1], Jacek M. Zurada[1]*,
Mariofanna Milanova[2], Sudeepa Bhattacharyya[3], and Larry J. Suva[4]

[1] Computational Intelligence Laboratory,
Department of Electrical and Computer Engineering,
University of Louisville, Louisville, KY
[2] Department of Computer Science, University of Arkansas at Little Rock,
Little Rock, AR
[3] Department of Orthopedic Surgery, Barton Research Institute,
University of Arkansas for Medical Sciences, Little Rock, AR
[4] Department of Physiology and Biophysics, Barton Research Institute,
University of Arkansas for Medical Sciences, Little Rock, AR

Abstract. Biomarkers are molecular parameters associated with presence and severity of specific disease states. Search for biological markers of cancer in proteomic profiles is a relatively new but very active research area. This paper presents a novel approach to feature selection and thus biomarker identification. The proposed method is based on blind separation of sources and selection of features from a reduced set of components.

1 Introduction

Early diagnosis is critical in cancer treatment and prevention. It is, therefore, essential to determine molecular parameters (so-called biomarkers) associated with presence and severity of specific disease states [1], [2], [3], [4]. Utilization of surface-enhanced laser desorption/ionization (SELDI) time-of-flight (TOF) mass spectrometry profiling of serum proteins (for description see [1], [2], [4]), combined with statistical or data mining methods, has been recently reported as a promising approach to identification of biomarkers. These techniques were successfully applied to identification of proteomic biomarkers of ovarian and prostate cancer: statistical Wilkinson p-value in [5], boosting algorithm in [6], and self organizing maps combined with genetic algorithm in [7]. Classical approach to feature selection was attempted by the authors in [8], [9]. Along the same line, we propose to utilize a signal decomposition technique to determine dissimilarities between different groups of protein samples and thus locate biomarkers. Protein samples are processed in a mass spectrometer (SELDI-TOF), which analyzes

* The work of this author was sponsored in part by the Systems Research Institute of the Polish Academy of Sciences, 01-447 Warszawa, Poland, ul. Newelska 6

L. Rutkowski et al. (Eds.): ICAISC 2004, LNAI 3070, pp. 486–491, 2004.
© Springer-Verlag Berlin Heidelberg 2004

substances based on mass to charge ratio (m/z) of its particle components. The result which is the table of intensities (amounts) of particle components with specific m/z is recorded and can be retrieved for manual or computer-assisted interpretation. The proteomic SELDI-TOF data were collected at the Barton Research Institute of University of Arkansas for Medical Sciences. The serum was obtained from patients with documented myeloma cancer and those that did not suffer from the disease. Values of m/z that discriminate between classes of cancerous and healthy serum are to be found. Very high dimensionality (30,000 elements in each profile) and variability of the data creates a need for nontraditional approaches to this problem.

2   Theoretical Background

The search for biomarkers in protein profiles can be viewed as a feature selection problem that can be formulated as follows: Given N data points $\mathbf{x}_i \in R^n$, $i = 1, \ldots, N$, with labels $y_i \in \{-1, 1\}$ select an L-element subset of features $\{x_{ik} | k \in S, S \subseteq 1, \ldots, N\}$ while preserving or possibly improving discriminative ability of a classifier. The number of relevant features L is usually chosen arbitrarily. The literature distinguishes between two types of algorithms to solve this problem: filter and wrapper [10]. Filter methods are understood as a preprocessing step to remove irrelevant features before classification. Popular filter methods measure the correlation between values of features and labels using Pearson correlation coefficient or mutual information. Wrapper method is a search through a space of feature subsets aimed at the maximization of some estimate of classification accuracy. Several filter algorithms have already been applied to the same data set by the authors [8], [9]. The nature of protein profiles allows for different approach to this problem. The profiles can be interpreted as signals in the m/z space that can be separated into statistically independent components. Magnitudes of those components denoted by $\mathbf{a}_i$ represent the original points $\mathbf{x}_i$ in a new feature space. Dimensionality of $\mathbf{a}_i$'s is usually much smaller than dimensionality of $\mathbf{x}_i$'s making classification and feature selection problem easier. The new feature set will then be reduced to attributes relevant to the given classification. Each attribute of $\mathbf{a}_i$ is associated with a computed component that is still in the m/z space. Therefore, relevant features point to relevant components where differences between protein profiles in m/z space can be observed. Optima of those components for a particular class indicate values higher or lower than usually. The following sections present a Blind Source Separation (BSS) technique used to compute components and their magnitudes in each profile, Rough Set (RS) based tools for reduction of the new feature set, and feature selection in m/z space.

2.1   Blind Source Separation

Each sequence of intensities $\mathbf{x}_i$ will be interpreted as a signal and will be denoted by a column vector. It is assumed here that each signal is a mixture of some underlying sources of activity. Identification of sources of a measured signal has been an active research area [11], [12], [13]. It is assumed that each input signal is a linear combination of some statistically independent sources (or basis functions):

$$\mathbf{x}_i = \mathbf{M}\mathbf{a}_i + \mathbf{e}_i, \tag{1}$$

where each column of $\mathbf{M} \in R^{n \times m}$ is a basis function $\mathbf{M}_j \in R^n, j = 1, 2, ..., m$, $\mathbf{a}_i \in R^m$ is a column vector of coefficients - magnitudes of each basis functions in the signal $\mathbf{x}_i$, and $\mathbf{e}_i \in R^n$ represents noise or error of the model. $\mathbf{M}$ and $\mathbf{a}$ are unknown parameters that need to be estimated. Statistical independence of the basis functions can be satisfied by minimizing mutual information between the basis functions. Thus $\mathbf{M}$ and $\mathbf{a}$ are estimated by solving the following:

$$\mathbf{M}, \mathbf{a} = \arg\min_{\mathbf{a}} \left(\arg\min_{\mathbf{M}} \left(I\left(\mathbf{M}_1, \mathbf{M}_2, ..., \mathbf{M}_m\right) + \lambda||\mathbf{x} - \mathbf{M}\mathbf{a}||^2 \right) \right), \tag{2}$$

where λ is a scaling factor, and $I(\mathbf{M}_1, \mathbf{M}_2, ..., \mathbf{M}_m)$ is mutual information between random variables $\mathbf{M}_1, \mathbf{M}_2, ..., \mathbf{M}_m$ defined as [14]:

$$I(\mathbf{M}_1, \mathbf{M}_2, ..., \mathbf{M}_m) = \sum_{j=1}^{m} H(\mathbf{M}_j) - H(\mathbf{M}_1, \mathbf{M}_2, ..., \mathbf{M}_m), \tag{3}$$

where $H(\mathbf{M}_j)$ is entropy of a random variable $\mathbf{M}_j$. Optimization using (2) may be performed with a gradient descent algorithm. The two quantities to be computed, $\mathbf{M}$ and $\mathbf{a}$, make this problem complex. The minimization can be solved by estimating only $\mathbf{M}$:

$$\mathbf{M} = \arg\min_{\mathbf{M}} \left(I\left(\mathbf{M}_1, \mathbf{M}_2, ..., \mathbf{M}_m\right) + \lambda||\mathbf{x} - \mathbf{M}\hat{\mathbf{a}}||^2 \right), \tag{4}$$

where the estimate $\hat{\mathbf{a}}$ of $\mathbf{a}$ in each step of the algorithm is the solution of the following:

$$\hat{\mathbf{a}} = \arg\min_{\mathbf{a}}||\mathbf{x} - \mathbf{M}\mathbf{a}||^2, \tag{5}$$

where the value of $\mathbf{M}$ is a partial solution of (4), similarly to [11].

2.2   Rough Sets

The theory of rough sets (RS) was introduced in the early 1980's by Zdzislaw Pawlak [15] [16]. Especially useful for a classification-relevant feature selection is the concept of reducts that is inherently embedded in the theory [17]. One of the most important notions of the rough sets theory is the indiscernibility relation, which is a binary equivalence relation that divides a given set of elements (objects) into a certain number of disjoint equivalence classes. An equivalence class of an element $\mathbf{a}_i \in X$ consists of all objects $\mathbf{a}_l \in X$ such that $\mathbf{a}_i R \mathbf{a}_l$, where R indicates a binary relation. Let $IS = (R^m, A)$ be an information system of objects from universe R^m described by the set of attributes A, then with any $B \subseteq A$ there is an associated equivalence relation $IND_{IS}(B)$:

$$IND_{IS}(B) = \{(\mathbf{a}_i, \mathbf{a}_l) \in R^{2m} | \forall j \in B, a_{ij} = a_{lj}\}. \tag{6}$$

$IND_{IS}(B)$ is called B-indiscernibility relation. If $(\mathbf{a}_i, \mathbf{a}_l) \in IND_{IS}(B)$, then objects $\mathbf{a}_i$ and $\mathbf{a}_l$ are indistinguishable from each other by attributes from B. Based on the concept of indiscernibility relation, a reduction in the space of attributes is possible. The idea is to keep only those attributes that preserve the indiscernibility relation. The rejected attributes are redundant since their removal cannot worsen the classification. There are usually several such subsets of attributes and those, which are minimal, are called reducts.

2.3 Feature Selection

The basis functions $\mathbf{M}_j$ associated with attributes a_{ij} of $\mathbf{a}_i$ selected as relevant reflect the change of intensity values specific to one of the given classes. The fact that the j-th attribute of $\mathbf{a}_i$ belongs to B indicates that the effect of $\mathbf{M}_j$ in any $\mathbf{x}_i$ will be different for the two classes. Statistical independence of basis functions ensures that their values are mostly different for the same m/z. In other words, $P(x_{ik} = x_{lk})$ is low for $i \neq l$. Thus, the biggest differences between intensity values are introduced by high values of the basis functions and the set of relevant features is equal to:

$$B_{m/z} = \{k | k = \arg\max_k \{M_{jk}\} \ \forall j \in B\}. \tag{7}$$

3 Experiments

The data set consisted of 19 protein profiles, 13 of which belonged to class *myeloma* and 6 to class *normal*. This was a preliminary study, so the computation was performed on a part of the profile – a subsequence of 100 elements that contained m/z values with highest Fisher Score (see [8]). The subsequence was separated into 5 source signals ($m = 5$). The RS-based tools reduced the extracted feature set to two elements. Values of the selected coefficients are presented in Fig. 1, where stars and open circles indicate objects that belong to classes myeloma and normal, respectively. One can see in Fig. 1 that the reduced set of coefficients can serve well as classification features. L values of k with the highest values of $\mathbf{M}_j$, $j \in B$ were selected as relevant features. A single linear neuron was trained on the intensity values selected by the described method. The training was performed several times on a set consisting of 6 profiles belonging to class myeloma and 8 from class normal. The original proportion 13:6 was causing a huge imbalance and poor training. The profiles from class myeloma were selected randomly for each training session. In each session the learning was repeated 14 times, leaving one profile as the testing set each time. The testing errors averaged over those 14 trainings were compared in order to examine generalization of training on selected features. The results, summarized in Table 1, indicate that there is a generalization improvement with a smaller number of selected features. Note that high values of test errors are due to the fact that only one neuron was trained. Reduction of error for smaller number of features is a result of high variability of the data and small size of the training set.

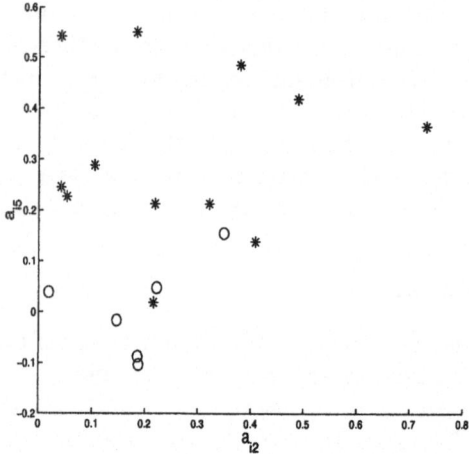

Fig. 1. Values of the selected coefficients for all training objects

Table 1. Analysis of neuron training with several sizes of feature set

Number of features	average testing error
100	4.2423
50	1.5376
20	0.7455
10	0.9643
5	0.5143

4   Conclusions

A new method of feature selection for signal-like data was proposed. BSS-based extraction of new features reduces dimensionality and simplifies the attribute selection problem in the original space. The basis functions selected by RS methods indicate differences between objects relevant for classification. Thus, an additional advantage of the described algorithm is the possibility of analysis of the results by specialists in an area associated with data. However, a few problems still need to be solved. A method for identifying best optima of the basis functions in terms of classification and generalization requires further investigation. Estimation of the number of needed basis functions, important from the computational point of view, should also be considered.

References

1. Srinivas, P. R., Srivastava, S., Hanash, S., and Wright Jr., G. L.: Proteomics in early detection of cancer. Clinical Chemistry **47** (2001) 1901 – 1911

2. Conrads, T. P., Zhou, M., III, E. F. P., Liotta, L., and Veenstra, T. D.: Cancer diagnosis using proteomic patterns. Future Drugs **4** (2003) 411 – 420
3. Diamandis, E. P.: Proteomic patterns in bilogical fluids: do they represent the future of cancer diagnostics? Clinical Chemistry **8** (2003) 1272 – 1278
4. Wulfkuhle, J. D., Liotta, L. A., and Petricoin, E. F.: Proteomic applications for the early detection of cancer. Nature Reviews **3** (2003) 267 – 275
5. Sorace, J. M. and Zahn, M.: A data review and re-assesment of ovarian cancer serum proteomic profiling. BMC Bioinformatics **4** (2003) 1471 – 2105
6. Yasui, Y., Pepe, M., Thompson, M. L., Adam, B.-L., Wright, Jr., G. L., Qu, Y., Potter, J. D., Winget, M., Thornquist, M., and Feng, Z.: A data-analytic strategy for protein biomarker discovery: profiling of high-dimensional proteomic data for cancer detection. Biostatistics **4** (2003) 449 – 463
7. Petricoin, E. F., Ardekani, A. M., Hitt, B. A., Levine, P. J., Fusaro, V. A., Steinberg, S. M., Mills, G. B., Simone, C., Fishman, D. A., Kohn, E. C., and Liotta, L. A.: Use of proteomic patterns in serum to identify ovarian cancer. Lancet **359** (2002) 572 – 577
8. Boratyn, G. M., Smolinski, T. G., Milanova, M., Zurada, J. M., Bhattacharyya, S., and Suva, L. J.: Scoring-based analysis of protein patterns for identification of myeloma cancer. In F. Valafar and H. Valafar, eds., Proceedings of the International Conference on Mathematics and Engineering Techniques in Medicine and Biological Sciences, METMBS'03, Las Vegas, NV, June 23 – 26 (2003) 60 – 65
9. Boratyn, G. M., Smolinski, T. G., Milanova, M., Zurada, J. M., Bhattacharyya, S., and Suva, L. J.: Bayesian approach to analysis of protein patterns for identification of myeloma cancer. In Proceeding of the Second International Conference on Machine Learning and Cybernetics, Xi-an, November 2 – 5, IEEE (2003) 1217 – 1221
10. Blum, A. and Langley, P.: Selection of relevant features and examples in machine learning. Artificail Intelligence **97** (1997) 245 – 271
11. Olshausen, B. A.: Sparse codes and spikes. In R. P. N. Rao, B. A. Olshausen, and M. S. Lewicki, eds., Probabilistic models of perception and brain function, MIT Press, Cambridge, MA (2001) 257 – 272
12. Amari, S.-I. and Cichocki, A.: Adaptive blind signal processing - neural network approaches. Proc. of the IEEE **86** (1998) 2026 – 2048
13. Comon, P.: Independent component analysis - a new concept? Signal Processing **36** (1994) 287 – 314
14. Cover, T. M. and Thomas, J. A.: Elements of information theory. John Wiley and Sons, Inc., New York (1991)
15. Pawlak, Z.: Rough sets. International Journal of Computer and Information Sciences **11** (1982) 341 – 356
16. Marek, W. and Pawlak, Z.: Rough sets and information systems. Fundamenta Matematicae **17** (1984) 105 – 115
17. Komorowski, J., Pawlak, Z., Polkowski, L., and Skowron, A.: Rough sets: A tutorial. In S. K. Pal and A. Skowron, eds., Rough Fuzzy Hybridization - A New Trend in Decision-Making (1999) 3 – 98

Inducing Jury's Preferences in Terms of Acoustic Features of Violin Sounds

Jacek Jelonek, Ewa Łukasik, Aleksander Naganowski, and Roman Słowiński

Institute of Computing Science,
Poznan University of Technology,
Piotrowo 3a, 60-965 Poznań, Poland
Roman.Slowinski@cs.put.poznan.pl

Abstract. A set of violins submitted to a competition has been evaluated by the jury from the viewpoint of several criteria and then ranked from the best to the worst. The sound of the instruments played by violinists during the competition has been recorded digitally and then processed to obtain sound attributes. Given the jury's ranking of violins according to sound quality criteria, we are inferring from the sound characteristics a preference model of the jury in the form of "if..., then..." decision rules. This preference model explains the given ranking and permits to build a ranking of a new set of violins according to this policy. The inference follows the scheme of an inductive supervised learning. For this, we are applying a special computational tool called Dominance-based Rough Set Approach (DRSA). The new set of attributes derived from the energy of consecutive halftones of the chromatic scales played on four strings has proved a good accuracy of the approximation.

1 Introduction

A set of violins submitted to the 10th International Henryk Wieniawski Violin-makers Competition in Poznań has been evaluated by the jury on a set of criteria [4]: a) volume of sound, b) timbre of sound, c) ease of sound emission, d) equal sound volume of strings, e) accuracy of assembly, f) individual qualities. Criteria a), b), d) refer to quality of the violin's sound while c), e), f) are related rather to quality of the violin's assembly. Various sounds of the competing instruments have been recorded digitally and then processed to obtain sound attributes.

Given the jury's rankings of violins according to sound quality criteria a), b), d), we have inferred in [2] a preference model of the jury in the form of "if..., then..." decision rules. This preference model explains the jury's ranking with respect to criteria a), b), d), in terms of the most relevant sound characteristics. It also permitted to build a ranking of a new set of violins in accordance with the jury's preference on the three criteria. The inference followed the scheme of an inductive supervised learning. For this, we applied a special computational tool called Dominance-based Rough Set Approach (DRSA)[1][7][8].

The approach is as follows. First, using the judgments of the members of the jury, we are constructing rough approximation of the preference relation known

L. Rutkowski et al. (Eds.): ICAISC 2004, LNAI 3070, pp. 492–497, 2004.
© Springer-Verlag Berlin Heidelberg 2004

from a ranking on criterion a), or b), or d). The rough approximation of the preference relation is a starting point for inducing the decision rules in terms of the acoustic features of the violins. The rules can serve to: (i) explain the decision policy of the jury, i.e. to reconstruct the ranking with respect to a given criterion by using rules to the violins from the competition, and (ii) build a new ranking for a new set of violins characterized by acoustic features. Application of a set of decision rules to a set of violins gives a preference graph where nodes correspond to violins and arcs are preference relations for pairs of violins. Positive and negative flows are calculated for each node (violin), giving arguments about its relative strength and weakness. Aggregation of both arguments leads to a final ranking of violins, either partial or complete. The approach can also be useful for discovering subsets of acoustic features being relevant for the final ranking.

In this paper we report the results of applying the above approach to a new set of features characterizing the same collection of instruments as in [2]. The new features are related to the energy calculated for individual semitone notes played in the chromatic scale. The same method has been used by F. Saunders [6] as an easy method of characterizing the acoustic features of violins.

The paper is organized as follows: in the next section, the dominance-based rough set approach is outlined; then, the acoustic data are characterized and, finally, the results are presented in terms of relevant acoustic features and decision rules.

2   The Rough Set Approach to Violin's Data Analysis

2.1   Pairwise Comparison Table (PCT) as Preferential Information and a Learning Sample

Let A be a set of objects (violins) evaluated by a finite set of criteria C. The preferential information concerning the multicriteria ranking of objects can be transformed to a pairwise comparison table (PCT) including *pairs of objects* from $A \times A$, described by preference relations on particular criteria and a comprehensive preference relation, for example, a large preference relation called *outranking relation*. The comprehensive preference relation is calculated from the jury's ranking of objects according to a given decision criterion. If for any pair of objects $(x, y) \in A \times A$, object x is placed not worse than object y in the ranking, then x outranks y; otherwise, x does not outrank y. In the following, xSy will denote the presence, while xS^cy the absence of the outranking relation for a pair $(x, y) \in A \times A$. S is reflexive, but neither necessarily transitive nor complete.

An $m \times (n + 1)$ Pairwise Comparison Table S_{PCT} is then created on the base of this information. Its first n columns correspond to criteria from set C. The last, $(n + 1)$-th column of S_{PCT}, represents binary relation S or S^c. The m rows are pairs from $A \times A$. Assuming the gain preference direction on each criterion $i \in [1; n]$, an inner element of S_{PCT} is a difference: calculated using evaluations $g_i(x)$ and $g_i(y)$ of objects x and y on criterion i. The difference $\Delta_i(x, y) = g_i(x) - g_i(y)$ is then translated to a degree of intensity of preference on the corresponding criterion.

2.2   DRSA Analysis of the PCT

Using the Dominance-based Rough Set Approach (DRSA) on the PCT, as described in [1][7][8], P-lower and P-upper approximations of comprehensive outranking relations S and S^c are defined, where $P \subseteq C$ ($P \neq \emptyset$). The P-lower approximation of relation S includes all pairs of objects from the PCT which are in relation S and such that they are not dominated by pairs of objects being in relation S^c. Such pairs are called consistent with the dominance principle. The P-upper approximation of relation S includes all pairs of objects from the PCT which are either in relation S or are in relation S^c while being dominated by a pair for which S holds. Analogical definition of approximations holds for relation S^c. The difference between P-lower and P-upper approximation of S and S^c is a joint boundary set including *inconsistent* pairs in the sense of the dominance principle.

The *quality of approximation* γ_P of S and S^c by $P \subseteq C$ is a measure expressing the ratio of all pairs of objects correctly assigned to S and S^c by the set P of criteria to all the pairs of objects contained in the PCT.

It is also possible to use the Variable Consistency Model on S_{PCT} [8] allowing that some of the pairs in positive or negative dominance sets belong to the opposite relation but at least l percent of pairs belong to the correct one.

2.3   Searching for Criteria with an Ordinal Scale

There is no explicit knowledge, whether a specified criterion has an ordinal scale or nominal only. In order to detect criteria with an ordinal scale, we propose to use a special coefficient Q_P within DRSA:

$$Q_p = (1 - \alpha)\gamma_P + \alpha \left[1 - \frac{|Edge(S)| + |Edge(S^c)|}{|A \times A|} \right] \tag{1}$$

It is a weighted sum of two components – the quality of approximation γ_P and the relative number of incomparable objects in each approximation expressed by the cardinality of edges: $EdgeP(S) = \{(x, y) \in S : (x, y) \text{ dominates itself only}\}$ and $EdgeP(S^c) = \{(x, y) \in S^c : (x, y) \text{ is dominated by itself only}\}$.

The weight $\alpha \in [0; 1]$ permits to tune the relative importance of the two components. The value of the coefficient Q_P, from the range $[0; 1]$, may be treated as a measure of the *semantic correlation* between the acoustic features and the decision criterion (ranking). We consider a feature as a criterion with an ordinal scale if the value of the coefficient Q_P is relatively high (close to 1.0). The search for the most relevant subset of criteria is made in a *wrapper loop* where groups are formed by adding features one by one. In each iteration, all groups (future subsets) are evaluated using the Q_P coefficient.

2.4   Use of Decision Rules for Decision Support

The decision rules induced from lower approximations of comprehensive outranking relations S and S^c from a given S_{PCT} represent a preference model of the jury. The syntax of the rules is the following [1][7][8]:

1. $D_{\geq}$-*decision rules*: *if* $x\ h^{\geq}(i_1)\ y\ and\ldots x\ h^{\geq}(i_e)\ y,\ then\ xSy$,
   where $\{i_1,\ldots,i_e\} = P \subseteq C$, and $h^{\geq}(i_1),\ldots,h^{\geq}(i_e)$ are degrees of intensity of preference on particular criteria by which x is **at least** preferred to y; these rules are supported by pairs of objects from the P-lower approximation of S only;
2. $D_{\leq}$-*decision rules*: *if* $x\ h^{\leq}(i_1)\ y\ and\ldots x\ h^{\leq}(i_f)\ y,\ then\ xS^cy$,
   where $\{i_1,\ldots,i_f\} = P \subseteq C$, and $h^{\leq}(i_1),\ldots,h^{\leq}(i_f)$ are degrees of intensity of preference on particular criteria by which x is **at most** preferred to y; these rules are supported by pairs of objects from the P-lower approximation of S^c only.

Application of these decision rules on a new set M of objects induces a specific preference structure on M. Exploitation of this structure with the Net Flow Score procedure [1][7][8] leads to the final ranking on M.

2.5   The Acoustic Attributes

The sounds for the analysis have been selected from the set of digital recordings gathered in AMATI database [4]. In [2] these were individual sounds played on open strings G, D, A, E. In this paper we analyze the entire range of semitone notes across a chromatic scale (two octaves) on G-string, from G3 to G5, on D-string, from D4 to D6, on A-string, from A4 to A6 and on E-string, from E5 to E7 (25 notes on each string). It is worth noting, that some of the semitones overlap, however played on different strings, they have different acoustical parameters [5] and may have different influence on machine perception of violin sound. Since each semitone note gives different, natural excitation for the whole violin body, the instruments response is also different – the sound is louder or more silent. The energy radiated by the instrument at each individual sound is calculated, in the result giving the curve representing instrument's response. The method is almost similar to the one introduced by F. Saunders in 1937 [6], called maximum level sound level curves. The compatible response obtained using various excitations methods are usually very carefully examined by specialists concerned with the quality of the instrument seeking for the cues for perfect sound.

Experiments concerned 25 instruments from the collection, ranked by the musicians as the best, average and the worst (the same as in [2]). Numbers that we use in the records stood for instruments identifiers during the competition.

2.6   The Results

Although cepstral coefficients gave good results in former experiments, the new set of data has been used in order to possibly improve generation of rules and also to yield more straightforward physical interpretation of data. As we present below, it is possible to approximate jury's rankings with an acceptable precision, using only a small subset of these all 100 values. The criteria were selected by using the algorithm described before.

These results were obtained for a selected group of 23 instruments, arranged in three different rankings, called A, B, D, according to sound quality criteria a), b), d) (see Section 1). For each ranking, one of the best subsets of criteria was chosen – the first letter corresponds to the string name. The quality was calculated for the S_{PCT} with *variable consistency* level equal to 0.95. Three sets of rules were generated on the base of these subsets using the *DomLEM* algorithm [7], which is a *minimal cover* rule induction algorithm. To reduce the size of the sets of rules, they were induced with *consistency level* equal to 0.9. A distance between the jury's original ranking and the ranking obtained by applying rules is calculated as an average position shift of each object.

The two data sets – cepstral coefficients and semitone energies – give close results, but some minor differences appeared. While the first approach best describes the timbre of sound, the second permits to characterise with the smallest error the equalisation of the sound volume. This conclusion is confirmed by the set of rules that is generated. The majority of rules contain sounds played on different strings in the conditional part. Since the rules are conjunctions of elementary conditions, they describe relations between strings.

The most frequent note that appears in the best criteria subsets is the G-string: $G^{\#}4$ (415 Hz) – in almost 64% subsets. For each ranking separately the frequency is as follows: ranking A – E-string: $A^{\#}5$ (932,3 Hz), 26%; ranking B – G-string: $G^{\#}4$, 19%; ranking C – G: $G^{\#}4$ - 33%. In the research reported by many authors, where various methods of instruments excitation are used, the importance of low frequency resonances for the quality of violins are discussed. In [5] important peaks have been found for Stradivarius violins between the notes B3 and D4 (247 and 293 Hz) and between E4 and G4 (329 and 392 Hz), raising up to A4 (440 Hz) for other old Italian violins. Important attributes found by the method roughly fall within the range recalled above. The other important sounds are of higher fundamental frequency from 1046 to 1661 Hz. This frequency space is less peaky, but also of importance for instruments quality.

Table 1. The results obtained using cepstral coefficients (string name and cepstral coefficient) [5]

Ranking	Subset of criteria	γ_P	No. of rules	Ranking distance
A	A-14, E-13, D-12, G-16	0.94	62	1.57
B	E-13, D-15, G-4, G-17, D-5	0.94	99	2.00
D	D-20, D-15, A-24, D-10	0.98	64	2.26

Table 2. Subsets obtained for the new data set (string name and semitone name)

Ranking	Subset of criteria	γ_P	No. of rules	Ranking distance
A	G:G$^\#$4, G:D5, A:F$^\#$6, A:G6, E:A$^\#$5	0.92	98	2.08
B	D:G4, A:D$^\#$6, A:G$^\#$6, E:F6, E:D$^\#$7	0.88	82	1.87
D	G:G$^\#$4, D:F5, D:A5, A:D6	0.91	57	1.70

2.7 Conclusions

The presented approach permits to create rankings of instruments that are almost identical to the original ones, which means that the jury's preferences are well approximated. The approach permitted, moreover, to discover a small but relevant subset of acoustic features ensuring a good approximation of the rankings. By induction of decision rules from available data, we are able to represent a decision policy of the jury in easily interpretable terms.

The rough set approach including the quality coefficient Q_P permits to deal with a set of features for which it is not explicitly known if attributes are criteria, i.e. attributes with preference-ordered domains. We are continuing this research to discover other interesting acoustic features than cepstral coefficients and energy of semitones (e.g. from [3]) on a larger set of violins.

Acknowledgements. The financial support from the State Committee for Scientific Research, the KBN grant no 4 T11F 002 22 is kindly acknowledged. The authors are grateful to Henryk Wieniawski Musical Society in Poznań for making accessible the judgments of the jury and for enabling recordings of violins.

References

1. Greco, S., Matarazzo, B., Słowiński, R.: Rough sets theory for multicriteria decision analysis. European J. of Operational Research **129** (2001) no.1, 1–47
2. Jelonek, J., Łukasik, E., Naganowski, A., Słowiński, R, Inferring Decision Rules from Jury's Ranking of Competing Violins, Proc. SMAC'03, Stockholm, 2003, 75–78
3. Kostek, B., Soft Computing in Acoustics, Physics Verlag, Heidelberg, 1999
4. Łukasik, E., Multimedia Database of Violin Sounds, Proc. SMAC'03, Stockholm, 2003, 79–82
5. Meyer, J., The tonal quality of violons, Proc. SMAC'83, Stockholm, 1985, 69–78
6. Saunders, F., The Mechanical Action of Violins, J. Acoust. Soc. Am, October 1937
7. Słowiński, R., Greco, S., Matarazzo, B.: Rough set based decision aiding. [In]: E. Burke and G. Kendall (eds.), Introductory Tutorials on Optimization, Search and Decision Support Methodologies, Kluwer Academic Publishers, Boston, 2003, chapter 16
8. Słowiński, R., Greco, S., Matarazzo, B.: Mining decision-rule preference model from rough approximation of preference relation. [In]: Proc. 26th IEEE Annual International Conference on Computer Software & Applications, 26-29 August 2002, Oxford, England, 1129–1134

Fuzzy Implication Operators in Variable Precision Fuzzy Rough Sets Model

Alicja Mieszkowicz-Rolka and Leszek Rolka

Department of Avionics and Control,
Rzeszów University of Technology,
ul. W. Pola 2, 35-959 Rzeszów, Poland
{alicjamr, leszekr}@prz.edu.pl

Abstract. This paper presents the variable precision fuzzy rough sets (VPFRS) model, which constitutes a generalisation of the extended variable precision rough set (VPRS) concept. The notion of the α-inclusion error based on the fuzzy implication operators will be introduced. Additionally to extending the basic definition of the fuzzy rough approximations, an idea of the weighted mean fuzzy rough approximations will be given. In an illustrating example the most popular residual implicators will be used.

1 Introduction

It is an interesting issue how to combine the fuzzy sets and rough sets paradigms together into one framework that allows to describe different aspects of uncertainty. A fuzzy rough approach that is mostly cited in the literature was given by Dubois and Prade [1].

Another important problem is an effective application of the rough sets theory [4] to analysis of real information systems. The idea of variable precision rough sets (VPRS) given by Ziarko [2] is a significant contribution in that direction.

The following paper presents a development of the fuzzy rough sets concept obtained by generalising the idea of the crisp VPRS model. The base of the proposed variable precision fuzzy rough set (VPFRS) model is the notion of the α-inclusion error, defined by means of fuzzy implication operators. Furthermore, a new method for determining the fuzzy rough approximations is given, in which the overall fuzzy set inclusion is inspected.

The presented approach can serve analysis of information systems with fuzzy attributes.

2 Variable Precision Fuzzy Rough Sets

The basic notion in VPRS is the inclusion error $e(A, B)$ of a nonempty (crisp) set A in a (crisp) set B defined by Ziarko as follows:

$$e(A, B) = 1 - \frac{\text{card}(A \cap B)}{\text{card}(A)} . \tag{1}$$

L. Rutkowski et al. (Eds.): ICAISC 2004, LNAI 3070, pp. 498–503, 2004.
© Springer-Verlag Berlin Heidelberg 2004

Our further considerations will be based on the extended version of VPRS proposed by Katzberg and Ziarko [2], in which two limits l and u for the required inclusion grade are used, with

$$0 \leq l < u \leq 1 . \tag{2}$$

The lower limit l and the upper limit u can be used to define the u-lower and the l-upper approximation of any subset A of the universe X by an indiscernibility (equivalence) relation R.

The u-lower approximation of A by R, denoted as $\underline{R}_u A$ is a set

$$\underline{R}_u A = \{x \in X:\ e([x]_R, A) \leq 1 - u\} \tag{3}$$

where $[x]_R$ denotes an indiscernibility class of R containing the element x.

The l-upper approximation of A by R, denoted as $\overline{R}_l A$ is a set

$$\overline{R}_l A = \{x \in X:\ e([x]_R, A) < 1 - l\} . \tag{4}$$

Let us consider a partition of the universe X, generated by a symmetric and reflexive fuzzy compatibility relation R. We denote the obtained family of fuzzy compatibility classes by $\Psi = \{X_1, X_2, \ldots, X_n\}$. Any fuzzy set F in X can be approximated by the family Ψ. The membership functions of the lower and upper approximation of F by Ψ are defined as follows [1]:

$$\mu_{\underline{\Psi}F}(X_i) = \inf_{x \in X} \mu_{X_i}(x) \to \mu_F(x) \tag{5}$$

$$\mu_{\overline{\Psi}F}(X_i) = \sup_{x \in X} \mathrm{T}(\mu_{X_i}(x), \mu_F(x)) \tag{6}$$

where: T denotes a t-norm operator [5] and $\to$ is an S-implication operator for that $x \to y = 1 - \mathrm{T}(x, 1 - y)$ [1].

The pair of sets $(\underline{\Psi}F, \overline{\Psi}F)$ is called a fuzzy rough set [1].

It is possible to evaluate the inclusion grade of a fuzzy set A in a fuzzy set B, regarding particular elements of A. We introduce to this end a notion called the fuzzy inclusion set of A in B denoted by A^B, which is based on an implication operator $\to$:

$$\mu_{A^B}(x) = \begin{cases} \mu_A(x) \to \mu_B(x) & \text{if } \mu_A(x) > 0 \\ 0 & \text{otherwise} \end{cases} \tag{7}$$

The extension of the VPRS idea on fuzzy sets requires a new measure of inclusion error that would be made, when the weakest elements of the approximating set (regarding their membership in the fuzzy inclusion set) were discarded. We will define it by applying the notion of α-cut (with $\alpha \in [0,1]$) by which, for any given fuzzy set A, a crisp set A_α can be obtained:

$$A_\alpha = \{x \in X :\ \mu_A(x) \geq \alpha\} . \tag{8}$$

The new measure, called α-inclusion error $e_\alpha(A, B)$ of any fuzzy set A in a fuzzy set B, is expressed as follows:

$$e_\alpha(A, B) = 1 - \frac{\mathrm{power}(A \cap A_\alpha^B)}{\mathrm{power}(A)} \tag{9}$$

where power denotes the cardinality of a fuzzy set (for any finite fuzzy set F defined in X: $\mathrm{power}(F) = \sum_{i=1}^{n} \mu_F(x_i)$).

We can allow some level of tolerance, in the sense of VPRS, by taking into account only the best elements of the approximating set for determination of the fuzzy rough approximations. According to this assumption, the u-lower approximation of the set F by R is a fuzzy set of X/R with a membership function, which we define as follows:

$$\mu_{\underline{R}_u F}(X_i) = \begin{cases} f_{i_u} & \text{if } \exists \alpha_u = \sup\{\alpha \in (0,1] : \ e_\alpha(X_i, F) \leq 1 - u\} \\ 0 & \text{otherwise} \end{cases} \tag{10}$$

where

$$f_{i_u} = \inf_{x \in S_{i_u}} \mu_{X_i}(x) \to \mu_F(x), \qquad S_{i_u} = \mathrm{supp}(X_i \cap X_{i_{\alpha_u}}^F) \, .$$

Similarly, it would be possible to define the l-upper approximation of the set F by R as a fuzzy set of X/R with a membership function:

$$\mu_{\overline{R}_l F}(X_i) = \begin{cases} f_{i_l} & \text{if } \exists \alpha_l = \sup\{\alpha \in (0,1] : \ \frac{\mathrm{power}(X_i \cap (X_i \cap F)_\alpha)}{\mathrm{power}(X_i)} > l\} \\ 0 & \text{otherwise} \end{cases} \tag{11}$$

where

$$f_{i_l} = \sup_{x \in S_{i_l}} \mu_{X_i}(x) * \mu_F(x), \qquad S_{i_l} = \mathrm{supp}(X_i \cap (X_i \cap F)_{\alpha_l}) \, .$$

Furthermore, one can observe that the fuzzy rough approximations given by (5) and (6) can be sensitive to disturbances, because they are expressed by means of limit values of the respective membership functions. In order to avoid this effect we propose an alternative definition of fuzzy rough approximations, which bases on the weighted mean value of membership (in the fuzzy inclusion set) for all used elements of the approximating class.

We introduce the u-lower approximation of the set F by R as a fuzzy set of X/R with a membership function based on the weighted mean membership expressed as:

$$\mu_{\underline{R}_u F}(X_i) = \begin{cases} f_{i_u} & \text{if } \exists \alpha_u = \sup\{\alpha \in (0,1] : \ e_\alpha(X_i, F) \leq 1 - u\} \\ 0 & \text{otherwise} \end{cases} \tag{12}$$

where

$$f_{i_u} = \frac{\mathrm{power}((X_i^F \cap X_{i_{\alpha_u}}^F) \cdot X_i)}{\mathrm{card}(X_{i_{\alpha_u}}^F)} \, . \tag{13}$$

The l-upper approximation of the set F by R is a fuzzy set of X/R with a membership function based on the weighted mean membership expressed as:

$$\mu_{\overline{R}_l F}(X_i) = \begin{cases} f_{i_l} & \text{if } \exists \alpha_l = \sup\{\alpha \in (0,1] : \ e_\alpha(X_i, F) < 1 - l\} \\ 0 & \text{otherwise} \end{cases} \tag{14}$$

where

$$f_{i_l} = \frac{\text{power}((X_i^F \cap X_{i_{\alpha_l}}^F) \cdot X_i)}{\text{card}(X_{i_{\alpha_l}}^F)}. \tag{15}$$

The operator $\cdot$ denotes here the product of fuzzy sets. Hence, the quantities f_{i_u} and f_{i_l} represent the weighted mean value of inclusion grade of X_i in F, determined by using only those elements of X_i, which are included in F at least to a degree α_u or α_l respectively.

3   Fuzzy Implicators for the VPFRS Model

We will use a criterion for selection of fuzzy implicators, which bases on a requirement regarding the grade of inclusion (7) of a fuzzy set A in a fuzzy set B. We say that the grade of inclusion of the set A in the set B, with respect to any element $x \in X$, is equal to 1, if the inequality $\mu_A(x) \le \mu_B(x)$ for that x is satisfied:

$$\mu_A(x) \to \mu_B(x) = 1, \quad \text{if } \mu_A(x) \le \mu_B(x). \tag{16}$$

This property does not hold for all implicators. It is satisfied for (residual) R-implicators that are defined using a t-norm operator T as follows:

$$x \to y = \sup\{\lambda \in [0,1] : \ T(x, \lambda) \le y\}. \tag{17}$$

We use in this paper three most popular R-implicators [5]:

- the implicator of Lukasiewicz: $x \to y = \min(1, 1 - x + y)$,
- the Gaines implicator: $x \to y = 1$ if $x \le y$ and y/x otherwise,
- the Gödel implicator: $x \to y = 1$ if $x \le y$ and y otherwise.

The implicator utilised by Dubois and Prade was the Kleene-Dienes (KD) S-implicator: $x \to y = \max(1 - x, y)$.

In the following example we apply the proposed concept of variable precision fuzzy rough approximations to analysis of a decision table with fuzzy attributes (Table 1). We use a compatibility relation [3] for comparing elements of the universe:

$$\mu_R(x, y) = \min_{q \in Q} \sup_{u \in U_q} \min(\mu_{V_q(x)}(u), \mu_{V_q(y)}(u)) \tag{18}$$

where: Q is a finite set of attributes, V_q is the fuzzy (linguistic) value given by a membership function μ_{V_q} defined on the original domain U_q of the attribute q, $V_q(x), V_q(y)$ are fuzzy values of the attribute q for x and y respectively.

Table 1. Decision table with fuzzy attributes

x	c_1	c_2	c_3	d
x_1	A_1	B_1	C_1	D_1
x_2	A_2	B_2	C_1	D_3
x_3	A_1	B_1	C_1	D_1
x_4	A_2	B_2	C_2	D_2
x_5	A_2	B_2	C_2	D_2
x_6	A_1	B_1	C_1	D_1
x_7	A_1	B_1	C_1	D_3
x_8	A_2	B_2	C_2	D_2
x_9	A_2	B_2	C_1	D_3
x_{10}	A_1	B_1	C_1	D_1

The linguistic values of all attributes are expressed by means of typical "triangular" membership functions. The intersection levels of different linguistic values for attributes are assumed as follows:

for A_1 and A_2: 0.30,   for B_1 and B_2: 0.25,   for C_1 and C_2: 0.25,
for D_1 and D_2: 0.20,   for D_2 and D_3: 0.20,
otherwise: 0.

We get a family $\Phi = \{F_1, F_2, F_3\}$ of compatibility classes with respect to the fuzzy decision attribute d:

$$F_1 = \{ \; 1/x_1, \quad 0/x_2, \quad 1/x_3, \quad 0.2/x_4, \quad 0.2/x_5, \quad 1/x_6, \quad 0/x_7,$$
$$0.2/x_8, \quad 0/x_9, \quad 1/x_{10} \; \},$$
$$F_2 = \{ \; 0.2/x_1, \quad 0.2/x_2, \quad 0.2/x_3, \quad 1/x_4, \quad 1/x_5, \quad 0.2/x_6, \quad 0.2/x_7,$$
$$1/x_8, \quad 0.2/x_9, \quad 0.2/x_{10} \; \},$$
$$F_3 = \{ \; 0/x_1, \quad 1/x_2, \quad 0/x_3, \quad 0.2/x_4, \quad 0.2/x_5, \quad 0/x_6, \quad 1/x_7,$$
$$0.2/x_8, \quad 1/x_9, \quad 0/x_{10} \; \},$$

and the following family $\Psi = \{X_1, X_2, X_3\}$ of compatibility classes with respect to the fuzzy condition attributes c_1, c_2, c_3:

$$X_1 = \{ \; 1/x_1, \quad 0.25/x_2, \quad 1/x_3, \quad 0.25/x_4, \quad 0.25/x_5, \quad 1/x_6, \quad 1/x_7,$$
$$0.25/x_8, \quad 0.25/x_9, \quad 1/x_{10} \; \},$$
$$X_2 = \{ \; 0.25/x_1, \quad 1/x_2, \quad 0.25/x_3, \quad 0.25/x_4, \quad 0.25/x_5, \quad 0.25/x_6, \quad 0.25/x_7,$$
$$0.25/x_8, \quad 1/x_9, \quad 0.25/x_{10} \; \},$$
$$X_3 = \{ \; 0.25/x_1, \quad 0.25/x_2, \quad 0.25/x_3, \quad 1/x_4, \quad 1/x_5, \quad 0.25/x_6, \quad 0.25/x_7,$$
$$1/x_8, \quad 0.25/x_9, \quad 0.25/x_{10} \; \}.$$

The Table 2 contains membership values of selected u-lower approximations for Gaines (G), Lukasiewicz (L), Gödel (Gö) and Kleene-Dienes (KD) implicator, and for the limit (inf) and the weighted mean (wm) based approach.

One can observe that the Lukasiewicz and Kleene-Dienes implicators are more sensitive to changes of the upper limit u than the Gaines and Gödel implicators. The Kleene-Dienes implicator produces in general slightly smaller membership values than the Lukasiewicz implicator. The Gaines implicator requires

Table 2. Selected u-lower approximations for different implication operators

		Method						
u	G-inf	G-wm	L-inf	L-wm	Gö-inf	Gö-wm	KD-inf	KD-wm
$\mu_{\underline{R}_u F_1}(X_1)$ 1	0.00	0.00	0.00	0.00	0.00	0.00	0.00	0.00
0.8	0.00	0.00	0.75	0.97	0.00	0.00	0.75	0.94
0.75	0.80	0.97	0.95	0.99	0.20	0.87	0.75	0.94
$\mu_{\underline{R}_u F_2}(X_2)$ 1	0.20	0.54	0.20	0.58	0.20	0.35	0.20	0.52
0.75	0.20	0.54	0.20	0.58	0.20	0.35	0.20	0.52
$\mu_{\underline{R}_u F_2}(X_3)$ 1	0.80	0.93	0.95	0.98	0.20	0.71	0.75	0.91
0.75	0.80	0.93	0.95	0.98	0.20	0.71	0.75	0.91
$\mu_{\underline{R}_u F_3}(X_2)$ 1	0.00	0.00	0.75	0.93	0.00	0.00	0.75	0.89
0.75	0.80	0.95	0.95	0.99	0.20	0.80	0.75	0.89

smaller values of u in order to increase the lower approximation. The implicator of Gödel is not suitable for the VPFRS model. The Lukasiewicz implicator turns out to be the most appropriate one.

4 Conclusions

After considering many examples we can confirm the usefulness of the Lukasiewicz implicator as the base for the variable precision fuzzy rough sets model. The proposed weighted mean approach produces results that are consistent with our expectations from a practical point of view.

References

1. Dubois, D., Prade, H.: Putting Rough Sets and Fuzzy Sets Together. In: Słowiński, R. (ed.): Intelligent Decision Support. Handbook of Applications and Advances of the Rough Sets. Kluwer Academic Publishers, Boston Dordrecht London (1992)
2. Katzberg, J.D., Ziarko, W.: Variable Precision Extension of Rough Sets. Fundamenta Informaticae, Vol. 27 (1996)
3. Mieszkowicz-Rolka, A., Rolka, L.: Fuziness in Information Systems. Electronic Notes in Theoretical Computer Science, Vol. 82, Issue No. 4. http://www.elsevier.nl/locate/entcs/volume82.html (2003)
4. Pawlak, Z.: Rough Sets. Theoretical Aspects of Reasoning about Data. Kluwer Academic Publishers, Boston Dordrecht London (1991)
5. Radzikowska, A.M., Kerre, E.E.: A Comparative Study of Fuzzy Rough Sets. Fuzzy Sets and Systems, Vol. 126 (2002) 137–155

Fuzzyfication of Indiscernibility Relation for Structurizing Lists of Synonyms and Stop-Lists for Search Engines

A. Niewiadomski[1], P. Kryger[1], and P.S. Szczepaniak[1,2]

[1] Institute of Computer Science, Technical University of Lodz,
ul. Wólczańska 215, 93-005, Lodz, Poland
[2] Institute of System Research, Polish Academy of Sciences,
ul. Newelska 6, 01-447, Warsaw, Poland

Abstract. The paper describes a method of creating a new information storage structure based on rough sets [1] and fuzzy sets [4]. The original element in the presented structure is a *fuzzy indiscernibility relation* between elements, which can be interpreted as *two elements are indiscernible with degree r*, where r is a number from the [1,4] interval. The authors show the implementation of the structure, and its application to intelligent searching of textual databases or Web resources, to improve and strengthen the existing searching mechanisms. The elements in the comparison process are words and sentences treated as sequences of letters and words, respectively. Given strings can be compared to other sequences of letters, Websites keywords, for instance. The important fact to be noted is that the described similarity does not concern the semantics of words or sentences it bases on letter subsequences only, but otherwise it can be used for finding semantic similarity also. The algorithm is used for partial structurizing the sets of synonyms for search engines. Finally, some remarks and comments on the further research are presented.

1 Basic Definitions

1.1 Rough Sets with Pawlak's Indiscernibility Relation

The concept of a *rough set* was proposed by Z. Pawlak in 1981 [1]. In his approach, he rejects the exact boundaries of a classic set and replaces them with upper and lower approximation of the set.

The *information system* is one of the base representations of data. Such a set is represented as a matrix, where each row symbolizes an object, and each column represents attributes of that object. Formally, an information set is a 4-tuple:

$$SI = \langle U, Q, V, f \rangle \tag{1}$$

where: U is a non-empty set called *Universe*, Q denotes a non-empty finite set of attributes, V stands for a domain of attributes and $f: U \rightarrow V$ is an information function. It is frequent to implement SI as a *table* in the relational database model.

L. Rutkowski et al. (Eds.): ICAISC 2004, LNAI 3070, pp. 504–509, 2004.
© Springer-Verlag Berlin Heidelberg 2004

It is possible to replace the information function f with a function called *information about an element* $f_x \colon Q \to V$ defined as follows:

$$f_x(q) = f(x, q) \quad \text{for each } q \in Q \text{ and } x \in U \text{ in } SI \text{ .} \tag{2}$$

The main relation in the rough set theory is the *indiscernibility relation*. For $x, y \in U$, $p \in P \subseteq Q$ we say that x and y are P-indiscernible if and only if $f_x(p) = f_y(p)$ (the elements x and y are indiscernible by attributes from P). Evidently, the indiscernibility relation is an equivalence relation.

What needs defining now is the lower and upper approximation of a set. Thus, the lower approximation of set $X \subseteq U$ is the set:

$$\underline{P}X = \{x \in U \colon [x]_P \subseteq X\} \tag{3}$$

and the upper approximation of set $X \subseteq U$ is:

$$\overline{P}X = \{x \in U \colon [x]_P \cap X \neq \emptyset\} \text{ .} \tag{4}$$

The above approach to the set definition gives rise to a new logic that reveals new opportunities for data mining and intelligent data analysis, and allows making conclusions basing on fuzzy and/or uncertain knowledge or inconsistent prerequisites.

1.2   Fuzzy Sets and Fuzzy Relations in the Sense of Zadeh

The fuzzy relation is defined on the base of a fuzzy set, the concept of which was given in 1965 by Zadeh [4]. The fuzzy relation R on the Cartesian product of two crisp and non-empty spaces of two spaces A and B is – per analogiam to classic relation – defined as:

$$R =_{\text{df}} \{\langle (a, b), \mu_R(a, b)\rangle \colon a \in A,\ b \in B,\ \mu_R \colon A \times B \to [0, 1]\} \tag{5}$$

where μ_R is called the *membership function*. The value of μ_R can be interpreted as a degree of connection between a and b (the closer to 1 that value is, the stronger association between those elements can be observed). One of the possible interpretations for $\mu_R(a, b)$ is the **similarity level between a and b**; the more similar the two elements are, the higher their membership degree to fuzzy relation is.

2   Rough Set with Fuzzy Indiscernibility Relation

Under the name of *"fuzzy indiscernibility relation"* the authors mean that two given elements are similar and – in the context of the given specific measure (see Sect. 3) – can be considered (almost) indiscernible. Indiscernibility of high – close to 1 – degree means that two elements are highly similar to each other, almost identical in fact. Otherwise, the r degree close to 0 means that two given elements can be considered similar only with significant tolerance to their distinctions.

Another approach to fuzzy solutions in the rough set theory is presented in [3], where Hadjimichael and Wong define the similarity of a considered object to the lower and/or upper approximation of a given rough set. Nevertheless, in the approach presented here the indiscernibility relation is redefined to create r-degree of the upper approximation (with respect to a given attribute). In this practical approach, a sample of a one-attribute information table is given (see Sect. 4).

Formally:

Rough set A with fuzzy indiscernibility relation in non-empty space X is the rough set constructed according to the following rules:

- *kern* or *lower approximation* of A – a single element of space X which is the constant parameter of the indiscernibility relation. In fact, the rough set is constructed to find all fuzzy similarity dependencies between the kern and the other elements of X,
- every element of X which is similar to the kern with r-degree belongs to r-approximation of A.
- The 1-approximation of A is the lower approximation of A in the sense of Pawlak.
- The 0-approximation is the set of elements completely different from the kern; that means that the similarity of the given element to the kern is exactly 0. In the case of words: the kern and the other word have no common letters, via (7) – see Sect. 3.

3   Fuzzy Similarity of Words

To compute the similarity of two given words, a fuzzy relation that shows *to what degree* these words are *indiscernible* is needed. In everyday language, by *indiscernible words* the words that can replace each other by sense are meant. It is a highly frequent situation in textual data mining that two similar but not necessarily identical words should be recognized with sufficiently close results.

Formally, the fuzzy relation for string comparison is of the form [2]:

$$R' = \{\langle (s_1, s_2), \mu_{R'}(s_1, s_2) \rangle : s_1, s_2 \in S, \ \mu_{R'} : S \times S \to [0,1]\} \qquad (6)$$

S – set of all strings,
$\mu_{R'}$ – the membership function given by the formula:

$$\mu_{R'}(s_1, s_2) = \frac{2}{(N^2 + N)} \sum_{i=1}^{N(s_1)} \sum_{j=1}^{N(s_1)-i+1} h(i,j) \qquad (7)$$

$h(i,j) = 1$ if an i-element long sub-string of word s_1 starting from the j-th position in word s_1 appears once (at least) in word s_2 (otherwise $h(i,j) = 0$);

$N(s_1), N(s_2)$ stand for the numbers of letters in words s_1 and s_2, respectively (called lengths of words);

$N = \max\{N(s_1), N(s_2)\}$.

The detailed example of comparisons and calculated results of similarity are presented in [2]. It is worth to mention here, that the fuzzy relation R' with the membership function (7) is reflexive. The other property of neighborhood relation – the symmetry – is necessary due to some approaches, if only the similarity between two given elements is to be modeled. In this particular sense the symmetry can be achieved within the operation "min" on $\mu_{R'}(s_1, s_2)$ and $\mu_{R'}(s_2, s_1)$, besides it doubles the cost of calculation.

4   Implementation

The following section demonstrates one of the possible implementations of "rough sets with fuzzy indiscernibility relation" as data-structure, which can be applied to Web search engine or another algorithm of intelligent textual information retrieval.

0.	program	1.000
1.	programmer	0.714
2.	programming	0.651
3.	programmist	0.651
4.	programmation	0.555
...	...	...
n.	hi	0.0

← Means, that similarity "program" to "programmer" is – via (7) – 0.714

Fig. 1. Sample structure implemented with definitions in Sect. 2

Notice that here the relation between words 2. and 3. ("programming" and "programmist") is the classical indiscernibility relation since both words are similar to the kern with the same grade.

In this context every word in the given language implies the existence of the rough set with fuzzy indiscernibility relation.

4.1   Implementation with Relational Database

Taking into account the resulting waste of memory as well as obvious ineffectiveness for searching, the keeping of information tables for all words in the system (data base) proves extremely inefficient. One of the possible solutions is the use of the reverse index method due to which, instead of storing each word in a separate table, a structure whose sample is shown below can be created:

wordId	word	references
1	friend	$< 2, 0.466 >, < 3, 0.636 >$
2	freindship	$< 1, 0.488 >, < 3, 0.423 >$
3	friendly	$< 1, 0.636 >, < 2, 0.403 >$

The first column *wordId* is the unique word identifier in the database. The second column *word* is just the described word. The most interesting is the third column: *references*. This is a finite, countable list of pairs:

$$< \text{secondary} Word Id \, , \; similarity >$$

where the *secondaryWordId* is the *wordId* of the word that was used to determine *similarity* to the word described by this row. The value of references should be recalculated each time when any word in the table is added, removed, or changed. If a pair with a specified *wordId* does not exist in the field of references, it is assumed that the specified word belongs to 0-approximation of the word described by this row.

4.2   Implementation with Object Oriented Database (OODB)

With the use of OODB the implementation is much simpler, even if it is based on the same concept. In OODB every single object has its unique id (it is ensured by the system), and its description does not base on very simple primitives, as it can have for example a collection of other objects as part of its structure.

Each word to be stored in the database may be represented by the structure shown below:

Word
≪ collection ≫ *references* < *secondaryWord, similarity* >

where *word* stands for the word described by this object, and *references* is a collection (hash, list or any other structure) of pairs – the same as described before (however, *secondaryWord* is just the reference not the *id*).

The example for the word "friend" is:

friend
≪ collection ≫ (< &friendship, 0.466 >, < &friendly, 0.636 >)

where &word means the reference (provided by the database) to the word.

5   Conclusions

The union of all possible information tables in a given language gives a structure enabling the effective search for words and phrases in textual information resources. Moreover, the structure is open and can be developed dynamically, "on-line". The authors are currently working on the application of the described structure to lexicon and stop-list tool supporting textual data searching and mining.

References

1. Pawlak, Z.: Rough Set Elements. In: Polkowski, L., Skowron, A.: Rough Sets in Knowledge Discovery. Springer Verlag (1998)
2. Niewiadomski, A.: Appliance of fuzzy relations for text document comparing. Proceedings of the 5th Conference NNSC (Zakopane, Poland, June 6-10) 347–352
3. Hadjimichael, M., Wong, M.: Fuzzy Representations in Rough Set Approximations. In: Ziarko W. (Ed.): Rough Sets, Fuzzy Sets and Knowledge Discovery. Springer Verlag (1994)
4. Zadeh L.A.: Fuzzy Sets. Information and Control **8** (1965) 338–353

Rough Sets in the Neuro-Fuzzy Architectures Based on Monotonic Fuzzy Implications

Robert Nowicki[1,2]

[1] Department of Computer Engineering, Częstochowa University of Technology,
Al. Armii Krajowej 36, 42-200 Częstochowa, POLAND,
rnowicki@kik.pcz.czest.pl,
http://kik.pcz.czest.pl
[2] Department of Artificial Inteligence, The Academy of Humanities and Economics
in Łódź, ul. Rewolucji 1905r. 64, 90-222 Łódź, POLAND

Abstract. In this paper we presented a general solution to compose rough-neuro-fuzzy architectures. Monotonic properties of fuzzy implications were assumed to derive fuzzy systems in the case of missing features. The fuzzy implications satisfying Fodor's lemma used in logical approach and t-norms used in Mamdani approach are discussed.

1 Introduction

In the last decade various neuro-fuzzy architectures [1], [4], [5], [6], [14], [15], [17] have been developed. They combine natural language description of fuzzy systems and learning properties of neural networks. Unfortunately, they are useless in the case of missing data, e.g. some attributes in a medical diagnostic system are not accessible. In order to overcome this problem the author [8], [9] proposed to combine the theory of rough sets [10] - [13] with neuro-fuzzy structures. The Mamdani approach in a combination with rough sets was studied in [8]. The logical approach was developed in [9] assuming the incorporation of S-implications into construction of neuro-fuzzy systems.

In this paper we present a novel approach to designing rough-neuro-fuzzy systems. The novelty is summarized as follows:
(i) A wide class of monotonic fuzzy implications satisfying Fodor's lemma [3] is applied to construct rough-neuro-fuzzy structures.
(ii) Due to the monotonic property of fuzzy implications we are able to generalize previous results [9], which were true for S-implications only.
(iii) It is shown that the lower and upper approximations of membership functions in the neuro-fuzzy structures allow to handle the problem of missing features.

As it was recently shown [16] the logical approach is more suitable for classification problems than the Mamdani approach. Therefore the results of the paper are potentially very useful when a designer of classification systems has to take into account missing data.

L. Rutkowski et al. (Eds.): ICAISC 2004, LNAI 3070, pp. 510–517, 2004.
© Springer-Verlag Berlin Heidelberg 2004

2   Preliminaries

In this section we present basic information concerning rough fuzzy sets and fuzzy implications.

2.1   Rough Fuzzy Sets

The concept of rough-neuro-fuzzy structures is based on definition of rough fuzzy set [2]. Briefly, the set of parameters Q defines an equivalence relation $\tilde{Q}$, which divides the universe X of objects x into equivalence classes. Given object $\hat{x}$ belongs to a class $[\hat{x}]_{\tilde{Q}}$. Thus, the membership function of lower approximation of a fuzzy set $A \subseteq X$ denoted as $\underline{\tilde{Q}}A$ is defined as

$$\mu_{\underline{\tilde{Q}}A}(\hat{x}) = \inf_{x \in [\hat{x}]_{\tilde{Q}}} [\mu_A(x)] \tag{1}$$

and membership function of upper approximation of fuzzy set $A \subseteq X$ denoted as $\overline{\tilde{Q}}A$ is defined as

$$\mu_{\overline{\tilde{Q}}A}(\hat{x}) = \sup_{x \in [\hat{x}]_{\tilde{Q}}} [\mu_A(x)]. \tag{2}$$

The pair $\{\underline{\tilde{Q}}A, \overline{\tilde{Q}}A\}$ is called a rough fuzzy set. The set Q is a set of known parameters. The rest of them are missing.

2.2   Monotonic Fuzzy Implications

In [3] the fuzzy implication is defined as a function $I\colon [0,1]^2 \mapsto [0,1]$, which satisfies the following conditions:
a) if $a_1 \leq a_3$, then $I(a_1, a_2) \geq I(a_3, a_2)$, for all $a_1, a_2, a_3 \in [0,1]$;
b) if $a_2 \leq a_3$, then $I(a_1, a_2) \leq I(a_1, a_3)$, for all $a_1, a_2, a_3 \in [0,1]$;
c) $I(0, a_2) = 1$, for all $a_2 \in [0,1]$;
d) $I(a_1, 1) = 1$, for all $a_1 \in [0,1]$;
e) $I(1, 0) = 0$. The common used functions that fulfill above conditions are Kleene-Dienes and Reichenbach implications.

The conditions a) and b) imply that all fuzzy implications are monotonic and we can write down as follows

$$\frac{\delta I(a_1, a_2)}{\delta a_1} \leq 0 \; ; \; \frac{\delta I(a_1, a_2)}{\delta a_2} \geq 0, \tag{3}$$

if drivatives exist.

Despite the definition, in implication part of the fuzzy system, we use functions which not fulfils above conditions as well. There are t-norms, called also T-implications or "engineering implications" and so-called Q-implications. The t-norm is defined as a function $T\colon [0,1]^2 \mapsto [0,1]$, which satisfies the following conditions:

a) if $a_1 \leq a_3$ and $a_2 \leq a_4$, then $T(a_1, a_2) \leq T(a_3, a_4)$, for all $a_1, a_2, a_3, a_4 \in [0, 1]$;
b) $T(a_1, a_2) = T(a_2, a_1)$, for all $a_1, a_2 \in [0, 1]$;
c) $T(T(a_1, a_2), a_3) = T(a_1, T(a_2, a_3))$, for all $a_1, a_2, a_3 \in [0, 1]$;
d) $T(a_1, 1) = a_1$, for all $a_1 \in [0, 1]$;
From above conditions stems also

$$T(a_1, 0) = 0. \tag{4}$$

The common used functions that fulfill above conditions are Larsen (product) Mamdni (min) relations.

The condition a) implies that all t-norms are monotonic and we can write down as follows

$$\frac{\delta T(a_1, a_2)}{\delta a_1} \geq 0 \; ; \; \frac{\delta T(a_1, a_2)}{\delta a_2} \geq 0. \tag{5}$$

The implications fulfils definition of fuzzy implication are used in logical approach of fuzzy reasoning. The T-implications are used in Mamdani approach of fuzzy reasoning. Then $I(a_1, a_2) = T(a_1, a_2)$.

3   Neuro-Fuzzy Architectures for Classification

The neuro fuzzy architectures [6], [7], [14], [15] comprise a fuzzifier, a fuzzy inference engine, a fuzzy rule base and a defuzzifier in one structure. In most solutions the fuzzifier uses the singleton fuzzification, the inference process is performed by the composition inference rule, the aggregation operator, applied in order to obtain the fuzzy set B' based on fuzzy sets $\overline{B}^k$. When we use the logical model, the aggregation is carried out by intersection, realized by any t-norm. The output value of a fuzzy system is determined in the process of defuzzification.

In classification task the fuzzy rule base could include rules in the form

$$R^k: \text{IF } v_1 \text{ is } A_1^k \text{ AND } v_2 \text{ is } A_2^k \text{ AND...}$$
$$... \text{ AND } v_n \text{ is } A_n^k \text{ THEN } x \in \omega_1(\overline{z}_1^k), x \in \omega_2(\overline{z}_2^k), ..., \tag{6}$$
$$...x \in \omega_m(\overline{z}_m^k)$$

where $\mathbf{v} = [v_1, v_2, ..., v_n]$ is the input linguistic variable, $\overline{\mathbf{v}} = [\overline{v}_1, \overline{v}_2, ..., \overline{v}_n]$ is the input, i.e. crisp value of $\mathbf{v}$, k is the number of a rule, $k = 1, ..., N$ and $\overline{z}_j^k$ is the membership degree of the object x to the j-th class ω_j. We assume that

$$\overline{z}_j^k = \begin{cases} 1 & \text{if } x \in \omega_j \\ 0 & \text{if } x \notin \omega_j \end{cases}. \tag{7}$$

We write just $x \in \omega_j$ when $\overline{z}_j^k = 1$ (what means that object x belongs to the j-th class, according to the k-th rule) in definition of the k-th rule. We can omit the part $x \in \omega_j(\overline{z}_j^k)$ when $\overline{z}_j^k = 0$ (what means that object x does not belong to the j-th class, according to the k-th rule).

The general complete description of the neuro-fuzzy system is derived as follows

$$\overline{z}_j = \frac{\sum\limits_{r=1}^{N} \overline{z}_j^r \cdot \overset{N}{\underset{k=1}{Agr}} I\left(\mu_{A^k}(\overline{\mathbf{v}}), \mu_{B^k}(\overline{z}_j^r)\right)}{\sum\limits_{r=1}^{N} \overset{N}{\underset{k=1}{Agr}} I\left(\mu_{A^k}(\overline{\mathbf{v}}), \mu_{B^k}(\overline{z}_j^r)\right)}, \tag{8}$$

where Agr realize the aggregation operation and is define as any T-norm in case of logical approach and any S-norm in case of Mamdani approach [15].

When we use assumption (7), we can write equation (8) in form

$$\overline{z}_j = \frac{\sum\limits_{\substack{r=1 \\ r\,:\,\overline{z}_j^r=1}}^{N} \overset{N}{\underset{k=1}{Agr}} I\left(\mu_{A^k}(\overline{\mathbf{v}}), \mu_{B^k}(\overline{z}_j^r)\right)}{\sum\limits_{r=1}^{N} \overset{N}{\underset{k=1}{Agr}} I\left(\mu_{A^k}(\overline{\mathbf{v}}), \mu_{B^k}(\overline{z}_j^r)\right)}. \tag{9}$$

When we assume that the consequent fuzzy sets B^k are normal, i.e. $\mu_{B^k}(\overline{z}_j^k) = 1$, and moreover that $\mu_{B^k}(\overline{z}_j^r) \approx 0$ for $k \neq r$, we can simplify (9) individualy for logical approach (and implications fulfiling definition of fuzzy implication) and for Mamdani approach. In the first case, using condition d) of fuzzy implication definition we get

$$\overline{z}_j = \frac{\sum\limits_{\substack{r=1 \\ r\,:\,\overline{z}_j^r=1}}^{N} \overset{N}{\underset{\substack{k=1 \\ k\neq r}}{T}} I\left(\mu_{A^k}(\overline{\mathbf{v}}), 0\right)}{\sum\limits_{r=1}^{N} \overset{N}{\underset{\substack{k=1 \\ k\neq r}}{T}} I\left(\mu_{A^k}(\overline{\mathbf{v}}), 0\right)}. \tag{10}$$

In case of Mamdani approach, using (4), we get

$$\overline{z}_j = \frac{\sum\limits_{\substack{r=1 \\ r\,:\,\overline{z}_j^r=1}}^{N} \mu_{A^r}(\overline{\mathbf{v}})}{\sum\limits_{r=1}^{N} \mu_{A^r}(\overline{\mathbf{v}})}. \tag{11}$$

Note, that we can write down

$$\mu_{\omega_j}(x) = \overline{z}_j. \tag{12}$$

4 Rough Sets in Neuro-Fuzzy Architectures

To find the rough fuzzy set of class ω_j we have to find

$$\mu_{\underline{\tilde{Q}}\omega_j}(\hat{x}) = \inf_{x\in[\hat{x}]_{\tilde{Q}}} [\mu_{\omega_j}(x)] = \inf_{\overline{\mathbf{v}}\in[\hat{\mathbf{v}}]_{\tilde{Q}}} [\overline{z}_j] = \underline{\overline{z}_j} \tag{13}$$

and

$$\mu_{\overline{\widetilde{Q}}\omega_j}(\hat{x}) = \sup_{x\in[\hat{x}]_{\overline{Q}}} [\mu_{\omega_j}(x)] = \sup_{\overline{v}\in[\hat{v}]_{\overline{Q}}} [\overline{z}_j] = \overline{\overline{z}}_j. \tag{14}$$

Let we assume that to calculate the value of (13) and (14) by (10) or (11) we can use the $\underline{\widetilde{Q}}A^k$ or $\overline{\widetilde{Q}}A^k$ instead of A^k. To decide which one, lower or upper approximation of A^k is necessary to use we test the sign of $\overline{z}_j$ derivatives.

4.1   Logical Approach

At first we test the sign of derivative $\overline{z}_j$ by membership function of this antecedent fuzzy sets which confirms that $x \in \omega_j$. When we use (3), it can be proved that

$$\frac{\delta}{\delta\mu_{A^l}(\overline{v})} \left. \frac{\displaystyle\sum_{\substack{r=1 \\ r:\,\overline{z}_j^r=1}}^{N} \mathop{T}_{\substack{k=1 \\ k\neq r}}^{N} I\left(\mu_{A^k}(\overline{v}),0\right)}{\displaystyle\sum_{r=1}^{N} \mathop{T}_{\substack{k=1 \\ k\neq r}}^{N} I\left(\mu_{A^k}(\overline{v}),0\right)} \right|_{l:\,\overline{z}_j^l=1} \geq 0. \tag{15}$$

Then we test the sign of derivative $\overline{z}_j$ by membership function of this antecedent fuzzy sets which confirms that $x \notin \omega_j$. In this case, using (3), we obtain

$$\frac{\delta}{\delta\mu_{A^l}(\overline{v})} \left. \frac{\displaystyle\sum_{\substack{r=1 \\ r:\,\overline{z}_j^r=1}}^{N} \mathop{T}_{\substack{k=1 \\ k\neq r}}^{N} I\left(\mu_{A^k}(\overline{v}),0\right)}{\displaystyle\sum_{r=1}^{N} \mathop{T}_{\substack{k=1 \\ k\neq r}}^{N} I\left(\mu_{A^k}(\overline{v}),0\right)} \right|_{l:\,\overline{z}_j^l=0} \leq 0. \tag{16}$$

Thus, to calculate $\mu_{\underline{\widetilde{Q}}\omega_j}(x) = \overline{z}_j$ we have to use $\underline{\widetilde{Q}}A^k$ when $x \in \omega_j$ and $\overline{\widetilde{Q}}A^k$ when $x \notin \omega_j$. We can finally write it as follows

$$\overline{\underline{z}}_j = \frac{\displaystyle\sum_{\substack{r=1 \\ r:\,\overline{z}_j^r=1}}^{N} \mathop{T}_{\substack{k=1 \\ k\neq r}}^{N} I\left(\mu_{A_L^k}(\overline{v}),0\right)}{\displaystyle\sum_{r=1}^{N} \mathop{T}_{\substack{k=1 \\ k\neq r}}^{N} I\left(\mu_{A_L^k}(\overline{v}),0\right)}, \tag{17}$$

where

$$A_L^k = \begin{cases} \underline{\widetilde{Q}}A^k & \text{if } \overline{z}_j^k = 1 \\ \overline{\widetilde{Q}}A^k & \text{if } \overline{z}_j^k = 0 \end{cases}. \tag{18}$$

To calculate $\mu_{\overline{\widetilde{Q}}\omega_j}(x) = \overline{\overline{z}}_j$ we have to use $\underline{\widetilde{Q}}A^k$ when $x \in \omega_j$ and $\underline{\widetilde{Q}}A^k$ when $x \notin \omega_j$. We can finally write it as follows

$$\overline{\overline{z}}_j = \frac{\sum\limits_{\substack{r=1 \\ r:\,\overline{z}_j^r=1}}^{N} \overset{N}{\underset{\substack{k=1 \\ k \neq r}}{T}} I\left(\mu_{A_U^k}(\overline{\mathbf{v}}), 0\right)}{\sum\limits_{r=1}^{N} \overset{N}{\underset{\substack{k=1 \\ k \neq r}}{T}} I\left(\mu_{A_U^k}(\overline{\mathbf{v}}), 0\right)}, \tag{19}$$

where

$$A_U^k = \begin{cases} \overline{\widetilde{Q}}A^k & \text{if } \overline{z}_j^k = 1 \\ \underline{\widetilde{Q}}A^k & \text{if } \overline{z}_j^k = 0 \end{cases}. \tag{20}$$

The concrete form of architecture depends on chosen fuzzy implication I.

4.2 Mamdani Approach

In case of Mamdani approach we also test the sign of derivative $\overline{z}_j$ by membership function of this antecedent fuzzy sets which confirms that $x \in \omega_j$. We get

$$\left. \frac{\delta}{\delta \mu_{A^l}(\overline{\mathbf{v}})} \frac{\sum\limits_{\substack{r=1 \\ r:\,\overline{z}_j^r=1}}^{N} \mu_{A^k}(\overline{\mathbf{v}})}{\sum\limits_{r=1}^{N} \mu_{A^k}(\overline{\mathbf{v}})} \right|_{l:\,\overline{z}_j^l=1} \geq 0. \tag{21}$$

Then we test the sign of derivative $\overline{z}_j$ by membership function of this antecedent fuzzy sets which confirms that $x \notin \omega_j$. In this case we have

$$\left. \frac{\delta}{\delta \mu_{A^l}(\overline{\mathbf{v}})} \frac{\sum\limits_{\substack{r=1 \\ r:\,\overline{z}_j^r=1}}^{N} \mu_{A^k}(\overline{\mathbf{v}})}{\sum\limits_{r=1}^{N} \mu_{A^k}(\overline{\mathbf{v}})} \right|_{l:\,\overline{z}_j^l=0} \leq 0. \tag{22}$$

Thus, as in logical approach, to calculate $\mu_{\underline{\widetilde{Q}}\omega_j}(x) = \underline{z}_j$ we have to use $\underline{\widetilde{Q}}A^k$ when $x \in \omega_j$ and $\overline{\widetilde{Q}}A^k$ when $x \notin \omega_j$. We can finally write it as follows

$$\underline{z}_j = \frac{\sum\limits_{\substack{r=1 \\ r:\,\overline{z}_j^r=1}}^{N} \mu_{A_L^r}(\overline{\mathbf{v}})}{\sum\limits_{r=1}^{N} \mu_{A_L^r}(\overline{\mathbf{v}})} \tag{23}$$

and, to calculate $\mu_{\widetilde{Q}\omega_j}(x) = \overline{\overline{z}}_j$ we have to use $\underline{\widetilde{Q}}A^k$ when $x \in \omega_j$ and $\overline{\widetilde{Q}}A^k$ when $x \notin \omega_j$. We can finally write it as follows

$$\overline{\overline{z}}_j = \frac{\sum\limits_{\substack{r=1 \\ r:\overline{\overline{z}}_j^r=1}}^{N} \mu_{A_U^r}(\overline{\mathbf{v}})}{\sum\limits_{r=1}^{N} \mu_{A_U^r}(\overline{\mathbf{v}})}. \tag{24}$$

In case of Mamdani approach we have one and only one form of architecture for every t-norm used in the implication part of the system.

5   Conclusion and Future Work

In this paper we presented a general solution to compose rough-neuro-fuzzy architectures. Monotonic properties of fuzzy implications were assumed to derive fuzzy systems in the case of missing features. The application of non-monotonic fuzzy implications will be a topic of our future work.

References

1. Czogała E., Łęski J.: Fuzzy and Neuro-Fuzzy Intelligent Systems, Physica-Verlag, A Springer-Verlag Company, Heidelberg, New York (2000)
2. Dubois D., Prade H.: Rough fuzzy sets and fuzzy rough sets, Internat. J. General Systems 17 (2-3), (1990) 191-209
3. Fodor J. C.: On fuzzy implication, Fuzzy Sets and Systems, vol. 42 (1991) 293-300
4. Lee K. M., Kwang D. H.: A fuzzy neural network model for fuzzy inference and rule tuning, International Journal of Uncertainty, Fuzziness and Knowledge-Based Systems, vol. 2, no. 3 (1994) 265-277
5. Lin C. T., Lee G. C. S.: Neural-network-based fuzzy logic control and decision system, IEEE Transactions on Computers, December, vol. 40, no. 12 (1991) 1320-1336
6. Nauck D., Klawonn F., Kruse R.: Foundations of Neuro-Fuzzy Systems, Wiley (997)
7. Nowicki R., Rutkowska D.: Competitice learning of neuro-fuzzy systems, Proc. 9th Zittau Fuzzy Colloquium 2001, Zittau, Germany, September 17-19 (2001) 207-213
8. Nowicki R., Rutkowski L.: Rough-Neuro-Fuzzy System for Classification, Proc. of Fuzzy Systems and Knowledge Discovery, Singapure (2002) 149
9. Nowicki R.: A neuro-fuzzy structure for pattern classification, Proceedings of the symposium on methods of artificial intelligence AI METH 2003, Gliwice, CD-ROM, (2003)
10. Pawlak Z.: Rough sets, International Journal of Information and Computer Science, Vol. 11, No. 341 (1982)
11. Pawlak Z.: Systemy informacyjne. Podstawy toeretyczne, WNT, Warszawa (1983)

12. Pawlak Z.: Rough Sets: Theoretical Aspects of Reasoning About Data, Dordrecht, Kluwer (1991)
13. Pawlak Z.: Rough sets, decision algorithms and Bayes' theorem, European Journal of Operational Research 136 (2002) 181-189
14. Rutkowska D., Nowicki R.: New neuro-fuzzy architectures, Proc. Int. Conf. on Artificial and Computational Intelligence for Decision, Control and Automation in Engineering and Industrial Applications, ACIDCA'2000, Intelligent Methods, Monastir, Tunisia, March (2000) 82-87
15. Rutkowska D., Nowicki R.: Implication - based neuro-fuzzy architectures, International Journal of Applied Mathematics and Computer Science, No.4 (2000) 675-701
16. Rutkowski L., Cpałka K.: Flexible Neuro-Fuzzy Systems, IEEE Trans. Neural Networks, May (2003)
17. Wang L. X.: Adaptive Fuzzy Systems and Control, PTR Prentice Hall, Englewood Cliffs (1994)

Rough Sets in the Neuro-Fuzzy Architectures Based on Non-monotonic Fuzzy Implications

Robert Nowicki[1,2]

[1] Department of Computer Engineering, Czestochowa University of Technology,
Al. Armii Krajowej 36, 42-200 Czestochowa, POLAND,
`rnowicki@kik.pcz.czest.pl`,
`http://kik.pcz.czest.pl`
[2] Department of Artificial Inteligence
The Academy of Humanities and Economics in Łódź,
ul. Rewolucji 1905r. 64, 90-222 Łódź, POLAND

Abstract. In this paper we presented a general solution to compose rough-neuro-fuzzy architectures. The fuzzy system in the case of missing features is derived without the assumption that used fuzzy implication is monotonic. The proposed solution is also suitable for the monotonic fuzzy implications satisfying Fodor's lemma. The architecture based on the Zadeh and Willmott fuzzy implications is derived as the special case of the proposed general solution.

1 Introduction

In the last decade various neuro-fuzzy architectures [1], [4], [5], [6], [15], [16], [19] have been developed. They combine natural language description of fuzzy systems and learning properties of neural networks. Unfortunately, they are useless in the case of missing data, e.g. some attributes in a medical diagnostic system are not accessible. In order to overcome this problem the author [8], [9] proposed to combine the theory of rough sets [11] - [14] with neuro-fuzzy structures. The Mamdani approach in a combination with rough sets was studied in [8]. The logical approach was developed in [9] assuming the incorporation of S-implications into construction of neuro-fuzzy systems and in [10] assuming all monotonic fuzzy implications satisfying Fodor's lemma [3].

In this paper we present a novel approach to designing rough-neuro-fuzzy systems. The novelty is summarized as follows:

(i) A wide class of range monotonic and non-monotonic fuzzy implications is applied to construct rough-neuro-fuzzy structures.

(ii) Due to departure from the monotonic assumption of fuzzy implications we are able to extend previous results [9], which were true only for S-implications and for monotonic implications [10] satisfying Fodor's lemma [3].

(iii) It is shown that the lower and upper approximations of membership functions in the neuro-fuzzy structures allow to handle the problem of missing features.

L. Rutkowski et al. (Eds.): ICAISC 2004, LNAI 3070, pp. 518–525, 2004.
© Springer-Verlag Berlin Heidelberg 2004

As it was recently shown [18] the logical approach is more suitable for classification problems than the Mamdani approach. The specific advantages of non-monotonic fuzzy implications such as the Zadeh implication was shown in [17]. Therefore the results of the paper are potentially very useful when a designer of classification systems has to take into account missing data.

2   Preliminaries

In this section we present basic information concerning rough fuzzy sets and fuzzy implications.

2.1   Rough Fuzzy Sets

The concept of rough-neuro-fuzzy structures is based on definition of rough fuzzy set [2]. Briefly, the set of parameters Q defines an equivalence relation $\widetilde{Q}$, which divides the universe X of objects x into equivalence classes. Given object $\hat{x}$ belongs to a class $[\hat{x}]_{\widetilde{Q}}$. Thus, the membership function of lower approximation of a fuzzy set $A \subseteq X$ denoted as $\underline{\widetilde{Q}}A$ is defined as

$$\mu_{\underline{\widetilde{Q}}A}(\hat{x}) = \inf_{x \in [\hat{x}]_{\widetilde{Q}}} [\mu_A(x)] \tag{1}$$

and membership function of upper approximation of fuzzy set $A \subseteq X$ denoted as $\overline{\widetilde{Q}}A$ is defined as

$$\mu_{\overline{\widetilde{Q}}A}(\hat{x}) = \sup_{x \in [\hat{x}]_{\widetilde{Q}}} [\mu_A(x)]. \tag{2}$$

The pair $\{\underline{\widetilde{Q}}A, \overline{\widetilde{Q}}A\}$ is called a rough fuzzy set.

2.2   Monotonic and Non-monotonic Fuzzy Implications

In [3] the fuzzy implication is defined as a function $I \colon [0,1]^2 \mapsto [0,1]$, which satisfies the following conditions:
a) if $a_1 \leq a_3$, then $I(a_1, a_2) \geq I(a_3, a_2)$, for all $a_1, a_2, a_3 \in [0,1]$;
b) if $a_2 \leq a_3$, then $I(a_1, a_2) \leq I(a_1, a_3)$, for all $a_1, a_2, a_3 \in [0,1]$;
c) $I(0, a_2) = 1$, for all $a_2 \in [0,1]$;
d) $I(a_1, 1) = 1$, for all $a_1 \in [0,1]$;
e) $I(1, 0) = 0$.
The common used functions that fulfill above conditions are Kleene-Dienes and Reichenbach implications.

   The conditions a) and b) imply that all fuzzy implications are monotonic and we can write down as follows

$$\frac{\delta I(a_1, a_2)}{\delta a_1} \leq 0 \; ; \; \frac{\delta I(a_1, a_2)}{\delta a_2} \geq 0, \tag{3}$$

if derivatives exist.

Despite that definition, in implication part of the fuzzy system, we use functions which not fulfil above conditions as well. There are t-norms and so-called Q-implications. The t-norms which are not regarded as a fuzzy implication and are called also T-implications and "engineering implications". They are monotonic. The Q-implications $I_R(a_1, a_2)$ are not monotonic for all $a_1, a_2 \in [0, 1]$. The one example of them - Zadeh implication

$$I_{\text{Zadeh}}(a_1, a_2) = \max\{\min\{a_1, a_2\}, 1 - a_1\} \tag{4}$$

does not fulfil conditions a) and d) in the definition of fuzzy implications. The second example - Willmott implication

$$I_{\text{Willmott}}(a_1, a_2) = \min\{\max\{1 - a_1, a_2\}, \max\{a_1, 1 - a_2, \min\{a_2, 1 - a_1\}\}\} \tag{5}$$

even does not fulfil condition b) and c).

3   Neuro-Fuzzy Architectures for Classification

The neuro fuzzy architectures [6], [7], [15], [16] comprise a fuzzifier, a fuzzy inference engine, a fuzzy rule base and a defuzzifier in one structure. In most solutions the fuzzifier uses the singleton fuzzification, the inference process is performed by the composition inference rule, the aggregation operator, applied in order to obtain the fuzzy set B' based on fuzzy sets $\overline{B}^k$. When we use the logical model, the aggregation is carried out by intersection, realized by any t-norm. The output value of a fuzzy system is determined in the process of defuzzification.

In classification task the fuzzy rule base could include rules in the form

$$R^k \colon \text{IF } v_1 \text{ is } A_1^k \text{ AND } v_2 \text{ is } A_2^k \text{ AND...}$$
$$\text{... AND } v_n \text{ is } A_n^k \text{ THEN } x \in \omega_1(\overline{z}_1^k), x \in \omega_2(\overline{z}_2^k), ..., \tag{6}$$
$$...x \in \omega_m(\overline{z}_m^k)$$

where $\mathbf{v} = [v_1, v_2, ..., v_n]$ is the input linguistic variable, $\overline{\mathbf{v}} = [\overline{v}_1, \overline{v}_2, ..., \overline{v}_n]$ is the input, i.e. crisp value of $\mathbf{v}$, k is the number of a rule, $k = 1, ..., N$ and $\overline{z}_j^k$ is the membership degree of the object x to the j-th class ω_j. We assume that

$$\overline{z}_j^k = \begin{cases} 1 & \text{if } x \in \omega_j \\ 0 & \text{if } x \notin \omega_j \end{cases}. \tag{7}$$

We write just $x \in \omega_j$ when $\overline{z}_j^k = 1$ (what means that object x belongs to the j-th class, according to the k-th rule) in definition of the k-th rule. We can omit the part $x \in \omega_j(\overline{z}_j^k)$ when $\overline{z}_j^k = 0$ (what means that object x does not belong to the j-th class, according to the k-th rule).

The general complete description of the neuro-fuzzy system is derived as follows

$$
\overline{z}_j = \frac{\sum\limits_{r=1}^{N} \overline{z}_j^r \cdot \mathop{T}\limits_{k=1}^{N} I\left(\mu_{A^k}(\overline{\mathbf{v}}), \mu_{B^k}(\overline{z}_j^r)\right)}{\sum\limits_{r=1}^{N} \mathop{T}\limits_{k=1}^{N} I\left(\mu_{A^k}(\overline{\mathbf{v}}), \mu_{B^k}(\overline{z}_j^r)\right)}
\tag{8}
$$

or using assumption (7)

$$
\overline{z}_j = \frac{\sum\limits_{\substack{r=1 \\ r:\, \overline{z}_j^r=1}}^{N} \mathop{T}\limits_{k=1}^{N} I\left(\mu_{A^k}(\overline{\mathbf{v}}), \mu_{B^k}(\overline{z}_j^r)\right)}{\sum\limits_{r=1}^{N} \mathop{T}\limits_{k=1}^{N} I\left(\mu_{A^k}(\overline{\mathbf{v}}), \mu_{B^k}(\overline{z}_j^r)\right)}.
\tag{9}
$$

Note, that we can write down $\mu_{\omega_j}(x) = \overline{z}_j$.

When we assume that the consequent fuzzy sets B^k are normal, i.e. $\mu_{B^k}(\overline{z}_j^k) = 1$, and moreover that $\mu_{B^k}(\overline{z}_j^r) \approx 0$ for $k \neq r$, we can simplify (9) for logical approach (not only for implications fulfiling the Fodor's definition of fuzzy implication). We get

$$
\overline{z}_j = \frac{\sum\limits_{\substack{r=1 \\ r:\, \overline{z}_j^r=1}}^{N} I\left(\mu_{A^r}(\overline{\mathbf{v}}), 1\right) \overset{T}{*} \mathop{T}\limits_{\substack{k=1 \\ k\neq r}}^{N} I\left(\mu_{A^k}(\overline{\mathbf{v}}), 0\right)}{\sum\limits_{r=1}^{N} I\left(\mu_{A^r}(\overline{\mathbf{v}}), 1\right) \overset{T}{*} \mathop{T}\limits_{\substack{k=1 \\ k\neq r}}^{N} I\left(\mu_{A^k}(\overline{\mathbf{v}}), 0\right)}.
\tag{10}
$$

4   Neuro-Fuzzy Architectures Uses Rough Sets

To find the rough fuzzy set of class ω_j we have to find

$$
\mu_{\underline{\widetilde{Q}}\omega_j}(\hat{x}) = \inf_{x \in [\hat{x}]_{\tilde{Q}}} [\mu_{\omega_j}(x)] = \inf_{\overline{\mathbf{v}} \in [\hat{\mathbf{v}}]_{\tilde{Q}}} [\overline{z}_j] = \underline{\overline{z}_j}
\tag{11}
$$

and

$$
\mu_{\overline{\widetilde{Q}}\omega_j}(\hat{x}) = \sup_{x \in [\hat{x}]_{\tilde{Q}}} [\mu_{\omega_j}(x)] = \sup_{\overline{\mathbf{v}} \in [\hat{\mathbf{v}}]_{\tilde{Q}}} [\overline{z}_j] = \overline{\overline{z}_j}.
\tag{12}
$$

We assume that to calculate the value of (11) and (12) by (9) or (10) we can use $\underline{\widetilde{Q}}A^k$ or $\overline{\widetilde{Q}}A^k$ instead of A^k.

In general case, we have to check all possible variants of using $\underline{\widetilde{Q}}A^k$ and $\overline{\widetilde{Q}}A^k$ instead of A^k and chose the minimal value of $\overline{z}_j$ to find $\mu_{\underline{\widetilde{Q}}\omega_j}(x) = \underline{\overline{z}_j}$ and maximal value $\overline{z}_j$ to find $\mu_{\overline{\widetilde{Q}}\omega_j}(x) = \overline{\overline{z}_j}$. We can write it down as follows

$$\underline{\overline{z}}_j = \min_{\varsigma=1..2^N} \frac{\sum\limits_{\substack{r=1 \\ r:\,\overline{z}_j^r=1}}^{N} \mathop{T}\limits_{k=1}^{N} I(\mu_{A^{k\varsigma}}(\overline{\mathbf{v}}), \mu_{B^k}(\overline{z}_j^r))}{\sum\limits_{r=1}^{N} \mathop{T}\limits_{k=1}^{N} I(\mu_{A^{k\varsigma}}(\overline{\mathbf{v}}), \mu_{B^k}(\overline{z}_j^r))} \tag{13}$$

and

$$\overline{\overline{z}}_j = \max_{\varsigma=1..2^N} \frac{\sum\limits_{\substack{r=1 \\ r:\,\overline{z}_j^r=1}}^{N} \mathop{T}\limits_{k=1}^{N} I(\mu_{A^{k\varsigma}}(\overline{\mathbf{v}}), \mu_{B^k}(\overline{z}_j^r))}{\sum\limits_{r=1}^{N} \mathop{T}\limits_{k=1}^{N} I(\mu_{A^{k\varsigma}}(\overline{\mathbf{v}}), \mu_{B^k}(\overline{z}_j^r))}, \tag{14}$$

where

$$A^{k\varsigma} = \begin{cases} \widetilde{\underline{Q}}A^k & \text{if } [(\varsigma-1) \text{ div } 2^{k-1}] \mod 2 = 0 \\ \widetilde{\overline{Q}}A^k & \text{if } [(\varsigma-1) \text{ div } 2^{k-1}] \mod 2 = 1 \end{cases}. \tag{15}$$

The number 2^N of all possible variants of using $\widetilde{\underline{Q}}A^k$ and $\widetilde{\overline{Q}}A^k$ instead of A^k, where N is the number of rules, could be quite big. So, the solution described by (13) and (14) is very expensive in use. In case of the monotonic fuzzy implication, both satisfying Fodor's lemma [3] and "engineering implications", we proved in [9] that to calculate $\mu_{\widetilde{\underline{Q}}\omega_j}(x) = \underline{\overline{z}}_j$ we have to use $\widetilde{\underline{Q}}A^k$ when $x \in \omega_j$ and $\widetilde{\overline{Q}}A^k$ when $x \notin \omega_j$. To calculate $\mu_{\widetilde{\overline{Q}}\omega_j}(x) = \overline{\overline{z}}_j$ we have to use $\widetilde{\overline{Q}}A^k$ when $x \in \omega_j$ and $\widetilde{\underline{Q}}A^k$ when $x \notin \omega_j$. In case of non-monotonic fuzzy implications, such as Zadeh (4) and Willmott (5) implication we will derive it below.

5 Rough-Neuro-Fuzzy Archtectures Based on Zadeh and Willmott Fuzzy Implication

In expression (10) the implication I occurs with second argument equals 0 or 1. We calculate it for Zadeh (4) and Willmott (5) implication. We get

$$I_{\text{Zadeh}}(a_1, 0) = 1 - a_1 \; ; \; I_{\text{Zadeh}}(a_1, 1) = \max\{a_1, 1 - a_1\} \tag{16}$$

for Zadeh, and

$$I_{\text{Willmott}}(a_1, 0) = 1 - a_1 \; ; \; I_{\text{Willmott}}(a_1, 1) = \max\{a_1, 1 - a_1\} \tag{17}$$

for Willmott implication. The result is the same. When we insert it to expression (10) we obtain

$$\overline{z}_j = \frac{\sum\limits_{\substack{r=1 \\ r:\,\overline{z}_j^r=1}}^{N} \max\{\mu_{A^r}(\overline{\mathbf{v}}), 1 - \mu_{A^r}(\overline{\mathbf{v}})\} \stackrel{T}{*} \mathop{T}\limits_{\substack{k=1 \\ k\neq r}}^{N} (1 - \mu_{A^k}(\overline{\mathbf{v}}))}{\sum\limits_{r=1}^{N} \max\{\mu_{A^r}(\overline{\mathbf{v}}), 1 - \mu_{A^r}(\overline{\mathbf{v}})\} \stackrel{T}{*} \mathop{T}\limits_{\substack{k=1 \\ k\neq r}}^{N} (1 - \mu_{A^k}(\overline{\mathbf{v}}))}. \tag{18}$$

We test the sign of expresion (18) derivate to decide whether it is necessary to use either lower $\underline{\widetilde{Q}}A^k$ or upper $\overline{\widetilde{Q}}A^k$ approximation of A^k. It can be proved that

$$\left.\frac{\delta\overline{z}_j}{\delta\mu_{A^l}(\overline{\mathbf{v}})}\right|_{l:\,\overline{z}_j^l=1} \geq 0\;;\;\left.\frac{\delta\overline{z}_j}{\delta\mu_{A^l}(\overline{\mathbf{v}})}\right|_{l:\,\overline{z}_j^l=0} \leq 0. \tag{19}$$

The meaning of value $\overline{z}_j^l$ in formulas (19) is explained in (7).

On the basis of sign of expressions (19) we can conclude that we have to use lower approximation $\underline{\widetilde{Q}}A^k$ instead of A^k when $x \in \omega_j$ and upper aproximation $\overline{\widetilde{Q}}A^k$ when $x \notin \omega_j$ to calculate $\mu_{\underline{\widetilde{Q}}\omega_j}(x) = \underline{z}_j$ as well as we have to use upper approximation $\overline{\widetilde{Q}}A^k$ instead of A^k when $x \in \omega_j$ and lower aproximation $\underline{\widetilde{Q}}A^k$ when $x \notin \omega_j$ to calculate $\mu_{\overline{\widetilde{Q}}\omega_j}(x) = \overline{z}_j$. These conclusions are analogous on conclusion obtained for monotonic fuzzy implications and "engineering implications" [9], [10]. For implication under consideration we can finaly write down

$$\underline{z}_j = \frac{\displaystyle\sum_{\substack{r=1 \\ r:\,\overline{z}_j^r=1}}^{N} \max\left\{\mu_{A_L^r}(\overline{\mathbf{v}}),1-\mu_{A_L^r}(\overline{\mathbf{v}})\right\} * \overset{T}{\underset{\substack{k=1 \\ k\neq r}}{\overset{N}{T}}}\left(1-\mu_{A_L^k}(\overline{\mathbf{v}})\right)}{\displaystyle\sum_{r=1}^{N} \max\left\{\mu_{A_L^r}(\overline{\mathbf{v}}),1-\mu_{A_L^r}(\overline{\mathbf{v}})\right\} * \overset{T}{\underset{\substack{k=1 \\ k\neq r}}{\overset{N}{T}}}\left(1-\mu_{A_L^k}(\overline{\mathbf{v}})\right)} \tag{20}$$

and

$$\overline{z}_j = \frac{\displaystyle\sum_{\substack{r=1 \\ r:\,\overline{z}_j^r=1}}^{N} \max\left\{\mu_{A_U^r}(\overline{\mathbf{v}}),1-\mu_{A_U^r}(\overline{\mathbf{v}})\right\} * \overset{T}{\underset{\substack{k=1 \\ k\neq r}}{\overset{N}{T}}}\left(1-\mu_{A_U^k}(\overline{\mathbf{v}})\right)}{\displaystyle\sum_{r=1}^{N} \max\left\{\mu_{A_U^r}(\overline{\mathbf{v}}),1-\mu_{A_U^r}(\overline{\mathbf{v}})\right\} * \overset{T}{\underset{\substack{k=1 \\ k\neq r}}{\overset{N}{T}}}\left(1-\mu_{A_U^k}(\overline{\mathbf{v}})\right)}, \tag{21}$$

where

$$A_L^k = \begin{cases}\underline{\widetilde{Q}}A^k & \text{if } \overline{z}_j^k = 1 \\ \overline{\widetilde{Q}}A^k & \text{if } \overline{z}_j^k = 0\end{cases}\;;\;A_U^k = \begin{cases}\overline{\widetilde{Q}}A^k & \text{if } \overline{z}_j^k = 1 \\ \underline{\widetilde{Q}}A^k & \text{if } \overline{z}_j^k = 0\end{cases}. \tag{22}$$

Equations (20) and (21) allow to construct the neuro-fuzzy architecture, which is able to classify patterns even in the case of missing features. This architectures based on Zadeh or Willmott fuzzy implications and uses the rough set theory to realize the main goal of the paper. It consists of a few type of elements, i.e. a division blocks, a sum blocks, a max blocks, a negation $(1-a)$ blocks, any t-norms blocks to perform Cartesian product, and any blocks to perform membership function for antecedent part of rule. The connection between elements depends on rules in knowledge database. The structure will be analogous to examples presented in [9].

6 Notes and Comments

The main result of the paper is defining the neuro-fuzzy architecture for classification based on exampled non-monotonic fuzzy implications (Zadeh and Willmott) which are able to classify patterns even in the case of missing features. This solution extends the class of neuro-fuzzy architectures. The obtained result is especially interesting because of peculiar properties of Zadeh and Willmott implications [17].

References

1. Czogała E., Łęski J.: Fuzzy and Neuro-Fuzzy Intelligent Systems, Physica-Verlag, A Springer-Verlag Company, Heidelberg, New York (2000)
2. Dubois D., Prade H.: Rough fuzzy sets and fuzzy rough sets, Internat. J. General Systems 17 (2-3), (1990) 191-209
3. Fodor J. C.: On fuzzy implication, Fuzzy Sets and Systems, vol. 42 (1991) 293-300
4. Lee K. M., Kwang D. H.: A fuzzy neural network model for fuzzy inference and rule tuning, International Journal of Uncertainty, Fuzziness and Knowledge-Based Systems, vol. 2, no. 3 (1994) 265-277
5. Lin C. T., Lee G. C. S.: Neural-network-based fuzzy logic control and decision system, IEEE Transactions on Computers, December, vol. 40, no. 12 (1991) 1320-1336
6. Nauck D., Klawonn F., Kruse R.: Foundations of Neuro-Fuzzy Systems, Wiley (997)
7. Nowicki R., Rutkowska D.: Competitice learning of neuro-fuzzy systems, Proc. 9th Zittau Fuzzy Colloquium 2001, Zittau, Germany, September 17-19 (2001) 207-213
8. Nowicki R., Rutkowski L.: Rough-Neuro-Fuzzy System for Classification, Proc. of Fuzzy Systems and Knowledge Discovery, Singapure (2002) 149
9. Nowicki R.: A neuro-fuzzy structure for pattern classification, Proceedings of the symposium on methods of artificial intelligence AI METH 2003, Gliwice, CD-ROM, (2003)
10. Nowicki R.: The Rough Sets in the Neuro-Fuzzy Architectures Based on Monotonic Fuzzy Implications, Seventh International Conference on Artificial Intelligence and Soft Computing, Lecture Notes in Artificial Intelligence, Springer-Verlag (2004)
11. Pawlak Z.: Rough sets, International Journal of Information and Computer Science, Vol. 11, No. 341 (1982)
12. Pawlak Z.: Systemy informacyjne. Podstawy toeretyczne, WNT, Warszawa (1983)
13. Pawlak Z.: Rough Sets: Theoretical Aspects of Reasoning About Data, Dordrecht, Kluwer (1991)
14. Pawlak Z.: Rough sets, decision algorithms and Bayes' theorem, European Journal of Operational Research 136 (2002) 181-189
15. Rutkowska D., Nowicki R.: New neuro-fuzzy architectures, Proc. Int. Conf. on Artificial and Computational Intelligence for Decision, Control and Automation in Engineering and Industrial Applications, ACIDCA'2000, Intelligent Methods, Monastir, Tunisia, March (2000) 82-87

16. Rutkowska D., Nowicki R.: Implication - based neuro-fuzzy architectures, International Journal of Applied Mathematics and Computer Science, No.4 (2000) 675-701
17. Rutkowska D., Nowicki R., Rutkowski L.: Neuro-Fuzzy System with Inference Process Based on Zadeh Implication, The Third International Conference on Parallel Processing & Applied Mathematics (PPAM'99), Kazimierz Dolny (1999) 597-602
18. Rutkowski L., Cpalka K.: Flexible Neuro-Fuzzy Systems, IEEE Trans. Neural Networks, May (2003)
19. Wang L. X.: Adaptive Fuzzy Systems and Control, PTR Prentice Hall, Englewood Cliffs (1994)

On L–Fuzzy Rough Sets*

Anna Maria Radzikowska[1] and Etienne E. Kerre[2]

[1] System Research Institute, Polish Academy of Science
ul. Newelska 6, 01-447 Warsaw, Poland
Anna.Radzikowska@ibspan.waw.pl

[2] Dept. of Applied Mathematics and Computer Science
Ghent University, Krijgslaan 281 (S9), B-9000 Gent, Belgium
Etienne.Kerre@UGent.be

Abstract. In this paper we introduce a new class of algebras, called *extended residuated lattices*. Basing on this structure we present an algebraic generalization of approximation operators and rough sets determined by abstract counterparts of fuzzy logical operations. We show formal properties of these structures taking into account several classes of fuzzy relations.

1 Introduction

In real world applications we usually deal with incomplete and imprecise information. Rough sets were proposed by Pawlak ([10],[11]) as a mathematical tool for representing incomplete information and soon evolved into the far–reaching methodology for processing and reasoning from incomplete data ([8],[12],[16]). Fuzzy set theory ([21]), on the other hand, offers a variety of techniques for analyzing imprecision. It seems therefore natural to combine methods developed within both theories in order to adequately modelling of incomplete and imprecise information. Many approaches to such hybrid systems were proposed in the literature ([3],[7],[9],[14],[18],[20]). In [13] and [14] we discussed a fuzzyfication of rough sets determined by triangular norms and fuzzy implications on the unit interval. However, as Goguen ([5]) pointed out, sometimes it may be impossible to use the linearly ordered set $[0,1]$ to represent degrees of membership, and the concept of an *L–fuzzy set* was then introduced. In ([15]), we have recently discussed algebraic characterization of fuzzy rough sets taking residuated lattices ([1],[2],[19]) as a basic structure. A residuated lattice is an extension of a bounded lattice by a monoid operation and its residuum, which are abstract counterparts of a triangular norm and a fuzzy residual implication, respectively. This algebra, however, does not give a sufficiently general counterpart of a fuzzy S–implication (the second main class of fuzzy implications). Consequently, basing on residuated lattices, we actually have only one class of fuzzy rough sets. Continuing our studies, in this paper we present a new class of algebras ([4]),

---

* The work was carried out in the framework of COST Action 274/TARSKI on *Theory and Applications of Relational Structures as Knowledge Instruments*.

L. Rutkowski et al. (Eds.): ICAISC 2004, LNAI 3070, pp. 526–531, 2004.
© Springer-Verlag Berlin Heidelberg 2004

called *extended residuated lattices* (ER–lattices). This is the extension of a residuated lattice by an antitone involution which corresponds to an involutive fuzzy negation. In contrast to residuated lattices, the signature of ER–lattices allows us to define algebraic counterparts of a triangular conorm and a fuzzy S–implication. Basing on this structure we present an algebraic generalization of approximation operators and rough sets determined by abstract counterparts of two classes of fuzzy implications. We show formal properties of these structures taking into account several classes of fuzzy relations.

2   Preliminaries

A *commutative monoid* is a system $(M, \otimes, e)$ such that $\otimes$ is an associative and commutative binary operation in M, $e \in M$ and $e \otimes x = x \otimes e = x$.

Typical examples of monoid operations are triangular norms (t–norms) and triangular conorms (t–conorms). A *t–norm* t (resp. *t–conorm* s) is an associative, commutative and non–decreasing in both arguments $[0, 1]^2 - [0, 1]$ mapping satisfying $t(x, 1) = t(1, x) = x$ (resp. $s(x, 0) = s(0, x) = x$) for any $x \in [0, 1]$. The most popular t–norms are: the Zadeh t–norm $t_Z(x, y) = \min(x, y)$, the algebraic product $t_P(x, y) = x \cdot y$ and the Łukasiewicz t–norm $t_L(x, y) = \max(0, x+y-1)$. Well-known t–conorms are: the Zadeh t–conorm $s_Z(x, y) = \max(x, y)$, the bounded sum $s_P(x, y) = x+y-x \cdot y$ and the Łukasiewicz t–conorm $s_L(x, y) = \min(1, x+y)$.

T–norms and t–conorms are the basis for constructing fuzzy implications. Recall that a *fuzzy implication* is a mapping $i : [0, 1]^2 \to [0, 1]$, non-increasing in the 1st and non-decreasing in the 2nd argument satisfying $i(0, 0) = i(0, 1) = i(1, 1) = 1$ and $i(1, 0) = 0$. Two main classes of these operations ([6]) are: a *residual implication*, based on a continuous t–norm t (R–implication, the residuum of t), is defined as: $i_t(x, y) = \sup\{z : t(x, z) \leqslant y\}$, and an *S–implication*, based on a t–conorm s and a fuzzy negation[1] n, is defined by: $i_{s,n}(x, y) = s(n(x), y)$. Typical R–implications are: the Gödel implication $i_Z(x, y) = 1$ if $x \leqslant y$ and $i_Z(x, y) = y$ elsewhere (the residuum of t_Z), the Gaines implication $i_P(x, y) = 1$ if $x \leqslant y$ and $i_P(x, y) = \frac{y}{x}$ elsewhere (the residuum of t_P), and the Łukasiewicz implication $i_L(x, y) = \min(1, 1-x+y)$ (the residuum of t_L). Typical S–implications are: the Łukasiewicz implication i_L (based on s_L and the standard fuzzy negation η), the Kleene–Dienes implication $i_{KD}(x, y) = \max(1-x, y)$ (based on s_Z and η) and the Reichenbach implication $i_R(x, y) = 1-x+x \cdot y$ (based on s_P and η).

Definition 1. *An **extended residuated lattice** (ER–lattice) is a structure* $(L, \wedge, \vee, \otimes, \to, \sim, 0, 1)$ *such that* (i) $(L, \wedge, \vee, 0, 1)$ *is a bounded lattice with the top element 1 and the bottom element 0,* (ii) $(L, \otimes, 1)$ *is a commutative monoid,* (iii) $\sim$ *is an antitone involution satisfying* $\sim 0 = 1$, $\sim 1 = 0$, *and* (iv) $\to$ *is a binary operation in L, called the residuum of $\otimes$, defined as follows:* $x \to y = \sup\{z \in L : x \otimes z \leqslant y\}$ *for all* $x, y \in L$.   □

An ER–lattice is *complete* iff the underlying lattice $(L, \wedge, \vee, 0, 1)$ is complete. Given an ER–lattice $(L, \wedge, \vee, \otimes, \to, \sim, 0, 1)$, we define the following operations in L: for all $x, y \in L$, $\neg x = x \to 0$, $x \oplus y = \sim(\sim x \otimes \sim y)$, and $x \Rightarrow y = \sim x \oplus y$.

---

[1] A fuzzy negation is a non-increasing mapping $n : [0, 1] \to [0, 1]$ satisfying $n(0) = 1$ and $n(1) = 0$. The standard fuzzy negation is $\eta(x) = 1-x$ for any $x \in [0, 1]$.

Observe first that $\otimes$ and $\to$ are algebraic counterparts of a t–norm and its residuum, respectively. Also, $\neg$ and $\sim$ correspond to fuzzy negations ($\neg$ need not be involutive). It is easy to check that $(L, \oplus, 0)$ is a commutative monoid, so $\oplus$ is the abstract counterpart of a t–conorm. Finally, observe that $\Rightarrow$ corresponds to a fuzzy S–implication.

An example of an ER–lattice is the algebra $([0,1], \min, \max, t, i_t, \eta, 0, 1)$, where t is an arbitrary continuous t–norm, i_t is its residuum and η is the standard fuzzy negation.

Basic properties of ER–lattices are given in the following proposition.

Proposition 1. *Let $(L, \wedge, \vee, \otimes, \to, \sim, 0, 1)$ be an ER–lattice and let $\twoheadrightarrow$ be either $\to$ or $\Rightarrow$. For all $x, y, z \in L$ and every indexed family $(v_i)_{i \in I}$ of elements of L,*

(i) $\to$ *and* $\Rightarrow$ *are antitone in the first and isotone in the second argument*
(ii) $\otimes$ *and* $\oplus$ *are isotone in both arguments*
(iii) $0 \otimes x = 0$, $1 \oplus x = 1$
(iv) $x \to 1 = 0 \to x = x \to x = 1$
(v) $1 \twoheadrightarrow x = x$
(vi) $x \to y = 1$ *iff* $x \leqslant y$
(vii) $x \otimes (x \to y) \leqslant y$
(viii) $x \twoheadrightarrow (y \twoheadrightarrow z) = (x \otimes y) \twoheadrightarrow z$
(ix) $(x \to y) \otimes (y \to z) \leqslant (x \to z)$
(x) $x \otimes \sup_{i \in I} v_i = \sup_{i \in I}(x \otimes v_i)$
(xi) $x \otimes \inf_{i \in I} v_i \leqslant \inf_{i \in I}(x \otimes v_i)$
(xii) $x \leqslant \neg\neg x$
(xiii) $x \to y \leqslant \neg y \to \neg x$
(xiv) $x \Rightarrow y = \sim y \Rightarrow \sim x$
(xv) $x \twoheadrightarrow \inf_{i \in I} v_i = \inf_{i \in I}(x \twoheadrightarrow v_i)$
(xvi) $\sup_{i \in I} v_i \twoheadrightarrow x = \inf_{i \in I}(v_i \twoheadrightarrow x)$
(xvii) $\sup_{i \in I} v_i = \sim \inf_{i \in I} \sim v_i$
(xviii) $\neg \sup_{i \in I} v_i = \inf_{i \in I} \neg v_i$
(xix) $\sup_{i \in I} \neg v_i \leqslant \neg \inf_{i \in I} v_i$. ∎

2.1 L–Fuzzy Sets and L–Fuzzy Relations

Let an ER–lattice $(L, \wedge, \vee, \otimes, \to, \sim, 0, 1)$ be given and let $\mathfrak{X}$ be a nonempty set. An L-*fuzzy set in* $\mathfrak{X}$ is a mapping $F : \mathfrak{X} \to L$. For any $x \in \mathfrak{X}$, $F(x)$ is the degree of membership of x in F. The class of all L–fuzzy sets in $\mathfrak{X}$ will be denoted by $\mathcal{F}_L(\mathfrak{X})$. Two specific L–fuzzy sets, $\emptyset$ and $\mathfrak{X}$, are respectively defined by: $\emptyset(x) = 0$ and $\mathfrak{X}(x) = 1$ for every $x \in \mathfrak{X}$. For any family $(A_i)_{i \in I}$ of L–fuzzy sets in $\mathfrak{X}$, we will write $\bigcup_{i \in I} A_i$ (fuzzy union) and $\bigcap_{i \in I} A_i$ (fuzzy intersection) to denote the L–fuzzy sets in $\mathfrak{X}$ defined by: $(\bigcup_{i \in I} A_i)(x) = \sup_{i \in I} A_i(x)$ and $(\bigcap_{i \in I} A_i)(x) = \inf_{i \in I} A_i(x)$, respectively. For any $A, B \in \mathcal{F}_L(\mathfrak{X})$, we will write $A \subseteq_L B$ iff $A(x) \leqslant B(x)$ for every $x \in \mathfrak{X}$, where $\leqslant$ is the natural ordering of the lattice L. Finally, using $\neg$ and $\sim$ we define two fuzzy complement operations: for any $A \in \mathcal{F}_L(\mathfrak{X})$ and any $x \in \mathfrak{X}$, $(\neg A)(x) = \neg A(x)$ and $(\sim A)(x) = \sim A(x)$.

An L-*fuzzy relation on* $\mathfrak{X}$ is a mapping $R : \mathfrak{X} \times \mathfrak{X} \to L$. For $x, y \in \mathfrak{X}$, $R(x, y)$ is the degree to which x is R-related to y. An L-fuzzy relation R is called (i) *serial* iff $R(x, y) \leqslant R(x, x)$ for all $x, y \in \mathfrak{X}$, (ii) *reflexive* iff $R(x, x) = 1$ for every $x \in \mathfrak{X}$, (iii) *symmetric* iff $R(x, y) = R(y, x)$ for all $x, y \in \mathfrak{X}$, (iv) $\otimes$-*Euclidean* iff $R(x, y) \otimes R(x, z) \leqslant R(y, z)$ for all $x, y, z \in \mathfrak{X}$, and (v) $\otimes$-*transitive* iff $R(x, y) \otimes R(y, z) \leqslant R(x, z)$ for all $x, y, z \in \mathfrak{X}$.

3   L–Fuzzy Rough Sets

Let $(L, \wedge, \vee, \otimes, \rightarrow, \sim, 0, 1)$ be a complete ER–lattice, $\mathfrak{X} \neq \emptyset$ and R be an L–fuzzy relation on $\mathfrak{X}$. A tuple $(L, \mathfrak{X}, R)$ is called an **L–fuzzy approximation space**.

Definition 2. *Given an L–fuzzy approximation space $(L, \mathfrak{X}, R)$, define the following mappings $\underline{R}, \overline{R} : \mathcal{F}_L(\mathfrak{X}) \rightarrow \mathcal{F}_L(\mathfrak{X})$ by: for any $A \in \mathcal{F}_L(\mathfrak{X})$ and any $x \in \mathfrak{X}$,*

$$\overline{R}(A)(x) = \sup_{y \in \mathfrak{X}}(R(x, y) \otimes A(y)) \tag{1}$$

$$\underline{R}(A)(x) = \inf_{y \in \mathfrak{X}}(R(x, y) \twoheadrightarrow A(y)), \tag{2}$$

where $\twoheadrightarrow$ stands for $\rightarrow$ or $\Rightarrow$. For any $A \in \mathcal{F}_L(\mathfrak{X})$, $\underline{R}(A)$ (resp. $\overline{R}(A)$) is called an **L–fuzzy lower** *(resp.* **L–fuzzy upper) rough approximation of** *A.   □*

Depending on the arrow operator used in (2), we have two classes of L–fuzzy lower rough approximations: (i) if $\twoheadrightarrow \, = \, \rightarrow$, then the operator (2) will be written $\underline{R}_r$ (it is determined by the algebraical counterpart of a fuzzy R–implication) and the class of all such operators will be denoted by $LRA_R(L)$, (ii) if $\twoheadrightarrow \, = \, \Rightarrow$, then (2) will be written $\underline{R}_s$ (it is determined by the abstract counterpart of a fuzzy S–implication) and the class of these operators will be denoted by $LRA_S(L)$. If either of these classes is considered, the symbol $\underline{R}$ will be used.

An **L–fuzzy rough set** is a pair $(L, U) \in \mathcal{F}_L(\mathfrak{X}) \times \mathcal{F}_L(\mathfrak{X})$, where $L = \underline{R}(A)$ and $U = \overline{R}(A)$ for some $A \in \mathcal{F}_L(\mathfrak{X})$. Similarly, we have two classes of L–fuzzy rough sets determined by $\underline{R}_r$ and $\underline{R}_s$, respectively.

Note that L–fuzzy rough approximation operations correspond to modal operators well–known in fuzzy modal logics. Namely, (1) coincides with the fuzzy diamond (possibility) operator and (2) corresponds to the fuzzy box (certainty) operator ([17]). We have then the following intuitive interpretation of the operations $\overline{R}$ and $\underline{R}$: for $A \in \mathcal{F}_L(\mathfrak{X})$ and $x \in \mathfrak{X}$, $\overline{R}(A)(x)$ (resp. $\underline{R}(A)(x)$) is the degree to which x *possibly* (resp. *certainly*) belongs to A.

The following theorem presents basic properties of L–fuzzy rough approximation operators.

Theorem 1. *For every complete ER–lattice $(L, \wedge, \vee, \otimes, \rightarrow, \sim, 0, 1)$ and for every L–fuzzy approximation space $(L, \mathfrak{X}, R)$, Then*

 (i) *$\overline{R}(\emptyset) = \emptyset$ and $\underline{R}(\mathfrak{X}) = \mathfrak{X}$*
 (ii) *for all $A, B \in \mathcal{F}_L(\mathfrak{X})$, $A \subseteq_L B$ implies $\underline{R}(A) \subseteq_L \underline{R}(B)$ and $\overline{R}(A) \subseteq_L \overline{R}(B)$*
 (iii) *for every $A \in \mathcal{F}_L(\mathfrak{X})$,*
  - *$\underline{R}_s(A) = \sim \overline{R}(\sim A)$ and $\overline{R}(A) = \sim \underline{R}_s(\sim A)$*
  - *$\underline{R}_r(A) \subseteq_L \neg \overline{R}(\neg A)$ and $\overline{R}(A) \subseteq_L \neg \underline{R}_r(\neg A)$*
 (iv) *for any indexed family $(A_i)_{i \in I}$ of L–fuzzy sets in $\mathfrak{X}$,*
  - *$\underline{R}(\bigcap_{i \in I} A_i) = \bigcap_{i \in I} \underline{R}(A_i)$ $\underline{R}(\bigcup_{i \in I} A_i) \,_L \!\!\supseteq \bigcup_{i \in I} \underline{R}(A_i)$*
  - *$\overline{R}(\bigcup_{i \in I} A_i) = \bigcup_{i \in I} \overline{R}(A_i)$ $\overline{R}(\bigcap_{i \in I} A_i) \subseteq_L \bigcap_{i \in I} \overline{R}(A_i)$.* ∎

Note that, regardless of the choice of the arrow operators, properties (i), (ii) and (iv) of the above theorem are straightforward generalization of the respective properties of Pawlak's rough sets. As regards duality (iii), it is satisfied for the class $LRA_S(L)$, but for the class $LRA_R(L)$ only its weaker form holds.

The next theorem presents properties of L–fuzzy rough approximation operators determined by some classes of fuzzy relations.

Theorem 2. *Let* $(L, \wedge, \vee, \otimes, \rightarrow, \sim, 0, 1)$ *be a complete ER–lattice and* $(L, \mathfrak{X}, R)$ *be an L–fuzzy approximation space. For every* $A \in \mathcal{F}_L(\mathfrak{X})$ *we have:*

(i) R *is serial*   *iff* $\underline{R}_r(A) \subseteq_L \overline{R}(A)$

(ii) R *is reflexive*   *iff* $\underline{R}(A) \subseteq_L A$ *iff* $A \subseteq_L \overline{R}(A)$

(iii) R *is symmetric*   *iff* $\overline{R}(\underline{R}_r(A)) \subseteq_L A$ *iff* $A \subseteq_L \underline{R}_r(\overline{R}(A))$

(iv) R *is* $\otimes$*–transitive*   *iff* $\overline{R}(\overline{R}(A)) \subseteq_L \overline{R}(A)$ *iff* $\underline{R}(A) \subseteq_L \underline{R}(\underline{R}(A))$

(v) R *is* $\otimes$*–Euclidean*   *iff* $\overline{R}(A) \subseteq_L \underline{R}_r(\overline{R}(A))$ *iff* $\overline{R}(\underline{R}_r(A)) \subseteq_L \underline{R}_r(A)$. ∎

Recall first that all equivalences mentioned in Theorem 2 hold for crisp rough approximation operators ([12]). Theorem 2 states that the class $LRA_R(L)$ generalizes most properties of the classical rough approximation operators. However, for the class $LRA_S(L)$ some properties do not hold. Specifically, equivalences (i), (iii) and (v) of Theorem 1 do not hold in general for $\underline{R}_s$. Consider, for example, the ER–lattice $([0,1], \min, \max, t_Z, i_Z, \eta, 0, 1)$. Now, $x \Rightarrow y = \max(1 - x, y)$, i.e. it is the Kleene-Dienes implication. Let R be a fuzzy serial relation on $\{a, b, c\}$ given in Table 1.

| Table 1. Relation R | | Table 2. Relation Q | |

<table>
<tr><td></td><td>a</td><td>b</td><td>c</td></tr>
<tr><td>a</td><td>0.8</td><td>0.1</td><td>0.6</td></tr>
<tr><td>b</td><td>0.1</td><td>1.0</td><td>0.7</td></tr>
<tr><td>c</td><td>0.6</td><td>0.1</td><td>0.9</td></tr>
</table>

<table>
<tr><td></td><td>a</td><td>b</td><td>c</td></tr>
<tr><td>a</td><td>0.4</td><td>0.6</td><td>0.5</td></tr>
<tr><td>b</td><td>0.4</td><td>0.6</td><td>0.8</td></tr>
<tr><td>c</td><td>0.4</td><td>0.6</td><td>0.9</td></tr>
</table>

Then $\underline{R}_s(\emptyset) = (\text{a}/0.2 \ \text{b}/0 \ \text{c}/0.1)$ and $\overline{R}(\emptyset) = \emptyset$, so $\underline{R}_s(\emptyset) \not\subseteq_L \overline{R}(\emptyset)$. Note that R is also symmetric. For $B = (\text{a}/0.1 \ \text{b}/0.9 \ \text{c}/0.7)$, $\overline{R}(\underline{R}_s(B)) = (\text{a}/0.4 \ \text{b}/0.7 \ \text{c}/0.7)$ and $\underline{R}_s(\overline{R}(B)) = (\text{a}/0.7 \ \text{b}/0.7 \ \text{c}/0.4)$, so $\overline{R}(\underline{R}_s(B)) \not\subseteq_L B$ and $B \not\subseteq_L \underline{R}_s(\overline{R}(B))$. It is also easy to check that the relation Q given in Table 2 is t_Z–Euclidean. For $C = (\text{a}/0 \ \text{b}/0 \ \text{c}/0.7)$, we easily get $\overline{Q}(C) = (\text{a}/0.5 \ \text{b}/0.7 \ \text{c}/0.7)$ and $\underline{Q}_s(\overline{Q}(C)) = (\text{a}/0.6 \ \text{b}/0.6 \ \text{c}/0.6)$. Again, $\overline{Q}(C) \not\subseteq_L \underline{Q}_s(\overline{Q}(C))$.

From Theorem 1 it follows that L–fuzzy equivalence relations (i.e. reflexive, symmetric and $\otimes$–transitive) are characterized by the equalities: $\underline{R}(\underline{R}(A)) = \underline{R}(A)$ and $\overline{R}(\overline{R}(A)) = \overline{R}(A)$ for every $A \in \mathcal{F}_L(\mathfrak{X})$. This is the straightforward generalization of the respective equalities satisfied for Pawlak's rough sets.

4 Conclusions

We have introduced a class of extended residuated lattices and, taking these structures as a basis, generalized the notions of rough approximations and rough sets. It has been pointed out that in the class of ER–lattices we have abstract counterparts of t–norms, t–conorms, fuzzy R–implications and fuzzy S–implications. Properties of L–fuzzy rough approximations have been presented. We have shown that most properties of classical rough approximations are preserved for the class of $LRA_R(L)$ of L–fuzzy lower rough approximations. However, for the class $LRA_S(L)$ some properties do not hold anymore. It seems then that the L–fuzzy lower rough approximations determined by the residuation operations of ER–lattices provide adequate generalization of the respective classical approximation operations.

References

1. Blount K., Tsinakis C. (2003), The structure of residuated lattices, Int. J. of Algebra Comput. **13(4)**, 437–461.
2. Dilworth R. P., Ward N. (1939), Residuated lattices, Transactions of the American Mathematical Society **45**, 335–354.
3. Dubois D., Prade H. (1990), Rough Fuzzy Sets and Fuzzy Rough Sets, Int. J. of General Systems **17**(2-3), 191–209.
4. Düntsch I. (2003), Private communication.
5. Goguen J. A. (1967), L–fuzzy sets, Journal of Mathematical Analysis and Applications **18**, 145–174.
6. Klir G. J., Yuan B. (1995), *Fuzzy Logic: Theory and Applications*, Prentice–Hall, Englewood Cliffs, NJ.
7. Nanda S., Majumdar S. (1992), Fuzzy rough sets, Fuzzy Sets and Systems **45**, 157–160.
8. Orłowska E. (ed) (1998), *Incomplete Information: Rough Set Analysis*, Physica–Verlag.
9. Pal S. K., Skowron A. (1999), Rough Fuzzy Hybridization: A New Trend in Decision Making, Springer–Verlag.
10. Pawlak Z. (1982), Rough sets, Int. Journal of Computer and Information Science **11**(5), 341–356.
11. Pawlak Z. (1991), *Rough Sets – Theoretical Aspects of Reasoning about Data*, Kluwer Academic Publishers.
12. Polkowski L., Skowron A. (eds) (1998), *Rough Sets in Knowledge Discovery*, Physica–Verlag.
13. Radzikowska A. M., Kerre E. E. (1999), Fuzzy Rough Sets Revisited, Proceedings of Eufit'99, published on CD.
14. Radzikowska A. M., Kerre E. E. (2002), A comparative study of fuzzy rough sets, Fuzzy Sets and Systems **126**, 137–155.
15. Radzikowska A. M., Kerre E. E. (2003), Fuzzy rough sets based on residuated lattices, submitted.
16. Słowiński R. (ed) (1992), *Decision Support by Experience – Applications of the Rough Set Theory*, Kluwer Academic Publishers.
17. Thiele H. (1993), On the definition of modal operators in fuzzy logic, Proceedings of ISMVL'93, 62–67.
18. Thiele H. (1998), Fuzzy Rough Sets versus Rough Fuzzy Sets – An Interpretation and a Comparative Study using Concepts of Modal Logics, Proceedings of EUFIT'97, 159–167.
19. Turunen E. (1999), *Mathematics Behind Fuzzy Logics*, Physica–Verlag.
20. Wei-Zhi Wu, Ju-Sheng Mi, Wen-Xiu Zhang (2003), Generalized fuzzy rough sets, Information Sciences **151**, 263–282.
21. L. A. Zadeh (1965), Fuzzy Sets, Information and Control **8**, 338–358.

Application of Rough Sets Techniques to Induction Machine Broken Bar Detection

M.R. Rafimanzelat and B.N. Araabi

Control and Intelligent Processing Center of Excellence
Department of Electrical and Computer Engineering
University of Tehran, Iran
m.rafimanzelat@ece.ut.ac.ir and araabi@ut.ac.ir

Abstract. A fault diagnosis system using rough sets based classification techniques is developed for cage induction machines broken bar detection. The proposed algorithm uses the stator current and motor speed as input. Several features are extracted from the frequency spectrum of the current signal resulting from FFT. A Rough Sets based classifier is then developed and applied to distinguish between different motor conditions. A series of experiments using a three phase 3 hp cage induction machine performed in different load and fault conditions are used to provide data for training and then testing the classifier. Experimental results confirm the efficiency of the proposed algorithm for detecting the existence and severity of broken bar faults.

1 Introduction

It is well known that induction motors dominate the field of electromechanical energy conversion. These machines find a wide role in most industries. Therefore, assessments of the running conditions and reliability of these drive systems is crucial to avoid unexpected and catastrophic failures. Consequently, the issue of preventive maintenance and noninvasive diagnosis of the condition of these induction motors is of great concern, and is becoming increasingly important [1].

In recent years, marked improvement has been achieved in the design and manufacture of stator winding. But cage rotor design has undergone little change. As a result, rotor failures (broken rotor bars and end rings) now account for a larger percentage of total induction motor failures [2].

To date, different methods have been proposed for rotor fault detection. For example, the most well-known approaches for diagnosis of broken rotor bars in induction machines are based on the monitoring and processing of the stator currents to detect sidebands around the fundamental present in the line current [3], [4], measuring harmonics in motor torque, speed [4], [5], and axial flux [6].

Current signals can easily be monitored for condition monitoring, control and purposes. The problem is how to extract different features from the current signal and discriminate among various machine conditions. Noise together with nonlinear behavior of machine with or without faults makes this task very

L. Rutkowski et al. (Eds.): ICAISC 2004, LNAI 3070, pp. 532–537, 2004.
© Springer-Verlag Berlin Heidelberg 2004

difficult. Most of the works on motor current signature analysis (MCSA) use second order based techniques like FFT analysis [3],[7] and a few time–frequency analysis such as wavelets [8].

Normally, the number of information available to reach the proper diagnosis is large enough to complicate fast human analysis. In this particular point the rough sets theory helps the human operator to cope with all available information and cluster it in a reasonable and comprehensive way. Our diagnosis procedure is based on a decision algorithm that is generated using the concepts of rough sets theory. In the following section, a brief review about the broken bar fault is presented. In section 3 the rough sets theory and the rough sets based classifier are introduced. An overview of the developed system and the implementation of the rough sets based classifier is explained in section 4. Experimental results are presented in section 5. Section 6 concludes the paper.

2   The Broken Bar Fault

The reasons for rotor bar and end-ring breakage are many. They can be caused by:

- Thermal stresses due to thermal overload and unbalance, hot spots or excessive losses, sparking (mainly fabricated rotors),
- Magnetic stresses caused by electromagnetic forces, unbalanced magnetic pull, electromagnetic noise and vibration,
- Residual stresses due to manufacturing problems,
- Dynamic stresses arising from shaft torques, centrifugal forces and cyclic stresses,
- Environmental stresses caused, for example, by contamination and abrasion of rotor material due to chemicals or moisture,
- Mechanical stress due to loose laminations, fatigued parts, bearing failure, etc [7].

Spectrum analysis of the machine line current show that the sideband components f_b around the fundamental of the line current spectrum usually appear when broken bar faults exist, where $f_b = (1 \pm 2s) f$, where f is the supply frequency and s is the slip.

3   Overview of Rough Set Theory

The objective of this section is to present basic concepts of rough set theory [9].

3.1   Information Systems

An information system is a pair A = (U, A), where U is a non-empty finite set of objects called the universe and A is a non-empty finite set of attributes such that $a : U \rightarrow Va$ for every a $\in$ A. The set V_a is called the value set of a. A is further partitioned into two disjoint subsets, condition attributes C and decision attributes D.

3.2   Indiscernibility

A decision system (decision table) may be unnecessarily large in part because it is redundant in at least two ways. The same or indiscernible objects may be represented several times, or some of the attributes may be superfluous.

For any equivalence relation R the equivalence class of an element x $\in$ X consists of all objects y $\in$ X such that xRy. Let $A = (U, A)$ be an information system, then with any B $\subseteq$ A there is associated an equivalence relation INDA(B):

$$IND_A(B) = \{(x, x') \in U^2 | \forall a \in B \; a(x) = a(x')\} \tag{1}$$

$IND_A(B)$ is called the B-indiscernibility relation. If (x, x') $\in IND_A(B)$, then objects x and x' are indiscernible from each other by attributes from B.

3.3   Set Approximation

Let $A = (U, A)$ be an information system and let B $\subseteq$ A and X $\subseteq$ U. We can approximate X using only the information contained in B by constructing the B-lower and B-upper approximations of X, denoted $\underline{B}X$ and $\overline{B}X$ respectively, where

$$\underline{B}X = \{Y \in U/B : Y \subseteq X\} \tag{2}$$

$$\overline{B}X = \{Y \in U/B : Y \cap X \neq \emptyset\} \tag{3}$$

The objects in $\underline{B}X$ can be with certainty classified as members of X on the basis of knowledge in B, while the objects in $\overline{B}X$ can be only classified as possible members of X on the basis of knowledge in B. The set $BNB(X) = \overline{B}X - \underline{B}X$ is called the B-boundary region of X, and thus consists of those objects that we cannot decisively classify into X on the basis of knowledge in B. The set U - $\overline{B}X$ is called the B-outside region of X and consists of those objects which can be with certainty classified as do not belonging to X (on the basis of knowledge in B).

3.4   Reduct and Core of Knowledge

Let R be a family of equivalence relations. The Reduct of R, RED(R), is defined as reduced set of relations that conserve the same inductive classification of set R. The Core of R, CORE(R), is set of relations that appears in all reducts of R, i.e. , the set of all indispensable relations to characterize the relation R. The concepts of core and reduct are of substantial significance to the process of Knowledge Base Reduction.

3.5   Knowledge Base Reduction

An important practical issue is whether some of the attributes in an information system are redundant with respect to enabling us to make the same object classifications as with the full set of attributes A. If an attribute subset $B \subseteq A$ preserves the indiscernibility relation R_A and hence our ability to form set approximations, then the attributes $A - B$ are said to be *dispensable*. Typically, an information system may have many such attribute subsets B.

The idea behind the knowledge base reduction is the simplification of a set of examples. An algorithm for reduction of conditions has been proposed in [10].

4   Rough Sets Based Classification System

The system developed in this work consists of 4 main steps shown in Fig. 1.

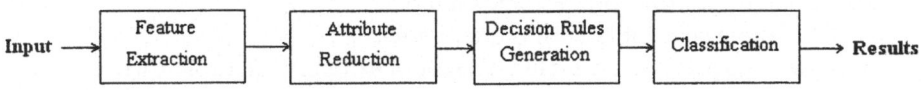

Fig. 1. System structure.

4.1   Feature Extraction and Examination

Various features describing the size or shape of sidebands could be used to distinguish healthy and faulty motors. Some considered in this work are listed below: 1. The area under the sidebands. 2. The amplitude of the sidebands. 3. The head angle of the sidebands.

The first two measures increase with the degree of fault (i.e. number of broken bars and extent of breakage). But the third feature decreases for faulty motors.

As there are two sideband harmonics, which can similarly account for the fault, the average values of the features calculated for the left and right sideband were used.

Table 1 presents a partial set of data obtained from some experiments showing the attributes and their values and the motor condition (decision attribute). The condition attribute A1, A2 and A3 are the 1st, 2nd and 3rd features introduced in previous section. The Boolean reasoning algorithm was used to convert continuous feature values to rough values. A1 takes the values: S (small), M (medium), and L (large). A2 has a value range of S (short), M (medium) and T

Table 1. Set of examples

Test No.	A1	A2	A3	A4	Dec
1	S	S	B	L	H
⋮	⋮	⋮	⋮	⋮	⋮
70	L	T	S	H	C

(tall). A3 may have the values: B (blunt), M (middle) and S (sharp). A4 describes the load level of the motor and is labeled by L for light, M for medium and H for heavy load condition. The Decision attribute, Dec, is the induction motor state that can have one of the values: H, I, W and C which stand for Healthy, Incipient Fault, Warning and Catastrophic respectively.

4.2   Knowledge Base Reduction and Decision Rule Generation

A knowledge base reduction technique proposed in [11] was used to filter out the redundant data in the decision table. The algorithm can be represented by the following steps:

Step 1: Eliminate the dispensable attribute.

Step 2: Compute the core of each example.

Step 3: Compose a table with reduct value.

Step 4: Merge possible examples. The set of examples in Table 1 when reduced generated the following set of rules:

Table 2. Reduced rules

if (A2 is S) *then* (Dec is H)
$\vdots$
If (A1 is L) *and* (A3 is S) *and* (A4 is H) *then* (Dec is C)

4.3   Classification

The rules generated in previous section established a rough sets based classifier which was used to classify input data coming from unknown motor conditions.

5   Experimental Results

Experimental results were obtained from a three phase, 3-hp, 50 Hz machine with a die-cast rotor having 28 bars made especially for this study. The broken-bar faults were created by drilling holes in the bars. The experiments were performed at 10 different loads varying from 10 to 100% of rated load and 7 different fault conditions form no broken bars to six broken bars that formed the 70 examples shown in table 1. The Fast Fourier Transform then was employed to get the frequency spectrum of current signals. The features described in section 4.1 then were calculated for all current data. 60 samples of the calculated attributes were used for training the rough sets based classifier as explained in previous section. The other 10 samples were used as hypothetically unknown motor conditions for testing the classifier. The rough sets based classifier responded correctly in all cases.

6   Conclusion

A diagnosis procedure to detect broken bar failures in induction machines was presented. Several features derived from the Fast Fourier Transform of the stator current signal were proposed and their relevance for fault detection was investigated and verified. A Rough Sets based classifier was utilized to distinguish between various broken bar and healthy conditions of motors. Experimental results from a three phase 3 hp cage induction motor confirmed the strength of the proposed method.

Acknowledgement. The authors would like to thank Emad Sharifi and Elham Khosroshahli from Niroo Research Institute for their technical support particularly in providing data for experimental results.

References

1. M. E. H. Benbouzid, "Bibliography on induction motors faults detection and diagnosis," IEEE Trans. Energy Conversion, vol. 14, no. 4, pp. 1065–1074, Dec. 1999.
2. A. H. Bonnett et al.,, "Rotor failures in squirrel cage induction motors," IEEE Trans. Ind. Applications, vol. 22, pp. 1165–1173, Nov./Dec. 1986.
3. G. B. Kliman, R. A. Koegl, J. Stein, R. D. Endicott, and M. W. Madden, "Noninvasive detection of broken rotor bars in operating induction motors," IEEE Trans. Energy Conversion, vol. 3, pp. 873–879, Dec. 1988.
4. N. M. Elkasabgy, A. R. Eastham, and G. E. Dawson, "Detection of broken bars in the cage rotor on an induction machine," IEEE Trans. Ind. Applications, vol. 22, pp. 165–171, Jan./Feb. 1992.
5. F. Filippetti, G. Franceschini, C. Tassoni, and P. Vas, "AI techniques in induction machines diagnosis including the speed ripple effect," in Conf. Rec. IEEE-IAS Annu. Meeting, San Diego, CA, Oct. 6–10, 1996, pp. 655–662.
6. P. J. Tavner and J. Penman, "Condition Monitoring of Electrical Machines". Letchworth, U.K.: Research Studies Press, 1987.
7. J. Milimonfared, H. M. Kelk, S. Nandi, A. D. Minassians, H. A. Toliyat, "A novel approach for broken-rotor-bar detection in cage induction motors", IEEE Trans. Ind. Applicat., Vol. 35 5, pp.1000–1006, Sept.-Oct. 1999.
8. C. Chao-Ming, K.A. Loparo, "Electric fault detection for vector controlled induction motors using the discrete wavelet transform", Proceeding of the 1998 American Control Conference, pp. 3297 –3301, Vol. 6.
9. Z. Pawlak, "Rough Sets", International Journal of Computer and Information Sciences, No. 11, 1982, pp. 341-356.
10. Z. Pawlak, "Rough Sets - Theoretical Aspects of Reasoning about Data", Kluwer Academic Publishers, Dordrecht, 1991.
11. A. Ohrn, "Discernibility and Rough Sets in Medicine: Tools and Applications", Ph.D. Thesis, Norwegian University of Science and Technology, Department of Computer and Information Science, 2000.

Application of Rough Sets and Neural Networks to Forecasting University Facility and Administrative Cost Recovery

Tomasz G. Smolinski, Darrel L. Chenoweth, and Jacek M. Zurada*

Computational Intelligence Laboratory, 319 Lutz Hall,
Department of Electrical and Computer Engineering,
University of Louisville,
Louisville, KY 40292, USA
{Tomasz.Smolinski,Chenoweth,Jacek.Zurada}@louisville.edu

Abstract. This paper presents a novel approach to financial time series analysis and prediction. It is mainly devoted to the problem of forecasting university facility and administrative cost recovery. However, it can also be used in other areas of a similar nature. The methodology incorporates a two-stage hybrid mechanism for selection of prediction-relevant features and for forecasting based on this selected sub-space of attributes. The first module of the methodology employs the theory of rough sets (RS) while the second part is based upon artificial neural networks (ANN).

1 Introduction

At all research-oriented universities throughout the United States, as well as many other countries, external funding plays a very important role in such institutions' budget planning. Many of externally funded research projects can produce significant revenue for a given university, in the form of the facilities and administrative (F&A) costs that can be recovered from the projects. Since F&A cost recovery is essential for supporting the university research enterprise, research administration units approach its accurate estimation very seriously, both in the short term and for long term planning.

Forecasting F&A is not a trivial problem. Even if all the external factors, such as the economic and political situation in the country, are to be ignored, many other variables that must be considered and accounted for in order to implement a trustworthy forecaster. For instance, the "success probability" of a given research proposal can strongly depend on the "success rate" of the principal investigator who is submitting the proposal, the nature and characteristics of the project and sponsor, and many other aspects.

Obviously, universities that are most concerned about accurately predicting F&A cost recovery are those that are highly involved in various research-oriented

---

* The work of this author was sponsored in part by the Systems Research Institute of the Polish Academy of Sciences, 01-447 Warszawa, Poland, ul. Newelska 6.

L. Rutkowski et al. (Eds.): ICAISC 2004, LNAI 3070, pp. 538–543, 2004.
© Springer-Verlag Berlin Heidelberg 2004

activities, and the volume of proposals that are being processed can be large. At those institutions, the number of project types, researchers, departments and sponsoring agencies that directly or indirectly influence the possible "success" of a given proposal is very high, and the interdependencies between those factors are very often quite complex. Some past data may prove helpful for extracting rules governing the mechanisms for proposals' funding or rejection. However, the volume of such data is typically extremely large, which makes it practically impossible to deal with the problem without adequate computational tools. This calls for use of suitable data mining or machine learning techniques that would be able not only to estimate the F&A cost recovery truthfully, but also provide additional interesting insight about the characteristics of the whole proposals/research projects environment.

The main goal of this research was to develop a methodology to forecast the amount of facilities and administrative F&A costs that will be recovered from funded research projects in a given period. The projects may either be currently funded or in a "pending" status at the moment but expected to contribute to the total F&A cost recovery. To achieve this goal, we propose to utilize the theory of rough set (RS) and artificial neural networks (ANN) in order to extract common characteristics of similar research projects and then, based on this "implicit clustering" of those projects, to perform a more detailed prediction, based on the conjecture that similar grants are expected to behave similarly.

2   Database and Frequency-Based General Approach

The data used in this project were a part of a real historical database provided by one of the research-oriented American universities. The database consisted of several datasets containing five-fiscal-year-worth information about the proposals as well as eight other directly involved entities (*i.e.*, parameters): *principal investigators, departments, colleges, proposal types* (*e.g.*, clinical trial, grant, subcontract, etc.), *project types* (*e.g.*, research, training/education), a *general classification* (*e.g.*, new project, continuation, competitive renewal, etc.), *sponsoring agencies*, and *sponsoring agencies' types* (*e.g.*, federal, industry, non-profit, etc.). For each proposal, its status was known (*i.e.*, funded or rejected), thus calculation of "success rates" for all the proposals' eight attributes enumerated above was straightforward - simply by using the ratio of funded proposals to the total number of submissions for each one of them. This was also the first general approach, proposed by the authors in [1], to the estimation of the "success rates" for the proposals themselves and, what follows, the forecast F&A recovery in a given period of time.

The calculation of the "success probability" for a given sponsored project was simply computed as the average of the ratios for those eight attributes. The final estimation of the F&A was based upon the sum of the F&A for the projects, for which the "success rate" exceeded some arbitrarily selected threshold, and discarded otherwise.

A computer program that was implemented for these experiments yielded the total predicted F&A recovery for a specified period of time (*e.g.*, fiscal year).

This simple frequency-based approach did not appear to be very useful. The error of the estimation was simply too large. Thus, the conclusion was drawn that there must be some additional aspects underlying the behavior of the system.

3   Sponsoring Agency-Dependent Frequency-Based Approach

Based on a detailed analysis of the preliminary results, a conclusion was drawn that the sponsoring agencies could not be considered "just another" parameter on the list of the entities determining the "fate" of a given proposal. Simply put, rather than describing the sponsors in the light of "success rates," one should probably view their frequency-based estimates as a sort of "willingness to spend money," and this, obviously, strongly depends on all the other parameters. A given agency may favor one investigator over another; may prefer researchers in one department than in other, etc. Thus the idea of removing the parameter *agency* from the list of "success rates" (as well as directly related *agency type*) was proposed. Instead of using the agency directly, agency-dependent success rates were to be calculated. It intuitively makes sense since if a given principal investigator is being favored by some agency and is strongly not by another, computing his or her total "success rate," would smear those subtleties, while the agency-dependent approach ought to clearly extract them.

Indeed, the results obtained with the agency-dependant frequency-based approach were much better than the ones obtained using all the eight attributes directly (for details see [1]). Therefore, this approach was used in the remaining part of the experiments.

4   Rough Sets-Based Approach to Selection of Prediction-Relevant Features

In order to further improve the accuracy of the prediction four additional attributes were introduced: *starting month of the project, ending month of the project, duration of the project in months*, and *magnitude of the requested funding* (*i.e.*, hundreds, thousands, millions of dollars, etc.). Also, the "success rate" of each one of the remaining six parameters introduced before was replaced by two numbers: the total number of submissions (for this particular investigator, department, college, etc., in the light of a given sponsoring agency) and the number of funded proposals. This allowed us to differentiate between a "success rate" of a principal investigator (or any other of the eight parameters, for that matter), who has submitted 1 proposal and has been awarded with 1 grant (100% rate!) and someone, who has submitted 100 proposals and has gotten 90 awards ("only" 90%, but chances may be higher).

The next step was to attempt to determine which of these eighteen attributes really mattered in terms of the proposals being awarded or rejected. In order to deal with this problem we have used the theory of rough sets introduced by Zdzislaw Pawlak [2], [3]. Especially useful for a classification-relevant feature selection is the concept of reducts that is inherently embedded in the theory [4].

One of the most important notions of the rough sets theory is the *indiscernibility relation*. Let $IS = (U, A)$ be an information system of objects from the universe U described by the set of attributes A, then with any $B \subseteq A$ there is an associated equivalence relation $IND_{IS}(B)$:

$$IND_{IS}(B) = \{(x, x') \in U^2 | \forall a \in B, a(x) = a(x')\}.$$

$IND_{IS}(B)$ is called *B-indiscernibility relation*. If $(x, x') \in IND_{IS}(B)$, then objects x and x' are indistinguishable from each other by attributes from B.

Based on the concept of indiscernibility relation, a reduction in the space of attributes is possible. The idea is to keep only those attributes that preserve the indiscernibility relation. The rejected attributes are redundant since their removal cannot worsen the classification (in the case of this project: differentiation between funded and rejected/withdrawn proposals is important). There are usually several such subsets of attributes and those, which are minimal, are called *reducts*.

5   Experiments and Results

In this part of the project, the rough set theory-based application ROSETTA and in particular the Johnson's reduction algorithm [5] were used. The algorithm yielded one reduct that consisted of nine attributes (50% reduction in complexity!): *starting month, duration in months, the total number of proposals for a given college, the number of funded proposals for a given college, the total number of proposals for a given principal investigator, the number of funded proposals for a given principal investigator, the magnitude of the requested funding, the total number of proposals for a given proposal type* (e.g., clinical trial, grant, subcontract, etc.), *the total number of proposals for a given general class* (e.g., new project, continuation, competitive renewal, etc.).

In an attempt to validate the feasibility of the reduct, a forecaster based on a feedforward neural network (FFNN) was implemented and investigated. A MATLAB environment with the Neural Networks Toolbox was used in this part of the project. A series of experiments was performed in order to determine the best possible configuration, *i.e.*, network's structure, activation functions, training algorithms, and selected results of those experiments will be presented in this section of the paper.

The main goal of this stage of the project was to perform a preliminary analysis and comparison of the behavior of the FFNN-based predictor supplied with all the 18 inputs and the forecaster that uses only those inputs that were included in the RS-derived reduct (9 attributes). In both cases, the "success probability" was to be predicted (between 0 and 1).

A feedforward neural network with one hidden layer was used. The number of neurons in the layer varied from the $\frac{1}{2}$ of the number of inputs to the double number of inputs + 1. The training algorithm that proved to be the most effective during preliminary experiments, and was used in final computations was the Bayesian regularization backpropagation algorithm (*trainbr*). For the output neuron, both *purelin* and *logsig* activation functions were used, and the latter one usually performed better.

Table 1. Test MSE for the *logsig* output activation function; a) complete set of inputs; b) reduced set of inputs

a.

# hidden neurons	Trial 1	Trial 2	Trial 3
4	0.0674	0.0838	0.0843
5	0.1073	0.1174	0.1115
6	0.0735	0.0802	0.1221
7	0.0761	0.0924	0.0794
8	0.0862	0.0846	0.0780
9	0.0645	0.0810	0.0840
10	0.0603	0.0548	0.0865
11	0.0726	0.0582	0.0591
12	0.0898	0.0715	0.0533
13	0.0617	0.0693	0.0578
14	0.0516	0.0679	0.0591
15	0.0619	0.0680	0.0486
16	0.0531	0.0675	0.0521
17	0.0656	0.0692	0.0572
18	0.0596	0.0603	0.0454
19	**0.0401**	0.0559	0.0472
20	0.0472	0.0555	0.0582
21	0.0537	0.0585	0.0609
22	0.0647	0.0443	0.0542
23	0.0506	0.0679	0.0534
24	0.0542	**0.0425**	0.0578
25	0.0499	0.0479	0.0579
26	0.0474	0.0543	0.0542
27	0.0574	0.0546	0.0507
28	0.0527	0.0536	**0.0449**
29	0.0481	0.0486	0.0573
30	0.0521	0.0455	0.0477
31	0.0526	0.0616	0.0502
32	0.0572	0.0559	0.0560
33	0.0573	0.0482	0.0543

b.

# hidden neurons	Trial 1	Trial 2	Trial 3
4	0.0741	0.0742	0.0733
5	0.0770	0.0779	0.0726
6	0.0716	0.0766	0.0939
7	0.0817	0.0994	0.0649
8	0.0789	0.1453	0.1037
9	0.0648	0.0993	0.0891
10	0.0658	0.0975	0.0713
11	0.0800	0.0831	0.0659
12	0.0675	0.0796	0.0502
13	0.0591	0.0717	0.0501
14	0.0849	0.0747	0.0605
15	0.0607	0.0605	0.0787
16	0.0535	0.0586	0.0538
17	0.0492	0.0513	**0.0451**
18	0.0598	0.0545	0.0519
19	0.0629	0.0618	0.0549
20	0.0540	0.0439	0.0550
21	0.0529	0.0575	0.0575
22	0.0567	0.0522	0.0572
23	0.0518	0.0587	0.0502
24	**0.0385**	0.0617	0.0502
25	0.0625	0.0579	0.0593
26	0.0562	0.0580	0.0565
27	0.0537	0.0536	0.0515
28	0.0538	0.0539	0.0559
29	0.0501	0.0485	0.0578
30	0.0526	0.0447	0.0555
31	0.0428	0.0552	0.0629
32	0.0435	**0.0436**	0.0484
33	0.0597	0.0513	0.0546

Table 1 shows the comparison of the mean square error on the testing dataset defined as $MSE = \frac{1}{n} \sum_{i=1}^{n} (P_e^i - P_a^i)^2$, where P_e^i is the success probability of the ith proposal estimated by the neural network, P_a^i is the actual probability of the ith proposal (*i.e.*, 1 for the awarded and 0 for the rejected proposals), and n is the total number of proposals in the testing set. The results were obtained during three separate trials of experiments. The lowest error values are shown in bold.

6   Conclusions

As can be seen based on the experiments described above, a hybridization of rough sets and artificial neural networks provides a useful and intuitively sound methodology for prediction of F&A cost recovery behavior. Even though the problem is non-trivial and virtually impossible to deal with "by hand," the solution delivered by the methodology is very straightforward and simple due to the two-stage approach.

The rough sets-based reduction of the attribute space not only improves the efficiency of the predictor itself, but also provides some additional information about the mechanisms governing the "award" or "reject" decision-making. The table above shows that the prediction error is at least comparable, if not smaller, when the set of inputs reduced via the rough sets-based methodology is used. Also, since it is possible to obtain it with a smaller neural network (*i.e.*, fewer inputs), the convergence time is significantly reduced. Most importantly, however, due to the application of the methodology, it is known which parameters play a significant role in terms of the process of proposal's approval or rejection. This information is very important to research administration officials since it may be used in the future for better preparation of grant proposals and thus increasing the chances of being funded. What naturally follows is increasing the institution's F&A cost recovery.

Acknowledgements. This project was sponsored by the Office of the Vice-President for Research, University of Louisville, KY, USA.

References

1. Smolinski, T.G., Chenoweth, D.L., Zurada, J.M.: Rough Set and Artificial Neural Networks-based Hybrid Approach to Financial Time Series Forecasting. Proc. of the IASTED International Conference on Neural Networks and Computational Intelligence (2003) 108–111
2. Pawlak, Z.: Rough Sets, Int. J. of Computer and Information Sciences 11 (1982) 341–356
3. Marek, W., Pawlak, Z.: Rough Sets and Information Systems, Fundamenta Matematicae 17 (1984) 105–115
4. Komorowski, J., Pawlak, Z., Polkowski, L., Skowron, A.: Rough Sets: A Tutorial. In: Pal, S.K., Skowron, A. (eds.): Rough Fuzzy Hybridization - A New Trend in Decision-Making (1999) 3–98
5. ROSETTA: A Rough Set Toolkit for Analysis of Data. Available: http://www.idi.ntnu.no/~aleks/rosetta

Selection of the Linearly Separable Feature Subsets

Leon Bobrowski[1,2] and Tomasz Lukaszuk[1]

[1] Faculty of Computer Science, Technical University Bialystok
[2] Institute of Biocybernetics and Biomedical Engineering, PAS, Warsaw, Poland

Abstract. We address a situation when more than one feature subset allows for linear separability of given data sets. Such situation can occur if a small number of cases is represented in a highly dimensional feature space.

The method of the feature selection based on minimisation of a special criterion function is here analysed. This criterion function is convex and piecewise-linear (*CPL*). The proposed method allows to evaluate different feature subsets enabling linear separability and to choose the best one among them. A comparison of this method with the *Support Vector Machines* is also included.[1]

1 Introduction

The linear separability of data sets is one of the basic concepts in neural networks and pattern recognition [1]. This concept provided fundamentals for the Perceptron's theory [2], [3]. More recently, the linear separability is intensively explored in the method of the *Support Vector Machines* [4].

The feature selection in pattern recognition means neglecting such measurements (features) which have no significant influence on the final decisions. The feature selection is particularly important when the data sets are composed of a small number of elements in a highly dimensional feature space. The situation when a small number of elements is represented in a highly dimensional feature space (*long feature vectors*) usually leads to the linear separability of data sets. The genomic data sets contain examples of the "long feature vectors".

The measures of linear separability of two data sets can be based on the minimal value of the convex and piecewise-linear (*CPL*) criterion functions [5]. The perceptron criterion function belongs to the *CPL* family in question. The linear separability measures with different properties can be achieved through modification of the *CPL* criterion functions. Recently proposed CPL criterion function allows to compare different feature subsets enabling linear separability and to choose the best one among them [6]. This criterion function contains the *CPL* penalty functions reflecting the costs of the particular features.

---

[1] This work was partially supported by the grant W/II/1/2004 from the Bialystok University of Technology and by the grant 16/St/2004 from the Institute of Biocybernetics and Biomedical Engineering PAS.

The minimal value of the *CPL* functions can be found efficiently through applying the basis exchange algorithms, which can be treated as special methods for the linear programming [7]. The Support Vector Machines are based on the algorithms of the quadratic programming [4].

This paper is an analysis of the properties of the feature selection based on the modified *CPL* criterion function. Particular attention is paid to the comparison of the *CPL* criterion functions to the *Support Vector Machine* approach.

2   Linear Separability of Data Sets

Let us consider data represented as the feature vectors $x_j[n] = [x_{j1}, ..., x_{jn}]^T$ $(j = 1, ..., m)$ of the same dimensionality n or as points in the n-dimensional feature space $F[n]$. The components x_i of the vectors $x_j[n]$ are called features. We are considering a situation, when the data can be a mixed (a qualitative-quantitative) type. Some components x_{ji} of the vectors $x_j[n]$ can be the binary $(x_i \in \{0,1\})$ and others the real numbers $(x_i \in \mathbf{R}^1)$.

Let us take into consideration two disjoined sets G^+ and G^- composed of m feature vectors x_j:

$$G^+ \cap G^- = \emptyset . \tag{1}$$

The *positive set* G^+ contains m^+ vectors x_j and the *negative set* G^- contains m^- vectors $(m = m^+ + m^-)$. We are considering the separation of the sets G^+ and G^- by the hyperplane $H(w, \theta)$ in the feature space $F[n]$

$$H(w, \theta) = \{x : \langle w, x \rangle = \theta\} \tag{2}$$

where $w = [w_1, ..., w_n]^T \in \mathbf{R}^n$ is the weight vector, $\theta \in \mathbf{R}^1$ is the threshold, and $\langle w, x \rangle$ is the inner product.

Definition 1. *The feature vector x is situated on the* positive side *of the hyperplane $H(w, \theta)$ if and only if $\langle w, x_j \rangle > \theta$ and the vector x is situated on the* negative side *of $H(w, \theta)$ iff $\langle w, x_j \rangle < \theta$.*

Definition 2. *The sets G^+ and G^- are* linearly separable *if and only if they can be fully separated by some hyperplane $H(w, \theta)$ (2):*

$$(\exists w, \theta) \quad (\forall x_j \in G^+) \langle w, x_j \rangle > \theta \quad and \quad (\forall x_j \in G^-) \langle w, x_j \rangle < \theta . \tag{3}$$

In accordance with the relation (3), all the vectors x_j belonging to the set G^+ are situated on the positive side of the hyperplane $H(w, \theta)$ (2) and all the feature vectors x_j from the set G^- are situated on the negative side of this hyperplane. It is convenient to replace the feature vectors x_j by the *augmented* vectors y_j, where

$$y_j = [1, x_j^T]^T = [1, w_1, ..., w_n]^T . \tag{4}$$

The inequalities (3) can be represented now as

$$(\exists v) \quad (\forall y_j \in G^+) \langle v, y_j \rangle > 0 \quad and \quad (\forall y_j \in G^-) \langle v, y_j \rangle < 0 \tag{5}$$

where $v = [-\theta, w^T]^T$ is the augmented weight vector [1].

3   From Linear Independence to Linear Separability

The linear separability of the sets G^+ and G^- can be defined equivalently to (5) in the following manner:

$$(\exists \boldsymbol{v}_1) \quad (\forall \boldsymbol{y}_j \in G^+)\langle \boldsymbol{v}_1, \boldsymbol{y}_j \rangle \geq 1 \quad \text{and} \quad (\forall \boldsymbol{y}_j \in G^-)\langle \boldsymbol{v}_1, \boldsymbol{y}_j \rangle \leq -1 \qquad (6)$$

Remark 1. (sufficient condition for linear separability). The sets G^+ and G^- are *linearly separable* (6), if the following matrix equality is fulfilled:

$$(\exists \boldsymbol{v}_2) \boldsymbol{A} \boldsymbol{v}_2 = \mathbf{1}' \qquad (7)$$

where $\boldsymbol{A}$ is the matrix of dimension $m \times (n+1)$, $m = m^+ + m^-$, and $\mathbf{1}'$ is the vector of dimension m. The rows of the matrix A constitute of the augmented feature vectors $\boldsymbol{y}_{j(i)}$. The vector yj(i) constitutes the i-th row of the matrix A. The i-th component of the vector $\mathbf{1}'$ is equal to 1 if $\boldsymbol{y}_{j(i)} \in G^+$ and equal to -1 if $\boldsymbol{y}_{j(i)} \in G^-$.

Remark 2. If the m vectors $\boldsymbol{y}_{j(i)}$ constituting the matrix $\boldsymbol{A}$ are linearly independent, then there exists at least one nonsingular submatrix $\boldsymbol{B}$ of dimension $m \times m$ made of m independent columns of $\boldsymbol{A}$.

In other words, the matrix $\boldsymbol{B}$ is composed of m independent vectors $\boldsymbol{y}'_{j(i)}$ of dimension m. The vectors $\boldsymbol{y}'_j$ are constructed from the feature vectors $\boldsymbol{y}_j$ by means of neglecting of the same components x_i. In this case, the below equation

$$\boldsymbol{B} \boldsymbol{v}'_2 = \mathbf{1}' \qquad (8)$$

has the following solution:

$$\boldsymbol{v}'_2 = \boldsymbol{B}^{-1} \mathbf{1}' . \qquad (9)$$

Let us remark that the solution $\boldsymbol{v}_2$ of the equation (7) also exists in this case. The solution $\boldsymbol{v}_2$ (7) can be derived from (8) by means of enlarging the vector $\boldsymbol{v}'_2$ with additional components equal to zero. The new components are put in those places, where the neglected components x_i of the vectors $\boldsymbol{y}_j$ have been situated. The existence of the solution $\boldsymbol{v}_2$ of the equation (7) means that the sets G^+ and G^- are linearly separable (9). The above remarks allow to prove the following Lemma.

Lemma 1. *The sets G^+ and G^- (8) composed of m linearly independent feature vectors $\boldsymbol{y}_j$ are linearly separable in at least one m-dimensional feature subspace $F_k[m]$ ($F_k[m] \subset F[n], m \leq n$).*

The Lemma 1 points out an important fact, that the linear separability of the sets G^+ and G^- (5) may result from the linear independence of the feature vectors $\boldsymbol{y}_j$ constituting these sets. Such case often occurs in practice, when the number m of the vectors $\boldsymbol{y}_j$ in the sets G^+ and G^- is no greater than dimensionality $(n+1)$ of these vectors ($m \leq n+1$).

4   Convex and Piecewise Linear (*CPL*) Criterion Function $\Phi_\lambda(v)$

The criterion function $\Phi_\lambda(v)$ is based on the *CPL* penalty functions $\varphi_j^+(v)$ or $\varphi_j^-(v)$ and $\phi_i(v)$. The functions $\varphi_j^+(v)$ are defined on the feature vectors y_j from the set G^+. Similarly $\varphi_j^-(v)$ are based on the elements y_j of the set G^-.

$$
\begin{aligned}
&\text{if}\ \ (y_j \in G^+)\ \ \text{and}\ \ (\langle v, y_j\rangle < 1)\ \ \text{then}\ \ \varphi_j^+(v) = 1 - \langle v, y_j\rangle\\
&\text{if}\ \ (y_j \in G^+)\ \ \text{and}\ \ (\langle v, y_j\rangle \ge 1)\ \ \text{then}\ \ \varphi_j^+(v) = 0
\end{aligned}
\tag{10}
$$

and

$$
\begin{aligned}
&\text{if}\ \ (y_j \in G^-)\ \ \text{and}\ \ (\langle v, y_j\rangle > -1)\ \ \text{then}\ \ \varphi_j^-(v) = 1 + \langle v, y_j\rangle\\
&\text{if}\ \ (y_j \in G^-)\ \ \text{and}\ \ (\langle v, y_j\rangle \le -1)\ \ \text{then}\ \ \varphi_j^-(v) = 0
\end{aligned}
\tag{11}
$$

The penalty functions $\phi_i(v) = |v_i|$ are related to particular features x_i.

$$
\begin{aligned}
&\text{if}\ \ (\langle e_i, v\rangle < 0)\ \ \text{then}\ \ \phi(v) = -\langle e_i, v\rangle\\
&\text{if}\ \ (\langle e_i, v\rangle \ge 0)\ \ \text{then}\ \ \phi(v) = \ \ \langle e_i, v\rangle
\end{aligned}
\tag{12}
$$

where $e_i = [0, ..., 0, 1, 0, ..., 0]^T$ are the unit vectors $(i = 1, ..., n + 1)$.
The criterion function $\Phi_\lambda(v)$ can be given in the following form:

$$
\Phi_\lambda(v) = \sum_{y_j \in G^+} \alpha_j \varphi_j^+(v) + \sum_{y_j \in G^-} \alpha_j \varphi_j^-(v) + \lambda \sum_{i \in I} \gamma_i \phi_i(v)
\tag{13}
$$

where $\alpha_j \ge 0$, $\lambda \ge 0$, $\gamma_i > 0$, $I = \{1, ..., n + 1\}$.
The nonnegative parameters α_j determine relative importance (*price*) of particular feature vectors $x_j(k)$. The parameters γ_i represent the *costs* of particular features x_i. We are using the minimal value of the criterion function $\Phi_\lambda(v)$:

$$
\Phi_\lambda(v*) = \min_v \Phi_\lambda(v)
\tag{14}
$$

The criterion function $\Phi_\lambda(v)$ (13) is the convex and piecewise linear (*CPL*) function as the sum of the *CPL* penalty functions $\alpha_j \varphi_j^+(v)$ (11), $\alpha_j \varphi_j^-(v)$ (12) and $\lambda \gamma_i \phi_i(v)$ (13). The basis exchange algorithm allows to find the minimum (18) efficiently, even in the case of large multidimensional data sets G^+ and G^- (1) [7]. The following *Lemma* can be proved:

Lemma 2. *If the sets G^+ and G^- (1) are linearly separable (5), and the prices γ_i are equal to 1 $((\forall i \in I)\gamma_i = 1)$, then there exists such value λ^+ that for a positive parameter λ which is no greater than λ^+ $(\forall \lambda \in (0, \lambda^+))$, the optimal vector $v*$ (14) separates (5) these sets and*

$$
\Phi_\lambda(v*) = \lambda \sum_{i \in I} |v_i *| = \lambda \| v* \|_{L1}
\tag{15}
$$

where $v* = [v_1*, ..., v_n*]^T$ and $\| v* \|_{L1} = \sum |v_i*|$ is the L_1 norm of the vector $v*$.

The proof of this Lemma is based on the fact, that for sufficiently small parameter λ the minimal value $\Phi_\lambda(v*)$ (14) of the function $\Phi_\lambda(v)$ (13) defined on the linearly separable sets G^+ and G^- (1) is equal to

$$\Phi_\lambda(v*) = \lambda \sum_{i \in I} \gamma_i \phi_i(v*) \tag{16}$$

The above equality results from the property, that the values of all the penalty functions $\varphi_j^+(v)$ and $\varphi_j^-(v)$ are equal to zero in the optimal point $v*$ for the linearly separable case.

As it results from the *Lemma 2*, in the case of linearly separable sets G^+ and G^- (1) minimisation of the function $\Phi_\lambda(v)$ (13) with a small parameter λ leads to the optimal vector $v*$ which not only separates these sets, but also has the minimal value of the L_1 norm of this vector.

5   Comparisons of the *Support Vector Machines* with the *CPL* Approach

The linear separability of the sets G^+ and G^- (5) by the vector $v*$ (14) can be formulated as:

$$\begin{array}{cl} (\forall y_j \in G^+) & \langle v*/\| v* \|, y_j \rangle \geq 1/\| v* \| \\ \textbf{and} \quad (\forall y_j \in G^-) & \langle v*/\| v* \|, y_j \rangle \leq 1/\| v* \| \end{array} \tag{17}$$

If the Euclidean norm ($\| v* \| = \langle v*, v* \rangle$) is used, the inequalities (17) mean that the sets G^+ and G^- (10) are separated by the hyperplane $H(v*) = \{y : \langle v*, y \rangle = 0\}$ (2) with the *margin* $\delta = 2/\| v* \|$. Minimization of the norm $\| v* \|$ means that the margin δ between the sets G^+ and G^- (10) becomes maximal. Such approach has been adopted in the *Support Vector Machine (SVM)* method in order to optimize location of the separating hyperplane $H(v*)$ (2) [7]. The quadratic programming is applied in order to find the minimal value of the margin $2/\| v* \|$ under the condition of the linear separability (17).

Let the symbols $G_l^+[m]$ and $G_l^-[m]$ stand for the positive and negative sets (1) composed of the m-dimensional feature vectors $y_j[m]$ from the subspace $F_k[m]$ ($F_k[m] \subset F(n)$). The sets $G_k^+[m]$ and $G_k^-[m]$ can be linearly separable (5) in the subspace $F_l[m]$. The minimal value $\Phi_\lambda(v_k^*[m])$ (14) of the *CPL* criterion function $\Phi_\lambda(v[m])$ (13) defined on the vectors $y'_j[m]$ can be used as the measure of the linear separability of the subspace $F_k[m]$. In other words, minimisation of the criterion function $\Phi_\lambda(v)$ (13) allows to compare different feature subspaces $F_k[m]$ and to choose the best one $F_k^*[m]$ from them.

The basis exchange algorithm adjusted to minimisation of the *CPL* criterion functions $\Phi_k(v[m])$ (13) in different subspaces $F_k[m]$ has been designed and implemented. This algorithm allows to find the best feature subspace $F_k^*[m]$ through the sequence of the below type:

$$F_1[m] \rightarrow F_2[m] \rightarrow \ldots\cdots \rightarrow F_k[m] = F_k^*[m] \tag{18}$$

where

$$\Phi_1^*(v[m]) \geq \Phi_2^*(v[m]) \geq \ldots \cdots \geq \Phi_k^*(v[m]) = \Phi_k^*(v[m]) \tag{19}$$

In accordance with the above relations, the sequence of the linearly separable feature subspaces $F_k[m]$ is designed in a such manner, that the minimal values $\Phi_k^*(v[m])$ of the criterion functions $\Phi_k(v[m])$ (13) in the successive subspaces $F_k[m]$ is decreasing. Each feature subspace $F_k[m]$ assures linear separability of the sets $G_k^+[m]$ and $G_k^-[m]$. In this case, the decreasing of the minimal values $\Phi_k^*(v[m])$ means the decreasing of the L_1 type distance (15), (17) between the sets $G_k^+[m]$ and $G_k^-[m]$.

6 Concluding Remarks

The proposed method of the selection of the optimal feature subspace $F_k^*[m]$ is based on directed search among linearly separable feature subspace $F_k[m]$. This search can be implemented as an efficient basis exchange procedure based on the sequence (18) with the property (19).

Selection of the feature subspaces $F_k^*[m]$ with best linear separability may be applied in solving many problems. One of the most interesting possibilities is gene extraction [8]. Another group of important applications is related to designing hierarchical neural networks and multivariate decision trees on the basis of the learning sets G_k (1) with a "long feature vectors". The ranked and the dipolar designing strategies can be combined with the procedure proposed here of the optimal feature subspace $F_k^*[m]$ selection [9].

References

1. Duda, O.R., Hart, P.E., Stork, D.G.: Pattern Classification, J.Wiley, New York (2001)
2. Bishop, Ch.M.: Neural Networks for Pattern Recognition, Clarendon Press, Oxford (1995)
3. Ripley, B.D.: Pattern Recognition and Neural Networks, Cambridge Univ. Press (1996)
4. Vapnik, V.N.: Statistical Learning Theory, J.Wiley, New York (1998)
5. Bobrowski, L.: Piecewise-Linear Classifiers, Formal Neurons and Separability of the Learning Sets, Proceedings of ICPR'96, 13th International Conference on Pattern Recognition, Wienna, Austria (August 25-29, 1996) 224–228
6. Bobrowski, L., The Method of the Feature Selection Based on the Linearly Separable Learning Sets, Proceedings of the 13th Internal Scientific Conference Biocybernetics and Biomedical Engineering, Edited by A. Nowakowski, Gdansk (2003) 237–242 (in Polish)
7. Bobrowski, L.: Design of Piecewise Linear Classifiers from Formal Neurons by Some Basis Exchange Technique, Pattern Recognition, 24(9), (1991) 863–870
8. Guyon, I., Weston, J., Barnhill, S., Vapnik, V.: Gene Selection for Cancer Classification using Support Vector Machines, Machine Learning, 46, (2002) 389–422
9. Bobrowski, L.: Strategies of Designing Neural Networks, Neural Networks, Vol. 6 in monography: Biocybernetics and Biomedical Engineering, Edited by M. Nalecz, Academic Publishing House Exit, Warsaw (2000) 295–321 (in Polish)

Short-Time Signal Analysis Using Pattern Recognition Methods

Piotr Boguś and Katarzyna D. Lewandowska

Department of Physics and Biophysics, Medical University of Gdańsk
Debinki 1, 80–210 Gdańsk, {piotr.bogus,kale}@amg.gda.pl

Abstract. The paper presents a method of signal analysis which is based on the parameter space consideration. The parameter space is created during the short-time analysis of the signal. The general schema of the approach consists of using a time window sliding in time along a signal. After choosing some particular parameters one observes their changes in a sliding window and analyzes the data in a multidimensional parameter space. For recognition and detection of different system states we propose to perform the clustering in the parameter space. The presented approach was used for analysis of EEG signals and some vibroacoustic signals taken form the combustion engine.

1 Introduction

The approach based on the application of some pattern recognition methods in short-time signal analysis was applied to EEG signals and some vibroacoustic signals taken from a combustion engines. The general schema of the method consists of using a window sliding in time along a signal. In a window one can perform any kind of analysis: from Fourier transformation, by statistical estimations to nonlinear methods. The idea of our approach is based on so called short-time Fourier analysis (window Fourier analysis) [1,8,11]. Choosing some particular parameters one can observe their changes in a sliding window. The clue of the method is the analysis of a multidimensional parameter space created by the parameter values. For identification and detection of different system states we propose to observe the evolution and to perform the clustering in the multidimensional parameter space [2,6,7].

2 Short-Time Signal Analysis Using Pattern Recognition Methods

The general signal characteristic (like Fourier spectrum) does not give us any information about local and instantaneous signal alterations that are more useful from a practical point of view.

The short-time Fourier spectrum analysis consists in calculating the instantaneous spectrum in sliding window. Hence for each moment we obtain the corresponding spectrum that can alter in time. The instantaneous continuous

L. Rutkowski et al. (Eds.): ICAISC 2004, LNAI 3070, pp. 550–555, 2004.
© Springer-Verlag Berlin Heidelberg 2004

spectrum can be defined in many ways. We present here the spectrum defined as the short-time Fourier transformation [1,8,11]. For discrete time function $u(i)$ we take the following definition

$$U(f,n) = \sum_{i=-\infty}^{\infty} u(i)h(n-i)e^{-j2\pi Ti} \; , \tag{1}$$

where $h(n)$ is a time function called a window function.

The spectrum calculated from (1) is a continuous spectrum and is periodic in frequency f. It depends on the window function form and the moment n. We assume that for the window function $h(n)$ a Fourier transformation exists. A window function should have a window shape, both in time ($h(n)$) and frequency domain ($H(f)$) [1,8,11].

In our approach we simply consider the particular parameters in the time window sliding along the signal. The general schema of proposed algorithm of short-time analysis is as follows [4,5]:

1. We choose the width of the time window.
2. In a sliding window we calculate the given signal parameters (in general one can take many of such parameters, e.g. FFT lines, statistical parameters, nonlinear parameters and others).
3. For the given window position the parameters values represent the point in the multidimensional data space (we called it a parameter space).
4. After sliding the window along the signal one has the set of points in the multidimensional parameter space.
5. For the comparison of different signals we perform the clustering in the parameter space and compare the cluster centers.
6. The values of parameters for the sliding time window give us the evolution in the parameter space.

In this paper we apply the classical hard c-means algorithm of clustering that is the simplest method among all the others and can be obtained by optimization of the objective function in a form [6,7]

$$J = \sum_{i=1}^{N} \sum_{j=1}^{c} p_{ij} E_{ij} \; , \tag{2}$$

where an energy E_{ij} is defined as an Euclidean distance $E_{ij} = |x_i - y_j|^2 = d_{ij}$ between the data point x_i and the centroid of cluster y_j and it is assumed that probabilities (membership values) p_{ij} that associates the data point x_i to cluster j are

$$\forall_{ij} \quad p_{ij} = \begin{cases} 1 & \text{if } x_i \in j \\ 0 & \text{if } x_i \notin j \end{cases} . \tag{3}$$

3   Results

3.1   EEG Signals

Electroencephalography (EEG) is a method of getting some quantitative information of the broad range of processes that take place in the brain (particularly brain cortex).

Table 1. The mean coordinates of centers in 7-dimensional parameter space for different types of EEG waves

	1	2	3	4	5	6	7
	Fourier 2	Fourier 3	Fourier 4	Fourier 5	Fourier 6	mean	variance
alpha wave	497.1	481.2	379.8	323.3	291.1	−0.3	20.9
beta wave	351.1	254.2	195.3	171.0	156.4	−1.0	9.5
muscle artefact	537.1	411.5	328.4	304.1	279.2	0.0	27.4
eye artefact	1433.5	1293.6	936.3	664.3	461.5	−0.1	29.5
theta wave	646.8	420.1	323.0	299.9	263.0	−1.0	16.6

In our experiments we first took into consideration the selected by the physician parts of EEG signals which represent the alpha waves, beta waves, theta waves (also called "slow" waves), muscle and eye artefacts [5]. Most of signals were sampled 256 per second, only theta waves had 128 sample per second, the time fragments more of 20 s. For all signals we applied the window of 1 s in width (256 or 128 samples). A window width was chosen as two periods of the typical lowest EEG frequency (2 Hz). For each window we calculated the seven parameters: FFT spectral lines from 2 till 6, mean and variance hence as the result we obtained the seven-dimensional parameter space. The mean centers values of the given EEG parts are presented in Tab.1. In turn, Fig.1 presents the exemplary 7-dimensional parameter space in projection into three and two-dimensional subspaces and results of their clustering into 2 and 3 clusters.

3.2   Vibroacoustic Signals

The vibroacoustic signals are often used in diagnosing of the mechanical devices like e.g. combustion engines. The most interesting was the comparison of the two engine states: normal cylinders work and the misfire state, when one or more of cylinders do not work [3,9,10].

The misfire was simulated by the disconnection of one cylinder of an engine. The measurements were preformed on exhaust locomotive 401Da–427. The acceleration sensor was fixed into the engine frame in the place, where one could define the measurement direction of acceleration. In measurements we used 16-channel digital recorder which bases on piezoelectric sensor [3,4].

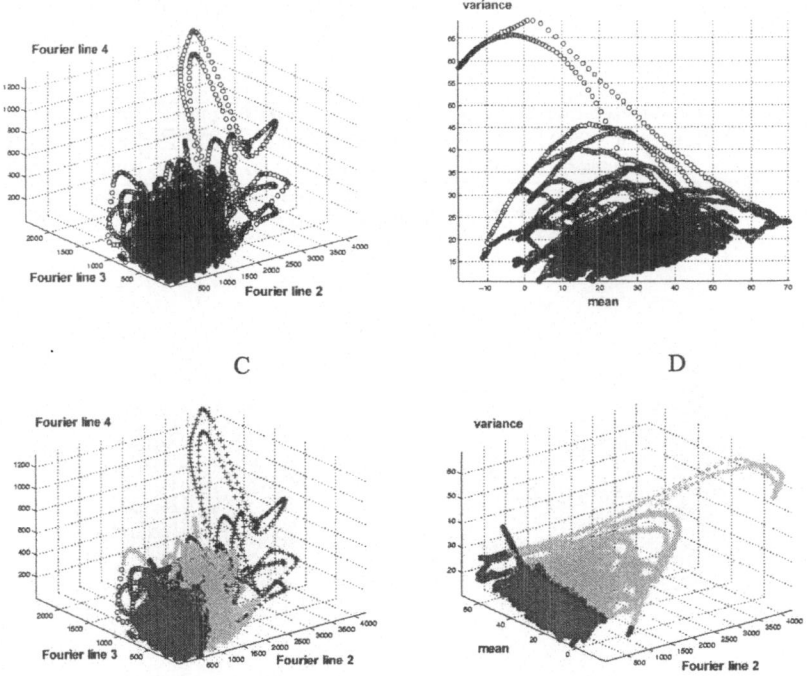

Fig. 1. Evolution in 7-dimensional parameter space in projection into three (A – Fourier line 2,3 and 4) and two dimensional (B – mean and variance) subspaces and the result of clustering into 2 and 3 groups in projection into subspace A.

The measurement of the locomotive engine was performed for three rotational velocities: $650 \div 680$ rev/min (idle run), 1100 rev/min, 1500 rev/min in three measurement phases

1. phase 1 – sensor is fixed on cylinder 1 – all cylinders are working,
2. phase 2 – sensor is fixed on cylinder 1 – cylinder 1 is disconnected,
3. phase 3 – sensor is fixed on cylinder 1 – cylinder 4 is disconnected.

The signal was registered in three channels, each channel represented a component in one of three directions: parallel to main locomotive axis, horizontal-transversal and vertical-transversal to main locomotive axis.

The sample frequency was 20 kHz. The window width was chosen as 0.1 s (2000 samples) and 0.01 s (200 samples). For each window we calculated the seven parameters: FFT spectral lines from 2 till 6, mean and variance hence we considered the 7-dimesnional parameter space. The mean centers values of the different signals are presented in Tab.1. In turn, Fig.2 shows an example of parameter space. Table 2 shows the significant difference between the centers for the proper and improper signals [4].

Table 2. The mean coordinates of centers in 7-dimensional parameter space for different types of signals.

	window	1 Fourier 2	2 Fourier 3	3 Fourier 4	4 Fourier 5	5 Fourier 6	6 mean	7 variance
all cylinders	0.1 s	628.93	526.62	550.79	660.96	513.13	3.50	365.10
work	0.01 s	428.42	652.82	1366.78	2854.60	1156.40	0.37	7.23
cylinder 1 does	0.1 s	552.87	537.14	819.78	703.86	460.463	−0.78	233.26
not work	0.01 s	542.48	869.75	1656.60	3487.70	1876.68	−0.08	69.00

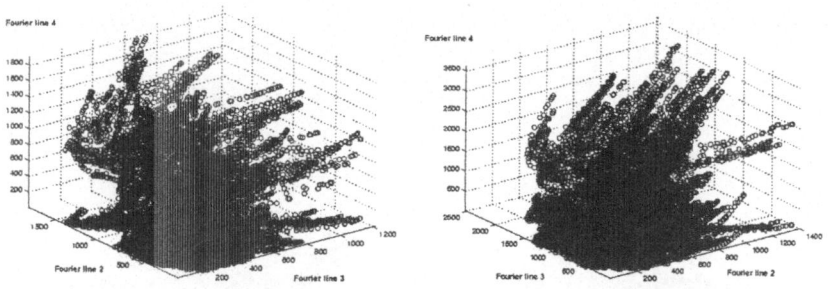

Fig. 2. The evolution in 7-dimensional parameter space projected on 3-dimesional subspace (FFT lines 2, 3 and 4) for signals 1500 rev/min for all cylinders work (A) and for cylinder 1 does not work (B) (for a window width 200 samples).

4 Conclusions

The approach presented in this paper can appear quite effective in the area where the main general aim is to discriminate and analyze the proper and improper signals that in EEG area are symptoms of pathology and artefacts and in vibroacoustic engine signals represent the misfire. The obtained results and observation of the multidimensional parameter space seem quite promising.

The general look at the parameter space allows us to distinguish the traces of window evolution. Parameter values sets calculated in a sliding window give us the points which coordinates evolve in the parameter space. Observing the parameter space one can find the massive center and some outside traces that can be treated as the improper behavior of signal fragments.

But taking into account the great complexity and variety of possible measurement schemes one should find our experiments only as the first and little fragment and the preliminary stage of the research.

We have used only the limited number of signals examples and the limited number of window parameters. It seems that using the higher number or different types of parameters may give us better classification and clustering results. Hence a future experiments should take more different parameters and higher or lower dimensional parameters space. In experiments we have used only the classical hard c-means clustering algorithm. The c-means algorithm of clustering suffers to problem of local minima and usually does not give satisfactory results in practice. Hence we expect an improvement of our experiment results by applying fuzzy c-means clustering algorithm, possibilistic clustering algorithm and statistical physics methods based clustering algorithms.

References

1. Allen, J. B., Rabiner, L. R.: A Unified Approach to Short-Time Fourier Analysis and Synthesis. Proceedings of the IEEE **65**,11 (1977) 1558–1564
2. Boguś, P., Massone, A. M., Masulli, F., Schenone, A.: Interactive Graphical System for Segmentation of Multimodal Medical Volumes Using Fuzzy Clustering. Machine GRAPHICS & VISION **7**,4 (1998) 781–791
3. Boguś, P., Merkisz, J., Grzeszczyk, R., Mazurek, S.: Nonlinear Analysis of Combustion Engine Vibroacoustic Signals for Misfire Detection. SAE Technical Paper Series. Electronic Engine Controls 2003–01–0354
4. Boguś, P., Merkisz, J., Waligórski, M.: Short-Time Methods of Signal Processing in Combustion Engine Diagnostic – OBDII/EOBD perspectives. Proceedings of 29th International Scientific Conference on Combustion Engines KONES 2003, Wisła, Poland (2003) 31–37
5. Boguś, P., Lewandowska, K., Jakitowicz, J.: Short-Time Methods in EEG Signals Analysis. Proceedings of 9th National Conference on Application of Mathematics in Biology and Medicine, Piwniczna, Poland (2003) 7–12
6. Bezdek, J. C.: Pattern Recognition with Fuzzy Objective Function Algorithms. Plenum Press (1987) 2nd edition
7. Duda, R., Hart, P.: Pattern Classification and Scene Analysis. Wiley Interscience, New York (1973)
8. Harris, F. J.: On the Use of Windows for Harmonic Analysis with the Discrete Fourier Transform. Proceedings of the IEEE **66**,1 (1978) 51–83
9. Merkisz, J., Boguś, P., Grzeszczyk, G.: Overview of Engine Misfire Detection Methods Used in On-Board Diagnostics. Journal of KONES – Internal Combustion Engines **8**,1–2 (2001) 326–341
10. Merkisz, J., Waligórski, M., Boguś, P., Grzeszczyk, R.: Misfire On-Board Diagnostic in Locomotive Engines (in Polish). Pojazdy Szynowe **4** (2002) 30–40
11. Portnoff, M. R.: Time-Frequency Representation of Digital Signals and Systems Based on Short-Time Fourier Analysis. IEEE Transactions on Acoustic, Speech, and Signal Processing, **ASSP–28**,1 (1980) 55–69

Application of Genetic Algorithms and Kohonen Networks to Cluster Analysis

Marian B. Gorzałczany and Filip Rudziński

Department of Electrical and Computer Engineering
Kielce University of Technology
Al. 1000-lecia P.P. 7, 25-314 Kielce, Poland
{m.b.gorzalczany,f.rudzinski}@tu.kielce.pl

Abstract. The paper presents two methods offering flexible solutions to cluster-analysis problems. The first one employs a genetic-algorithm-based Travelling-Salesman-Problem-solution, and the second one - self-organizing Kohonen networks. The operation of both techniques has been illustrated with the use of synthetic data set and then they have been tested by means of real-life, multidimensional *Mushrooms Database* (8124 records) available from the FTP server of the University of California at Irvine (ftp.ics.uci.edu).

1 Introduction

Cluster analysis is an important topic in various problems of classification, pattern recognition, association, intelligent decision support, etc. The performance of the majority of existing clustering methods is influenced by several more or less subjective factors such as the choice of the number of clusters (usually unknown in advance), the choice of the "similarity" measure, the initial cluster centers, different cluster-validity criteria, and so on [2].

This paper outlines two methods offering more flexible solutions to cluster-analysis problems. These methods aim at providing the user with an image (in two-dimensional space) of the cluster distribution in a given data set. The first approach employs a genetic-algorithm-based solution of the Travelling Salesman Problem, and the second one - a self-organizing Kohonen network. First, both techniques have been presented by means of an exemplary, synthetic data set and then they have been tested using a real-life, multidimensional data set (the so-called *Mushrooms Database*) [7]. The considerations presented in this paper are continued in paper [1] included in this volume.

2 Cluster Analysis by Means of Genetic Algorithms

Travelling Salesman Problem (TSP for short), conceptually, can be formulated as follows: the travelling salesman must visit every city in the area of his activity exactly once and then return to the starting point. There is also a variant of TSP without the demand of returning to the starting point - it of the interest

L. Rutkowski et al. (Eds.): ICAISC 2004, LNAI 3070, pp. 556–561, 2004.
© Springer-Verlag Berlin Heidelberg 2004

in the present paper. Given the cost of travel between all cities, the salesman must plan his itinerary so as to achieve the minimal total cost of the entire tour [5]; in our approach it is equivalent to designing the minimal (shortest) route connecting all cities).

Application of a genetic-algorithm-based TSP-solution method to cluster analysis consists of two main stages. In the first stage, a minimal route connecting all the points of the considered data set should be determined. An analysis of distances between neighbouring points along the route obtained in such a way provides the user with an image of the internal structure of the data set. It also gives the basis for the inference regarding the number and position of clusters within a given data set, which is an essence of cluster analysis.

Therefore, in the second stage of the proposed methodology, a histogram of distances between neighbouring points along the route is determined and then the corresponding histogram of "nearness" is calculated. The distance $d_{i,j}$ between two points $A_i, A_j \in R^n$ ($A_i = (a_{i1}, a_{i2}, \ldots, a_{in})$, $A_j = (a_{j1}, a_{j2}, \ldots, a_{jn})$) can be determined, e.g., by means of the Euclidean norm as follows

$$d_{i,j} = d(A_i, A_j) = \|A_i - A_j\| = \sqrt{\sum_{k=1}^{n}(a_{ik} - a_{jk})^2} \qquad (1)$$

The histogram of distances H_i^{dist} between two neighbouring points A_i, A_{i+1} along the route ($i = 1, 2, \ldots, r-1$, r - number of points along the route) is defined by $H_i^{dist} = d_{i,i+1}$ and the corresponding histogram of nearness H_i^{near} - by the following

$$H_i^{near} = (\max_{j=1,2,\ldots,r-1} H_j^{dist}) - H_i^{dist} = (\max_{j=1,2,\ldots,r-1} d_{j,j+1}) - d_{i,i+1}, \quad i = 1, 2, \ldots, r-1 \qquad (2)$$

The higher the bars of the nearness histogram are, the closer the corresponding data points are situated (they belong to a more compact clusters).

Fig. 1a presents a synthetic data set (250 points on the plane) for the purpose of illustration of the proposed technique. Using genetic algorithm, a minimal route connecting all the points has been determined as shown in Fig. 1b. In turn, in Fig. 2, the histogram of nearness - calculated according to (2) - has been presented. Although the histogram shows the existence of 3 clusters in the data set, sometimes (including the present case) it is worth to subject the histogram a filtering or smoothing action. Fig. 3 shows an approximation of nearness histogram of Fig. 2 by means of a set of second-order polynomials [4].

An analysis of either original histogram or the approximated one gives an image of the cluster distribution in the given data set. A simple criterion for determining the number and locations of clusters may be a cut-off of the histogram at some level of nearness (see Fig. 3) associated with the degree of compactness of the clusters obtained. The higher the histogram cut-off level, the more compact (characterized by small and close-to-each-other distances between data points) clusters in data set are generated. On the other hand, the lower the histogram cut-off level, the more fuzzy clusters are produced. This technique also allows us to define membership functions for fuzzy relations formally representing particular clusters.

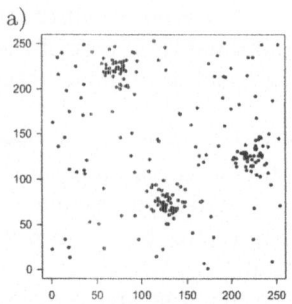 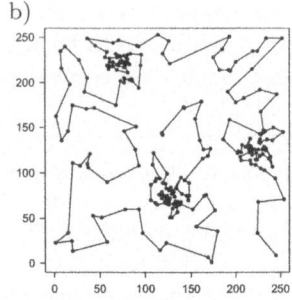

Fig. 1. Exemplary, synthetic data set (a) and a minimal route in it determined by a genetic algorithm (b)

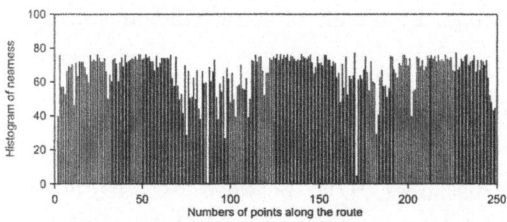

Fig. 2. Histogram of nearness between neighbouring points along the route of Fig. 1b

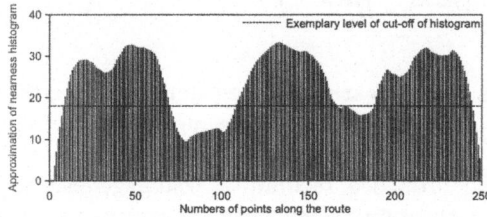

Fig. 3. Approximation of the nearness histogram of Fig. 2

There is one drawback of the proposed technique (although not affecting - in a significant way - the results obtained): not always remote points along the route generated by genetic algorithm in a given data set are remote in the original data set. In order to alleviate this problem, the afore-presented technique can be treated, conceptually, as a "point of departure" to other approach. Instead of looking for the route crossing all the original data points, it is worth considering to find shorter, simplified, "averaged" route coming through low-level, locally defined (by the method itself) clusters in the original data space. An excellent tool for performing this task is offered by self-organizing Kohonen networks [3].

3   Cluster Analysis with the Use of Kohonen Networks

In this paper, a self-organizing Kohonen network with one-dimensional neighbourhood is used. The network has an input layer with n units $x_1, x_2, \ldots, x_n$ and an output layer with m neurons arranged in a chain; their outputs are $y_1, y_2, \ldots, y_m$, where $y_j = \sum_{i=1}^{n} w_{ji} x_i$, $j = 1, 2, \ldots, m$ and w_{ji} are weights connecting the output of j-th neuron with i-th input. Using vector notation $(\boldsymbol{x} = (x_1, x_2, \ldots, x_n)$, $\boldsymbol{w}_j = (w_{j1}, w_{j2}, \ldots, w_{jn}))$, $y_j = \boldsymbol{w}_j \boldsymbol{x}$. In the learning process, the network aims - through the competition of neurons - to such an arrangement of neurons (that is, the selection of their weight vectors) to minimize a global error E of approximation of particular input vectors $\boldsymbol{x}_l$ $(l = 1, 2, \ldots, L)$ by the weight vectors $\boldsymbol{w}_{w_l}$ of neurons w_l winning in the competition when $\boldsymbol{x}_l$ is presented. Applying the Euclidean norm (1), global error E can be expressed as follows: $E = \frac{1}{L} \sum_{l=1}^{L} \| \boldsymbol{x}_l - \boldsymbol{w}_{w_l} \|$. Assuming the normalization of input vector $\boldsymbol{x}_l$ and using the Euclidean norm, the winning neuron w_l for the input vector $\boldsymbol{x}_l$ is selected such that $\| \boldsymbol{x}_l - \boldsymbol{w}_{w_l} \| = \min_{j=1,2,\ldots,m} \| \boldsymbol{x}_l - \boldsymbol{w}_j \|$.

In practice, Winner-Takes-Most (WTM) learning algorithms are applied, in which not only the winning neuron but also neurons from its specific neighbourhood update their weights. However, the further a given neuron in the neighbourhood of the winning one is located, the lesser update of its weights takes place. The learning rule can be formulated as follows: $\boldsymbol{w}_j(k + 1) = \boldsymbol{w}_j(k) + \eta_j(k) N(j, w_{\boldsymbol{x}}, k)[\boldsymbol{x}(k) - \boldsymbol{w}_j(k)]$, where $\eta_j(k)$ is the learning coefficient, $N(j, w_{\boldsymbol{x}}, k)$ is the neighbourhood function (both shrink while the learning progresses) and k is the iteration number. There are various WTM learning algorithms with different neighbourhood functions $N(j, w_{\boldsymbol{x}}, k)$. In this paper, a linear neighbourhood function has been used:

$$N(j, w_{\boldsymbol{x}}, k) = \begin{cases} 1 - |j - w_{\boldsymbol{x}}| \eta_j(k), & \text{for } |j - w_{\boldsymbol{x}}| \leq \lambda, \\ 0, & \text{for } |j - w_{\boldsymbol{x}}| > \lambda, \end{cases} \tag{3}$$

where λ is the number of neurons belonging to the neighbourhood of the winning neuron and, obviously, $|j - w_{\boldsymbol{x}}| \eta_j(k) \leq 1$ is always fulfilled for $|j - w_{\boldsymbol{x}}| \leq \lambda$.

Fig. 4 shows the route determined by the self-organizing network with 50 neurons arranged in the chain for the data set of Fig. 1a. Fig. 6 presents a polynomial approximation of the nearness histogram for the route of Fig. 4. An analysis of the histogram gives a clear image of the cluster distribution in the original data set. Introducing - as in the previous section of the paper - a cut-off of the histogram at some level of nearness (see Fig. 6) allows us to determine either more compact or more fuzzy clusters.

4   Application of Both Techniques to Multidimensional Cluster-Analysis Problems

Both techniques that have been presented in previous sections of the paper, now will be tested with the use of a real-life, multidimensional data set (the so-called *Mushrooms Database*) [7]. It is worth mentioning that the number of classes

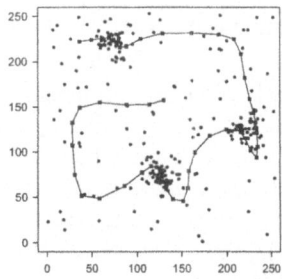

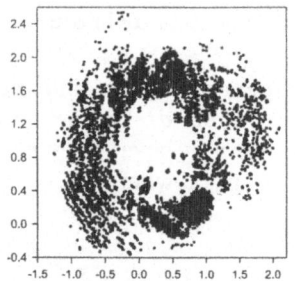

Fig. 4. Minimal route determined by 50-neuron self-organizing network for data set of Fig. 1a

Fig. 5. Sammon's planar mapping of multidimensional attribute space of *Mushrooms Database*

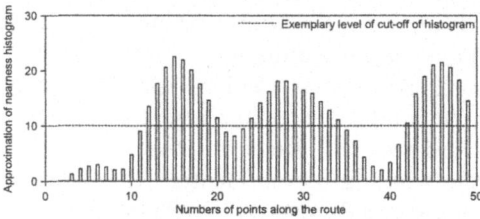

Fig. 6. Approximation of the nearness histogram between neighbouring points along the route of Fig. 4

(equal to 4) and the class assignments are known here; it allows us for direct verification of the results obtained.

The *Mushrooms Database* is the data set that contains as many as 8124 records (mushroom descriptions); each record is described by 22 nominal attributes. Due to high dimensionality of the attribute space, an important issue is graphical presentation of the distribution of these data in a way the human being is able to comprehend. For this purpose, a well-known Sammon's mapping [6] for the presentation of multi-dimensional data on the plane has been used. Fig. 5 presents the Sammon's planar mapping of multidimensional attribute space of *Mushrooms Database*. Fig. 7 shows the envelope of the polynomial approximation of the nearness histogram for the minimal route - determined by means of genetic algorithm - connecting all the data points. Three local minima of the plot of Fig. 7 indicate the boundaries between particular four clusters (classes). The percentage of correct decisions regarding the assignment of data points to particular classes is very high (91.6%).

In turn, the self-organizing network with 100 neurons arranged in a chain has been applied to determine a simplified, "averaged" route through the attribute space of *Mushrooms Database*. Fig. 8 presents the nearness histogram for this route. Without performing a polynomial approximation, four bar clusters - corresponding to four clusters (classes) in original data space - are clearly visible in Fig. 8. The percentage of correct decisions is also very high (93.2 %).

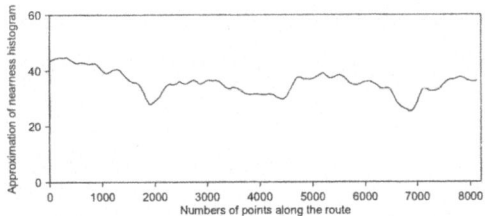

Fig. 7. Envelope of the approximation of the nearness histogram for minimal route in attribute space of *Mushrooms Database* determined by genetic algorithm

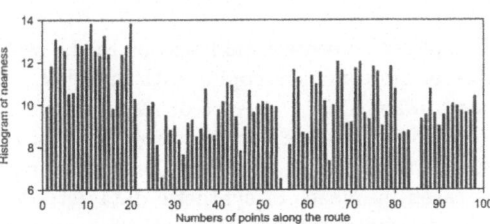

Fig. 8. Histogram of nearness for minimal route in attribute space of *Mushroom Database* determined by 100-neuron self-organizing network

5   Conclusions

Two methods offering flexible solutions to cluster-analysis problems have been presented in this paper. The first one employs the genetic-algorithm-based TSP-solution, and the second one - the self-organizing Kohonen networks. The operation of both techniques has been illustrated with the use of synthetic data set and then they have been tested by means of real-life, multidimensional *Mushrooms Database* (8124 records) [7]. The considerations presented in this paper are continued in paper [1] included in this volume.

References

1. Gorzałczany M.B., Rudziński F.: Modified Kohonen networks for complex cluster-analysis problems, in Proc. of Seventh Int. Conference on Artificial Intelligence and Soft Computing IEEE ICAISC 2004, Zakopane, 2004, in this volume.
2. Höppner F., Klawon F., Kruse R., Runkler T.: Fuzzy Cluster Analysis. J. Wiley & Sons, Chichester, 1999.
3. Kohonen T.: Self-organizing Maps. Springer-Verlag, Berlin, 1995.
4. Mathcad 2001 Professional (Polynomial regression). MathSoft, Inc., 1986-2000.
5. Michalewicz Z.: Genetic Algorithms + Data Structures = Evolution Programs. Springer-Verlag, Berlin, Heidelberg, 1996.
6. Sammon J.: A nonlinear mapping for data structure analysis. IEEE Trans. on Computers 18, 1969, pp. 401-409.
7. Machine Learning Database Repository, University of California at Irvine (ftp.ics.uci.edu).

Modified Kohonen Networks for Complex Cluster-Analysis Problems

Marian B. Gorzałczany and Filip Rudziński

Department of Electrical and Computer Engineering
Kielce University of Technology
Al. 1000-lecia P.P. 7, 25-314 Kielce, Poland
{m.b.gorzalczany,f.rudzinski}@tu.kielce.pl

Abstract. The paper presents a modification of the self-organizing Kohonen networks for more efficient coping with complex, multidimensional cluster-analysis problems. The essence of modification consists in allowing the neuron chain - as the learning progresses - to disconnect and later to reconnect again. First, the operation of the modified approach has been illustrated by means of synthetic data set. Then, this technique has been tested with the use of a real-life, complex, multidimensional data set (*Pen-Based Recognition of Handwritten Digits Database*) available from the FTP server of the University of California at Irvine (ftp.ics.uci.edu).

1 Introduction

This paper is a continuation of work [1] included in this volume. The paper [1] presents two methods offering flexible solutions to cluster-analysis problems by providing the user with an image (in two-dimensional space) of the cluster distribution in a given, multidimensional data set. The first method employs a genetic-algorithm-based solution of the Travelling Salesman Problem, and the second method - a self-organizing Kohonen network with one-dimensional neighbourhood (the neurons are arranged in a chain). The main idea behind the first method is to find a minimal route coming through all the data points. Then, a histogram of nearness of the neighbouring points along the route is determined. This histogram reveals an image of the data structure and cluster distribution in a given data set.

In order to get a proper image of the cluster distribution, the following condition should be fulfilled by both methods: the route determined by either method must cross only once a given data group being a candidate for a final cluster. If this condition is not fulfilled (e.g., due to complexity of the cluster distribution in a given data set), both methods overestimate the number of clusters.

This paper, first, illustrates the above-mentioned issue by means of an example. Then, a modification of the self-organizing Kohonen networks is formulated. It allows the networks to generate proper image of cluster distributions even in very complex problems; examples illustrating this issue are also provided. Finally, the benefits of using the modified self-organizing networks are demonstrated with the use of a real-life, complex and multidimensional data set (*Pen-Based Recognition of Handwritten Digits Database*) [2].

L. Rutkowski et al. (Eds.): ICAISC 2004, LNAI 3070, pp. 562–567, 2004.
© Springer-Verlag Berlin Heidelberg 2004

2   Illustration of Drawback of Conventional Kohonen Networks in Some Cluster-Analysis Problems

Fig. 1 shows a synthetic data set (1024 points on the plane) with three visible "parallel" clusters and the route in this set determined by 100-neuron self-organizing network (the neuron chain). Due to complexity of the cluster distribution, the route comes through some clusters more than once which results in an overestimation of the number of actual clusters. It is confirmed by the histogram of nearness (see [1] for details) for the route of Fig. 1. This histogram - shown in Fig. 2 - suggests the occurrence of four or five clusters.

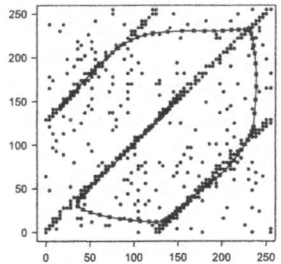

Fig. 1. Synthetic data set and the route in it determined by 100-neuron self-organizing network

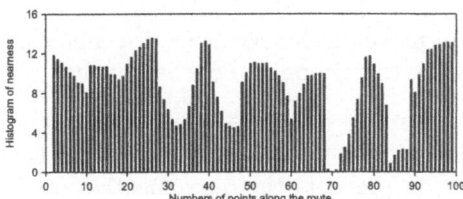

Fig. 2. Histogram of nearness for the route of Fig. 1

3   Modification of Self-Organizing Kohonen Networks

The main goal of modification of self-organizing networks is to allow the neuron chain of the network to fit the data structure (the cluster distribution) as good as possible. In order to achieve this goal, the following three-stage learning scenario can be employed:

Stage 1. Train the network in a conventional way.

Stage 2. Allow the network - under some conditions - to disconnect (in one or more points) its neuron chain. Continue the training of the network (to be more specific, two or more neuron sub-chains) in a conventional way.

Stage 3. Allow some of the neuron sub-chains - under some conditions - to reconnect and continue the final phase of training in a conventional way.

The first stage of the proposed scenario brings the original neuron chain (with neurons connected by the neighbourhood mechanism) to the point beyond which the network is not able to better fit the data structure. What's even worse, if the network encounters in the data space two comparable in size areas of data points (two candidates for clusters), the neurons from the first area are attracted to the second area, and vice-versa. Allowing the neuron chain to disconnect at some point between these clusters (the second stage of the proposed scenario) is a natural solution to the problem at hand. In turn, two or more sub-chains of the original neuron chain are subject to learning in a conventional way. These sub-chains are better suited to more precisely fit the data structure. In the course of further learning, it may happen that some sub-chains approach each other (they may represent different parts of the same data cluster). Therefore, it is reasonable to allow some of these sub-chains to reconnect (the third stage). After such actions, the conventional learning of the whole system should be continued for some time.

As far as the second stage of the afore-outlined learning scenario is concerned, the following four conditions - based on experimental investigations - allowing the neuron chain to disconnect have been formulated. Possible disconnection takes place between neuron no. i and neuron no. $i+1$; $i \in \{1, 2, \ldots, r-1\}$, where r represents the number of neurons either in an original neuron chain, or in a given sub-chain subject to further disconnection.

Condition 1: $d_{i,i+1} > \alpha_1 \dfrac{\sum_{j=1}^{r-1} d_{j,j+1}}{r}$, where: $d_{i,i+1}$ - distance between neurons no. i and no. $i+1$ (see [1] for details) and α_1 - experimentally selected coefficient (usually $\alpha_1 \in [1.5, 2]$).

The first condition prevents the excessive disconnection of the neuron chain or sub-chain by allowing to disconnect only relatively remote neurons.

Condition 2: win_i, $win_{i+1} < \alpha_2 \dfrac{\sum_{j=1}^{r} win_j}{r}$, where: win_i - number of wins of i-th neuron and α_2 - experimentally selected coefficient (usually $\alpha_2 \in [0.1, 0.2]$).

The second condition prevents the disconnection of the neuron chain (sub-chain) within the group of close-to-each-other data, that is, between the neurons characterized by a relatively high level of wins.

Condition 3: r_{s1}, $r_{s2} > \alpha_3 r$, where: r_{s1}, r_{s2} - number of neurons in first ($s1$) and second ($s2$) sub-chain, respectively, of the r-element neuron chain to be disconnected $(r_{s1} + r_{s2} = r)$ and α_3 - experimentally selected coefficient (usually $\alpha_3 \in [0.1, 0.2]$).

The third condition prevents the disconnection of short sub-chains from a given chain. Experiments show a tendency of chain-end neurons to escape from data groups they are in (chain-end neurons have fewer neighbours and are weakly attracted by the winning neurons). Without the third condition, undesirable, short chain-end sub-chains would occur.

Condition 4: $\dfrac{\sum_{j=1}^{r_{s1}} win_{s1j}}{r_{s1}}$, $\dfrac{\sum_{j=1}^{r_{s2}} win_{s2j}}{r_{s2}} > \alpha_4 \dfrac{\sum_{j=1}^{r} win_j}{r}$, where: win_{s1j}, win_{s2j} - number of wins of j-th neuron from first ($s1$) and second ($s2$) sub-chain, respectively, and α_4 - experimentally selected coefficient (usually $\alpha_4 \in [0.1, 0.2]$).

The fourth condition prevents the disconnection of sub-chains of rarely winning neurons corresponding to areas of data loosely scattered outside more compact data groups.

Experimental investigations leading to formulation of criteria for the third stage of the earlier-outlined learning scenario (reconnection of some neuron subchains) are underway.

Fig. 3 shows the performance of the modified self-organizing network - at several steps - applied to the synthetic data set of Fig. 1. Conventional self-organizing network has not been able to correctly cope with these data, as shown in Figs. 1 and 2. The present approach - as it can be seen in Fig. 3d and Fig. 4 showing the nearness histogram for the route of Fig. 3d - provides a clear and correct image of the cluster distribution in the problem considered.

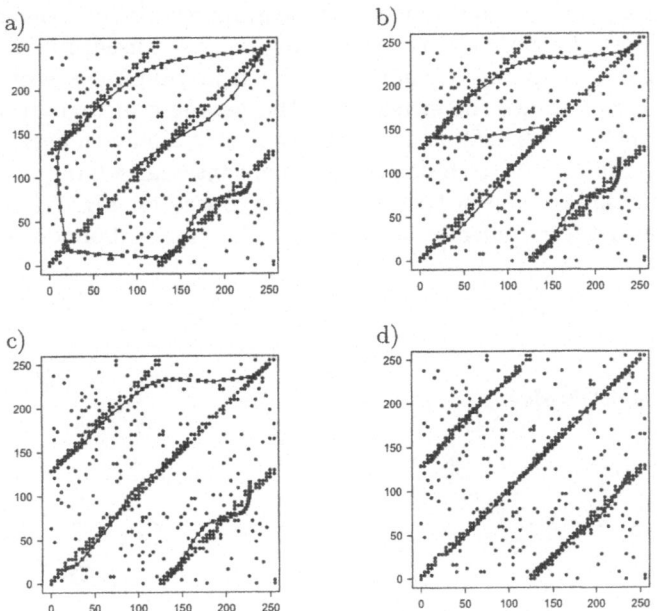

Fig. 3. Performance of the modified self-organizing network for the synthetic data set of Fig. 1

4 Application to Complex, Multidimensional Cluster-Analysis Problem

The technique that has been presented in previous section of the paper, now will be tested with the use of a real-life, complex, multidimensional data set (*Pen-Based Recognition of Handwritten Digits Database*) [2]. The number of classes (equal to 10: digits 0 through 9) and the class assignments are known here, which allows us for direct verification of the results obtained.

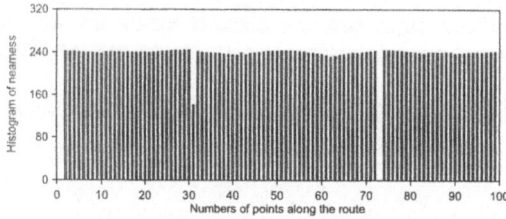

Fig. 4. Histogram of nearness for the route of Fig. 3d

The database under consideration contains as many as 7494 records (hand-written digits); each record is described by 16 nominal attributes. Due to high dimensionality of the attribute space, for the graphical presentation of these data - as in [1] - a well-known Sammon's mapping has been used. Fig. 5 presents the Sammon's planar mapping of multidimensional attribute space of the data set considered. Fig. 7 shows the envelope of the nearness histogram for the route determined in this set by 500-neuron self-organizing Kohonen network. It is easy to see that - due to data complexity - the conventional self-organizing network simply is not able to cope with this problem. Based on Fig. 7 it is difficult to determine both the number of clusters and the cluster boundaries in a given data set.

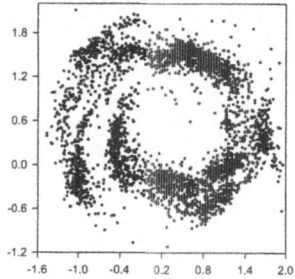

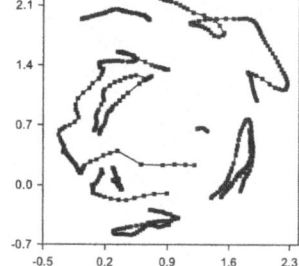

Fig. 5. Sammon's planar mapping of multidimensional attribute space (*Pen-Based Recognition of Handwritten Digits Database*)

Fig. 6. The route in data set of Fig. 5 determined by 500-neuron modified self-organizing network

In turn, Fig. 6 presents a route in this data set determined by the modified self-organizing network of Section 3 of this paper, and Fig. 8 - the envelope of the nearness histogram for the route of Fig. 6. This time a perfectly clear image of the cluster distribution, including the number of clusters and the cluster boundaries (determined by 9 local minima on the plot of Fig. 8), is revealed. The percentage of correct decisions, equal to 85.7%, regarding the class assignments is also very high.

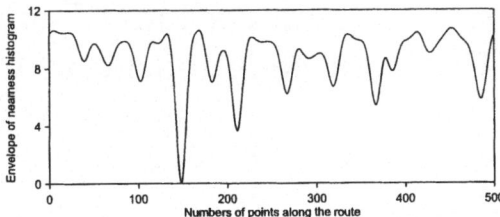

Fig. 7. Envelope of nearness histogram for the route in attribute space of Fig. 5 determined by 500-neuron conventional self-organizing network

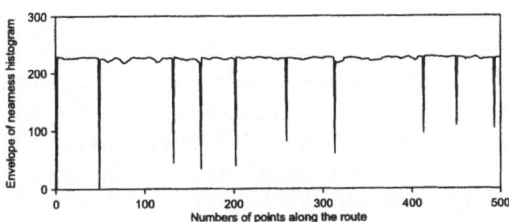

Fig. 8. Envelope of nearness histogram for the route of Fig. 6

5 Conclusions

The modification of the self-organizing Kohonen network with one-dimensional neighbourhood for efficient coping with complex, multidimensional cluster-analysis problems has been presented in this paper. The concept of modification consists in allowing - under some conditions - the neuron chain to disconnect in the course of learning. As the learning progresses, some sub-chains of neurons - under some other conditions - could be allowed to reconnect again. This enables the modified network to fit much better the structures "encoded" in data. First, the operation of the modified self-organizing network has been illustrated by means of synthetic data set. Then, this technique has been tested with the use of real-life, complex, multidimensional data set (*Pen-Based Recognition of Handwritten Digits Database*) [2]. The superiority of the modified approach in comparison to conventional self-organizing network has been clearly demonstrated.

References

1. Gorzałczany M.B., Rudziński F.: Application of genetic algorithms and Kohonen networks to cluster analysis, in Proc. of Seventh Int. Conference on Artificial Intelligence and Soft Computing IEEE ICAISC 2004, Zakopane, 2004, in this volume.
2. Machine Learning Database Repository, University of California at Irvine (ftp.ics.uci.edu).

Reducing the Computational Demands for Nearest Centroid Neighborhood Classifiers

Szymon Grabowski

Computer Engineering Department, Technical University of Lodz,
Al. Politechniki 11, Lodz, 90-924
SGrabow@kis.p.lodz.pl

Abstract. The k Nearest Centroid Neighbor (k-NCN) is a relatively new powerful decision rule based on the concept of so-called surrounding neighborhood. Its main drawback is however slow classification, with complexity $O(nk)$ per sample. In this work, we try to alleviate this disadvantage of k-NCN by limiting the set of the candidates for NCN neighbors for a given sample. It is based on an intuition that in most cases the NCN neighbors are located relatively close to the given sample. During the learning phase we estimate the fraction of the training set which should be examined only to approximate the "real" k-NCN rule. Similar modifications are applied also to ensemble of NCN classifiers, called voting k-NCN. Experimental results indicate that the accuracy of the original k-NCN and voting k-NCN may be preserved while the classification costs significantly reduced.

1 Introduction

The standard k Nearest Neighbors (k-NN) rule is known for half a century, but still there are few classifiers superior in terms of accuracy. One of those rare successful proposals is the idea of k *Nearest Centroid Neighbors* (k-NCN) [9]. As in k-NN, a set of k neighbors of a test sample is selected, and the class with the greatest number of votes among those neighbors defines the output label.

The k nearest centroid neighbors of a query sample q are obtained as follows: the first neighbor of q is its nearest neighbor, n_1; the i-th neighbor, $n_i, i \geq 2$, is such that the centroid (i.e., the mean) c_i of this and previously selected neighbors, $n_1, \ldots, n_{i-1}$, is the closest to q.

Several works have pointed out high accuracy of k-NCN [9,10,2,4]. Its main drawback of k-NCN is however slow classification, with complexity $O(nk)$ per sample. Finding each successive NCN neighbor requires examining all the samples from the learning set, which is often prohibitively costly.

In this paper, we propose a modified decision rule, which limits the set of the candidates for NCN neighbors for each sample. The rate of such reduction and hence the potential classification speedup rate is determined during the learning phase, i.e., is known before the actual classification. We adapt the idea not only to the original k-NCN, but also to its voting variant proposed in our earlier work [5,4].

L. Rutkowski et al. (Eds.): ICAISC 2004, LNAI 3070, pp. 568–573, 2004.
© Springer-Verlag Berlin Heidelberg 2004

2   The Proposed Algorithms

Intuitively, the NCN neighbors should be located close to the query sample. However, the experimental results are somewhat counterintuitive. In [5], we counted the number of distance based neighbors within radius associated with the farthest among the k nearest centroid neighbors. Those nearest neighbor counts are surprisingly high: for example, for a single partition of the Ferrite dataset (to be described in Section 4), within the radius of the ball induced with 10 NCN neighbors there are on average about 140 distance based neighbors. Similar results were obtained on other data-sets. This phenomenon has two consequences. First, it suggests that the importance of neighbors' proximity could be overrated. Moreover, if for a given NCN neigh-borhood so many samples are located closer to the query than the most distant NCN neighbor, then there may exist many ways to "improve" the set of neighbors to predict the label of the query sample [5]. The second conclusion is less optimistic: if NCN neighbors are often quite far from the tested sample, then there is not much hope for a significant speedup of the search process. We however decided to take a closer look at this question.

A basic idea for speeding up the classification of query sample q is to sort the learning set samples according to their distance to q, and then look for NCN neighbors only in a fraction of the learning set containing the closest samples. But what fraction? Datasets vary a lot in their characteristics and consequently any fixed percentage of samples (significantly less than 100%) may be inappropriate for many real datasets. Regarding that, it is advisable to determine the fraction in the learning phase.

The simplest idea is to find the farthest of k NCN neighbors for each sample in the learning set in a leave-one-out manner, calculate its rank according to the distance (for example, the third nearest neighbor would get rank 3) and finally find the maximum m over all those ranks. The ratio $m/(n-1)$, where n is the learning set count, is the desired fraction. Such an idea is however sensitive to the presence of such atypical training samples for which at least one of its k NCN neighbors has a large rank.

We devised a more robust variant of the presented idea. Let us define m_{robust} rank as the minimal value such that for, e.g., 95% samples from the training set the farthest of their k NCN neighbors has its distance rank not exceeding m_{robust}. Now the fraction of closest samples used in the classification phase will be equal to $m_{robust}/(n-1)$, which of course never exceeds the previously discussed fraction $m/(n-1)$. This variant will be called *limited k-NCN v1* in the test section.

Another extension is possible. Instead of finding the proper rank for all k neighbors, such a parameter may be estimated from the training set for each i-th neighbor ($i=1, \ldots, k$) separately. We denote this variant with *limited k-NCN v2*.

In an earlier work [4], we proposed the *voting k-NCN* classifier, which is an ensemble of k-NCN components with the decision obtained via plurality voting. The desired diversity in the ensemble is achieved by taking varying counts of neighbors k for the component k-NCN classifiers. The component classifiers are trained on random partitions of the whole learning set. The learning set is divided L times at random into halves, and one half is used as the "real" training set and the other as the validation set. In this way, L values: $k_1, \ldots, k_L$, are obtained. The classification stage works with the k_i-NCN components, which refer (as opposed to the training phase) to the whole learning set. We set L to 10 in our experiments.

Adapting the neighborhood limiting ideas to the voting k-NCN is straightforward. The rank m_{robust} is now defined as the minimal value such that for, e.g., 95% samples from the training set the farthest of their k_{max} NCN neighbors has its distance rank not exceeding m_{robust}, where k_{max} denotes the maximum among the $k_1, \ldots, k_L$ values. In this way, the variants v1 and v2 for limited voting k-NCN can be defined analogously to the respective variants for the limited k-NCN.

3   Implementation Issues

The set of candidate neighbors for a given query sample q may be obtained via sorting the training set samples according to the distance to q, but in fact full sorting is not necessary. In the limited k-NCN v1, it is enough to divide the learning set into two disjoint subsets of specified size, one such that any sample from this subset is located in the closer or equal distance to q than any sample from the other subset. The well-known *randomized-select* algorithm [1], based on quick sort, serves this purpose.

In the limited k-NCN v2 variant, more "sortedness" is required for the training set. For simplicity, we decided to sort fully the subset of $m_{robust} \cdot n/(n-1)$ nearest samples to q, where m_{robust} is the minimal value such that for f=95% samples from the training set the farthest of their k NCN neighbors has its distance rank not exceeding m_{robust}. As it appears, the computational increase in this phase of classification in v2 is more than compensated with the savings in distance calculations in the NCN search phrase.

During our experiments we noticed quite a surprising phenomenon. A very simple distance calculation trick, namely: rejecting the candidate sample if already after the first half of examined features it may be concluded the sample is located too far (a trick viable for both k-NN and k-NCN), had a major speed impact for the used datasets. For example, for Ferrite dataset and k-NCN, in about 90% of cases the given criterion was satisfied.

Another practical trick for k-NCN-like classification is to avoid multiplications/divisions as the real centroids of found-so-far neighbors are not actually necessary. Instead of the centroid of i neighbors, $i = 1 \ldots k$, we can store their sum (which obviously is the centroid vector multiplied by i) and consequently refer to the query vector multiplied by the same i. In this way, all the distances are scaled, which does not hinder finding the NCN neighbors. Additionally, some temporary values may be cached in k-NCN routines for further speedup of a few percent.

4   Experimental Results

We conducted experiments on two real datasets: one concerning quality control of ferrite cores [7,8] and one taken from a remote sensing application [11]. For Ferrite dataset ten unbalanced partitions were made: 1400 samples (training sets) and 4503 samples (test sets). The dataset has 30 features and 8 classes. The available remote sensing dataset contained 5124 samples (5 classes, 9 features). Again, ten partitions were used: the learning sets had 1250 samples each time.

The tested classifiers were k-NN, k-NCN, voting k-NCN and the proposed limited k-NCN and limited voting k-NCN in two variants: v1 and v2. As we have men-tioned the significant impact of the two simple distance calculation tricks, we decided to compare the classifiers in two implementations: *plain* and *fast* (both described tricks used for k-NCN based classifiers, and only the former one for k-NN). For the voting k-NCN variants, we present the results of the fast implementations only. Learning sessions are identical for k-NCN and its "limited" variants, and so is for the voting k-NCN case. That means the learned values of k are identical for a given task, which is a potential deficiency of our idea.

The average value of k for k-NN over 10 partitions was 4.5 for Ferrites and 10.8 for Remotes. For k-NCN, the respective values of k were 5.9 and 14.2.

In limited k-NCN v1, it was enough to consider on average 16.3% of all samples for NCN candidates for Ferrites. The respective fraction for Remotes was 45.1%. In v2, the fractions for individual i-th ($i = 1 \ldots k$) neighbors vary of course, but on average are much lower. Taking the average fraction for each partition, and again the average over all the partitions, we obtain 5.0% for Ferrites and 14.3% for Remotes.

All the program codes were compiled in Delphi 3.0. The tests were run on an Athlon 2400+ machine with 256 MB RAM under Windows 98 SE. Each 10-partition series was tested several times and the best total timing was taken for the comparison. Tables 1 and 2 present average errors and timings for both datasets. The rightmost column indicates the slowdown factor in comparison to the fast k-NN implementation.

It is easy to notice that the limited k-NCN v2 is much faster than original k-NCN (1.73x for Ferrites and 2.69x for Remotes, comparing the fast implementations) and also achieves (perhaps accidentally) slightly greater accuracies. The results are quite stable over the partitions showing that the ad hoc fraction parameter f=95% was quite a good choice. The limited k-NCN v1 variant was less beneficial, anyway in comparison with original k-NCN it still looks competitively. It is also noteworthy how profitable simple implementation tricks may be; a fair speed comparison of original k-NN and k-NCN was one of the purposes for this work. Nevertheless, k-NN is still much faster than any of the k-NCN based classifiers, so it depends on the application whether the expected accuracy boost with limited k-NCN is worth the additional classification time. This question pertains to the limited voting k-NCN as well, where further improvements in accuracy also imply classification 7-9x slower than k-NN. Still, the v2 variant

Table 1. Ferrites. Classification errors and timings

classifier	error (%)	classif. time (s)	time rel. to k-NN, fast
k-NN, plain	10.96	2.50	2.66
k-NN, fast	10.96	0.94	1.00
k-NCN, plain	10.18	19.57	20.82
k-NCN, fast	10.18	5.99	6.37
limited k-NCN v1, plain	10.17	6.33	6.73
limited k-NCN v1, fast	10.17	4.33	4.61
limited k-NCN v2, plain	10.10	4.30	4.57
limited k-NCN v2, fast	10.10	3.47	3.69
voting k-NCN, fast	9.69	21.70	23.11
limited voting k-NCN, v1, fast	9.66	12.18	12.97
limited voting k-NCN, v2, fast	9.68	6.67	7.10

of limited voting k-NCN is about 3x faster than the original rule at a similar accuracy rate.

Table 2. Remotes. Classification errors and timings

classifier	error (%)	classif. time (s)	time rel. to k-NN, fast
k-NN, plain	21.63	0.38	1.36
k-NN, fast	21.63	0.28	1.00
k-NCN, plain	20.77	7.99	28.54
k-NCN, fast	20.77	3.98	14.21
limited k-NCN v1, plain	20.78	4.40	15.71
limited k-NCN v1, fast	20.78	2.78	9.93
limited k-NCN v2, plain	20.67	2.02	7.21
limited k-NCN v2, fast	20.67	1.48	5.29
voting k-NCN, fast	20.11	7.59	27.50
limited voting k-NCN, v1, fast	20.10	5.37	19.44
limited voting k-NCN, v2, fast	20.19	2.54	9.21

The appropriate value of the fraction f can possibly be estimated from the training set, nevertheless after the preliminary attempts we do not expect a breakthrough in accuracy or speed. Some more experiments are required with the *randomized-select* routine; currently it is implemented in the simplest form.

5   Conclusions and Future Plans

We presented the idea of limiting the set of neighbors for k-NCN decision rules. In practice, such a limitation does not change much in the classification, except for a significant speed improvement. We also presented several simple but surprisingly efficient implementation tricks for NN and NCN based classifiers. As the next step, we intend to perform the comparison tests on a broader collection of datasets. Of interest should also be to incorporate the presented ideas into several cascade classifiers [4], where NCN components are expected to be triggered on relatively few samples only. It is our hope that the modified schemes will become faster, but the classification accuracy will be preserved.

References

[1] T. H. Cormen, Ch. E. Leiserson and R. L. Rivest: Introduction to Algorithms, MIT Press, 1990.

[2] Sz. Grabowski: Experiments with k-NCN decision rule, IX Konferencja Sieci i Systemy Informatyczne (9th Conf. "Networks and IT Systems"), Lodz, Poland, 2001, pp. 307–317.

[3] Sz. Grabowski: A family of cascade NN-like classifiers, Proc. 7th Int. IEEE Conf. TCSET'2002, Lviv-Slavsk, Ukraine, Feb. 2002, pp. 223–225.

[4] Sz. Grabowski, A. Jozwik and C.-H. Chen: Nearest neighbor decision rule for pixel classification in remote sensing, a chapter in Frontiers of Remote Sensing Info Processing, ed. S. Patt, World Scientific Publishing Co. Pte. Ltd., Singapore, July 2003.

[5] Sz. Grabowski: A family of cascade NN-like classifiers, Proc. 7th Int. IEEE Conf. on Experience of Designing and Application of CAD Systems in Microelectronics (CADSM), Lviv-Slavsk, Ukraine, Feb. 2003, pp. 503–506.

[6] Sz. Grabowski: Towards decision rule based on closer symmetric neighborhood, Biocybernetics and Biomedical Engineering, Vol. 23, No. 3, pp. 39–46, July 2003.

[7] A. Jozwik, L. Chmielewski, W. Cudny and M. Sklodowski: A 1-NN preclassifier for fuzzy k-NN rule, Proc. 13th Int. Conf. on Pattern Recognition, vol. IV, track D, Parallel and Connectionist Systems, Vienna, Austria, 1996, pp. 234–238.

[8] M. Nieniewski, L. Chmielewski, A. Jozwik and M. Sklodowski: Morphological detection and feature-based classification of cracked regions in ferrites, Machine Graphics and Vision, Vol. 8, No. 4, 1999.

[9] J. S. Sanchez, F. Pla and F. J. Ferri: On the use of neighbourhood-based nonparametric classifiers, Pattern Recognition Letters, Vol. 18, No. 11–13, pp. 1179–1186, 1997.

[10] J. S. Sanchez, F. Pla and F. J. Ferri: Improving the k-NCN classification rule through heuristic modifications, Pattern Recognition Letters, Vol. 19, No. 13, pp. 1165–1170, 1998.

[11] S. B. Serpico, F. Roli: Classification of multisensor remote sensing images by structured neural networks, IEEE Trans. on Geoscience Remote Sensing, Vol. 33, No. 3, pp. 562–578, 1995.

SSV Criterion Based Discretization for Naive Bayes Classifiers

Krzysztof Grąbczewski
kgrabcze@phys.uni.torun.pl

Department of Informatics, Nicolaus Copernicus University,
ul. Grudziądzka 5, 87-100 Toruń, Poland.
http://www.phys.uni.torun.pl/kmk

Abstract. Decision tree algorithms deal with continuous variables by finding split points which provide best separation of objects belonging to different classes. Such criteria can also be used to augment methods which require or prefer symbolic data. A tool for continuous data discretization based on the SSV criterion (designed for decision trees) has been constructed. It significantly improves the performance of Naive Bayes Classifier. The combination of the two methods has been tested on 15 datasets from UCI repository and compared with similar approaches. The comparison confirms the robustness of the system.

1 Introduction

There are many different kinds of algorithms used in computational intelligence for data classification purposes. Different methods have different capabilities and are successful in different applications. For some data sets, really accurate models can be obtained only with a combination of different kinds of methodologies.

Decision tree algorithms have successfully used different criteria to separate different classes of objects. In the case of continuous variables in the feature space they find some cut points which determine data subsets for further steps of the hierarchical analysis. The split points can also be used for discretization of the features, so that other methods become applicable to the domain or improve their performance.

The aim of the work described here was to examine the advantages of using the Separability of Split Value (SSV) criterion for discretization tasks. The new method has been analyzed in the context of the Naive Bayes Classifier results.

2 Discretization

Many different approaches to discretization can be found in the literature. There are both supervised and unsupervised methods. Some of them are very simple, others – quite complex.

The simplest techniques (and probably the most commonly used) divide the scope of feature values observed in the training data into several intervals of equal width or equal data frequency. Both methods are unsupervised – they operate with no respect to the labels assigned to data vectors.

L. Rutkowski et al. (Eds.): ICAISC 2004, LNAI 3070, pp. 574–579, 2004.
© Springer-Verlag Berlin Heidelberg 2004

The supervised methods are more likely to give high accuracies, because the analysis of data labels may lead to much better separation of the classes. However, such methods should be treated as parts of more complex classification algorithms, not as means of data preprocessing. When a cross-validation test is performed and a supervised discretization is done in advance for the whole dataset, then the CV results may get strongly affected. Only performing the discretization of the trainig parts of data for each fold of the CV will guarantee reliable results.

One of the basic supervised methods is discretization by histogram analysis. The histograms for all the classes displayed as a single * plot provide some visual tool for manual cut points selection (but obviously this technique can also be automated).

Some of the more advanced methods are based on statistical tests: ChiMerge [1], Chi2 [2]. There are also supervised discretization schemes based on the information theory [3]. Decision trees which are capable of dealing with continuous data can be easily used to recursively partition the scope of a feature into as many intervals as needed, but it is not simple to specify the needs. The same problems with adjusting parameters concern all the discretization methods. Some methods use statistical tests to decide when to stop further splitting, some others rely on the Minimum Description Length Principle. The way features should be discretized can depend on the classifier which is to deal with the converted data. Therefore it is most advisable to use wrapper approaches to determine the optimal parameters values for particular subsystems. Obviously, wrappers suffer from their complexity, but in the case of fast discretization methods and fast final classifiers, they can be efficiently applied to medium-sized datasets (in particular to the UCI repository datasets [4]).

There are already some comparisons of different discretization methods available in the literature. Two broad studies of the algorithms can be found in [5] and [6]. They are good reference points for the results presented here.

3   SSV Criterion

The SSV criterion is one of the most efficient among criteria used for decision tree construction [7]. Its basic advantage is that it can be applied to both continuous and discrete features. The *split* value (or *cut-off point*) is defined differently for continuous and symbolic features. For continuous features it is a real number and for symbolic ones it is a subset of the set of alternative values of the feature. The *left side* (LS) and *right side* (RS) of a split value s of feature f for a given dataset D is defined as:

$$\text{LS}(s, f, D) = \begin{cases} \{x \in D : f(x) < s\} & \text{if } f \text{ is continuous} \\ \{x \in D : f(x) \notin s\} & \text{otherwise} \end{cases} \quad (1)$$

$$\text{RS}(s, f, D) = D - \text{LS}(s, f, D)$$

where $f(x)$ is the f's feature value for the data vector x. The definition of the *separability of a split value* s is:

$$\text{SSV}(s) = 2 * \sum_{c \in C} |\text{LS}(s, f, D_c| * |\text{RS}(s, f, D - D_c)|$$
$$- \sum_{c \in C} \min(|\text{LS}(s, f, D_c|, |\text{RS}(s, f, D_c|) \quad (2)$$

where C is the set of classes and D_c is the set of data vectors from D assigned to class $c \in C$.

Decision trees are constructed recursively by searching for best splits (with the largest SSV value) among all the splits for all the features. At each stage when the best split is found and the subsets of data resulting from the split are not completely pure (i.e. contain data belonging to more than one class) each of the subsets is analyzed in the same way as the whole data. The decision tree built this way gives maximal possible accuracy (100% if there are no contradictory examples in the data), which usually means that the created model overfits the data. To remedy this a cross validation training is performed to find the optimal parameters for pruning the tree. The optimal pruning produces a tree capable of good generalization of the patterns used in the tree construction process.

3.1 SSV Based Discretization

The SSV criterion has proved to be very efficient not only as a decision tree construction tool, but also in other tasks like feature selection [8] or discrete to continuous data conversion [9].

The discretization algorithm based on the SSV criterion operates for each of the continuous features separately. For given training dataset D, selected continuous feature f and the target number n of splits, it acts according to the following:

1. Build SSV decision tree for the dataset obtained by projection of D to one-dimentional space consisting of the feature f.
2. Prune the tree to have no more than n splits. This is achieved by pruning the outermost splits (i.e. the splits with two leaves), one by one, in the order of increasing value of the reduction of the training data classification error obtained with the node.
3. Discretize the feature using all the split points occurring in the pruned tree.

Obviously, the discretization with n split points leads to $n+1$ intervals, so the sensible values of the parameter are integers greater than zero.

The selection of the n parameter is not straightforward. It depends on the data being examined and the method which is to be applied to the discretized data. It can be selected arbitrarily as it is usually done in the case of equal width or equal frequency intervals methods. Because the SSV discretization is supervised, the number of intervals will not need to be as large as in the case of the unsupervised methods. If we want to look for the optimal value of n, we can use a wrapper approach which, of course, requires more computations than a single transformation, but it can better fit n to the needs of the particular symbolic data classifier.

4 Results

To test the advantages of the presented discretization algorithm, it has been applied to 15 datasets available in the UCI repository [4]. Some information about the data is presented in table 1. The datasets are defined in spaces with continuous features, which facilitates testing discretization methods. The same sets were used in the comparison presented in [5]. Although Dougherty et al. present many details about their test, there is still some uncertainty, which suggests some caution in comparisons, for example it is not specified whether the discretization was performed as a part of classification system or at the data preprocessing stage, also the way of treating unknown values is not reported. The results presented here ignore the missing values when estimating probabilities i.e. for given interval of given features only vectors with known values are given consideration to. When classifying a vector with missing values, the corresponding features are excluded from calculations.

For each of the datasets a number of tests has been performed and the results placed in table 2. All the results are obtained with the Naive Bayes Classifier run on differently prepared data. The classifier function is $argmax_{c \in C} P(c) P(x_i|c)$, where x_i is the value of i'th feature of the vector x being classified. $P(c)$ and $P(x_i|c)$ are estimated on the basis of the training data set (neither Laplace correction nor m-estimate was applied). For continuous features $P(x_i|c)$ is replaced by the value of Gaussian density function with mean and variance estimated from the training samples.

In table 2, the **Raw** column reflects the results obtained with no data preprocessing, **10EW** means that 10 equal width intervals discretization was used, SSV_4 reflects the SSV criterion based discretization with 4 split points per feature and SSV_O corresponds to the SSV criterion based discretization with a search for optimal number of split points. The best value of the parameter was searched in the range from 1 to 25, in accordance with the results of 5-fold cross-validation test conducted within the training data. The table presents classification accuracies placed above their standard deviations calculated for 30 repetitions[1] of 5-fold cross-validation (the left one concerns the 30 means and the right one is the average internal deviation of the 5-fold CVs). The **-P** suffix means that the discretization was done at the data preprocessing level, and the **-I** suffix, that the transformations were done internally in each of the CV folds.

Using supervised methods for data preprocessing is not reasonable – it offends the principle of testing on unseen data. Especially when dealing with a small number of vectors and a large number of features, there is a danger of overfitting and attractively looking results may turn out to be misleading and completely useless. A confirmation of these remarks can be seen in the lower part of table 3. Statistical significance of the differences was examined with the paired t test.

5 Conclusions

The discretization method presented here significantly improves the Naive Bayes Classifier's results. It brings a statistically significant improvement not only to the basic NBC formulation, but also in relation to the 10 equal-width bins technique and other methods examined in [5]. The results presented in table 2 also facilitate a comparison of the proposed algorithm with the methods pursued in [6]. Calculating average accuracies over 11 datasets (common to both studies) for the methods tested by Yang et al. and for SSV based algorithm shows that SSV offers lower classification error rate than all the others but one – the Lazy Discretization (LD), which is extremely computationally expensive.

---

[1] The exception is the last column which because of higher time demands shows the results of 10 repetitions of the CV test. One should also notice that the results collected in [5] seem to be single CV scores.

Table 1. Datasets used for the comparisons.

Dataset	Vectors	Classes	Features		Missing values	
			continuous	discrete	number	percent
Annealing	898	5	6	12	5907	36.54
Australian credit approval	690	2	6	8	0	0
Wisconsin breast cancer	699	2	9	0	16	0.25
Cleveland heart disease	303	2	5	8	7	0.18
Japanese credit screening (crx)	690	2	6	9	67	0.65
Pima Indian diabetes	768	2	8	0	0	0
German credit data	1000	2	24	0	0	0
Glass identification	214	6	9	0	0	0
Statlog heart	270	2	13	0	0	0
Hepatitis	155	2	6	13	167	5.67
Horse colic	368	2	7	15	1927	23.80
Hypothyroid	3163	2	7	18	5329	6.74
Iris	150	3	4	0	0	0
Sick-euthyroid	3163	2	7	18	5329	6.74
Vehicle silhouettes	846	4	18	0	0	0

Table 2. Comparison of the classification results.

Dataset	Raw	10EW-P	10EW-I	SSV_4-P	SSV_4-I	SSV_O-P	SSV_O-I
Annealing	90,99	96,06	95,97	97,58	97,64	97,69	97,54
	0,83/2,45	0,29/1,53	0,39/1,39	0,22/1,06	0,30/1,13	0,28/1,10	0,33/0,92
Australian credit	77,16	84,43	84,71	85,86	85,86	85,99	85,68
	0,33/3,34	0,48/2,80	0,62/2,74	0,40/2,63	0,40/2,51	0,48/2,85	0,47/3,12
Wisconsin breast cancer	95,97	96,62	96,54	96,54	96,54	97,41	97,30
	0,11/1,45	0,14/1,41	0,15/1,58	0,21/1,37	0,24/1,35	0,05/1,31	0,11/1,32
Cleveland heart disease	83,62	81,28	81,79	83,77	83,26	83,92	83,30
	0,57/4,78	0,96/4,50	0,68/4,39	0,57/4,65	0,68/4,64	0,86/4,33	1,24/3,67
Japanese credit (crx)	77,39	84,18	83,92	85,90	85,64	85,90	85,67
	0,33/2,97	0,48/2,94	0,55/3,16	0,50/2,55	0,47/2,68	0,50/2,55	0,66/3,07
Pima Indian diabetes	75,56	75,70	75,85	75,34	75,07	76,35	74,91
	0,47/3,32	0,74/3,49	0,74/3,17	0,41/3,45	0,78/3,09	0,36/2,90	0,75/3,60
German credit data	72,41	75,08	74,94	76,20	76,04	76,20	75,53
	0,61/3,12	0,51/2,78	0,58/2,75	0,48/2,77	0,44/2,84	0,48/2,77	0,58/2,88
Glass identification	46,02	57,84	60,73	69,59	66,09	68,97	64,40
	2,14/6,88	1,44/6,22	2,45/7,17	1,45/6,75	2,30/7,40	1,84/6,42	1,76/6,63
Statlog heart	84,22	80,94	81,60	83,28	82,70	84,06	83,07
	0,85/4,21	1,02/4,89	0,95/4,41	0,69/4,64	0,84/4,84	0,57/5,47	0,61/5,59
Hepatitis	85,05	86,52	86,75	86,65	85,01	86,83	85,10
	0,85/5,49	1,02/5,71	1,85/5,11	1,00/5,11	1,12/5,80	0,87/5,51	0,88/5,62
Horse colic	79,35	79,44	79,23	78,82	78,39	79,00	78,86
	0,73/4,48	0,74/4,83	0,93/4,95	0,69/4,58	0,94/4,46	0,66/5,11	0,50/5,43
Hypothyroid	97,74	96,49	96,55	98,25	98,17	98,49	98,26
	0,08/0,43	0,15/0,51	0,20/0,70	0,08/0,38	0,13/0,37	0,09/0,48	0,10/0,45
Iris	95,44	92,76	92,36	93,44	93,13	93,78	92,93
	0,47/3,52	1,05/4,56	1,36/4,77	0,84/4,00	0,93/4,40	1,16/3,85	1,00/3,98
Sick-euthyroid	85,52	91,53	90,62	95,10	94,86	95,65	95,51
	0,36/2,04	0,19/1,05	0,69/2,05	0,17/0,68	0,21/0,67	0,12/0,69	0,24/0,72
Vehicle silhouettes	45,65	61,99	61,71	59,00	57,61	62,49	61,64
	0,85/3,27	1,00/2,88	1,05/3,26	0,62/3,54	0,71/3,96	1,04/3,44	0,97/3,75
Average	79,47	82,72	82,88	84,35	83,73	84,85	83,98

Table 3. Statistical significance of the results differences.

Methods	Nominally			Significantly		
	better	same	worse	better	same	worse
10EW-I vs Raw	10	0	5	8	3	4
SSV_4-I vs Raw	9	0	6	9	5	1
SSV_O-I vs Raw	12	0	3	9	6	0
SSV_4-I vs 10EW-I	10	1	4	4	10	1
SSV_O-I vs 10EW-I	11	0	4	5	10	0
10EW-P vs 10EW-I	8	0	7	0	15	0
SSV_4-P vs SSV_4-I	12	2	1	0	15	0
SSV_O-P vs SSV_O-I	15	0	0	3	12	0

Moreover, the high result of the LD methods is a consequence of 13% lower error for the glass data, and it seems that the two approaches used different data (the reported numbers of classes are different). The 13% difference is also a bit suspicious, since it concerns all the other methods too and is the only one of that magnitude.

There is still some area for future work: it would be interesting to have a criterion to determine the optimal number of split points without an application of a wrapper technique. Moreover, to simplify the search a single n determines the number of intervals for each of the continuous features. It could be more accurate to treat the features independently and, if necessary, use different numbers of splits for different features.

References

1. Kerber, R.: Chimerge: Discretization for numeric attributes. In: National Conference on Artificial Intelligence, AAAI Press (1992) 123–128
2. Liu, H., Setiono, R.: Chi2: Feature selection and discretization of numeric attributes. In: Proceedings of 7th IEEE Int'l Conference on Tools with Artificial Intelligence. (1995)
3. Fayyad, U.M., Irani, K.B.: Multi-interval discretization of continuous-valued attributes for classification learning. In: Proceedings of the 13th International Joint Conference on Artifficial Intelligence, Morgan Kaufmann Publishers (1993) 1022–1027
4. Merz, C.J., Murphy, P.M.: UCI repository of machine learning databases (1998) http://www.ics.uci.edu/~mlearn/MLRepository.html.
5. Dougherty, J., Kohavi, R., Sahami, M.: Supervised and unsupervised discretization of continuous features. In: Proceedings of the ICML. (1995) 194–202
6. Yang, Y., Webb, G.I.: A comparative study of discretization methods for Naive-Bayes classifiers. In: Proceedings of PKAW 2002: The 2002 Pacific Rim Knowledge Acquisition Workshop. (2002) 159–173
7. Grąbczewski, K., Duch, W.: The Separability of Split Value criterion. In: Proceedings of the 5th Conference on Neural Networks and Their Applications, Zakopane, Poland (2000)
8. Duch, W., Winiarski, T., Biesiada, J., Kachel, A.: Feature ranking, selection and discretization. In: Proceedings of the Internatijonal Conference on Artificial Neural Networks 2003. (2003)
9. Grⁱbczewski, K., Jankowski, N.: Transformations of symbolic data for continuous data oriented models. In: Proceedings of the ICANN 2003, Springer (2003)

Comparison of Instance Selection Algorithms II. Results and Comments

Marek Grochowski and Norbert Jankowski

Department of Informatics, Nicholaus Copernicus University
ul. Grudziądzka 5, 87-100 Toruń, Poland, http://www.phys.uni.torun.pl/kis
{grochu|norbert}@phys.uni.torun.pl

Abstract. This paper is an continuation of the accompanying paper with the same main title. The first paper reviewed instance selection algorithms, here results of empirical comparison and comments are presented. Several test were performed mostly on benchmark data sets from the machine learning repository at UCI. Instance selection algorithms were tested with neural networks and machine learning algorithms.

1 Introduction

The survey of different algorithms for instance selection was presented in the accompanying article with the same main title.

The performance of instance selection methods is tested here using k-nearest neighbors model, support vectors machine, SSV decision tree, NRBF (a normalized version of RBF network), FSM model and IncNet (see the accompanying paper for references).

Instance selection algorithms were grouped into noise filters (ENN [1], ENRBF [2,3]), condensation algorithms (CNN [4], CA [5], RNN [6], IB3 [7], GE, RNGE [8], ICF [9], ENRBF2, DROP1-5[10]) and prototype selection algorithms (LVQ [11], MC1 & RMHC [12], ELH, ELGrow and Explore [13], DEL [10]).

2 Results

To test the reliability of instance selection algorithms the performance on several datasets was checked. Nearly all tests were prepared on databases from the Machine Learning Repository at UCI Irvine [14]. One database (skin cancer – 250 train and 26 test instances, 14 attributes, 4 classes) was obtained from Z. Hippe [15]. Each benchmark was tested with 10-fold cross-validation, except for the skin cancer dataset which has separate test file. Cross-validation results were repeated and averaged over 10 runs. Standardization of all data was performed before learning. The following UCI repository datasets were used in tests: Wisconsin breast cancer (699 instances, 9 attributes and two classes), Cleveland heart disease (303 instances, 13 attributes, 2 classes), appendicitis (106

L. Rutkowski et al. (Eds.): ICAISC 2004, LNAI 3070, pp. 580–585, 2004.
© Springer-Verlag Berlin Heidelberg 2004

instances, 8 attributes, two classes), Iris (150 instances, 4 attributes, two classes), wine (178 instances, 13 attributes, 3 classes), Pima indians diabetes (768 instances, 8 attributes, two classes).

Figures 1–6 present information about accuracy on the unseen data and on the compression provided by the selection algorithms. Each figure corresponds to a single classification algorithm (kNN, NRBF, FSM, IncNet, SSV, SVM) tested with several instance selection algorithms (single point); results were averaged over all benchmarks. The horizontal axis shows the compression of the training set in percents (100% = the whole training set). The vertical axis corresponds to accuracy changes on **the test set** for a given instance selection algorithm. The *zero level* is defined by the accuracy obtained by a given classification algorithm trained on the whole training set (kNN, NRBF, etc.). For example "+2" on vertical axis means that the average test accuracy is 2% better than the base algorithm trained using the whole dataset.

In the *dataset reduction* category at the top are MC1, RMHC, LVQ with 1.3% of training set instances left, next are ELGrow (1.35%), Explore (1.43%), DEL (4.91%). It is important that the first three algorithms had compression factor fixed (one instance per class), while algorithms ELGrow, Explore and DEL estimate optimal reduction level automatically depending only on the complexity of the training dataset. As can be seen especially in figures 1 and 2 the performance of the ELH or the ELGrow is worse than that of Explore, and the performance of DEL algorithm falls between them. Next to algorithms Explore and DEL are algorithms ICF, DROP3 and DROP5. Algorithms like LVQ, RMHC, Explore, MC1, DEL and DROP2-4 have got the best performance taking into account accuracy and dataset reduction performance – the upper left parts of figures 1 and 2 – for kNN and NRBF classifiers. It is very important that prototypes extracted from algorithms such as the Explore or RMHC algorithm, that leave only a few instances, can be considered as really simple knowledge representation through prototypes. In most cases Explore extracts extremely small set (a few) of instances and they are very effective (accuracy on unseen data is very high); in cases where Explore is not at the top of accuracy on the unseen data it may be substituted by RMHC, MC1 or DROP2-4 algorithms. For example on the appendicitis database the accuracy of kNN with selection algorithm Explore was 82.7%, and with MC1 was 86.7% (the base performance of kNN was 86.4%)

For kNN and NRBF interesting results were obtained for some prototype selection algorithms, condensation algorithms, as well as for some noise reduction filters, but for FSM, IncNet, SSV or SVM models it is clear that only some noise reduction algorithms (like ENRBF or ENN) can be used, and without any significant gain in accuracy. The selection algorithm ENRBF2 may be considered for models FSM, IncNet or SVM. Noise reduction for these models may stabilize the learning process, however it is not necessary for most of the benchmark. Note that algorithms like Explore, RMHC, ELGrow lead to a complete collapse when used with SSV or SVM.

For tests presented in figures 1–6 LVQ, MC1 and RMHC were configured with one instance per one class.

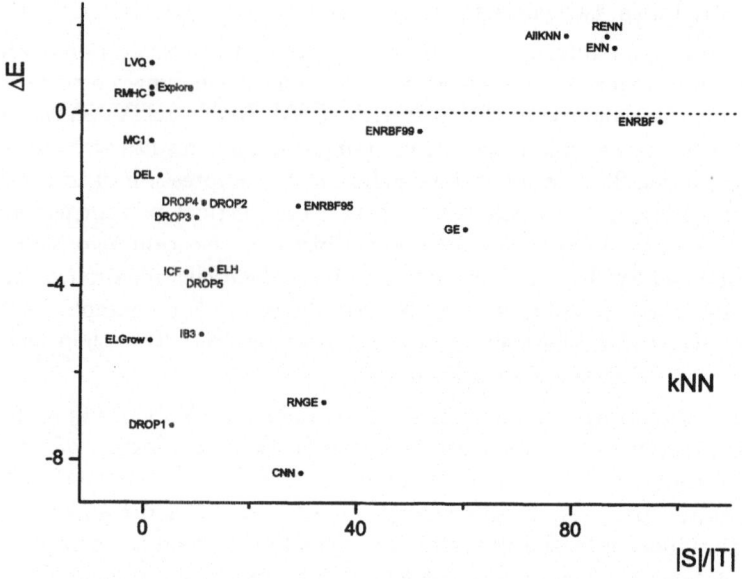

Fig. 1. Classifier: kNN ($\Delta E = 0$ corresponds to accuracy 85.77%)

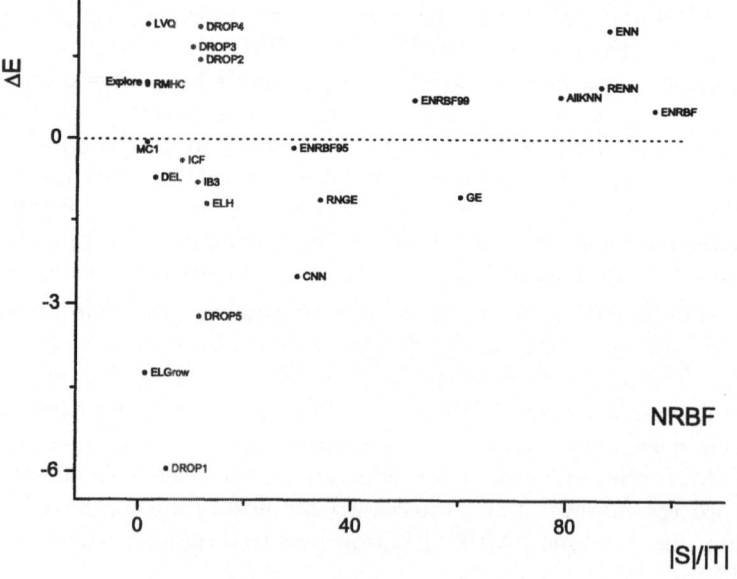

Fig. 2. Classifier: NRBF ($\Delta E = 0$ corresponds to accuracy 84.87%)

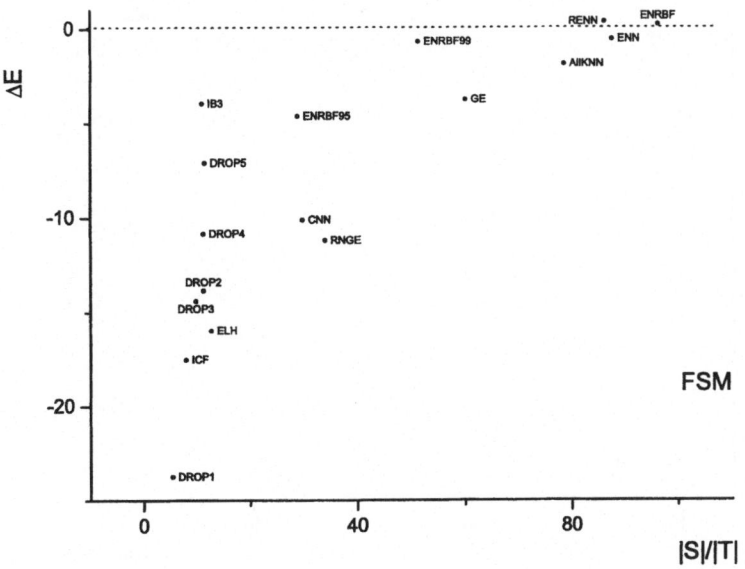

Fig. 3. Classifier: FSM ($\Delta E = 0$ corresponds to accuracy 89.18%)

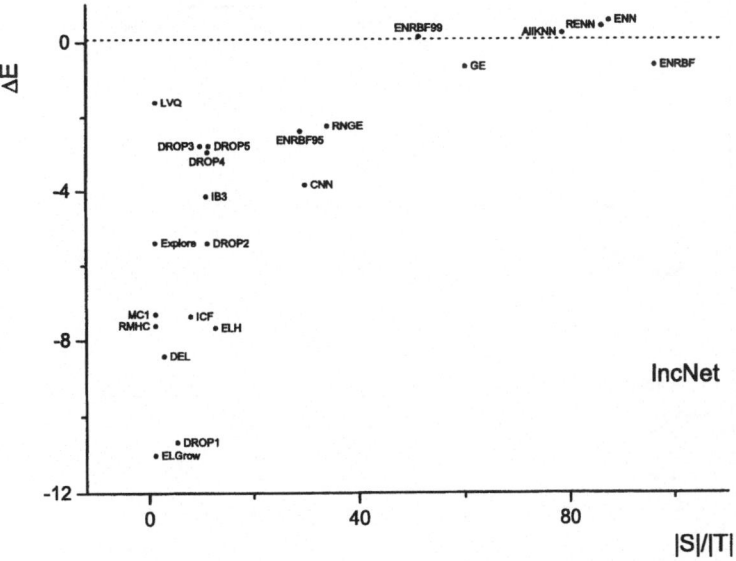

Fig. 4. Classifier: IncNet ($\Delta E = 0$ corresponds to accuracy 88.01%)

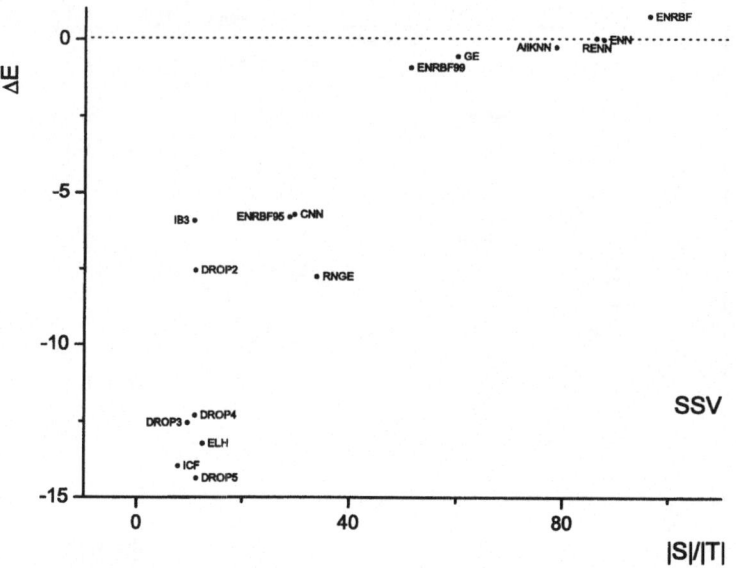

Fig. 5. Classifier: SSV ($\Delta E = 0$ corresponds to accuracy 88.18%)

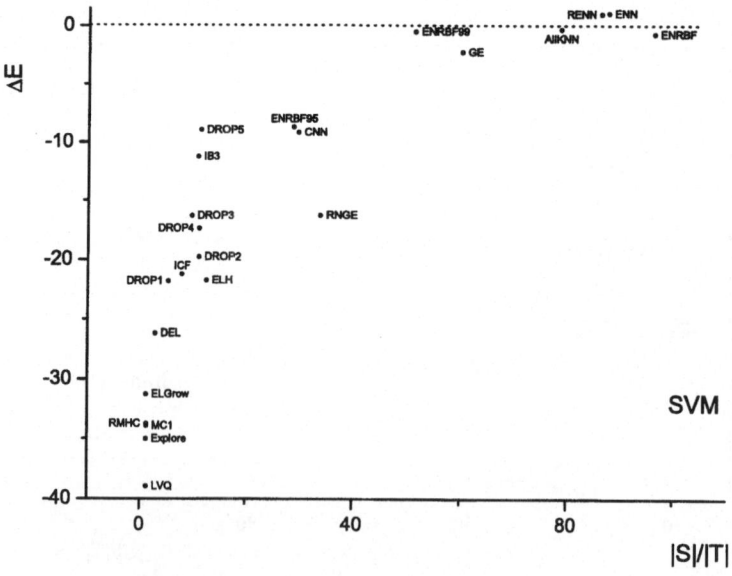

Fig. 6. Classifier: SVM ($\Delta E = 0$ corresponds to accuracy 86.35%)

3   Conclusions

Some of the instance selection algorithms tested in this paper are very interesting. Between the prototype selection algorithms Explore, RMHC, MC1, LVQ, DROP2-4 and DEL, are the most effective. They automatically estimate the number of instances for optimal compression of the training set and reach high accuracy on the unseen data. The RMHC and LVQ algorithms also finished tests with high level of accuracy on the unseen data.

In the group of noise filters ENN algorithm came at the top, especially for kNN & NRBF and ENRBF. These algorithm may stabilize the learning process, except the SSV or SVM models.

References

1. Wilson, D.: Asymptotic properties of nearest neighbor rules using edited data. IEEE Transactions on Systems, Man, and Cybernetics **2** (1972) 408—421
2. Grochowski, M.: Wybór wektorów referencyjnych dla wybranych method klasyfikacji. Master's thesis, Department of Informatics, Nicholas Copernicus University, Poland (2003)
3. Jankowski, N.: Data regularization. In Rutkowski, L., Tadeusiewicz, R., eds.: Neural Networks and Soft Computing, Zakopane, Poland (2000) 209–214
4. Hart, P.E.: The condensed nearest neighbor rule. IEEE Transactions on Information Theory **14** (1968) 515—516
5. Chang, C.L.: Finding prototypes for nearest neighbor classifiers. IEEE Transactions on Computers **23** (1974) 1179—1184
6. Gates, G.: The reduced nearest neighbor rule. IEEE Transactions on Information Theory **18** (1972) 431—433
7. Aha, D.W., Kibler, D., Albert, M.K.: Aha,. Machine Learning **6** (1991) 37—66
8. Bhattacharya, B.K., Poulsen, R.S., Toussaint, G.T.: Application of proximity graphs to editing nearest neighbor decision rule. In: International Symposium on Information Theory, Santa Monica (1981)
9. Brighton, H., Mellish, C.: Advances in instance selection for instance-based learning algorithms. Data Mining and Knowledge Discovery **6** (2002) 153–172
10. Wilson, D.R., Martinez, T.R.: Reduction techniques for instance-based learning algorithms. Machine Learning **38** (2000) 257—286
11. Kohonen, T.: Learning vector quantization for pattern recognition. Technical Report TKK-F-A601, Helsinki University of Technology, Espoo, Finland (1986)
12. Skalak, D.B.: Prototype and feature selection by sampling and random mutation hill climbing algorithms. In: International Conference on Machine Learning. (1994) 293—301
13. Cameron-Jones, R.M.: Instance selection by encoding length heuristic with random mutation hill climbing. In: Proceedings of the Eighth Australian Joint Conference on Artificial Intelligence. (1995) 99—106
14. Merz, C.J., Murphy, P.M.: UCI repository of machine learning databases (1998) http://www.ics.uci.edu/~mlearn/MLRepository.html.
15. Hippe, Z.S., Iwaszek, G.: From research on a new method of development of quasi-optimal decision trees. In Kopotek, M., Michalewicz, M., Wierzcho, S.T., eds.: Intelligent Information Systems IX, Warszawa, Institute of computer science (2000) 31–35

SBL-PM-M: A System for Partial Memory Learning

Karol Grudziński

Department of Physics, Academy of Bydgoszcz
Plac Weyssenhoffa 11, 85-072 Bydgoszcz, Poland
kagru@ab-byd.edu.pl

Abstract. Partial Memory Learning (PML) is a machine learning paradigm in which only a subset of cases generated from an original training set is used for classification. This paper concerns a new method for partial memory learning. The SBL-PM-M method is a completely new model. We evaluate the performance of the new algorithm on several real-world datasets and compare it to a few other PML systems and to the base classifier.

1 Introduction

Partial Memory Learners (PML) [1,2,3,4,5,6] are usually on-line learning systems that select and store a portion of the past learning examples. This paper concerns a new method for partial memory learning.

The SBL-PM-M is a completely new method and is based on minimization of the cost function, which returns the number of errors the classifier makes.

The paper consists of five sections. First the old SBL-PM-B algorithm is briefly described. In the third section a new partial-memory algorithm which we call SBL-PM-M is described. In the fourth section the generalization abilities of all classifiers are compared on real world datasets. The last section concludes the paper.

2 The SBL-PM-B System

SBL-PM-B (formerly SBL-PM) is our own algorithm that has already been described earlier [7,8]. The name SBL-PM-B is slightly misleading as it imposes connection of this algorithm to Similarity Based Methods. SBL is the name of our package, Similarity Based Learner [9], in which this algorithm had been first implemented. PM stands for Partial Memory and B for Basic. This algorithm is however universal and can be built on top of an arbitrary classifier. A description of SBL-PM-B follows.

Cases are removed from the training set taking into account the leave-one-out classification accuracy value on the training set and the value computed by classifying the training set as the test set, given partial memory as the training set. A quotation from our earlier paper, [7], provides the best description of the SBL-PM-B algorithm:

L. Rutkowski et al. (Eds.): ICAISC 2004, LNAI 3070, pp. 586–591, 2004.
© Springer-Verlag Berlin Heidelberg 2004

1. 'Set the partial memory of the system (reference set) to the entire training set, $\mathcal{R}=\mathcal{T}=\{R_i\}, i = 1..N$.
2. Set the target accuracy Δ performing the leave-one-out test on $\mathcal{T}$; lowering the target accuracy will reduce the final number of the reference vectors.
3. For $i = 1$ to N
   a) Set the temporary reference set to $\mathcal{R}'=\mathcal{R}-\{R_i\}$.
   b) Using the leave-one-out test and the current reference set $\mathcal{R}'$ calculate the prediction accuracy A_c on the whole training set $\mathcal{T}$.
   c) If $A_c \geq \Delta$ set $\mathcal{R}=\mathcal{R}'$

Vectors are sequentially eliminated from the reference set. If the classification accuracy drops below the accuracy Δ obtained in the leave-one-out test on the entire training set, the case from the reference set must be retained, otherwise it can be eliminated. The threshold value $(0 < \Delta < 100)$ (in percents) may also be given by the user, allowing for some degradation of the performance as a penalty for reduction of the reference set. The final reference set should be significantly smaller than the original training set with minimal degradation of the prediction accuracy. By setting the value of Δ at the beginning of calculations the number of cases that will remain in the partial memory is controlled to a certain extent. Δ can be optimized by running the SBL-PM procedure for several values of Δ'.

3   The SBL-PM-M Algorithm

The idea of SBL-PM-M is very simple. Each training vector is assigned a binary weight with the value of 1 indicating that this case takes part in the classification process and otherwise is not taken into account. The number of weights is equal to the number of samples in the training set which are optimized with a non-gradient minimization routine. The cost function returns the number of errors the classifier makes. This process corresponds to selection of attributes through minimization (also possible with the SBL software). So far we have tried only the simplex minimization method [10].

Such a minimization process is much harder than in the case of the weighting of attributes [11,12] since the number of adaptive parameters in the reference selection is usually much higher than in the case of weighting of attributes. However proper construction of the minimization termination criterion allows us to arrive at a reasonable solution already after 150 – 200 cost evaluations. The total number of cost evaluations is increased by the number equal to the number of training samples + 1 which is required to initialize the simplex. Similarly to SBL-PM-B, in SBL-PM-M there is a way to roughly control the number of cases retained by initializing the simplex (randomly) with zeros and ones generated with a different probability. The probability of the number of ones with which we initialize simplex is given as the input parameter. The value of 0.5 indicates that we start the learning with approximately the half of the size of the training set. The number of samples retained depends on this parameter, the greater the number of ones, the more samples will be retained. It is hard to estimate the number of samples retained as is depends on the initial number of training samples we start from, the classifier, the maximal number of the cost evaluations (which is also the input parameter) and data itself. The output of the model is the reference set with which the unseen cases are classified.

Time consumption of SBL-PM-M is directly proportional to the number of cost evaluations and the number of training samples used. The larger is the training dataset, the more cost evaluations is needed to assure low variance of the model. To many cost evaluations may lead to overfitting.

4   Numerical Experiments

The results of SBL-PM-M are presented here and compared to our SBL-PM-B model and our base classifier (k-NN). The results of Wilson's and Martinez implementation of k-NN, and their models: RT1, RT2, RT3 and H-IB3 are taken from [4] and are placed below ours. Our aim is to illustrate the influence of the reduction of the training set size on classification. The results in tables are sorted with respect to the accuracy attained by systems on test sets. Our k-NN training results have been obtained by performing leave-one-out cross-validation on training partitions. The SBL-PM-B and SBL-PM-M training results come from performing the k-NN test on the reduced training set ($\mathcal{T}$- $\mathcal{R}$) taking the partial-memory set ($\mathcal{R}$) as a training set. In all our experiments 10-fold stratified cross-validation test repeated 10 times has been used. For every SBL-PM-M result the probability with which ones (i.e. the weights of cases taking part in the classification) are inserted in the simplex is given right after the method name. Following this number, in the square brackets, the restriction on the maximum number of the cost evaluations is given. In the case of Wilson's and Martinez experiments, the average number of samples retained has been calculated by us from the available parameters. What concerns the SBL-PM-B method, the letter 'A' following the name of this model denotes that the parameter Δ was set to the leave-one-out value attained by k-NN on the training set.

The first dataset used for our study is the well known iris dataset [13]. It consists of four attributes (without a class), 150 cases belonging to three classes, there are 50 cases per class. The SBL-PM-M results on the test set are comparable to the ones attained by the other classifiers. The SBL-PM-B model stores much fewer cases in the partial memory than other methods. The summary of the results obtained for this data is given in Table 1.

Promoters is the second dataset that has been used in our experiments [13]. There are 106 samples equally distributed in two classes, 57 attributes. The data is purely symbolic. In this case SBL-PM-M performs much better than SBL-PM-B and comparable to the other methods. The results from our experiments on this dataset are given in Table 2.

The last dataset used for our study is the well-known breast-cancer (Wisconsin) database [13]. It consists of 699 records, 11 attributes (including class). Vectors belonging to the majority class constitute about 66% of the size of the entire dataset. The SBL-PM-M results are comparable to those achieved by Wilson and Martinez. The summary of the results obtained for this data is given in Table 3.

Table 1. Results for the 10-fold CV Test on Iris Data.

System	Train %, Size			Test %
k-NN, k=1, Euclidean	95.4 ± 0.9	135.0	(100%)	95.6 ± 0.6
SBL-PM-B-A, k=1, Euclidean	96.2 ± 0.9	4.9	(3.6%)	94.7 ± 1.7
SBL-PM-M-0.5-[250] k=1, Euclidean	93.4 ± 1.2	39.2	(29%)	94.1 ± 1.4
SBL-PM-M-0.1-[1000] k=1, Euclidean	91.4 ± 2.5	17.1	(12.7%)	92.3 ± 1.9
SBL-PM-M-0.05-[2000] k=1, Euclidean	90.0 ± 2.3	12.4	(9.2%)	90.2 ± 2.3
RT3, k=3, HVDM	?	20.0	(14.8%)	95.3 ± ?
RT2, k=3, HVDM	?	22.8	(16.9%)	95.3 ± ?
k-NN, k=3, HVDM	?	135.0	(100%)	94.0 ± ?
H-IB3, k = 3, HVDM	?	14.9	(11.0%)	92.0 ± ?
RT1, k=3, HVDM	?	15.8	(11.7%)	89.3 ± ?

Table 2. Results for the 10-fold CV Test on Promoters Data.

System	Train %, Size			Test %
k-NN, k=1, VDM	90.2 ± 0.5	96.0	(100%)	90.3 ± 1.6
SBL-PM-M-0.5-[250], k=1, VDM	90.6 ± 1.0	44.8	(47.0%)	87.4 ± 1.7
SBL-PM-M-0.3-[250], k=1, VDM	90.8 ± 1.2	30.5	(31.8%)	86.5 ± 3.1
SBL-PM-M-0.2-[250], k=1, VDM	88.4 ± 1.5	10.1	(10.5%)	84.2 ± 3.4
SBL-PM-B-A, k=1, VDM	90.7 ± 0.5	22.0	(22.9%)	77.1 ± 3.3
k-NN, k=3, HVDM	?	96.0	(100%)	94.0 ± ?
RT1, k=3, HVDM	?	7.9	(8.2%)	85.0 ± ?
RT3, k=3, HVDM	?	16.0	(16.7%)	86.8 ± ?
RT2, k=3, HVDM	?	17.1	(17.8%)	87.9 ± ?
H-IB3, k = 3, HVDM	?	9.6	(10.0%)	88.6 ± ?

5   Conclusions and Further Research

The algorithms described in this paper are designed to provide an alternative, case-based way of data explanation to the rule discovery analysis. They can also serve as a preprocessing step for large datasets in order to speed up classification and learning of other models. In the last case, a sufficiently large number of samples should be retained to avoid a 'curse of dimensionality' problem.

It is not a surprise that partial memory systems described here usually do not improve but degrade the performance of the classifiers employed, as most of

Table 3. Results for the 10-fold CV Test on Breast-Cancer (Wisconsin) Data.

System	Train %	Size		Test %
k-NN, k=1, Euclidean	95.7 ± 0.1	630.0	(100%)	95.7 ± 0.4
SBL-PM-B-A, k=1, Euclidean	96.0 ± 0.3	5.4	(0.9%)	95.7 ± 0.7
SBL-PM-M-0.025-[250], k=1, Euclidean	93.0 ± 1.7	17.5	(2.7%)	93.1 ± 2.2
SBL-PM-M-0.01-[500], k=1, Euclidean	91.9 ± 1.5	9.2	(1.5%)	91.6 ± 1.5
SBL-PM-M-0.005-[250], k=1, Euclidean	89.5 ± 5.3	6.4	(1.0%)	89.5 ± 5.3
SBL-PM-M-0.001-[500], k=1, Euclidean	89.3 ± 4.3	5.1	(0.8%)	89.5 ± 4.2
k-NN, k=3, HVDM	?	630.0	(100%)	96.3 ± ?
RT3, k=3, HVDM	?	22.7	(3.6%)	96.1 ± ?
RT2, k=3, HVDM	?	36.5	(5.8%)	96.1 ± ?
H-IB3, k = 3, HVDM	?	16.4	(2.6%)	95.7 ± ?
RT1, k=3, HVDM	?	16.4	(2.6%)	94.0 ± ?

the partial memory learning algorithms do. However, after inclusion of them in the similarity based metalearning model [14,15] they could lead to increase of the prediction ability of the methods based on the SBM framework.

So far only the preliminary numerical experiments had been done with the k-nearest neighbors algorithm which had been used as a classification engine. Experiments with other classifiers are in preparation and will be a subject of a separate paper.

SBL-PM-M can give comparable results to other methods and is a valuable PML model but requires tuning the parameters very carefully to get optimal results. Relatively high variance of the results obtained with this method can be eliminated by increasing the number of cost evaluations.

Acknowledgments. Support by Department of Physics, Academy of Bydgoszcz, which made taking part of the author of this paper in this conference possible is gratefully acknowledged.

References

1. Maloof, M. A., Michalski, R. S.: AQ-PM: A System for Partial Memory Learning. Intelligent Information Systems, Ustroń, Poland (1999) 70-79
2. Maloof, M., Michalski, R. S.: Selecting Examples for Partial Memory Learning. Machine Learning, **41**, (2000) 27-52
3. Maloof, M., Michalski, R. S.: Incremental Learning with Partial Instance Memory. Proceedings of the Thirteenth International Symposium on Methodologies for Intelligent Systems, Lyon, France, (2002), In Foundations of Intelligent Systems, Lecture Notes in Artificial Intelligence, (2366), Berlin:Springer-Verlag, 16-27
4. Wilson, D. R., Martinez, T. R.: Instance Pruning Techniques. In Fisher, D.: Machine Learning: Proceedings of the Fourteenth International Conference. Morgan Kaufmann Publishers, San Francisco, CA, (1997), 404-417.

5. Wilson, D. R., Martinez, T. R.: Reduction Techniques for Instance-Based Learning Algorithms. Machine Learning, **38**, (2000), 257-286
6. Grochowski, M.: Selecting Reference Vectors in Selected Methods of Classification. MSc. Thesis, Nicholaus Copernicus University, Department of Applied Informatics, Toruń, Poland, (2003) (In Polish)
7. Grudziński, K., Duch, W.: SBL-PM: A Simple Algorithm for Selection of Reference Instances for Similarity-Based Methods. Intelligent Information Systems, Bystra, Poland (2000), in Advances in Soft Computing, Physica-Verlag (Springer), 99-108
8. Duch, W.: Similarity Based Methods: a general framework for classification, approximation and association. Control and Cybernetics 29 4, (2000), 1-30
9. SBL, Similarity Based Learner, Software Developed by Karol Grudziński. Nicholaus Copernicus University, 1997-2002, Academy of Bydgoszcz 2002-2004
10. Nelder, J. A., Mead, R.: A simplex method for function minimization. Computer Journal **7** (1965), 308-313
11. Duch, W., Grudziński, K.: The weighted k-NN method with selection of features and its neural realization. Fourth Conference on Neural Networks and Their Applications, Zakopane, Poland (1999), 191-196
12. Duch, W., Grudziński, K.: Weighting and Selection of Features in Similarity-Based Methods. Intelligent Information Systems, Ustroń, Poland, (1998), 32-36
13. Mertz, C. J., Murphy, P. M.: UCI repository of machine learning databases. http://www.ics.uci.edu/pub/machine-learning-data-bases
14. Duch, W., Grudziński, K.: Meta-Learning: searching in the model space. Proceedings of the International Conference on Neural Information Processing, Shanghai, (2001), Vol. I, 235-240
15. Duch, W., Grudziński, K.: Meta-learning via search combined with parameter optimization, Intelligent Information Systems, Sopot, Poland, (2002), In Advances in Soft Computing, Physica-Verlag (Springer), 13-22

Relevance LVQ versus SVM

Barbara Hammer[1], Marc Strickert[1], and Thomas Villmann[2]

[1] Department of Mathematics/Computer Science,
University of Osnabrück, D-49069 Osnabrück, Germany
[2] Clinic for Psychotherapy and Psychosomatic Medicine, University of Leipzig,
Karl-Tauchnitz-Straße 25, D-04107 Leipzig, Germany

Abstract. The support vector machine (SVM) constitutes one of the most successful current learning algorithms with excellent classification accuracy in large real-life problems and strong theoretical background. However, a SVM solution is given by a not intuitive classification in terms of extreme values of the training set and the size of a SVM classifier scales with the number of training data. Generalized relevance learning vector quantization (GRLVQ) has recently been introduced as a simple though powerful expansion of basic LVQ. Unlike SVM, it provides a very intuitive classification in terms of prototypical vectors the number of which is independent of the size of the training set. Here, we discuss GRLVQ in comparison to the SVM and point out its beneficial theoretical properties which are similar to SVM whereby providing sparse and intuitive solutions. In addition, the competitive performance of GRLVQ is demonstrated in one experiment from computational biology.

1 Introduction

Starting with the pioneering work of Vapnik and Chervonenkis, empirical risk minimization and structural risk minimization have been identified and quantified as the two goals when training a supervised machine learning classifier [15]. Thereby, the structural risk is not necessarily directly connected to the number of parameters; rather the interior capacity of the function class implemented by the respective model measured in terms of the VC dimension, for example, is the relevant quantity. Because of this fact, effective machine learning models can be designed also for very high dimensional data and complex underlying regularities.

The support vector machine constitutes a prime example of a machine learner which directly aims at structural risk minimization during training [3]. The structural risk of the SVM is given by the classification margin. A large margin ensures good mathematical generalization bounds and, in practice, excellent generalization ability of SVMs. Two further benefits of the SVM can be observed: the dual Lagrangian problem of SVM training can be solved optimum in polynomial time, thus SVM training is guaranteed to converge to a global optimum. Input data are implicitly mapped to a high dimensional feature space by a kernel, which offers a natural interface to adapt the model to specific settings and to integrate prior knowledge [5]. However, one drawback of the SVM is the expansion of a solution in terms of the dual Lagrangian variables: given training data $(x^i, y_i) \in \mathbb{R}^n \times \{-1, 1\}$ and a kernel $k : \mathbb{R}^n \times \mathbb{R}^n \to \mathbb{R}$, the final SVM classifier into the two classes -1 and 1 is of the form

$$x \mapsto \begin{cases} 1 & \text{if } \sum_i \alpha_i y_i k(x^i, x) \geq \theta \\ -1 & \text{otherwise} \end{cases}$$

L. Rutkowski et al. (Eds.): ICAISC 2004, LNAI 3070, pp. 592–597, 2004.
© Springer-Verlag Berlin Heidelberg 2004

where α_i are the dual Lagrangian variables optimized during training, and θ is the bias. The Lagrangian variables α_i are nonvanishing for support vectors x^i. Support vectors are all points which are errors, all points which have a too small margin, and points which are correctly classified but have a minimum margin, i.e. 'extreme' points of the training set. Thus the solution is not formulated in terms of 'typical' points but in terms of 'atypical' training examples. In addition, the number of support vectors is usually given by a fraction of the training set, i.e. the size of the found solution scales linearly with the size of the training set. Thus training is quadratic with respect to the training set size, and classification is linear. Alternatives to the SVM which expand solutions in terms of typical vectors have been proposed, such as Bayes-point machines [10].

Here, we focus on another very intuitive learning model which is based on a different training paradigm: prototype based learning vector quantization (LVQ) as proposed by Kohonen [11]. We discuss a recent extension of simple LVQ which integrates an adaptive metric, and we show that the new model has the same beneficial properties as SVM: it converges to a global optimum, it allows to integrate prior knowledge in a kernelized version, and it can be interpreted as a large margin optimizer for which mathematical dimensionality independent generalization bounds exist. In contrast to SVM, the method provides an expansion in terms of typical vectors, and the solution does not scale with the size of the training set, thus training time is linear in the number of training patterns and the classification effort is constant. In addition, we demonstrate that the method is competitive to SVM in one experiment.

2 GRLVQ

Generalized relevance learning vector quantization (GRLVQ) has been proposed in [9] as an extension of simple LVQ. Assume a finite set of training data $(x^i, y_i) \in \mathbb{R}^n \times \{1, \ldots, C\}$ is given, C being the number of different classes. A GRLVQ network represents every class c by a finite set of prototypes in $\mathbb{R}^n$. A prototype is denoted by w^r, c_r being its class. A new signal is classified by the winner-takes-all rule $x \mapsto c(x) = c_r$ such that $d^\lambda(x, w^r)$ is minimum, whereby $d^\lambda(x, w^r)$ is the scaled squared Euclidean distance $d^\lambda(x, w^r) = \sum_i \lambda_i (x_i - w_i^r)^2$ with relevance terms $\lambda_i \geq 0$ for each dimension i which add up to 1, i.e. $\sum_i \lambda_i = 1$.

Training adapts the prototypes and the relevance terms according to the given data. The training rule is formally derived as a stochastic gradient descent method on the cost function

$$E_{\mathrm{GRLVQ}} = \sum_i \mathrm{sgd}\left(\frac{d_{r+} - d_{r-}}{d_{r+} + d_{r-}}\right)$$

where $\mathrm{sgd}(x) = (1 + \exp(-x))^{-1}$ is the logistic function, the sum is over all training vectors x^i, d_{r+} denotes the distance of x^i from the closest prototype w_{r+} with the same class as x^i, and d_{r-} denotes the distance of x^i from the closest prototype w_{r-} with a different class label than x^i. Note that the nominator $d_{r+} - d_{r-}$ is negative if and only if the point x^i is classified correctly. Thus minimization of the cost function aims at maximizing the number of correctly classified points.

The learning rule of GRLVQ can be derived thereof taking the gradients of the summands. The qualitative form of the update rules is the same as for basic LVQ: having presented a point x^i, the closest correct prototype is adapted by $\triangle w_{r+} = \eta \cdot c_1 \cdot$

$(w^{r^+} - x^i)$, where η is the learning rate. c_1 is a factor the precise form of which is of no importance for this article. The closest incorrect prototype is adapted by $\triangle w_{r-} = -\eta \cdot c_2 \cdot (w^{r^-} - x^i)$, c_2 being another factor, and the relevance terms are adapted by $\triangle \lambda_l = -\eta \cdot (c_3 \cdot (w_l^{r^+} - x_l^i)^2 - c_4 \cdot (w_l^{r^-} - x_l^i)^2)$, followed by normalization, c_3 and c_4 being additional factors. It has been discussed in [9] that this update scheme can be interpreted as a straightforward application of Hebbian learning, as used for basic LVQ. As pointed out in [9], where also the precise update formulas can be found, the additional scaling terms c_i and the adaptation of the metric via relevance terms leads to a stable and efficient alternative of original LVQ which can also deal with very high dimensional and heterogeneous data.

Unlike SVM, a GRLVQ classifier is formulated in terms of prototypes. These are adapted during training such that typical positions of the data set are found; thus they provide a very intuitive classification. In addition the number of prototypes is fixed and it has to be chosen according to the number of modes of the underlying distribution, but it does not depend on the number of concrete training examples.

2.1 Local Optima

GRLVQ as introduced above constitutes a stochastic gradient descent method on a cost function, thus it might converge to a local optimum of the cost function. This fact can be prevented introducing neighborhood cooperation of the prototypes as proposed in [6]. In the article [6], the cost function of GRLVQ is merged with the cost function of Neural Gas (NG), which constitutes an unsupervised and very reliable clustering algorithm [12]. NG introduces a data optimum neighborhood cooperation of the prototypes such that initialization of the prototypes has almost no effect on the training result and the prototypes spread faithfully among the data points. As demonstrated in [6], the combination of NG with GRLVQ allows to apply GRLVQ also to highly multimodal settings, and the modification reliably converges to global optima of the GRLVQ cost function.

2.2 Kernelization

GRLVQ relies on the weighted Euclidean metric. Because of adaptive relevance terms, irrelevant and noisy dimensions can automatically be detected and the method can also deal with high dimensional input data. However, nonlinear transformations of the input data and correlations of the input dimensions are not accounted for and the weighted Euclidean metric might be an inappropriate similarity measure for such situations. GRLVQ (and also the combination with NG) is formulated in an abstract way as cost minimization. Therefore we can achieve greater flexibility of the method by just substituting the Euclidian similarity measure d^λ by another problem dependent differentiable similarity measure with possibly adaptive parameters λ in the cost function. For every such choice the update formulas of GRLVQ can formally be derived taking the derivatives. Thus prior knowledge can be integrated into GRLVQ using a different similarity measure in the cost function. This new version with similarity measure $\tilde{d}^\lambda$ instead of d^λ can be interpreted as a kernelized of standard GRLVQ iff a function Φ exists such that $\tilde{d}(x,y) = d^\lambda(\Phi(x), \Phi(y))$ holds. The article [13] discusses conditions under which such Φ can be found. A sufficient condition is, for example, that $\tilde{d}$ is symmetric with $\tilde{d}(0,0) = 0$, and $-\tilde{d}$ being conditionally positive definite. Examples for alternative kernels especially suited e.g. for time series data have been proposed in [7].

2.3 Large Margin Bounds

Generalization bounds for standard LVQ have recently been presented in the article [4]. GRLVQ differs from LVQ in the essential property that the metric is also adapted during training, thus its capacity is larger. Nevertheless, it is possible to derive dimensionality independent large margin bounds for GRLVQ networks: assume the class of GRLVQ classifiers with p prototypes, two classes, adaptive squared Euclidean metric, and weights and inputs restricted to the length b is considered. The empirical loss of a given training set is the number of misclassified points. To derive a large margin bound, this loss is modified in analogy to [1] in the following way: we fix a margin parameter $\rho > 0$. The 'security' or margin of the classification of a point x^i is given by the quantity $-d_{r+} + d_{r-}$, the distance of the point from the closest correct prototype compared to the closest incorrect one. If this term is negative, the classification is incorrect. If it is positive, it is correct, but possibly only with a small margin. We define the loss function

$$L : \mathbb{R} \to \mathbb{R}, \ t \mapsto \begin{cases} 1 & \text{if } t \leq 0 \\ 1 - t/\rho & \text{if } 0 < t \leq \rho \\ 0 & \text{otherwise} \end{cases}$$

and the empirical error including the margin, given m training points x^i,

$$\hat{E}_m^L := \sum_{i=1}^{m} L(-d_{r+} + d_{r-})/m$$

This error collects all misclassification and it also punishes all classifications which are correct, but which have a margin smaller than ρ. We are, of course, not interested in this empirical loss, but in the generalization ability of a given GRLVQ network, i.e. the quantity

$$E := P(-d_{r+} + d_{r-} \leq 0)$$

for an arbitrary data point (x, y) chosen according to a fixed probability measure P on $\mathbb{R}^n \times \{0, 1\}$. If the training points (x^i, y_i) are chosen independent and identically distributed according to P, one can show that the error E deviates from the empirical error $\hat{E}_m^L$ by a term of order

$$\frac{p^2}{\rho \cdot \sqrt{m}} \cdot (b^3 + \sqrt{\ln 1/\delta})$$

with confidence δ [8]. This bound does not depend on the input dimensionality, thus GRLVQ is well suited also for high dimensional input data. Rather, the larger the margin ρ, the better the generalization bound. Remarkably, the margin is the security according to which the classification is done, i.e. the term $-d_{r+} + d_{r-}$. This term is included in the nominator of the cost function of GRLVQ. Thus GRLVQ directly aims at margin optimization during training.

3 Experiments

Having discussed the analogy of GRLVQ and SVM with respect to large margin generalization bounds, convergence to a global optimum, and flexibility by a different choice

Table 1. Accuracy (in %) of various methods achieved on the IPsplice dataset, the classification accuracy on the test set is reported for the models. The results for alternatives to GRLVQ are taken from [14].

$GRLVQ_{EUC}$	$GRLVQ_{LIK}$	HMM	SVM_{LIK}	SVM_{TOP}	SVM_{FK}
95.6	96.5	94	96.3	94.6	94.7

of the similarity measure, we add an experiment where we compare several recent classification results achieved by the SVM with GRLVQ networks. The task is to distinguish pieces of human DNA according to the three classes donor, acceptor, or neither. These classes refer to the borders between coding and non-coding regions of the DNA. The data set is the publicly available IPSplice data set from the UCI repository [2], containing 765 acceptors, 767 donors, and 1654 decoys. The inputs are given by 60 nucleotides around a potential splice site, whereby we encode the 4 nucleotides T, C, G, A in $\mathbb{R}^3$ Thus the input dimensionality is 180.

GRLVQ is trained with 8 prototypes per class, the standard weighted Euclidean metric, and, alternatively, the locality improved metric (LIK) which is designed to take local correlations of time series into account. LIK first adds up the distances of entries in small consecutive windows (in our case windows of radius 3 to account for potential reading frames). The accumulated distances within windows are taken to the power of $d = 3$, thus local correlations are computed. The result of all windows is afterwards accumulated weighted with adaptive relevance terms λ_i. Training has been done for 2000 epochs and the learning rates have been optimized for this data set. Initial neighborhood cooperation of NG has been included to ensure convergence to a global optimum.

Results of a 10-fold crossvalidation of GRLVQ with the standard metric (EUC) and LIK are reported in Table1. The result is compared to the classification accuracy achieved by hidden Markov models (HMM), and the SVM with different kernels, the locality improved kernel, and two kernels derived from a statistical model (TOP and FK) [14]. Note that the accuracy of our method is competitive to the solutions found by SVM, whereby the achieved classifiers are very sparse for our setting (only 8 prototypes per class) and the training complexity is only linear in the size of the training set.

Interestingly, the relevance profile achieved by GRLVQ mirrors biological knowledge. As depicted in Fig. 1, the relevance terms are maximum in the direct neighborhood of the potential splice site (place 0), indicating consensus strings at this region. In addition, the left part is emphasized a bit more than the right one, corresponding to a pyrimidine rich region before potential acceptors.

4   Conclusions

We have discussed the classifier GRLVQ in comparison to the SVM and we have pointed out its similar theoretical properties: it constitutes a large margin optimizer with convergence to a global optimum and large flexibility due to a general metric. Thereby, GRLVQ provides more intuitive solutions in terms of typical vectors than SVM, and the size of the found classifier does not scale with the size of the training set. These theoretical facts have been accompanied by one experiment. Thus, GRLVQ constitutes a valuable alternative to SVMs.

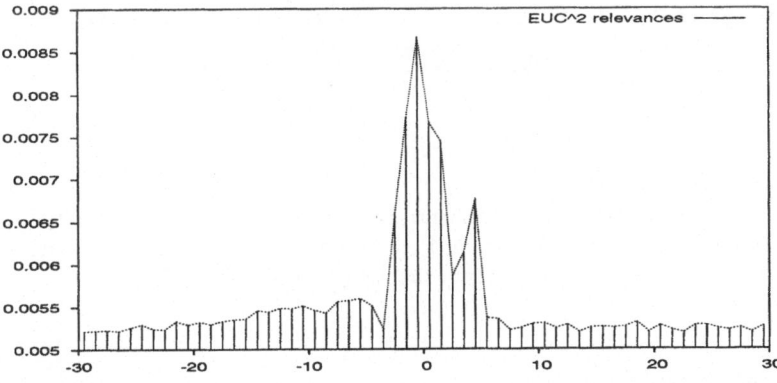

Fig. 1. Relevance profile for the weighted Euclidean similarity measure for the IPSplice data set. Each position shows the average over the successive relevance factors for the four nucleotides at one position of the window.

References

1. P.L. Bartlett and S. Mendelson. Rademacher and Gaussian complexities: risk bounds and structural results. *Journal of Machine Learning and Research* 3:463-482, 2002.
2. C.L. Blake and C. J. Merz, UCI Repository of machine. learning databases, Irvine, CA: University of California, Department of Information and Computer Science.
3. C. Burges. A tutorial on support vector machines for pattern recognition. *Knowledge Discovery and Data Mining*, 2(2), 1998.
4. K. Crammer, R. Gilad-Bachrach, A. Navot, and A. Tishby. Margin analysis of the LVQ algorithm. In: *NIPS 2002*.
5. T. Gärtner. A survey of kernels for structured data. *SIGKDD Explorations* 5(2):49-58, 2003.
6. B. Hammer, M. Strickert, and T. Villmann. Learning vector quantization for multimodal data. In J.R. Dorronsoro, editor, *ICANN'02*, pages 370-375. Springer, 2002.
7. B. Hammer, M. Strickert, and T. Villmann. Supervised Neural Gas with General Similarity Measure. To appear in Neural Processing Letters.
8. B. Hammer, M. Strickert, and T. Villmann. On the generalization ability of GRLVQ networks. Osnabrücker Schriften zur Mathematik, Preprint, no. 249, 10/2003.
9. B. Hammer and T. Villmann. Generalized relevance learning vector quantization. *Neural Networks*, 15:1059–1068, 2002.
10. R. Herbrich, T. Graepel, and C. Campbell. Bayes point machines. *Journal of Machine Learning Research*, 1:245–279, 2001.
11. T. Kohonen. *Self-Organizing Maps*. Springer, 1995.
12. T. Martinetz, S.G. Berkovich, and K.J. Schulten. 'Neural-gas' networks for vector quantization and its application to time-series prediction. *IEEE Transactions on Neural Networks*, 4(4):558–569, 1993.
13. B. Schölkopf. *The kernel trick for distances*. Technical Report MSR-TR-2000-51. Microsoft Research, Redmond, WA, 2000.
14. S. Sonnenburg, G.Rätsch, A. Jagota, and K.-R. Müller. New methods for splice site recognition. In: J. R. Dorronsoro (ed.), *ICANN'2002*, pages 329–336, Springer, 2002.
15. V. Vapnik and A. Chervonenkis. On the uniform convergence of relative frequencies of events to their probabilities. *Theory of Probability and its Applications* 16(2):264-280, 1971.

Comparison of Instances Seletion Algorithms I. Algorithms Survey

Norbert Jankowski and Marek Grochowski

Department of Informatics, Nicholaus Copernicus University
ul. Grudziądzka 5, 87-100 Toruń, Poland, http://www.phys.uni.torun.pl/kis
{norbert|grochu}@phys.uni.torun.pl

Abstract. Several methods were proposed to reduce the number of instances (vectors) in the learning set. Some of them extract only *bad* vectors while others try to remove as many instances as possible without significant degradation of the reduced dataset for learning. Several strategies to shrink training sets are compared here using different neural and machine learning classification algorithms. In part II (the **accompanying paper**) results on benchmarks databases have been presented.

1 Introduction

Most algorithms to train artificial neural networks or machine learning methods use all vectors from the training dataset. However, there are several reasons to reduce the original training set to smaller one. The first of them is to reduce the noise in original dataset because some learning algorithms may be noise-fragile (for example, plain linear discrimination methods [1]). The second reason to shrink the training set is to reduce the amount of computation, especially for instance-based learning (or lazy-learning) algorithms [2] such as the k-nearest neighbors [3], or for huge training sets. The third and relatively new reason to use vector selection appeared together with new prototype selection algorithms. These algorithms shrink training sets sometimes even below 1% of original size keeping the accuracy for unseen vectors high. As the results of shrinking good prototype vectors are selected. Such prototypes may be seen as knowledge representation — each prototype represent a cluster in simple[1] Voronoi diagram.

Probably the first instance selection algorithm was proposed by Hart in the Condensed Nearest Neighbor Rule (CNN) [4]. As will be shown below CNN condenses on the average the number of vectors three times. The performance of CNN algorithm is not good, but this model inspired construction of new methods such as SNN by Ritter et al. [5], RNN by Gates [6] or ENN by Wilson [7]. A group of three algorithms were inspired by *encoding length* principle [8]. Other algorithms were derived from graph theory [9], sets theory [10] or Monte Carlo sampling [11].

Typically the performance of selection methods has been tested usually only on the k-nearest neighbors model. Tests of the performance of instance selection

---

[1] Simple because of few prototypes.

L. Rutkowski et al. (Eds.): ICAISC 2004, LNAI 3070, pp. 598–603, 2004.
© Springer-Verlag Berlin Heidelberg 2004

methods is carried in this paper on machine learning algorithms and neural network algorithms. From the ML group of algorithms the k-nearest neighbor, support vectors machine [12] and SSV decision tree [13] has been chosen. From the artificial neural network domain the NRBF (a normalized version of RBF network), FSM model [14] and IncNet [15] algorithms have been selected.

2   Short Survey of Instance Selection Algorithms

Algorithms for selection of instances may be divided in three application-type groups: noise filters, condensation algorithms and prototype searching algorithms. Because of space limitation full description cannot be given here but details of algorithms presented below may be found in the bibliographical links. Let's assume that there is a training set $\mathcal{T}$ which consists of pairs $\langle \mathbf{x}_i, y_i \rangle, i = 1, \dots, n$, where $\mathbf{x}_i$ defines input vector of attributes and y_i defines the corresponding class label.

2.1   Noise Filters

Edited Nearest Neighbor (ENN) algorithm was created in 1972 by Wilson [7]. The main idea of ENN is to remove given instance if its class does not agree with majority class of its neighbors. ENN starts from original training set.

Repeated ENN was also proposed by Wilson. The only difference is that the process of ENN is repeated as long as any changes are made in the selected set.

All k-NN presented by Tomek in [16] is another modification of ENN algorithm: the ENN is repeated for *all k* (k=1,2, ... ,l).

ENRBF is an *Edited* version of NRBF[17,18]. NRBF is defined as normalized version of RBF. NRBF estimates probability of k-th class given vector $\mathbf{x}$ and training set $\mathcal{T}$:

$$P(k|\mathbf{x}, \mathcal{T}) = \sum_{i \in I^k} \bar{G}_i(\mathbf{x}; \mathbf{x}_i), \tag{1}$$

where $I^k = \{i : \langle \mathbf{x}_i, y_i \rangle \in \mathcal{T} \wedge y_i = k\}$, and $\bar{G}_i(\mathbf{x}; \mathbf{x}_i)$ is defined by

$$\bar{G}_i(\mathbf{x}; \mathbf{x}_i) = \frac{G(\mathbf{x}; \mathbf{x}_i, \sigma)}{\sum_{j=1}^{n} G(\mathbf{x}; \mathbf{x}_j, \sigma)}, \tag{2}$$

and $G(\mathbf{x}; \mathbf{x}_i, \sigma)$ (σ is fixed) is defined by $G(\mathbf{x}; \mathbf{x}_i, \sigma) = e^{-\frac{||\mathbf{x} - \mathbf{x}_i||^2}{\sigma}}$.
   The ENRBF eliminates all vectors if only:

$$\exists_{k \neq y_i} \quad P(y_i|\mathbf{x}, \mathcal{T}^i) < \alpha P(k|\mathbf{x}, \mathcal{T}^i), \tag{3}$$

where $\mathcal{T}^i = \mathcal{T} - \{\mathbf{x}_i, y_i\}$, and $\alpha \in (0, 1]$.

2.2   Condensation Algorithms

Condensed Nearest Neighbor Rule (CNN) was made by Hart [4]. The CNN algorithm starts new data set from one instance per class randomly chosen from training set. After that each instance from the training set that is wrongly classified using the new dataset is added to this set. This procedure is very fragile in respect to noise and the order of presentation.

Reduced Nearest Neighbor (RNN) described in [6] by Gates was based on the same idea as CNN. However RNN starts from original training set and rejects only those instances that do not decrease accuracy.

IB3 was described by Aha et al. in [2]. IB3 is an incremental algorithm. Instance x from the training set is added to a new set S if the nearest *acceptable* instance in S (if there are no acceptable instance a random one is used) has different class than x. Acceptability is defined by the confidence interval

$$\frac{p + \frac{z^2}{2n} \pm z\sqrt{\frac{p(p-1)}{n} + \frac{z^2}{2n^2}}}{1 + \frac{z^2}{n}} \tag{4}$$

z is confidence factor (in IB3 0.9 is used to accept, 0.7 to reject). p is the classification accuracy of a given instance (while added to S). n is equal to a number of classification-trials for given instance (while added to S). See [2] for more details.

Gabriel Editing (GE) and Relative Neighborhood Graph Editing (RNGE) — two algorithms based on graph theory – were constructed by Bhattacharya et al. [9]. Decision surface of the 1-NN algorithm creates Voronoi diagram. It can be observed that instances on the border between classes are important in classification process. The complexity of building Voronoi diagrams is $O(N^{d/2})$, that is too expensive for real datasets. Because of that authors decided to use Gabriel graphs. The complexity of this algorithm is $O(n^3)$. Stronger instance–shrinking can be obtained using a modification of GE method called RNGE.

Iterative Case Filtering (ICF) was proposed by Brighton & Mellish in [10]. ICF defines *local set* $\mathcal{L}(\mathbf{x})$ which contain all cases inside largest hypersphere centered in $\mathbf{x}$ such that the hypersphere contains only cases of the same class as instance $\mathbf{x}$. Authors define two properties, *reachability* and *coverage*:

$$Coverage(x) = \{\mathbf{x}' \in \mathcal{T} : \mathbf{x} \in \mathcal{L}(\mathbf{x}')\}, \tag{5}$$

$$Reachability(x) = \{\mathbf{x}' \in \mathcal{T} : \mathbf{x}' \in \mathcal{L}(\mathbf{x})\}. \tag{6}$$

In the first phase ICF uses ENN algorithm to remove the noise from the training set. In the second phase ICF algorithm removes each instance $\mathbf{x}$ for which the $Reachability(x)$ is bigger than the $Coverage(x)$. This procedure is repeated for each instance in $\mathcal{T}$. After that ICF recalculates *reachability* and *coverage* properties and restarts the second phase (as long as any progress is observed).

ENRBF2 is also based on NRBF defined by Eq. 1. ENRBF2 removes given instance $\mathbf{x}_i$ from the training set if the criterion below is satisfied:

$$P(y_i|\mathbf{x}_i; \mathcal{T})\beta < P(y_i|\mathbf{x}_i; \mathcal{T}^i) \tag{7}$$

$\beta \in (0, 1]$. This means that if removing instance $\mathbf{x}_i$ probability that this instance belongs to the class y_i is not significantly reduced then such instance can be removed.

DROP1–5 models were developed by Wilson & Martinez [19]. Let's define $\mathcal{A}(\mathbf{x})$ as a set of instances for which instance $\mathbf{x}$ is one of the k nearest neighbors. DROP1 removes instance $\mathbf{x}$ from the training set if it does not change classification of instances from $\mathcal{A}(\mathbf{x})$ (only those instances depend on $\mathbf{x}$). The performance of DROP1 was really bad. The second version — DROP2 — starts the process from sorting instances according to their distances from the nearest opposite class instance. The DROP3 additionally run the ENN algorithm before starting the DROP2 algorithm. DROP4-5 are another version of DROP2 – see [19] for details.

2.3   Prototype Selection

Prototypes methods are very interesting because original training set may be transformed even to a few prototypes, therefore it can be treated as an approach for knowledge representation. Each of the prototypes represents one field covering its Voronoi diagram. Such field in highly compressed dataset (few vectors) corresponds to a cluster. If prototypes are used with 1NN the prototypes may be seen as prototype rules because each prototype is assigned to a single class. For example if $\mathcal{S}$ contains prototype vectors $\mathbf{p}_i$ and its corresponding classes are c_i than the decision process of instance $\mathbf{x}$ is simplified to find i:

$$i := \arg \max_{\mathbf{p}_j \in \mathcal{S}} ||\mathbf{p}_j - \mathbf{x}|| \tag{8}$$

which points to the winner class c_i.

Learning Vectors Quantization (LVQ) is well known model proposed by Kohonen in [20]. In contrary to all previous algorithms (except CA) LVQ changes the positions of codebook vectors (neurons) during learning and finally neurons have different values than original instances of the training set. See [20] for more.

Monte Carlo 1 (MC1) and Random Mutation Hill Climbing (RMHC). These two methods described in [11] by Skalak are based on stochastic behavior. MC1 in each iteration use Monte Carlo to draw new set of instances and to test the accuracy. Only the best drawn set of instances is remembered. RMHC use mutation in place of Monte Carlo.

Encoding length — ELH, ELGrow and Explore: these three algorithms (Cameron-Jones [8]) use cost function defined by:

$$J(m, n, x) = F(m, n) + m \log_2 c + F(x, n - m) + x \log_2(c - 1), \tag{9}$$

where n and m are numbers of instances in the training set and in the new data set S respectively. x defines the number of badly classified vectors (basing on S), and $F(m, n)$ is defined by

$$F(m, n) = \log^* \left(\sum_{i=0}^{m} \frac{n!}{i!(n-i)!)} \right), \tag{10}$$

$\log^* n = \arg\min_k F(k) \geq n$, k – is integer, and $F(0) = 1, F(i) = 2^{F(i-1)}$.

ELH starts from the empty set and adds instances if only they minimize the cost function $J(\cdot)$. ELGrow additionally tries to remove instances if it helps to minimize the cost function $J(\cdot)$. Explore extend the ELGrow by 1000 iterations of stochastic addition or deletion of instances if only it minimizes the costs. Those methods are very effective.

The algorithm DEL is another modification of ELH. It can be seen as decremental version of ELH [19].

2.4 Classification of Algorithms

Instance selection algorithms work in different ways; some of them belong to incremental or decremental family, while others try to mix both strategy.

Instance dataset creation strategy	
Incremental	CNN, IB3, ELH
Decremental	RNN, SNN, ENN, CA (Chang), ENRBF, DROP1-5, Del
Mixed	RENN, All k-NN, LVQ, MC1, RMHC, ELGrow(!), Explore

However, more important than strategy of the dataset building presented above is the complexity of presented algorithms. In the table below complexity comparison can be found.

ENN	RENN All-kNN	CNN RNN	IB3	GE RNGE	ICF	EN- RBF(2)	DROP 1-5	LVQ	MC1 RMHC	ELH ElGrow Explore Del
$O(n^2)$	$O(in^2)$	$O(n^3)$	$O(n^2 \log_2 n)$	$O(n^3)$	$O(in^2)$	$O(n^2)$	$O(n^3)$	$O(in^2)$	$O(n^2)$	$O(n^2)$

Another feature which distinguish between groups of model is their "scene analysis". Some algorithms try to preserve the border points. This can be observed especially with algorithms based on graph theory – GE and RNGE. In contrary are algorithms which try to estimate cluster centers, like the LVQ. In the next group models which remove the noise can be placed. Instances that remained have clusters with smoother shapes. More sophisticated behavior can be observed in such algorithms as ICF, DROP3-5, Encoding Length or MC1.

References

1. Duda, R.O., Hart, P.E., Stork, D.G.: Patter Classification and Scene Analysis. 2 edn. Wiley (1997)
2. Aha, D.W., Kibler, D., Albert, M.K.: Aha,. Machine Learning **6** (1991) 37–66
3. Cover, T.M., Hart, P.E.: Nearest neighbor pattern classification. Institute of Electrical and Electronics Engineers Transactions on Information Theory **13** (1967) 21–27
4. Hart, P.E.: The condensed nearest neighbor rule. IEEE Transactions on Information Theory **14** (1968) 515–516
5. Ritter, G.L., Woodruff, H.B., Lowry, S.R., Isenhour, T.L.: An algorithm for a selective nearest neighbor decision rule. IEEE Transactions on Information Theory **21** (1975) 665–669
6. Gates, G.: The reduced nearest neighbor rule. IEEE Transactions on Information Theory **18** (1972) 431–433
7. Wilson, D.: Asymptotic properties of nearest neighbor rules using edited data. IEEE Transactions on Systems, Man, and Cybernetics **2** (1972) 408–421
8. Cameron-Jones, R.M.: Instance selection by encoding length heuristic with random mutation hill climbing. In: Proceedings of the Eighth Australian Joint Conference on Artificial Intelligence. (1995) 99–106
9. Bhattacharya, B.K., Poulsen, R.S., Toussaint, G.T.: Application of proximity graphs to editing nearest neighbor decision rule. In: International Symposium on Information Theory, Santa Monica (1981)
10. Brighton, H., Mellish, C.: Advances in instance selection for instance-based learning algorithms. Data Mining and Knowledge Discovery **6** (2002) 153–172
11. Skalak, D.B.: Prototype and feature selection by sampling and random mutation hill climbing algorithms. In: International Conference on Machine Learning. (1994) 293–301
12. Schölkopf, B., Smola, A.: Learning with Kernels. MIT Press, Cambridge, MA (2002)
13. Grąbczewski, K., Duch, W.: A general purpose separability criterion for classification systems. In: 4th Conference on Neural Networks and Their Applications, Zakopane, Poland, Polish Neural Networks Society (1999) 203–208
14. Adamczak, R., Duch, W., Jankowski, N.: New developments in the feature space mapping model. In: Third Conference on Neural Networks and Their Applications, Kule, Poland, Polish Neural Networks Society (1997) 65–70
15. Jankowski, N., Kadirkamanathan, V.: Statistical control of RBF-like networks for classification. In: 7th International Conference on Artificial Neural Networks, Lausanne, Switzerland, Springer-Verlag (1997) 385–390
16. Tomek, I.: An experiment with the edited nearest-neighbor rule. IEEE Transactions on Systems, Man, and Cybernetics **6** (1976) 448–452
17. Grochowski, M.: Wybór wektorów referencyjnych dla wybranych method klasyfikacji. Master's thesis, Department of Informatics, Nicholas Copernicus University, Poland (2003)
18. Jankowski, N.: Data regularization. In Rutkowski, L., Tadeusiewicz, R., eds.: Neural Networks and Soft Computing, Zakopane, Poland (2000) 209–214
19. Wilson, D.R., Martinez, T.R.: Reduction techniques for instance-based learning algorithms. Machine Learning **38** (2000) 257–286
20. Kohonen, T.: Learning vector quantization for pattern recognition. Technical Report TKK-F-A601, Helsinki University of Technology, Espoo, Finland (1986)

Lecture Notes in Artificial Intelligence 3070

Edited by J. G. Carbonell and J. Siekmann

Subseries of Lecture Notes in Computer Science

Springer-Verlag Berlin Heidelberg GmbH

Leszek Rutkowski   Jörg Siekmann
Ryszard Tadeusiewicz   Lotfi A. Zadeh (Eds.)

Artificial Intelligence and Soft Computing - ICAISC 2004

7th International Conference
Zakopane, Poland, June 7-11, 2004
Proceedings

 Springer

Series Editors

Jaime G. Carbonell, Carnegie Mellon University, Pittsburgh, PA, USA
Jörg Siekmann, University of Saarland, Saarbrücken, Germany

Volume Editors

Leszek Rutkowski
Technical University of Czestochowa, Department of Computer Engineering
Al. Armii Krajowej 36, 42-200 Czestochowa, Poland
E-mail: lrutko@kik.pcz.czest.pl

Jörg Siekmann
German Research Center for Artificial Intelligence (DFKI)
Stuhlsatzenhausweg 3, 66123 Saarbrücken, Germany
E-mail: Joerg.Siekmann@dfki.de

Ryszard Tadeusiewicz
AGH University of Science and Technology, Institute of Automatics
Al. Mickiewicza 30, 30-059 Kraków, Poland
E-mail: rtad@agh.edu.pl

Lotfi A. Zadeh
University of California
Computer Science Division and the Electronics Research Laboratory
Department of EECs
Berkeley, CA 94720-1776, USA
E-mail: zadeh@cs.berkeley.edu

Library of Congress Control Number: 2004106909

CR Subject Classification (1998): I.2, F.4.1, F.1, F.2, I.4

ISSN 0302-9743
ISBN 978-3-540-22123-4   ISBN 978-3-540-24844-6 (eBook)
DOI 10.1007/978-3-540-24844-6

This work is subject to copyright. All rights are reserved, whether the whole or part of the material is
concerned, specifically the rights of translation, reprinting, re-use of illustrations, recitation, broadcasting,
reproduction on microfilms or in any other way, and storage in data banks. Duplication of this publication
or parts thereof is permitted only under the provisions of the German Copyright Law of September 9, 1965,
in its current version, and permission for use must always be obtained from Springer-Verlag. Violations are
liable to prosecution under the German Copyright Law.

springeronline.com

© Springer-Verlag Berlin Heidelberg 2004
Originally published by Springer-Verlag Berlin Heidelberg New York in 2004.

Typesetting: Camera-ready by author, data conversion by PTP-Berlin, Protago-TeX-Production GmbH
Printed on acid-free paper   SPIN: 11010999   06/3142   5 4 3 2 1 0

Preface

This volume constitutes the proceedings of the 7th Conference on Artificial Intelligence and Soft Computing, ICAISC 2004, held in Zakopane, Poland, June 7–11, 2004. The conference was organized by the Polish Neural Network Society in cooperation with the Department of Computer Engineering at the Technical University of Częstochowa, WSHE University in Łódź and IEEE Neural Networks Society. The previous conferences took place in Kule (1994), Szczyrk (1996), Kule (1997) and Zakopane (1999, 2000, 2002) and attracted a large number of papers and internationally recognized speakers: Prof. Lotfi A. Zadeh, Prof. Robert Marks, Prof. Enrique Ruspini, Prof. Zdzisław Bubnicki, Prof. Jacek Żurada, Prof. Shun-ichi Amari, Prof. Kaoru Hirota, Prof. Ryszard Tadeusiewicz, Prof. Shiro Usui, Prof. Włodzisław Duch, Prof. Erkki Oja, Prof. Syozo Yasui, Prof. Witold Pedrycz, Prof. Janusz Kacprzyk, Prof. Laszlo T. Koczy, Prof. Soo-Young Lee and Prof. Daniel Amit. The aim of this conference is to build a bridge between traditional artificial intelligence techniques and recently developed soft computing techniques. It was pointed out by Prof. Lotfi A. Zadeh that "Soft Computing (SC) is a coalition of methodologies which are oriented toward the conception and design of information/intelligent systems. The principal members of the coalition are: fuzzy logic (FL), neurocomputing (NC), evolutionary computing (EC), probabilistic computing (PC), chaotic computing (CC), and machine learning (ML). The constituent methodologies of SC are, for the most part, complementary and synergistic rather than competitive". This volume presents both traditional artificial intelligence methods and soft computing techniques presented in 14 parts:

1. Invited Papers
2. Neural Networks and Their Applications
3. Fuzzy Systems and Their Applications
4. Evolutionary Algorithms and Their Applications
5. Rough Sets and Their Applications
6. Soft Computing in Classification
7. Image Processing
8. Robotics
9. Multiagents Systems
10. Various Problems of Artificial Intelligence
11. Control, Modelling and System Identification
12. Medical Applications
13. Mechanical Applications
14. Various Applications

The conference attracted a total of 250 submissions from 35 countries and after the review process, 175 papers were accepted.

I would like to thank our participants, invited speakers and reviewers of the papers for their scientific and personal contribution to the conference. I also thank Alfred Hofmann editor-in-chief of Springer-Verlag's Lecture Notes in Computer Science/Artificial Intelligence series and Christine Günther from the LNCS Editorial for their cooperation in the preparation of this volume. Finally I thank my co-workers Jarosław Bilski, Marcin Gabryel, Marcin Korytkowski and Rafał Scherer, for their enormous efforts to make the conference a very successful event.

June 2004   Leszek Rutkowski
                          President of the Polish Neural Network Society

Organization

ICAISC 04 was organized by the Polish Neural Network Society and the Department of Computer Engineering at Częstochowa University of Technology in cooperation with WSHE University in Łódź and the IEEE Neural Network Society.

Chairpersons

Honorary chairmen	Lotfi Zadeh (USA)
	Zdzislaw Bubnicki (Poland)
	Zdzisław Pawlak (Poland)
	Jacek Żurada (USA)
General chairman	Leszek Rutkowski (Poland)
Co-chairmen	Włodzisław Duch (Poland)
	Janusz Kacprzyk (Poland)
	Józef Korbicz (Poland)
	Ryszard Tadeusiewicz (Poland)

Program Committee

S. Amari (Japan)
J. Arabas (Poland)
R. Babuska (The Netherlands)
A. Bargiela (UK)
I. Batyrshin (Russia)
E. Bayro-Corrochano (Mexico)
M. Białko (Poland)
L. Bobrowski (Poland)
L. Bolc (Poland)
P. Bonissone (USA)
B. Bouchon-Meunier (France)
J.J. Buckley (USA)
T. Burczyński (Poland)
A. Cader (Poland)
W. Cholewa (Poland)
B. De Baets (Belgium)
N. Derbel (Tunisia)
E. Dudek-Dyduch (Poland)
L. Dymowa (Poland)
J. Fodor (Hungary)
D. Fogel (USA)

R. Galar (Poland)
M. Gorzałczany (Poland)
J.W. Grzymała-Busse (USA)
P. Hajek (Czech Republic)
S. Halgamuge (Australia)
R. Hampel (Germany)
Z. Hasiewicz (Poland)
T. Hendtlass (Australia)
Y. Hayashi (Japan)
K. Hirota (Japan)
Z. Hippe (Japan)
J. Józefczyk (Poland)
T. Kacprzak (Poland)
T. Kaczorek (Poland)
W. Kamiński (Poland)
N. Kasabov (New Zealand)
O. Kaynak (Turkey)
V. Kecman (New Zealand)
J. Kluska (Poland)
M. Kłopotek (Poland)
L.T. Koczy (Hungary)

L. Kompanec (Poland)
R. Kosiński (Poland)
W. Kosiński (Poland)
J.M. Kościelny (Poland)
Z. Kowalczuk (Poland)
R. Kruse (Germany)
J.L. Kulikowski (Poland)
R. Kulikowski (Poland)
V. Kurkova (Czech Republic)
M. Kurzyński (Poland)
J. Kusiak (Poland)
H. Kwaśnicka (Poland)
S.Y. Lee (Korea)
A. Ligęza (Poland)
J. Łęski (Poland)
B. Macukow (Poland)
K. Madani (France)
W. Malina (Poland)
K. Malinowski (Poland)
J. Mańdziuk (Poland)
A. Materka (Poland)
R. Mesiar (Slovakia)
Z. Michalewicz (USA)
W. Moczulski (Poland)
W. Mitkowski (Poland)
D. Nauck (Germany)
E. Nawarecki (Poland)
A. Niederliński (Poland)
E. Oja (Finland)
S. Osowski (Poland)
M. Partyka (Poland)
W. Pedrycz (Canada)

A. Piegat (Poland)
E. Rafajłowicz (Poland)
S. Raudys (Lithuania)
R. Rojas (Germany)
I. Rudas (Hungary)
D. Rutkowska (Poland)
E.H. Ruspini (USA)
N. Sano (Japan)
R. Setiono (Singapore)
P. Sewastianow (Poland)
J. Siekmann (Germany)
P. Sincak (Slovakia)
A. Skowron (Poland)
E. Skubalska-Rafajłowicz (Poland)
R. Słowiński (Poland)
P. Szczepaniak (Poland)
P. Strumiłło (Poland)
M. Sugeno (Japan)
J. Świątek (Poland)
H. Takagi (Japan)
R. Takahashi (Japan)
B. Turksen (Canada)
S. Usui (Japan)
M. Wagenknecht (Germany)
Z. Waszczyszyn (Poland)
B.M. Wilamowski (USA)
M. Wygralak (Poland)
R. Wyrzykowski (Poland)
J. Yen (USA)
R. Yager (USA)
J. Zieliński (Poland)

Referees

R. Adamczak
R. Babuska
A. Bargiela
L. Bobrowski
J. Buckley
T. Burczyński
A. Cader
K. Cetnarowicz
W. Cholewa

R. Cierniak
B. De Baets
W. Duch
L. Dymowa
M. Flasiński
D.B. Fogel
R. Galar
A. Gawęda
M. Giergiel

M.B. Gorzałczany
W. Greblicki
M. Grzenda
J.W. Grzymala-Busse
K. Grąbczewski
Z. Hasiewicz
Y. Hayashi
T. Hendtlass
Z. Hendzel

K. Hirota
A. Janczak
N. Jankowski
J. Józefczyk
J. Kacprzyk
W. Kamiński
O. Kaynak
V. Kecman
J. Kluska
L. Kompanets
J. Korbicz
P. Korohoda
R. Kosiński
W. Kosiński
J.M. Kościelny
R. Kruse
V. Kurkova
M. Kurzyński
J. Kusiak
H. Kwaśnicka
M.A. Kłopotek
S.-Y. Lee
J. Lęski
A. Ligęza

B. Macukow
K. Madani
W. Malina
A. Materka
J. Mańdziuk
J.M. Mendel
R. Mesiar
Z. Michalewicz
Z. Mikrut
W. Mitkowski
W. Moczulski
M. Mrugalski
E. Nawarecki
R. Nowicki
A. Obuchowicz
E. Oja
S. Osowski
K. Patan
W. Pedrycz
A. Pieczyński
A. Piegat
V. Piuri
E. Rafajłowicz
S. Raudys

I.J. Rudas
R. Scherer
R. Setiono
P. Sevastjanov
A. Skowron
E. Skubalska-Rafajłowicz
P. Strumiłło
P.S. Szczepaniak
E. Szmidt
P. Śliwiński
J. Świątek
H. Takagi
B. Turksen
S. Usui
M. Wagenknecht
T. Walkowiak
B.M. Wilamowski
M. Witczak
M. Wygralak
R.R. Yager
S. Zadrożny
J.S. Zieliński

Table of Contents

Invited Papers

Evolutionary Design of Information Systems Architectures 1
  Danilo Ardagna, Chiara Francalanci, Vincenzo Piuri, Fabio Scotti

Clifford Support Vector Machines for Classification 9
  Eduardo Bayro-Corrochano, Nancy Arana-Daniel,
  J. Refugio Vallejo-Gutiérres

Uncertain Variables and Systems – New Problems and Results 17
  Zdzislaw Bubnicki

Blind Signal Separation and Extraction: Recent Trends, Future
Perspectives, and Applications 30
  Andrzej Cichocki, Jacek M. Zurada

Visualization of Hidden Node Activity in Neural Networks:
I. Visualization Methods 38
  Włodzisław Duch

Visualization of Hidden Node Activity in Neural Networks:
II. Application to RBF Networks 44
  Włodzisław Duch

Rough Set Approach to Incomplete Data 50
  Jerzy W. Grzymala-Busse

Neural Networks of Positive Systems 56
  Tadeusz Kaczorek

Support of Natural, by Artificial, Intelligence Using Utility
as Behavioral Goal 64
  Roman Kulikowski

Top-Down Selective Attention for Robust Perception
of Noisy and Confusing Patterns 73
  Soo-Young Lee

On ANN Based Solutions for Real-World Industrial Requirements 79
  Kurosh Madani

ActiveMath: An Intelligent Tutoring System for Mathematics 91
  Erica Melis, Jörg Siekmann

Inference Rules and Decision Rules 102
  Zdzisław Pawlak

Survival of Intelligent Agents in Changing Environments 109
  Šarūnas Raudys

Inducing Robust Decision Rules from Rough Approximations
of a Preference Relation 118
  Roman Slowinski, Salvatore Greco

The New Concept in Computer Vision:
Automatic Understanding of the Images 133
  Ryszard Tadeusiewicz, Marek R. Ogiela

Neural Networks and Their Applications

Dynamic High Order Neural Networks: Application for Fault Diagnosis .. 145
  Eugen Arinton, Józef Korbicz

Momentum Modification of the RLS Algorithms 151
  Jarosław Bilski

Parallel Realisation of QR Algorithm for Neural Networks Learning 158
  Jarosław Bilski, Sławomir Litwiński, Jacek Smoląg

Rainfall-Runoff Modelling Using Three Neural Network Methods 166
  H. Kerem Cigizoglu, Murat Alp

Probability Distribution of Solution Time in ANN Training
Using Population Learning Algorithm 172
  Ireneusz Czarnowski, Piotr Jędrzejowicz

Parallelization of the SOM-Based Integrated Mapping 178
  Gintautas Dzemyda, Olga Kurasova

Training Radial Basis Functions by Gradient Descent 184
  Mercedes Fernández-Redondo, Carlos Hernández-Espinosa,
  Mamen Ortiz-Gómez, Joaquín Torres-Sospedra

Generalized Backpropagation through Time for Continuous Time
Neural Networks and Discrete Time Measurements 190
  Krzysztof Fujarewicz, Adam Galuszka

Experiments on Ensembles of Radial Basis Functions 197
  Carlos Hernández-Espinosa, Mercedes Fernández-Redondo,
  Joaquín Torres-Sospedra

Orthodoxy Basis Functions and Convergence Property in
Procedure Neural Networks 203
  Jiong Jia, Jiuzhen Liang

Confidence Estimation of GMDH Neural Networks 210
    Józef Korbicz, Mihai F. Metenidis, Marcin Mrugalski,
    Marcin Witczak

On Some Factors Influencing MLP Error Surface..................... 217
    Mirosław Kordos, Włodzisław Duch

Discovery of Linguistic Rules by Means of RBF Network
for Fault Detection in Electronic Circuits 223
    Jan Koszlaga, Pawel Strumillo

Combining Space-Filling Curves and Radial Basis Function Networks ... 229
    Adam Krzyżak, Ewa Skubalska-Rafajłowicz

Chaotic Itinerancy for Patterns Separation 235
    Paweł Matykiewicz

Dynamic Search Trajectory Methods for Neural Network Training 241
    Y.G. Petalas, D.K. Tasoulis, M.N. Vrahatis

Visualizing and Analyzing Multidimensional Output
from MLP Networks via Barycentric Projections 247
    Filip Piękniewski, Leszek Rybicki

Optimization of Centers' Positions for RBF Nets
with Generalized Kernels 253
    E. Rafajłowicz, M. Pawlak

Fixed Non-linear Combining Rules versus Adaptive Ones 260
    Sarunas Raudys, Zidrina Pabarskaite

Learning and System Modeling via Hamiltonian Neural Networks 266
    Wieslaw Sienko, Wieslaw Citko, Dariusz Jakóbczak

Recurrent Network Structure for Computing Quasi-inverses
of the Sierpiński Space-Filling Curves............................... 272
    Ewa Skubalska-Rafajłowicz

Fuzzy Systems and Their Applications

Comparison of Reasoning Methods for Fuzzy Control 278
    Bohdan Butkiewicz

Fuzzy Modelling with a Compromise Fuzzy Reasoning 284
    Krzysztof Cpalka, Leszek Rutkowski

A Self Tuning Fuzzy Inference System for Noise Reduction 290
    Nevcihan Duru, Tarik Duru

Fuzzy-Neural Networks in the Diagnosis
of Motor-Car's Current Supply Circuit............................ 296
  Stanisław Gad, Mariusz Łaskawski, Grzegorz Słoń,
  Alexander Yastrebov, Andrzej Zawadzki

Fuzzy Number-Based Hierarchical Fuzzy System 302
  Adam E. Gaweda, Rafał Scherer

Stock Trend Prediction Using Neurofuzzy Predictors
Based on Brain Emotional Learning Algorithm 308
  Mahdi Jalili-Kharaajoo

Digital Implementation of Fuzzy Petri Net Based on Asynchronous
Fuzzy RS Flip-Flop 314
  Jacek Kluska, Zbigniew Hajduk

Fuzzy Calculator – Useful Tool for Programming with Fuzzy Algebra 320
  Roman Koleśnik, Piotr Prokopowicz, Witold Kosiński

On Defuzzyfication of Ordered Fuzzy Numbers 326
  Witold Kosiński

Information Criterions Applied to Neuro-Fuzzy Architectures Design 332
  Robert Nowicki, Agata Pokropińska

On Hesitation Degrees in IF-Set Theory 338
  Anna Pankowska, Maciej Wygralak

Fuzzy Cognitive Maps Learning through Swarm Intelligence 344
  E.I. Papageorgiou, K.E. Parsopoulos, P.P. Groumpos, M.N. Vrahatis

Application of the General Gaussian Membership Function
for the Fuzzy Model Parameters Tunning 350
  Andrzej Pieczyński, Andrzej Obuchowicz

Are Linguistic Evaluations Used by People
of Possibilistic or Probabilistic Nature? 356
  Andrzej Piegat

Fuzzy Linear Programming in Ship Trajectory Optimization
in a Restricted Area 364
  Zbigniew Pietrzykowski

Application of Fuzzy Weighted Feature Diagrams
to Model Variability in Software Families 370
  Silva Robak, Andrzej Pieczyński

Neuro-Fuzzy Relational Classifiers................................ 376
  Rafał Scherer, Leszek Rutkowski

What Differs Interval Type-2 FLS from Type-1 FLS? 381
  Janusz T. Starczewski

A Similarity Measure for Intuitionistic Fuzzy Sets
and Its Application in Supporting Medical Diagnostic Reasoning 388
  Eulalia Szmidt, Janusz Kacprzyk

Evolutionary Algorithms and Their Applications

Multi-criterion Evolutionary Algorithm with Model of the Immune
System to Handle Constraints for Task Assignments 394
  Jerzy Balicki

Parallel Genetic Algorithm for Minimizing Total Weighted
Completion Time 400
  Wojciech Bożejko, Mieczysław Wodecki

Adaptive Evolutionary Computation –
Application for Mixed Linear Programming 406
  Ewa Dudek-Dyduch, Dominik Jarczyk

Adaptive Evolutionary Computation
of the Parametric Optimization Problem 414
  Tadeusz Dyduch

Concentration of Population in Phenotypic Evolution 420
  Iwona Karcz-Dulęba

An Evolutionary Clustering Algorithm 426
  Marcin Korzeń

An Evolutionary Algorithm for Oblique Decision Tree Induction 432
  Marek Kretowski

Propagation of Building Blocks in SGA and MPGA 438
  Grzegorz Kusztelak, Marek Rudnicki, Sławomir Wiak

Selection Pressure and an Efficiency
of Neural Network Architecture Evolving 444
  Halina Kwaśnicka, Mariusz Paradowski

Rule Extraction from Neural Network by Genetic Algorithm
with Pareto Optimization 450
  Urszula Markowska-Kaczmar, Paweł Wnuk-Lipiński

Graph Transformations in Evolutionary Design 456
  Piotr Nikodem, Barbara Strug

A Genetic Algorithm for Probabilistic SAT Problem 462
  Zoran Ognjanović, Uroš Midić, Jozef Kratica

Design and Optimization of Combinational Digital Circuits
Using Modified Evolutionary Algorithm 468
    Adam Słowik, Michał Białko

Modified Version of Roulette Selection for Evolution Algorithms
– The Fan Selection 474
    Adam Słowik, Michał Białko

New Genetic Crossover Operator for the TSP 480
    Sang-Moon Soak, Byung-Ha Ahn

Rough Sets and Their Applications

Hybridization of Blind Source Separation and Rough Sets
for Proteomic Biomarker Indentification 486
    Grzegorz M. Boratyn, Tomasz G. Smolinski, Jacek M. Zurada,
    Mariofanna Milanova, Sudeepa Bhattacharyya, Larry J. Suva

Inducing Jury's Preferences in Terms of Acoustic Features
of Violin Sounds 492
    Jacek Jelonek, Ewa Łukasik, Aleksander Naganowski,
    Roman Słowiński

Fuzzy Implication Operators in Variable Precision Fuzzy Rough
Sets Model 498
    Alicja Mieszkowicz-Rolka, Leszek Rolka

Fuzzyfication of Indiscernibility Relation for Structurizing
Lists of Synonyms and Stop-Lists for Search Engines 504
    A. Niewiadomski, P. Kryger, P.S. Szczepaniak

Rough Sets in the Neuro-Fuzzy Architectures Based on Monotonic
Fuzzy Implications 510
    Robert Nowicki

Rough Sets in the Neuro-Fuzzy Architectures Based on
Non-monotonic Fuzzy Implications 518
    Robert Nowicki

On L–Fuzzy Rough Sets 526
    Anna Maria Radzikowska, Etienne E. Kerre

Application of Rough Sets Techniques to Induction Machine Broken
Bar Detection 532
    M.R. Rafimanzelat, B.N. Araabi

Application of Rough Sets and Neural Networks to Forecasting
University Facility and Administrative Cost Recovery.............. 538
    Tomasz G. Smolinski, Darrel L. Chenoweth, Jacek M. Zurada

Soft Computing in Classification

Selection of the Linearly Separable Feature Subsets................... 544
Leon Bobrowski, Tomasz Lukaszuk

Short-Time Signal Analysis Using Pattern Recognition Methods 550
Piotr Boguś, Katarzyna D. Lewandowska

Application of Genetic Algorithms and Kohonen Networks
to Cluster Analysis 556
Marian B. Gorzałczany, Filip Rudziński

Modified Kohonen Networks for Complex Cluster-Analysis Problems 562
Marian B. Gorzałczany, Filip Rudziński

Reducing the Computational Demands
for Nearest Centroid Neighborhood Classifiers 568
Szymon Grabowski

SSV Criterion Based Discretization for Naive Bayes Classifiers 574
Krzysztof Grąbczewski

Comparison of Instance Selection Algorithms II.
Results and Comments 580
Marek Grochowski, Norbert Jankowski

SBL-PM-M: A System for Partial Memory Learning 586
Karol Grudziński

Relevance LVQ versus SVM 592
Barbara Hammer, Marc Strickert, Thomas Villmann

Comparison of Instances Seletion Algorithms I. Algorithms Survey 598
Norbert Jankowski, Marek Grochowski

Towards Grammatical Inferencing of GDPLL(k) Grammars
for Applications in Syntactic Pattern Recognition-Based
Expert Systems 604
Janusz Jurek

Intelligent Layer of Two-Way Voice Communication
of the Technological Device with the Operator 610
Wojciech Kacalak, Maciej Majewski

A Neural Network Based Method for Classification
of Meteorological Data 616
K. Kaminski, W. Kaminski, P. Strumillo

An Empirical Test Suite for Message Authentication Evaluation
in Communications Based on Support Vector Machines 622
    D.A. Karras

Efficient Digital Fingerprint Production and Evaluation
for Secure Communication Systems Based on Genetic Algorithms 628
    D.A. Karras

On Chinese Web Page Classification 634
    Jiuzhen Liang

A New Fuzzy Clustering Method with Constraints in Time Domain 640
    Jacek Leski, Aleksander Owczarek

Special Cluster Analysis and Basic Feature Estimation
with a Modification of Self-Organizing Map 646
    Janusz Morajda

An Unsupervised Cluster Analysis and Information
about the Modelling System 652
    Izabela Rejer

Cursive-Character Script Recognition Using Toeplitz Model
and Neural Networks 658
    Khalid Saeed, Marek Tabedzki

Learning with an Embedded Reject Option 664
    Ramasubramanian Sundararajan, Asim K. Pal

Image Processing

Impulsive Noise Suppression from Highly Corrupted Images by Using
Resilient Neural Networks 670
    Erkan Beşdok, Pınar Çivicioğlu, Mustafa Alçı

A New Methodology for Synthetic Aperture Radar (SAR) Raw Data
Compression Based on Wavelet Transform and Neural Networks 676
    Giacomo Capizzi, Salvatore Coco, Antonio Laudani,
    Giuseppe Pappalardo

Fuzzy Processing Technique for Content-Based Image Retrieval 682
    Ryszard S. Choraś

Human Ear Identification Based on Image Analysis 688
    Michał Choraś

Automatic Change Detection Based on Codelength Differences
in Multi-temporal and Multi-spectral Images 694
    Joselíto J. Chua, Peter E. Tischer

Estimating Face Direction via Facial Triangle........................ 700
  Min Gyo Chung, Jisook Park, Jiyoun Dong

An Image Compression Algorithm Based on Neural Networks 706
  Robert Cierniak

Fuzzy Nonparametric Measures for Image Matching 712
  Boguslaw Cyganek, Jan Borgosz

Neural Computation of the Fundamental Matrix 718
  Boguslaw Cyganek

Face Detection Using CMAC Neural Network........................ 724
  H. Fashandi, M.S. Moin

A Biologically Inspired Active Stereo Vision System Using a
Bottom-Up Saliency Map Model 730
  Bum-Soo Jung, Sang-Bok Choi, Sang-Woo Ban, Minho Lee

Problems Connected with Application of Neural Networks
in Automatic Face Recognition 736
  Rafal Komanski, Bohdan Macukow

Czestochowa-Faces and Biometrics of Asymmetrical Face 742
  Leonid Kompanets, Mariusz Kubanek, Szymon Rydzek

Wafer Die Position Detection Using Hierarchical Gray Level
Corner Detector 748
  Jae Hyung Na, Hae Seok Oh

On Fuzzy Labelled Image Segmentation Based on
Perceptual Features 754
  Pilar Sobrevilla, Eduard Montseny

Generalized Multi-layer Kohonen Network and Its Application to
Texture Recognition... 760
  A. Tomczyk, P.S. Szczepaniak, B. Lis

Robotics

Translation STRIPS Planning in Multi-robot Environment
to Linear Programming 768
  Adam Galuszka, Andrzej Swierniak

Fuzzy Combiner of Behaviors for Reactive Control
of Wheeled Mobile Robot 774
  Zenon Hendzel

Artificial Intelligence of the Decision Unit of a Mobile Robot 780
  Jan Kazimierczak

Finding Location Using a Particle Filter and Histogram Matching 786
  Bogdan Kwolek

Calculation of Model of the Robot by Neural Network
with Robot Joint Distinction 792
  J. Możaryn, J.E. Kurek

Multi-robot Coordination Based on Cooperative Game 798
  Krzysztof Skrzypczyk

Model Based Predictive Robotic Manipulator Control
with Sinusoidal Trajectory and Random Disturbances 804
  Hasan Temurtas, Fevzullah Temurtas, Nejat Yumusak

Multiagent Systems

Performance Evaluation of Multiagent Personalized
Information System 810
  Tomasz Babczyński, Zofia Kruczkiewicz, Jan Magott

A Neural-Based Agent for IP Traffic Scanning and Worm Detection 816
  Andrzej Bielecki, Paweł Hajto

Evolutionary Neural Networks in Collective Intelligent
Predicting System... 823
  Aleksander Byrski, Jerzy Bałamut

Development of a Personalized Digital Library System Based on the
New Mobile Multi Agent Platform 829
  Young Im Cho

FOOD: An Agent-Oriented Dataflow Model 835
  Nicolas Juillerat, Béat Hirsbrunner

Flock-Based Architecture for Distributed Evolutionary Algorithms 841
  Marek Kisiel-Dorohinicki

Quickprop Neural Network Short-Term Forecasting Framework
for a Database Intrusion Prediction System 847
  P. Ramasubramanian, A. Kannan

Various Problems of Artificial Intelligence

The New Concepts in Parallel Simulated Annealing Method 853
  Wojciech Bożejko, Mieczysław Wodecki

Simulated Annealing with Restart to Job Shop Scheduling Problem
Using Upper Bounds 860
  Marco Antonio Cruz-Chavez, Juan Frausto-Solis

Requirements and Solutions for Web-Based Expert System 866
    Maciej Grzenda, Marcin Niemczak

Information Structuring in Natural Language Communication:
Syntax versus Semantic 872
    Wladyslaw Homenda

Strategic Planning through Model Checking of ATL Formulae 879
    Wojciech Jamroga

On a Special Class of Dempster-Shafer Theories 885
    Mieczysław Alojzy Kłopotek

A Computer Based System Supporting Analysis
of Cooperative Strategies 891
    Lech Kruś

Application of Soft Computing Techniques to Rescue
Operation Planning 897
    Jiří Kubalík, Jiří Kléma, Miroslav Kulich

Reduction of Tabular Systems 903
    Antoni Ligęza, Marcin Szpyrka

Temporal Difference Approach to Playing Give-Away Checkers 909
    Jacek Mańdziuk, Daniel Osman

Artificial Neural Networks for Solving Double Dummy Bridge Problems . . 915
    Krzysztof Mossakowski, Jacek Mańdziuk

On Application of Ant Algorithms to Non-bifurcated Multicommodity
Flow Problem 922
    Krzysztof Walkowiak

A Parallel Clustering Algorithm for Categorical Data Set 928
    Yong-Xian Wang, Zheng-Hua Wang, Xiao-Mei Li

Intensive versus Non-intensive Actor-Critic Reinforcement
Learning Algorithms 934
    Pawel Wawrzynski, Andrzej Pacut

Virtual Modeling and Optimal Design of Intelligent
Micro-accelerometers 942
    Slawomir Wiak, Andrzej Cader, Pawel Drzymala, Henryk Welfle

Control, Modelling, and System Identification

Local Pattern-Based Interval Models 948
    Wojciech Cholewa

Implementation of Two-Stage Hopfield Model and Its Application in
Nonlinear Systems 954
    Ivan Nunes da Silva, Jose Alfredo C. Ulson, Andre Nunes de Souza

Genetic Algorithm Based Fuzzy Sliding Mode with Application
to Building Structures 960
    Kambiz Falsafian, Mahdi Jalili-Kharaajoo

Influence of the Training Set Selection on the Performance of the
Neural Network State Variables Estimators in the Induction Motor 966
    Jerzy Jelonkiewicz, Andrzej Przybył

LMI-Based Design of Optimal Controllers
for Takagi-Sugeno Fuzzy Systems 972
    J. Park, Y. Park, K. Kwak, J.H. Hong

Design of Multi-objective Evolutionary Technique Based
Intelligent Controller for Multivariable Nonlinear Systems 978
    Farzan Rashidi, Mehran Rashidi

Design of a Robust Sliding Mode Fuzzy Controller
for Nonlinear HVAC Systems 984
    Farzan Rashidi, Behzad Moshiri

Global Identification of Complex Systems with Cascade Structure 990
    Jerzy Swiatek

Medical Applications

Diagnosis of Melanoma Using IRIM, a Data Mining System 996
    Jerzy W. Grzymala-Busse, Jay Hamilton, Zdzislaw S. Hippe

Detection of Spiculated Masses in Mammograms Based on Fuzzy
Image Processing 1002
    Aboul Ella Hassanien, Jafar M. Ali, Hajime Nobuhara

Artificial Neural Networks in Identifying Areas
with Homogeneous Survival Time 1008
    Małgorzata Krętowska, Leon Bobrowski

Multistage Diagnosis of Myocardial Infraction Using a Fuzzy Relation ... 1014
    Marek Kurzynski

Application of SVM to Ovarian Cancer Classification Problem 1020
    Maciej Kusy

ROC Analysis for Fetal Hypoxia Problem by Artificial Neural Networks.. 1026
    Lale Özyılmaz, Tülay Yıldırım

The Challenge of Soft Computing Techniques
for Tumor Characterization 1031
   E.I. Papageorgiou, P.P. Spyridonos, C.D. Stylios, P. Ravazoula,
   G.C. Nikiforidis, P.P. Groumpos

A Multi-stage Classification Method in Application to Diagnosis
of Larynx Cancer 1037
   Danuta Rutkowska, Jacek K. Klimala

Multi-neural Network Approach for Classification of Brainstem
Evoked Response Auditory 1043
   Mariusz Rybnik, Saliou Diouf, Abdennasser Chebira,
   Veronique Amarger, Kurosh Madani

The Study of Hierarchy Importance of Descriptive Attributes in
Computer Assisted Classification of Melanocytic Skin Lesions 1050
   Aleksander Sokołowski, Alicja Dereń

Medical Knowledge Representation in Terms of IF-THEN Rules and
the Dempster-Shafer Theory 1056
   Ewa Straszecka

Online Neural Network Training for Automatic Ischemia
Episode Detection.. 1062
   D.K. Tasoulis, L. Vladutu, V.P. Plagianakos, A. Bezerianos,
   M.N. Vrahatis

Mechanical Applications

Sequential and Distributed Evolutionary Computations
in Structural Optimization 1069
   Tadeusz Burczyński, Wacław Kuś, Adam Długosz,
   Arkadiusz Poteralski, Mirosław Szczepanik

Neural Analysis of Concrete Fatigue Durability by the
Neuro-fuzzy FWNN 1075
   Magdalena Jakubek, Zenon Waszczyszyn

Neural and Finite Element Analysis of a Plane Steel Frame Reliability
by the Classical Monte Carlo Method................................ 1081
   Ewa Pabisek, Joanna Kaliszuk, Zenon Waszczyszyn

The Solution of an Inverse Problem in Plates by Means of
Artificial Neural Networks 1087
   Grzegorz Piątkowski, Leonard Ziemiański

Filtering of Thermomagnetic Data Curve Using Artificial Neural
Network and Wavelet Analysis...................................... 1093
   Łukasz Rauch, Jolanta Talar, Tomáš Žák, Jan Kusiak

Various Applications

Evolutionary Negotiation Strategies in Emerging Electricity Markets 1099
  Salem Al-Agtash

Evolutionary Algorithm for Scheduling of CHP Plant with Urban
Heat Distribution Network 1105
  Krzysztof Dziedzicki, Andrzej Augusiak, Roman Śmierzchalski

Semi-mechanistic Models for State-Estimation – Soft Sensor for
Polymer Melt Index Prediction 1111
  Balazs Feil, Janos Abonyi, Peter Pach, Sandor Nemeth, Peter Arva,
  Miklos Nemeth, Gabor Nagy

Neural Approach to Time-Frequency Signal Decomposition 1118
  Dariusz Grabowski, Janusz Walczak

ANN Based Modelling and Correction in Dynamic
Temperature Measurements 1124
  Lidia Jackowska-Strumiłło

One Day Prediction of NIKKEI Index Considering Information
from Other Stock Markets 1130
  Marcin Jaruszewicz, Jacek Mańdziuk

Application of Neural Network Topologies in the Intelligent Heat
Use Prediction System 1136
  Leszek Kiełtyka, Robert Kucęba, Adam Sokołowski

Genetic Algorithm for Database Indexing 1142
  Marcin Korytkowski, Marcin Gabryel, Robert Nowicki, Rafał Scherer

Application of Neural Networks and Two Representations of Color
Components for Recognition of Wheat Grains Infected by *Fusarium
Culmorum* Fungi 1148
  Aleksander Kubiak, Zbigniew Mikrut

Hybrid Neural Model of the Sea Bottom Surface 1154
  Jacek Lubczonek

Fuzzy Economic Analysis of Simulated Discrete Transport System....... 1161
  Jacek Mazurkiewicz, Tomasz Walkowiak

A Survey on US Economic Sanction Effects on Iranian High Tech
Industries: Fuzzy Logic Approach 1168
  Mohammad R. Mehregan, Hossein Safari, Parviz Naseri,
  Farshid Hosseini, Kumars Sharifi

Modeling of Optoelectronic Devices through Neuro-Fuzzy Architectures .. 1175
  Antonio Vanderlei Ortega, Ivan Nunes da Silva

Neural Network Based Simulation of the Sieve Plate Absorption
Column in Nitric Acid Industry 1181
    Edward Rój, Marcin Wilk

Artificial Neural Networks for Comparative Navigation 1187
    Andrzej Stateczny

Predicting Women's Apparel Sales by Soft Computing 1193
    Les M. Sztandera, Celia Frank, Balaji Vemulapali

Model Improvement by the Statistical Decomposition 1199
    Ryszard Szupiluk, Piotr Wojewnik, Tomasz Zabkowski

Author Index 1205

Towards Grammatical Inferencing of GDPLL(k) Grammars for Applications in Syntactic Pattern Recognition-Based Expert Systems*

Janusz Jurek

Institute of Computer Science, Jagiellonian University
Nawojki 11, 30-072 Cracow, Poland

Abstract. The recent results of the research into construction of syntactic pattern recognition-based expert systems are presented. The model of syntactic pattern recognition has been defined with the use of GDPLL(k) grammars and parsers, and the model has been successfully applied as an efficient tool for inference support in several expert systems. Nevertheless, one of the main problems of practical application of GDPLL(k) grammars consists in difficulties in defining the grammar from the sample of a pattern language. In the paper we present the first achievement in the field of grammatical inferencing of GDPLL(k) grammars: an algorithm of automatic construction of a GDPLL(k) grammar from a so-called polynomial specification of the language.

1 Introduction

DPLL(k) grammars and parsers (syntax analysers) have been introduced [3] as efficient tools for inference support in syntactic pattern recognition-based real-time expert systems. The research into DPLL(k) grammars and parsers have been started for the purpose of an on-line analysis of complex patterns representing trend functions related to the behaviour of a very complex industrial-like equipment [2]. These trend functions have been treated in an analogous way, as it is made while applying syntactic pattern recognition for ECG or EEG analysis. DPLL(k) grammars have been proven to be a suitable tool not only for describing the trend functions (the grammars are stronger descriptively than context-free grammars), but for analysing them as well (the DPLL(k) parser is of linear computational complexity [7]).

Although we have already achieved very good results of the research, the model of DPLL(k) grammars and parsers is still being developed. During few past years we have been verifying the possibility of practical use of the model in several different application areas. The model has been successfully embedded in an expert system for evaluating of organ of hearing in neonates in electric response audiometry (a common project led by Chair of Applied Computer

* This work was supported by the Polish State Committee for Scientific Research (KBN) under Grant No. 3 T11C 054 26.

L. Rutkowski et al. (Eds.): ICAISC 2004, LNAI 3070, pp. 604–609, 2004.
© Springer-Verlag Berlin Heidelberg 2004

Science, Jagiellonian University, and Otolaryngological Clinic, Jagiellonian University Medical College [4]). Now, the model is to be applied as a part of an on-line expert system running at the Polish Power Grid Company, one of the biggest companies in Poland which is responsible for the whole Polish power system.

However, as it turned out the model should be improved to fulfil the strong requirements of the applications mentioned above. The main problem of practical applications of the model consists in difficulties in defining the grammar from the sample of a pattern language. Therefore, a grammatical inference algorithm is needed to automate a very complex process of constructing suitable grammars. The problem of grammatical inferencing is a well-known issue in syntactic pattern recognition area. There are many approaches and methods developed since seventies [5,9,6]. Nevertheless there is still lack of general models of inferencing context-sensitive grammars since inference algorithms have been constructed only for some particular subclasses of context-sensitive languages and grammars (e.g. [1]). The generative power of DPLL(k) is "almost" as big as context-sensitive grammars [3], and developing a method of grammatical inference for this kind of grammars is of big importance.

In the paper we present the first achievement in the field of grammatical inferencing of GDPLL(k) grammars. GDPLL(k) grammars are "enhanced" DPLL(k) grammars — GDPLL(k) grammars are stronger descriptively and computationally than DPLL(k) grammars [8]. We present an algorithm of automatic construction of a GDPLL(k) grammar from a so-called polynomial specification of a language.

2   Basic Definitions

Let us introduce a few basic definitions [3,8] needed to discuss the inference algorithm.

Definition 1.   A *generalised dynamically programmed context-free grammar* is a six-tuple:

$$G = (V, \Sigma, O, P, S, M),$$

where V is a finite, nonempty alphabet; $\Sigma \subset V$ is a finite, nonempty set of terminal symbols (let $N = V \setminus \Sigma$); O is a set of basic operations on the values stored in the memory (assignment, addition, subtraction, multiplication); $S \in N$ is the starting symbol; M is the memory (the memory is defined as such a memory structure that integer numbers can be stored in it and each element of the memory can be accessed in a constant time); P is a finite set of productions of the form: $p_i = (\mu_i, L_i, R_i, A_i)$ in which $\mu_i : M \longrightarrow \{TRUE, FALSE\}$ is the predicate of applicability of the production p_i defined with the use of operations ($\in O$) performed over M; $L_i \in N$ and $R_i \in V^*$ are left- and right-hand sides of p_i respectively; A_i is the sequence of operations ($\in O$) over M, which should be performed if the production is to be applied. $\square$

A derivation for generalised dynamically programmed grammars is defined in the following way. Apart from testing whether L_i occurs in a sentential form derived, we check the predicate of applicability of a production p_i. The predicate in generalised dynamically programmed grammars is defined as an expression based on variables stored in the memory. The evaluation of the predicate can need some calculations over integer values. If the predicate is true, we replace L_i with R_i and then we perform the sequence of operations over the memory. The execution of the operations changes the contents of the memory (memory variables). It is done with the help of arithmetical and assignment instructions.

Definition 2.   Let $G = (V, \Sigma, O, P, S, M)$ be a generalised dynamically programmed context-free grammar. The grammar G is called a *Generalised Dynamically Programmed LL(k) grammar*, GDPLL(k) grammar, if: 1) the LL(k) condition of deterministic derivation is fulfilled, and: 2) the number of steps during derivation of any terminal symbol is limited by a constant. (Formal specifications of the two conditions is included in [3]). □

3   Model of Inferencing GDPLL(k) Grammars

Our approach to the inferencing GDPLL(k) grammars is based on the following method. We divide the inference process into two phases:

1. The first phase is responsible for extraction of the features of the sample, and generalisation of the sample. A so-called *polynomial specification of the language* is obtained as the result of the phase.
2. In the second phase, a GDPLL(k) grammar is generated on the basis of polynomial specification of the language.

Both phases are independent of each other. The second phase is well-defined, i.e. the result of this phase is strictly determined by the input data (a polynomial specification of language). On the contrary, the first phase is not well-defined since there may be many approaches to the generalisation of the sample and the "quality" of an approach depends on a particular application and a particular sample of the language.

In the paper we show the algorithm of automatic generation of a GDPLL(k) grammar from the polynomial specification of a language. Although the algorithm corresponds only to the second phase, it is the essential part of our grammatical inference method.

Firstly, let us present the following definition:

Definition 3.   Let A is a set of all (terminal) symbols which appear in the sample, N set of integer variables. *Polynomial specification of a language* is of the form:

$$L_p(A, N) = S_i^{p_j(n_k)}$$

where: p_j is a polynomial of a variable $n_k \in N$; variable n_k can be assigned only values greater or equal 1 ($n_k \geq 1$); S_i, called *polynomial structure*, is defined in a recursive way:

1) $S_i = (a_{i_1}...a_{i_r})$, where $a_{i_j} \in A$
   (S_i is called a *basic* polynomial structure) or

2) $S_i = (S_{i_1}^{p_{i_1}(n_{i_1})}...S_{i_r}^{p_{i_r}(n_{i_r})})$, where S_{i_k} is defined as in 1) or 2).
   (S_i is called a *complex* polynomial structure.) $\square$

Example 1. Let $A = \{a, b, c\}$ be a set of terminal symbols, $N = \{n, m\}$ be a set of integer variables. Then: $L_p(A, N) = ((ab)^{2n+1}c^{m^2})^{n+2}(ab)^{m^3}$ is an example of polynomial specification of a language. The polynomial structures in the specification are the following:

$S_1 = ((ab)^{2n+1}c^{m^2})^{n+2}(ab)^{m^3}$	$p_1 \equiv 1$
$S_{1_1} = (ab)^{2n+1}c^{m^2}$	$p_{1_1}(n) = n+2$
$S_{1_2} = ab$	$p_{1_2}(m) = m^3$
$S_{1_{1_1}} = ab$	$p_{1_{1_1}}(n) = 2n+1$
$S_{1_{1_2}} = c$	$p_{1_{1_2}}(m) = m^2$

Now, we can define the algorithm of automatic generation of a GDPLL(k) grammar from the polynomial specification of the language.

Algorithm 1. Let $L_p(A, N)$ be a polynomial specification of a language. We will construct a GDPLL(k) grammar $G = (V, \Sigma, O, P, S, M)$ generating the language.

Step 1. Let $\Sigma := A$.

Step 2. For each variable $n \in N$ in $L_p(A, N)$ we define two variables: v_n and d_n in the grammar memory M.

Step 3. For each polynomial structure S in $L_p(A, N)$ we define: a nonterminal symbol $X_S \in V$, and two memory variables c_S and e_S in M.

Step 4. For each $S^{p(n)}$ structure in $L_p(A, N)$ we define productions in P.

- if S is a *basic* polynomial structure, i.e. $S = (a_1...a_r)$, we define productions in the following way:

i	μ_i	core	operations on M
1_S	$c_S = 0$	$X_S \longrightarrow a_1...a_r X_S$	$c_S := 1; e_S := p(v_n)$
2_S	$c_S < e_S$	$X_S \longrightarrow a_1...a_r X_S$	$c_S := c_S + 1$
3_S	$(c_S = e_S)$ and $(d_n = true)$	$X_S \longrightarrow \lambda$	$c_S := 0;$
4_S	$(c_S = e_S)$ and $(d_n = false)$	$X_S \longrightarrow \lambda$	$c_S := 0; d_n := true$
5_S	$(c_S = e_S)$ and $(d_n = false)$	$X_S \longrightarrow a_1...a_r X_S$	$c_S := c_S + 1; v_n := v_n + 1;$ $e_S := p(v_n)$

- if S is a *complex* polynomial structure, i.e. $S = (S_1^{p_1(n_1)}...S_r^{p_r(n_r)})$, we define productions in the following way:

i	μ_i	core	operations on M
1_S	$c_S = 0$	$X_S \longrightarrow X_{S_1}...X_{S_r}X_S$	$c_S := 1; e_S := p(v_n)$
2_S	$c_S < e_S$	$X_S \longrightarrow X_{S_1}...X_{S_r}X_S$	$c_S := c_S + 1$
3_S	$(c_S = e_S)$ and $(d_n = true)$	$X_S \longrightarrow \lambda$	$c_S := 0;$
4_S	$(c_S = e_S)$ and $(d_n = false)$	$X_S \longrightarrow \lambda$	$c_S := 0; d_n := true$
5_S	$(c_S = e_S)$ and $(d_n = false)$	$X_S \longrightarrow X_{S_1}...X_{S_r}X_S$	$c_S := c_S + 1; v_n := v_n + 1;$ $e_S := p(v_n)$

Step 5. Let the starting symbol of the grammar G be S (a nonterminal symbol which has not been used yet). Let X_{S_1} be the nonterminal symbol defined for the first polynomial structure (being the root of the structures' tree). We define the initial production in P in the following way:

i	μ_i	core	operations on M
1	$true$	$S \longrightarrow X_{S_1}$	$c_{S_1} := 0; ...; c_{S_q} := 0; \; e_{S_1} := -1; ...; e_{S_q} := -1$ $v_{n_1} := 1; ...; v_{n_t} := 1; \; d_{n_1} := false; ...; d_{n_t} := false$

The definition of the initial production is the last step in the algorithm. $\square$

The idea of the algorithm is the following. We use memory variables to implement "loops" during derivation. Current value of n (in exponent expression) is stored in v_n. Variable c_S is a counter of repetitions of S structure. Variable e_S contains the current evaluation of exponent expression for S structure. Boolean variable d_n stores information whether n is fixed or not (i.e. if the value of n has been determined before). Operations on the memory defined for each production are responsible for "programming" proper number of repetitions during derivation.

4   Concluding Remarks

In the paper we have presented the algorithm of automatic generation of a GDPLL(k) grammar from the polynomial specification of a language. The algorithm is the main part of our grammatical inference model. The model has been developed for the purposes of the construction of syntactic pattern recognition-based expert systems.

As we have mentioned in the introduction, there are several possible applications of the model. As the first practical verification, it has has been successfully embedded in an expert system for evaluating of organ of hearing in neonates in electric response audiometry [4]. An example of a window in the parser module is shown in Figure 1. Thanks to the grammatical inference algorithm, it is possible to automatically construct complex GDPLL(k) grammars describing very sophisticated medical symptoms in ERA.

Although the algorithm presented is the basis of our grammatical inference method, there are still some research to be done. Our next goal is the automatic generation of the polynomial specification of a language from the sample. The results of the research will be a subject of further publications.

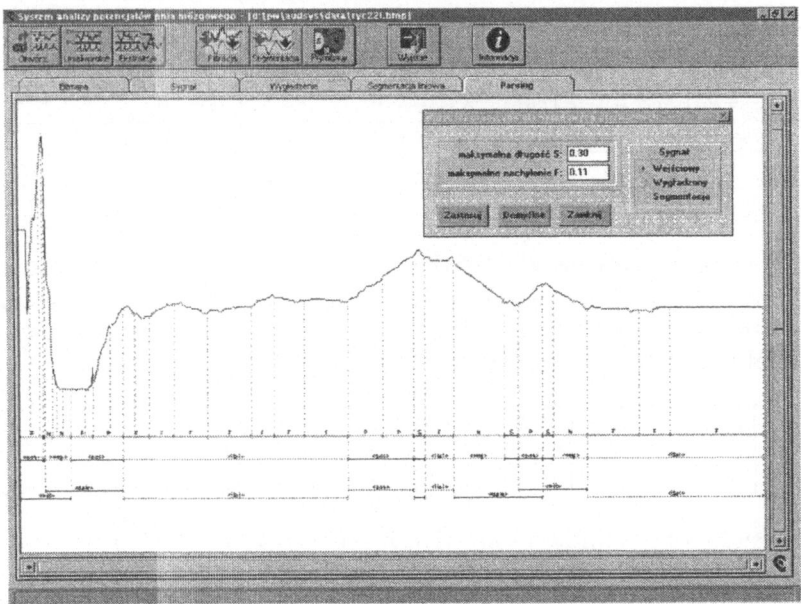

Fig. 1. Parsing of brainstem ERA charts for the purpose of medical diagnostics.

References

1. Alquezar, R., Sanfeliu, A.: Recognition and learning of a class of context-sensitive languages described by augmented regular expressions. Pattern Recognition, vol. 30, no. 1 (1997) 163–182.
2. Behrens, U., Flasiński, M., Hagge, L., Jurek, J., Ohrenberg, K.: Recent developments of the ZEUS expert system ZEX. IEEE Trans. Nucl. Sci., NS-43, (1996) 65–68.
3. Flasiński, M., Jurek, J.: Dynamically Programmed Automata for Quasi Context Sensitive Languages as a Tool for Inference Support in Pattern Recognition-Based Real-Time Control Expert Systems. Pattern Recognition, vol. 32, no. 4 (1999) 671–690.
4. Flasiński, M., Reroń, E., Jurek, J., Wójtowicz, P., Atłasiewicz, K.: Mathematical linguistics model for medical diagnostics of organ of hearing in neonates. Accepted for publication in Lecture Notes in Computer Science (LNAI).
5. Fu, K.S.: Syntactic Pattern Recognition and Applications, Prentice Hall, Englewood Cliffs, (1982).
6. Higuera De La, C.: Current Trends in Grammatical Inference. Lecture Notes in Computer Science, vol. 1876 (2000) 28–31.
7. Jurek, J.: On the Linear Computational Complexity of the Parser for Quasi Context Sensitive Languages. Pattern Recognition Letters, no. 21 (2000) 179–187.
8. Jurek, J.: The Generalised Model of DPLL(k) Automata for Applications in Real-Time Expert Systems. Proc. 3rd Conf. On Computer Recognition Systems, KO-SYR'03, Miłków, Poland, 26-29 May 2003, 321–326.
9. Sakakibara, Y.: Recent Advances of Grammatical Inference. Theoretical Computer Science, vol. 185, no. 1 (1997) 15–45.

Intelligent Layer of Two-Way Voice Communication of the Technological Device with the Operator

Wojciech Kacalak and Maciej Majewski

Department of Mechanical Engineering
Technical University of Koszalin
Raclawicka 15-17
75-620 Koszalin, Poland

{kacalakw,mmaj}@tu.koszalin.pl

Abstract. In this paper there is a review of the selected issues on recognition and safety estimation of voice commands in natural language given by the operator of the technological device. A view is offered of the complexity of the recognition process of words and commands using neural networks made of a few layers of neurons. The paper presents some research results of speech recognition and automatic command recognition with artificial neural networks. The first part of the paper introduces a new conception of an intelligent layer of two-way voice communication of the technological device with the operator and discusses the general topics and issues. The second part is devoted to a discussion of more specific topics of the automatic command recognition and safety estimation that have led to interesting new approaches and techniques.

1 Introduction

Speech is the natural mode of communication for humans. It is a singularly efficient way for humans to express ideas and desires. Therefore, it is not surprising that we have always wanted to communicate with and command various technical devices by voice. Voice control is particularly appealing when the human's hands or eyes are otherwise occupied. In the future, speech unquestionably will become the primary means of communication between humans and machines.

The advantages of intelligent two-way voice communication of the technological devices with the operator include the following [KM03b]:

1. More resistance from the operator's errors and more efficient supervising of process with the chosen level of supervision automation.
2. Elimination of scarcities of the typical co-operation between the operator and the technological device.
3. Reaching a higher level of organising realization of a technological process equipped with the intelligent two-way voice communication system, which is relevant for its efficiency and production humanization.
4. No need of an operator being present at the work stand by the technological device (any distance from the technological device) [O'S00].

L. Rutkowski et al. (Eds.): ICAISC 2004, LNAI 3070, pp. 610–615, 2004.
© Springer-Verlag Berlin Heidelberg 2004

2   Intelligent Two-Way Communication by Voice

According to the new conception, the intelligent layer of two-way voice communication of the technological device with the operator presented in Fig. 1, is equipped with the following intelligent mechanisms: operator identification, recognition of words and complex commands, command syntax analysis, command result analysis, command safety assessment, technological process supervision, and also operator reaction assessment [KM03a].

If the operator is identified and authorized by the intelligent voice communication layer, a produced command in continuous speech is recognized by the speech recognition module and processed to the text format. Then the recognised text is analysed with the syntax analysis subsystem. The processed command is sent to the word and command recognition modules using artificial neural networks to recognise the command, which next is sent to the effect analysis subsystem for analysing the status corresponding to the hypothetical command execution, consecutively assessing the command correctness, estimating the process state and the technical safety, and also possibly signalling the possible error caused by the operator. Then the command is sent to the safety assessment subsystem for assessing the grade of affiliation of the command to the correct command category and making corrections. Next the command execution subsystem signalises commands accepted for executing, assessing reactions of the operator, defining new parameters of the process and run directives. The subsystem for voice communication produces voice commands to the operator.

3   Command Recognition and Safety Estimation

In the automatic command recognition system as shown in Fig. 2, the speech signal is processed to text and numeric values with the module for processing voice commands to text format using the speech recognition engine. The separated words of the text are the input signals of the neural network for recognizing words. The network has a training file containing word patterns. As the work result, the network recognizes words as the operator's command components, which are represented by its neurons. The recognized words are sent to the algorithm for coding words. Next the coded words are transferred to the command syntax analysis module. It is equipped with the algorithm for analyzing and indexing words. The module indexes words properly and then they are sent to the algorithm for coding commands. The commands are coded as vectors and they are input signals of the command recognition module using artificial neural network. The module uses the 3-layer Hamming neural network either to recognize the operator's command or to produce the information that the command is not recognized. The neural network is equipped with a training file containing patterns of possible operator's commands.

The recognised command given by the operator is processed and sent from the command syntax subsystem to the verification subsystems of effects and safety. The effect analysis module, shown in Fig. 3a, makes analysis of the recognised command. The technical safety of the technological device is checked by analysing the state of execution of the commands required to have been done as

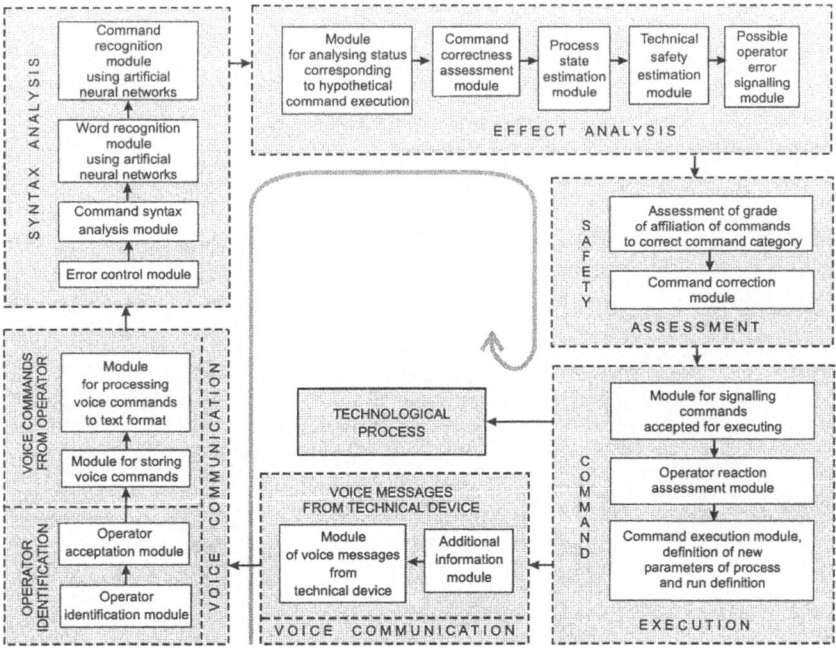

Fig. 1. Scheme of the intelligent layer of two-way voice communication of the technological device with the operator

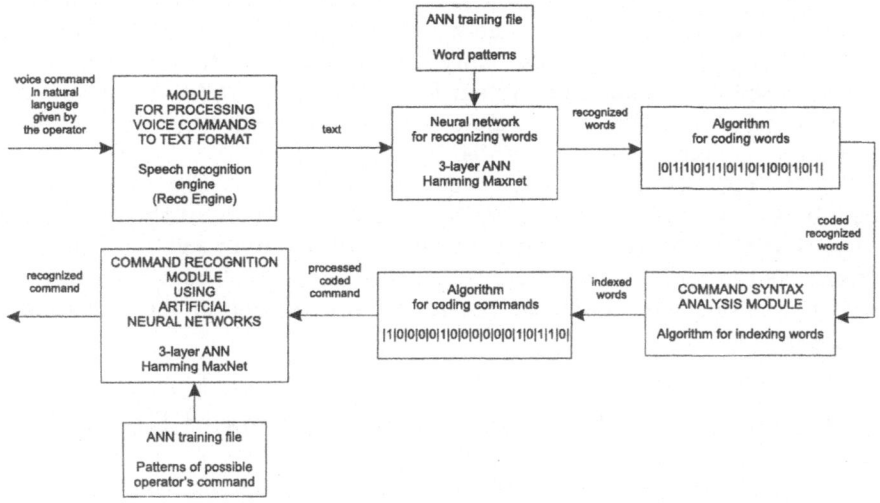

Fig. 2. Scheme of the automatic command recognition system

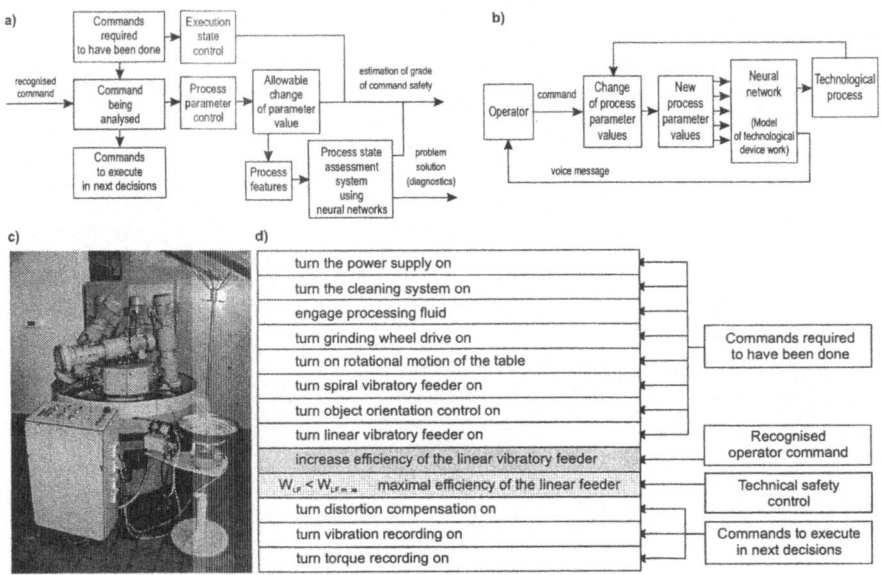

Fig. 3. Scheme of the command effect analysis and safety assessment system

well as the commands to execute in next decisions. The process parameters to be modified by executing the command are checked and the allowable changes of the parameter values are determined. The analysis of the parameter values is based on the technological process features. The values of the parameter changes are the input signals of the neural network of the process state assessment system. The neurons of the neural network represent solutions to the diagnostics problem. The neural network also makes an estimation of the grade of safety of the recognised command. The system for checking the state of the automatic device for grinding of small ceramic elements that is shown in Fig. 3c, before executing next commands is presented in Fig. 3d.

The technological safety assessment system, shown in Fig. 3b, is based on a neural network which is trained with the model of work of the technological device. New values of the process parameters are the input signals of the neural network. As the work result of the system, voice messages from the technological device to the operator about the possibility of executing of the command are produced.

4   Research Results of Automatic Command Recognition

For the evaluation of research results of the automatic speech recognition, it has to be defined how to calculate the command recognition rate. The calculation is done after performing each case of recognition event. The recognition rate is calculated from the formula for the total number of errors and the error rate. The total number of errors is the sum of the insertion errors and the out-of-context errors. The error rate equals to the total number of errors divided by the total number of commands in a case.

As shown in Fig. 4a, the speech recognition module recognizes 85-90% of the operator's words correctly. As more training of the neural networks is done, accuracy rises to around 95%. For the research on word recognition at different

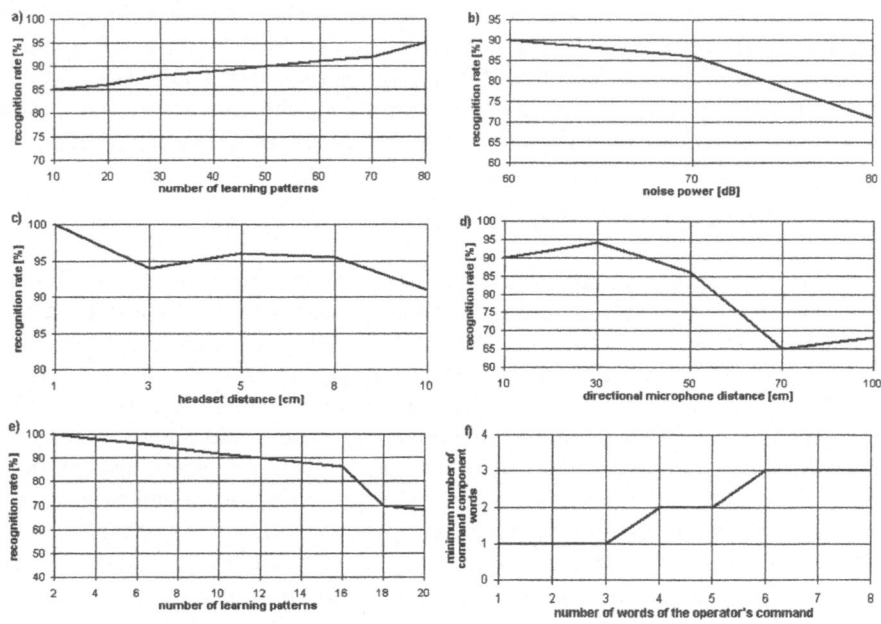

Fig. 4. Speech and command recognition rate

noise power, the microphone used by the operator is the headset. As shown in Fig. 4b, the recognition performance is sensitive to background noise. The recognition rate is about 86% at 70 dB and 71% at 80 dB. Therefore, background noise must be limited while giving the commands. For the research on word recognition at different microphone distances, the microphone used by the operator is the headset. As shown in Fig. 4c, the recognition rate decreases when the headset distance increases. The recognition rate has been dropped for 9% after the headset distance is changed from 1 to 10 cm. Also for the research on word recognition at different microphone distances, the microphone used by the operator is the directional microphone. As shown in Fig. 4d, the recognition rate after 50 cm decreases reaching rate about 65%.

The command recognition module using Hamming Maxnet neural networks is capable of recognizing different commands of the same meaning in natural language. The ability of the 3-layer neural network to learn to recognise commands depends on the number of learning patterns of possible operator commands.

The specified number of the patterns enables the network to learn and work efficiently and quickly. Based on the research, the following conclusion has been reached in Fig. 4e. It could be said that the fewer patterns the neural network is trained with, the faster it works and learns. If the Hamming Maxnet network was trained with the number of patterns bigger than 16, it begun to mix up and overlay the gathered experience information. It is caused by the limited number of neurons storing the training patterns. As a consequence of that fact, there are sometimes considerable errors while recreating the knowledge by the neural network. As shown in Fig. 4f, the ability of the neural network to recognise the command depends on the number of command component words. Depending on the number of component words of the command, the neural network requires the minimal number of words of the given command as its input signals.

5   Conclusions and Perspectives

In the future, voice messages in natural language will undoubtedly be the most important way of communication between humans and machines. In the automated processes of production, the condition for safe communication of the technological device with the operator is analyzing the state of the technological device and the process before the command is given and using artificial intelligence for assessment of the technological effects and safety of the command. In operations of the automated technological processes, many process states and various commands from the operator to the technological device can be distinguished. A large number of combined technological systems characterize the realization of that process. In complex technological processes, if many parameters are controlled, the operator is not able to analyse a sufficient number of signals and react by manual operations on control buttons. The research aiming at developing an intelligent layer of two-way voice communication is very difficult, but the prognosis of the technology development and its first use shows a great significance in efficiency of supervision and production humanisation.

Acknowledgements. The support of the Polish State Committee for Scientific Research (KBN grant 5 T07D 036 24) is highly appreciated.

References

[KM03a] W. Kacalak and M. Majewski. Intelligent two-sided voice communication system between the machining system and the operator. *Proceedings of the Artificial Neural Networks in Engineering ANNIE 2003 Conference, St. Louis USA, ASME Press New York*, pages 969–974, 2003.

[KM03b] W. Kacalak and M. Majewski. Supervising of technological process using two-sided voice communication between the machining system and the operator. *Modern Trends in Manufacturing CAMT2003 Wroclaw*, pages 175–182, 2003.

[O'S00] D. O'Shaughnessy. Speech communications: Human and machine. *IEEE Press New York*, 2000.

A Neural Network Based Method for Classification of Meteorological Data

K. Kaminski[1], W. Kaminski[1], and P. Strumillo[2]

[1] Faculty of Process and Environmental Engineering, Technical University of Łódź,
Wólczańska 213, 93-005 Łódź, Poland. kaminski@wipos.p.lodz.pl
[2] Institute of Electronics, Technical University of Łódź, Wólczańska 223, 90-924
Łódź, Poland. pstrumil@p.lodz.pl

Abstract. A neural network based method for classification of meteorological data is proposed in the paper. The method consists of two phases. First, a non-linear projection of the data space is performed by means of radial basis functions. The neural gas algorithm is used for determining locations of the basis functions. Second, a nonlinearly projected data is allocated to different classes by means of a competitive network layer. Nonlinear data transformation was necessary for obtaining linear separability of 6 classes of the meteorological data defined in 8 dimensions.

1 Introduction

Vast amounts of data can be stored nowadays thanks to developments in computer technology. The task of extracting meaningful information from large sets of data becomes the major challenge of a research field termed data mining. Various statistical techniques have been proposed for description of large data sets (e.g. correlation methods or ARMA - auto-regressive moving average models), that usually assume that a collection of analysed data is due to a linear process. Moreover, if this is a parametric data model additional a priori knowledge about the analysed data is required. Artificial neural network (ANN) paradigms overcome these two limitations, i.e. linearity assumption and a priori knowledge requirement about the analysed data. This is due to ANN universal flexibility in building complex nonlinear models and both supervised or un-supervised capability in searching for statistical structure in data. A hybrid neural network concept for analysis of meteorological data is proposed. First, a set of radial basis functions (RBF) is used for nonlinear transformation of multidimensional input data space. Then, so generated feature space is processed further by means of self-organised network playing the role of a cluster detector and data classifier.

2 Description of the Method

The proposed method that proved effective for classification of meteorological data consists of the following data processing steps:

L. Rutkowski et al. (Eds.): ICAISC 2004, LNAI 3070, pp. 616–621, 2004.
© Springer-Verlag Berlin Heidelberg 2004

1. Application of the neural-gas algorithm for determining RBF receptive filed.
2. Nonlinear projection of data by means of RBF.
3. Self-organised data classification.

Radial basis functions of type given in (1) are used for nonlinear projection of the input data space into multidimensional feature space:

$$u_{ij} = \exp\left[\frac{-\parallel z_i - z_{cj}\parallel^2}{\delta}\right], j = 1,\ldots,M, i = 1,\ldots,p \tag{1}$$

where:
u_{ij} – j-th coordinate of i-th input data vector in a feature space,
z_i – i-th input data vector,
δ – scaling factor,
z_{cj} – centre coordinate of j-th basis function,
M – number of basis functions (feature space dimension),
p – number of training vectors.

In theory, the number of basis functions (i.e. feature space dimension) can be arbitrarily large. This requires, however, excessively large training sets. In engineering practice, the number of basis functions needs to be chosen considerably smaller than the number of training patterns (vectors). The size of feature space dimension should strongly depend on data complexity, data classification task, and the adopted classifier. In the presented work the criterion for choosing a minimum number of basis functions for which inter-class data separability in the feature space is achieved was employed [2,3,4].

There have been many methods proposed for selection of radial basis function centres, e.g. at random, by means of self-organising algorithms, or other probabilistic methods [1,2]. In the presented application a neural-gas algorithm search of centres was used. This method takes its name after the manner in which the centres migrate (similarly as Brownian gas particles movements) before they settle into stable locations [2,5]. In the neural-gas algorithm each RBF centre is represented by a neural node. Each such node is connected to each element of input patterns via randomly pre-assigned weight coefficients. The following distance measure is computed for all the nodes in each training iteration:

$$d_{ij} = \parallel z_i - w_j \parallel \tag{2}$$

where: z_i – denotes i-th training pattern and w_j – is the weight corresponding to j-th RBF centre. Then, following the concept of the neural gas algorithm, the nodes are ranked according to an increasing distance (2) and are assigned a parameter given by:

$$H(s(j)) = \exp\left(-\frac{s(j)}{\lambda}\right) \tag{3}$$

where: λ – is the scaling coefficient, and $s(j)$ – the position number $1,\ldots,M$ of j-th node in a sorted series of nodes. In the neural-gas algorithm, as opposed to the other competitive algorithms, connection weights of all nodes are modified according to the formula:

$$w'_j = w_j + \eta H\left(s\left(j\right)\right)\left(z_i - w_j\right) \tag{4}$$

where η is the training rate that is decreased with each training iteration.

Note, that the winning node (i.e. for which (2) is the smallest) obtains the largest value of factor (3). For other nodes this factor decreases with a decreasing rank. The training process is halted once the weight corrections for all nodes drop below a predetermined threshold. So obtained weight vectors determine coordinates of basis functions centres in the input space.

Basis functions distributed by means of the neural-gas algorithm are used for nonlinear projection of the input data space into feature space. The transformed data is then classified by means of a competitive algorithm with the "winner takes all" mechanism. Thus, in the training iterations only the winning neuron (i.e. whose weight vector w_j^* is the closest in an inner product sense to the vector u_i in the feature space) has its weights updated:

$$w_j^* = \alpha u_i + \left(1 - \alpha\right) w_j = w_j + \alpha \left(u_i - w_j\right) \tag{5}$$

The learning rate parameter α is decreased linearly to zero with each training iteration. Training vectors are picked at random without repetitions in each training epoch. A track of the number of times each neuron wins the competition is kept. If there are "dead" neurons (i.e. poor winners) they are removed and training is restarted with a smaller number of neurons.

The following supervised method is proposed for evaluating separability of data in the feature space. It is based on the Euclidean distance measure $d_{ij} = \| u_{ij} - w_j \|$ between j-th class prototype w_j and u_{ij}, i.e., i-th feature vector associated with j-th class. First an average class "radius" is computed from:

$$r_j = \frac{\sum_{i=1}^{P_j} d_{ij}}{P_j} \tag{6}$$

where P_j is the number of feature vectors associated with j-th class. Then, the following decision about inter class separability is taken: if $\delta_{jm} > \| w_j - w_m \| - \left(r_j + r_m\right)$, i.e., distance between class prototypes is larger than the sum of class radii it is conjectured that classes j and m are sufficiently separated.

3   Case Study – Classification of Meteorological Data

The proposed nonlinear transformation was applied for inter-class data separation of meteorological data collected at Lublinek Airport in the years 1976-1995. In climatology a number of different atmospheric circulation types are identified. The aim of the study was identification of weather vectors that characterise different types of circulations. The considered circulation types are listed in Table 1.

Table 1. Classification of atmospheric circulation types

Symbol	Circulation type	Circulation subtype	Number of training vectors for years 1976-1995
A	Western	cyclone	587
B	Southern	cyclone	354
BE	Southern	intermediate	184
C2D	Western	anticyclone	679
CB	North-Western	cyclone	1107
D	South-Western	cyclone	469
D2C	South-Western and Southern	anticyclone	261
E	North-Eastern	anticyclone	1025
E0	North-Eastern and Eastern	cyclone	763
E1	South-Eastern and Eastern	anticyclone	570
E2C	North-Western	anticyclone	322
F	South-Eastern	cyclone	330
G	Central	anticyclone	431
X	other	other	223

Table 2. Factors of the "weather" vector (average values for 24 hours)

No.	Weather vector factor	Variability range
1.	average temperature	$-22{,}2°C - 29{,}0°C$
2.	precipitation	$0 - 99{,}8\ mm$
3.	average wind direction	$0 - 353\ °$
4.	average wind velocity	$0 - 13\ ^m/_s$
5.	average cloudiness	$0 - 8{,}6$
6.	average air humidity	$34{,}3 - 100\ \%$
7.	average atmospheric pressure	$950{,}15 - 1022{,}36\ hPa$
8.	hours of insolation	$0 - 16{,}4\ h$

Table 2 lists factors of the weather vector taken into account in defining weather circulation type.

Collections of vectors characterising different circulation types were tested for inter-class separability. Results obtained from the proposed data separation methods were compared to earlier studies in which different linear concepts of data classifications were used including Principal Component Analysis (PCA) approach for reducing weather vector dimension [7]. In that work a considerable number of input weather vectors associated with different circulations featured similar locations in the input space.The proposition of employing a non-linear transformation of data as opposed to linear methods has enabled a better inter class separability of patterns.

Table 3 lists values of the inter-class separability criterion δ_{jm} obtained for CB circulation class (the most typical for Polish winter).

Table 3. Values of separability criterion δ_{jm} obtained after RBF transformation of input data

Winter, Circulation CB	I class	II class	III class	IV class	V class	VI class
I class	-	0.0171	0.0119	0.3917	0.1024	0.2153
II class	0.0171	-	0.0439	0.4594	0.0137	0.4925
III class	0.0119	0.0439	-	0.2126	0.0415	0.2746
IV class	0.3917	0.4594	0.2126	-	0.2266	0.1302
V class	0.1024	0.0137	0.0415	0.2266	-	0.3718
VI class	0.2153	0.4925	0.2746	0.1302	0.3718	-

Note that all table entries are positive. Thus, a good separation of weather circulation classes was obtained in the feature space generated by radial basis functions. This result was obtained for all circulation types. Unfortunately, there is no physical interpretation of the features in the so generated space. The correspondence between the input data space and the feature data space can be identified by noting indices of the vectors in both spaces.

4   Summary

A method for nonlinear transformation of input data space aimed at improving their separability was proposed. The transformation was implemented by means of radial basis functions whose locations in the input space were optimised by employing a neural-gas algorithm. A competitive training rule was used for identifying prototypes of predefined data classes in the feature space. The method was tested on a collection of meteorological data and proved effective in obtaining good separability of atmpspheric circulation types.

Acknowledgement. This work was carried out as a part of the research project No. 4T09C00522 sponsored by the Polish Ministry of Scientific Research and Information Technology in 2002-2004.

References

[1] Strumillo P., Kaminski W.: Radial Basis Function Neural Networks. Theory and Applications, Proceedings of the Sixth International Conference on Neural Networks and Soft Computing, Zakopane, 2002, pp. 107-119.
[2] Osowski S.: Neural network algorithms (in Polish). WNT, Warszawa, 1996.
[3] Kohonen T.: Self-organizing maps. Berlin, Springer-Verlag, 1995.
[4] Haykin S.: Neural Networks, a comprehensive foundation. Prentice Hall, 1999.
[5] Martinez T.M., Berkovich S .G., Schulten K. J.: "Neural-gas" network for vector quantization and its application to time-series prediction. IEEE Trans. Neural Networks, vol. 4, no. 4, 1993, pp. 558-569.

[6] Osuchowska-Klein B.: Catalogue of atmospheric circulation types. (in Polish) (1976-1990). IMGW, Warszawa, 1991.

[7] Kaminski W., Strumillo P., Skrzypski J.: Evaluation of climatic air pollution by means of principal component analysis. Chemical Industry and Environment III. 1, 1999, pp. 71-78.

An Empirical Test Suite for Message Authentication Evaluation in Communications Based on Support Vector Machines

D.A. Karras

Chalkis Institute of Technology & Hellenic Open Univ., Rodu 2, Ano Iliupolis,
Athens 16342, Greece,
dakarras@usa.net

Abstract. The strength of data integrity, message authentication and pseudonym generation mechanisms in the design of secure multimedia communication applications relies on the quality of the message digest algorithms used. In this paper, we propose Support Vector Machines based evaluation benchmarks to assess the message digest function quality since there is lack of practical tests to be applied to message digest algorithms in the emerging field of designing secure information and communication systems especially for the delivery of multimedia content, where the issues of copyright protection and security in transactions are outstanding.

1 Introduction

A one way hash function or message digest is a digital fingerprint created from a plaintext block, that is part of a message. All the information of the message is used to construct the Message Digest hash, but the message cannot be recovered from the hash. For this reason, Message Digests are also known as one way hash functions. While the mainstream analysis of hash functions involves theoretical investigation of their properties, the designer of security protocols in communication systems doesn't occupy a comprehensive framework for applying computationally feasible and of practical value evaluation tests to assess such hash values. Actually such theoretical analysis leads to tests needing non polynomial time to be conducted.

Message and user authentication, data integrity as well as digital signature generation techniques may make use of un-keyed or keyed message digest (hash) functions. Un-keyed message digest functions take as input strings of variable length and produce, according to their mapping algorithm, output of fixed length, generally smaller than the input string, called digest or message digest value [1,2,3,4,5,6,7]. On the other hand, keyed message digest functions take as input additionally a secret key. Hereafter, we deal mainly with un-keyed message digest functions and use for them the key-word message digest functions. In this section, we outline some aspects of well-known message digest functions as well as the contribution of this paper. In the second section, we describe the proposed

L. Rutkowski et al. (Eds.): ICAISC 2004, LNAI 3070, pp. 622–627, 2004.
© Springer-Verlag Berlin Heidelberg 2004

methodology and in the third section its application to MD4, MD5 and SHA. Finally, we conclude the paper and outline future work on this subject.

The MD5 algorithm handles messages of arbitrary length and produces digests consisting of 128 bits [8, 9, 10]. Each message after it has been appended by padding bits and its length is processed in blocks of 512 bits. The Secure Hash Algorithm (SHA, [8, 9, 10, 11]) is a variant of the MD4 algorithm, like the MD5 algorithm. However, the algorithm produces digests of 160 bits in length, although it takes as input messages of arbitrary length as the MD5 does.

There exists a multitude of applications of Artificial Neural Networks (ANN) in communications and information systems. The design, however, of secure such systems has not been considered so far involving ANN. Moreover, the design of improved hash functions algorithms to be applied to security mechanisms and protocols of information and communication systems makes necessary the development of a practical evaluation methodology of such algorithms. So far only theoretical tests exist in the literature, as for instance in [12]. The novel aspect of this work relies on the fact that for the first time, a set of practical benchmarks is proposed to deal with this requirement. These tests are mainly based on Support Vector Machines (SVM) ANNs properties concerning classification and function approximation, as well as on statistical and information theoretic methods.

The main concept of the proposed methodology is to produce sets of hash values applying the corresponding different hash function algorithms. Then, on each such set we sequentially apply the neural, statistical and information theoretic benchmarks. The result is the production of the set of relevant test statistics. By comparing these statistics with previously defined thresholds we might conjecture the strength of the associated hash function algorithm.

Before proceeding with the proposed methodology we recall the required characteristics of hash functions, that are the following. It is computationally easy to extract the digest from the message, hard to find the message from the digest, hard to find another message that lead to a given digest and hard to find two or more messages that lead to the same digest (birthday attack, [8]). ('Easy' might mean polynomial time and space; or more practically, within a certain number of machine operations or time units. On the other hand, "hard" might mean requiring effort far exceeding affordable resources or a lower bound on the number of operations or memory required in terms of a specified security parameter or the probability that a property is violated be exponentially small.)

The requirement for rapid execution of the algorithm leads to the selection of simple sets of operations, as in the case of MD5 and SHA, which, designed for 32-bit architectures, base on addition modulo 2^{32}. Furthermore, rapid execution implies the selection of simple data structures and operations to program and the avoidance of large substitution tables.

The second and the third desired characteristics, namely the hardness to invert the function and to find another message for a given digest, are of comparable difficulty to achieve, since choosing appropriate nonlinear function operations it makes these problems hard to solve. Therefore, the avoidance of structural flaws that are vulnerable to crypto-analytic attacks and the use of nonlinear operations with good statistical (uniform) behavior prevent the attacker of employing other methods than brute-force [8]. In the case of brute-force attacks, the length of the digests is critical, since it indicates the maximum number of trials to find a message that lead to a given digest, provided each possible digest has equal probability to occur.

2   A Suite of SVM Neural Network Benchmarks for Quality Assessing Hash Functions

In this research effort, we propose five SVM [13] neural-network-based modeling benchmarks. These neural modeling benchmarks should show the impossibility to model the message digest function by neural network architectures. Otherwise, it would indicate feasibility in modeling the message digest functions by artificial intelligence techniques and consequently in reducing the processing effort required to attack them. The application of the five practical tests based methodology to the well known MD5 and SHA message digest algorithms confirmed the good quality of them, though not as good as supposed theoretically. The proposed suite of five neural modeling benchmarks is based on SVM neural network's ability to map any input-output function onto network's structure and therefore, to model any input-output mapping implied by a set of training samples. Therefore, to perform each of these tests, a suitable set of training samples is constructed by applying the message digest function under consideration to a set of input messages. Each training sample consists of the pair of the input message (pattern) and a subset of the associated digest bits (pattern). This latter pattern is considered as the desired output one. Then, either the same or another independent set of test samples of the same type is produced and the generalization ability of the SVM is calculated by assessing the average error bits for all the test samples. If this average error is equal to digest's length then, it is maximum, and of course it is an indication that the SVM cannot model such a message digest function.

More formally, concerning the first one of the SVM based message digest function evaluation tests, let us assume a training set of input messages X_i with length n and their associated digests d_i with length m. The one way message digest function under evaluation could be considered as a set of m boolean functions f_k, $f_k : F_{n2} \to F_2$ where, F_{n2} is the set of all boolean vectors with length n and F_2 is the set $\{0,1\}$. We, therefore, consider a set of m neural networks of SVM type with which we attempt to model each of the boolean functions f_k. Each such function f_k estimates the k-th bit of the message digest, which is associated with an input message X_i. The k-th SVM is trained using its own training set of pairs (X_i, k_i), where k_i is the k bit of the message digest corresponding to the input message X_i. R such pairs comprise the training sets of the m SVMs. We then consider T similar pairs produced by input messages X_i with $R+1 \leq i \leq R+T$, and we estimate the generalization capability of each one of the m SVMs in the set of T test samples (X_i, k_i), $R+1 \leq i \leq R+T$, $1 \leq k \leq m$.

That is, the average generalization error, measured as the number of wrongly predicted bits, is given as follows

GE = (1/T) $\sum$i,k (||ki- [ki]||), R+1¡=i¡=R+T, 1¡=k¡=m and [ki] is the predicted by the k-th SVM bit ki, of the digest di. GE is maximum when GE = m, where m is the length of di. This evaluation test provides an indication of whether each digest bit can be modeled or not.

Concerning the second and the third of the SVM based message digest function evaluation benchmarks, their goal is to provide digest block modeling results instead of single bit modeling outcomes. The importance of these tests comes from the requirements that every message should have its own unique digest, from which the input message cannot be produced and that it should be impossible to find two or more messages with the same digest. These hash function specifications demand that not only each digest bit be unpredictable by following a uniform distribution but, also, every digest sub-block be unpredictable and thus, consist of independent bits and follow again a uniform distribution. Otherwise, sub-blocks with correlated bits would be easily predictable. This evaluation concept is, also, investigated in the entropy related tests [12], where the entropy of 2-byte digest sub-blocks might be considered, since it is practically impossible to consider the entropy of 128 or 160-bits blocks, that is the full digest length (for MD5 and SHA message digest algorithms respectively). The second and third evaluation tests proposed here involving SVMs, investigate predictability of 2-byte digest sub-blocks as well as of the whole digest, respectively. As in the previous test, let us assume a training set of input messages **X**i with length n and their associated digests di with length m. In the case of the second SVM based test, the one way message digest function under evaluation could be considered as a set of m-7 boolean functions fk , fk : Fn2 $\rightarrow$ F82 where, Fk2 is the set of all boolean vectors with length k. We, therefore, consider a set of m-7 neural networks of SVM type with which we attempt to model each of the boolean functions fk. Each such function fk estimates the k-th byte of the message digest, which is associated with an input message **X**i. It is obvious that overlapping bytes are considered with regards to the digest bits (a total of m-8+1 bytes). The k-th SVM is trained using its own training set of pairs (**X**i, ki), where ki is the k byte of the message digest corresponding to the input message **X**i. R such pairs comprise the training sets of the m-7 SVMs. We then, consider T similar pairs produced by input messages **X**i with R+1¡=i¡=R+T, and we estimate the generalization capability of each one of the m-7 SVMs in the set of T test samples (**X**i, ki), R+1¡=i¡=R+T, 1¡=k¡=m-7. That is, the average generalization error is measured as

GE = (1/T) $\sum$i,kr (||ki_r- [ki_r]||), R+1¡=i¡=R+T, 1¡=k¡=m-7, 1¡=r¡=8 and [ki_r] is the predicted by the k-th SVM r bit of the byte ki of the digest di. GE is maximum when GE = 8(m-7), where m is the length of di. Similarly, in the third SVM based evaluation test we consider only one SVM trained to estimate the predictability of the whole digest. Actually, this is the case where the SVM based evaluation test approach is the only practical one. Indeed, rigorous statistical and information theoretic tests can evaluate the quality of only small sub-blocks of the whole digest since the number of possible events is 2 powered in 128 (or 160 for the SHA algorithm). In such a case SVMs offer an empirical solution, at least an indication of the quality of the digest, despite the known fact that they cannot generalize well in problems where the number of outputs is too high. Therefore, this third SVM based evaluation test involves only estimation of the SVM training error. In the fourth SVM based evaluation benchmark we investigate whether the digest is invertible, that is whether the message can be predicted from the digest or not. To this end, we consider again the structure of the first SVM based evaluation test and we form n (message length) SVMs with m inputs (determined by the digest di) and one output (each message bit). The generalization error GE, given by the same formula, becomes maximum if GE = n and this is the highest score for the message digest algorithm under investigation.

Finally, in the last SVM based evaluation benchmark we aim at examining the structural flaws of the digests produced by message digest algorithms. To this end, we consider an auto-associative SVM with m inputs (determined by the digest di) and the same m outputs. The goal is to find the minimum number of hidden units with which the SVM can encode the digest. Therefore, the less the digest is compressed the highest the score of the corresponding message digest algorithm. Thus, the compression ratio equal to the number of hidden units/digest length is a measure of the structural flaws of the digest. The maximum score is of course 1 (=m/m, where m the digest length). The above suite of five benchmarks is applied to two of the most well known message digest algorithms, namely, MD5 and SHA as well as to MD4 for comparison reasons. The results obtained indicate the validity of the proposed message digest function evaluation framework.

3   Practical Evaluation of MD4, MD5, and SHA

We have conducted a series of experiments to illustrate the performance of the proposed methodology for evaluation of message digest functions. Namely, we have considered the MD4, MD5 algorithms and SHA with input messages of 512 bits. MD4/ MD5 produce digests of 128 bits and SHA of 160 bits.

In the experimental study herein outlined we have considered 5000 input messages for constructing the training sets of all the SVMs involved. The test set has been constructed from another different set of 5000 input messages. The average generalization error GE for MD4/ MD5, estimated from the test set, as determined in the previous section was $\cong$ 94/ 124 bits and for SHA $\cong$ 155 bits, concerning the first and the second neural benchmark. Regarding the third neural test the results obtained are GE=90/ 120 and GE=152 respectively. Regarding the fourth neural test the results obtained are GE=480/ 502 for the MD4/ MD5 and GE=508 for the SHA. Finally, concerning the last neural benchmark we have obtained compression ratios of 0.7712, 0.9385 and 0.956 respectively.

4   Conclusions and Prospects

We proposed and described an evaluation methodology for unkeyed message digest functions to be used for secure communication systems. The methodology consists of five neural-network-based modeling tests based on SVM. This suite of tests has been applied to MD4/ MD5 and SHA algorithms and the results obtained are quite promising concerning the quality of the test suite. The required computation time is not as large to be infeasible to apply for modern computer systems. The suggested hash function quality assessment benchmark suite reveals weaknesses for MD4 hash values while the results for MD5 and SHA do not show statistically significant weaknesses. We intend to extent the methodology by introducing further tests based on artificial intelligence techniques (genetic algorithms) and to apply them to keyed message digest functions as well. Moreover, we intend to design better such algorithms in terms of passing these benchmarks and integrate them in secure communication protocols.

References

1. I.B. Damgard, 'Collision Free Hash Functions and Public Key Signature Schemes', Advances in Cryptography, Eurocrypt '87, Lecture Notes in Computer Science 304, Springer Verlag, 1987, pp. 203-216.
2. I.B. Damgard, 'A Design Principle for Hash Functions', Advances in Cryptography, Crypto '89, Lecture Notes in Computer Science 435, Springer Verlag, 1989, pp. 416-427.
3. B. Preenel, 'Cryptographic Hash Functions', Transactions on Telecommunications, vol. 5, 1994, pp. 431-448.
4. M.N. Wegman, J.L. Carter, 'New Hash Functions and Their Use in Authentication and Set Quality', J. of Computer and System Sciences, vol. 22, 1981, pp. 265-279.
5. B. Schneier, Applied Cryptography, John Willey and Sons, 1996.
6. M. Peyravian, A. Roginsky, A. Kshemkalyani, 'On Probabilities of Hash Value Matches', J. Computers & Security, Vol. 17, No. 2, 1998, pp. 171-176.
7. D. Stinson, 'Combinatorial Techniques for Universal Hashing', J. of Computer and System Sciences, vol. 48, 1994, pp. 337-346.
8. W. Stallings, Network and Internetwork Security, Prentice Hall, 1995.
9. C. P. Pfleeger, Security in Computing, Prentice Hal, 1997.
10. G. J. Simmons (editor), Contemporary Cryptology, The Science of Information Integrity, IEEE Press, 1992.
11. FIPS PUB 180-1, Secure Hash Standard, 1995.
12. E.P Dawson and H.M. Gustafson, "A method for measuring entropy of symmetric cipher key generators", J. of Computers & Security vol. 17, no 2, 1998, pp. 177-184.
13. Haykin, S., "Neural Networks. A Comprehensive Foundation", Prentice Hall, 1999.

Efficient Digital Fingerprint Production and Evaluation for Secure Communication Systems Based on Genetic Algorithms

D.A. Karras

Chalkis Institute of Technology & Hellenic Open University., Rodu 2, Ano Iliupolis, Athens 16342, Greece, dakarras@usa.net

Abstract. A novel procedure based on genetic algorithms is presented for the evaluation and production of digital fingerprints in the design of secure communication systems. These digital fingerprints are computed using the methodology of un-keyed one-way functions (hash functions). The problem of evaluating the quality of such functions is formulated as a global optimization one in the space spanned by all possible messages and is approached from a practical viewpoint by involving genetic algorithms, contrary to the very few similar research efforts existing in the literature that are of only theoretical interest. Moreover, the problem of producing digital fingerprints of good quality for use in communication systems is formulated in terms of a hash function constructed by involving the genetic algorithm procedure, exclusively utilizing the crossover operator and the steady-state reproduction method and omitting its random components. The promising results herein obtained illustrate the importance of applying genetic algorithms in communication systems security design.

1   Introduction

Digital fingerprints use mathematical algorithms to generate a string of digits and numbers that represents the contents of an electronically-transmitted message. If the message is tampered with, the digital fingerprint will change to reflect changes in the content. The fingerprint of the received message can then be compared with the digital fingerprint of the original message to ensure that the contents have not been altered. The sequences produced by the digital fingerprint functions are short, fixed-length strings of bits, referred to as "digital fingerprints" or "hash values," that uniquely represent a single piece of digital message. Digital fingerprints are unique in the sense that two different pieces of data-when run through a one-way hash function-can never create the same digital fingerprint. Because the hash functions are one-way, no portion of the original data can be reconstructed from the digital fingerprint. One-way hash functions produce results so unique that changing a single bit in the original piece of digital data changes the calculated fingerprint completely. Thus, these digital fingerprints are ideally suited for use as "stand-ins" for the digital data

L. Rutkowski et al. (Eds.): ICAISC 2004, LNAI 3070, pp. 628–633, 2004.
© Springer-Verlag Berlin Heidelberg 2004

from which they are produced [1]. Their basic properties required include easiness in computing the digital fingerprints and hardness in computing the message from a given digital fingerprint and in finding another message with the same hash value. However, these characteristics are not sufficient for the digital fingerprint functions to be applied in cryptographic protocols. Therefore, collision resistance is required, which means that it is hard to find two or more random messages to have the same digital fingerprint [1,2]. Several digital fingerprint functions have been proposed and are, in the meantime, extensively used in security mechanisms, such as MD5 and SHA [1]. The MD5 algorithm handles messages of arbitrary length and produces hash values consisting of 128 bits [1]. Each message after it has been appended by padding bits and its length is processed in blocks of 512 bits. The Secure Hash Algorithm (SHA, [1]) is a variant of the MD4 algorithm, like the MD5 algorithm. However, the algorithm produces hash values of 160 bits in length, although it takes as input messages of arbitrary length as the MD5 does.

The contribution of this paper lies on applying genetic algorithms modeling for evaluating and producing digital fingerprints for the first time in the literature. Actually, there are very few research efforts in the literature with the goal to evaluate the quality of digital fingerprints from a practical point of view. The results provided are mainly of theoretical interest [3,4] and of little practical value. The main goal of this paper is, therefore, to investigate how genetic algorithms, a widely accepted tool of computational intelligence for use in optimization problems, could become a tool of practical value in evaluating digital fingerprints.

In this section, we discussed some aspects of known digital fingerprint functions as well as the contribution of this paper. In the second section, we describe the proposed methodology for evaluating and producing digital fingerprint functions based on genetic algorithms and in the next section its application to SHA/MD5 is illustrated. Finally, we conclude the paper and outline the future work.

2   The Genetic Algorithms Based Methodology for Evaluating and Producing Digital Fingerprints

The problem of evaluating one-way functions is formulated as a global optimization one. The goal of the suggested novel approach is to indicate that it is not possible to find a message having the same hash value as a given one. Namely, the strategy followed is next presented. First, a message M1 of 512 bits is considered, which leads to the computation of a hash value D1. D1 is determined as the given hash value, involved as the target value in the proposed approach. Then, starting from a neighborhood of M1 and thinking of it as the initial population, the genetic algorithm is applied to this initial population and spans the whole message space by trying to minimize the distance (Hamming distance) D1' – D1. In this case, D1' is the hash value corresponding to any message M1'. So, the children of the initial population are evaluated in terms of the hash values they produce. After N steps the probability of finding another message M2 with hash value equal to or near to D1 is considered. In the next paragraphs we outline the proposed algorithm for evaluating the quality of digital fingerprints from a practical point of view, which is, also, illustrated in figure 1.

1) The first step is to create an initial population of R=500 messages computed by considering alterations of the original message M1. The original message M1, which could be located in a text file, is considered to be unknown to the genetic algorithm, thus, in the population produced the resulting messages must be different from M1. This requirement is obvious, since, otherwise the genetic algorithm would stop given that M1 is included in the initial population and its hash value is the target one, namely, the D1. We could achieve it by changing the first character in the original message and then producing the population. The resulting message M1' is recombined randomly K=500 times but always keeping the first character constant. The recombination of M1 is achieved by replacing the characters of the messages with random characters from the Matlab character set (Matlab is used throughout this implementation). At the end, a population of R=500 messages is created, all different from the original message.

2) Then, a function is created, which evaluates the Hamming distance between the hash value of M1 and the hash value of the rest of the messages of the initial population. From that point forward, the genetic algorithm is applied to the population and tries to minimize the distance between the hash values. After the initial population is produced, it is necessary to find a way to calculate the Hamming distance. The Hamming distance between two strings is defined as the number of bits, for which the two strings are different. Thus, the fitness function outputs the Hamming distance between two hash values. The first hash value is the known hash value of the original message. To produce it, the executable file of SHA/ MD5 runs. The second hash value is the hash value corresponding to the input message of the fitness function. This fitness function accepts as input a string, which in this case is a message from the initial population. Again, SHA/ MD5 executable file runs in order to calculate the hash value of the input message. The next step is to convert both hash values in binary form. Finally, each bit of these hash values is compared in order to find their associated Hamming distance.

3) After the creation of the initial population and the calculation of the Hamming distances, it is time to apply the genetic algorithm. The genetic algorithm is used at this stage for optimization. Genetic algorithms are direct search methods and use only the function values, which in this case are the Hamming distances. Once the initial population has been created, the genetic algorithm enters a loop. At the end of each iteration a new population will be created applying a certain number of stochastic operators to the previous population. One such iteration is referred to as a generation.

The first operator to be applied is selection.

In order to create a new intermediate population of two "parents", two independent extractions of an individual from the old population are performed, where the probability for each individual of being extracted is linearly proportional to its fitness. The parents are selected using tournament selection. Therefore, above average individuals will expectedly have more copies in the new population, while below average individuals will risk extinction. Once the population of parents, that is, of individuals that have been selected for reproduction, has been extracted, the individuals for the next generation will be produced through the main two reproduction operators: crossover and mutation.

To apply the crossover operator, couples are formed with all parent individuals. Then, with a certain probability, called crossover rate Pcross, each couple actually undergoes crossover: the two strings are cut at the same random position and their second halves are swapped between a single individual, called "child", thus yielding a novel individual, containing characters from both parents. After crossover, all individual messages undergo mutation. The purpose of mutation is to simulate the effect of transcription errors that can happen with a very low probability (Pmut).

The crossover and mutation operators can affect the best member of the message population, which does not produce offspring in the next generation. Thus, the algorithm also includes a version of elitism: take the best individual (i.e. the message with the smaller hamming distance) and compare it with a random individual of the new population. If the new individual is worse, replace it with the best individual from the old population.

In addition to the proposed evaluation methodology using genetic algorithm modeling, we apply genetic algorithm modeling too in the production of digital fingerprints that could improve SHA performance. To this end, we involve an in principle similar procedure with the one previously outlined.

a) Given a message M1 of 512 bits and the corresponding SHA D1 hash value of 160 bits, its associated initial population is defined and produced as previously.

b) Application of the Genetic algorithm modeling, after a pre-specified number of generations Max_gener, leads to the final population. In such an application the random component of the algorithm that is, the mutation operator is excluded since a digital fingerprint should be a deterministic one-way hash function. The goal of the optimization process is the same as before, that is to minimize the fitness function herein defined.

c) From the final population with Max_pop = R =500 members we construct a 160 bits hash value by considering its 160 members with the max Hamming distances from D1 and extracting the middle bit from each message bit sequence. We select the maximum Hamming Distance from SHA D1 members of the final population since we assume in this derivation that the SHA D1 hash value has structural flaws and therefore, it is attempted to minimize such flaws by examining the combination of other D1 "similar" hash values (in some kind of "vicinity", but not so "close" to D1, although these "similar" hash values might have large distances due to the uniform distribution property of hash functions. We remind that the optimization process minimizes D1'-D1). Of course such an approach is heuristic and can be validated only if good results might be experimentally obtained. Fortunately this is the case as it is next demonstrated.

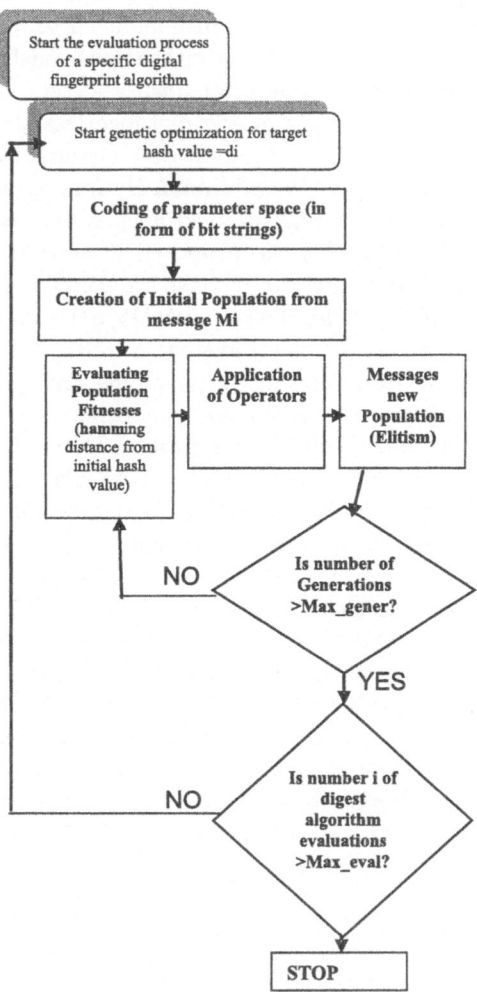

Fig. 1. Overview of the proposed methodology for evaluating digital fingerprints

3   Discussion of the Results and Conclusions

The framework for implementing the proposed evaluation methodology is as outlined in figure 1, while for implementing the suggested hash value derivation procedure is as outlined in section 2. In order to achieve statistically significant results the proposed methodology comprises max_eval number of evaluations.

In the experiments herein presented the most important parameters used were: max_eval=100, Max_gener (Number of max generations) = 300, Probability of crossover - Pcross = 0.8, Probability of mutation - Pmut = 0.02, Mutation scale- Mut_scale = 0.99, Probability of tournament - Ptour = 0.7

Then, considering the MD5/SHA algorithm with hash value length equal to 128/160, the best and worst generations are selected. Best generations are considered the generations with Hamming distance less than B=105/135 bits, and worst generations those with Hamming distance greater than W=110/140 bits. What has been found is that the minimum Hamming distance is on average 72/125 for the traditional MD5/SHA derived hash values, corresponding to 100 initial populations for 100 runs of the proposed in section 2 evaluation procedure associated with 100 different target hash values. The respective minimum for the suggested genetic algorithm based on MD5/SHA digital fingerprint derivation (as described in section 2) is on average 81/137. On the other hand, the respective minima of the Hamming distances of the final populations produced from the genetic algorithm running for 300 generations on the initial populations specified in the previous result, is on average 59/104 bits for the traditional MD5/SHA hash value derivation and 75/132 bits for the suggested genetic algorithm based on MD5/SHA digital fingerprint derivation (as described in section 2). This result clearly indicates that genetic algorithm processing, viewed as a global optimization approach, might be used to strengthen digital fingerprint derivation. In addition it is clear that they can find minima of the Hamming distance which are much better than the minima found when running on the initial population. Such results might illustrate deficiencies in MD5 digital fingerprint, which makes easier its attack. The practical interest of this research effort for an attack of MD5 or a different digital fingerprint algorithm, like SHA, is that the application of the genetic algorithm leads to better starting points for a brute force attack. Therefore, at these points, the attacker starts searching not a 2 128 space but a 2 59, for instance space, which is much easier to search and attack.

References

1. B. Schneier, *Applied Cryptography*, John Willey and Sons, 1996.
2. M. Peyravian, A. Roginsky, A. Kshemkalyani, On Probabilities of Hash Value Matches, *J. Computers & Security*, Vol. 17, No. 2, 1998, pp. 171-176.
3. D. Stinson, 'Combinatorial Techniques for Universal Hashing', *J. of Compute & System Sciences*, vol. 48, 1994, pp. 337-346.
4. E.P Dawson and H.M. Gustafson, A method for measuring entropy of symmetric cipher key generators, *J. of Computers & Security* vol. 17, no 2, 1998, pp. 177-184.

On Chinese Web Page Classification

Jiuzhen Liang

Institute of Computer Science, Zhejiang Normal University, Jinhua, China, 321004
liangjiuzhen@yahoo.com

Abstract. This paper deals with Chinese web page classification based on text contents. It includes setting up dictionary, departing words, extracting feature, designing classifiers, etc. First, feature compression problem is discussed in detail, which several methods are introduced reducing the feature dimension from more than 120,000 to 5,000. Second, several classifiers are selected to pattern training, such as linear neural perceptron, self-organization mapping networks, radial basis function neural networks, and support vector machine. In the last of this paper experiments on *Chinese people daily* web version are illustrated and classification results are compared.

1 Introduction

In recent years, web page automatic classification is one of popular research work in the information process area. More and more people engage themselves in this research domain. Web automatic classification includes web text information, structure information and super link information [1]. Most people now pay their attentions on the web page text automatic classification, i.e. classification based on text content [2]. Due to the variety of web page text content, the complexity of web page structure, and so on, it is difficult to improve the classification accuracy. Although there are all kinds of classifiers that are created, such as Naive Bayes classifier [3], K-neighbor clustering [4], self-organization neural networks [5], these classifiers almost have special underground and application conditions, respectively. In detail, Naive Bayes classifier needs hypothesis that all features used to classification are submitted to polynomial independent distribution. K-neighbor clustering can be only applied to the case that there is no other class sample in the neighbor of one class. Self-organization neural networks can hold order mapping, but need long training time. For neural network classifier, it needs fewer hypotheses for sample distribution model than Naive Bayes classifier. So it depends little on special problem, but needs large training samples and more repetition in training to determine neural network's parameters. In the case of large samples and high dimension of sample features, learning is the most difficult problem. If the number of samples is almost in the scale of feature dimension, for example, text classification problem, the number of samples and the dimension of features are all in thousands, the sample is very sparse in the distribution space and this must have bad effect to generalization of classifier. In this case it becomes more important to introduce prior knowledge of samples

L. Rutkowski et al. (Eds.): ICAISC 2004, LNAI 3070, pp. 634–639, 2004.
© Springer-Verlag Berlin Heidelberg 2004

into the selection of neural network's structure and sample training. For web page classification problem and considering the case of classification based on keyword frequency, the prior knowledge is the statistical information, especially the keyword frequency for each different classes and the keyword concentration degree information in each web page classes. These of statistical information are important to web page classification and much usefulness to feature selection.

The following contents include mainly three parts. The first part discusses web page text feature extracting and selecting based on keyword frequency. The second introduces some classifiers, which is now convinced effective to Chinese web page categorizing. These classifiers include linear neural perceptron, naive Bayes statistic model, self-organize function mapping (SOFM), redial basis function (RBF), support vector machine (SVM), etc. The third part gives some experiment results and contrasts for the above classifiers mentioned. The corresponding classification problem comes from the web version of *Chinese people's daily* . The last part is the conclusion of the whole paper.

2   Feature Extraction for Chinese Web Page

Feature extracting based on keyword is mainly including the following two points. The first aspect is that whether one keyword appears in any document belonging to a certain class. The second is the frequency of this word appeared. This work is completed by word parsing system, i.e. making a keyword dictionary, scanning web page by keyword dictionary, and calculating the frequency of each keyword. Usually there are large words in the keyword dictionary, and there are many useless words that have even bad effects on classification. So it is very important to select keywords from the dictionary. Feature compression is one of important way for feature selecting, and there many methods for these kinds of work, such as primary component analysis, rough set reduction, information entropy gain, keyword threshold bound, etc [6].

Recently, Vector Space Model (VSM) is considered one of most popular model for representing the feature of text contents. In this model, a document is regarded as a vector composed of a serial of cross words,which can be expressed as $V(d) = (t_1, x_1(d); \cdots ; t_i, x_i(d); \cdots ; t_n, x_n(d))$, where t_i denotes the i-th keyword and $x_i(d)$ is the weight of t_i in document d. Usually $x_i(d)$ is defined as the frequency function $tf_i(d)$ of t_i appeared in document d, denote as $x_i(d) = (tf_i(d))$. Some common useful function forms of ϕ are listed as following.

$$Boolean function : \phi = \begin{cases} 1 , tf_i(d) \geq 1 \\ 0 , tf_i(d) = 0 \end{cases} \tag{1}$$

$$Square root function : \phi = \sqrt{tf_i(d)} \tag{2}$$

$$Logarithm function : \phi = log(tf_i(d) + 1) \tag{3}$$

$$TFIDF function : \phi = tf_i(d) \times log(\frac{N}{n_i}) \tag{4}$$

In formula (4), N is the number of total documents and n_i is the number as documents in which i-th keyword appears. In practice, we choose the following four forms of document vector feature.

(1) Word frequency database: each record corresponds to a vector $V_j = (x_{j1}, x_{j2}, \cdots, x_{jn})$, here x_{ji} denotes the frequency of i-th keyword in j-th document.

2) Document length processing word frequency database: each record corresponds to a vector $V_j = (x_{j1}/L_j, x_{j2}/L_j, \cdots, x_{jn}/L_j)$, here x_{ji} denotes the frequency of i-th keyword in j-th document and L_j is the text length of j-th document.

(3) ID/TIF feature database: each record corresponds to a vector $V_j = (x_{j1}/v_1, x_{j2}/v_2, \cdots, x_{jn}/v_n)$, here x_{ji} denotes the frequency of i-th keyword in j-th document and v_i is the number of documents in which i-th keyword appears (also called inverse document frequency).

(4) Frequency unitary feature database: each record corresponds to a vector $V_j = (x_{j1}/S_j, x_{j2}/S_j, \cdots, x_{jn}/S_j)$, here x_{ji} denotes the frequency of i-th keyword in j-th document and $S_j = \sqrt{\sum_{i=1}^{n} x_{ji}^2}$.

In order to filtrate the redundancy keyword feature, we introduce the concept of word frequency covering rate, as denoting

$$x_{ij} = \frac{f_{ij}}{\sum_{j=1}^{n} f_{ij}} \cdot \frac{d_{ij}}{N_j} \tag{5}$$

Where f_{ij} is the frequency of i-th keyword in j-th document, d_{ij} is number of j-th class documents in which i-th keyword appears and N_j is number of j-th class documents. Variant x_{ij} reflects the correlation between i-th keyword and j-th class document. The more x_{ij} is large, the more it reflects the feature of j-th class, and the more it is useful to classification. While the little x_{ij} is, the little frequency is which i-th keyword appears in j-th class documents. For this reason, we set a threshold T for filtrating the redundancy keyword feature.

$$\bar{x}_i = \max_j \{x_{ij}\} \tag{6}$$

If $\bar{x}_i > T$ then i-th keyword is reserved, otherwise delete this keyword.

3   Classifier Design

Classifier design is the main part of classification and it behaves as the most important part in showing the classification results. Clearly, there are many classifiers to choose for a pattern recognition problem. Such as the simplest K-mean clustering, self-organize mapping clustering if we do not know the label of each sample. In the case of pattern label known, some classical supervised learning method can be considered such as linear neural perceptron, RBF, SVM, Na?ve

Bayes statistic model, etc. Also there are many other classifiers to choose surely. But considering the particularity of text categorizing, i.e. with huge dimension of feature and large amount of sample, we can not choose those classifiers that need long time training and have complex computing in constructing them. For example, feedforward neural network with hidden layers usually needs long time training in the stage of learning; hiberarchy-clustering method needs computing complexity as $N(N-1)\cdots 2\cdot 1$ with N samples. So for the practical text classification problems classifier accuracy is one important and the computation complexity is another important problem that we can not avoid. In this section we introduce four kinds of classifiers to the web text-categorizing problem, respectively.

3.1 Linear Neural Perceptron

Linear classifier, also called perceptron, is very famous as almost the simplest classifier in solving the linear separated problem. According to Vapnik's statistic learning theory, simple classifier model has good generalization ability in all models with the same level of training accuracy [7]. So we can suppose that web text classification problem is linear separate with certain category error (e.g. with 10% error permitted). For detail describing of linear classifier dues to [8].

3.2 SOFM-LVQ Classifier

Among the existing SOM models, Kohonen's model is the famous SOM neural network. which also called feature-mapping model. SOM neural network can process none ordered set and apparently show the topology relationship of objects by neuron's self-organize behaves, such as the distribution of clustering centers. Among the total input vectors, the weights corresponding to the winner output neuron is the clustering center. Actually, the self-organizing procedure is that finding the optimal matching weight to the input vector. SOM is an unsupervised learning algorithm. If the labels of training samples are known, one of the improved strategies is helped by LVQ (Learning Vector Quantization), which can adjust the clustering center farther. For detail describing of SOMF-LVQ classifier dues to [5].

3.3 RBF Neural Networks

Redial basis function neural network is a classical three layers feedforward neural network with the input layer accepting the outside information, the second layer called hidden layer, which finished a mapping from input space to a high vector space by nonlinear function , and the output layer. In the second layer we hope that the nonlinear function can transform a nonlinear problem to a linear one in the high vector space. It is worth mentioned that the dimension of hidden space is not must higher than that of input layer. For detail describing of RBF classifier dues to [9].

3.4 SVM Classifier

In a SVM, the original vector x is mapped into Hilbert space vector $\mathbf{z}$ and the samples in the Hilbert space is linear separated. In the Hilbert space one can construct an optimal interface plane as the following form.

$$f(x) = sgn(\sum_{i=1}^{N} \alpha_i^* y_i K(\mathbf{x_i}, \mathbf{x}) + b^*) \tag{7}$$

Here α_i^* is the optimal solution that enables the following function take the maximum value.

$$Q(\alpha) = \sum_{i=1}^{N} \alpha_i - \frac{1}{2} \sum_{j=1}^{N} \alpha_i \alpha_j y_i y_j K(\mathbf{x_i}, \mathbf{x_j}) \tag{8}$$

Where $K(\mathbf{x_i}, \mathbf{x}) = < \phi(\mathbf{x_i}), \phi(\mathbf{x}) >$ is called kernel function. For detail describing of SVM classifier dues to [7].

4   Experiment and Analysis

In this paper, the sample set is supplied by the web version of People's Daily [5]. The whole set includes 8 classes with 5096 samples, i.e. 594 samples of International Class (IC), 524 samples of Environment Protection class (EP), 820 samples of Economy Class (EC), 777 samples of Military Affairs class (MA), 701 samples of Science Education class (SE), 713 samples of Current Affair class (CA), 495 samples of Life Class (LC), and last 472 samples of ENtertainment class (EN). After the word separating process, the web page text vector dimension is 59682, and this number can be reduced to 5575 by filtrating of class covering rate threshold. At last, by filtrating of stop word dictionary, the dimension of sample used to classification is 4904. The web page vector set is build up by the 4904 words dictionary, scanning each web page text and counting the frequency of every word. And so a 4904 dimensions vector is corresponding to a web page. Through large mount of training samples the classifier is constructed reflecting the relationship between web page features and web page class. Also by test samples the classification ability of classifier can be evaluated.

In the following experiments the ratio of training samples to test samples is 2:1, i.e. 3398 samples is used in training and 1698 samples for testing. Four classifications of testing results are listed as in table 1.

5   Conclusion

The problem of web page classification is of large scale either in the dimension of features or in the total number of samples, which is a severe trial both for the training time and the storing space in the classifier's design. Some traditional and very complex classifiers, such as multi-layer BP neural network and degree

Table 1. Comparing results of six classification precision(%)

Classifier	IC	EP	EC	MA	SE	CA	LC	EN	Total
Perceptron	85.28	97.99	83.97	87.39	92.5	35.92	91.04	96.83	82.24
SOFM-LVQ	79.97	91.22	93.90	91.51	89.16	90.74	85.05	95.76	89.85
RBF	69.70	91.38	90.88	88.42	88.84	89.50	81.82	88.54	86.51
SVM	81.31	96.55	90.15	92.66	91.85	89.92	84.24	90.45	89.81

clustering, are hard to implement under existing experiment conditions. So we need such classifiers that guarantee high classifying precision while on the other hand are feasible to design. Perceptron and SVM are such ideal classifiers, among which the latter is our first choice.

References

1. Yao J.T. and Yao Y.Y., Information granulation for Web based information retrieval support systems, Data Mining and Knowledge Discovery: Theory, Tools, and Technology V, Orlando, Florida, USA, April 21-22, 2003, Dasarathy, B.V. (Ed.), The International Society for Optical Engineering, pp. 138-146, 2003
2. Zhu M.,Wang J. and Wang J.P., On The Feature Selection of Web Page Classification,(In Chinese) Computer Engineering, 2000, 26(8): 35 37
3. Fan Y.,Zheng C.,Wang Q.Y.,Cai Q.S.,Liu J., Web Page Classification Based on Naive bayes Method,(In Chinese) Journal of Software, 2001, 12(9): 1386 1392
4. Shi Z.Z., Knowledge Discovering (In Chinese), Beijing: Tsinghua University Press, 2002.
5. Zhang Y.Z., The Automatic Classification of Web Pages Based on Neural Networks, Neural information processing, ICONIP2001 Proceedings, November 14-18,2001 Shanghai, China, Vol.2, 570 575.
6. Sebastiani F.,Machine Learning in Automated Text Categorization, ACM Computing Surveys, Vol. 34, No. 1, March 2002, pp. 1 47.
7. Vapnik V.N.,Statistical Learning Theory, J. Wiley, New York, 1998.
8. Liang J.Z.,Feature compression and linear classifier design of web page based on prior knowledge, The 12th National Conference on Neural Networks Proceedings, Beijing, Posts & Telecom Press. Dec. 2002.
9. Haykin S., Neural Networks-A Comprehensive Foundation, Second Edition, Prentice Hall, 1999.

A New Fuzzy Clustering Method with Constraints in Time Domain

Jacek Leski[1,2] and Aleksander Owczarek[2]

[1] Institute of Electronics, Silesian University of Technology
Akademicka 16, 44-100 Gliwice. Poland. jl@boss.iele.polsl.gliwice.pl
[2] Department of Computer Medical Systems, Institute of Medical Technology and
Equipment. Roosevelt St. 118A, 41-800 Zabrze. Poland. aleck@itam.zabrze.pl

Abstract. This paper introduces a new fuzzy clustering method with
constraints in time domain which may be used to signal analysis. Proposed method makes it possible to include a natural constraints for signal
analysis using fuzzy clustering, that is, the neighbouring samples of signal belong to the same cluster. The well-known from the literature fuzzy
c-regression models can be obtained as a special case of the method proposed in this paper.

1 Introduction

The Fuzzy C-Means (FCM) method is one of the most popular clustering methods based on the minimization of a criterion function [1]. In the literature
there are many modifications of the FCM method. These modifications may be
treated as inclusion of an additional information into the process of clustering.
A first group of modifications of the FCM method includes information about
shapes of clusters. A second group of modifications includes information about
non-Gaussian distribution of data and the presence of noise and outliers. An
other group of modifications which use numerous variants of incorporating additional information into the process of fuzzy clustering has been introduced by W.
Pedrycz, c.f. conditional fuzzy c-means, fuzzy clustering with partial supervision,
collaborative clustering [3].

The above-mentioned fuzzy clustering algorithms are successfully applied to
a wide variety of problems. However, a few applications to the signal analysis
may be find in the literature. If clustered objects represents the consecutive
in time domain samples of a signal, then the following constraint seems to be
natural. It is great possibility that the neighbouring samples of signal belong to
the same cluster. The above constraint may be called a time-domain-constraint.
The goal of this work is to introduce time-domain-constrained fuzzy c-regression
models clustering method.

L. Rutkowski et al. (Eds.): ICAISC 2004, LNAI 3070, pp. 640–645, 2004.
© Springer-Verlag Berlin Heidelberg 2004

2   Time-Domain-Constrained Fuzzy c-Regression Models Method

Suppose we have a set, $\mathrm{Tr}^{(N)} = \{(\mathbf{x}_k, y_k)\}_{k=1}^{N}$, where each independent datum $\mathbf{x}_k \in \mathbb{R}^t$ has a corresponding dependent datum $y_k \in \mathbb{R}$. We assume that data pairs from $\mathrm{Tr}^{(N)}$ set are unlabeled and drawn from switching regression model, that consist of c models in the following linear form: $y_k = w_0^{(i)} + \widetilde{\mathbf{w}}^{(i)\top} \mathbf{x}_k + e_k$ for $k = 1, 2, \cdots, N$ where e_k represents uncertainty for kth pair, $\mathbf{w}^{(i)} = \left[w_0^{(i)}, \widetilde{\mathbf{w}}^{(i)\top} \right]^{\top} \in \mathbb{R}^{t+1}$ are parameters of ith model. We have not any information about membership degree of kth data pair to the ith model $u_{i,k}$ and parameters of these models $\mathbf{w}^{(i)}$. It follows, that simultaneous estimation of c-partition of the data pairs set and parameters of models are needed. This problem, called Fuzzy C-Regression Models (FCRM), is solved in [2]. The FCRM method is a perfect tool for nonstationary signal analysis. If analyzed discrete-time signal is denoted by $s(k\Delta)$, where k is discrete time and Δ is sampling period, then, in this case, y_k denotes an amplitude of signal for kth sample ($y_k = s(k\Delta)$) and $\mathbf{x}_k$ stands for a discrete time index ($\mathbf{x}_k = x_k = k\Delta$) or amplitudes of previous ξ samples ($\mathbf{x}_k \in [s((k-1)\Delta), s((k-2)\Delta), \cdots, s((k-\xi)\Delta)]^{\top}$). After the FCRM clustering of the above data, we obtain both signal models and membership degree of each sample to these models.

The set of all possible fuzzy partitions of N data pairs into c-regression models is defined by [1]

$$\mathcal{P}_{fc} = \left\{ \mathbf{U} \in \mathbb{R}^{c \times N} \,\Big|\, \underset{\substack{1 \le i \le c \\ 1 \le k \le N}}{\forall}\, u_{i,k} \in [0,1]; \sum_{i=1}^{c} u_{i,k} = 1; 0 < \sum_{k=1}^{N} u_{i,k} < N \right\}. \quad (1)$$

The criterion function of the fuzzy c-regression models is given in the form [2]

$$J_m(\mathbf{U}, \mathbf{W}) = \sum_{i=1}^{c} \sum_{k=1}^{N} (u_{i,k})^m \left(y_k - \mathbf{w}^{(i)\top} \mathbf{x}_k' \right)^2, \quad (2)$$

where $\mathbf{W} = [\mathbf{w}^{(i)}, \mathbf{w}^{(2)}, \cdots, \mathbf{w}^{(c)}] \in \mathbb{R}^{(t+1) \times c}$, $\mathbf{x}_k' \triangleq [1, \mathbf{x}_k^{\top}]^{\top}$ is the augmented input vector. The parameter m influences a fuzziness of the regression models. A larger m results in fuzzier models. Usually $m = 2$ is used.

A new criterion function of time-domain-constrained fuzzy c-regression models is proposed in the following form

$$J_m'(\mathbf{U}, \mathbf{W}) = \sum_{i=1}^{c} \sum_{k=1}^{N} (u_{i,k})^m \left(y_k - \mathbf{w}^{(i)\top} \mathbf{x}_k' \right)^2 \quad (3)$$

$$+ \gamma \sum_{i=1}^{c} \sum_{k=1}^{N-1} (u_{i,k} - u_{i,k+1})^m \left(y_k - \mathbf{w}^{(i)\top} \mathbf{x}_k' \right)^2.$$

In the case of signal analysis the second term in (3) imposes time-domain constraints, which may be interpreted as: the neighbouring samples of a signal belong to the same model. Thus, in (3) we have two terms: a standard error term from the FCRM method and a regularizing term depending on smoothness of membership degrees $u_{i,k}$. Parameter $\gamma \geq 0$ controls the trade-off between the smoothness of membership degrees and the amount up to which clustering errors are tolerated. For $\gamma = 0$ the original FCRM method is obtained. The larger γ the more smoothness membership degrees and greater clustering errors. Finally, it may also be noted that the criterion (3) is similar to criterion used in the collaborative clustering method [3]. However, in (3) the difference of membership degrees representing the neighbouring samples is minimized instead of minimizing a difference between partition matrices for two different datasets.

If we define the following vector and matrices: $\mathbf{y} = [y_1, y_2, \cdots, y_N]^\top = [\tilde{\mathbf{y}}^\top, y_N]^\top$, $\mathbf{X} = [\mathbf{x}'_1, \mathbf{x}'_2, \cdots, \mathbf{x}'_N]^\top = \left[\tilde{\mathbf{X}}^\top, \mathbf{x}'_N\right]^\top$, $\mathbf{D}_1^{(i)} = \text{diag}((u_{i,1})^m, (u_{i,2})^m, \cdots, (u_{i,N})^m) \in \mathbb{R}^{N \times N}$ and $\mathbf{D}_2^{(i)} = \text{diag}((u_{i,1} - u_{i,2})^m, (u_{i,2} - u_{i,3})^m, \cdots, (u_{i,N-1} - u_{i,N})^m) \in \mathbb{R}^{(N-1) \times (N-1)}$ for $i = 1, 2, \cdots, c$, then criterion function (3) may be written in the following matrix form

$$J'_m(\mathbf{U}, \mathbf{W}) = \sum_{i=1}^{c} \left\{ \left(\mathbf{y} - \mathbf{X}\mathbf{w}^{(i)}\right)^\top \mathbf{D}_1^{(i)} \left(\mathbf{y} - \mathbf{X}\mathbf{w}^{(i)}\right) \right. \tag{4}$$
$$\left. + \gamma \left(\tilde{\mathbf{y}} - \tilde{\mathbf{X}}\mathbf{w}^{(i)}\right)^\top \mathbf{D}_2^{(i)} \left(\tilde{\mathbf{y}} - \tilde{\mathbf{X}}\mathbf{w}^{(i)}\right) \right\}.$$

The following theorem may be formulated for the weighting exponent equal to 2.

Theorem 1. If $m = 2$, $1 < c < N$ and $\gamma \geq 0$ are fixed parameters, and $I_k, \tilde{I}_k$ are sets defined as: $I_k = \left\{ i \,\middle|\, 1 \leq i \leq c; \; \left(y_k - \mathbf{w}^{(i)\top}\mathbf{x}'_k\right)^2 = 0 \right\}$, $\tilde{I}_k = \{1, 2, \cdots, c\} \backslash I_k$, then $(\mathbf{U}, \mathbf{W}) \in (\mathcal{P}_{fc} \times \mathbb{R}^{(t+1) \times c})$ may be globally minimal for (4) only if

$$\bigvee_{\substack{1 \leq i \leq c \\ 1 \leq k \leq N}} u_{i,k} = \begin{cases} \dfrac{1}{\displaystyle\sum_{j=1}^{c} \dfrac{\left(y_k - \mathbf{w}^{(i)\top}\mathbf{x}'_k\right)^2}{\left(y_k - \mathbf{w}^{(j)\top}\mathbf{x}'_k\right)^2}}, & k = N \\[20pt] \dfrac{1 + \gamma u_{i,k+1} \displaystyle\sum_{j=1}^{c} \dfrac{\left(y_k - \mathbf{w}^{(i)\top}\mathbf{x}'_k\right)^2}{\left(y_k - \mathbf{w}^{(j)\top}\mathbf{x}'_k\right)^2}}{(1+\gamma) \displaystyle\sum_{j=1}^{c} \dfrac{\left(y_k - \mathbf{w}^{(i)\top}\mathbf{x}'_k\right)^2}{\left(y_k - \mathbf{w}^{(j)\top}\mathbf{x}'_k\right)^2}}, & k = N-1, \cdots, 1 \\[24pt] \begin{cases} 0, & i \in \tilde{I}_k \\ \displaystyle\sum_{i \in I_k} u_{i,k} = 1, & i \in I_k \end{cases}, & I_k \neq \emptyset. \end{cases} \tag{5}$$

where $I_k = \emptyset$,

and

$$\bigvee_{1 \leq i \leq c} \mathbf{w}^{(i)} = \left(\mathbf{X}^\top \mathbf{D}_1^{(i)} \mathbf{X} + \gamma \tilde{\mathbf{X}}^\top \mathbf{D}_2^{(i)} \tilde{\mathbf{X}}\right)^{-1} \left(\mathbf{X}^\top \mathbf{D}_1^{(i)} \mathbf{y} + \gamma \tilde{\mathbf{X}}^\top \mathbf{D}_2^{(i)} \tilde{\mathbf{y}}\right). \tag{6}$$

Proof. If $\mathbf{W} \in \mathbb{R}^{(t+1) \times c}$ is fixed then criterion function (3) can be written as

$$J_2'(\mathbf{U}, \mathbf{W}) = \sum_{k=1}^{N} g_k(\mathbf{U}), \tag{7}$$

where

$$g_k(\mathbf{U}) = \begin{cases} \sum\limits_{i=1}^{c} \left\{ (u_{i,k})^2 \left(y_k - \mathbf{w}^{(i)\top} \mathbf{x}_k' \right)^2 \right. \\ \left. + \gamma \sum\limits_{i=1}^{c} (u_{i,k} - u_{i,k+1})^2 \left(y_k - \mathbf{w}^{(j)\top} \mathbf{x}_k' \right)^2 \right\}, & k = 1, 2, \cdots, N-1, \\ \sum\limits_{i=1}^{c} (u_{i,k})^2 \left(y_k - \mathbf{w}^{(i)\top} \mathbf{x}_k' \right)^2 & k = N. \end{cases} \tag{8}$$

Thus, for the last column of $\mathbf{U}$ ($k = N$) only the minimization of (7) may be performed independently to other columns of $\mathbf{U}$. The Lagrangian of (8) for $k = N$ with constraints from (1) is

$$G_N(\mathbf{U}, \lambda) = \sum_{i=1}^{c} (u_{i,N})^2 \left(y_N - \mathbf{w}^{(i)\top} \mathbf{x}_N' \right)^2 - \lambda \left[\sum_{i=1}^{c} u_{i,N} - 1 \right], \tag{9}$$

where λ is the Lagrange multiplier. Setting the Lagrangian's gradient to zero we obtain

$$\frac{\partial G_N(\mathbf{U}, \lambda)}{\partial \lambda} = \sum_{i=1}^{c} u_{i,N} - 1 = 0, \tag{10}$$

and

$$\underset{1 \le s \le c}{\forall} \quad \frac{\partial G_N(\mathbf{U}, \lambda)}{\partial u_{s,N}} = u_{s,N} \left(y_N - \mathbf{w}^{(s)\top} \mathbf{x}_N' \right)^2 - \lambda = 0. \tag{11}$$

From (11) we get

$$u_{s,N} = \frac{\lambda}{\left(y_N - \mathbf{w}^{(s)\top} \mathbf{x}_N' \right)^2}. \tag{12}$$

From (10), (12) we obtain

$$\underset{1 \le s \le c}{\forall} \quad u_{s,N} = \frac{1}{\sum\limits_{j=1}^{c} \dfrac{\left(y_N - \mathbf{w}^{(s)\top} \mathbf{x}_N' \right)^2}{\left(y_N - \mathbf{w}^{(j)\top} \mathbf{x}_N' \right)^2}}. \tag{13}$$

If all elements of Nth column of the partition matrix $\mathbf{U}$ are calculated, then the elements of $(N-1)$th column may be calculated, then the elements $(N-2)$th column, and so on. Thus, we calculate the elements of kth column assuming that all elements of $(k+1)$th column are already calculated. The Lagrangian of (8) for $k \in \{1, 2, \cdots, N-1\}$ with constraints from (1) is

$$G_k(\mathbf{U}, \lambda) = \sum_{i=1}^{c} (u_{i,k})^2 \left(y_k - \mathbf{w}^{(i)\top} \mathbf{x}_k' \right)^2 \tag{14}$$

$$+ \gamma \sum_{i=1}^{c} (u_{i,k} - u_{i,k+1})^2 \left(y_k - \mathbf{w}^{(i)\top} \mathbf{x}_k' \right)^2 - \lambda[\sum_{i=1}^{c} u_{i,k} - 1],$$

where λ is the Lagrange multiplier. Setting the Lagrangian's gradient to zero we obtain

$$\frac{\partial G_k(\mathbf{U}, \lambda)}{\partial \lambda} = \sum_{i=1}^{c} u_{i,k} - 1 = 0, \tag{15}$$

and

$$\underset{1 \le s \le c}{\forall} \quad \frac{\partial G_k(\mathbf{U}, \lambda)}{\partial u_{s,k}} = u_{s,k} \left(y_k - \mathbf{w}^{(s)\top} \mathbf{x}_k' \right)^2 \tag{16}$$

$$+ \gamma (u_{s,k} - u_{s,k+1}) \left(y_k - \mathbf{w}^{(s)\top} \mathbf{x}_k' \right)^2 - \lambda = 0.$$

From (16) we get

$$u_{s,k} = \frac{\lambda + \gamma u_{s,k+1} \left(y_k - \mathbf{w}^{(s)\top} \mathbf{x}_k' \right)^2}{\left(y_k - \mathbf{w}^{(s)\top} \mathbf{x}_k' \right)^2}. \tag{17}$$

From (15), (17) we obtain

$$\lambda = \frac{1 + \gamma - \sum_{j=1}^{c} u_{j,k+1}}{\sum_{j=1}^{c} \dfrac{1}{\left(y_k - \mathbf{w}^{(j)\top} \mathbf{x}_k' \right)^2}}. \tag{18}$$

Combination of (17), (18) and taking into account (15) yields

$$\underset{1 \le s \le c}{\forall} \quad u_{s,k} = \frac{1 + \gamma u_{s,k+1} \displaystyle\sum_{j=1}^{c} \dfrac{\left(y_k - \mathbf{w}^{(s)\top} \mathbf{x}_k' \right)^2}{\left(y_k - \mathbf{w}^{(j)\top} \mathbf{x}_k' \right)^2}}{(1+\gamma) \displaystyle\sum_{j=1}^{c} \dfrac{\left(y_k - \mathbf{w}^{(s)\top} \mathbf{x}_k' \right)^2}{\left(y_k - \mathbf{w}^{(j)\top} \mathbf{x}_k' \right)^2}}. \tag{19}$$

If $I_k \ne \emptyset$, then the choice of $u_{i,k} = 0$ for $i \notin I_k$ and $\sum_{i \in I_k} u_{i,k} = 1$ for $i \in I_k$ results in minimization of the criterion value in (3), because elements of the partition matrix are zeros for non-zero $\left(y_k - \mathbf{w}^{(i)\top}\mathbf{x}_k'\right)^2$, and non-zero for $\left(y_k - \mathbf{w}^{(i)\top}\mathbf{x}_k'\right)^2$ equal to zero. The necessary conditions for minimization of (3) with respect to the parameters vectors $\mathbf{w}^{(i)}$, $i = 1, 2, \cdots, c$ are easily obtained from the matrix form of the criterion function (4). If matrix $\mathbf{U}$ is fixed and the criterion function's (4) gradient with respect to the cluster centers $\mathbf{w}^{(s)}$ is set to zero, then we obtain

$$\frac{\partial J_m'\left(\mathbf{W}\right)}{\partial \mathbf{w}^{(s)}} = -2\mathbf{X}^\top \mathbf{D}_1^{(i)}\left(\mathbf{y} - \mathbf{X}\mathbf{w}^{(i)}\right) - 2\gamma\widetilde{\mathbf{X}}^\top \mathbf{D}_2^{(i)}\left(\widetilde{\mathbf{y}} - \widetilde{\mathbf{X}}\mathbf{w}^{(i)}\right) = \mathbf{0}. \quad (20)$$

After some simple matrix algebra we have (6).   □

It is worth noting that from (5) and (6) for $\gamma = 0$ the necessary conditions for traditional fuzzy c-regression models are obtained. The optimal partition is obtained by iterating through: (5) and (6). This method can be called Time-Domain-Constrained Fuzzy C-Regression Models (TDCFCRM):

1° Fix c $(1 < c < N)$, $m = 2$ and $\gamma \geq 0$. Initialize $\mathbf{U}^{(0)} \in \mathcal{P}_{fc}$. Set the iteration index $\ell = 1$.
2° Calculate the parameters matrix $\mathbf{W}^{(\ell)}$ for ℓth iteration using (6) and $\mathbf{U}^{(\ell-1)}$.
3° Update the fuzzy partition matrix $\mathbf{U}^{(\ell)}$ for ℓth iteration using (5) and $\mathbf{W}^{(\ell)}$.
4° If $\left\|\mathbf{U}^{(\ell)} - \mathbf{U}^{(\ell-1)}\right\|_F > \xi$ then $\ell \leftarrow \ell + 1$ and go to 2° else stop.

$\|\cdot\|_F$ denotes the Frobenius norm and ξ is a pre-set parameter. From experiments may be concluded that the reasonable choice of parameter γ includes $\gamma \in [0.02N, 0.08N]$.

3   Conclusions

In this paper, a new time-domain-constrained fuzzy clustering method is proposed. Incorporation of additional information into the clustering process, i.e. in signal analysis the neighbouring samples belong to the same cluster, is described by a new component in the criterion function. The necessary conditions (with proof) to obtain a local minimum of the criterion function are shown. The well-known from the literature fuzzy c-regression models can be obtained as a special case of the method proposed in this paper.

References

1. J.C. Bezdek, "*Pattern Recognition with Fuzzy Objective Function Algorithms*" New York, Plenum Press, 1982.
2. R.J. Hathaway, J.C. Bezdek, "*Switching Regression Models and Fuzzy Clustering*" IEEE Trans. Fuzzy Systems, Vol. 1, No. 3, pp. 195–204, 1993.
3. W. Pedrycz, "*Distributed Collaborative Knowledge Elicitation*" Computer Assisted Mechanics and Engineering Sciences, Vol.9, pp.87–104, 2002.

Special Cluster Analysis and Basic Feature Estimation with a Modification of Self-Organizing Map

Janusz Morajda

Cracow University of Economics, Department of Computer Science, Rakowicka 27,
31-510 Cracow, Poland
eimorajd@cyf-kr.edu.pl

Abstract. The paper describes a proposed method of modification of self-organizing map and its application to special cluster analysis (delivering the information about selected essential feature, which values derive from an ordered set) and also to estimation of the selected (basic) feature for newly occurring patterns. The utilization of this technique in the issue of real estate appraisal has been described. The visualizations of a cluster map, selected estimation maps and numerical results for this problem have been presented.

1 Introduction

Self-organizing map (SOM), proposed by Kohonen, is a well-known neural network architecture used for cluster analysis [1], [5]. SOM includes two fully connected layers and is trained in an unsupervised way. For a given input pattern $\mathbf{x}$, weights modification is performed for a second-layer neuron with minimal distance between its weight vector $\mathbf{w}$ and vector $\mathbf{x}$, and for the cells belonging to its certain topological neighbourhood. The learning process is iteratively repeated.

SOM is regarded as a tool that executes non-linear transformation of any metric space into 2-dimensional discrete space, and as the method of non-parametric regression that fits code vectors (weight vectors) $\mathbf{w}$ to the pattern distribution in a feature space. The training process orders the map so as similar patterns are represented by neighbouring neurons in the map. Consequently SOMs are applied to cluster analysis and also to its 2-dimensional visualisation. Many of such applications of SOMs to various problems have been reported in literature (see e.g. [3], [4], [5]).

The LVQ (Learning Vector Quantization) neural network has a similar to SOM, 2-layer structure and performs a pattern recognition (classification) process for *a priori* known classes. Each class is represented by one or a few arbitrarily assigned neurons in the second layer. The class for input vector $\mathbf{x}$ is indicated by a neuron with minimal distance between its weight vector $\mathbf{w}$ and vector $\mathbf{x}$. The LVQ training procedure utilizes a supervised technique based on

L. Rutkowski et al. (Eds.): ICAISC 2004, LNAI 3070, pp. 646–651, 2004.
© Springer-Verlag Berlin Heidelberg 2004

delivered information of the correct class for each learning pattern [5]. Graphical visualization does not have application in LVQs.

Although these types of neural networks can effectively perform standard cluster analysis or pattern recognition problems, there are some specific issues that can require somewhat more advanced techniques of analysis together with results visualization. Let us consider a cluster analysis problem that requires a separate consideration of a selected, fundamentally meaningful feature v. We assume that values of v belong to an ordered set (e.g. a range of real numbers). The problem may also concern future evaluation of feature v for newly occurring cases with unknown value of v. Let us here note that if we divide the set of values v into sufficient number of (ordered) subsets, the problem of evaluation of v amounts to the pattern recognition issue, where classes of input vectors $\mathbf{x}$ are determined by subsequent subsets of v.

The paper presents a method, based on a certain modification of SOMs and also inspired by LVQ training techniques, which can effectively deal with such kinds of problems and, moreover, enables useful visualization of results. The study also demonstrates the research concerning the method application to the real estate appraisal issue.

2   The Method of Self-Organizing Map Modification

Let us consider a set of patterns (feature vectors) in a n-dimensional metric space. Let us assume that each vector is described by $n-1$ "common" features and one basic feature v represented by values from a certain range (generally belonging to a certain ordered set). The proposed modification of SOM consists in the orientation of 2-dimensional map (output layer) so as its vertical axis represents only the feature v (see Fig. 1), while the horizontal axis represents the rest of feature vector. As the vertical axis of the neural map (with a finite number of cell rows) constitutes the values set of the discrete transformation of v, the subsequent rows of cells in the map are assigned to certain subsets (subranges) of v that are increasingly ordered on this axis. The feature v is not directly included in network input vector (input layer).

The learning procedure for such maps is similar to SOM training, however the winning neuron for a given learning input pattern *must* belong to the row representing the value of v (i.e. sufficient subset of v) for that pattern. Weight vector modification (according to the rule used in SOMs) is performed not only for the winner, but also for a certain number of cells belonging to its horizontal and vertical neighborhood[1]. So modified training technique is in principle a supervised learning method, somewhat similar to LVQ, however differs from LVQs about the network structure and use of neighborhood. Let us name here such modified SOM networks as MSOM.

---

[1] Advisability of use of vertical neighbourhood results from the fact that values of v come from an ordered set and the discrete transformation performed by the neural map preserve this order.

The developed MSOM maps allow cluster analysis of patterns with presentation of special information about the feature v for particular clusters, which is shown on the vertical axis of the map. The method enables also the reconstruction of typical patterns for the clusters connected with given values of v.

The developed MSOM can be also effectively utilized in the process of estimation of unknown values of feature v for newly occurring patterns. When a certain pattern $\mathbf{x}$ (that includes remaining, i.e. known features of a certain object) is delivered to the network input, the map neurons generate signals indicating distances between vector $\mathbf{x}$ and their own weight vectors $\mathbf{w}$. Cells reacting with low signals "recognize" the pattern $\mathbf{x}$. The row of the map, where a neuron generating the lowest signal is placed, indicates the estimated value (actually the subset of values) of v. Moreover, the visual (or numerical) analysis of all map signals may deliver more sophisticated possibilities of estimation and allows its uncertainty evaluation.

Similar neural nets (called visual prediction maps) have been presented by Morajda in [3] and applied for time series (stock index) forecasting and its visual analysis.

3   The Research and Obtained Results

The problem that has been considered in the research concerns the real estate appraisal with use of comparative method. The data applied include the information about previously evaluated estate objects and come from the census carried out in 1970 in the USA [2] and consist of 400 selected cases connected with particular census areas in Boston.

The 14 numeric features describe each case. The considered essential feature v is the median of the estate values in the given census area. The remaining 13 features comprise: average (in the area) number of rooms, percentage of objects developed before 1940, a factor indicating percentage of Black people living in the area, percentage of low social status people, number of committed crimes per capita, percentage of estates occupying more than 25000 square feet, percentage of industrial zones, real estate tax ratio, number of pupils per one teacher, binary factor that equals 1 if the area borders on Charles River and 0 otherwise, weighted distance to 5 basic employment zones in Boston, a factor expressing ease of access to ring roads around the city, and the indicator of air pollution. These 13 variables, after classical min-max normalisation to the range of [0, 1], constitute the input vector to MSOM.

The applied MSOM parameters have been selected as follows:
- map dimensions: horizontal: 25, vertical: 20 (total 500 neurons in the map),
- initial neighbourhood (horizontal × vertical): rectangle 5 × 17,
- neighbourhood gradually decreasing during the learning stage,
- neighbourhood function decreasing for the increasing distance between neurons,
- total number of learning epochs: 200,
- initial learning coefficient $\eta = 0.02$, decreasing during the learning stage,
- initial weights: randomly selected from the range [0, 1].

The 380 of 400 cases have been utilized as a learning set, while the remaining 20 cases have been applied to the testing procedure. The particular cases from the learning set have been assigned to the subsequent rows in the map on the basis of the equal division of increasing estate values v between particular rows. As the constructed map includes 20 rows of neurons, 19 learning cases have been assigned to each row (19 patterns with the lowest v - to the first row and so on, 19 cases with the highest v - to the last, i.e. the highest row). Such division method, however not obligatory, ensures better cluster visualization. As a result, each row represents a certain range of v, but for the purpose of presented research a given row is characterized by the average value v of the patterns assigned to it.

The training and testing of MSOM have been implemented with utilization of the author's computer program, written in C. According to the accepted assumption, during the learning stage the winning neuron for a given case was chosen from the row that had been assigned to the value v for this case. Nevertheless the neighbouring map cells (with reference to the winner) have also undergone training in a given step.

Figure 1 presents the distribution of clusters in the trained map. It should be noted that obtained weight vector for the central neuron of a given cluster represents the typical pattern connected with corresponding class of cases.

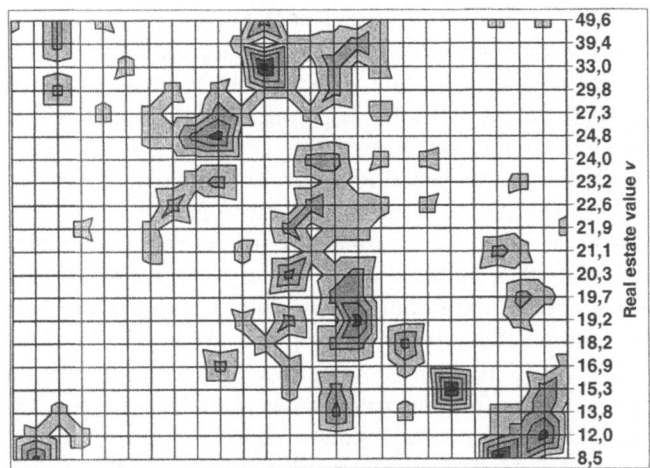

Fig. 1. The map of pattern clusters in the developed MSOM. White area represents "void" neurons having assigned 0 or 1 pattern. The more shaded area, the more learning cases have been assigned to corresponding neurons. As a result of such an assignment, clusters of patterns can be clearly identified; moreover, appropriate real estate value v (in 1000s dollars) for particular clusters is indicated on the vertical axis of the map

The developed MSOM can be also applied to fundamental feature v estimation (i.e. variable presented on the vertical axis) for newly occurring cases with unknown value of v. For such an issue, a pattern should be delivered to the input of developed MSOM and map of output signals should be analyzed. These signals represent the distances between the weight vectors and the input vector, consequently the "winning" neuron generating the lowest signal "recognizes" the pattern. The value v assigned to the map row including this neuron can be assumed as an evaluated value for the case. Moreover, the analysis of the size of the map area, which generates low signals (similar to the winner signal), may deliver information about the uncertainty of such evaluation.

The results of evaluation of real estate value for the first and the second test cases (not included in learning set) has been graphically shown in Fig. 2.

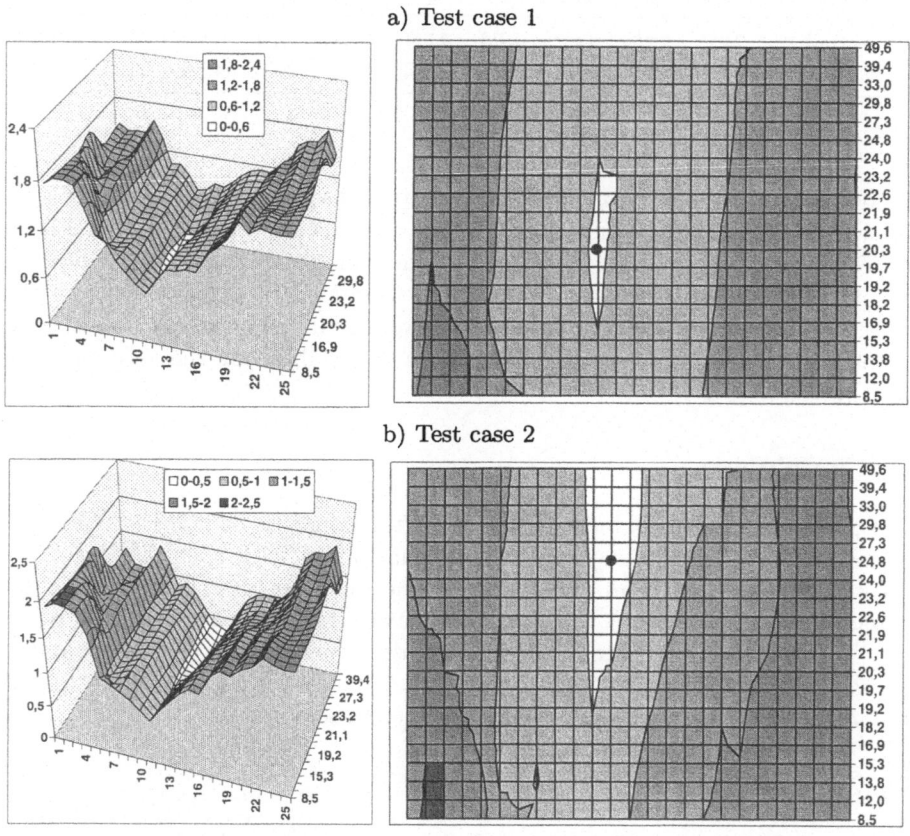

Fig. 2. Three- and two-dimensional maps of output signals for the first test case (upper charts) and the second test case (lower charts). The winning neurons (marked by black points) for particular cases belong respectively to: the row representing value $v = 20.3$ for the test case 1 (actual value $v = 18.9$), and the row representing the value $v = 24.8$ for the test case 2 (actual value $v = 24.8$); values v expressed in 1000s dollars

It is worth noting that for test case 2 the MSOM model shows a high possibility of obtaining higher estate values v than the price indicated by the winning neuron (consider the white area of low output signal in Fig. 2b). This observation was also confirmed by the experiment with use of perceptron neural networks.

Table 1 presents estimated by MSOM values of v (appraised estate values) for all 20 test patterns, with comparison to actual price data.

Table 1. Actual and evaluated by the MSOM winning neuron values v for 20 test cases

Estate values in 1000s dollars for 20 cases included in test set									
Actual	18.9	24.8	24.5	18.3	42.3	19.3	19.3	12.7	36.1	23.2
Evaluated	20.3	24.8	24.8	18.2	39.4	20.3	21.1	8.5	33.0	23.2
Actual	21.2	15.7	18.2	18.8	11.9	14.3	28.4	43.5	21.2	20.6
Evaluated	21.9	20.3	21.1	21.1	21.9	15.3	29.8	49.6	21.1	21.9

The obtained test root of mean squared error **RMSE = 3.302** and is slightly worse than the corresponding error (RMSE = 3.286) achieved by the multilayer perceptron (mainly due to occurrence of significant error for case 15). The mean absolute error **MAE = 2.254** and is better than MAE = 2.440 achieved by the perceptron. However, the calculated here errors could be even less because they are partially caused by discrete quantization of variable v on the vertical axis of MSOM.

4   Conclusions

The proposed method, which derives from the concepts of SOM an LVQ networks, enables cluster analysis and its visualization with special respect to a selected key feature. The developed MSOM network can also effectively evaluate (numerically and visually) values of this feature for new patterns. The results obtained for the issue of real estates appraisal confirm the usefulness and effectiveness of the method. Further research, however, should be devoted to an important problem of proper MSOM parameters selection.

References

1. Kohonen T.: 'Self-organizing Maps'. Springer-Verlag, Berlin (1995)
2. Lula P.: 'Feed-forward Neural Networks in the Modelling of Economic Phenomena' (in Polish). Cracow University of Economics, Cracow (1999)
3. Morajda J.: 'Neural Networks and Their Economic Applications', in 'Artificial Intelligence and Security in Computing Systems' - Proc. of the 9th International Conference ACS'2002, Kluwer Academic Publishers, Boston/Dordrecht/London (2003)
4. Witkowska D.: 'Artificial Neural Networks in Economic Analyses' (in Polish). Lódź (1999)
5. Zieliński J.S. (ed.): 'Intelligent Systems in Management - Theory and Practice' (in Polish). Scientific Publishing House PWN, Warsaw (2000)

An Unsupervised Cluster Analysis and Information about the Modelling System

Izabela Rejer

Szczecin University, Poland,
i_rejer@uoo.univ.szczecin.pl

Abstract. The aim of the article is to present a possible way of joining
the information coming from the modelling system with the unsupervised
clustering method, fuzzy c–means method. The practical application of
the proposed approach will be presented via problem of bankruptcy prediction.

1 Introduction

The problem that will be presented in the article arose during a survey on
bankruptcy prediction which was led in the last year at the University of Szczecin
[4]. The most important goal of the survey was to build a neural network model
which would have been able to predict whether a firm described by a set of chosen
financial factors would fail in a next year or not. So the problem was defined
as: *find a classifier which would be able to isolate firms that would bankrupt in a
next year from firms that would be still alive in that year.*

The base of the modelling process was a data set U consisted of 1091 data
vectors $v : \{x_1 \dots x_{55}, y\}$, where: x_i denoted input variables and y denoted output
variable. The input variables represented the condition of a firm in a year *k-1*
and the output variable informed whether a firm failed in a year *k*. The values
of the output variable were established by the Economy Courts.

At first look the set U seemed to be good enough for the classification task.
However, during the survey it turn out that the classification made from the
low point of view was very ambiguous so it could not be used as a base of an
effective model. This ambiguousness caused that both classes existed in the data
set interfered so tightly that it was impossible to isolate clusters composed of
data belonged only to one class. The problem is illustrated in the fig. 1 (fig. 1a
shows the original ambiguous classes and fig. 1b shows the classes obtained after
the reorganization process which will be discussed later in the article).

Since the data from the original data set could not be a base of an effective model, a question arose what could be done in order to improve the data
describing the analysed system? For answering this question the data set was
once more carefully analysed. Of course the input values could not be changed
because they represented the actual condition of analysed firms. Theoretically
also the output classes were unchangeable because they were established by the
most reliable authority — by the court. However, when the chosen subset of data

L. Rutkowski et al. (Eds.): ICAISC 2004, LNAI 3070, pp. 652–657, 2004.
© Springer-Verlag Berlin Heidelberg 2004

triangle: bankrupt firm, square: sound firm, point: firm of an unknown state

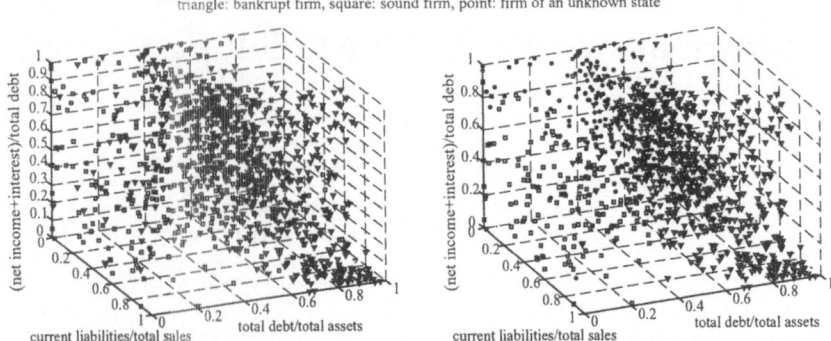

Fig. 1. The bankruptcy data classification: original (a), after reorganization (b)

was presented to an auditor it turn out that about 30% of the examples were classified by him in an opposite way. This disagreement in classification had its source in the type of firms submitted to the judgement. Expert-auditor had a possibility to judge all firms existed in the chosen subset of firms while the court judged only these firms which wanted to get a bankruptcy status. That means the court had no possibility to evaluate any firm, even if it was in a very bad condition, which was artificially kept in life by its owners. So, after the expert's evaluation it became clear that for building an effective model of the analysed system the original data set had to be reorganized.

In order to reorganize the original data set a modified fuzzy c-means method was used. The modification of the classic fuzzy c-means method described in the article was based on the union of this unsupervised method with the information existed in the original data set.

2 The Classic Fuzzy C-Means Method

Classic fuzzy c-means method divides a data set into set of clusters which centres minimized a chosen distance measure between data points and clusters centres [3]. When the Euclidean distance is taken into consideration, the objective function is given as:

$$\text{Min} \sum_{i=1}^{c} \sum_{j=1}^{n} (\mu_{ij})^q \|x_j - m_j\|^2 \ , \tag{1}$$

where: μ_{ij} a degree of membership of the data point j to the cluster i, q a degree of fuzziness of the membership function, x_j the value of the data point j, m_i the centre of the cluster i, c number of clusters, n number of data points.

The optimisation of the objective function is executed through the iterative algorithm which in every step t modifies clusters' centres according to the equation:

$$m_{xl,i} = \frac{\sum_{j=1}^{n} \mu_{ij}^{q}(t) * x_{l,j}}{\sum_{j=1}^{n} \mu_{ij}^{q}(t)} \quad , \tag{2}$$

where: $l = 1, \ldots, d$, d the dimension of the input vector.

The degrees of membership μ_{ij} are calculated in each step of the algorithm according to the equation:

$$\mu_{ij}(t+1) = \frac{1}{\sum_{k=1}^{c} [\frac{d_{ij}(t)}{d_{kj}(t)}]^{\frac{2}{q-1}}} \quad , \tag{3}$$

where: $d_{ij}(t)$ the Euclidean distance between data point i and the cluster j, $d_{kj}(t)$ the Euclidean distance between data point i and all c clusters.

Since the objective function (1) mostly has a highly non-linear characteristic, the process of adjusting the clusters' centres can easily stall in a local minima. So, it is necessary to carry on the algorithm many times, with different number of clusters and different starting positions of the clusters' centres.

Assuming the same amount of clusters, results obtained with different starting positions of the clusters' centres theoretically are easily to compare. The most advisable is this set of clusters which is characterised by the smallest value of the objective function. According to this statement the sets of clusters characterised by same values of the distance measure should be treated as identical. Unfortunately this theoretical rule cannot be used in most real high-dimensional systems, in which two sets of clusters described by the same value of the objective function can contain completely different data. The reason of this situation is that the distance which is minimized (1) is the total distance calculated on the base of all dimensions of the analysed system.

So, the distance measure allows only for choosing the sets of clusters which are characterised by the smallest multi-dimensional distances between the clusters' centres and the data points but do not allow to decide which of these sets guarantees the most reasonable content of each cluster. This set has to be chosen in another way. One possibility of choosing it is to use the additional knowledge existed in the data set describing the analysed system. Such approach can be used in systems similar to the system analysed in this article — it means to the systems which were previously divided into ambiguous classes. Of course the original classification can not be totally incorrect. In the analysed system the original classification was in 70% in agreement with the expert's evaluation so the information came from it could be used in the clustering process.

3   The Cluster Analysis with an Additional Information

The algorithm which was used to the reclassification of the data set was performed in two steps. The first step was concentrated on the cluster analysis and the second was aimed at defining the proper class label for each cluster from the chosen clusters' set.

In the cluster analysis step, the fuzzy c-means method, described in the second part of the article, was used. The adjustment of the positions of the clusters' centres was carried on according to the objective function given in (1) with the fuzziness parameter q set to 1.5. The stop condition for the algorithm was set as follows:

$$\frac{1}{c*n}\sum_{i=n}^{c}\sum_{j=1}^{n}|\mu_{ij}(t+1)-\mu_{ij}(t)| \leq 10^{-5} \ . \tag{4}$$

The algorithm was performed 1.000 times for different amount of clusters and different starting positions of each cluster. The results of each algorithm realisation were not compared as in the classic fuzzy c-means method – according to the value of the Euclidean distance (1) – but according to the measure which was based on the information originated from the original data set. The measure D was defined as an average difference between the number of bankrupt and sound firms existed in each cluster from the analysed clusters' set:

$$D = \frac{1}{c}\sum_{i=1}^{c}|b_i - s_i| \ , \tag{5}$$

where: b_i the number of bankrupt firms in the cluster i, s_i the number of sound firms in the cluster i.

Larger values of the measure D denoted more desirable set of clusters.

One of the most important problems which can be encountered during the cluster analysis is to find the appropriate number of clusters. It is not possible to use the original distance measure as a guide in a process of looking for it. It is also impossible to use the measure proposed above. The reason of it is that the more clusters are taken into consideration the better values of both measures can be obtained. So, the best values (the smallest Euclidean distance (1) and the largest difference measure (5)) can be achieved when the number of clusters is equal to the number of data points. Of course creating such clusters' set has no sense because it introduces nothing to our knowledge of the analysed system.

The problem mentioned above was solved by setting up the minimal number of data points per cluster. It was assumed that the minimal number of data points per each cluster could not be smaller than the dimension of the input vector, which was equal to 55. When at least one cluster from the clusters set contained less data points than chosen value, the whole set was eliminated from the study. So, only these sets of clusters which fulfilled above condition were taken into consideration during the comparison process.

As it was mentioned before, the whole algorithm was executed 1.000 times. At the end of the analysis 786 correct sets of clusters were compared. The best one consisted of 10 clusters and was characterized by the greatest discrimination abilities: D=51.1 (tab. 1).

The raw cluster analysis allows to divide the whole data set into some separable subsets but it does not give any information on the meaning of the data belonged to each subset. In some applications such result is sufficient but when the data set has to be used as a base of a classification model, the clusters interpretation has to be performed.

In order to deal with this task once again the primary classification existed in the original data set was used. The rule for the reclassification was as follows: the clusters consisted in more than 66.67% of bankrupt firms were regarded as bankrupt (class 0), the clusters consisted in less than 33.33% of bankrupt firms were regarded as sound (class 2), the rest clusters were regarded as "difficult to determine" (class 1).

After the new classification the reorganized data set consisted of 215 failed firms, 696 non-failed firms and 180 firms of an unknown state (tab. 1). As it can be observed via chart presented in the fig. 1, the process of the data set reorganisation brought large improvement in the data classification.

Table 1. The chosen clusters set ($D = 51.1$)

Number of cluster	Number of failed firms	Number of non-failed firms	% of failed firms	Class label
1	50	20	71.43	0
2	66	27	70.97	0
3	21	115	15.44	2
4	36	55	39.56	1
5	13	103	11.21	2
6	52	139	27.69	2
7	53	36	59.55	1
8	38	18	69.23	0
9	35	83	28.57	2
10	32	99	24.43	2

4   The Verification of the New Classification

The results of the reclassification were verified by building a neural model, based on the data from the reorganized data set, and by comparing the model's results with the expert's evaluation. The model's inputs were chosen via the hierarchical method [5]. The parameters of the neural networks that was used for building models needed in every stage of the hierarchical method were as follows: flow of signals: one-way, architecture of connections between layers: all to all, hidden layers: 1 hidden layer with 6-10 sigmoid neurons, output layer: 1 sigmoid neuron, training method: backpropagation algorithm with momentum and changing learning rates [1,2]. The neural models were trained on the base of 80% of the data chosen randomly from the whole data set. The remaining 20% of the data were used in the testing process. Each neural model was trained five times. The modelling process was stopped with the five-input model, characterised by the testing error 3.56%. The results obtained in succeeding steps of the hierarchical method are shown in the tab. 2.

In order to verify the behaviour of the final model, 25 new examples were presented to the model and to the expert-auditor. It occurred that the model's

Table 2. The results of the hierarchical method

Name of chosen variable	training error %	testing error %
total debt/total assets	15.98	15.62
current liabilities/total sales	10.41	10.30
(net income + interest)/total debt	7.79	7.80
invested capital (logic variable)	5.80	4.85
EBIT/current liabilities	3.47	3.56

performance was in 92% in agreement with the expert's evaluation. Such good result proved that the reorganization of the data set was performed in a correct way and that the final model can be used in practical applications.

5   Conclusion

It is not a rare situation that the original classes isolated from the whole data set describing a real multi–dimensional system are not truly separable. Of course the data set consisted of non–separable classes cannot be a base of an effective model. So, if the model of such system has to be built, first the cluster analysis has to be performed. However, the raw cluster analysis allows only for dividing the data set into subsets but does not allow to assign any interpretation to those subsets. Required interpretation can be made, as was proposed in the article, by taking into account the information coming from the original classification. Of course proposed approach can be used only when there is a possibility of evaluating the error of the original classification and when the value of this error is reasonable.

The aim of the article was to present a possible way of joining the information coming from the original data set with the unsupervised clustering method, fuzzy c-means method. As it was shown via the neural model and its expert's verification, proposed approach allowed to build very precise and reliable model of the analysed, highly-dimensional system.

References

1. Demuth H. Beale M.: Neural Network Toolbox User's Guide. The Math Works Inc., Natick MA USA (2000)
2. Masters T.: Practical Neural Network Recipes in C++. Scientific-Technical Publishing Company, Warsaw (1996)
3. Piegat A.: Fuzzy Modelling and Control. Physica-Verlag, New York (1999)
4. Rejer I.: How to deal with the data in a bankruptcy prediction modelling. Kluwer Academic Publisher (to appear)
5. Sugeno M., Yasukawa T.: A Fuzzy-Logic-Based Approach to Qualitative Modelling. IEEE Transaction on Fuzzy Systems vol. 1, no. 1 (1993)

Cursive-Character Script Recognition Using Toeplitz Model and Neural Networks

Khalid Saeed and Marek Tabedzki

Computer Engineering Department, Faculty of Computer Science, Bialystok Technical University, Bialystok, Poland.*
aidabt@ii.pb.bialystok.pl
http://aragorn.pb.bialystok.pl/~zspinfo/

Abstract. This paper presents a hybrid method to use both the idea of projection and Toeplitz Matrix approaches to describe the feature vectors of an image and hence identifying it. The method applies two different tools. The main one is Toeplitz forms and the second is Neural Networks. The image model considered in this work are some selected Arabic scripts. The letter is first projected on 12 axes, then the lengths of these axes are measured and afterwards for the sake of classification and recognition these lengths are compared with the ones in the data base. The method has proved its high efficiency upon the other known approaches. Toeplitz model has shown its successful role in improving the description of the image feature vectors and hence increasing the rate of recognition. The overall algorithm has reached a very low rate of misclassification. Both machine and hand written cases have been studied. In this paper, examples of handwritten scripts are considered.

Introduction

The method of projection has been known since a long time ago [1–3]. Its algorithm is based on the idea of projecting the pixels forming the letter-image onto axes surrounding the script. The number of the projection axes has been modified and changed from two to four and then to 12 [1]. Fig.1 (a) shows the Arabic letters ﺑ - pronounced B and ﺡ - pronounced HH, thinned in (b) and projected onto four axes in the 4-axis model in (c).

The obtained feature vectors are not qualified to satisfy perfect description of the original image. A similar approach, but in a distribution of 13 axes [1, 2], has been conducted. Experiments have shown that the optimal number of projection axes or segments is 12 [1]. Fig.1 (d) shows the letters put into a window-frame with 12 axes. The window is designed to contain one script-image. Therefore, if a word is considered, then it should be segmented into letters before entering the testing window. The idea of segmentation is beyond the topics of this work.

Another important preprocessing step preceding the projection is the image pixelization to thin the letter-image to one-pixel-width skeleton [4]. This simplifies the whole procedure of projection and feature extracting.

---

* This work is supported by the Rector of Bialystok Technical University.

L. Rutkowski et al. (Eds.): ICAISC 2004, LNAI 3070, pp. 658–663, 2004.
© Springer-Verlag Berlin Heidelberg 2004

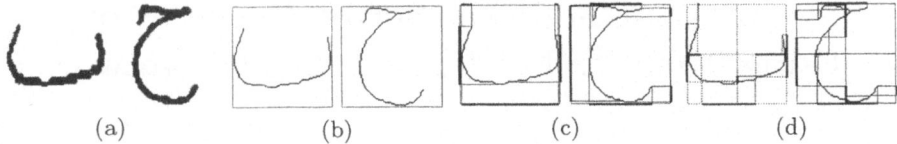

Fig. 1. (a) Two Arabic letters: ﺏ - B without dot and ح - HH. (b) Their thinned shapes. (c) Their possible ways of projection onto 4 axes. (d) Projection onto 12 axes.

Basic Database

A 16-Arabic-script base has been used with ten samples each. The hand-written letters are shown in Table1. For all script samples, 30% of the base contents are for training and the remaining for testing.

Table 1. 16 Arabic scripts given in their hand and machine forms

Seq.	1	2	3	4	5	6	7	8	9	10	11	12	13	14	15	16
Machine	ﺏ	ح	ﺩ	ﺭ	ﺱ	ﺹ	ﻁ	ﻉ	ﻑ	ﻩ	ﻷ	ﻭ	ﻡ	ﻝ	ﻱ	ﺍ
Hand	ﻭ	ح	ﺩ	ﺭ	ﺱ	ﺹ	ﻁ	ﻉ	ﻑ	O	ﻷ	ﻭ	ﻡ	ﻝ	ﺱ	ﺍ
Pronunciation	B	HH	D	R	S	SS	DD	AA	F	H	LA	W	M	L	Y	A

Projection Art

The main aspect of this work is to add the use of the suggested in [5, 6] model of minimal eigenvalues to the method of projection in [1]. They are extended in this paper to act together with the designed for-this-purpose neural networks in order to work out a general method of projection and identification.

The Algorithm of Projection

1. The first step is to thin the script.
2. Then each pixel of the thinned image is projected onto the nearest two of the 12 axes, on one horizontal and one vertical axis.
3. For each of the resulting axis-bars of pixels the fraction of bar-length to axis-length is calculated.
4. This is repeated until all script-pixels are projected.
5. Now we have 12 bars with lengths of values between zero (when no pixel is on the axis) and one (when the axis is full of pixels).
6. A 12-element feature vector is formed whose elements are the values of the bar-lengths fractions in the range $\langle 0, 1 \rangle$.
7. This vector gives a good description of the script and is used for further analysis as the input to the system of classification.

Example of Feature Vector Verification and Script-Image Description

The letter ‍ح HH is projected onto 12 axes (Fig.2) according to the algorithm given in Section 3.1. As seen, the projected pixels form 12 bars of different values. They are the elements of the given letter ‍ح feature vector FV defined in Eq.(1) and is unique for the given letter.

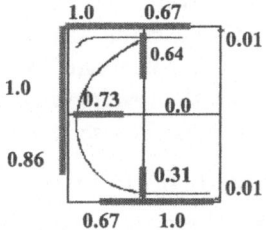

Fig. 2. The Arabic letter ‍ح - HH projected on 12 axes

This is why the projection method describes the image well in a given definite class and hence forms the basic part for classification process of an image in such a class.

$$FV = (1.0, 0.67, 0.73, 0.0, 0.67, 1.0, 1.0, 0.86, 0.64, 0.31, 0.01, 0.01) \qquad (1)$$

Experiments and Results

A number of experiments have been done on all letters of the Arabic and Latin alphabets for both machine and handwritten scripts. Here are shown the results of the experiments applied on Arabic-letters. The Latin alphabet, however, is simple and the projection results have shown no difficulties at all [7]. After projecting the classification takes place.

Image Classification

The feature vector obtained in Section 3.2 is the characteristic vector describing an image in a definite class. The classifying and identifying methods considered in this work are:

Element-to-Element Classification. This means we are comparing the feature vector elements of the tested script with those in the database. Although the method gives very high efficiency, it is awkward and time-consuming. It also implies the necessity of storing large database and continual iterating through it. Moreover, in real application it becomes much bigger than the size presented in the experiments shown in this work.

Classification by Neural Networks. An artificial Neural Network is used [8–10] to prevent the necessity of storing huge database and searching through it for each analyzed letter. The feature vectors train the neural network, which in turn gives the last decision of classification and recognition in a fast and efficient way. The applied three-layer NN is trained by the method of backpropagation. The log-sigmoid transfer function $F(n) = \frac{1}{1+e^{-bn}}$ with $b = 2$ is used.

The elements of the vector FV in Eq.(1) are treated as the input to the neural network. The two-hidden-layer network has 16 outputs representing the letters given in Table 1. After the learning stage, a test set is used to verify the accuracy of the method. An efficiency average of 93% correctly recognized letters has been obtained. Table 2 shows the results of Network method. There still are some cases which need improvement. The script ر R, for example, is recognized 73% while the compound script لا (LA to mean L and A, two letters in one) is recognized 76%. This decreases the whole efficiency average.

Table 2. Results of Neural Network Classification

Script	ب	ح	د	ر	س	ص	ط	ع	ف	ه	لا	و	م	ل	ي	ا
Recognition rate	100	96	100	73	97	100	96	87	84	100	76	96	100	100	87	91

Classification by Neural Networks and Toeplitz Matrices - Hybrid Approach. Vector elements of Eq.(1) obtained from projection are used to form Toeplitz matrices, according to the algorithm of minimal eigenvalues described in [5, 6] with some modification. The details of the algorithm are not within the topics of this work. Here, however, the algorithm modification is given. Simply, the vector lengths of Eq.(1) define the coefficients c_i of Taylor series in Eq.(2), which in turn, are the determinants' elements of Toeplitz matrices.

$$T(z) = c_0 + c_1 z + c_2 z^2 + ... + c_n z^n + ... \quad (2)$$

$$D_i = \begin{vmatrix} c_0 & c_1 & \cdots & c_i \\ c_1 & c_2 & \cdots c_{i-1} \\ \cdots & \cdots & \cdots & \cdots \\ c_i & c_{i-1} & \cdots & c_0 \end{vmatrix}, \quad i = 0, 1, 2, ..., n \quad (3)$$

The minimal eigenvalues $(\lambda_0, \lambda_1, \lambda_2, ..., \lambda_n)$ of these determinants form a nonincreasing series (Fig.3). They furnish a good description of the image they represent, even when the image is very complicated [11]. Fig.3a,b,c shows the behavior of the λ's for three different letters; they are ب - B, ح - HH and س - S. The curves of one script-image are too similar. Fig.3d, however, shows the three average curves of these scripts. They differ from each other.

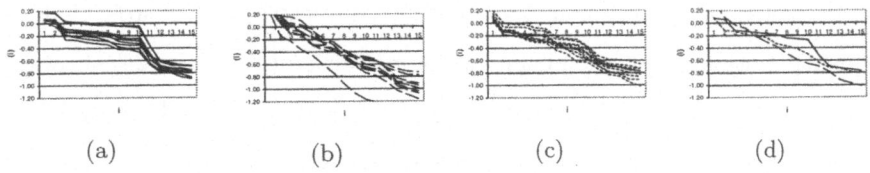

(a)   (b)   (c)   (d)

Fig. 3. Series of minimal eigenvalues for the scripts ب - B (a), ح - HH (b) and س - S (c), minimal eigenvalues average-series for the three script-images (d).

Although the Toeplitz-form approach is itself a good classifier [6], it does not show flexible applications as a decision maker. Its role is the best when acting as an image descriptor [5]. To make this way of image description useful, the output of the minimal eigenvalues algorithm after projection is used as the input to the NN instead of direct application. This has improved the rate of recognition of some scripts. The incorrectly recognized characters with other methods are properly classified with this hybrid one (Table 3). Despite the misclassification of some script samples causing a lower rate of only 85%, the hybrid method has proved to be more effective in recognizing what other methods fails to do because of script complexity (rate of recognition of the compound script لا - LA increases from 76% to 100%).

Table 3. Comparison between Neural Network and Hybrid Classification

Method of Classification (all with Projection)	Selected Scripts Classification Rate%							
	ر	ص س	ط	ف	ه	لا	و	ل
Element-to-element	100	100	100	86	100	86	86	100
Toeplitz	86	100	100	14	57	86	100	100
NN	73	100	96	84	100	76	96	100
Hybrid	97	97	83	63	100	100	100	100

Conclusions

A hybrid method depending on previous ideas to describe and identify cursive-scripts is used in this paper. It makes use of both the projection approach and minimal eigenvalues model as image descriptors while neural networks as classifiers and decision makers. The steps of applying all models are given in details showing how the classification rate is increasing after perfect analysis of the cursive script character and certain modifications to the previous models. Although using only neural networks showed the best results, it is advised, however, to use them together with minimal eigenvalues of Toeplitz matrices for better recognition of misclassified scripts by other methods. A general look at the tables of results proves this conclusion. For example, the letter Ɣ̌ - LA and ﺝ - R were frequently misclassified when using neural network only - Ɣ̌ was 24% times classified as ﺝ while ﺝ was 27% times classified as Ɣ̌. The use of Toeplitz matrices improved the classification rate of these two letters - now the letter Ɣ̌ was recognized properly 100% and the letter ﺝ 97% times. Some other letters have also shown some increase in efficiency.

References

1. K. Saeed, "A Projection Approach for Arabic Handwritten Characters Recognition," P. Sincak and J. Vascak (Eds), Quo Vadis Computational Intelligence? New Trends and App. in Comp. Intelligence, pp. 106-111, Physica-Verlag: Berlin 2000.
2. D. Burr, "Experiments on Neural Net Recognition of Spoken and Written Text, IEEE Trans. On Acoustic, Speech and Signal Proc., 36, no. 7, 1162-1168, 1988.
3. J. Zurada, M. Barski, W. Jedruch, "Artificial Neural Networks," PWN, Warszawa 1996 (In Polish).
4. K. Saeed, M. Rybnik, M. Tabedzki, "Implementation and Advanced Results on the Non-interrupted Skeletonization Algorithm," 9th CAIP Int. Conference on Computer Analysis of Images and Patterns, 5-7 Sept., Warsaw 2001. Proceedings published in: Lecture Notes in Computer Science - W. Skarbek (Ed.), Computer Analysis of Images and Patterns, pp. 601-609, Springer-Verlag Heidelberg: Berlin 2001.
5. K. Saeed, "Computer Graphics Analysis: A Method for Arbitrary Image Shape Description." MGV - International Journal on Machine Graphics and Vision, Institute of Computer Science, Volume 10, Number 2, 2001, pp. 185-194, Polish Academy of Sciences, Warsaw 2001.MGV
6. K. Saeed, M. Tabedzki, M. Adamski, "A New Approach for Object-Feature Extract and Recognition," 9th International Conference on Advanced Computer Systems - ACS'02, pp. 389-397, 23-25 October, Miedzyzdroje 2002.
7. K. Saeed, "New Approaches for Cursive Languages Recognition: Machine and Hand Written Scripts and Texts," Advances in Neural Networks and Applications, pp. 92-97, WSES Press: Tenerife 2001.
8. M. Riedmiller, H. Braun, "RPROP - A Fast Adaptive Learning Algorithm," Technical Report, Karlsruhe University, 1992.
9. H. Goraine, "Application of Neural Networks on Cursive Text Recognition," Advances in Signal Processing and Computer Technologies, pp. 350-354, WSES/IEEE, WSES Press: Crete 2001.
10. R. Tadeusiewicz, "Neural Networks," AOW, Cracow 1992 (in Polish).
11. K. Saeed, M. Kozlowski, "An Image-Based System for Spoken-Letter Recognition," Lecture Notes in Computer Science - M. Pietkov (Ed.), Computer Analysis of Images and Patterns, pp. 494-502, Springer-Verlag Heidelberg: Berlin 2003.

Learning with an Embedded Reject Option

Ramasubramanian Sundararajan[1]* and Asim K. Pal[2]

[1] Information & Decision Technologies Lab
GE India Technology Centre Pvt. Ltd.
Plot 122, EPIP Phase 2, Hoodi Village, Whitefield Road, Bangalore 560066, India
ramasubramanian.sundararajan@geind.ge.com
[2] Professor of Information Systems & Computer Science
Indian Institute of Management Calcutta
D. H. Road, Joka, Kolkata 700104, India
asim@iimcal.ac.in

Abstract. The option to reject an example in order to avoid the risk of a costly potential misclassification is well-explored in the pattern recognition literature. In this paper, we look at this issue from the perspective of statistical learning theory. Specifically, we look at ways of modeling the problem of learning with an embedded reject option, in terms of minimizing an appropriately defined risk functional, and discuss the applicability thereof of some fundamental principles of learning, such as minimizing empirical risk and structural risk. Finally, we present some directions for further theoretical work on this problem.

1 Introduction

The primary focus of learning theory with regard to pattern recognition problems has been on algorithms that return a prediction on every example in the example space. However, in many real life situations, it may be prudent to reject an example rather than run the risk of a costly potential misclassification.

The issue of introducing a reject option in a learning machine has been dealt with extensively in the pattern recognition community. Typically, a learning algorithm first finds the optimal hypothesis on the entire example space, and the optimal rejection region is then calculated. The rejection region is usually defined in terms of a threshold on the strength of the output [1]; however, other methods such as ambiguity and distance-based thresholds [2], class-related thresholds [3] and voting schemes for ensembles of classifiers have been explored in the literature.

At the end of the training process, the example space is divided into regions where the hypothesis returns a prediction (of one of m classes in a pattern recognition problem), and a region where it does not return a prediction at all. The generalization performance of the classifier depends on the way the example space is divided into these regions. Therefore, it is intuitive that an approach that determines these regions in an integrated manner would give better performance as compared to one that determines these regions in a decoupled manner as described above. We shall refer to the integrated approach as an *embedded rejection scheme*. Learning algorithms for training perceptrons and support vector machines with an embedded rejection scheme have been recently proposed [4,5].

---

* This work was done as part of a fellow (doctoral) program at IIM Calcutta

L. Rutkowski et al. (Eds.): ICAISC 2004, LNAI 3070, pp. 664–669, 2004.
© Springer-Verlag Berlin Heidelberg 2004

The focus of this paper is to look at the underlying mechanism for learning with an embedded reject option. Specifically, we ask the question: *How do we formulate an inductive principle for learning with an embedded reject option from a set of examples?*

2   The Problem of Learning with an Embedded Reject Option

Let $S = ((x_1, y_1), \ldots (x_\ell, y_\ell))$ be a labeled i.i.d. sample drawn from an unknown but fixed joint distribution $F(x, y)$, $x \in X$, $y \in Y = \{1, \ldots m\}$, where m is the number of classes. A learning algorithm L uses the sample S to arrive at a hypothesis $h \in H$, which, in case a reject option is permitted, will output $h(x) \in \{0\} \cup Y$, where 0 represents the reject option.

Let us consider a scenario wherein the rationale for rejection of an example comes from the fact that the cost of rejection is lower than the cost of misclassification. We shall assume that the costs of misclassification and rejection (as well as the gain from correct classification) do not vary across classes. A simple version of the loss function $L_1(x, y, h)$ for a given example can therefore be represented as:

$$L_1(x, y, h) = \begin{cases} 0 & \text{if } h(x) = y \\ \gamma & \text{if } h(x) = 0 \\ 1 & \text{if } h(x) \neq y, \ h(x) \neq 0 \end{cases} \tag{1}$$

where $0 < \gamma < 1$ is the cost of rejection. The above formulation implicitly treats rejection as another class in the problem. However, in many cases, a more intuitive notion would be to look at a hierarchical setup wherein one stage would decide whether or not a prediction is made (in which case a loss of γ is applied), and the other stage would determine the loss (0 or 1) on a predicted example.

In order to formulate the risk function for such a method, we approach the problem by introducing the concept of locality of a hypothesis. The idea of locality has been dealt with earlier through the Local Risk Minimization principle by Vapnik [6]; however, this principle does not account for the possibility of differential costs between rejection and misclassification. Therefore, we present a modified formulation here on the basis of differential costs.

Let $h^p \in H^p$ be the hypothesis that returns a prediction for any given example, and $\theta \in \Theta$ be an indicator function, whose value is 1 when the hypothesis rejects a particular example, and 0 otherwise. Thus

$$h(x) = (1 - \theta(x, h^p))h^p(x)$$

Let the loss function for the hypothesis h^p be:

$$L_2(x, y, h^p) = \begin{cases} 0 & \text{if } h^p(x) = y \\ 1 & \text{if } h^p(x) \neq y \end{cases} \tag{2}$$

L_1 can therefore be rewritten as:

$$L_1(x, y, h) \equiv L_3(x, y, h) = \gamma\theta(x, h^p) + (1 - \theta(x, h^p)) L_2(x, y, h^p) \tag{3}$$

The risk of the compound hypothesis h is given by the expectation of L_3 over the example space:

$$R(h) = \int L_3(x, y, h) \, dF(x, y) \tag{4}$$

Note that this formulation allows the rejection hypothesis θ to have a complexity that is independent of the prediction hypothesis h^p (see Section 4).

The learning problem can therefore be stated as one of finding the hypothesis h_{opt} that minimizes the risk functional R. To minimize this risk, learning algorithms may use as an inductive principle, the objective of minimizing the empirical version of R for a sample of size ℓ, thereby obtaining the hypothesis h_ℓ. It is intuitive to see that such a learning algorithm would have to minimize the risk due to both h^p and θ simultaneously. This would not have been possible had we applied the local risk minimization principle, which uses the loss function $(1 - \theta(x, h^p))L_2(x, y, h^p)$.

3   The ERM Principle for Learning with an Embedded Reject Option

The ERM principle states that, in order to arrive at the optimal hypothesis that minimizes the risk functional R, one should choose the hypothesis that minimizes the empirical risk R^{emp} measured over the given sample S, as follows:

$$h_\ell = \arg\min_{H(H^p, \Theta)} R^{emp}(S, h) = \arg\min_{H(H^p, \Theta)} \frac{1}{\ell} \sum_{i=1}^{\ell} L_3(x_i, y_i, h) \tag{5}$$

Two of the key questions regarding the applicability of the above inductive principle are examined below:

Consistency. As the number of examples increases to infinity, does the empirical risk of the optimal hypothesis chosen by the above principle should converge to the minimum possible value of risk for the hypothesis class. A key theorem by Vapnik [6] states that, for bounded risk functionals, the necessary and sufficient condition for this happening is the uniform one-sided convergence of the empirical risk to the actual risk.

Bounds on the actual risk of h_ℓ. We wish to provide a non-asymptotic upper bound for the risk of the hypothesis chosen by the ERM principle. Also, since the underlying distribution of the examples is unknown, the bounds should be distribution-free. In order to arrive at this bound, we shall extend a key result due to Vapnik [6]:

Let $R(\alpha)$ be the actual risk of a hypothesis $\alpha \in \Lambda$ (without a reject option), defined on the set of real-valued bounded loss functions $0 \le L(x, y, \alpha) \le B$ with VC dimension d. Let $R^{emp}(\alpha)$ be the empirical risk. Then, with confidence $1 - \eta$, the inequality

$$R(\alpha) \le R^{emp}(\alpha) + \frac{B\varepsilon(\ell)}{2}\left(1 + \sqrt{1 + \frac{4R^{emp}(\alpha)}{B\varepsilon(\ell)}}\right) \tag{6}$$

holds true, where

$$\varepsilon(\ell) \le 4\frac{G^\Lambda(2\ell) - ln\frac{\eta}{4}}{\ell} \le 4\frac{d(ln\frac{2\ell}{d} + 1) - ln\frac{\eta}{4}}{\ell} \tag{7}$$

where G^Λ is the growth function of the set of loss functions L (parametrized by α), and d is the corresponding VC dimension.

To bound the risk functional R (in (4)), we require a bound on the growth of the loss function L_3. Through an application of Sauer's lemma, we can show that the growth function $G^H(\ell)$ for L_3 is bounded by:

$$G^H(\ell) \leq \ln\left(3\left(\frac{e\ell}{d_r}\right)^{d_r}\left(\frac{e\ell}{d_p}\right)^{d_p}\right) \tag{8}$$

where d_r and d_p are the VC dimensions of the rejection hypothesis class Θ, and the loss function L_2 (based on the prediction hypothesis class H^p) respectively. The growth function bound here is computed in a manner analogous to the one used for computing growth function bounds for neural networks [7], wherein the growth function of the network is bounded by the product of the growth function of its components. Using the above result, we can substitute the quantity $\varepsilon(\ell)$ by the quantity

$$\xi(\ell) = \varepsilon_r(\ell) + \varepsilon_p(\ell) + \frac{4}{\ell}\ln\left(3\eta/4\right)$$

where the bound on $\varepsilon_.(\ell)$ is defined as in equation (7) using the corresponding VC dimension. The relevant bound on the risk, with probability $1 - \eta$, is therefore given by:

$$R(h_\ell) \leq R^{emp}(S, h_\ell) + \frac{\xi(\ell)}{2}\left(1 + \sqrt{1 + \frac{4R^{emp}(S, h_\ell)}{\xi(\ell)}}\right) \tag{9}$$

We shall now bound the difference between the actual risk of the hypothesis h_ℓ and the best possible hypothesis h_{opt}. From Hoeffding's bounds [8], we know that, with confidence $1 - \eta$, the inequality

$$R(h_{opt}) > R^{emp}(S, h_{opt}) - \sqrt{\frac{-ln\,\eta}{2\ell}} \tag{10}$$

holds true. Since $R^{emp}(S, h_\ell) \leq R^{emp}(S, h_{opt})$, from equations (9) and (10), we see that with confidence $1 - 2\eta$, the bound is given by:

$$R(h_\ell) - R(h_{opt}) \leq \left(\frac{\xi(\ell)}{2}\left(1 + \sqrt{1 + \frac{4R^{emp}(S, h_\ell)}{\xi(\ell)}}\right) + \sqrt{\frac{-ln\,\eta}{2\ell}}\right) \tag{11}$$

3.1 Example

We present here, an example of applying the risk bounds derived above, on the results of an algorithm for perceptron learning with an embedded reject option. The hypothesis learnt here is a hyperplane with asymmetric bandwidths for rejection. The learning algorithm arrives at the hypothesis by gradient descent on a criterion function based on the distance of an example from both bandwidths, weighted by the differential cost applicable therein. For details of the algorithm, see [4].

To arrive at these risk bounds, we need to find d_p and d_r for this compound hypothesis. We know that the VC dimension of a perceptron is equal to $n + 1$, where n is the dimensionality of X; it is easy to see that the VC dimension of a system of asymmetric bandwidths around a hyperplane is equal to 2. Using these values, the risk bound can be computed as described in Section 3.

The algorithm was run on the Pima Indians diabetes benchmark dataset taken from the UC Irvine machine learning data repository. The dataset contains information about 768 patients (in the form of 8 real-valued attributes), and the output is one of 2 classes. 568 data points were used for training, and 200 for testing. The attained risk on the training sample, and the corresponding risk bounds, are shown in Figure 1 below, for varying values of the rejection cost γ. The algorithm has been found to produce an acceptable solution with non-zero bandwidth only for $\gamma \leq 0.5$; hence, the results have been shown only for those values. We can see here that these risk bounds are fairly loose as a result of the number of examples being small compared to the complexity of the class. When the number of examples increases, this bound becomes much tighter.

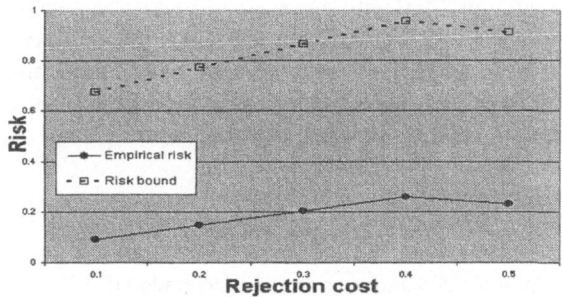

Fig. 1. Risk bounds - example (Pima Indians diabetes dataset)

4   Minimizing Structural Risk

Here we briefly discuss the concept of capacity control for our learning problem. It is clear from equation (9) that the tightness of the bound on the actual risk of the hypothesis h_ℓ depends on two factors: the empirical risk, and the complexity of the hypothesis classes. To optimize the bound in (9) with respect to both the empirical risk and the complexity of the compound hypothesis class H (parametrized by H^p and Θ), we look at a nested series of hypothesis classes H_i wherein $G^{H_{i-1}}(\ell) \leq G^{H_i}(\ell) \leq G^{H_{i+1}}(\ell)$ for a given sample size ℓ. The optimal hypothesis $h_{opt(i)} \in H_i$ is therefore the one which achieves the tightest bound on the risk, both in terms of the empirical risk and the complexity term. In the context of the problem of learning with a reject option, this implies that one could improve this trade-off both by optimizing the complexity of the prediction hypothesis h^p and the rejection hypothesis θ. Also, it is possible to perform a comparative analysis of the effect of a complex prediction hypothesis *vis-a-vis* a complex rejection scheme.

5   Scope for Further Work

In this paper, we have approached the problem of learning with an embedded reject option from the point of view of statistical learning theory. To this end, we have presented a new formulation of the learning problem, and derived the bounds on the risk of the solution obtained through ERM on the given sample. Our formulation depends on the representation of the compound hypothesis h in terms of h^p and θ; however, there are algorithms such as grid-search methods (with a reject option applied on empty grid cells) that do not necessarily have such a hierarchical structure. In such cases, one can also attempt to directly estimate the VC dimension of L_1 and obtain the bounds thereof, or apply risk bounds derived using other notions of dimension for multi-valued functions, such as the Natarajan dimension [9]. However, it must be noted that, in cases where the hypothesis can be viewed in terms of h^p and θ, the method provided in this paper gives an easier way of arriving at the bounds.

In this paper, we have looked at only one way of formulating the problem of arriving at an optimal cost solution. Typically, in many real situations wherein a reject option is required, the learning problem is expressed in a constrained sense: for instance, one may wish to maximize the accuracy of a learning algorithm while allowing for a certain percentage of rejections. The appropriate bounds for such formulations may also be derived using methods similar to the ones discussed in this paper.

References

1. Chow, C.K.: On optimum recognition error and reject trade-off. IEEE Transactions on Information Theory **16** (1970) 41–46
2. Le Cun, Y.e.a.: Handwritten digit recognition with a backpropagation network. In: Advances in Neural Information Processing Systems. Volume 2., Morgan Kaufmann (1990) 396–404
3. Fumera, G., Roli, F.: Multiple reject thresholds for improving classification reliability. Technical report, Univ. of Calgary (1999)
4. Sundararajan, R., Pal, A.K.: A conservative approach to perceptron learning. Accepted at 5th WSEAS International Conference on Neural Networks & Applications (NNA'04) (2004)
5. Fumera, G., Roli, F.: Support vector machines with embedded reject option. In Lee, S.W., Verri, A., eds.: Pattern Recognition with Support Vector Machines - First International Workshop, Proceedings, Springer (2002)
6. Vapnik, V.N.: Statistical Learning Theory. John Wiley & Sons (1998)
7. Sontag, E.: Vapnik-chervonenkis dimension of neural networks. In Bishop, C., ed.: Neural Networks and Machine Learning. Springer (1998)
8. Hoeffding, W.: Probability inequalities for sums of bounded random variables. Journal of the American Statistical Association **58** (1963) 13–30
9. Natarajan, B.K.: On learning sets and functions. Machine Learning **4** (1989) 67–97

Impulsive Noise Suppression from Highly Corrupted Images by Using Resilient Neural Networks

Erkan Beşdok[1], Pınar Çivicioğlu[2], and Mustafa Alçı[3]

[1] Erciyes University, Institute of Science, Computer Engineering Dept., Kayseri,
Turkey, ebesdok@erciyes.edu.tr
[2] Erciyes University, Civil Aviation School, Avionics Dept.,Kayseri, Turkey,
civici@erciyes.edu.tr
[3] Erciyes University, Engineering Faculty, Electronic Eng. Dept., Kayseri, Turkey,
malci@erciyes.edu.tr

Abstract. A new impulsive noise elimination filter, entitled Resilient Neural Network based impulsive noise removing filter (RF), which shows a high performance at the restoration of images corrupted by impulsive noise, is proposed in this paper. The RF uses Chi-square goodness-of-fit test in order to find corrupted pixels more accurately. The corrupted pixels are replaced by new values which were estimated by using the proposed RF. Extensive simulation results show that the proposed filter achieves a superior performance to the other filters mentioned in this paper in the cases of being effective in noise suppression and detail preservation, especially when the noise density is very high.

1   Introduction

Noise is one of the undesired factors causing the corruption of images and therefore recovery of an image from noisy data is a fundamental step in every image analyzing process. Degradation of images by impulsive noise is usually caused by the errors originating from noisy sensors or communication channels.

Order statistics based nonlinear filters have demonstrated excellent robustness properties at the suppression of impulsive noise and they are conceptually simple and easy to implement. The first and the well-known member of the order statistics based filters is the standard median filter (SMF) [1], which has been proved to be a powerful method in removing impulsive noise. SMF uses the rank-order information of the input data to remove impulsive noise by changing the considered pixel with the middle-position element of the reordered input data. The problem with the SMF is that it tends to alter pixels undisturbed by impulsive noise and remove fine details in the image, such as corners and thin lines, especially when the noise ratio is high. Recently, different modifications of the median filter [2, 3, 4, 5, 6] have been developed in order to overcome this drawback. Furthermore, detection-based median filters with thresholding operations have been proposed and the switching scheme is introduced by some

L. Rutkowski et al. (Eds.): ICAISC 2004, LNAI 3070, pp. 670–675, 2004.
© Springer-Verlag Berlin Heidelberg 2004

of the recently published papers where the algorithms of impulse detection are employed before filtering and the detection results are used to control whether a pixel should be modified or not [2]. The method proposed in this paper, RF, differs from the other impulsive noise removal filters by performing the restoration of degraded images with no blurring even when the images are highly corrupted by impulsive noise.

In this paper, the proposed filter is compared with SMF [1], and the recently introduced complex structured impulsive noise removal filters: Iterative Median Filter (IMF) [2], Progressive Switching Median Filter (PSM) [2], Signal Dependent Rank Order Mean Filter (SDROM) [3], Two-state Recursive Signal Dependent Rank Order Mean Filter (SDROMR) [3], Impulse Rejecting Filter (IRF) [4], Non-Recursive Adaptive-Center Weighted Median Filter (ACWM) [5], Recursive Adaptive-Center Weighted Median Filter (ACWMR) [5], and the Center Weighted Median Filter (CWM) [6].

The rest of the paper is organized as follows: The detail of the *Artificial Neural Networks and Surface Fitting* is given in Section 2. The *Proposed Filter* is defined in Section 3 and finally, *Experiments* and *Conclusions* are presented in Sections 4 and 5, respectively.

2 Artificial Neural Networks and Surface Fitting

2.1 Artificial Neural Networks (ANNs)

An ANN is a nonlinear information processing tool that is inspired by the way of biological nervous systems [7, 8, 9, 10, 11]. ANNs have seen an explosion of interest over the last few years, and are being successfully applied across an extraordinary range of problem domains, in areas as diverse as finance, medicine, engineering, geology, image processing, pattern recognition and optics. There are various types of neural network applications available in the literature for image restoration [7, 8, 9, 10, 11].

Resilient Neural Networks (RPROP) were developed by Riedmiller and Braun [8, 9]. In contrast to other gradient algorithms, this algorithm does not use the magnitude of the gradient. It is a direct adaptation of the weight step based on local gradient sign. The RPROP algorithm generally provides faster convergence than most other algorithms [7, 8, 9]. More details about the RPROP algorithm can be found in [8, 9].

2.2 Surface Fitting

Surface fitting is a useful tool to preserve huge amount of information in the spatial data [12]. An image surface is a representation of the pixel values that are continuous over image space and surfaces can be created to represent any kind of measure of thematic information such as intensity of electromagnetic field, elevation, temperature, and pixel data of an image. ANNs have been used in a number of applications for surface fitting [12] and impulsive noise suppression [13].

Descriptive Surface Fitting (DSF) methods are the most commonly used methods for surface fitting. The DSF methods do not use statistical models and do not explicitly recognize spatial dependence [14]. Furthermore, error estimates cannot be achieved in DSF methods and also predictions for corrupted pixel values with the lowest error cannot be produced [7, 12, 14]. Therefore, the DSF methods for image surfaces are really exploratory methods, not formal predictors. In real-time applications, the DSF methods are often used for prediction of surfaces, due to their ease of use and simplicity in computational requirements. There are many techniques introduced to create DSF surfaces [7, 12, 14].

3   Proposed Filter

Image pixels do not scatter randomly in real images. Therefore the gray value of a pixel is more related with the neighbor pixels than distant ones. *Creation of image surface from the data of uncorrupted pixels is based on this observation, which is a reflection of the spatial dependence of the uncorrupted pixels in real images.* The proposed filter, RF, is a finite-element-based filter [7, 11, 12] and it uses the Delaunay triangles [7, 12], as finite elements. The RF involves four main steps: image padding, delaunay triangulation, interpolation and image reconstruction. For the implementation of RF, the image was padded with 5 pixels reflected copy of itself on the sides in order to cover the whole image with Delaunay network. Then the triangulation phase was achieved by using the spatial positions of the non-uniformly scattering pixels. The convex-hull and Delaunay triangles were both obtained over the image after the Delaunay triangulation phase as expressed in [7]. Then RPROP was used as an interpolant for each Delaunay triangle to get the estimated gray values of uniformly scattering pixels. The spatial positions of the non-uniformly scattering pixels, which are at the corners of the Delaunay triangles, have been used as the inputs of the RPROP and the corresponding gray values have been used as the output. Undesired factors affect the image acquisition sensor systems uniformly and impulsive noise has a uniform characteristic aspect of its position over the image. Therefore estimations of gray values were made for only uniformly scattering pixels. The original gray values of the non-uniformly scattering pixels and the estimated gray values of the corrupted pixels were reorganized in order to obtain the restored image. The well-known *Chi-square goodness-of-fit* test has been used in order to find out the uniformly scattering gray levels within corrupted image.

The corrupted image surface was divided into [*32x32*] pixels sized unoverlapping blocks and the total amount of each gray level within these blocks were counted. Then, for each gray level the significance probability of *Chi-square goodness-of-fit* test was computed by using the total amount of gray levels for each block. Extensive simulations, which were conducted on more than 100 *real images* all of which are 256x256 pixels sized and 8 bpp (bits/pixel) images, with different noise densities, exposed that the significance probability of *Chi-square goodness-of-fit* test [15] values greater than *0.001±0.0005* correspond to uniformly scattering gray values and are suspected to be corrupted pixels.

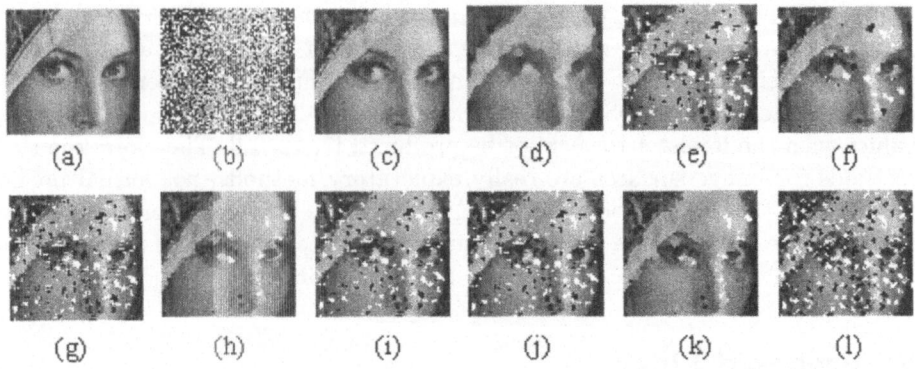

Fig. 1. The restored images of the Noisy Lena for noise density=50%: (a) The noise-free Lena, (b) Noisy Lena for noise density=50%, (c) **RF (Proposed)**, (d) IMF, (e) SMF, (f) PSM, (g) SDROM, (h) SDROMR, (i) IRF, (j) ACWM, (k) ACWMR, (l) CWM.

Table 1. Restoration results in MSE for The Lena Image.

Method	Noise Density					
	10%	20%	30%	40%	50%	60%
Noisy Image	1852.70	3767.60	5563.60	7451.50	9268.40	11152.00
RF (Proposed)	**12.00**	**22.56**	**40.42**	**57.17**	**83.60**	**109.84**
IMF	124.05	140.06	158.84	203.36	261.87	491.57
SMF	87.09	148.82	353.46	958.83	2046.10	3856.60
PSM	54.92	85.76	132.48	272.63	647.30	1938.30
SDROM	60.52	136.35	408.80	1105.70	2339.10	4322.30
SDROMR	56.79	91.21	171.88	287.33	553.76	1071.80
IRF	61.15	127.84	366.24	981.06	2098.80	3918.50
ACWM	51.97	121.51	367.27	993.73	2119.40	3951.00
ACWMR	46.95	85.67	170.71	299.57	536.23	1007.80
CWM	76.27	259.94	727.17	1729.30	3273.40	5431.60

Table 2. Restoration results in MSE for The Peppers Image.

Method	Noise Density					
	10%	20%	30%	40%	50%	60%
Noisy Image	1940.10	3988.80	5897.70	7914.50	9960.80	11929.00
RF (Proposed)	**11.96**	**25.92**	**43.58**	**65.84**	**89.95**	**117.43**
IMF	123.82	149.80	190.54	249.05	335.41	667.77
SMF	77.69	160.17	389.36	1021.90	2161.00	4151.50
PSM	55.24	94.58	159.79	301.41	714.25	1952.20
SDROM	63.70	195.43	482.43	1240.30	2528.90	4674.00
SDROMR	61.34	149.97	268.08	474.06	750.02	1568.00
IRF	60.14	182.08	437.96	1126.40	2299.90	4309.50
ACWM	55.70	181.99	442.58	1139.30	2317.90	4333.40
ACWMR	54.51	142.14	259.92	463.44	727.67	1395.30
CWM	84.55	303.75	818.32	1860.70	3557.80	5858.40

4   Experiments

A number of experiments were realized in order to evaluate the performance of the proposed RF in comparison with the recently introduced and highly approved filters for impulsive noise suppression. The experiments were carried out on more than 100 *real images* which also include the well-known test images; *The Lena* and *The Peppers* images, which are [*256x256*] pixels sized and 8 bpp images. The Test Images were corrupted by impulsive noise at various noise densities ranging from 10% to 60%. The *Noise Density* term denotes the proportion of corruption of image pixels. If the noise density is equal to 10%, then it means that 10% of the image pixels were corrupted. The restoration results for the noise density of 50% are illustrated in Fig. 1. It is easily seen from Fig. 1 that, noise suppression and detail preservation are satisfactorily compromised by using the proposed RF even if the noise density is high. The restoration performance is quantitatively measured by the Mean-Squared-Error (MSE) [11]. The SMF, IMF, PSM, SDROM, SDROMR, IRF, ACWM, ACWMR and CWM have been simulated as well for performance comparison. The major improvement achieved by the proposed filter has been demonstrated with the extensive simulations of the mentioned test images corrupted at different noise densities. It is seen from Tables 1-2 that the RF provides a substantial improvement compared with the simulated filters, especially at the high noise density values. Impulsive noise removal and detail preservation are best compromised by the RF. Robustness is one of the most important requirements of modern image enhancement filters and the Tables 1-2 indicate that RF provides robustness substantially across a wide variation of noise densities.

5   Conclusions

It is seen from the Tables 1-2 that the proposed RF, gives absolutely better restoration results and a higher resolution in the restored images than the restoration results of the comparison methods, mentioned in this paper. The proposed RF yields satisfactory results in suppressing impulsive noise with no blurring while requiring a simple computational structure.

The effectiveness of the proposed filter in processing different images can easily be evaluated by appreciating the Tables 1-2 which are given to present the restoration results of RF and the comparison filters for images degraded by impulsive noise, where noise density ranges from 10% to 60%. As can be seen clearly from the Tables 1-2 that the MSE values of the proposed RF is far more smaller than the MSE values of comparison filters for all of the test images. In addition, the proposed RF supplies more pleasing restoration results aspect of visual perception and also provides the best trade-off between noise suppression and image enhancement for detail preservation as seen in Fig.1.

References

[1] J.W. Tukey, Nonlinear (nonsuperposable) methods for smoothing data, in Cong. Rec. EASCON'74, (1974), 673.

[2] Z. Wang, D. Zhang, Progressive switching median filter for the removal of impulse noise from highly corrupted images, IEEE Trans. on Circuits and Systems-II: Analog and Digital Signal Processing, **46** (1), (1999), 78-80.

[3] E. Abreu, M. Lightstone, S. K. Mitra, K. Arakawa, A new efficient approach for the removal of impulse noise from highly corrupted images, IEEE Trans. on Image Processing, **5** (6), (1996), 1012-1025.

[4] T. Chen, H.R. Wu, A new class of median based impulse rejecting filters, IEEE Int. Conf. on Image Processing, **1**, (2000), 916-919.

[5] T. Chen, H. R. Wu, Adaptive impulse detection using center weighted median filters, IEEE Signal Processing Letters, **8** (1), (2001), 1-3.

[6] S.J. Ko, Y. H. Lee, Center weighted median filters and their applications to image enhancement, IEEE Trans. on Circuits and Systems II, **43** (3), (1996), 157-192.

[7] MathWorks, MATLAB the language of technical computing, MATLAB Function Reference. New York: The MathWorks, Inc., (2002).

[8] M. Riedmiller, H. Braun, A direct adaptive method for fester backpropogation learning: The Rprop algorithm. Proceedings of the IEEE Int. Conf. on Neural Networks, San Francisco, CA, (1993), 586-591.

[9] M. Riedmiller, Rprop- Description and implementation details:Technical Report, University of Karlsruhe, Germany, (1994).

[10] S. Haykin, Neural networks, A comprehensive foundation, NY, Macmillan College Publishing Company, (1994).

[11] G.K. Knopf, J. Kofman, Adaptive reconstruction of free-form surfaces using bernstein basis function networks, Engineering Application of Artificial Intelligence, **14**, (2001), 557-588.

[12] D.F. Watson, Contouring: A guide to the analysis and display of spacial data, Pergamon, New York, (1994), 101-161.

[13] L. Guan, Image restoration by a neural network with hierarchical cluster architecture, Journal of Electronic Imaging, **3** (2), (1994), 154-163.

[14] S. Price, Surface interpolation of apartment rental data: Can surfaces replace neighborhood mapping, The Appraisal Journal, **70** (3), (2002), 260-273.

[15] G.W. Snedecor, W.G. Cochran, Statistical Methods, Eighth Edition, Iowa State University Press, (1989).

A New Methodology for Synthetic Aperture Radar (SAR) Raw Data Compression Based on Wavelet Transform and Neural Networks

Giacomo Capizzi[1], Salvatore Coco[1], Antonio Laudani[1], and
Giuseppe Pappalardo[2]

[1] Università di Catania, Dipartimento Elettrico Elettronico e Sistemistico,
Viale Andrea Doria 6, I-95125 Catania, Italy
{gcapizzi,coco}@diees.unict.it
[2] Università di Catania, Dipartimento di Matematica e Informatica,
Viale Andrea Doria 6, I-95125 Catania, Italy

Abstract. Synthetic Aperture Radar (SAR) raw data are characterized
by a high entropy content. As a result, conventional SAR compression
techniques (such as block adaptive quantization and its variants) do not
provide fully satisfactory performances. In this paper, a novel methodology for SAR raw data compression is presented, based on discrete wavelet transform (DWT). The correlation between the DWT coefficients
of a SAR image at different resolutions is exploited to predict each coefficient in a subband mainly from the (spatially) corresponding ones
in the immediately lower resolution subbands. Prediction is carried out
by classical multi-layer perceptron (MLP) neural networks, all of which
share the same, quite simple topology. Experiments carried out show
that the proposed approach provides noticeably better results than most
state-of-the-art SAR compression techniques.

1 Introduction

Synthetic aperture radar (SAR) is a very efficient instrument for obtaining a
better understanding of the environment [1]. Due to the high entropy of SAR raw
data, conventional compression techniques (see [2] for an overview) fail to ensure
acceptable performances, in that lossless ones do not in fact succeed to compress,
while general purpose lossy ones (e.g. JPEG) provide some compression degree
only at the price of unacceptable image quality degradation. In any case, in SAR
data compression, a tolerable degree of image deterioration is unavoidable, and
a fundamental issue in the compression system design is therefore the trade-
off between the complexity of the algorithms employed and the image quality
requirements, which will of course be typically application-dependent. Memory
and time computational requirements are particularly critical in on board space
applications. State-of-the-art SAR data compression (lossy) techniques, based
on block adaptive quantization (BAQ) and its variants [3], are rather simple to
implement but do not provide fully satisfactory compression performances.

L. Rutkowski et al. (Eds.): ICAISC 2004, LNAI 3070, pp. 676–681, 2004.
© Springer-Verlag Berlin Heidelberg 2004

In this paper, a novel methodology for SAR raw data lossy compression is presented, based on discrete wavelet transform (DWT) [4]. Specifically, we exploit the correlation exhibited by the DWT coefficients of a SAR image at different resolutions [5]. This allows the coefficients for each of the LH, HL and HH subbands at a given resolution to be predicted based mainly on the (spatially) homologue ones in the same subband at the immediately inferior resolution. Prediction is carried out by classical multi-layer perceptron (MLP) neural networks, all of which share the same, quite simple topology (6 neurons with 21 connections, over two layers), but may have different weights. This approach will be shown to afford noticeably better results than conventional SAR compression techniques.

2 Methodology

2.1 SAR Compression

The input SAR image is partitioned into 512×512 blocks (smaller blocks can be employed to trade time for memory). The generic block is decomposed by DWT at three increasingly lower resolutions, as shown in Figure 1. As noted, each subband LLIJ (for $IJ =$ LH, HL, HH) can be obtained, by a suitable MLP$_{LLIJ}$, from the three lower resolution subbands LLLLLH, LLLLHL, LLLLHH; subsequently, each subband IJ (again for $IJ =$ LH, HL, HH) can be predicted from LLLH, LLHL, LLHH by a suitable MLP$_{IJ}$.

As a result, the information associated with the input block can be compressed by storing the weights characterizing the six MLPs employed and the DWT coefficients in the lowest resolution LLLLLL, LLLLLH, LLLLHL, LLLLHH subbands. The latter four 64×64 DWT coefficient sets, as well as the 21×6 MLP weights, are scalarly quantized, and the data thus obtained represent the compressed image. Compression essentially results from the use of prediction to reconstruct the original 512×512 DWT coefficients at the original resolution, from solely 4·(64×64)=128×128 DWT coefficients and just 21x6 weights at a resolution that is twice as lower.

2.2 Prediction and Reconstruction

Our prediction methodology is mainly based on employing each DWT coefficient in a subband, to predict the four spatially corresponding coefficients to which it expands in the corresponding subband, at the immediately superior resolution. As an example, we illustrate how DWT coefficient LLLH$[x, y]$ for row x and column y in subband LLLH allows prediction of coefficients LH$[2x, 2y]$, LH$[2x + 1, 2y]$, LH$[2x, 2y+1]$, LH$[2x+1, 2y+1]$. More specifically, the predicting MLP$_{LH}$ is fed the inputs specified below.

- To predict LH$[2x, 2y]$, we use LLLH$[x, y]$ and its homologues in the other subbands LLHL and LLHH, i.e. LLHL$[x, y]$ and LLHH$[x, y]$;

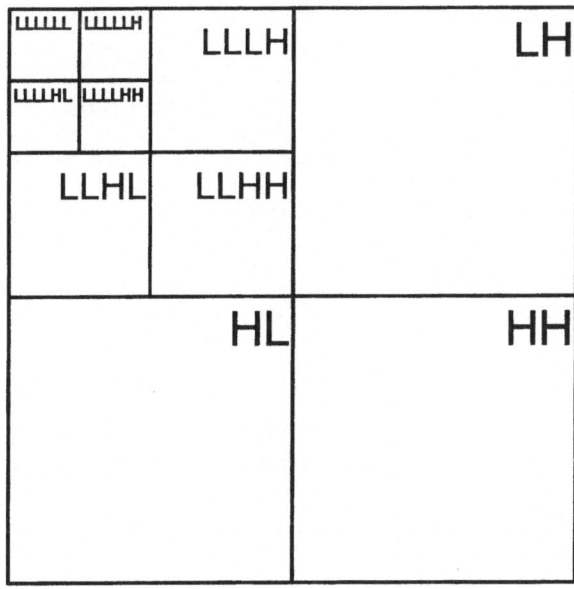

Fig. 1. DWT decomposition iterated three times

- to predict LH[$2x + 1, 2y$], we use LLLH[x, y] and its "horizontal" neighborhood LLLH[$x - 1, y$] and LLLH[$x + 1, y$];
- to predict LH[$2x, 2y + 1$], we use LLLH[x, y] and its "vertical" neighborhood LLLH[$x, y - 1$] and LLLH[$x, y + 1$];
- to predict LH[$2x + 1, 2y + 1$], we use LLLH[x, y] and its "diagonal" neighborhood LLLH[$x - 1, y - 1$] and LLLH[$x + 1, y + 1$];

As noted above, a classical multi-layer perceptron (MLP) is employed for prediction. All the six perceptrons MLP$_{LLIJ}$, MLP$_{IJ}$ (IJ = LH, HL, HH) share the same topology, which consists in:

- 3 inputs (the DWT lower resolution subband coefficients);
- 2 hidden layers with 3 neurons each;
- 1 output layer containing 1 neuron with linear activation function (its output is the predicted DWT cowfficient in the higher resolution subband).

3   Experimental Results

The SAR raw data employed to test the proposed compression system originated from four different X-SAR acquisition sessions performed in April 1994. Data were later stored in accordance with the format defined by CEOS, the Committee on Earth Observation Satellites of the German Processing and Archiving Facility (D-PAF/DLR). Typical features for some of these data are reported in Table 1.

Table 1. Typical SAR raw data features

Location	Jesolo (Italy)
Data Take ID	018.21
Quantization I/Q (bit)	6
Number of lines (azimuth)	22320
Pixels per line(I/Q)	2496
Archive ID	44624
D-PAF Job Number	Order 510107

SAR signal appears to be very random-like (cf. Figure 2) and exhibits a low correlation between magnitude and phase. Its entropies of various orders, measured as described in [6], approach the number of quantization bits used for the raw signal. This indicates that such data are prone to be hardly compressible with lossless schemes.

Given the high number of lines and pixels per line, it is clear that an acquisition, although typically lasting few seconds, involves a large amount of data (in the order of hundreds of megabytes) This explains why the image is better processed in data blocks of a manageable size, which we have set to 512×512. This applies especially in view of deploying our compression system on board a where computing and storage resources are critical.

Experiments have been conducted on image portions exhibiting significant statistical features, discarding instead regions that might make the compressor to perform too favourably. Input SAR data are processed in their polar representation, as magnitude-phase pairs. Typical compression ratios obtained are

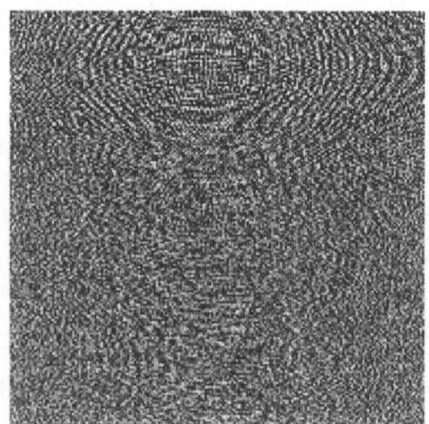

Fig. 2. Magnitude (right) and phases (left) of a typical raw SAR image block

47 with a PSNR of 36dB for the phase and 1.5 with a PSNR of 19 dB for the magnitude. The worse performance obtained on magnitude data is due to the fact that, since neural prediction does not perform well in the reconstruction of the LLHH and HH subbands, these are better stored directly, without any processing.

Table 2. Phase results

Block	Compression ratio	PSNR	MSE
128×128	45.2	37.20dB	0.78
256×256	46.5	35.79dB	1.08
512×512	47.0	37.55dB	0.72

Table 3. Magnitude results

Block	Compression ratio	PSNR	MSE
128×128	1.38	19.32dB	47.87
256×256	1.47	19.08dB	50.62
512×512	1.51	19.20dB	49.19

4   Conclusions

Performance of the proposed compression system are significantly higher than those ensured by state-of-the-art SAR compression techniques. E.g., on the same dataset employed for our experiments, FBAQ algorithms typically yield a PSNR of about 9 dB for a compression rate 3, or a PSNR of about 13 dB for a compression rate 2. Other methods recently proposed in the literature [7,8,9] do not substantially improve on these results. In contrast, our technique typically attains a compression ratio of about 3, combining the phase ratio (typically very high) and the (lower) magnitude ratio (cf. Tables 2 and 3), with PSNRs that never drop below 20 dB. A compression ratio of about 2 and a PSNR better than 50dB (cf. again the tables) can be achieved applying our technique to the phase alone, and leaving the magnitude uncompressed. This would also halve the computational effort required for compression.

Finally, it is worth noting that a potential advantage of the neural predictor employed is that it easily lends itself to a hardware or a DSP parallel implementation.

References

1. Curlander, J., McDonough, R.: Synthetic Aperture Radar. Wiley, New York (1991)
2. Sayood, K.: Introduction to Data Compression, 2nd edition. Morgan Kaufmann, San Francisco, California (2000)
3. Benz, U., Strodl, K., Moreira, A.: A comparison of several algorithms for SAR raw data compression. IEEE Trans. On Geoscience and Remote Sensing **33** (1995) 1266–1276
4. Mallat, S.: A Wavelet Tour of Signal Processing. Academic Press, New York (1999)
5. Shapiro, J.: Embedded image-coding using zerotrees of wavelet coefficients. IEEE Transactions on Signal Processing **41** (1993) 3445–3462
6. Capizzi, G., Coco, S., Lanza, P., Mottese, S.: Nth order entropy computation algorithms for lossless data compression. In: Proceedings of the DSP98 Conference, Noordwijk, The Netherlands (1998)
7. El Boustani, A., Branham, K., Kinsner, W.: An optimal wavelet for raw SAR data compression. In: Proceedings of IEEE CCECE 2003. Volume 3. (2003) 2071–2074
8. Fischer, J., Benz, U., Moreira, A.: Efficient SAR raw data compression in frequency domain. In: Proceedings of IGARSS '99. Volume 4. (1999) 2261–2263
9. Pascazio, V., Schirinzi, G.: SAR raw data compression by subband coding. IEEE Transactions on Geoscience and Remote Sensing **41** (2003) 964–976

Fuzzy Processing Technique for Content-Based Image Retrieval

Ryszard S. Choraś

Faculty of Telecommunications & Electrical Engineering
University of Technology & Agriculture
S. Kaliskiego 7, 85-791 Bydgoszcz
choras@mail.atr.bydgoszcz.pl

Abstract. Current technology allows the acquisition, transmission, storing, and manipulation of large collections of images. Images are retrieved basing on similarity of features where features of the query specification are compared with features from the image database to determine which images match similarly with given features. Feature extraction is a crucial part for any of such retrieval systems.
In this paper we propose effective method for image representation which utilizes fuzzy features such as color and fuzzy radial moments.

1 Introduction

Research has been focused on the automatic extraction of the visual content of image to enable retrieval (CBIR - content-based image retrieval). Efficient retrieval is based on automatically derived features. These features are typically extracted from color, texture and shape properties of query image and images in the database. In the retrieval process, these features of the query specification are compared with features of the image database to determine which images match similarly (correctly) with the given features (Fig. 1). There are several similarity measures but measures based on fuzzy logic would appear to be naturally better suited. Efficient retrieval is based on automatically derived features. Images are retrieved basing on similarity of features.

Let $\{\mathbf{F}(x,y); x,y = 1, 2, \ldots . N\}$ be a two-dimensional image pixel array. For color images $F(x,y)$ denotes the color value at pixel (x,y) i.e.,

$\mathbf{F}(x,y) = \{F_R(x,y), F_G(x,y), F_B(x,y)\}$. For black and white images, $\mathbf{F}(x,y)$ denotes the gray scale intensity value of pixel (x,y).
Let f represent a mapping function from the image space to n-dimensional feature space $\mathbf{x} = \{x_1, x_2, \ldots, x_n\}$

$$f : \mathbf{F} \to \mathbf{x} \tag{1}$$

where n is the number of features used to represent the image.
The problem of retrieval is as follows:
for a query image Q, we find image S from the image database such that distance between corresponding feature vectors is less than specified threshold, i.e.,

$$D(f(Q), F(S)) \leq t \tag{2}$$

L. Rutkowski et al. (Eds.): ICAISC 2004, LNAI 3070, pp. 682–687, 2004.
© Springer-Verlag Berlin Heidelberg 2004

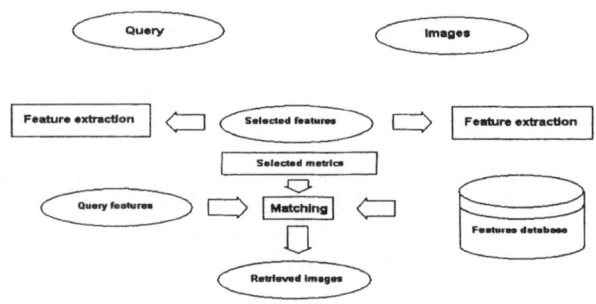

Fig. 1. Schematic diagram of the image retrieval process.

Humans use color shape to understand and recollect the contents of an image. Therefore it is natural to use features based on these attributes for image retrieval. This paper demonstrates the effectiveness of using simple color and shape features for image retrieval.

In this paper we propose fuzzy processing technique to the content description and effective method for image representation which utilizes fuzzy radial moments as shape features.

This paper has been organised as follows. The next section presents fuzzy image segmentation and fuzzy edge detection which generalizes region-growing segmentation and edge detection. Next, we describe fuzzy radial moments. Finally, query processing is described and conclusion is given.

2   Fuzzy Image Segmentation

Color is one of the most widely used features for image similarity retrieval. This is not surprising given the fact that color is an easily recognizable element of an image and the human visual system is capable of differentiating between infinitely large numbers of colors.

A region-based retrieval system segments images into regions and retrieves images based on the similarity between regions. Applying fuzzy processing techniques to CBIR, we represent each region as a multidimensional fuzzy set - fuzzy feature in the feature space of color, texture and shape. Each image is characterized by a class of fuzzy features. Each fuzzy feature of the database image is matched with all fuzzy features of the query image.

The query image and all images in the database are first segmented into regions. Regions are then represented by multidimensional fuzzy sets in the feature space. Clustering techniques identify homogeneous clusters of points in the feature space e.g color space and then label each cluster as a different region. The homogeneity criterion is usually that distance from one cluster to another cluster in the color feature space should be smaller than a threshold.

Firstly, we initialize the membership levels of each pixel $F(x, y)$ as

$$\mu_{xy} = \frac{F(x, y)}{maxF(x, y)} \tag{3}$$

Image segmentation partitions an image into a set of homogeneous regions. It outlines objects in an image. Fuzzy rules are presented below:

1 IF the color difference σ between pixel and the neighboring pixels is SMALL AND the pixel has LOW discontinuity D, THEN merge the pixel into the region,

2 IF a segmented region is SMALL, THEN merge the region into the neighboring region.

We can write
R_i - homogeneous region in image **F**

$$\mathbf{F} = \bigcup_{i=1}^{m} R_i; \qquad R_i \cap R_j = 0 \qquad for \quad i \neq j \tag{4}$$

$\overline{F}_{R_i}$ - average intensity level of the region R_i,
$n(R_i)$ - number of pixels in R_i,
$N(R_i)$ - neighborhood of R_i.

We have

1. $\overline{F}_{R_1} = F(0, 0), \quad n(R_1) = 1$
2. If $F(x, y) \in N(R_i)$ and $F(x, y)$ satisfies homogeneity criterion H on R_i, then merge $F(x, y)$ into R_i

$$\overline{F}(R_i) = \frac{\overline{F}(R_i) \cdot n(R_i) + F(x, y)}{n(R_i) + 1}, \qquad n(R_i) = n(R_i) + 1 \tag{5}$$

Update $N(R_i)$ and repeat for every $F(x, y) \in N(R_i)$ satisfies H
3. Repeat step 2 for each R_i.

For fuzzy image segmentation, the homogeneity H is a fuzzy variable.

The homogeneity consists of two parts: the standard deviation and the discontinuity of the intensities at each pixel of the image. The standard deviation $\sigma_{x, y}$ at pixel $F(x, y)$ can be written

$$\sigma_{x, y} = \frac{1}{W^2} [\sum_{m=-w}^{w} \sum_{n=-w}^{w} [f(x + m, j + n) - \overline{f}(x + m, y + n)]^2]^{\frac{1}{2}} \tag{6}$$

where $W = 2w + 1$ and

$$\overline{f}(x, y) = \frac{1}{W^2} \sum_{m=-w}^{w} \sum_{n=-w}^{w} f(x + m, y + n) \tag{7}$$

A measure of the discontinuity $D_{x, y}$ at pixel $F(x, y)$ can be written as

$$D_{x, y} = \sqrt{G_x^2 + G_y^2} \tag{8}$$

where G_x and G_y are gradients at pixel $F(x, y)$ in the x and y direction.

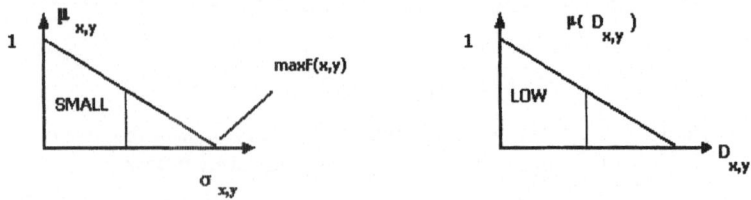

Fig. 2. Fuzzy sets used in homogeneity criterion.

3   Fuzzy Moments

The centroid of the segmented image is found and furthermore, m concentric circles are drawn with the centroid of the image as the center. The radius ρ_j of the jth circle is as follows

$$\rho_j = \sqrt{\frac{j}{m}} \rho_m \tag{9}$$

where ρ_m - distance from the centroid to the furthest pixel of the image.

We use the surrounding circle of f for partitioning it to $K \times L$ sectors, where K is the number of radial partitions and L is the number of angular partitions. This is given by

$$\theta = \frac{2\pi}{L} \qquad \rho = \frac{R}{K} \tag{10}$$

The radial and angular fuzzy moments of the segment contained between angles α and $\alpha + \theta$ and between circles of radius ρ_j and ρ_{j+1} are defined as follows

$$\Psi^{\rho_j, \alpha}(k, p, q) = \sum_{\rho_j}^{\rho_{j+1}} \sum_{\alpha}^{\alpha+\theta} \rho^k \mu(F(\rho, \theta)) \cos^p \theta \sin^q \theta \tag{11}$$

where k is order of the radial moments and $(p + q)$ is the order of the angular moments and (Fig.3)

$$\mu = \begin{cases} 0 & f \leq a \\ 2 \times [\frac{(f-a)}{(c-a)}]^2 & a \leq f \leq b \\ 1 - 2 \times [\frac{(f-a)}{(c-a)}]^2 & b \leq f \leq c \\ 1 & x \geq c \end{cases} \tag{12}$$

4   Query Processing

The color image retrieval must be researched in the certain color space. The RGB space is selected to research the color image retrieval, therefore we must

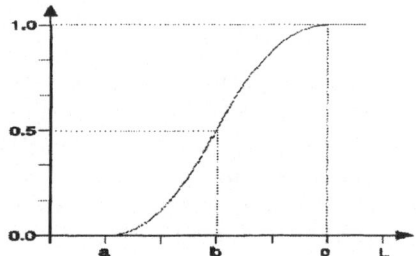

Fig. 3. A standard S-function .

perform all the operations (initialize membership, segmentations, compute fuzzy moments) according to the R,G,B components.

The general algorithm for color image retrieval is as follows:

1. Calculate the three component images of the color image in the certain color space (i.e. RGB)
2. Calculate membership of each component image
3. Segmenting each component image - we extract the region corresponding to each component according to homogeneity criterium.
4. Calculate the fuzzy moments for each component image
5. Each component image corresponds to feature vectors
   $V_{comp_i\ image} = [\overline{F}(R_i)_{comp\ image}, n(R_i)_{comp\ image}, \Psi^{\rho_j, \alpha}(k, p, q)_{comp\ image}]$
6. Feature vector for color image is
   $V_{image} = [V_{comp_1\ image}, V_{comp_2\ image}, V_{comp_3\ image}]$
7. Calculate the distance between each subfeature of one image to the other images and the minimum is selected as the feature distance between color images
8. Take the feature distance as the image similarity to perform the color image retrieval.

Three similarity functions $sim_R(Q, D)$, $sim_G(Q, D)$ and $sim_B(Q, D)$, respectively accounting for RGB image components are computed. Each function $simX(Q, D)$ between a database image feature, defined by the tuple $D = (d_0, d_1, \ldots, d_n)$, and the query image feature, also defined by a tuple $Q = (q_0, q_1, \ldots, q_n)$ is computed using the cosine similarity coefficient, defined as:

$$sim(Q, D) = \frac{\sum d_i q_i}{\sqrt{\sum d_i^2 \times \sum g_i^2}} \qquad (13)$$

The resulting coefficients are merged to form the final similarity function as:

$$sim(Q, D) = a \times sim_R(Q, D) + b \times sim_G(Q, D) + c \times sim_B(Q, D) \qquad (14)$$

where a, b and c are weighting coefficient empirically set.

5   Conclusion

Currently available large images repositories require new and efficient methodologies for query and retrieval. Content based access appears to be a promising direction to increase the efficiency and accuracy of unstructured data retrieval. We have introduced a system for similarity evaluation based on the extraction of simple features such as color and fuzzy image moments. We considered these features as a simple set perceptually useful in the retrieval from thematic databases, i.e. limited to a common semantic domain.

6   References

1. V. V. Gudivada, V. V. Raghavan, Guest Editors' Introduction: Content-Based Image Retrieval Systems, *IEEE Computer*,28, 9, 1995.
2. IEEE Computer, special issue on Content Based Image Retrieval, 28, 9, 1995.
3. Niblak et al., The QBIC project: Querying images by content using color, texture, and shape, *Proceedings of the SPIE: Storage and Retrieval for Image and Video Databases* vol. 1908, 1993.
4. M. Flickner et al., Query by Image and Video Content: The QBIC System, *IEEE Computer*, 28, 9, 1995
5. Y. Gong and M. Sakauchi, Detection of regions matching specified chromatic features, *Computer vision and image understanding*, 61,2, 1995.
6. G. Wyszechi, W. S. Stiles, *Color science: concepts and methods, quantitative data and formulas*, Wiley, NewYork, 1982.
7. Y. Chen, J.Z. Wang, A region-Based Fuzzy Feature Matching Approach to Content-Based Image Retrieval, *IEEE Trans. on PAMI*, vol.24, no.9, pp.1252-1267,2002.
8. H. Wang, D. Suter, Color Image Segmentation Using Global Information and Local Homogeneity, *Proc. 7th Digital Computing Techniques and Applications (eds. C. Sun, H. Talbot, S. Ourselin, T. Adriaansen)*, pp. 89-98, Sydney,2003.

Human Ear Identification Based on Image Analysis

Michał Choraś

Faculty of Telecommunications & Electrical Engineering
University of Technology & Agriculture
S. Kaliskiego 7, 85-791 Bydgoszcz
chorasm@mail.atr.bydgoszcz.pl

Abstract. Biometrics identification methods proved to be very efficient, more natural and easy for users than traditional methods of human identification. The future of biometrics leads to passive physiological methods based on images of such parts of human body as face and ear. The article presents a novel geometrical method of feature extraction from human ear images in order to perform human identification.

1 Introduction

There are many known methods of human identification based on image analysis. In general, those biometrics methods can be divided into behavioral and physiological regarding the source of data, and can be divided into passive and invasive biometrics, regarding the way the data is acquired. The major advantage of physiological biometrics is that it is passive and the implemented systems work only with the acquired images of specific body parts. All the user has to do is to place his face or ear in front of the camera or alternatively touch the sensor with his fingers and wait for the identification process to take place. But some systems can verify the identity of humans even without their cooperation and knowledge, which is actually the future of biometrics. Such systems can either use face or ear biometrics, however, it seems that the human ear is the most promising method of human identification. In the next section we explain the advantages of ear biometrics over face recognition. Then in section 3 we present the geometrical approach to feature extraction and classification.

2 Ear Identification

Human ears have been used as major feature in the forensic science for many years. Recently so called earprints, found on the crime scene, have been used as a proof in over few hundreds cases in the Netherlands and in the United States. Human ear contains more specific and unique features than any other part of the body and there are many advantages of using ear in comparison with face.

Firstly, ear does not change during human life, and face changes more significantly with the age than any other part of human body. Face can also change due

L. Rutkowski et al. (Eds.): ICAISC 2004, LNAI 3070, pp. 688–693, 2004.
© Springer-Verlag Berlin Heidelberg 2004

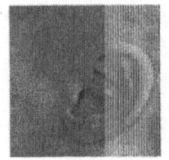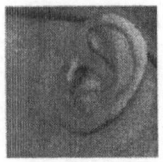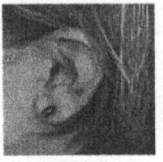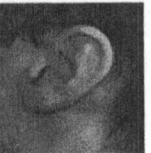

Fig. 1. Some examples of various ear images from our database.

to cosmetics, facial hair and hair styling. Secondly, face changes due to emotions and expresses different states of mind like sadness, happiness, fear or surprise. In contrast, ear features are fixed and unchangeable. Moreover, the color distribution is more uniform in ear than in human face, iris or retina. Thanks to that fact, not much information is lost while working with the grayscale or binarized images, as we do in our method. Ear is also smaller than face, which means that it is possible to work faster and more efficiently with the images with the lower resolution. Ear images cannot be disturbed by glasses, beard nor make-up. However, occlusion by hair or earrings is possible (Figure 1c). The first, manual method, used by Iannarelli in the research, in which he examined over 10000 ears and proved their uniqueness, was based on measuring the distances between specific points of the ear. The major problem in ear identification systems is discovering automated method to extract those specific, key points. In our work, the feature extraction step is divided into image normalization, contour extraction, calculation of the centroid, coordinates normalization and geometrical feature extraction, as described in the next section. We treat the centroid as the specific point in our method, even though it is not a specific point within the ear topology.

3 Feature Extraction

We propose a straightforward method to extract features needed to classification. Our method represents the geometrical approach, but it is fully automated and no manual operations are needed. Our method consists of the following steps:

- contour detection
- binarization
- coordinates normalization
- feature extraction and classification

3.1 Contour Detection

First we perform the edge detection step. In our case it is a crucial operation since it is obvious that lines are the most prominent features that could be obtained from the ear image, and our goal is to detect major outer and inner curves of the earlobe. We propose to use the local method which examines illumination

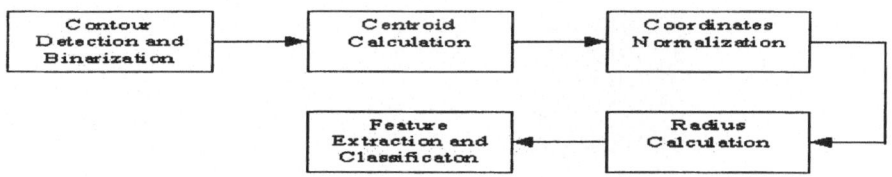

Fig. 2. Block diagram of our method.

changes within the chosen window $n \times n$. We usually use 3×3 window and we divided the image into many overlapping regions of that size. For each of those regions we calculate mean μ and standard deviation σ of the pixel intensity values in 8-pixel neighborhood.

$$\mu = \frac{1}{n^2} \sum_{i=1}^{n} \sum_{j=1}^{n} I(i,j) \qquad \sigma = \sqrt{\frac{1}{(n^2-1)} \sum_{i=1}^{n} \sum_{j=1}^{n} \left(I\left(i,j\right) - \mu \right)^2} \qquad (1)$$

Then we perform decision if the center pixel of the examined region belongs to the line or to the background. We propose the usage of mean and standard deviation of pixel intensities in calculation of the threshold value $T(x,y)$ used in contour detection, as given in equation:

$$T(i,j) = \mu - k * \sigma \qquad (2)$$

where k is a certain constant.
If S is a difference between the maximum value of the pixel intensity and the minimum value of the pixel intensity in each region the rule for obtaining the binary contour image $g(i,j)$ is:

$$g(i,j) = \begin{cases} 1 & if \quad S(i,j) \geq T(i,j) \\ 0 & if \quad S(i,j) < T(i,j) \end{cases} \qquad (3)$$

Some examples of the edge detection are shown in the Figure 3.

3.2   Size and Coordinates Normalization

Given the binary image $g(i,j)$, we search for the centroid which later becomes the reference point for feature extraction. We obtain the centroid such as (Fig. 4):

$$I = \frac{\sum_i \sum_j i\, g\left(i,j\right)}{\sum_i \sum_j g\left(i,j\right)} \qquad J = \frac{\sum_i \sum_j j\, g\left(i,j\right)}{\sum_i \sum_j g\left(i,j\right)} \qquad (4)$$

Because the features for a recognition algorithm should be invariant to ear translation and scale change, the coordinates normalization is performed. Therefore we normalize coordinates in such a way that the centroid becomes the

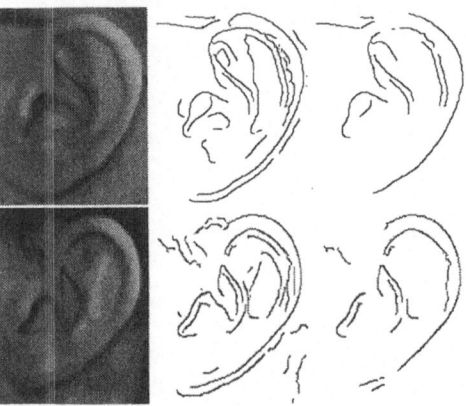

Fig. 3. Acquired ear images and two corresponding images after contour detection (with different values of constant k.)

center of the image. Suppose that the image with pixel coordinates (i, j) undergoes geometric transformations to produce an invariant image with coordinates (x, y).

This transformation may be expressed as:

$$[x, y, z] = [i, j, 1] \begin{bmatrix} 1 & 0 & 0 \\ 0 & 1 & 0 \\ -I & -J & 1 \end{bmatrix} \begin{bmatrix} \frac{1}{\sigma_i} & 0 & 0 \\ 0 & \frac{1}{\sigma_i} & 0 \\ 0 & 0 & 1 \end{bmatrix} \quad (5)$$

where:

- I, J - centroid
- σ - standard deviation of i and j respectively:

$$\sigma_i = \sqrt{\frac{\sum_i \sum_j i^2 g(i,j)}{\sum_i \sum_j g(i,j)} - I^2} \qquad \sigma_j = \sqrt{\frac{\sum_i \sum_j j^2 g(i,j)}{\sum_i \sum_j g(i,j)} - J^2} \quad (6)$$

Furthermore, our method is also invariant to rotation, as all the rotated images of the same object have the same centroid. That is the major reason that we chose the centroid of the image to be the reference point in the feature extraction algorithm. Such approach allows successful processing of RST queries.

3.3   Feature Extraction and Classification Algorithm

There are many possible geometrical methods of feature extraction and shape description, such as Fourier Descriptors, Delaunay Triangles and methods based on combination of angles and distances as parameters. We propose a method, which is based on number of pixels that have the same radius in a circle with the center in the centroid. The algorithm for feature extraction is presented below:

1. we create a set of circles with the center in the centroid (Figure 4)
2. number of circles Nr is fixed and unchangeable
3. we create circles in such a manner that the corresponding radiuses are α pixels longer from the previous radius
4. since each circle is crossed by the contour image pixels, we count the number of intersection pixels l_r
5. next, we calculate all the distances between neighboring pixels; we proceed in the counter-clockwise direction
6. we build the feature vector that consists of all the radiuses with the corresponding number of pixels belonging to each radius and with the distances between those pixels

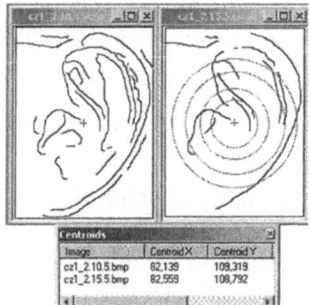 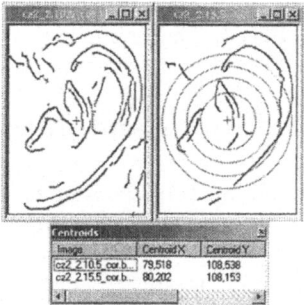

Fig. 4. Ear images with the extracted edges and with the centroid marked with a cross. Circles represent the radius values for calculation of number of pixels intersecting each circle. The table below shows the centroid values for each binary image.

The algorithm for Nr=3 is symbolically presented in the Figure 5. The general rule for forming feature vector is presented below:

$$V = \{[r_{min}, l_{r_{min}}, d^0_{r_{min}}, d^1_{r_{min}}, ..., d^{l_{r_{min}}}_{r_{min}}] ...$$
$$... [r_{max}, l_{r_{max}}, d^0_{r_{max}}, d^1_{r_{max}}, ..., d^{l_{r_{max}}}_{r_{max}}]\}. \tag{7}$$

For each image stored in the database, the feature vector is obtained and stored in the database to be compared with the input image. The algorithm for recognition of an input image is following:

1. the feature vector of the input image is obtained
2. the feature vectors are of the same length, as the number of circles is fixed
3. for each radius, we search the database feature vectors that have the same number of intersections
4. in the next step we check if the difference between corresponding distances is less than a certain threshold value
5. otherwise the input image is rejected

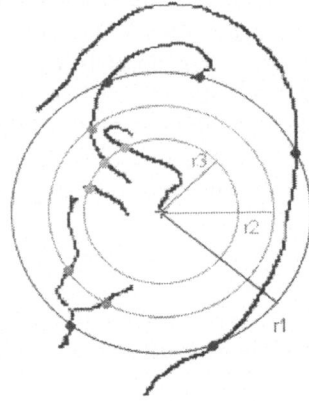

Fig. 5. The symbolic representation of our algorithm for $N_r = 3$.

4   Conclusions and Future Work

In the article we propose a novel human identification method based on human ear. We believe that human ear is unique and has many advantages over other biometrics methods. We suggested geometrical method in order to extract features needed to classification. First we perform contour detection algorithm, then size normalization. Thanks to placing the center of the new coordinates system in the centroid, our method is invariant to rotation, translation and scaling, which will allow RST queries. The centroid is also a key reference point in the feature extraction algorithm. We create circles centered in the centroid and we count the number of intersection points for each radius and all the distances between neighboring points. So far we have worked with images of very high quality and with the ideal conditions of recognition, without illumination changes. For such images we obtained very high recognition ratio.

References

1. Burge M, Burger W., *Ear Biometrics*, Johannes Kepler University, Linz, Austria 1999.
2. Choraś M, *Human Identification Based on Image Analysis - New Trends*, Proc. Int. IEEE Workshop Signal Processing'03, pp. 111-116, Poznan 2003.
3. Iannarelli A., *Ear Identification*, Forensic Identification Series, Paramont Publishing Company, California 1989.
4. Safar M., Shahabi C., Sun X., *Image Retrieval By Shape: A Comparative Study*, University of Southern California, November 1999.

Automatic Change Detection Based on Codelength Differences in Multi-temporal and Multi-spectral Images

Joselíto J. Chua and Peter E. Tischer

School of Computer Science and Software Engineering
Monash University, Victoria 3800, Australia
{jjchua,pet}@mail.csse.monash.edu.au

Abstract. We propose a technique for detecting significant changes in a scene automatically, based on images acquired at different times. Compared to conventional luminance difference methods, the proposed technique does not require an arbitrarily-determined threshold for deciding how much change in pixel values amounts to a significant change in the scene. The technique can be used to detect the changes that occured in the scene, even when the images are of different spectral domains.

1 Introduction

We consider the problem of automatic change detection in multi-temporal images. Given two images of the same scene, acquired at different times, the problem involves obtaining a *change-detection map*, which is a binary image indicating regions where significant changes have occured between the two images. A solution to this problem has a number of important applications in computer vision [1,2], medical imaging [3,4], remote sensing [5,6], and video coding [7].

Conventional change detection methods can be divided into three steps: (i) pre-processing of the images to be compared; (ii) a pixel-by-pixel comparison of the images in order to generate a difference image; and (iii) thresholding the difference image to obtain a change-detection map [5].

Pre-processing involves rendering the images in a comparable spatial domain. In a vision-based road navigation system, for example, image stabilization techniques can be used to attenuate the effect of the movements and vibrations of the vehicle [1]. A number of standard automatic image registration techniques can be used to obtain maximal spatial alignment of the images to be compared [8]. Pre-processing may also involve rendering the images in a comparable spectral domain. In some applications, for example, it may be possible to re-scale the pixel intensities to compensate for the differences in lighting conditions at the time when the images were taken.

The focus of this paper is on generating the difference image, and obtaining a change-detection map from the difference image.

L. Rutkowski et al. (Eds.): ICAISC 2004, LNAI 3070, pp. 694–699, 2004.
© Springer-Verlag Berlin Heidelberg 2004

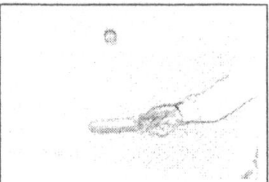

Image A: frame003   Image B: frame004   Image D: difference

Fig. 1. The luminance difference image between two consecutive frames in the image sequence "tennis," where $f_\mathbf{D}(x) = |f_\mathbf{A}(x) - f_\mathbf{B}(x)|$ for every $x \in X$.

2 Luminance Difference

Let $\mathbf{A} = (X, f_\mathbf{A})$ and $\mathbf{B} = (X, f_\mathbf{B})$ represent the two images being compared, where X is the set of spatial coordinates, and $f_\mathbf{A}$ and $f_\mathbf{B}$ are the luminance functions. If the images have R rows and C columns, then $X = \{\langle i, j \rangle \mid i = 1, \dots, R$ and $j = 1, \dots, C\}$. Given a pixel coordinate $x \in X$, the pixel value in $\mathbf{A}$ at x is given by $f_\mathbf{A}(x)$. Similarly, the pixel value at the same coordinate in $\mathbf{B}$ is given by $f_\mathbf{B}(x)$.

Difference images are often obtained by taking the difference in luminance values of corresponding pixels [1,7]. For example, the difference image $\mathbf{D} = (X, f_\mathbf{D})$ in Figure 1 has pixel values $f_\mathbf{D}(x) = |f_\mathbf{A}(x) - f_\mathbf{B}(x)|$ for every $x \in X$. This approach, however, has a number of limitations. It assumes that the pixel values have been normalised such that the scale of their differences correspond to the magnitude of the changes between the images. The approach does not allow comparison of images from different spectral domains. In medical imaging applications, for example, the same anatomical structure in the brain can appear as bright pixels in one modality, but as dark pixels in another modality.

Another major drawback is the difficulty in generating the change-detection map from the luminance difference image. Thresholds are often used on the difference in pixel values to determine which pixels should be labeled "changed" in the change-detection map. As [9] pointed out, there is a lack of automatic and non-heuristic methods for determining the thresholds. Classical techniques are often based on empirical strategies or manual trial-and-error procedures, which can affect the resulting change-detection map significantly [9].

3 Codelength Difference

The technique proposed in this paper determines the change-detection map based on the differences in the length of the codewords in an entropy-based coding of the images.

Let G be the set of possible pixel values in the images. In 8-bit greyscale images, for example, $G = \{0, 1, 2, \dots, 255\}$. Given $g \in G$, let $\Pr(g)$ denote the probability estimate for that pixel value based on the relative frequency distribution of the pixel values in an image. In an entropy-based coding of the pixel values in $\mathbf{A}$, the length of the codeword for the pixel at x is given by:

$$\mathcal{L}_A(x) = -\log \Pr(f_\mathbf{A}(x)) \tag{1}$$

where the logarithm is base 2. We then consider the codelength for the same pixel, given a probability model which is conditional on the corresponding pixel in the image $\mathbf{B}$:

$$\mathcal{L}_{A|B}(x) = -\log \Pr(f_\mathbf{A}(x) \mid f_\mathbf{B}(x)) \tag{2}$$

where $\Pr(f_\mathbf{A}(x) \mid f_\mathbf{B}(x))$ denotes the conditional probability of a pixel value in $\mathbf{A}$, given the pixel value at the same location in $\mathbf{B}$.

Our criteria for comparing the codelengths $\mathcal{L}_A(x)$ and $\mathcal{L}_{A|B}(x)$ is based on a basic data compression principle: better models yield shorter average codelengths. The difference between Equations 1 and 2, given by:

$$h(x) = \mathcal{L}_A(x) - \mathcal{L}_{A|B}(x) \tag{3}$$

$$= \log \frac{\Pr(f_\mathbf{A}(x) \mid f_\mathbf{B}(x))}{\Pr(f_\mathbf{A}(x))} \tag{4}$$

$$= \log \frac{\Pr(f_\mathbf{B}(x) \mid f_\mathbf{A}(x))}{\Pr(f_\mathbf{B}(x))} \tag{5}$$

$$= \mathcal{L}_B(x) - \mathcal{L}_{B|A}(x) \tag{6}$$

represents the information gained when image $\mathbf{B}$ is used to obtain a conditional model for the pixels in $\mathbf{A}$, and vice versa. Pixels where $h(x)$ is negative indicate regions where the model conditional on $\mathbf{B}$ does not offer more information about $\mathbf{A}$ than the simple model for $\mathbf{A}$. These regions can be regarded as areas where significant changes in the scene occured.

The technique detects changes by comparing the pixel codelengths resulting from two models: (1) the relative frequency distribution of the pixel values in the $\mathbf{A}$; and (2) the conditional probability of a pixel value in $\mathbf{A}$, given the corresponding pixel value in the $\mathbf{B}$. If a pixel's codelength resulting from model (1) is shorter than the codelength resulting from model (2), then the pixel is marked as "changed" in the change-detection map. This yields a natural threshold for determining the change-detection map, $\mathbf{M}$, as follows:

$$f_\mathbf{M}(x) = \begin{cases} 1 & \text{if } h(x) < 0 \\ 0 & \text{otherwise} \end{cases} \tag{7}$$

Figure 2 shows the codelength-based difference image and change-detection map for images $\mathbf{A}$ and $\mathbf{B}$ in Figure 1. Figure 2(a) shows the normalised codelength-based difference image, $\mathbf{D}$, whose pixel values are given by:

$$f_\mathbf{D}(x) = 255 \times \frac{h(x) - h_{\min}}{h_{\max} - h_{\min}} \tag{8}$$

where $h_{\min} = \min_{x \in X} h(x)$ and $h_{\max} = \max_{x \in X} h(x)$.

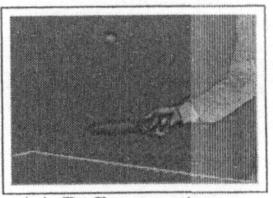
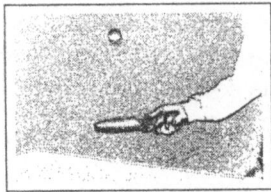
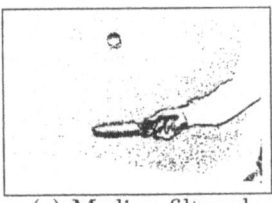

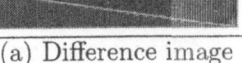

| (a) Difference image | (b) Change detection | (c) Median filtered |

Fig. 2. The codelength-based difference image and change-detection map for images **A** and **B** in Figure 1.

Figure 2(b) shows the binary image **M**, where black pixels indicate regions where changes were detected. Note that the change detection process can be sensitive to mis-registration noise [10]. In the case of Figure 2(b), the changes detected in the background were caused by camera movement over the textured surface that fills the background. Models based on the relative frequency distribution of the pixel values are sensitive to mis-registration noise because the models do not take the spatial relationship of the pixels into account [11]. In order to compensate for this defficiency, a median filter is applied on the initial change-detection map to obtain the final map. Figure 2(c) is the result of applying a median filter with radius 1 to image **M**. A better solution would be to use high-order models, such as those used in [11], to take the spatial relationship of the pixels into account during change detection.

An advantage of the proposed technique is that it can be used to compare multi-spectral images. The technique is based on the correspondence of the pixel values, rather than the difference in their intensities. This ability to compare images from different spectral domains is illustrated in Figure 3. Image **A** is the popular test image "lenna." Image **B** is obtained by replacing the region of the face of **A** with pixels from another popular test image known as "mandrill." Image **C** is the negative mode of **B**. Although the difference in luminance values can be used to detect the changes between **A** and **B**, the different modality in **C** makes luminance differences unsuitable to detect the changes (Figure 3(b)). On the other hand, the change-detection map based on the proposed technique is able to identify the changed pixels correctly, even though **A** and **C** are of different modalities (Figure 3, (c) and (d)). This capability is useful in applications such as geo-spatial imaging, where images from various spectral domains need to be compared in order to identify features which may be apparent in one spectrum but not in another.

4   Conclusion

We proposed a technique for automatic change detection in multi-temporal images of the same scene. The proposed technique has two important advantages over conventional luminance difference methods: (1) the decision threshold is

(a) Test Images:

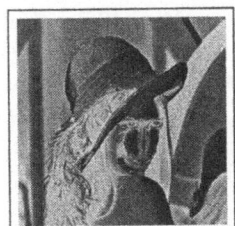

Image A   Image B   Image C

(b) Luminance Difference:

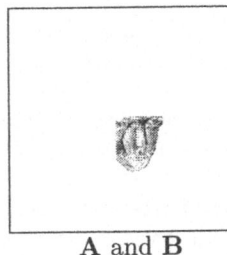

A and B   A and C

(c) Codelength-based Change-Detection:

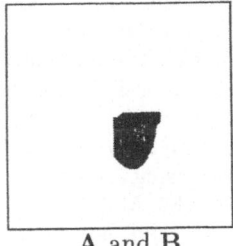
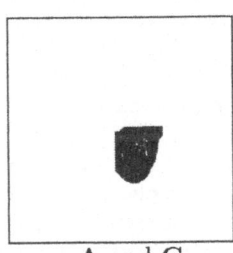

A and B   A and C

(d) Codelength-based Change-Detection Map (Median Filtered):

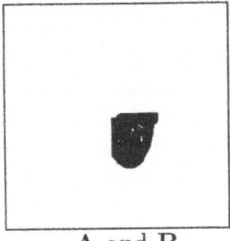
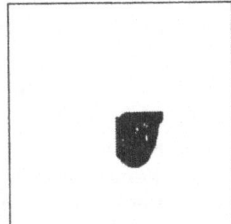

A and B   A and C

Fig. 3. Comparison of luminance difference and codelength-based change-detection map in multi-spectral images.

inherent in the technique, thus disposing the need for arbitrarily-determined thresholds; and (2) the technique is able to detect the changes even when the images are of different modalities (spectral domains). The technique can be used as a component in multi-spectral computer vision systems.

Work is currently underway towards improving the technique by considering high-order Markov models that can take advantage of the spatial relationship of the pixels. Although high-order models often perform better, they also require larger amounts of computation and storage space [5]. The challenge is to make such high-order techniques sufficiently "fast and lean" to be of practical use in applications involving remote autonomous agents.

References

1. C.-Y. Fang, S.-W. Chen, and C.-S. Fuh. Automatic change detection of driving environments in a vision-based driver assistance system. *IEEE Trans. Neural Networks*, 14(3):646–657, May 2003.
2. Y. Kameda and M. Minoh. A human motion estimation method using 3-successive viedo frames. In *Proc. of the Int'l. Conf. on Visual Systems and Multimedia '96*, pages 135–140, Gifu City, Japan, September 1996.
3. M. Holden, J.A. Schnabel, and D.L.G. Hill. Quantification of small cerebral ventricular volume changes in treated growth hormone patients using nonrigid registration. *IEEE Trans. Medical Imaging*, 21(10):1292–1301, October 2002.
4. C.R. Maurer, Jr., D.L.G. Hill, A.J. Martin, H. Liu, M. McCue, D. Rueckert, D. Lloret, W.A. Hall, R.E. Maxwell, D.J. Hawkes, and C.L. Truwit. Investigation of intraoperative brain deformation using a 1.5T interventional MR system: Preliminary results. *IEEE Trans. Medical Imaging*, 17(5):817–825, October 1998.
5. L. Bruzzone and D.F. Prieto. An adaptive semiparametric and context-based approach to unsupervised change detection in multitemporal remote-sensing images. *IEEE Trans. Image Processing*, 11(4):452–466, April 2002.
6. T. Yamamoto, H. Hanaizumi, and S. Chino. A change detection method for remotely sensed multispectral and multitemporal images using 3-D segmentation. *IEEE Trans. Geoscience and Remote Sensing*, 39(5):976–985, May 1999.
7. M. Kim, J.G. Choi, D. Kim, H. Lee, M.H. Lee, C. Ahn, and Y.-S. Ho. A VOP generation tool: Automatic segmentation of moving objects in image sequences based on spatio-temporal information. *IEEE Trans. Circuits and Systems for Video Technology*, 9(8):1216–1226, December 1999.
8. A.A. Goshtasby and J. Le Moigne. Special issue on image registration. *Pattern Recognition*, 32(1), January 1999.
9. L. Bruzzone and D.F. Prieto. Automatic analysis of the difference image for unsupervised change detection. *IEEE Trans. Geoscience and Remote Sensing*, 38(3):1171–1182, May 2000.
10. X. Dai and S. Khorram. The effects of image misregistration on the accuracy of remotely sensed change detection. *IEEE Trans. Geoscience and Remote Sensing*, 36(5):1566–1577, September 1998.
11. J.J. Chua and P.E. Tischer. A similarity measure based on causal neighbours and mutual information. In A. Abraham, M. Köppen, and K. Franke, editors, *Design and Application of Hybrid Intelligent Systems*, volume 104 of *Frontiers in Artificial Intelligence and Applications*, pages 842–851. IOS Press, 2003.

Estimating Face Direction via Facial Triangle

Min Gyo Chung, Jisook Park, and Jiyoun Dong

Dept. of Computer Science, Seoul Women's University, Seoul, Korea
{mchung,jspark,dongji79}@swu.ac.kr

Abstract. In this paper, we propose a vision-based approach to detect a face direction from a single monocular view of a face by using a facial feature called *facial triangle*. Specifically, the proposed method introduces formulas to detect face rotation, horizontally and vertically, using the facial triangle. Our method makes no assumption about the structure of the face and produces an accurate estimate of face direction.

1   Introduction

The recent rapid development of human-computer interaction and surveillance technologies has brought great interests in application systems to process faces. Research and development efforts in these systems have been primarily focused on such areas as facial feature extraction, face recognition, and facial expression analysis [1,2,3,4,5].

However, very few approaches have been reported toward face direction detection. Even existing methods to face direction detection have serious limitations. For example, Gee and Cipolla [6] assume a specific model for the geometry of faces with three model ratios, Minagawa et al. [7] require two stereo images captured by two cameras, and the work of Ballard and Stockman [8] is subject to a condition that the inter-point distances between three 3D coordinates (corresponding to three feature points in a 2D image) are known a priori.

In this paper, we propose a vision-based approach to detect a face direction from a single monocular view of a face by using a face feature called *facial triangle*, which is formed by two eyebrows (or eyes) and the lower lip. The proposed method introduces formulas to detect face rotation, horizontally and vertically, using the facial triangle. And it makes no assumption about the structure of a face and produces an accurate estimate of face direction.

2   Direction Detection Scheme

The proposed scheme consists of three major steps: *preprocessing, extraction of facial triangle*, and *face direction detection* steps.

In the preprocessing step, the face region in an input image is first located and separated from the background using any well-known region segmentation algorithms. A gradient operator such as Sobel operator is then applied to the segmented face region to detect the edges. The edge map is thresholded into

L. Rutkowski et al. (Eds.): ICAISC 2004, LNAI 3070, pp. 700–705, 2004.
© Springer-Verlag Berlin Heidelberg 2004

a binary image and then noise is eliminated from the binary image by using morphological transformations such as binary dilation (See Fig. 1).

The facial triangle extraction step chooses two eyebrows and the lower lip as three feature points to build facial triangle. Facial triangle is basically a virtual polygon drawn upon a *facial plane*, which is defined by the three feature points. In addition to locating the feature points, we also construct three imaginary *facial axes* on a face as follows: horizontal axis connecting two eyebrows, and both horizontal and vertical axes passing through the center of the lower lip. The facial triangle is now constructed by connecting the center of the lower lip and the two intersection points between the face contour and the horizontal axe going through the eyebrows (See Fig. 2). The vertical axis plays a role of dividing the facial triangle into two smaller triangles (corresponding to left and right cheeks).

Finally, the last step takes some measurements on the facial triangles, and simply computes the rotation angle of the face by using those measurements as an input to the facial direction formulas proposed in this work.

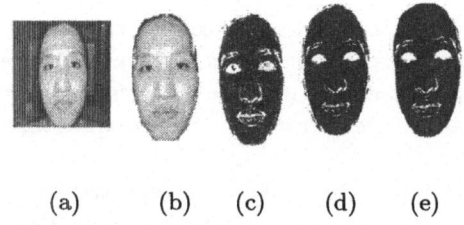

(a)   (b)   (c)   (d)   (e)

Fig. 1. Intermediate images produced at each phase of the preprocessing step: (a) Original image, (b) Image without background, (c) Detected edge image, (d) Binarized edge image, and (e) Morphological transformation applied to the binary image to eliminate noise and enhance facial features

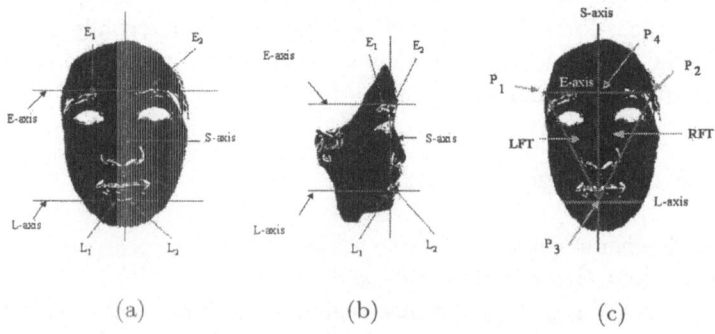

(a)   (b)   (c)

Fig. 2. (a) Facial model: front view, (b) Facial model: profile view, and (c) Facial triangle: the whole facial triangle contains two smaller facial triangles, LFT and RFT

2.1   Facial Triangle Construction

A more detailed explanation will be given here about how to construct facial triangle, using the resulting image shown in Fig. 1 (e). Two eyebrows and the lower lip are chosen as natural feature points for the construction of facial triangle.

Consider the facial model in Fig. 2 (a) and (b). Assuming that the face image is scanned vertically from bottom to top, then L_1 indicates the first white point to be encountered when each row is scanned from left to right, whereas L_2 is the location of the first white point obtained when the scanning direction is reversed. Conceptually, L_1 and L_2 represent two bottommost points on the lower lip. Similarly, two topmost points on the eyebrows (one point for each left and right eyebrow) can be found and denoted as E_1 and E_2. Based on the four detected points L_1, L_2, E_1, and E_2, three imaginary facial axes, named as L(Lip)-axis, E(Eyebrow)-axis, and S(Symmetry)-axis, can be built as shown in Fig. 2 (a) and (b). L-axis and S-axis are horizontal and vertical axes, respectively, both passing through the midpoint of the lower lip $\frac{L_1+L_2}{2}$. E-axis runs parallel to L-axis and goes through the midpoint of the eyebrows, $\frac{E_1+E_2}{2}$.

Figure 2 (c) illustrates the construction of facial triangle using the above three facial axes. Points P_1 and P_2 are the two intersection points between the face contour and the E-axis. The S-axis crosses the E-axis at point P_4 as well as the L-axis at point P_3. The facial triangle is now defined by the three points P_1, P_2 and P_3. Further, the entire facial triangle can be broken down into two smaller triangles, each corresponding to left and right cheeks. The left smaller triangle, symbolized as LFT (Left Facial Triangle), consists of points P_1, P_3, and P_4 and its area is represented by a symbol A_{LFT}. Similarly, the right smaller triangle, symbolized as RFT (Right Facial Triangle), consists of points P_2, P_3, and P_4 and a symbol A_{RFT} is used to denote the area of RFT.

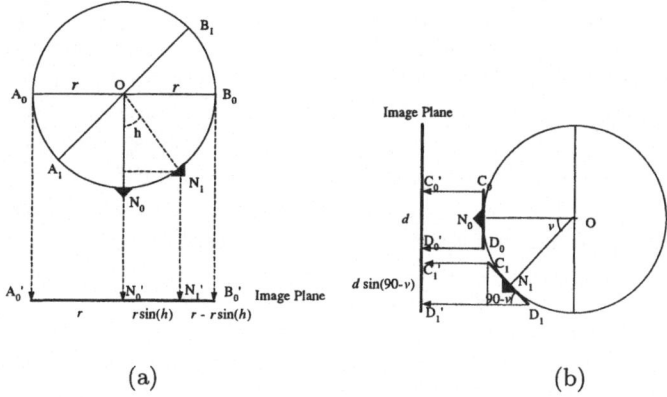

(a)   (b)

Fig. 3. Geometrical configuration for face orientation detection: (a) Horizontal rotation and (b) Vertical rotation

2.2   Direction Detection

Consider the method for estimating face direction based on the facial triangle. Figure 3 (a) and (b) illustrate the simplified geometry for the detection of horizontal and vertical head rotation, respectively. Figure 3 (a) is a top view of a human head. Assume the two points A_0 and B_0 denote the position of the ears and the point N_0 symbolizes the nose. Assume further that these three points on the face are mapped into corresponding points A_0', B_0', and N_0' on the camera image plane. Now, when the face is rotated horizontally by an arbitrary angle h, the three points moves to the new positions A_1, B_1, and N_1. Especially, for the rotation of the nose from N_0 to N_1 in 3D space, the imaged nose point translates from N_0' to N_1' on the image plane by the distance of $r\sin(h)$. Since the nose is a point on the S-axis, the translation of the imaged nose point actually corresponds to the horizontal shift of the S-axis, thus leading to a shift along E-axis(or L-axis) of the facial triangle points P_3 and P_4 in Fig. 2 (c). Ultimately this shift will cause the areas of the left and right facial triangles to be changed.

Let s be the distance between P_3 and P_4. Then, the relationship between the rotation angle and the areas of the left and right facial triangles can be expressed as follows:

$$A_{LFT} = \frac{1}{2}sr(1 + \sin h), \quad A_{RFT} = \frac{1}{2}sr(1 - \sin h)$$

$$A_{RFT} - A_{RFT} = sr\sin h, \quad A_{LFT} + A_{RFT} = sr$$

Now, the horizontal rotation angle h can be calculated as follows by introducing a ratio R_{area} between the areas of the facial triangles:

$$R_{area} = \frac{A_{LFT} - A_{RFT}}{A_{LFT} + A_{RFT}} = \sin h$$

$$h = \sin^{-1}(R_{area}) \tag{1}$$

To understand how to compute the vertical rotation angle of a face, now take a look at the facial triangle in Fig. 2 (c) again. The basic idea is that when the face is rotated vertically, the length of the vertical line segment $\overline{P_3P_4}$ varies a lot while the length of the horizontal line segment $\overline{P_1P_2}$ remains unchanged. Figure 3 (b) shows the side view of a face, where we suppose that the line segment $\overline{C_0D_0}$ corresponds to the vertical line segment $\overline{P_3P_4}$ in the facial triangle. The line segment $\overline{C_1D_1}$ is a rotation of angle v from the line segment $\overline{C_0D_0}$. Then, the projected length of the line segment $\overline{C_1D_1}$ becomes $d\sin(90-v) = d\cos v$, where d is the actual length of the line segment $\overline{C_1D_1}$. Based on these observations, we can derive the formula to compute the vertical rotation angle as follows:

$$\hat{d} = d\cos v$$

$$v = \cos^{-1}(\frac{\hat{d}}{d}) = \cos^{-1}(\frac{\hat{d}}{\hat{c}k}), \tag{2}$$

where $\hat{d}$, the projected length of the line segment $\overline{C_1D_1}$, can be obtained by measuring the distance from P_3 to P_4 on the facial triangle, $\hat{c}$ is a measured distance from P_1 to P_2, and k is a constant (we used $\frac{2}{3}$). Here, we use tha fact that $d = ck \simeq \hat{c}k$, because the length of the horizontal line segment $\overline{P_1 P_2}$ remains unchanged irrespective of vertical rotations: that is, $c \simeq \hat{c}$.

3   Experimental Results

Face images were captured by Canon IXUS 400 digital camera. The image capturing was made on five subjects, each in 13 different horizontal orientations: 0, ±15, ±30, ±45, ±60, ±75, and ±90 degrees, and in 10 different vertical orientations: 0, ±10, ±20, ±30, ±40, 50 degrees. Figure 4 shows the faces of the five subjects, which are typical Korean women.

To assess the validity of the horizontal face direction formula in Equation (1), we measured the area of LFT, A_{LFT}, as well as the area of RFT, A_{RFT}, and then computed the ratio R_{area} for each of the 65(= 13*5) images. The plot of the ratio R_{area} vs. rotation angle reveals a sine curve relationship between those two quantities as shown in Fig. 5 (a). Indeed, this sort of relationship verifies that Equation (1) can be reliably used to provide accurate estimates of facial orientation across many different subjects. More error analyses and experiments show that our approach makes it possible to obtain the ratios R_{area} within an error tolerance of $\pm0.085\%$, as well as the face orientation angle within an error tolerance of $\pm1.67°$.

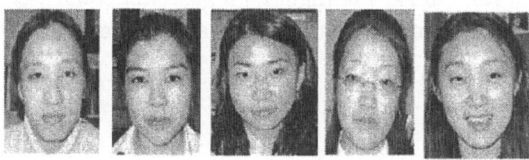

Fig. 4. The faces of the five subjects used for the experiment

The errors when using the vertical face direction formula in Equation (2), are presented in Figure 5 (b). The y-axis represents an error, which is the absolute value of the difference between the correct angle and the angle estimated by the Equation (2). Compared with the Equation (1), Equation (2) reports quite noticeable errors due to some uncertainties such as inaccurate feature locations and simplified camera model. However, it performs better as the magnitude of vertical rotation angle gets greater.

4   Conclusion

In this paper, we propose a vision-based approach to detect a face direction from a single monocular view of a face by using a facial feature called *facial triangle*.

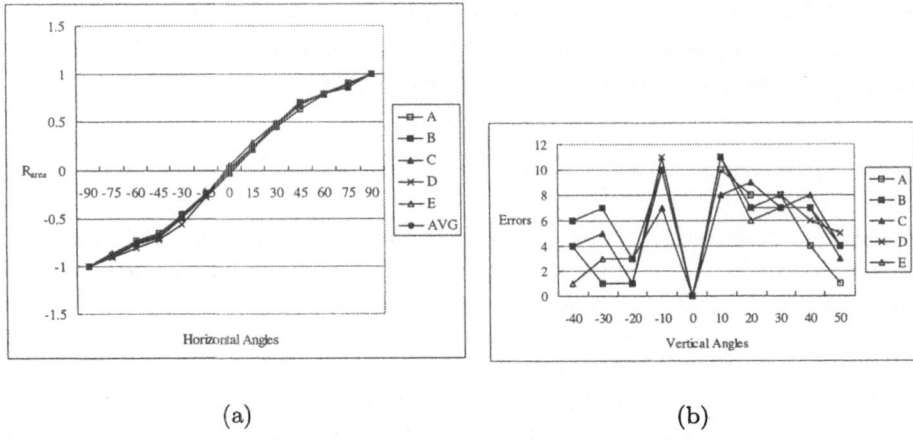

(a)   (b)

Fig. 5. (a) Plot of ratio R_{area} vs. horizontal rotation angles for each subject, and (b) Plot of errors vs. vertical rotation angles for each subject

For the construction of the facial triangle, two eyebrows and the lower lip are chosen as three natural feature points. Based on the facial triangle, we can derive facial direction formulas for horizontal and vertical face rotations. Our approach can be effectively used not only for applications in human-computer interaction, but also potential applications such as searching for images with similar face direction or automatic photo arrangement systems that will often need to set the different left or right margin of a photo according to the face direction of a person in the photo.

References

1. B. Moghaddam, "Principal manifolds and bayesian subspaces for visual recognition," ICCV, 1131-1136, 1999.
2. M. A. Turk and A. P. Pentland, "Eigenfaces for recognition," J. Cognitive Neurosci., vol. 3, no. 1, 71-86, 1991.
3. C. Liu and H. Wechsler, "Probabilistic reasoning models for face recognition," in Proc. of Computer Vision and Pattern Recognition, 827-832, 1998.
4. G. Guo, S. Li, and K. Chan, "Face recognition by support vector machines," Proc. of the International Conferences on Automatic Face and Gesture Recognitions, 196-201, 2000.
5. H. Sahbi and N. Boujemaa, "From coarse to fine skin and face detection," The 8th ACM International Conference on Multimedia, 2000.
6. Andrew Gee and Robert Cipolla, "Determining the gaze of faces in images," Image and Vision Computing, Vol.12. No. 10, pp.639-647, 1994.
7. T. Minagawa, H. Saito and S. Ozawa, "Face-direction estimating system using stereo vision," IECON97, New Orleans, 1997.
8. Philippe Ballard and G. Stockman, "Controlling a computer via facial aspect," IEEE Transactions on Systems, Man, and Cybernetics, Vol.25. No. 4, pp.669-677, 1995.

An Image Compression Algorithm Based on Neural Networks

Robert Cierniak

Department of Computer Engineering, Czestochowa University of Technology,
Al. Armii Krajowej 36, 42-200 Czestochowa,
Poland
cierniak@kik.pcz.czest.pl

Abstract. In this paper a combination of algorithms useful for image compression standard is discussed. The main algorithm, named predictive vector quantization (PVQ), is based on competitive neural networks quantizer and neural networks predictor. Additionally, the noiseless Huffman coding is used. The experimental results are presented and the performance of the algorithm is discussed.

1   Introduction

Among methods for image compression proposed in the literature the vector quantization (VQ) technique has emerged as an effective tool [1],[2]. One of approaches to image compression combines the VQ technique with differential pulse code modulation (DPCM) leading to the predictive vector quantization (PVQ). The design of the PVQ scheme requires both a predictor and a VQ codebook determination. In this paper we develop the so-called modified closed-loop methodology to solve above problem. The vector quantizer will be based on competitive neural networks, whereas the predictor will be designed as the non-linear neural network - contrary to a heuristic method presented in [1] and linear predictors developed in our previous papers [3],[5]. To improve the compression ratio without any additional distortions the Huffman coding is included. The combination of PVQ and Huffman algorithms could be an interesting base to create a new image compression standard.

2   Preprocessing

Let us assume that an image is represented by an $N_1 \times N_2$ array of pixels $y_{n_1 n_2}, n_1 = 1, 2, ..., N_1, n_2 = 1, 2, ..., N_2$. The image is portioned into continuous small blocks of the dimension $n_1 \times n_2$.

$$
\mathbf{Y}(m_1, m_2) = \begin{bmatrix} y_{11}(m_1, m_2) \cdots y_{1, n_2}(m_1, m_2) \\ \vdots \quad \ddots \quad \vdots \\ y_{n_1, 1}(m_1, m_2) \cdots y_{n_1, n_2}(m_1, m_2) \end{bmatrix}, \tag{1}
$$

L. Rutkowski et al. (Eds.): ICAISC 2004, LNAI 3070, pp. 706–711, 2004.
© Springer-Verlag Berlin Heidelberg 2004

where: $\mathbf{Y}(m_1, m_2)$, $m_1 = 1, 2, ..., N_1/n_1$, $m_2 = 1, 2, ..., N_2/n_2$. The arrays (1) will be represented by the corresponding vectors

$$\mathbf{V}(m_1, m_2) = [v_1(m_1, m_2), v_2(m_1, m_2), ..., v_q(m_1, m_2)]^T, \qquad (2)$$

where we identify: $q = n_1 \cdot n_2$, $m_1 = 1, 2, ..., M_1$, $m_2 = 1, 2, ..., M_2$, $v_1(m_1, m_2) = y_{11}(m_1, m_2), ..., v_q(m_1, m_2) = y_{n_1, n_2} m_1, m_2$. That means that the original image is represented by $\frac{N_1 \cdot N_2}{q}$ vectors $\mathbf{V}(m_1, m_2)$. The successive input vectors to the encoder $\mathbf{V}(t)$, $t = 1, 2, ..., \frac{N_1 \cdot N_2}{q}$ (see Fig. 1), correspond to vectors $\mathbf{V}(m_1, m_2)$ in the line-by-line order.

3   Neural PVQ Algorithm

The architecture of the predictive vector quantization algorithm (PVQ) is depicted in Fig.1. This architecture is a vector extension of the scalar differential pulse code modulation (DPCM) scheme [3],[5] plus Huffman coding.

The block diagram of the PVQ algorithm consists of an encoder and decoder, each containing an identical neural-predictor, codebook and neural vector quantizer, Huffman coder The successive input vectors $\mathbf{V}(t)$ are introduced to the encoder and the difference $\mathbf{E}(t) = [e_1(t), e_2(t), ..., e_q(t)]^T$ given by the equation

$$\mathbf{E}(t) = \mathbf{V}(t) - \overline{\mathbf{V}}(t) \qquad (3)$$

is formed, where: $\overline{\mathbf{V}}(t) = [\bar{v}_1(t), \bar{v}_2(t), ..., \bar{v}_q(t)]^T$ is the predictor of $\mathbf{V}(t)$. Statistically, the difference $\mathbf{E}(t)$ requires fewer quantization bits than the original subimage $\mathbf{V}(t)$. The next step is vector quantization of $\mathbf{E}(t)$ using the set of reproduction vectors $\mathbf{G} = [\mathbf{g}_0, \mathbf{g}_1, ..., \mathbf{g}_J]$ (codebook), where $\mathbf{g}_j = [g_{1j}, g_{2j}, ..., g_{qj}]^T$.(codewords). For every q-dimensional difference vector $\mathbf{E}(t)$, the distortion (usually the mean square error) between $\mathbf{E}(t)$ and every codeword $\mathbf{g}_j$, $j = 0, 1, ..., J - 1$ is computed. The codeword $\mathbf{g}_{j^0}(t)$ is selected as the representation vector for $\mathbf{E}(t)$ if

$$d_{j^0} = \min_{0 \leq j \leq J} d_j, \qquad (4)$$

a measure d in expression (4) we can take e.g. the Euclidean distance. Observe that by adding the prediction vector $\overline{\mathbf{V}}(t)$ to the quantized difference vector $\mathbf{g}_{j^0}(t)$ we get the reconstructed approximation $\widetilde{\mathbf{V}}(t)$ of the original input vector $\mathbf{V}(t)$, i.e.

$$\widetilde{\mathbf{V}}(t) = \overline{\mathbf{V}}(t) + \mathbf{g}_{j^0}(t). \qquad (5)$$

The prediction vector $\overline{\mathbf{V}}(t)$ of the input vector $\mathbf{V}(t)$ is made from past observation of reconstructed vector $\widetilde{\mathbf{V}}(t-1)$. The predictor in our approach is a

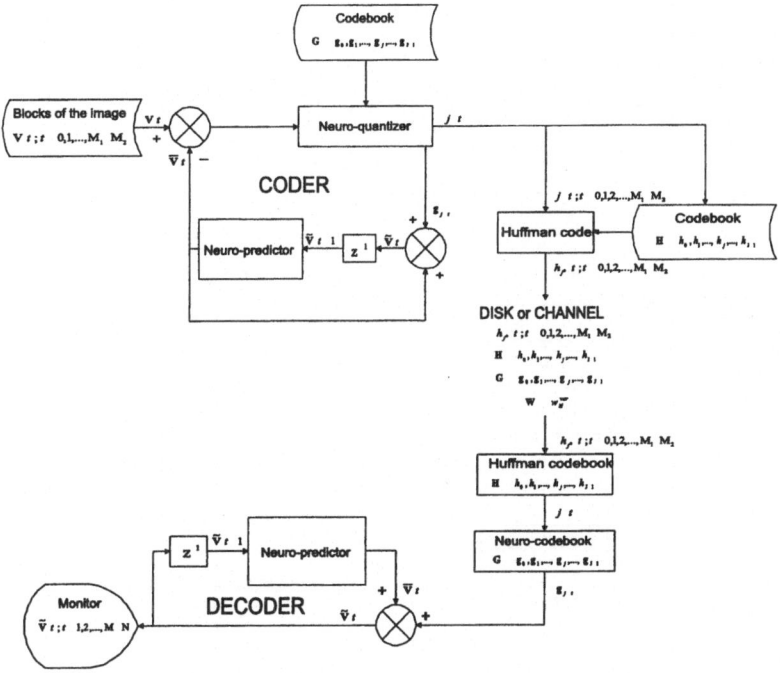

Fig. 1. PVQ+Huffman compression algorithm

nonlinear neural network specially designed for this purpose. Finally, the set of the $j^0(t)$ is coded by Huffman coder. The codebook of the Huffman coder is designed using set of counters f_j which count how frequently given label $j^0(t)$ araises after presentation of all vectors $\mathbf{V}(t)$. The appropriate codewords $h^0(t)$ from the Huffman codebook are broadcasted via the transmission channel to the decoder. In the decoder, first the codewords $h^0(t)$ transmitted by the channel are decoded using the Huffman codebook and then inverse vector-quantized. Next, the reconstructed vector $\widetilde{\mathbf{V}}(t)$ is formed in the same manner as in the encoder (see formula (5)).

3.1   The Modified Closed-Loop Procedure

The design of the presented compression algorithm requires first a parallel predictor and a codebook design and next a determination of the Huffman coder. The modified closed-loop methodology of this procedure is shown in Fig 2. This approach contains several steps: a)Design of the initial neural predictor based on the residuals; b)Generation of an initial codebook using open-loop methodology; c)Sequentially performed procedure of the new codebook calculation using unsupervised learning algorithm and then adjustment of the neural predictor through the supervised learning. The process is stopped after achieving the satisfied low level of the compression error. d)Determination of the Huffman codebook.

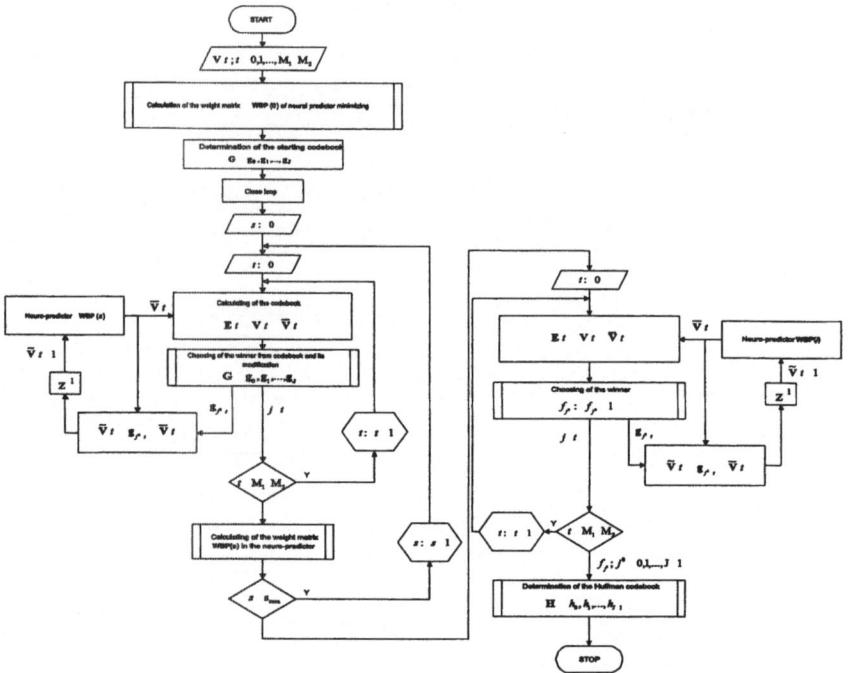

Fig. 2. Diagram of the modified closed-loop methodology

Predictor based on neural networks. The supervised neural network is proposed to design a nonlinear predictor [4]. The first structure is a three layer network with forward propagation This neural network is designed as follows: number of inputs and outputs is equal $q = 16$, the structure of the net is 16-8-16 neurons in particular layers, and the sigmoid activation function of the neurons in the output layer is scaled by 255. The second neural network structure is a single layer network with 8 neurons In both cases, during the learning process we attempt to minimize the mean square error taking the following form

$$Q = \sum_{t=1}^{M_1 M_2} \sum_{i=1}^{q} \left(y_i(t) - \tilde{v}_i(t) \right)^2, \tag{6}$$

where $y_i(t)$ is the k-th neural network output. Obviously, the input of the net is $\tilde{v}_i(t-1)$; $i = 1, 2, ..., q$. The weights matrix $\mathbf{WBP}(s)$ can be found by the back-propagation method.

Generation of an initial codebook. We will find the codebook $\mathbf{G}(0) = [\mathbf{g}_0, \mathbf{g}_1, ..., \mathbf{g}_J]$, $\mathbf{g}_j = [g_{1j}, g_{2j}, ..., g_{qj}]^T$, $j = 0, 1, ..., J-1$, where J = size of the code-book, minimizing the performance measure

$$D = \sum_{t=1}^{M_1 M_2} d\left[\mathbf{E}\left(t\right), \mathbf{g}_{j^o}\left(t\right)\right]^2, \tag{7}$$

where:

$$d\left[\mathbf{E}\left(t\right), \mathbf{g}_{j^o}\left(t\right)\right] = \min_{0 \le j \le J}\left\{d\left[\mathbf{E}\left(t\right), \mathbf{g}_j\right]\right\}, \tag{8}$$

and d is the distortion (usually chosen as the mean square error) between the vector $\mathbf{E}\left(t\right)$ and the code vector $\mathbf{g}_j$. The code-vector $\mathbf{g}_{j^o}\left(t\right)$ with the minimum distortion is called the "winner". Because of its properties, the neural network is able to create the code-book $\mathbf{G}$ as a result of learning. For this purpose we can use a single-layer neural network.

The elements of the input vector $\mathbf{E}\left(t\right) = \left[e_1\left(t\right), e_2\left(t\right), ..., e_q\left(t\right)\right]^T$ are connected to every neural unit having the weights $\mathbf{W}_j\left(0\right) = \left[w_{1j}\left(0\right), w_{2j}\left(0\right), ..., w_{qj}\left(0\right)\right]^T$ and the output z_j, $j = 0, 1, ..., J$. The weights $\mathbf{W}_j$ are considered to be the code-vectors, i.e.

$$\mathbf{G}\left(0\right) = \left[\mathbf{g}_0\left(0\right), \mathbf{g}_1\left(0\right), ..., \mathbf{g}_J\left(0\right)\right] = \left[\mathbf{W}_1\left(0\right), \mathbf{W}_2\left(0\right), ..., \mathbf{W}_J\left(0\right)\right], \tag{9}$$

and the number of neural units J+1 is the size of the codebook.

The weights $\mathbf{W}_j\left(0\right)$ will be determined by making use of the unsupervised neural networks. We used the frequency-sensitive competitive learning (FSCL) network [3],[5] where F is a suitably chosen function of the counter f_j. The recursive procedure takes the form

$$\mathbf{W}_{j^o}\left(0\right)\left(t+1\right) = \mathbf{W}_{j^o}\left(0\right)\left(t\right) + H\left(f_{j^o}\right)\left(\mathbf{E}\left(t\right) - \mathbf{W}_{j^o}\left(0\right)\left(t\right)\right), \tag{10}$$

where H is another function of the counter f_{j^o}. The counter f_{j^o} counts how frequently the neural unit j is the "winner".

4   Experimental Results

The tested image was a standard picture "Lena" ($N_1 \times N_2 = 512 \times 512$ frame of size, 256 grey levels for each pixel and blocks of image 4×4 pixels). The experiment shows realisation of the presented compression scheme: with nonlinear neural predictors described in this paper. In Fig. 3a we show the original and in Fig. 3b the reconstructed image "Lena" image for the code-book size = 512, twenty loops and the FSCL algorithm. In this case MSE = 32,70 and SNR = 23.33.

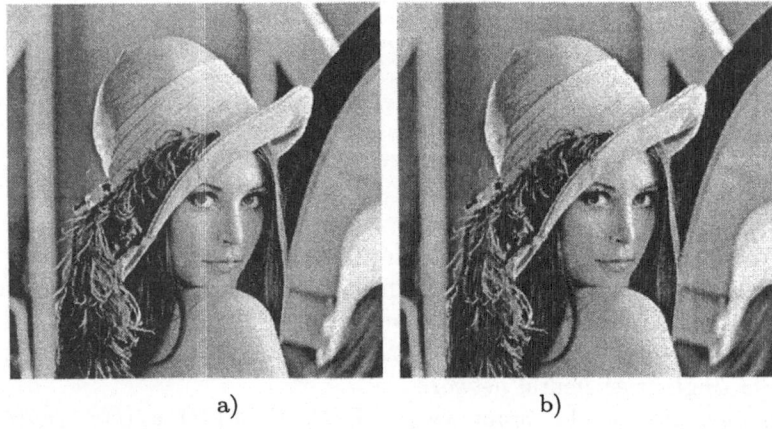

a)   b)

Fig. 3. The original image "Lena" a), the reconstructed image "Lena" b)

References

[1] Gray R.: Vector quantization. IEEE ASSP Magazine (1984) 4-29
[2] Gersho A., Gray R. M.: Vector quantization a. signal compression, Kluwer Academic Publishers (1992)
[3] Rutkowski L., Cierniak R.: Image compression by competitive learning neural networks and predictive vector quantization, Applied Mathematics and Computer Science. **6** (1996)
[4] Manikopoulos C. N.: Neural networks approach to DPCM system designe for image coding. IEE Proceedings-I (1992)
[5] Cierniak R., Rutkowski L.: On image compression by competitive neural networks and optimal linear predictors. Signal Processing: Image Communication - a Eurosip Journal, Elsevier Science B. V., **15** (2000) 559-565

Fuzzy Nonparametric Measures for Image Matching

Boguslaw Cyganek and Jan Borgosz

AGH - University of Science and Technology,
Al. Mickiewicza 30, 30-059 Krakow, Poland
{cyganek,borgosz}@agh.edu.pl

Abstract. Many correlation measures have been already proposed for image matching. The special group with quite different statistical properties constitute the nonparametric measures. Their virtue in the task of image matching lies mostly in the known distribution function and resistance against local image fluctuations and outliers. In this paper the fuzzy enhancement of the nonparametric measures is proposed. It allows for better representation of the local relations among image pixels. The presented concepts are underpinned by many experiments which results are also provided and discussed.

1 Introduction

The key concept behind the nonparametric correlation measures lies in changing a given value from a statistical sample by its rank among all the other values in that sample. This way, the resulting list of new values has the *uniform* distribution function. Therefore the correlating statistics deals only with uniform sets of integers. The two examples of such correlation measures are Spearman's rank-order or Kendall's τ [7].

The nonparametric measures were introduced to image processing by Zabih and Woodfill [9] and Bhat and Nayar [2]. Their Census and Rank measures are computed from the local neighborhoods of pixels based on relations among neighboring pixels. Their values are then compared to find out the correlation measure. They have proved great usefulness in stereo image matching [1],[3] and also in image processing with neural networks [4].

In this paper the fuzzy [10],[6] enhancement to the nonparametric measure for image matching is proposed. Its "fuzziness" comes from the fuzzy rules for pixel comparisons. These rules comprise also an expert knowledge on "importance" of pixels differences and possible saturations.

2 Fuzzy Nonparametric Measures for Local Neighborhoods

The local 3×3 neighborhood of pixels is shown in Fig. 1. The key role plays a central pixel at index c. All other pixels have to be set in an ordered fashion, for which an exemplary ordering is proposed in Fig. 1.

L. Rutkowski et al. (Eds.): ICAISC 2004, LNAI 3070, pp. 712–717, 2004.
© Springer-Verlag Berlin Heidelberg 2004

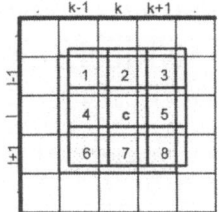

Fig. 1. Explanation of the 3×3 neighborhoods of pixels *P(i)*. Visible pixel ordering. The central pixel, denoted as **c**, is a reference pixel

For the central pixel *P(c)* and each other pixel *P(i)* from its closest neighborhood we define a fuzzy relation: $R_f(P(c), P(i))$ in a form presented in Table 1. The proposed rules were set based on the observation on "closeness" of pixels intensities and the phenomenon of saturation for large discrepancies in intensity values. In many experiments it was observed that it is important to distinguish cases where pixels are identical (taking into an account noise) or "a little" different. At the same time for "much bigger" differences it was usually sufficient to provide information on direction of such change.

Table 1. Fuzzy rules for relation between pixels based on their relative intensity value

	Fuzzy rule for relation between pixels: $R_f(P(c), P(i))$
1	strongly smaller
2	smaller
3	little smaller
4	equal
5	little greater
6	greater
7	strongly greater

The piecewise-linear membership function $\mu_F(i)$ realizing the rules in Table 1 can be constructed simply by providing appropriate threshold values. However, a set of at least six thresholds is cumbersome in many practical implementations. Therefore in this paper a more compact membership function is proposed as follows:

$$\mu_F^{(1)}(i) = \frac{1}{1 + e^{-\alpha(P(c) - P(i))}} \tag{1}$$

where $P(i)$ is an intensity value for a pixel at position i in the neighborhood, c is a position of the central pixel, α is a constant. Alternatively, the following membership function can be used:

$$\mu_F^{(2)}(i) = \frac{1}{2} + \frac{1}{2} \tanh\left[\alpha\left(P(c) - P(i)\right)\right] \tag{2}$$

where the parameters are the same as in (1). The sigmoidal function (1) and hyperbolic (2) change rapidly (with a rate determined by the coefficient α) if the pixels are "close" and get into saturation in cases of significant differences – see Fig. 2. The both functions return values in a range: 0 to 1. The parameter α is arbitrarily set based on experiments – usually from 0.5 to 5.0.

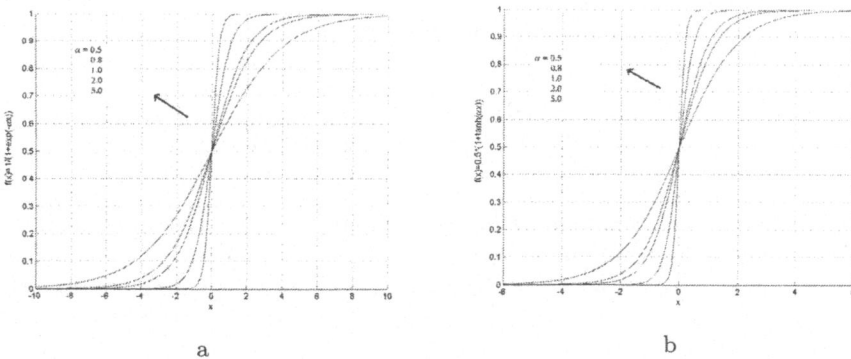

Fig. 2. Plots of the fuzzy membership functions $\mu_F(i)$ for comparison of pixel intensities: the sigmoidal function (a), the hyperbolic function (b)

Applying (1) or (2) to all pixels from a given neighborhood results in a membership vector $\mu_F(c)$.

3   Correlation with Fuzzy Nonparametric Measures

Image correlation follows computation of fuzzy membership vectors for each pixel of the images. The fuzzy rules can be applied to solve this task [8].

Let us assume some matching window W conceived as a set of indexes of pixels belonging to a certain compact sub-area of a given image. Taking two such windows, each in an image to be compared, we can determine their correlation as follows:

$$C^{(i)}(W_1, W_2) =$$
$$= \frac{1}{1+N_1+N_2} \sum_{(p_1,q_1)\in W} \sum_{(p_2,q_2)\in W_2} \left| \mu_1^{(i)}(p_1, q_1) - \mu_2^{(i)}(p_2, q_2) \right| \qquad (3)$$

where W_1 and W_2 are pixel windows in the two images, $\mu_r^{(i)}(p_k, q_k)$ is the i–th membership function for image r, determined at pixel of indexes $(p_k, q_k)\in W_k$, N_1 and N_2 are normalizing values determined as follows:

$$N_r^{(i)} = \sum_{(p_k,q_k)\in W_k} \left| 2\mu_r^{(i)}(p_1, q_1) - 1 \right| \qquad (4)$$

An addition of 1 in (3) assures values different from 0 in the denominator.

For each pixel in the reference window the formula (3) assumes computation of its absolute difference with *each* pixel in the second window. Such computation is very time consuming. Therefore the simplified version of (3) and (4) is proposed which assumes the same size of the two comparison windows W_1 and W_2, as follows:

$$C^{(i)}(p_0, q_0, K, L) =$$
$$= \frac{1}{1+N_1+N_2} \sum_{k=0}^{K} \sum_{l=0}^{L} \left| \mu_1^{(i)}(p_0 + k, q_0 + l) - \mu_2^{(i)}(p_0 + k, q_0 + l) \right| \quad (5)$$

$$N_r^{(i)} = \sum_{k=0}^{K} \sum_{l=0}^{L} \left| 2\mu_r^{(i)}(p_0 + k, q_0 + l) - 1 \right| \quad (6)$$

where K and L are constants defining a rectangular pixel window in the two images with its top-left corner at (p_0, q_0).

Based on the measure (5) we have to decide on a degree of "similarity" of the compared regions. This can be done in a fuzzy fashion - Table 2.

Table 2. Fuzzy rules for relation between pixels based on their relative intensity value

	Fuzzy rule for similarity	Condition on the membership function (7)
1	similarity	$\mu_S(C^{(i)}) = 1$
2	questionable similarity	$\mu_S(C^{(i)}) > \frac{1}{2}$
3	dissimilarity	$0 \leq \mu_S(C^{(i)}) \leq \frac{1}{2}$

The fuzzy reasoning described in Table 2 is realized by the following piecewise-linear membership function $\mu_S(C^{(i)})$ and its complement $1-\mu_S(C^{(i)})$ describing fuzzy degree of similarity and dissimilarity, respectively.

$$\mu_S\left(C^{(i)}\right) = \begin{cases} 1 \text{ if } C^{(i)} \leq \vartheta_1 \\ \frac{\vartheta_2 - C^{(i)}}{\vartheta_2 - \vartheta_1} \text{ if } C^{(i)} > \vartheta_1 \end{cases} \quad (7)$$

where ϑ_1 and ϑ_2 are threshold values and $C^{(i)}$ is defined by (5).

Having defined the fuzzy comparison measure $\mu_S(C^{(i)})$ and its complement we can say that two regions *can* be considered as matching if and only if $\mu_S(C^{(i)}) > [1-\mu_S(C^{(i)})]$, i.e. when the following condition holds:

$$\mu_S\left(C^{(i)}\right) > \frac{1}{2} \quad (8)$$

Finally, taking (7) and (8) together we obtain the fuzzy assignments in the last column of Table 2. It is also a result of (7) that the condition on the "strong" similarity, i.e. $\mu_S(C^{(i)}) = 1$, holds if $C^{(i)} \leq \vartheta_1$.

4   Experimental Results

All of the presented fuzzy algorithms were implemented in C++ and built into the software processing platform, presented at the previous ICNNSC [5]. The test stereo pairs are presented in Fig. 3.

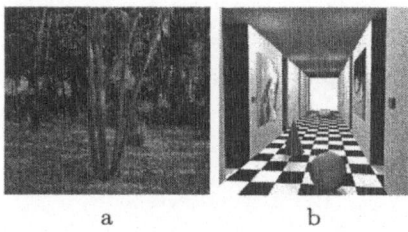

a   b

Fig. 3. Test stereo pairs: "Trees" (real) (a), "Corridor" (art.) (b)

Resulting disparity maps for "Trees" are presented in Fig. 4. The first disparity map (Fig. 4a) was obtained with the SAD measure. Visible are many false matches. The second disparity map (Fig. 4b) was computed with the Census 3×3 measure. Disparity maps obtained with the proposed fuzzy measure are presented in Fig. 4c and median filtered in Fig. 4d. The better quality of the last disparity maps is evident. However, this is at the cost of computation time which is 44 s for the latter.Fig. 5a contains the disparity maps for the artificial pair "Corridor". Fig. 5b presents this disparity map filtered by the 3×3 median filter to remove false matches. However, in the case of artificial images quality of the resulting disparity maps is very similar for the "classical" and fuzzy measures.

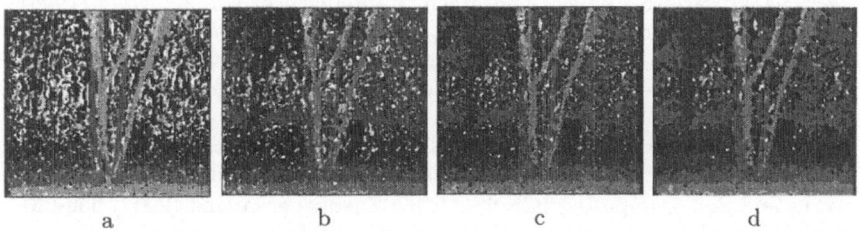

a   b   c   d

Fig. 4. Disparity maps of the stereo pair "Trees". Comparison with the SAD measure (a), comparison with the Census 3×3 measure (b). Comparison with the fuzzy measure from Table 1 (c), disparity map filtered with the median filter (d)

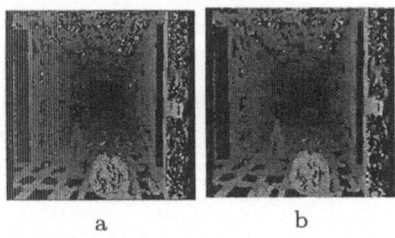

a   b

Fig. 5. Disparity maps of the stereo pair "Trees". Comparison with the fuzzy measure from Table 1 (a), disparity map filtered with the median filter (b)

5   Conclusions

This paper presents the fuzzy nonparametric transformation of local neighborhoods of pixels, as well as fuzzy rules for image matching. This novel approach allows for better representation of pixel relations in the local neighborhoods of pixels. Such a transformation changes statistical distribution of data and allows for elimination of local image distortions and noise. In effect, the more reliable matching is possible what was shown based on experiments with stereo matching.

This paper is a result of research work registered in KBN The State Committee for Scientific Research of Poland at number 4 T11D 005 25 and its publication is sponsored from KBN founds.

References

1. Banks J., Bennamoun M., Corke P.: Non-Parametric Techniques for Fast and Robust Stereo Matching. CSIRO Manufacturing Science and Technology, Australia (1997)
2. Bhat D.N., Nayar S.K.: Ordinal Measures for Image Correspondence. IEEE Transactions on Pattern Analysis and Machine Intelligence, Vol. 20, No. 4 (1998)
3. Cyganek, B., Borgosz, J.: A Comparative Study of Performance and Implementation of Some Area-Based Stereo Algorithms. LNCS 2124 (2001) 709-716
4. Cyganek, B.: Three Dimensional Image Processing (in Polish). EXIT Warsaw (2002)
5. Cyganek, B., Borgosz J.: A Software Platform for Evaluation of Neural Algorithms for Stereo Image Processing. IEEE Sixth International Conference on Neural Networks and Soft Computing ICNNSC-2002, Zakopane, Poland (2002) 656-661
6. Kecman, V.: Learning and Soft Computing. MIT Press (2001)
7. Press W.H., Teukolsky S.A., Vetterling W.T., Flannery B.P.: Numerical Recipes in C. The Art of Scientific Computing. Second Edition. Cambridge University Press (1999)
8. Shankar, B.U., Ghosh, A. , Pal, S.K.: On Fuzzy Thresholding of Remotely Sensed Images in Soft Computing for Image Processing. Springer (2000) 130-161
9. Zabih, R., Woodfill, J.: Non-Parametric Local Transforms for Computing Visual Correspondence. Proc. Third European Conf. Computer Vision (1994) 150-158
10. Zadeh, L.A.: Fuzzy sets. Information and Control, 8 (1965) 338-353

Neural Computation of the Fundamental Matrix

Boguslaw Cyganek

AGH - University of Science and Technology,
Al. Mickiewicza 30, 30-059 Krakow, Poland
{cyganek}@agh.edu.pl

Abstract. The fundamental matrix combines the mutual relation of the corresponding points in the two images of an observed scene. This relation, known also as an epipolar geometry, allows for a further depth reconstruction, image rectification or camera calibration. Thus, computation of the fundamental matrix has been one of the most important problems of computer vision. Many linear and non-linear methods were already proposed to solve this problem. However, due to the nature of image processing there is no unique solution and each method exhibits some exclusive properties. In this paper a neural approach to the computation of the fundamental matrix is proposed. For this purpose, the special configuration of the back-propagation neural network was developed. Both, linear and non-linear versions are also discussed.

1 Introduction

The fundamental matrix plays a central role in computer vision. This is caused by the fact that the fundamental matrix determines the epipolar geometry of observed scene. The fundamental matrix can be then used for scene reconstruction, image rectification, computation of projective invariants or stereo matching [7],[4],[2].

There are many methods to compute the fundamental matrix. They can be divided into linear and nonlinear ones [8],[4]. The fundamental matrix can be determined linearly by providing eight corresponding points [8] or even seven points with some additional computations [7]. Further Hartley showed that a special normalization procedure can make the linear methods more numerically stable and robust in respect to outliers [6]. The nonlinear methods are usually more accurate but at the cost of computation time and numerical complexity. The most common are: the algebraic minimization method, the iterative-minimization method with Sampson cost function, the Gold Standard algorithm or RANSAC [1],[7],[8],[9],[4].

All of the mentioned methods have some advantages and peculiarities. It is very interesting whether the fundamental matrix can be estimated by neural networks and what would be the results of such an approach. This paper tries to answer these questions by providing appropriate neural networks and related experimental results.

L. Rutkowski et al. (Eds.): ICAISC 2004, LNAI 3070, pp. 718–723, 2004.
© Springer-Verlag Berlin Heidelberg 2004

2   Epipolar Geometry and the Fundamental Matrix

The stereo setup of the two cameras is presented in Fig. 1.

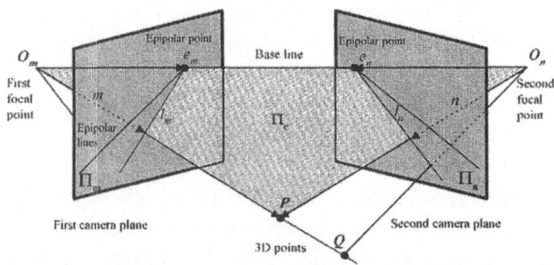

Fig. 1. Epipolar geometry of a stereo camera setup. All images of 3D points of opaque objects can lie only on corresponding epipolar lines. Π_l and Π_r are left and right camera planes

It is assumed that the cameras can be represented by a pinhole model. For each non occluded 3D point, belonging to an opaque object, we obtain two image points, each on a different camera plane, Π_m or Π_n. The image points are related by the formula:

$$\mathbf{m}^{\mathbf{T}}\mathbf{F}\mathbf{n} = 0 \tag{1}$$

where $m = [m_1, m_2, m_3]$ and $n = [n_1, n_2, n_3]$ are left and right image points expressed in the homogeneous (thus three components in a 2D point representation; usually $m_3 = n_3 = 1$) coordinate systems associated with their image planes, F is a fundamental matrix which determines an epipolar geometry associated with a given camera setup [2].

Thus, knowledge of the matrix F allows us to find epipolar lines in the forms: $l_m = Fn$, $l_n = F^T m$, for the left and right cameras, respectively. In a case of a stereo correspondence this limits the search to one dimension.

Taking into account homogeneous representation of points, the formula (1) for a given single pair of matched points, can be expressed in the following form:

$$\mathbf{u}^{\mathbf{T}}\mathbf{f} = \sum_{i=1}^{9} u_i f_i = 0 \tag{2}$$

where

$$\mathbf{u} = [m_1 n_1, m_2 n_1, n_1, m_1 n_2, m_2 n_2, n_2, m_1, m_2, 1]^{\mathbf{T}} \tag{3}$$

$$\mathbf{f} = [F_{11}, F_{12}, F_{13}, F_{21}, F_{22}, F_{23}, F_{31}, F_{32}, F_{33}]^{\mathbf{T}} \tag{4}$$

Solution to the (2) and (3, 4) can be found linearly when at least eight point correspondences are known, since the matrix F has rank eight, although it has nine parameters. This can be done by a simple SVD decomposition, however, the input coordinates should be normalized to assure better numerical stability [6]. In practice, due to image noise and inaccuracies in point matching, the matrix F has rank nine what in a case of simple linear method unfortunately leads to the trivial zero solution. In this case, and also in a overspecified system of equations – when more than eight point correspondences exits – (2) can be found in a least-squares sense as follows [7]:

$$\min_{\|\mathbf{f}\|=1} \|\mathbf{Uf}\|^2 = \min_{\|\mathbf{f}\|=1} (\mathbf{f}^T \mathbf{U}^T \mathbf{Uf}) \tag{5}$$

where rows of the matrix U are created from the point correspondences in a form of vectors u^T. The solution to (5) is the unit eigenvector corresponding to the smallest eigenvalue of $U^T U$. The formulas (2) and (5) create foundation for neural processing.

3   Neural Networks for Computation of the Fundamental Matrix

The formula (2) can be directly used to construct *a fundamental neural network* with one input layer fed by the input signals u (3), one output neuron and synaptic weights formed by the sought coefficients of the matrix f - see Fig. 2a.

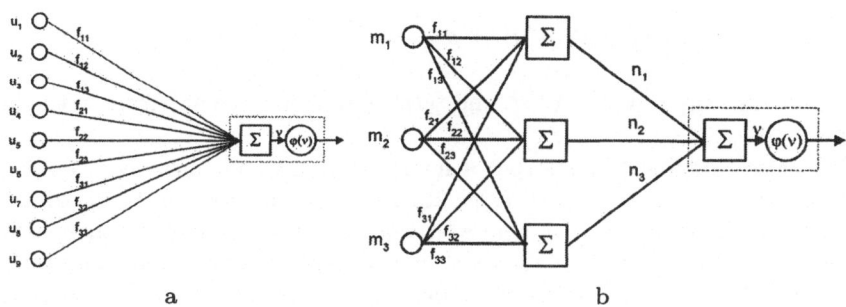

Fig. 2. Neural network for computation of the fundamental matrix (a fundamental neural network). The input signal u is composed from homogeneous coordinates of the corresponding points. The matrix elements are obtained as weights of the input layer after training (a),Neural network for direct computation of the fundamental matrix. It holds that $m_3 = n_3 = 1$ (b)

The role of an additional processing element $\varphi(\nu)$ can be comprehended applying $\varphi(.)$ to (2):

$$\varphi\left(\mathbf{u}^T \mathbf{f}\right) = \varphi(\sum_{i=1}^{9} u_i f_i) = \varphi(0) \tag{6}$$

where $\varphi(.)$ is the perceptron activation function. If $\varphi(.)$ is linear then we obtain directly (2) as a special case.

It was already pointed out that in practice the point matching process is burdened with inaccuracies in position measurements and image noise. Therefore let us analyze (6) in respect to a small change h of the input parameter u. Such a scrutiny can be easily done with help of the Taylor expansion as follows:

$$\varphi\left((\mathbf{u_0}+\mathbf{h})^\mathbf{T}\mathbf{f}\right) = \varphi\left(\mathbf{u_0^T}\mathbf{f}\right) + \mathbf{h^T}\nabla\varphi\left(\mathbf{u_0^T}\mathbf{f}\right) + \frac{1}{2}\mathbf{h^T}\left[\nabla^2\varphi\left(\mathbf{u_0^T}\mathbf{f}\right)\right]\mathbf{h} + \Re \quad (7)$$

where $\Re$ is the remainder term. Assuming that $\varphi(\text{x})=1/(1+e^{-\alpha x})$ is the logistic function and disregarding all higher series terms, we obtain the following approximation:

$$\varphi\left((\mathbf{u_0}+\mathbf{h})^\mathbf{T}\mathbf{f}\right) = \varphi\left(\mathbf{u_0^T}\mathbf{f}\right) + \mathbf{h^T}\mathbf{f}\alpha\varphi\left(\mathbf{u_0^T}\mathbf{f}\right)\left[1 - \varphi\left(\mathbf{u_0^T}\mathbf{f}\right)\right] \quad (8)$$

where α is a slope parameter of the sigmoid. Now comparing (8), where it was assumed that $\varphi(.)$ is the logistic function, with a case when $\varphi(.)$ is linear, we observe that the second term of expansion (8) differs by a multiplicative coefficient ρ:

$$\rho = \alpha\varphi\left(\mathbf{u_0^T}\mathbf{f}\right)\left[1 - \varphi\left(\mathbf{u_0^T}\mathbf{f}\right)\right] \quad (9)$$

Assuming further that the network is trained (or closed to be trained) then from (2) and (6) for the sigmoid we find that:

$$\varphi\left(\mathbf{u_0^T}\mathbf{f}\right) \to \varphi(0) \Rightarrow \rho \to \alpha\varphi(0)\left[1 - \varphi(0)\right] = \frac{\alpha}{4} \quad (10)$$

Therefore, as long as $\alpha < 4$ the second term is attenuated comparing to the linear case.

It is also possible to construct a neural network that directly realizes (1). Such a network is presented in Fig. 2b. However, in practice it appeared that the network shown in Fig. 2a exposed better training parameters (such as faster convergence and smaller dependence on initial weight parameters). It was already mentioned that it is possible to construct a fundamental neural network starting from (5) instead of (2). We easily perceive that such a formulation directly leads to the PCA problem, formulated for search of the eigenvector corresponding to the *smallest* eigenvalue. Thus, it can be realized by a feedforward network with the Hebbian-based minimum eigenfilter [10]. Alternatively, the APEX or kernel-based PCA algorithms [5] can be used to solve for the fundamental matrix. In all cases, the fundamental matrix is formed from weights of the neural network *after* this network is fully trained.

4   Experimental Results

All of the presented algorithms were implemented in C++ and built into the neural processing platform, presented at the previous ICNNSC [3]. Experiments were done with about ten different stereo pairs. Fig. 3 presents one stereo pair

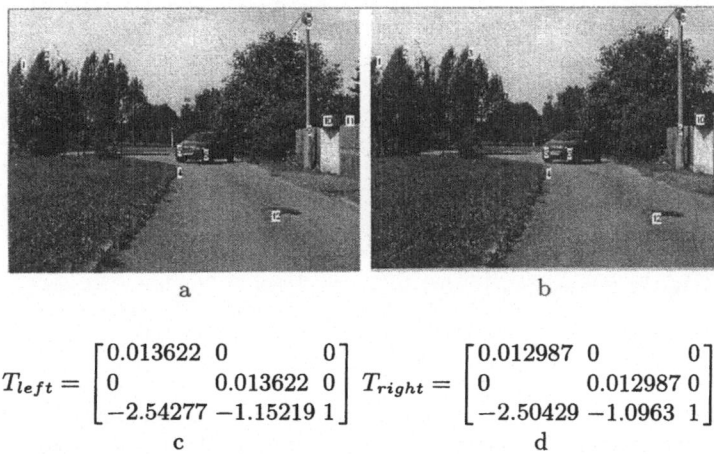

$$T_{left} = \begin{bmatrix} 0.013622 & 0 & 0 \\ 0 & 0.013622 & 0 \\ -2.54277 & -1.15219 & 1 \end{bmatrix} \quad T_{right} = \begin{bmatrix} 0.012987 & 0 & 0 \\ 0 & 0.012987 & 0 \\ -2.50429 & -1.0963 & 1 \end{bmatrix}$$

c   d

Fig. 3. The pair "Fiat" with matching points: left image (a), right image (b), left points transformation matrix T_{left} (c), right points transformation matrix T_{right} (d)

"Fiat". As alluded to previously, coordinates of the matched points are normalized before matrix F is computed so that the centroid of the points is at the origin and the average distance from the origin is equal to $\sqrt{2}$. The transformation matrixes are in Fig. 3(c-d). For both topologies the back-propagation learning method in a sequential mode (i.e. weights update is performed on each training example) was used. Choice of initial weight values is very important for the further network operation. They were generated by a uniform random generator in the range close in magnitude to the range of transformed point coordinates. Due to proper data normalization the network convergence was always achieved. Learning parameters are presented in Fig. 4. The computed fundamental matrix computed by means of the network from Fig. 2a is visible in Fig. 5(a), and for network from Fig. 2b in Fig. 5(b).

5 Conclusions

This paper concerns application of the neural networks to the computer vision problem of finding the fundamental matrix. To the best of our knowledge, it is the first such a report. The two feedforward configurations of the neural networks have been presented and discussed. The first one is a single nonlinear perceptron. The second one, due to an additional hidden layer, directly accepts point coordinates. In both networks the sigmoidal activation function was applied as a nonlinear element. For this case it was shown theoretically that a nonlinear processing element stabilizes network response on small changes in the input signal. This increases system robustness on point outliers when the network approaches a stable point. The additional structures of fundamental neural networks were also proposed: the feedforward Hebbian-based eigenfilter, the APEX and

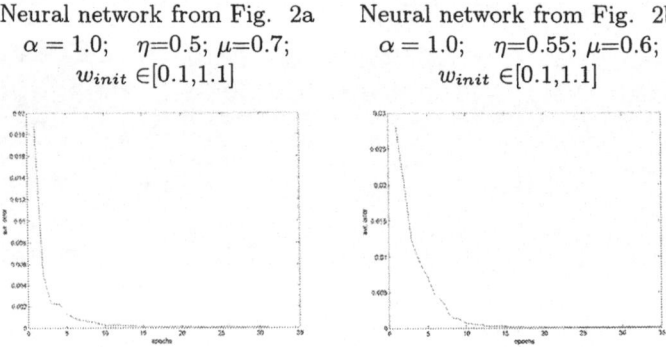

Neural network from Fig. 2a   Neural network from Fig. 2b
$\alpha = 1.0$; η=0.5; μ=0.7; $\alpha = 1.0$; η=0.55; μ=0.6;
$w_{init} \in [0.1, 1.1]$ $w_{init} \in [0.1, 1.1]$

Fig. 4. Training parameters of the two neural networks (α - parameter of the sigmoid, η - training parameter, μ - momentum; w_{init} – initial values of weights)

$$\mathbf{F} = \begin{bmatrix} -0.03341 & -0.009806 & 0.01269 \\ -0.02030 & -0.0067 & 0.007814 \\ 0.013787 & 0.004134 & -0.005248 \end{bmatrix} \quad \mathbf{F} = \begin{bmatrix} -0.03897 & -0.024073 & 0.01535 \\ -0.01062 & -0.007828 & 0.004129 \\ 0.01550 & 0.009562 & -0.006107 \end{bmatrix}$$

a   b

Fig. 5. Computed fundamental matrixes for the stereo pair "Fiat": Neural network from Fig. 2a (a), Neural network from Fig. 2b (b)

kernel-based PCA neural network. These can pave a way for further research on fundamental neural networks.

References

1. Chesi G., Garulli A., Vicino A., Cipolla R.: On the Estimation of the Fundamental Matrix: A Convex Approach to Constrained Least-Squares. ECCV (2000)
2. Cyganek, B.: Three Dimensional Image Processing (in Polish). EXIT Warsaw (2002)
3. Cyganek, B., Borgosz J.: A Software Platform for Evaluation of Neural Algorithms for Stereo Image Processing. IEEE ICNNSC-2002, Poland (2002) 656-661
4. Faugeras, O.D., Luong, Q.-T.: The Geometry of Multiple Images. MIT Press (2001)
5. Haykin, S.: Neural Networks. A Comprehensive Foundation. Prentice Hall (1999)
6. Hartley, R.I.: In Defense of the Eight-Point Algorithm. PAMI, V.19, No. 6 (1997) 580-593
7. Hartley, R.I., Zisserman A.: Multiple View Geometry in Computer Vision. CUP (2000)
8. Luong Q.-T., Faugeras O.D.: The Fundamental matrix: theory, algorithms, and stability analysis. INRIA (1995)
9. Luong Q.-T., Deriche R., Faugeras O.D., Papadopoulo T.: On Determining the Fundamental Matrix: INRIA Technical Report No. 1894 (1993)
10. Tadeusiewicz R.: Neural Networks. RM Academic Publishing House, Warsaw (in Polish) (1993)

Face Detection Using CMAC Neural Network

H. Fashandi and M.S. Moin

Biometrics Research Laboratory, Information Society Group
Iran Telecommunication Research Center, P.O.Box 14155-3961, Tehran, Iran
{fashandi,moin}@itrc.ac.ir

Abstract. We present a new method based on CMAC neural network, used as classifier in a frontal face detection system. The gray level and the position of the pixels of an input image are directly presented to the network. Due to the simple structure of CMAC, with only one trainable layer, the training phase is very fast. The proposed method has been tested on a data set containing 960 faces and 20000 non-faces, selected among difficult face and non-face patterns. The results of experimentations exhibit an error rate of 8.5%, which is a reasonable result considering the simple structure of system and the important number of difficult patterns in the test dataset.

1 Introduction

Face detection is the process of determining whether or not there is (are) any face(s) in a given image, and then calculating the location of each detected face, or simply classifying the image into face or non-face classes. Face detection is the first step in almost any face processing system, including face identification, face verification and facial feature extraction. Due to the high degree of variations in face images, such as pose, facial expressions, lighting conditions, image orientations and imaging conditions, there are several challenges related to the problem of face detection. Obviously, the presence of color and motion in an image could facilitate the process of face detection; however, since these parameters are not common in face detection problems, to cover a wider range of applications, we focused our attention on still and gray level images.

Face detection methods can be classified in two main categories: feature-based and image-based [1][2]. Feature-based methods use explicit facial information as features and the decision is made based both on these features and the relation between them, such as geometrical distance between facial components, e.g. eyes [3]. Image based approaches use training algorithms, incorporating facial information implicitly into the system through mapping and training schemes. Examples of this category are neural networks [4][5], statistical approaches such as Hidden Markov Models [6] and Bayesian methods [7], Support Vector Machines [8], Linear subspace methods such as Principal Component Analysis (PCA) [9], Fisher Linear Discriminant and Factor Analysis [10][11].

In this paper we present a new method for face detection based on the CMAC neural network. The gray level and position of the image pixels are used as

L. Rutkowski et al. (Eds.): ICAISC 2004, LNAI 3070, pp. 724–729, 2004.
© Springer-Verlag Berlin Heidelberg 2004

network's inputs. Thus, there is no need to an additional feature extraction phase. This is a salient point of our approach, which helps to simplify the system's structure.

The rest of this paper is organized as follows: Section 2 describes CMAC neural network. Section 3 is dedicated to the process of face detection with CMAC. Section 4 contains experimental results and Section 5 is the conclusion.

2   CMAC Neural Network

The CMAC (Cerebellar Model Articulation Controller) was first introduced by Albus in 1975 as a simple model of the cortex of the cerebellum [12]. CMAC is a linear combination of overlapped basis functions. In CMAC, a set of neurons are activated locally by a particular input. Due to its properties such as local generalization, rapid computation, function approximation capability, and output superposition, CMAC has been widely used in a variety of applications, such as robot control, pattern recognition and signal processing systems.

Figure 1 shows a CMAC neural network with 3 overlapped layers in a bidimensional input space. The input space is quantized using a set of overlapping tiles (receptive fields). Each input vector activates only one tile in each layer and each tile has a unique address. In practical applications, the total number of tiles in input space can be extremely large. Thus, a majority of applications using CMAC are based on a hashing method, which requires a mapping between the virtual addresses of activated tiles and their corresponding physical addresses. The output of the network is the sum of the physical active weights.

During the training phase, only the weights of active tiles are updated as follows:

$$\Delta W_i = b \times (y_d - y) \ , \quad i = 1, \cdots, C \tag{1}$$

where W_i is the i-th weight in the physical memory, y_d is the desired output of the network, y is the current output of the network, b is the learning rate and C which is called generalization parameter determines the number of overlapping layers.

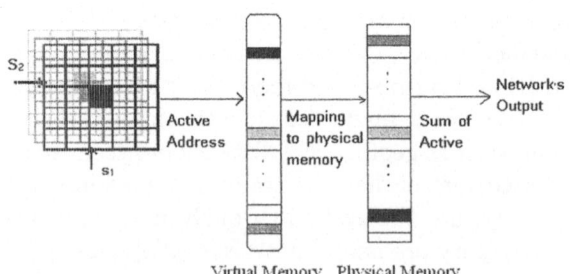

Fig. 1. Structure of a CMAC neural network

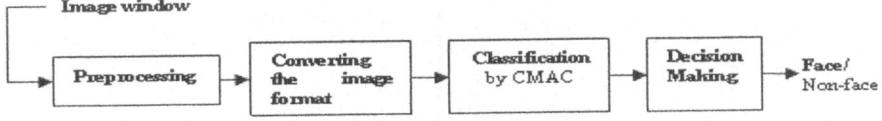

Fig. 2. Overview of our face detection system

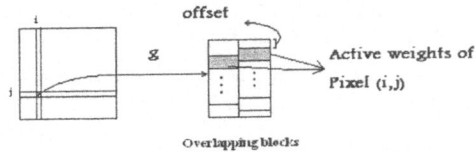

Fig. 3. Mapping a pixel to CMAC input space

3   System Overview

Figure 2 shows an overview of the system we implemented for face detection. In this section, we explain different parts of the system. **Image windowing:** To scan the input image, like many other face detection systems, we have used 19×19 pixel windows. This size is appropriate to maintain the dimensionality of the window vector space manageably small, without discarding distinctive visual features of face patterns. To locate faces with different sizes, this procedure is applied to different scales of the input image.

Preprocessing: The input image's details do not contain useful information for face detection and on the contrary, could also lead the procedure to false results. Thus, during the preprocessing phase, in addition to histogram equalization, an averaging mask of the size 3×3 is applied to each window to eliminate the high frequency components of the input image.

Converting the image format: In order to present an image to the CMAC neural net, first the $h \times w$ pixel image is converted to a vectorized format. Each pixel has a gray level between 0 and 255 and its position in the output vector depends on its position in input image, which is important information in the classification procedure. Each pixel is related to C overlapping blocks. The gray level range (between 0 and 255) is quantized into q levels. The gray level of an input pixel is located in one of these levels and thus, its corresponding weight in each layer is activated as shown in Figure 3. The overall structure of this part is shown in Figure 4-(a). If the input image has $h \times w$ pixels, the network would also have $h \times w$ blocks shown in Figure 3. **CMAC for Classification:** CMAC can be used as a classifier by making a suitable mapping between output space Z and the class label c. This mapping can be expressed as:

$$c = \begin{cases} face & , \quad z > 0 \\ non-face & , \quad z <= 0 \end{cases} \tag{2}$$

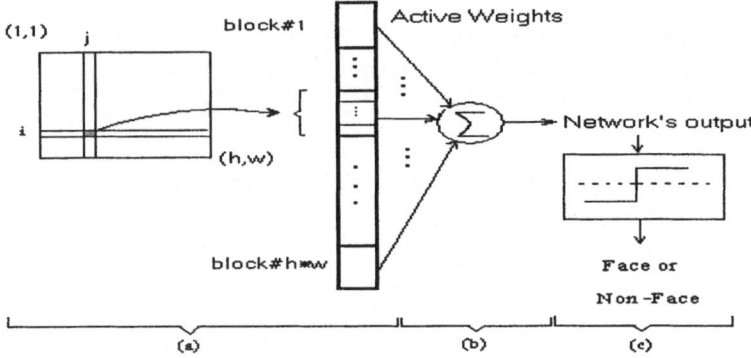

Fig. 4. Overall structure of the system: (a)Converting image format and presenting to the network, (b) Calculating network's output, (c) Decision Making

This step is shown in Figure 4-(c). Obviously, for multi-class problems, two thresholds should be fixed for each class to determine a region of acceptance. These threshold values may be set such as to divide up the scalar range of z into the number of classes to be represented [13].

At the beginning of the training phase, all the weights are set to zero. During the training phase, active weights of the network are updated as follows:

$$\Delta W_i = \beta_1 \times (y_d(S) - y(S)) + \beta_2 \times (y(S) - W[A_i]) \ , \ \ i = 1, \cdots, C \qquad (3)$$

where β_1 and β_2 are training gains, y_d is the desired value for input S, $y(S)$ is the network output, W is the physical memory and A_i is the address of active weights. Since the CMAC output is a sum over multiple weights, appropriate magnitude regularization is used to penalize individual weights, depending on their deviation from the sum. The desired values for face and non-face classes are set to 1 and -1, respectively.

4   Experimental Results

The initial training set for training the CMAC network contained 7000 face samples taken from CBCL[1] , ORL[2] and BioID[3] databases and 6548 non-face samples taken from non-face samples from CBCL database. We have used bootstrap technique to represent the difficult non-face samples once again to the network.

In order to determine the resolution of the network, i.e. the number of quantization levels, we have done multiple experiments on a data set of 960 faces and

---

[1] http://www.ai.mit.edu/projects/cbcl
[2] http://www.uk.research.att.com/facedatabase.html
[3] http://www.humanscan.de/support/downloads/facedb.php

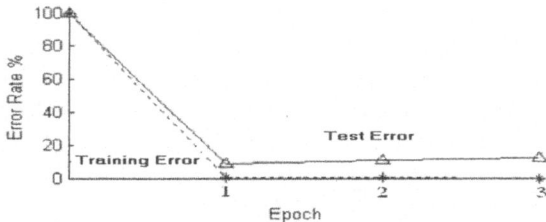

Fig. 5. Training and test errors

Fig. 6. Some samples of test data set

1000 non-faces. This resolution has been set to 70, which belongs to the network with the best result obtained on this test set.

We obtained an error rate of 8.5% on a test dataset containing 20000 non-face samples and 960 face samples. Figure 6 shows some samples of the test set. The diagram of training and test errors has been shown in Figure 5. As it is depicted in this figure, the training error reaches its minimum value after only two epochs, which indicates that the training phase is accomplished very fast. This is a result of the very simple structure of the network (with only one layer) and also its local generalization property. On the other hand, the error rate of 8.5% is obtained on a dataset containing difficult face and non-face samples, especially some non-faces that are very similar to faces (Fig. 6).

5   Conclusions

Face detection is a very complicated task, since: (1) there are a considerable number of non-face categories, and some of them are very similar to faces and (2) there are wide variations in face images, due to the different poses, facial expressions, lighting conditions, image orientations and imaging conditions. In this paper we have presented a new approach based on CMAC neural network for face detection. The network has only one layer and due to its simplicity and local generalization property, its training phase is very fast, taking only one epoch to reach an error of 0.6%. In order to test the network, we have used a completely different dataset containing a large number of faces and non-faces and including a remarkable number of difficult patterns. Despite the inherent difficulties of the face detection problems and the presence of this amount the test dataset, the network obtained an error rate of 8.5% which is a reasonable result, making CMAC neural networks with their fast training and test performances, good candidate for real time face detection problems.

References

1. Ming-Hsuan Yang, David Kriegman and Narendra Ahuja, "Detecting Faces in Images: A Survey", *IEEE Transactions on Pattern Analysis and Machine Intelligence*, Vol. 24, No. 1 (2002) 34–58.
2. Erik Hjelmas and Boon Kee Low, "Face Detection: A Survey", *Computer Vision and Image Understanding*, 83 (2001) 236-274.
3. K. C. Yow and R. Cipolla, "Feature-based human face detection", *Image and vision computing*, Vol. 15, No. 9 (1997) 713-735.
4. Rowley, Baluja, and Kanade, "Neural Network-Based Face Detection", *IEEE Transaction on Pattern Analysis and Machine Intelligence*, Vol. 20, No. 1(1998) 23-38.
5. Dan Roth, Ming-Hsuan Yang and Narenda Ahuja, "A SNoW-Based Face Detector", *Neural Information Processing Systems*, Vol. 12, MIT Press (2000) 855-861.
6. A. V. Nefian and M. H. Hayes, "Face detection and recognition using Hidden Markov Models", *International Conference on Image Processing (ICIP98)*, Vol. 1, (1998), 141-145.
7. L. Meng, T. Q. Nguyen, D. A, Castanon, "An Image-based Bayesian Framework for Face Detection", *Proceedings of IEEE Intl. Conf. on Computer Vision and Pattern Recognition*, (2000).
8. E. Osuna, R. Freund, and F. Girosi, "Training support vector machines: An application to face detection", *Proceeding of IEEE conference on Computer Vision and Pattern Recognition* (1997) 130-136.
9. K. K. Sung, T. Poggio, "Example-Based Learning for view based human face detection", *IEEE Transaction on Pattern Analysis and Machine Intelligence*, Vol. 20, No. 1 (1998) 39-51.
10. M. H. Yang, D. Kriegman and N. Ahuja, "Face Detection Using Multimodal Density Models", *Computer Vision and Image Understanding*, Vol. 84 (2001) 264-284.
11. T. Kurita and T. Taguchi, "A Modification of Kernel-based Fisher Discriminant Analysis for Face Detection", *Proceedings of the 5th International Conf. on Automatic Face and Gesture Recognition* (2002) 300-305.
12. J. S. Albus, "A New Approach to manipulator Control: the Cerebellar Model Articulation Controller (CMAC)", *Trans. ASME, Series G. Journal of Dynamic Systems, Measurement and Control*, Vol. 97 (1975) 220-233.
13. D. Cornforth, "Building Practical Classifiers Using Cerebellar Model Associative Memory Neural Networks", *Proc. Conf Artificial Neural Networks and Expert Systems, Otago*, (2001).

A Biologically Inspired Active Stereo Vision System Using a Bottom-Up Saliency Map Model

Bum-Soo Jung[1], Sang-Bok Choi[2], Sang-Woo Ban[1], and Minho Lee[1]

[1] School of Electronic and Electrical Engineering,
[2] Department of Sensor Engineering,
Kyungpook National University,
1370 Sankyuk-Dong, Puk-Gu, Taegu 702-701, Korea
mholee@knu.ac.kr
http://abr.knu.ac.kr

Abstract. We propose a new active stereo vision system using a human-like vergence control method. The proposed system uses a bottom-up saliency map model with a human-like selective attention function in order to select an interesting region in each camera. This system compares the landmarks as to whether the selective region in each camera finds the same region. If the left and right cameras successfully find the same landmark, the implemented vision system focuses on that landmark. Using motor encoder information, we can automatically obtain depth data even when occlusion problem occurs. Experimental results show that the proposed convergence method is very effective in implementing an active stereo system and it can also can be applied to a visual surveillance system for discriminating between a real human face and a photograph.

1 Introduction

When the human eye searches for something in a natural scene, the left and right eyes converge on an interesting object. This mechanism is divided into two attention processes. In a top-down process, the human visual system determines salient locations through perceptive processing. On the other hand, with a bottom-up process, the human visual system determines salient locations from primitive features such as intensity, color, and orientation. Using the bottom-up process, humans selectively focus on a salient area according to various stimuli in the input scene [1]. If we can apply this human-like vergence function considered human attention process to an active stereo vision system, an efficient and intelligent vision system can be developed.

Since Krotkov organized the stereo system [2], many researchers have been developing the vergence stereo system [3,4]. Even though these approaches provided interesting results, the developed systems needed a high computation load to attain vergence control. Also, they didn't consider the advantages of a human-like vergence control mechanism. Therefore, we need a new method not only to sufficiently reflect a biological vergence control mechanism, but also to reduce the computation load during vergence control. Recently, Conradt et al. proposed

L. Rutkowski et al. (Eds.): ICAISC 2004, LNAI 3070, pp. 730–735, 2004.
© Springer-Verlag Berlin Heidelberg 2004

a stereo vision system using a biologically inspired saliency map (SM) [5]. They detected landmarks in both images with interaction between the feature detectors and the SM, and obtained their direction and distance. They, however, only considered a simple SM model to reflect the roles of neurons in the hippocampus which responded to mainly depth information. They didn't consider the brain-like visual processing mechanism nor did they tackle the occlusion problem which is a difficult but important hurdle in trying to implement a stereo vision system.

In this paper, we propose a new biologically motivated active stereo vision system that reflects the processes of a biological stereo visual signal from the retinal operation to the visual cortex. This system is based on the biologically inspired bottom-up SM model [6]. In each camera, we obtained a salient object in a natural scene using the SM model and compared the salient regions in each camera. If the difference in the salient region's values is sufficiently small, we regard the salient region as a landmark in each camera in order to make a vergence. Then the stereo vision system moves to each landmark point by a series of motors, the result of which becomes the vergence. When the disparity between the two vergence points is minimized by the salient region comparison, a depth estimation algorithm is performed in the vergence point and this provides an opportunity to solve the occlusion problem. To prevent it from being a repetitively attended region in the vision system, the converged region is masked by an inhibition of return (IOR) function [7]. Then the above procedure is repeated when the vision system continuously searches a new converged region.

2   The Bottom-Up Saliency Map Model

We used the SM model which reflects the functions of the retina cells, the LGN and the visual cortex [6]. We considered the intensity, edge and color opponent coding as the basic features of the SM model to reflect the role of the retina [6]. We also considered symmetry information as an addition basis to reflect the role of the LGN. We used a Gaussian pyramid with a scale from 0 to 9, and constructed a "conspicuity" map that uses 5 feature maps such as intensity, edge, symmetry, RG and BY [6]. Finally, the function of the visual cortex is considered as a redundancy reduction based on Barlow's hypothesis [6,8]. We used an independent component analysis (ICA) algorithm to model the roles of the visual cortex because the ICA is the best way to reduce the redundancy [6, 9]. After the convolution between the channel of the feature maps and the ICA filters, we finally attained the saliency map [6].

3   Vergence Control Algorithm Using the Bottom-Up SM Model

3.1   Selection and Verification of Landmarks

During an infant's development, binocular disparity by binocular fixation is comprised of three different mechanisms; alignment of the eyes, convergence, and sensory binocularity [10]. According to this fact, the single eye alignment should be the first factor considered regarding convergence that needs binocular fixation. In order to accomplish the single eye alignment, we use successive salient regions by the SM model in each camera image. Most of the stereo vision systems fix one of two cameras in the master eye. Humans, however, probably do not perform single eye alignment in this manner. The eye that has the dominant landmark may be considered the master eye, and the other eye is the slave eye that aligns itself to the landmark of the master eye. In our model, the SM model generates the maximum salient value for the dominant landmark in each camera image. Comparing the maximum salient values in the two camera images, we can adaptively decide which one is the master eye that has a camera with a larger salient value.

In order to verify the candidate as a landmark, we need to compare the salient region of the master eye with that of the slave eye. The regions obtained by the IOR function, which is to avoid duplicating the selection of the most salient region, are compared in order to decide on a landmark. If the IOR region of the master eye is similar to that of the slave eye, we regard the IOR regions as a landmark in order to make convergence. The comparison of the histogram values of the IOR regions between the left and right cameras are used for the verification of a landmark. In our model, the IOR function is implemented by noise-tolerant generalized symmetry transformation (NTGST) [11].

3.2   Depth Estimation Using Vergence Control

After the vergence control is successfully finished, we are able to get depth information. Fig. 1 shows the top view of the verged cameras. First, we have to obtain the two camera angles. Considering the limitation of the field of view (F) in the horizontal axis and the motor encoder resolution (U), we can acquire the encoder value (E) for the limited field of view of the horizontal axis. Eq. (1) shows the encoder value (E). This encoder value is used to calculate the value (x_t) of the horizontal axis motor for the alignment of each camera to a landmark as shown in Eq. (2). In Eq. (2), R denotes the x-axis resolution of the image

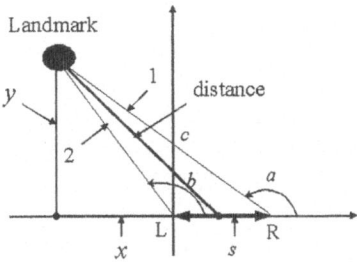

Fig. 1. Top view of the verged cameras where 'L' and 'R' are the focus center of the left and right cameras, respectively, and 'a' and 'b' are camera angles for the right and left cameras, respectively. 'C' is an intercept of line 1, and 's' is the distance between the two cameras. Lines 1 and 2 show straight lines from the right and left cameras to a landmark, respectively.

and T denotes the x coordinates of a landmark. The encoder value which moves each camera to the landmark point is translated to the angel (x_d) by Eq. (3). As a result, the angles a and b are obtained by Eq. (3) by substituting T for the x coordinates of the left and right cameras. We don't need to consider the y coordinates for which the values of the IOR regions of the two cameras are almost the same.

$$E = (F \cdot 360^0)/U \tag{1}$$

$$x_t = -E + (E \cdot T)/R \tag{2}$$

$$x_d = 90^0 - (R \cdot x_t)/U \tag{3}$$

The vertical distance (y) is obtained by the following equations:

$$tan(a) \cdot x - s \cdot tan(a) = y \tag{4}$$

$$tan(b) \cdot x = y \tag{5}$$

$$y = \frac{tan(a) \cdot tan(b)}{tan(a) - tan(b)} \cdot s \tag{6}$$

Eqs. (4) and (5) show the formulas for the straight lines between the cameras and the landmark, respectively. Eq. (6) is the equation by which the vertical distance (y) can be calculated in Fig. 1. Using the vertical distance (y) and a simple equation of triangular function, we can obtain the distance information.

4   Hardware Setup

Figs. 2 (a) and (b) show the block diagram of the developed active stereo vision system and a picture of the implemented active stereo vision system with five degrees of freedom, respectively.

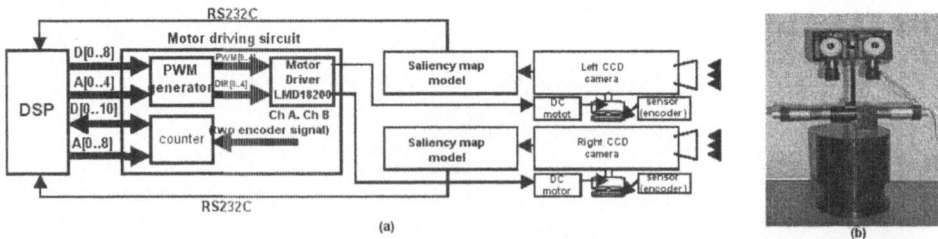

Fig. 2. The hardware construction of active stereo vision system; (a) Block diagram (b) The implemented hardware system.

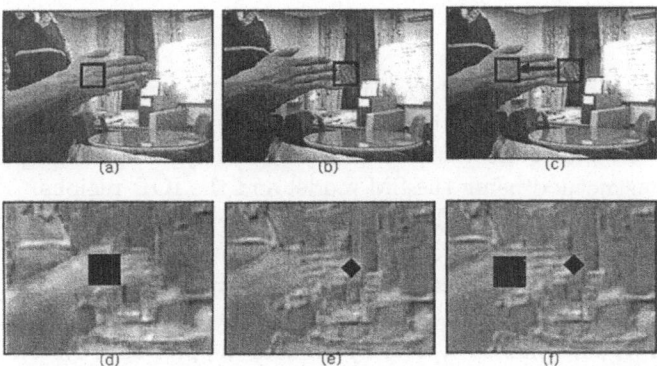

Fig. 3. The verification of a landmark by comparing the IOR regions in occlusion region. (a) The most salient region of the master camera (b) The most salient region of the slave camera (c) The second salient region of the slave camera (d) The IOR region of most salient region in the master camera (e) The IOR region of occlusion region and the IOR region of the most salient region in the slave camera (f) The IOR region of the second salient region in the master camera.

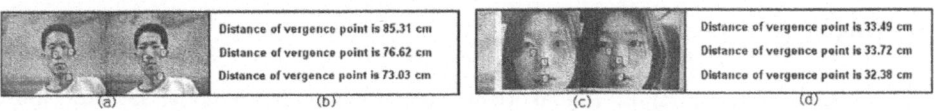

Fig. 4. The depth map formation of real image; (a) Real image (b) Depth information in real image (c) Photograph (d) Depth information in photograph.

5   Computer Simulation and Experimental Results

Figs. 3 (a) and (b) show a salient region of a master and slave eye, respectively. Figs. 4 (d) and (e) show the SM with the IOR functions. As shown in these figures, the y coordinates of the salient regions for the master and the slave eye are almost the same, but the comparison of the IOR regions gives a different landmark because of occlusion. In this case, we consider the next salient region in the same y coordinate, in which the IOR function prevents the duplicate selection of the most salient region. Figs. 3 (c) and (f) show the second salient region of the slave eye and the SM with the IOR function, respectively. Comparing Fig. 3 (d) with Fig. 3 (f), the IOR region is almost the same. As a result, we can obtain a landmark for convergence even when the occlusion problem occurs. Fig. 4 shows the depth map information of a real image and photograph, respectively. As shown in these figures, the proposed system can identify which scene contains a real face, and it also can be applied to a visual surveillance system by discriminating a real human face and photograph using distance information.

6   Conclusion

We proposed a new biologically motivated active stereo vision system that mimics human-like bottom-up visual attention. We used a saliency map model that reflects the biological visual pathway In the system, we proposed a landmark selection method using the SM model and the IOR regions. Also, a depth estimation method was applied after the convergence of the two cameras. Based on the proposed algorithm, we implemented a human-like active stereo vision system with five degrees of freedom. From the experimental results, we showed the effectiveness of the proposed vergence control method by solving the occlusion problem. A surveillance system which uses the proposed system is currently under investigation.

Acknowledgement. This research was supported by the Brain Science and Engineering Research Program of the Ministry of Korea Science and Technology and Grant (No.R05-2003-000-11399-0(2003)) from the Basic Research Program of the Korea Science and Engineering Foundation.

References

1. Navalpakkam, V., Itti, L.: A goal oriented attention guidance model. Lecture Notes in Computer Science **2525** (2002) 472–479
2. Krotkov, E.: Exploratory visual sensing for determining spatial layout with an agile stereo camera system. Tech. Rep. MS-CIS-87-29 (1987)
3. Yamato, J.: A layered control system for stereo vision head with vergence. IEEE International Conference on Systems, Man, and Cybernetics **2** (1999) 836–841
4. Peng, J., Srikaew, A., Wilkes, M., Kawamura, K., Peters, A.: An active vision system for mobile robots. IEEE International Conference on Systems, Man, and Cybernetics **2** (2000) 1472– 1477
5. Conradt, J., Pescatore, M., Pascal, S., Verschure, P.: Saliency maps operating on stereo images detect landmarks and their distance. International Conference on Artificial Neural Networks (2002)
6. Park, S.J., Shin, J.K., Lee, M.: Biologically Inspired Saliency Map Model for Bottom-up Visual Attention,. Lecture Notes in Computer Science **2525** (2002) 418–426
7. Itti, L., Koch, C.: Computational Modeling of Visual Attention, Nature Reviews Neuroscience **2(3)** (2001) 194–203
8. Barlow, H.B., Tolhust, D.J.: Why do you have edge detectors?. Optical society of America Technical Digest **23** (1992) 172
9. Bell, A.J., Sejnowski, T.J.: The independent components of natural scenes are edge filters. Vision Research **37** (1997) 3327–3338
10. Thorn, F., Gwiazda, J., Cruz, A.A.V., Bauer, J.A., Held, R.: The development of eye alignment, convergence, and sensory binocularity in young infants. Investigative Ophthalmology and Visual Science **35** (1994) 544–553
11. Park, S.J., An, K.H., Lee, M.: Saliency map model with adaptive masking based on independent component analysis. Neurocomputing **49** (2002) 417–422

Problems Connected with Application of Neural Networks in Automatic Face Recognition

Rafal Komanski and Bohdan Macukow

Faculty of Mathematics and Information Science, Warsaw University of Technology
00-661 Warsaw, Poland, Pl.Politechniki 1

Abstract. One of possible solutions in creating an automatic system of face recognition is application of auto-associative neural networks for remembering and recognise two-dimensional face images. Experiments with applying the Hopfield network and twolayer perceptron confirmed the possibility of remembering and reproducing face images, even if partially covered or disturbed. Limited technical possibilities enable using only low definition images. It is due to the fact that computations take a long time, and the number of remembered faces is relatively small. Proper working of the network is influenced in a significant way by light and facial expressions.

1 Introduction

Face is a unique feature of every person, the same applies to fingerprint and pupil. Improvement of computers and of their processor capacity resulted in introducing informatics into this area. Automatic face recognition has been drawing a lot of attention in the recent years. Digital identification possibility has found broad application in safety systems and improvement of communication between a man and digital computers. From among biometric identification systems using unique characteristics of people face recognition systems draw a lot of attention. This results among others from the method specificity. People being identified may not be aware of the fact that there is such a system working next to them and recognising scanning them. Face recognition systems are limited to obtaining a face image, then to analysing the image and deciding whether the person is included in their data base or not. The work concentrates only on the face recognition problem, in particular on using auto-association neural networks for this purpose.

2 Basic Notions

Automatic face processing includes numerous issues, i.e. face detection in a picture, face recognition, analysis of facial expression, and classification based on facial features. The first problem is the face detection. In some cases conditions in which a picture is taken can be fully controlled. For example the face position can be easily specified in passport photographs. Yet in many situations position, size

L. Rutkowski et al. (Eds.): ICAISC 2004, LNAI 3070, pp. 736–741, 2004.
© Springer-Verlag Berlin Heidelberg 2004

Fig. 1. Face detection in a picture. Detected faces are marked with frames. One of the faces in the picture, tilted right, has not been detected.

and orientation of a face are not known in advance. First step in face detection is checking if a given picture includes any faces. After that the number, situating and size of particular faces are specified. Nevertheless we should differentiate at this point between face detection and face localisation. The second of the problems deals with finding a face situating when it is known that in a given picture there is exactly one face. Figure 1 shows the issue of face detection in a picture [4]. The next step is recognising the face found in the picture. The main task here is to compare and to match the unknown face in the picture with the faces in the database. One of possibilities here is the application of neural networks.

Next problems in face processing, although not directly associated with face recognition, are also very important. The first of them is the facial expression analysis. Basing on the information included in the way a given face looks one can specify if a person is e.g. happy, sad, surprised or frightened. Different facial expressions create a difficulty in face recognition.

Another problem is the classification on the basis of facial features. Classifications can be based on the person's sex, age, race, etc. Yet the mechanisms working here are not known.

One of the basic notions is a face representation. All faces must be stored in the basis in the same format. A new face to recognise must be also converted into the same format. Methods based on neural networks directly use two-dimensional face images in grey scale. In studies devoted to face recognition it is assumed that the starting point are pictures with nothing but faces on them, so there is no need for detection. Such a format was used for the tests the results of which are described further in this article. The images can be stored in various resolutions and use different numbers of the grey colour levels.

The application of neural networks solves one of the most important problems, i.e. an economical way of storing faces in memory. An important feature of associative memory is the ability to remember the input data in order to reproduce them even if the input to the network is their disturbed or partially damaged version. Associative memories function as content addressable memories. In such a memory information is remembered in the connections weights. The first person to use auto-associative memory to remember and reproduce face

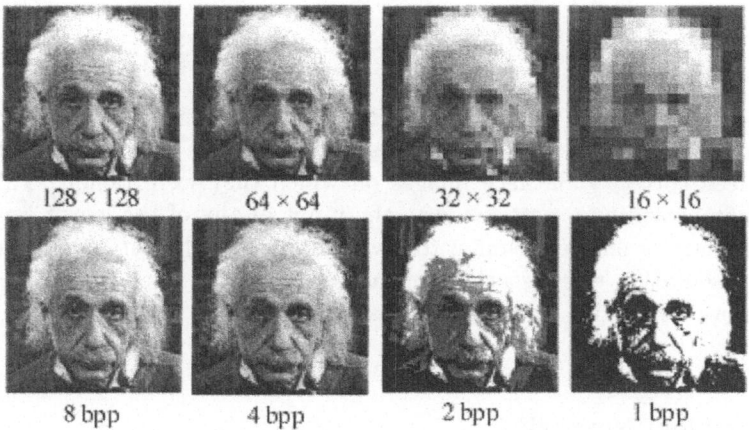

Fig. 2. A face image in various resolutions (scaled to the same size) and in various number of grey colour levels.

images was Kohonen. He proved that an auto-associative network can be used as a content addressable memory for storing face images [2].

3   Networks Used in the Tests

In the simulation programme used for carrying out the experiments two models of auto-associative memory were applied. The first of them is the model of auto-associative memory proposed by Hopfield in 1982 [1]. The second model of auto-associative memory is a twolayer network, taught with the method of a scaled conjugate gradient algorithm.

A discrete Hopfield network is a single-layer recurrent network. In the learning mode the values of weights are specified in accordance with the Hebbian Learning Rule. In the reproducing mode the values of weights are frozen and the network can work synchronously or asynchronously. The Hopfield network functioning in the synchronous mode and with bipolar neurones has been implemented in the simulation programme.

The second type of auto-associative memory used in the tests is a twolayer perceptron. In order to specify the weights of the network's hidden layers a special strategy called a backpropagation algorithm should be applied. The most efficient methods of learning are the optimisation methods based on developing the objective function into the Taylor's series. The process of learning by the network means an iterative choice of minimisation directions, so that the error function is minimised. In order to determine the minimisation direction one can use the algorithm of the highest descent, the algorithm of variable metric, and the most effective for big networks scaled conjugate gradient algorithm. This algorithm was proposed by Moller [3], and it combines determining the minimisation direction with the optimum pace of learning.

4 Results

The tests have proved that the Hopfield network as well as a twolayer perceptron can be used as a content addressable associative memory. The networks reproduced correctly the face images on which they were taught. This means that when providing a network with the input of any of the learnt images, the original image or one very similar to it was received as the output. Also when the input presentation was disturbed or partial, networks generated correct images with recovered missing parts of faces as the output.

4.1 Hopfield Network

Enormous demands concerning memory are a serious limitation to the Hopfield network. That is why carrying out the tests with this type of memory has been limited to images not exceeding $32 \times 32 \times 8$ bpp. Exemplary results obtained with the use of Hopfield network are presented in Fig. 3. The network also did very good when partially covered or disturbed images were presented as the input.

Another limitation in case of Hopfield network is the fact that computations during learning and iterative computations in the reproducing mode take a long time.

Even if only several face images were used to teach one network the computation time was counted in minutes and hours. It was necessary to introduce a limitation of the maximum number of iterations. Consequently the obtained results were not always satisfying, because there was not enough time for the network's state to stabilise.

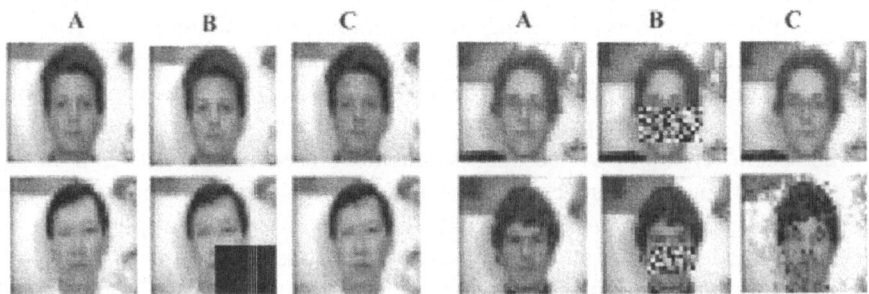

Fig. 3. Exemplary results of operation of the simulation programme for Hopfield network taught $32 \times 32 \times 8$ bpp images. A original images, B input to network, C network response.

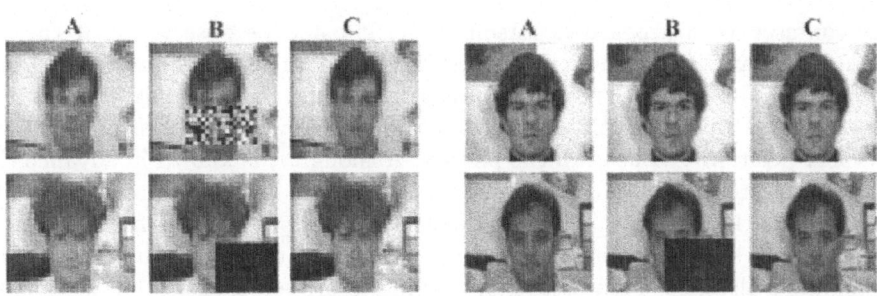

Fig. 4. Exemplary results for twolayer network, on the left $32 \times 32 \times 8$ bpp images, on the right $64 \times 64 \times 8$ bpp images. A original images, B input to network, C network response.

4.2 Twolayer Perceptron

The tests on twolayer network also confirmed possibility of applying it as a content addressable memory for face images. The network reproduced the images from the teaching file correctly. The exemplary results of the operation of simulation programme for the twolayer network are presented in Fig. 4. Also in cases when the images presented as the input to network were slightly modified, i.e. disturbed or partially covered, the network reproduced the images in a satisfactory way.

4.3 Differences and Similarities

There are differences in functioning of both the types of tested memories. The twolayer network is a feedforward network. Hence the computing time during reproduction is relatively short. There are no such problems with huge memory demand as in the case of Hopfield network. Yet the time of computation during learning is much longer. What is more the process of learning is not always successful. It depends on the network's structure and initial values of weights. It was indispensable to introduce a limit for the maximum number of iterations during learning. Thus it happened that the network finished learning with a high level of energy. In such a case the network responded with a noise. Better results were achieved when the level of energy after finishing learning was lower. The number of elements in the hidden layer can be set in a simulation programme. The appropriate tests were carried out with a few to a few dozen neurones in the hidden layer.

Both the types of the tested networks did very well during tests with images saved in smaller number of the grey colour levels. Yet with lower resolutions of picture cutting down on the quality of photos resulted in making them hard to distinguish even by a human.

The common problem for both types of memory was an incorrect reproduction of face images produced with the use of a different light than in the images on which the network was taught. To give an example, a partially shadowed face was confused with a bearded person's face. It could be observed that the network simply aimed at finding the closest picture in terms of Hamming's distance. Nevertheless in such a situation even a person could make a mistake.

Another problem worth paying attention to is a wrong recognition in case of different position of a head in the picture. Although it is known in advance that the picture presents one face, the face can be in frontal position, in semiprofile, or in profile. Besides the head can be turned up, down, to the front or can be tilted to the side. Networks aiming at finding the closest picture in terms of Hamming's distance. They were more willing to present rather other faces in the given position than the correct faces as the output.

5 Summary

Face recognition is a difficult and complex problem. It can be divided into a few subproblems: detection, identification, analysis of the facial expression and categorisation on the basis of facial expressions. The article presents a discussion on the possibilities of using neural networks to recognise faces. Experiments carried out with the use of Hopfield network and a twolayer perceptron taught with the method of a scaled conjugate gradient algorithm have proved that the networks can be used as a context addressable memory for the images of faces. The main two problems that drew the author's attention were the facts of incorrect recognition when the light and the position of head in photographs are variable. A serious problem is also different appearance of faces depending on people's emotional states. Additional limitations are relatively small capacities of network, slow speed of computations and high demand for memory.

References

1. Hopfield J.J.: Neural network and physical systems with emergent collective computational abilities. Proc. National Academy of Science, USA, 79:2554-2558, 1982
2. Kohonen T.: Associative Memory: A System Theoretic Approach. Springen, Berlin 1977
3. Moller M.F.: A scaled conjugate gradient algorithm for fast supervised learning. Neural Networks, Vol. 6, pp. 525-533, 1993
4. Samal A., Iyengar P.A.: Automatic recognition and analysis of human faces and facial expressions: A survey. Pattern Recognition, Vol. 25, no. 1, pp. 65-77, 1992

Czestochowa-Faces and Biometrics of Asymmetrical Face

Leonid Kompanets, Mariusz Kubanek, and Szymon Rydzek

Czestochowa University of Technology
Institute of Computer and Information Sciences
Center for Intelligent Multimedia Techniques
Dabrowskiego Street 73, 42-200 Czestochowa, Poland
{leonid.kompanets,mariusz.kubanek,szymon.rydzek}@icis.pcz.pl

Abstract. Traditionally, in face authentication/identification methods the presumption concerning face/head symmetry is used. For novel applications that concern creating techniques by means of which it is possible to reproduce the extraordinary complexity of skin, muscle, eye and hair movements, which convey emotion, gesture, psychological state or psycho-sociological traits, we begin to create new research direction called *Biometrics of Asymmetrical Face*.

In the paper, it is presented a novel type of 2D precise normalized model of a face for modern and prospect authentication/identification techniques creation in live biometrics that called *Czestochowa-face* model. Result of creating the ophthalmogeometrical technique, which is based on Czestochowa-face model, is also given. Some attention has been drawn to interdisciplinary research context. Beside the first-hand usage, the new type of face model and the technique may be employed in the areas of human-computer interaction, identification of cognition-psyche type of personality for personnel management, and so on.

1   Problem Statement

In this paper, the result of development of a novel model of a human face taking into consideration the ophthalmogeometry, face asymmetry, and brain asymmetry phenomena are presented. The model and the ophthalmogeometrical technique development are concerned with the processing and interpretation of face and eyes part of facial image features as information resources in algorithmic manner.

This study is based on two theses: 1) A value of cornea diameter (the only known constant of human body after 4-5 years old) equals $10\pm0,56$ mm [2]. So for purpose of face image normalization it was introduced a new unit called *Muld* (1 Muld = $10\pm0,56 \times 10\pm0,56$ mm^2); for current scale of the image, 1 *Muld* evaluates as *?N* pixels). 2) Primary source of face asymmetry effect is brain asymmetry phenomenon [3]. This information can be used as a valuable live biometric and/or as a specific cognition psyche information.

There are some inter- and trans-disciplinary "bottlenecks", which quantitatively hold back the development in a particular direction [6-9]. A) Informational

L. Rutkowski et al. (Eds.): ICAISC 2004, LNAI 3070, pp. 742–747, 2004.
© Springer-Verlag Berlin Heidelberg 2004

objects, which are beginning to be dealt with, are "non-mathematical" and having intelligent behavior. B) The known models of face and head [1] built on the basis of the thesis of their geometrical symmetry. (Having the author's evaluation done, the error of parameters measurement is reduced by about 5-8 % in comparison with the potential accurateness boarder.) C) In the modern fields [3, 4, 8, 9] an interesting aspect is the cognition-psyche interpretation of the information gained by means of algorithmic methods.

During the creation of the model and the technique, and their approval on the basis of pictures of about 150 people, the described problem was successfully solved to some extent. The issue analysis has shown that, to achieve the aim, numerous, necessary, mutually connected problems should be solved and adequate algorithmic examination tools should be created. These partial rich in content, algorithmic problems are:

1. Finding (discovering) a "truthful" vertical axis Y of a face.
2. Creation of the *Muld*-normalization procedure of a frontal view facial image.
3. Constructing a combine (two polar and one Cartesian) facial coordinate system Y-$O1$-$X1$-$O2$-$X2$ based on the "truthful" axis Y, and a special virtual coordinate system Y^*-O^*-X^* for eyes area.
4. Visualization in Y^*-O^*-X^* of person's ophthalmologeometrical pattern.
5. (Synthesis of special facial images (left-left and right-right composites) for face asymmetry features evaluation.)
6. The Czestochowa-face creation.
7. Creation of the ophthalmogeometrical authentication technique.
8. (Creation of an algorithm for precise mapping and evaluating similarity of a pair of compared facial components or given component set in a holistic manner.)
9. (Formulation of some theses concerning the cognition-psyche interpretation of gained ophthalmogeometrical, face asymmetry and other features.)

2   On the Ophthalmogeometry and Brain Asymmetry Phenomena

According to E. Muldashev [2], person's psychological and other states are described with 22 parameters of an eyes part of a face. We use information that is included in some planar ophthalmogeometrical figures, which are produced with tangents of four eye corners, appropriate eye silhouettes, wrinkles over eyes, and some other facial components (Fig.1, 2). Face asymmetry phenomenon has been known for long and researched by painters, psychologists [5]. However, in live biometrics, psychological testing [4], human resources management, the phenomenon is not widely used. At the moment, the original interpretation of face asymmetry is based on the technical and psychological formalization of the brain hemispheres asymmetry phenomenon, being dealt with in [3].

The primary information of the enumerated phenomena is presented by means of a 2D single frontal image of a face. Biometrics and/or cognition-psyche

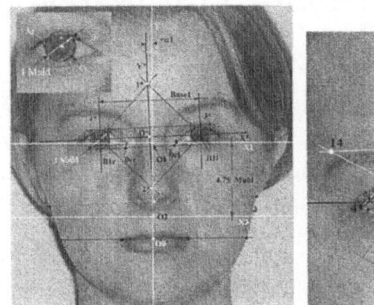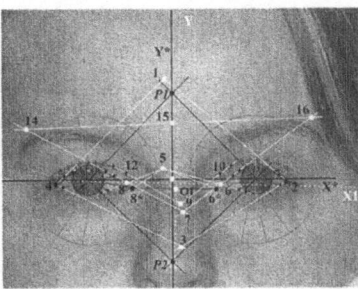

Fig. 1 and 2. Illustration of the preparatory and content-related stages of an ophthalmogeometrical pattern estimation, accordingly

features of a person may be drawn out of this information in a nonintrusive way. The main aim of the paper is to verify the thesis that the effects of ophthalmogeometry and face asymmetry may serve as new valuable biometrics especially in case of their fusion. Below in the form of a sketch, the result of the study is given. The lack of space allows only to focus on the graphic and algorithmic means of contents transmission.

3   "Truthful" Vertical Axis, *Muld*-Normalization, Two Special Coordinate Systems of a Face

Human face is an example of the new class of information objects – non-rigid, dynamic, intelligent ones, mathematic or algorithmic description of which is an art and challenge for programmers. The idea of finding a "truthful" vertical axis Y of a face and constructing the special virtual coordinate system $Y^*\text{-}O^*\text{-}X^*$ for eyes area are illustrated in Fig.1.

In the course experiments for finding the "real" vertical face axis, there were chosen anthropometrics points $O1$ (the center of a line linking interior eye corners Ocr, Ocl in Fig.1 (points 8* and 6* in Fig.2)) and $O0$ (the center of a line linking mouth corners in Fig.1). (In the case of the assignation of point $O0$ being impossible this way, there has been constructed reserve procedure).

For strict face mapping and/or face components comparison (silhouette, eyes, brows, mouth, nose, ears, wrinkles of different kind, unique traits) uses necessary quantity of rays coming from points $O1$ and/or $O2$ whole facial coordinate system, as well as the necessary quantity of parallels to Y and/or $X1$ lines (Fig.3, 4). De fault, all measurements here and below are done in *Mulds*.

4 Ophthalmogeometrical Pattern Visualization (and Composite Synthesis)

As proven in [2, 8, 9], person's ophthalmogeometrical pattern has a unique appearance from birth till human death. But it is not ordinary visible. Example of the pattern are given in Fig.2. The sequence of calculating steps is as follows.
INPUT: 2D single frontal view facial image.
OUTPUT: Person's ophthalmogeometrical pattern (Fig.2, 3, 4).

1. Find the placement of two circles described around the eyes cornea (iris) and measure the amount $?N$ of pixels that constitutes 1 *Muld* (Fig.1).
2. Build the coordinate system Y^*-O^*-X^* and the figure including points $P1^*,P2^*$ (Fig.2). If points $P1^*$ and $P2^*$ are placed on the Y^* line, **then**
3. Build the external figures 1,2,3,4 and internal - 5,6,7,8, the triangles 5,8,8* and 5,6,6*, 7,14,15,16, the angle 10,9,12 (Fig.2).
4. Find point $O1$. Construct the system Y-$O1$-$X1$-$O2$-$X2$.
5. Adjust the system Y^*-O^*-X^* and system Y-$O1$-$X1$-$O2$-$X2$ as in Fig.1.
6. Measure the ophthalmogeometrical parameters (see Tab. 1):
   $[\pm x0^*, \pm y01^*; \pm \alpha \ [^\circ] \ ; B1, x3^*, y3^*, x1^*, y1^*, y15^*, x5^*, y5^*, x7^*, y7^*, x9^*, y9^*]$

Example of the Czestochowa-Faces

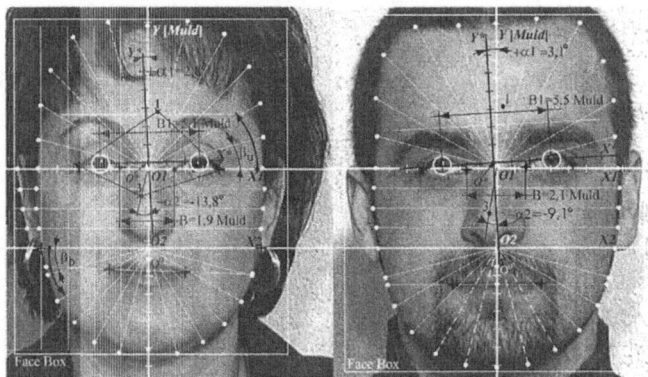

Fig. 3 and 4. Illustration of the *Muld*-normalization and mapping procedures for woman's and man's facial images

5 Constructing Czestochowa-Faces

The main Czestochowa-faces feature are: 1) the "truthful" vertical axis Y of an asymmetrical face, 2) the special combined system Y-$O1$-$X1$-$O2$-$X2$ and adjusted to it the special virtual coordinate system Y^*-O^*-X^* for eyes area of a face, 3) the 2D *Muld*-normalization procedure and construction of *"Face Box"* (Fig.3, 4), 4) the ophthalmogeometrical pattern of a person, face asymmetry feature, and brain asymmetry phenomenon background, 5) procedure of precise evaluating of (pseudo-information) similarity for any pair of facial components, sets of components, and faces [6-9], 6) algorithmic realization of the model, 7) measured features interpretation in biometrics, brain asymmetry, and cognition-psyche terms, 8) presenting the possibility of exact facial image mapping and/or its proper component set in the uniformed *absolute* values.

The Czestochowa-faces were presented in this form in analogy to the existing types of Fisher-, Eigen-, Chernoff-, Wavelet-faces. In respect to the fact that this model regards the modern knowledge about face asymmetry phenomena, brain asymmetry and ophthalmogeometry, as well as having the possibility of precise and scaled in *Mulds* asymmetric faces mapping, this model can be classified as an interdisciplinary face model of a new generation.

6 Ophthalmogeometric Authentication Technique Experimenting

The idea of using of ophtalmogeometric pattern for authentication, and also the result of experiment in calibrating mode is presented in Tab.1.

At the first stage, a sign vectors **2** and **4** produced by the ophthalmogeometrical pattern parameter vectors of basic (**1**) and comparing ($\leftarrow$**6**) images are compared. If necessary, the mean square distances σ_{ij} of parameters **x3 - y9** are calculated. If Hamming distance **3** is non-zero, further comparing is not needed. We can assume that the precision ϵ of pattern values measuring is near to σ_{12}.

Tab. 1. Result of the ophalmogeometrical authentication technique experiment

The same person image 1 (accordingly after 1st and 2nd clicking procedures)							
1st Input of image 1[1] $\rightarrow$			???			2nd Input of image 1[2] $\leftarrow$	
Feature	1	2	3	4	5 $\downarrow$	$\leftarrow$ 6	7
XO[*] [Muld]	0,0897	+	0	+	0,0897	0,0897	0
YO[*] -"-	0,3077	+	0	+	0,3077	0,3077	0
$\pm\alpha$[°]	-2,3282	−	0	−	-2,3282	-2,3282	0
Base1 -"-	5,1929	+	0	+	5,1929	5,1929	0
X3 -"-	-0,1673	−	0	−	-0,6418	-0,6418	0,4745
Y3 -"-	-1,6652	−	0	−	-1,6710	-1,6710	0,0058
X1 -"-	-0,1670	−	0	−	-0,4745	-0,4745	0,3075
Y1 -"-	-1,4760	−	0	−	-1,4934	-1,4934	0,0174
Y15 -"-	1,6275	+	0	+	1,6275	1,6275	0
X5 -"-	0,0399	ε	0	ε	-0,0016	-0,0016	0,0415
Y5 -"-	0,5754	+	0	+	0,3324	0,3324	0,2430
X7 -"-	-0,1761	−	0	−	-0,1244	-0,1244	-0,0518
Y7 -"-	-1,3446	−	0	−	-1,3069	-1,3069	-0,0377
X9 -"-	-0,2594	−	0	−	-0,2206	-0,2206	-0,0388
Y9 -"-	-0,8177	−	0	−	-0,7926	-0,7926	-0,0251
					$\sigma_{12} = \rightarrow$		0,166

Legend: **1** and $\leftarrow$ **6** - pattern parameter vectors of basic and comparing images; **5**$\downarrow$ - parameter vector of normalized pattern $\leftarrow$**6**; **2** and **4** - sign masks of the vectors **1** and **5**$\downarrow$; **3** - Hamming distance vector for the comparing vectors **2** and **4**.

7   Conclusion

In this paper, it has been verified the thesis that the phenomena of ophthalmogeometry and face asymmetry may serve as new very valuable biometrics especially in case of their fusion. Moreover, it has been verified these biometrics contain information about cognitive and psychological features of a person, which can make them be interesting for future applications.

(Some interesting novelties of joint researching the ophthalmogeometry and facial asymmetry phenomena have been noticed: the uniqueness of the facial asymmetry and ophthalmogeometry characteristics; topological non-changeability of person's pattern considering emotional states; the possibility of using point 3 of the pattern as an indicator of the dominant brain hemisphere; the uniqueness and significant prevalence of the face image normalization using the *Muld*; etc.)

The paper may be qualified as an exploring new research direction.

Acknowledgments. This work is sponsored by the Polish State Committee for Scientific Research under Grant No. 4 T11C 003 25.

References

[1] "Research Videos". Available at http://seeingmachines.com/videos/research
[2] Muldashev Ernst: *Whom did we descend from?*, "OLMA-PRESS", Moscow 2002 (In Russian)
[3] Anuashvili Avtandil: *Fundamentals of Psychology. Scientific, Philosophic and Spiritual Fundamentals of Psychology*. The Institute for Control Problems Press, Moscow, 2001 (In Russian)
[4] Anastasi Anna, Urbina Susan: *Psychological Testing*. Prentice-Hall, Inc., 1997
[5] Carter Rita: *Mapping the Mind*. California, 1998
[6] Kompanets Leonid, Valchuk Tetiana: "Identification/Authentication of Person Cognitive Characteristics". The IEEE AutoID'02 Proc. 3rd Workshop on Automatic Identification Advanced Technologies, 14-15 March 2002, Tarrytown, New York, USA, 12-16
[7] Valchuk Tetiana, Wyrzykowski Roman, Kompanets Leonid: "Mental Characteristics of Person as Basic Biometrics". Post-ECCV'02 Workshop on Biometric Authentication. 1st June 2002, Copenhagen. In: LNCS # 2359, 78-90
[8] Kompanets Leonid, et al.: "Based on Pseudo-Information Evaluation, Facial Asymmetry and Ophthalmologic Geometry Techniques for Human-Computer Interaction, Person Psyche Type Identification, and Other Applications". Proc. 7th Multi-Conference on Systemics, Cybernetics and Informatics: SCI'03 and ISAS'03, Vol. XII, Information Systems, Technologies and Applications II,.235-240. July 27-30, 2003 - Orlando, Florida, USA.
[9] Kompanets Leonid: "Counterterrorism-Oriented Psychology and Biometrics Techniques: Part 2/2. Based on Brain Asymmetry, Eyes "Fingerprints", Face Asymmetry, and Person Psyche Type Identification Information Techniques". Pre-proc. SCI'03, Symposium on The Role of Academy in the War on Terrorism, Eds: Callaos Nagib, Kompanets Leonid, Takeno Junishi, Wej Huaqiang, July 29, 2003 - Orlando, Florida, USA, 18-21.

Wafer Die Position Detection Using Hierarchical Gray Level Corner Detector

Jae Hyung Na and Hae Seok Oh

Soongsil University, Sangdo 5 dong Dongjak Gu, Seoul, Korea

Abstract. In this paper, we will introduce a method for wafer die position detection using corner detector. We present a hierarchical gray level corner detector (HGLCD) to detect die position accurately. HGLCD divides the corner region into many homocentric circles and get corner response and angle about each circle. The experiments have shown that the new corner detector is more accurate and more efficient in its performance than other two popular corner detectors.

1 Introduction

These days the application of WSCSP (Wafer Scale Chip Scale Packaging) technology is the general trend in the semiconductor industry. WSCSP technology requires marking procedure that marks product information on the backside of the wafer that is according to the die location. It is an important procedure but until now human operator detects the die position using eye or teaching all kind of die pattern and then do pattern matching. Consequently the need of automation in marking process is very significant. To automate marking process, it is necessary to detect die position automatically and accurately. We propose a method to recognize die position precisely and speedily using a new corner detector based on hierarchical gray level corner model.

1.1 Wafer Image

In this section, we will consider the characteristic of wafer image. A great of variety of Wafers are produced now. So it is impossible to recognize all kinds of die pattern. So to detect die position we should detect the cross point of "saw street", not die itself. We can classify wafer according to the shape of saw street as follows.

a. Single line saw street
b. Double line saw street
c. Variable width saw street
d. Complex pattern saw street

Fig. 1 shows the example of each type of saw street. Most of wafer has a, b, c type and our domain is a, b, c type wafer.

L. Rutkowski et al. (Eds.): ICAISC 2004, LNAI 3070, pp. 748–753, 2004.
© Springer-Verlag Berlin Heidelberg 2004

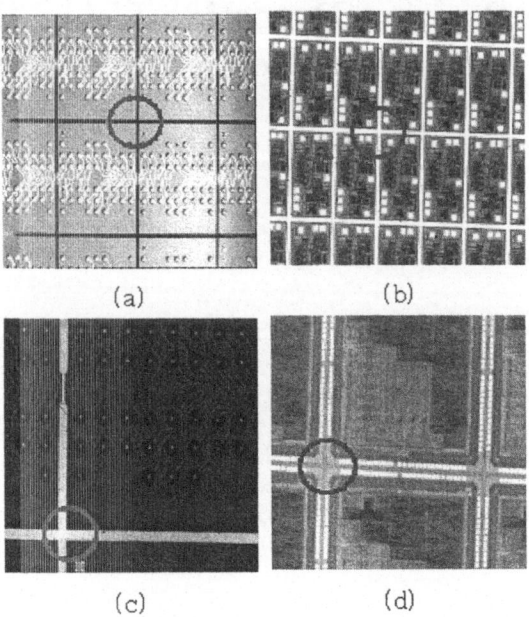

Fig. 1. Classification of wafer by saw street shape, (a) Single line, (b) Double line, (c) Variable width, (d) Complex pattern

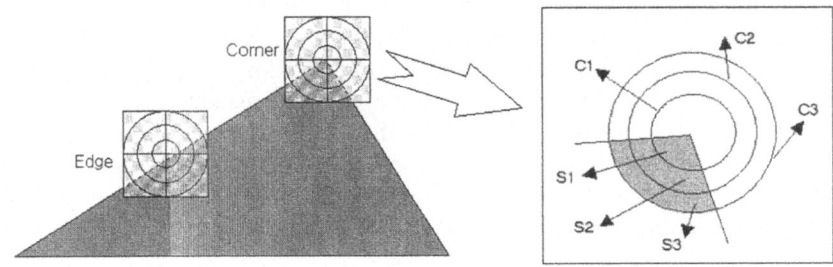

Fig. 2. Hierarchical Corner model

2   Hierarchical Gray Level Corner Detector (HGLCD)

In this chapter we will introduce a hierarchical gray level corner detector (HGLCD). We can divide the corner region into many homocentric circles, $C_1, C_2, C_3 ..., C_n$ like Fig. 2. The gray region represents the corner region and the white region represents the background region.

Let S_i be the corresponding cirque of corner region with C_i. If every i-th circle satisfies equation 1, we can say that the central point fits the requirement of hierarchical corner structure and it can be regarded as a corner candidate.

$$\frac{S_i}{C_i} = \frac{\theta}{360} < 0.5 \tag{1}$$

Where θ represents corner angle. Equation 1 is calculated form C_1 to C_n. If C_i does not meet equation 1 then the calculation is stopped. So HGLCD can process more quickly than other gray level corner detector. Equation 1 is very efficient, but it cannot distinguish noise from corner point. So we must consider the difference of gradient about each homocentric circles C_1, C_2, C_3 using equation 2.

$$|\theta_{i-1} - \theta_i| \leq t_d \tag{2}$$

Where the threshold value t_d decides the continuity of angle. t_d converges on zero if i is increased.

The angle of i-th circle can be calculated as following equation.

$$\theta = ArcTan\frac{C_x - S_{ix}}{C_y - S_{iy}} \tag{3}$$

C_x, C_y represent the center coordination of homocentric circle C_i and S_{ix}, S_{iy} represent the central coordination of S_i.

The brightness of each pixel within the mask is compared with that of the nucleus to calculate the similarity. Originally a simple equation determined this comparison.

$$C_i(P_i, P_0) = [1 \; if \; I(P_i) - I(P_0) < t_b, \; 0 \; if I(P_i) - I(P_0) \geq t_b] \tag{4}$$

Where P_0 is the position of the nucleus in the two dimensional image, P_i is the position of any other point within the mask, $I(P_i)$ is the brightness of any pixel, t_b is a brightness difference threshold.

$$C_i(P_i, P_0) = e^{-(\frac{I(P_i)-I(P_0)}{t_b})^6} \tag{5}$$

The Equation 5 was chosen to give a "smoother" version of Equation 4. This allows a pixel's brightness to vary slightly without having too large an effect on $C_i(P_i, P_0)$.[1]

The equation is implemented as a look up table for speed. According to SUSAN principle, reasonable value of t_b is 25.[1] But in the wafer image the value is not suitable because of the reflection of light. So we chose the deviation of intensity as a brightness difference threshold t_b using equation 6.

$$t_b = \sqrt{\frac{1}{n}\sum_{i=1}^{n}(P_i - m)^2}, \; m = \frac{\sum_{i=1}^{n}P_i}{N} \tag{6}$$

Finally the corner response R is described as equation 7.

$$R = \sqrt{\frac{1}{n}\sum_{i=1}^{n}(P_i, P_0)}, \; N = MASK \; SIZE \tag{7}$$

We can get candidates for a corner point using equation 1 and 2. And a pixel that has local maxima value of r is selected as a corner point.

In the real work, the mask size N is very important. If we use a small mask, it will be some sensitive to strong edges and noise. If we use a big mask, only significant corners will be reported and some small corners will be ignored. Usually a circular 7 by 7 mask is used to detect corner point[1][3], but HGLCD uses square mask to compute corner angle and uses a multi level mask. First we adjust a big mask and equation 2 prevents false positive detection. And then we use small mask again for a good localization of a corner point.

3   Detection of Wafer Die Position

Corner detector which used to die position recognition should satisfy a number of important criteria. [2]

1) All the true corners should be detected.
2) No false corners should be detected.
3) Corner points should be well localized.
4) Corner detector should be robust with respect to noise.
5) Corner detector should be efficient.

We noticed that "the cross of a saw street" represents a die position. So we detect the cross of a saw street using HGLCD and then composed the array of die using corner position information. Edge based corner detectors are too week with noise and takes long time. On the other hand gradient based corner detector like Plessy is not localized well.[3][4]
New corner does not require any preprocessing. Fig. 4 shows the die detection procedure using HGLCD. In automation, die detection process is followed by pre-align process. Generally the tolerance of pre-aligner is less than 3 degrees. So we can detect corner point accurately using equation 3.

4   Experimental Results

In this part, we examine the performance of three corner detectors, our new corner detector (HGLCD), SUSAN, IPAN99. We tested with Pentium III 550MHz PC with Windows 2000 environment. We tested the detection result with various die pattern images. In case of simple die pattern, all corner detectors detected corner point well. But in the case of complex die pattern, HGLCD detected corner point well more than other two detectors. Fig. 3 shows the corner detection result for the complex die pattern image. In all case SUSAN shows good result but it has more false positive than HGLCD. On the other hand edge based corner detector (IPAN99) shows very poor result in the complex pattern images because it is difficult to get edge exactly. We can see that the computational cost of the new corner detector is lower than SUSAN because HGLCD has a hierarchical structure.

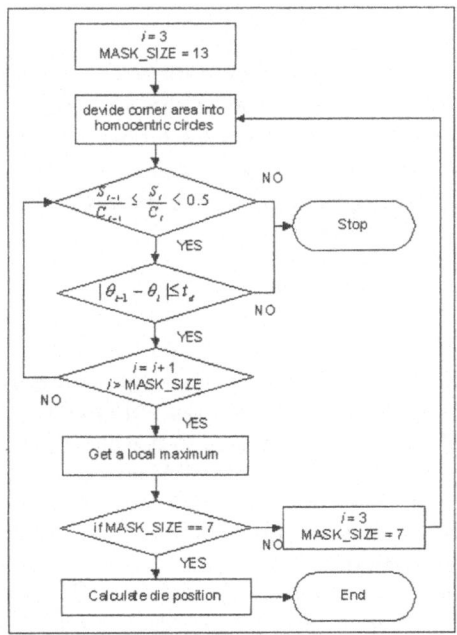

Fig. 3. Wafer die position detection

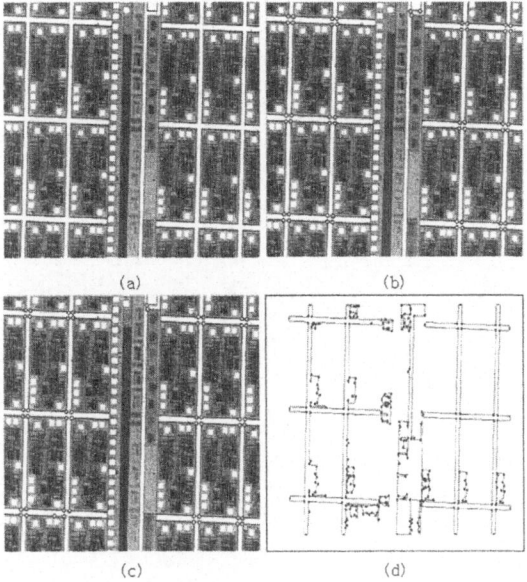

Fig. 4. Outputs of corner detectors for a given complex wafer image, (a) Input image
(b) HGLCD (c) SUSAN (d) IPAN99

5   Conclusion

We have proposed a new corner detector for wafer die position recognition. It assumes that each circle of a corner point should have same corner degree and intensity. The new corner detector achieves high processing speed using hierarchical search scheme. Also it can estimate the corner angle, which reduces false positive. HGLCD can be used not only as a die position detector but also as a general purpose corner detector.

References

1. Smith, SM. , Brady, M.: SUSAN - a new approach to low level image processing International Jounal of Computer Vision **vol.23(1)** (1997) 45–78
2. Mokhatian, F., Ekeland, I.: Robust image corner detection through curvature scale space IEEE Trans on Patern Analysis and Machine Intelligence , **20(12)** (1998) 1376–1381
3. Zheng, Z., Wang, H., Teoh,K.: Analysis of gray level corner , Pattern Recognition Letters **vol.20** (1999) 149–162
4. Arrebola, F., Bandera, A., Camacho, P., Sandova, A.: Corner detection by local histograms of contour chain code. **33(21)** (1997) 769–1771

On Fuzzy Labelled Image Segmentation Based on Perceptual Features*

Pilar Sobrevilla[1] and Eduard Montseny[2]

[1] Applied Mathematics II Department
[2] Computer Engineering and Industrial Systems Deptartment,
Technical University of Catalonia, Pau Gargallo 5, 08028 Barcelona, Spain,
{pilar.sobrevilla,eduard.montseny}@upc.es

1 Introduction

One of the monolithic goals of Computer Vision (CV)is to automatically interpret general digital images of arbitrary scenes. Although this goal has produced a vast array of research, a solution to the general problem has not been found. The difficulty of this goal has caused the field to focus on smaller, more constrained problems related with the different tasks involved, such as: noise removal, smoothing, and sharpening of contrast -*low-level*-; segmentation of images to isolate objects and regions, and description and recognition of the segmented regions -*intermediate-level*-; and interpretation of the scene -*high-level*-.

Uncertainty abounds in every phase of CV. Problems coming up from not handling of uncertainty at low and intermediate levels made still more difficult automation of high level tasks. It compelled researchers to look for solutions with which designing computer vision algorithms whose models were close to the Marr's principles [9]: *1.- Principle of Least Commitment*: "Don't do something that may later have to be undone"; *2.- Principle of Graceful Degradation*: "Degrading the data will not prevent the delivery of at least some of the answer".

Although usually uncertainty has been associated to random components, and has been analyzed using probabilistic methods, there exist a lot of cases wherein source of uncertainty is also dependant of other kind of factors ([12]). Fuzzy set theory and fuzzy logic provide the tools needed for modelling the algorithms according with aforementioned principles, but it doesn't means that algorithms designed using membership functions will preserve those principles.

Fuzzy sets have developed an innovative methodological and algorithmic framework to cope with complex and ill-defined systems, contributing to pattern recognition algorithms development making easier the design of algorithms based on interpretable models. As Keller states in ([8]), rule-based systems have gained popularity in CV applications, particularly in high-level vision activities. He also point out that these systems are suitable for modelling algorithms related with low and intermediate levels of CV systems, asserting that *"fuzzy logic offers numerous approaches to translate such rules and to make inferences from the rules and facts modelled similarly"*.

---

* Work partially supported by the Spanish CICYT Project TIC2002-02791.

L. Rutkowski et al. (Eds.): ICAISC 2004, LNAI 3070, pp. 754–759, 2004.
© Springer-Verlag Berlin Heidelberg 2004

2   Benefits of Considering Vagueness and Experts' Knowledge in Boundary Detection

Probably is at low and intermediate levels where the effects of data uncertainty and vagueness, within the considered concepts, are more noticeable. As known, features always are fulfilled at a certain degree, and natural objects' shapes display certain similarity degree. Fuzzy sets theory and fuzzy logic provide with the necessary set of tools for analyzing, according with a set of rules, a set of features so as to get the degree to which two shapes are similar. It must be also emphasized that fuzzy theory allows the use of interpretable models that are more easily improvable than non-interpretable models.

These reasons have impelled many researchers to use fuzzy set theory and fuzzy logic for solving problems connected with low and intermediate CV levels. Moreover, if expert's knowledge is considered within the base of rules for carrying out a specific kind of analysis, an usually intuitive way of behavior (heuristic rules), highly non-linear by nature, and hardly describable using traditional mathematical models, is being introduced.

Boundaries give information of image's objects location, describing their shape and size. In ideal images edges correspond to object boundaries, but definition of what constitutes an edge is rather vague, heuristic, and even subjective. So, we can say that: *"An edge point locates a pixel where there is significant local intensity change; an edge fragment is a collection of edge points; and an edge detector produces either a set of edge points or edge fragments"*. Because of *intensity* and *location* are related to concepts defined in an imprecise way, next questions unavoidably come up:

1. When can we say that a *local intensity change* is sufficiently meaningful as to take the decision that it is an edge?

2. If an edge fragment is made up of a set of pixels, when can we assert that an *edge is located* in a specific pixel and not in one of its neighborhoods?

In correct image data, these questions could be tackled performing an analysis of the information provided by a pixel and its local neighbors (i.e. in a 3x3 window). However, as image data contain vagueness, the only knowledge we can get from their analysis refers to the degree to which a significant level intensity change can be noticed at a pixel, being necessary a more regional analysis for checking the existence of an edge fragment. Some edge detection algorithms that take into account image vagueness are given in [1], [5], [6], [14], and [16].

3   *FLSPF*, a Robust Image Segmentation Algorithm

Segmentation is fundamental, and one of the most difficult steps in computer vision ([1] and [7]), as well as in model-based object recognition systems, because subsequent tasks rely heavily on the quality of its results.

Image segmentation consists in dividing the image into regions that must be homogeneous with regard to some image features, avoiding the influence of illumination artifacts (shadows, highlights, etc.) or object pose (occlusions, orientation, etc.). One of the main decisions for designing a robust image segmentation algorithm is choosing the features to be considered in the region analysis.

For getting more accurate results, and improve vagueness treatment, some techniques or characteristics emulating human beings' image segmentation skills can be taken into account, as color, texture, and brightness,although last one is very difficult to be considered by classic computer vision systems.

Our efforts are addressed to develop an algorithm that, considering aforementioned problems and restrictions, be useful for a wide range of detection and segmentation applications. We design a method for *Fuzzy Labelled Segmentation based on Perceptual Features* (*FLSPF*), adaptable to monochrome and color image segmentation. It is based on the use of a fuzzy rule base that incorporates expert knowledge, heuristics, and probability to possibility transformations.

3.1   *FLSPF* for Monochrome Images

In real-world applications constant gray values characterizing image's objects and background are seldom met due to intensity variability, that can be caused by image formation process (noise, non-uniform illumination, or inhomogeneous background). So, considering an individual pixel it is not possible to deduce whether it is located in a region, but it is required to analyze a local neighborhood. Moreover, since digital images are displayed as discrete sets of brightness points, if the ability of the eye to discriminate brightness levels is considered within the vision system design, image-processing results could be improved.

This is way, in [15] a first attempt was made of introducing the capability of human vision system for recognizing brightness levels considering, as long as possible, the variability introduced by the different sources. The model was a *Fuzzy Rule-based Gray-level Histogram Analysis* (*FRGHA*), wherein the rules formalized experts' knowledge and experience, but avoided their subjectivity.

Here we propose a *FRGHA* algorithm developed from the data to the algorithm wherein, extending our framework, the *Generic Possibility Functions* for the *Linguistic Brightness' labels* are obtained at the training stage, what makes necessary a suitable trackdown of the training imagery.

Given a test image, its *Brightness Histogram* is automatically obtained evaluating the Brightness feature. Once the local minimums have been obtained, the *Histogram* is *Segmented*. To do it, the membership degree of the peaks to the *Mixed* and *Border-Peaks* fuzzy sets are obtained based on a set of rules that has been lightened, with regard our previous work, by using a structural element.

Figure 1 shows the six peaks located within the histogram of a real image. After applying the rules, peaks 5 and 6 are associated to the label *Clear*, peak 4 is related to label *Medium*, and peaks 1, 2, and 3 are associated to label *Dark*. The *Characteristics* and *Parameters* associated to the *Brightness' labels* are derived from the *Peaks' Features*. Last row of Table 1 depicts the intervals related with the three labels obtained applying the rules to the peaks of Fig.1.

Finally, the *Membership Functions* of the *Labels Fuzzy Sets* are derived applying the *Features* of the *Brightness' labels* and the *Generic membership functions*.

3.2   *FLSPF* for Color Images

After studying the behavior of some color spaces, in front of noise and illumination variations, we have chosen the (*HSI*) space because, as its components

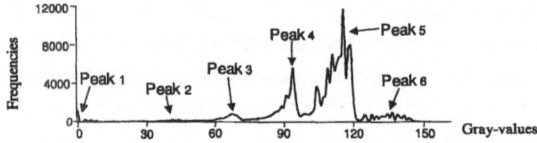

Fig. 1. Relevant peaks obtained for the histogram of a real image.

Table 1. Intervals associated to the labels

	Peak1	Peak2	Peak3	Peak4	Peak5	Peak6
I_{Peak}	$[0, 12]$	$[15, 48]$	$[50, 71]$	$[74, 97]$	$[100, 122]$	$[100, 122]$
I_{Peak75}	$[0, 5]$	$[30, 48]$	$[61, 70]$	$[88, 96]$	$[110, 119]$	$[110, 119]$
Labels	$I_{Dark} = [0, 71]$; $I_{Dark75} = [0, 70]$			$I_{Medium} = [74, 97]$; $I_{Medium75} = [88, 96]$	$I_{Clear} = [100, 147]$; $I_{Clear75} = [110, 139]$	

represent the dye-H-, the purity-S-, and the brightness-I- of any color, they are closer to the human perception of color. Specifically, we have selected the Smiths' *HSI* space because: it shows the maximum component reliability under illumination variations; provides high independence between their color components; codes human meaningful information,; and allows to isolate physical illumination phenomenon efficiently (shades, highlights, etc.).

We use the H and S components for representing the color feature of the scene objects, while the I component is interpreted as a color-independent feature, measuring the intensity of the light reflected by the objects. As a consequence segmentation is slightly affected by lightening variations, as shadowing and shadows, because they almost don't modify the object surface color feature.

The proposed *Labelled Image Segmentation algorithm*, classify (*label*) each image pixel to the most suitable (similar) pattern of a previously defined patterns' set. It allows recognizing the same object color on unconnected regions, and provides a clue for the following stages (i.e.: object recognition tasks), as pixel labels refer not only to image regions but also to object features.

The proposed *FLSPF* algorithm is based on what we say *Relevant Colors* (*RCs*), or chromatic patterns to be detected on the image. Each *RC* depicts not a single point but a certain distribution within the H-S space. So, after performing the *Relevant Colors Identification* and *Characterization*, the image pixels are *Labelled* according to their similarities with the characterized patterns.

1. *Relevant Colors Identification.*- As the algorithm is intended to deal with controlled lab environment, and outdoors natural scenes, it assumes the presence of illumination intensity artifacts as well as signal noise. So, once the *RGB* noise propagation through the Smiths' *HS* components is modelled ([13]) depending on the color position in the *HSI* space , the H and S *Stability Functions* providing the degree of confidence of any H-S pair are defined by Eq.1. Using these functions, we have described a method that computes a fuzzy (soft) histogram of the image pixels' H-S values, according to their uncertainty. It means that unstable color pixels will account less to the histogram distribution than stable ones.

Definition 1. *If x_H, x_S, x_I are the Hue, Saturation and Intensity values of pixel x, its H and S Stability degrees are given by:*

$$F_H\left(x_S, x_I\right) = \min\left(\frac{(k_H \cdot x_S \cdot x_I)}{20000}, 1\right); \quad F_S\left(x_I\right) = \min\left(\frac{(k_H \cdot x_S)}{500}, 1\right) \ . \quad (1)$$

Wherein scalar factors k_H and k_S can be chosen to suitably fit real data variability range.

Then, the fuzzy histogram is analyzed, using our specific watershed-based algorithm, to detect their predominant peaks that are supposed to correspond with the image relevant colors.

Figure 2-(a) depicts the projections, over the H-S domain, of three *potential distributions-pds-* associated to pixel-colors having the same measured I value, but different H and S values. As can be observed in 2-(a), as well as in the 3-D representation of 2-(b), *pds'* height decrease as pixel-color saturation decrease.

2. *Relevant Colors Characterization:* Once the colors have been defined, the system has to characterize their chromatic pattern. So, per each relevant color, two membership functions are obtained representing its typicality at each chromatic component value. This step is automatically carried out from the H and S histograms of each color pattern, an example is shown in Fig.3.

3. *Image Pixel Classification:* Finally, each pixel gets a global membership degree to each relevant color, so that the final *labelling* corresponds to the relevant color providing the maximum value. Moreover, to improve the classification rate in presence of unstable color values, the membership degrees can be modified by the pixels and color patterns stability. Equations (2) and (3) provide the similarity degrees of the H and S values of the pixel and the corresponding H and S values of a color C_k. In these expressions h_k and s_k are the central values

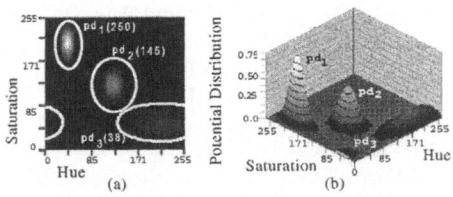

Fig. 2. *Potential distributions* of three pixels having the same measured I-value, but different H and S values. (a) Projection over the H-S domain; (b) 3-D representation.

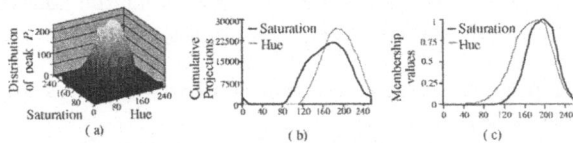

Fig. 3. (a) H-S histogram of Relevant Peak P_j; (b) Projections over the H and S axis; (c) *Hue* and *Saturation* membership functions of Relevant Color RC_j.

of the corresponding H and S membership functions, and $F_H(p_{ij})$ and $F_S(p_{ij})$ are the H and S *stability values* of pixel p_{ij}.

$$\mu_{C_k}'^H(p_{ij}) = \mu_{C_k}^H(h_k - (h_k - h_{ij}) \cdot F_H(p_{ij})) \ . \tag{2}$$

$$\mu_{C_k}'^S(p_{ij}) = \mu_{C_k}^S(s_k - (s_k - s_{ij}) \cdot F_H(p_{ij})) \ . \tag{3}$$

Then, the color patterns membership values are obtained by substituting the values obtained using expressions (2) and (3) within next expression

$$\mu_{C_k}(p_{ij}) = \sqrt{\mu_{C_k}'^H(p_{ij}) \cdot \mu_{C_k}'^S(p_{ij})} \ . \tag{4}$$

4 Results

For lack of space it has been impossible to include some results of the proposed algorithm, you can see them in: http://cubisme.upc.es/regofucov.

References

1. Bezdek, J. C., Chandrasekhar, R., Attikouzel, Y.: A geometric approach to edge detection. IEEE Trans. on Fuzzy Systems. **60(1)** (1998) 52–75
2. Bezdek, J., Keller, J., Krishnapuran, R., Pal, N.: Fuzzy Models and Algorithms for Pattern Recognition and Image Processing. Kluwer Publish., Norwell, MA. (1999)
3. Cheng, H. D., Jiang, X. H., Sun, Y., Wang,J.L.: Color image segmentation: advances and prospects. Pattern Recognition, **34(12)** (2001) 2259–2281
4. Chien, B. C., Cheng, M. C.: A color image segmentation approach based on fuzzy similarity measure. Proc. of the FUZZ-IEEE 02. (2002) 449–454
5. Dave, R. N.; Boundary detection through fuzzy clustering. Proc. of the FUZZ-IEEE 92. (1992) 127–134
6. Garcia-Barroso, C., Sobrevilla, P., Larre, A., Montseny, E.: Fuzzy contour detection based on a good approximation of the argument of the gradient vector. Proc. of the NAFIPS-FLINT 2002. (2002) 255–260
7. Haralick, R. M., Shapiro, L. G.: Image segmentation techniques. Computer Vision, Graphics and Image Processing. **29** (1985) 100–132
8. Keller, J. M.: Fuzzy Logic in Computer Vision. Proc. of the 6th Int. Fuzzy System Association World Congress (IFSA 95). (1995) 7–10
9. Marr, D.: Vision. San Francisco, CA:W.H. Freeman and Company. (1982)
10. Montseny, E., Sobrevilla, P.: On the Use Image Data Information for Getting a Brightness Perceptual Fuzzy Model. Proc. of the FUZZ-IEEE 02. (2002) 1086–1091
11. Pal, N. R., Pal, S. K.: A Review of Image Segmentation Techniques. Pettern Recognition. **26(9)** (1993) 1277–1294
12. Pao, Y. H.: Vague Features and Vague Decision Rules: The Fuzzy-Set Approach. Adaptive Patt. Recog. and Neural Networks. Ed. Addison Wesley. (1989) 51–81
13. Romani, S., Montseny, E., Sobrevilla, P.: Obtaining the Relevant Colors of an image through Stability-based Fuzzy Color Histograms. Proc. of the FUZZ-IEEE 03. (2003) 914–919
14. Russo, F., Ramponi, G.: Edge Extraction by FIRE Operators. Proc. of the FUZZ-IEEE 94. (1994) 249–253
15. Sobrevilla, P., Keller, J., Montseny, E.: Using a Fuzzy Morphological Structural Element for Image Segmentation. Proc. of the NAFIPS'00. (2000) 95–99
16. Tizhoosh, H. R.: Fast fuzzy edge detection. Proc. of NAFIPS'02. (2002) 239–242.

Generalized Multi-layer Kohonen Network and Its Application to Texture Recognition

A. Tomczyk[1], P.S. Szczepaniak[1,2], and B. Lis[1]

[1] Institute of Computer Science, Technical University of Lodz
Wolczanska 215, 93-005, Lodz, Poland
[2] Systems Research Institute, Polish Academy of Sciences
Newelska 6, 01-447 Warsaw, Poland

Abstract. In the paper a *multi-layer neural network* and its application to texture segmentation is presented. The generalized network is built using two types of elements: CU - clustering units and DCB - data completion blocks. Clustering units are composed of Kohonen networks. Each Kohonen network is a *self-organizing map* (SOM) trained to be able to distinguish, in an unsupervised way, certain clusters in the input data. Data completion blocks are placed between CU and their aim is to prepare data for the CU. This paper presents a sample application of a *double-layer network* to automatic texture segmentation. The method has been evaluated on both artificial and real images, and the results achieved are presented.

1 Introduction

The aim of the segmentation is to divide an image into regions that exhibit similar characteristic. Most of the segmentation techniques can be classified as either *edge-based* or *region-based* methods. The methods of the first type are aimed at detection of discontinuities between homogeneous areas while those of the second type try to group image pixels into regions that meet a given homogeneity criterion. The most popular approaches in the *region-based* segmentation are *region growing and splitting* methods, and more general *features vector clustering* methods. The latter are discussed in this paper.

The purpose of the clustering is to take a given set of object and assign a label to each object. This assignment is not random, that is similar objects (according to some actually considered similarity measure) should obtain the same label. Numerous known algorithms grouping objects into clusters can be divided into two main groups: *hierarchical clustering* methods and *partitioning clustering* methods. The first ones successively merge smaller clusters into larger or split larger (e.g. *single linkage procedure*). The methods of the second group, on the other hand, decompose data set into clusters directly (e.g. *k-means algorithm*). In image segmentation pixels are the usual objects that are being grouped (but in general objects can be larger structures). The different approaches to that problem can be found in the literature. For example in [8] *Gabor filters* are used for extracting features and *simulated annealing* for optimization of the

L. Rutkowski et al. (Eds.): ICAISC 2004, LNAI 3070, pp. 760–767, 2004.
© Springer-Verlag Berlin Heidelberg 2004

clustering objective function. In [9], however, texture features were extracted with *2-D moving average model* and a *fuzzy clustering* method was proposed for unsupervised segmentation. *Image block moments* and *growin regions* combined with *radial basis neural network* are another possible propositions ([7]).

The clustering method discussed here is a *multi-layer Kohonen network*. The idea of the *multi-layer architecture* as an advanced clustering method is not entirely new. Kaski and Kohonen in [3] used *double-layer architecture* for clustering large amount of text documents from the newsgroups, Lampinen and Oja in [5] discussed formal description of *double layer architecture*, and Koh, Suk and Bhandarkar in [4] utilised *multi-layer architecture* to hierarchical range image segmentation. As shown in the sequel, architecture presented here generalizes all the mentioned ideas which enables its use in a variety of other applications.

The article is organized as follows: section 2 presents motivation for the presented work, section 3 describes the proposed generalised architecture, section 4 contains description of the method of the sample neural network application to texture segmentation, and finally the last section presents a short discussion of the outcomes together with the main ideas for the future research directions.

2 Motivation

For proper clustering of the object set O, the most important issue is the choice of the object features. This choice (apart from the clustering algorithm itself) determines resulting clusters. Moreover Kohonen networks ([1,2,6,7,13,14]) require that the objects should be encoded in the form of *features vectors*; each ne becomes an input of the neurons. The encoding can be understood as a function e that assigns a vector from certain set F to a given object ($e : O \rightarrow F$, $F \subset \mathbb{R}^N$ and N is a number of features). Sometimes however, in more complex tasks, it proves to be very complicated to choose a proper set of features that leads to satisfactory clustering results. This can be caused by insufficient knowledge about the problem domain or by difficulty with utilising the existing, accessible knowledge while using a single *features vector*.

As an example, a simple situation can be considered where objects can be described by two features of the same type and additionally it is known that for the similarity of the objects the order of the values in the *features vector* does not matter. A *single-layer Kohonen network* is not able to give satisfactory results because it will rather assign different labels to objects encoded with the same values but in different order. It does not mean that there are no such features that can give satisfactory results but finding them can be a non-trivial task. In such a situations the *double-layer architecture* can be of use.

Generalizing the problem described above a hierarchical clustering algorithm can be built which can be a solution to some clustering problems where the *single-layer Kohonen network* fails because of difficulties with defining the proper *features vector*.

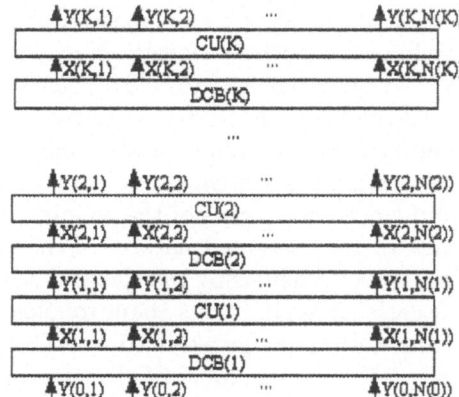

Fig. 1. The architecture of the proposed multi-layer, hierarchical clustering system (first index denotes layer number and the second a successive number of the element in the layer)

3 Architecture

The architecture proposed in this article is presented in Fig. 1. There are two main elements forming a hierarchical, *multi-layer structure*: DCB - data completion block and CU - clustering unit (K is the number of layers).

The aim of the CU elements is to independently assign label Y to each corresponding input vector X ($N(k)$ denotes number of the corresponding pairs in the k-th layer). Each label Y can also be a vector (it can be anything that can act as a unique label of the cluster e.g. index, generalized index, weight vector). The aim of the DCB is to prepare input vectors X basing on the outputs from the previous layer. Vectors $Y(0,n)$ ($n = 1, \ldots, N(0)$) are direct components of the *features vector* of the currently processed object ($Y(0,1) \times \ldots \times Y(0, N(0)) \in F$).

Each $CU(k)$ can be a set of the $N(k)$ independent Kohonen networks denoted as $KN(k,n)$ where $n = 1, \ldots, N(k)$ (Fig. 2a) or if all $X(k,n)$ vectors represent the same type of the *features vector* it can be composed of one $KN(k,1)$ that works successively on all input vectors giving corresponding labels (Fig. 2b). Other solutions may also be proposed.

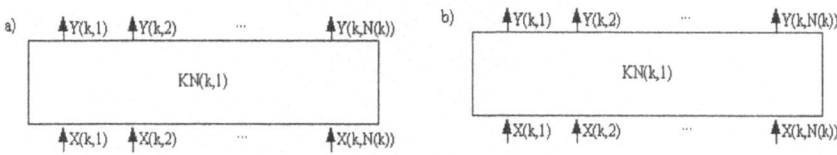

Fig. 2. Sample $CU(k)$ with a set of Kohonen networks (a) and $CU(k)$ where all $X(k,n)$ can be treated in the same way (b)

Such architecture generalizes the solutions mentioned above and met in the literature. In [3] the architecture with two layers ($K = 2$) was proposed, $Y(1, n)$ ($n = 1, \ldots, N(1)$) was the winner index and $DCB(2)$ generated a histogram from the outputs of $CU(1)$ ($N(2) = 1$). In [5] $K = 2$ as well but $N(1) = N(2) = 1$ and $Y(1, 1)$ was the multidimensional index of the winner neuron from the first layer. In [4], there was a *multi-layer architecture*, where $Y(k, n)$ ($k = 1, \ldots K$, $n = 1, \ldots, N(k)$) were the current weights of the winning neuron in $KN(k, n)$.

Because all the units of the presented network architecture can work independently all the KN can be trained using the classical algorithms ([1,2,11,12]). This architecture makes also no assumptions about topology of the KN. Further the following additional notation will be assumed: $NN(k, n)$ number of neurons in $KN(k, n)$, $NX(k, n)$, $NY(k, n)$ - number of elements in vectors $X(k, n)$ and $Y(k, n)$ respectively (thus for example $N = NY(0, 1) + \ldots + NY(0, N(0))$).

4   Sample Application and Results

The main problem in pixel clustering is proper definition of the *feature vector*. Usually the choice of homogenity criterion is more complicated than the simple choice of the pixel color and the task of choosing a proper pixel features becomes non-trivial. One of the most challenging tasks in that field is texture recognition.

Texture in the image analysis has no formal definition. For real images it can be understood as a way of the intensity variation that allows to distinguish such properties of the areas as smoothness, coarseness, regularity, etc. ([15,17]). The three main approaches used to describe textures are statistical, spectral, and structural. Here the third approach will be in the focus of attention.

Structural techniques describe texture as composed of simple primitives which are texture elements. Those elements, called *texels*, are regularly arranged on a surface according to certain rules (Fig. 3). Sometimes those rules can be really simple, e.g. in artificial images where *texels* are often uniformly distributed. In general, however, the rules are more complicated and grammars of various types must be used to formalize their description.

To define *features vectors* the concept of *frames* proposed in [16] can be used. Each *frame* decides which image points should be considered together with clustered pixel. The simplest *frame* is a rectangular one where points lie

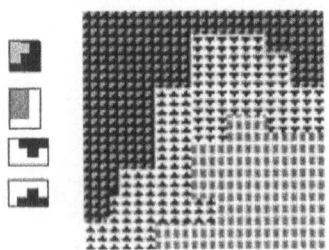

Fig. 3. Artificial image with four types of textures (on the left corresponding *texels*)

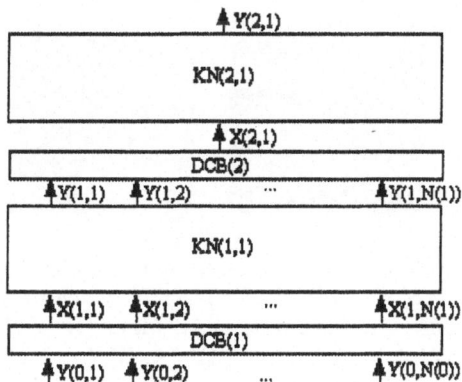

Fig. 4. Architecture used for texture segmentation ($Y(0,n) = X(1,n)$ - the *frames*, $Y(1,n)$ - label of the *frame* $X(1,n)$, $X(2,1)$ - histogram of the labels $Y(1,n)$, $Y(2,1)$ - final label of the pixel)

in the intersection points of the rectangular grid (W - width and H - height) with center in the currently considered pixel. Another type of frame could be a *linear-polar frame* where points lie in the intersection point of the concentric circles and equally distributed radii (C - number of circles, R - number of radii, A - distance between circles) ([16]).

A traditional *single-layer Kohonen network* is not able to cope with a segmentation process using any of those *frames* as an input vector because each pixel in a single *texel* can have a different *frame* (Fig. 5a). That is why the *double-layer architecture* ($K = 2$) can be of use here ([16]). In the proposed algorithm not only frame of the currently considered pixel is presented but also the *frames* of some pixels from the *neighbourhood* e.g. rectangular *neighbourhood* (further WN and HN denote dimensions of that ractangle). Each vector $Y(0,n)$ ($n = 1,\ldots,N(0)$ where $N(0)$ is a number of the elements in the *neighbourhood*) represents a single *frame*. $DCB(1)$ returns the unchanged input vectors as its outputs ($N(0) = N(1)$ and $X(1,n) = Y(0,n)$) (the same result can be obtained otherwise when there is only one input vector $Y(0,1)$ that contains pixel values for all the pixels from *neighbourhood* and the aim of $DCB(1)$ is to decompose it into frames $X(1,n)$). $CU(1)$ is composed of a single KN (Fig. 2b) whose aim is to cluster coming *frames* for all pixels from *neighbourhood* independently and return ($Y(1,n)$) the number of the winning vector (it encodes possible patterns of incoming frames in weight vectors of its neurons). $DCB(2)$ completes the number of the winners and builds histogram of those values $X(2,1)$ ($N(2) = 1$). $CU(2)$ is a single KN and its aim is to find clusters among those histograms.

The results achieved using described above method are promising. Fig. 5b and Fig. 5c present results obtained using *double-layer architecture* with *rectangular* and *linear-polar frame*. Both gave satisfactory results. However, the latter was always presented only in its basic orientation. That is why both output images are similar and two areas with texels rotated by 180 degrees were grouped into two different clusters which could be acceptable if in the considered problem

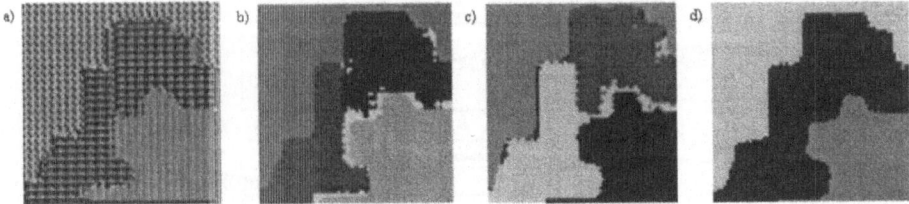

Fig. 5. Segmentation results for: *single-layer Kohonen network* $(NN(1,1) = 100)$ with *rectangular frame* $(W = H = 5)$ (a), *double-layer Kohonen network* $(NN(1,1) = 100,$ $NN(2,1) = 5, WN = HN = 5)$ with *rectangular frame* $(W = H = 5)$ (b), *double-layer Kohonen network* $(NN(1,1) = 100, NN(2,1) = 5, WN = HN = 5)$ with *linear-polar frame* $(C = 6, R = 8, A = 1)$ without rotations (c) and *double-layer Kohonen network* $(NN(1,1) = 100, NN(2,1) = 5, WN = HN = 5)$ with *linear-polar frame* $(C = 6,$ $R = 8, A = 1)$ with rotations (d)

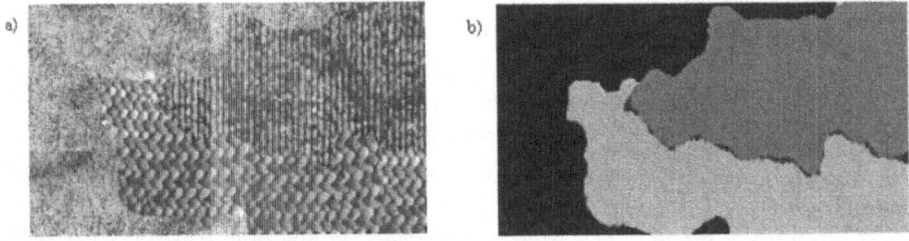

Fig. 6. Image with fabric textures (a) and results obtained for *rectangular frame* $(NN(1,1) = 100, NN(2,1) = 4, W = H = 9, WN = HN = 9)$ (b)

those two areas represented two different objects. However, if the orientation of texels was not important and these areas should be treated as one object the additional presentations must be used in *linear-polar frame* (Fig. 5d) as described in [16].

The method gives also satisfactory results for real images where strict patterns of texels cannot be distinguished and where even the same texels can differ slightly (Fig. 6b).

5   Conclusions

The architecture presented in this paper can be of use there, where the problems with proper choice of the features of the objects that are to be grouped together into clusters exists and additionally there are known some other relations between already known features or between groups of those features. It does not make any assumptions about type of the grouped objects and about labels assigned to them so it can be utilised in any kind of clustering problem. Moreover it generalizes the other types of the similar architectures that can be found in the literature ([3,4,5,14]).

In this article the double-layer version of this architecture was utilised in a practical problem. Even though not fully automated, the segmentation technique presented in this article is able to cope with texture recognition. The discussion of the parameters of this method can be found in [16]. The main advantage of this technique is the fact that only a little a priori knowledge about considered image is needed. Moreover using a proper *frame* it can cope with texture rotations. The problem of scale invariance was not solved in this approach but idea of *logarithmic-polar frame* ([16]) seems to be promising for further research. The main drawback of this method (and potentially of all the methods basing on this architecture) can be a number of calculations that makes the whole process of clustering time-consuming. However, it could be overcome using either parallel calculations (some units of the network can work independently) or simply by caching some results whose calculation can be repeated during clustering process (e.g. the same *frames* are used for clustering different pixels). In similiar form the method can be used for images described on a higher level of abstraction where image is described by larger structures then pixels. All these aspects are being still thoroughly investigated.

References

1. Kohonen T.: Self-organized formation of topologically correct feature maps. Biological Cybernetics **43** (1982) 59–69
2. Kohonen T.: Self-organizing maps. Springer Berlin (1995)
3. Kohonen T., Kaski S., Lagus K., Honkela T.: Very Large Two-Level SOM for the Browsing of Newsgroups. ICANN'96 Bochum Germany, Lecture Notes in Computer Science, Springer Berlin, vol. **1112** (1996) 269–274
4. Koh J., Suk M., Bhandarkar S. M.: A Multi-Layer Kohonen's Self-Organizing Feature Map for Range Image Segmentation. Neural Networks, vol. **8**, no. **1** (1995) 67–86
5. Lampinen J., Oja E.: Clustering Properties of Hierarchical Self-Organizing Maps. Journal of Mathematical Imaging and Vision, vol **2** (1992) 261–272
6. Haykin S.: Neural Networks. A comprehensive Foundation. Macmillan Publ. Comp., Englewood Cliffs (1994)
7. Looney C. G.: Pattern recognition using Neural Networks. Oxford University Press, New York, Oxford (1997)
8. Hoffmann T., Puzicha J., Buchmann J. M.: Deterministic annealing for unsupervised texture segmentation. Lecture Notes in Computer Science: Proc. Int. Workshop on Energy Minimazation Methods in Computer Vision and Pattern Recognition, Venice, Springr-Verlag Berlin (1997) 213–228
9. Eom K.: Segmentation of monochrome and color textures using moving average modelling approach: Image Vis. Comput. J. **17(3-4)** (1999) 233–244
10. Won C. S., Derin H.: Unsupervised Segmentation of Noisy and Textured Images Using Markov Random Fields. CVGIP: Graphical Models and Image Processing, vol. **54**, no. **4** (1992) 306–328
11. Jain A. K., Forokhnia F.: Unsupervised Texture Segmentation Using Gabor Filters: Pattern Recognition, vol. **24**, no. **12** (1991) 1167–1186
12. Mirmehdi M., Petrou M.: Segmentation of Color Textures. IEEE Transactions on Pattern Analysis and Machine Intelligence, vol. **22**, no. **2** (2000) 142–159

13. Tadeusiewicz R.: Sieci neuronowe (Neural networks). Akademicka Oficyna Wydawnicza RM, Warsaw (1993) (in Polish)
14. Osowski S.: Sieci neuronowe do przetwarzania informacji (Neural networks in information processing). Oficyna Wydawnicza Politechniki Warszawskiej, Warsaw (2000) (in Polish)
15. Zielinski K. W., Strzelecki M.: Komputerowa analiza obrazu biomedycznego, wstep do morfometrii i patologii ilosciowej (Computer analysis of biomedical image, an introduction to morphometry and quantitative pathology). PWN, Warsaw-Lodz (2002) (in Polish)
16. Lis B., Szczepaniak P. S., Tomczyk A.: Multi-layer Kohonen Network and Texture Recognition. WISSC-2'03 Warsaw International Seminar on Soft Computing, Systems Research Institute, Polish Academy of Sciences (2003)
17. Pal S. K., Mitra S.: Neuro-Fuzzy Pattern Recognition. John Wiley & Sons, New York (1999)

Translation STRIPS Planning in Multi-robot Environment to Linear Programming

Adam Galuszka and Andrzej Swierniak

Silesian University of Technology, 44-100 Gliwice, Poland
agaluszka@ia.polsl.gliwice.pl

Abstract. In the paper multi-robot environment with STRIPS representation is considered. Under some assumptions such problems can be modelled as a STRIPS system (for instance Block World environment) with one initial state and disjunction of goal states. If STRIPS planning problem is invertible then it is possible to apply machinery for planning in the presence of incomplete information to solve the inverted problem and then to find a solution for the original problem. To reduce computational complexity of this approach a transformation to Linear Programming problem is proposed. Simulations illustrate the reduced problem.

1 Introduction

In multi-agent (multi-robot) environment each agent tries to achieve its own goal [2]. It leads to complications in problem modelling and searching for a solution: in most cases agent goals are conflicting, agents have usually different capabilities and goals preferences, agents interact with problem environment simultaneously. In our case problem environment was modelled as Block World with STRIPS representation. This domain is often used to model planning problems ([2], [9], [13], [5]) because of complex actions definition and simple physical interpretation. Starting from 1970s STRIPS formalism [10] seems to be the most popular for planning problems [14]. Planning problems algorithms usually are at least NP-hard, even in Block World environment (here the problem of optimal planning is NP-complete). Block World today stated an experimentation benchmark for planning algorithms [7]. Also more realistic situations can be presented as Block World problems, where moving blocks corresponds to moving different objects like packages, trucks and planes [11]. The case of Block World problem where the table has a limited capacity corresponds to a container loading problem [12].

1.1 Problem Definition

We focus on the following situation:
- in the initial state there are a finite number of blocks and a table with unlimited place;
- two (or, in general case, more) robots want to rebuilt the initial state, each in its own way (each robot wants to achieve its own desired goal situation);

L. Rutkowski et al. (Eds.): ICAISC 2004, LNAI 3070, pp. 768–773, 2004.
© Springer-Verlag Berlin Heidelberg 2004

- goal of each robot consists of subgoals;
- each subgoal has its preference (subgoals are more or less important for robots). This is not considered in this paper;
- robots have different capabilities (i.e. each robot is not able to move all blocks);
- robots can not cooperate (this assumption is justified in the case where in the environment the communication is not allowed or communication equipment is broken down).

We are interested in the following two problems:
- to find a solution for above situation;
- to reduce computational complexity of searching for this problem solution.

1.2   Method of Finding a Solution

The problem where there are some possible initial states and one goal state is called problem of planning in the presence of incompleteness. The inverted problem is the situation with one initial state and more possible goal states. It corresponds to multi-robot Block World problem where each robot wants to achieve its own goal. If we are able to find a plan for problem of planning in the presence of incompleteness, then it is possible to extract solution for multi-agent problem.

1.3   Organization of This Paper

In section 2 STRIPS planning problem and property of invertability of such problem are defined. In section 3 a transformation of STRIPS planning to Linear Programming is described. In section 4 simulation results are presented. All is concluded.

2   STRIPS Planning Problem and Its Invertability

In general, STRIPS system is represented by four lists $(C;\ O;\ I;\ G)$ ([3], [10]):
- a finite set of ground atomic formulas (C), called conditions;
- a finite set of operators (O);
- a finite set of predicates that denotes initial state (I);
- a finite set of predicates that denotes goal state (G).

Initial state describes physical configuration of the blocks. Description should be complete i.e. should deal with every true predicate corresponding to the state. Goal situation is a conjunction of predicates. In multi-agent environment each agent defines own goal. The algorithm result is an ordered set of operators which transforms an initial state into a goal situation. This set is called a plan. Operators O in STRIPS representation consist of three sublists: a precondition list , a delete list and an add list. The precondition list is a set of predicates that must be satisfied in world-state to perform this operator. The delete list is a set of predicates that stay false after performing the operator and the add list is a set that stay true. Two last lists show effects of operator performing in problem state.

Now consider the situation where for a given STRIPS planning problem and for a given plan that solves this problem one is interested in a new problem: to find a plan that transforms now the goal state into the initial one. If such plan exists then the problem is called invertible. This property is connected with the invertability of the operators. Under closed world assumption applying an inverse operator leads back to the previous state. It is proved that if there exists an inverse operator for each operator, then the problem is invertible [8].

Without loss of generality for defined in section 1 multi-robot environment Block World as STRIPS planning problem limited to only completely decomposed initial state (i.e. all blocks are on the table) will only be considered. Then the inverted problem is to decompose all possible initial states (i.e. goal definition consists only of 'on-table' predicates). The number of possible initials corresponds to number of robots. So the inverted problem is planning in the presence of incompleteness.

In general planning with complete information is a NP-complete problem (optimal planning in Block World environment is NP-complete [6]). Planning in the presence of incompleteness belongs to the next level in the hierarchy of completeness [1]. That is why polynomial transformation of defined problem to Linear Programming problem and is proposed. Then the solution of the problem with incomplete information will be analyzed.

3   Transformation to Linear Programming Problem

Following [4] the transformation from planning to Linear Programming is based on mapping of conditions and operators in each plan step to variables. Truth values of conditions are mapped to 0 and 1 for the planning without incompleteness, and to any values between 0 and 1 for planning with incomplete information. The objective function reaches the maximum if the goal situation is true in last step of planning.

As an example consider the problem of planning in Block World environment with 4 blocks (called A, B, C, D). The goal is to decompose the initial state. It is assumed one STRIPS operator that moves the block x from the block y to the table:

   $move$-to-$table(x,y)$:
   $preconditions$: $on(x,y)$, $clear(x)$
   del: $not(on(x,y))$
   add: $clear(y)$

The goal is reached if the following conditions are true:

   $clear(A)$, $clear(B)$, $clear(C)$, $clear(D)$

Assume 2 steps of planning (states indexes are: 0, 1, 2). So (16+16+16) variables are needed for conditions:

   $on(A,B)(i)$, $on(A,C)(i)$, $on(A,D)(i)$, $on(B,A)(i)$, $on(B,C)(i)$, $on(B,D)(i)$, $on(C,A)(i)$, $on(C,B)(i)$, $on(C,D)(i)$, $on(D,A)(i)$, $on(D,B)(i)$, $on(D,C)(i)$, $clear(A)(i)$, $clear(B)(i)$, $clear(C)(i)$, $clear(D)(i)$
   for $i = 0, 1, 2$.

In addition (12+12) variables are needed for operators (12 for transformation from state 0 to 1 and 12 from 1 to 2):

move-to-table(A,B)(i),   *move-to-table(A,C)(i)*,   *move-to-table(A,D)(i)*, *move-to-table(B,A)(i)*, *move-to-table(B,C)(i)*, *move-to-table(B,D)(i)*, *move-to-table(C,A)(i)*,   *move-to-table(C,B)(i)*,   *move-to-table(C,D)(i)*,   *move-to-table(D,A)(i)*, *move-to-table(D,B)(i)*, *move-to-table(D,C)(i)* for $i = 0, 1$.

The objective function is:

$$Max \ (\ clear(A)(2) \ + \ clear(B)(2) \ + \ clear(C)(2) \ + \ clear(D)(2) \ )$$

If the goal is reached then the objective function is equal to 4 (4 conditions are true in the goal state).

Constraints for Linear Programming problem are:

- at most 1 operator can be applied in each planning step (for the problem with complete information) or the sum of operators truth degrees in each step is equal to 1 (for the problem with incomplete information):

$$\sum move\text{-}to\text{-}table(x,y)(i) \leq 1$$

for $i = 0, 1$.

Operator can not be applied unless its preconditions are true:

$on(x,y)(i) \geq move\text{-}to\text{-}table(x,y)(i)$
(for all 12 operators in each planning step)

$clear(A)(i) \geq move\text{-}to\text{-}table(A,B)(i) + move\text{-}to\text{-}table(A,C)(i) +$
$move\text{-}to\text{-}table(A,D)(i);$

$clear(B)(i) \geq move\text{-}to\text{-}table(B,A)(i) + move\text{-}to\text{-}table(B,C)(i) +$
$move\text{-}to\text{-}table(B,D)(i);$

$clear(C)(i) \geq move\text{-}to\text{-}table(C,A)(i) + move\text{-}to\text{-}table(C,B)(i) +$
$move\text{-}to\text{-}table(C,D)(i);$

$clear(D)(i) \geq move\text{-}to\text{-}table(D,A)(i) + move\text{-}to\text{-}table(D,B)(i) +$
$move\text{-}to\text{-}table(D,C)(i)$

for $i = 0, 1$.

Next group of constraints describe changes of the state after applying an operator. These are equality constraints:

$clear(A)(i+1) = clear(A)(i) + move\text{-}ta\text{-}table(B,A)(i) + move\text{-}to\text{-}table(C,A)(i)$
$+ move\text{-}to\text{-}table(D,A)(i)$

and similar for blocks: *B*, *C* and *D*, and:

$on(A,B)(i+1) = on(A,B)(i) - move\text{-}to\text{-}table(A,B)(i).$

Finally constraints for variables are needed: these should be mapped between 0 and 1 values what corresponds to truth degree of the variables.

4   Simulation Results

Two test cases have been implemented in MATLAB. In first case problem with complete information has been solved, in second case - problem with incomplete information. For both cases transformation to Linear Programming results the problem with 72 variables, 34 inequality constraints and 32 equality constraints.

In the first case the problem was to decompose the initial state defined below:

on(A,B), on(D,C), clear(A), clear(D).

The solution of Linear Programming algorithm is the set of variables values that gives optimal (maximal) value of objective function. These corresponds to truth values of operators: *move-to-table(D,C)*(0)=1 and *move-to-table(A,B)*(1)=1 that solve planning problem in 2 steps.

In the second case represents the problem with incomplete information in initial state (then the inverted problem corresponds to problem with two robots with conflicting goals). The initial state now consists of two possible initial situations:

(on(A,B), on(D,C), clear(A), clear(D)) or (on(A,C), on(D,B), clear(A), clear(D)).

In the initial state the truth values of variables *on(A,B)(0)*, *on(D,C)(0)*, *on(A,C)(0)*, *on(D,B)(0)* are equal to 0.5 what represents the uncertainty whether block *A* is on *C* or *B* and block *D* is on *C* or *B*.

Now the solution corresponds to truth values of operators: *move-to-table(A,B)(0)*=0.5 and *move-to-table(A,C)(0)*=0.5 and *move-to-table(D,B)(1)*=0.5 and *move-to-table(D,C)(1)*=0.5 that solve planning problem also in 2 steps. The interpretation of this solution is as follow: first move block A to the table (from B or C) then move block D (from B or C). The inversion of this solution leads to solution of 2 robots problem with conflicting goals.

5   Conclusion

Defining Block World environment as an invertible STRIPS planning problem allows to apply planning in the presence of incompleteness as a machinery of searching for a solution of inverted multi-agent problem and then extraction of a solution for the primary multi-robot problem. The approach presented in the paper is applicable only to the work block model. It should be interesting to extend this work to other domains. The group of robots which move blocks is an agent based system (not multi agent system) because there is no communication among the constituent agents.

Translation to Linear Programming allows to reduce computational complexity of searching for the solution. That is because planning in the presence of incompleteness is usual at least NP-complete problem, Linear Programming is polynomial-time complete problem and transation from STRIPS to Linear Programming is also polynomial [4]. The cost of this approach is that algorithm can results in non-interpretable solutions for some initial states (what is followed by assumption N $\neq$ NP).

Acknowledgement. This work was supported by State Committee for Scientific Research (KBN) grant No. 4 T11A 012 23 in the year 2004.

References

1. Baral Ch., Kreinovich V., Trejo R.: Computational complexity of planning and approximate planning in the presence of incompleteness. Artificial Intelligence **122** (2000) 241–267
2. Boutilier C., Brafman R.I.: Partial-Order Planning with Concurrent Interacting Actions. Journal of Artificial Intelligence Research **14** (2001) 105–136
3. Bylander T.: The Computational Complexity of Propositional STRIPS Planning. Artificial Intelligence **69** (1994) 165–204
4. Bylander T.: A Linear Programming Heuristic for Optimal Planning. Conf. American Association for Artificial Intelligence (1997)
5. Galuszka A., Swierniak A.: Planning in multi-agent environment as inverted STRIPS planning in the presence of uncertainty. Recent Advances in Computers, Computing and Communications, WSEAS Press (Ed. July 2002) 58–63
6. Gupta N., Nau D.S.: On the complexity of Blocks-World Planning. Artificial Intelligence bf 56(2-3) (1992) 223–254
7. Howe A.E., Dahlman E.: A Critical Assessment of Benchmark Comparison in Planning. Journal of Artificial Intelligence Research **17** (2002) 1–33
8. Koehler J., Hoffmann J.: On Reasonable and Forced Goal Orderings and their Use in an Agenda-Driven Planning Algorithm. Journal of Artificial Intelligence Research **12** (2000) 339–386
9. Kraus S., Sycara K., Evenchik A.: Reaching agreements through argumentation: a logical model and implementation. Artificial Intelligence **104** (1998) 1–69
10. Nilson N.J.: Principles of Artificial Intelligence. Toga Publishing Company, Palo Alto (1980)
11. Slaney J., Thiebaux S.: Block World revisited. Artificial Intelligence **125** (2001) 119–153
12. Slavin T.: Virtual port of call. New Scientist (June 1996) 40–43
13. Weld D.S., Anderson C.R., Smith D.E.: Extending Graphplan to Handle Uncertainty and Sensing Actions. Proc. 15th National Conf. on AI (1998) 897–904
14. Weld D.S.: Recent Advantages in AI Planning. Technical Report UW-CSE-98-10-01, AI Magazine (1999)

Fuzzy Combiner of Behaviors for Reactive Control of Wheeled Mobile Robot

Zenon Hendzel

Rzeszow University of Technology,
Department of Applied Mechanics and Robotics,
Powstancow Warszwy 8, 35-959 Rzeszow, Poland
zenhen@prz.rzeszow.pl

Abstract. This paper proposes a sensor based navigation method with fuzzy combiner for navigation of mobile robot in uncertain environments. The proposed navigator consists of two main behaviors: a reaching the middle of a collision-free space behavior, and goal-seeking behavior. The fuzzy combiner can fuse low-level behaviors so that the mobile robot can go for the goal position without colliding with obstacles. The fuzzy combiner is a soft switch that chooses more then one low-level action to be active with different degrees through fuzzy combination at each time step. The output of the navigation level is fed into a fuzzy tracking controller that takes into account the dynamics of the mobile robot. Computer simulation have been conducted to illustrate the performance of the proposed fuzzy combiner of behaviors by a series of experiments on the emulator of wheeled mobile robot $Pioneer - 2DX$.

1 Introduction

Several researchers have already argued the importance of looking at a mobile robot as a set of elementary behaviors [1,3,6,8]. Elementary behaviors are important components of reactive control in which mobile robot must continuously interact with their environment. By reactive control is means that all decisions are based on the currently perceived sensory information [2,4,6,7]. An important consequence of the reactive approach is that for the high level in hierarchical structure, we don't need any environmental modelling. The fundamental idea of behavioral control is to view a mobile robot missions as the simultaneous and temporal execution of a set of elementary behaviors. Numerous behavior co-ordination mechanisms have been proposed. For a detailed overview, discussion, and comparison of behavior co-ordination mechanisms see [3,9]. Behavior co-ordination mechanisms can be divided into two main classes: arbitration and command fusion [3]. Command fusion mechanisms provides for a co-ordination scheme that allows all behaviors to simultaneously contribute to the control of the system in a co-operative manner. Command fusion approach, with fuzzy mechanism, which allow for weighted combination of behaviors [3,9], is using in this work to solve the task of reactive navigation of mobile robot in uncertain

L. Rutkowski et al. (Eds.): ICAISC 2004, LNAI 3070, pp. 774–779, 2004.
© Springer-Verlag Berlin Heidelberg 2004

environments. The proposed navigator consists of two main behaviors: a reaching the middle of a collision-free space behavior, and goal-seeking behavior. It
is assumed, that each low-level behavior has been well designed at design stage
and then fused by fuzzy combiner of behaviors to determine a proper actions
acting on the environment at running stage.

2   Fuzzy Combiner of the Behaviors

This section introduces the structures and functions of the proposed fuzzy navigator and its key component fuzzy combiner of two behaviors: obstacle avoidance and goal seeking. In this research, the scheme of the mobile robot used,
like $Pioneer - 2DX$, is shown in figure 1. Presented robot has two degrees of
freedom. In the word co-ordinates a posture is defined as $[x_A, y_A, \beta]^T$ where
(x_A, y_A) is the position of the point A, and β is the heading angle of the robot
with respect to absolute co-ordinates (x, y). The mobile robot's kinematics is
defined by

$$\begin{bmatrix} \dot{x}_A \\ \dot{y}_A \\ \dot{\beta} \end{bmatrix} = \begin{bmatrix} V_{Am}\cos\beta & 0 \\ V_{Am}\sin\beta & 0 \\ 0 & \omega_m \end{bmatrix} \begin{bmatrix} u_v \\ u_\beta \end{bmatrix} \qquad (1)$$

with the maximum linear V_{Am} and angular ω_m speeds, where u_v is the multiplying coefficient applied to the maximum linear velocity of point A of the robot
and u_β is the multiplying coefficient applied to the maximum angular velocity
of the frame. Described mobile robot is equipped with eight an ultrasonic sensor
ring as depicted in figure1. The radius of the sensors s_i, is L_i and sensors are divided into three group. A group is composed of three, two and three neighboring
sensors, gives a distance to the obstacle d_{Li}, d_{Fi}, d_{Ri}, in its field of view, where
$d_{min} \le d_{(.)} \le d_{max}$ and each sensor covers an angular view which are oriented by
angles $\alpha_{Li}, \alpha_{Fi}, \alpha_{Ri}$ respectively. The navigation task is defined as navigating the

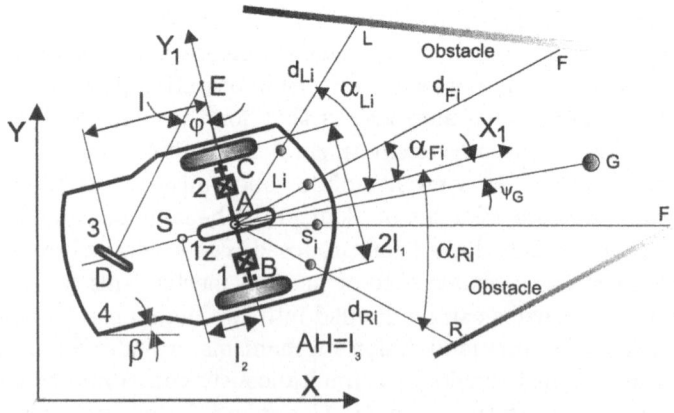

Fig. 1. The scheme of the mobile robot

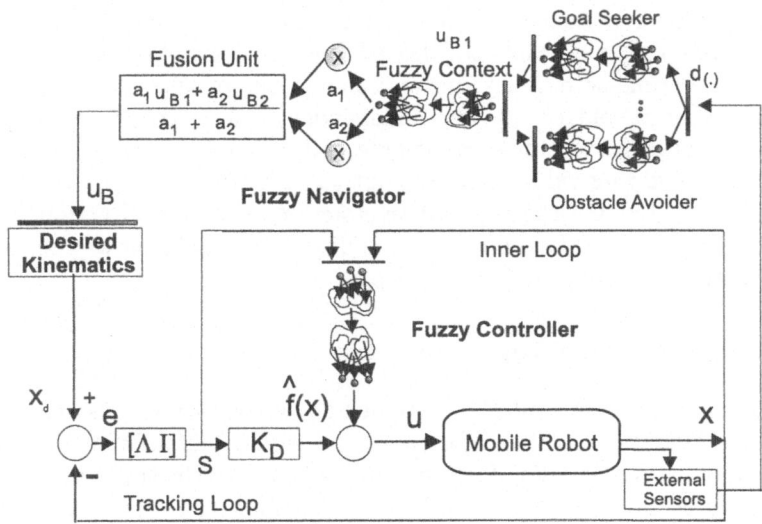

Fig. 2. Navigator and controller architecture

mobile robot from a start co-ordinate to its goal without colliding with obstacles in between. To solving this control problem for non-holonomic mobile robot with considering the vehicle dynamics [4,5,7], it is assumed that the current configuration of the mobile robot $x_d = [x_A, y_A, \beta]^T$ (desired kinematics) is generated at each time step, by fuzzy navigator which generates vector of multiplying coefficient $u_B = [u_v, u_\beta]^T$, based on the environment information, $d_{(.)}$ as depicted in figure 2. When the mobile robot encounters a obstacle which obstructs the goal, these two behaviors are in conflict. In this paper we adopt the concept of gating architecture [3,9] to solve this conflict. In the proposed multi objective fuzzy navigator we use fuzzy combiner (FC) to combine low-level modules which are denoted as obstacle avoider (OA) and goal seeker (GS) in figure 2. Each module receives distances sensed by the ultrasonic sensors and produce output signals. The OA determines the action $u_{B2} = [u_{vOA}, u_{\beta OA}]^T$ for the behavior of obstacle avoidance, while the GS determines the action, $u_{B1} = [u_{vGS}, u_{\beta GS}]^T$ for the behavior of goal seeking. These two behavioral modules work independently and their actions are fused by the FC to produce action $u_B = [u_v, u_\beta]^T$ for the navigation. It is assumed that each low-level module has been well designed to serve a particular objective of the required multiple objectives. Many techniques have been development to design single objective. This techniques include fuzzy modeling, neural network, etc. As shown in figure 2, the proposed FC is composed of two elements, a fuzzy context unit and an integration unit. The fuzzy context decides a set of the weights for the two low-level module action according to two control status signal $J(the'context')$ generated by environment feedback signal at each time step. The control status signals indicate the status of the control objectives and are defined by

$$J_i = degree \, (distance \, of \, goal_i) \,, i = 1, 2 \tag{2}$$

where any proper distance measure can be used. The control status signal J defined in the above indicates the degree that i-th control objective is achieved at the current time step. Such information can be obtained by simply checking the status of each control objective independently. The weights a_i produced by the fuzzy context determines the degree of the low-level control action u_{Bi} . With these weighting values, the integration unit will do the linearly weighted summation to combine the two low-level actions into a final action u_B as the output of the FC. Due to the powerful ability fuzzy modeling we consider fuzzy techniques to realize the FC in this paper.

3   Design Fuzzy Combiner

In this section, the proposed FC is applied to two behaviors: obstacle avoidance and goal seeking, to show its performance and applicability. Before design an FC for the fuzzy navigator, using fuzzy technique based on the trial-and-error design approach, it is assumed that each low-level module has been well designed [6, 7].To design the proposed FC, first we need to define two control status signals J_1 and J_2 . Let the inputs variables of a fuzzy navigator are respectively a measured distances on the right, $d_R = max\,(s_6, s_7, s_8)$ on the left, $d_L = max\,(s_1, s_2, s_3)$ and in the front, $d_F = min\,(s_4, s_5)$, and d is the distance between point A and G. Let us define the errors: $e_R = d_R - d$, $e_L = d_L - d$, $e_F = d_F - d$, and ψ_G is the angular deviation needed to reach the goal G. Control status signals are defined as follows according to the two control objectives

$$J_1 = [e_L, e_R, e_F]^T, J_2 = \psi_G \qquad (3)$$

They are normalized to be in $e_{min} \le e_{(.)} \le e_{max}$ and $-\pi \le \psi_G \le \pi$ respectively. The used FC is build with fuzzy inference systems based on a set of rules such as: $If(e_{(.)}isA_i)$ and $(\psi_G isB_i)$ Then $(a_i isC_i)$ and $If(e_{(.)}isA_i)$ and $(\psi_G$ is $B_i)$ Then $(a_i is \neg C_i)$ where A_i, B_i, C_i are linguistic labels of the inputs $e_{(.)}, \psi_G$ and of the outputs a_1, a_2. The shape of the membership functions is triangular and the whole rule-base is depicted in figure 3 in six decision tables. The term set for J_1 and J_2 is $(N - negative, P - positive)$ and $(N - negative, Z - zero, P - positive)$ respectively and the term set for a_i and a_2 is $(S - small, L - large)$. In the FC the inputs are the control status signals J_1 and J_2, and the output are the weighting values of low-level modules 1 and 2, a_1, a_2 . From rule tables we observe that module 1 will be activated, i.e. $a_1 = L$,when $J_{11} > 0$ and $J_2 < 0$ or $J_{12} > 0$ and $J_2 > 0$ or $J_{13} > 0$ and $J_2 = 0$. At the same times module 2 is suppressed i.e. $a_2 = S$. We also observe that module 2 is activated, i.e. $a_2 = L$ only when the first goal is suppressed i.e. $a_1 = S$. The design method for the FC is straightforward. It relies heavily on expert knowledge and the precise analysis of discussions problem.

4   Simulation

To illustrate the performance of the proposed fuzzy combiner for path planning and control, first it was build simulator of the mobile robot and workspace

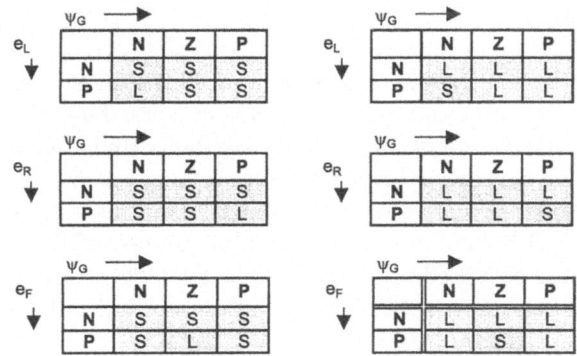

Fig. 3. Rule table for a_1 and a_2

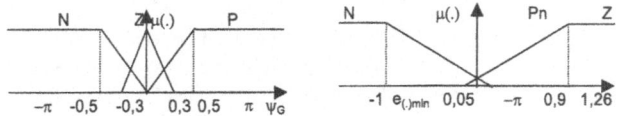

Fig. 4. Membership functions of fuzzy terms in Fig.3

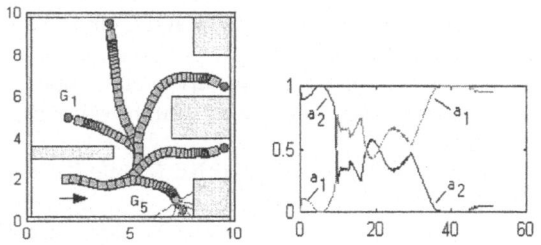

Fig. 5. Trajectories of point A and weights a_i

in Matlab/Simulink [6]. We performed simulation in which, the rule-base tables depicted in figure 3 were put into the $Max - Min$ inference algorithm to evaluate the rules and the center average method is used for the defuzzification a_1, a_2, where $L = 1, S = 0$. The shape of the membership functions is triangular and is depicted in figure 4. An example of the resulting fuzzy combiner is shown in figure 5. The mobile robot had received mission to reach a given goal position G_i from given start position with reaching the middle of a collision-free space. The environment was consider as fixed and completely unknown.

The successive activation of the different behaviors can be observed in figure 5. As depicted in figure 5 for given goal position G_5, more than a behavior is active at the same time, that permits a soft transition.

5   Conclusion

We have presented a fuzzy navigator, which is based on expert knowledge, that performs well in complex and unknown environments. The principle of the navigator is built on the fusion of the obstacle avoidance and goal seeking behaviors. The output of the navigation level is fed into a fuzzy tracking controller that takes into account the dynamics of the mobile robot. The numerical experimental results obtained with emulator of mobile robot Pioneer-2DX confirmed also the effectiveness of the proposed path planning and control strategy. Future research will concentrate on applying proposed solution as a priori knowledge used in a reinforcement learning approach.

References

1. Arkin R.C.: Behaviour-Based Robotics. The MIT Press (1998)
2. Berenstain J.,Koren J.: Real-Time Obstacle Avoidance for Fast Mobile Robots. IEEE Transaction on Systems Man and Cybernetics Vol.19 (1989) No.5 1179–1186
3. Driankov D., Saffiotti, A., Ed.: Fuzzy Logic Techniques for Autonomous Vehicle Navigation. Springer-Verlag (2001)
4. Hendzel Z.: Adaptive Fuzzy Controller of Wheeled Mobile Robot. Proc. of the 5-th Conference Neural Networks and Their Applications, Zakopane (2000) 395–400
5. Giergiel M., Hendzel Z., Zylski W.: Modelling and Control of Wheeled Mobile Robots. WNT Warsaw (2002) (in Polish).
6. Hendzel Z.: Neural Network Reactive Navigation and Control of Wheeled Mobile Robot. Neural Network and Soft Computing Rutkowski, Kacprzyk Eds. Springer-Verlag (2003) (686–691)
7. Hendzel Z.: Fuzzy Reactive Control of Wheeled Mobile Robot. Journal of Theoretical and Applied Mechanics (to appear)
8. Latombe J.C.: Robot Motion Planning. Kluwer Academic Publishers (1991)
9. Lin C.,T., Chung I.F. A Reinforcement Neuro-Fuzzy Combiner for Multi Objective Control. IEEE Transaction on Systems, Man. and Cybernetics Vol.29 No.6 (1999) 726–744

Artificial Intelligence of the Decision Unit of a Mobile Robot

Jan Kazimierczak

Wroclaw University of Technology
Wyb. Wyspianskiego 27
50-370 Wrocław, Poland
kazim@ict.pwr.wroc.pl

Abstract. In this paper, it is indicated that the decision unit of mobile robot should be performed in the form of a hardware which owns some features of intelligence. For this reason, the synthesis of the decision unit should be executed in such a way in order to achieve these features in its logical structure. In the paper, the process of robot moving, over the plane with obstacles, is treated as an extensive game with the nature. In this game the decision unit chooses its moving strategies in the same manner as a human being in the identical situation. The synthesis of a symbolic expression representing the game tree, performing by the computer, is introduced. In the symbolic expression some features of intelligence are taken into consideration. It is shown that this symbolic expression is transformed by the computer into another symbolic expressions which unequivocally indicates on the logical structure of the hardware playing the role of the decision unit.

1 Introduction

One of trends in constructing mobile robot indicates that the decision unit of it should be made in the form of hardware instead software [1], [2]. Taking into account of the artificial intelligence idea, the decision unit made in the form of hardware should has some features of the intelligence. According to this such features should be taken into consideration during synthesis of the decision unit. One of formal tools useful for this purpose is the formal model of two-person extensive game with the nature. As an example we assume that the mobile robot moves over a plane with heterogeneous configuration of obstacles. The task of the robot is to carry out the exploration of whole plane and to determine the configuration of obstacles. In this game the walk-strategies of the robot are moves in the determined directions. The strategies of the nature are obstacles appearing on the road of robot moving.

Because the decision unit does not know which obstacles the robot meets on its road, therefore in each state of the game it considers all admissible in the given state moving strategies and arranges them according to succession of their using. This succession depends on of the robot trajectory executed so far and on obstacles met on this trajectory. In order to determine the succession of the

L. Rutkowski et al. (Eds.): ICAISC 2004, LNAI 3070, pp. 780–785, 2004.
© Springer-Verlag Berlin Heidelberg 2004

moving strategies in every state of the game the decision unit should has some features of intelligence. Namely, the reasoning of the decision unit should to be as the reasoning of a man who is to explore whole restricted area of the ground with obstacles.

In order to design the robot decision unit with the above mentioned intelligence it is necessary to perform the synthesis of the game tree describing the robot moving on the plane. It should be early performed by the computer in the form of a symbolic expression representing the game tree.

2   Synthesis of the Game Tree

It is assumed that the plane of the robot moving is the square divided into sixteen identical smaller squares as it is shown in Figure 1. In each smaller square e_i the central point x_i is distinguished. During the moving over the real plane the robot treats one as the virtual plane from Figure 1. It is assumed that the robot moves along straight lines. Motion of robot along a given straight line we call moving strategy or a walk strategy. The moving strategies are illustrated in Figure 1. They form the set:

$$Y = \{y_1, y_2, \dots, y_i, \dots, y_{16}\}.\tag{1}$$

Strategies y_i indexed by odd numbers denote a move forward, while strategies y_i labeled by even numbers denote a move backward. The set of walk strategies of the nature consists of four elements

$$Z = \{z_1, z_2, z_3, z_4\}\tag{2}$$

where z_1 denotes that there no obstacles when moving "forward"; z_2 denotes that there has appeared an obstacle when moving "forward"; z_3 denotes the lack

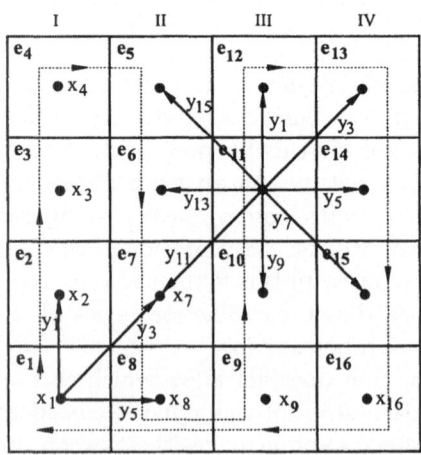

Fig. 1. Partition of the plane by squares and moving strategies of the robot

of obstacle when moving "backward"; z_4 denotes an appearance of an obstacle when moving "backward".

In order to perform synthesis of the game tree to each square e_i the set of all possible moving strategies from this square is determined. Below we introduce only some of these sets.

$$
\begin{aligned}
e_1 &\leftrightarrow E_1 = \{y_1e_2, y_3e_7, y_5e_3\} \\
e_2 &\leftrightarrow E_2 = \{y_1e_3, y_3e_6, y_5e_7, y_7e_8, y_9e_1\} \\
e_3 &\leftrightarrow E_3 = \{y_1e_4, y_3e_5, y_5e_6, y_7e_7, y_9e_2\} \\
e_4 &\leftrightarrow E_4 = \{y_5e_5, y_7e_6, y_9e_3\} \\
e_5 &\leftrightarrow E_5 = \{y_9e_6, y_7e_{11}, y_5e_{12}, y_{11}e_3, y_{13}e_4\} \\
e_6 &\leftrightarrow E_6 = \{y_9e_7, y_7e_{10}, y_5e_{11}, y_3e_{12}, y_{11}e_2, y_{13}e_3, y_{15}e_4, y_1e_5\}
\end{aligned}
\tag{3}
$$

The elements y_ie_r included in the sets (3) are used to determine actual paths of robot moving over the plane. We assume that when lack of obstacles the path of robot moving should be such as it is shown brocken line in Fig. 1. This path will be disturbed when some obstacles appear over the plane and another path will be realized. In each situation arising in the game from every set E_i being under consideration only strategies y_ie_r admissible in the given situation are chosen. Then the chosen strategies are arranged according to priorities of their using. For example, the strategies y_ie_r belonging to the set E_1 will be arranged as follows: y_1e_2 (1), y_3e_7 (2), y_5e_8 (3). The element y_1e_2 in this sequence denotes that the moving strategy y_1 is performed in the first order and, if lack of an obstacle during performing y_1, the robot reaches central point x_2 in the square e_2. The element y_3e_7 denotes that the moving strategy y_3 is performed in the second order in the case when during performing the strategy y_1 the robot met an obstacle. Similarly, the strategy y_5 is performed in the third succession.

On the basis of the sets (3) and some rules used to designate moving strategies priorities the computer constructs a symbolic expression representing the game tree. The beginning part of this expression has the form as follows:

$$
\begin{aligned}
E^+ = {}^0(e_1^1(y_5e_8, y_3e_7, y_1e_2^2(y_9e_1, y_7e_8, y_5e_7, y_3e_6, y_1e_3^3(\\
y_9e_2, y_7e_7, y_5e_6, y_3e_5, y_1e_4^4(\ldots
\end{aligned}
\tag{4}
$$

After the open bracket $^1($ there are pairs y_ie_r belonging to the set E_1. These pairs are ordered according to their priorities. This order is performed from right to left. The same interpretation have pairs y_re_i included in the terms $^2(\ldots^3(\ldots^4(\ldots$. The pairs y_ie_r appearing in E^+ after any open bracket and ended with comma are extended. This extension is realized in such a way that to symbol e_i appearing in the considered pair all admissible in the given situation pair $(y_re_j) \in E_i$ are assigned. As an example let's suppose that during moving from the square e_2 to square e_3 the robot met an obstacle. In this situation the robot returns to the central point x_2 of the square e_2 and perform the moving strategy y_3. Hence, the pair y_3e_6 appearing in the expression E^+ (4) between open brackets $^2($ and $^3($ should be extended. This extension is performed by the computer in such a way that the set E_6 is considered, the pair $y_{13}e_3$ in E_6 is

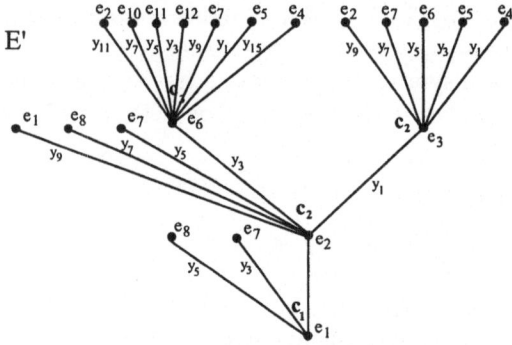

Fig. 2. The beginning part of game tree

eliminated and then remaining pairs $y_r e_i$ belonging to the set E_6 are ordered. After performing this operation the expression E^+ obtains the following form:

$$E^+ = {}^0(e_1 \ {}^1(y_5 e_8, y_3 e_7, y_1 e_2 \ {}^2(y_9 e_1, y_7 e_8, y_5 e_7, y_3 e_6 \ {}^3(y_{11} e_2, y_7 e_{10}, y_5 e_{11}, \\ y_3 e_{12}, y_9 e_7, y_1 e_5, y_{15} e_4)^3, y_1 e_3 \ {}^4(y_9 e_2, y_7 e_7, y_5 e_6, y_1 e_4 \ {}^5(\ldots$$

(5)

On the basis of the symbolic expression E^+ (5) one can draw the beginning part of the game tree, which is shown in Figure 2. In this tree to each vertex the symbol c_j denoting the sequence of edges y_r which come out from it is assigned. There are many vertices with the same symbol c_j.

3   Synthesis of the Decision Unit

On the complete symbolic expression E^+ some operations are performed which are equivalent to splitting the game tree into some parts.

Notice that many vertices of the game tree will be denoted by the same symbol e_i. However, in order to determine states of robot moving, vertices should be marked by symbols of states q_i $(i = 1, 2, \ldots)$. Hence, the expression E^+ (5) is transformed into the symbolic expression Q^+ representing the graph Q'.

$$Q^+ = {}^0(q_1^1(y_5 q_4, y_3 q_3, y_1 q_2^2(y_9 q_9, y_7 q_8, y_5 q_7, y_3 q_6^3(\ldots$$

(6)

Having the expression Q^+ the computer assigns to every symbol q_i, the symbol c_j representing the sequence of edges y_r coming out from the given vertex q_i. Hence the expression Q^+ is transformed into the expression C^+.

$$C^+ = {}^0(c_1 q_1^1(\ldots, y_1 c_2 q_2^2(\ldots, y_3 c_3 q_6, y_1 c_2 q_5^3(\ldots$$

(7)

On the basis of the complete symbolic expression C^+ we can draw a graph C'. The graph C' is divided into subgraphs C_i. Each subgraph C_i contains only nodes with different symbols c_j. Hence the expression C^+ is divided into

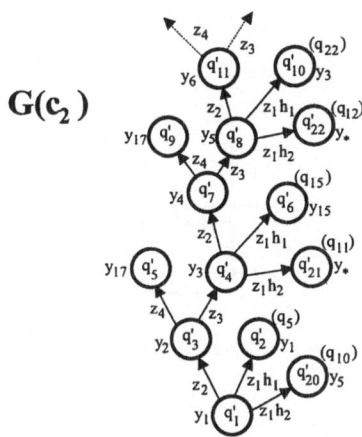

$$G(c_2)$$

Fig. 3. A fragment of the graph $G(c_2)$ illustrating the behavior of the robot in states denoted by the symbol c_2 representing the sequence y_1, y_3, y_5, y_7, y_9

subexpressions C_i^{++}. Each subexpression C_i^{++} obtains symbolic name h_i. For example, the expression C_2^{++} with name h_2 has the form as follows:

$$C_2^{++} =^0 (c_2^1(y_1 h_2 c_5^2(y_9 h_2 c_6^3(y_9 h_2 [h_5]c_6)^3)^2)^1)^0 \tag{8}$$

Then, the subexpressions C_i^{++} are combined each other. This operation results in the symbolic expression C'^+, representing transition-state diagram of a sequential circuit $< C >$ generating the signal c_j.

Then on the basis of the expression C'^+ and subexpressions $C_i'^+$ the expression H'^+ is obtained

$$H'^+ =^0 (h_1^1(c_2 y_1 h_2, c_3 y_5 h_4, \ldots, h_2^1(c_6 y_9 h_5, \ldots, h_4^1(c_9 y_9 h_6, \ldots \tag{9}$$

The expression H'^+ represents a graph H' treated as transition-state diagram of the sequential circuit $< H >$ which generates the signal h_r.

Notice that to all edges of the graphs E' and Q' the symbol z_1 of the nature strategy (no obstacle) has been assigned. Hence, in order to determine the behaviour of the robot at the nature strategies z_2, z_3 and z_4, from those vertices q_i of the graph Q' to which the same symbol c_j is assigned only one is chosen and it is considered as a graph $G(c_j)$. The structure of such a graph for $c_j = c_2$ is shown in Figure 3.

The vertices q_i' of the graph $G(c_2)$ are treated as states of a finite automaton which generates the strategies y_r belonging to the sequence c_2. For synthesis of the decision part of the decision unit, the sets $\tilde{Q}_r$ including vertices q_i' to which the same symbol y_r is assigned are completed. Symbols q_i' belonging to the given set $\tilde{Q}_r$ are treated as one state b_r of the automaton $< B >$. All graphs $G(c_j)$ are collapsed and combined together so that vertices q_i' with the same symbol b_r coincide at one vertex b_r. The result of this operation is the symbolic expression B'^+,

$$B'^+ =^0 (b_1^1(z_1 c_3 h_3 b_5, z_2 c_3 b_2, \ldots, z_2 c_2 b_2^2(z_3 c_3 b_3, \ldots, z_3 c_2 b_3^3(\ldots \tag{10}$$

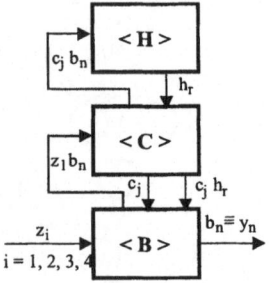

Fig. 4. The block structure of the decision part of the mobile robot decision unit

The complete symbolic expression B'^+ represents the transition-state diagram of the automaton $< B >$. Taking into account relations existing between automata $< C >$, $< H >$ and $< B >$ we can draw a block diagram of the decision unit of the mobile robot. This diagram is shown in Figure 4.

4   Conclusions

In this paper the possibility of performing the decision unit of the mobile robot in the form of hardware possessing of some feature of artificial intelligence has been proved. The process of the robot moving over the plane with obstacles has been introduced as the realization of a game with the nature. The most important point in this game is the arrangement of the robot moving strategies according to priorities of their using.

References

1. Kazimierczak J., Łysakowska B.: Intelligent adaptive control of a mobile robot: The automaton with an internal and external parameter approach, Robotica (1988), volume 6, pp. 319-326, Cambridge 1988.
2. Kazimierczak J.: A Technique to Transform Programs into Circuits, Microprocessing and Microprogramming, volume 22, pp. 125-140, North-Holland 1988.
3. Kazimierczak J.: From some Tasks to Biology and then to Hardware [in]: Evolvable Systems: From Biology to Hardware, Lecture Notes in Computer Science, pp. 359-376, Springer-Verlag, Tokyo 1997.

Finding Location Using a Particle Filter and Histogram Matching*

Bogdan Kwolek

Rzeszów University of Technology, 35-959 Rzeszów, Poland
bkwolek@prz.rzeszow.pl

Abstract. This paper considers the problem of mobile robot localization. The localization is done using a particle filter built on a highly accurate probabilistic model of laser scan and a histogram based representation of sensor readings. A histogram matching exploits sensor data coming from the laser and data obtained from the existing map. Experimental results indicate feasibility of the proposed approach for navigation.

1 Introduction

The problem of determining the position that is occupied by the robot is a central issue in robotics and has been deeply investigated in the literature. Mobile robots cannot rely solely on dead-reckoning to determine their location because of cumulative nature of errors in odometry readings. Self-localization techniques are utilized as a way to compensate the errors that accumulate during the robot movement by comparing the acquired sensor data with the pre-stored model of the environment in form of a map. For this reason the mobile robot should be equipped with sensors that allow determining the location. The most commonly used sensors are sonar, laser range finders and CCD. Recently Monte Carlo based algorithms have become a very popular framework to cope with the self-localization of mobile robots. A family of probabilistic algorithms known as Monte Carlo Localization [2][4] is one of the very few methods capable of localizing the robot globally. Global position estimation is the ability to determine the robot's position in a prepared in advance map, given no other information than that the robot is somewhere on the map. Once the robot has been localized in the map within some certainty, a local tracking is performed during maneuvering with aim to keep the track of the robot position over time. Monte Carlo based algorithms represent a robot's belief by a set of weighted particles to approximate the posterior probability of robot location by using a recursive Bayesian filter. The key idea of Bayes filtering is to estimate a probability density over the state space conditioned on the sensor data. Algorithms that deal with the global localization are relatively recent, although the idea of estimating the state recursively using particles is not new. The application of

---

* This work has been supported by the Polish Committee for Scientific Research.

L. Rutkowski et al. (Eds.): ICAISC 2004, LNAI 3070, pp. 786–791, 2004.
© Springer-Verlag Berlin Heidelberg 2004

particle filters to mobile robot localization [2][4] was motivated by the CONDEN-SATION algorithm [5], a particle filter that has been applied with a remarkable success to visual tracking problems [5][6].

The basic MCL algorithm performs poorly if the proposal distribution contains not enough samples in the right target location. MCL also performs poorly when the sensor noise level is too small taking into account uncertainty coming from the discretized map of the environment. A simple strategy based on adding artificial noise to the sensor readings has been applied in work [4]. The approach presented in [7] overcomes the degradation to small sample sets by integrating two complementary ways of generating samples in the estimation and using a kernel density tree in fast sampling. The approach we present in this paper utilizes the histogram based techniques to compare a laser scan with the scan representation obtained from an existing map. It is based on the concept of correlation between the scan extracted from the map taking into account the location of the considered particle and the sensor scan. A high similarity of histograms indicates a good match between laser readings and scans which represent considered map pose. Due to the statistical nature, a histogram based representation holds sufficient statistics for the sensor distributions and introduces desirable uncertainty. The histogram can be pre-computed and stored for every possible robot orientation and position. In a slower version of the algorithm the histogram at the considered map pose can be computed on-line. We show that histogram based map representation has powerful capability and can be used to distinguish sensor scans in a fast manner. Our experimental results indicate feasibility of the algorithm in which the highly accurate observation model from work [7] and histogram based one are combined within a particle filter in order to perform localization of the robot.

2   Monte Carlo Localization and Bayesian Filtering

The typical problem in partially observable Markov chains is to obtain a posterior distribution over the state x_t at any time t taking into account all available sensor measurements $z_0, ..., z_t$ and controls $u_0, ..., u_t$. The state x_t depends on the previous state x_{t-1} according to stochastic transition model $p(x_t \mid x_{t-1}, u_{t-1})$ for a control signal u_{t-1} which moves the robot from state x_{t-1} to state x_t. Such a motion model generalizes exact mobile robot kinematics by a probabilistic component and expresses the probability for certain actions to move the robot to certain relative positions. The state in the Markov chain is not observable. At each time step t a robot makes observation z_t which is a probabilistic projection of the robot state x_t through a stochastic observation model $p(z_t \mid x_t)$. The observation model describes the probability for taking certain measurements at certain locations. We assume that observations z_t are conditionally independent given the states x_t and that the initial distribution at time $t = 0$ is $p(x_0)$.

The posterior density $p(x_t \mid z_t)$ over the state space $\mathcal{X}$ characterizes the belief of the subject about its current state at time t given its initial belief and the sequence of observations $z_0, ..., z_t$. Bayes filters estimate the belief recursively.

The initial belief characterizes the initial knowledge about the system state, which in global localization corresponds to a uniform distribution reflecting an unknown initial pose. In the prediction phase the following motion model is used to obtain the predictive density

$$Bel(x_t) = \int p(x_t \mid x_{t-1}, u_{t-1}) Bel(x_{t-1}) dx_{t-1} \tag{1}$$

The parameter u may be an odometry reading or a control command. In the second phase a measurement model is used to utilize sensor information in order to obtain the posterior

$$Bel(x_t) \propto (z_t \mid x_t) Bel(x_t) \tag{2}$$

This term expresses the likelihood of the state x_t given that z_t was observed. The above two formula describe an iterative scheme for Bayesian filtering.

Monte Carlo Localization relies on the sample based representation of the belief $Bel(x_t)$ by a set of N weighted samples distributed according to $Bel(x_t)$

$$Bel(x_t) \approx \{x_t^{[i]}, w_t^{[i]}\}_{i=1,\dots,N} \tag{3}$$

and the sampling/importance resampling algorithm. Each particle is represented by a state of the mobile robot (x, y, ϕ) and a weight that reflects the contribution of particular particle to belief of the robot. A sample set constitutes a discrete distribution and if the number of samples goes to infinity such distributions approximate the correct posterior density smoothly. From the samples we can always approximately reconstruct the posterior density using a histogram or a kernel based density estimation technique [3]. The population of samples evolves as new action is executed and new sensor observations are obtained. The prediction phase uses the probabilistic motion model to simulate the effect of the action on the set of particles. When the new sensory information is available we use Bayes rule in order to update the probability density function of the moving robot with the latest observation.

One of the practical difficulties that is associated with particle filters is degeneration of the particle population after a few iterations because weights of several particles are negligible to contribute to the probability density function. The aim of resampling is to eliminate particles with low importance weights and multiply particles with high importance weights. The resampling selects with higher probability samples that have a high likelihood associated with them. Without resampling the variance of the weight increases stochastically over time. An algorithm to perform the resampling from a set of particles in $O(N)$ time has been proposed in [1]. The sensor readings are typically incorporated in two phases having on regard the outlined above resampling. In the first phase each importance factor is multiplied by $p(z_t \mid x_t)$. In the second one the resampling is conducted and afterwards the importance factors are normalized so that they sum up to 1 and for this reason they constitute a discrete probability distribution. As it was mentioned above the initial pose in the global localization is unknown and therefore the initial prior is uniform over the space of possible poses.

3   Scan Matching Using Histogram

A grid based map represents environment by regularly spaced grid cells. Each grid cell indicates the presence of an obstacle in the corresponding region of the environment. If a robot occupies a certain pose in the map we can compute expected laser scan readings using the well known ray-tracing. The scan readings obtained in such a way can be then used in comparison with robot scan readings.

Fig. 1a. illustrates the map of the office environment in which localization experiments have been conducted. This office-like environment is 560 by 460 cm and it has been discretized into 280x230x90 cells. A single scan of the laser range finder which was used in experiments returns a hemicircle of 180 readings with 1 degree incrementation. The distance error of range measurement using this sensor is 1 cm. A sample laser scan is depicted in the Fig. 1b. A reference scan which has been obtained on the basis of the map for the corresponding robot pose from Fig. 1b. is demonstrated in the Fig. 1c.

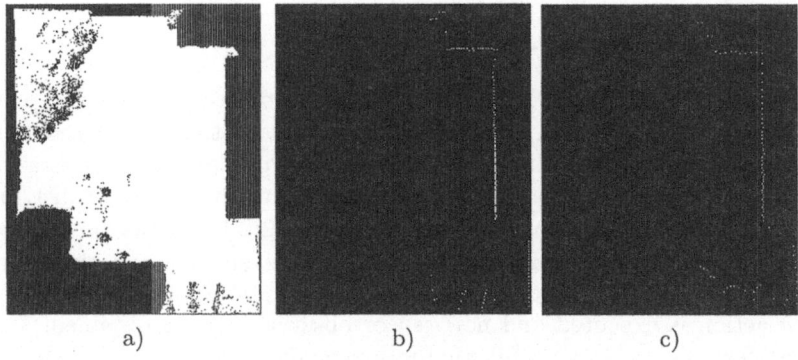

a)   b)   c)

Fig. 1. Map, sample laser data from the environment, corresponding reference scan

A histogram is obtained by quantizing the scan distances into L bins and counting the number of times each distance occurs in the single scan. Due to the statistical nature, a scan histogram can only reflect the environment shape in a limited way. Two scan shapes taken at close whereabouts appear very similar to each other and taking the above into account the number of histograms needed for environment representation is reasonably small. If the number of bins L is too high, the histogram is noisy. If L is too low, the density structure of the scan shape is smoothed. The histogram based techniques are effective only when L can be kept relatively low and where sufficient data amounts are available. The reduction of bins makes the comparison of two histograms faster and additionally such a compact representation reduces memory requirements. That aspect is particularly important considering on the one hand a limited computational power of the on-board computer and on the other hand the necessity of work with a rate which enables the mobile robot to utilize localization results during a maneuvering.

In order to compare two histograms we need a similarity or dissimilarity metric. For a given pair of histograms I and M each containing l values, the intersection of the histograms is defined as follows:

$$H_\cap = \frac{1}{\sum_{j=1}^{L} I_j} \sum_{j=1}^{L} \min(I_j, M_j) \qquad (4)$$

The terms I_j, M_j represent the number of particular scan values inside the j-th bucket of the current and the model histogram, respectively, whereas L the total number of buckets. The result of the intersection of two histograms is the percentage of scans which share the same distances in both histograms.

4 Robot Localization Using Particles

The probabilistic search for the best pose is realized in the utilized particle filter on the basis of the motion as well as the observation model. Any arbitrary mobile robot motion $[\triangle x, \triangle y]^T$ can be carried out as a rotation followed by a translation. The noise is applied separately to each of the two motions because they are independent. When the robot rotates about $\triangle \phi$ the odometry noise can be modeled as a Gaussian with experimentally established mean and standard deviation proportional to $\triangle \phi$. During a forward translation the first error is related to the traveled distance and the second one is associated with changes of the orientation attending the forward translation. The simple way to obtain the translation model is to discretize the motion into K steps and to cumulate the simulated effect of noise from each step. The sensor model describes the probability of obtaining a particular scan shape given the laser's pose and a geometrical map of the environment. In the histogram based version of the particle filter the following observation model $p(z_t \mid x_t) = H_\cap(I_t, M(x_t))$ has been utilized.

In order to obtain an estimate of the pose the weighted mean ($\sum_i w^{[i]} x^{[i]}$), in a small sub-cube around the best particle has been utilized. The orientation of the robot has been determined on the basis of sum of direction vectors of particles from the sub-cube as $\phi = arctan(\sum_i \sin \phi^{[i]}, \sum_i \cos \phi^{[i]})$. The effect of probabilistic search for the best position has additionally been enhanced via a local move of particles according to their probability. The more probable the particle is, the less it is moved.

5 Experimental Results

All experiments were carried out in an office environment with our experimental Pioneer [8] based platform which is equipped with a laser range finder as well as an on-board 850 MHz laptop computer. The goal of the first group of tests was experimental verification of efficiency of particle filter utilizing histogram models when the robot is continuously moving. Two 4-bins histograms representing the x and y-components of the scans ensure the high efficiency with relatively low computational burden. During experiments which typically took about 10 minutes the position has been determined 5 times per sec. and the maximal velocity was 0.8 m/s. The number of particles used was between 500 and 5000. Assuming stationary particles between consecutive motions, we observed that a cloud consisting of 5000 particles forms a boundary around the robot in which minimum two successive positions of the robot are always contained. The goal of the second group of experiments was to evaluate the precision of determining the position in certain points. In order to record data in known positions the robot has been manually moved several times on a rectangular path of 10 m. Next, the particle filters utilizing the histogram and the accurate probabilistic models of the laser have been compared on recorded data. The histogram based algorithm reports the position of the robot anywhere from ten to twenty iterations from the start of the global localization. In the second algorithm the position is known after a few iterations. The square root of the sum of squared errors of 100 measurements on the mentioned above path was about 1000 cm and 750 cm, respectively. The overall performance of the histogram based algorithm is poorer than that of the conventional one. However, each approach has complimentary strengths and weaknesses. The particle filter which merges both approaches yields superior localization performance. The square root of the sum of squared errors was about 800 cm.

6 Conclusion

We have presented a method that robustly localizes a robot in an office. The histogram based representation of the environment is very useful in particle filters relying on laser readings. Initial results show that our combined method outperforms the method using highly accurate probabilistic model of the laser scan.

References

1. Carpenter, J., Clifford, P., Fearnhead, P., An improved particle filter for non-linear problems, IEE Proceedings - Radar, Sonar and Navigation, **146** (1999) 2-7
2. Dellaert, F., Fox, D., Burgard, W., Thrun, S., Monte Carlo localization for mobile robots. In Proc. of IEEE Int. Conf. on Robotics and Automation (1999) 1322-1328
3. Dellaert, F., Burgard, W., Fox, D., Thrun, S., Using the condensation algorithm for robust, vision-based mobile robot localization. In Proc. of the IEEE Int. Conf. on Computer Vision and Pattern Recognition (1999) 588-594
4. Fox, D., Burgard, W., Dellaert, F., Thrun S., Monte Carlo localization: Efficient position estimation for mobile robots. In Proc. of the Sixteenth National Conference on Artificial Intelligence (AAAI), Orlando FL (1999) 343-349
5. Isard M., Blake, A., Contour tracking by stochastic propagation of conditional density, European Conf. on Computer Vision, Cambridge UK (1996) 343-356
6. Perez, P., Hue, C., Vermaak, J., Gangnet, M., Color-based probabilistic tracking, European Conference on Computer Vision (2002) 661-675
7. Thrun, S., Fox, D., Burgard, W., Dellaert, F., Robust Monte Carlo localization for mobile robots, Artificial Intelligence, **128** (2001) 99-141
8. Pioneer 2 mobile robots-Operations manual. ActivMedia Robotics, LLC (2001)

Calculation of Model of the Robot by Neural Network with Robot Joint Distinction

J. Możaryn and J.E. Kurek

Warsaw University of Technology,
Institute of Automatic Control and Robotics,
Warszawa, ul. Sw.Andrzeja Boboli 8, 02-525,
J.Mozaryn@mchtr.pw.edu.pl

Abstract. There is presented the design of the feedforward neural network for calculation of coefficients of the robot model. Proposed method distinguishes the degrees of freedom and improves the performance of the network using information about the control signals. A numerical example for calculation of the neural network model of Puma 560 robot is presented.

1 Introduction

Mathematical model of industrial robots can be calculated using the Lagrange-Euler or d'Alambert equations [1]. However, it is rather difficult to obtain the data of physical properties of the robot: inertia momentums, masses, etc. without disassembling of the robot.

The mathematical model of robot is highly nonlinear and it is very difficult to identify its coefficients. For the reason the neural networks can be used for calculation of the model coefficients [3], [5], [6]. This technique has advantages such as approximation and generalization.

One of the problems in designing the neural network structures for robot model calculation is the distinguishing between the degrees of freedom. This information is significant for proper identification of the coefficients of equations describing the dynamics of each degree of freedom. In the paper we present the method for the neural networks design using data from the positions of robot links and control signals. The proposed method can be used for coefficients identification for each degree of freedom of robot.

The organization of the paper is as follows. The discrete time robot model based on the Lagrange-Euler equations is given in the Sect. 2. Then, in Sect. 3 and Sect. 4 the neural network structures for identification of the robot model coefficients are presented. In the Sect. 5 the computer simulations are described. The conclusions are given in Sect. 6.

L. Rutkowski et al. (Eds.): ICAISC 2004, LNAI 3070, pp. 792–797, 2004.
© Springer-Verlag Berlin Heidelberg 2004

2   Discrete Time Robot Model

The discrete time model of robot with n degrees of freedom, based on Lagrange-Euler equations can be presented as follows [6]

$$q(k+1) = T_p^2 M^{-1}(k)(\tau(k) - V(k) - G(k)) + 2q(k) - q(k-1), \qquad (1)$$

where $\tau(k) \in R^n$ is a vector of input signals, $q \in R^n$ is a vector of generalized joint coordinates, $M(k) = M[q(k)] \in R^{n \times n}$ is a robot inertia matrix, $V(k) = V[q(k), q(k-1)] \in R^n$ is a vector of Coriolis and centrifugal effects, $G(k) = G[q(k)] \in R^n$ is a vector of gravity loading, k is a discrete time, T_p is sampling time, $t = kT_p$.

3   Neural Network Robot Model

Using (1) and the following notation

$$E(k) = [e_i(k)]_{n \times 1} = -T_p^2 M^{-1}(k)(V(k) + G(k)) + 2q(k) - q(k-1) \qquad (2)$$

$$X(k) = [x_{ij}(k)]_{n \times n} = T_p^2 M^{-1}(k) \qquad (3)$$

the equation for m-th degree of freedom can be written as follows

$$q_m(k+1) = e_m(k) + \sum_{i=1}^{n} x_{mi}(k)\tau_i(k) \qquad (4)$$

where $e_m(k) = e_m[q(k), q(k-1)]$ and $x_{mi}(k) = x_{mi}[q(k)]$. The neural network structure which will be used for calculation of the model (4) coefficients is shown in the Fig. 1.

4   Neural Network Robot Model with Robot Joint Distinction

Usually it is impossible to distinguish which degree of freedom is modelled using the neural networks structure based on (4). The trajectories in each degree of freedom used in training process can be the same, and therefore each structure of neural networks does not model the exact coefficients of (2).

In order to distinguish the degrees of freedom there is proposed to consider the additional information about the control signal of the link which is modelled. This information is unique for this degree of freedom. Therefore the both sides of (4) we multiply by the control signal $\tau_m(k)$ for the modelled joint

$$q_m(k+1)\tau_m(k) = e_m(k)\tau_m(k) + \sum_{i=1}^{n} x_{mi}(k)\tau_i(k)\tau_m(k) \qquad (5)$$

This equation will next be used for calculation of robot model coefficients. The neural networks structure for calculation of coefficients of the (5) is shown in the Fig. 2.

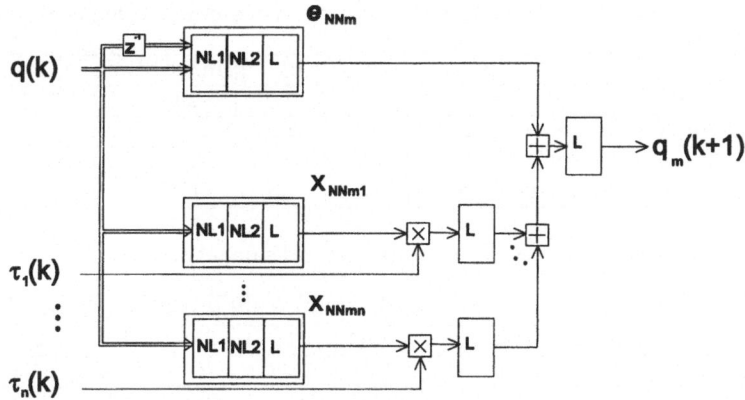

Fig. 1. Feedforward neural network structure proposed for calculation of coefficients of (4)

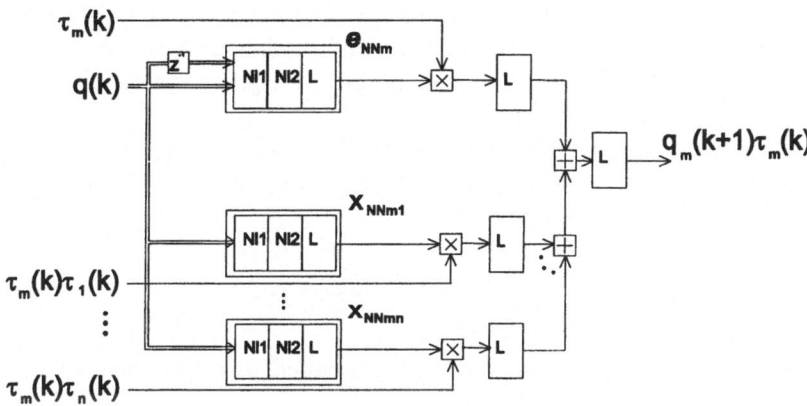

Fig. 2. Feedforward neural network structure proposed for calculation of coefficients of (5)

5   Computer Simulations

In order to train and test the proposed neural network there were generated the data of inputs and outputs of the robot Puma 560 with 6 degrees of freedom [4]. The robot was simulated with given trajectory in time interval $T = 10[sec]$, with sampling time $T_p = 0.01[sec]$. Thus, there were 1000 data samples for training and 1000 data samples for testing of the neural models.

For calculation of the training and testing data, the trajectory for every joint was set according to the following formula:

$$
\begin{aligned}
q_i(k) &= acos(sk) + a + q_{i2} && \text{if } q_{i1} > q_{i2} \\
q_i(k) &= acos(sk + \pi) + a + q_{i1} && \text{if } q_{i1} < q_{i2} \\
q_i(k) &= q_{i1} && \text{if } q_{i1} = q_{i2}
\end{aligned}
\tag{6}
$$

Table 1. Values of the lowest and highest positions in every degree of freedom

links	$link_1[°]$	$link_2[°]$	$link_3[°]$	$link_4[°]$	$link_5[°]$	$link_6[°]$
q_1, *training trajectories*	-20	10	-180	-20	20	-100
q_2, *training trajectories*	160	45	225	170	100	266
q_1, *testing trajectories*	-20	140	-180	-20	90	120
q_2, *testing trajectories*	86	10	30	40	20	-100

Table 2. Values of the neural networks quality indexes Q_i

Q_i	$link_1[°]$	$link_2[°]$	$link_3[°]$	$link_4[°]$	$link_5[°]$	$link_6[°]$
NN Model of (4), training trajectories	0.0011	115	65	10	60	106
NN Model of (5), training trajectories	1.7	0.05	2	0.03	0.02	2.14
NN Model of (4), testing trajectories	1623	414	364	428	1551	715
NN Model of (5), testing trajectories	149	407	347	269	147	537

where $a = |\frac{q_{i1}-q_{i2}}{2}|$, q_{i1} is the start position in the link i, $s = 2\pi\frac{Tp}{T}$. The values of the q_{i1}, q_{i2} are different for the training and testing trajectories and are given in the Table 1. The training and testing data are presented in the Fig. 3 and Fig. 4.

Both models, that are presented in the Fig. 1 and Fig. 2, were trained with the same number of neurons. In all nonlinear layers (NL) the neurons described by the sigmoid function (7) were used:

$$y = f_{nl}(x) = \frac{1}{1+e^{-x}} - 1 \tag{7}$$

In linear layers (L) there are neurons described with the linear function:

$$y = f_l(x) = x \tag{8}$$

There were 2 neurons in each nonlinear layer and 1 neuron in each linear layer.

Neural networks were trained using the backpropagation method and the Levenberg-Marquardt method to update weights in all layers [2].

The performance of each neural network model for each degree of freedom of the robot was checked. Good performance was obtained, if the input-output data for both neural network structures was the same. Thus, in the neural network from Fig.2 the control signal $\tau_m(k) = 1$. The quality index for the models was the maximum absolute difference between the trajectory in i-th link q_i and output of the network y_i:

$$Q_i = max|y_i(k) - q_i(k+1)|, \tag{9}$$

where k is the number of the data sample.

The values of Q_i for neural network models of (4), (5) and each degree of freedom of robot Puma 560 are given in the Table 2.

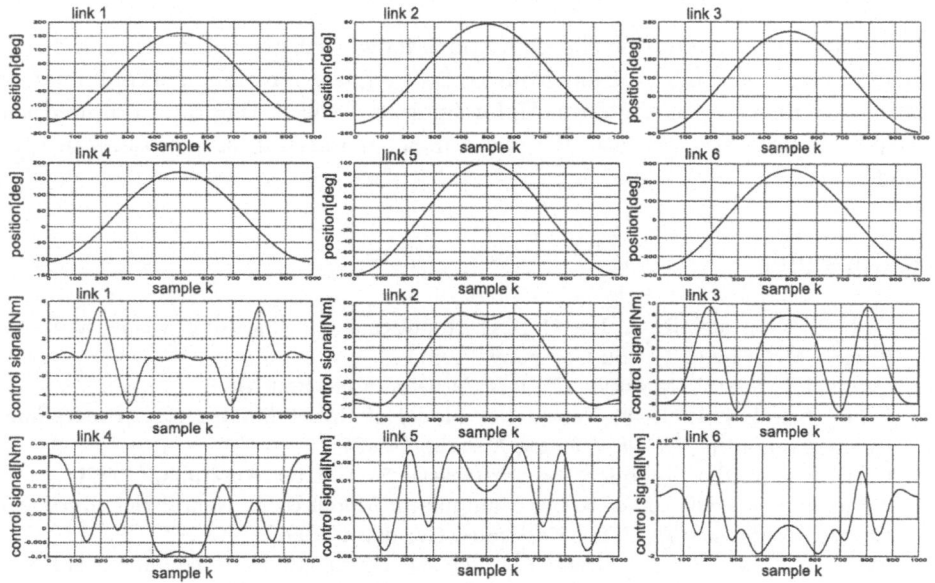

Fig. 3. Training trajectories in every degree of freedom

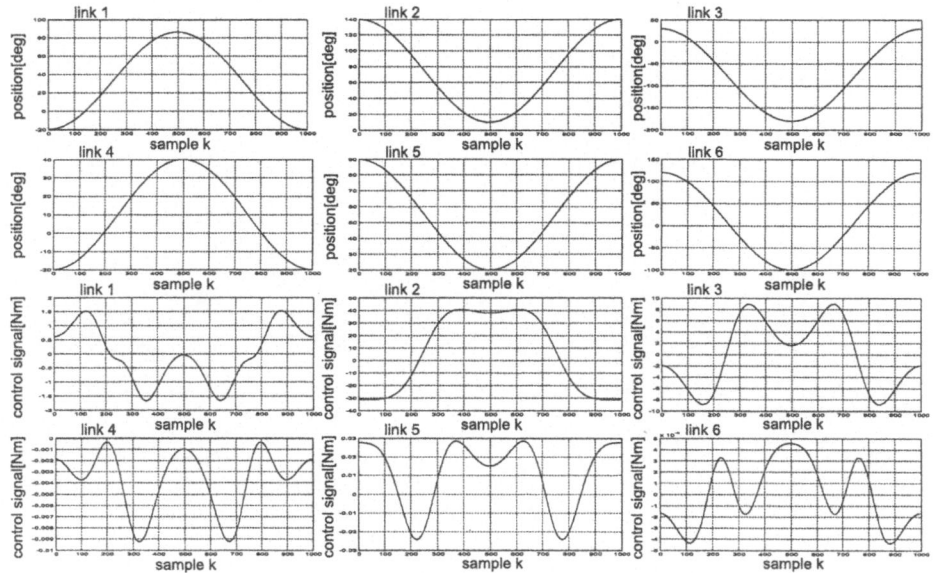

Fig. 4. Testing trajectories in every degree of freedom

6   Concluding Remarks

The results obtained during the simulations show, that presented neural network models which use information from control signals have good approximation properties for the training data. Unfortunately if the testing data are used the results are not very accurate. We plan further research in order to improve the model.

References

1. Fu K. S., Gonzalez R. C., Lee C. S. G. Robotics: control, sensing, vision, and inteligence, McGraw-Hill Book Company, (1987)
2. Osowski S. Neural Networks, OWPW, Warszawa (In Polish)
3. (1994) Kurek J. E.(1998) Neural Net Model of Robot Manipulator, Proceedings Neural Computing NC'98, Vienna, Austria, (1998)
4. Corke P. I. Matlab Robotics Toolbox (release 5), CSIRO, Australia, (1999)
5. Kurek J. E. Calculation of Robot Manipulator Model Using Neural Net, European Control Conference ECC '99, Karlsruhe, Germany, (1999)
6. Możaryn J., Wildner C., Kurek J.E. Calculation of the Model of the Industrial Robot Using Neural Networks, XIV National Control Conference KKA 2002, Zielona Gora, Poland, (2002)(In Polish)

Multi-robot Coordination Based on Cooperative Game

Krzysztof Skrzypczyk

Department of Automatic Control, Silesian University of Technology,
44-100 Gliwice, Poland
kskrzypczyk@ia.polsl.gliwice.pl

Abstract. The paper addresses the problem of a real time collision-free movement coordination in a multi-robot environment. An architecture of the control system that is designed to control a movement of a team of mobile robots performing their navigational tasks is presented. The proposed approach to the problem of coordination utilize the normal form games. The cooperative concept of solution that provides a "fair" distribution of costs is used. An arbiter was introduced to provide unique solution when multiple ones exist. Results of simulation of the proposed method, made for two robots are presented.

1 Introduction

The key issue in a problem of controlling a team of robots is coordination of movements of individual team-mates. In a mobile robotics domain the basic problem that is often considered is the simple point-to-point navigation task, execution of which requires motion planning. The mutual interactions between individual robots sharing a common workspace, even if the workspace is free of obstacles make the problem of motion planning non trivial. The game theory seems to be a convenient tool for modelling and solving multi-robot interaction problems. Therefore the game theory is often used in this context and a lot of works have been reported in the literature. In [2] some aspects of the coordination problem faced by a population of self-interested interacting agents, from the perspective of 2-players repeated game are presented. The criterion based on the maxi-max concept were used to find the solution of the problem. The zero-sum game was also proposed as a tool for modelling the sensor based motion planning for mobile robots in [1]. A saddle point concept was used as a solution of the problem. In [3] a method for analyzing and selecting time-optimal coordination strategies for n robots whose configurations are constrained to lie on C-space road map is presented. The *maximal Nash equilibria* concept were used to find favorable strategies for each robot. The next work [4] presents the algorithm that computes the complete set of Pareto-optimal coordination strategies for two translating polygonal robots in the plane. All of the works present methods that could be applied in an off-line mode due to their large computational complexity. In this paper a method of coordination that utilize elements of game theory is

L. Rutkowski et al. (Eds.): ICAISC 2004, LNAI 3070, pp. 798–803, 2004.
© Springer-Verlag Berlin Heidelberg 2004

presented. We discuss repetitive use of normal form, non zero sum games. We present an architecture of the control system that is based on centralized sensory sub-system, and is able to navigate many mobile robots from their initial to target locations. The solution based on cooperation between robotic-agents is proposed. The solution is obtained by minimizing the performance index that provides "fair" cost distribution between robots. Different robot cost preferences related to a distance of robots to their targets and their energetic efficiency are modelled. It is worth noticing that solution obtained with the proposed method is inside of a set of pareto-optimal solutions. The main advantage of this approach is that is fast enough to cope with a real-time robots coordination and is robust to some extent to unprecise and uncertain sensory information.

1.1   The System Overview

We consider the problem of coordination under a few assumptions: The position and orientation of robots and obstacles that are recognizable by sensors are known in each discrete moment of time;The target location in the discrete moment of time t_n is known;The robots actions are synchronized with the incoming sensory information. The block diagram of the control system that meets above requirements is presented in the fig.1.

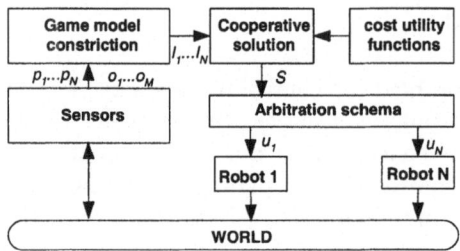

Fig. 1. General block diagram of the control system

The idea of the system could be described as follows: *Sensors* provide information of positions of robots and the obstacles. Next linear velocities of robots are set. Then the coordination problem is modelled as a N-person, non-zero-sum game according to the rules presented further in the section 3,basing on this model, computation of solution sets according to the *cooperative solution* concept is made. If there are multiple solutions the unique solution is obtained as a result of arbitration process made according to an *arbitration schema*.

1.2 Problem Formulation

Let us denote a state of the i-th robot, provided by sensory system in a discrete moment t_n of time by $p_i(t_n)$ and a state of the j-th obstacle by $o_j(t_n)$:

$$p_i(t_n) = \left[x_i, y_i, \hat{\Theta}_i\right]; \quad o_j(t_n) = \left[x_j, y_j, \hat{\Theta}_j\right] \tag{1}$$

where x, y are location coordinates of robots and obstacles in a coordinates frame fixed to the workspace. The $\hat{\Theta}$ is an estimation of heading of the given robot or obstacle obtained on the basis of current and previous position data. The target location of the i-th robot is defined by:

$$g_i = [x_g \ y_g] \tag{2}$$

Since each robot is assumed to be a differential driven one, the movement of this kind of mobile platform is controlled by changing the velocity of a right and left wheel. However for the purpose of this work it is convenient to consider the control as changing an angular ω_i and a linear velocity v_i. Thus we denote a control of the i-th robot by $u_i = [\omega_i \ v_i]$. The aim of the system is to guide each robot in a collision free way from its initial location to the target one. That means in every moment we look for a control u_i that applied to the i-th robot push it toward its target.

2 Model of the Game

The problem of coordination of movements of multiple robots that share the workspace could be perceived as a conflict situation between individual decision-makers(robots). The robots share the workspace which implies the interactions between robots have to be considered. Moreover, the existence of obstacles inside the workspace makes the problem more complex. The game theory is a convenient framework for modelling and solving the problems of conflict nature and was applied here to model the problem stated above.

2.1 Discretization

The set of possible controls of the i-th robot is defined as a cartesian product:

$$U_i = \Omega_i \times V_i \quad U_i = \{(\omega_i, v_i) : \omega_i \in \Omega_i \cap v_i \in V_i\} \tag{3}$$

where Ω_i and V_i denote finite sets of possible values of the angular and the linear velocity. This method of discretization leads to large decision sets and in consequence to large size of a problem. Therefore we propose to discretize only one control variable - angular velocity. We have:

$$U_i = \{(\omega_i, v_i) : \omega_i \in \Omega_i \cap v_i = f(d_T, d_{\min}, d_{\max})\} \tag{4}$$

The linear velocity is set according to a heuristic rule, which is that the robot should slow down in a proximity of other robots or obstacles to prevent safe manoeuvring. When robot is close to its target the velocity of the robot should be decreased. Therefore we model this rule as a heuristic function of the distance to the target d_T, and distance to the nearest object d_{min}.

2.2   Cost Function

We have to determine for each robot the cost function, value of which depends on movements of other robots, distance to the obstacles and the distance to the target - $I_i(d_1, ...d_N) = f_i(U, O)$, where $U = \left[u_1^{k_1}, u_2^{k_2}, ...u_N^{k_N}\right]$ and $O = [o_1, ...o_M]$. The control made by i-th robot is a selection of the k-th element from the set (4). Let us first define predicted position of the i-th robot, associated with its decision d_i:

$$
\begin{aligned}
\hat{x}_i^{d_i} &= x_i + v_i^{t-1}T_o\cos(\hat{\Theta}_i + \omega_i^{t-1}T_o) + \\
&\quad + v_i(\Delta t - T_o)\cos(\hat{\Theta}_i + \omega_i^{t-1}T_o + \omega_i^{d_i}(\Delta t - T_o)) \\
\\
\hat{y}_i^{d_i} &= y_i + v_i^{t-1}T_o\sin(\hat{\Theta}_i + \omega_i^{t-1}T_o) + \\
&\quad + v_i(\Delta t - T_o)\sin(\hat{\Theta}_i + \omega_i^{t-1}T_o + \omega_i^{d_i}(\Delta t - T_o))
\end{aligned}
\tag{5}
$$

We assume that there exists a delay between moment of receiving sensory information and the moment of decision making. Therefore we introduce the time of delay T_0 which is a worst-case estimation of a time of computing and sending information. The $\omega_i^{t-1}, v_i^{t-1}$ are the previous controls applied to the i-th robot that still influences the robot by the time T_0. Now we can define predicted distance of the i-th robot to its target $\hat{L}_{t,i}(d_i)$, and predicted distance between robot i-th and j-th - $\hat{L}_{r,ij}(d_i, d_j)$. The distances are computed according to the Manhattan Norm. Analogously the predicted distance between i-th robot and k-th obstacle $\hat{L}_{o,i,k}$ is determined. The idea of constructing the cost function is that the robot should minimize its predicted distance to the target, and maximize the distance to the nearest object. Therefore we propose the following form of the cost function, associated with the set of decisions $\{d_1, d_2, ..., d_N\}$ adopted by a team of robots:

$$
I_i(d_1, d_2, ..., d_N) = w_t\hat{L}_i(d_i) + w_o\frac{1}{\min_{\substack{j=1...N \\ k=1...M \\ j\neq i}}\left(\hat{L}_{r,i,j}(d_i, d_j), \hat{L}_{o,i,k}(d_i, d_k)\right)}
\tag{6}
$$

The w_t, w_o in (6) are weighting factors that adjust influences of the target and a nearest object.

3   Solution

We look for a solution of the problem as a set of actions for which costs are satisfactory for each robot. Since we think of a group of robots as of a team therefore the cooperation between agents can be considered. The one, well known concept of cooperative solution is the Pareto one. Unfortunately, the problem is that an unique Pareto solution occurs extremely rarely. In general there can be infinitely many Pareto optima for any complicated game. In some cases, when the outcomes of the players have common physical interpretation and they are

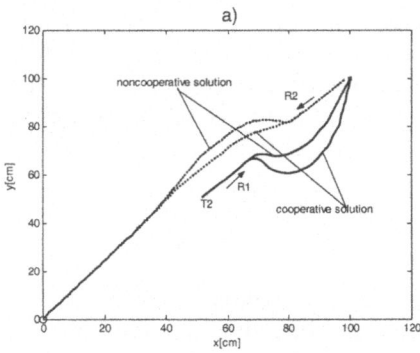 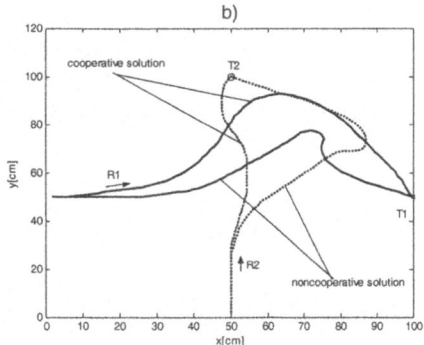

Fig. 2. Exemplary results of simulations made for two navigational problems

comparable another solution concept can be introduced that provides "fair" distribution of costs among the players. In order to make the costs comparable we have to define cost preferences for each robot expressed by so called utility function $f(I_i)$. We define the utility function as the linear one $f(I_i) = \beta I_i$. The solution of the cooperative problem is the one that minimize the performance index J:

$$\{d_{10}, d_{20}, ..., d_{N0}\} = \min_{d_1, d_2, ..., d_N} (J) \tag{7}$$

where

$$J = \sum_{i=1}^{N} \beta_i I_i + \max_{i=1...N} \beta_i \left(\left(\frac{1}{N} \sum_{i=1}^{N} I_i \right) - I_i \right) \tag{8}$$

The solution proposed above gives "fair" distribution of costs among agents simultaneously take into account different preferences of each robot.

4   Simulation

A number of simulations were made to verify the effectiveness of proposed approach. However in this section we present two exemplary ones. The fig.2 presents results of two point-to-point navigational experiments. The motion plans in both cases were obtained with two solution concepts: a noncooperative (presented in [5]) and the cooperative, discussed in the previous section. The experiments were carried out for decision sets $U_1 = U_2 = [-225, -112.5, 0, 112.5, 225]$ and the sample time $\Delta t = 0.1s$. The linear velocities were set to $v_{opt,1} = v_{opt,2} = 20cm/s$. The cost utility functions coefficients in both experiments were $\beta_1 = 0.5, \beta_2 = 1$. In the first one they are related to the initial distances of robots to their targets however in the second with robots energetic efficiency. We can see that the cooperation allows to reduce the length of the path of the robot 2 (R2), by increasing the length of the path of the robot 1 which has shorter initial distance to its target (in the case presented in the fig. 2a) or higher energetic efficiency (fig. 2b). The results show that the cooperation between agents allows to complete team-mission even if one of teammates has worse parameters or starts at worse initial conditions. Both cases have strict relation to energetic efficiency. For example, if one agent has low batteries then the other goes off his optimal path what causes the first agent is able to complete its task.

5   Conclusion

In this paper a methodology based on normal form cooperative game was used for motion planning of a team of robots operating in a dynamic environment. This methodology was illustrated by simulation made for a team of 2 mobile robots with different cost preferences. Although in the paper only two simulation experiments were presented, a great number of simulations were made and a lot of robots configurations, parameters were tested. The experiments prove that the proposed approach gives good results, under considered assumptions. Presented solution concept gives even cost distribution between agents and simultaneously takes into account different cost preferences of agents. It is worth noticing, that computation time of the solution is small enough to consider the method as a real-time one. Therefore our future researches shall be focused on applying the method in the real multi robot system.

Acknowledgments. This work has been supported by the KBN grant no 4T11A 01223 in the year 2004.

References

1. Esposito J., Kumar V.: Closed loop motion plans for mobile robots. Proc. IEEE Intl Conf. On Robotics and Automation (2000) 1020-1025
2. Golfarelli M.,Meuleu N.: Multi Agent Coordination in Partially Observable environments. Proceedings of the IEEE Int. Conf. of Robot and Automation, San Francisco (2000) 2777-2782
3. LaValle S., Hutchinson S.: Path selection and coordination for multiple robots via Nash equilibria. Proc. 1994 IEEE Intl Conf. Robot. and Automation (1994) 1847–1852
4. LaValle S., Hutchinson S.: Optimal Motion Planning for Multiple Robots Having Independent Goals. IEEE Trans. On Robotics and Automation 14(6) (1998) 912-925
5. Skrzypczyk K.: Noncooperative Games Based Collision Free Movement Planning in Multiagent Systems. Proc. of the V-th Phd Workshop, Vol.1. Istebna-Zaolzie (2003) 63-68

Model Based Predictive Robotic Manipulator Control with Sinusoidal Trajectory and Random Disturbances

Hasan Temurtas[1], Fevzullah Temurtas[2], and Nejat Yumusak[2]

[1] Dumlupinar University, Electric-Electronic Engineering, Kutahya, Turkey
[2] Sakarya University, Computer Engineering, Adapazari, Turkey

Abstract. In this study, the application of the single input single output (SISO) neural generalized predictive control (NGPC) of a three joint robotic manipulator with the comparison of the SISO generalized predictive control (GPC) is presented. Dynamics modeling of the robotic manipulator was made by using the Lagrange-Euler equations. The frictional effects, the random disturbance, the state of carrying and falling load were added to dynamics model. The sinusoidal trajectory principle is used for position reference and velocity reference trajectories. The results show that the NGPC-SISO algorithm performs better than GPC-SISO algorithm and the influence of the load changes and disturbances to the NGPC-SISO is less than that of the GPC-SISO with sinusoidal trajectory.

1 Introduction

In recent years, robotic manipulators have been used increasingly in the manufacturing sector and in applications involving hazardous environments for increasing productivity, efficiency, and worker safety. The use of conventional linear control techniques limits the basic dynamic performance of manipulators. The dynamic characteristics of general spatial manipulators are highly nonlinear functions of the positions and velocities of the manipulator elements. And the dynamic performance characteristics of manipulators are degraded by the inertial properties of the objects being manipulated. Dynamic control of the manipulator is realized by generating the necessary inputs (torque/voltage) which supply the motion of the manipulator joints according to desired position and velocity references and applying these inputs to the joints [1,2,3,4].

One of the applied manipulator control techniques is generalized predictive control (GPC) [4,5]. GPC had been originally developed with linear plant predictor model which leads to a formulation that can be solved analytically. If a nonlinear model is used, a nonlinear optimization algorithm is necessary. This affects the computational efficiency and performance by which the control inputs are determined. For nonlinear systems, the ability of the GPC to make accurate predictions can be enhanced if a neural network is used to learn the dynamics of the system instead of standard nonlinear modeling techniques [6].

L. Rutkowski et al. (Eds.): ICAISC 2004, LNAI 3070, pp. 804–809, 2004.
© Springer-Verlag Berlin Heidelberg 2004

A priori information needed for manipulator control analysis and manipulator design is a set of closed form differential equations describing the dynamic behavior of the manipulators. Various approaches are available to formulate the robot arm dynamics, such as Lagrange-Euler, Newton-Euler and Recursive Lagrange [7,8]. In this study, Lagrange-Euler is used for dynamics modeling of the three joints robotic manipulator. Furthermore, by adding the effects of the joint frictions and loads to the Lagrange-Euler equation sets, the simulation results are performed for the most general situations.

2   Neural Generalized Predictive Control

The neural generalized predictive control (NGPC) system [6] for the robotic manipulator [4] can be seen in Figure 1.a. It consists of four components, the robotic manipulator or its simulator, a tracking reference signal that specifies the desired trajectory of the manipulator, a neural network for prediction, and the cost function minimization (CFM) algorithm that determines the input needed to produce the desired trajectory of the manipulator. In the single input single output (SISO) NGPC method, one independent NGPC-SISO algorithm is used for each individual joint as seen in Figure 1.b. In Figure 1, torque, u, is the control input to the manipulator system and the trajectory, y, is the output, ym is the reference output and yn is the predicted output of the neural network.

The NGPC algorithm operates in two modes, prediction and control. The CFM algorithm produces an output which is either used as an input to the robotic manipulator or the manipulator's neural network model. The switch position is set to the robotic manipulator when the CFM algorithm has solved for the best input, $u(n)$, that will minimize a specified cost function. Between samples, the switching position is set to the manipulator's neural network model where the CFM algorithm uses this model to calculate the next control input, $u(n+1)$, from predictions of the response from the manipulator's model. Once the cost function is minimized, this input is passed to the manipulator. The computational issues of the NGPC are addressed in [6]. In this study, the GPC_SISO algorithm was also used to control the robotic manipulator for comparison. Detailed information about GPC_SISO algorithm can be found in [4,5].

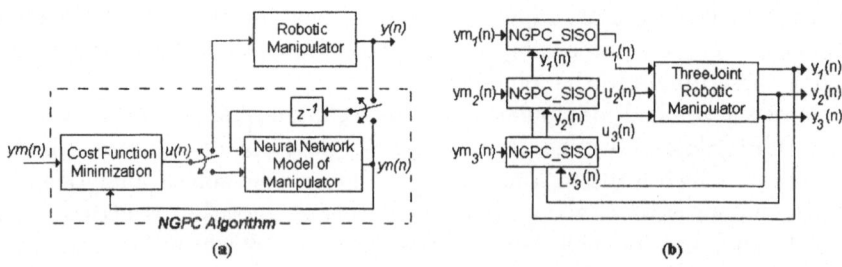

Fig. 1. Block diagram of the NGPC system (a) and application of NGPC-SISO algorithm (b)

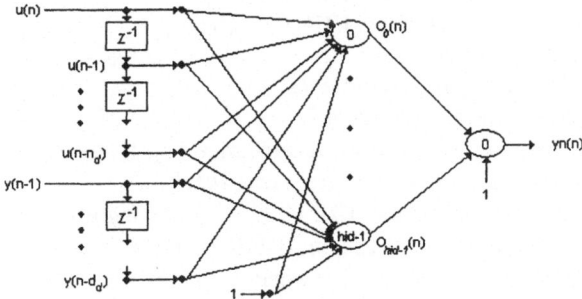

Fig. 2. Multi-layer feed-forward neural network model with a time delayed structure

2.1 Robotic Manipulator Neural Network Model

A multi-layer feed-forward network (MLFN) with tapped time delays was used for the robotic manipulator neural network model. The network structure shown in Figure 2 depicts the SISO structure with the linear model embedded into the weights. The torque, u, is the control input to the manipulator system and the trajectory, y, is the output. The inputs to the network are torque, past values of the torque, and the past values of the manipulator's trajectory. The network has a single hidden layer with multiple hidden layer nodes and a single output node. The activation function for the hidden layer nodes is tangent-sigmoid transfer function and the activation function for the output node is linear transfer function [4]. The back propagation algorithm was used for training of neural network model [9].

3   Simulation Parameters

A three joints robotic manipulator system has three inputs and three outputs. Inputs are the torques applied to the joints and outputs are the velocities of the joints. In this study, the three joints robotic manipulator system is controlled according to SISO control methods. In these control methods one independent SISO algorithm is used for each individual joint. The robotic arm dynamics are interactive, but, these interactions influence the individual joint velocities. Because of these influences, there is no obstruction at the using of the three independent SISO algorithms [4].

To perform the useful tasks, a robot arm must move from an admissible initial position/orientation to an admissible final position/orientation. This requires that the robot arm's configurations at both the initial and final positions must be known before the planning of the motion trajectory [4]. In this study, position reference and velocity reference trajectories for each limb are determined according to the sinusoidal trajectory principles to control the manipulator simulator. Detailed information about sinusoidal trajectory can be found in [4].

The following control states and values were used for the GPC-SISO and NGPC-SISO.

The control states used in this study;
A. Only friction effects
B. Friction and carrying load effects
C. Friction and falling load effects
D. Friction and falling load and disturbance (up to max. ± 0.5 Nm) effects
The control values used in the simulation;
- The masses of the limbs are 13.134 *Kg*, 10.332 *Kg* and 6.444 *Kg*.
- The lengths of limbs are 0.154 *m*, 0.445 *m* and 0.396 *m*.
- Torques applied to joints are between -225 *Nm* and +225 *Nm*.
- The Coulomb friction [10] effect is *0.5 Nt.m.*
- The viscous friction [10] effect is *1.0 Nt.m/rad.s-1.*
- Total simulation time is *1 s.* and total step number is *500.*
- The robotic manipulator caries *10 Kg* load at the state of falling load.
- The load is falling in step *300* (at time *0.6 s.*
- Runge-Kutta integration number for each step is *4.*
- Each joint angle is changing from *0 rd* to *0.78539 rd*.

4   Results and Discussions

Some sample control results of the three joints robotic manipulator which use
GPC-SISO and NGPC-SISO algorithms are given in the Figure 3 and Figure 4
respectively. Comparison of the GPC-SISO and NGPC-SISO algorithms control
results are summarized and demonstrated in the table 1, and table 2. As seen
in the Figure 3 and 4, torque and angular velocity graphics are much smooth
in the NGPC-SISO that those in the GPC-SISO for sinusoidal trajectory. So,
motion of the manipulator is more smooth and flexible in the NGPC-SISO for
this trajectory principle. In the same figures, it is shown that the influence of
load change to the NGPC-SISO is less than that of the GPC-SISO. This shows
that NGPC-SISO is much stable than GPC-SISO to the load changes for the
sinusoidal trajectory. As seen in the table 1, and table 2, angle location errors,
and x, y, z axis errors of the end point are smaller in the NGPC-SISO than

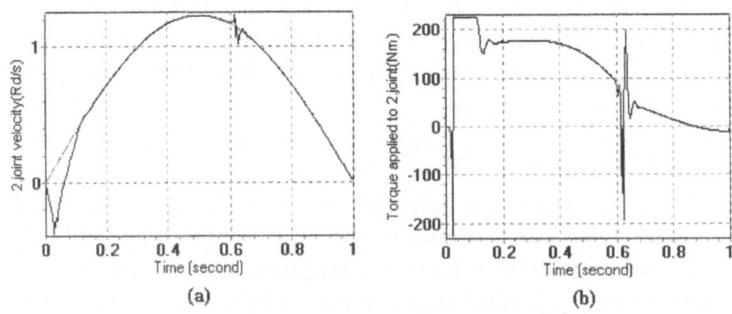

(a)   (b)

Fig. 3. Sample control results of the three joint manipulator controlled by GPC-SISO
algorithms for joint 2 at the state of falling load

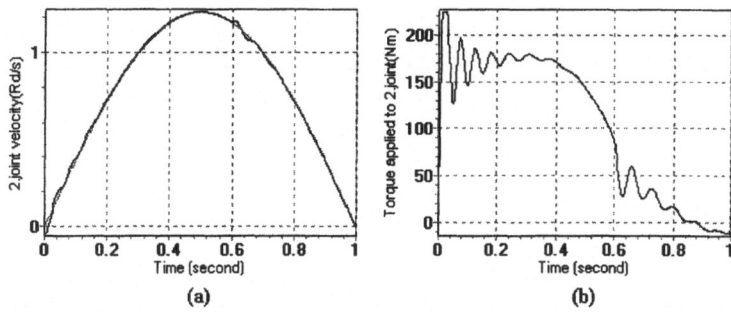

Fig. 4. Sample control results of the three joint manipulator controlled by NGPC_SISO algorithms for joint 2 at the state of falling load

Table 1. Angle location errors

Control state	Control	1.Joint	2.Joint	3.Joint	Unit
A	GPC-SISO	0.000014	-0.007872	-0.001717	
	NGPC-SISO	0.000013	0.000187	-0.000062	
B	GPC-SISO	-0.000149	-0.022124	0.005929	
	NGPC-SISO	0.000227	0.003584	0.000442	(Rd)
C	GPC-SISO	-0.000246	-0.023795	0.004551	
	NGPC-SISO	0.000058	0.000911	0.000017	
D	GPC-SISO	-0.000041	-0.028890	0.006487	
	NGPC-SISO	0.000062	0.000909	0.000019	

Table 2. x, y, z axis errors of the end point

Control state	Control	X coordinate	Y coordinate	Z coordinate	Unit
A	GPC-SISO	1.722898	1.740392	-6.285419	
	NGPC-SISO	-0.049617	-0.033657	0.108382	
B	GPC-SISO	4.923169	4.738716	-13.454184	
	NGPC-SISO	-0.940756	-0.661756	2.721265	(mm)
C	GPC-SISO	5.331456	5.026672	-15.199823	
	NGPC-SISO	-0.238576	-0.167058	0.653774	
D	GPC-SISO	6.289884	6.238179	-18.095953	
	NGPC-SISO	-0.240427	-0.164531	0.653842	

those in the GPC-SISO. The difference between control results for the no-load, the carrying load and the falling load states and the states with disturbances can be easily shown. These values for the NGPC-SISO are less than that of the GPC-SISO. In these tables, it's also shown that the influence of load change to the NGPC-SISO is less than that of the GPC-SISO. This result is similar to the result which is shown from figures. The same tables show also that while the influence of the disturbances to the GPC-SISO can be easily shown, the influence of the disturbances to the NGPC-SISO is negligibly small. Based on the simulation results shown in the figures and tables, it is seen that NGPC-SISO algorithm performs better than GPC-SISO algorithm for the robotic manipulator control with sinusoidal trajectory. This can be because of that the robotic manipulator is a non-linear system and NGPC-SISO is non-linear system model while GPC-SISO is linear system model. The NGPC-SISO algorithm combines also the advantages of predictive control and neural network.

References

[1]   Eskandarian, A., Bedewi, N.E., Kramer, B.M., Barbera, A.J.: Dynamics Modeling of Robotic Manip. using An Artif.icial Neural Net. , Journal of Robotic Systems, **11**(1) (1994) 41-56.

[2]   De, N.M., Gorez, R.: Fuzzy and Quantitative Model-Based Control System for Robotic Manipulators , International Journal of System Sci., **21** (1993).

[3]   Hosogi, S., Watanabe, N., Sekiguchi, M.: A Neural Network Model of the Cerebellum Performing Dynamic Control of a Robotic Manipulator by Learning , Fujitsi Sci. and Technical Journal, **29** (1993).

[4]   Temurtas, F., Temurtas, H., Yumusak, N., Oz, C.: Effects of the Trajectory Planning on the Model Based Predictive Robotic Manipulator Control , ISCIS'03, Lectures Notes in Computer Science, **2869** (2003).

[5]   Hu, H., Gu, D.: Generalized Predictive Control of an Industrial Mobile Robot , IASTED International Conference, Intelligent Systems And Control, Santa Barbara, California, USA,October 28-30, (1999) 234-240 .

[6]   Soloway, D., Haley, P.J.: Neural Generalized Predictive Control: A Newton-Raphson Implementation, IASTED International Conference, Proceedings of the IEEE CCA/ISIC/CACSD, IEEE Paper No. ISIAC-TA5.2, (1996) .

[7]   Silver, W. M.: On the Equivalence of Lagrangian and Newton-Euler Dynamics for Manipulators, The International Journal of Robotics Research, **1**(2) (1982) 60-70.

[8]   Lee, C. S. G.: Robot Arm Kinematics- Dynamics, and Control, Computer, **15**(12) (1982) 62-80.

[9]   Haykin, S.: Neural Networks, A Comprehensive Foundation, Macmillan Publishing Company, Englewood Cliffs, N.J. (1994).

[10] Seraji, H.: A New Approach to Adaptive Control of Manipulators, Journal of Dynamic Systems, Measurement, and Control, **109** (1987) 193-202.

Performance Evaluation of Multiagent Personalized Information System

Tomasz Babczyński, Zofia Kruczkiewicz, and Jan Magott

Institute of Engineering Cybernetics, Wrocław University of Technology

Abstract. An agent-oriented architecture for personalized information system is considered in this paper. This architecture is composed of four types of agents and is based on FIPA standard. The emphasis is put on performance evaluation, which is based on system dynamics. In FIPA, the most extensive models of dynamics are statecharts. Performance statecharts are such statecharts that are extended by probability distributions of activity duration times and probability distribution for solving non-determinism. Performance analysis of the personalized information system using performance statecharts is carried over in the paper.

1 Introduction

The classical information systems do not adapt to their users and do not keep in their memory a history of each user requests. The intelligent agent information system can assist the users by learning their preferences. Such systems should manage the users profiles, i.e., the systems have to acquire new knowledge about the users, to classify them. The architecture of personalized information system that is considered in the paper is based on the system described in paper [5]. This system is combined from four types of agents: Assistant, Searcher, Co-ordinator, and Learning. The Learning agent collects information about users profiles. The main goal of our paper is to analyze the performance of this system.

Performance analysis of systems can be done by: experiments with real-system or examination of system models. In literature, performance evaluation of the following multiagent systems (MASs): ZEUS [2], JADE [2], Skeleton Agents [2], IBM_Aglets [3], Concordia [3], Voyager [3] is presented. When the new MAS is designed, then according to performance engineering of software systems [6], performance requirements have to be considered at each phase of life cycle. Software performance engineering (SPE) examines the performance implications of software requirements (e.g., mean response time) and design alternatives, and enables assessing performance before coding. It is an alternative to the "fix it later" approach, which defers performance concerns to integration testing what can result in delivery delays or interior product quality.

In SPE, performance models are required. Performance evaluation is mainly based on system dynamics. In FIPA [4], the most extensive models of dynamics are statecharts. Performance statecharts [1] are such an extension of FIPA statecharts that contains probability distributions of activity duration times and

L. Rutkowski et al. (Eds.): ICAISC 2004, LNAI 3070, pp. 810–815, 2004.
© Springer-Verlag Berlin Heidelberg 2004

probability distribution for solving non-determinism. In paper [1], performance evaluation of multiagent information retrieval system with then following type of agents: Manager, Bidder, and Searcher, using performance statecharts has been carried over. In present paper, we evaluate the performance of the personalized information system using performance statecharts.

The organization of the paper is as follows. In section 2 analyzed multiagents personalized information system is described. In next section, its performance model is discussed. In section 4 results of simulation experiments with the system are given. Then conclusions are presented.

2   Multiagent Personalized Information System

In Fig.1 diagram of communication protocol [4] between the application agents is shown. In Fig.2 the performance statecharts of the co-ordinator type agent (CTA), mapped from this protocol diagram is shown.

In protocol shown in Fig. 1, the assistant type agent (ATA) receives a succeeding search request from the user and sends the *inform-of-announce* message to the CTA about the need of search task realization - it makes the transition (T) *c1* in Fig.2. Then the ATA sends the *cfp-request-i* message with task to the CTA (it causes the T *c2*), starts the ATA timer for the termination time (TT) *ta1* and waits for the *propose-the-result* message from the CTA not longer than *ta1*=21 time units.

During this time the CTA, when passing through the T *c2*, sends the *cfp-profile-i* message (the user-i profile in request) to the learning type agent (LTA). When the LTA has finished, it gives the CTA the found user profile - it makes the T *c3*. The CTA sends the *request-to-search* message of search task to the searcher type agents (STAs) and starts the timer of the TT *tc1* - these two actions have occurred when the T *c3* has been made. These actions generate trigger events, e.g. t-c-1, that will make another Ts, e.g., the t-c-1 will make the T *c6* after *tc1* time units - so they are named delayed events. When STAs have finished, they send *inform-the-result* message with the found information (it makes the T *c4*) or they send the *failure-search* message with the failure result of searching (it makes the T *c5*). The co-operation between STAs and the CTA is completed immediately when the CTA receives responses from all STAs co-operating with them (they make the T *c7*) or when the TT *tc1* has elapsed (it makes the T *c6*). The CTA can wait for the message not longer then *tc1*=18 time units. The CTA aggregates any good responses and the user profile versus the assumed criterions or if it has received the *failure-search* message or has not received responses before the TT *tc1* has elapsed, it estimates the result from the user profile. The CTA sends the *propose-the-result* message as the result to the ATA and starts the timer for the TT *tc2* - these delayed events have started when the T *c8* has been made. It can wait for the *inform-accept-result* or *inform-no-accept-result* message from the ATA not longer than *tc2*=45 time units.

When the ATA has received the *propose-the-result* message (first one) before the TT *ta1* will elapse, it has started this message evaluation with participation

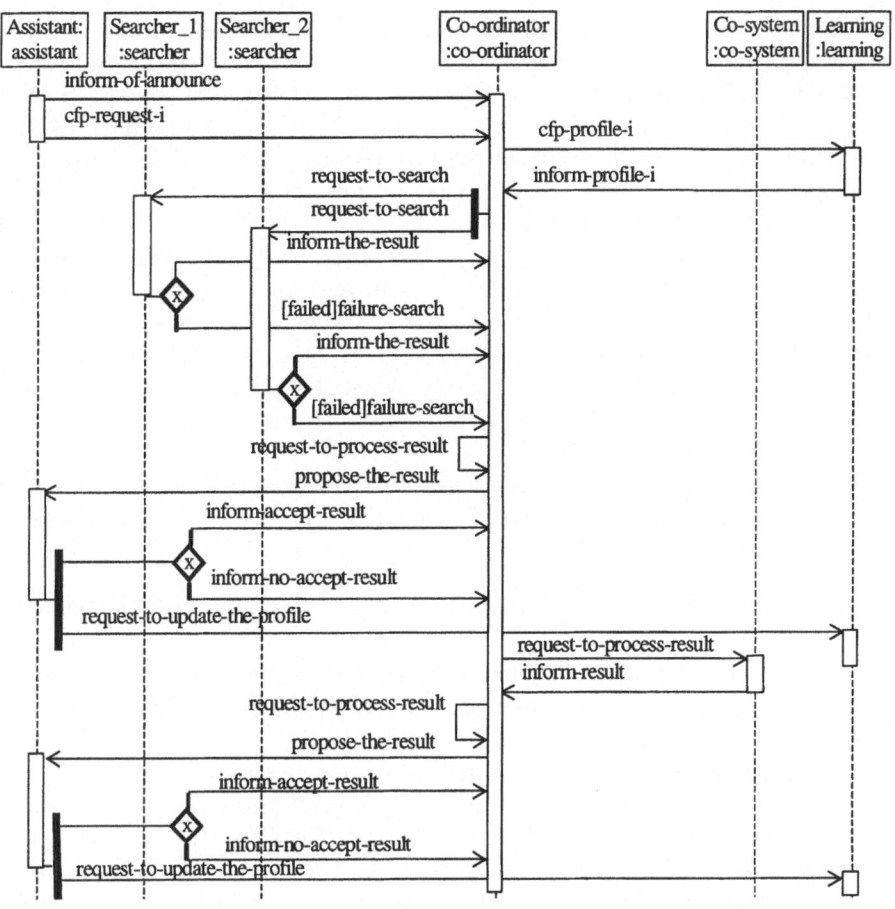

Fig. 1. The-user-defined interaction protocol diagram, named personalized-net.

of the user. The ATA can wait for the result of the user evaluation not longer than $ta2=40$ time units and has sent the *inform-accept-result* message (it makes the T $c12$) or the *inform-no-accept-result* message (it makes the T $c10$), starts the timer for the TT $ta3$ and can wait for the second *propose-the-result* not longer than $ta3=9$ time units. The co-operation between the CTA and ATA is completed immediately, when the CTA receives the *inform-accept-result* message from the ATA. When the CTA has received the *inform-no-accept-result* message indicating the rejection of the first *propose-the-result* message (it makes the T $c10$) or $tc2$ has elapsed (it makes the T $c11$), the CTA has sent the *request-to-process-result* message as the request of the processing the searching result to the *Co-ordination System* and starts the timer for the TT $tc3$ (these delayed events have started when the T $c10$ or $c11$ has been made). The CTA can wait for the *inform-result* message from *the Co-ordination System* not longer than $tc3=10$ time units. When the CTA has received the *inform-result* message from

Co-ordination System (it makes the T *c9*), it has aggregated these results by performing the *request-to-process-result* activity and has sent the second *propose-the-result* message with aggregated result to the ATA and starts the timer for the TT *tc2* - these delayed events have started when it has made the T *c9*. If the CTA has received no response from the *Co-ordination System* before the TT *tc3* has elapsed (it makes the T *c15*) or the TT *ta3* has elapsed, the co-operation with the ATA and the CTA ends.

When the ATA has received the *propose-the-result* message for the second time, it has evaluated this information again and has sent the *inform-accept-result* message as the approval (it makes the T *c12*) or the *inform-no-accept-result* message as the rejection (it makes the T *c14*). The co-operation between the CTA and ATA is completed immediately, when the CTA receives the approval or rejection from the ATA or the TT *tc2* has elapsed (it makes the T *c13*) or the TT *ta2* has elapsed.

When the ATA has sent the approval or the rejection to the CTA for first and second time, the LTA has received the *request-to-update-the-profile* message.

3   Performance Model of Analyzed Multiagent Systems

The performance statecharts of the examined multiagent system contains AND type state with substates, representing the ATA, the CTA, the *Co-ordination System*, two STAs and the LTA.

The following performance parameters model messages transmission times (MTTs): MTTs between the CTA and the *Co-ordination System* and between the CTA and STAs through wide area network (WAN), which are expressed by two stage Erlang distribution with parameter $\lambda = 1$ for each stage (erl(2,1)); MTTs between the CTA and the ATA through the local area network (LAN), which is given by exponential distribution with parameter $\lambda = 10$ (exp(10)), e.g., the MTT of the *propose-the-result* message, sent when the T *c8* or *c9* has been made.

Another parameters characterized activities times of agents are: the searching time of the STA described by the uniform distribution over the interval [0,16), i.e., the mean searching time is equal to 8 time units, while the maximal time is equal to 16; the probability that the STA finds required information is equal to 0.6; the time of preparing the user profile by the LTA is equal to 2 time units, i.e., the time between receiving the *cfp-profile-i* and sending the *inform-profile-i* messages; the time of preparing the answer to the CTA by the *Co-ordination System* described by the uniform distribution over the interval [0,2), i.e., the time between receiving the *request-to-process-result* message from the CTA and sending the *inform-result* message to the CTA; the time of evaluating the result from the CTA by the ATA with participation of the user is given by exponential random variable time with parameter $\lambda = 0.05$ (mean time is equal to 20 time units), i.e., the time between receiving the *propose-the result* message from the CTA and sending the *inform-accept-result* or *inform-no-accept-result*. Execution times of the other activities are supposed to be equal to zero.

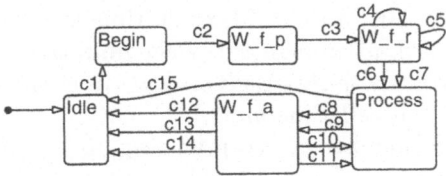

Fig. 2. Performance model of the CTA

At Fig. 2 performance statechart for the CTA is given, which contains: the termination times, the random variables modeling the time parameters of the CTA and netware. The labels of the performance statecharts are partially described in section 2. For example, the label c10 describes the transition by the following components (c10:<<i-n-a-r>,<<r-t-p-r,erl(2,1)>,<t-c-3,$tc3$>>>): the trigger event indicates the *inform-no-accept-result* message (i-n-a-r) sent by the *ATA* after evaluating the result by the user, the list of delayed events includes: the *request-to-process-result* message (r-t-p-r) sent by the CTA to *the Co-ordination System* with MTT erl(2,1) and start initialization of the timer for tc3. The TT $tc3$ generates the trigger event t-c-3, that makes the T $c15$ (c15:<<t-c-3>,<>>). The response to the r-t-p-r is the trigger event *inform-result* (i-r) of the T $c9$ (c9:<<i-r>,<<p-t-r,exp(10)>,<t-c-2,$tc2$>>>) etc.

4   Results of Experiments

Now we present some results of simulation experiments for time and probability of receiving an accepted response by the ATA. The goal of the experiments is to optimize the system metrics by tuning the termination times.

First *propose-the-result* message is prepared by the CTA after co-operation with STSs. Second *propose-the-result* message is prepared by the CTA after co-operation with the *Co-ordination System*. TTs are equal to values given in

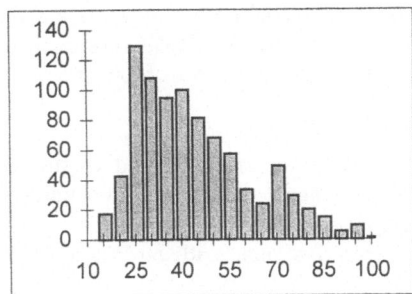
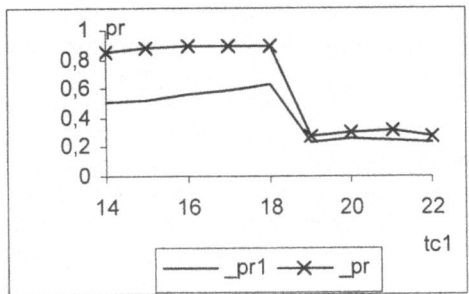

Fig. 3. Number of accepted responses as a function of time of receiving the response by the ATA (left); Probabilities *pr*, *pr1* as a function of termination times *tc1 of the CTA* (right)

section 3 axcept *tc1* at Fig. 3 right. Maximal time from time instance when the ATA has sent the *inform-of-announce* message until time instance when the user will evaluate the first *propose-the-result* message from the CTA is approximately equal to $ta1+ta2=21+40=61$ time units.

At Fig. 3 left, the number of accepted responses is increasing for response time equal to 70 time units. This is caused by second *propose-the-result* message. In Fig. 3 right, *pr* denotes the probability of receiving an accepted response in first or second *propose-the-result* message, while *pr1* denotes the probability of receiving an accepted response in first *propose-the-result* message. During time interval of length $ta1=21$, the ATA has sent *inform-of-announce* and *cfp-request-i* messages to the CTA, the LTA has prepared *inform-profile-i* message in 2 time units, co-operation between the CTA and the STAs has to be completed, and the CTA has sent *propose-the-result* message from to the ATA. Therefore, the probabilities *pr*, *pr1* are much smaller for *tc1*>19 than for *tc1*<18.

5 Conclusions

Performance analysis of multiagent personalized information system has been done. Performance models of agents are expressed by performance statecharts. The following performance metrics: the time and the probability of receiving an accepted response by user have been examined by simulation. These experiments can be used for tuning of values of agent termination times in order to optimize performance metrics.

References

1. T. Babczyński, Z. Kruczkiewicz, J. Magott, Performance evaluation of multiagent information retrieval system, accepted for publication in Foundations of Computing and Decision Sciences
2. D.Camacho, R.Aler, C.Castro, J. M. Molina, Performance evaluation of ZEUS, JADE, and SkeletonAgent frameworks, in: Proc. IEEE Systems, Man, and Cybernetics Conference, 2002
3. M.Dikaiakos, M.Kyriakou, G.Samaras, Performance evaluation of mobile-agent middleware: A hierarchical approach, In Proceedings of the 5th IEEE International Conference on Mobile Agents, J.P. Picco (ed.), Lecture Notes in Computer Science series, vol. 2240, pages 244-259, Springer, December 2001
4. FIPA system documentation, *http://www.fipa.org/specs/*
5. C. Petit-Roze, E. G.-L. Strugeon, Intelligent agents to structure and to process personalized information system, in: in: Proc. Intelligent Agents Web Technologies and Internet Commerce - IAWTIC 2003, Vienna, Austria, 165-174.
6. C. U. Smith, Performance Engineering of Software Systems, Addison-Wesley, 1990

A Neural-Based Agent for IP Traffic Scanning and Worm Detection*

Andrzej Bielecki and Paweł Hajto

Institute of Computer Science
Jagiellonian University
Poland, Nawojki 11, 30-072 Cracow
{bielecki,hajto}@ii.uj.edu.pl

Abstract. We present a neural approach to worm detection designed as a part of a multi-agent system intended to manage IP networks. The efficiency of virus recognition is about 95%.

1 Introduction

The creation of a multi-agent system (MAS) serving, optimizing and securing an IP network is our aim. The system is planned to consist of at least two types of agents. The first class will be dedicated to be executed on routers while the second one is intended to manage client machine resources. Tasks of the complete MAS can be specified as follows:

- traffic flow optimization;
- security control (detection of abuses);
- quality of service (client service in dependence of their contract value);
- early detection of viruses and exchange of information concerning infected hosts;
- interaction with users;
- client processes management: specification and satisfaction of their necessities, negotiations concerning the way and time of fulfilment.

To allow the MAS complete the above tasks, the system has to posses the following functional possibilities:

- prediction of network load;
- real time effective activity while critical situations;
- classical properties of MASes like learning abilities, social abilities (for instance possibility of information exchange), mobility etc.;
- pattern recognitions possibilities for instance in the context of malicious traffic detection;
- data mining possibilities.

* This work was supported by the Polish State Committee for Scientific Research (KBN) under Grant No. 3 T11C 054 26.

L. Rutkowski et al. (Eds.): ICAISC 2004, LNAI 3070, pp. 816–822, 2004.
© Springer-Verlag Berlin Heidelberg 2004

In this work we present a part of an agent dedicated to run on an IP router. Its task is to gather and analyze SMTP (e-mail) traffic focusing on worm detection. Due to high CPU demand of usual antiviral scanners we propose a solution based on statistical analysis and neural classification. It achieves a good accuracy and has a low computational cost, which is critical for real time applications.

2   Motivation

Internet Service Providers (ISPs) have to deal with different classes of problems, like economical, related to law and technical ones. In the technical domain network state is one of their main concerns. It regards the physical layer: lines, modems, access points, routers, etc. and logical, i.e. traffic generated by clients, limited bandwidth resources, bandwidth guarantees, security policies, servers load. A typical headache cause for a network administrator is observing the network being congested by a new Internet worm spreading itself from thousands of client machines. It is often impossible to remotely remove a worm or to get in touch with an unexperienced user to give virus removal instructions. It is also not a good idea to drop all traffic send to, let's say, TCP port no. 25. The obvious choice would be to start a virus scanner on a dedicated machine and analyze all traffic from/to clients. Then drop the "suspicious" packets. This would involve huge CPU resources in case of high network load and is not effective. That is why we want to use neural networks and statistical analysis. The advantages are: good accuracy, low CPU power consumption and detection of unknown worms and viruses. Our method can be easily adapted to track hosts, that generate heavy traffic not related to viruses, but which can also be malicious, like P2P applications.

3   Neural Networks and TCP/IP Traffic Statistical Analysis

We will focus on packets travelling through an IP router and its interfaces. Each packet has a source and destination address and in case of the most important TCP and UDP protocols a source and destination port. In this chapter we present a method for collecting and classifying packets coming from the client computers of a hypothetical ISP.

Artificial Neural Networks are eagerly used, because of their good fitness for approximation and classification purposes [6], [11], [12]. Neural applications lie in areas of pattern recognition, expert systems, control theory, etc. The ANNs in scope of our interest are Multilayer Perceptrons.

3.1   Gathering Data and Host Classification

The method bases on the fact, that viruses and worms generate an intensive network traffic in order to multiply themselves, because they try to infect as many machines as possible. There were many famous worm outbreaks, as e.g. Blaster, which performed denial of service attacks to windowsupdate.com.

Let us assume, that the network we would like to monitor is called N. We know the IP address space assigned to the clients. We need to have information from every packet travelling from N to internet. This can be easily accomplished e.g. if the main router is a unix system. In this case we can use one machine for routing and analyzing.

The main idea of data collection algorithm can be expressed as follows:

```
//Example: Watch outgoing SMTP (email) data
PROTO_TO_OBSERVE = TCP; DEST_PORT_TO_OBSERVE = 25
sub collect(srcIP, destIP, srcport, destport, payloadlen, proto) {
    if (proto=PROTO_TO_OBSERVE and destport=DEST_PORT_TO_OBSERVE) {
        stat_Amin[srcIP].set_of_hosts_contacted += destIP;
        stat_Amin[srcIP].total_bytes_send += payloadlen;
        stat_Bmin[srcIP].set_of_hosts_contacted += destIP;
        stat_Bmin[srcIP].total_bytes_send += payloadlen;
        stat_Cmin[srcIP].set_of_hosts_contacted += destIP;
        stat_Cmin[srcIP].total_bytes_send += payloadlen;
    }
    every_Amin {
        clear(history_Amin);
        history_Amin[srcIP].number_of_hosts_contacted =
            amount(stat_Amin[srcIP].set_of_hosts_contacted);
        history_Amin[srcIP].total_bytes_send =
            stat_Amin[srcIP].total_bytes_send;
        clear(stat_Amin);
    }
    every_Bmin {
        clear(history_Bmin);
        history_Bmin[srcIP].number_of_hosts_contacted =
            amount(stat_Bmin[srcIP].set_of_hosts_contacted);
        history_Bmin[srcIP].total_bytes_send =
            stat_Bmin[srcIP].total_bytes_send;
        clear(stat_Bmin);
    }
    every_Cmin {
        clear(history_Cmin);
        history_Cmin[srcIP].number_of_hosts_contacted =
            amount(stat_Cmin[srcIP].set_of_hosts_contacted);
        history_Cmin[srcIP].total_bytes_send =
            stat_Cmin[srcIP].total_bytes_send;
        clear(stat_Cmin);
    }
}
```

The "Xmin" denotation represents a time interval. For instance, we can choose to collect data during 1 minute, 5 minutes and 10 minutes intervals. Then "Amin" stands for "1 minute interval", "Bmin" for "5 minutes interval", etc. A data structure stat_Xmin is indexed by srcIP and contains for each srcIP a set of hosts contacted during last X minutes and amount of bytes send to all this hosts. If srcIP didn't send any packets during the X minutes time interval, then stat_Xmin[srcIP] is undefined. The structure stat_Xmin has to be cleared every X minutes. Information from the last X minutes interval is saved in history_Xmin data structure. The purpose of this proceeding is to evaluate the state of a host as a function of amount of data send and number of contacted IPs during different time periods. This parameters take part in ANN training process.

The choice of time intervals length has influence on detection accuracy. The intervals can overlap or be disjunctive, which involves slight changes in the code presented above. However, the main idea remains the same - collect history of host activity.

Having a tool for defining each client's activity we can train a neural network to act as a detector of hosts sending malicious data. This ANN can be regarded as a function $f : \mathbb{R}^6 \to \mathbb{R}$, which classifies a srcIP by information from history_Amin[srcIP], history_Bmin[srcIP] and history_Cmin[srcIP] as healthy or infected. Obviously, first we need to train the network to realize this mapping, which can be accomplished by an usual antivirus scanner. As soon as the network is trained, the scanner is not needed.

```
//General neural scanner algorithm
CYCLE=0; RESPOK=0; TRAINING = TRUE;
while () {
    packet = get_packet();
    collect(packet.srcIP, packet.destIP,
            packet.srcport, packet.destport,
            packet.payloadlen, packet.proto);
    CYCLE++;
    nn = ANN.insert(history_Amin[srcIP].number_of_hosts_contacted,
                    history_Amin[srcIP].number_of_bytes_send,
                    history_Bmin[srcIP].number_of_hosts_contacted,
                    history_Bmin[srcIP].number_of_bytes_send,
                    history_Cmin[srcIP].number_of_hosts_contacted,
                    history_Cmin[srcIP].number_of_bytes_send);
    //if ANN response is > 0.5 we classify the packet as viral
    if (nn > 0.5) nnvir = VIRUS; else nnvir = NOVIRUS;
    if (virus_scan(packet.payload)==nnvir) RESPOK++;
    //switch off training if > 90% of packets are good classified
    if (CYCLE>MAX_TRAINING_CYCLE AND RESPOK/CYCLES>0.9)
        TRAINING=FALSE;
    if (TRAINING)
        ANN.train(history_Amin[srcIP].number_of_hosts_contacted,
                  history_Amin[srcIP].number_of_bytes_send,
                  history_Bmin[srcIP].number_of_hosts_contacted,
                  history_Bmin[srcIP].number_of_bytes_send,
                  history_Cmin[srcIP].number_of_hosts_contacted,
                  history_Cmin[srcIP].number_of_bytes_send,
                  vir);
}
```

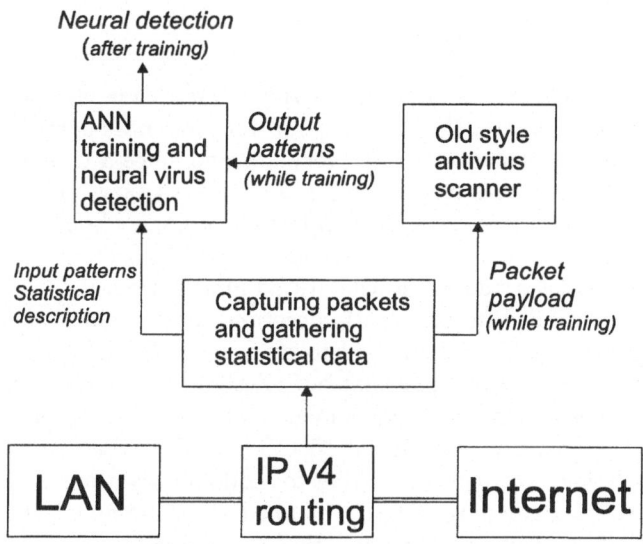

Fig. 1. Cybernetic model of the neural virus scanner

3.2   Test Configuration and Results

The described algorithm has been tested in a small ISP company. It was implemented in C++ (packet capturing, ANN library) and Perl (collecting statistical information). The application run on a linux router. Its cybernetic model is shown on fig. 1.

We have focused on outgoing SMTP packets and were using a simple scanner to detect the Win32/Gibe.B@mm worm. We have chosen 1 minute (A), 5 minutes (B) and 10 minutes (C) time intervals. During 3 hours the program captured 2000 packets, of which 132 were part of the worm's code. After 500 initial training presentations of statistical descriptions (input patterns) and scanner responses (output patterns) a two layer perceptron (2 hidden neurons, 1 output neuron) was able to detect 94% of remaining 50 viral packets and 97.6% of 1450 clean packets. Details are presented in table 1.

Table 1. Neural scanner accuracy

	False detection	True detection
With worm	6%	94%
Without worm	2.4%	97.6%

The CPU usage on a Duron 600MHz machine during testing procedure raised about 6%. The machine was simultaneously routing about 2 mbit/s intense traffic through 3 network interfaces.

4   Concluding Remarks

A neural scanner can be used for improving network management. The above presented results indicate, that it is a good tool for mass spreading worms detection. The computational costs are very low and since a trained scanner does not analyze content of the packets it can early detect new, unknown worms. In case of huge networks it is extremely important to know about possible dangers. Information from our neural scanner can be used in firewall or traffic control policies. It can assist a human in network administration.

As it was mentioned in introduction section, the presented solution is intended to be a part of a MAS dedicated to manage an IP network. The theory of MASes still lacks a good basement for both designing them on a cybernetic level and implementing in software environments. That is why the problem has been being studied intensively (e.g. [1], [4], [5]). Some of approaches rely on achievements of psychology, for instance trying to model motivations and emotions [3], [10]. Our network managing MAS is planned to be designed according to the paradigm of information metabolism - the theory created by polish psychiatrist A. Kępiński in late sixties [7], [8]. The information metabolism theory was used by the author to describe the structure and dynamics of human psyche both in a normal state and in pathology. It seems, that the significance of Kępiński's concepts goes far beyond psychology and psychiatry and can be applied to a very wide class of cybernetic objects - self controlling open systems. The usefulness of the theory in application to MASes has been discussed in [2].

References

1. Bielecki A., *Some aspects of Theoretical Foundations of a Neural Agent Process*, LNAI, vol. 2296, 2002, p. 47-53.
2. Bielecki A., Nowak D., *A Multiagent System based on the Information Metabolism Theory*, LNCS, accepted.
3. Canamero D., *Modelling Motivations and Emotions as a basis for Intelligent Behaviour*, Proc. 1st Int. Conf. on Autonomous Agents, Marina del Rey, California USA, 1997, p. 148-155.
4. Cetnarowicz K., Gruer P., Hilaire V., Koukam A., *A Formal Specification of M-Agent Architecture*, LNAI, vol. 2296, 2002, p. 62-72.
5. Ferber J., *Multi-Agent Systems. An Introduction to Distributed Artifical Intelligence*, Addison Wesley Longmann, Harlow, 1999.
6. Hertz J., Krogh A., Palmer R. G., *Introduction to the Theory of Neural Computation*, Addison Wesley Publ. Co., Massachusetts, 1991.
7. Kokoszka A., Bielecki A., Holas P., *Mental organization according to metabolism of information and its mathematical description*, Int. Journal of Neuroscience, vol. 107, 2001, p. 173-184.
8. Kępiński A., *Melancholy*, PZWL, Warsaw, 1972 (in Polish).
9. *Linux Advanced Routing And Traffic Control HOWTO*, http://www.lartc.org.
10. Velasquez J.D., Maes P., *Cathexis: A Computational Model of Emotions*, Proc. 1st Int. Conf. on Autonomous Agents, Marina del Rey, California USA, 1997, p. 518-519.

11. Zurada J.M., *Introduction to Artifical Neural Systems*, West Publ. Co., St. Paul, 1992.
12. Tadeusiewicz R., *Neural Networks*, Academic Publishing House, Warsaw, 1993 (in Polish).

Evolutionary Neural Networks
in Collective Intelligent Predicting System

Aleksander Byrski and Jerzy Bałamut

AGH University of Science and Technology
Mickiewicz Avenue 30, 30-059 Kraków, Poland,
olekb@agh.edu.pl, jurekb@acchsh.com

Abstract. In the paper a hybrid, agent-based system of evolving neural networks dedicated to time-series prediction is presented. First the idea of a multi-agent predicting system is introduced. Second some aspects of the system concerning management of collective intelligence and evolutionary design of a predicting neural network are discussed. Then a hybrid solution – an evolutionary multi-agent system (EMAS) is proposed. Finally selected results of the experiments are presented.

1 Introduction

Looking for the optimal neural network one may consider performing multiple experiments, in order to find desired values of the neural model. Such process is a very time consuming job and can be conducted only by an expert, who is forced to repeat all his tasks when new application of the neural network emerges.

The parameters describing neural network (architecture, learning coefficients e.a.) may be encoded in a chromosome and thus be a subject of evolutionary optimisation, that can be seriously improved by using intelligent agent-based systems. Agents managed in specific way, may become a source of *collective intelligence.*

Combining evolutionary computation with multi-agent systems (MAS) leads to decentralisation of the evolutionary optimisation process. Training of a neural network may be entrusted to an autonomously acting agent. Such defined *evolutionary multi-agent system* (EMAS) may help in search for the optimal configuration of a neural network for the given problem, or at least help to establish a starting point for further network structure development.

This paper presents the concept and implementation of such a hybrid, collective intelligent system. The main task of the system is time-series prediction, and at the same time, to optimise the architecture and parameters of predicting neural networks.

2 MAS for Time-Series Prediction

Time-series predicting system may be considered as a black box with some input sequences, and predictions of successive values of (some of) these sequences as

L. Rutkowski et al. (Eds.): ICAISC 2004, LNAI 3070, pp. 823–828, 2004.
© Springer-Verlag Berlin Heidelberg 2004

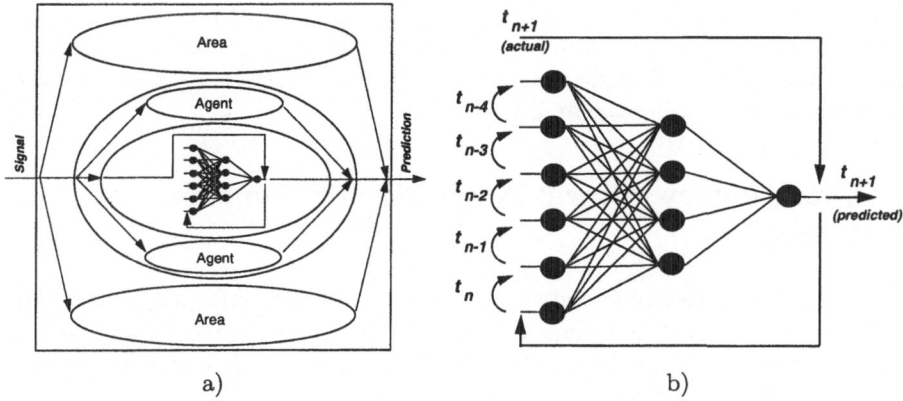

Fig. 1. a) Predicting neural MAS, b) Predicting neural network

output. Some mechanism inside that box should be able to discover hidden regularities and relationships in and between the input sequences. Assuming that the characteristics of the signal(s) may change in time, this mechanism should be also able to dynamically adapt to these changes ignoring different kinds of distortion and noise.

2.1 Predicting MAS

When the signal to be predicted is much complicated (e.g. when different trends change over time or temporal variations in relationships between particular sequences are present) the idea of a *multi-agent predicting system* may be introduced. The predicting MAS may be viewed as the box with a group of intelligent agents inside (fig. 1). Subsequent elements of input sequence(s) are supplied to the environment, where they become available for all agents. Each agent may perform analysis of incoming data and give predictions of the next-to-come elements of input. Specialisation in function or time of particular agents allow for obtaining better results by cooperation or competition in the common environment. Based on predictions of all agents, prediction of the whole system may be generated.

2.2 Managing Collective Intelligence of a Population of Agents

One may notice that a group of autonomous yet cooperating intelligent agents can exhibit a kind of *collective intelligence*. While dealing with such a system an important problem arises: how to determine the answer of the whole system to given problem. For mentioned time-series prediction problem, it should be decided how to select an agent which output is the best or most representative and thus may be presented as the output of the whole system, or how to combine more than one agent's answers to produce the desired output value.

In the particular system, the way of combining multiple individuals' answers can be based on probability analysis (combined with voting strategy where the answer of the group of experts comes as a weighted answer of every member of the group) as shown in section 4.2.

3   Evolutionary Neural Networks for Time-Series Prediction

Many techniques were invented that allow for automatic design of a neural network that fulfills the requirements of the problem. The search for the desirable neural network can be made by an evolutionary algorithm[4,6], and this approach is presented in this paper.

3.1   Prediction with Neural Networks

A neural network may be used by an agent as a particular mechanism to model the characteristics of a signal in a system for time-series prediction [3]. Usually the next value of a series is predicted based on a fixed number of previous ones (fig. 1). Thus the number of input neurons correspond to the number of values the prediction is based on, and the output neuron(s) give prediction(s) of the next-to-come value(s) of the series. The feed-forward network on (fig. 1) should predict t_{n+1} value of the series, based on a fixed number of previous values, which are given on the inputs of the first layer. When t_{n+1} value is predicted, the inputs are shifted, and the value t_{n+1} is given as the input to the last neuron of the first layer.

3.2   Evolutionary Design of Neural Network

In order to design optimal network for given problem, the structure of the network and/or the parameters of their learning should be encoded into a chromosome which is a subject of the evolution process.

Chromosome can be constructed simply as a vector of different parameters describing the process of learning and working of neural network, as well as its architecture.

Search for optimal design of neural network can be enhanced using of classical architecture optimisation methods like pruning [2]. The parameters of the pruning process can be evolved, while architecture of the network can be refined using pruning.

4   Neural EMAS for Time-Series Prediction

The configuration of the agents in a predicting MAS (kind of specialisation or method of cooperation) is often difficult to specify. What is more, when dynamic changes of the characteristics of the signal are possible, the configuration of the agents should reflect these changes, automatically adapting to the new characteristics. The mechanisms of evolution may help to transform the whole population of agents (by means of mutation and/or recombination) so as it fits best current profile of the input signal (proper selection/reproduction) – this evolutionary development of predicting MAS meets the general idea of an evolutionary agent system (EMAS).

4.1 Evolutionary Multi-agent Systems

The key idea of EMAS is the incorporation of evolutionary processes into a multi-agent system (MAS) at a population level [1]. It means that besides interaction mechanisms typical for MAS (such as communication) agents are able to reproduce (generate new agents) and may die (be eliminated from the system). A decisive factor of an agent's activity is its fitness, expressed by the amount of possessed non-renewable resource called life energy. Selection is realised in such a way that agents with high energy are more likely to reproduce, while low energy increases the possibility of death.

In EMAS training of a neural network may be entrusted to an agent while the search for a suitable network architecture may be realised as the process of evolution occurring in the whole population. A genotype describing architecture and parameters of neural network, posessed by an agent, is modified by genetic operators when inherited by its offspring. Evaluation of agents is based on the quality of prediction.

4.2 A Population of Agents as a Dynamic Modular Neural Network

In the above-described system every agent contains a neural network, which acts as a computational model for the given (prediction) problem. This is similar to the approach of modular neural networks such as the model of PREdictive MOdular Neural Network. PREMONN is a group (team) of neural networks, which solve the same problem, and their responses are combined together to yield the final result [5].

Applying PREMONN algorithm, every prediction of the given time-series may be assigned a certain probability, which can be used to determine the answer of the whole group of predicting individuals. After every prediction step, every individual based on its predictions and errors:

$$y_t^k = f_K(y_{t-1}, y_{t-2}, \ldots, y_{t-M})$$

$$e_t^k = y_t - \hat{y}_t^k$$

computes its credit function:

$$p_t^k = \frac{p_{t-1}^k \cdot e^{-\frac{|e_t^k|^2}{2\sigma^2}}}{\sum_{n=1}^{K} p_{t-1}^n \cdot e^{-\frac{|e_t^k|^2}{2\sigma^2}}}$$

Based on this function the response of the group of individuals can be a weighted combination of the answers or even can be the result of the winner-take-all combination (choosing the best individual in the meaning of credit function).

5   Experimental Results

System was implemented using distributed evolutionary applications platform Ant.NET developed at AGH-UST (*http://antnet.sourceforge.net*).

Neural networks used in the experiments were multi-layer perceptrons with three layers. There were 6 neurons in the input layer and 15 neurons in the first and the second hidden layer. The sigmoid activation function was used in hidden layers and linear function in the output layer. The learning rates for hidden and output layers, momentum, penalty function parameters and weight cut-off threshold were the subject of evolution process. The networks were trained with standard backpropagation method with momentum.

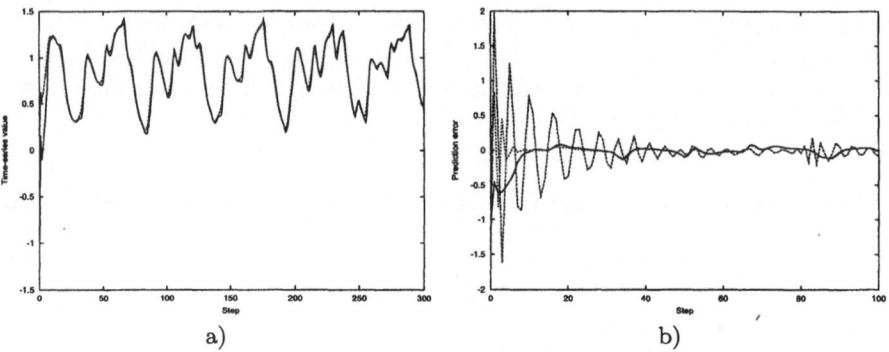

Fig. 2. a) Original and predicted time series, b) Error of prediction

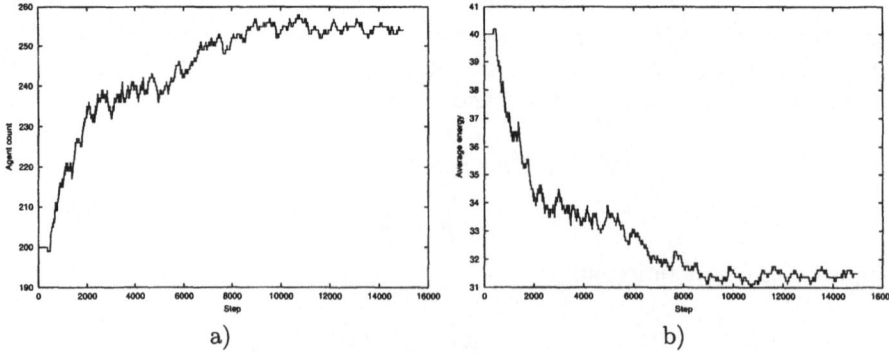

Fig. 3. a) Number of agents in the population, b) Average agent energy

The results described below were obtained for Mackey-Glass time series with delay parameter equal to 30 and step parameter equal to 10. The signal range was from 0, 2 to 1, 4.

In the first graph original and predicted time series are presented (fig. 2a) and absolute prediction error of selected agents (fig. 2b). The learning process tends to be faster at the beginning and slows down after few hundreds of steps. PREMONN classification mechanism allows to keep the global prediction error quite small after few dozens of learning epochs, although prediction of particular agents may not be accurate.

A crucial task in these kind of systems is to maintain stable number of the agents in the population in order to continue the evolution process. In the conducted experiments the agent population seems to be stable, as it can be observed in the graph (fig. 3a), where the number of agents in the system is presented. It is to notify that the number of agents at the beginning of the evolution process changes very fast, then begins to stabilize. As the processes of evolution and death are based on the life energy of agents, it can be seen in the graph (fig. 3b), that amount of this resource is also stable during the operation of the system, which proves that mechanisms of resource distribution agents (prices and penalties) are satisfactory.

6   Conclusions

Evolutionary design of neural networks may lead to obtaining faster and better results than these designed by a man from scratch. At the same time a population of cooperating agents may produce much more reliable results than even the best (as it may seem) agent at a time, which may be perceived as an example of collective intelligence. Combination of the answers of particular predicting models with use of PREMONN algorithm leads to obtaining accurate prediction even if not every neural network is able to predict given time series.

After satisfactory results obtained for the prediction of the Mackey-Glass time-series, attempts will be made to predict more complicated, real-world ones.

References

1. A. Byrski, M. Kisiel-Dorohinicki, and E. Nawarecki. Agent-based evolution of neural network architecture. In M. Hamza, editor, *Proc. of the IASTED Int. Symp.: Applied Informatics.* IASTED/ACTA Press, 2002.
2. S. Haykin. *Neural networks: a comprehensive foundation.* Prentice Hall, 1999.
3. T. Masters. *Neural, Novel and Hybrid Algorithms for Time Series Prediction.* John Wiley and Sons, 1995.
4. M. Mitchell. *An Introduction to Genetic Algorithms.* MIT Press, 1998.
5. V. Petridis and A. Kehagias. *Predictive Modular Neural Networks – Application to Time Series.* Kluwer Academic Publishers, 1998.
6. X. Yao and Y. Liu. Evolving artificial neural networks through evolutionary programming. In L. J. Fogel, P. J. Angeline, and T. Bäck, editors, *Evolutionary Programming V: Proc. of the 5th Annual Conf. on Evolutionary Programming.* MIT Press, 1996.

Development of a Personalized Digital Library System Based on the New Mobile Multi Agent Platform

Young Im Cho

Dept. of Computer Science, Pyongtaek University
111 Yongi-dong, Pyongtaek, Kyongki-do, KOREA, 450-701
Tel : +82-31-659-8342
yicho@ptuniv.ac.kr

Abstract. In this paper, I propose a Personalized Digital Library System (PDLS) based on a new mobile multi agent platform. This new platform is developed by improving the DECAF (Distributed Environment-Centered Agent Framework) which is one of the conventional distributed agent development toolkits. Also, a mobile ORB (Object Request Broker), Voyager, and a new multi agent negotiation algorithm are adopted to develop the new platform. The new mobile multi agent platform is for mobile multi agents as well as the distributed environment, whereas the DECAF is for the distributed and non-mobile environment. From the results of the simulation, the searched time of PDLS is lower, as the numbers of servers and agents are increased. And the user satisfaction is four times greater than the conventional client-server model. Therefore, the new platform has some optimality and higher performance in the distributed mobile environment.

1   Introduction

Recent developments of the internet and network technologies evoke the technical change of the data processing from a conventional centralized and local processing system to the distributed processing system. The research about this network and the various approaches have been studied in order to efficiently manage mutual operations in such a network environment.

Many studies have been actively carried out in a distributed processing environment by using agent systems for efficient network management [1].

There are so many application areas of agents in the real world. One of these areas is a digital library system. This is a library developed to replace the conventional library, in order to serve information from databases on the web to users, according to the development of computers and the related fields.

However, there are several problems in the searching of data of the existing digital libraries. First, as the searching method is one dimensional and distinguishes the existence of the searching keyword from the database, the result is very simple. Secondly, the results may contain unnecessary information under

L. Rutkowski et al. (Eds.): ICAISC 2004, LNAI 3070, pp. 829–834, 2004.
© Springer-Verlag Berlin Heidelberg 2004

a condition that was not given the prior information about the user. Thirdly, whenever a client connects to the servers, he has to receive the certification and be under the dominant power of the influence of network.

To overcome such problems, I proposed a new platform of mobile multi agents for a personal digital library in this paper. For developing a new platform, I combined the existing DECAF (Distributed Environment Centered Agent Framework) multi agent framework [2] with Voyager which is a mobile ORB (Object Request Broker). Also a new negotiation algorithm and a scheduling algorithm are proposed, so that I developed a PDLS (Personal Digital Library System) using this new platform. Although the partial studies for a personal digital library have been carried out, there has been none about the integrated and systemized personal digital library. For the higher relationship among searched documents from mobile servers, an unsupervised neural network is applied. For the user's preference, some modular clients are applied to a neural network. A multi agent platform and a mobile agent platform are combined to develop a new mobile multi agent platform so as to decrease a network burden. Also, a new negotiation algorithm and a scheduling algorithm are activated for the effectiveness of PDLS. PDLS is different from the electronic paper service system which is supplied only to members. It is a more intelligent system that is capable of establishing a database in users' computer by learning the interests of those individuals. In this paper, I tried to set up the theoretical structure of the multi mobile agents and develop an algorithm of the modified intelligent negotiation agent for inducing interaction among multi agents.

This paper is composed of five chapters. Multi agents and DECAF framework is explained in chapter 2. PDLS based on a new mobile multi agent platform is explained in chapter 3. The simulation results of PDLS are explained in chapter 4, and finally the conclusions are in chapter 5.

2   Multi Agent System

DECAF (Distributed Environment-Centered Agent Framework) is a conventional framework to design a lot of intelligent agents [2]. DECAF is a kind of operating system including agent communication, planning, scheduling, monitoring, coordination, diagnosis, and learning among agents. DECAF makes a socket program by itself, and presents some building blocks which makes messages and communicates between agents. Therefore, users or programmers can produce agents without having some knowledge about API approaches. Also, users or programmers do not need to make the communication codes directly to communicate among agents. DECAF produces a KQML protocol automatically which sends messages and searches other agents and interacts between agents. Agent systems have been developed using various languages and platforms, and they are classified into so many types by purpose. In DECAF, many agents' tasks are divided by both GPGP (Generalized Partial Global Planning) and TAEMS (Task Analysis Environment Modeling and Simulation) algorithms.

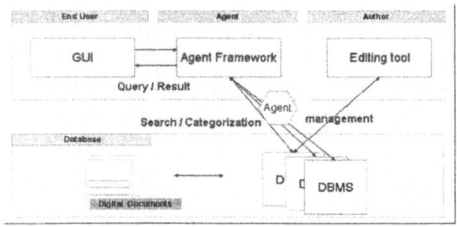

Fig. 1. Agent based Digital Library

GPGP is for improving of PGP which acts as a coordination algorithm of multi agents [3]. The first advantage of GPGP is that it reduces the system overhead which occurs by overlapping interaction among agents. And the second advantage of GPGP is that it is independent from some specific domain areas. Therefore, GPGP can make heterogeneous multi agents system having different functions. User's requirements can be decomposed by GPGP, and be structured by TAEMS [4]. In TAEMS task structure, the root task can be decomposed into subtasks, and the subtasks can be decomposed into methods. The leaf node acts as a method that becomes an activated element.

Voyager [5] is a distributed mobile agent's framework for developing agent's applications, whereas DECAF is a non-mobile agent's framework. Voyager is an interactive framework with Java programming. Also, Voyager can activate any Java class in remote sites, and it makes use of network bandwidths effectively. A digital library serves a lot of information on-line [5],[7]. The advantages of digital libraries are user friendly, on-site service and accessibility. However, in case of not having standardized platform, the search of heterogeneous information from digital libraries may be hard, as well as impossible. If it does not have or learn about the user's information, unnecessary or useless information will appear in the searched results from the digital library.

Figure 1 shows the concept of an agent based digital library which is proposed in this paper. This is based on the proposed mobile multi agent framework to search many servers concurrently, using multi agents. Also user's profile can be produce into a database in this system.

3 Personal Digital Library System Based on a New Mobile Agent Platform

The proposed system, in Figure 2(a), is a Personalized Digital Library System (PDLS) based on a new multi mobile agent platform. The system combines a mobile system and a distributed processing system to make an optimization of behaviors in a distributed environment. To establish a distributed environment, DECAF is used, and to activate a mobile framework, Voyager is used here. The PDLS is composed of two parts: client group and server group. The client group is composed of three modules. First, a user interface module lets

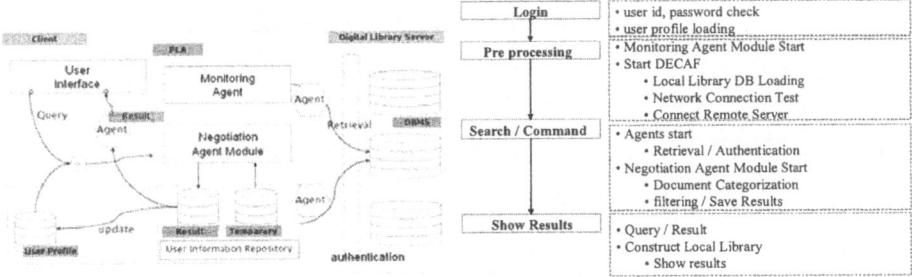

(a) PDLS Structure   (b) Interactions among Detailed Modules in PDLS

Fig. 2. PDLS Structure and Interactions among Modules

users make use and control the library. Second, a user profile control module learns the user's preferences by neural network (SOM [8]), and makes databases accordingly. Third, a PLA (Personal Library Agent) module makes multi agents in real time, and searches information from the library according to the user's profile, and stores the searched results into a database. The interactions among detailed modules in PDLS are explained in Figure 2(b).

As shown in Figure 3(a), PLA has two modules and two databases. The monitoring agent module is composed of Voyager and DECAF, and it monitors the agents' movements and controls their executions. When the user's requirements are transferred to the PLA, the monitoring agent module checks whether the servers are available or not. After that, it makes some agents, and passes them to the servers. The searched results are saved in a temporary repository. They are filtered by negotiation agents, and the final results are saved in the result repository. In the proposed platform, the relationship among multi agents in negotiation agent module in Figure 3(b). Agent-Task Group generates Task-1, Task-2 and Task-3 according to Agent 1, Agent 2, and Agent 3. Tasks are automatically decomposed into methods and do their assigned tasks. Each method has five types of methods' relationships. Add-R is to add the results of actions to the results of the other methods. Activate-R is to let the running method run continuously, Compensate-R is the relationship that the results among methods need to be compensated. Replace-R is to replace the results of receiving methods with the results of sending methods. Contradict-R is to disregard the results of receiving methods. Also, there are lots of relationships between methods and tasks and between methods and resources, such as Enable, Facilitate, Produce, Consume, Limits and so on. In the negotiation algorithm, if the agents in the same levels do the different actions, then max operation is operated to produce the output of the agents, and if the agents in the lower levels do the different actions, then min operation is operated.

The construction of the initial user's profile is constructed by the user's first input information. According to the user's searched results, PDLS endows the

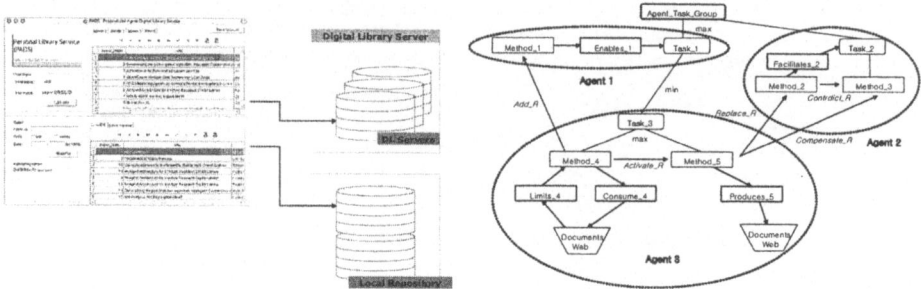

(a) User Interface and Module Relations

(b) Agents Negotiation

Fig. 3. PDLS Interface and Negotiation

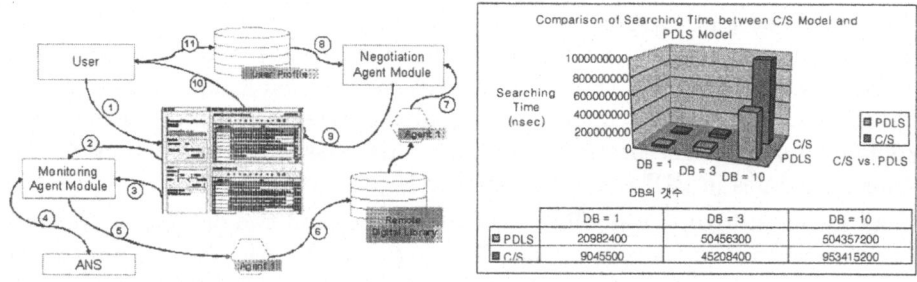

(a) PDLS Simualation Scenario

(b) Simulation Results

Fig. 4. Simulation Results

user's keywords to weight values, and updates user's profile information by SOM (self organizing map) network in real time [7]. The user interface is composed of four windows. The user's window is for entering the user's information and for recalling the user's profile from databases. The monitoring window is for checking agent's activities. The remote window shows the final results, and finally the local window shows the constructed hard disk information of the user's computer by PDLS.

4 Simulation Results

The user interface is composed of four panes, and each pane is interconnected. The login window and query window is for user login. The user pane is for checking the agents' activation states including monitoring. The remote pane is for representing the information of remote servers and searched results. The local pane is for representing the building states of a local library. The scenario for PDLS simulation is in Figure 4(a).

The searching times between the proposed PDLS and the traditional client-server model are shown in Figure 4(b). As time passed, PDLS showed a faster search time as well as a much safer search than the client-server model. The result showed that as the numbers of servers were increased, the searching time was decreased in PDLS.

5 Conclusion

In this paper, I proposed a Personal Digital Library System. PDLS is designed based on a new mobile multi agent platform using Voyager and DECAF agent framework. The new platform is a hybrid system of a mobile and a distributed system in order to achieve an optimality in distributed Environments, and to make it operate effectively by the propose of a new negotiation algorithm and a new scheduling algorithm. From the simulation results of PDLS, the performance and the user's satisfaction of this system is higher than any other information search systems as of now. Also, as the numbers of servers and agents are increased, the searched time of PDLS is lowered. And the degree of the user's satisfaction is increased four times than the conventional client-server model. In the future, PDLS needs to be compensated in order to be activated in the real world.

References

1. David C., Colin H., Aaron Kershenbaum, Mobile Agents: Are They a Good Idea?, 1995
2. John R. Graham, Keith S. Decker, Michael Mersic, DECAF - A Flexible Multi Agent System Architecture, Appearing in Autonomous Agents and Multi-Agent Systems. Accepted, to appear, 2003
3. Keith S. Decker, Victor R. Lessor Generalizing the partial global algorithm. Intelligent Cooperative Information Systems, 1(2), pp.319 346. 1992
4. Keith S. Decker, Task Environment Centered Simulation, 1996
5. ObjectSpace, Voyager Core Technology 2.0 User Guide, ObjectSpace, 1998
6. Sanchez, AGS: Introducing Agents as Services Provided by Digital Libraries, 1997
7. Jonas Holmstrom, A framework for Personalized Library Services, October 2002
8. Kohonen, Self Organizing Feature Map, 1995

FOOD: An Agent-Oriented Dataflow Model

Nicolas Juillerat and Béat Hirsbrunner

University of Fribourg, Department of Computer Sciences, 1700 Fribourg,
Switzerland,
{nicolas.juillerat,beat.hirsbrunner}@unifr.ch,
http://diuf.unifr.ch/pai

Abstract. This paper introduces FOOD, a new Dataflow model that
goes beyond the limitations of the existing models, and targets the implementation of multi-agent systems. The central notion of FOOD, the
Dataunit, which expresses all the dynamics that are required in multi-
agent systems, is presented in details. Then it is shown how the FOOD
model, despite its simplicity, has an expression power that goes beyond
object-oriented languages in term of dynamics and mutability.

1 Introduction

Traditional Dataflow models have advantages over textual languages, such as
their implicit parallelism, which makes them good candidates for the implementation of multi-agent systems. Unfortunately, most of the existing Dataflow
models are also limited to flows of data, which are static entities that are unable
to express the dynamics required by multi-agent systems [11].

The FOOD model that is presented in this paper extends the traditional,
demand-driven Dataflow model with a new notion that is able to express the dynamics and mutability of agents, and overcomes the limitations of the existing
models. The expression power of FOOD is then stated, by presenting how it
can express the notions of object-oriented languages without adding them explicitly (unlike most existing object-oriented Dataflow models [2]), and how it goes
beyond them by allowing controlled mutation of both data and functionalities.

2 The Traditional Dataflow Models

Dataflow languages are visual languages where the different steps of computation
are represented visually by black boxes, the *Units*[1]; and the flows of data are
represented by *connections* between Units. The figure 1 shows an example of a
Dataflow and its components. The various existing Dataflow models and languages, their structures, semantics and applications are described in the literature
[3,4,7,9,10,12].

Despite their advantages, traditional Dataflow models also have serious limitations. Figure 2 shows both an advantage and a limitation of the traditional

---

[1] Also called *function boxes*, *components* or simply *operators* in the literature.

L. Rutkowski et al. (Eds.): ICAISC 2004, LNAI 3070, pp. 835–840, 2004.
© Springer-Verlag Berlin Heidelberg 2004

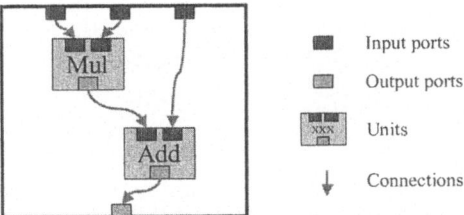

Fig. 1. A Dataflow and its components.

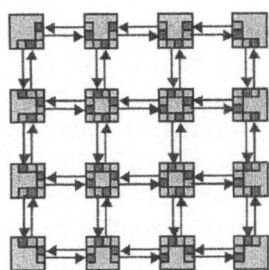

Fig. 2. A grid-like environment implemented by a Dataflow. Each cell is implemented by a Unit. Connections can transport the data representing an agent from one cell to another.

Dataflow models: The fact a Dataflow is a special case of a graph makes it possible for the topology of a Dataflow to match the topology of the problem it solves. However, distributed computing often implies high dynamics. The agent programming methodology reflect this requirement by encapsulating behaviors with data structures, i.e. using active entities. But in this example, an agent can only be implemented by a flow of data, a possibly structured, but passive entity. What we would like is to have flows of agents, that is, flows of entities consisting of *both data and functionalities*. We would also like agents to be able to adapt themselves, that is, both their data and functionalities should be *modifiable* at runtime. The FOOD[2] model presented in this paper addresses these wishes.

3   The FOOD Model

While the traditional Dataflow models are based on the notions of Units, connections and data flows, a Dataflow in the FOOD model is built only with two notions: connections and *Dataunits*.

The notion of connection in FOOD is similar to that of traditional Dataflow models. The notion of Dataunit is between the notions of data and Unit, and has the following characteristics:

---

[2] First-class Object Oriented Dataflow

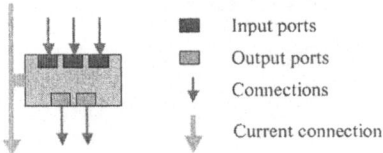

■	Input ports
▦	Output ports
↓	Connections
↓	Current connection

Fig. 3. A possible representation of a Dataunit call. The current connection holds the called Dataunit and the other connections supply arguments and collect results.

- Dataunits are used like data: they flow through the connections of the Dataflow, they can be used as argument to a function and returned as a result. Like data, Dataunits can only exist in connections and ports.
- Dataunits can be called (evaluated), like Units. As a Dataunit can only exist in connections and ports, a call to a Dataunit occurs in a connection that is holding it, which is named the *current connection*. Other connections are used like in the traditional Dataflow models to transmit arguments and results (which are Dataunits too). An example is shown in figure 3.
- Dataunits can be simple, in which case they have a single functionality, whose implementation is given by a *reference to a Dataflow*. But they can also be *structured*: a structured Dataunit is composed of zero or more fields that are Dataunits as well. Like with structured data, any field of a Dataunit can be replaced at runtime by another compatible Dataunit. A call to a structured Dataunit can only evaluate one of the simple Dataunits it contains and must therefore statically define which one. A possible representation of a call to a structured Dataunit is shown in figure 4.
- Dataunits, like data structures, are typed. The type of a simple Dataunit is given by the types of its input and output ports. The type of a structured Dataunit is given by the types of all its fields.
- Assignment compatibility between Dataunits is defined as follow: a Dataunit is assignment compatible with another one if they have the same type, or if the later *contains* a field that have the same type as the former. This definition is less restrictive than the common definition of compatibility between structured data types.
- Dataunit can optionally have a static property: the *enclosing type*. A Dataunit that has an enclosing type can only be used as a *field* in a structured Dataunit whose type is compatible with the enclosing type. This Dataunit is the *enclosing Dataunit* and can dynamically change at runtime. While a Dataunit without an enclosing type can only access its own fields, a Dataunit with an enclosing type can also access the fields of its enclosing Dataunit.[3]

---

[3] The assignment compatibility between Dataunits includes the compatibility of the enclosing types, if any. The absence of enclosing type is defined to be compatible with any enclosing type.

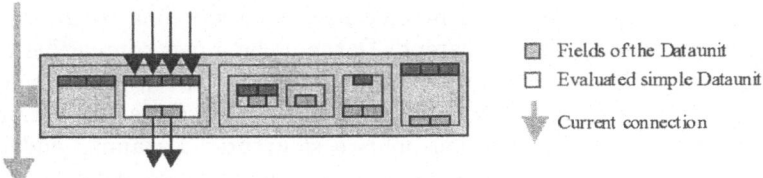

Fig. 4. A possible representation of a call on a structured Dataunit. In this representation the entire structure of the Dataunit is displayed.

4   The Expression Power of FOOD

In this section, we first show that the notion of Dataunit in FOOD can be used to represent, or simulate an object and therefore that FOOD expresses all the semantics of object-oriented languages. In the second part we present other possibilities of FOOD that can not be expressed directly by most object-oriented languages[4] but are required for the implementation of multi-agent systems.

4.1   Object-Oriented Semantics

A Dataunit is composed of fields that are Dataunits themselves. This is the only way of structural composition that exists in FOOD. An object, on the other hand, is structured in four ways that all have different restrictions and characteristics [8]: an object has *fields*, *parents* (inheritance), *methods* and *inner classes*. Fields and inheritance are *mono-directional* compositions: an object has access to its parents and fields, but the reverse is not true. Methods and inner classes are *bi-directional* compositions because they both have access to their enclosing object. Inheritance, methods and inner classes are all *static* compositions, i.e. they can not be changed at runtime. Fields, whose values are modifiable, therefore constitute the only dynamic composition in object-oriented languages.

Fields are implicitly expressed by ports and connections in FOOD, just like variables in traditional Dataflow models [4,6]. The three other ways of composition in object-oriented languages can be expressed using the single way of composition of the Dataunits in FOOD: an object that inherits one ore more parent objects is expressed by a Dataunit that is composed by one or more "parent" Dataunits that have no enclosing type. The methods and inner classes of an object are expressed in the same way, but in that case, the enclosed Dataunits (expressing the methods or inner classes) have an enclosing type that matches the type of the enclosing Dataunit (expressing the enclosing object). Therefore, they can access the fields of the enclosing Dataunits, just like a method or an instance of an inner class can access the fields and methods of their enclosing object.

Recall that in FOOD, each field of a Dataunit can be replaced at any time with a compatible one. Overriding a method of a parent object can therefore

---

[4] Except, in a limited way, using Aspect programming [1], which goes in a similar direction.

be expressed in FOOD by replacing the field corresponding to the method in the field corresponding to the "parent" Dataunit by a new compatible Dataunit that implements the new version of the method. The current connection, which is associated to each Dataunit call, can be used to express the notion of the current object. As this connection holds a structured Dataunit, and that the parent objects are expressed by fields, they can be accessed as well.

A first interpreter of a language following the FOOD model has been realized, with functionalities to convert any Java object into an equivalent Dataunit (as discussed above) whose implementations are provided by the methods of the underlying Java object. Work is still in progress to provide Dataunits with implementations based on real Dataflows.

4.2 Mutability Semantics

The only way of composition used in FOOD allows any field to be replaced at *runtime*, therefore FOOD can express even more dynamics than object-oriented language: each functionality of a structured Dataunit can be modified at any time by replacing the corresponding field with another compatible Dataunit that provides a different implementation. The use of fields for composition, static typing and compatibility rules, ensure that these "mutations" are not chaotic. Other programming practices such as self-modifying code can express the same level of mutability but are very hard to control and are only possible in assembly languages and, surprisingly, in LISP[5]; these practices are usually strongly discouraged [5]. The main difference between the FOOD approach and self-modifying code is that in FOOD only Dataunits are mutable; that is, only *references* to Dataflows are mutable; the Dataflows themselves are not.[6]

If it were possible to express the possibilities of FOOD in an object oriented language, like we have previously transposed the possibilities of object-oriented languages to FOOD, we would have an object oriented language with facilities such as: replacing one of the parent of an object at runtime by another one that is compatible, or replacing the method of an object at runtime by another one with the same signature.

5 Conclusion

The FOOD model inherits the advantages of traditional Dataflow models, which makes it a well-suited model for the implementation of distributed applications. But it also overcome their limitations by introducing a new notion, the *Dataunit*, which can express all the dynamics and mutability that are necessary to implement the notion of agent. The expression power of the Dataunit has

---

[5] LISP can manipulate lists, and then evaluate a list as if it were a LISP expression using the **eval** keyword

[6] An indirect, but crucial consequence is that FOOD is a Dataflow model where, although the Dataunits are passed by value, their real contents (that is, their implementations, i.e. the referenced Dataflows) are in reality passed by reference.

been proved to go even beyond the possibilities of object-oriented languages for capturing some advanced features of multi-agent systems, namely structural dynamics, adaptability of behaviors and composition [11]. This makes FOOD a new and modern computation model of choice for the implementation of multi-agent systems, in particular dynamical and re-configurable systems.

References

1. The AOSD Steering Committee: Aspect-oriented Software Development, http://aosd.net/ (last visited on January 2004)
2. M. Burnett, A. Goldberg, T. Lewis: Visual Object-Oriented Programming, Manning Publications (1995)
3. M. Burnett et al.: Forms/3: A First-Order Visual Language to Explore the Boundaries of the Spreadsheet Paradigm, CiteSeer Scientific Literature Digital Library (2001)
4. M. Boshernitsan, M. Downes: Visual Programming Languages: A Survey, CiteSeer Scientific Literature Digital Library (1997)
5. Commodore Business Machines: Amiga ROM Kernel Reference Manual: Libraries, Addison-Wesley, 3rd edition (1991)
6. G. Gao, L. Bic, J.-L. Gaudiot: Advanced Topics in Dataflow Computing and Multithreading, Wiley-IEEE Computer Society Press (1995)
7. D. Ingalls, S. Wallace, Y. Chow, F. Ludolph, K. Doyle: Fabrik, A Visual Programming Environment, ACM/SIGPLAN 00PSLA '88 Conference Proceedings, 23, (1988) 176–190
8. B. Meyer: Object-Oriented Software Construction, Prentice Hall, 2nd edition (2000)
9. R. Mark Meyer, T. Masterson: Towards a better Programming Language: Critiquing Prograph's Control Structures, The Journal of Computing in Small Colleges, Volume 15, Issue 5 (2000) 181–193
10. K. Pingali and Arvind: Efficient Demand-Driven Evaluation, ACM Transactions on Programming Languages and Systems, Volume 7, Issue 2 (1985) 311–333
11. A. Tafat-Bouzid, M. Courant and B. Hirsbrunner: A Coordination Model for Ubiquitous Computing, Proceedings of the 3rd WSEAS International Conference on Multimedia, Internet and Video Technologies (2003)
12. W. Wadge, E. Ashcroft: Lucid, the Dataflow Programming Language, Academic Press (1985)

Flock-Based Architecture
for Distributed Evolutionary Algorithms*

Marek Kisiel-Dorohinicki

Institute of Computer Science
AGH University of Science and Technology, Kraków, Poland
doroh@agh.edu.pl

Abstract. The paper presents an agent-based architecture facilitating impleme-
tation of parallel evolutionary algorithms, utilising the novel concept of a *flock*.
The model proposed is an extension to classical regional parallel evolutionary
algorithm. Flocks introduce additional level of organisation of the system,
allowing for separation of distribution and evolution issues, and thus opening
possibility of dynamic reconfiguration of subpopulations adequately to the
structure of the problem being solved. Selected experimental results illustrate the
idea "at work".

Keywords: Parallel evolutionary algorithms, multi-agent systems.

1 Introduction

Evolutionary algorithms (EA) are used today for more and more complex problems often requiring long computational time. Parallel implementations seem to be a promising
answer to this problem, particularly because of natural parallelism of evolutionary processes. What is more, it turns out that some parallel models of evolutionary computation
are able to provide even better solutions than comparably sized classical evolutionary
algorithms – considering not only the quality of obtained solutions and convergence rate,
but first of all the convergence reliability.

Even though many variants of *parallel evolutionary algorithms* (PEA) are discussed
in the literature [2], recently *coarse-grained* (*regional*) models seem to gain more and
more interest, which is mainly because they may be easily implemented on any distributed architecture. Yet the classical version of coarse-grained PEA suffers from the
problem of dynamic reconfiguration of regions. Some hybrid approaches try to address
this shortage – for example a *dual individual* distributed genetic algorithm [4] differen-
tiates between nodes (units of distribution) and regions (units of evolution). A similar
structure of several organisational levels was adopted in the *flock-based* approach described in this paper. The proposed architecture also utilizes agent paradigms to facilitate
the implementation of the system.

The paper is organised as follows. In section 2 a short presentation of different
variants of parallel evolutionary algorithms with emphasis on coarse-grained models

---

* This work was partially sponsored by State Committee for Scientific Research (KBN) grant
no. 4 T11C 027 22.

L. Rutkowski et al. (Eds.): ICAISC 2004, LNAI 3070, pp. 841–846, 2004.
© Springer-Verlag Berlin Heidelberg 2004

and the above-mentioned hybrid approach (a dual individual DGA) constitutes a point of departure for further considerations. Then (section 3) after a few words of introduction on agent-based modelling and evolutionary phenomena, a flock-based architecture is described. The considerations are illustrated by experimental results obtained for two typical test functions (section 4).

2 Parallel Evolutionary Algorithms

Evolutionary algorithms, as an abstraction of natural evolutionary processes, are apparently easy to parallelize and thus many models of parallel implementations have been proposed [2]. The standard approach (sometimes called a *global parallelisation*) does not require any change to the conceptual algorithm and consists in distributing selected steps of the sequential algorithm among several processing units. In this case a population is unstructured (*panmictic*) and both selection and mating are global (performed over the whole population).

Decomposition approaches are characterised by non-global selection/mating and introduce some spatial structure of a population. In a *coarse-grained* PEA (also known as *regional* or *multiple-deme* model) a population is divided into several subpopulations (regions, demes). In this model selection and mating are limited to individuals inhabiting one region and a migration operator is used to move (copy) selected individuals from one region to another. In a *fine-grained* PEA (also called a *cellular* model) a population is divided into a large number of small subpopulations with some neighbourhood structure. Here selection and mating are performed in the local neighbourhood (overlapping subpopulations). It is even possible to have only one individual in each subpopulation (this is sometimes called a *massively* parallel evolutionary algorithm).

And finally there are also methods which utilise some combination of the models described above (*hybrid* PEAs), such as a dual individual DGA described in more detail below.

Regional Models

Regional models introduce coarse-grained spatial structure of a population, suitable for implementation in a distributed architecture. Each node has its own (sub)population and runs a separate thread of evolution, thus conceptually subpopulations 'live' on geographically separated regions (fig. 1). A new operator – migration – controls the process of exchanging individuals between regions. The model is usually described by a few parameters: a number of regions, a number of individuals in each region, as well as migration topology, rate/interval and a strategy of choosing individuals to migrate.

Migration topology describes how individuals migrate from one region to another. This often depends on the software architecture and the most common are hypercube, ring, or k-clique. In an *island* model individuals can migrate to any other subpopulation, while in a *stepping stone* model individuals can migrate only to neighbouring region(s). Migration rate and interval denote how many and how often individuals migrate. Of course migration rate should be greater if migration interval is longer. Typically the

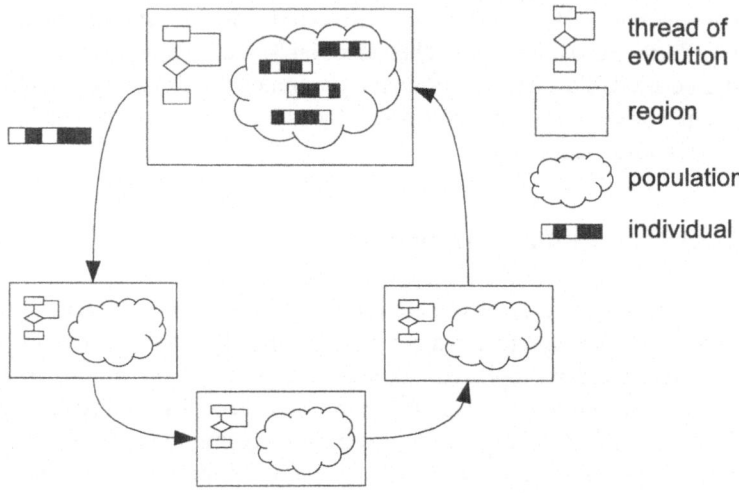

Fig. 1. A regional PEA – arrows indicate possible migration in stepping stone topology

best individuals are chosen for migration and immigrants replace the worst individuals in a destination region. Other possibility is that immigrants replace the most similar individuals (e.g. using Hamming distance as a measure) or just replace emigrants.

Hybrid Systems – Dual Individual DGA

A *dual individual* distributed genetic algorithm (DGA) is an example of a hybrid model of PEA for cluster systems [4]. Here a population is divided into regions (like in an island model) but in each region there are only two individuals. In each node there are several regions. Migration is performed at two levels: individuals move between regions in one node (a stepping stone model), and regions move between nodes. This method is slower than a pure island model but is said to reach better solutions.

3   Flock-Based Multi-agent Model of Evolutionary Computation

At first sight evolutionary computation and multi-agent systems seem to have nothing in common – the former is a search and optimisation technique, while the latter is a general concept of modelling decentralised systems. A key concept in the multi-agent approach is that of an agent – a software entity, which is situated in some environment and autonomously acts on it so as to satisfy its own goals. A multi-agent system (MAS) is designed and implemented as a set of interacting agents and the interactions (e.g. cooperation, coordination or negotiation) turn out to be the most characteristic and powerful component of the paradigm [5].

Since the processes of evolution are decentralised by nature, multi-agent systems turn out to be a perfect tool for modelling them [6]. Depending on whether agents represent individuals or populations of them, two different agent-based architectures of

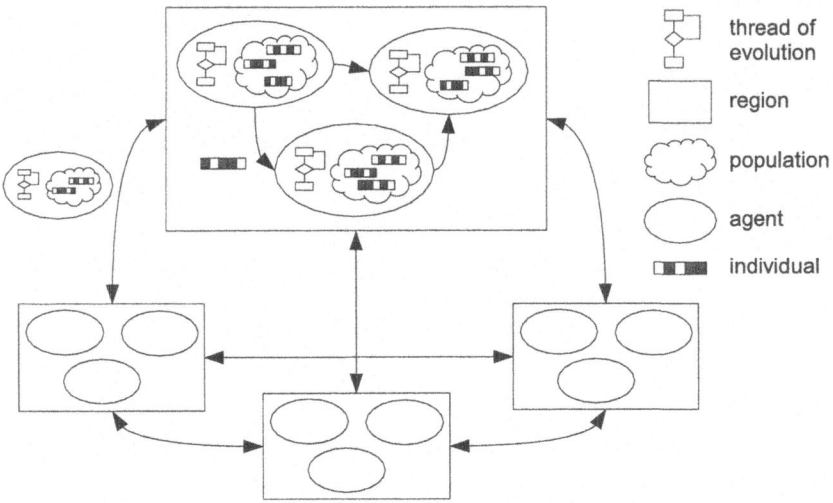

Fig. 2. Flock-based approach to multi-agent evolutionary computation

evolutionary computation systems may be distinguished: in an evolutionary multi-agent system (EMAS) an agent acts as an individual [3, and later], while in a flock-based one an agent manages a group of individuals inhabiting one region (a flock).

A flock-based architecture extends the classical island model of PEA providing additional level of organisation of the system. Subpopulations on the islands (distribution units) are divided into flocks, where independent processes of evolution (e.g. some classical sequential EAs) are managed by agents. It is possible to distinguish two levels of migration, just like in dual individual DGA described in the previous section:

- exchange of individuals between flocks on one island,
- migration of flocks between islands.

Also merging of flocks containing similar individuals or dividing of flocks with large diversity allows for dynamic changes of population structure to possibly well reflect the problem to be solved (the shape of fitness function, e.g. location of local extrema). Management of agents-flocks may be realised with the use of non-renewable resources, just like selection in EMAS.

4 Experimental Studies

Preliminary experimental studies of the described-above approach was based on GAVaPS (Genetic Algorithm with Varying Population Size), which introduces a flexible selection mechanism based on the individual (chromosome) lifetime [7].

The implementation was realised with the use of AgWorld platform [1] – a software framework based on PVM, facilitating agent-based implementations of distributed evolutionary computation systems (for further reference see *http://agworld.sf.net/*).

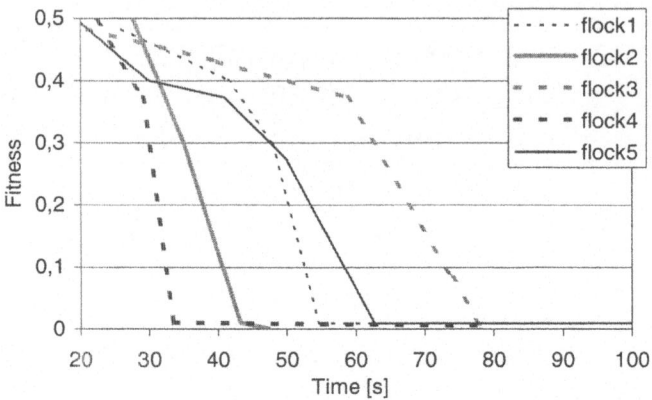

Fig. 3. Fitness of the best individual in different flocks for Schaffer F6 test function

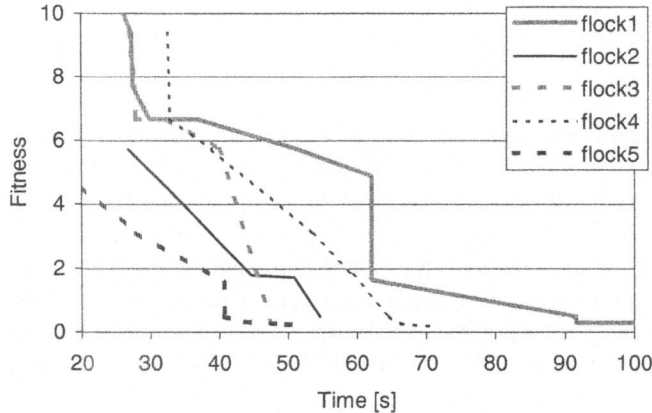

Fig. 4. Fitness of the best individual in different flocks for Schaffer F7 test function

Figures 3 and 4 show the convergence rate in different flocks in terms of fitness of the best individual in consecutive steps of computation for Schaffer F6 and F7 test functions. One may notice different convergence rate in different flocks, which is achieved by low individual migration rate. The flocks where evolution process is stopped by too low genetic diversity of individuals (premature convergence) die. Yet other flocks may take over the necessary resources and continue their evolution. The solution found is always very close to the global optimum, so the computation reliability of the presented solution seems to be high, as expected. Of course deeper analysis of this phenomenon needs further experiments. Also the mechanisms responsible for merging of flocks have not been verified yet.

5 Concluding Remarks

Parallelisation of classical evolutionary algorithms is a conceptually easy task, since evolution is a parallel process by nature. Yet agent-based models of evolutionary computation provide a more complex model of evolution – closer to its natural prototype. This entails the following features:

- local selection allows for intensive exploration of the search space, which is similar to classical parallel evolutionary algorithms,
- behaviour of an agent (the flock) depends on its interaction with the environment, which allows for adaptive reconfiguration of subpopulations,
- explicitly defined living space facilitates implementation in a distributed computational environment.

However it still remains an open question whether these models are more powerful then these of classical (parallel) evolutionary algorithms considering their computational properties. The goal of further research is thus to compare the features of the proposed approach with other implementations known from literature.

References

1. A. Byrski, L. Siwik, and M. Kisiel-Dorohinicki. Designing population-structured evolutionary computation systems. In T. Burczyński, W. Cholewa, and W. Moczulski, editors, *Methods of Artificial Intelligence (AI-METH 2003)*, Silesian Univ. of Technology, Gliwice, Poland, 2003.
2. E. Cantú-Paz. A summary of research on parallel genetic algorithms. *IlliGAL Report No. 95007. University of Illinois*, 1995.
3. K. Cetnarowicz, M. Kisiel-Dorohinicki, and E. Nawarecki. The application of evolution process in multi-agent world (MAW) to the prediction system. In M. Tokoro, editor, *Proc. of the 2nd Int. Conf. on Multi-Agent Systems (ICMAS'96)*. AAAI Press, 1996.
4. T. Hiroyasu, M. Miki, M. Hamasaki, and Y. Tabimura. A new model of distributed genetic algorithm for cluster systems: Dual individual DGA. In *Proceedings of he Third International Symposium on High Performance Computing*, 2000.
5. N. R. Jennings, K. Sycara, and M. Wooldridge. A roadmap of agent research and development. *Journal of Autonomous Agents and Multi-Agent Systems*, 1(1):7–38, 1998.
6. M. Kisiel-Dorohinicki. Agent-oriented model of simulated evolution. In W. I. Grosky and F. Plasil, editors, *SofSem 2002: Theory and Practice of Informatics*, Lecture Notes in Computer Science. Springer-Verlag, 2002.
7. Z. Michalewicz. *Genetic Algorithms + Data Structures = Evolution Programs*. Springer-Verlag, 1996.

Quickprop Neural Network Short-Term Forecasting Framework for a Database Intrusion Prediction System

P. Ramasubramanian and A. Kannan

Department of Computer Science and Engineering
Anna University, Chennai 600025, India.
suryarams@cs.annauniv.edu, kannan@annauniv.edu

Abstract. This paper describes a framework for a statistical anomaly prediction system using Quickprop neural network forecasting model, which predicts unauthorized invasions of user based on previous observations and takes further action before intrusion occurs. The experimental study is performed using real data provided by a major Corporate Bank. A comparative evaluation of the Quickprop neural network over the traditional neural network models was carried out using mean absolute percentage error on a prediction data set and a better prediction accuracy has been observed. Further, in order to make a legitimate comparison, the dataset was divided into two statistically equivalent subsets, viz. the training and the prediction sets, using genetic algorithm.

1 Introduction

In today's business world, information is the most valuable asset of organizations and thus requires appropriate management and protection. Security policies do not sufficiently guard data stored in a database system against "privileged users". In database systems, the primary security threat comes from insider abuse and from intrusion. So, it is essential to establish a second line of defense for a distributed database environment in the form of an intrusion detection system (IDS).

Anomaly detection approaches [2][3] must initially baseline the normal behavior of the user on the database object being monitored and then use deviations from this baseline to detect possible intrusions. The main advantage of anomaly detection systems is that they can detect novel intrusion, as well as variations of known intrusions. The challenge in such systems is defined as "normal behavior" in a way that minimizes the false alarm rate and maximizes the detection efficiency. In our work, a statistical anomaly prediction system which uses a Quickprop prediction algorithm to predict the future on-line behavior of the user, based on previous observations. The trained model is then used to detect future attacks against the system.

L. Rutkowski et al. (Eds.): ICAISC 2004, LNAI 3070, pp. 847–852, 2004.
© Springer-Verlag Berlin Heidelberg 2004

2   Related Works

The existing Intrusion detection systems [2][4] operate in real time, capturing the intruder when or after intrusion occurs. From the existing methods of detecting the intrusion, we observed that all intrusion detection systems were lacking a vital component: that they take action, after an intrusion has been detected [3]. This serious weakness has led to the research on forecasting models. However, though the Intrusion Detection system is real-time, it can detect the intrusion after the action, but never before. To address the problem of detecting intrusions after they take place, we utilize a Quickprop prediction algorithm, which takes into account user behavior and generates a predicted profile to foresee the future user actions.

Existing works on Intrusion Detection has focused largely on network [5] and host intrusion [2]. Most of the research on database security revolves around access policies, roles, administration procedures, physical security, security models and data inference [4]. Little amount of work is done on database IDSes even though most emphasis in literature has been found for Network IDSes [3]. To the best of the author's knowledge, this is the only work using statistical forecasting model to predict database intrusions.

3   Database Auditing

Auditing is monitoring and recording of selected user database actions. We need an utility to capture the submitted database transactions in order to compare them with those in the legitimate user profile. Oracle provides the sql_trace utility that can be used to trace all database operations in a database session of an user. We make use of its capability to log SQL transactions executed by the database engine [4].

The following attributes are included in each audit trail record:

- User ID
- Session ID
- Host ID & IP address
- Rel Var(s)/Tuple(s)/Attribute(s) ID
- **Action:** It describes the operation performed or attempted.
- **Completion:** It describes the result of an attempted operation. A successful operation returns the value zero, and unsuccessful operations returns the error code describing the reason for the failure.
- **Transaction Time:** The time at which the events or state changes are registered in the computer system. The total value of the user session is calculated based on this transaction time.
- **Valid Time:** It includes two values namely start_time and end_time representing the interval during which the tuple in the audit record is valid. The prediction values that are generated by our 'Statistical prediction engine', past observations and on-line behavior of user are stipulated using valid time attribute.

The following metrics are considered to audit the user behaviors:

- Audit the frequency of certain commands execution (Command Stroke Rate) by an user on an object in a session
- Audit Execution Denials or Access Violations on an object in a session
- Audit the Object utilization by an user for certain period
- Audit the overt requests for a data object in a session

4   Prediction Algorithm

Quickprop neural network forecasting model makes periodic short-term forecasts, since long-term forecasts cannot accurately predict an intrusion [3]. In this we use a multivariate time series technique to forecast the hacker's behavior effectively. This algorithm consists of three phases: detection of number of inputs, determination of the number of neurons in hidden layer(s) and construction of a Quickprop forecaster. In the detection phase, autocorrelation analysis is used to identify the number of inputs of time series for training. A rule of thumb, known as the Baum-Haussler rule, is used to determine the number of hidden neurons.

In order to carry out prediction, a d:n:n:1 four layer feed-forward Quickprop neural network method(d input units, n hidden units, and a single unit) has been considered. In order to check the most appropriate parameters for prediction, we carried out a sweeping in the number of neurons of the hidden layer. It can be observed that the successive increase in the number of neurons in the hidden layer hardly diminishes the training error, and also that the validation error increases considerably. After few rigorous experiments, the following Quickprop net model was selected for prediction: 10 nodes in the input layer, 12 in the first middle layer, 10 in the second middle layer, and one output layer. For our study, a Quickprop network of the commercially available artificial neural network simulator QwikNet was used. The learning rate value of 0.1 and the momentum factor value around 0.5 would produce the fastest learning for this problem. In this test, the weights were initialized for each of the networks with random values within the range [-0.5,0.5] and the number of iterations that were carried out was 15,000. Bounding the weights can help in preventing the network from becoming saturated.

5   Experimental Results

5.1   Model Development and Selection of Model Inputs

This study uses audit data were provided by a major corporate bank, SBI, Chennai, India. The database objects considered are (1) Customer Deposit Accounts(CDAcc) and (2) Customer Loan Accounts(CLAcc) as well as (3) Ledger Reports related to each transactions on the Customer Accounts(LRep). The database objects is used by Tellers(Tlr), Customer_Service_Reps(CSR) and Loan

Officers(LO) to perform various transactions. It is also used by Accountants(Acc), Accounting_Managers(AccMr) and Internal_Auditors(IntAud) to post, generate and verify accounting data. Branch_Manager(BrM) has the ability to perform any of the functions of other roles in times of emergency and to View all transactions, Account Statuses and Validation Flags.

1. Audit metrics 2. Authorization(High, Medium, Low) 3. Hours off(% of total) 4. Days off(% of total) like holidays and weekend 5. Hour-of-day(candidate variable) 6. Day-of-week(candidate variable) 7. Daily Periodicity(High, Medium, Low and Insignificant) 8. Weekly Periodicity (High, Medium, Low and Insignificant) 9. Mean weekly consumption are considered as input variables in order to train the forecasting model. In this model only one output is needed for indicating the value of forecasted data resource consumption of an user.

5.2   Training and Testing Data

The observations were measured from May 5, 2003 to Dec 5, 2003 for all the users. We use the data from 5th May, 2003 to 3rd Aug, 2003 as training examples and data ranges from 4th Aug.2003 to 2nd Nov, 2003 as testing examples. The time interval is user definable, but we chose the time between observations is one hour. The global data from each user is split into two equal sets. Each set was used to train the forecasting models, then they were interchanged to test the performance of models(i.e., the data set 1 was used to test the model that had been trained with data set2, and vice-versa). Furthermore, training pairs were randomly ordered before presenting them to the prediction model. The final forecast accuracy was obtained as a simple average of the results from those two test sets. This approach does cross validation, ensure certain data set independence and can avoid over-training. However, for a legitimate comparison of a neural network model, training and prediction data sets should be chosen in such a way that they are statistically similar. In this paper, we have used Genetic Algorithm(GA) for such division of the data that has been explored by Bowden et al [1].

5.3   Experimental Topology

Fig. 1 shows a piece of the actual and predicted behavior curve for user Customer_Service_Reps(CSR), using Quickprop as a forecasting model.Fig. 1 shows the actual values for real observations and the associated single-step forecasts. The X-axis specifies the real observations with our forecasting results and the Y-axis defines the usage of an object for an hour. For example, 0.2 ensures that the user has used that particular object for 12 minutes, in a specific hour of the object usage. We present a comparative graph(Fig. 1) of the data resource consumption by CSR for 100 validation patterns, which gives the real values versus the predicted values.

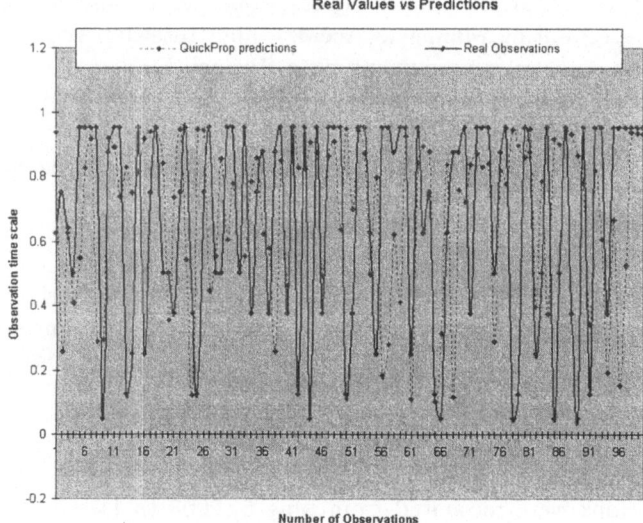

Fig. 1. Real values versus predicted values of the user

6 Performance Analysis

In order to evaluate the accuracy of our forecasting model, a widely accepted quantitative measure, such as Mean Absolute Percentage Error(MAPE) has been used. The performance analysis of the Quickprop forecaster was measured in terms of Mean Absolute Percentage Error (MAPE)=
$\frac{1}{N}\sum_{i=1}^{N}|\frac{Forecast_i - Target_i}{Target_i}|$, where N = Number of observations. MAPE will
be employed in this paper as the performance criterion, for its easy understanding and simple mathematical computation. The mean absolute percentage error determines the mean percentage deviation of the predicted outputs from the target outputs. This absolute deviation places greater emphasis on errors occurring with small target values as opposed to those of larger target values. Table 1 compares the MAPE computed for the QuickProp and the other neural network predictors.

Table 1. Error Measurement. RProp: Resilient propagation; RP: Randomize Patterns; DBD: Delta Bar Delta

Models	Tlr	CSR	LO	Acc	AccMr	IntAud	Avg. of MAPE(%)
QuickProp	1.9747	3.9965	0.0713	4.1780	9.1140	26.5326	7.64452
RProp	2.0667	4.9716	0.0873	5.2297	10.5408	30.3359	8.8720
BackProp(RP)	3.5841	5.0164	0.0912	5.5522	14.4856	37.2338	10.9939
BackProp(DBD)	4.2786	5.7335	0.1208	6.0443	15.5016	45.7680	12.9078
BackProp(Online)	5.1448	7.6308	0.1392	7.8316	18.8750	48.4673	14.6814

7   Conclusions and Future Works

7.1   Conclusions

In this paper, a statistical database anomaly prediction system has been presented to learn previously observed user behavior in order to prevent future intrusions in database systems. Quickprop NN is investigated as a tool to predict database intrusions and this method gave improved results i.e., decreased MAPE as compared to any traditional NN model.

7.2   Future Works

From the results it can be seen that neither of the neural network methods provide high confidence for prediction. In fact, more advanced intervention analysis can be incorporated which would, most likely, produce even better results. Hence for the future we'll incorporate other NN models and ensemble techniques further to improve the predictability of database intrusion and reduce the rate of false negative alarms.

Acknowledgments. The authors gratefully acknowledge the anonymous reviewers for their useful comments.

References

1. Bowden, G.J., Maier, H.R., Dandy, G.C.: Optimal division of data for neural network models in water resources applications. Water Resources Research. **38** (2002) 1–11.
2. Michael, C.C., Anup Ghosh.: Simple, State-Based Approaches to Program-Based Anomaly Detection. In ACM Transactions on Information and System Security. **5** (2002) 203–237.
3. Pikoulas, J., Buchanan, W.J., Manion, M., Triantafyllopoulos, K.: An intelligent agent intrusion system. In Proceedings of the 9th IEEE International Conference and Workshop on the Engineering of Computer Based Systems - ECBS, IEEE Comput. Soc., Luden, Sweden. (2002) 94–102.
4. Sin Yeung Lee, Wai Lup Low and Pei Yuen Wong.: Learning Fingerprints For A Database Intrusion Detection System. In Proceedings of the 7th European Symposium on Research in Computer Security, Zurich, Switzerland. (2002) 264–280.
5. Triantafyllopoulos, K., Pikoulas, J.: Multivariate Bayesian regression applied to the problem of network security. Journal of Forecasting. **21** (2002) 579–594.

The New Concepts in Parallel Simulated Annealing Method[*]

Wojciech Bożejko[1] and Mieczysław Wodecki[2]

[1] Institute of Engineering, Wrocław University of Technology
Janiszewskiego 11-17, 50-372 Wrocław, Poland
wbo@ict.pwr.wroc.pl
[2] Institute of Computer Science, University of Wrocław
Przesmyckiego 20, 51-151 Wrocław, Poland
mwd@ii.uni.wroc.pl

Abstract. New elements of the parallel simulated annealing method are proposed to solve the permutation flow shop scheduling problem with the criterion of total completion time ($F^*||C_{Sum}$). This problem is more difficult to optimize than $F^*||C_{max}$ (minimizing the makespan). Simulated annealing belongs to the artificial intelligence methods, which are commonly used to solve NP-hard combinatorial optimization problems. In the parallel algorithm, we propose a new acceptance probability function, multi-step technique, dynamic long-term memory and backtrack-jump. Computational experiments (for Taillard's benchmarks ta001-ta050, [8]) are given and compared with results yielded by the best algorithms discussed in literature [10]. We also present new referential solutions for ta051-ta080 instances (published on our benchmark page [1]), which so far have no solutions.

1 Introduction

Finding optimal solutions to the NP-hard combinatorial problem is not generally realistic. For large-size problems, an exact algorithm may not be useful since it is computationally too expensive. Approximate algorithms, which do not guarantee finding an optimal solution, are a good alternative. Some popular metaheuristics are: simulated annealing, taboo search and genetic methods.

The simulated annealing (SA) is a stochastic heuristic method approach designed to find a near-optimal solution of the combinatorial optimization problem, motivated by the physical process of crystallization. This method was first introduced by Metropolis et al. [6], while Kirkpatrick et al. [4] and Cerny [2] applied the technique to optimization problems. It has gained popularity and there are many papers in literature on the subject with successfully implemented scheduling problems.

The simulated annealing algorithm starts from an initial solution. Each iteration randomly selects a solution from the neighborhood and evaluates its objective function. If the solution is superior then it is accepted, if the solution

---

[*] The work was supported by KBN Poland, within the grant No. T11A01624.

L. Rutkowski et al. (Eds.): ICAISC 2004, LNAI 3070, pp. 853–859, 2004.
© Springer-Verlag Berlin Heidelberg 2004

is interior, it is accepted with some probability. This probability is calculated by an acceptance function depending on the parameter called temperature. The accepted element becomes the initial in the next iteration of the algorithm. Therefore, there are three essential steps of the SA method: (1) neighborhood, (2) acceptance function, (3) cooling scheme.

Basic problems which appear during designing of local improvement algorithms (simulated annealing and tabu search), are: (a) intensification of calculations – rapid attaining of local minimum, and (b) diversification of calculations – after reaching the local minimum, jumping into another 'good' region of the feasible solutions space.

We take under consideration the permutation flow shop scheduling problem described as follows. A number of jobs are to be processed on a number of machines. Each job must go through all the machines in exactly the same order and the job order is the same on every machine. Each machine can process at most one job at any point of time, and each job may be processed on at most one machine at any time. The objective is to find a schedule that minimizes the sum of completion time of the jobs.

In this paper we describe the parallel simulated annealing algorithm for the flow shop scheduling with the objective of minimizing the sum of completion times, and we propose many modifications of the classical simulated annealing method. The new elements of the method: are acceptance probability function, multi-step, dynamic long term memory and backtrack-jump. Computational experiments are compared with the results yielded by the best algorithms discussed in literature. New benchmarks,not available in literature, are published in [1].

2   Problem Formulation

Each of n jobs from the set $J=\{1,2,\ldots,n\}$ has to be processed on each of m machines from the set $M=\{1,2,\ldots,m\}$ in succession. Job $j \in J$ consists of a sequence of m operations $O_{j1}, O_{j2},\ldots,O_{jm}$. Operation O_{jk} corresponds to the processing of job j on machine k during an uninterrupted processing time p_{jk}. We want to find such a schedule that the sum of the job's completion times is minimal.

Let $\pi =(\pi(1), \pi(2),\ldots,\pi(n))$ be a permutation of jobs $\{1,2,\ldots,n\}$ and let $\varPi$ be the set of all permutations. Each permutation $\pi \in \varPi$ defines a processing order of jobs on each machine. We wish to find a permutation $\pi^* \in \varPi$ that:

$$C_{sum}(\pi^*) = \min\{C_{sum}(\pi): \ \pi \in \varPi\}$$

where $C_{sum}(\pi) = \sum_{i=1}^{n} C_{i,m}(\pi)$ and $C_{i,j}(\pi)$ is the time required to complete job i on the machine j in the processing order given by the permutation π. In literature there are a few papers discussing this problem. Wang [9] shows some constructive algorithms based on the heuristic rule such as LIT and SPD. In the paper of Yamada et al. [10] a metaheuristic method is proposed to solve the problem. The representative neighborhood in this method incorporates the stochastic sampling and tabu search combined with genetic local search. The algorithm is applied to Taillard's benchmark problems t001-t050 from [8].

3   Simulated Annealing Method

A combinatorial optimization problem can be defined as a problem with well defined finite solution space Ω and objective function $F(\pi)$, $\pi \in \Omega$. The problem consists in finding an element π^* such that $F(\pi^*) = \min\{F(\pi): \pi \in \Omega\}$.

For every element $\pi \in \Omega$ we call a ***move*** transformation $r : \pi \rightarrow r(\pi) \in \Omega$. Let $M(\pi)$ be a fixed set of moves on element $\pi \in \Omega$, and let $M(\Omega) = \bigcup_{\pi \in \Omega} M(\pi)$ be a set of all moves. We call a ***neighborhood*** $N(\pi)$ of element π a set of elements generated by moves from $M(\Omega)$, i.e. $N(\pi) = \{r(\pi): r \in M(\Omega)\}$.

Simulated annealing is a randomized local improvement method, which accepts solutions depending on the value of the cost function. In each iteration of the SA algorithm a random perturbation is made to the current solution $\pi \in \Omega$, giving rise to the set $N(\pi)$ of neighbors. The neighbor $\beta \in N(\pi)$ is accepted as the next configuration with probability function $\Psi(\pi, \beta, T)$. The $\Psi(\pi, \beta, T)$ is known as *accepting function* and depends on control parameter T (*temperature*). Its value changes at suitably chosen intervals. In practice the function $\Psi(\pi, \beta, T)$ is chosen in such way that solutions corresponding to large increases in cost have a small probability of being accepted, whereas solutions corresponding to small increases in cost have a larger probability of being accepted.

Sequential Simulated Annealing Algorithm sSA
Let π be any feasible solution, $N(\pi)$ – the neighborhood of π, π^* – the best known solution, L – the number of iterations for fixed value of temperature T.

> ***Step 0***: $\pi^* \leftarrow \pi$;
> ***Step 1***: <u>for</u> $k = 1, 2, \ldots, L$ <u>do</u>
> Select at random $\beta \in N(\pi)$;
> <u>if</u> $F(\beta) < F(\pi^*)$ <u>then</u> $\pi^* \leftarrow \beta$;
> <u>if</u> $F(\beta) < F(\pi)$ <u>then</u> $\pi \leftarrow \beta$
> <u>else if</u> $\Psi(\pi, \beta, T) > \text{random}([0,1))$ <u>then</u> $\pi \leftarrow \beta$;
> ***Step 2***: Modify the temperature;
> ***Step 3***: If stop criterion is not true then go to Step 1.

Change of temperature follows according to the cooling scheme. Initial T_0 is determined experimentally. The most common acceptance function in SA algorithms is Boltzman function $\Psi(\pi, \beta, T) = \exp(-[(F(\beta) - F(\pi))/T])$, geometrical cooling scheme $T \leftarrow c \cdot T$ $(0 < c < 1)$ and moves: insert or swap.

3.1   Intensification and Diversification of Calculations

In this chapter we present a new acceptance function and cooling scheme. In order to intensify calculations we introduce:

a) backtrack jump – return to the neighborhood where improvement of the current solution takes place,
b) changes of temperature – enable on exact exploration of the promising region.

For better diversification of calculations we will apply:

a) multi-step – moving computations to an other remote region of solutions,
b) changes (increasing) of temperature enabling approval of considerably worse solutions.

Acceptance function and cooling scheme. If for randomly determined permutation $\beta \in N(\pi)$ there occur $C_{\max}(\beta) < C_{\max}(\pi)$, then β is the base solution in the next iteration. Contrarily, i.e. when $C_{\max}(\beta) \geq C_{\max}(\pi)$, the probability of acceptance in place of the base solution in the next iteration is determined by the acceptance function. We propose a new acceptance function:

$$\Psi_{\alpha,\lambda}(\pi,\beta) = \exp\left[\left(\frac{C_{Sum}(\beta) - C_{Sum}(\pi)}{C_{Sum}(\pi^*)}\right) \cdot \frac{\ln \lambda}{\alpha}\right],$$

which also depends on the best solution π^* determined until now. Parameters α i λ $(0 < \lambda < 1, \alpha > 0)$ act the role of changing the temperature in the classical acceptance function. We can intensificate or diversificate calculations changing these parameters (cooling scheme). By reducing them we intensificate calculations, whereas by enlarging them we make it possible to move away from the current local minimum (diversification of computations).

Backtrack-jump. Let π be the current base solution, T_π the temperature and π^* the best solution determined until now. By **LM** we denote long-term memory. On **LM** we will record certain attributes of the algorithm's iteration: base solution and temperature. If for randomly chosen permutation $\delta \in N(\pi)$, $F(\delta) < F(\pi)$ then we record on **LM** the pair (π, T_π), in other words $LM \leftarrow LM \cup (\pi, T_\pi)$.

If 'return condition' comes out (e.g. lack of improvement of the best solution after execution of a fixed number of iterations), then we get the pair (β, T_β) from the **LM** memory. In place of the current base solution of the algorithm we take permutation β, and T_β becomes the current temperature. In SA algorithms long-term memory **LM** is implemented using stack or queue.

Multi-step. If during a certain number of iterations the value of objective function is growing, then we execute a multi-step: generating distant permutation (in the sense of the number of moves) from the current base solution.

Let $\beta_s, \beta_{s+1}, \ldots, \beta_t$ be a search trajectory, i.e. sequence of consecutive base solutions. If $F(\beta_s) < F(\beta_{s+1}) <, \ldots, < F(\beta_t)$ and $|t - s| > Lbp$, where Lbp is a fixed parametr, then we execute the multi-step. For fixed parameter k we generate permutation $\delta = r_k(r_{k-1}(, \ldots, r_1(\beta_t), \ldots,))$, where $r_1, r_2, \ldots, r_k$ are randomly generated moves. We take permutation δ as a base solution and $T_\delta \leftarrow T_0$.

4   Parallel Simulated Annealing pSA

The first parallelizations of the simulated annealing method were based on the crossing along a single trajectory through the solution's space (co called single-walk strategy). There were two ideas used in this strategy: move acceleration and parallel moves. Kravitz and Rutenbar [5] described one of the first examples of this type of parallelization of the simulated annealing metaheuristics.

Another method, crossing along a multiple trajectory through the solution's space (multiple-walk strategy), was proposed by Miki ed al. [7] and Czech [3]. This method is based on the execution of several threads (independent, semi-independent or cooperative) running simulated annealing at different temperatures. Such a model was the base of our researches.

New elements of the pSA method: intensification and diversification, multi-step and long-term memory were implemented in parallel as follows. A master - slave model was used in implementation of the parallel algorithm. The master process keeps shared data, such as the best known solution and backtrack-jump heap. Slave processes $i = 1, 2, \ldots, p$ run its own simulated annealing threads with different temperatures $T^i = (\alpha^i, \lambda^i)$. If one process finds a new best solution π^*, then it sends it to the master process and runs an intencification procedure for next $S = 10$ iterations. Slave processes obtain up-to-date π^* from the master process every $K = 10$ iterations. If the process has no improvement of its own search procedure for $R = 20$ 'big' iterations (without modification of temperature), it runs the backtrack-jump procedure, consisting of getting new current solutions from the backtrack heap of the master process. Both, sequential and parallel algorithms, make n iterations without modification of the temperature inside one 'big' iteration.

5   Computational Results

The algorithm was coded in Ada95 and run on 4-processors Sun Enterprise 4x400MHz, tested on the benchmark problems taken from the literature (see OR-Library [8] for more details). Main tests were based on 50 instances with 100, ..., 500 operations. Every instance of the test problems was executed 8 times, and the average and minimal result was used for comparing. The standard deviation of results was computed too – it was the measure of algorithm stability.

Results of tests are shown in Table 1. Starting solutions for the first process were taken from the quick approximate algorithm NEH, other processes start with random solutions. For all tested algorithms, the number of iterations was counted as a sum of iterations on processors. All algorithms, sequential and parallel, make 20.000 iterations, so the 4-processor implementations make 5.000 iterations on each of 4 processors.

Table 1. Relative distances to reference solutions [10].

$n \times m$	1 processor (sSA)			4 processors (pSA)		
	average	minimal	std. dev.	average	minimal	std. dev.
20×5	0.23%	0.05%	0.16%	0.08%	0.00%	0.08%
20×10	0.27%	0.04%	0.17%	0.05%	0.00%	0.05%
50×5	0.14%	0.01%	0.12%	0.04%	0.00%	0.04%
50×10	1.51%	1.25%	0.19%	1.25%	0.91%	0.20%
50×20	1.97%	1.56%	0.26%	1.54%	1.09%	0.29%
average	0.82%	0.58%	0.18%	0.59%	0.40%	0.13%

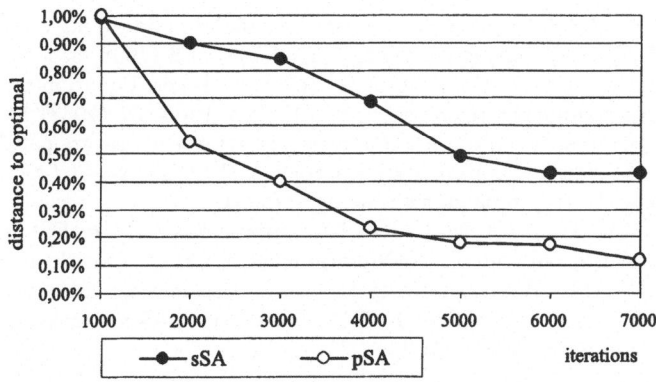

Fig. 1. Comparison of convergence for sSA and pSA algorithms.

As we can see in Table 1 the average distance to reference solutions for sequential sSA and parallel pSA was at the level of 0.82% for 1-processor implementation and at the level of 0.59% for 4-processors implementation. All algorithms have the same number of iterations and comparable costs. Additionally, the results of the parallel algorithm in 8 runs was more stable: standard deviations of the result equaled to 0.13%, compared to 0.18% for the sequential algorithm. Another test was made for comparing algorithms in the matter of convergence's speed. Tests were made on the first 10 instances of the benchmarks [8], the average distance to reference solutions was used for comparison. As we can see in Figure 1 the parallel algorithm achieves better results than the sequential algorithm after the same number of iterations (as the sum of iterations on each processor).

6   Conclusions

We have discussed a new approach to parallel simulated annealing based on asynchronous multiple-walk strategy. As we can see parallelization increases the quality of the solutions obtained. The idea of the backtrack-jump and the multistep was used. Computer experiments show, that the parallel algorithm is considerably more efficient and stable in comparison to the sequential algorithm.

References

1. Benchmark library: http://www.ii.uni.wroc.pl/~mwd/wobz.html
2. Černy V.: Thermodynamical approach to travelling salesman problem: An efficient simulation algorithm. J. Optim. Theory Appl. **45** (1985) 41–51
3. Czech Z.: Three parallel algorithms for simulated annealing. Lecture Notes in Computer Science **2328**, Springer Verlag (2002) 210–217
4. Kirkpatrick S., Gellat C.D., Vecchi M.P.: Optimization by simulated annealing. Science **220** (1983) 671–680

5. Kravitz S.A., Rutenbar R.A.: Placement by simulated annealing on a multiprocessor. IEEE Transactions on Computer Aided Design **6** (1998) 534–549
6. Metropolis N., A.W. Rosenbluth, A.H. Teller, E. Tellet: Equation of state calculation by fast computing machines. Jurn. Of Cem. Phys. **21** (1953) 1187–1191
7. Miki M., Hiroyasu T., Kasai M.: Application of the temperature parallel simulated annealing to continous optimization problems. IPSL Trans. **41** (2000) 1607–1616
8. OR-Library: http://mscmga.ms.ic.ac.uk/info.html
9. Wang C., Chu C., J. Proth J.: Heuristic approaches for $n|m|F|\sum C_i$ scheduling problems. European Journal of Operational Research (1997) 636–644
10. Yamada T., C.R. Reeves: Solving the C_{sum} Permutation Flowshop Scheduling Problem by Genetic Local Search. IEEE International Conference on Evolutionary Computation ICEG 98 (1998) 230–234

Simulated Annealing with Restart to Job Shop Scheduling Problem Using Upper Bounds

Marco Antonio Cruz-Chavez[1] and Juan Frausto-Solis[2]

[1] Faculty of Chemical Sciences and Engineering, Autonomous University of Morelos
State Av. Universidad 1001, Col. Chamilpa, 62270, Cuernavaca, Morelos, MÉXICO
mcruz@buzon.uaem.mx
[2] Department of Computer Science, ITESM, Campus Cuernavaca Paseo de la
Reforma 182-A, 62589, Temixco, Morelos, MÉXICO
juan.frausto@itesm.mx

Abstract. An algorithm of simulated annealing for the job shop scheduling problem is presented. The proposed algorithm restarts with a new value every time the previous algorithm finishes. To begin the process of annealing, the starting point is a randomly generated schedule with the condition that the initial value of the makespan of the schedule does not surpass a previously established upper bound. The experimental results show the importance of using upper bounds in simulated annealing in order to more quickly approach good solutions.

1 Introduction

The job shop scheduling problem (JSSP) is considered to be one of the most difficult to solve in combinatorial optimization. It is also one of the most difficult problems in the NP-hard class [1].

The JSSP consists of a set of machines that each carry out the execution of a set of jobs. Each job consists of a certain number of operations, which must be carried out in a specific order. Each operation is carried out by a specific machine and has a specific time of execution. Each machine can execute a maximum of one operation at any given point in time. A single machine is unable to carry out more than one operation of the same job. The objective of the problem is to find the makespan. The makespan is defined as the time it takes to complete the last operation in the system. An immense number of models exist that represent the JSSP, but the two most important and influential models are those of disjunctive formulation [2] and disjunctive graph [2] and [3].

The simulated annealing algorithm (SA) [4] is an analogy between the annealing process of solids and the problem of solving combinatorial optimization problems. This algorithm has been used with high rates of success for JSSP by several researchers [5], [6], [7], [8], [9], and [10]. For the JSSP, S is a schedule obtained by using a randomly generated initial point. S' is in the neighborhood of S, which is obtained by a small perturbation of S. T_0 and T_f are the intial and final temperatures of the process. β is the coefficient of temperature that controls the cooling of the system. $f(S)$ is the energy of the configuration S, which is

L. Rutkowski et al. (Eds.): ICAISC 2004, LNAI 3070, pp. 860–865, 2004.
© Springer-Verlag Berlin Heidelberg 2004

generally the makespan. One of the ways of perturbing the neighborhood of S is proposed by Balas [3], and involves exchanging a pair of adjacent operations that are within critical blocks of operations. This form of altering the neighborhood is known as N_1. The critical blocks of operations are the operations that form the longest path of the schedule. Each critical block of operations that form this path are performed by a common machine. N_1, have been used previously in SA with good results by [5], [6], [7], [8], and [10]. N_1 is what is used in this work due to ease of implementation.

Other researchers have developed variations of N_1. The algorithm of Matsuo et al. [7] is a derivation of N_1, called N_{1a}. This type of change to the neighborhood involves changing the placement of three pairs of adjacent operations simultaneously, where each operation pair is performed by a different machine. The algorithm of Aart et al. [5], also a derivation of N_1, called N_{1b}, involves reversing three adjacent pairs of operations that are all performed by the same machine, and with the condition that one of the pairs does not form the longest path.

Another type of derivation of N_1 is the neighborhood of critical block (CB), which is called N_2. In this type of neighborhood, one operation in the block is changed for either the initial or final operation of the block. It is not required that the operations that change places be adjacent. The algorithms that use N_2 are the CBSA of Yamada et al. [10] and the CSBA+CB of Yamada and Nakano [9]. This last algorithm uses a deterministic local search called shifting bottleneck (SB) [11]. It uses SB when the schedule S', which is a perturbation of S, is rejected in the SA. When the rejection occurs, the shifting bottleneck is applied to S' in order to improve it. Once S' is improved, although $f(S')$ come to be greater than $f(S)$, the solution is accepted. In this type of neighborhood, the shifting bottleneck must be used whenever S' is rejected in the algorithm. The implementation of the SB is not easy because it requires that the release time and due dates are calculated. Here, an algorithm is proposed which is easy to implement and produces high quality solutions; it is a simulated annealing algorithm with restart [12].

2   Simulated Annealing with Restart Using Upper Bounds

The proposed algorithm of simulated annealing with restart (SAR) consists of executing a set of SA. The SAR algorithm using upper bound can be seen in Figure 1. Each simulated annealing that is executed involves the iteration of the SAR algorithm. Each repetition begins using a different schedule. The idea of beginning with different schedules for each repetition of SAR came about because of experimental tests that were carried out. In the experimental tests, it was detected that even though SA allows the search for a global optimum, at some point low temperatures eliminate this possibility and the search finds a local optimum. By beginning with different schedules, more variability of solutions is obtained than by beginning with only a single schedule. It is seen that the restart

---

1. Given initial iteration $k = 0$, initial values of S_f, T_f, β
2. Beginning of annealing $k = k + 1$:
    3. $S = S_0 \leq Upper\ Bound$, $T = T_0$, initial S_c
    4. While the final temperature Tf is not reached,
        5. While equilibrium is not reached:
        •Generate a state $S\prime$ by means of a perturbation in S
        •if $f(S\prime) - f(S) \leq 0$ then $S = S\prime$
        •if $f(S\prime) - f(S) > 0$ the state is accepted with
                the probability: $P_{accept} = e^{-\left(\frac{f(S\prime)-f(S)}{T}\right)}$
        •With a randomly generated number α
                        evenly distributed between $(0, 1)$
        •if $\alpha < P_{accept}$ then $S = S\prime$
        •if $S < S_c$ then $S_c = S$
        •If the equilibrium does not exist, return to 5
    $T = T * \alpha$
    The best configuration is stored, if $S_c < S_f$ then $S_f = S_c$
    If $T \geq T_f$, return to 4
If $k < maxiter$, return to 2 to begin a new annealing
The solution is S_f

Fig. 1. The simulated annealing algorithm with restart to JSSP using an upper bound

of the simulated annealing algorithm leaves a different point in the solution space each time it is repeated.

The restarting of the algorithm allows for the search of global optimums by using a new schedule in each repetition of SAR. This allows for a different part of the solution space to be explored when SAR is at a local optimum. This not only increases the probability of finding a global optimum, but also increases the time of the search. In the SAR algorithm, at the beginning of each simulated annealing, an UB (Upper Bound) is established in order to randomly obtain the schedule with which to start the process. The value of the makespan of this schedule may not be greater than the UB, or the schedule is not accepted as the initial configuration of the annealing. The UB was established by trial and error, so that the algorithm took no longer than 15 seconds to find an I-SCHED (initial schedule) that could be used to begin the repetitions of the SAR algorithm. In order to obtain an I-SCHED that did not surpass the UB, a random procedure was used. First, a random sequence of operations was formed for each machine. Next, a scheduling algorithm [13] was used to eliminate global cycles. Finally, this schedule is improved by using the Giffler and Thompson algorithm [14] that obtains active schedules [6]. With the proposed procedure, obtaining good initial solutions that they don't surpass an UB in a short period of time could be assured.

In each iteration of the SAR algorithm, SA is fully completed. The best configuration after all the repetitions are completed is the final solution. The number of annealings carried out, that is, the number of repetitions of the algorithm, is a function of time of execution and depends on the problem.

Other form of restart with SA is proposed by Yamada and Nakano [9], Yamada et al. [10] and Aydin and Fogarty [15].

3   Computational Results

The proposed algorithm was proven with two benchmark registered in the OR library [16], FT10 of 10x10 and LA40 of 15x15. For the FT10, ten trials were done with an UB = 1570, generating the initial schedules with the procedure I-SCHED, and ten trials were done without an UB, but also using the procedure of I-SCHED. The parameters of T_0 = 32*(Makespan of I-SCHED), T_f = 1.0, β = 0.98, and N_1 as the type of neighborhood were equal in each test performed, whether there was an UB or not. In both cases, a maximum time of four hours was used to obtain the results. When the UB is used, the optimum (930) is obtained in 80% of trials, the quickest being obtained in 44 minutes, 55 seconds. The standard deviation is 2.95 with an average makespan of 931.4. If an UB is not used, the obtained results are of poor quality (the optimum could not be obtained), with a standard deviation of 4.97 and an average makespan of 941.9. We also compared the results obtained with the algorithms ASSA using N_1 and CBSA N_2, of Yamada et al. [10] because they have obtained some of the best results for the problem FT10. They also carried out ten trials. It can be seen that ASSA presents a greater standard deviation of 5.10 and a higher average makespan of 939.5. The worst result obtained by the SAR algorithm for the makespan was 937 and by ASSA 951. It is obvious that the SAR algorithm is more effective than ASSA in obtaining the optimum for the problem FT10. For the CBSA algorithm, in ten trials, and average makespan of 930.8 was obtained and a standard deviation of 2.4. Only in one trial was CBSA unable to obtain the optimum result, this trial gave a makespan of 938. These results indicate that CBSA, by a small margin, is better able to find accurate solutions than SAR. It is believed that the CBSA obtains better results due to the neighborhood it uses, because the only difference between ASSA and CBSA is the type of neighborhood used.

It is important to emphasize that a great number of tests were generated, with sequences of slower cooling in both cases, with and without UB. The results of all the performed tests slower cooling were farther from the global optimum. In addition, there was a considerable increase in the time of execution of the algorithm in order to find these solutions.

Table 1 shows the results of several algorithms of SA for the problem FT10. In the table, the type of neighborhood each author used is specified. None of these algorithms involve restarting the annealing so their time of execution is small. It can also be observed that most of the results are poorer than those obtained by the SAR when an upper bound is not applied. Table 2 shows the best performance of several algorithms of SA, including the SAR algorithm, for the benchmark LA40 of JSSP.

The parameters in SAR for LA40 were fixed to: UB = 2300, T_0 = 25, T_f = 5.0 and β = 0.99. In the same table 2 it can be observed that the result obtained by SAR with a 0.90% relative error is better than all of the other algorithms that use N_1 and derivatives of N_1. SAR also surpasses the CBSA N_2. SAR is surpassed only by CBSA+SB. The CBSA+SB algorithm use the neighborhood N_2 and im-

Table 1. Results of several simulated annealing algorithms for the problem FT10

FT10 , 10 x 10, optimum = 930		
Authors	$t = seg$	Makespan
Aart et al. (N_1)	99	969
Aart et al. (N_{1b})	99	977
Van Laarhoven (N_1)	3895	951
Matsuo et al. (N_{1a})	987	946

Table 2. Results of several simulated annealing algorithm for the problem LA40

LA40, 15 X 15, optimum = 1222		
Algorithm	Makespa	%ER
CBSA+SB(N_2)	1228	0.49
SAR(N_1)	1233	0.90
VanLaarhoven(N_1)	1234	0.98
Matsuo et al.(N_{1a})	1235	1.06
CBSA(N_2)	1235	1.06
Aart et al.(N_{1b})	1254	2.62
Aart et al.(N_1)	1256	2.78

plements the procedure of deterministic local search, called shifting bottleneck, for the re-optimization of schedules obtained in each repetition of the algorithm.

4   Conclusion

The use of upper bounds in the algorithm allows the solution of the problem FT10 to be found in almost all trials. This indicates that for this problem, in the SAR algorithm, starting with the good schedules that do not surpass an UB, improves the solution considerably. Also, it is recommended that the simulated annealing be restarted in several points with good schedules. By doing this, better solutions are obtained which are nearer to the global optimum.

The quality of the solution of SAR (N_1) for the problem LA40 is comparable to the CBSA+SB (N_2). One advantage that SAR has over the CBSA+SB is that for the CBSA+SB, it is necessary to find the machines with the shifting bottleneck in each repetition. To find all of this information, it is necessary to calculate the release times and due dates of each operation that is involved in the problem. Thus, because of the similar quality and simpler implementation, SAR appears to be of more interest from a scientific point of view. It is thought that SAR would have better performance with large problems than CBSA+SB due to the fact that SAR does not use deterministic local search procedures. Better performance would be possible in SAR using N_2.

References

1. Garey, M.R., Johnson, D.S. and Sethi, R., The complexity of Flow shop and Job shop Scheduling. Mathematics of Operations Research, Vol. I, No 2, USA, 117-129, May, 1976.
2. Conway, R. W., Maxwell, W.L. and Miller, L. W., Theory of Scheduling, Addison-Wesley, Reading, Massachusetts, 1967.
3. Balas, E., Machine sequencing via disjunctive graphs: an implicit enumeration algorithm, Oper. Res., 17:941-957, 1969.
4. Kirkpatrick, S., Gelatt Jr., S. D. and Vecchi, M. P., Optimization by simulated anneal-ing. Science, 220(4598), 13 May, 671-680, 1983.
5. Aarts, E.H.L., Van Laarhoven, P.J.M., Lenstra, J.K. and Ulder, N.L.J., A computational study of local search algorithms for job shop scheduling, ORSA Journal on Computing 6, 118-125, 1994.
6. Pinedo, M., Scheduling Theory, Algorithms, and Systems, Prentice Hall, U.S.A., 1995.
7. Matsuo, H., Suii, C.J. and Sullivan, R.S., A controlled search simulated annealing method for the general job shop scheduling problem, Working paper 03-04-88, Graduate School of Business, University of Texas, Austin, 1988.
8. Van Laarhoven, P.J.M. , Aarts, E.H.L. and Lenstra, J.K., Job shop scheduling by simulated annealing. Oper. Res., 40(1):113-125, 1992.
9. Yamada, T., and Nakano, R., Job-shop scheduling by simulated annealing combined with deterministic local search, Meta-heuristics: theory and applications, Kluwer academic publishers MA, USA, pp. 237-248, 1996.
10. Yamada, T., Rosen, B. E. and Nakano, R., A simulated annealing approach to job shop scheduling using critical block transition operators, IEEE, 0-7803-1901-X/94, 1994.
11. Adams, J., Balas, E. and Zawack, D., The shifting bottleneck procedure for job shop scheduling, Mgmt. Sci., 34, 1988.
12. Ingber, L., Simulated annealing: Practice versus theory, Mathematical Computer Modelling, 18(11), 29-57, 1993.
13. Nakano, R. and Yamada, T., Conventional Genetic Algorithm for Job-Shop. Problems, in Kenneth, M. K. and Booker, L. B. (eds) Proceedings of the 4th International Conference on Genetic Algorithms and their Applications, San Diego, USA, pp. 474-479, 1991.
14. Zalzala, P. J. and Flemming, Zalsala, A.M.S. (Ali M.S.), ed., Genetic algorithms in engineering systems /Edited by A.M.S. Institution of Electrical Engineers, London, 1997.
15. Aydin, M. E. and Fogarty, T. C., Modular Simulated annealing algorithm for job shop scheduling running on distributed resource machin (DRM), South Bank University, SCISM, 103 Borough Road, London, SE1 0AA, UK, 2002.
16. Beasley, J.E., OR Library, Imperial College, Management School, http://mscmga.ms.ic.ac.uk/info.html, 1990.

Requirements and Solutions for Web-Based Expert System

Maciej Grzenda[1] and Marcin Niemczak[2]

[1] Warsaw University of Technology, Faculty of Mathematics and Information Science,
Pl. Politechniki 1, 00-661 Warszawa, POLAND
grzendam@mini.pw.edu.pl,
http://www.mini.pw.edu.pl/~grzendam
[2] Warsaw University of Technology,
Faculty of Electronics and Information Technology
ul. Nowowiejska 15/19, 00-665 Warszawa
marcin.niemczak@wp.pl

Abstract. The advent of the Internet has strongly influenced modern software systems. Existing intranet solutions are being gradually replaced with www services available everywhere and at any time. The availability of the wide area network has resulted in unprecedented opportunities of remote and distributed cooperation of large groups of people and organizations.

Originally expert systems have been used for internal purposes in different organizations. The purpose of this work is to summarize the results of the project aiming to revise the functionality and architecture of traditional expert systems in terms of modern trends in web-based systems. Both knowledge representation, development of the knowledge base and interface solutions have been reconsidered. The proposed solutions are based on the pilot implementation of the internet expert system.

1 Introduction

Expert systems (ES) have been successfully applied in many organizations. In most cases they have been used for internal purposes of scientific laboratories [6,8], medical centers [6] or commercial organizations [3]. At the same time the growing importance of web-based systems can be observed. Initial static web services have grown up to support the database layer, server-side scripting languages and portable data representation in the form of eXtensible Markup Language (XML) [2]. As a consequence, the functionality of the IT systems available previously only internally on the limited number of workstations, has been spread out all over the world through the use of www technology. Not only does it allow for remote work of the organization's associates, but also it makes it possible for the external organizations and people to cooperate in this work. The same advantages influence the development of expert systems.

The purpose of this paper is to provide an overview of different aspects of implementing internet-aware expert systems. Both new opportunities and

L. Rutkowski et al. (Eds.): ICAISC 2004, LNAI 3070, pp. 866–871, 2004.
© Springer-Verlag Berlin Heidelberg 2004

possible drawbacks have been discussed. These relate to typical problems of expert system design and implementation including knowledge representation, inference methods, development of the knowledge base, the rules for constructing expert system shell with www interface, the requirements posed by the need for the integration of the expert system with the remaining part of the web service.

The primary objective of the research project was to investigate the requirements and solutions for expert system available across the Internet for distributed group of experts and end users working for non-commercial organizations in different knowledge domains. In other words, no a priori specific knowledge could be adopted in the system.

The solutions proposed in this work are supported by the results of implementing web-based shell for the Jess expert system [1].

2 Knowledge Representations and Inference Strategies towards Internet Architecture

Design stage of expert system cannot be underestimated. There are many ways of representing knowledge base and many ways of using that knowledge for inference. Having assumed that the Internet expert system should allow for distributed knowledge acquisition from experts working in distant locations, we have to provide these domain experts with the tool that does not require the assistance of knowledge engineers. Thus, different knowledge base representations and reasoning strategies listed below were included in the research on designing and implementing Internet Expert System Shell (IES) that can be widely accessed and used by users that are not experts in the domain of expert systems:

- *Propositional and Predicate Logic* [8] allows storing the knowledge in the form of strictly defined mathematical rules. Users of IES are not necessarily mathematicians or scientists and it would be difficult for them to translate their knowledge to the form of well-defined mathematical constructs. Taking into account the qualifications of prospective users, theoretically propositional and predicate logic could be used as a knowledge base for IES. However, having in mind that the system will be available through the Internet interface to the broad audience that is not always scientific oriented, it is worth considering to choose other more suitable knowledge representation.
- *Frames and Semantic Networks* [6,8] are quite complex structures with built in inheritance mechanisms and semantic connections. To define the knowledge base with usage of frames several preliminary steps would be required: frame definition, inheritance identification and finally data filling. Beside difficulty with designing proper structures it would be also difficult to keep the user interface on intermediate level and simultaneously provide all functionality needed during designing frame and semantic net IES.
- *Procedural Programs* [5] can be used whenever computer experts maintain expert system and what is also important these experts possess programming skills. Comparing procedural programs to predicate logic or semantic nets

and frames it is clearly visible that this kind of knowledge representation cannot be used in the case of designed IES and is far from what IES users could expect.

- *Production Rules* [8,1] in the form IF premises THEN actions fit exactly reasoning manner of real human expert. As premises one can put answers obtained during interview, as actions goals to obtain and by applying some way of reasoning simulate giving advice or explanation process of real human expert. Production rules are quite easy to define and suit the best broad knowledge domain that the IES will be required to serve. To create knowledge base with usage of production rules the expert should perform several quite simple tasks: define premises, define actions and finally create rules. Each of these steps does not require advanced interface and can be easily implemented on intermediate user level. By defining above constructs expert user can create knowledge bases from almost all domains and what is important do it quickly and easily.

To sum up, production rules appeared to be the most promising representation and were used as the heart of designed IES. To make use of the knowledge stored in production rules several reasoning strategies were considered:

- *Backward Chaining* as a goal driven process tries to prove the goal analyzing the premises. With usage of backward chaining IES can simulate in the natural way the case of interview in which user has already defined problem to solve. By back processing rules in given knowledge base system can find and ask necessary questions to collect the facts and then present solution to the user.
- *Forward Chaining* as a data driven process tries to find new goals by analyzing the premises. With usage of forward chaining IES can simulate the case of interview in which user wants to explore given domain. While collecting facts system can present already found solutions to the user.
- *Hybrid Chaining* is a way of combining forward and backward chaining altogether. Some expert systems find it useful because in specific cases it can provide the solution quicker. IES system does not implement Hybrid Chaining because the order of processing rules in the knowledge base might be not natural and could confuse some users.

Finally, after analysis of IES requirements and available reasoning strategies forward and backward inference strategies have been implemented in the IES.

3   Applied IES – Architecture and Solutions

Web-based expert systems have gained gradual acceptance in different domains. These include expert systems playing the role of IT help desk, performing forecasts of financial markets, supporting the maintenance of mobile and telecommunication services or library catalogs [7]. However, in many cases these systems concentrate on specific domain problems or require the user to deploy the software using APIs rather then ready-to-use tools. The purpose of this section is to provide an overview of different aspects of preparing web-based expert system and highlight some of the solutions proposed in the implementation stage of our research, assuming expected application of the IES in different domains.

Implementation stage of IES as a system for Internet users forced consideration of specific requirements that normally could be omitted in standard ES. First of all, the system was intended to be available from any place with Internet connection and 24 hours a day with usage of Internet browser. That demand caused that IES was implemented on the base of web application architecture. Expert users of the system were recognized as experts in specified domain but not necessarily in the field of ES. For end user target group no assumptions could be made either. These conditions influenced development of expert user and end user interfaces that were kept on intermediate and easy level respectively. IES based on Web Application model can be widely accessed by people of different nationalities. Therefore multilingual features played great role in designing the knowledge repository of the system. System internationalization was separated from business logic so that the expert users after defining facts and rules do not have to change given knowledge base in case of translation to different language. On the contrary, translator role has been introduced to enable separating the design of the knowledge base from translating already defined content into different languages.

Developed IES was designed to be universal and was not targeted on any particular knowledge domain or organization. It can store any knowledge that can be put into the form of production rules. Statistics included in the system allow experts to observe how users use the system so as to find weak and strong points of knowledge bases. Expert user using expert's web service can trace what kind of knowledge end user is eager to obtain and what causes that sometimes the user is presented with not satisfactory solution. Flexible presentation layer was also important feature in design of IES. Almost each organization sharing its knowledge would like to customize the presentation of the system for the end user without touching the system business logic or writing some additional code. IES provides great flexibility producing XML output for end user interface that can be translated to any other document with usage of XSLT transformations. All functionality of end user module can be embedded into larger functioning web application or other systems by calling directly IES and therefore the system may be easily used to provide expert functionality when necessary.

Web architecture beside all its advantages described above possesses also some disadvantages. Internet as a public place is always less secure then local area network. If data stored in knowledge base is confidential and the system does not require sharing it among many users then probably it will be better to choose another solution. Still, additional measures including encryption can be applied to prevent the communication from being intercepted or disclosed by third parties.

The architecture of the implemented expert system is depicted on fig. 1. The overall design is based on MVC (Model View Controller) paradigm and is divided into several parts:

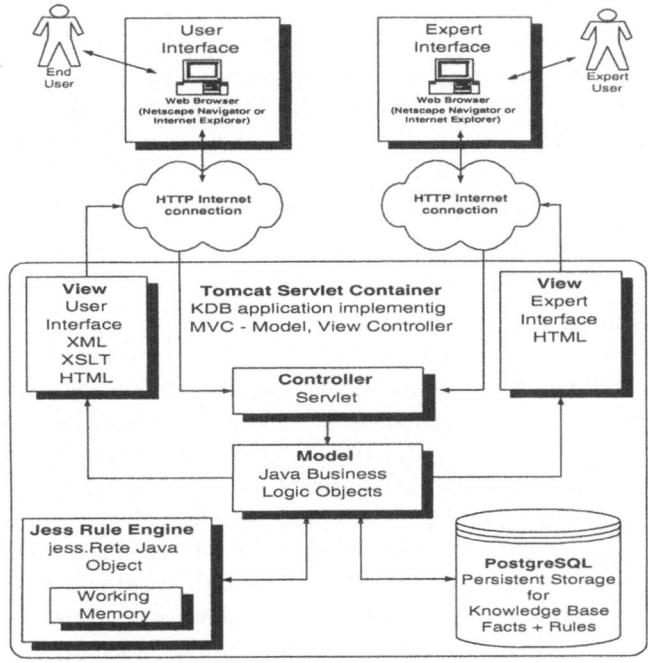

Fig. 1. The architecture of Internet Expert System

- *View* part of the system is responsible for rendering output from business logic to expert and end user interface. Expert Interface is rendered as HTML pages. User Interface is based on XML output. In order to present XML results to end users, XSLT transformations have to be applied to transform XML documents to HTML documents. IES expert system provides the structure of basic XSLT transforms [2] that can be easily extended by organizations depending on individual needs.
- *Controller* is responsible for dispatching requests from browser to proper business logic objects. It also controls authorization and proper sequence of execution of IES web application.
- *Model* is the most important part of IES expert system. It contains business logic objects responsible for serving every request dispatched from controller. Beside business logic objects, Model part contains jess.Rete [1] object serving as the interface to Jess rule engine and objects responsible for interaction with persistent storage for knowledge bases, facts and rules. Persistent storage is implemented using RDBMS .
- *Jess* is a rule engine and scripting language developed at Sandia National Laboratories in Livermore, CA [4]. Numerous projects have been already built using Jess. These include expert systems that evaluate insurance claims and mortgage applications, network intrusion detectors and security auditors, design assistants that help mechanical engineers. See [4] for complete reference.

Jess possesses the rule compiler and inference engine to reason on the rules that must be supplied in Jess syntax. Although Jess itself provides console for programming and enables basic input and output it cannot be used directly by experts or end users of designed IES because these people are not programmers and probably they never will be ones. The second reason is that the users of the system could not reach it because it is impossible to distribute the Jess with proper rules to every user and then teach the users how to maintain Jess.

4   Conclusions

Growing availability of the Internet makes it possible for multiple users to cooperate in order to achieve common goals. Consequently it enables domain experts to share their knowledge at convenient time from any location. This perspective also creates new opportunities for non-profit and educational organizations.

In our research expert systems have been reevaluated in terms of their suitability for web access. Both the requirements for internal knowledge representation and tight, but straightforward integration with existing services have been examined. The internet expert system has been developed to verify the assumptions made in the project. Using web interface, multiple experts can contribute to the knowledge base content and end users can find the solutions to their problems. At the same time users' activity can be monitored and saved to be accessed by the experts in order to find insufficient rules or determine typical users' profiles.

Acknowledgements. The authors would like to thank Sandia National Laboratories and the Jess Team that develops and manages the Jess Expert System software [4] for their support in realizing this project.

References

1. Friedman-Hill, E., Jess in Action - Rule-Based Systems in Java, Manning, 2003
2. Holzner, S., Inside XSLT, New Riders Publishing, 2002
3. Jackson, P., Reichgelt, H., Van Harmelen, F.: Logic-Based Knowledge Representation, MIT Press, 1988
4. Jess Home Page - http://herzberg.ca.sandia.gov/jess
5. Krishnamoorthy, C.S., Rajeev, S. : Artificial Intelligence and Expert Systems for Engineers, CRC Press LLC, 1996
6. Liebowitz, J.: The Handbook of Applied Expert Systems, CRC Press LLC, 1999
7. Poo C.C., Toh T.K., Khoo S.G.: Design and Implementation of the E-Referencer, Data and Knowledge Engineering Journal, **Vol. 32**, 2000, pp. 199-218.
8. Rich, E.: Artificial Intelligence, McGraw-Hill Inc., 1990
9. Russell, S.J., Norvig, P. : Artificial Intelligence: Modern Approach, Prentice Hall, 1995

Information Structuring in Natural Language Communication: Syntax versus Semantic

Wladyslaw Homenda

Faculty of Mathematics and Information Science
Warsaw University of Technology, 00-661 Warsaw, Poland
homenda@mini.pw.edu.pl

Abstract. The paper introduces an approach to natural language processing based on perceiving natural language as a tool of human communication, tool describing subjects of this communication. This approach reveals parallel syntactic and semantic attempts to natural language processing. Both attempts are reflected in the paradigms of information granulation and granular computing. Duality of granular spaces derived from syntax and semantic of natural language statements is considered. The directions for future research are outlined

1 Introduction

Natural languages are tools used in human communication. They enable us to express all sorts of things in all sorts of situations in surrounding and dynamically evolving world. Therefore, natural languages have to be powerful and accurate enough to allow for precise communication. On the other hand, natural languages have to evolve together with the world they are used to describe.

The tasks of information representation and exchange are fundamental subjects of science, research and technology in the computerized information era. For that reason natural languages as tools of communication raise temptation and force attempts to formalize natural languages and automate their processing as well as processing of information supported by them.

After decades of fruitful development of methods of natural language processing, it is clear that formalization of a full natural language and automation of its processing is far from complete. Natural language formalization and processing is usually restricted by different factors, for instance restricted with regard to syntax, semantics, knowledge, style, etc. Even in these local subsets of natural language automation of natural language processing is still defective. As a result it is assumed in this paper that only a subset of English natural language is investigated, subset that will not maliciously generate incorrect examples.

The paper is structured as follow. Section 2 briefly refers to state of the art in the field of natural language processing: lexical analysis and syntactic structuring. The meaning of semantic utilized in the paper is defined in Section 3.2. The parallel between syntax, semantic and knowledge granularity is developed in Section 3.

L. Rutkowski et al. (Eds.): ICAISC 2004, LNAI 3070, pp. 872–878, 2004.
© Springer-Verlag Berlin Heidelberg 2004

2   Natural Language Processing

Having a text of mother language human being at a glance captures structure of a sentence, meaning of its components and of a sentences as a whole. Process of understanding information expressed by consecutive sentences is simple, easy and fast. No conscious analysis of separate words, their morphology, individual relations is needed to recover information encoded in the sentences, c.f. [4,5,12, 13]. Unlike, automation of this process is neither easy, nor simple. Automatic analysis of information supported by a sentence of natural language needs acquisition of elementary items of a text, detailed and accurate information about grammatical behavior of individual words, formation of more complex language structures, analysis of relations between components of a separate sentence as well as cross sentence implicit information ties. The most important stages of natural language processing: lexical analysis, syntactic structuring, and semantic interpretation are briefly discussed below.

2.1   Lexical Analysis

Automation of natural language processing requires separation of analysed construction (a phrase, a sentence, a text) into elementary items that are words in case of written language statements. Selection of words is associated with acquiring detailed, accurate information about the grammatical, statistical, uncertain and contextual behavior of them. Data acquisition of this stage is founded at a typical language dictionary supplemented by additional information about words as, for instance, grammatical classification and features, syntactic patterns, idioms, statistics of words, relations of given word to other items, a level of certainty of such relations. These relations are defined in the language dictionary and may be subjected to incremental updates along with processing of consecutive texts. For given text being processed an extract of the language dictionary - so called *text vocabulary* - is created and then developed during next stages of text processing.

Let us consider a simple sentence *The best students were operating the optical equipment*, c.f. [3]. The text vocabulary created at the basis of this sentence includes entries as, for instance:

student noun, ((undergraduate, 0.5), (graduate, 0.5), (best, 0.2), ...)

operate, verb transitive, verb intransitive, regular conjugation, sentence patterns 6A, 2A, 2C, 4A, ((<something> , 0.5), (<somebody> <something>, 0.5), (<someone> on <someone>, 0.4), ...)

2.2   Syntactic Structuring

The syntactic approach to natural language processing was extensively explored in the past. Syntactic structuring of language statements is solely based on context free methods. An algorithm of syntactic analysis is provided with a context free grammar of a local area of natural language as well as with a text vocabulary created at the stage of lexical analysis. Context free grammars employed in syntactic structuring allow for recognizing structures of analysed language construction and extracting information entities up to a sentence level.

Let us consider the sentence *"The best students were operating the optical equipment"*. This sentence is based on the sentence pattern in [8] denoted by 6A. This pattern defines a kernel of a sentence *Student operates equipment*. The kernel has the verb *operates* relating two nouns: subject *student* and direct object *equipment*. These elements were then developed to the more complex verb and noun phrases. The verb *operate* was transformed to past continues form *were operating*. The noun *student* was transformed do plural form and supplemented by determinant and adjective to create the noun phrase *The best students*. This additions wrap items of sentence kernel in extra element defining more specific meaning of the verb and noun phrases.

3 Information Structuring

Natural language processing, as described Section 2, leads to extracting information from statements subjected to the processing. A collection of information items creates an ocean of data that has to be subjected into a process of mining conceptual entities of information. This process finally leads to overall understanding of processed statements. The process of structuring space of information fits the paradigms of granular computing and information granulation. Granular computing paradigm "raised from a need to comprehend the problem and provide with a better insight into its essence rather than get buried in all unnecessary details. In this sense, granulation serves as an abstraction mechanism that reduces an entire conceptual burden. As a matter of fact, by changing the *size* of the information granules, we can hide or reveal a certain amount of details one intends to deal with during a certain design phase". It is worth stressing that information granules not only support conversion of clouds of detailed data into more tangible information granules but, very importantly, afford a vehicle of abstraction that allows to think of granules as different conceptual entities; see [2,10] and the references therein.

3.1 Granular Space Formation

Syntactic structuring is efficient in analyzing statements up to separate sentences. It also has its powerful contribution to information extraction from natural language and - subsequently - to the process of information structuring and formation of a space of granular information. According to fundamental works of Chomsky [4,5] syntactical structuring recognizes phrases of different levels of complication. It stems from lexical analysis which creates basis of granule space of information. Based on elementary items created from unique words syntactic structuring enlarges them to expanded plain phrases which can be recursively developed into nested hierarchy of phrases. Syntactic structuring recognizes and distinguishes a number of classes of such complex phrases.

For instance noun phrase *the equipment* is built from text vocabulary words and then is included into a more complex noun phrase *the optical equipment* which - in turn - may be a part of the prepositional phrase *with the optical equipment*. A new, more complex, entities attached to text vocabulary create next levels of information structure, levels that dynamically depend on further text analysis. The process of lexical analysis is a kind of low level computation done for entered text and aimed in extraction of elementary items of the text. This stage creates a lowest level of information granule pyramid based on text vocabulary items. The collection of all syntactic structures of a given text create a *text lexicon* The stage of syntactic structuring adds next levels of this pyramid respective to growing complexity of these structures.. Granules of higher levels bring abstraction of lower level granules. Consequently, as it was outline in [2], these phrases create further levels of information granule pyramid. The methodology used for granule pyramid creation for music notation was studied in [7]. This methodology could be adopted to natural language information structuring.

3.2   Semantic Interpretation

People use different natural languages to express the same subjects of communication like, for instance, describing things and beings and relations between them, expressing ideas and feelings, communicating thoughts and reflections. Alternatively, people use tools different then natural languages for communication: programming languages, artificial languages, language of gesture, drawings, photographs, music notation. All these tools allow for information exchange. Different tools of human communication support different spaces of information. A language of gesture covers a space of information that is not the same as a space covered by a language of drawings. Natural languages are most universal tools of communication. In general, they cover most parts of information spaces spanned by other tools.

Considering these observations it becomes clear that natural language is a tool rather than a subject of human communication. Therefore, syntactic approach to natural language processing is a workout of a projection of a space of information being exchanged onto a space of natural language constructions: words, phrases, sentences, texts. On the other hand, natural language texts are deeply context sensitive, c.f. [1,2,6,9]. For that reason study on human communication with natural language utilized as a tool, if restricted to pure syntactic approach based on context free methods, will not give a complete perspective on the information space being exchanged. We can consider a switch to context sensitive methods to solve the problems of incompleteness of syntactic methods in natural language communication. However, context sensitive methods are not feasible due to their complexity. Therefore, semantic approach to natural language communication mutually utilized with syntactic structuring would actually allow for coping with (some) unsolvable problems of incompleteness and inexactness.

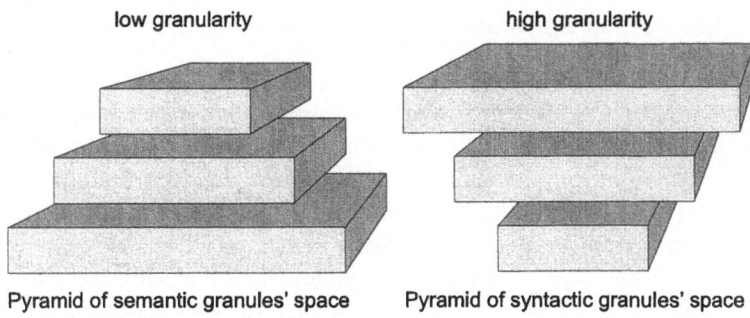

Fig. 1. Duality of syntax and semantic

In this paper the study of natural language carried out into a space of communication subjects is understood as semantic approach to natural language processing. Formally, the mapping V describes semantic of natural language constructions:

$$V : L \to W$$

where: L is a text lexicon, W is real world described by a text.

The mapping V assigns objects of real world W to statements stored in the text lexicon L. For instance, the noun *student* is assigned a set of students of the world W (all students of a country, of a town, of a university, of a campus, of a student's group - depending on information already collected). The value $V(student)$ is one student chosen from this set. On the other hand, the same set of students, as in case of singular noun *student*, is assigned to the plural noun *students*. However, in case of plural noun the value $V(students)$ is equal to the whole set of students. More complex phrase *the best student* restricts the set of students defined by the phrase *student* to a proper subset of it. And, finally, a phrase *the first student on the list* is assigned one student.

Verb phrase creates a crisp relation on subject and, if present in a sentence, on direct and indirect objects. Formally, verb phrase defines a relation (with domain of one, two or three arguments) on sets of objets of real world defined by noun phrases, c.f. [6]. The verb *operate* defines in general a broad range of relations *V(operate)* that, for instance, are defined with respect to particular patterns *"the man operates the machine"*, *"the new law operates"*, c.f. [8]. In case of the sentence *"The best students were operating the optical equipment"* the verb *were operating* defines a relation *V(were operating)* on two sets *V(The best students)* and *V(the optical equipment)* of real world objects. Other relations derived from this sentens start from simplest one *V(operate)(V(students), V(equipment))* and ending with the most specific and most important one: *V(were operating)(V(the best students), V(the optical equipment))*.

3.3   Syntax versus Semantic – Duality of Granular Pyramids

Granular computing as opposed to numeric computing is knowledge-oriented. Information granules exhibit different levels of knowledge abstraction what strictly corresponds to different levels of granularity. Depending upon the problem at hand, we usually group granules of similar *size* (that is granularity) together in a single layer. If more detailed (and computationally intensive) processing is required, smaller information granules are sought. Then these granules are arranged in another layer. In total, the arrangement of this nature gives rise to the information pyramid. In granular processing we encounter a number of conceptual and algorithmic layers indexed by the *size* of information granules. Information granularity implies the usage of various techniques that are relevant for the specific level of granularity, c.f. [11]. Referring to natural language processing, we can refine syntactic structures by associating the layers of the information processing pyramid with the size of their information granules.

The meaning of granule size is defined accordingly to real application and should be consistent with common sense and with the knowledge base of the application. The size of this papers does not permits a discussion on the topic of granule size. Roughly speaking size of syntactic granules is a function of the number of words and of depth of the syntactic structure. The size of the syntactic granule *equipment* is smaller then the size of the granule *the equipment* which in turn has smaller size then the granule *the optical equipment*. On the other hand, we can define size of semantic granule as a quantity of real world objects or a length of continue concept. The size of semantic granule $V(equipment)$ is greater than the size of semantic granule $V(the\ optical\ equipment)$. Likewise the size of semantic granule $V(operate)$ is greater than the size of semantic granule $V(were\ operating)$. Amazingly, greater size of syntactic granule correspond to smaller size of respective semantic granule. The relevance between syntactic and semantic granules is shown in the Figure 1. This relevance is a manifestation of well know and widely utilized duality phenomenon between closely related spaces.

4   Conclusions

A novel framework of the natural language processing based on unified syntactic and semantic analysis were discussed in the paper. Syntactic approach to information structuring in natural language processing as discussed in [2] was supplemented by semantic inquiry of natural language statements. It was outlined that both syntactic and semantic attempts create dual structures of information. The scope and size of the paper allowed for brief presentation of the proposed new framework, so then further research is needed to investigate the methodology of building granular spaces of information. The two important direction of further inquiry that need to be undertaken are 1) context sensitivity of natural language statements approximated by unified exploration of syntax and semantic of statements and 2) syntactic inconsistencies and semantic ambiguities solving in this new framework.

References

1. J. F. Allen, C. F. Perrault, Analysing Intension in Utterances, Artificial Intelligence 15 (1980) 143-178.
2. A. Bargiela, W. Homenda, Information structuring in natural language communication: syntactical approach, Proc. of the International Conference on Fuzzy Systems and Knowledge Discovery, Singapore, November 18-22, 2002.
3. C. Beardon, D. Lumsden, G.Holmes, Natural Language and Computational Linguistics, an introduction, New York, 1991.
4. N. Chomsky, Aspects of a theory of syntax, MIT Press, Cambridge, Massachusetts, 1965.
5. N. Chomsky, Rules and representations, Columbia University Press, New York, 1980.
6. W. Homenda, Databases with Alternative Information, IEEE Transactions on Knowledge and Data Engineering, vol. 3, no. 3, September 1991.
7. W. Homenda, Granular Computing as an Abstraction of Data Aggregation - a View on Optical Music Recognition, Archives of Control Sciences, Vol. 12 (XLVIII), 2002 No. 4, pp 433-455.
8. A. S. Hornby, Oxford Advanced Learner's Dictionary of Current English, Oxford University Press, 1980.
9. R. I. Kittradge, Semantic Processing of Text in Restricted Sublanguages, Computers and Mathematics, 9 (1983) 45-58.
10. W. Pedrycz, Computational Intelligence: An Introduction, CRC Press, Boca Raton, FL, 1997.
11. W. Pedrycz, Granular Computing: An introduction, Proc. of the Joint 9th IFSA World Congress and 20th NAFIPS Internat. Conf., Vancouver, July 25-28, 2001.
12. G. Sampson, Educating Eve, Continuum International, London, New York, 1999.
13. T. Winograd, Language as a cognitive process, Addison Wesley, Readings, Massachusetts, 1983.
14. L. A. Zadeh, Fuzzy logic = Computing with words, IEEE Trans. on Fuzzy Systems, vol. 4, 2, 1996, 103-111.

Strategic Planning through Model Checking of ATL Formulae

Wojciech Jamroga

Parlevink Group, University of Twente, Netherlands
jamroga@cs.utwente.nl
http://www.cs.utwente.nl/~jamroga

Abstract. Model checking of temporal logic has already been proposed for automatic planning. In this paper, we introduce a simple adaptation of the ATL model checking algorithm that returns a strategy to achieve given goal. We point out that the algorithm generalizes minimaxing, and that ATL models generalize traditional game trees. The paper ends with suggestions about other game theory concepts that can be transfered to ATL-based planning.

Keywords: Multi-agent systems, multi-agent planning, model checking.

1 Introduction

Logic-based approaches to Artificial Intelligence seem to be presently undervalued by most AI practitioners. However, we believe that mathematical logic – while probably not the best tool for engineering – should still be important in AI research for at least two reasons. First, mathematical models provide a conceptual apparatus for *thinking* about systems, that can be as well used outside mathematical logic. The second reason is that creating a formal model of a problem makes one realize many (otherwise implicit) assumptions underlying his or her approach to this problem. Having made them explicit, one can strive to relax some of them and still use a part of the formal and conceptual machinery – instead of designing solutions completely ad hoc.

Model checking is an interesting idea that emerged from the research on logic in computer science. The model checking problem asks whether a particular formula φ holds in a particular model M. This seems especially useful in the case of dynamic or temporal logics, whose models can be interpreted as game models, transition systems, control flow charts, data flow charts etc. Moreover, model checking turns out to be relatively cheap in computational terms. It has been already proposed that the model checking of computation tree logic (CTL) formulae can be used for generating plans in deterministic as well as non-deterministic domains [6,7]. ATL is an extension of CTL that includes notions of agents, their abilities and strategies (conditional plans) explicitly in its models. Thus, ATL seems even better suited for planning, especially in multi-agent systems, which was already suggested in [8]. In this paper, we introduce a simple adaptation of

L. Rutkowski et al. (Eds.): ICAISC 2004, LNAI 3070, pp. 879–884, 2004.
© Springer-Verlag Berlin Heidelberg 2004

the ATL model checking algorithm from [1] that – besides checking if a goal can be achieved – returns also an appropriate strategy to achieve it. We point out that this algorithm generalizes the well-known search algorithm of minimaxing, and that ATL models generalize turn-based transition trees from game theory. The paper ends with some suggestions about other game theory concepts that seem worth studying in the context of ATL.

2   Multi-agent Planning through ATL Model Checking

Alternating-time Temporal Logic ATL [1] is an extension of CTL [3], and inherits from the latter several operators for describing temporal properties of systems: A *(for all paths)*, E *(there is a path)*, $\bigcirc$ *(at the next moment)*, $\Diamond$ *(sometime)*, $\Box$ *(always)* and $\mathcal{U}$ *(until)*. Typically, paths are interpreted as sequences of successive states of computations. An example CTL model (transition system), together with the tree of possible computations, is displayed in Figure 1. A CTL formula A$\Diamond$halt, for instance, expresses the property that the the system is bound to terminate (which is true if the initial state is either q_2 or q_3, but false for q_1 and q_2). Another formula, E($\neg$halt)$\mathcal{U}$win, means that it is possible achieve a winning position before the system halts (which is true for all states except q_4).

ATL replaces E and A with a class of *cooperation modalities* $\langle\langle A \rangle\rangle$ (where A is a group of agents). The common-sense reading of $\langle\langle A \rangle\rangle\Phi$ is: "*The group of agents A have a collective strategy to enforce Φ regardless of what all the other agents do*". ATL models include a set of players Σ, a set of (global) system states Q, valuation of propositions π (specifying which propositions are true in which states), and decisions available to every player at each particular state; finally, a complete tuple of decisions and a state imply a deterministic transition according to the transition function δ. We will be writing $\delta(q, \sigma_A, \sigma_{\Sigma\backslash A})$ to denote the system transition from state q when the agents from A decide to proceed with (collective) action σ_A, and $\sigma_{\Sigma\backslash A}$ is the collective choice from their opponents.

It is worth noting that the complexity of ATL model checking is linear in the number of transitions in the model and the length of the tested formula, so the checking should terminate in a sensible time even for *huge* models and formulae.

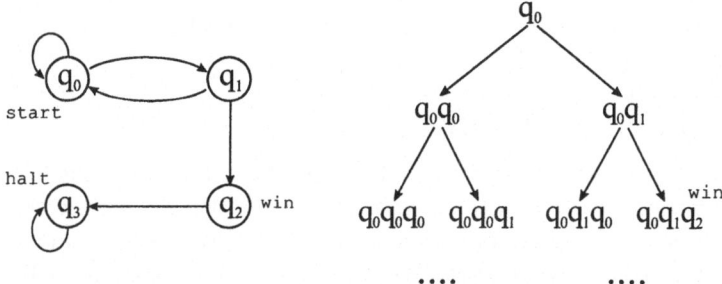

Fig. 1. Transition system and the tree of possible computations.

function $plan(\varphi)$.
Returns a subset of Q for which formula φ holds, together with a (conditional) plan to achieve φ. The plan is sought within the context of concurrent game structure $S = \langle \Sigma, Q, \Pi, \pi, \delta \rangle$.

case $\varphi \in \Pi$: return $\{\langle q, - \rangle \mid \varphi \in \pi(q)\}$
case $\varphi = \neg \psi$: $P_1 := plan(\psi)$; return $\{\langle q, - \rangle \mid q \notin states(P_1)\}$
case $\varphi = \psi_1 \vee \psi_2$:
   $P_1 := plan(\psi_1)$; $P_2 := plan(\psi_2)$;
   return $\{\langle q, - \rangle \mid q \in states(P_1) \cup states(P_2)\}$
case $\varphi = \langle\!\langle A \rangle\!\rangle \bigcirc \psi$: return $pre(A, states(plan(\psi)))$
case $\varphi = \langle\!\langle A \rangle\!\rangle \Box \psi$:
   $P_1 := plan(true)$; $P_2 := plan(\psi)$; $Q_3 := states(P_2)$;
   while $states(P_1) \not\subseteq states(P_2)$
   do $P_1 := P_2|_{states(P_1)}$; $P_2 := pre(A, states(P_1))|_{Q_3}$ **od**;
   return $P_2|_{states(P_1)}$
case $\varphi = \langle\!\langle A \rangle\!\rangle \psi_1 \mathcal{U} \psi_2$:
   $P_1 := \emptyset$; $Q_3 := states(plan(\psi_1))$; $P_2 := plan(true)|_{states(plan(\psi_2))}$;
   while $states(P_2) \not\subseteq states(P_1)$ **do** $P_1 := P_1 \oplus P_2$; $P_2 := pre(A, states(P_1))|_{Q_3}$ **od**;
   return P_1
end case

Fig. 2. Adapted model checking algorithm for ATL formulae. Cases of $\psi_1 \vee \psi_2$ and $\langle\!\langle A \rangle\!\rangle \Diamond \psi$ are omitted, because the first can be re-written as $\neg(\neg\psi_1 \vee \neg\psi_2)$, and the latter as $\langle\!\langle A \rangle\!\rangle true \, \mathcal{U} \psi$.

2.1 Planning Algorithm

In this section, a simple modification of the ATL model checking algorithm [1] is proposed, as shown in Figure 2. Function pre is used here to go "one step back" while constructing a plan for some coalition of agents. Thus, $pre(A, Q_1)$ takes as input a coalition A and a set of states $Q_1 \subseteq Q$ and returns as output the set Q_2 of all states such that when the system is in one of the states from Q_2, the agents A can cooperate and force the next state to be one of Q_1 (together with A's collective choices that accomplish this). Function $states(P)$ returns all the states for which plan P is defined. $P_1 \oplus P_2$ refers to augmenting plan P_1 with all new subplans that can be found in P_2; finally $P|_{Q_1}$ denotes plan P restricted to the states from Q_1 only. More formally:

- $pre(A, Q_1) = \{\langle q, \sigma_A \rangle \mid \forall \sigma_{\Sigma \backslash A} \delta(q, \sigma_A, \sigma_{\Sigma \backslash A}) \in Q_1\}$;
- $states(P) = \{q \in Q \mid \exists_\sigma \langle q, \sigma \rangle \in P\}$;
- $P_1 \oplus P_2 = P_1 \cup \{\langle q, \sigma \rangle \in P_2 \mid q \notin states(P_1)\}$;
- $P|_{Q_1} = \{\langle q, \sigma \rangle \in P \mid q \notin Q_1\}$.

Note that the algorithm returns a (non-empty) plan only if the outmost operator of the checked formula is a cooperation modality (i.e. it specifies explicitly *who* is to execute the plan and what is the objective). In consequence, our approach to negation is *not* constructive: for $\neg\langle\!\langle A \rangle\!\rangle \Phi$, the algorithm will not return a strategy for the rest of agents to actually avoid Φ (although $\neg\langle\!\langle A \rangle\!\rangle \Phi$ implies that such a strategy exists). Similar remark applies to alternative, conjunction, and nesting of strategic formulae. This approach is more natural than it seems at the first glance – even if the subformulae refer to the same set of agents for whom plans are needed. Consider, for instance, the transition system from Figure 1, and suppose that there is only one agent a in the system, who executes the transitions. Formula $\langle\!\langle a \rangle\!\rangle \Box \mathtt{start} \wedge \langle\!\langle a \rangle\!\rangle \Diamond \mathtt{halt}$ holds in q_1; however, it is hard to see what plan should be generated in this case. True, a has a plan to remain in q_1 for ever, and he has a plan to halt the system eventually, but these are *different* plans and cannot be combined. Similarly, $\langle\!\langle a \rangle\!\rangle \Box \langle\!\langle a \rangle\!\rangle \Diamond \mathtt{win}$ holds in q_0, but it does not mean that a has a plan to win infinitely many times. He can always see a way to win; however, if he chooses that way, he will be unable to win again!

2.2 Rocket Example

As an example, consider a modified version of the Simple Rocket Domain from [2]. The task is to ensure that a cargo eventually arrives in Paris (proposition $\mathtt{atCP}$); there are three agents with different capabilities who can be involved, and a single rocket that can be used to accomplish the task. Initially, the cargo may be in Paris, at the London airport ($\mathtt{atCL}$) or it may lie inside the rocket ($\mathtt{inCR}$). Accordingly, the rocket can be moved between London ($\mathtt{atRL}$) and Paris ($\mathtt{atRP}$).

There are three agents: x who can load the cargo, unload it, or move the rocket; y who can unload the cargo or move the rocket, and z who can load the cargo or supply the rocket with fuel (action *fuel*). Every agent can also decide to do nothing at a particular moment (the *nop* – "no-operation" action). The agents act simultaneously. The "moving" action has the highest priority (so, if one agent tries to move the rocket and another one wants to, say, load the cargo, then only the moving is executed). "Loading" is effected when the rocket does not move and more agents try to load than to unload. "Unloading" works in a similar way (in a sense, the agents "vote" whether the cargo should be loaded or unloaded). If the number of agents trying to load and unload is the same, then the cargo remains where it was. Finally, "fueling" can be accomplished alone or in parallel with loading or unloading. The rocket can move only if it has some fuel ($\mathtt{fuelOK}$), and the fuel must be refilled after each flight. We assume that all the agents move with the rocket when it flies to another place. The concurrent game structure for the domain is shown in Figure 3.

$$plan(\langle\!\langle x \rangle\!\rangle \Diamond \mathtt{atCP}) = \{\langle 9, - \rangle, \langle 10, - \rangle, \langle 11, - \rangle, \langle 12, - \rangle\} \tag{1}$$

$$plan(\langle\!\langle x, y \rangle\!\rangle \Diamond \mathtt{atCP}) = \{\langle 2, x\!:\!load \cdot y\!:\!nop \rangle, \langle 6, x\!:\!move \cdot y\!:\!nop \rangle, \langle 7, x\!:\!unload \cdot y\!:\!unload \rangle, \tag{2}$$
$$\langle 8, x\!:\!unload \cdot y\!:\!unload \rangle, \langle 9, - \rangle, \langle 10, - \rangle, \langle 11, - \rangle, \langle 12, - \rangle\}$$

$$plan(\langle\!\langle x, z \rangle\!\rangle \Diamond \mathtt{atCP}) = \{\langle 1, x\!:\!load \cdot z\!:\!load \rangle, \langle 2, x\!:\!load \cdot z\!:\!load \rangle, \langle 3, x\!:\!nop \cdot z\!:\!fuel \rangle, \tag{3}$$
$$\langle 4, x\!:\!move \cdot z\!:\!nop \rangle, \langle 5, x\!:\!load \cdot z\!:\!fuel \rangle, \langle 6, x\!:\!move \cdot z\!:\!nop \rangle,$$
$$\langle 7, x\!:\!unload \cdot z\!:\!nop \rangle, \langle 8, x\!:\!unload \cdot z\!:\!nop \rangle, \langle 9, - \rangle, \langle 10, - \rangle, \langle 11, - \rangle, \langle 12, - \rangle\}$$

Plans to eventually achieve $\mathtt{atCP}$ – for x alone, x with y, and x with z, respectively – are shown above. In the first case, x cannot guarantee to deliver

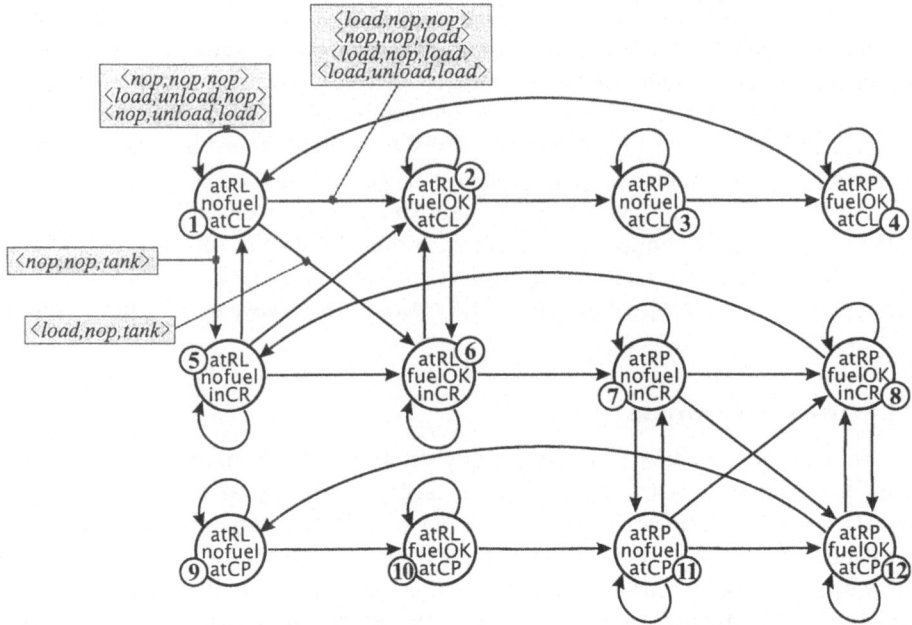

Fig. 3. A version of the Simple Rocket Domain. States of the system are labeled with natural numbers. All the transitions for state 1 (the cargo and the rocket are in London, no fuel in the rocket) are labeled. Output of agents' choices for other states is analogous.

the cargo to Paris (unless the cargo already *is* there), because y and z may prevent him from unloading the goods (2). The coalition of x and y is more competent: they can, for instance, deliver the cargo from London if only there is fuel in the rocket (2). However, they have no infallible plan for the most natural case when 1 is the initial state. Finally, $\{x, z\}$ have an effective plan for any initial situation (3).

2.3   Minimaxing as Model Checking

It is easy to see that the algorithm from Figure 2 can be used for emulating the well known search algorithm of minimaxing. To find the best plan for A, we should label the final positions with the payoff values $p_1, p_2, ...$, then check which $plan(\langle\!\langle A \rangle\!\rangle \Diamond p_i)$ returns a decision for the initial state, and pick the one for maximal p_i. The resulting procedure is still linear in the number of states, transitions and different payoff values. Note that the algorithm proposed here is more general than the original minimaxing: the latter can be applied only to finite turn-based game trees (i.e. systems in which the number of states is finite, there are no cycles, and players cannot act simultaneously), while the model checking-based approach deals also with models in which players act in parallel, and with infinite trees that can be generated by a finite transition system.

Let us also observe that the planning algorithm, proposed in this paper, looks for a plan that must be successful against every line of events – hence the algorithm generalizes minimaxing in zero-sum (i.e. strictly competitive) games. It can be interesting to model the non-competitive case within the scope of ATL as well: while checking $\langle\langle A \rangle\rangle\varphi$, the opponents $\Sigma \setminus A$ may be assumed different goals than just to prevent A from achieving φ. Then, assuming optimal play from $\Sigma \setminus A$, we can ask whether A have a strategy to enforce φ provided that $\Sigma \setminus A$ intend (or desire) to bring about ψ.

3   Conclusions and Future Work

In this paper, an adaptation of ATL model checking is proposed. The algorithm looks for infallible conditional plans to achieve objectives that can be defined via ATL formulae. The algorithm generalizes minimaxing in zero-sum games, extending it to (possibly infinite) games in which agents can act in parallel.

It seems that the link between model checking and minimaxing can be exploited to enrich the framework of ATL, too. First (as already mentioned in the previous section), ATL might be extended so that it can be used to model non-competitive games. Next, efficient pruning techniques exist for classical minimaxing – it may be interesting to transfer them to ATL model checking. Moreover, game theory has developed more sophisticated frameworks, like games with incomplete information and games with probabilistic outcomes (including temporal models, best defense criteria etc.). Investigation of similar concepts in the context of ATL can prove worthwhile, and lead to new research questions, concerning phenomena like non-locality [4] and design of efficient suboptimal algorithms [5] in the scope of logics for multi-agent systems.

References

1. R. Alur, T. A. Henzinger, and O. Kupferman. Alternating-time temporal logic. *Journal of the ACM*, 49:672–713, 2002.
2. A. L. Blum and M. L. Furst. Fast planning through graph analysis. *Artificial Intelligence*, 90:281–300, 1997.
3. E. A. Emerson. Temporal and modal logic. In J. van Leeuwen, editor, *Handbook of Theoretical Computer Science*, volume B, pages 995–1072. Elsevier, 1990.
4. I. Frank and D. Basin. Search in games with incomplete information : A case study using bridge card play. *Artificial Intelligence*, 100(1-2):87–123, 1998.
5. I. Frank, D.A. Basin, and H. Matsubara. Finding optimal strategies for imperfect information games. In *Proceedings of AAAI/IAAI*, pages 500–507, 1998.
6. F. Giunchiglia and P. Traverso. Planning as model checking. *ECP*, pp. 1–20, 1999.
7. M. Pistore and P. Traverso. Planning as model checking for extended goals in non-deterministic domains. In *Proceedings of IJCAI*, pages 479–486, 2001.
8. W. van der Hoek and M. Wooldridge. Tractable multiagent planning for epistemic goals. In *Proceedings of AAMAS-02*, pages 1167–1174. ACM Press, 2002.

On a Special Class of Dempster-Shafer Theories

Mieczysław Alojzy Kłopotek

Institute of Computer Science, Polish Academy of Sciences
ul. Ordona 21, 01-237 Warszawa, Poland
klopotek@ipipan.waw.pl
http://www.ipipan.waw.pl/~klopotek

Abstract. In this paper we want to draw Reader's attention to the issue of impact of separate measurement of features (attributes) from which we want to make inferences. It turns out, that the fact of separate measurements implies algorithmic simplifications for many forms of reasoning in DST. Basic theorems and algorithms exploiting this are given.

1 Introduction

The Dempster-Shafer Theory (DST) [3] has long ago been established as a way to express both uncertainty and incompleteness of information (see [2]-[5] and references therein). However, for reasoning purposes, efficiency of computation for larger sets of variables is a vital issue. In the past, this issue has been addressed from various perspectives, including decomposition in valuation based systems (see [4] and follow-up papers). In this paper we want to draw Reader's attention to the issue of impact of separate measurement of features (attributes) from which we want to make inferences. It turns out, as will be visible subsequently, that the fact of separate measurements implies algorithmic simplifications for many forms of reasoning in DST. Let us first remind basic definitions of DST:

Definition 1. *Let Ξ be a finite set of elements called elementary events. Any subset of Ξ be a composite event. Ξ be called also the frame of discernment. A basic probability assignment function is any function $m{:}2^{\Xi} \to [0,1]$ such that $\sum_{A\in 2^{\Xi}} |m(A)| = 1$, $m(\emptyset) = 0$, $\forall_{A\in 2^{\Xi}}\ \ 0 \le \sum_{A\subseteq B} m(B)$ (|.| - absolute value). A belief function be defined as $Bel{:}2^{\Xi} \to [0,1]$ so that $Bel(A) = \sum_{B\subseteq A} m(B)$ A plausibility function be $Pl{:}2^{\Xi} \to [0,1]$ with $\forall_{A\in 2^{\Xi}}\ Pl(A) = 1 - Bel(\Xi - A)$ A commonality function be $Q{:}2^{\Xi} - \{\emptyset\} \to [0,1]$ with $\forall_{A\in 2^{\Xi}-\{\emptyset\}}\ \ Q(A) = \sum_{A\subseteq B} m(B)$*

Furthermore, a Rule of Combination of two Independent Belief Functions Bel_1, Bel_2 Over the Same Frame of Discernment (the so-called Dempster-Rule), denoted $Bel_{E_1,E_2} = Bel_{E_1} \oplus Bel_{E_2}$ is defined as follows: :

$$m_{E_1,E_2}(A) = c \cdot \sum_{B,C;A=B\cap C} m_{E_1}(B) \cdot m_{E_2}(C)$$

(c - constant normalizing the sum of $|m|$ to 1).Furthermore, let the frame of discernment Ξ be structured in that it is identical to cross product of

L. Rutkowski et al. (Eds.): ICAISC 2004, LNAI 3070, pp. 885–890, 2004.
© Springer-Verlag Berlin Heidelberg 2004

domains Ξ_1, Ξ_2, ...Ξ_n of n discrete variables $X_1, X_2, \ldots X_n$, which span the space Ξ. Let $(x_1, x_2, \ldots x_n)$ be a vector in the space spanned by the variables $X_1, X_2, \ldots X_n$. Its projection onto the subspace spanned by variables $X_{j_1}, X_{j_2}, \ldots X_{j_k}$ ($j_1, j_2, \ldots j_k$ distinct indices from the set 1,2,...,n) is then the vector $(x_{j_1}, x_{j_2}, \ldots x_{j_k})$. $(x_1, x_2, \ldots x_n)$ is also called an extension of $(x_{j_1}, x_{j_2}, \ldots x_{j_k})$. A projection of a set A of such vectors is the set $A^{\downarrow X_{j_1}, X_{j_2}, \ldots X_{j_k}}$ of projections of all individual vectors from A onto $X_{j_1}, X_{j_2}, \ldots X_{j_k}$. A is also called an extension of $A^{\downarrow X_{j_1}, X_{j_2}, \ldots X_{j_k}}$. A is called the vacuous extension of $A^{\downarrow X_{j_1}, X_{j_2}, \ldots X_{j_k}}$ iff A contains all possible extensions of each individual vector in $A^{\downarrow X_{j_1}, X_{j_2}, \ldots X_{j_k}}$. The fact, that A is a vacuous extension of B onto space $X_1, X_2, \ldots X_n$ is denoted by $A = B^{\uparrow X_1, X_2, \ldots X_n}$

Definition 2. *Let m be a basic probability assignment function on the space of discernment spanned by variables $X_1, X_2, \ldots X_n$. $m^{\downarrow X_{j_1}, X_{j_2}, \ldots X_{j_k}}$ is called the projection of m onto subspace spanned by $X_{j_1}, X_{j_2}, \ldots X_{j_k}$ iff*

$$m^{\downarrow X_{j_1}, X_{j_2}, \ldots X_{j_k}}(B) = c \cdot \sum_{A; B = A^{\downarrow X_{j_1}, X_{j_2}, \ldots X_{j_k}}} m(A) \quad (c \text{ - normalizing factor})$$

Definition 3. *Let m be a basic probability assignment function on the space of discernment spanned by variables $X_{j_1}, X_{j_2}, \ldots X_{j_k}$. $m^{\uparrow X_1, X_2, \ldots X_n}$ is called the vacuous extension of m onto superspace spanned by $X_1, X_2, \ldots X_n$ iff*

$$m^{\uparrow X_1, X_2, \ldots X_n}(B^{\uparrow X_1, X_2, \ldots X_n}) = m(B)$$

and $m^{\uparrow X_1, X_2, \ldots X_n}(A) = 0$ for any other A. We say that a belief function is vacuous iff $m(\Xi) = 1$ and $m(A) = 0$ for any A different from Ξ.

Projections and vacuous extensions of *Bel*, *Pl* and *Q* functions are defined with respect to operations on m function. Notice that by convention if we want to combine by Dempster rule two belief functions not sharing the frame of discernment, we look for the closest common vacuous extension of their frames of discernment without explicitly notifying it.

Definition 4. *Let B be a subset of Ξ, called evidence, m_B be a basic probability assignment such that $m_B(B) = 1$ and $m_B(A) = 0$ for any A different from B. Then the conditional belief function $Bel(.\|B)$ representing the belief function Bel conditioned on evidence B is defined as: $Bel(.\|B) = Bel \oplus Bel_B$.*

2 Definition and Computations of DS-Theories with Separately Measurable Attributes (SMA-DST)

Generally, if we have n variables $X_1, X_2, ..., X_n$ with respective domains $\Xi_1, \Xi_2, ..., \Xi_n$, then the frame of discernment is $2^{\Xi_1 \times \Xi_2 \times ... \times \Xi_n}$. So if we have $n = 3$ variables with domain sizes $card(\Xi_i) = 4$ for each i=1,2,3, then the number of possiable focal points of a belief function defined over this space is more than 10 000 000 000 000 000. We propose a restriction of the Dempster-Shafer theory only to so called separately measurable attributes that is

Definition 5. *A belief function Bel fulfills the requirement of separately measurable variables iff its only focal points are such (nonempty) sets $A \subseteq 2^{\Xi_1 \times \Xi_2 \times \cdots \times \Xi_n}$ for which $A = A_1 \times A_2 \times \ldots \times A_n$ with $A_i \subseteq \Xi_i$ for $i = 1, \ldots, n$.*

A belief function with separately measurable attributes in the above example may possess at most 3300 focal points. Clearly this reduction dimensionality cannot be a sufficient reason to support this class of belief functions. It shall only indicate potential losses in expressive power on the one hand and the manageability gains on the other hand. Further properties of separately measurable belief functions are:

Theorem 1. *if Bel is a separately measurable belief function in variables $X_1, \ldots, Xn$, then also $Bel^{\downarrow X_{i_1}, \ldots, X_{i_k}}$ for any set of indices $i_1, \ldots, i_k$ is also a separately measurable belief function. Any empty extension of this function is also a separately measurable belief function. If Bel_1, Bel_2 are separately measurable belief functions, then also $Bel_1 \oplus Bel_2$ is also a separately measurable belief function*

Let us define the pseudo-conditional belief function as follows [5,1]:

Definition 6. *if Bel is a belief function in variables $X_1, \ldots, Xn$, then the conditional belief function $Bel^{|X_{i_1}, \ldots, X_{i_k}}$ (Bel conditioned on $X_{i_1}, \ldots, X_{i_k}$) for any set of indices $i_1, \ldots, i_k$ is defined as any pseudo-belief function (that is a "belief" function allowing for negative masses m, however keeping Q's non-negative) fitting the following rquation:$Bel = Bel^{\downarrow X_{i_1}, \ldots, X_{i_k}} \oplus Bel^{|X_{i_1}, \ldots, X_{i_k}}$*

Theorem 2. *if Bel is a separately measurable belief function in variables $X_1, \ldots, Xn$, then for every set of indices $i_1, \ldots, i_k$ there exists always a conditional belief function $Bel^{|X_{i_1}, \ldots, X_{i_k}}$ which is also separately measurable.*

As with general type belief functions, we have:

Theorem 3. *if Bel is a separately measurable belief function in variables $X_1, \ldots, Xn$, then we can calculate any measure m, Bel, Pl, Q from any measure m, Bel, Pl, Q for focal points reusing the same storage cells for storing the target measure as used for the source measure.*

3   Algorithmic Implications

Subsequent recalculation procedures demonstrate this possibility. For calculation of Bel from m and vice-versa we use the defining equation for Bel. Theoretical foundation of algorithms recalculating between Q and Pl is given by the easily checkable formula

$$Pl(A) = (-1)^{card(A)+1}Q(A) + \sum_{j=1}^{card(A)-1} \sum_{B; B \subseteq A, card(B)=j} (-1)^{j+1}Q(B)$$

The procedure texts use C-styled syntax (as they are taken from C-implementation). SET is assumed to be a data type holding separately measurable sets. The ordering of focal points in the vector is assumed to agree with sub-set partial order (if $SET[i] \subset SET[j]$ then $i < j$)

struct DISTRIBUTION

{unsigned Space; /* number of focal points */
float *Dist; /* measures m,Bel,Pl or Q for the focal points indicated by corresponding sets Set[i] */ (depending on Type) */
SET *Set; /* focal sets ordered in accordance with subset partial ordering */
char Type ; /* 'm' - m, 'B' - Bel, 'P' - Pl, 'Q' - Q */ };

void **Type_Conversion**(struct DISTRIBUTION *v, char new_Type)/* FU: Conversion of type of representation of Dempster-Shafer distribution from m,Bel,Pl or Q to m,Bel,Pl or Q */
{switch(v− >Type)
  {case 'm': /* the original type: 'm' */
switch(new_Type) {case 'B': m_to_Bel(v); break; case 'P': m_to_Q(v); Q_to_Pl(v); break;case 'Q': m_to_Q(v); break;}break;
  case 'B': /* the original type: 'B' - Bel */
  switch(new_Type) {case 'm': Bel_to_m(v); break; case 'P': Bel_to_m(v); m_to_Q(v); Q_to_Pl(v); break; case 'Q': Bel_to_m(v); m_to_Q(v); break; }break;
  case 'P': /* the original type: 'P' - Pl */
  switch(new_Type) {case 'm': Pl_to_Q(v); Q_to_m(v); break; case 'B': Pl_to_Q(v); Q_to_m(v); m_to_Bel(v); break; case 'Q': Pl_to_Q(v); break;
}break;
  case 'Q': /* the original type: 'Q' - Q */
  switch(new_Type) {case 'm': Q_to_m(v); break; case 'B': Q_to_m(v); m_to_Bel(v); break; case 'P': Q_to_Pl(v); break; }break;
}}
void **m_to_Bel**(struct DISTRIBUTION *v) /* Conversion from m to Bel */
{int j,k; float sum;
  for (j=v− >space-1;j≥0;j−)
  {for (sum = 0,k=j-1; k≥0; k−)
    if (v− >Set[k] ⊆v− >Set[j]) then sum += v− >Dist[k];
    v− >Dist[j]+=sum;
  }
  v− >Type = 'B'; }
void **Bel_to_m**(struct DISTRIBUTION *v) /* Conversion from Bel to m */
{int j,k; float sum;
  for (j=0; j <v− >space;j++)
  {for (sum = 0,k=j-1; k≥0; k−)
    if (v− >Set[k] ⊆v− >Set[j]) then sum += v− >Dist[k];
    v− >Dist[j]-=sum;
  }
  v− >Type = 'm'; }

```
void m_to_Q(struct DISTRIBUTION *v) /* Conversion from m to Q */
{int j,k; float sum;
  for (j=0; j<v− >space;j++)
  {for (sum = 0,k=j+1; k<v− >space;k++)
     if (v− >Set[j] ⊆v− >Set[k]) then sum += v− >Dist[k];
   v− >Dist[j]+=sum;
  }
  v− >Type = 'Q'; }
void Q_to_m(struct DISTRIBUTION v) /* Conversion from Q to m */
{int j,k; float sum;
  for (j=v− >space-1;j≥0;j−)
  {for (sum = 0,k=j+1; k<v.space;k++)
     if (v.Set[j] ⊆v.Set[k]) then sum += v.Dist[k];
   v.Dist[j]-=sum;
  }
  v.Type = 'm'; }
void Pl_to_Q(struct DISTRIBUTION *v) /* Conversion from Pl to Q. */
{int j,k;
  for (j=0; j<v− >space;j++)
    for (k=j+1; k<v− >Space;k++)
     if (v.Set[j] ⊆v.Set[k]) then v− >Dist[k]-= v− >Dist[j];
  for (j=0; j<v− >Space;j++)
   if ( v− >Dist[j]<0.) then v− >Dist[j]= -v− >Dist[j];
  v− >Type = 'Q'; }
void Q_to_Pl(struct DISTRIBUTION *v)
/* Conversion from Q to Pl. */
{int j,k;
  for (j=0; j<v− >space;j++)
    for (k=j+1; k<v− >Space;k++)
     if (v.Set[j] ⊆v.Set[k]) then v− >Dist[k]-= v− >Dist[j];
  for (j=0; j<v− >Space;j++)
   if ( v− >Dist[j]<0.) then v− >Dist[j]= -v− >Dist[j];
  v− >Type = 'P'; }
```

These algorithms have also an immediate impact on calculations of DST belief combination. DST combination is easily expressed in terms of multiplication of Q measures. Hence an efficient transformation of m to Q and back radically improves the efficiency of DST rule of evidence combination.

Let us now briefly mention what we are loosing when restricting the category of belief functions under consideration. We cannot express information depending on some logical relationship between attributes. We may have attributes SEX with domain {male, female} and a medical index PARAM with domain {low, normal, high}. If we measure a physical attribute related to this index then it may turn out that this value lies within a range ust too low for a male but normal for a woman (e.g. some red blood cell count). If we happen not to know the sex of patient under consideration, we may express this information in a general-type DST as m({(male,low),(female,normal)})=1. No expression for this exists within the class of separately measured belief functions. However, we shall demonstrate subsequently that the assumption of separate measurability is implicit in many techniques for handling belief functions.

4   Justification of SMA-DST

One of the well known methods for propagation of uncertainty for the Dempster-Shafer Theory is the method of local computations developed by Shenoy and Shafer [4]. A pre-requisite for application of this method is existence of decomposition (factorization) of a joint belief function Bel in n variables into a "product" $Bel = Bel_1 \oplus Bel_2 \oplus \ldots \oplus Bel_k$ such that each component function is in a radically smaller number of variables. Such a factorization may be imagined as a decomposition along a hypergraph. Essentially, the method consists of two stages.

1. transformation of the hypergraph into a hypertree (or a Markov tree) representation
2. propagation of uncertainty along this hypertree for a given set of observations

It is due to the fact that stage one does not need to be re-run for new observations that the method is considered as highly efficient. But if we study carefully the paper [4] then we see immediately that the form of observations is really limited. In fact, only *separately measurable* belief functions are allowed, because the complex fact mentioned at the end of the previous section {(male,low),(female,normal)} would require (possibly radical) change of hypertree structure before a correct propagation of uncertainty can be done.

Still another justification of separate measurability may be derived from relationship between empty extension and statistical independence [5]. As stated in that monograph, empty extensions are equivalent to statistical independence only for SMA-DST.

References

1. Kłopotek, M.A., Wierzchoń, S.T.: Conditional Belief Functions versus Proper Belief Functions. In: Rutkowski, L., Kacprzyk, J., (Eds.): *Neural Networks and Soft Computing.* Springer-Verlag 2003, ISBN 3-7908-0005-8, pp. 614-619
2. Kłopotek, M.A., Wierzchoń, S.T.: In search for new applications of evidence theory. Zeszyty Naukowe AP - Studia Informatica. Nr1, 2003, pp. 27-36
3. Shafer, G.: *A Mathematical Theory of Evidence.* Princeton University Press, Princeton, 1976
4. Shenoy, P.P., Shafer, G.: Axioms for probability and belief-function propagation. In: Shachter R.D., Levitt T.S., Kanal L.N., Lemmer J.F. (eds): Uncertainty in Artificial Intelligence 4, Elsevier Science Publishers B.V. (North Holland), 1990,
5. S.T.Wierzchoń, M.A.Kłopotek: Evidential Reasoning. An Interpretative Investigation. Wydawnictwo Akademii Podlaskiej, Siedlce, 2002 PL ISSN 0860-2719.

A Computer Based System Supporting Analysis of Cooperative Strategies

Lech Kruś

Systems Research Institute, Polish Academy of Sciences
Newelska 6, 01-447 Warsaw, krus@ibspan.waw.pl

Abstract. The paper deals with ideas of decision support with use of computer based systems. A negotiation problem is considered related to joint realization of a risky innovative project by two parties. The utility function approach and cooperative game concepts are utilized in the decision support. An experimental system has been constructed and selected computational results are presented.

Keywords: Computer-based systems, decision support, negotiations, innovations, financial analysis

1 Introduction

This paper illustrates ideas presented by Roman Kulikowski in the plenary lecture [3]. A cooperation problem is considered related to joint realization of a research project aimed to construct a new, innovative product or a new technology. Let two parties, for example a research institute and a firm interested in the product, negotiate conditions of the project realization. The project is realized in the presence of risk. It can give a large rate of return on the invested capital if it will succeed, but there is also a risk that it can fail. The negotiation problem relates to participation of the parties in investment cost of the project as well as in expected benefits and in the risk. The parties have also to fix jointly the planned time of the project realization, the overall stream of expenditures and other conditions of the project realization. Each party has his own preferences regarding the financial reward from the project and the risk. In the paper a computer based system is considered which supports the parties in the cost-benefit-risk analysis of the project and aids the negotiation process. Attached references relate to investment analysis [10], utility function approach and its applications [1,2,4,6,8], cooperative solution concepts [9,7], ideas of decision support in negotiations [5].

2 Formulation of Cooperation Problem

A representative of a research institute and a representative of a firm called further investor discuss joint realization of a research project aimed to construct a new innovative product. The project requires resources concentrated within a

L. Rutkowski et al. (Eds.): ICAISC 2004, LNAI 3070, pp. 891–896, 2004.
© Springer-Verlag Berlin Heidelberg 2004

time period $[0, T]$ to accomplish the research activity and implement production of the product. After that a harvesting period $[T, T_1]$ is considered, when the product will be sold on the market and when a cash flow is expected. The research institute and the investor are partners in the joint venture and jointly participate in the investment expenditures. The research institute covers the cost of working time of the research team with adequate knowledge and experience as well as suitable scientific environment. The investor covers other cost. Let $q_r(t)$ and $q_i(t)$ denote stream of expenditures per time unit covered by the research institute and by the investor respectively. Then the present discounted value of investment costs covered by the research institute $I_r(T)$ and by the investor $I_i(T)$ can be calculated by:

$$I_r(T) = \int_0^T q_r(t)e^{-r_d t}dt, \qquad I_i(T) = \int_0^T q_i(t)e^{-r_d t}dt,$$

where r_d - is a discount rate.

The costs are compared to the present value of the cash flow in the harvesting period:

$$P_1(T) = \int_T^{T_1} p_1 e^{-r_a t}dt$$

where p_1 - denotes the cash flow which could be obtained in the initial time unit, r_a - represents discount and "aging" of innovative product, T_1 is given.

The project can succeed, but there is also a risk that it can fail. According to [2] a simple two scenario model is assumed to analyze the risk. The first scenario assumes that the project will be accomplished with success in the given time T. It can occur with a probability $p(T)$. The second scenario of failure can occur with the probability $1 - p(T)$. The probabilities depend on planed time of the project realization. In the paper [8] a proposal has been presented enabling calculation of the probability as a function of the accomplishment time for complex projects consisting of some number of risky operation and stages. A calculation algorithm has been proposed utilizing expert opinions about values of basic probabilities of realization of particular operations in a given time and applying the Bernoulli scheme. Having the probability $p(T)$, the expected rate of return and the expected benefit obtained from the project realization can be calculated for a given stream of investment expenditures. Let $I(T) = I_r(T) + I_i(T)$, then the rate of return will be $R^u(T) = [P_1(T) - I(T)]/I(T)$ in the case of success, and $R^d(T) = -1$ in the case of failure. Let the respective benefits be denoted by $B^u(T) = P_1(T) - I(T)$ and $B^d(T) = -I(T)$. The expected values and variances of the benefit and of the rate of return can be also calculated.

Each partner invests in the project only a part of his capital, carrying in the time also other activities. The research institute invests $I_r(T)/P_r(T)$ part of his overall capital $P_r(T)$. The investor engages $I_i(T)/P_i(T)$ part of his overall capital $P_i(T)$. The decision making problem deals with a joint selection of the planned time T and an agreement about the division of the benefit. Let us see that the benefit is a random variable and the parties can have different attitudes with respect to the risk. The methodology presented in [3] enables analysis of the problem with use of Utility Sustainable Development (U.S.D.) concept. Denote the profit division strategy by $y, 0 \le y \le 1$. It defines the part of the benefit directed to the research institute. The other part $(1-y)$ is directed to the investor. The expected rates of return and the variances can be calculated as functions of the decision variables, denoted respectively by $R_r(T, y)$ and $\sigma_r^2(T, y)$ in the case of the institute, and by $R_i(T, y)$ and $\sigma_i^2(T, y)$ in the case of investor.

According to the formula (15) in [3] the utility of the research institute

$$U_r(T, y) = \bar{I}_r R_r(T, y)(S_r(T, y))^{1-\beta_r}, \quad \bar{I}_r = P x_r^{\beta_r} = P_r \left(\frac{I_r}{P_r} \right)^{\beta_r} \quad (1)$$

can be calculated as well as the utility $U_i(T, y)$ of the investor.

In the above utility representations the quantities β_r, β_i are subjective parameters characterizing the entrepreneurship of the research institute and the investor respectively. The notion $S = 1 - \kappa * \sigma / R$ is called safety index (the quantities S, κ, R are presented in the above formulas with subscripts r or i for the research institute and the investor respectively). The safety index takes values from the interval $[0, 1]$. It represents a risk in the above utility functions and in general is different for each party. The parameter κ characterizes the fear of failure of the considered party and is subjective. In [3] the detailed explanation of the parameters can be found, as well as procedures enabling their evaluation.

Each party tries to select the decision variables, i.e. T and y, maximizing his individual utility. The opinions about the optimal decision variables are in general contradictory. We deal with a bargaining problem considered in general form in the theory of cooperative games. The set of attainable values of the utilities U_r and U_i is called further the agreement set and is denoted by $S \in R^2$. It is defined in the space of utilities of negotiating parties. The set is defined by the model relations and constraints. Particular points from the set can be obtained under the unanimous agreement of the parties. The points are compared to a given "status quo" point $d = (d_r, d_i) \in R^2$. The status quo point defines the utilities the parties can obtain when they do not decide to realize jointly the research project. It can be defined by utilities of alternative, traditional activities $U_{rT}(T)$ and $U_{iT}(T)$, so the status quo $d_r = U_{rT}(T)$, $d_i = U_{iT}(T)$. It is obvious that each of the perspective partners will decide to cooperate if the utility obtained from the joint project will be grater then from the competitive traditional activity. The problem consists in a selection of a point from the set S that could be unanimously accepted by both parties.

3   Computer Based Decision Support

A computer based system is proposed having the following three general options.

The first one supports an evaluation of the model parameters and a general analysis of the model. It is dedicated to the model analyst, who implements the model in the system, assumes values of the model parameters and introduces data to the system. The option enables analysis of output variables for assumed sequences of the decision variables, required to check a general consistence of the implemented model.

The second option supports a unilateral analysis of the decision-making problem made by each of the parties negotiating the contract. Each party can assume sequences of values for the decision variables, can assume different values for the parameters of the utility functions and check sequences of output variables. Each party makes the analysis independently, without any interaction of the other party. Using this option the optimal decision variables can also be found maximizing the utility of particular party. The optimum, useful in the analysis, can however not take into account real preferences of the other party, and in general can be hardly accepted as a consensus. The analysis should allow each of the parties to learn and understand relations among the decision and the output variables, to understand also its own preferences. After such an analysis the party will be better prepared for negotiations.

The third option enables generation of mediation proposals presenting possible results of cooperation. The proposals can be calculated on the base of solution concepts of cooperative game theory. Such a solution is considered in the theory as a function $f(\cdot)$ defining a unique point $f(\mathcal{S}, d) = \hat{U} = (\hat{U}_r, \hat{U}_i) \in \mathcal{S}, \hat{U} \geq d$, which could be jointly accepted by the parties. The pair $(\mathcal{S}, d)$ is called the bargaining problem. Nash in [9], looking for the solution which could be accepted by two parties as fair, has proposed a set of properties (called also axioms) the solution should fulfill. He has shown that there is a unique solution which is Independent on Equivalent Utility Representations, Pareto Optimal, Independent on Irrelevant Alternatives, Symmetric. The properties of the solution can not be rejected by a reasonable party. The Nash solution is defined by the function f^N: $f^N(\mathcal{S}, d) = U^N = (U_r^N, U_i^N)$, such that $U^N \geq d$, and $(U_r^N - d_r)(U_i^N - d_i) > (U_r - d_r)(U_i - d_i), \forall U = (U_r, U_i) \in \mathcal{S}$ and $U \neq U^N$.

In our case the mediation proposal based on Nash solution concept can be derived by solving the following optimization problem:

$$\max_{T,y}(u_r - d_r) \cdot (u_i - d_i), \text{ subject to the constraints:}$$

$u_r \leq U_r(T, y), u_i \leq U_i(T, y), T \geq 0, y \in [0, 1]$, where T, y are decision variables, negotiated by the parties, $U_i(T, y)$ defines investor utility. It is dependent on his expected rate of return and safety index. $U_r(T, y)$ defines utility of the research institute and also depends on his expected rate of return and safety index (see formula (1)). In this option, for assumed scenarios of input quantities and given parameters of utility functions of the parties, the system solves optimization problem mentioned above and calculates optimal values of decision variables and corresponding output variables. The results are presented as a mediation proposal for joint analysis made by the parties. The parties can modify scenarios about initial input data, obtain new mediation proposal from the system and repeat analysis. Interactive procedures are considered facilitating finding the consensus.

To make the above functions the system, in its construction, consists of modules including model representation, utility function evaluator, solver, respective data base, procedures enabling interactive sessions, graphical interface.

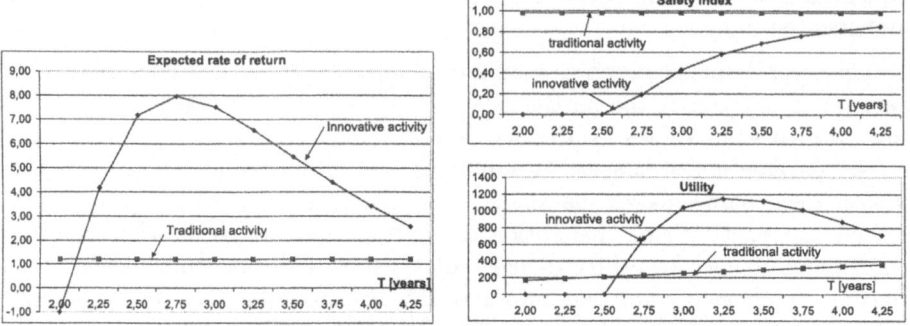

Fig. 1. Unilateral analysis made by the research institute

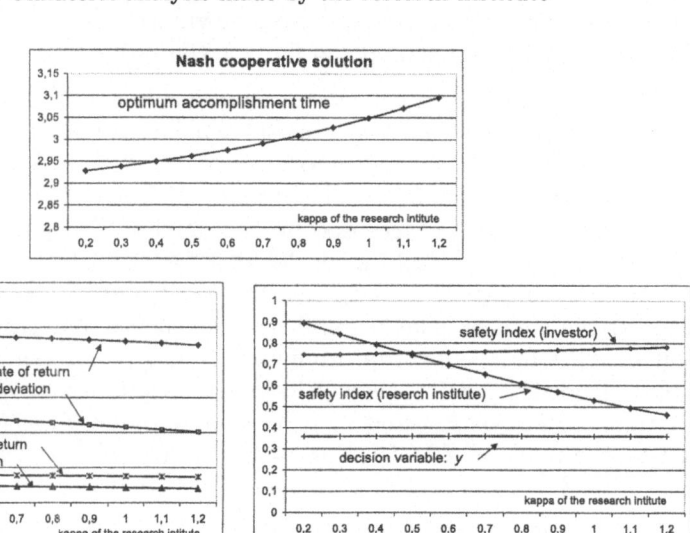

Fig. 2. Mediation proposals

An experimental version of the system has been constructed and some calculation runs have been made. Selected results are presented in figures 1, 2. Fig. 1 illustrates unilateral analysis made by the research institute representative. It includes selected quantities presented to the representative for changed accomplishment time T of the project. They were obtained for assumed investment streams $q_r(t)$ and $q_i(t)$, given decision variable y and assumed model parameters.

The representative can see how the expected rate of return, the safety index and the utility resulting from investments in the innovative project depend on the time T in comparison to a traditional activity. The increasing time T results in the increasing safety index. There is an optimal time T maximizing the utility. The similar relations can be observed in the case of the investor, however the time T maximizing his utility is in general different.

Fig. 2 illustrates mediation proposals based on Nash cooperative solution concept. They were calculated for assumed investment expenditures covered in 10%

by the research institute and 90% by the investor. The parameters $\beta_r = \beta_i = 0.5$. Selected quantities are presented by curves in the figure. They were obtained for different, changed κ_r parameter. Each point of the curves was derived by solving the optimization problem mentioned before. The increasing κ_r means that the research institute invests greater part of its liquid capital (see [3], relations 3-5) in the innovative project which is more risky than the traditional activity. Therefore the safety index decreases. The decision variable is almost the same, but the optimal accomplishment time increases so that a decrease of expected rate of return and of standard deviation is rather mild. One can also observe that the expected rate of return related to the investor is lightly decreasing. It means that according to the Nash solution an increasing risk of the research institute is partly recompensed by the investor.

4   Final Remarks

The proposed computer based system supports overall analysis of the project, supports unilateral analysis made independently by each party and enables also derivation of mediation proposals. The mediation proposals are based on cooperative solution concepts formulated in the theory of games. In the presented example the Nash solution concept has been used. The decisions and outputs related to the solution concepts are derived by solving appropriate optimization problems. The Kulikowski's concept of two factors utility has been applied to describe multicriteria goals of parties. An experimental version of such a system has been constructed and computational results have been obtained.

References

1. Coombs, C.H., et al.: Mathematical Psychology, Prentice Hall, Inc. (1970).
2. Kulikowski, R.: On General Theory of Risk Management and Decision Support Systems, Bull. of Polish Academy of Sci., Ser. Techn. **51** (2003)213–226.
3. Kulikowski R.: Support of Natural, by Artificial, Intelligence Using Utility as Behavioral Goal. Proc. of the 7th ICAISC Conference (2004)(In this volume).
4. Kulikowski, R., Kruś, L.: Support of Education Decisions in Group Decisions and Voting. Ed. J.Kacprzyk, D.Wagner. AOW EXIT, Warsaw (2003)154–168.
5. Kruś, L.: Multicriteria Decision Support in Negotiations. Control and Cybernetics, **25**(1996) 1245–1260.
6. Kruś, L.: A system Supporting Financial Analysis of an Innovation Project in the case of Two Negotiating Parties. Bull. of Polish Academy of Sci., Ser. Techn., **50** (2002) 93–108.
7. Kruś, L., Bronisz P.: Cooperative game solution concepts to a cost allocation probem. EJOR, **122** (2000) 258–271.
8. Kruś, L.: Financial Analysis of Innovative Activity. In: Modeling of Preferences and Risk '03, (T. Trzaskalik ed.) AE Katowice, Poland (2003) (In Polish)
9. Nash J.; The Bargaining Problem. Econometrica, **18** (1950) 155–162.
10. Sharpe W., G. Alexander, J. Bailey : Investments. 5th edition. Englewood Cliffs: Prentice Hall (1995).

Application of Soft Computing Techniques to Rescue Operation Planning

Jiří Kubalík, Jiří Kléma, and Miroslav Kulich

Department of Cybernetics, CTU Prague, Technicka 2,
166 27 Prague, Czech Republic
{kubalik,klema,kulich}@labe.felk.cvut.cz

Abstract. This paper presents an application of ant colony optimisation and genetic algorithm to rescue operation planning. It considers the task as the multiple travelling salesmen problem and proposes suitable heuristics in order to improve the performance of the selected techniques. Then it applies the implemented solutions to a real data. The paper concludes with comparison of the implementations and discussion on the aspects of the utilisation of the proposed heuristics.

1 Introduction

Recently, significant research initiatives have been undertaken, that specifically focus on the problem of developing systems to support search and rescue operations mainly in urban environments. The aim of these operations is activity coordination and planning for a rescue squad in case of emergencies or catastrophes in order to search for injured persons and to review of all specified places.

The main task (searching for survived persons or objects with an unknown position) is in the literature mentioned as the exploration problem: plan a tour for each squad member so that every point in the environment can be visible by at least one member. This problem can be solved in two steps. Locations for sensing (the sites, from which all points of the environment are visible) are found in the first step, followed by finding an optimal strategy how to connect these cities by m squad members. Such a problem can be restated as the Multiple Travelling Salesmen Problem (MTSP): given N cities and A agents, find an optimal tour for each agent so that every city is visited exactly once. A typical criterion to be optimized is the overall time spent by the squad (i.e., the slowest team member) during the task execution. The ability to solve the MTSP in a fast and optimal way therefore plays an important role in the rescue scenario.

During the last decade, a big number of applications of *ant colony optimisation* (ACO) and *genetic algorithms* (GA) to the combinatorial problems were published showing that the techniques are capable of solving those problems and in particular the TSP, see [6], [2].

Next section briefly introduces ACO and GA and describes implementations with heuristics designed for solving MTSP. The experiments on real data are presented in Section 3. The paper concludes with discussion on the performance of the used techniques.

L. Rutkowski et al. (Eds.): ICAISC 2004, LNAI 3070, pp. 897–902, 2004.
© Springer-Verlag Berlin Heidelberg 2004

2   Applied Soft Computing Techniques

2.1   Hybrid Genetic Algorithm

Genetic algorithms (GAs) are probabilistic search and optimisation techniques, which operate on a population of chromosomes, each representing a potential solution to the given problem [5], [6]. Each chromosome is assigned a fitness value expressing its quality. Such a population is evolved by means of reproduction and recombination operators in order to breed near optimal solutions. The evolution is running until some termination-condition is fulfilled and the fittest chromosome encountered during the evolution is returned as the found solution.

Representation. In our work we chose the natural path representation [6] for encoding the agents tours in the form of the linear string. This means that the tour is represented by a sequence of integer numbers, where each number represents the name of the city and the order of numbers is the order of cities in the tour. Here we consider the number of agents A to be greater than one, so the complete plan should represent A tours. This is simply ensured so that the starting city receives A copies in each legally structured chromosome.

Crossover and Mutation. We used the edge recombination crossover operator introduced in [7]. This operator is based on the fact that the links between cities represent an important information that should be transferred from parental solutions to their offspring. Thus the operator builds the offspring so that it tries to use as much of the links present in the parents as possible.

Besides the mutation involved in the crossover operation we used a mutation operator as well. The operator finds a sequence of cities within the whole plan by random and applies the inversion operation on it.

Single Tour Optimisation – STO. GAs have been shown to be powerful optimisation techniques. However when using GAs for any problem one should try to incorporate the knowledge of the problem into the GA as much as possible. In this work we use techniques for local optimisation of the plan. The single tour optimisation takes as an input the set of N cities assigned to one agent and generates the optimised tour through the cities as follows

1. Sort the cities according to their distance from the *depot* in ascending order and store them in array $C[]$. The *depot* is $C[1]$.
2. Take the first two cities (the closest to the *depot*) and make the tour

$$C[1] - - - C[2] - - - - C[3]$$

   Set the counter of used cities to $k = 3$.
   Calculate the length of the partial tour.
3. If $k == N$ then end.
4. Take the next unused city $next = C[k+1]$.
5. For all links $(C[i], C[j])$ present in the partial tour calculate the added value

$$AV = length(C[i], next) + length(C[j], next) - length(C[i], C[j])$$

6. Insert the city *next* into the tour in between cities $C[i]$ and $C[j]$), for which the added value is minimal.
7. Increment the counter k.
8. Goto step 4.

Note, that this algorithm does not guarantee finding an optimal tour through the given set of cities so the tour generated by the algorithm is accepted only if it is shorter than the original tour.

Longest Tour Shortening – LTS. The second optimisation routine used in our implementation tries to shorten the longest tour of the plan. First, it selects some city C of the longest tour by random. Then it adds the city C into all other tours using the strategy described in the algorithm above - steps 5.-6. Finally if there exist one or more tours with the node C such that they are shorter than the original longest tour, then the city C is removed from the current longest tour and is placed to the tour, which has the shortest length with the city C. Put simply, this routine tries to delegate a part of the load of the most busy agent to some other one.

Note that the changes made by the LTS routine are accepted only if they improve the whole plan. Contrary to that the *single tour optimisation* routine does not necessarily have to improve the whole plan to be accepted. Its role is to make all the individual tours shorter and possibly without crossings.

Evaluation Function. Generally the evaluation function is the only information the GA has to direct the search for promising solutions. So it has to cover all the aspects of the sought solution. In our case we are seeking the plan such that (1) the total time needed to complete all the tours is minimal and (2) all agents must be involved. For evaluation of potential solution i we used the fitness function defined as follows

$$fitness(i) = max\_tour(i) * (All\_Agents/Involved\_Agents),$$

where $max\_tour(i)$ is the length of the longest tour of the whole plan i, All_Agents is the number of agents we want to use, and $Involved\_Agents$ is the number of agents with non-zero length tour in the plan. The goal is to minimise this function. The function is designed so that if two solutions have the longest tour of the same length then the one with more agents involved have smaller fitness value. In other words, the term $All\_Agents/Involved\_Agents$ represents a penalty for each agent with zero-length tour in the plan. The term $All\_Agents/Involved\_Agents$ pushes the GA towards solutions with all agents involved.

Evolutionary Model. We used a genetic algorithm with the steady-state evolutionary model. This means that is operates on a single population. The whole population is randomly initialised first. Then the population is modified through the steps – selection of parents,cross the parents over, and applying the mutation, STO and LTS to the offspring – until the stopping criterion is fulfilled. The currently worst individual of the population is replaced by the newly generated solution in each generational cycle.

2.2   Ant Colony Optimisation

Ant algorithms are multi-agent systems in which the behavior of each single agent called ant is inspired by the behavior of real ants. The basic ant colony optimization (ACO) idea is that a large number of simple artificial agents are able to build good solutions to hard optimization problems via low-level based communications. Real ants cooperate in their search for food by depositing chemical traces (pheromones) on the floor while artificial ants cooperate by using a common memory that corresponds to the pheromone of real ants [3].

Basic implementation. The basic implementation (denoted as ACO) is based on proposals and recommendations published in [1], [3]. The problem is approached to the traditional TSP as follows: the depot is duplicated a number of times equal to the number of agents, $k = 1, ..., N + A - 1$ ants has to visit all the cities exactly once constructing a plan consisting of A tours. The next city to be visited is selected by a random propositional rule [2] based on the pheromone trails and visibility (reciprocal of the true distance) connected to the individual arcs. The pheromone trails are updated as proposed in [4]. The final plan length used to select the best ant and to update the pheromone trails has to be adjusted to MTSP task. In our implementation it is calculated as follows:

$$plan\_length(k) = max\_tour(k) + tour\_sum(k)/2 - min\_tour(k),$$

where $max\_tour(k)$ and $min\_tour(k)$ are the true lengths of the longest and shortest tours of the plan, $tour\_sum$ is the total length of all the tours. The ant has not only to minimise the longest tour but also optimise distribution of tours among agents and also the rest of the plan in order to update the pheromone trails correctly.

Heuristic Plan Optimisation. Hybrid ant colony optimization (hACO) uses *the 2-opt-heuristic*, which is often applied in TSP like tasks [1]. The heuristics generates a so called 2-optimal tour, i.e., the tour in which there is no possibility to shorten the tour by exchanging two arcs.

The second heuristic applied in hACO is *the longest tour shortening* described in Section 2.1. The resulting hybrid algorithm can be described as follows:

1. For each iteration do:
   a) For each ant $k = 1, ..., N + A - 1$ placed at different starting city generate a new plan using ACO outlined above.
   b) For each ant improve all tours using the 2-opt-heuristic.
   c) For each ant try the random LTS routine once.
   d) Select the best ant and use it to update the pheromone trails (the iteration best strategy).
2. Take the best ant over all the iterations and try the random LTS routine repeatedly until no change appears for $2 * N/A$ trials.

3   Experiments and Results

This section presents an empirical analysis of ACO and hGA. The comparisons are based on the quality of the solutions achieved after the same number of

Table 1. Comparison of ACO and GA with and without heuristics on the real data

| | 3 agents | | | 4 agents | | | 5 agents | | |
	avg best	stdev	best	avg best	stdev	best	avg best	stdev	best
GA	7300	365	6964	6859	204	6681	6341	146	6118
hGA	6962	24	**6952**	6550	65	**6413**	6117	44	**6016**
ACO	7476	79	7266	6936	61	6835	6623	150	6326
hACO	6957	16	**6952**	6545	86	**6379**	6146	72	**5970**

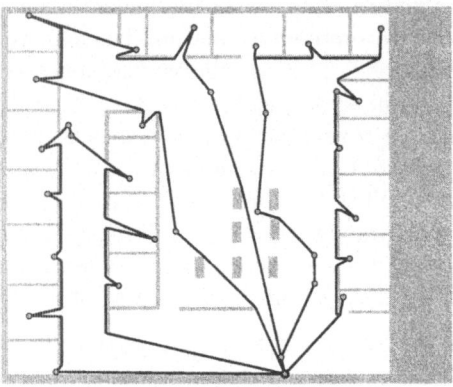

Fig. 1. The best solution found for three agents

fitness function evaluations (34000 were used here), which is a commonly used condition when comparing different techniques. Each experiment was replicated 20 times and the results were averaged.

The configuration of ACO:

- initial learning step $\alpha_i = 0.05$, linearly increased during learning up to $2 * \alpha_i$
- initial explore/exploit parameter $q_0 = 0.9$, linearly increased up to 1
- discount factor $\gamma = 0.3$
- plan evaluations: $(N + A - 1) * 1000$ (i.e., 34 000 for 3 agents etc.)

The configuration of hGA:

- population size: 1000
- selection: tournament selection with $N = 3$
- crossover operator: edge recombination operator, probability of crossover 1.0
- mutation: simple city-pair swapping mutation operator, $P_m = 10\%$
- heuristic rates: $P_{STO} = 10\%$, $P_{LTS} = 10\%$

4   Conclusions

The results show that the heuristic routines used for post-processing of the potential solutions make the GA faster at finding highly-fit plans. This is in agreement with the intuition that the heuristics represent efficient means for local tuning of the raw solutions processed by the plain GA. On the other hand the effect of the heuristics can be negative as well. The utilisation of the heuristic might cause reduction of the search space in an undesirable manner so that it makes finding an optimal solution difficult. For example the *single tour optimisation* generates for a given set of cities always the same tour. Since the heuristic is not optimal there might exist better tour for the cities, which is unreachable when the heuristic is applied. This might explain the distribution of results obtained with hGA for five agents. Out of 20 runs even 10 runs ended up at a strong attractor represented by the solution of the length 6137.

ACO shows slower convergence to a single highly-fit plan. This characteristic makes the plain ACO results worse when compared with the plain implementation of GA. On the other hand, utilisation of heuristics brings more focus into the ant colony without early reduction of the search space, which probably results in the observed minimisation of the overall time spent by the squad (hACO outputs the best plans found in the discussed task). This assumption is supported by comparison of distributions of results for hACO and hGA. Under comparable settings as reported in the previous paragraph, hACO ended up at the strong attractor 6137 only 3 times out of 20 runs. This phenomenon can be further explored by dealing with the identical heuristics for both the applied soft computing techniques in future.

Acknowledgments. This research work was supported by the Grant Agency of the Czech Republic within the project No. 102/02/0132.

References

1. Bullnheimer B., Hartl R., Strauss C.: *Applying the Ant System to the Vehicle Routing Problem.* 2nd Metaheuristic Int. Conference, Sophia-Antipolis, France, 1997.
2. Dorigo M., Gambardella L. M.: *Ant Colony System: A Cooperative Learning Approach to the Traveling Salesman Problem.* IEEE Transactions on Evolutionary Computation Vol.1, No. 1, pp. 53-66, 1997.
3. Gambardella L. M., Taillard E., Agazzi G.: *MACS-VRPTW: A Multiple Ant Colony System for Vehicle Routing Problems with Time Windows.* In Corne, Dorigo, Glover (Eds.), New Ideas in Optimization. McGraw-Hill, London, UK, pp. 63-76, 1999.
4. Gambardella L. M., Dorigo M.: *Ant-Q: A Reinforcement Learning Approach to The Traveling Salesman Problem.* Proceedings of 12th Int. Conference on Machine Learning, A. Prieditis and S. Russell (Eds.), Morgan Kaufmann, pp. 252-260, 1995.
5. Goldberg D. E.: *Genetic Algorithms in Search, Optimization, and Machine Learning.* Addison-Wesley, 1989.
6. Michalewicz Z.: *Genetic Algorithms + Data Structures = Evolution Programs.* Springer-Verlag, Berlin Heidelberg, Second edition, 1994.
7. Whitley D., Starkweather T., Fuguay D.: *Scheduling Problems and Traveling Salesman.* The Genetic Edge Recombination Operator. In Proceedings of the Third ICGA, San Mateo, CA, Morgan Kaufmann Publishers, pp. 133-140, 1989.

Reduction of Tabular Systems

Antoni Ligęza and Marcin Szpyrka

AGH University of Science and Technology, Kraków, Poland,
{ligeza,mszpyrka}@agh.edu.pl

Abstract. A tabular system takes the form of a table with columns described by attributes and rows specifying rules. Systems with non-atomic values are considered since they expressive power is much higher than the one of classical attributive decision tables. Such system can reduced to concise form through gluing of rows with similar values. Efficient reduction can lead to minimization, which can be performed with or without overlapping. The paper gives the idea of such reduction, provides two algorithms and presents some numerical results.[1]

Keywords: Tabular rule-based systems, reduction, granular systems, granular sets, granular relations

1 Introduction

Rule-based systems encoded in the form similar to attributive decision tables [Pawlak 1991] and extended to incorporate non-atomic attribute values constitute simple yet powerful knowledge specification tool, i.e. the so-called *Extended Tabular Systems* or *Extended Attributive Decision Table* [Ligęza 2001, Ligęza 2001]. The scheme of such a tabular system consists of a sequence of (distinct) attributes, say $A_1, A_2, \ldots, A_n, H$, selected as common characteristics of data items; H is the decision attribute (if present). For any attribute A_i there is defined its domain D_j, for $j = 1, 2, \ldots, n$. The basic data and knowledge representation structure is just a table with the columns labeled with the attributes and the rows specifying the rules.

In classical RDB format the data are represented in the form of the following table:

$$
\mathbf{T} =
\begin{array}{|c|c|c|c|c|c||c|}
\hline
A_1 & A_2 & \ldots & A_j & \ldots & A_n & H \\
\hline
t_{11} & t_{12} & \ldots & t_{1j} & \ldots & t_{1n} & h_1 \\
t_{21} & t_{22} & \ldots & t_{2j} & \ldots & t_{2n} & h_2 \\
\vdots & \vdots & \vdots & \vdots & \vdots & \vdots & \vdots \\
t_{m1} & t_{m2} & \ldots & t_{mj} & \ldots & t_{mn} & h_m \\
\hline
\end{array}
\tag{1}
$$

The above table $\mathbf{T}$ represents m uniformly structured rule specified with m *records*, one for each rule. In case of classical attributive decision tables each $t_{ij} \in D_j$ is an *atomic value* of the appropriate attribute. The extended tabular

[1] Research supported by KBN Research Project No 4 T11C 035 24.

L. Rutkowski et al. (Eds.): ICAISC 2004, LNAI 3070, pp. 903–908, 2004.
© Springer-Verlag Berlin Heidelberg 2004

systems allow for non-atomic values of attributes: the elements t_{ij} can be *subsets* of the attribute domains (in case of discrete nominal sets) or *intervals* in case of numbers. In fact, they can be admitted any *lattice* elements [Ligęza 2001, Ligęza 2002]. The main goal to prefer extended tabular systems with complex attribute values is that such specifications are much more concise than the ones with atomic values. In fact, a system having a large number of atomic rules can be reduced to one which is *logically equivalent*, but simultaneously having only few rules. The main goal of this paper is to discuss some two ways of reducing tabular systems.

2   An Example

For intuition, let us consider a simple tabular system with the following specification of rules.

$$\mathbf{T_1} = \begin{array}{|c|c||c|}
\hline
A_1 & A_2 & H \\
\hline
[0,1] & [2,3] & h \\
\hline
[1,2] & [0,1] & h \\
\hline
[1,2] & [1,2] & h \\
\hline
[1,2] & [2,3] & h \\
\hline
[2,3] & [0,1] & h \\
\hline
[2,3] & [1,2] & h \\
\hline
[2,3] & [2,3] & h \\
\hline
[3,4] & [0,1] & h \\
\hline
\end{array} \tag{2}$$

The above system may constitute a part of some bigger specification of a decision support system, control system or a monitoring system. Since the system incorporates non-atomic values forming in fact granules of attribute domains and granules in the Cartesian product of these domains, we shall refer to such systems as *granular* ones. For intuition, reduction of granular systems consists in gluing selected granules so that less but bigger ones are obtained.

Note that all the presented rules have the same value of the conclusion attribute, i.e. $H = h$. Obviously, the system can be reduced by *gluing* the preconditions of selected rules. Without going into details we show below some possible reduction results in a simple graphical form.

The graphical representation of the system (or, more precisely, of its preconditions) is given leftmost of the picture. The next step shows two different reduction possibilities. The rightmost forms specify the so-called *canonical forms*, i.e. equivalent representations composed from some maximal sets (in this case – rectangles) such that the projection of them on any attribute do not overlap or are identical [Ligęza 2002].

Note that both the reduced forms are results of *gluing without overlapping*; this means that two subsets can be joined only if their projection on all but one attribute are identical while the values of the one attribute are simply summed up. In case of rectangles (boxes in a multidimensional space) one can glue only adjacent rectangles (boxes). Example results for *gluing with overlapping* are given in the next picture.

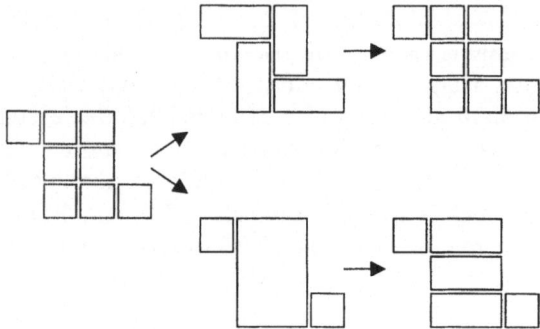

Fig. 1. Example tabular system and its reduced forms – gluing without overlapping

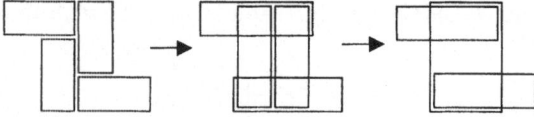

Fig. 2. Example tabular system and its reduced forms – gluing with overlapping

Note that gluing without overlapping is conceptually simpler, however the final result is not unique. Gluing with overlapping is computationally more complex, but the results may be better since less rules can be generated. In the next section some basic mathematics background for discussing reduction is provided.

3   Granular Sets, Relations, and Tables

The notion of granular sets and relations are presented in some details in [Ligęza 2002]; here only the most important ideas are outlined in brief. Consider a set V and several subsets of it, say $V_1, V_2, \ldots, V_k$. A *semi-partition* of V [Ligęza 2002] is any collection of its subsets $V_1, V_2, \ldots, V_k$. A semi-partition is normalized (in normal form) iff $V_i \cap V_j = \emptyset$ for all $i \neq j$. A semi-partition is also called an s-partition or sigma-partition (σ-partition) for short. An s-partition of V will be denoted as $\sigma(V)$. In extended tabular systems, instead of using atomic values of attribute domains, we prefer to consider the domains as granular sets, within which the elements of s-partitions are specified.

For a given set S (e.g. the domain of an attribute) a granular set over S can be defined as follows.

Definition 1 *A granular set $G(S)$ is a pair $G(S) = \{S, \sigma(S)\}$, where $\sigma(S)$ is any s-partition defined on S. If the s-partition $\sigma(V)$ is unnormalized, then the granular set is also determined as an unnormalized one.*

Granular sets can be used to analyze and manipulate certain domains with a variable degree of details. Using the idea of granular set a granular relation can be defined as follows. Consider some collection of sets $D_1, D_2, \ldots, D_n$. Let there be defined some granular sets on them, i.e. $G_1 = (D_1, \sigma_1(D_1)), G_2 = (D_2, \sigma_2(D_2)), \ldots, G_n = (D_n, \sigma_n(D_n))$.

Definition 2 *A* granular relation $R(G_1, G_2, \ldots, G_n)$ *is any set* R_G *such that* $R_G \subseteq U_G$ *where*

$$U_G = \sigma_1(D_1) \times \sigma_2(D_2) \times \ldots \times \sigma_n(D_n). \tag{3}$$

The set U_G *will be referred to as* granular universe *or* granular space.

The elements (rows) of a granular relation will be called *boxes*; in fact they constitute granules in the Cartesian product U_G. A granular relation is specified in the form of extended tabular system and it defines a kind of meta-relation, i.e. one based on sets instead of single elements. In fact, if R is a relation defined as $R \subseteq D_1 \times D_2 \times \ldots \times D_n$, then any tuple of R_G is composed of a number of finer tuples of R. And this is the basic idea behind reduction – to glue together the finer specifications.

4   Reduction of Granular Tables

Some theoretical foundations of reduction of granular tables are presented in [Ligęza 2003]. The main idea of reduction of rules is to minimize the number of rules (records, rows) while preserving logical equivalence. An interesting possibility consists in replacing some two (or a number of) rules having the same conclusions with a single equivalent rule.

Using the tabular knowledge representation, reduction takes the following form:

rule	A_1	A_2	...	A_j	...	A_n	H
r^1	t_1	t_2	...	t_{1j}	...	t_n	h
r^2	t_1	t_2	...	t_{2j}	...	t_n	h

rule	A_1	A_2	...	A_j	...	A_n	H
r	t_1	t_2	...	$t_{1j} \cup t_{2j}$	...	t_n	h

provided that $t_{1j} \cup t_{2j}$ can be found (in case of intervals, only adjacent or overlapping intervals are normally glued).

The above reduction requires that the selected rules are identical on all but one attributes. It is simple, but its application may sometimes be limited. It describes in fact the reduction without overlapping.

In a more general case the one can consider reduction with overlapping which takes the following form::

rule	A_1	A_2	...	A_j	...	A_n	H
r^1	t_1^1	t_2^1	...	t_j^1	...	t_n^1	h
r^2	t_1^2	t_2^2	...	t_j^2	...	t_n^2	h

rule	A_1	A_2	...	A_j	...	A_n	H
r	$t_1^1 \cap t_1^2$	$t_2^1 \cap t_2^2$	...	$t_j^1 \cup t_j^2$	...	$t_n^1 \cap t_n^2$	h

Of course, the operation gives some result only if all the intersections are non-empty. This operation is more general than the above gluing without overlapping; for the case $t_i^1 = t_i^2$ for all $i \neq j$ it becomes the former one.

5   Two Reduction Algorithms

Two reduction algorithms are presented below. The first one performs reduction without overlapping; the second one allows for overlapping.

```
/* Reduction without overlappig */

1.  Enumerate the rules from 1 to m.
    max:=m, i:=2.
2.  If exists rule Ri such that
    for j=1,..i-1, if exists rule Rj and gluing of Ri and Rj is possible
    then:
      - delete rules Ri and Rj,
      - insert the resulting rule as Rmax+1,
      - max:=max+1,
      - goto 4.
3.  If i=max exit.
4.  i:=i+1, go to 2.
```

```
/* Reduction with overlappig */

1.  Enumerate the rules from 1 to m, enumerate attributes from 1 to k.
    max:=m, i:=2.
2.  If does not exist rule Ri goto 10.
3.  j:=1
4.  If does not exist rule Rj goto 9.
5.  a:=1.
6.  Glue rules Ri and Rj with respect to attribute a; if empty, goto 8.
7.  Check the new rule for subsumption; if it is not subsumed, insert it
    as Rmax+1.
8.  If a<k set a:=a+1 and goto 6.
9.  If j<i-1 set j:=j+1 and goto 4.
10. If i<max set i:=i+1 and goto 2.
```

The above algorithms were implemented in Prolog [Rokita 2003] and tested on a number of examples.

6   Conclusions

Reduction is an important operation which allows for transformation of rule based systems and tabular systems to some minimal form. The proposed approach can be considered as an extension of the minimization algorithms known for reduction of combinatorial logical circuits (ones based on use of Karnaugh Tables

System	Decision	No. of rules	Non-over	Complexity	Over	Complexity
Lenses	1	4	2	179	2	3517
	2	5	2	316	2	5600
	3	15	5	1410	3	168 542
Mycology	be	12	1	1576	1	41 539
	sg	24	1	3 054	1	138 497
And-Or	0	27	8	3 790	8	380 308
	1	37	7	6 174	3	1 741 026
Iris	se	50	39	18 475	40	217 533
	ve	50	46	21 059	46	110 774
	vi	50	47	20 320	47	87 524
Mushroom	p	3916	1441	57 007 507	–	–
	e	4208	1539	64 990 577	–	–

or Quine-McCluskey approach) over attributive and first-order logic. An important feature is that the resulting system is logically equivalent to the initial one. This means that the proposed approach is safe – no over-generalization takes place. Simultaneously, one cannot expect to obtain reduction comparable to the one in case of rule induction.

References

[Ligęza 2001] Ligęza, A., I. Wojnicki and G.J. Nalepa: Tab-Trees: a CASE tool for the design of extended tabular systems. In: Proceedings of DEXA'2001, LNCS **2113** (2001) 422–431

[Ligęza 2001] Ligęza A.: Toward Logical Analysis of Tabular Rule-Based Systems. Int J of Intelligent Systems **16** (2001) 333-360

[Ligęza 2002] Ligęza A.: Granular sets and granular relations. An algebraic approach to knowledge representation and reasoning. In: M.A. Kłopotek, S.A. Wierzchoń and M. Michalewicz (Eds.) Intelligent Information Systems 2002. Advances in Soft Computing. Physica-Verlag. (2002) 331-340

[Ligęza 2003] Ligęza A.: Dual resolution for logical reduction of granular tables. In: M.A. Kłopotek, S.A. Wierzchoń and K. Trojanowski (Eds.) Intelligent Information Systems 2003. Advances in Soft Computing. Springer (2003) 363-372

[Pawlak 1991] Pawlak, Z.: Rough Sets. Theoretical Aspects of Reasoning about Data. Kluwer Academic Publishers (1991)

[Rokita 2003] Rokita, L.: Selected metods for analysis of tabular rule-based systems. M.Sc.Thesis, UST-AGH, Kraków (2003) (in Polish)

Temporal Difference Approach to Playing Give-Away Checkers

Jacek Mańdziuk and Daniel Osman

Faculty of Mathematics and Information Science, Warsaw University of Technology,
Plac Politechniki 1, 00-661 Warsaw, POLAND
mandziuk@mini.pw.edu.pl, dosman@prioris.mini.pw.edu.pl

Abstract. In this paper we examine the application of temporal difference methods in learning a linear state value function approximation
in a game of give-away checkers. Empirical results show that the TD(λ)
algorithm can be successfully used to improve playing policy quality in
this domain. Training games with strong and random opponents were
considered. Results show that learning only on negative game outcomes
improved performance of the learning player against strong opponents.

1 Introduction

The temporal difference algorithm TD(λ) [1] has been successfully used in many
games: backgammon [2], checkers [3,4], chess [5], go [6], othello [7] and other. It
was first used by A.L. Samuel in 1959 [3] but received it's name after the work
of R. Sutton [1].

In this paper we apply the TD(λ) method to the US variant of give-away
checkers (GAC). The rules of GAC [8] are exactly the same as in ordinary
checkers, the only difference between these two games is the goal. In GAC a
player that *loses* all his pieces is considered a winner. Formally a player wins if
in his turn no legal move can be made. Although computer checkers have achieved world class game play [9], there is no known GAC program able to compete
with the best human players. The game at first glance may seem trivial or at
least not interesting, however a closer look reveals that it may be even a harder
game to play than checkers. For example a simple piece disadvantage isn't a
good estimation of in-game player's performance. A player left with one king
can easily be forced to eliminate all of the opponent's pieces.

2 Value Function

In order to assign values to non-terminal states $s \in S$ the following state value
function approximation was used:

$$V(s,w) = a \cdot \tanh \left(b \cdot \sum_{k=1}^{K} \omega_k \cdot \phi_k(s) \right), \qquad a = 99,\ b = 0.027 \qquad (1)$$

L. Rutkowski et al. (Eds.): ICAISC 2004, LNAI 3070, pp. 909–914, 2004.
© Springer-Verlag Berlin Heidelberg 2004

where $\phi_1(s),\ldots,\phi_K(s)$ are state to integer mapping functions also called basis functions or the elements of a state feature vector. $w = [\omega_1,\ldots,\omega_K]^T \in \mathbb{R}^K$ is the tunable weight vector. $a = 99$ to guarantee that $V(s,w) \in (-99;+99)$ and $b = 0.027$ so that $a \cdot \tanh(b \cdot 99) \approx 99$. The $tanh(\cdot)$ function was used only for technical reasons. Besides this the value function $V(s,w)$ can be seen as a weighted sum of basis functions $\phi_i(s)$. For terminal states $s \in T$ the values of $V(s,w)$ are $+100$ for win, 0 for tie and -100 for loss for any $w \in \mathbb{R}^K$.

The value function is used to assign values to leaf nodes of a fixed-depth d-ply mini-max game search tree. After that a move is executed following the best line of play found. In this case it is said that a player follows a greedy policy because at every state always the best move according to the program is made.

3   Temporal Difference Algorithm. Learning a Policy

The TD(λ) algorithm is used to modify weights. At time t the weight update vector Δw_t is computed from the following equation:

$$\Delta w_t = \alpha \cdot \delta_t \cdot e_t \tag{2}$$

where $\alpha \in (0,1)$ is the learning step-size parameter. The second component $\delta_t = r_{t+1} + \gamma V(s_{t+1}^{(l)}, w) - V(s_t^{(l)}, w)$ represents the temporal difference in state values. r_{t+1} is the scalar reward obtained after a transition from state s_t to s_{t+1}. $\gamma \in (0;1)$ is the discount parameter. In our experiments $\gamma = 1$ and $r_t = 0$ for all t, although a small negative value of r_t could have been used in order to promote early wins. $s_t^{(l)}$ is the principal variation leaf node obtained after performing a d-ply mini-max search starting from state s_t (the state observed by the learning player at time t). In other words $V(s_t^{(l)}, w)$ is the mini-max value of state s_t or a d-step look-ahead value of s_t. The last component of equation (2) is the eligibility vector e_t updated in the following recursive equation:

$$e_0 = 0, \qquad e_{t+1} = \nabla_w V_{t+1} + (\gamma\lambda)e_t \tag{3}$$

where $\lambda \in (0,1)$ is the decay parameter. $\nabla_w V_k$ is the gradient of $V(s_k,w)$ relative to weights w. Formally the i-th element of this gradient equals:

$$(\nabla_w V_k)_i = \frac{\partial V(s_k,w)}{\partial w_i} = \phi_i(s_k) \quad i = 1,\ldots,K, \quad k = 1,2,\ldots \tag{4}$$

where K is the size of the weight vector and s_k is the state observed at time k. The eligibility vector holds the history of state features encountered. The elements of this vector (unless they are encountered again) decay exponentially according to the decay parameter λ. The features in e_t are thought to be significant while performing weight updates at time t. The eligibility vector is the main tool used by delayed reinforcement learning for assigning credit to past actions [10].

In TD(λ) weight updates are usually computed on-line after every learning player's move. However in this paper the learning player's weights are changed only after the game ends (off-line $TD(\lambda)$). This enables us to condition weight replacement with the final result of the game (win, loss or tie).

The weight vector determines the value function which in turn determines the player's policy $\pi : (S, \mathbb{R}^K) \to A$. Policy $\pi(s, w)$ is a function that for every state $s \in S$ and some weight vector $w \in \mathbb{R}^K$ maps an action $a \in A$. Thus tells the computer player which move to perform at state s. Our goal is to learn an optimal policy that maximizes the chance of a win (learning control). This is achieved indirectly by learning to predict the final outcome of being in state s.

4   Experiment Design and Results

The computer player that has his weights changed (trained) after every game by the $TD(\lambda)$ algorithm is called the learning player. There were 10 learning players each having it's own set of 25 opponents. All weights for players 1 and 6 where initialized with 0. The rest of the players had their vectors initialized with random numbers $r \in (-10.0, +10.0)$. Each of the 250 opponents also had their weight vector initialized with random numbers. All the opponent's weight vectors were pairwise different and were never changed during learning. In training game number i the learning player played against opponent $(i \bmod 25) + 1$. Players 1 to 5 always played using white pieces (they performed the first move). Players 6 to 10 played using black pieces. For every win the learning player received 1 point, for a tie 0.5 and for a loss 0 points.

The game tree search depth $d = 4$ mainly due to time limitations. The size of the weight vector $K = 22$. In games marked with LL (learn on loss) the learning player's weights were modified only in the case of its loss or tie. In games marked with LB (learn on both) the weights were modified after every game no matter the final outcome.

In order to check if the performance in the training phase really reflects policy improvement, a testing phase was introduced. In the testing phase one weight vector achieved by the learning player in some point in time is taken and used by the testing player to play against 1,000 new random opponents. These opponents were not encountered earlier by the learning players. The same set of 1,000 opponents was used in all testing phases mentioned in this paper.

4.1   Tuning α and λ

Over 300,000 initial games were played in order to observe performance with different values of parameters α and λ chosen. The results in this phase showed that applying a good pair of parameters in the right moment can substantially shorten the learning time and increase results. Finally the following scheme for decreasing α and λ was chosen: in games $1 - 2,500$: ($\alpha = 1E - 4, \lambda = 0.95$), in games $2,501 - 5,000$: ($\alpha = 2E - 5, \lambda = 0.7$), in games $5,001 - 7,500$: ($\alpha = 1E - 5, \lambda = 0.5$) and in games $7,501 - 10,000$: ($\alpha = 5E - 6, \lambda = 0.2$). All the following results are based on games played using this scheme.

Table 1. Training and test phase performance. Each result is averaged over 10 passes, one for each learning player.

(a) Training phase. Random opponents

games	LL	LB
1 - 2,500	64.9%	64.7%
2,501 - 5,000	70.5%	70.2%
5,001 - 7,500	72.0%	72.2%
7,501 - 10,000	70.8%	69.1%

(b) Training phase. Strong opponents

games	LL	LB
1 - 2,500	61.8%	52.9%
2,501 - 5,000	64.3%	54.9%
5,001 - 7,500	71.9%	51.8%
7,501 - 10,000	62.8%	52.3%

(c) Test phase. Random opponents

after game	LL	LB
7,500	70.2%	68.8%
10,000	69.8%	68.7%

(d) Test phase. Strong opponents

after game	LL	LB
7,500	72.3%	69.1%
10,000	72.9%	68.9%

4.2   Learning on 25 Random Opponents

Table 1(a) presents the results of training the learning players on 25 random opponents. It can be seen that both the LL and LB methods achieved comparable results. The highest average result (72.2%) was obtained using the LB method during games 5,001-7,500. In subsequent games the performance decreased.

Results of the learning players during training were observed after every 25 games. Performance history of the best players learning with the LL and LB methods on 25 random opponents are presented in Figs. 1(a) and 1(b), resp. The best overall result was achieved by player 9-LB some time after the 6000-th game (Fig. 1(b)) and exceeded 88% of the possible maximum. The worst overall result was a fall to 56% for player 7-LL after 10,000 games (not presented).

4.3   Learning on 25 Strong Opponents

After 10,000 games with 25 random opponents, the learning players were trained against 25 strong opponents during another 10,000 games. This time the opponents used the weight vectors of the 20 learning players trained using the LL and LB methods in the first 10,000 games. The additional 5 opponents were initialized with random weight vectors. Like before, the opponents did not change during training. This set of opponents was the same for all learning players in this phase. The results are presented in Table 1(b). This time the LL method was superior to LB one. The difference in performance was about 10 to 20 percent points in favor of LL during all the games played. The history of performance changes for the best LL and LB players is presented in Figs. 1(c) and 1(d), resp.

Results from the test phase are presented in Tables 1(c) and 1(d). They confirm the superiority of the LL method used for training with strong opponents. In this case however, unlike in the case of training with random opponents, the fall in training performance during games 7,500-10,000 was not observed. Further investigation of this phenomenon is one of our future research goals.

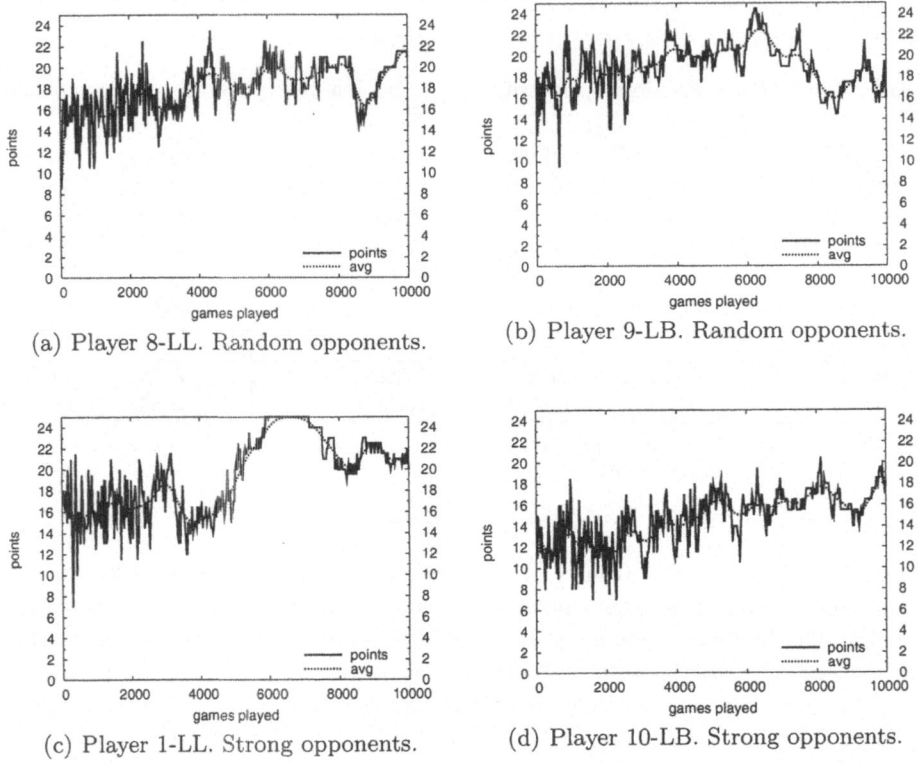

(a) Player 8-LL. Random opponents.

(b) Player 9-LB. Random opponents.

(c) Player 1-LL. Strong opponents.

(d) Player 10-LB. Strong opponents.

Fig. 1. History of performance changes for the best players in LL and LB methods playing against random and strong opponents.

5 Conclusions

A similar approach to the LL method presented in this paper was used earlier by Baxter [5]. In his chess learning program (KnightCap), there was no weight update in the case when the learning player won with a lower ranked opponent. As of our knowledge however, no one compared the LL and LB methods directly. The superiority of the LL method can be explained in the following way. A loss or a tie of the learning player means that the weight vector is not optimal and a weight update is recommended. A win however probably means only that the opponent was not good enough and a different one could have performed better. Learning on such outcomes can be misleading. The LL method showed its superiority only while learning on strong opponents. The reason behind this could be that while learning on random (weak) opponents no special care has to be taken in order to achieve good results and an ordinary TD(λ) algorithm is sufficient. Another explanation is that frequent weight updates may be desirable when playing against random opponents that share no common strategy. Frequent weight changing in this case could compensate for the superiority of LL learning.

In the experiment also a variant of LL method (called 3L) consisted in training with the same opponent for up to 3 games in a row in case of losses was introduced. The idea of 3L method was to focus more on the opponents that "with no doubt" were stronger than the learning player. This method however appeared to be inferior to LL one.

A variant of the TD(λ) algorithm called TDLeaf(λ) was proposed in [5] for applications using a game tree search. Comparing the performance of this algorithm with the results presented in this paper is one of our future goals.

References

1. Sutton, R.: Learning to predict by the method of temporal differences. Machine Learning **3** (1988) 9–44
2. Tesauro, G.: Temporal difference learning and td-gammon. Communications of the ACM **38** (1995) 58–68
3. Samuel, A.L.: Some studies in machine learning using the game of checkers. IBM Journal of Research and Development **3** (1959) 210–229
4. Schaeffer, J., Hlynka, M., Jussila, V.: Temporal difference learning applied to a high-performance game-playing program. In: International Joint Conference on Artificial Intelligence (IJCAI). (2001) 529–534
5. Baxter, J., Tridgell, A., Weaver, L.: Knightcap: A chess program that learns by combining td(lambda) with game-tree search. In: MACHINE LEARNING Proceedings of the Fifteenth International Conference (ICML '98), Madison WISCONSIN (1998) 28–36
6. Schraudolph, N.N., Dayan, P., Sejnowski, T.J.: Learning to evaluate go positions via temporal difference methods. In Baba, N., Jain, L., eds.: Computational Intelligence in Games. Volume 62. Springer Verlag, Berlin (2001)
7. Walker, S., Lister, R., Downs, T.: On self-learning patterns in the othello board game by the method of temporal differences. In: Proceedings of the 6th Australian Joint Conference on Artificial Intelligence, Melbourne, World Scientific (1993) 328–333
8. Alemanni, J.B.: Give-away checkers.
http://perso.wanadoo.fr/alemanni/give_away.html (1993)
9. Schaeffer, J., Lake, R., Lu, P., Bryant, M.: Chinook: The world man-machine checkers champion. AI Magazine **17** (1996) 21–29
10. Singh, S.P., Sutton, R.S.: Reinforcement learning with replacing eligibility traces. Machine Learning **22** (1996) 123–158

Artificial Neural Networks for Solving Double Dummy Bridge Problems

Krzysztof Mossakowski and Jacek Mańdziuk

Faculty of Mathematics and Information Science, Warsaw University of Technology,
Plac Politechniki 1, 00-661 Warsaw, POLAND
{mossakow,mandziuk}@mini.pw.edu.pl

Abstract. This paper describes the results of applying artificial neural networks to the double dummy bridge problem. Several feedforward neural networks were trained using resilient backpropagation algorithm to estimate the number of tricks to take by players NS in fully revealed contract bridge deals. Training deals were the only data presented to the networks. The best networks were able to perfectly point the number of tricks in more than one third of deals and gained about 80% accuracy when one trick error was permitted. Only in less than 5% of deals the error exceeded 2 tricks.

1 Introduction

This paper presents the first step on the way to construct a computer program playing the game of contract bridge, using artificial neural networks. The first step relies on a verification of neural networks' ability to estimate the number of tricks that can be taken by one pair of players in a deal, in assumption of optimal play of all players. The problem is simplified by revealing all hands - the so-called *double dummy problem*.

The next step in a construction of a contract bridge program, will be an estimation of a number of tricks during and after bidding. In this step only partial information about other players' hands will be available.

The most important, and also the most interesting issue in contract bridge, is a play. A game strategy, good enough to win, or to have the biggest chance to win, regardless of opponents play, should be developed. The play would be the third part of a construction of a computer program playing contract bridge.

There are many computer programs playing the game of a contract bridge, unfortunately most of them are much worse than human players. To the best of our knowledge there are only two of them that can win against strong amateur-level players: Bridge Baron [1] and GIB [2]. GIB, Ginsberg's Intelligent Bridge-player, also succeeded in playing against professionals. We are not aware of any program developed based on neural networks playing at the "decent" level.

L. Rutkowski et al. (Eds.): ICAISC 2004, LNAI 3070, pp. 915–921, 2004.
© Springer-Verlag Berlin Heidelberg 2004

2   The Data

The data used in solving double dummy bridge problems was taken from GIB Library [3], which includes 717, 102 deals with revealed all hands. Additionally the library provides a number of tricks taken by the pair NS for each deal under the assumption of a perfect play of both parties. In all experiments the attention was fixed on a number of tricks taken by a pair NS with W player defender's lead for notrump play.

The set of deals was divided into three groups. The first 500, 000 deals were assigned to training. Deals numbered from 500, 001 to 600, 000 were assigned to validation, and the rest of deals to testing. Usually the training set contained 10, 000 deals, however for some number of networks 100, 000 deals were used.

3   Neural Networks

In all experiments feed-forward networks created, trained and tested using JNNS (Java Neural Network Simulator) [4] were used. In most cases logistic (unipolar sigmoid) activation function was used for all neurons except for the case of representation of data using negative numbers, where the hyperbolic tangent (bipolar sigmoid) activation function was applied.

The number of input neurons was specified by the chosen method of deal's representation. The numbers of hidden layers and neurons varied. In most of the experiments the output layer was composed of a single neuron representing the estimated number of tricks taken by a pair NS. All networks were trained using Rprop algorithm[5], with the following choice of method's parameters: initial and maximum values of an update-value factor were equal to 0.1 and 50.0, resp., and weight decay parameter was equal to $1E - 4$.

4   Experiment Description and Results

In this section results of several experiments with various ways of coding a deal (hands' cards) and the ways of coding an estimated number of tricks to be taken are described. All results are presented in the form: $[(A \mid B \mid C), (D \mid E \mid F)]$. The first three numbers represent resp. the fractions *in percent* of training deals for which the network was mistaken by no more than 2 tricks ($A\%$), no more than 1 trick ($B\%$) and was perfectly right ($C\%$). The other three numbers indicate analogous results for testing data.

4.1   Coding a Deal

Two approaches to coding a deal as a set of real numbers suitable for neural network input representation were applied.

In the first approach each card of each hand was represented by two real numbers: the value (2, 3,..., *King*, *Ace*) and the suit (*Spades*, *Hearts*, *Diamonds*,

Table 1. Results obtained for various coding schemes and network architectures. Column denoted by D represents the number of training deals.

Network type	Results (in %)	D
(26x4)-(13x4)-1	[(94.77 | 77.45 | 31.91), (94.77 | 77.50 | 32.05)]	100,000
(26x4)-(13x4)-(7x4)-13-1	[(96.02 | 80.14 | 33.57), (93.87 | 75.70 | 31.04)]	10,000
52-1	[(94.17 | 76.22 | 31.06), (94.15 | 76.15 | 31.29)]	100,000
52-25-1	[(96.27 | 81.02 | 34.60), (95.81 | 79.95 | 34.02)]	100,000
104-1	[(94.81 | 77.62 | 32.19), (94.76 | 77.52 | 32.19)]	100,000
104-30-4-1	[(97.04 | 82.84 | 36.25), (95.64 | 79.63 | 33.74)]	100,000
104-14	[(84.76 | 63.75 | 26.72), (84.72 | 63.28 | 24.79)]	100,000
104-33-14	[(93.59 | 76.96 | 35.61), (93.58 | 76.23 | 31.82)]	100,000

Clubs). Both real numbers were calculated using a uniform linear transformation to the range $[0.1, 0.9]$ (ranges $[0, 1]$ and $[0.2, 0.8]$ were also tested, but no significant difference was noticed). Representation of each hand required 26 values, so the total number of input values was 104 (26x4). The simplest neural network, without hidden neurons - (26x4)-1, accomplished result [(75.86 | 51.63 | 18.37), (75.90 | 51.78 | 18.56)].

More complex network - (26x4)-(13x4)-(7x4)-13-1, presented in Fig. 1(a), yielded much better results: [(96.02 | 80.14 | 33.57), (93.87 | 75.70 | 31.04)]. Comparably good results were also accomplished by simpler network without the two last hidden layers, i.e. (26x4)-(13x4)-1: [(94.77 | 77.45 | 31.91), (94.77 | 77.50 | 32.05)].

In the other way of coding a deal each card had its own input neuron assigned, which input value denoted the hand containing this card. The hands were coded as follows: $N : 1.0$, $S : 0.8$, $W : -1.0$, $E : -0.8$. The following order of cards was used: $2S$ (two *Spades*), $3S$, $4S$, ..., KS (king of *Spades*), AS and so on for *Hearts*, *Diamonds* and *Clubs* (other orders were also tested, but no significant difference in results was observed). The simplest neural network without hidden neurons, i.e. 52-1 accomplished the result [(94.17 | 76.22 | 31.06), (94.15 | 76.15 | 31.29)]. Adding one hidden layer: 52-25-1 improved the result to [(96.27 | 81.02 | 34.60), (95.81 | 79.95 | 34.02)].

A slight modification of the above way of coding a deal was done by extending the input representation to 104 neurons. The first 52 input neurons represented assignment to a pair (value 1.0 for NS pair and -1.0 for WE), and the other 52 ones represented a hand in a pair (1.0 for N or W and -1.0 for S or E). The simplest network: 104-1 accomplished the result [(94.81 | 77.62 | 32.19), (94.76 | 77.52 | 32.19)], and two-hidden layer network $104 - 30 - 4 - 1$, presented in Fig. 1(b), yielded the result [(97.04 | 82.84 | 36.25), (95.64 | 79.63 | 33.74)].

4.2   The Way of Coding the Number of Tricks

The first approach to coding the number of tricks was the use of a linear transformation from integer values: $0, \ldots, 13$ to the range of real values $[0.1, 0.9]$.

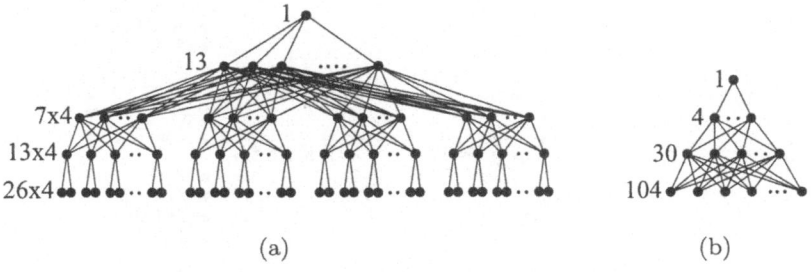

Fig. 1. Sample neural network architectures.

Alternative way of coding consisted in providing one output neuron per each possible number of tricks, i.e. a total of 14 output neurons. Here the idea was to treat the prediction problem as the type of pattern classification/clustering problem with only one output being active. During training value 1.0 was used to indicate the correct output class (number of tricks), and 0.0 (or −1.0) to represent the other (incorrect) output classes. The simplest network: 104-14 accomplished the result [(84.76 | 63.75 | 26.72), (84.72 | 63.28 | 24.79)]. Adding one hidden layer: 104-33-14 improved the results significantly to [(92.70 | 74.21 | 34.85), (92.54 | 73.74 | 29.78)] and [(93.59 | 76.96 | 35.61), (93.58 | 76.23 | 31.82)], resp. for the case of using −1.0 and 0.0 to represent incorrect outputs in the training phase.

5   Analysis of Results

The number of iterations required to learn the training set without overfitting depended mostly on the way of coding a deal. The networks with coding (26x4) needed a few tens of thousands iterations, and networks with coding by cards assignment (52 or 104) only several hundred ones.

Results obtained for various input codings and neural architectures described in section 4 are summarized in Table 1. The best results were accomplished by networks with coding a deal by card assignment, but results achieved for the other coding are only slightly worse. The conclusion drawn from the table could be, that achieving the results at the level of (96 | 80 | 34) on the testing set seems to be a difficult task. At first glance, the result of 34% of the faultless prediction may seem discouraging. However it must be emphasized, that neural networks were trained using information about deals only. Actually, no information about the rules of the play was explicitly provided. In particular, no information about some nuances of the play, e.g. finesses or squeezes was coded in the input. Only cards in hands and numbers of tricks to be taken were presented in the training data.

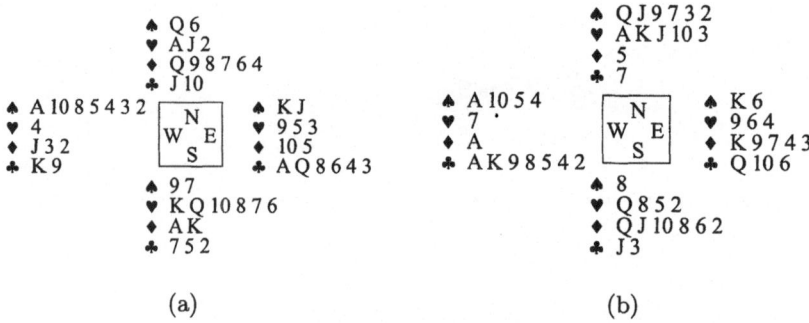

(a)   (b)

Fig. 2. Sample deals.

5.1   Simple Estimator of the Number of Tricks

To have a point of reference very simple, naive estimator of the number of tricks
was proposed. It was based on Work point count for the pair NS (ace - 4 points,
king - 3, queen - 2, jack - 1; total number of points in a deal - 40). The number of
tricks to take by NS was estimated by $(13/40) * points\_of\_NS$. This estimator
for the testing set of 100,000 deals achieved the result of (86.19 | 61.32 | 22.52).

5.2   Hand Patterns

Work point count is widely used to estimate the power of a hand, but one of
its most important drawbacks is omitting hand patterns. Short and long suits
are very important during the play. Table 2 presents medium values of standard
deviation values for hand suits' lengths. A general conclusion, which can be
drawn from this statistics is that true values of very short and very long suits
are quite difficult to be estimated by neural networks used in the experiments.

On the other hand, comparing the results of naive estimator (see Section 5.1)
with the ones presented in Table 1 indicates that the networks definitely go
beyond the naive Work point - based estimation of the hand's strength.

5.3   Sample Deals

In this section two examples of sample deals from [3] are presented - see Fig. 2.

The first deal (Fig. 2(a)) is the deal for which the number of tricks taken by
NS in notrump play can be either 12 (when N or S makes defender's lead) or
0 (when the opponent player makes the defender's lead). The network's output
was 6. Since in all data presented in the experiments W always made a defender's
lead the expected result was 0. Therefore the network highly overestimated hands
NS. Certainly the naive estimator also made a big mistake, it claimed 7 tricks
for NS. This example shows that in solving even a double dummy problem there
may be several nuances that should be carefully taken into account, e.g. defining
the hand that makes defender's lead.

Table 2. Mean values of standard deviations for hand suits' lengths (columns M) in the training set for (26x4)-(13x4)-(7x4)-13-1 network composed of 10,000 deals. Columns D represent the difference between network's output and the target number of tricks.

D	Number of deals	M	D	Number of deals	M
−4	23	1,803186	1	2303	1,379000
−3	150	1,577670	2	754	1,467983
−2	834	1,424109	3	178	1,611750
−1	2354	1,353548	4	40	1,724390
0	3357	1,318973	5	6	1,607476
			6	1	1,879716

The second sample deal (Fig. 2(b)) shows that long suits not always caused problems for trained networks. The network predicted 2 tricks for NS when W makes a defender's lead, which is a correct value. Naive estimator claimed 6 tricks for NS.

6   Conclusions

In this piece of research the underlying assumption is to reduce human's influence on neural networks to the minimum. This is the reason of avoiding special preprocessing of deals. It seems to be reasonable to present to networks information about short suits (e.g. humans add 2 points for a void and 1 point for a singleton) but authors decided to let the networks discover this information by themselves if it is really important. The difference between results of neural networks and naive estimation of hands' strengths shows, that neural networks were able to notice hand patterns as important information. However statistics presented in Table 2 show that there is still some room for improvement in this area.

Based on the assumption that only raw data is presented to the network the result of (95.81 | 79.95 | 34.02) on the test set achieved in the experiments looks promising. Only in less than 5% of deals the network was wrong by more than 2 tricks.

Several other experiments with double dummy problem are planned. First of all some other neural network architectures would be tested, e.g. Self-Organizing Maps. There is also a need to test plays other than notrump.

In the next step of research only one hand will be fully presented along with some incomplete information about other hands. This part of research will simulate bidding. The last stage will be the play phase.

References

1. Smith, S., Nau, D., Throop, T.: Computer bridge: A big win for ai planning. AI Magazine **19** (1998) 93–105
2. Ginsberg, M.: Gib: Imperfect information in a computationally challenging game. Journal of Artificial Intelligence Research **14** (2001) 303–358
3. Ginsberg, M. (http://www.cirl.uoregon.edu/ginsberg/gibresearch.html)
4. (http://www-ra.informatik.uni-tuebingen.de/software/JavaNNS/welcome_e.html)
5. Riedmiller, M., Braun, H.: A fast adaptive learning algorithm. Technical report, University Karslruhe, Germany (1992)

On Application of Ant Algorithms to Non-bifurcated Multicommodity Flow Problem

Krzysztof Walkowiak

Chair of Systems and Computer Networks, Faculty of Electronics, Wroclaw University of Technology, Wybrzeze Wyspianskiego 27, 50-370 Wroclaw, Poland
`Krzysztof.Walkowiak@pwr.wroc.pl`

Abstract. Our discussion in this article centers on the application of ant algorithms to the non-bifurcated multicommodity flow problem. We propose a general framework of ant algorithm that can be applied to the design of static flows in connection-oriented computer networks. Next, through numerical simulation, we study the influence of algorithm's parameters setting on the quality of solutions. We compare and discuss two variants of the algorithm: without and with feasible initial solution.

1 Introduction

Many computer network optimization problems are NP-complete. Therefore, heuristic algorithms are developed to solve these problems. The most substantial examples of soft-optimization algorithms are: genetic, simulated annealing, machine learning, tabu-search, neural nets and ant systems [1], [2], [5], [6], [8]. In this work we concentrate on ant algorithms, a method proposed in 1991 by Dorigo *et al.* [2], called also ant system (AS) or ant colony optimization (ACO). The AS is a simulation of agents that cooperate to solve an optimization problem by means of uncomplicated communications. The motivation comes from research on the behavior of real ants. Ants can cooperate effectively in a group to perform some tasks for the whole colony. It was observed that an ant lays some pheromone (in variable quantities) on the ground marking the path it follows. Next, ants moving toward the feeding area can detect the pheromone left by previous ants, make a decision to follow it, and reinforce the selected trail with its own pheromone. This form of indirect communication mediated by pheromone placing is called stigmergy. An additional aspect of real ants' behavior is the coupling between autocatalityc (positive feedback) mechanism and the implicit evaluation of solutions, i.e. the more ants follow a trail, the more attractive that trail becomes for being followed.

In this paper we propose two ant algorithms to solve the well-known non-bifurcated multicommodity (m.c.) flow assignment problem commonly encountered in connection-oriented (c-o) networks using techniques like Asynchronous Transfer Mode (ATM) or MultiProtocol Label Switching (MPLS) [4], [7].

The remainder of the paper is organized as follows. In Section 2 we formulate the non-bifurcated flow assignment (NBFA) problem. Section 3 includes the ant algorithm. Section 4 contains results. Last section concludes this work.

L. Rutkowski et al. (Eds.): ICAISC 2004, LNAI 3070, pp. 922–927, 2004.
© Springer-Verlag Berlin Heidelberg 2004

2 Non-bifurcated Multicommodity Flow Problem

We are given a network (G,c) where $G=(N,A)$ is a directed graph with n nodes and m arcs, $c : A \rightarrow R^+$ is a function that defines capacities of the arcs. All commodities included in a set P are numbered from 1 to p, where p is the number of all commodities. Each commodity of flow requirement Q_k must be routed from the source to the destination node through a given network. We use the link-path representation of the non-bifurcated m.c. flow denoted as vector $\underline{f}$. For each commodity $i \in P$ a set of routes $\Pi_i = \left\{ \pi_i^k : k = 1, ..., l_i \right\}$ from the source of i to the destination of i. Binary variable x_i^k indicates which route is used for commodity i. Another binary variable a_{ij}^k indicates whether or not the route π_i^k uses the arc $j \in A$. The NBFA problem is formulated as follows

$$\min_{\underline{f}} K(\underline{f}) = \sum_{j=1}^{m} f_j \tag{1}$$

subject to

$$\sum_{k=1}^{l_i} x_i^k = 1 \qquad \forall i \in P \tag{2}$$

$$x_i^k \in \{1,0\} \qquad \forall i \in P; \pi_i^k \in \Pi_i \tag{3}$$

$$f_j = \sum_{i=1}^{p} \sum_{k=1}^{l_i} a_{ij}^k x_i^k Q_i \tag{4}$$

$$f_j \leq c_j \qquad \forall j \in A \tag{5}$$

The objective (1) is the overall network flow. However, also other functions like network cost or delay can be used in the problem. Important is the capacity constraint (5), which ensures that flow cannot exceed capacity of arc.

For the sake of simplicity we introduce the following function

$$\varpi(x) = \begin{cases} 0 & for \quad x \leq 0 \\ x & for \quad x > 0 \end{cases} \tag{6}$$

Constraints in the problem tackled by the ant algorithm either must be introduced to the objective function using the penalty method or the formulation of algorithm should guarantee that all constraints are satisfied. To introduce the constraint (5) we change the objective function in the following way

$$K'(\underline{f}) = \sum_{j=1}^{m} (f_j + Pn(\varpi(f_j - c_j))^2) \tag{7}$$

The parameter Pn is a penalty factor. The algorithm should be encouraged to find feasible solutions through suitable selection of Pn. Other constraints of NBFA problem hold due to the formulation of ant algorithm presented below.

3   The Ant Algorithm for the NBFA Problem

The outline of the algorithm presented in this section was proposed in [6]. We assume that each commodity has its own ant that deposits its individual type of pheromone. Each ant possesses memory to store the route being traversed. Algorithm's iteration starts with placing each ant in its source node.

```
1  InitializePheromoneValues()
2  for n=1 to NOI do
3    for i=1 to p do InitializeAnt(i)
4    while(ExistAnts()==TRUE) do
5      for i=1 to p do
6        if (ExistAnt(i)==TRUE) then
7          MoveAnt(i)
8        end if
9      end for
10     end while
11     PheromoneUpdate()
12     DaemonActions()
13 end for
```

The main loop of the above algorithm (lines 2-13) is done for a given number of iterations. The loop 4-10 is repeated until each ant reaches its destination. Index t, used in the following as superscript, denotes the number of current iteration. Other termination criteria, like evaluation of the best-found solution can be also applied. Significant elements of the algorithm are explained below.

InitializePheromoneValues(): We consider two variants of ant algorithm. In the first algorithm - called ANB - all pheromone values are initially set to 1. In the second method - called ANBIS (ANB with Initial Solution) - also initially all pheromone values are set to 1. Then, each ant follows the path given by the feasible solution found by another algorithm. Next, we update the pheromone according to formulas given below.

MoveAnt(i): This procedure is responsible for moving of the ant through the network. The ant continues its trip across the network until it reaches the destination node. According to current state and position in the network, the ant applies its decision policy and selects next node to move to. The ant is attracted to a node of those adjacent to its current node and included in the set of allowed nodes A_i^t [5]. Let τ_{ij}^t denote amount of the i-th ant pheromone laid on the arc to the j-th node. The weight of attraction of node j for the i-th ant is as follows

$$\epsilon_{ij}^t = \frac{\tau_{ij}^t}{\sum_{j \in A_i^t} \tau_{ij}^t} \tag{8}$$

Moreover, we apply some local heuristic information η_{ij}^t of selecting node j by ant i. To find η_{ij}^t we use information on residual capacity of arcs and the distance to the destination node. Values of η_{ij}^t are normalized similarly to ϵ_{ij}^t.

The ant decision probability of selecting node j by the i-th ant is as follows

$$\gamma_{ij}^t = \frac{(\epsilon_{ij}^t)^\alpha \cdot (\eta_{ij}^t)^\beta}{\sum_{j \in A_i^t} ((\epsilon_{ij}^t)^\alpha \cdot (\eta_{ij}^t)^\beta)} \qquad (9)$$

Parameters α and β are applied to obtain a trade-off between local heuristic information and pheromone intensity. To solve the problem of loop mentioned in [5], we allow the ant to backtrack to the source node and find the shortest route using the shortest path algorithm skipping the pheromone information.

PheromoneUpdate(): If we assume that in time cycle t the ant i uses the route π_i^t, the variable L_i^t denoting the length of the ant's route is as follows

$$L_i^t = \sum_{k=1}^m a_{ik}^t (f_k + Pn(\varpi(f_k - c_k))^2) \qquad (10)$$

The pheromone information is updated after all ants complete their routes [2], [5]. Knowing each ant's route, we can calculate L_i^t according to (10) and update the pheromone according to the following formula

$$\tau_{ij}^{t+1} = \tau_{ij}^t + \frac{R}{L_i^t} \qquad (11)$$

Pheromone evaporation reduces the level of pheromone on all links by a factor ρ (evaporation coefficient) at the end of each iteration t [5].

DaemonActions(): When the ant arrives at the destination node it dies, i.e., it is removed from the system. However, memory of ant's route it transferred to the Global Daemon. Using this information the objective function and statistics are computed.

The algorithm presented above and applied to the NBFA problem differs from previous ant systems. It is a direct consequence of optimization problem considered here. The most significant characteristics of NBFA that influences the algorithm are: static and connection-oriented flow, capacity constraint.

4   Results

The objective of the simulation study is twofold. First, we want to find the best values of algorithms' parameters. Next, we plan to compare the performance of the ANB and ANBIS with other heuristics developed for the NBFA problem. Both algorithms are coded in C++. Results are obtained from simulations on 3 sample networks: 1866, 1874 and 1882. All networks have 18 nodes and 66, 74, 82 arcs, respectively. Arc's capacity is in the range from 150 to 300 BU (bandwidth units). It is assumed in the simulation that there is requirement to establish a connection for each direction of every node pair. Thus, the total number of ants in each network is 306. To evaluate performance of algorithms for growing traffic load, for each topology we consider 4 various traffic demand patterns.

To make tuning of algorithms' parameters we change for single simulation only value of one parameter while holding all other parameters constant. The tested values are similar to [2]: $Pn \in \{0, 1, 2, 5, 10, 20\}$, $R \in \{1, 100, 10000\}$, $\rho \in \{0.3, 0.5, 0.7, 0.9, 0.999\}$, $\alpha \in \{0, 0.5, 1, 5\}$, $\beta \in \{0, 1, 2, 5, 10, 20\}$. In all simulations, the number of iterations is fixed to 50. The result obtained for a particular simulation is the best result over 50 iterations. Analysis of ANB results shows that parameters Pn, R and ρ generally do not have a strong effect on the value of the objective function given by (7). In contrast, the influence of parameters α and β on the objective function is significant. The most excellent results are obtained for $\alpha \in \{0, 0.5, 1\}$, $\beta = 20$. An interesting comment, with regard to earlier work in the field of ant algorithms, is that ANB yields high-quality results for $\alpha = 0$. According to the depiction of the algorithm, setting α to 0 indicates that the pheromone is not applied and only local heuristic formula is used. It is due to the fact that local heuristic information is calculated using a complex procedure that utilizes a lot of information on the current network state. The second potential explanation is that relatively many commodities are set up between neighbor nodes. However, we verified the hypothesis by considering only routes between remote nodes (at least 3 hops) and the results were comparable.

Parameters' setting for ANIBS differs from ANB. The best results are obtained for the following values: $Pn = 0$, $R = 10000$, $\alpha \in \{1, 5\}$, $\beta = 20$. ANBIS is little affected by ρ. Recall that in ANBIS we start with a feasible solution, for which the capacity constraint is satisfied. Therefore, the penalty factor Pn, which is significant in searching for a feasible solution, is set to 0. The importance of R grows because the algorithm should stay in the feasible regions of the solution space. Comparison of ANB and ANBIS parameters' tuning indicates that the major issue in the considered problem is feasibility of results. ANB algorithm must be encouraged to search the feasible solution. ANBIS pays more attention to improving the existing feasible solution.

Table 1. Performance of ANB and ANBIS against other heuristics for network 1882

Demand	ANB	ANBIS	FDInit	FD	AlgNB
22	14388	13948	14234	14036	14014
21	13629	13314	13566	13398	13377
20	12860	12680	12680	12680	12680
19	12122	12046	12046	12046	12046

We compare results of ANB and ANBIS with results obtained for the Flow Deviation (FD) algorithm [3] and another heuristic AlgNB depicted in [7]. The FD consists of two phases: FDInit that finds a feasible starting solution and FD that tries to improve the result. It must be noted that as an initial solution in ANBIS we have used the result of FDInit. Results for 4 traffic demand patterns in network 1882 are reported in Table 1. We can see that ANBIS outperforms all other algorithms. However, the gap between ANBIS and AlgNB is only 0.25%. ANBIS yields much better results than ANB. In confirms the usefulness of starting solution. Nevertheless, ant algorithms are much slower than FD and AlgNB - the execution of ant algorithm is about 20 times longer.

5   Conclusions

In this work we have proposed and discussed a novel ant algorithm for the static non-bifurcated multicommodity flow assignment problem. Due to the fact that the considered problem differs from problems solved by ant algorithms before, it was impossible for us to re-implement existing ant system approaches. We have examined some subjects that occur in tackling the NBFA problem by ant algorithm. The key issue is tuning of the algorithm. We have noticed that some parameters influence the performance of ANB and ABNIS much more significantly than others. We have selected the best values of parameters. We have evaluated ANB and ANBIS in comparison with other heuristics. There are not many papers on the application of ant systems to the problem of static flow assignment. Most of previous works in the field of ant algorithms concentrates on dynamic routing. This work confirms that ant algorithm can be applied also to static optimization problems of c-o computer networks with objective function using additive arc metric. In future we plan to develop ant algorithms for optimization of functions using bottleneck metrics in c-o networks.

References

1. Dorigo, M., Di Caro, G., Gambardella, L.: Ant Algorithms for Discrete Optimization. Artificial Life 5(2), (1999) 137-172
2. Dorigo, M., Maniezzo, V., Colorni, A.: Positive Feedback as a Search Strategy. Technical Report No. 91-016, Politecnico di Milano, Italy (1991)
3. Fratta, L., Gerla, M., Kleinrock, L.: The Flow Deviation Method: An Approach to Store-and-Forward Communication Network Design. Networks Vol. 3. (1973) 97-133
4. Kasprzak, A.: Designing of Wide Area Networks. Wroclaw Univ. of Tech. Press, (2001) (In Polish)
5. Varela, N., Sinclair, M.: Ant Colony Optimisation for Virtual-Wavelength-Path Routing and Wavelength Allocation. In Proc. of the Congress on Evolutionary Computation (1999)
6. Walkowiak, K.: Ant Algorithms for Design of Computer Networks. In Proc. of 7th International Conference on Soft Computing MENDEL 2001, Brno (2001) 149-154
7. Walkowiak, K.: Heuristic algorithms for assignment of non-bifurcated multicommodity flows. In Proc. of Advanced Simulation of Systems ASIS, (2003) 243-248
8. Wozniak, M.: Application of the confidence measure in knowledge acquisition process. Lectures Notes In Computer Science, LNCS 2659, (2003) 635-643

A Parallel Clustering Algorithm
for Categorical Data Set*

Yong-Xian Wang[1], Zheng-Hua Wang[1], and Xiao-Mei Li[2]

[1] School of Computer, National University of Defense Technology,
410073 Changsha, China
{yongxian_wang,zhwang}@yahoo.com
[2] College of Command and Technology of Equipment,
101416 Beijing, China
lxmcjh@sohu.com

Abstract. During modeling protein structure prediction, it is a fundamental operation and often as a preprocess of in specific tasks that a very large categorical data sets are partitioned into disjoint and homogeneous clusters. The classical k-modes algorithm is a partial solution to such problems. This work presents a parallel implementation of the k-modes algorithm based on the message passing model. The proposed algorithm exploits the inherent data-parallelism in the k-means style algorithm. Tested with the amino acid data sets on a maximum of 8 nodes the algorithm has demonstrated a very good relative speedup and scaleup in the size of the data set.

1 Introduction

Clustering or grouping of similar objects is one of the most widely used procedures in data mining. Clustering algorithms have been widely studied in various fields including machine learning, neural networks and statistics. Traditionally, k-means algorithm is one of the most popular clustering algorithms based on the partition strategy. However, the main limitation to numeric data restricts its usage scope in various applications. Huang [1] proposed a k-modes algorithm which extends the clustering algorithm to categorical domains. In this paper, as our main contribution, we propose a parallel k-modes clustering algorithm on distributed memory multiprocessors, that is, on a shared-nothing parallel machine, and analytically and empirically validate our parallelization strategy. Specifically, we extend the k-modes clustering algorithm from online-update style to batch-update style and propose a parallel version based on the message-passing model of parallel computing [2,3]. Our focus is on parallelizing directly the extension version of original k-modes algorithm.

The rest of the paper is organized as follows. The sequential k-modes algorithm to categorical data is briefly discussed in Sect. 2. We carefully analyze its computational complexity and design a parallel k-modes algorithm in Sect. 3. Application to the problems of protein secondary structure prediction and its performance, speedup and

* This work is supported partially by the National Natural Science Foundation of China (NSFC) under grant: 69933030.

L. Rutkowski et al. (Eds.): ICAISC 2004, LNAI 3070, pp. 928–933, 2004.
© Springer-Verlag Berlin Heidelberg 2004

scaleup, of our parallel k-modes algorithm are demonstrated in Sect. 4. Finally Sect. 5 gives concluding remarks and future work.

2   The Classical k-Modes Algorithm

Let $\Omega_1, \Omega_2, \ldots, \Omega_d$ be d attribute sets, where $\Omega_j = \{\omega_1, \omega_2, \ldots, \omega_{\rho_j}\}$ is a finite, unordered set and $\rho_j = \mathrm{card}(\Omega_j)$ is the cardinality of set Ω_j. The attribute space is defined by $\Omega = \Omega_1 \times \Omega_2 \times \ldots \times \Omega_d$. If an object $X \in \Omega$, we call it a *categorical object*.

Given a set of n categorical objects $\Theta = \{X_i\}_{i=1}^n \subset \Omega$. To cluster these n objects into k groups, the essence of k-modes algorithm is to minimize the cost function

$$E = \frac{1}{n} \sum_{i=1}^{n} \left\{ \min_{1 \leq j \leq k} d(X_i, M_j) \right\}, \tag{1}$$

where $d(\cdot, \cdot)$ denotes the dissimilarity measure between two categorical object. The appropriate k objects $\{M_j\}_{j=1}^k$ are known as *cluster modes*. The objective of clustering Θ is to find those modes such that (1) arrives at minimal value.

As an easy-to-implement approximate solution to (1), the classical k-modes algorithm consists of the following steps:

1. Select k initial modes, one for each cluster.
2. Calculate the dissimilarities between objects and modes, and allocate each object to the cluster whose mode is the nearest to the object, if necessary.
3. Recalculate k modes of clusters in a batch-update style.
4. Repeat steps 2 and 3, until some convergence reaches.

Fig. 1(a) illustrates the details of the (sequential) k-modes algorithm above. In next section, we analyze its computational complexity in detail and propose a parallel implementation.

3   Parallel k-Modes Algorithm

The parallel k-modes algorithm proposed here is mainly based on the Single Program Multiple Data (SPMD) model using message-passing method MPI (Message Passing Interface) for computing on distributed memory multiprocessors. Table 1 gives the summary of a few MPI routines used in our parallel version of k-modes described in the following sections [2].

At first we analyze in detail the computational complexity of the sequential implementation of the k-modes algorithm in Fig. 1(a). We count each addition, multiplication, or comparison as one floating point operation (flop). From Fig. 1(a) we can estimate the computation of the sequential implementation of the k-modes algorithm as $(nkd + nd + kd\rho) \cdot \tau \cdot T^{\mathrm{flop}}$. where $\rho = \max\{\rho_j\}_{j=1}^d$ and τ denotes the number of k-modes iterations and T^{flop} denotes the time (in seconds) for a floating point operation. In this paper, we are interested in the case $n \gg k, d, \rho$. Under this condition the serial complexity of the k-modes algorithm is dominated by

$$T_1 \sim nkd \cdot \tau \cdot T^{\mathrm{flop}}. \tag{2}$$

Table 1. MPI routines used in parallel k-modes algorithm.

MPI Routine	Description
MPI_Comm_size()	returns the number of processes
MPI_Comm_rank()	returns the process identifier for the calling process
MPI_Bcast(msg,root)	broadcast msg from process root to all of the processes
MPI_Allreduce(A,B,MPI_SUM)	sums all the local copies of A in all the processes and places the result in B on all of the processes

By implementing a version of k-modes on a distributed memory machine with P processors, we hope to reduce the total computation time by nearly a factor of P. A simple, but effective, parallelization strategy is to divide the n data points into P blocks (each of size roughly n/P) and compute lines 14-22 for each of these blocks in parallel on a different processor. This is the our implementation in Fig. 1(b).

For simplicity, assume that P divides n. In Fig. 1(b), for $\mu = 0, 1, \ldots, P - 1$, we assume that the process identified by μ has access to the data subset $\{X_i : i = \mu \cdot (n/P) + 1, \ldots, (\mu + 1) \cdot (n/P)\}$. Observe that each of the P processes can carry out the "dissimilarity calculations" in parallel or asynchronously, if the modes $\{m_j\}_{j=1}^k$ are available to each process. To enable this, a local copy of the modes $\{m_j\}_{j=1}^k$ is maintained for each process. Under this parallelization strategy, each process needs to handle only k/P data points, and hence we expect the total computation time for the parallel k-modes to decrease to

$$T_P^{\text{comp}} = T_1/P \sim nkd \cdot \tau \cdot T^{\text{flop}}/P. \tag{3}$$

That is, we expect that the computational burden will be shared equally by all the P processors. However, there is also a price attached to this benefit, namely, the associated communication cost. Before each new iteration of k-modes can begin, all the P processes must communicate to recompute the modes $\{m_j\}_{j=1}^k$. This global communication (and hence synchronization) is represented by lines 25-32 of Fig. 1(b). Since, in each iteration, there are roughly $kd\rho$ "MPI_Allreduce" operator, and we can estimate the communication time for the parallel $k$modes algorithm to be

$$T_P^{\text{comm}} \sim kd\rho \cdot \tau \cdot T_P^{\text{reduce}}, \tag{4}$$

where T_P^{reduce} denotes the time (in seconds) required to "MPI_Allreduce" a floating point number on P processors.

As a conclusion, each iteration of our parallel k-modes algorithm consists of an asynchronous computation phase followed by a synchronous communication phase. Combine (3) and (4) we can estimate the computational complexity of the parallel k-modes algorithm as

$$T_P = T_P^{\text{comp}} + T_P^{\text{comm}} \sim nkd \cdot \tau \cdot T^{\text{flop}}/P + kd\rho \cdot \tau \cdot T_P^{\text{reduce}}. \tag{5}$$

It can be seen also that the relative cost for the communication phase T_P^{comm} is insignificant compared to that for the computation phase T_P^{comp}, if

$$\frac{n}{\rho} \gg \frac{P \cdot T_P^{\text{reduce}}}{T^{\text{flop}}}. \tag{6}$$

1:		1:	MPI_Comm_size()
2:		2:	μ = MPI_Comm_rank()
3:	COST = Large Number	3:	COST = Large Number
4:		4:	**if** $\mu = 0$ **then**
5:	Select initial modes $\{m_j\}_{j=1}^k$	5:	Select initial modes $\{m_j\}_{j=1}^k$
6:		6:	**end if**
7:		7:	MPI_Bcast($\{m_j\}_{j=1}^k$)
8:	**repeat**	8:	**repeat**
9:	oldCOST = COST	9:	oldCOST = COST
10:	COST' = 0	10:	COST' = 0
11:	$q_{j,l}(\omega) = 0(\omega \in \Omega_l, 1 \leq l \leq d, 1 \leq j \leq k)$	11:	$q_{j,l}(\omega) = 0(\omega \in \Omega_l, 1 \leq l \leq d, 1 \leq j \leq k)$
12:		12:	
13:	**for** $i = 1$ to n **do**	13:	**for** $i = \mu \cdot n/P + 1$ to $(\mu + 1) \cdot n/P$ **do**
14:	**for** $j = 1$ to k **do**	14:	**for** $j = 1$ to k **do**
15:	Calculate the dissimilarity $d(X_i, m_j)$	15:	Calculate the dissimilarity $d(X_i, m_j)$
16:	**end for**	16:	**end for**
17:	Find the nearest mode m_{j^*} to X_i	17:	Find the nearest mode m_{j^*} to X_i
18:	COST' = COST' + $d(X_i, m_{j^*})$	18:	COST' = COST' + $d(X_i, m_{j^*})$
19:	**for** $l = 1$ to d **do**	19:	**for** $l = 1$ to d **do**
20:	$q_{j^*,l}(X_{i,l}) = q_{j^*,l}(X_{i,l}) + 1$	20:	$q_{j^*,l}(X_{i,l}) = q_{j^*,l}(X_{i,l}) + 1$
21:	**end for**	21:	**end for**
22:	**end for**	22:	**end for**
23:		23:	
24:		24:	$q' = q$
25:	**for** $j = 1$ to k **do**	25:	**for** $j = 1$ to k **do**
26:	**for** $l = 1$ to d **do**	26:	**for** $l = 1$ to d **do**
27:		27:	**for all** $\omega \in \Omega_l$ **do**
28:		28:	MPI_Allreduce($q'_{j,l}(\omega), q_{j,l}(\omega)$, MPI_SUM)
29:		29:	**end for**
30:	$m_{j,l} = \arg\max\{q_{j,l}(\omega) : \omega \in \Omega_l\}$	30:	$m_{j,l} = \arg\max\{q_{j,l}(\omega) : \omega \in \Omega_l\}$
31:	**end for**	31:	**end for**
32:	**end for**	32:	**end for**
33:	COST = COST'	33:	MPI_Allreduce(COST', COST, MPI_SUM)
34:	**until** COST $\geq$ oldCOST	34:	**until** COST $\geq$ oldCOST
	(a)		(b)

Fig. 1. Sequential versus Parallel k-modes Algorithm. (a) Sequential version. (b) Parallel version

Since the right-hand side of the above condition is a machine constant, as the ratio of n to ρ increases, we expect the relative cost for the communication phase compared to the computation phase to progressively decrease.

4   Data Experiments and Performance Analysis

4.1   Experimental Setup

We run all of our experiments on a cluster system with a maximum of 8 Intel Pentium 4 PC nodes. The processor in each node runs at 2.5GHz with 1 gigabytes of main memory. The processors communicate with each other through Ethernet network with 100M bits of bandwidth. The implementation is in C and MPI.

In order to test the speedup and the scalability of parallel k-modes algorithm above, we design two groups of data experiment for our modeling the protein secondary structure prediction [4]. The data set used in these experiments are extracted from the PDB [5]. In clustering procedure, each protein chain is divided into lots of "fragment blocks" with a uniform length and each block is regarded as a categorical object with multiple attributes characterized by various physicochemical and biological properties of amino acids. The dissimilarity of two amino acid is derived from substitution matrix PAM250 [6]. To evaluate the performance of k-modes algorithm, in each group of our experiments, we vary the length of blocks n, the number of desired clusters k, the number of dimension d, solely and respectively, and remain other parameters fixed.

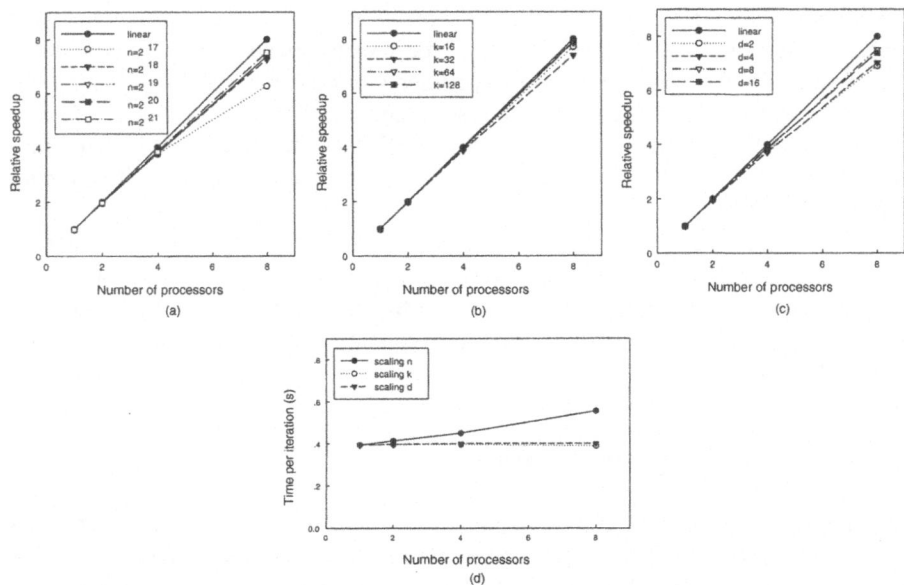

Fig. 2. Relative speedup and scaleup curves. (a) Relative speedup for $n = 2^{17}, 2^{18}, 2^{19}, 2^{20}, 2^{21}$ with fixed $k = 32$ and $d = 16$. (b) Relative speedup for $k = 16, 32, 64, 128$ with fixed $n = 2^{21}$ and $d = 16$. (c) Relative speedup for $d = 2, 4, 8, 16$ with fixed $n = 2^{21}$ and $k = 32$. (d) Scaleup for the "scaling n" curve, the value of n is scaled by the number of processors, while k and d are fixed. There is an analogy in the curves "scaling k" and "scaling d".

4.2 Speedup and Scaleup

Relative speedup is a summary of the efficiency of the parallel algorithm and scaleup mainly captures how well the parallel algorithm handles larger data sets when more processors are available. Using Eq. (2) and (5), we can write relative speedup and the relative scaleup with respect to n of the parallel k-modes algorithm roughly as following:

$$\text{Speedup} = \frac{n \cdot T^{\text{flop}}}{n \cdot T^{\text{flop}}/P + \rho \cdot T_P^{\text{reduce}}}, \tag{7}$$

$$\text{Scaleup} = \frac{nkd \cdot T^{\text{flop}}}{nPkd \cdot T^{\text{flop}}/P + kd\rho \cdot T_P^{\text{reduce}}}. \tag{8}$$

Relative scaleup with respect to either k or d can be defined analogously and we omit the details for brevity.

From (8) we can see the relative scaleup will approach the constant 1 if

$$\frac{n}{\rho} \gg \frac{T_P^{\text{reduce}}}{T^{\text{flop}}}. \tag{9}$$

It's clear that condition (6) implies condition (9), so condition (9) is more easily satisfied for large number of objects n.

We report three sets of experiments, where we vary n, k and d, respectively, to evaluate the speedup of our algorithm. In all these experiments, the ρ has been taken the fixed value 20. We also design three experiments to study the scaleup of our parallel k-modes algorithm. In all of these three data sets, the same data set with $n = 2^{18}$, $k = 16$ and $d = 2$ is used when running on 1 processor. We vary the n, k and d in proportion to the number of processors P when $P = 2, 4, 8$. The execution times per iteration are reported in Fig. 2(d).

As shown in Fig. 2, our parallel k-modes algorithm has a good size up behavior in the number of data objects. All these empirical facts are consistent with the theoretical analysis presented in the previous section; in particular, see condition (6). At the same time, the results show that our algorithm has excellent linear scaleup in k and d, but a little poorer in n.

5   Conclusions and Future Work

In this paper, we present a parallel implement of k-modes algorithm for distributed memory multiprocessors. The proposed algorithm exploits the inherent data-parallelism in the sequential k-modes algorithm and adopts the batch-updating strategy instead of on-line updating strategy like in Huang [1] in iteration. Tested with the data sets of protein the algorithm has demonstrated a very good relative speedup and scaleup in the size of the data set.

Our future work will include: (1) Our algorithm is also easily adapted to shared memory multiprocessors where all processors have access to the same memory space. (2) Another future work is to combine our k-modes algorithm with the fuzzy system together, say, fuzzy k-modes clustering approach, in our modeling for protein structure prediction. Because of the similarity between k-modes algorithm and k-means algorithm, we believe that the k-modes fuzzy clustering has similar characteristic to the fuzzy k-means clustering algorithm.

References

1. Huang, Z.: Extensions to the k-means algorithm for clustering large data sets with categorical values. Data Mining and Knowledge Discovery 2 (1998) 283–304
2. Shit, M., Otto, S., Huss-Lederman, S., Walker, D., Dongarra, J.: MPI: The Complete Reference. The MIT Press, Cambridge, Massachusetts (1998)
3. Li, X., Fang, Z.: Parallel clustering algorithms. Parallel Computing 11 (1989) 275–290
4. Wang, Y.X., Chang, H.Y., Wang, Z.H., Li, X.M.: Input selection and rule generation in Adaptive Neuro-Fuzzy Inference System for protein structure prediction. Lecture Notes in Computer Science 2690 (2003) 514–521
5. Berman, H., Westbrook, J., Feng, Z., Gilliland, G., Bhat, T., Weissig, H., Shindyalov, I., Bourne, P.: The protein data bank. Nucleic Acids Research 28 (2000) 235–242
6. Altschul, S.: A protein alignment scoring system sensitive at all evolutionary distances. Journal of Molecular Evolution 36 (1993) 290–300

Intensive versus Non-intensive Actor-Critic Reinforcement Learning Algorithms

Pawel Wawrzynski and Andrzej Pacut*

Institute of Control and Computation Engineering
Warsaw University of Technology
00–665 Warsaw, Poland
P.Wawrzynski@elka.pw.edu.pl, http://home.elka.pw.edu.pl/~pwawrzyn
A.Pacut@ia.pw.edu.pl, http://www.ia.pw.edu.pl/~pacut

Abstract. Algorithms of reinforcement learning usually employ consecutive agent's actions to construct gradients estimators to adjust agent's policy. The policy is then the result of some kind of stochastic approximation. Because of slowness of stochastic approximation, such algorithms are usually much too slow to be employed, e.g. in real-time adaptive control.

In this paper we analyze replacing the stochastic approximation with the estimation based on the entire available history of an agent-environment interaction. We design an algorithm of reinforcement learning in continuous space/action domain that is of orders of magnitude faster then the classical methods.

Keywords: Reinforcement learning, model-free control, importance sampling

1   Introduction

The most popular algorithms of reinforcement learning such as *Q-Learning* [11] and actor-critic methods [1], [10], [3] are constructed as a sequence of loops. A single loop comprises (i) observing the agent's state, (ii) suggesting an action to perform, (iii) observing the consequence of the action, (iv) performing some finite (usually very small) set of operations on algorithm's parameters. For example, if the algorithm uses a neural network, weights of the network are modified along a certain gradient. Convergence of such algorithms is then as slow as slow is the network's training. The slowness is not a problem when we think of reinforcement learning as a tool for determining the policy in simulation tasks. If, however, we think of reinforcement learning as a tool for adaptive control, the slowness becomes disturbing.

Obviously, the rationing of computational expense discussed above is not the only possible approach. In [8], Sutton introduces an architecture that is much more computationally intensive. The architecture explores the dynamics of the

---

* *Senior Member, IEEE*

L. Rutkowski et al. (Eds.): ICAISC 2004, LNAI 3070, pp. 934–941, 2004.
© Springer-Verlag Berlin Heidelberg 2004

environment to build its model. In the meantime, the model is utilized to design a policy with the use of asynchronous dynamic programming. In [5], the *prioritized sweeping* is employed to optimize such an approach.

Building the model of environment and its use with some form of dynamic programming may be satisfying in the case of finite state and action spaces. In such a setting, the resulting model can be precise. In the case of continuous environment, the precise model is usually impossible to obtain and the idea of determining the policy directly from the experience is tempting. Such the approach has already been utilized, see e.g. [4]. In this paper we follow the same direction, however a solution we provide is different.

To show our motivation, let us discuss the following problem. We are given samples $X_1, X_2, \ldots$ from some unknown scalar distribution. After each i-th sample, we are to provide an approximation m_i of the median of the distribution. One way is to employ the stochastic approximation, namely

$$m_i = m_{i-1} + \beta_i \begin{cases} -1 \text{ if } X_i < m_{i-1} \\ 1 \quad \text{if } X_i \geq m_{i-1} \end{cases}$$

where β_i is decreasing sequence which satisfies some standard conditions.

Another way is to employ a "batch" estimate, i.e. to take $\lceil i/2 \rceil$-th highest value among $X_1, \ldots, X_i$. Obviously the second way provides better approximations. It, however, requires remembering the entire history of sampling and is more computationally expensive.

In this article, we analyze a simple actor-critic algorithm [10], [3] and discuss an issue of achieving a policy as a result of direct estimation, rather then as a result of stochastic approximation. The paper is devoted to a discussion of certain concepts, while the details of derivations are left to [13].

2   An Actor-Critic Algorithm

We discuss a discounted Reinforcement Learning problem [9] with continuous (possibly multi-dimensional) states $s \in \mathcal{S}$, continuous (possibly multi-dimensional) actions $a \in \mathcal{A}$, rewards $r \in \mathbb{R}$, and discrete time $t \in \{1, 2, \ldots\}$.

2.1   Actor

At each state s, the action a is drawn from the density $\varphi(.; \theta)$. The density is parameterized by the vector $\theta \in \Theta \subset \mathbb{R}^m$ whose value is determined by parametric approximator $\widetilde{\theta}(s; \mathbf{w}_\theta)$. The approximator is parameterized by the weight vector $\mathbf{w}_\theta$. Let φ satisfy the following conditions:
a) $\varphi(a; \theta) > 0$ for $a \in \mathcal{A}, \theta \in \Theta$,
b) for every $a \in \mathcal{A}$, the mapping $\theta \mapsto \ln \varphi(a; \theta)$ is continuous and differentiable.

For example, $\varphi(a; \theta)$ may be the normal density with the mean equal to θ and a constant variance, whereas $\widetilde{\theta}(s, \mathbf{w}_\theta)$ can by a neural network. In this example, the output of the network determines a center of the distribution the action is drawn from.

For the given φ and $\widetilde{\theta}$, the discussed action selection mechanism forms a policy which depends only on $\mathbf{w}_\theta$. We denote this policy by $\pi(\mathbf{w}_\theta)$. For each fixed $\mathbf{w}_\theta$, the sequence of states $\{s_t\}$ forms a Markov chain. Suppose $\{s_t\}$ has stationary distribution $\eta(s, \mathbf{w}_\theta)$.

To determine our objective, let us define in a standard manner the value function for a generic policy π, namely $V^\pi(s) = \mathcal{E}\left(\sum_{i \geq 0} \gamma^i r_{t+1+i} \big| s_t = s; \pi\right)$. The ideal but not necessary realistic objective is to find $\mathbf{w}_\theta$ that maximizes $V^{\pi(\mathbf{w}_\theta)}(s)$ for each s. The realistic objective is to maximize the averaged value function, namely

$$\Phi(\mathbf{w}_\theta) = \int_{s \in S} V^{\pi(\mathbf{w}_\theta)}(s)\,\mathrm{d}\eta(s, \mathbf{w}_\theta).$$

2.2   Critic

In general, actor-critic algorithms employ some estimators of the gradient $\nabla\Phi(\mathbf{w}_\theta)$ to maximize $\Phi(\mathbf{w}_\theta)$. In order to construct such the estimators, we employ the approximator $\widetilde{V}(s; \mathbf{w}_V)$ of the value function $V^{\pi(\mathbf{w}_\theta)}(s)$ for the current policy. The approximator (e.g., a neural network) is parameterized by the weight vector $\mathbf{w}_V$. For the approximator $\widetilde{V}$ to be useful in policy improvement, it should minimize the mean-square error

$$\Psi(\mathbf{w}_V, \mathbf{w}_\theta) = \int_{s \in S} \left(V^{\pi(\mathbf{w}_\theta)}(s) - \widetilde{V}(s; \mathbf{w}_V)\right)^2 \mathrm{d}\eta(s, \mathbf{w}_\theta)$$

with respect to $\mathbf{w}_V$.

The action-value function $Q^\pi : S \times A \mapsto \mathbb{R}$ is typically defined as the expected value of future discounted rewards the agent may expect starting from the state s, performing the action a, and following the policy π afterwards [11], namely

$$Q^\pi(s, a) = \mathcal{E}\left(r_{t+1} + \gamma V^\pi(s_{t+1}) \big| s_t = s, a_t = a\right) \tag{1}$$

We are interested in the parameter that governs the action selection rather then the action itself. Let us define the pre-action-value function $U^\pi : S \times \Theta \mapsto \mathbb{R}$, as the expected value of future discounted rewards the agent may expect starting from the state s, performing an action drawn from the distribution characterized by the parameter θ, and following the policy π afterwards [12]:

$$U^\pi(s, \theta) = \mathcal{E}\left(r_{t+1} + \gamma V^\pi(s_{t+1}) \big| s_t = s; a_t \sim \varphi(.; \theta)\right) = \mathcal{E}_\theta Q^\pi(s, \mathbf{Y}) \tag{2}$$

where $\mathcal{E}_\theta$ denotes the expected value calculated for the random vector $\mathbf{Y}$ drawn from $\varphi(.; \theta)$. Note that by definition, $V^{\pi(\mathbf{w}_\theta)}(s) = U^{\pi(\mathbf{w}_\theta)}\left(s, \widetilde{\theta}(s; \mathbf{w}_\theta)\right)$.

Summing up, the considered problem is to find $\mathbf{w}_\theta$ that maximizes

$$\Phi(\mathbf{w}_\theta) = \int_{s \in S} U^{\pi(\mathbf{w}_\theta)}\left(s, \widetilde{\theta}(s; \mathbf{w}_\theta)\right) \mathrm{d}\eta(s, \mathbf{w}_\theta) \tag{3}$$

This in turn requires to solve the auxiliary problem of minimization of

$$\Psi(\mathbf{w}_V, \mathbf{w}_\theta) = \int\limits_{s \in S} \left(U^{\pi(\mathbf{w}_\theta)}(s, \widetilde{\theta}(s; \mathbf{w}_\theta)) - \widetilde{V}(s; \mathbf{w}_V) \right)^2 d\eta(s, \mathbf{w}_\theta) \qquad (4)$$

with respect to $\mathbf{w}_V$.

3   Two Alternative Approaches to the Problem

Both approaches we discuss are based on *policy iteration*: they alternate two steps: (i) modification of $\mathbf{w}_\theta$ to optimize the first step of each trajectory, i.e. to maximize $U^{\pi(\mathbf{w}_\theta)}(s, \widetilde{\theta}(s; \mathbf{w}_\theta))$ with $\pi(\mathbf{w}_\theta)$ fixed and (ii) improvements of the estimates of $U^{\pi(\mathbf{w}_\theta)}$.

3.1   Non-intensive Approach Based on Stochastic Approximation

An actor-critic algorithm based on the standard (*non-intensive*, as it might be called) approach comprises the following operations at consecutive t:

1. Regard s_t as drawn from $\eta(., \mathbf{w}_\theta)$. Draw the control action $a_t \sim \varphi(.; \widetilde{\theta}(s_t; \mathbf{w}_\theta))$. Observe r_{t+1} and s_{t+1}.
2. *Policy improvement.* Modify $\mathbf{w}_\theta$ along the direction of some estimator of

$$\frac{d}{d\mathbf{w}_\theta} U^\pi(s_t, \widetilde{\theta}(s_t; \mathbf{w}_\theta))$$

   for fixed $\pi = \pi(\mathbf{w}_\theta)$.
3. *Policy evaluation.* Modify $\mathbf{w}_V$ along the direction of

$$\left(v_t - \widetilde{V}(s_t; \mathbf{w}_V) \right) \frac{d\widetilde{V}(s_t, \mathbf{w}_V)}{d\mathbf{w}_V}$$

   where v_t is some ,,better" estimation of $V^{\pi(\mathbf{w}_\theta)}(s_t)$. In the simplest case, $v_t = r_{t+1} + \gamma \widetilde{V}(s_{t+1}; \mathbf{w}_V)$.

The estimator utilized in step 2. has the form

$$\frac{d\widetilde{\theta}(s; \mathbf{w}_\theta)}{d\mathbf{w}_\theta} g_t$$

where g_t is some estimator of

$$\frac{dU(s_t, \widetilde{\theta}(s_t; \mathbf{w}_\theta))}{d\widetilde{\theta}(s_t; \mathbf{w}_\theta)}$$

and U is in turn an approximation of $U^{\pi(\mathbf{w}_\theta)}$ for a fixed $\pi(\mathbf{w}_\theta)$. A way to construct the estimator g_t is known since the Williams' REINFORCE algorithm [14]. It is based on the following generic property:

$$\nabla_\theta \mathcal{E}_\theta f(\mathbf{Y}) = \mathcal{E}_\theta \left((f(\mathbf{Y}) - c) \nabla_\theta \ln \varphi(\mathbf{Y}; \theta) \right) \qquad (5)$$

where $\mathbf{Y}$ is drawn from the distribution $\varphi(.; \theta)$. The equation holds for any function f and constant c if certain liberal regularity conditions are satisfied. Why is this property so important? We draw $\mathbf{Y}$ acording to $\varphi(.; \theta)$ (i.e., perform the action a_t) and obtain the return $f(\mathbf{Y})$ (or an estimation of $Q^{\pi(\mathbf{w}_\theta)}(s_t, a_t)$). The larger is the return, the higher is the need to change the parameter θ to make generating of this $\mathbf{Y}$ more plausible. Equation (5) states that in order to maximize $\mathcal{E}_\theta f(\mathbf{Y})$, θ should be adjusted along the direction of $(f(\mathbf{Y}) - c)\nabla_\theta \ln \varphi(\mathbf{Y}; \theta)$. An implementation in reinforcement learning is straightforward: the larger is the estimate of $Q^{\pi(\mathbf{w}_\theta)}(s_t, a_t)$, the larger should be the change of $\widetilde{\theta}(s_t; \mathbf{w}_\theta)$ to make the action a_t more plausible. The g_t estimator should be then something like

$$(Q(s_t, a_t) - c(s_t))\nabla \ln \varphi(a_t; \widetilde{\theta}(s_t; \mathbf{w}_\theta))$$

where $Q(s_t, a_t)$ is an estimator of $Q^{\pi(\mathbf{w}_\theta)}(s_t, a_t)$ and c is any function. In [12], we propose to employ:

$$g_t = (r_{t+1} + \gamma \widetilde{V}(s_{t+1}; \mathbf{w}_V) - \widetilde{V}(s_t; \mathbf{w}_V))\nabla \ln \varphi(a_t; \widetilde{\theta}(s_t; \mathbf{w}_\theta))$$

which gives a satisfying behavior.

3.2   Intensive Approach Based on Direct Estimation

An algorithm based on the alternative approach comprises two activities performed simultaneously:

1. Exploration of the environment by performing consecutive actions based on the current policy $\pi(\mathbf{w}_\theta)$.
2. Approximation of the policy iteration:
   a) *Policy evaluation.* Adjustment of $\mathbf{w}_\theta$ to maximize an estimate $\widehat{\Phi}_t(\mathbf{w}_\theta, \mathbf{w}_V)$, of $\Phi(\mathbf{w}_\theta)$ based on all events up to the current step t.
   b) *Policy improvement.* Adjustment of $\mathbf{w}_V$ to minimize an estimate $\widehat{\Psi}_t(\mathbf{w}_V, \mathbf{w}_\theta)$, of $\Psi(\mathbf{w}_V, \mathbf{w}_\theta)$ based on all events up to the current step t.

The policy employed in step 1. is the one repeatedly modified by the process 2.

Worth noting is a similarity between the above policy determination and the maximum likehood estimation. In the former, we look for the parameter that maximizes the probability of generating the available data. Here, we look for the parameters most plausible to generate the data we would like to draw.

In order to construct $\widehat{\Phi}_t(\mathbf{w}_\theta, \mathbf{w}_V)$, we treat all previous states s_i as drawn from $\eta(., \mathbf{w}_\theta)$ and replace the integral with the average value

$$\widehat{\Phi}_t(\mathbf{w}_\theta, \mathbf{w}_V) = \frac{1}{t} \sum_{i=1}^{t} \widehat{U}(s_i, \widetilde{\theta}(s_i; \mathbf{w}_\theta))$$

where $\widehat{U}$ is an estimator of $U^{\pi(\mathbf{w}_\theta)}$. The estimator utilizes $\widetilde{V}$ (otherwise the critic would be useless) and hence $\widehat{\Phi}_t$ depends also on $\mathbf{w}_V$.

In the same way we construct $\widehat{\Psi}_t$, namely

$$\widehat{\Psi}_t(\mathbf{w}_V, \mathbf{w}_\theta) = \frac{1}{t}\sum_{i=1}^{t}\widehat{e_i^2}$$

where $\widehat{e_i^2}$ is an estimator of $\left(U^{\pi(\mathbf{w}_\theta)}\left(s_i, \widetilde{\theta}(s_i; \mathbf{w}_\theta)\right) - \widetilde{V}(s_i; \mathbf{w}_V)\right)^2$.

To construct particular forms of $\widehat{U}$ and $\widehat{e_i^2}$, one must take into consideration that each action a_i has been drawn from the distribution $\varphi(.; \theta_i)$, where, in general, $\theta_i \neq \widetilde{\theta}(s_i; \mathbf{w}_\theta)$ for the current value of $\mathbf{w}_\theta$. In other words, the action has been drawn from a "wrong" distribution. The construction of the appropriate estimators may be based on importance sampling and the ideas developed by Precup *et al.* in e.g. [6], [7]. We discuss the details in [13].

4   Illustration: Cart-Pole Swing-Up

The discussion above leads to two algorithms of reinforcement learning. First, the *non-intensive* algorithm can be treated as a special version of the generic algorithm discussed in [10]. We call it Randomized Policy Optimizer (RPO). The second, the *intensive* one, is based on direct estimation and we call it the Intensive Randomized Policy Optimizer (IRPO). We discuss its implementation in more details in [13].

In this section, we briefly illustrate a behavior of RPO and IRPO algorithms used to control the Cart-Pole Swing-Up [2], which is a modification of the *inverted pendulum* frequently used as a benchmark for reinforcement learning algorithms. The control objective is to, by moving cart, swing up the pendulum attached to the cart and stabilize it upwards.

The algorithms employed by Doya [2] utilize the exact model of the plants dynamics. They control the plant sufficiently well after 700 trails.

The learning curves for our algorithms are presented in Fig. 1. The RPO algorithm, a simple model-free actor-critic algorithm learns a good behavior

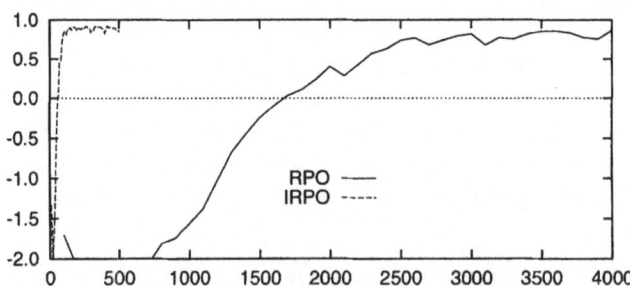

Fig. 1. RPO and IRPO applied to the Cart-Pole Swing-Up: The average reinforcement as a function of the trail number. Each point averages the reinforcements in 10 consecutive trails and each curve averages 10 runs (IRPO) or 100 runs (RPO).

after about 3000 trails (see [12] for details of its implementation). The IRPO achieves a satisfying behavious after about 100 trails (see [13]), which makes about 15 minutes of the real time of the plant. Our algorithms do not use the Cart-Pole Swing-Up model and yet RPO behavior is comparable to the one obtained in [2] with the model, while IRPO behaves better then model-based technique. Furthermore, IRPO performs all the computation in the real time of the plant; the entire process of learning lasts for about 15 minutes.

5   Conclusions and Further Work

We replaced the stochastic approximation in actor-critic algorithms with estimation based on the entire available history of actor-environment interactions. The resulting algorithm of reinforcement learning in continuous space of states and actions seems to be powerful enough to be used in adaptive control tasks in real time. The algorithm does not use nor build a model of the environment.

Most algorithms of reinforcement learning suppress the randomization as the learning continues. This is of course also possible for the IRPO. Extension of the presented methodology that incorporates a decreasing exploration is a topic of our current research.

References

1. A. G. Barto, R. S. Sutton, and C. W. Anderson, "Neuronlike Adaptive Elements That Can Learn Difficult Learning Control Problems, " *IEEE Trans. Syst., Man, Cybern.*, vol. SMC-13, pp. 834-846, Sept.-Oct. 1983.
2. K. Doya, "Reinforcemente learning in continuous time and space," *Neural Computation,* 12:243-269, 2000.
3. V. R. Konda and J. N. Tsitsiklis, "Actor-Critic Algorithms," *SIAM Journal on Control and Optimization,* Vol. 42, No. 4, pp. 1143-1166, 2003.
4. M. G. Lagoudakis and R. Paar, "Model-free least-squares policy iteration," *Advances in Neural Information Processing Systems,* volume 14, 2002.
5. A. W. Moore and C. G. Atkeson, "Prioritized Sweeping: Reinforcement Learning with Less Data and Less Real Time," *Machine Learning,* Vol. 13, October, 1993.
6. D. Precup, R. S. Sutton, S. Singh, "Eligibility Traces for Off-Policy Policy Evaluation," *Proceedings of the 17th International Conference on Machine Learning,* Morgan Kaufmann, 2000.
7. D. Precup, R. S. Sutton, S. Dasgupta, "Off-policy temporal-difference learning with function approximation," *Proceedings of the Eighteenth International Conference on Machine Learning,* 2001.
8. R. S. Sutton, "Integrated Architectures For Learning, Planning, and Reacting Based on Approximating Dynamic Programming," *Proceedings of the Seventh Int. Conf. on Machine Learning,* pp. 216-224, Morgan Kaufmann, 1990.
9. R. S. Sutton, A. G. Barto, *Reinforcement Learning: An Introduction,* MIT Press, Cambridge, MA, 1998.
10. R. S. Sutton, D. McAllester, S. Singh, and Y. Mansour, "Policy Gradient Methods for Reinforcement Learning with Function Approximation," *Advances in Information Processing Systems 12,* pp. 1057-1063, MIT Press, 2000.

11. C. Watkins and P. Dayan, "Q-Learning," *Machine Learning*, vol. 8, pp. 279-292, 1992.
12. P. Wawrzynski, A. Pacut, "A simple actor-critic algorithm for continuous environments," submitted for publication, available at http://home.elka.pw.edu.pl/~pwawrzyn, 2003.
13. P. Wawrzynski, A. Pacut, "Model-free off-policy reinforcement learning in continuous environment," submitted for publication, available at http://home.elka.pw.edu.pl/~pwawrzyn, 2004.
14. R. Williams, "Simple statistical gradient following algorithms for connectionist reinforcement learning," *Machine Learning*, 8:299-256, 1992.

Virtual Modeling and Optimal Design of Intelligent Micro-accelerometers

Slawomir Wiak[1], Andrzej Cader[2], Pawel Drzymala[3], and Henryk Welfle[4]

[1] Institute of Mechatronics and Information Systems,
Technical University of Lodz,
90-924 Lodz, ul. Stefanowskiego 18/22
and Academy of Humanities and Economics,
Rewolucji 1905 r. 64, 90-222 Lodz, Poland
wiakslaw@p.lodz.pl
[2] Academy of Humanities and Economics,
Rewolucji 1905 r. 64, 90-222 Lodz, Poland
acader@wshe.lodz.pl
[3] Institute of Mechatronics and Information Systems,
Technical University of Lodz,
90-924 Lodz, ul. Stefanowskiego 18/22
pdrzymal@p.lodz.pl
[4] Institute of Mechatronics and Information Systems,
Technical University of Lodz,
90-924 Lodz, ul. Stefanowskiego 18/22
welfle@p.lodz.pl3

Abstract. Recently, we observe rapid growth of methodologies and their applications in creating 3D virtual object structures. The aim of this paper is to carry out the solid modeling ensures better flexibility of the software in creating the 3D structures of intelligent Micro-ElectroMechanical (MEMS). This paper deals with modelling of 3D structure of surface micromachined accelerometers. Keeping knowledge about predefined accelerometer structure we start optimisa-tion procedure exploiting deterministic optimisation technique.

1 Introduction

The aim of this paper is to carry out the comparative study of two commonly used techniques exploited in building 3-D structures of virtual objects. The most sophisti-cated CAD software could offer two following methods of building up 3D geometry of the object, generating the data files (proposed by authors the block diagram of creating the 3D structures by use of two technologies - see Fig. 1):

- Solid Modeling - which uses geometric simple (even primitive) volumes and Boolean operations to construct the model. Solid modeling allows generating, assembling and editing any defined objects through operations such as transformations and combinations. Basic objects (blocks, cylinders, discs, spheres, cones, pyramids and toroids) can be created at any position in the

L. Rutkowski et al. (Eds.): ICAISC 2004, LNAI 3070, pp. 942–947, 2004.
© Springer-Verlag Berlin Heidelberg 2004

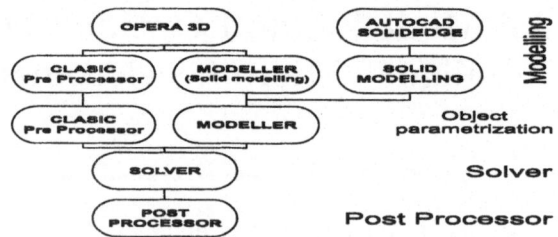

Fig. 1. Block diagram of CAD packages

space. These objects can also be merged, intersected or subtracted from other objects in space to create more complex geometry.

– Classical preprocessor - which uses extrusion from 2D cross-section (predefined the base plane) into 3rd dimension. In the pre processor, there is the concept of a base plane , which can be created using general polygons in the predefined coordinate system (Oxy, Oyz or Oxz). The plane object geometry, on the base plane, is then extruded to form volumes (by moving to next lay-ers).

Both modules (methods of 3D structures generation) allow the user to create the fi-nite element mesh (while Finite Element Method is employed as one of the approxi-mate method), specify subdomain geometry, define material characteristics including also non-linear and anisotropic material properties, and graphically examine and dis-play the data. Moreover, the post processor provides facilities necessary for displaying the vector quantities, and as well displaying field quantities as graphs, contour maps, etc. The post processor could provide the calculation and displaying many derived quantities and could plot particle trajectories through the calculated fields.

2   Solid Modeling of Micro-accelerometer 3D Structures by Use of Geometric Modeller

Building of the geometry could be arranged by use of simple parameterized vol-umes like: BLOCK, CYLINDER, DISC, SPHERE, TORUS and PRISM / PYRAMID combining with Boolean Operations (like: Union With Regularization, Union Without Regularization, etc.). Boolean operations are performed on bodies, not cells. The main distinction between a cell and a body is that a cell is a volume of the model, while a body is a hierarchical assembly of cells, faces, edges and points. Hence, it is necessary to pick the new cylinders created as bodies not cells. In the next step it is possible to select from each volume the following parts: Bodies, Cells, Faces, Edges. Additionally we could also define transformation operations, sweeping and morphing operations.

Solid modeling could be arranged as two stage process. Surfaces of volumes (cells) are initially discretized into triangles. Controls are available to define the exactness of the representation of curved surfaces. Then, using the surface mesh, each cell is meshed automatically into tetrahedral elements. Element size can be controlled by defining a maximum element size on vertices, edges, faces or cells within a model. This allows the mesh to be concentrated in areas of interest, where high accuracy is required, or where the field is changing rapidly.

One of the most sophisticated software exploiting Boolean operations and prede-fined parameterized volumes is OPERA code (an OPerating environment for Elec-tromagnetic Research and Analysis, by Vector Fields Ltd.). Finite element discretiza-tion forms the basis of the methods used in these analysis programs. This widely ap-plicable technique for the solution of partial differential equations requires special enhancements to make it applicable to vector field calculations, one of them could be electromagnetic vector field. Access to these features is supported by the Geometric Modeller or classical pre processor. This modeling technique allows many models to be created from the basic building blocks. Other more advanced techniques allow the geometry to be enhanced by e.g. sweeping an existing face. Exploiting any COMMAND, from the COM-MANDS FAMILY, allows the user to define the follow-ing variables: direction, name, and type of volume. It is arranged in the sequence of defining: as the first object or set of objects, then variables defining object.

Designing devices of complex geometry, such sensors, actuators, motors, trans-formers, Intelligent MicroElectromechanical Systems (IMEMS), etc. requires accurate calculation of the forces and torques. In the last decade wide group of engineers and scientists have focused their interest on solving an increasingly huge number of alge-braic equations using the software packages. Efficiency of the device development is also due to design flexibility, developing of simulation tools and CAD systems, inte-gration of mircodevices and microelectronics, etc.

In general, multi-layer surface mircoactuator fabrication process is enough flexible to produce advanced device structures. MEMS structure development requires reliable fabrication processes and flexible CAD/(analysis and optimal design) tools. A wide variety of micromechanical structures (devices typically in the m range) have been built recently by using processing techniques known from VLSI industry. Accelerometers are important devices in the range of variety applications such as air bag actuation (by Analog and Berkeley Sensor and Actuator Center), microrobots, etc. The electrostatic comb accelerometer is fabricated by use of different techniques like CDV, RIE, Wet etching, etc. The relationship between input voltage and output displacement has been widely analyzed experimentally and theoretically in the litera-ture [1]. The accelerometer consists of a moving comb teeth, suspended by spring beams on both sides, and fixed teeth. The suspension is designed to be compliant in the x direction of motion and to be stiff in the orthogonal direction (y) to keep the comb fingers aligned. The applied voltages on the force unit causes a net electrostatic force to pull the movable part in the desired direction.

Such a sophisticated software could allow creating 3D structure of the device, full model analysis (structural mechanics, electrostatics, fluid flow, vibration, etc.). Mod-eling in terms of hexahedral elements is very time consuming. This is

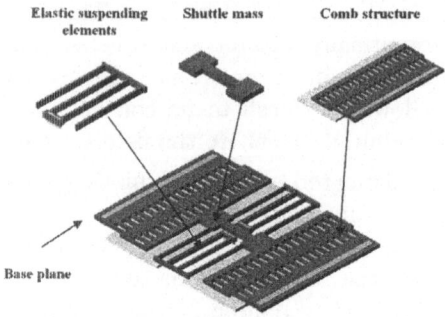

Fig. 2. IMEMS example - accelerometer [4-7].

an ideal situa-tion for using tetrahedral elements, created automatically by the Modeller (see Fig. 2). Generally, the solvers allow mixed linear and quadratic elements in the same problem, and are recommended for locally improving the accuracy within a model. The previous steps have defined the geometry of each subdomain. The free space that surrounds the object must also be included as part of the model. In the real world, this space extends to infinity.

3   Single Criteria Problems of Comb Accelerometer

In a design problem from real-life engineering, the presence of a single design cri-terion is rather an exception than a rule; often, the designer has to cope with the mini-mization of two or more conflictual criteria. It is reasonable to state that design or inverse - problems are multiobjective problems by their very na-ture and imply the simultaneous minimization of a number of objectives being in mutual conflict. Tradi-tionally, multicriteria problems are reduced to single criterion problems, for instance by means of one of the following procedures:
i) the use of a penalty function composed of the various criteria;
ii) the separate solutions of single criterion problems and their trade-off;
iii) the solution of a single criterion problem, taking the other criteria as con-straints.

This approach leads to classical methods of multiobjective optimization and gives a solution which is supposed to be the optimum.

A much more satisfactory way to tackle the problem of multicriteria opti-mization consists of applying the Pareto optima theory in connection with a suitable minimiza-tion algorithm. These improved analytical formulas are in the next step of accelerome-ter design introduced to optimal design procedure. Aut-hors have defined the following optimization criteria being partially conflictual criteria:

• Maximum of accelerometer drag force,
• Maximum of accelerometer force sensitivity,
• Minimum stress response. As the test problem optimisation, while two crietria

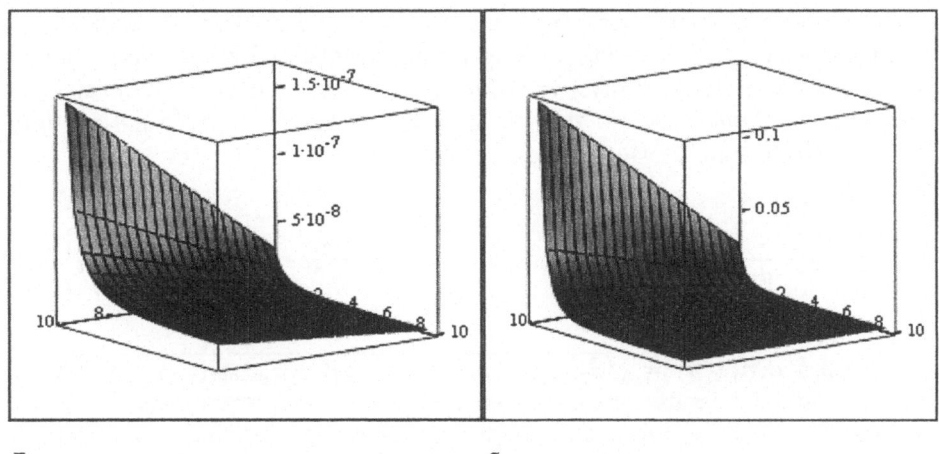

$$F_{ah} \qquad\qquad\qquad S_{ah}$$

Fig. 3. Force and sensitivity curves in y axis corresponding to geometry con-straints (d, n, p) and variables (a, h).

are defined (1 and 2 as separate criteria), the comb drive with movement in one direction (y) is taken.

In the first step of optimization procedure it is expected to evaluate first two crite-ria, whether they are influencing each other or not. In order to carry out the above the dedicated software exploiting gradient methods has been elaborated to carry out opti-mization process. In order to realize the defined goal virtual model of accelerometer is necessary to be defined by use of solid modeller. Energy stored for the device is de-fined as follows (where C means equivalent object capacitance being function of the set of variables, and U means supply voltage):

$$W = \frac{1}{2}CU^2 \tag{1}$$

Sensitivity of equivalent circuit model along X and Y are expressed as follows:

$$s_y = \frac{\partial C}{\partial y} \qquad s_x = \frac{\partial C}{\partial x} \tag{2}$$

Basing on the stored energy evaluation (see expression 1) the acting force in Y di-rection is expressed by the following formula:

$$F_y = -\frac{\partial W}{\partial y} = \frac{1}{2}U^2\frac{\partial C}{\partial y} \tag{3}$$

and finally (s-symmetrical structure):

$$F_{y,s}\frac{1}{2}aU^2\left((n-2)(\frac{1}{p+x}) + (n-1)(\frac{1}{m-x}) + 2(n-3)\frac{d}{(h+y)^2})\right. \tag{4}$$

The list of accelerometer basic variables to be introduced into optimization algorithm for selected: pole configurations, air gap length and geometric parameter variations are as follows: $a_{min} := 1\mu m, a_{max} := 10\mu m, p_{min} := 2\mu m, p_{max} := 5\mu m, d_{min} := 1\mu m, d_{max} := 5\mu m, h_{min} := 1\mu m, h_{max} := 10\mu m, z_{min} := 10\mu m, z_{max} := 50\mu m, n_{min} := 10\mu m, n_{max} := 15\mu m$
Max sensitivity

$$S_s(y) := -\frac{d}{dy}F_s(x_0, y) \qquad S_{opt}(a, h, d, n, y) := \frac{\varepsilon a U^2}{2}\left[(2n - 3)\frac{d}{(h + y)^3}\right] \quad (5)$$

Max force:
$$S_{optd}(a, p, h, d, n, x, y) := \sqrt{S_{xs\_opt}(a, p, h, d, n, x, y)^2 + S_{ys\_opt}(a, p, h, d, n, x, y)^2}$$
The preliminary results are displayed in Figure 3 confirming that both first and sec-ond criterion are not in conflict, moreover the maximum values (optimization crite-rion) are for almost the same accelerometer structure. When we tackle with third op-timization criterion this would be done in a straightforward way using the theory of Pareto optimality. $F_{ah}(a, h) := F_{s\_opt}(a, p, h, d, n, x_0, y_0)$
$S_{ah}(a, h) := S_{s\_opt}(a, h, d, n, y_0)$

References

1. Wiak S.: Intelligent Micro-Electro-Mechanical Systems (IMEMS) - Modelling and Optimal Design, AI-METH 2003 - Artificial Intelligence Methods, Gliwice, Poland (2003).
2. OPERA-3D User Guide, Vector Fields Limited, Oxford, England, ver. 9.0, (2004).
3. Wiak S., Rudnicki M.: Optimisation and Inverse Problems in Electromagnetism. Kluwer, Academic Publisher (2003).
4. Brown K.S.: On the Feasibility of Integrated Optical Waveguidebased In-Situ Monitoring of Microelectromechanical Systems (MEMS), dissertation Phd in engineering, Department of Computer Science and Electrical Engineering Morgantown, West Virginia 2000.
5. Tang W. C., Nguyen T.-C. H., Judy M. W., and Howe R. T.: Electrostatic Comb Drive of Lateral Polysilicon Resonators, Sensors and Actuators A, 21 (1990) 328-331.
6. Yong Zhou (advisor: prof. Gary K. Fedder, co-advisor: dr. Tamal Mukherjee): Layout Syn-thesis of Accelerometers, MS Project Report, Department of Electrical and Computer Engi-neering, Carnegie Mellon university, August, 1998
7. Wiak S., Smolka K.: Electrostatic Comb Accelerometer - Field and Equivalent Circuit Mod-eling, COMPUMAG 2003, Saratoga Springs, USA, July 2-5, 2003.

Local Pattern-Based Interval Models

Wojciech Cholewa

Silesian University of Technology
Faculty of Mechanical Engineering
44-100 Gliwice, Poland
`wojciech.cholewa@polsl.pl`

Abstract. This paper aims to inform about special diagnostic models designed for reasoning about causes of observed symptoms, e.g. a state of an object. The paper introduces the general idea of inverse models produced by numerical inversion of simulation results, where the simulation is being run by known cause-effect models transforming state features into diagnostic symptoms. Special attention has been drawn to a strict and interval modelling as well as to global and local models. Suggested methodology is focused on the identification of local models such as pattern based models, i.e. models spanned on particular sets of selected data. Although the presented approach is addressed to diagnostics it may be easily extended to other applications.

1 Introduction

The paper presents some results from research on methods of technical diagnostics. Generic diagnostic task consists among others of measurements, estimation of signal features and reasoning on the basis of the values of such features about a state of an investigated object. The accuracy of diagnoses depends strongly on the quality of diagnostic rules and models forming the knowledge base of reasoning systems. Unfortunately, this kind of diagnostic knowledge is concerned with incomplete, imprecise and even erroneous domain knowledge, mainly because of that it is acquired directly from experts.

An approach discussed in this paper results from the assumption that the diagnostic models can be acquired indirectly from examples representing different conditions of running machinery. The examples may be collected as monitoring results for running objects and may be calculated as results of simulation carried out with the use of the known and carefully validated dynamic cause-effect models of considered objects.

An important question discussed indirectly in this paper is *"How to develop an efficient diagnostic model by means of simulation data?"*.

2 Assumptions

Let us consider a causal object O with given inputs s and outputs u. Let M be an unknown mathematical model of the object O. The model M sets the mapping of all inputs s expressing causes into all outputs u expressing effects

L. Rutkowski et al. (Eds.): ICAISC 2004, LNAI 3070, pp. 948–953, 2004.
© Springer-Verlag Berlin Heidelberg 2004

$$u = M(s) \tag{1}$$

Outputs are written down as vector values of observed (i.e. not all) output features $u0$ (e.g. temperature, amplitude of vibration). Inputs are written down as vectors s merged of the following components (projections)

- values $s0$ of state features (values representing the expected diagnoses),
- values $s1$ of features determining operating conditions of the object,
- values $s2$ of features, which are constant for the object
- values $s3$ of features considered to be very difficult (or even impossible) to estimate or measure. Leaving out these values equation (1) converts into

$$u0 = M(s0, s1, s2) \tag{2}$$

The mapping (2) may be inexact because not all independent variables (eg. $s3$) are considered. The goal is to find a mapping N

$$y = N(x) \text{ where } y = s0 \text{ and } x = (u0, s1, s2) \tag{3}$$

where the mapping (3) may be inexact, too.

Data determined through measurements on real objects or calculated as results of simulations are collected as tuples $w = (x, y)$. The general set of data fitted to the considered object or a family of similar objects is called the learning data set $W_L = \{w_1, w_2, \cdots\}$ which includes a subset of training data $W_D \subseteq W_L$, a subset of test data $W_T \subseteq W_L$ and an optional subset of pattern data (subset of patterns) $W_P \subseteq W_L$ which may be included directly into the definition of the model (for an example-based model only).

There are reasons to suppose that an exact and unique inverse model N (3) does not exist when the considered inputs and outputs do not take into account all features. Moreover, from the assumption dealing with the model M (2) it does not follow than an inverse model exists at all. There is no any other choice but to accept that the considered relations are the reason of inaccuracies and errors. The problem may be discussed in the scope of granular computing [1], e.g. by means of intervals. Intervals are subsets in $\mathbb{R}$, denoted by lowercase letters enclosed in square brackets, e.g. $[x]$. The intervals $[x]$ can be characterised by their lower ^-x and upper ^+x bounds, allowing introducing an alternative notation $[x] \equiv [^-x, {}^+x]$. Intervals introduced for real values can be extended into n-dimensional vectors of intervals

$$[x] \equiv [^-x, {}^+x] \equiv \{x \in \mathbb{R}^n : {}^-x \leq x \leq {}^+x\} \tag{4}$$

Intervals can be characterised by their centre, width and radius

$$\text{center}([x]) = ({}^+x + {}^-x)/2 \tag{5}$$

$$\text{width}([x]) = {}^+x - {}^-x \tag{6}$$

$$\text{radius}([x]) = ({}^+x - {}^-x)/2 = \text{width}([x])/2 \tag{7}$$

3 Models of Mappings

One can classify the models due to the types of relationships identified among model inputs and outputs. The most common way is to consider mappings from inputs' values into outputs' values. This kind of models is discussed in a huge number of papers and books. The main objective of this chapter is to compare selected properties of global and local versions of such models. A *global model* is valid over the whole learning data set, or equivalently over the whole range of input and output data. Its identification means identification of the function N in (3). It is useful to assume that each component y_h of $\boldsymbol{y} = [y_1, y_2, \cdots]$ depends only on the variables $\boldsymbol{x}$. This assumption simplifies the task and allows us to consider each component y_h separately and independently of other $\boldsymbol{y}$ components, substituting equation (3) with a set of equations

$$y_h = N_h(\boldsymbol{x}) \tag{8}$$

A *local model* is distinct from the global one. It is valid in a neighbourhood of a selected element $\boldsymbol{x}$ only.

3.1 Global Strict Models

The basic example of global strict models of mappings is a class of approximation models. They are given in the form of functions N_h (8) with identified parameters capable to approximate the training data set $\boldsymbol{W_D}$ within the specified accuracy. To identify the functions N_h (8) a generic form of these functions and a relevant quality criterion are required. In general, such criterion depends on the data underlying the model, as well as on the modelling purposes, but the following two classes of criteria are frequently applied

- the so-called minimal distance criterion (with e.g. $q = 2$ for the well known least-squares criterion)

$$\sum\nolimits_{(\boldsymbol{x},\boldsymbol{y})\in W_D;\ \hat{\boldsymbol{y}}(\boldsymbol{x})=N(\boldsymbol{x})} \|\boldsymbol{y} - \hat{\boldsymbol{y}}(\boldsymbol{x})\|^q \longrightarrow \min \tag{9}$$

- full fit criterion (for a given set of training data W_D)

$$\forall_{(\boldsymbol{x},\boldsymbol{y})\in W_D;\ \hat{\boldsymbol{y}}(\boldsymbol{x})=N(\boldsymbol{x})} (\boldsymbol{y} = \hat{\boldsymbol{y}}(\boldsymbol{x})) \tag{10}$$

The most general way to solve the discussed task is application of neural networks. This approach is attractive, since due to existing software, the required domain specific knowledge as well as knowledge of neural networks theory and training strategies are minimal. One should take care only on selection of the proper size of the neural network, i.e. the number of network parameters.

3.2   Global Interval Models

The main disadvantage of strict models of mappings discussed in chapter 3.1 is the lack of information about the quality of approximation and the accuracy of the models in such cases where the accuracy varies across the range of the independent variable x. One of possibilities for representing local inaccuracies of the model is substitution of the strict function $N_h(x)$ (8) taking values $\hat{y}_h(x) \in \mathbb{R}$ with a function taking interval values $[\hat{y}_h(x)] \subset \mathbb{R}$, such that

$$\text{Prob}\,(y_h(x) \in [\hat{y}_h(x)]) = \text{Prob}\left(^-\hat{y}_h(x) \leq y_h(x) \leq^+ \hat{y}_h(x)\right) \geq \alpha \qquad (11)$$

where Prob$(\cdot)$ denotes the probability function, and α is its threshold value. Interval value $[\hat{y}_h(x)]$ consists of two boundaries $^-\hat{y}_h(x)$ and $^+\hat{y}_h(x)$ setting models called the unilateral data models [2], because each of them limits the data set from one side. Let us assume that the interval $[\hat{y}_h(x)]$ is symmetric with respect to the function $\hat{y}_h(x)$ which is equal to its centre (5)

$$\text{center}([\hat{y}_h(x)]) = \hat{y}_h(x) \qquad (12)$$

The radius (7) of this interval

$$\text{radius}([\hat{y}_h(x)]) = \left(^+\hat{y}_h(x) - \,^-\hat{y}_h(x)\right)/2 \qquad (13)$$

may be interpreted as the particular local deviation. The radius (13) depends on local values of independent variable x.

An interval model $[\hat{y}(x)]$ represented by (12) and (13) may be identified by means of an algorithm consisting of the following steps:

1. identify the strict model $\hat{y}(x)$ for the given training data W_D,
2. for all training data W_D by means of the identified strict model $\hat{y}(x)$, calculate the absolute values of deviations

$$\Delta y\,(x) = |\hat{y}\,(x) - y\,(x)| \qquad (14)$$

3. identify the strict model $\Delta\hat{y}(x)$ for absolute deviations (14), in a similar way as suggested in chapter 3.1 and assume that radius$([\hat{y}(x)])$ equals to $\beta\Delta\hat{y}(x)$, where β is the relative width of the identified symmetric interval.
4. set the interval model considering equation (12) and identified models $\hat{y}(x)$, $\Delta\hat{y}(x)$, as follows

$$[\hat{y}(x)] = [\,\hat{y}(x) - \beta\Delta\hat{y}(x)\,,\,\hat{y}(x) + \beta\Delta\hat{y}(x)\,]\;\text{ with }\beta > 0 \qquad (15)$$

3.3   Local Strict Models

The main difficulty during the identification of global models is connected with required quality of models. Instead of looking for a global model for all the learning data, which is capable to substitute such data, we can save the data and form a local model which of course requires permanent access to pattern data.

Local models are valid in a cylindrical neighbourhood of a selected element in the learning data set W_L and not over the whole this set. Frequently applied local models belong to interpolation models, spanning over the set of pattern examples $W_P \subseteq W_L$, which play the role of model parameters. The most common approach for local modelling within a bounded neighbourhood of a point under examination is focused on linear in parameters interpolation with respect to least-squares criterion (9).

An another group of interesting interpolation algorithms may be presented [4] in the form of weighted averages of known values of the function, calculated in the neighbourhood $\epsilon(x)$ of the point x. Equation (16) presents an example of such average with weights $\nu(d)$ defined as functions (17) decreasing monotonically with the distance $d(x, x_p)$ between x and pattern x_p taken from $(x_p, y_p) \in W_P$

$$\hat{y}(x) = \frac{\sum_{x_p \in \epsilon(x)} \nu(x, x_p) \, y(x_p)}{\sum_{x_p \in \epsilon(x)} \nu(x, x_p)} \tag{16}$$

where for the distance $d(x, x_p)$ the function $\nu(x, x_p)$ may be considered as $\nu(d(x, x_p))$. For example

$$\nu(d) = \exp\left(-d^2/r^2\right) \quad \text{or} \quad \nu(d) = r^2/\left(d^2 + r^2\right) \tag{17}$$

where r is a parameter interpreted as the radius of the neighbourhood $\epsilon(x)$. Extending weights (17) interpreted as the *importance measure* for pattern data, it is possible to take into account the different accuracy of patterns.

Some considerations should be given to the tuning of scaling of x as it might lead to a better fitting of the model outcome. A convenient place to apply scaling preprocessing and make use of its interesting side effects is the general definition of the distance, necessary for (17)

$$d^2(x, x_p) = (x - x_p)^T C (x - x_p) \tag{18}$$

with a scaling matrix C, which may be set as diagonal one in the simplest case. Considering discussed local models this matrix should be global to the whole model i.e. common to all considered cases.

Suggested methodology should be distinguished from radial basis function networks [3] and support vector machines [5] which possess all drawbacks of global models. The discussed weighted average (16) is a raw local model even in such a case when the global scaling matrix C should be applied.

3.4   Local Interval Models

Taking into account advantages of local models as well as advantages of interval models it may be interesting to couple the both solutions together. It is possible to adapt the procedure for identification of the interval model, presented in chapter 3.2 in such a way that deviations $\Delta y(x)$ will be modelled by means of weighted averages (16). This can be done in the following steps

1. for considered value of an independent variable x select pattern data x_p belonging to the neighbourhood $\epsilon(x)$ of x
2. for each $x_p \in \epsilon(x)$ apply the local model (16) to calculate $\hat{y}(x_p)$ and apply (14) to calculate $\Delta y(x_p)$
3. introduce the local model for $\Delta\hat{y}(x)$ in a form similar to (16).

Local interval models allow us to identify the model just when it is needed. Such the models are particular suitable for task requiring permanent modifications of pattern data. An example of such tasks is programming of simulation tasks.

4 Conclusions

It has been shown that an effect-cause diagnostic model, designed for reasoning about a state of an object based on observed symptoms can be developed as a pattern based model i.e. the model spanned on particular sets of selected pattern data. It was assumed that such data results from the simulation done by means of known and correctly validated cause-effect models transforming state features into diagnostic symptoms.

Generally, the numerical inversion of simulation results, i.e. transformation from cause-effect into effect-cause relation, is possible by means of interval modelling and may result in global and local interval models. The local models possess important advantages that they are identified when they are needed. Suggested effective procedure for identifying such models uses a particular interpolation of examples consisting of pattern data. Elaborated procedure may be applied to strict models as well as interval models.

It should be pointed out that the general conclusion drawn from this paper is a recommendation to use local, interval, pattern based models in greater extend. Although the presented approach is addressed to diagnostics it may be easily extended to other applications.

Acknowledgement. The support from the Polish State Committee for Scientific Research (KBN) in Warsaw is gratefully acknowledged.

References

1. Bargiela A., Pedrycz W.: Granular Computing - An Introduction. Kluwer Academic Publishers. Boston 2003.
2. Cholewa W.: Unilateral Diagnostic Models. 2nd International Conference on Acoustical and Vibratory Surveillance Methods and Diagnostic Techniques. Senlis (1995). Proceedings vol.2, 805–815.
3. Howlett R. J., Jain L. C.: Radial Basis Function Networks. Part 1 - Recent Developments in Theory and Applications. Part 2 - New Advances in Design. Physica-Verlag, Heidelberg 2001.
4. Powell M. J. D.: A Review of Methods for Multivariable Interpolation at Scattered Data Points. In: Duff I. S., Watson G. A.: The State of the Art in Numerical Analysis, Clarendon Press, Oxford (1997) 283–309.
5. Vapnik V.N.: The Nature of Statistical Learning Theory. Springer. 2000.

Implementation of Two-Stage Hopfield Model and Its Application in Nonlinear Systems

Ivan Nunes da Silva, Jose Alfredo C. Ulson, and Andre Nunes de Souza

São Paulo State University - UNESP/FE/DEE
School of Engineering, Department of Electrical Engineering
CP 473, CEP 17033.360, Bauru-SP, Brazil

Abstract. This paper presents an efficient neural network for solving constrained nonlinear optimization problems. More specifically, a two-stage neural network architecture is developed and its internal parameters are computed using the valid-subspace technique. The main advantage of the developed network is that it treats optimization and constraint terms in different stages with no interference with each other. Moreover, the proposed approach does not require specification of penalty or weighting parameters for its initialization.

1 Introduction

In the neural networks literature, there exist several approaches used for solving constrained nonlinear optimization problems. The first neural approach applied in optimization problems was proposed by Tank and Hopfield in [1], where the network was used for solving linear programming problems.

More recently, it was proposed in [2] a recurrent neural network for nonlinear optimization with a continuously differentiable objective function and bound constraints. In [3], it was developed a multilayer perceptron for nonlinear programming, which transforms constrained optimization problems into a sequence of unconstrained ones by incorporating the constraint functions into the objective function of the unconstrained problem. Basically, most of these neural networks presented in the literature for solving nonlinear optimization problems contain some penalty or weighting parameters. The stable equilibrium points of these networks, which represent a solution of the constrained optimization problems, are obtained only when those parameters are properly adjusted, and in this case, both the accuracy and the convergence process can be affected. In this paper, we have developed a two-stage neural network not depending on penalty or weighting parameters.

2 The Two-Stage Neural Network Architecture

The mapping of constrained optimization problems using a Hopfield network consists of determining the weight matrix T and the bias vector i^b to compute

L. Rutkowski et al. (Eds.): ICAISC 2004, LNAI 3070, pp. 954–959, 2004.
© Springer-Verlag Berlin Heidelberg 2004

equilibrium points. A modified energy function $E^m(t)$ composed by two terms is used here, which is defined as follows:

$$E^m(t) = E^{conf}(t) + E^{op}(t) \tag{1}$$

where $E^{conf}(t)$ is a confinement term that groups all the constraints imposed by the problem, and $E^{op}(t)$ is an optimization term that conducts the network output to the equilibrium points. Thus, the minimization of $E(t)$ of this network is conducted in two stages:

i) Minimization of the Term $E^{conf}(t)$:

$$E^{conf}(t) = -\frac{1}{2} v(t)^T \cdot T^{conf} \cdot v(t) - v(t)^T \cdot i^{conf} \tag{2}$$

where: $v(t)$ is the network output, T^{conf} is weight matrix and i^{conf} is bias vector belonging to $E^{conf}(t)$. This corresponds to confinement of $v(t)$ into a valid subspace that confines the inequality and equality constraints imposed by the problem. A detailed explanation on the valid-subspace technique can be found in [4].

ii) Minimization of the Term $E^{op}(t)$:

$$E^{op}(t) = -\frac{1}{2} v(t)^T \cdot T^{op} \cdot v(t) - v(t)^T \cdot i^{op} \tag{3}$$

where: T^{op} is weight matrix and i^{op} is bias vector belonging to $E^{op}(t)$. This moves $v(t)$ towards an optimal solution (equilibrium points).

Thus, as shown in Figure 1, the operation of the two-stage neural network consists of three main steps, which are defined as follows:

Step (I): Minimization of E^{conf}, corresponding to the projection of $v(t)$ in the valid subspace defined by:

$$v(t+1) = T^{conf} \cdot v(t) + i^{conf} \tag{4}$$

where: T^{conf} is a projection matrix $T^{conf} \cdot T^{conf} = T^{conf}$ and $T^{conf} \cdot i^{conf} = 0$. This operation corresponds to an indirect minimization process of $E^{conf}(t)$ using orthogonal projection de $v(t)$ on the feasible set [4].

Step (II): Application of a *symmetric-ramp* activation function constraining $v(t)$ in a hypercube, i.e. $g(v_i) = v_i$, where $v_i(t) \in [lim_i^{inf}, lim_i^{sup}]$. For those cases in that $v \in \Re^n$, we can assume $lim_i^{inf} = -\infty$ and $lim_i^{sup} = +\infty$.

Step (III): Minimization of E^{op}, which involves updating of $v(t)$ in direction to an optimal solution (defined by T^{op} and i^{op}), which corresponds to network

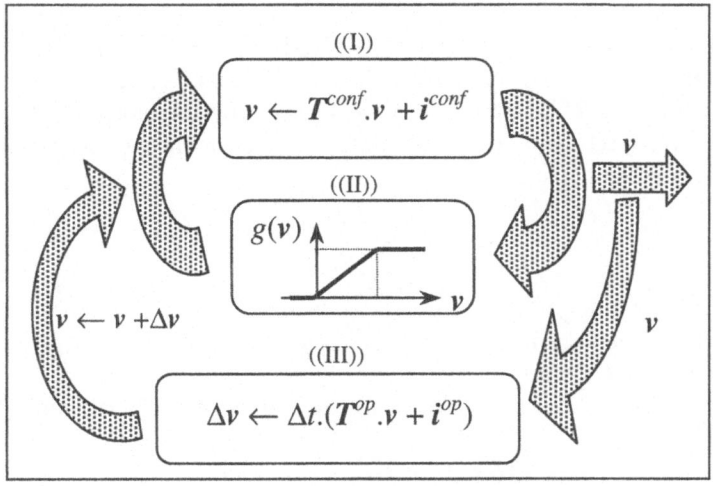

Fig. 1. Two-stage neural network model.

equilibrium point that represents a solution for the constrained optimization problem, by applying the gradient in relation to the energy term E^{op}, i. e.:

$$\frac{dv(t)}{dt} = \dot{v} = -\frac{\partial E^{op}(t)}{\partial v} \tag{5}$$

$$\Delta v = -\Delta t \cdot \nabla E^{op}(v) = \Delta t \cdot (T^{op} \cdot v + i^{op}) \tag{6}$$

Therefore, minimization of E^{op} consists of updating $v(t)$ in the opposite direction of the gradient of E^{op}. These results are also valid when sigmoid-type activation functions are used.

As seen in Figure 1, each iteration represented by the above steps has two distinct stages. First, as described in step ((III)), v is updated using the gradient of the term E^{op} alone. Second, after each updating given in step ((III)), v is projected directly in the valid subspace.

3   Formulation of Constrained Optimization Problems through the Two-Stage Neural Network

Consider the following constrained optimization problem, with m-constraints and n-variables, given by the following equations:

$$\text{Minimize } E^{op}(v) = f(v) \tag{7}$$

$$\text{subject to } E^{conf}(v): \; h_i(v) \leq 0 , \; i \in 1..m \tag{8}$$

$$z^{min} \leq v \leq z^{max} \tag{9}$$

where v, z^{min}, $z^{max} \in \Re^n$; $f(v)$ and $h_i(v)$ are continuous, and all first and second order partial derivatives of $f(v)$ and $h_i(v)$ exist and are continuous. The vectors z^{min} and z^{max} define the bounds on the variables belonging to the vector v.

The parameters T^{conf} and i^{conf} are calculated by transforming the inequality constraints in (8) into equality constraints by introducing a slack variable $w \in \Re^n$ for each inequality constraint:

$$h_i(v) + \sum_{j=1}^{m} \delta_{ij} \cdot w_j = 0 \tag{10}$$

where w_j are slack variables, treated as the variables v_i, where $\delta_{ij} = 1$ for $i = j$ and $\delta_{ij} = 0$ for $i \neq j$.

After this transformation, the problem defined by (7), (8) and (9) can be rewritten as:

$$\text{Minimize } E^{op}(v^+) = f(v^+) \tag{11}$$

$$\text{subject to } E^{conf}(v) : \; h^+(v^+) = 0 \tag{12}$$

$$z_i^{min} \leq v_i^+ \leq z_i^{max} , \;\; i \in (1..n) \tag{13}$$

$$0 \leq v_i^+ \leq z_i^{max} , \;\; i \in (n+1)..N \tag{14}$$

where $N = n + m$, and $v^{+T} = [v^T \; w^T] \in \Re^N$ is a vector of extended variables. It is important to observe that E^{op} does not depend on the slack variables w. A projection matrix [5] to the system defined in (12) can be given by:

$$T^{conf} = I - \nabla h(v^+)^T \cdot (\nabla h(v^+) \cdot \nabla h(v^+)^T)^{-1} \cdot \nabla h(v^+) \tag{15}$$

where:

$$\nabla h(v^+) = \begin{bmatrix} \frac{\partial h_1(v^+)}{\partial v_1^+} & \frac{\partial h_1(v^+)}{\partial v_2^+} & \cdots & \frac{\partial h_1(v^+)}{\partial v_N^+} \\ \frac{\partial h_2(v^+)}{\partial v_1^+} & \frac{\partial h_2(v^+)}{\partial v_2^+} & \cdots & \frac{\partial h_2(v^+)}{\partial v_N^+} \\ \vdots & \vdots & \ddots & \vdots \\ \frac{\partial h_p(v^+)}{\partial v_1^+} & \frac{\partial h_p(v^+)}{\partial v_2^+} & \cdots & \frac{\partial h_p(v^+)}{\partial v_N^+} \end{bmatrix} \tag{16}$$

Inserting the value of (15) in the expression of the valid subspace in (4), we have the following equation:

$$v^+ = [I - \nabla h(v^+)^T (\nabla h(v^+) \cdot \nabla h(v^+)^T)^{-1} \nabla h(v^+)] \cdot v^+ + i^{conf} \tag{17}$$

Results of the Lyapunov stability theory [6] can be used in order to develop a deeper understanding of the equilibrium condition. By the definition of the Jacobian, when v leads to equilibrium point $v^e = 0$ ($\|i^{conf}\| \to 0$), $h(v^+)$ may be approximated as follows:

$$h(v^+) \approx h(v^e) + J \cdot (v^+ - v^e) \tag{18}$$

where $J = \nabla h(v^+)$.

In the proximity of the equilibrium point $v^e = 0$, we obtain the following equation:

$$\lim_{v \to v^e} \frac{\|h(v^+)\|}{\|v^+\|} = 0 \tag{19}$$

Finally, introducing the results from (18) and (19) in equation given by (17), it is obtained the following iterative expression:

$$v^+ \leftarrow v^+ - \nabla h(v^+)^T \cdot (\nabla h(v^+) \cdot \nabla h(v^+)^T)^{-1} \cdot h(v^+) \tag{20}$$

Thus, the expression defined by step ((I)) in Figure 1 is similar to the above equation. The parameters T^{op} and i^{op} in this case are such that the vector v^+ is updated in the opposite gradient direction that of the energy function E^{op}. Thus, the equilibrium points of the network, which represent those minimum points, can be calculated by assuming the following values to T^{op} and i^{op}:

$$i^{op} = - \left[\frac{\partial f(v)}{\partial v_1} \quad \frac{\partial f(v)}{\partial v_2} \quad \cdots \quad \frac{\partial f(v)}{\partial v_N} \right]^T \tag{21}$$

$$T^{op} = 0 \tag{22}$$

To demonstrate the advanced behavior of the two-stage neural network derived in this section and to validate its properties, some simulation results are presented in the next section.

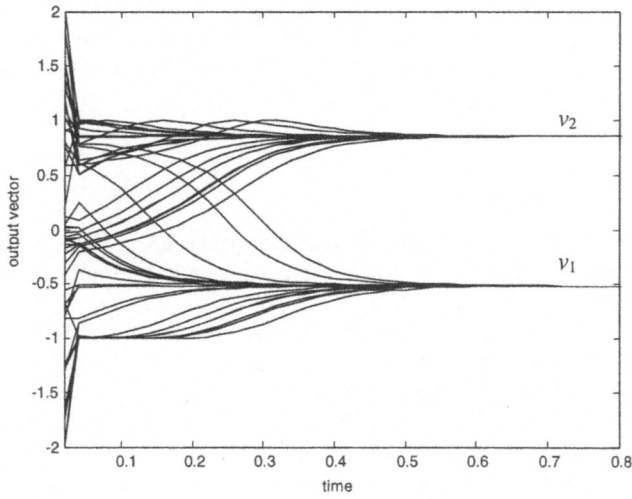

Fig. 2. Trajectories of the two-stage neural network for 20 initial points.

4   Simulation Results

Consider the following constrained optimization problem, which is composed by inequality constraints:

$$\text{Min } f(v) = v_1^3 + (v_1 - 2v_2)^3 + e^{v_1 + v_2} \tag{23}$$

$$\text{subject to}: \ v \in V \tag{24}$$

where $V = \{v \in \Re^2 \mid v_1^2 + v_2^2 \leq 1\}$. This problem has a unique optimal solution given by $v = [-0.5159 \quad 0.8566]^T$ with $f(v^*) = -9.8075$. All simulation results provided by the two-stage neural network show that it is globally asymptotically stable at v^*.

To illustrate the global convergent behavior of the two-stage neural network, Figure 2 shows the trajectories of v starting from several initial points.

It is important to observe that all trajectories starting from the inside or outside of the feasible region V converge to v^*. Thus, the proposed approach always converges to the optimal solution, independently whether the chosen initial point is located in the feasible region or not.

5   Conclusion

From the simulation results we can conclude that the two-stage neural network proposed in this paper has the advantages of global convergence and high accuracy of solutions. Some particularities of the neural approach in relation to primal methods normally used in nonlinear optimization are the following: i) it is not necessary the computation, in each iteration, of the active set of constraints; ii) the neural approach does not compute Lagrange's multipliers; and iii) the initial solution used to initialize the network can be outside of the feasible set defined from the constraints.

References

1. Tank, D. W., Hopfield, J. J.: Simple neural optimization networks: an A/D converter, signal decision network, and a linear programming circuit. IEEE Transactions on Circuits and Systems. **33** (1986) 533–541
2. Liang, X. B. , Wang, J.: A recurrent neural network for nonlinear optimization with a continuously differentiable objective function and bound constraints. IEEE Transactions on Neural Networks. **11** (2000) 1251–1262
3. Reifman, J., Feldman, E. E.: Multilayer perceptron for nonlinear programming. Computers & Operations Research. **29** (2002) 1237–1250
4. Aiyer, S. V. B. et al.: A theoretical investigation into the performance of the Hopfield model. IEEE Transactions on Neural Networks. **1** (1990) 53–60
5. Luenberger, D. G.: Linear and Nonlinear Programming. Addison-Wesley (1984)
6. Vidyasagar, M.: Nonlinear Systems Analysis. Prentice-Hall (1988)

Genetic Algorithm Based Fuzzy Sliding Mode with Application to Building Structures

Kambiz Falsafian[1] and Mahdi Jalili-Kharaajoo[2]

[1] Technical Collage of Marand (Civil Eng. Group), University of Tabriz, Iran
kfalsafian@tabrizu.ac.ir
[2] Young Researchers Club, Islamic Azad University, Tehran, Iran
mahdijalili@ece.ut.ac.ir

Abstract. In this paper, the design of Fuzzy Sliding Mode Control (FSMC) based on Genetic Algorithms (GAs) is studied. Using the proposed approach, a robust controller is designed for building structures under earthquake excitation. It is found that the building structure under the proposed control method could sustain in safety and stability when the system is subjected to external disturbances.

1 Introduction

This work presents a FSMC based on GAs to control civil engineering structures under dynamic loading [1-4]. To improve the performance of the sliding mode control (SMC), based fuzzy controller, [5-7] we adopt optimal searching algorithms, that is, the genetic algorithms (GAs). The GAs have been demonstrated to be a powerful tool for automating the definition of the fuzzy control rule base and membership functions, because that adaptive control, learning, and self-organization can be considered in a lot of cases as optimization or searching processes.

The proposed control strategy attempts to reduce cumulative structural responses during earthquakes by applying the active pulse control force. The effectiveness of the proposed controller is investigated for a three-storey building subjected to the El Centro earthquake. The simulation results show the ability of the proposed controller in the attenuation of the effect of the earthquake excitation.

2 Equation of Motion of Structural Systems

Consider an n-storey building. The building is idealized by an n degree-of-freedom linear system and is subjected to environmental loads $w(t)$ and control forces $u(t)$. The vector equation of motion is given by

$$M\ddot{x}(t) + C\dot{x}(t) + Kx(t) = B_1 u(t) + E_1 w(t) \tag{1}$$

where $x(t) = [x_1, x_2, ..., x_n]^T$ is a vector of order n with $x_i(t)$ being the displacement of the ith storey relative to ground. M, C, K are $n{\times}n$ mass, damping and

L. Rutkowski et al. (Eds.): ICAISC 2004, LNAI 3070, pp. 960–965, 2004.
© Springer-Verlag Berlin Heidelberg 2004

stiffness matrices, respectively, B_1 is an $n \times m$ location matrix of control forces, E_1 is an $n \times p$ location matrix of external loads, $u(t) = [u_1, u_2, ..., u_m]^T$ is a vector of m control forces, and $w(t) = [w_1, w_2, ..., w_p]^T$ is a vector of p environmental loads. Equation (1) can be converted into the state equation as in the form

$$\dot{z}(t) = Az(t) + Bu(t) + Ew(t) \tag{2}$$

3   Fuzzy Sliding Mode Control Design Based on GAs

Consider the design of a sliding mode controller for the following system

$$\dot{z}(t) = A(z(t) - z_d) + Bu(t) + f(z, u, t) \tag{3}$$

where z_d is reference trajectory and $u(t)$ is the input to the system. We choose m switching functions as follows

$$s_i(z) = c_i z = c_{i1} z_1 + c_{i2} z_2 + ... + c_{i2n} z_{2n} \tag{4}$$

where c_i is a sliding vector. We rewrite Equation (4) in the form

$$s(z) = cz; c = [c_1, c_2, ..., c_m]^T. \tag{5}$$

The following is a possible choice of the structure of a sliding mode controller [8,9]

$$u = u_k + u_{eq}; u_{eq} = -(cB)^{-1} cAz, u_k = -(cB)^{-1} (\gamma + \sigma) \frac{s}{\|s\|} \tag{6}$$

According to the control law (6) with one switching function, we have the fuzzy control rule j [5] as

R^j: If s is A^j, then u is u^j.

where for $j = -q, -q+1, ..., q$, the value of s is obtained from Equation (5) for one switching function, and A^j is a linguistic value with respect to s of rule j. The definition of membership function is

$$\mu_{A^i}(s) = \{ \frac{s - \sigma_{j-1}}{\sigma_j - \sigma_{j-1}}, \sigma_{j-1} < s < \sigma_j; \frac{\sigma_{j+1} - s}{\sigma_{j+1} - \sigma_j}, \sigma_j < s < \sigma_{j+1} \} \tag{7}$$

where σ_j is the center of jth membership function. The triangle membership function is determined by three parameters σ_{j-1}, σ_j and σ_{j+1}. The definition of membership functions is symmetrical, that is, $\sigma_0 = 0, \sigma_{-1} = -\sigma_1, ..., \sigma_{-q} = -\sigma_q$. The control law u_j is

$$u_j = k_j sgn(s_j) + u_{eqj}; u_{eqj} = G_j z \tag{8}$$

With respect to the SMC, the parameters are assumed as follows

$$q = 1, \sigma_0 = 0, \sigma_{-1} = \sigma_1 = \epsilon(\epsilon \to 0), G_{-1} = G_0 = G_1 = -(cB)^{-1} cA,$$
$$tk_{-1} = (cB)^{-1}(\gamma + \sigma), k_0 = 0, k_1 = -(cB)^{-1}(\gamma + \sigma) \tag{9}$$

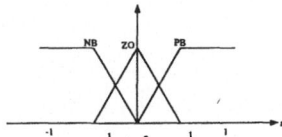

Fig. 1. The membership function of fuzzy sets

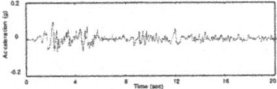

Fig. 2. The El Centro earthquake with a PGA of 0.1

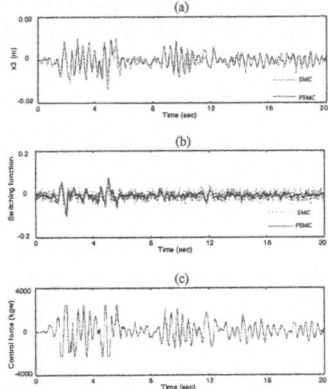

Fig. 3. (a) Time history of displacement using SMC and FSMC: top storey, (b) time history of switching function s for SMC and FSMC, (c) time history of control force for FSMC

Fitness as a qualitative attribute measures the reproductive efficiency of living creatures according to the principle of survival of the fittest. In the FSMC design, the parameters of controller are determined and optimized through assessing the individual fitness. In order to employ the GAs to optimize the FSMC for the system, we establish the fitness function according to the objective of active vibration control. For the active vibration control, we define the performance index [6] as

$$J = \frac{1}{M} \sum |s_k| \tag{10}$$

where s_k is the value of switching function s at the kth time step, $M = int(t_{max}/\triangle t)$ denotes the number of computing steps, t_{max} is the running time, and $\triangle t$ is the sampling period. The fitness function can then be defined as

$$F = \frac{1}{J + \tau} \tag{11}$$

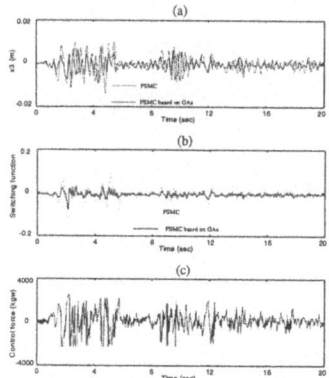

Fig. 4. (a) Time history of displacement using FSMC and FSMC based on GAs: top storey, (b) time history of switching function s for FSMC and FSMC based on GAs, (c) time history of control force for FSMC based on GAs

where τ is a small positive constant used to avoid the numerical error of dividing by zero.

In this paper, the linear encoding form is used. Here, a 16-bit binary coding is used for each parameter. Crossover and mutation rates are not fixed during evolution period. At the beginning, crossover and mutation rates are, respectively, fixed to 0.9 and 0.1, then decrease 10 percent in each generation until crossover rate is 0.5 and mutation rate is 0.01. The population size has to be an even number and is kept fixed throughout. Generally, the bigger the population size, the more design features are included. The population size should not be too small, but the procedure of optimizing will be slow when the population size is big.

4   Simulation Example

To assess the FSMC based on GAs for a building structure, simulation results of a three-storey building model are obtained. In this study, we discuss an active bracing system with two dynamic actuators installed diagonally between the ground and first floor, which is the same as that of Reference [10]. The capacity of actuator is 2.5 ton. The control objective is to apply a proper force to track the desired trajectories to the origin, i.e. $z_d = 0$. The relevant parameters of the system can be found in [10].

At first stage, we set the following parameters

$c = [1...1], u_{eq} = [2395 - 8455 + 30288 - 5595 - 562 - 551], u_k = 2500sgn(s)$

Then, we have the following three control rules (q=1)

R^{-1}: If s is NB, then u is $G_{-1}z + k_{-1}$.

R^0: If s is NB, then u is $G_0z + k_0$.

R^1: If s is NB, then u is $G_1z + k_1$.

where the membership functions with respect to fuzzy sets NB, ZO, and PB are shown in Fig. 1.

The El Centro earthquake ground acceleration with a PGA of 0.1g as shown in Fig. 2 is used as the input excitation. In order to study the performance of the controllers, the response of displacement of the third order, x3, will be studied. In the case of using FSMC, the peak response at location of x3 is 1.165cm, and the rms of control force is 899.8kgw (Fig. 4). Figures 5(a)-(c) show the time histories of displacement x3, For the FSMC based on the GAs, the peak response is 0.7855cm, and the rms of control force is 760.6kgw.

From the simulation results, it is found: The FSMC based on the GAs has the same effect with the SMC, but has a smaller rms of control force than that of the FSMC without the GAs. Hence, the performance of the FSMC based on the GAs is better than that of the SMC and the FSMC.

5   Conclusion

In this paper, the FSMC based on the GAs for structural buildings has been developed. First, the SMC-based fuzzy controller is introduced. Designing an equivalent control and a hitting control give the membership functions of consequent part. The membership functions of antecedent part are defined for stability requirement. Secondly, a fuzzy sliding mode controller is developed through the GAs, i.e. we design the optimal parameters of the FSMC without any experts' knowledge. The dynamic simulations of a three-storey building subjected to the El Centro earthquake show that the proposed three different control methods are effective in reducing the responses of the building structure. It is found that the FSMC based on the GAs has the same effect with the SMC and the FSMC, but has the smallest rms of control force.

References

1. Spencer, J., S. J. Dyke and H. S. Deoskar, Benchmark problems in structural control. Part I: active mass driver system. in Proc. 1997 ASCE Structures Congr., Portland, Oregon, 13-16 April, 1997.
2. Aldemir1, U, M. Bakioglu1 and S. S. Akhiev, Optimal control of linear buildings under seismic excitations, Earthquake Engineering and Structural Dynamics, 30, pp.835-851, 2001.
3. Guenfaf, L., M. Djebiri, M. S. Boucherit and F. Boudjema, Generalized minimum variance control for buildings under seismic ground motion, Earthquake Engineering and Structural Dynamics, 30, pp.945-960, 2001.
4. Lynch, J.P. and Law, K.H. Market-based control of linear structural systems, Earthquake Engineering and Structural Dynamics, 31, pp.1855-1877, 2002.
5. Lu YS, Chen JS. A self-organizing fuzzy sliding mode controller design for a class of nonlinear servo systems. IEEE Transactions of Industrial Electronics, 41, pp.492-502, 1994.
6. Chen JY. Expert SMC-based fuzzy control with genetic algorithms. Journal of the Franklin Institute, 6, pp.589-610, 1999.
7. Lin SC, Chen YY. Design of self-learning fuzzy sliding mode controllers based on genetic algorithms. Fuzzy Sets and Systems, 86, pp.139 -153, 1997.

8. Young, D. K., Utkin,V. I. & Özgüner, A control engineer's guide to sliding mode control. IEEE Transaction on Control System Technology 7(3), May, 1999.
9. J.J. Slotine and W. Li, Applied Nonlinear Control, Englewood Cliffs, NJ: Prentice-Hall, 1991.
10. Lu LY, Chung LL, Huang SK. A test program for using active member concept in seismic structural control. Proc. 2nd World Conf. on Structural Control, Japan, Wiley: New York, pp.1891-1900, 1998.

Influence of the Training Set Selection on the Performance of the Neural Network State Variables Estimators in the Induction Motor

Jerzy Jelonkiewicz and Andrzej Przybył

Częstochowa University of Technology
Dąbrowskiego 69, 42-200 Częstochowa, Poland
{jelon,przybyl}@kik.pcz.czest.pl

Abstract. In the paper three neural networks state variables estimators of the induction motor are considered, which recreate rotor angular speed, rotor flux and stator current components in the rotor flux reference frame. Input variables for the neural estimators are the components of stator current and voltage to allow for sensor less control of induction motor drive. Performance of the estimators is compared for the networks trained using static, dynamic and mixed sets of data. Intention of the analysis is to find the best way the training data are obtained that assures possibly high accuracy of the estimators.

1 Introduction

Eliminating of mechanical sensors in induction motor drives by novel sensor less control methods has been a field of research for many years. However it is a common feature of many sensor less techniques that they require high computational effort and the accuracy of speed estimation is not satisfying. Amongst varied techniques of sensor less speed estimation of induction motor the Model Reference Adaptive System (MRAS) approach looks to be the most promising because of good accuracy to computational effort ratio [1,2,3]. On the other hand, these relatively simple state variable estimators for the induction motor suffer from some severe drawbacks like integration drift (MRAS 1)[1], sensitivity to noise in measured stator current (MRAS 3), necessity to adapt settings for the PI controller for the operating point (MRAS 2, 3, 4). Therefore the neural networks estimators were proposed to improve the quality and accuracy of the motor state variables recreation. Positive results of the previously presented neural networks estimators encourage authors to work on their accuracy improvement considering different data set used for off-line training of the selected networks. To previously used data sets obtained only for static operating points of the motor, two more data sets were added - first obtained only for dynamic operating points of the motor and second with mixed static and dynamic vectors. The paper presents the results of comparison of the above mentioned three neural networks estimators. The main objective of the paper is to find possibly

L. Rutkowski et al. (Eds.): ICAISC 2004, LNAI 3070, pp. 966–971, 2004.
© Springer-Verlag Berlin Heidelberg 2004

efficient solution for the data sets composition used for training the state variables neural networks estimators in the induction motor. Selected structures are then tested to evaluate their accuracy in the static and dynamic operating points in the wide speed range.

2   Neural Networks State Variables Estimators

In the field oriented control of the induction motor drive, some state variables must be measured, calculated or estimated. In this control method, the decomposition of the control variables is possible only when the position and amplitude of the rotor flux is known. This leads to further decomposition of the stator current into the components that are responsible for motor torque and flux. Moreover, in the applications where the rotor speed is controlled, rotor angular speed must be known. Therefore, amongst variety of different estimators, three were selected that recreate state variables, crucial for rotor flux oriented control. The first one estimates rotor angular speed, the second recreates rotor flux and finally the third structure calculates the stator current components in the rotor flux reference frame. In all considered structures the input vector consists of the components of the stator current and voltage with their delayed values as other configuration of this vector influences the performance of the estimator [3,4].

2.1   Rotor Angular Speed Estimator

Features of the MRAS-based rotor speed estimators depend strongly on the selected state variable used to compare reference and adaptive models and create the tuning signal for adaptive model. With the help of neural network features, these two stage estimators can be replaced by one structure. Such an neural networks estimator, described in [1], reveals good accuracy in the run-up speed, while for the rotor–flux–oriented control achieved accuracy (MSE $= 3 \times 10^{-3}$ after 40 epochs) does not seem to be satisfying. The solution considered in the paper follows the above mentioned idea trying to find out how dynamic and static accuracy of the rotor speed estimator depends on the way the training vectors were obtained. The neural network estimator that recreates rotor angular speed was constructed according to the scheme in Fig. 1.

2.2   Rotor Flux Estimator

The rotor flux components in the stationary reference frame can be calculated in the following way:

$$\Psi_{rd} = \frac{L_r}{L_m} \left[\int (u_{sD} - R_s i_{sD}) dt - L'_s i_{sD} \right] \tag{1}$$

$$\Psi_{rq} = \frac{L_r}{L_m} \left[\int (u_{sQ} - R_s i_{sQ}) dt - L'_s i_{sQ} \right] \tag{2}$$

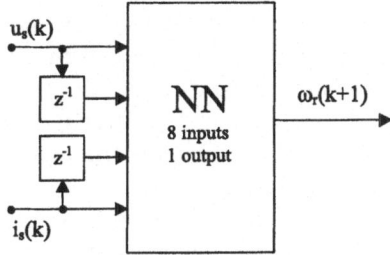

Fig. 1. Rotor speed estimator scheme

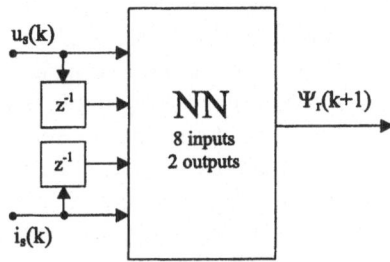

Fig. 2. Rotor flux estimator scheme

where: L_r, L_m and L_s' are rotor, main and stator transient inductances, R_s is stator resistance and $u_{sD,Q}$, $i_{sD,Q}$ represent stator voltage and current components in the stationary reference frame. Unfortunately, direct implementation of this estimator faces known problem with the integration drift. Proposed neural network that estimates the flux components [3,5] proved to be an interesting solution. Although trained using input vectors obtained for static operating points of the motor, revealed good enough static and average dynamic features. As dynamic features of the estimator are especially important for the rotor-flux-oriented control, the neural network structure according to Fig. 2 will be tested using static, dynamic and mixed sets of the input vectors.

2.3 Stator Current Components Estimator in Rotor Flux Reference Frame

The stator current components in the rotor flux reference frame can be obtained when the stator current vector is projected to the axis fixed to the rotor flux as follows:

$$i_{sx} = i_s \cos \delta \tag{3}$$

$$i_{sy} = i_s \sin \delta \tag{4}$$

where i_s is the current amplitude and δ is the angle between the current vector and the rotor flux. Assuming that stator current vector is known (amplitude i_s and angle), i_{sx}, i_{sy} components can be calculated when the angle δ is available.

This angle is defined as the difference between the stator current vector angle and rotor flux vector angle, which is determined by the rotor flux components (1,2). Estimation of these current components is particularly important in the rotor-flux-oriented control as they can be directly used for the rotor flux and torque value stabilization. For this estimator the neural network has the layout identical to that one shown in Fig. 2.

The data sets generation for training as well as all the simulation tests were carried out in the Matlab–Simulink environment. The data were recorded for the supply voltage frequency range (10 Hz, 50 Hz) with the 10 Hz step. For the tests the standard induction motor was considered with the following parameters: $P_n = 1100W$, $U_n = 380V$, $R_s = 6.88\Omega$, $R_r = 6.35\Omega$, $L_{ls} = 34 \times 10^{-3}H$, $L_{lr} = 34 \times 10^{-3}H$, $L_m = 450 \times 10^{-3}H$ and rated torque $T_n = 7,6Nm$. Each data samples were obtained for the combination of the supply voltage frequency and load torque values: 2, 5, 8 Nm. For the dynamic data sets, the data samples consisted of 320 vectors obtained in the transients related to loading and unloading the motor. In this way 6 samples were created for each frequency, giving 30 samples all together containing 9600 vectors. Static data sets were obtained only for the static operating points of the motor considering the same frequency values as for the dynamic data sets. In the mixed data sets both previous selections were represented equally including dynamic data only for loading the motor while for static conditions, data samples were added for 2, 5, 8 Nm step load.

3   Results of Training and Simulation

Considering the results obtained in the previous papers related to the network structure, the neural networks used for training had two 10 node hidden layers activated by the tansig transfer function. Results of training concerning three neural networks estimating rotor speed, flux and stator current components in the rotor flux reference frame shows Table 1. The abbreviations in the first row stand for static (S), dynamic (D), mixed (M) and reduced dynamic (RD) data sets. The numbers presented in the table signify the error obtained in the trained network after 500 epochs (MSE).

It is clearly seen in Table 1 that the lowest error values were achieved for the static data sets. The error values for the mixed data sets were placed between results for static and dynamic data sets but closer to the latter although the samples for the considered data sets were taken equally from the static and dynamic source.

Table 1. Neural networks training errors

	S	D	M	RD
ω_r	1.48×10^{-7}	4.02×10^{-6}	4.80×10^{-6}	2.18×10^{-6}
Ψ_r	1.12×10^{-7}	1.29×10^{-5}	1.64×10^{-6}	2.28×10^{-6}
i_{sxy}	4.35×10^{-6}	6.87×10^{-5}	3.85×10^{-5}	3.69×10^{-5}

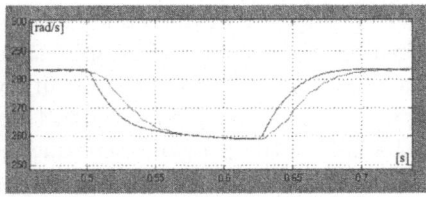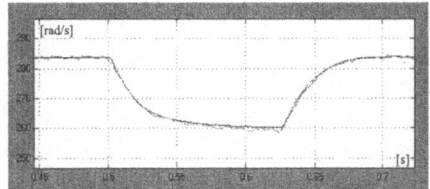

Fig. 3. Rotor angular speed for step load and unload transients ($T_L = 8Nm$) for static (left), dynamic data sets (right)

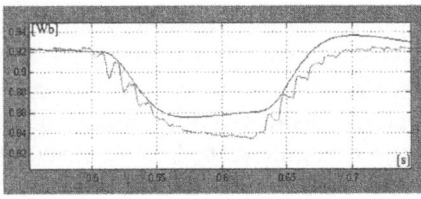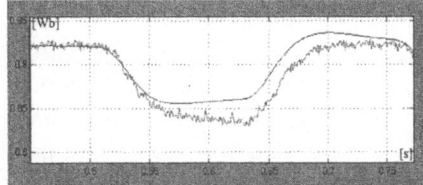

Fig. 4. Rotor flux amplitude for step load and unload transients ($T_L = 8Nm$) for static (left), dynamic data sets (right)

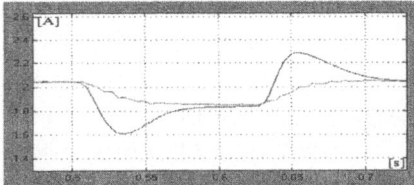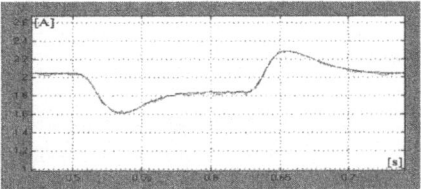

Fig. 5. Flux component of the stator current for step load and unload transients ($T_L = 8Nm$) for static (left), dynamic data sets (right)

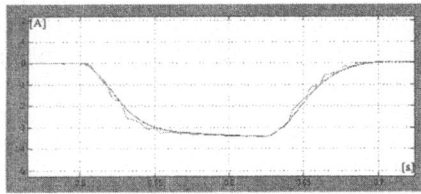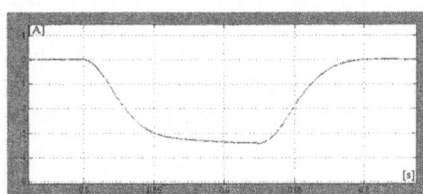

Fig. 6. Torque component of the stator current for step load and unload transients ($T_L = 8Nm$) for static (left), dynamic data sets (right)

Fig. 3-6 show how the training results of the neural network estimators transfer to their features in the simulation tests. To save space in the paper, the diagrams present results of the simulation of the trained estimators for supply frequency 45 Hz that is also representative for other frequencies in the considered range. Although the training error for the rotor speed estimator is much lower for the static data sets, its ability to follow the load and unload transients is rather poor. When dynamic data sets is used for training, the estimator shows good static and dynamic features. Two other attempts with different data sets generation were only partly successful. For the first one with mixed samples some improvement in the transients is observed at the cost of lower static accuracy. Another test considered only dynamic samples obtained for the step load transient, reducing number of training vectors the half of the previous set (marked as RD in Table 1). Unfortunately, also in this case the results are clearly worse.

4 Conclusions

Although the static data sets, used for training of the induction motor state variables neural networks estimators, are easy to create and can be small, they do not reflect the complete feature of the machine. Especially for the rotor speed and the flux component of the stator current the delay or even inability of the NN output signal to follow the pattern in the dynamic state is noticeable. On the other hand the accuracy of the state variables recreation for the dynamic data sets is satisfying. Other attempts with the mixed and reduced data sets failed or were rather disappointing. Presented approach encourages to look for possibly small, optimal data set as it transfers to a shorter training process.

References

1. Vas P.: Artificial–Intelligence–Based Electrical Machines and Drives, Monographs in Electrical and Electronic Engineering nr 45, Oxford University Press, (1999)
2. Seong-Hwan Kim, Tae-Sik Park, Ji-Yoon Yoo, Gwi-Tae Park: Speed-Sensorless Vector Control of an Induction Motor Using Neural Network Speed Estimation, IEEE Trans. on Ind. Electr., vol. 48, no 3, (2001) 609-614
3. Jelonkiewicz J., Przybył A.: Neural Networks Implementation of Model Reference Adaptive Systems in Induction Motor Drive, Proc. EPE'01, Graz (2001) on CD
4. Orłowska-Kowalska T., Kowalski C.: Neural network application for flux and speed estimation in the sensorless induction motor drive Proc. of ISIE'97, IEEE (1997)
5. Jelonkiewicz J.: Neural Network Improvement of Model Reference Adaptive System in Induction Motor Drive. PEMC'02, Dubrownik (2002) on CD

LMI-Based Design of Optimal Controllers for Takagi-Sugeno Fuzzy Systems

J. Park[1]*, Y. Park[2], K. Kwak[3], and J.H. Hong[1]**

[1] Department of Control and Instrumentation Engineering, Korea University,
Jochiwon, Chungnam, 339-700, Korea
[2] Division of Aerospace Engineering, Department of Mechanical Engineering,
Korea Advanced Institute of Science and Technology, Daejeon, 305-701, Korea
[3] Fire Control Lab, Agency for Defense Development, Daejeon, 305-600, Korea

Abstract. This paper considers the problem of designing optimal stabilizing controllers for the systems that can be modelled by the Takagi-Sugeno (TS) fuzzy model. Contrary to difficult optimal control problems dealing with fixed cost functions directly, we pursue the strategy in which the cost function is determined during the design process. This approach makes the problem easy to solve and yields stabilizing controllers which satisfy the inherent robustness of optimal controllers. The design procedure of this paper consists of solving LMIs (linear matrix inequalities). The applicability of the proposed method is illustrated via an example.

1 Introduction

There have been many recent studies concerning the fuzzy modelling and fuzzy control. Particularly pertinent to this paper are results which provide systematic design procedures for robust and stabilizing fuzzy controllers [1]. In this paper, we present a new design procedure yielding robust and stabilizing controllers for the nonlinear systems described by the TS (Takagi-Sugeno) fuzzy model [2]. Based on the well-known fact that the robustness achieved as a result of the optimality is largely independent of the particular choice of a certain part of the cost function, we address the problem of designing robust and stabilizing controllers for the TS fuzzy systems in the framework of the optimal control theory. Also, it is shown that to find the parameters of the optimal controllers can be represented as an LMI (linear matrix inequality) problem. Formulation of the controller synthesis problems with LMIs is of great practical value because they can be solved by efficient convex optimization tools [3]-[4].

This paper is organized as follows: In Section 2, preliminaries are provided regarding the TS fuzzy model and optimal control theory. Our main results on the design of optimal controllers for the TS fuzzy systems are presented in Section 3. In Section 4, a controller is designed for the inverted pendulum

* Corresponding author. E-mail: parkj@korea.ac.kr
** J.H. Hong and J. Park wish to acknowledge the financial support of the Korea Ministry of Commerce, Industry and Energy (Grant 1008490).

L. Rutkowski et al. (Eds.): ICAISC 2004, LNAI 3070, pp. 972–977, 2004.
© Springer-Verlag Berlin Heidelberg 2004

system to illustrate the proposed method. Finally, concluding remarks are given in Section 5.

2   TS Fuzzy Model and Optimal Control

In this paper, we are concerned with the design of optimal controllers for the systems described by the TS fuzzy model. The IF-THEN rules of the TS fuzzy model are given in the following form [5]: *Plant Rule l:*

$$\text{IF } x_1(t) \text{ is } M_1^l \text{ and } \cdots x_n(t) \text{ is } M_n^l, \text{ THEN } \dot{x}(t) = A_l x(t) + B_l u(t) + a_l \quad (1)$$

$l = 1, \cdots, m$.

Here, $x_i(t), i = 1, \cdots, n$ and $M_i^l, i = 1, \cdots, n, l = 1, \cdots, m$ are state variables and fuzzy sets, respectively, $x(t) \in D \subset \mathbb{R}^n$ and $u(t) \in \mathbb{R}^p$ are the state and input vector, respectively, m is the number of IF-THEN rules, and (A_l, B_l, a_l) is the lth local model of the fuzzy system. Following the usual inference method, we have the following state equation for the TS fuzzy system [5]:

$$\dot{x}(t) = \sum_{l=1}^{m} \mu_l(x(t))\{A_l x(t) + B_l u(t) + a_l\}, \quad (2)$$

where the normalized weight functions μ_l satisfy $\mu_l(x) \geq 0, \forall l \in \{1, \cdots, m\}$, and $\sum_{l=1}^{m} \mu_l(x) = 1$ for any $x \in D$. For simplicity, we will denote the normalized weight function $\mu_l(x(t))$ by μ_l from now on. Let $L \triangleq \{1, \cdots, m\}$ be the index set for the local models (1), and let $S_l \subset D$ denote the cell where the l-th local model plays a dominant role, i.e.,

$$S_l \triangleq \{x \in D \mid \mu_l(x) \geq \mu_i(x) \text{ for } \forall \, i \in L\}, \, l \in L.$$

Also, let L^* denote the index set for cells which do not contain the origin. Since the origin is an equilibrium point, it is assumed throughout this paper that $a_l = 0$ for all $l \in L \setminus L^*$.

In general, the TS fuzzy controller is described by the following IF-THEN rules [1]: *Controller Rule l:*

$$\text{IF } x_1(t) \text{ is } M_1^l \text{ and } \cdots \text{ and } x_n(t) \text{ is } M_n^l, \text{ THEN } u(t) = K_l x(t)$$

$l = 1, \cdots, m$.

Note that the IF part of the above controller rule shares the same fuzzy sets with that of (1). The usual inference method for the TS fuzzy model yields the following representation for the TS fuzzy controller [1]:

$$u(t) = \sum_{l=1}^{m} \mu_l K_l x(t). \quad (3)$$

Here, the μ_l are the same as in (2), and the state feedback gains K_l need to be found so that design requirements such as stability and robustness may be met. Our main strategy for finding a satisfactory set of the K_l is to utilize the optimal control theory (see [6], for example).

One of the most important problems in the area of optimal control is to find an optimal feedback control law for the nonlinear system described by

$$\dot{x}(t) = f(x(t)) + g(x(t))u(t). \tag{4}$$

In the problem, we wish to find a control law $u(t) = u(x(t))$ which can achieve the following: (1) Asymptotic stability of the equilibrium point $x = 0$. (2) Minimization of the cost function

$$J = \int_0^\infty \{l(x(t)) + u(t)^T R(x(t))u(t)\} \, dt, \tag{5}$$

where $l(x)$ is a positive definite function and $R(x) = R(x)^T$ is a positive definite matrix for all $x \in D$. For a given feedback control $u(x)$, the value of cost J depends on the initial state $x(0)$. Thus, we write the value of J as $J(x(0))$, or simply $J(x)$. When J is at its minimum, $J(x)$ is called the optimal value function. As is shown in the next lemma [6], the above optimal control problem can be reduced to solving the HJB (Hamilton-Jacobi-Bellman) equation.

Lemma 1. *Suppose that there exists a positive definite function $V(x) \in C^1(\mathbb{R}^n)$ which satisfies the HJB equation*

$$l(x) + L_f V(x) - (L_g V(x))R^{-1}(x)(L_g V(x))^T/4 = 0, \ V(0) = 0, \tag{6}$$

and the feedback control $u^* = -R^{-1}(x)(L_g V(x))^T/2$ achieves the asymptotic stability of the equilibrium point $x = 0$ for the system (4). Then u^* is the optimal stabilizing control which minimizes the cost function (5) over all $u(t)$ guaranteeing $\lim_{t\to\infty} x(t) = 0$, and $V(x)$ is the optimal value function.

Many optimal control problems deal with the fixed cost functions. However, to solve their corresponding HJB equations is not a feasible task in general. On the other hand, it is well-known that the robustness achieved as a result of the optimality is largely independent of the particular choice of $l(x)$ when $R(x) = I$. Hence, it is motivated to pursue the strategy in which the positive definite function $l(x)$ is *a posteriori* determined in the process of controller design. More precisely, we use the following lemma [6]:

Lemma 2. *A stabilizing control u^* solves an optimal control problem for system (4) if it is of the form*

$$u^* = -(L_g V(x))^T/2, \tag{7}$$

where $V(x) \in C^1(\mathbb{R}^n)$ is a positive definite function such that

$$l(x) \triangleq -L_f V(x) + (L_g V(x))(L_g V(x))^T/4 > 0 \tag{8}$$

for any $x \neq 0$.

In this paper, Lemma 2 is utilized in the following manner. First, we find a positive definite function $V(x) \in C^1(\mathbb{R}^n)$ satisfying the inequality (8). Then, it is obvious that the function $V(x)$ satisfies the HJB equation (6) with $l(x)$ defined as in (8) and $R(x) = I$. Moreover, note that when $V(x) \in C^1(\mathbb{R}^n)$ is a positive definite function satisfying (8), the following holds true for any $x \neq 0$:

$$\dot{V}(x)\,|_{u=u^*} = L_f V(x) - (L_g V(x))(L_g V(x))^T/2 = -l(x) - \|u^*\|^2 < 0.$$

Thus, from the Lyapunov stability theorem, we see that u^* of (7) is a stabilizing control. Therefore, we can conclude that under the condition of Lemma 2, u^* of (7) is the optimal stabilizing feedback minimizing $J = \int_0^\infty (l(x) + u^T u)dt$.

3 LMI-Based Design Procedure

In this section, we establish a design procedure for the optimal control of the TS fuzzy systems. First, note that the TS fuzzy system (2) is an example of the class represented by the canonical form (4) with $f(x) = \sum_{l=1}^m \mu_l (A_l x + a_l)$ and $g(x) = \sum_{l=1}^m \mu_l B_l$; thus Lemma 2 is applicable to our problem. Next, for the sake of convenience in controller design, restrict focus only on the cases that the optimal value function $V(x)$ can be expressed in the quadratic form $x^T P x$ where $P > 0$. Then the controller u^* of (7) can be reduced to

$$u^* = -(L_g V(x))^T/2 = \sum_{l=1}^m \mu_l(-B_l^T P)x. \tag{9}$$

A remarkable observation here is that the optimal controller (9) takes the form of the TS fuzzy controller (3) with $K_l = -B_l^T P$. For more details on this observation and related material, please refer to the authors' previous paper [7]. Applying Lemma 2 to the quadratic value function case, we see that the TS fuzzy controller u^* of (9) becomes an optimal stabilizing controller for the TS fuzzy system (2) if the following hold:

$$
\begin{cases}
P > 0 \\
l(x) \triangleq -L_f V(x) + (L_g V(x))(L_g V(x))^T/4 \\
\quad = -x^T \{\sum_{l=1}^m \mu_l(A_l^T P + PA_l)\}x - \sum_{l=1}^m \mu_l(x^T Pa_l + a_l^T Px) \\
\quad\quad + x^T \{P(\sum_{l=1}^m \mu_l B_l)(\sum_{l=1}^m \mu_l B_l)^T P\}x \\
\quad > 0 \text{ for } \forall x \in D \setminus \{0\}.
\end{cases} \tag{10}
$$

Thus, we have the following:

Theorem 1. *Consider the TS fuzzy system (2). If there exists $P \in \mathbb{R}^{n \times n}$ satisfying (10), then $u^* = \sum_{l=1}^m \mu_l(-B_l^T P)x$ is the optimal stabilizing control which minimizes the cost function $J = \int_0^\infty (l(x(t)) + \|u(t)\|^2)dt$.*

In order to find a matrix P satisfying (10), the method of this paper proceeds as follows: First, we introduce the following bounds for each cell S_l:

$$-(\sum_{l=1}^m \mu_l a_l)(\sum_{l=1}^m \mu_l a_l)^T \leq -E_{la}E_{la}^T, \quad -(\sum_{l=1}^m \mu_l B_l)(\sum_{l=1}^m \mu_l B_l)^T \leq -E_{lB}E_{lB}^T. \tag{11}$$

Note that since all the information for the μ_l, a_l, and B_l are given precisely, the above bounds can be easily obtained. For a hint on how to obtain these bounds, see [5] for example. Next, define $N_l \triangleq \{i \in L \mid \mu_i(x) > 0 \text{ for some } x \in S_l\}$. Then with $Q \triangleq P^{-1}$, we can easily show that for each $l \in L \setminus L^*$, $A_iQ + QA_i^T - E_{lB}E_{lB}^T < 0$, $\forall i \in N_l$ guarantees $l(x) > 0$ for $\forall x \in S_l$. Finally, suppose that for each $l \in L^*$, we have matrices Y_l and y_l such that $S_l \subset \{x \in \mathbb{R}^n \mid \|Y_lx + y_l\| \leq 1\}$. Then, utilizing the S-procedure [3] and some strategy of [8], we can show that the following holds true for each $l \in L^*$: If there exists $v_l > 0$ and $Q > 0$ such that $A_iQ + QA_i^T - E_{lB}E_{lB}^T - v_lE_{la}E_{la}^T - (QY_l^T - v_la_iy_l^T)(v_lI - v_ly_ly_l^T)^{-1}(Y_lQ - v_ly_la_i^T) < 0$, $\forall i \in N_l$, then $l(x) > 0$ for $\forall x \in S_l$. Therefore, we have the following:

[Design Procedure]
(1) Find $v_l > 0$, $l \in L^*$, and $Q = Q^T > 0$ satisfying

$$\begin{cases} A_iQ + QA_i^T - E_{lB}E_{lB}^T < 0, \; l \in L \setminus L^*, \; i \in N_l \\ \begin{bmatrix} A_iQ + QA_i^T - E_{lB}E_{lB}^T - v_lE_{la}E_{la}^T & QY_l^T - v_la_iy_l^T \\ Y_lQ - v_ly_la_i^T & v_l(I - y_ly_l^T) \end{bmatrix} < 0, \; l \in L^*, \; i \in N_l \end{cases}$$
$$(12)$$

(2) Compute $K_l = -B_l^TQ^{-1}, l = 1, \cdots, m$, and set $u^* = \sum_{l=1}^m \mu_lK_lx$.

4   A Numerical Example

In this section, we applied the proposed design procedure to the problem of balancing an inverted pendulum on a cart, in which the system is approximated by the following TS fuzzy model [5]:

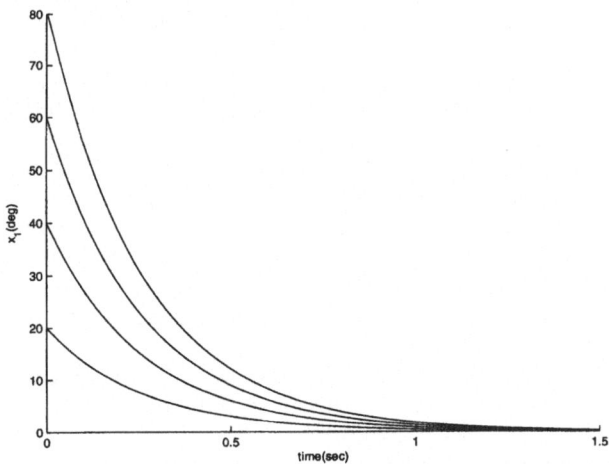

Fig. 1. Simulation results for initial conditions $x_1(0) = 20, 40, 60, 80$, and $x_2(0) = 0$

Rule 1: IF x_1 is *about* 0, THEN $\dot{x} = A_1 x + B_1 u + a_1$,
Rule 2: IF x_1 is *about* $-\pi/2$, THEN $\dot{x} = A_2 x + B_2 u + a_2$,
Rule 3: IF x_1 is *about* $+\pi/2$, THEN $\dot{x} = A_3 x + B_3 u + a_3$,

where $A_1 = \begin{bmatrix} 0 & 1 \\ 17.2941 & 0 \end{bmatrix}$, $B_1 = \begin{bmatrix} 0 \\ -0.1765 \end{bmatrix}$, $A_2 = A_3 = \begin{bmatrix} 0 & 1 \\ 0.2395 & 0 \end{bmatrix}$, $B_2 =$

$B_3 = \begin{bmatrix} 0 \\ -0.0052 \end{bmatrix}$, $a_1 = \begin{bmatrix} 0 \\ 0 \end{bmatrix}$, $a_2 = \begin{bmatrix} 0 \\ 0.3679 \end{bmatrix}$, $a_3 = \begin{bmatrix} 0 \\ -0.3679 \end{bmatrix}$, and the norma-

lized weight functions are $\mu_1 = 1 - 2|x_1|/\pi$, $\mu_2 = (-2x_1/\pi) * 1_{\{x_1 < 0\}}$, and $\mu_3 = (2x_1/\pi) * 1_{\{x_1 > 0\}}$. For the remaining parameters, we used $E_{2a} = E_{3a} = a_2/2$, $E_{1B} = (B_1 + B_2)/2$, $E_{2B} = E_{3B} = B_2$, $Y_2 = Y_3 = [8/\pi \; 0]$, $y_2 = 3$, and $y_3 = -3$. From the proposed design procedure, we obtained the following state feedback gains: $K_1 = 10^5 * [2.77 \; 0.953]$, $K_2 = K_3 = 10^3 * [8.21 \; 2.83]$. The simulation results in Fig. 1 shows that the designed controller $u = (\mu_1 K_1 + \mu_2 K_2 + \mu_3 K_3)x$ yields satisfactory performance for various initial conditions.

5   Concluding Remarks

In this paper, we addressed the problem of designing controllers for the TS fuzzy systems in the framework of the optimal control. Our design procedure is given in the form of an LMI problem. Since LMIs can be solved efficiently within a given tolerance by the interior point methods, the proposed design method is useful in practice. Further investigations yet to be done include the extension of the proposed method toward the use of piecewise quadratic value functions.

References

1. K. Tanaka and H. O. Wang, Fuzzy Control Systems Design and Analysis: A Linear Matrix Inequalities Approach, John Wiley & Sons, Inc., New York, 2001.
2. T. Takagi and M. Sugeno, "Fuzzy identification of systems and its applications to modeling and control," IEEE Transactions on Systems, Man and Cybernetics, vol. 15, pp. 116-132, 1985.
3. S. Boyd, L. ElGhaoui, E. Feron, and V. Balakrishnan, Linear Matrix Inequalities in Systems and Control Theory, SIAM Studies in Applied Mathematics, vol. 15, SIAM, Philadelphia, 1994.
4. P. Gahinet, A. Nemirovski, A. J. Laub, and M. Chilali, LMI Control Toolbox, MathWorks Inc., Natick, MA, 1995.
5. G. Feng, "H_∞ controller design of fuzzy dynamic systems based on piecewise Lyapunov functions," IEEE Transactions on Systems, Man, and Cybernetics - Part B: Cybernetics, vol. 34, pp. 283-292, 2004.
6. R. Sepulchre, M. Jankovic, and P. V. Kokotovic, Constructive Nonlinear Control, Springer-Verlag, New York, 1997.
7. Y. Park, M.-J. Tahk, and J. Park, "Optimal stabilization of Takagi-Sugeno fuzzy systems with application to spacecraft control," Journal of Guidance, Control, and Dynamics, vol. 24, pp. 767-777, 2001.
8. M. Johansson, Piecewise Linear Control Systems, Lecture Notes in Control and Information Sciences, vol. 284, Springer-Verlag, Berlin, 2003.

Design of Multi-objective Evolutionary Technique Based Intelligent Controller for Multivariable Nonlinear Systems

Farzan Rashidi[1] and Mehran Rashidi[2]

[1] Control Research Department, Engineering Research Institute,Tehran, Iran
P.O.Box: 13445-754, Tehran
f.rashidi@ece.ut.ac.ir
[2] Hormozgan Regional Electric Co., Bandar-Abbas, Iran
mrashidi@mehr.sharif.edu

Abstract. The main objective of this paper is to present a new method based on Multiobjective evolutionary algorithm for control of the multivariable and nonlinear systems. Problem design considers time domain specifications such as overshoot, rising time, settling time and stationary error as well as interaction effects. Genetic algorithms are employed to satisfy time domain design specifications, that are not considered in an explicit way in the standard nonlinear control theory. Adaptation, setpoint tracking and satisfaction of temporary response specifications are the advantages of this method that be shown by some simulations.

1 Introduction

The theory of linear dynamic systems is now well understood and is widely applied to many field of engineering such as robotics, processes control, ship stirring and many others. However, the theory of nonlinear systems has received less attention, the reason being the diversity and complexity of the nonlinear systems [1]. Nonlinear behaviors are very common in practice and usually are approximated by linearization around the operating point. This procedure may not be acceptable for complex and highly reliable systems. However, with the advent of fast and powerful digital computer many nonlinear control system design methods allow optimization of controller parameters by simulating the closed loop system and evaluating the response according to some quantitative performance or fitness criterion [2]. A controller structure is postulated, then simulated with a model of the plant, and the controller parameters are estimated so as to give a good system response. Several optimization techniques, denominated as intelligent(genetic algorithms, neural networks, simulated annealing, tabu search) and classic(gradients, Hessians, linearity, and continuity), can be used for obtaining controller parameters directly, or in order to select design parameters [3]. Genetic Algorithms (GAs) are a family of intelligent algorithms which explore the search space by fitness evaluations and then guide the search by "survival-of-the-fittest" evolutionary principles. In system theory, robustness, specifications for setpoint

L. Rutkowski et al. (Eds.): ICAISC 2004, LNAI 3070, pp. 978–983, 2004.
© Springer-Verlag Berlin Heidelberg 2004

tracking and disturbance attenuation are considered in the frequency domain by means of weighting transfer functions. Nevertheless, temporary response specifications are not considered "a priori" or explicitly, so that this one must be taken into account after the controller has been obtained in a trial and error procedure. In this paper we propose a new method based on Multiobjective evolutionary algorithm for control of multivariable and nonlinear systems. Time responses specifications as well as interaction effects are considered for a multivariable, nonlinear and non minimum phase system using genetic algorithms for tuning controllers with time domain specifications (overshoot, stationary error, and rise time). In the subsequent sections, we discuss our proposed controller, and its application in the closed loop control of multivariable and nonlinear systems, simulation and some concluding remarks.

2   Multiobjective Evolutionary Algorithms

2.1   Genetic Algorithm

The GAs are the stochastic global search method that mimic the metaphor of natural biological evolution. These algorithms maintain and manipulate a population of solutions and implement the principle of survival of the fittest in their search to produce better and better approximations to a solution. This provides an implicit as well as explicit parallelism that allows for the exploitation of several promising areas of the solution space at the same time. The implicit parallelism is due to the schema theory developed by Holland, while the explicit parallelism arises from the manipulation of a population of points [4]. The implementation of GA involves some preparatory stages. Having decoded the chromosome representation into the decision variable domain, it is possible to assess the performance, or fitness, of individual members of a population. This is done through an objective function that characterizes an individual's performance in the problem domain. During the reproduction phase, each individual is assigned a fitness value derived from its raw performance measure given by objective function. Once the individuals have been assigned a fitness value, they can be chosen from population, with a probability according to their relative fitness, and recombined to produce the next generation. Genetic operators manipulate the genes. The recombination operator is used to exchange genetic information between pairs of individuals. The crossover operation is applied with a probability px when the pairs are chosen for breeding. Mutation causes the individual genetic representation to be changed according to some probabilistic rule. Mutation is generally considered to be a background operator that ensures that the probability of searching a particular subspace of the problem space is never zero. This has the effect of tending to inhibit the possibility of converging to a local optimum.

Multiobjective Evolutionary Algorithms (MOEA) are based on multiobjective Genetic Algorithms (MOGA). The MOEA begins with a population of possible solutions, called strings. Each string is fed into a model as the candidate solution, in this case these strings are the parameters of the configured controller model. This model is usually a computer program representation of the solution to the problem. The compensator model with initialize parameters is then implemented in a cascade with the nonlinear system model which returns the overall time response. From these time responses the objectives are evaluated and the cost function (fitness) calculated and returned to MOEA. Based on these cost functions, MOEA selects strings for evolution to create the next generation of strings. Multi-objective simply means that there is more than one objective involved [1]. For each string, each objective represents a separate cost. The manner in which a string is deemed superior or inferior to other strings is carried out by a selection mechanism. The selected strings undergo the evolutionary process where the traits of the selected strings (which may or may not be good) are selected and combined to form new strings for the next generation. In theory, with each generation, the strings in the population should return better and better cost functions by obtaining strings (controller parameters) nearer to the optimal solutions. In practice, often there are limits to the values of cost functions that can be achieved. This depends on the objective functions and the constraints imposed on the model parameters. Further, there may be serious conflicts between the objectives, such that some of the objectives may not be met. In this case the domain knowledge of the designer must be employed to effect the appropriate trade offs between the conflicting objectives.

2.2   Proposed MOEA for Nonlinear Systems Control

In conventional applications of nonlinear MIMO system theory, controller is designed for robustness and performance specifications expressed in the frequency domain, but the typical indicators of the time response (overshoot, rise time, settling time and etc.) are not considered "a priori". In practice, it is difficult to obtain adequate time responses using this approach[5]. In this paper we present a new method based on MOEA to satisfy time responses specifications as well as interaction effects between loops. We have implemented the following algorithm for the controller design based on evolutionary algorithm for MIMO nonlinear systems:

1. The target close loop time domain specifications (for example: rise time, overshoot, settle time, stationary error) are established.
2. The structure of weighting matrices is selected (design parameters).
3. The parameters values intervals are set.
4. The control problem is solved aided with GA for obtaining design specifications (the target feedback loop).
5. Cost functions are calculated in order to evaluate the control system.

3   Simulation Results

The following simulation results illustrate the capabilities of proposed method. In these simulations we have chosen a nonlinear model of HVAC system which it has delayed behavior and also is a multivariable, nonlinear and non minimum phase. The actual plant model involves four inputs and three output processes, of which two inputs can be manipulated for achieving desired performance levels. The state space equations governing the model are as follows [6]:

$$
\begin{aligned}
\dot{x}_1 &= 60u_1\alpha_1(x_3 - x_1) - 60u_1\alpha_2(W_s - x_2) + \alpha_3(Q_0 - h_{fg}M_0) \\
\dot{x}_2 &= 60u_1\alpha_1(W_s - x_2) + \alpha_4 M_0 \\
\dot{x}_3 &= 60u_1\beta_1(-x_3 + x_1) + 15u_1\beta_1(T_0 - x_1) \\
&\quad -60\,u_1\beta_3(0.25W_0 + 0.75x_2 - W_s) \\
y_1 &= x_1, \quad y_2 = x_2
\end{aligned} \tag{1}
$$

In which y_1 and y_2 are the outputs and the other parameters are as follows:

$$
u_1 = f, u_2 = g_{mp}, x_1 = T_3, x_2 = W_3, x_3 = T_2, \alpha_1 = \frac{1}{V_s}, \alpha_2 = \frac{h_{fg}}{C_p V_s}
$$

$$
\alpha_3 = \frac{1}{\rho C_p V_s}, \alpha_4 = \frac{1}{\rho V_s}, \beta_1 = \frac{1}{V_{he}}, \beta_2 = \frac{1}{\rho C_p V_{he}}, \beta_3 = \frac{h_w}{C_p V_{he}} \tag{2}
$$

The actuator's transfer function can be considered as:

$$
G_{act}(s) = \frac{k}{1 + \tau s} \tag{3}
$$

In which k and τ are the actuator's gain and time constant. Due to knowledge based on experimental data, the structured selected for the weighting matrices $W(s)$ are given by

$$
W(s) = diag(\frac{a_i s + b_i}{c_i s + d_i}), \quad i = 1, 2, ... \tag{4}
$$

where the parameters of the matrices are obtained by minimization through GAs with objective function $Fitness$:

$$
J = w_1 t_r + w_2 t_s + w_3 M_p + w_4 ITAE + w_5 I_{jk} \tag{5}
$$
$$
Fitness = 1/(1 + J)
$$

in which $ITAE$, t_r, t_s, M_p and w_i ($i = 1, 2, ..., 5$) are the integral of time multiplied by absolute error, rising time, settling time, overshoot for step change in the setpoint, and the weighting factors respectively. I_{jk} denotes the interaction effects between loop j and k and is defined as:

$$
I_{jk} = \frac{y_{jk}(t_\infty)}{y_{jj}(t_\infty)} \quad \text{for} \quad j \neq k \tag{6}
$$

where y_{jk} denotes the loop interaction.

In order to implement our design methodology, Matrices structure and range of the design parameters are selected as are given before. Also parameters of

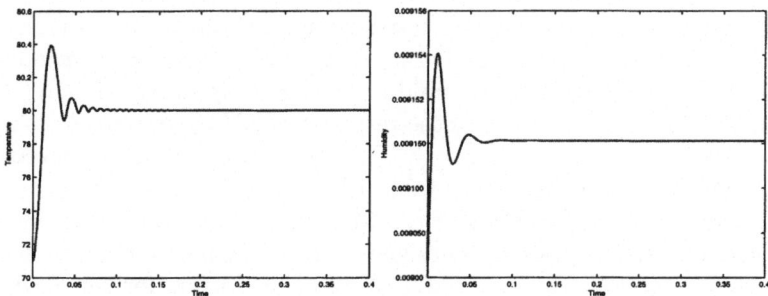

Fig. 1. HVAC system responses for the specifications given in Table 1.

Table 1. Performance characteristics of HVAC system, (for fig.1)

Name of objectives	Desired objectives $y_1 - y_2$	Obtained objectives $y_1 - y_2$
t_r	$0.07 - 0.07$	$0.04 - 0.04$
M_p	$5\% - 5\%$	$4.63\% - 2.66\%$
t_s	$0.2 - 0.2$	$0.1 - 0.1$
$ITAE$	$0.1 - 0.1$	$0- $ ¡0.1
I_{jk} $j, k = 1, 2$	$0.1 - 0.1$	$0.035 - 0$

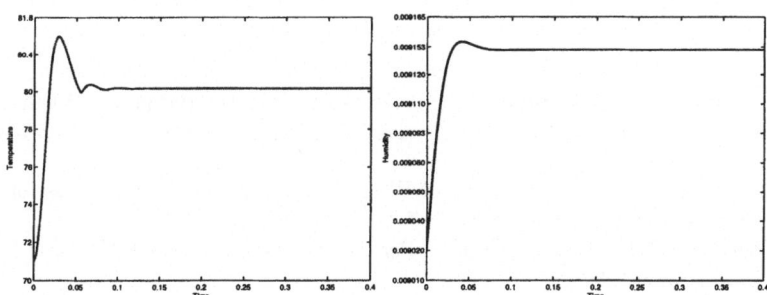

Fig. 2. HVAC system responses for the specifications given in Table 2.

Table 2. Performance characteristics of HVAC system, (for fig.2)

Name of objectives	Desired objectives $y_1 - y_2$	Obtained objectives $y_1 - y_2$
t_r	$0.07 - 0.07$	$0.025 - 0.029$
M_p	$5\% - 5\%$	$8.8\% - 3.7\%$
t_s	$0.2 - 0.2$	$0.1 - 0.1$
$ITAE$	$0.1 - 0.1$	$0- $ ¡0.1
I_{jk} $j, k = 1, 2$	$0.1 - 0.1$	$0.037 - 0$

the weighting transfer functions are adjusted by means of GA optimization. We apply proposed method with time response specifications $t_r \leq 0.1$, $M_p \leq 5\%$, $t_s \leq 0.2$, $ITAE \leq 0.1$ and $I_{jk} \leq 0.1$ $(j, k = 1, 2, \quad j \neq k)$ respectively. We wish to track temperature and humidity to their respecting set point levels of $80°F$ and 0.00915. Figure 1 shows the response of HVAC system. As it is clearly obvious, results are very satisfactory. The performance levels achieved via the proposed approach are outlined in table 1.

To illustrate the capabilities of the MOEA to affect the trade off between the objectives. we Supposed the designer requires reducing the rise time of y_1 (temperature) too less than 0.05. MOEA was called again for this new requirement. Table 2 and Figure 2 show that the new criterion is satisfied only on the expense of increased overshoot.

4   Conclusion

In this paper a new method based on multiobjective evolutionary algorithm for control of nonlinear MIMO systems was presented. The controller was designed for time domain specifications requirements. Adaptation, setpoint tracking and satisfaction of temporary response specifications are the most important advantages of the proposed method that are shown in the simulation results. Other important advantage of this method is relative independency to plant model that makes it more interesting for real application.

References

1. S.D Katebi and M.R Katebi: Control Design for Multivariable Multi-valued nonlinear systems. Journal of System Analysis Modeling and Simulation (SAMS), vol. 15,13–37, 1994.
2. Man K.F., K.S. Tang, S. Kwong and W.A. Halang: Genetic Algorithms for Control and Signal Processing, Springer, 1997.
3. Goldberg, D: Genetic Algorithms in Search, Optimisation, and Machine Learning, Addison-Wesley, 1989.
4. P. J. Flemming and R. C. purshouse: Genetic Algorithms in Control Engineering, Research report NO. 789. Dept. of Automatic and System Eng, University of Sheffield, UK, 2001.
5. Rashidi, F., Rashidi, M., Hosseini, A.H.: Intelligent Control Strategis for speed regulation of DC Motors, IEEE International Conference on Control Application, 2003.
6. Alber, T. P., Chan, W. L., Chow, T. T.: A Neural Network-Based Identifier/Controller for Modern HVAC Control, ASHRAE Transaction, 1994.

Design of a Robust Sliding Mode Fuzzy Controller for Nonlinear HVAC Systems

Farzan Rashidi[1] and Behzad Moshiri[2]

[1] Control Research Department, Engineering Research Institute,Tehran, Iran
f.rashidi@ece.ut.ac.ir
[2] Center of Excellence for Control and Intelligent Processing, Department of
Electrical and Computer Engineering, Tehran University
moshiri@ut.ac.ir

Abstract. Heating, Ventilating and Air Conditioning (HVAC) plant, is a multivariable, nonlinear and non minimum phase system, that its control is very difficult. In this paper, we apply a robust sliding mode fuzzy controller to HVAC system. Our proposed method can achieve very robust and satisfactory performance and could be used to get the desired performance levels. The response time is also very fast despite the fact that the control strategy is based on bounded rationality. To evaluate the usefulness of the proposed method, we compare the response of this method with PID controller. The simulation results show that proposed method has the better control performance than PID controller.

1 Introduction

The energy consumed by heating, ventilating and air conditioning (HVAC) equipment constitutes fifty percent of the world total energy consumption [1]. HVAC systems include all the air conditioning systems used for cooling (heating) the buildings and keeping their conditions in a favorable range. The problem of HVAC control can be posed from two different points of view. In the first, one aims at reaching an optimum consumption of energy. In the second, that is more common in HVAC control, the goal is keeping moisture, temperature, pressure and other air conditions in an acceptable range. Several different control and intelligent strategies have been developed in recent years to achieve the stated goals fully or partially. Among them, PID controllers [2], DDC methods [3], optimal [4], nonlinear [5] and robust [6] control strategies, and neural and/or fuzzy [7,8] approaches are to be mentioned. The purpose of this paper is to suggest another control approach, based on hybrid of fuzzy logic and sliding mode control, to achieve faster response with reduced overshoot and rise time. In the subsequent sections, we discuss the HVAC system, our proposed controller, and its application in the closed loop control system, simulation and some concluding remarks.

L. Rutkowski et al. (Eds.): ICAISC 2004, LNAI 3070, pp. 984–989, 2004.
© Springer-Verlag Berlin Heidelberg 2004

2   Sliding Mode Fuzzy Control

A Sliding Mode Controller is a Variable Structure Controller (VSC) [13]. Basically, a VSC includes several different continuous functions that can map plant state to a control surface, and the switching among different functions is determined by plant state that is represented by a switching function Consider the design of a sliding mode controller for the following system [12]:

$$x^{(n)} = f(x, \dot{x}, ..., x^{(n-1)}, t) + bu(t) \tag{1}$$

here we assume $b > 0$. $u(t)$ is the input to the system. The following is a possible choice of the structure of a sliding mode controller [14]:

$$u = k \tanh(\frac{s}{\phi}) + u_{eq} \tag{2}$$

Where u_{eq} is called equivalent control which is used when the system state is in the sliding mode. k is a constant and it is the maximal value of the controller output. s is called switching function because the control action switches its sign on the two sides of the switching surface $s = 0$ and constant factor ϕ defines the thickness of the boundary layer. s is defined as:

$$s = \dot{e} + \lambda e \tag{3}$$

Where $e = x_d - x$ and x_d is the desired state. λ is the constant. $\tanh(.)$ is a hyperbolic tangent function. The control strategy adopted here will guarantee the system trajectories move toward and stay on the sliding surface $s = 0$ from any initial condition if the following condition meets:

$$s\dot{s} \leq -\eta|s| \tag{4}$$

where η is a positive constant that guarantees the system trajectories hit the sliding surface in finite time.

In a Takagi-Sugeno (TS) type FLC, the rule output function typically is a liner function of controller inputs. The mathematical expression of this function is similar to a switching function. This similarity indicates that the information from a sliding mode controller can be used to design a fuzzy logic controller, resulting in a Sliding Mode Fuzzy Controller (SMFC). In fact, since a fuzzy system can seamless connects different control strategies into one system, one can directly incorporate sliding mode controllers into a fuzzy logic controller. Each rule in an FLC can be a sliding mode controller. The sliding mode controller in each rule can have various forms. The boundary layer and the coefficients of the sliding surface become the coefficients of the rule output function and have their physical meanings. The ith rule for a Sliding Mode Fuzzy Controller is expressed as follows:

$$\text{if} \quad e \quad \text{is} \quad A_i \quad \text{and} \quad \dot{e} \quad \text{is} \quad B_i \quad \text{then} \quad u_i = k \tanh \frac{\dot{e} + \lambda_i e + c_i}{\phi_i} \tag{5}$$

The constant coefficients of λ_i and c_i are determined by the open loop data. They are determined in such a way that the slop of the nonlinear switching curve is followed.

3   Mathematical Model of HVAC System

In this paper we used the model developed in [1] since it aims at controlling the temperature and humidity of the Variable Air Volume (VAV) HAVC system. Below, we describe the mathematical structure of a MIMO HVAC model used throughout this paper. The state space equations governing the model are as follows:

$$
\begin{aligned}
\dot{x}_1 &= 60u_1\alpha_1(x_3 - x_1) - 60u_1\alpha_2(W_s - x_2) + \alpha_3(Q_0 - h_{fg}M_0) \\
\dot{x}_2 &= 60u_1\alpha_1(W_s - x_2) + \alpha_4 M_0 \\
\dot{x}_3 &= 60u_1\beta_1(-x_3 + x_1) + 15u_1\beta_1(T_0 - x_1) \\
&\quad -60\,u_1\beta_3(0.25W_0 + 0.75x_2 - W_s) \\
y_1 &= x_1, \quad y_2 = x_2
\end{aligned}
\tag{6}
$$

In which the parameters are:

$$
u_1 = f, u_2 = g_{mp}, x_1 = T_3, x_2 = W_3, x_3 = T_2, \alpha_1 = \frac{1}{V_s}, \alpha_2 = \frac{h_{fg}}{C_p V_s}
$$

$$
\alpha_3 = \frac{1}{\rho C_p V_s}, \alpha_4 = \frac{1}{\rho V_s}, \beta_1 = \frac{1}{V_{he}}, \beta_2 = \frac{1}{\rho C_p V_{he}}, \beta_3 = \frac{h_w}{C_p V_{he}}
\tag{7}
$$

The actuator's transfer function can be considered as:

$$
G_{act}(s) = \frac{k}{1 + \tau s}
\tag{8}
$$

In which k and τ are the actuator's gain and time constant. The HVAC system has delayed behavior which is represented via linearized, first order and time delay system. Furthermore, the model represents a MIMO system in which one of the I/O channels has a right half plane zero, meaning that it is non-minimum-phase.

4   Simulation Results

The actual plant model involves four inputs and three output processes, of which two inputs can be manipulated for achieving desired performance levels. We wish to track temperature and humidity to their respecting set point levels of $73°F$ and 0.009, while maintaining the supply air temperature within the range of $40°F$ to $100°F$. A sliding mode fuzzy temperature controller and a sliding mode fuzzy humidity controller have been designed for the HVAC system. The inputs for the temperature controller are temperature error and temperature error rate. Figure 1 shows the response of HVAC system. As it is clearly obvious, results are very satisfactory. In fig. 2, the response of HVAC system with PID controller is shown. The performance levels achieved via the two alternative approaches are outlined in table 1.

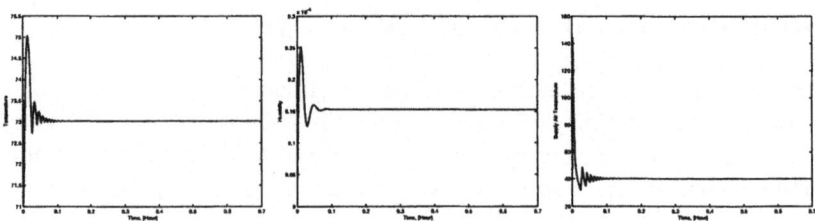

Fig. 1. HVAC system responses with sliding mode fuzzy controller

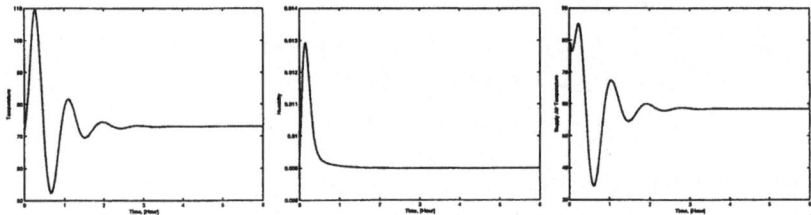

Fig. 2. HVAC system responses with PID controller

Table 1. Performance characteristics of HVAC system with SMFC and PID controller

	SS-Error (Temp-Humi)	RiseTime (Temp-Humi)	POS (Temp-Humi)
SMFC	$0.00 - 1.50$	$0.001 - 0.0007$	02.050 - 0.00
PID	0.00 - 0.00	0.009 - 0.002	49.96 - 43.33

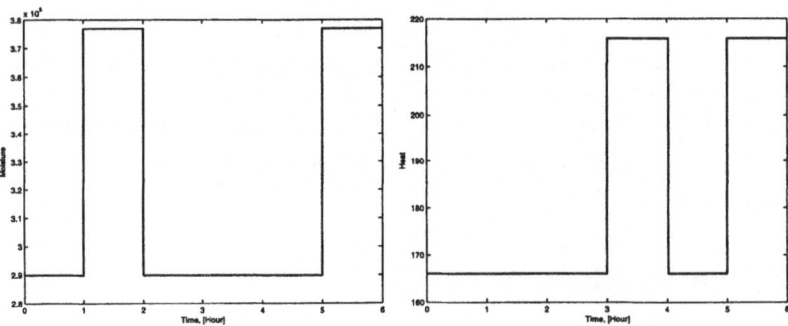

Fig. 3. The heat and moisture disturbance signals for robustness consideration

We examined the robustness of this controller with respect to external disturbances. To do that, we fed the plant with time-variable heat and moisture disturbance signals in the form given in figure 3. As observed in the figure 3, there is some deterioration from the nominal amounts of the two external disturbances. The response of the SMFC and PID controller are given in the figure 4 and 5, respectively. As shown figure 4 and 5, the SMFC shows the better control performance than PID controller in terms of settling time, overshot and rise

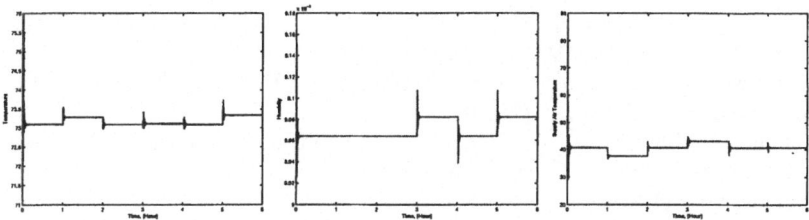

Fig. 4. HVAC system responses with SMFC with the presence of disturbance variations

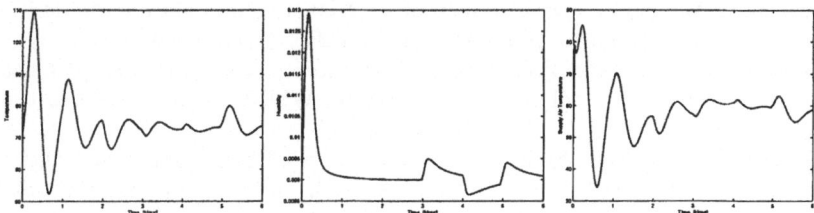

Fig. 5. HVAC system responses with PID controller with the presence of disturbance variations

time. The outputs of the system, with the presence of disturbance variations, show that the SMFC can track the inputs suitably. But the performance of PID controller is poor.

5 Conclusion

In this paper the applicability of the SMFC to the fulfillment of complex tasks of adaptive set point tracking and disturbance rejection of a HVAC system was shown. The control of the non-minimum phase, multivariable, nonlinear and nonlinearizable plant with constraints on its supply air temperature is indeed a demanding task from control theoretic viewpoint. The controller presented in this paper possessed excellent tracking speed and robustness properties.

References

1. Serrano, B. A., Velez-Reyes, M.: Nonlinear Control of A Heating Ventilation and Air Conditioning Systems with Thermal Load Estimation IEEE Transaction on Control Systems Technology, Volume 7, (1999).
2. Geng, G., Geary, G. M.: On Performance and Tuning of PID Controllers in HVAC Systems. Conference on Control Application, (1993).
3. Newman, H. M.: Direct Digital Controls for Building Systems. John Wiley pub., (1994)
4. Zaheeruddin, M.: Optimal Control of A Single Zone Environment Space. Building and Environment, (1992).

5. Tigrek, T., Dasgupta, S., Smith, T. F.: Nonlinear Optimal Control of HVAC Systems. Proceeding of IFAC Conference, (2002)
6. Underwood, C.P.: Robust Control of HVAC Plant II: Controller Design. Proceeding of CIBSE, Vol. 21, No. 1, (2000).
7. Osman, A., Mitchell, J. W., Klein, S. A.: Application of General Regression Neural Network in HVAC Process Identification and Control. ASHRAE Transaction, Volume 102, (1996).
8. Curtiss, P. S., Kreider, J. F., Branenuehl, M. J.: Local and Global Control of Commercial Building HVAC Systems Using Artificial Neural Networks. American Control Conference (ACC), (1994).
9. Jian, W., Wenjian, C.: Development of an Adaptive Neuro-Fuzzy Method for Supply Air Pressure Control in HVAC System IEEE Trans., (2000).
10. Rashidi, F., Lucas, C.: Applying CBRL (Context Based Reinforcement Learning) to Multivariable Control of a HVAC System. WSEAS Trans. on Circuit and Systems, (2003).
11. Semsar, E., Yazdanpanahm M. J., Lucas, C.: Nonlinear Control and Disturbance Decoupling of an HVAC System via Feedback Linearization and Back-Stepping, IEEE Conference on Control Application, (2003)
12. J.J. Slotine and S.S. Sastry: Tracking control of nonlinear systems using sliding surfaces with application to robot manipulators. International Journal of Control, vol.38, no.2, (1983),465–492
13. J.S. Glower and J. Munighan: Designing Fuzzy Controllers from a Variable Structures Standpoint. IEEE Transactions on Fuzzy Systems, vol.5, no.1, (1997), 138–144.
14. John Y. Hung, Weibing Gao and James C. Hung: Variable Structure Control: A Survey. IEEE Transactions on Industrial Electronics, vol.40, no.1, (1993), 2–21.

Global Identification of Complex Systems with Cascade Structure

Jerzy Swiatek

Institute of Control and Systems Engineering, Wroclaw University of Technology,
Wyb. Wyspianskiego 27, 50-370 Wroclaw, Poland. `jerzy.swiatek@pwr.wroc.pl`

Abstract. In this paper, a problem of input-output complex systems identification is presented. The description of a complex system is given by a description of each system element and structure. Local and global identification problems are formulated, and a different approach to the identification problem is discussed. Based on the multi-criteria concept, the globally optimal model with respect to the quality of local models is presented.

Keywords: Identification, modelling, complex systems

1 Introduction

The design of computer aided management systems for a complex plant generates new tasks of complex system identification. Similar problems can be encountered in the design of computer control systems for complex process or the modelling of complex systems of a different nature (for example: biological plants). In such a system, the elementary processes are usually defined and connection between elements is usually given. In the production process, the elementary operations are elements of complex systems, and the structure of the system is dictated by time schedule of operations, in turn dictated by technological conditions. In this case, we have problem of modelling the complex of an operation system [1,3]. Investigation of technical or biological plants [1,4,5,6] usually gives us identification of complex input-output system. In this case, we can distinguish a sub-process (elementary process) with some inputs and outputs which can operate separately. The connection between the inputs and outputs of each element gives us a complex system. The modelling of such a system is connected with the modelling of each process separately, taking into account the connection between elements. Such a formulation of the problem gives us new tasks of identification of complex systems. Sometimes in such a system, some inner inputs and outputs could not be measured. We can have a problem of identification with restricted measurement possibilities [6]. We have another problem when analyzing a two-level (generally multi-level) management or control process. Dependent on the level, we expected a model of different quality. At the lower level, it is better to prepare locally optimal model, but at the upper level, globally optimal description is required. In this paper the local and global identification problem is discussed. The multi-criteria approach is used to formulate the globally optimal model.

L. Rutkowski et al. (Eds.): ICAISC 2004, LNAI 3070, pp. 990–995, 2004.
© Springer-Verlag Berlin Heidelberg 2004

2   A Description of a Complex System

Let us consider that an input-output complex system consists of M subsystems $O_1, O_2, \ldots, O_M$. Let:

$$\bar{y}_m = \Phi_m(u_m, a_m) \tag{1}$$

denote an m system elements model with input u_m and output y_m, where: $\bar{y}_m$ is the vector of the model output, a_m is the vector of the model parameters of the m-th element, $m = 1, 2, \ldots, M$. Input, output and model parameters are vectors from respective spaces, i.e.: $u_m \in U \subseteq \mathbb{R}^{S_m}$, $y_m, \bar{y}_m \in Y \subseteq \mathbb{R}^{L_m}$, $a_m \in A \subseteq \mathbb{R}^{R_m}$. Let $u, y, \bar{y}, a$ denote vectors of all inputs, plant and model outputs and model parameters, respectively, i.e.:

$$u^T = \begin{bmatrix} u_1 \ldots u_M \end{bmatrix}, \ y^T = \begin{bmatrix} y_1 \ldots y_M \end{bmatrix}, \ \bar{y}^T = \begin{bmatrix} \bar{y}_1 \ldots \bar{y}_M \end{bmatrix}, \ a^T = \begin{bmatrix} a_1 \ldots a_M \end{bmatrix}.$$

The structure of the complex system is given by the connection between the inputs and outputs of each element. It is necessary to define which input of a particular element is the output of the other element. Let us note that some system input is not the output of any other elements. Those inputs are called external inputs — x. Furthermore, let us distinguish some plant outputs which are important for model application, for example outputs which are used to formulate a control problem at the upper level. We call those outputs global outputs — v. Now the structure of the system may be described by the following equations:

$$u = Ay + Bx \tag{2}$$

$$v = Cy, \tag{3}$$

where: A, B are a zero-one coincidence matrix and matrix C shows global outputs.

Let:

$$\bar{y}^T = \begin{bmatrix} \bar{y}_1 \ldots \bar{y}_M \end{bmatrix} = \begin{bmatrix} \Phi_1(u_1, a_1) \ \Phi_2(u_2, a_2) \cdots \Phi_M(u_M, a_M) \end{bmatrix} = \Phi(u, a). \tag{4}$$

Substituting (2) in the place of u in (4), we have:

$$\bar{y} = \Phi(A\bar{y} + Bx, a). \tag{5}$$

Solution (5) with respect to $\bar{y}$ is:

$$\bar{y} = \Phi^{-1}(x, a; A, B). \tag{6}$$

Taking into account (3), we have:

$$\bar{v} = C\bar{y} = \Phi^{-1}(x, a; A, B) = \bar{\bar{\Phi}}(x, a). \tag{7}$$

Equation (7) is the global model of a complex with external inputs x and global outputs v.

3   Complex System Identification

To determine the optimal model parameters of a complex system, the measurements of input and output of each element are collected. The choice of the best model parameter in this case is reduced to the determination of such values of the parameters for which the identification performance index is minimal. The performance index is a measure of the difference between model outputs and respective measurements. Because of the complexity of the system, there are different possibilities to define identification performance index. On the one hand, it is possible to determine an optimal model for each system element separately, and on the other hand, we can define performance index for the system as a whole. In the first case, we obtain the locally optimal models for each element separately not taking into account the structure of the system. The second case gives the globally optimal model for the whole system.

3.1   Globally Optimal Model

Let us consider now the global approach, i.e. the comparison of only a selected plant output with global model output defines the globally optimal model. In this case, the global identification performance index measures the difference between selected plant output and global model output v. The global identification performance index has the form:

$$Q(a) = \sum_{n=1}^{N} q\left(v_n, \overline{\overline{\Phi}}(x_n, a)\right),\tag{8}$$

where: q is a measure of the difference between the selected output of the complex plant, and respective model global outputs, v_n, x_n denote the n-th measurements of global plant outputs and external inputs, respectively.

The globally optimal parameters of the complex system model — $\tilde{a}$, are obtained by minimization of the performance index (8) with respect to a, i.e.:

$$\tilde{a} \to Q(\tilde{a}) = \min_a Q(a).\tag{9}$$

Equations (1) and (4) with parameters $\tilde{a}$ obtained in (9) are globally optimal models of the separate elements. Equation (7) with parameters $\tilde{a}$ is a globally optimal model of the complex system as a whole.

3.2   Cascade Structure

In practical applications, a very popular case of complex system is a system with cascade structure. All complex systems can be transferred to the mentioned structure without feedback. The respective global model (9) for this structure has the form:

$$\begin{bmatrix} \overline{v}^{(1)} \\ \overline{v}^{(2)} \\ \vdots \\ \overline{v}^{(M)} \end{bmatrix} = \begin{bmatrix} \Phi_1(x, a_1) \\ \Phi_2(\Phi_1(x, a_1), a_2) \\ \vdots \\ \Phi_M(\cdots \Phi_2(\Phi_1(x, a_1), a_2) \cdots a_M) \end{bmatrix}\tag{10}$$

The global identification performance index (9) is:

$$Q(a) = \sum_{n=1}^{N} \sum_{m=1}^{M} q(v_n^{(m)}, \overline{v}_n^{(m)}). \tag{11}$$

Notice that model (10) may be given in the recursive fom:

$$\overline{v}^{(m+1)} = \Phi_m(\overline{v}^{(m)}, a_m), \qquad m = 0, 1, \ldots, M, \tag{12}$$

where $\overline{v}^{(0)} = x$.

To determine the globally optimal model parameters, dynamic programming methods may be used.

4   An Identification Algorithm Based on Dynamic Programing

Step 1. Determine $\tilde{a}_M$ such that:

$$\tilde{a}_M = \Psi_M(V_N^{(M)}, \overline{V}_N^{(M-1)}) \rightarrow \min_{a_M} \sum_{n=1}^{N} q_M(\overline{v}_n^{(M-1)}, a_M)) = \overline{Q}_M(V_N^{(M)}, \overline{V}_N^{(M-1)}),$$
$$\tag{13}$$

where: $V_N^{(M)} = \left[v_1^{(M)} v_2^{(M)} \cdots v_N^{(M)}, \right]$ is a sequence of measurements of M-th global output, and $\overline{V}_N^{(M-1)}$ is the sequence of outputs of the $(M-1)$-th element in cascade structure:

$$\overline{V}_N^{(M-1)} = \left[\overline{v}_1^{(M-1)} \overline{v}_2^{(M-1)} \cdots \overline{v}_N^{(M-1)} \right]. \tag{14}$$

Inserting (12) into (14), we obtain

$$\overline{V}_N^{(M-1)} = \left[\Phi_{M-1}(\overline{v}_1^{(M-2)}, a_{M-1}) \, \Phi_{M-1}(\overline{v}_2^{(M-2)}, a_{M-1}) \cdots \Phi_{M-1}(\overline{v}_N^{(M-2)}, a_{M-1}) \right]$$
$$= \overline{\Phi}(\overline{V}_N^{(M-2)}, a_{M-1}). \tag{15}$$

Consequently, result (13) may be rewritten:

$$\overline{Q}_M(V_N^{(M)}, \overline{V}_N^{(M-1)}) = \overline{Q}_M(V_N^{(M)}, \overline{\Phi}_{M-1}(\overline{V}_N^{(M-2)}, a_{M-1})).$$

Step 2. Determine $\tilde{a}_{M-1}$ such that:

$$\tilde{a}_{M-1} = \Psi_{M-1}(V_N^{(M)}, V_N^{(M-1)}, \overline{V}_N^{(M-2)}) \rightarrow$$

$$\min_{a_{M-1}} \left\{ \sum_{n=1}^{N} q_{M-1}(v_n^{(M-1)}, \Phi_{M-1}(\overline{v}_n^{(M-2)}, a_{M-1})) \right.$$

$$\left. + \overline{Q}_M(V_N^{(M)}, \overline{\Phi}_M(V_N^{(M-2)}, a_{M-1})) \right\} = \overline{Q}_{M-1}(V_N^{(M)}, V_N^{(M-1)}, \overline{V}_N^{(M-2)}), \tag{16}$$

where: $V_N^{(M-1)} = \left[v_1^{(M-1)} v_2^{(M-1)} \cdots v_N^{(M-1)}\right]$ is a sequence of measurements of $(M-1)$-th global output, and $\overline{V}_N^{(M-2)}$ is the sequence of outputs of the $(M-2)$-th element in cascade structure:

$$\overline{V}_N^{(M-2)} = \left[\overline{v}_1^{(M-2)} \overline{v}_2^{(M-2)} \cdots \overline{v}_N^{(M-2)}\right] \tag{17}$$

Inserting (12) into (17), we obtain:

$$\overline{V}_N^{(M-2)} = \left[\Phi_{M-2}(\overline{v}_1^{(M-3)}, a_{M-2})\Phi_{M-2}(\overline{v}_2^{(M-3)}, a_{M-2}) \cdots \Phi_{M-2}(\overline{v}_N^{(M-3)}, a_{M-2})\right]$$

$$= \overline{\Phi}_{M-2}(\overline{V}_N^{(M-3)}, a_{M-2}). \tag{18}$$

Consequently, result (16) may be rewritten:

$$\overline{Q}_{M-1}(V_N^{(M)}, V_N^{(M-1)}, \overline{V}_N^{(M-2)}) = \overline{Q}_{M-1}(V_N^{(M)}, V_N^{(M-1)}, \overline{\Phi}_{M-2}(\overline{V}_N^{(M-3)}, a_{M-2})).$$

Step $M - 1$. Determine $\tilde{a}_2$ such that:

$$\tilde{a}_2 = \Psi_2(V_N^{(M)}, V_N^{(M-1)}, \ldots, V_N^{(2)}, \overline{V}_N^{(1)}) \rightarrow$$

$$\min_{a_2}\left\{\sum_{n=1}^{N} q_2(v_n^{(2)}, \Phi_2(\overline{v}_n^{(1)}, a_2)) + \overline{Q}_3(V_N^{(M)}, V_N^{(M-1)}, \ldots, V_N^{(2)}, \overline{V}_N^{(1)})\right\} \tag{19}$$

where: $V_N^{(2)} = \left[v_1^{(2)} v_2^{(2)} \cdots v_N^{(2)}\right]$ is a sequence of measurements of the second global output, $\overline{V}_N^{(1)}$ is the sequence of outputs of the first element in cascade structure,

$$\overline{V}_N^{(1)} = \left[v_1^{(1)} v_2^{(1)} \cdots v_N^{(1)}\right]. \tag{20}$$

Inserting (12) into (20) we obtain:

$$\overline{V}_N^{(1)} = \left[\Phi_1(\overline{v}_1^{(0)}, a_1) \Phi_1(\overline{v}_2^{(0)}, a_1) \cdots \Phi_1(\overline{v}_N^{(0)}, a_1)\right]$$

$$= [\Phi_1(x_1, a_1) \Phi_1(x_2, a_1) \cdots \Phi_1(x_N, a_1)] = \overline{\Phi}_1(X_N, a_1), \tag{21}$$

where:

$$\overline{V}_N^{(0)} = \left[v_1^{(0)} v_2^{(0)} \cdots v_N^{(0)}\right] = [x_1 x_2 \cdots x_N] = X_N, \tag{22}$$

X_N is the sequence of the external input. Consequently, result (19) may be rewritten:

$$\overline{Q}_2(V_N^{(M)}, V_N^{(M-1)}, \ldots, V_N^{(2)}, \overline{V}_N^{(1)}) = \overline{Q}_2(V_N^{(M)}, V_N^{(M-1)}, \ldots, V_N^{(2)}, \overline{\Phi}_1(X_N, a_1)).$$

Step M. Determine $\tilde{a}_1$ such that:

$$\tilde{a}_1 = \Phi_1(V_N^{(M)}, V_N^{(M-1)}, \ldots, V_N^{(1)}, X_N) \rightarrow$$

$$\min_{a_1}\left\{\sum_{n=1}^{N} q_1(v_n^{(1)}, \Phi_2(x_n, a_1)) + \overline{Q}_2(V_N^{(M)}, V_N^{(M-1)}, \ldots, V_N^{(2)}, \overline{\Phi}_2(X_N, a_1))\right\}$$

$$= \overline{Q}_1(V_N^{(M)}, V_N^{(M-1)}, \ldots, V_N^{(1)}, X_N), \tag{23}$$

where: $V_N^{(1)} = \left[v_1^{(1)} v_2^{(1)} \cdots v_N^{(1)} \right]$ is the sequence of measurements of the first global output.

Now we can come back to (21) and determine:

$$\overline{V}_N^{(1)} = \overline{\Phi}_1(X_N, \tilde{a}_1) = \overline{\Phi}_1(X_N, \Psi_1(V_N^{(M)}, V_N^{(M-1)}, \ldots, V_N^{(1)}, X_N)),$$

which is necessary to determine:

$$\tilde{a}_2 = \Psi_2(V_N^{(M)}, V_N^{(M-1)}, \ldots, V_N^{(2)}, \overline{V}_N^{(1)})$$
$$= \Psi_2(V_N^{(M)}, V_N^{(M-1)}, \ldots, V_N^{(2)}, \overline{\Phi}_1(X_N, \Phi_1(V_N^{(M)}, V_N^{(M-1)}, \ldots, V_N^{(1)}, X_N))).$$

Similarly $\tilde{a}_3$, $\tilde{a}_4$ and so on. Finally $\tilde{a}_M = \Psi_M(V_N^{(M)}, \overline{V}_N^{(M-1)})$. Sequence (14) will be determined at the previous step as $\overline{V}_N^{(M-1)} = \overline{\Phi}_{M-1}(\overline{V}_N^{(M-2)}, \tilde{a}_{M-1})$.

5 Final Remark

In this paper, the problem of complex input-output systems is discussed. The locally and globally optimal models are introduced. It has been shown that based on the multi-criteria approach, the other models may be defined. It has been shown that for cascade structure, the dynamic programming approach may be used for global modelling. The same approach may be used for globally optimal modelling with respect to the quality of local models [7]. The presented approach is useful for the investigation of computer control systems for complex plant.

References

1. Bubnicki Z., *Identification of Control Plants*, Oxford, N. York, Elsevier, 1980.
2. Bubnicki Z., *Problems of complex systems identification*, Proc. of International Conference on Systems Engineering, Lanchester Politechnic, Coventry, 1980.
3. Bubnicki Z., *Global modelling and identification of network systems,* Proc. of 3rd International Conference on Systems Engineering, Wright State University, Dayton, USA, 1984.
4. Drałus G., Swiatek J., *Global modelling of complex systems by neural networks,* Proc. of 7th International Symposium on Artificial Life and Robotics, Oita, Japan, 2002.
5. Swiatek J., *Two stage identification and its technical and biomedical applications,* Wydawnictwo Politechniki Wrocławskiej, Wrocław, 1987 (in Polish)
6. Swiatek J., *Identification,* Problems of Computer Science and Robotics. Grzech A., editor, Zakład Narodowy im Ossolińskich — Wydawnictwo PAN, Wrocław, 1998. (in Polish)
7. Swiatek J., *Global and local modelling of complex input output systems.* Proc. of Sixteen International Conference on Systems Engineering, September 9-11 2003, Coventry University, Coventry, England pp. 669-671.

Diagnosis of Melanoma Using IRIM, a Data Mining System

Jerzy W. Grzymala-Busse[1], Jay Hamilton[2], and Zdzislaw S. Hippe[3]

[1] Department of Electrical Engineering and Computer Science, University of Kansas,
Lawrence, KS 66045, USA
and
Institute of Computer Science Polish Academy of Sciences, 01-237 Warsaw, Poland
Jerzy@ku.edu
http://lightning.eecs.ku.edu/index.html

[2] Department of Electrical Engineering and Computer Science, University of Kansas,
Lawrence, KS 66045, USA
CSJay@ku.edu

[3] Department of Expert Systems and Artificial Intelligence, University of
Information Technology and Management, 35-225 Rzeszow, Poland
ZHippe@wenus.wsiz.rzeszow.pl

Abstract. Melanoma is a very dangerous skin cancer. In this paper we
present results of experiments on three melanoma data sets. Two data
mining tools were used, a new system called IRIM (Interesting Rule Induction Module) and well established LEM2 (Learning from Examples
Module, version 2), both are components of the same data mining system LERS (Learning from Examples based on Rough Sets). Typically
IRIM induces the strongest rules that are possible for a data set. IRIM
does not need any preliminary discretization or preprocessing of missing
attribute values. Though performance of IRIM and LEM2 is fully comparable, IRIM provides an additional opportunity to induce unexpected
and strong rules supplying an important insight helpful for diagnosis of
melanoma.

1 Introduction

Melanoma is a very dangerous skin cancer. Moreover, the number of diagnosed
cases increase each year. Any improving melanoma diagnosis will save human
lives.

In our research we used three versions of a basic data set with 410 cases that
was collected at the Regional Dermatology Center in Rzeszow, Poland [6]. This
data set describes every case in terms of thirteen attributes: Asymmetry, Border,
six binary attributes associated with Color, five binary attributes associated with
Diversity, and an additional attribute called TDS (Total Dermatoscopic Score),
computed on the basis of the ABCD formula [12].

We used a new component of LERS (Learning from Examples based on
Rough Sets) called IRIM (Interesting Rule Induction Module). Rough set theory

L. Rutkowski et al. (Eds.): ICAISC 2004, LNAI 3070, pp. 996–1001, 2004.
© Springer-Verlag Berlin Heidelberg 2004

was initiated in 1982 [9]. IRIM does not induce rule sets in a conventional fashion as standard rule induction algorithms such as LEM1 or LEM2 (Learning from Examples Module, version 1 and 2, respectively) [2]. IRIM resembles the ALL RULES algorithm, part of the LERS [2] and the EXPLORE algorithm [11]. First of all, rules created by IRIM may not cover all positive cases of the concept. Secondly, there is a lot of overlapping and even subsuming between rules induced by IRIM. Instead, IRIM induces the strongest possible rules, covering the most positive cases of the concept. Such rules have a potential to be not only new but also interesting and surprising to experts in the area, hence the name of the module.

An approach to data mining based on inducing very few rules, for example, a single rule, was introduced in [8], and then was continued in a number of papers, see, e.g., [7]. Rule truncation [8], i.e., removal of weak rules while keeping stronger rules in the rule set belongs to the same category. This technique proved its applicability in diagnosing melanoma [3]. A similar technique, pruning of decision trees, wee, e.g., [10], is used in tree generation systems as well.

The main objective of our research was to check usefulness of IRIM in melanoma diagnosis by comparing the performance of IRIM versus a standard rule induction module LEM2. As it is known [3], [4], performance of LEM2 is fully comparable with that of melanoma diagnosticians. Results of our experiments show that performance of IRIM is comparable with performance of LEM2.

2   Data Mining Tools

The main tool for our experiments was a recent addition to LERS, called IRIM, created for inducing the strongest rules describing a concept. For every concept IRIM creates a rule set with rules satisfying some pre-defined input parameters: the minimum rule length (i.e., number of rule conditions), the maximum rule length, and minimum of conditional probability of the concept given rule domain. The rule domain is the set of all cases satisfying the left hand side of the rule. For brevity, the minimum of conditional probability of the concept given rule domain will be called a *ratio* parameter.

The algorithm LEM2 needs discretization, a preprocessing, to deal with numerical attributes. Discretization is a process of converting numerical attributes into symbolic attributes, with intervals as values. On the other hand, IRIM induces rules during discretization. IRIM computes first the set of blocks for all attribute-value pairs (a, v). If $t = (a, v)$ is an attribute-value pair then a block of t, denoted $[t]$, is a set of all cases from U that for attribute a have value v, where U denotes the set of all cases. IRIM recognizes integer and real numbers as values of attributes, and labels such attributes as numerical. For numerical attributes IRIM computes blocks in a different way than for symbolic attributes. First, it sorts all values of a numerical attribute. Then it computes cutpoints as averages for any two consecutive values of the sorted list. For each cutpoint c IRIM creates two blocks, the first block contains all cases for which values of the numerical attribute are smaller than c, the second block contains remaining cases, i.e., all cases for which values of the numerical attribute are larger than

c. The search space of IRIM is the set of all blocks computed this way, together with blocks defined by symbolic attributes. Then IRIM combines attribute-value pairs relevant to a concept and creates rules describing the concept, taking into account pre-defined, by the user, input parameters. In addition, IRIM handles missing attribute values during rule induction. For any attribute with missing values, blocks are computed only from the existing attribute-value pairs [5].

The classification system of LERS [6] is a modification of the bucket brigade algorithm. The decision to which concept a case belongs is made on the basis of three factors: strength, specificity, and support. They are defined as follows: *Strength* is the total number of cases correctly classified by the rule during training. *Specificity* is the total number of attribute-value pairs on the left-hand side of the rule The third factor, *support*, is defined as the sum of scores of all matching rules from the concept, where the score of the rule is the product of its strength and specificity. The concept for which the support is the largest is the winner and the case is classified as being a member of that concept. Every rule induced by LERS is preceded by three numbers: specificity, strength, and rule domain size.

The output of IRIM is the set of all rules satisfying input parameters. In general, IRIM generates very big rule sets. The worst time complexity of IRIM is exponential with respect to the number of attributes. Hence, in our experiments, we selected the maximum rule length to be equal to two or three and the ratio to equal to at least 0.8.

3   Experiments

We conducted our experiments on three data sets on melanoma. Two data sets were discretized using divisive cluster analysis [4]. The third was the original data set, with original numerical attributes. In the first discretized data set, in [1] denoted by "0-0", the attribute TDS was optimized by using a new ABCD" formula [1]. In the second discretized data set, denoted by "div", the attribute TDS before discretization was computed using the traditional ABCD formula. In the original, not discretized data set, called "original", the TDS attribute was computed using the traditional ABCD formula. In all of our experiments for testing data the LERS classification system was applied.

In our first sequence of experiments the number of errors, out of 410 cases, was determined using ten-fold cross validation. Results are presented in Table 1. Note that the number of errors for "0-0" and "div" data sets and LEM2 system were equal to 10 and 15, respectively.

In the third, original data set, some attributes were numerical. This causes very time-consuming rule induction by IRIM. However, during ten-fold cross validation we observed that in different folds the same strong rules were consistently induced. Due to this observation, an additional experiment was conducted, to compare the number of errors determined by ten-fold cross validation and resubstitution. In resubstitution the same data are used for training and testing. Obviously, resubstitution is much less time-consuming than ten-fold cross vali-

Table 1. Rule sets induced by IRIM

	Number of errors			
	Data set "0-0"		Data set "div"	
Number of rules	Max. rule length = 2	Max rule length = 3	Max rule length = 2	Max. rule length = 3
1	22	22	9	9
2	25	33	11	9
3	35	34	10	9
4	36	35	10	9
5	36	37	10	9
6	36	37	10	9
7	36	36	10	10
8	36	36	10	10
9	36	36	9	10
10	36	36	9	10

Table 2. Errors determined by ten-fold cross validation versus errors determined by resubstitution for data set "0-0"

	Number of errors			
	Ten-fold cross validation		Resubstitution	
Number of rules	Max. rule length = 2	Max rule length = 3	Max rule length = 2	Max. rule length = 3
1	22	22	22	22
2	25	33	22	36
3	35	34	34	36
4	36	35	37	36
5	36	37	37	36

Table 3. Errors determined by ten-fold cross validation versus errors determined by resubstitution for data set "div"

	Number of errors			
	Ten-fold cross validation		Resubstitution	
Number of rules	Max. rule length = 2	Max rule length = 3	Max rule length = 2	Max. rule length = 3
1	9	9	9	9
2	11	9	11	9
3	10	9	10	9
4	10	9	10	9
5	10	9	11	9

dation. Since we wanted to test up to five strongest rules induced by IRIM from the original data, we compared ten-fold cross validation with resubstitution for up to five rules, see Tables 2 and 3.

Goodness-of-fit test returns $\chi^2 = 1.027$, this value is smaller than $\chi^2_{0.05} = 3.073$ for $(4-1)(5-1) = 12$ degrees of freedom, so the null hypothesis cannot be

Table 4. Errors determined by IRIM and resubstitution from the original data set

Number of rules	Number of errors
1	9
2	13
3	11
4	11
5	10

rejected at the level 0.05 of significance and we conclude that the approximate test, using resubstitution, provided a good fit for ten-fold cross validation.

The results of using resubstitution for the strongest rules induced by IRIM from the original data are presented in Table 4. Due to enormous computational complexity we restricted our attention to rules of the maximal length equal to two and the ratio equal to 0.9. Also, selection of rules to the rule sets was not automatic, as in the previous experiments, with discretized data sets. This time, selection was conducted manually since consecutive rules in the sorted list differed only slightly. For example, for rules describing benign cases of melanoma, the two strongest rules, at the beginning of the sorted list, were

2, 144, 149

(C_BLUE, 0) & (TDS, 1..4.85) -> (MELANOMA, Benign_nev)

2, 144, 149

(C_BLUE, 0) & (TDS, 1.25..4.85) -> (MELANOMA, Benign_nev)

Obviously, the second rule does not introduce a lot of new knowledge, so that rule was ignored in the process of identifying the strongest rules.

4   Conclusions

From the results of our experiments it is clear that IRIM may induce high quality rules. For the data set "0-0" IRIM was worse than LEM2, but for the data set "div" it was better. The two data sets differ by the way TDS was computed. Since in the data set "0-0" the optimal ABCD formula was selected particularly for LEM2, it explains why the performance of LEM2 was better.

Moreover, inducing rule sets directly from raw data, not discretized, IRIM again performed very well. It is surprising that the number of errors may grow with the number of rules in the data set. Nevertheless, IRIM has a potential to induce the best possible rule set, because the rule set induced by any other rule induction system is a subset of the set of all possible rules induced by IRIM, the only problem is selecting this rule set from a very large rule set induced by IRIM. Thus, the problem needed to be solved in the future is how to automate selection of the best rule set from the superset of all rules induced by IRIM. Finally, rules induced by IRIM may be used not only for classification but also to provide a new insight into the problem for domain experts. Such experts may learn strong regularities, hidden in the data, that were not known before use of data mining.

References

1. Alvarez, A., Brown, F. M., Grzymala-Busse, J. W., and Hippe, Z. S.: Optimization of the ABCD formula used for melanoma diagnosis. Proc. of the IIPWM'2003, Int. Conf. On Intelligent Information Processing and WEB Mining Systems, Zakopane, Poland, June 2–5, 2003, 233–240.
2. Grzymala-Busse, J. W.: LERS—A system for learning from examples based on rough sets. In Intelligent Decision Support. Handbook of Applications and Advances of the Rough Sets Theory. Slowinski, R. (ed.), Kluwer Academic Publishers, Dordrecht, Boston, London (1992) 3–18.
3. Grzymala-Busse J. W. and Hippe Z. S.: Postprocessing of rule sets induced from a melanoma data set. Proc. of the COMPSAC 2002, 26th Annual International Conference on Computer Software and Applications, Oxford, England, August 26–29, 2002, 1146–1151.
4. Grzymala-Busse J. W. and Hippe Z. S.: A search for the best data mining method to predict melanoma. Proceedings of the RSCTC 2002, Third International Conference on Rough Sets and Current Trends in Computing, Malvern, PA, October 14–16, 2002, Springer-Verlag, Berlin, Heidelberg, New York (2002) 538–545.
5. Grzymala-Busse, J. W. and Wang A. Y.: Modified algorithms LEM1 and LEM2 for rule induction from data with missing attribute values. Proc. of the Fifth International Workshop on Rough Sets and Soft Computing (RSSC'97) at the Third Joint Conference on Information Sciences (JCIS'97), Research Triangle Park, NC, March 2–5, 1997, 69–72.
6. Hippe, Z. S.: Computer database NEVI on endargement by melanoma. *Task Quarterly* **4** (1999) 483–488.
7. R. C. Holte. Very simple classification rules perform well on most commonly used datasets. *Machine Learning* **11** (1993) 63–90.
8. R. S. Michalski, I. Mozetic, J. Hong, N. Lavrac.: The AQ15 Inductive Learning System: An Overview and Experiments. Intelligent System Group, University of Illinois at Urbana-Champaign, ISG 86–20, 1986.
9. Pawlak, Z.: Rough Sets. *International Journal of Computer and Information Sciences* **11** (1982) 341–356.
10. Quinlan, J. R.: C4.5: Programs for Machine Learning, Morgan Kaufmann Publishers, San Mateo, CA (1988).
11. Stefanowski, J.: Algorithms of Decision Rule Induction in Data Mining (in Polish). Poznan University of Technology Press, Poznan, Poland (2001).
12. Stolz, W., Braun-Falco, O., Bilek, P., Landthaler, A. B., Cogneta, A. B.: Color Atlas of Dermatology, Blackwell Science Inc., Cambridge, MA (1993).

Detection of Spiculated Masses in Mammograms Based on Fuzzy Image Processing

Aboul Ella Hassanien[1], Jafar M. Ali[1], and Hajime Nobuhara[2]

[1] Kuwait University, Collegue of Business Administration,
Quantitative Methods and Information Systems Department,
P.O. Box 5969 Safat, code no. 13060 Kuwait,
Abo@cba.edu.kw
http://www.cba.edu.kw/abo
[2] Hirota Lab., Dept. of Computational Intelligence and Systems Science
Interdisciplinary Graduate School of Science and Engineering
Tokyo Institute of Technology
4259 Nagatsuta, Midori-ku, Yokohama, 226-8502, JAPAN
Phone: +81-45-924-5682, Fax: +81-45-924-5676

Abstract. This paper presents an efficient technique for the detection of spiculated masses in the digitized mammogram to assist the attending radiologist in making his decisions. The presented technique consists of two stages, enhancement of spiculation masses followed by the segmentation process. Fuzzy Histogram Hyperbolization (FHH) algorithm is first used to improve the quality of the digitized mammogram images. The Fuzzy C-Mean (FCM) algorithm is then applied to the preprocessed image to initialize the segmentation. Four measures of quantifying enhancement have been developed in this work. Each measure is based on the statistical information obtained from the labelled region of interest and a border area surrounding it. The methodology is based on the assumption that target and background areas are accurately specified. We have tested the algorithms on digitized mammograms obtained from the Digital Databases for Mammographic Image Analysis Society (MIAS)[1].

1 Introduction

Breast cancer is the type of cancer with highest incidence rates in women. It is the most common cause of cancer death in women in many countries. Recent statistics show that breast cancer affects one of every 10 women in Europe and one of every eight in the United States [4]. Early detection of cancer helps save lives. Currently, screening mammography is the most effective tools for early detection of abnormalities like lesions which are characteristic by their shape and margin. Spiculated lesions are highly suspicious sign of breast cancer. It is characterized by spiculation radiating from the margins of the mass. Mammography is a specific type of imaging that uses a low-dose X-ray system and high-contrast, high-resolution film for examination of the breasts. It can depicts most of the

---

[1] This work was supported by Kuwait university, Research Grant No.[IQ01/03]

L. Rutkowski et al. (Eds.): ICAISC 2004, LNAI 3070, pp. 1002–1007, 2004.
© Springer-Verlag Berlin Heidelberg 2004

significant changes of breast disease [8]. The primary radiographic signs of cancer are masses (its density, size, shape, borders), spicular lesions and calcification content. These features may be extracted according to their coherence and orientation and can provide important visual cues for radiologists to locate suspicious areas without generating false positives. The objective of this research is not to construct a high-tech radiologist. The introduced technique is intended to serve as a second opinion for the radiologist. We focus our effort on the detection of cancerous masses from mammograms. Our goal is to locate suspicious regions in the mammogram for more detail examination by the attending physicians. This paper introduces fuzzy image processing [7] technique for detection of spiculated lesions in Mammograms. It is based on the fuzzy Histogram Hyperbolization (FHH) conjunction with the fuzzy C-Mean algorithm.

The rest of this paper is organized as follows. Section (2) discusses the contrast enhancement algorithm based on Fuzzy Histogram Hyperbolization. In Section (3) mammogram clustering algorithm using Fuzzy C-mean is explained. Section (4) introduces the four quantitative measures. Experimental results are given and discussed in section (5). The paper is concluded in section (6).

2 Contrast Improvement with Fuzzy Histogram Hyperbolization (FHH)

Fuzzy based contrast enhancement [1,9], some parameters in each neighborhood for adjacent of the membership function such as minimum and maximum gray levels in the image is needed. Then, we can find the parameters of the membership function for some subimages and interpolate these values to obtain corresponding values for each pixel. In many cases, the global adaptive implementation is necessary to achieve better results. Fuzzy-based local contrast is very fast compared to global and classical image enhancement algorithms. The Gary level transformation through the fuzzy histogram Hyperbolization for generating new gray levels is defined as follows:

$$\acute{g}_{mn} = \frac{L-1}{e^{-1}-1} \cdot (e^{-\mu(g_{mn})^{\beta}-1}) \tag{1}$$

The constant L denotes the maxumm number of gray levels in an image, $\mu(g_{mn})$ is the membership value of gray levels g_{mn}, and $\beta \in [0.5, 2]$ is a parameter to modify the meaning of a fuzzy set. We setting the shape of membership function as a triangular and setting the value of fuzzifier β as a linguistic edge such that: $\beta = -0.75\mu + 1.5$.

The contrast improvement with fuzzy histogram hyperbolization algorithm contains of four phases. It starts by initialization the parameters of the image phase. Then by fuzzification of the gray levels phase (i.e., membership values to the dark, gray and bright) sets of gray levels. It followed by the grey level modification phase. Finally, generation of a new gray levels phase.

3   Fuzzy C-Mean Clustering Algorithm

Because tumor tissues in a mammogram have different textures and gray levels other than the normal ones; it is possible to use image segmentation methods to differentiate them from the background. However, image segmentation of cancerous tumors is reported to be very difficult not only due to their high variance of size and texture, but also due to disturbances from the fatty tissues, veins and glands in the background. In order to avoid these disturbances, we introduce a Fuzzy C-Mean algorithm for segmentation of the mammogram [2,5]. It attempts to cluster feature vectors by searching for local minima of the following objective function with respect to each fuzzy membership grade U_{ij} and each cluster center:

$$minimize : J_m(U, v) = \sum_{k=1}^{N} \sum_{i=1}^{C} (U_{ki})^m (wA + C) \qquad (2)$$

Where w is the wight, $A = (Y_k(x) - v_i(x))^2 + (Y_k(y) - v_i(y))^2$ is the pixel coordinates, $C = \sum_{D=R,G,B} (Y_k(D) - v_i(D))^2$ is the pixel intensity on RGB color space, $Y = \{y_1, y_2, \cdots, y_N\} \subset R^n$ is the data sets; c number of clusters in Y; $2 \leq c < n$; m is a weighting exponent: $1 \leq m < \infty$; $U = \{U_{ki}\}$ is the fuzzy c-partition of Y; $\|y_k - v_i\|A$ is an induced a-norm on R^n.

The weight exponent m has the effect of reducing the square distance error by an amount that depends on the observations membership in the cluster. The partitions that minimize J_m become increasingly hard. Conversely, higher values of m tend to soften a samples cluster membership, and the partition becomes increasingly blurred. Generally m must be selected by experimental means. The fine step of FCM algorithm is to generate an initial random membership matrix and use this random membership matrix as weight of each sample to belong to each cluster, then computes the centroid of each cluster. The new cluster centers are used to update the membership matrix . the updated membership matrix is compared with the previous ones. If the difference is greater than some threshold, then another iteration is computed, otherwise the algorithm is stopped.

4   Quantitative Measures

In this section we will introduce and describe four different quantitative measures [3] to evaluate the enhancement results. (1)Target to Background Contrast Measure based on Standard Deviation; (2)Target to Background Contrast Measure Based on Entropy; (3)Index of Fuzziness; and (4) Fuzzy Entropy. A key object of a contrast enhancement is to maximize the difference between the background and target mean grey scale level and ensure that the homogeneity of the mass is increased aiding the visualization of its boundaries and location. Using the ratio of the standard deviation of the grey scales within the target before and after enhancement, we can quantify this improvement using the target to background contrast enactment based on the standard deviation. This measure is initially computed by determining the difference between ratios of the mean grey scales in the target and background images in the original and enhances images as:

$$TBC_{SD} = \{\frac{(m_t^e/m_b^e) - (m_t^o/m_b^o)}{\sigma_t^e/\sigma_t^o}\} \tag{3}$$

Where $m_t^e, m_b^e, m_t^o, m_b^o$ are the mean of the grey scales comprising the target and background respectively of the original image before and after enhancement and where σ_t^e, σ_t^o the standard deviations of the grey scales are before and after enhancement. Within the mammogram image, the target has a greater density within the mammogram thus having higher mean grey scale intensity compared to the surrounding background. A good enhancement algorithm should aim to enhance the contrast between target and background by increasing the mean grey scale of the target area and then reducing the mean grey of the background area, thereby increasing the value of TBC_{SD}. The background contrast ratio can also be calculated using the entropy E of target and background areas within an image. This measure is computed in a similar manner to TBC_{SD} by determining the difference between ratios of the mean grey scales in the target and background areas in both original and enhanced images as:

$$TBC_{Entropy} = \{\frac{(m_t^e/m_b^e) - (m_t^o/m_b^o)}{E_t^e/E_t^o}\} \tag{4}$$

Where E_t^e and E_t^o are the entropy of the target in the original and enhancement image, respectively. An effective enhancement algorithm will lead to a large value of $TBC_{Entropy}$.

5   Results and Discussion

To study the performance of the introduced algorithm, first we present the results of the Fuzzy Histogram Hyperbolization. Next, we evaluate the enhancement results based on the four pre-discussed measurements. Finally, fuzzy C-Mean segmentation results is then presented. In this implementation, we will consider four spiculated masses images with different parameters . The images were selected from the Digital Databases for Mammographic Image Analysis Society (MIAS) [6]. Figure 1: illustrates the enhancement results; (a) Represents the original image (b) Represent Fuzzy Histogram Hyperbolization enhancement result.

Table (1) illustrates TPC_{SD}, $TBC_{Entropy}$, indexes of fuzziness (H) and Entropy (γ) parameters for enhancement results, we consider five images with different cancer parameters. We have to note that a good enhancement technique should aim to increase the contrast between target and background by increasing the ratio of mean grey in these areas. This background contrast ratio is calculated in a similar manner to the previous measure as the difference between the ratios of the mean grey in the target and background areas. An effective enhancement technique should aim to reduce the entropy of the target compared with

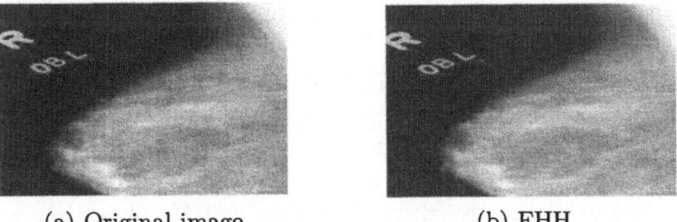

(a) Original image   (b) FHH

Fig. 1. Fuzzy Histogram Hyperbolization Enhancement results

Table 1. TBC_{SD}, TBC_{Entroy}, H,γ parameters for the enhancement results

Measures	TBC_{SD}		$TBC_{Entropy}$		H		γ	
	Original	Fuzzy	Original	Fuzzy	Original	Fuzzy	Original	Fuzzy
mdb145	0.01	0.51	0.011	0.63	0.2893	0.258	0.2177	0.1981
mdb148	0.82	0.96	−0.34	0.16	0.0211	0.0082	0.0056	0.0051
mdb175	0.52	0.79	0.16	0.87	0.4231	0.3909	0.2314	0.2001
mdb179	0.36	0.63	0.22	0.87	0.0528	0.0061	0.4101	0.3190

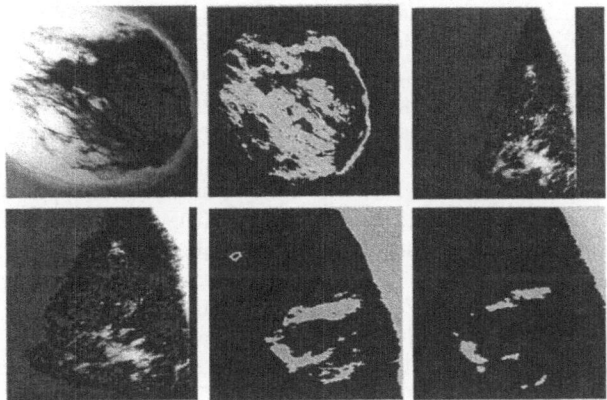

Fig. 2. FCM segmentation results with different number of clusters

the original. The final value of will be larger for an effective enhancement technique. In addition the enhancement technique should aim to reduce the spread of grey scales in the enhanced target image compared with original. The final value of will be larger for an effective enhancement technique. also, we observed that the index of fuzziness and the entropy decrease with enhancement. Figure (2) represents Fuzzy C-Mean with different initiation parameters. The weight parameter of cost function is ranging from 0.001 to 0.0000001 and the clusters numbers ranging form three to sis clusters. From the obtained results, we observe that the good results come with high number of clustering with small weight of the cost function.

6 Conclusion

This paper presents an application of the fuzzy set theory in image processing for the detection of spiculated masses in digitized mammogram. The introduced technique consists of two stages, enhancement of spiculations followed by the detection of the location via clustering the region of interest. For the enhancement algorithm, Fuzzy Histogram Hyperbolization (FHH) algorithm is introduced. For the clustering process, a fuzzy c-mean (FCM)clustering algorithm is used to provide a fuzzy partition of the images. By evaluating the reliability of the measures using the fuzzy based approach and histogram equalization techniques, the results support the qualitative assessment of images that the fuzzy technique has a higher utility in the enhancement process. The results proved that the proposed algorithm is very successful and has high detection accuracy.

References

1. Aboul ella Hassanien and Amr Bader: A comparative study on digital mamography Enhancement algorithms based on Fuzzy Theory. International Journal of Studies in Informatics and Control, SIC - Volume 12 Number 1,pp. 21-31, 2003.
2. Bezdek, J.C., Ehrlich, R., and Full, W.: FCM: the Fuzzy c-Means clustering algorithm. Computers and Geosciences, 10, pp.191-203,1984.
3. Bovis, K. J. and Singh, S.: Enhancement technique evaluation using quantitative measures on digital mammograms. Proc. 5th International Workshop on Digital Mammography Toronto, Canada, M.J. Yaffe (ed.), Medical Physics Publishing, pp. 547-553, 11-14 June, 2000.
4. Cancer Net Home Page of the National Cancer Institute http://biomed.nus.sg, 2002.
5. Cannon, R.L., Dave, J.V., and Bezdek, J.C.: Efficient implementation of the Fuzzy c-Means clustering algorithms. IEEE Trans. Pattern Anal. Mach. Intel., 8(2), pp. 248-255,1986.
6. http://www.wiau.man.ac.uk/services/MIAS/MIASmini.htm.: The Mammographic Image Analysis Society: Mini Mammography Database, 2003.
7. Kerre, E. and Nachtegael, M.: Fuzzy techniques in image processing: Techniques and applications. Studies in Fuzziness and Soft Computing, vol. 52, Physica Verlag: Heidelberg 2000.
8. Nico K., Martin T., Jan H., Leon V. E.: Digital Mammography: Computational Imaging and Vision. In: Kluwer academic publication, 1998.
9. Tizhoosh, H.R.: Fuzzy image enhancement: an overview. Kerre, E., Nachtegael, M. (Eds.): Fuzzy Techniques in Image Processing, Springer, Studies in Fuzziness and Soft Computing, pp. 137-171, 2000.

Artificial Neural Networks in Identifying Areas with Homogeneous Survival Time

Małgorzata Krętowska[1] and Leon Bobrowski[1,2]

[1] Faculty of Computer Science, Białystok Technical University, Wiejska 45a, 15-351 Białystok, Poland
[2] Institute of Biocybernetics and Biomedical Engineering PAS, Ks. Trojdena 4, Warsaw, Poland
mmac@ii.pb.bialystok.pl, leon.bobrowski@ibib.waw.pl

Abstract. In the paper an artificial neural network designed for prediction of survival time is presented. The method aims at identifying areas in the feature space homogeneous from the point of view of survival experience. The proposed method is based on minimization of a piecewise linear function. Appropriately designed dipolar criterion function is able to cope with censored data. Additional pruning phase prevents the network from over-fitting.

1 Introduction

Survival analysis is concerned mainly with prediction of failure occurrence. In medicine, the failure usually represents death or disease relapse. Failure time prediction is done on the base of datasets, which are gathered within the space of several years. The data, describing the analyzed phenomenon, contains patients characteristics (e.g. sex, age, outcomes of laboratory tests) and the failure time t. One of the most important and distinguishing features of survival data is censoring. For *uncensored* patients the failure occurred exactly at the time t (failure indicator $\sigma = 1$). *Censored* cases ($\sigma = 0$) contain incomplete information of the failure occurrence. The only information is that the failure did not occur before t.

Statistical methods used in analysis of survival data require some additional assumptions about the analyzed phenomenon. If the requirements are difficult to obey some other techniques are adopted. Among them artificial neural networks are considered as one of the most promising tools. Application of ANN in survival data analysis may be assess from the point of view of several criteria. One of the most common approach is based on the prediction of failure occurrence before a given time e.g. 5 years [6,9]. Other authors divide survival time into several disjoint intervals and the neural network task is to choose the interval in which the failure is most likely to occur. The problem that appears in all proposed techniques is how to treat censored cases. The most popular idea is simply to omit them, another one is to impute the failure time using such methods as Cox regression models [7], decision trees [12] or Kaplan-Meier method [11]. The neural network models that are able to cope with censored cases directly are a

L. Rutkowski et al. (Eds.): ICAISC 2004, LNAI 3070, pp. 1008–1013, 2004.
© Springer-Verlag Berlin Heidelberg 2004

small part of all the proposed techniques. They are developed as a generalization of regression models and were used mainly to estimate the hazard function [2,10].

In this paper we propose a neural network model aims at prediction of survival time. This is equivalent to identifying subgroups of patients with homogeneous response for a given treatment. The technique is able to deal with censored cases and do not require artificial division of survival time. The additional optimizing phase allows receiving the network with better generalization ability.

2   Learning Phase

A neural network model, considered in the paper, consists of two layers: input and output layer. The output layer is built from neurons with binary activation function. From geometrical point of view a neuron divides feature space into two subspaces by using a hyper-plane $H(\mathbf{w}, \theta) = \{\mathbf{x} :< \mathbf{x}, \mathbf{w} >= \theta\}$, where $\mathbf{x}$ is a feature vector, $\mathbf{w}$ - a weight vector and θ is a threshold. The neuron is activated (the output $z = 1$) if the input vector $\mathbf{x}$ is situated on the positive site of the hyper-plane H. The layer of formal neurons divides N-dimensional feature space into disjoint areas. Each area is described by single output vector $\mathbf{z} = [z_1, z_2, \ldots, z_L]^T$, where $z_i \in \{0,1\}$, L is the number of neurons in the layer. The network works correctly if all the areas are homogeneous from the point of view of analyzed problem. In case of survival data each area should include patients with similar survival times.

The proposed learning procedure is based on the concept of dipoles [3]. The dipole is a pair of different covariates vectors $(\mathbf{x}_i, \mathbf{x}_j)$ from the learning set. We distinguish mixed and pure dipoles. Mixed dipoles are formed between objects, which should be separated while pure ones between objects which are similar from the point of view of an analyzed criterion. In our approach pure dipoles are created between pairs of feature vectors, for which the difference of failure times is small, mixed dipoles - between pairs with distant failure times. Taking into account censored cases the following rules of dipole construction can be formulated:

1. a pair of feature vectors $(\mathbf{x}_i, \mathbf{x}_j)$ forms the pure dipole, if
   - $\sigma_i = \sigma_j = 1$ and $|t_i - t_j| < \eta$
2. a pair of feature vectors $(\mathbf{x}_i, \mathbf{x}_j)$ forms the mixed dipole, if
   - $\sigma_i = \sigma_j = 1$ and $|t_i - t_j| > \zeta$
   - $(\sigma_i = 0, \sigma_j = 1$ and $t_i - t_j > \zeta)$ or $(\sigma_i = 1, \sigma_j = 0$ and $t_j - t_i > \zeta)$

Parameters η and ζ are equal to quartiles of absolute values of differences between uncensored survival times. The parameter η is fixed as 0.2 quartile and ζ - 0.6.

We introduce two types of piece-wise linear and convex (CPL) penalty functions $\varphi_j^+(\mathbf{v})$ and $\varphi_j^-(\mathbf{v})$:

$$\varphi_j^+(\mathbf{v}) = \begin{cases} \delta_j - < \mathbf{v}, \mathbf{y}_j > & \text{if } < \mathbf{v}, \mathbf{y}_j > \leq \delta_j \\ 0 & \text{if } < \mathbf{v}, \mathbf{y}_j >> \delta_j \end{cases} \tag{1}$$

$$\varphi_j^-(\mathbf{v}) = \begin{cases} \delta_j + <\mathbf{v}, \mathbf{y}_j> & \text{if } <\mathbf{v}, \mathbf{y}_j> \geq -\delta_j \\ 0 & \text{if } <\mathbf{v}, \mathbf{y}_j> < -\delta_j \end{cases} \tag{2}$$

where δ_j is a margin $(\delta_j = 1)$, $\mathbf{y}_j = [1, x_1, \ldots, x_N]^T$ is an augmented covariate vector and $\mathbf{v} = [-\theta, w_1, \ldots, w_N]^T$ is an augmented weight vector. Each mixed dipole $(\mathbf{y}_i, \mathbf{y}_j)$, which should be divided, is associated with a function $\varphi_{ij}^m(\mathbf{v})$ being a sum of two functions with opposite signs $(\varphi_{ij}^m(\mathbf{v}) = \varphi_j^+(\mathbf{v}) + \varphi_i^-(\mathbf{v})$ or $\varphi_{ij}^m(\mathbf{v}) = \varphi_j^-(\mathbf{v}) + \varphi_i^+(\mathbf{v}))$. For pure dipoles, which should stay undivided, we associate a function $\varphi_{ij}^p(\mathbf{v})$ $(\varphi_{ij}^p(\mathbf{v}) = \varphi_j^+(\mathbf{v}) + \varphi_i^+(\mathbf{v})$ or $\varphi_{ij}^c(\mathbf{v}) = \varphi_j^-(\mathbf{v}) + \varphi_i^-(\mathbf{v}))$. A dipolar criterion function is a sum of penalty functions associated with each dipole:

$$\Psi_d(\mathbf{v}) = \sum_{(j,i)\in I_p} \alpha_{ij}\varphi_{ij}^p(\mathbf{v}) + \sum_{(j,i)\in I_m} \alpha_{ij}\varphi_{ij}^m(\mathbf{v}) \tag{3}$$

where α_{ij} determines relative importance (price) of the dipole $(\mathbf{y}_i, \mathbf{y}_j)$, I_p and I_m are the sets of pure and mixed dipoles, respectively. The parameters of neurons in a layer are obtained by sequential minimization (basis exchange algorithms [5]) of the dipolar criterion functions. The function is built from all the pure dipoles and those mixed dipoles which were not divided by previous neurons. The learning phase is finished when all the mixed dipoles are divided.

3   Optimization and Neurons Reduction Phase

The neural network model created according to the procedure described in the previous paragraph may be over-fitted. To improve the generalization ability of the network the second phase of learning procedure - optimization - is proposed. The optimization (pruning) phase consists of two steps. The first step is aimed at distinguishing and enlargement of prototypes, and the other at reduction of redundant neurons.

The prototypes are the areas which contain the largest number of feature vectors $\mathbf{x}$. The number of prototypes is not fixed, but they should cover the assumed fraction of uncensored cases from the learning set (in the experiments 50%). Each prototype P is characterized by median survival time $Me(P)$ and 95% confidence interval for median survival time. The estimators of survival functions are calculated by using Kaplan-Meier method [8].

For each observation $o(\mathbf{x}, t, \sigma)$ from the learning set that is situated outside distinguished areas we need to choose the prototype to which the observation should belong. The prototype is chosen according to following rules:

1. determine the set of prototypes SP for which the observation o will not increase 95% confidence interval for median survival time
2. if $\sigma = 1$ choose the prototype $P_i \in SP$, for which

$$|t - Me(P_i)| = \min_{P_j \in SP} |t - Me(P_j)|$$

3. if $\sigma = 0$ choose the prototype $P_i \in SP$, for which $t - Me(P_i) < 0$ and

$$||\mathbf{x} - P_i|| = \min_{P_j \in SP} ||\mathbf{x} - P_j||$$

where $||\mathbf{x} - P_i||$ means the distance of the vector $\mathbf{x}$ to the prototype P_i

Location of the vectors $\mathbf{x}$ in the chosen prototypes is equivalent to minimizing a pice-wise linear criterion functions $Q_l(\mathbf{v}_l)$ $(l = 1, 2, \ldots, L)$ connected with all the neurons. As a results of minimization new prototypes are received. Whole procedure is repeated unless the global criterion function:

$$Q(\mathbf{v}_1, \mathbf{v}_2, \ldots, \mathbf{v}_L) = Q_1(\mathbf{v}_1) + Q_2(\mathbf{v}_2) + \ldots + Q_L(\mathbf{v}_L) \qquad (4)$$

stops decreasing [4].

The other step of optimization phase causes the reduction of neurons which divide areas with similar survival times. As a similarity measure between two areas the log-rank test is used. The test verifies the hypothesis about no differences between survival times of two analyzed areas. The neuron is eliminated if in all the tests (number of tests is equal to the number of pairs of areas which will be joint after neuron reduction) the hypothesis was not rejected at 0.05 significance level.

After reduction of one neuron the whole optimization procedure is repeated from the beginning.

4   Experimental Results

The analysis was conducted on the base of two data sets. The first data set is from the Veteran's Administration (VA) lung cancer study [8]. In this trial, male patients with advanced inoperable tumors were randomized to either standard (69 subjects) or test chemotherapy (68 subjects). Only 9 subjects from 137 are censored. Information on performance status at baseline (Karnofsky rating - KPS), disease duration in months, age in years at randomization, prior therapy (yes, no), and cell type (large, squamous, small, adeno), is available. The other dataset contains the information on 205 patients (148 censored cases) with malignant melanoma following radical operation. The data was collected at Odense University Hospital in Denmark by K.T. Drzewiecki [1]. Each patient is described by 4 features: sex, age, tumor thickness and ulceration.

The artificial neural network received for *VA lung cancer* data contains three formal neurons. Four areas were distinguished in the six dimensional feature space (see table 1). The best prediction is for patients belonging to the first area for which median survival time is equal to 200 days. For patients who belong to the area no. IV median survival time is equal to 19 days only. Survival functions calculated for all the areas are presented in figure 1a.

In *Malignant melanoma* dataset five homogeneous subgroups of patients were found. For the first three areas it is impossible to calculate median survival time because of the large fraction of censored cases in the data. Analyzing the survival

Table 1. Characteristics of the received patterns

Dataset	Pattern	Median (95% CI)	n (censored)
VA lung	I	200 (162; 250)	25(3)
cancer	II	117 (95; 132)	41(4)
	III	51 (35; 73)	40(0)
	IV	19 (13; 21)	31(2)
Malignant	I	-	50(44)
melanoma	II	-	19(16)
	III	-	69(48)
	IV	2567 (1228; ...)	16(9)
	V	793 (693; ...)	26(10)

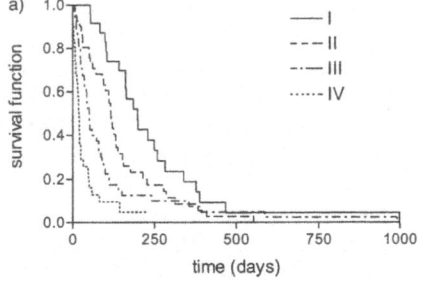
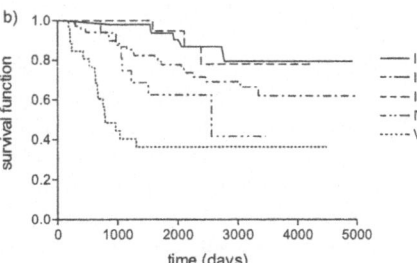

Fig. 1. Kaplan-Meier survival functions for distinguished areas: a) *VA lung cancer*; b) *Malignant melanoma*

functions (fig. 1b) we can see that the patterns no. I and III are very similar. They are represented by $[1,1,0]^T$ and $[1,0,1]^T$ network outputs respectively. The patters do not border directly on each other. It may suggest that there are two different areas with similar, long survival time in the feature space. In opposite to these two areas is subgroup no. V. The median survival time is equal to 793 days. The risk of failure for the patients belonging to this area is high.

5   Conclusions

The artificial neural network approach was proposed to identify areas in feature space which are homogeneous from the point of view of survival time. The main advantage of the method is lack of artificial division of survival time into disjoint intervals. The method based on the information received from the data identifies the subgroups of patients with similar survival experience. The algorithm both in the first and the other phase is able to deal with censored cases. Additional two-step optimization phase allows improving the generalization ability of the network. Distinguished patters are defined by the rules possible to interpret also by people who are not closely related to the neural network methodology.

Acknowledgements. This work was supported by the grant W/WI/1/02 from Białystok Technical University.

References

1. Andersen P.K., Borgan O., Gill R. D., Statistical Models based on Counting Processes. Springer (1993)
2. Biganzoli E., Boracchi P., Mariani L., Marubini E., Feed forward neural networks for the analysis of censored survival data: a partial logistic regression approach. Statistics in Medicine **17**(10) (1998) 1169–1186
3. Bobrowski L., Krętowska M., Krętowski M., Design of neural classifying networks by using dipolar criterions. Proc. of the Third Conference on Neural Networks and Their Applications, Kule, Poland (1997) 689–694
4. Bobrowski L., Krętowska M., Dipolar pruning of neural layers. Proc. of the 5th Conference on Neural Network and Soft Computing, Zakopane, Poland (2000) 174–179
5. Bobrowski L., Niemiro W., A method of synthesis of linear discriminant function in the case of nonseparability. Pattern Recognition **17** (1984) 205–210
6. Burke H.B., Goodman P.H., Rosen D.B., Henson D.E., Weinstein J.N., Harrell F.E., Marks J.R., Winchester D.P., Bostwik D.G., Artificial neural networks improve the accuracy of cancer survival prediction. Cancer **79** (1997) 857–862
7. De Laurentiis M., Ravdin, P.M., A technique for using neural network analysis to perform survival analysis of censored data. Cancer Letters **77** (1994) 127–138
8. Kalbfleisch J. D., Prentice R. L., The Statistical Analysis of Failure Time Data. John Wiley & Sons (1980)
9. Kappen H.J., Neijt J.P., Neural network analysis to predict treatment outcome. Annals of Oncology Suppl. **4** (1993) 31–34
10. Liestol K., Andersen P.K., Andersen U., Survival analysis and neural nets. Statistics in Medicine **13** (1994) 1189–1200
11. Mani D. R., Drew J.,Betz A., Datta, P., Statistics and data mining techniques for lifetime value modeling. Proc. of KDD (1999) 94–103
12. Ripley, B.D., Ripley, R.M., Neural networks as statistical methods in survival analysis. Artificial Neural Networks: Prospects for Medicine, Dybowski R., Grant V. (eds.), Landes Biosciences Publishers (1998)

Multistage Diagnosis of Myocardial Infraction Using a Fuzzy Relation

Marek Kurzynski

Wroclaw University of Technology, Faculty of Electronics, Chair of Systems and
Computer Networks, Wyb. Wyspianskiego 27, 50-370 Wroclaw, Poland
Marek.Kurzynski@pwr.wroc.pl

Abstract. This paper presents decision algorithm based on fuzzy relation developed for the multistage pattern recognition. In this method - assuming that the learning set is given - first we find fuzzy relation in the product of feature and decision space as solution of an optimisation problem and next this relation is used in decision algorithm. The application of presented method to the computer-aided diagnosis of myocardial infraction is discussed and compared with algorithms based on statistical model.

1 Introduction

One of the most often used instruments for the computer-aided medical diagnosis are pattern recognition methods. The most familiar structure of the classifier decison logic is the single-level tree, where the distinction among all classes is made in one stage. In practical situations however, this "one-shot" structure may not be the most appropriate scheme. When the number of features is quite large and classes are numerous, an efficient approach is multistage recognition system based on a multilevel decision tree scheme. This method has many remarkable advantages [3] (e.g. natural division of classes, the use of different features at different nodes) over the conventional one-stage classifier.

A decison-tree consists of a root-node, a number of nonterminal nodes. Associated with the root-node is the entire set of classes into which a pattern may be classified. A nonterminal node is an intermediate decision and its immediate descendant nodes represent the outcomes of that decision. A terminal node corresponds to a terminal decision, i.e. the decision procedure terminates and the unknown pattern being classified is assigned to the class associated with that node. Thus, in order to classify the pattern into a class, one has to traverse a path of the tree starting at the root-node and at each encountered nonterminal node one ought to take a decision on the further path in the tree, until a terminal node is reached. This terminal node represents the final classifiction and its label (number) indicates to which class the unknown pattern is assigned.

The paper is a sequel of the author's earlier publications [1], [2], [4], [5], [6], and it yields new results dealing with the algorithms of multistage recognition for the case when fuzzy inference procedures are applied as diagnostic algorithm.

L. Rutkowski et al. (Eds.): ICAISC 2004, LNAI 3070, pp. 1014–1019, 2004.
© Springer-Verlag Berlin Heidelberg 2004

2   Preliminaries and the Problem Statement

If we adopt a probabilistic model of the recognition task and assume that the *a priori* probabilities of disease units and conditional probability density functions of symptoms $f_j(x)$, $x \in X$, $j \in M = \{1, 2, ..., M\}$ there exist, then appropriate diagnostic algorithms at particular stages of the classification procedure can be obtained by solving a certain optimization problem. Now, however, in contrast to one-stage recognition, the optimality criterion can be formulated in different ways, and various manners of action of the algorithms can be assumed, which in effect gives different optimal decision rules for the particular stages of classification [3]. Let us consider two cases.

The globally optimal strategy(GOS)
The minimization of the mean probability of misclassification of the whole multistage decision process leads to an optimal decision strategy, whose recognition algorithm at the n-th stage is the following [1]:

$$\Psi^*_{i_{n-1}}(x_{i_{n-1}}) = i_n \quad if$$
$$P_c(i_n) \sum_{j \in M_{i_n}} p_j(x_{i_{n-1}}) = \max_{k \in M^{(i_{n-1})}} P_c(k) \sum_{j \in M_k} p_j(x_{i_{n-1}}), \quad (1)$$

where $M^{(i_{n-1})}$ denotes the set of decision numbers at the n-th stage determined by the decision i_{n-1} made at the previous stage, M_{i_n} denotes the set of class numbers (final diagnoses) accessible after the decision i_n at the n-th stage is made. $P_c(i_n)$ is the probability of correct classification at the next stages if at the n-th stage decision i_n is made and $p_j(x)$ denotes *a posteriori* probability of disease unit which can be calculated from given data (learning set) using empirical Bayes rule.

What is interesting is the manner of operation of the above decision rule. Namely, its decision indicates this node for which *a posteriori* probability of set of classes attainable from it, multiplied by the respective probability of correct classification at the next stages of recognition procedure, is the greatest one. In other words, the decision at any interior node of a tree depends on the future to which this decision leads.

The locally optimal strategy (LOS)
Formally, the locally strategy can be derived minimizing the local criteria, which denote probabilities of misclassification for particular nodes of a tree. Its recognition algorithm at the n-th stage is as in (1), but without probabilities $P_c(i_n)$. The LOS strategy does not take into regard the context and its decision rules are mutually independent.

In the real world there is often a lack of exact knowledge of *a priori* probabilities and class-conditional probability density functions, whereas only a learning set (the set of case records provided with a firm diagnosis), is known, viz.

$$S = \{(x_1, j_1), (x_2, j_2), ..., (x_L, j_L)\}. \quad (2)$$

In these cases we can to estimate appropriate probabilities and conditional densities from (2) and then to use these estimators to calculate discriminant functions of rules GOS and LOS strategies.

In the next section, assuming that the learning set (2) is given, we present the fuzzy inference engine procedure for multistage recognition (diagnosis), which - in some way - correspond to LOS and GOS strategies.

3   Algorithms

In the presented method of multistage recognition, on the base of learning set (2), first we find for each nonterminal node fuzzy relation between fuzzified feature space and class numbers set, as a solution of appropriate optimization problem. Next this relation, expressed as matrix, can be used to make decision in multistage recognition procedure in twofold manner.

More precisely, this method leads to the following steps for i_{n-1}th node of decision-tree:

1. Divide the spaces of features $x^{(i_{n-1})}$ into fuzzy regions. In the further example we use triangular fuzzy sets with 3 partitions. Usually, these fuzzy sets corresponds with the linguistic values of features, which state space $\overline{X}^{(i_{n-1})}$.

2. Calculate observation matrix $O^{(i_{n-1})}$ (fuzzy relation in the product of feature space $\overline{X}^{(i_{n-1})}$ and learning subset $S^{(i_{n-1})}$) - the i-th matrix row contains grades of membership of features $x^{(i_{n-1})}$ of i-th learning pattern from $S^{(i_{n-1})}$ to the fuzzy sets created at the previous step.

3. Determine decision matrix $D^{(i_{n-1})}$ (relation in the product of learning subset $S^{(i_{n-1})}$ and the set of decision numbers $M^{(i_{n-1})}$) - its i-th row contains 0's and the figure one at position corresponding to decision number $i_{n-1}^{(j)}$, for which the class number of i-th learning pattern from $S^{(i_{n-1})}$ belongs to the set $M_{i_{n-1}^{(j)}}$.

4. Find matrix $E^{(i_{n-1})}$, so as to minimize criterion

$$\rho(O^{(i_{n-1})} \circ E^{(i_{n-1})}, D^{(i_{n-1})}). \tag{3}$$

Operator $\circ$ denotes $max - t-$norm composition of relations, i.e. multiplication of matrices O and E with $*$, $+$ operators replaced by t-norm and max [8]. Criterion evaluates difference between matrices A and B, $\rho(A, B) \geq 0$ and $\rho(A, B) = 0$ iff $A = B$. In the further example, we adopt

$$\rho(A, B) = \sum_{i,j} (a_{ij} - b_{ij})^2 \tag{4}$$

and as method of minimization (3) the genetic algorithm will be applied. Matrix $E^{(i_{n-1})}$ is a fuzzy relation in product of decision set $M^{(i_{n-1})}$ and feature space $\overline{X}^{(i_{n-1})}$. Its elements (grades of membership) represent intensity of fuzzy features (symptoms in medical diagnosis, for example) for each class (disease). The manner of using the expert-matrix to make decision at i_{n-1} node is obvious. Namely, from given feature vector $x^{(i_{n-1})}$ of pattern to be recognized, first me must determine the observation row-matrix $O_0^{(i_{n-1})}$ (like in step 2 of the method) and next calculate the decision row-matrix $D_0^{(i_{n-1})}$, as the max-t-norm composition of relations (see step 3), viz.

$$O_0^{(i_{n-1})} \circ E^{(i_{n-1})} = D_0^{(i_{n-1})}. \tag{5}$$

As a decision we choose this number from the set $M^{(i_{n-1})}$, which corresponds to the maximum value of elements of row-matrix $D_0^{(i_{n-1})}$ (Algorithm 1) or row-matrix $D_0^{(i_{n-1})} P_c(i_{n-1})$ (Algorithm 2), where $P_c(i_{n-1})$ denotes diagonal-matrix of empirical probabilities defined in (1). It is obvious, that Algorithm 1 corresponds to LOS of probabilistic approach, whereas Algorithm 2 is related to GOS strategy.

In the next section we present results of comparative analysis of proposed algorithms using reach enough set of real-life data that concerns multistage diagnosis of myocardial infraction.

4   Diagnosis of Myocardial Infraction (MI)

4.1   Material and Methods

In the Computer Centre of the Wroclaw Medical Academy the set of clinical information was collected. It contains 231 case records of patients admitted to the cardiological unit with chest pain of acute onset. Each case history contains administrative data and values of 26 clinical data [2] presented in Table 1 and the firm diagnosis from the following set: (1) Angina prectoris, (2) Angina prectoris - Prinzmetal variant, (3) Myocardial infraction - transmural, (4) Myocardial infraction - subendocardial (5) Pain of non-heart origin. The classes have been organized into two-stage classifier according to the following schema: (1)+(2)=(B) - Angina prectoris, (3)+(4)=(C) - Myocardial infraction, (B)+(C)+(5)=(A) - Chest pain.

Table 1. Clinical features considered

1. General: (1) Sex, (2) Age
2. Pain: (3) Site at onset, (4) Chest pain radiation, (5) Pain character, (6) Onset of pain, (7) Number of hours since onset, (8) Duration of the last episode
3. General examination: (9) Systolic blood pressure, (10) Diastolic blood pressure, (11) Heart rate, (12) Respiration rate, (13) Rales, (14) Cyanosis, (15) Chest wall tenderness, (16) Smoker index
4. Biochemical tests: (17) CK, (18) LDH, (19) a-HBDH (20) AspAT
5. ECG examination: (21) HRV, (22) ST segment elevation (depression), (23) ST segment slope, (24) T wave time, (25) T wave inverse, (26) new Q wave

First, we have selected the best feature subset for each non-terminal node (the continuous features were avaliable for selection) using Kolmogorov criterion [9]. At each non-terminal node the features were used from the best single one to the set of 4 features, successively. In order to find expert-matrices for non-terminal nodes the genetic algorithm was applied, which is a popular method in optimization and can improve the search procedure.

The genetic algorithm proceeded as follows [10].

Coding method - the values of elements of matrix E were directly coded to the chromosome.

The fitness function - was defined as follows:

$$Fit = Q - \rho(A, B) \tag{6}$$

where ρ is as in (4) and Q is suitably selected positive constant.

Initialization - the initial population of chromosomes with which the search begins was generated randomly. The size of population - after trials - was set to 40.

Reproduction - roulette wheel.

Crossover and mutation - a two-point crossover was used and probability of mutation was 0.05.

Stop procedure - evolution process was terminated after 1000 generations.

4.2   Results

In order to study the performance of the proposed recognition concepts and evaluate its usefulness to the computer-aided diagnosis of ARF some computer experiments were made using the resubstitution method [9].

Results for Algorithm 1 (A1) and Algorithm 2 (A2) are presented in Table 2. Additionally results for probabilistic algorithms GOS and LOS are also given.

Table 2. The results of classification accuracy in percent

Algorithm	Number of features per node			
	1	2	3	4
LOS	52.8	60.7	66.0	70.5
GOS	51.5	60.1	68.5	73.3
A1	49.4	58.3	65.7	74.4
A2	51.1	61.2	67.5	75.1

These results imply the following conclusions:

1. There occurs a common effect within each algorithm group: algorithms that do not take into regard the context of decision procedure in multistage process (LOS and Algorithm 1) are always worse than those that treat multistage procedure as a compound decision process (GOS and Algorithm 2). This confirms the effectiveness and usefulness of the conceptions and algorithm construction principles presented above for the needs of multistage diagnosis.

2. The difference between probabilistic algorithms and fuzzy methods is insignificant.

5   Conclusions

In this paper we focus our attention on the fuzzy approach to the multistage pattern recognition and application of elaborated methods to the diagnosis of acute renal failure. In order to study the performance of the proposed recognition concepts and evaluate their usefulness to the computer-aided diagnosis some computer experiments were made using real data. The objective of our experiements was to measure quality of the tested algorithms that was defined by the frequency of correct decisions.

The comparative analysis presented above for the multistage diagnosis is also of the experimental nature. The algorithm-ranking outcome cannot be treated as one having the ultimate character as a that of a law in force, but it has been achieved for specific data within a specific diagnostic task. However, although the outcome may be different for other tasks, the presented research may nevertheless suggest some perspectives for practical applications and - as it seems - has proved rightness of proposed concepts.

References

1. Kurzynski M.: Probabilistic algorithms, neural networks, and fuzzy system applied to the multistage diagnsis of acute abdominal pain - a comparative study of methods. Proc. 1st Int. Conference on Fuzzy Systems and Knowledge Discovery, Singapore (2002) (CD ROM)
2. Kurzynski M.: Multistage empirical Bayes approach versus artificial neural network to the computer aided myocardial infraction diagnosis. Proc. IEEE EMBS Conference, Vienna (2002) 762-766
3. Kurzynski M.: On the multistage Bayes classifier. Pattern Recognition, 21 (1988) 355-365
4. Kurzynski M., Puchala E.: Hybrid pattern recognition algorithms with the statistical model applied to the computer-aided medical diagnosis. Lecture Notes in Computer Science, Medical Data Analysis, (2001) 133-139
5. Kurzynski M.: Fuzzy inference systems for multistage pattern recognition - applicatoion to medical diagnosis. Proc. 3rd IASTED Int. Conf. on Artificial Inelligence and Applications, Benalmadena (Spain) (2003) 348-353
6. Kurzynski M: Fuzzy inference systems for multistage diagnosis of acute renal failure in children. Lecture Notes in Computer Science, Medical Data Analysis, LNCS 2868 (2003) 99- 108
7. L-X Wang L-X.: A course in fuzzy systems and control, New York: Prentice-Hall (1998)
8. Czogala E., Leski J.: Fuzzy and neuro-fuzzy intelligent systems, New York: Physica-Verlag (2000)
9. Gyorfi P., Lugossi G.: A probabilistic theory of pattern recognition, New York: Springer Verlag, (1996)
10. Goldberg D.: Genetic algorithms in search, optimization and machine learning, New York: Addison-Wesley (1989)

Application of SVM to Ovarian Cancer Classification Problem

Maciej Kusy*

Faculty of Electrical and Computer Engineering,
Rzeszow University of Technology, W. Pola 2, 35-959 Rzeszow, Poland,
mkusy@prz.rzeszow.pl

Abstract. In this article Sequential Minimal Optimization (SMO) approach as the solution of Support Vector Machines (SVMs) algorithm is applied to the ovarian cancer data classification problem. The comparison of different SVM models is presented in order to determine the chance of 60 months survival for a woman to be treated ovarian cancer. A cross-validation procedure is used for this purpose.

1 Introduction

Support Vector Machines (SVM) introduced by Vapnik [13], [14] are, among many applications, used in tasks of medical data classifications helpful in the diagnosis statements. This article presents the application of SVM to real medical data classification problem. The usage of this particular algorithm can be justified by the fact that SVM provide an optimal separating hyperplane in case of classification, have small number of learning parameters, and that by means of SMO, they solve the problem fast [13].

The task relies on finding the best parameters of the SV machine that can give the lowest error on the unseen data set, called validation set [2], [6], [8], being taught on the known training data set. The standard *k-fold* cross-valildation procedure is used to this problem [2], [6], [8]. The input data set consists of 199 vectors each of the length of 17. This input space represents the population of 199 women who were treated ovarian cancer disease. 17 different parameters were registered on each single case of the sick person [11]. The binary classification problem is faced because the information relevant to the physicians is whether the patient can survive 60 months or not. As the solution of SVM algorithm, Platt's SMO approach is applied [5], [9], [10].

* Author appreciates the assistance of prof. Andrzej Skret, dr.Tomasz Lozinski of Obstetrics and Gynecology Department, State Hospital Rzeszow, Rzeszow (Poland) in rendering the ovarian cancer learning data accessible and detailed explanation of the problem of the ovarian cancer disease, and dr. Jacek Kluska of Faculty of Electrical and Computer Engineering, Rzeszow University of Technology, Rzeszow (Poland) in providing valuable comments and discussions concerning the cross validation procedure and SVM algorithm.

L. Rutkowski et al. (Eds.): ICAISC 2004, LNAI 3070, pp. 1020–1025, 2004.
© Springer-Verlag Berlin Heidelberg 2004

Due to the complexity and diversity of the patients and their sickness parameters measured, this kind of classification results may provide a lot of medical hints, which in turn, can be helpful in diagnostic decision making, treatment applications, and confirmation that the curing process is correct. The importance of such insights can be measured by the fact that the ovarian cancer is most often occurring cancer disease of women genital organs in Poland whose morbidity still grows up.

This paper is structured as follows. Sections 2 and 3 briefly introduce the SVM theory and the SMO algorithm respectively. In section 4 the problem of the disease known as ovarian cancer is explained. Later on, in section 5, one verifies using cross-validation procedure, how the SMO algorithm can predict unseen data using different complexity SVMs. Finally, section 6 presents the conclusions.

2   Overview of Support Vector Machines

The classification task analyzed in this article is solved by means of SVMs and amounts to the solution of the following Quadratic Programming (QP) optimization problem:

$$
\begin{cases}
\max_{\alpha_i} W(\boldsymbol{\alpha}) = \sum_{i=1}^{l} \alpha_i - \dfrac{1}{2} \sum_{i=1}^{l} \sum_{j=1}^{l} \alpha_i \alpha_j y_i y_j k(\mathbf{x}_i, \mathbf{x}_j) \\
\sum_{i=1}^{l} \alpha_i y_i = 0, \qquad 0 \le \alpha_i \le C, \qquad i = 1, \dots, l
\end{cases}
\tag{1}
$$

where Lagrange multipliers α_i, are the coefficients to be found, $\mathbf{x}_i$ and y_i are given input-output pairs, and $k(\mathbf{x}_i, \mathbf{x}_j)$ is the kernel function between the input examples. For completeness, refer to [1], [4], [7], [13]. Different kinds of kernel functions can be used in this problem (see: [3], [12] for details).

3   Sequential Minimal Optimization

The method developed for training the SVMs for large data sets, created by Platt is called Sequential Minimal Optimization (SMO) [5], [9], [10]. It solves the QP problem given by (1). The solution is found under necessary and sufficient Karush-Kuhn-Tucker (KKT) conditions [3], [10]. SMO performs the decomposition of the overall QP problem into the series of the smallest possible optimization problems. Only two Lagrange multipliers are involved in this problem. To solve (1) SMO first computes the constraints on two multipliers and then finds the constraint maximum using these coefficients. The algorithm always optimizes and alters two Lagrange multipliers at every step with at least one coefficient violating KKT conditions. Some criteria are used for the selection of multipliers in order to ensure the large increase of the objective function. These are two separate heuristics of choice - one for the first Lagrange multiplier and one for the second. Detailed explanation is given in [10].

4   The Ovarian Cancer Data for Classification Problem

Ovarian cancer is most often occurring cancer disease of women genital organs in Poland. The reason is found in gene mutation and the existence of this sickness among the ancestors of a sick person. The ovarian cancer's morbidity still keeps on increasing. Its occurrence is estimated with the frequency of 3/100000 of registered women under the age of 37 and 40/100000 over this age.

According to [11], the exploration and treatment comprised 199 women. Every single patient was examined with 17 different parameters which are used for this classification problem. Below, the set of these parameters is presented. In parentheses the numerical labels are provided in order to conduct SMO:

1. figo staging of the ovarian cancer $\in \{1, 2, 3, 4\}$;
2. observation-examination $\in \{0, 1\}$; 60 months - complete (1), less than 60 - incomplete (0);
3. hospital $\in \{0, 1\}$; state clinical hospitals (1), others (0);
4. age of hospitalized woman $\in \{22, 25, ..., 81\}$;
5. hysterectomy - removal of uterus $\in \{0, 1\}$; performed (1), not performed (0);
6. adnexectomy - complete removal of ovary and salpinx $\in \{0, 1\}$; performed (1), not performed (0);
7. full exploration of abdomen $\in \{0, 1\}$; possible (0), performed (1);
8. kind of surgery $\in \{1, 2, 3\}$; hysterectomy (1), adnexectomy (2), only exploration (3);
9. appendectomy - removal of appendix $\in \{0, 1\}$; performed (1), not performed (0);
10. removal of intestine $\in \{0, 1\}$; performed (1), not performed (0);
11. degree of debulking $\in \{1, 2, 3\}$; entire (3), up to $2cm$ (1), more than $2cm$ (2);
12. mode of surgery $\in \{1, 2, 3\}$; intraperitoneal (1), extraperitoneal (2), trans-tumor resection (3);
13. histological type of tumor $\in \{1, 2, 3, 4, 5\}$;
14. grading of tumor $\in \{1, 2, 3, 4\}$; GI (1), GII (2), GIII (3), data unavailable (4);
15. kind of chemotherapy $\in \{1, 2, 3\}$;
16. radiotherapy $\in \{0, 1\}$; performed (1), not performed (0);
17. "second look" surgery $\in \{0, 1\}$; performed (1), not performed (0);

The analysis on ovarian cancer treatment are studied thoroughly in [11].

5   SMO Application

In order to find solution to SVM algorithm the software based on Platt's SMO was created. The software was used to solve this particular ovarian cancer classification problem.

The input data set is (199x17) matrix which represents the population of 199 women who were treated ovarian cancer disease with 17 different parameters registered on each single case of the sick person. In given task the binary classification problem is faced since the information relevant to the physicians is whether the patient survives 60 months or not. Therefore the target values of the input examples are applied as the labels of **0** and **1**.

The goal is to find such a parameter of the SV machine that can give the lowest number of misclassified unseen data points. This number can be expressed by means of unseen data prediction error. It means that, once such a parameter is found, one is capable of applying the algorithm to new data classification problem with some percentage of certainty. This section is devoted determining such a percentage.

In order to find a SVM, that predicts to unseen data in the best way, the technique that compares different machines is used. It can find the model that provides the lowest percentage of incorrect prediction of new data. In cases of SVMs, one can teach various machines on a *training* set, by altering their kernel function parameter. The performance of such machines can then be compared by evaluating the prediction error using an independent *validation* set. The SVM with the smallest error with respect to validation set is selected. Such an approach is called hold out method. Since this procedure can itself lead to some over-fitting to the validation set, the performance of the selected model should be confirmed by measuring its performance on a third independent set, called a *test* set [2]. This procedure requires large training data set.

Unfortunately, when data set is small, a part of the data cannot be kept aside for model comparing purposes. Therefore, a k-fold cross-validation approach is often applied. In this technique one divides the training set into k-subsets. The model is then trained on all subsets except for one, and the validation error is measured by testing it on the subset left out. This procedure is repeated for a total of k trials, each time using a different subset for validation. The performance of the model is assessed by averaging the error under validation set over all trials of the experiment [6]. Then a different model is used (*e.g.* with learning parameters changed) and the procedure is repeated. A typical choice for k is $k = 10$.

In case of ovarian cancer classification problem the k-fold cross-validation procedure is also used. The k parameter is set to $k = 10$. Exponential SVM is applied with kernel function:

$$k(\mathbf{x}_i, \mathbf{x}_j) = \exp\left(-\frac{\|\mathbf{x}_i - \mathbf{x}_j\|}{2\sigma^2}\right) . \tag{2}$$

Different SVM models are tested according to the change of sigma parameter. The values of this parameter are indicated in Fig. 1. The constraint C is set to $C = 10^6$ (see [10] and [13] for details). For every σ and fixed C value, ($k = 10$)-fold cross validation is run. The results are averaged over k. The formula in (3) is used to calculate the unseen (cross-validating) data prediction error:

$$E = \frac{1}{k}\sum_{n=1}^{k}(i_n) \tag{3}$$

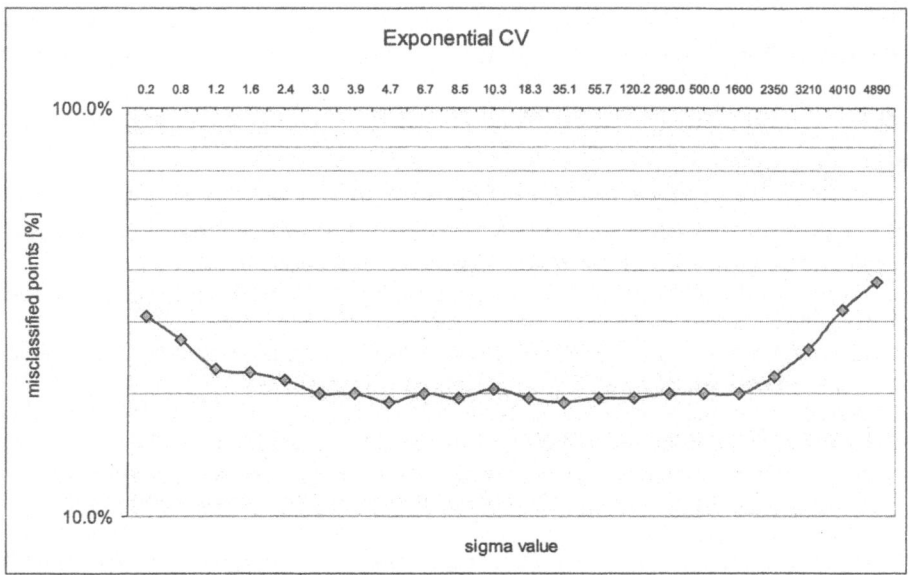

Fig. 1. The percentage of misclassified examples within the cross-validation procedure for exponential kernel training versus sigma σ value

where i_n is the the number of misclassified vectors of the input matrix for a given σ and fixed C within a single k-separation. The total prediction error is then calculated. Fig. 1 presents the outcome average (over k) prediction errors expressed in terms of percentage of misclassified points calculated on the cross-validating data sets for different values of sigma parameter.

Only these SVMs for which sigma ranges from the values of 3.0 to 1600.0 provide clearly low percentage of incorrect prediction of new data. Additionally there are two values of this parameter, namely: $\sigma = 4.7$ and $\sigma = 35.1$ that give the lowest percentage of misclassified examples, i.e. 19.0%. This gives us the 81% confidence of classifying correctly an unknown example, a patient, in this case.

6 Conclusions

The results presented in this paper prove that the cross-validation procedure used to train SV machines can bring very important information to the problem of classification of new patients suffering from ovarian cancer disease. If one finds, by means of this procedure, an appropriate value of sigma parameter of the kernel function, (*i.e.* $\sigma = 4.7$ and $\sigma = 35.1$), and apply it to SVM, the following can be concluded: the woman, to be treated ovarian cancer, has 81.0% chance of 60 months survival. This, in turn, may provide a lot of medical hints that can be useful in making decision on treatment process, sort of diagnosis to be stated.

Generally, the influence of particular parameters for the woman who is trea-ted ovarian cancer is known. However, what is shown in this paper, this kind of analysis for a population of women for 60-months survival has prediction feature. The use of SVM in medical exploration is currently tested. The goal is to create the women's treating model which implements SVM.

References

1. Burges, J.C.: A Tutorial on Support Vector Machines for Pattern Recognition, Vol.2., No.2. In: Data Mining and Knowledge Discovery (1998)
2. Bishop, C.M.: Neural Networks for Pattern Recognition. Oxford University Press Inc., New York (1995)
3. Cristianini, N., Taylor, J.S.: An Introduction to Support Vector Machines and Other Kernel Based Methods. Cambridge University Press, Cambridge (2000)
4. Gunn, S.: Support Vector Machines for Classification and Regression. ISIS Technical Report, Southampton (1998)
5. Hearst, M. A., Schölkopf, B., Dumais, S., Osuna, E., Platt, J.: Trends and Controversies - Support Vector Machines, 13(4). In IEEE Intelligent Systems (1998) 18-28
6. Haykin, S.: Neural Networks: A Comprehensive Foundation. Prentice Hall Inc., New Jersey (1999)
7. Kecman, V.: Learning and Soft Computing: Support Vector Machines, Neural Networks, and Fuzzy Logic Models. MIT Press. Massachusetts (2001)
8. Mitchell, T.M.: Machine Learning. The McGraw-Hill Companies Inc., New York London Madrid Montreal Singapore Sydney Tokyo (1997)
9. Platt, J.C.: Sequential Minimal Optimization: A Fast Algorithm for Training Support Vector Machines. Technical Report MSR-TR-98-14, Microsoft Research (1998)
10. Platt, J.: Fast Training of Support Vector Machines Using Sequential Minimal Optimization. In: Schölkopf, B., Burges, J.C., Smola, J. (eds.): Advances in Kernel Methods - Support Vector Learning. MIT Press, Cambridge (1999) 185-208
11. Skret, A., Lozinski, T., Samolyk, S., Chrusciel, A., Krol, P., Fabisiak, W.: Current Place of Debulking Surgery And Staging in the Treatment of Ovarian Cancer. Recommendations, Reality And Survival. In: New Technologies for Gynecologic And Obstetric Investigation. CIC International Edition, Rome (1999) 23-30
12. Stitson, M.O., Wetson, J.A.E., Gammerman, A., Vovk, V., Vapnik, V.: Theory of Support Vector Machines. Technical Report Royal Holloway University, London (1996)
13. Vapnik, V.N.: The Nature of Statistical Learning Theory. Springer-Verlag, New York (1995)
14. Vapnik, V.N.: An Overview of Statistical Learning Theory, Vol.10, No.5. In: IEEE Trans. Neural Networks (1998) 988-999

ROC Analysis for Fetal Hypoxia Problem by Artificial Neural Networks

Lale Özyılmaz and Tülay Yıldırım

Department of Electronics & Comm. Eng.,
Yıldız Technical University, İstanbul 34349, Turkey
{ozyilmaz,tulay}@yildiz.edu.tr

Abstract. As fetal hypoxia may damage or kill the fetus, it is very important to monitor the infant so that any signs of fetal distress can be detected as soon as possible. In this paper, the performances of some artificial neural networks are evaluated, which eventually produce the suggested diagnosis of fetal hypoxia. Multilayer perceptron (MLP) structure with standard back propagation, MLP with fast back propagation (adaptive learning and momentum term added), Radial Basis Function (RBF) network structure trained by orthogonal least square algorithm, and Conic Section Function Neural Network (CSFNN) with adaptive learning were used for this purpose. Further more, Receiver Operating Characteristic (ROC) analysis is used to determine the accuracy of diagnostic test.

1 Introduction

Fetal hypoxia, oxygen deficiency in the tissues, of any cause leads to a conversion from aerobic to anaerobic metabolism, which produces less energy and more acid [1]. Oxygen exchange between mother and fetus occurs in the placenta. Therefore, the cause of hypoxia can originate in either area. Oxygenated blood enters the fetus from the placenta through the umbilical vein and circulates through the fetus with the majority of the blood bypassing the lungs. The blood then returns to the placenta through the two umbilical arteries [2]. If the oxygen supply is not restored, the fetus dies. Fetal hypoxia may result from [1]:

1. Reduced placental perfusion with maternal blood and consequent decrease in fetal arterial blood oxygen content due to low $pO2$ (hypoxemic hypoxia);
2. Reduced arterial blood oxygen content due to low fetal hemoglobin concentration (anemic hypoxia);
3. Reduced blood flow to the fetal tissues (ischemic hypoxia). Maternal risk factors that may lead to fetal hypoxia include [2]:
   - Diabetes
   - Pregnancy-induced or chronic hypertension
   - Rh sensitization from a previous pregnancy
   - Maternal infection
   - Sickle cell anemia

L. Rutkowski et al. (Eds.): ICAISC 2004, LNAI 3070, pp. 1026–1030, 2004.
© Springer-Verlag Berlin Heidelberg 2004

- Chronic substance abuse
- Asthma
- Seizure disorders
- Post-term or multiple-gestation pregnancy
- Pre-term birth

Doppler ultrasonography is a noninvasive technique used to assess the hemodynamic components of vascular impedance. Umbilical artery Doppler flow velocimetry has been adapted for use as a technique of fetal surveillance, based on the observation that flow velocity waveforms in the umbilical artery of normally growing fetuses differ from those of growth-restricted fetuses. Specifically, the umbilical flow velocity waveform of normally growing fetuses is characterized by high-velocity diastolic flow, whereas with intrauterine growth restriction, there is diminution of umbilical artery diastolic flow. Commonly measured flow indices, based on the characteristics of peak systolic frequency shift (S), end-diastolic frequency shift (D), and mean peak frequency shift over the cardiac cycle (A), include the following:

- Systolic to diastolic ratio (S/D)
- Resistance index (S-D/S)
- Pulsatility index (S-D/A)

Randomized studies of the utility of umbilical artery Doppler velocimetry generally have defined abnormal flow as either absent end diastolic flow, or a flow index greater than two standard deviations above the mean for gestational age.[3]

There is considerable interest in the use of computational techniques to aid in the diagnosis of medical problems. In this paper, the performances of some artificial neural networks are evaluated, which eventually produce the suggested diagnosis of fetal hypoxia. Furthermore, Receiver Operating Characteristic (ROC) analysis is used to determine the accuracy of diagnostic test.

2   ROC Analysis

Receiver Operating Characteristic (ROC) analysis is commonly used in medicine and healthcare to quantify the accuracy of diagnostic test. The basic idea of diagnostic test interpretation is to calculate the probability a patient has a disease under consideration given a certain result. Without ROC analysis, it is difficult to summarize the performance of a test with a manageable number of statistics and to compare the performance of different tests.[4]

The diagnostic performance is usually evaluated in terms of sensitivity and specificity. Sensitivity is the proportion of patients with disease whose tests are positive. Specificity is the proportion of patients without disease whose tests are negative. The measures are defined as [5]:

$$sensitivity = \frac{number\ of\ true\ positives}{number\ of\ true\ positives\ +\ number\ of\ false\ negatives} \quad (1)$$

$$specivity = \frac{number\ of\ true\ negatives}{number\ of\ true\ negatives\ +\ number\ of\ false\ positives} \quad (2)$$

where #true positives and #false negatives are the number of fetal hypoxia case correctly classified and incorrectly classified as normal case, respectively. Similarly, #true negatives and #false positives are the number of normal case correctly classified and incorrectly classified as fetal hypoxia case.

3   Artificial Neural Network Implementation Issues

There is considerable interest in the use of artificial neural network techniques to aid in the diagnosis of medical problems. In this work, the performances of Multilayer Perceptron (MLP), Radial Basis Function (RBF) networks and Conic Section Function Neural Network (CSFNN) were evaluated, which eventually produce the suggested diagnosis of fetal hypoxia.

Multilayer perceptrons (MLPs) are the most known feedforward neural network structure trained by many different algorithms. They are supervised networks so they require a desired response to be trained. They learn how to transform input data into a desired response. With one or two hidden layers, they can achieve any input-output map.

Radial Basis Function (RBF) network is a type of artificial neural network for application to problems of supervised learning (e.g. regression, classification and time series prediction). RBF has traditionally been associated with radial functions in a single-layer network. Radial functions are simply a class of functions. In principle, they could be employed in any sort of model (linear or nonlinear) and any sort of network (single-layer or multi-layer). An RBF network is nonlinear if the basis functions can move or change size or if there is more than one hidden layer.

Conic Section Function Neural Network (CSFNN) is an algorithm to unify perceptron and radial basis function units in a multilayer network. The basic idea is that decision regions of MLPs and RBFNs are two special cases of conic section functions. The units are made adaptive to decide themselves between the two extremes (open and close decision boundaries), which can lead to better data fitting. Thus, the propagation rule of a CSFNN is based on a cone that can fold or unfold between these two cases. This algorithm combines the advantages of multilayer perceptrons and radial basis function networks, which have proven to often be complementary for real-world applications. Faster learning and/or improved performance can be obtained [6].

4   Diagnosing Fetal Hypoxia

Pulsatility index (S-D/A), Resistance Index (R1), and Systolic/Diastolic ratio (S/D) measurements obtained from Doppler ultrasound examinations and gestational age of the mother (as week) were used in the evaluation of performances of artificial neural networks. All data samples were represented by these four parameters. These were given to neural networks as input data. Outputs of the networks represented normal and hypoxic cases of fetus. In the application, a total of 210 patient data were used. 68% of total samples were belonged to normal and the remaining 32% were belonged to fetuses with hypoxia. The data were partitioned into the training and test sets in such a way that samples in the sets could represent both cases; 147 of the available 210 data were used for the training of networks in order to withhold the remaining 63 data for testing.

4.1   Diagnostic Results of Artificial Neural Networks

Multilayer perceptron (MLP) structure with standard back propagation, MLP with fast back propagation (adaptive learning and momentum term added), Radial Basis Function (RBF) network structure trained by OLS algorithm, and Conic Section Function Neural Network (CSFNN) with adaptive learning have been trained and tested with the appropriate data. Classification accuracies of these networks for both training and test sets were given in Table 1.

Table 1. Diagnostic performances of artificial neural networks

Networks	Classification accuracy of training set (%)	Classification accuracy of test set (%)
MLP with standart bp	100	96.8
MLP with fast bp	100	96.8
RBF	100	87.3
CSFNN	100	100

Table 2. Results of ROC analysis

Networks	Train		Test	
	Sensitivity	Specificity	Sensitivity	Specificity
MLP with standart bp	1	1	1	0.9523
MLP with fast bp	1	1	1	0.9523
RBF	1	1	0.9523	0.8333
CSFNN	1	1	1	1

5   Conclusions and Discussion

As fetal hypoxia may result in damaging or death of the fetus, it is very important to monitor the infant so that any signs of fetal distress can be detected as soon as possible. In this paper, the performances of some artificial neural networks are evaluated, which eventually produce the suggested diagnosis of fetal hypoxia.

In this work, Doppler ultrasound measurements and gestational age of mother were used in conjunction to detect fetal hypoxia. With this aim, three different neural network architectures were used with appropriate training algorithms. Results showed that all networks were 100% successful for the training set. However, the real performance can be measured when unknown samples presented to network, that is the case of test. RBF network showed the worst classification accuracy in test stage. MLP network was trained by two different training algorithms. Results of those were same but the algorithm with adaptive learning rate and momentum was faster than the standard one. The best performance was belonged to CSFNN. This network classified all test samples correctly.

For many medical problems, high classification accuracy is less important than the high sensitivity and/or specificity of a classifier system. As ROC analysis allows to quantify the accuracy of diagnostic tests, sensitivity and specificity values of neural networks have been considered for both training and test sets separately to show real performances. After ROC analysis applied to training set, it was seen that all sensitivity and specificity values were 1 for all networks as expected since they classified all training samples correctly. For test set, regarding to sensitivity and specificity values, the performance of CSFNN was the best one, by matching with the classification accuracy.

As a result, it was seen that the artificial neural networks, especially CSFNN, can be successfully used in evaluating the performances for diagnosing fetal hypoxia.

References

1. Nicolaides K., Rizzo G., Hecker K. and Ximenes R.: Doppler in Obstetrics, http://www.centrus.com.br/DiplomaFMF/SeriesFMF/doppler/capitulos-html (2002)
2. Washington J.: Fetal and Neonatal Hypoxia, available in http://www.continuing education.com/resptherapist/fetalnh/index.html (2004)
3. Umbilical Artery Doppler Velocimetry, available in http://www.medem.com/MedLB/ (2004)
4. Provost F., Fawcett T., Kohavi R.: The Case Against Accuracy Estimation for Comparing Induction Algorithms, Proc. 15th International Conf. on Machine Learning (Madison), (1998) 445–553
5. Sboner A., Eccher C., Blanzieri E., Bauer P., Cristofolini M., Zumiani G., and Forti S.: A multiple classifier system for early melanoma diagnosis. AI in Medicine, (2003) Vol.27: 29-44.
6. Özyılmaz L., Yıldırım T., Köklü K.: Comparison of neural algorithms for function approximation, Pakistan Journal of Applied Sciences, (2002) Vol.2 (2): 288-294

The Challenge of Soft Computing
Techniques for Tumor Characterization

E.I. Papageorgiou[1], P.P. Spyridonos[2], C.D. Stylios[3], P. Ravazoula[4],
G.C. Nikiforidis[2], and P.P. Groumpos[1]

[1] Department of Electrical and Computer Engineering, University of Patras,
GR–26500 Patras, Greece, {epapageo,groumpos}@ee.upatras.gr
[2] Computer Laboratory, School of Medicine, University of Patras,
GR–26500 Patras, Greece {spyridonos,gnikf}@med.upatras.gr
[3] Department of Computer Science, University of Ioannina,
GR–1186, Ioannina, Greece, stylios@cs.uoi.gr
[4] Department of Pathology, University Hospital of Patras, GR–26500, Patras, Greece

Abstract. Computational diagnosis tools are becoming indispensable
to support modern medical diagnosis. This research work introduces an
hybrid soft computing scheme consisting of Fuzzy Cognitive Maps and
the effective Active Hebbian Learning (AHL) algorithm for tumor characterization. The proposed method exploits human experts' knowledge
on histopathology expressed in descriptive terms and concepts and it is
enhanced with Hebbian learning and then it classifies tumors based on
the morphology of tissues. This method was validated in clinical data
and the results enforce the effectiveness of the proposed approach.

1 Introduction

Histological examination is used to evaluate the degree of tumor malignancy.
In superficial urinary bladder tumors, the modality of therapy highly depends
on the morphological tumor characterization [1]. World Health Organization
(WHO) tumor-grading protocols classify tumors as low-grade or high-grade [1].
The final categorization for tumor grade relies on the complex interplay of disci-
pline histopathological variables and measurements related to tissue architecture
and appearance. Correct evaluation of histological material is mainly depending
on the pathologists' experience since all these diagnostic variables are combined
synergistically, but with a rather vague way. Taking into account the inherent
subjectivity of decision process, the reproducibility of grading tumors performed
by pathologists is questioned [2]. Previous efforts to standardize classification
and grading of tumors using computer-aided grade diagnosis were based on pattern recognition techniques [3]. In this research work the main effort is to exploit
and utilize human specialized knowledge on histopathology expressed in descriptive terms and concepts and to develop an advanced grading tool that can advise
doctors in the tumor grading during daily clinical practice. The proposed method
is based on FCMs [4] and the implementation of AHL algorithm [5]. In the medical application area, FCMs have been successfully used for decision-making in

L. Rutkowski et al. (Eds.): ICAISC 2004, LNAI 3070, pp. 1031–1036, 2004.
© Springer-Verlag Berlin Heidelberg 2004

radiation therapy planning systems [6]. This paper is structured in the following sections: Section 2 presents some fundamental aspects of FCMs and the AHL algorithm. Section 3 describes the development of the FCM Tumour Grading Tool (FCM-TG). In section 4 the FCM grading tool is used to classify and evaluate clinical test cases. Section 5 discusses the results, outlines the conclusions and future research directions are proposed.

2   Fuzzy Cognitive Maps and Activation Hebbian Learning Algorithm

The FCM represents the human knowledge and experience at the kind of concepts and weights of the interconnections between concepts. Each concept represents one of the key-factors of the model and it is characterized by its value A_i. Between concepts there are cause and effect relationships that are illustrated in the FCM graph with the weighted arc w_{ji} from one concept towards another. The value of w_{ji} indicates how much concept C_j influences concept C_i. The sign of w_{ji} indicates whether the relationship between concepts C_j and C_i is direct or inverse, either expresses positive causality between two concepts ($w_{ji} > 0$) or negative causality ($w_{ji} < 0$). The direction of causality indicates whether concept C_j causes concept C_i, or vice versa. These three parameters have to be considered when assigning a weight value w_{ji} to an interconnection [4]. Generally, the value of each concept is calculated by applying the following calculation rule:

$$A_i(k+1) = f\left(A_i(k) + \sum_{\substack{j=1 \\ j \neq i}}^{N} A_j(k) * w_{ji}\right), \tag{1}$$

where $A_i(k+1)$ is the value of concept C_i at simulation step $k+1$, $A_j(k)$ is the value of concept C_j at time k , w_{ji} is the weight of the interconnection between concept C_j and concept C_i and f is the sigmoid threshold function. The methodology for developing FCMs is based on a group of experts who are asked to define the concepts and describe the relationships among concepts. Every expert describes each one of the interconnections with a fuzzy IF-THEN rule, with the following form, where B, D and E are fuzzy linguistic variables:
IF a change B occurs in the value of concept C_j **THEN** a change D in the value of concept C_i is caused.
Infer: The influence from concept C_j to C_i is E.
The inference of the rule is a linguistic variable E, which determines the grade of causality between the two concepts [7]. All the fuzzy weights suggested by the group of experts are summed (through SUM technique) and an overall linguistic weight is produced, which with the defuzzification method of Center of Area (CoA) [8], is transformed to a crisp weight, belonging to the interval $[-1, 1]$.

The AHL algorithm has been proposed to create advanced FCMs with better modelling and classification abilities [5]. The AHL introduces the asynchronous updating for the concepts and weights of FCM, defines the activation and activated concepts as well as the Activation Decision Concepts (ADCs), which are the observable outputs of the system. This learning algorithm is based on the premise that one (or more) of the concepts, at each iteration, is considered as the activated concept(s) which triggers the interrelated concepts causing to them a change in their values. According to the infrastructure of the FCM, experts initially determine the activated and activation concepts for every simulation step and determine the way, with which factors-concepts affect the ADCs. During this activation process the weight w_{ji} of the causal interconnection of the related concepts is modified and is updated for each iteration step k using the following discrete type, as they suggested and described in [5]:

$$w_{ji}(k+1) = (1-\gamma) * w_{ji}(k) + n * A_j^{act}(k) * [A_i(k) - A_j^{act}(k) * w_{ji}(k)], \quad (2)$$

where n, γ are the learning rate parameters. These parameters take positive values in the range $[0, 0.1]$ and they are exponentially attenuated according to the number of simulation cycles. Eq. (1) that calculates the value of each concept of FCM is updating, taking into consideration the value of weight $w_{ji}(k)$ which is now modified at every iteration step according to Eq. (2). This AHL algorithm improves the FCM grading ability and enhances the FCM modeling capabilities; the AHL adjusts the weights ensuring that the FCM will classify successfully.

3   Description of the FCM Tumor Grading (FCM-TG) Model

The FCM model for tumor grading (FCM-TG) is developed by experts using the methodology described in [7]. For this specific medical application our experts were histopathologists with deep knowledge and great clinical experience. Experts defined the main histopathological features (concepts) that play important role in the final grade diagnostic decision [9]. Each variable can take two, three or four possible discrete values (Table 1). Values of concepts were described using five positive linguistic variables depending on the characteristics of each particular concept, such as very high, high, medium, weak and zero. Furthermore, histopathologists were asked to explain the degree of influence among these concepts, which was represented by a linguistic variable of the set {positive very high, positive high, positive medium, positive weak, zero, negative weak, negative medium, negative low, negative very low}. Following the FCM developing algorithm [7], the FCM-TG model was constructed (Fig 1).

Then the AHL can be used to modify the weights of the general FCM-TG according to the initial values of concepts for each case of urinary bladder tumor. According to the AHL algorithm, experts were asked to select the sequence of activation concepts, the steps and the cycle of simulation. The ninth concept of 'Grade' was defined as the ADC, which determines the tumor grade. Experts defined that concepts C_8 and C_7 are the first activated concepts, which at next iteration step trigger simultaneously the concepts C_1, C_2, C_3 and C_4, behaving as second activated concepts. C_5 and C_6, are triggered by the second activation concepts and are the third activated concepts, which all together fire the C_9

Table 1. Histological features for coding tumors' malignancy

Histological features	Assessment
C_1:Cell Distribution	Even, clustered
C_2: Cell size	Uniform, pleomorphic
C_3: Cell number	Numerous, variable
C_4: Cytoplasm	Homogeneous, variable
C_5: Nuclei	Uniform, irregular, very irregular, bizarre
C_6: Nucleoli	Inconspicuous, evident, prominent
C_7: Necrosis	Inconspicuous, frequent
C_8: Mitosis	Absent–rate, occasional, numerous

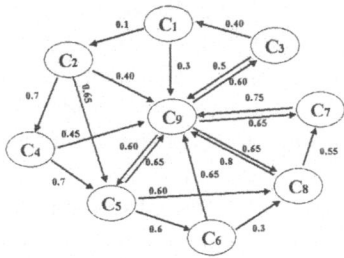

Fig. 1. The FCM tumor grading model

(Grade). The proposed sequence of activated and activation concepts mimic the way with which experts examine the histological material microscopically when they assign the grade of tumor. They start by 'scanning' the tissue sample under the microscope in order to assess the tissue appearance as a whole, and then they focus on regions with marked nuclear atypia, assessing morphological nuclear features and so on [3].

4   Implementation of FCM-TG Model

After FCM-TG development and the determination of necessary specifications for the implementation of the AHL , the FCM-TG was used to examine cases and assign grade to the tumors. The classification task requires the determination of the decision margin; for this reason ninety–two cases of urinary bladder cancer were used. The same cases were used to evaluate the performance of the FCM-TG model in categorizing tumors as low grade or high grade. The cases were collected at the Department of Pathology, University Hospital of Patras Greece. Histopathologists had diagnosed 63 cases as low-grade and 29 as high-grade follo-wing conventional WHO grading system [1]. In order to use the FCM-TG model, histopathologists were asked to examine each tissue section retrospectively and estimate the value of the eight histopathological variables (Table 1); these va-lues were transformed in the range [0, 1], and were assigned to the corresponding concepts. The initial value 'Grade' ('G') of the concept C_9 was randomly selected but was kept the same value for all cases. FCM-TG model was able to give distinct different values for the majority of high-grade and low-grade cases. However, some of the high grade and low-grade cases appear to have similar 'G' values. This is reasonable because it is very difficult for the doctors to clearly classify some cases and there is a certain region called 'Grey' region, where the diagnostic criteria overlap and for cases belonging to this region there is a degree of diagnostic uncertainty. Subsequently, the definition of a sharp decision line to categorize 'G' values as low or high seems to not fit reasonably well to the assumption of continuous grade and the continuous spectrum of biological changes in tumors' appearance. For this reason, we introduced a 'Grey' region defined by two decision lines for the diagnostic categories instead of using one sharp decision line. To construct the decision margin for the 'Grey' region we employed the minimum distance method; the mean 'G' values m1 and m2, for each grade category, were estimated and a decision line was determined as the perpendicular bisector of the line joining m1 and m2. We randomly selected 60 cases out of the 92 and we implemented the minimum distance method. We repeated this procedure one hundred times. The mean value (m) and the standard deviation (std) of the derived one hundred decision lines were estimated.

The decision margin of the 'Grey' zone was set by the 'G' values belonging in the region defined by the m± 3std (0.915 ± 0.025). 'G' values lower than 0.915 − 0.025 were set to belong to the low-grade cases and values greater than 0.915 + 0.0025 were set to belong to high-grade cases. After the determination of the decision margin, the FCM-TG model performance was evaluated for all the 92 cases. 87.3% of the low grade cases were found to belong in a region less than 0.9125 and 93.10% of the high grade cases were found in a region greater than 0.9175. For high-grade cases the estimated 'G' values are represented by □ and for low grade the estimated 'G' values are represented by ∇ (Fig. 2). Using the FCM-TG model with the same initial weights and retaining the AHL algorithm

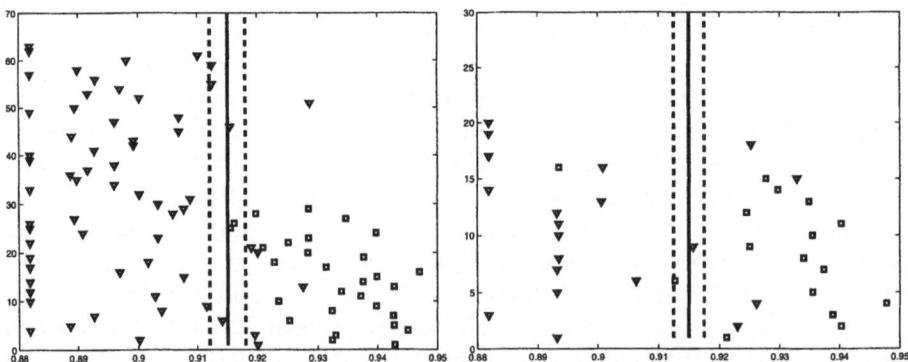

Fig. 2. Decision regions defined by 92 cases (left) Categorization of 36 new clinical cases (right) after defining the decision margin

36 new urinary bladder cancer cases were evaluated. Cases have been previously diagnosed as 20 low-grade cases and 16 high-grade. Cases categorized using the decision margin previously determined. The success rate for the low-grade cases was 80%. For the high-grade the FCM-TG accuracy was 87.5%.

5   Conclusion

In this paper an hybrid soft computing approach to support medical diagnosis is presented. The method incorporates experts' knowledge in developing the FCM-TG and determining the AHL algorithm and so it achieves characterization of tumor malignancy. In terms of sensitivity and specificity, the accuracy for the high-grade cases was 87% and for the low-grade cases was 80%. Concluding, the FCM-TG is fast, easily implemented in clinical practice and performs with reasonably high accuracy, rendering the FCM-TG an accessible alternative solution in automatic grade characterization.

References

1. Bostwick, D., Ramnani, D., Cheng, L.: Diagnosis and grading of bladder cancer and associated lesions. Urologic Clinics of North America **26** (1999) 493–507
2. Ooms, E., Anderson, W., Alons, C., Boon, M., Veldhuizen, R.: Analysis of the performance of pathologists in grading of bladder tumours. Human Pathology **26** (1983) 140–143
3. Spyridonos, P., Cavouras, D., Ravazoula, P., Nikiforidis, G.: A computer-based diagnostic and prognostic system for assessing urinary bladder tumour grade and predicting cancer recurrence. Med Inform Internet Medic **27** (2002) 111–122
4. Kosko, B.: Fuzzy cognitive maps. Int. J. Man-Machine Studies **24** (1986) 65–75
5. Papageorgiou, E., Stylios, C., Groumpos, P.: Active hebbian learning algorithm to train fuzzy cognitive maps. In: Int J Approx Reasoning, accepted for publication (2004)
6. Papageorgiou, E., Stylios, C., Groumpos, P.: An integrated two-level hierarchical decision making system based on fcms. IEEE Trans Biomed Engin **50** (2003) 1326–1339
7. Stylios, C., Groumpos, P.: Fuzzy cognitive maps in modelling supervisory control systems. Intelligent and Fuzzy Systems **8** (2000) 83–98
8. Lin, C., Lee, C.: Neural Fuzzy Systems: A Neuro-Fuzzy Synergism to Intelligent Systems. N.J. Prentice Hall, Upper Saddle River (1996)
9. Murphy, W., Soloway, S., Jukkola, A., Crabtree, W., Ford, K.: Urinary cytology and bladder cancer, the cellular features of transitional cell neoplasms. Cancer **53** (1984) 1555–1565

A Multi-stage Classification Method in Application to Diagnosis of Larynx Cancer

Danuta Rutkowska[1,2] and Jacek K. Klimala[3]

[1] Department of Computer Engineering, Technical University of Częstochowa
Armii Krajowej 36, 42-200 Częstochowa, Poland
drutko@kik.pcz.czest.pl
http://kik.pcz.pl
[2] Department of Artificial Intelligence, WSHE University in Łódź
Rewolucji 1905, 52, 90-213 Łódź, Poland
http://www.wshe.lodz.pl
[3] Department of Laryngology and Dental Surgery,
District General Hospital, PCK 1, 42-200 Częstochowa, Poland

Abstract. In this paper, a multi-stage classification method is applied to a problem of larynx cancer diagnosis. The biochemical tumor markers, called CEA and SCC, as well as ferritin, and other factors, are used in order to produce the diagnosis. A neuro-fuzzy network is employed at every stage of the classification method. The networks reflect fuzzy IF-THEN rules, formulated based on the data containing measurements of the particular factors (attributes). The classification method is proposed to support a medical doctor decision, and provide additional useful information concerning the diagnosis.

1 Introduction

A classification problem is usually the main task of diagnosis systems. Results of the classification depend on the data, i.e. the measurements of the attributes. The data vectors represent records of the attribute values, which characterize objects being classified. A number of various classification methods can be found in the literature; see e.g. [1], [6].

With regard to medical diagnosis applications, it is very important to employ a method that does not accept misclassifications. Therefore, a multi-stage classification algorithm is proposed [9]. The idea of this method is to classify only those data vectors which can be assigned to proper classes without mistakes. Otherwise, the "I do not know" answer is produced by the classifier, with an additional information about (more than one) classes to which the data vectors may belong.

In this paper, the multi-stage classification method is applied to support the medical diagnosis of larynx cancer. The problem is described in Section 2, and the classification algorithm is presented in Section 3. Results of the diagnosis are discussed in Sections 4 and 5. Conclusions are included in Section 6.

L. Rutkowski et al. (Eds.): ICAISC 2004, LNAI 3070, pp. 1037–1042, 2004.
© Springer-Verlag Berlin Heidelberg 2004

2   Medical Diagnosis Problem

The problem of larynx cancer diagnosis, considered in this paper, was a subject of work by Klimala [3]. The data records of 25 patients have been gathered; 23 men and 2 women, 39-65 years old, affected by the disease. Histopathological examination showed the larynx cancer in all these patients. Four degrees of the disease have been distinguished, and 6, 5, 7, 7 patients have been classified to 1st, 2nd, 3rd, 4th degree of advance of the disease, respectively. The patients were hospitalized for surgical treatment, and cobalt therapy, but first — biochemical tumor markers, CEA, SCC, and ferritin level had been determined.

The role of the tumor markers in the larynx cancer diagnosis was studied in [3], [4], [5]. CEA is the carcinoembryonic antigen, SCC is the squamous cell carcinoma antigen, and ferritin is the main protein that stores and transports ferrum in the human body.

Apart from the CEA, SCC, and ferritin, other laboratory tests, such as global protein, and alpha1, alpha2, beta globulins had been used for the larynx cancer patients. Based on the measurements of these factors, a comparison of classification by use of several methods, including neural networks, is shown in [2].

In this paper, the tumor markers, CEA, SCC, and ferritin, as well as the global protein, and alpha1, alpha2, beta globulins, are taken into account with regard to the diagnosis of the larynx cancer. In addition, the influence of cigarettes smoked by the patients, and alcoholic drinks, can be investigated.

3   Multi-stage Classification Method

In this section, the classifier that performs the so-called perception-based multi-stage classification, proposed in [9], is considered.

The classification system is composed of M classifiers corresponding to M stages of the classification process. Each of these classifiers is a neuro-fuzzy system, in the form of a connectionist network, that reflect fuzzy IF-THEN rules, which are perception-based rules [9]. The perception-based approach refers to the computational theory of perceptions, introduced by Zadeh [10]. This means that perceptions about the features (attributes) are described by words, and represented by fuzzy sets. The fuzzy IF-THEN rules are formulated in the following form

$$R^{(k)} : \textbf{IF } x_1 \text{ is } A_1^k \text{ AND } x_2 \text{ is } A_2^k \text{ AND } \ldots \text{ AND } x_n \text{ is } A_n^k$$
$$\textbf{THEN Class } j \tag{1}$$

where $\mathbf{x} = [x_1, \ldots, x_n]^T \epsilon \mathbf{X} \subset \mathbf{R}^n$ is a vector of linguistic variables corresponding to the input values (attributes), $k = 1, \ldots, K$, and $j = 1, \ldots, C$. Of course, $K = C$, if the number of rules equals to the number of classes. The fuzzy sets A_i^k, for $i = 1, \ldots, n$, represent linguistic descriptions of the perceptions about attribute values, e.g. *low, medium, high*.

The fuzzy sets are assumed to be characterized by trapezoidal membership functions, which are determined based on granulation of the ranges of attribute

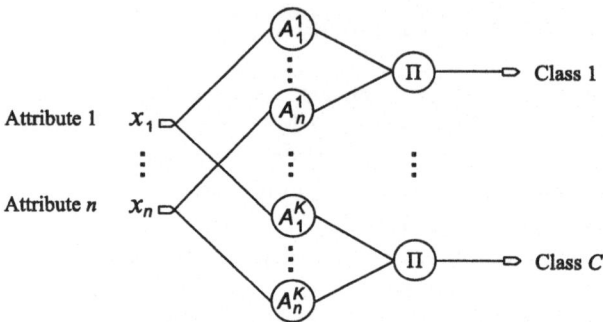

Fig. 1. Neuro-fuzzy classifier

values. For details concerning the fuzzy granulation, applied in the multi-stage classification method, see [9].

The neuro-fuzzy classifiers, at every stage, are represented in the form of connectionist networks portrayed in Fig. 1. The components of the input vectors are values of the attributes that characterize objects to be recognized (classified). The output values correspond to the classes, and the maximal output value points out the class to which the input vector belongs, according to the inference performed by the neuro-fuzzy system. The nodes (neurons) of the first layer of this network realize membership functions of the fuzzy sets, A_i^k, for $i = 1, \ldots, n$, in the antecedent parts of the rules (1). The nodes of the second layer perform the multiplication which realizes the Cartesian product of the antecedent fuzzy sets, $A^k = A_1^k \times \cdots \times A_n^k$. Thus, the output values of these nodes express the so-called degree of rule activation (firing strength), so the maximal value of the rule activation corresponds to the rule with the proper class, which is indicated in the consequent (conclusion) part of this rule. The inference process, in the neuro-fuzzy classifiers, is based on the fuzzy IF-THEN rules; see [7], for details.

The main advantage of the perception-based, multi-stage, neuro-fuzzy classifier is its performance without misclassifications. This means that the classifier produces either correct responses or the "I do not know" answers. The data vectors which are not classified at the 1st stage (because of the "I do not know" answers) are transmitted to the 2nd stage classifier. Then, the data vectors with the "I do not know" answer produced by the 2nd stage neuro-fuzzy classifier are allowed to enter the 3rd stage classifier, and so on.

4   Diagnosis of Larynx Cancer

The multi-stage classification method, described in Section 3, has been applied to the medical diagnosis problem, introduced in Section 2.

The data records of 25 patients, examined with regard to the larynx cancer, have been considered. As mentioned in Section 2, four degrees of the disease, i.e. four classes, have been distinguished. Thus, $K = C = 4$, concerning rules

(1) and the corresponding neuro-fuzzy network, in the multi-stage classification method, discussed in Section 3.

The data records contain measurements of the biochemical tumor markers, such as CEA, SCC, and ferritin, but as explained in Section 2, also include global protein, alpha1, alpha2, beta globulins, as well as information about cigarettes and alcoholic drinks consumed by the patients. The medical doctor's diagnosis, based on the histopathological examination, and other factors, is assigned to each record. Thus, the records can be treated as the examples, which are called learning data for neural networks and other intelligent systems [7], [11].

In order to solve the medical diagnosis problem by use of the multi-stage classification method, the perception-based fuzzy IF-THEN rules should be formulated based on the data set. At every stage, the number of the rules equals to the number of the classes, so 4 rules should be reflected by the corresponding neuro-fuzzy network, shown in Fig.1. Of course, at each stage the fuzzy sets A_i^k, for $i = 1, \dots, n$, in the rules (1), are different. The number of stages and the fuzzy sets depend on the data values.

As mentioned in Section 3, the fuzzy sets are characterized by trapezoidal membership functions, determined based on granulation of the ranges of attribute values. In [9], fuzzy granulation is proposed to perform the classification. An alternative method of the classification that applies the perception-based rules with Gaussian membership functions is proposed in [8]. However, this is not the multi-stage algorithm, so some percetage of misclassifications may occur.

The idea of the perception-based classification is to employ the fuzzy IF-THEN rules, formulated based on the perceptions about the attributes, described by words, and characterized by the fuzzy sets. The classification is performed by use of the fuzzy logic inference [10].

In order to formulate the fuzzy IF-THEN rules, the ranges of attribute values are granulated with regard to the classes. Thus, the data vectors belonging to the same class are associated with the same rule. The problem is with the data vectors that belong to more than one class. It is difficult to classify the data vectors from the overlapping classes. In this case, more than one rule is activated during the inference process.

The multi-stage classification method first (at the first stage) tries to classify the data vectors that are easiest to be classified. Then, more rules are created for the data vectors belonging to overlapping classes, so the data items that are more difficult to be classified are taken into account at the next stages. If a data vector belongs to overlapping classes, and the system cannot infer a decision about the class to which it belongs, the "I do not know" answer is produced. Then, this data vector enters the next stage, to be classified. The "I do not know" answer is better than a misclassification, so we do not need to expect all data vectors assigned to a class by the system. Instead, we are interested in the information that the data vectors may belong, e.g. to class 1 or 2.

It should be emphasized that the multi-stage method always performs without misclassifications on the learning data, i.e. the data items employed to formulate the IF-THEN rules. We can observe very good performance (without misclassifications) also on other data that do not belong to the learning data set. Of course, the fuzzy granulation should be done properly, with appropriate range of fuzziness, so the shapes of the membership functions should allow to perform the generalization by means of the rules. It seems obvious that the more data items we can use to create the rules the better generalization ability we obtain, similarly to neural networks [11].

In the problem of larynx cancer diagnosis, we have only 25 data items, so we cannot expect very good generalization ability of the classification system. However, we can apply the multi-stage classification method in order to provide a useful information concerning the diagnosis. As mentioned in Section 1, the multi-stage method is employed to support the medical diagnosis of larynx cancer. This means that this method gives more specific information that tells how difficult is to classified particular data items. In addition, the influence of the attributes can be observed by means of this method. The detailed information is presented in Sections 5 and 6.

5   Experiments on the Larynx Cancer Data

As explained in Section 4, with so small amount of data records, we cannot expect the system decision, concerning the diagnosis, without misclassifications, on other data that those belonging to the learning data set. Of course, the multi-stage classification method performs perfectly (without misclassifications) on the learning data set. However, in this case, the crisp (not fuzzy) granulation is sufficient. This means that fuzzy sets A_i^k, for $i = 1, \ldots, n$, in rules (1), become crisp sets. These sets are characterized by the membership functions, which as a matter of fact are characteristic functions, taking value equal 1 within the granulated range and 0 out of the range. The same result (without misclassifications) is obtained, for the learning data, when the fuzzy sets are represented by trapezoidal membership functions with very small range of fuzziness. In this case, the trapezoidal functions are very close to the corresponding characteristic functions.

Three experiments have been done for the larynx cancer data, using the multi-stage classification method. Firstly, the CEA, SCC, and ferritin were taken into account as the attributes that characterize degrees of the patient's disease, i.e. the advance of the tumor. Secondly, the global protein, and alpha1, alpha2, beta globulins were considered as the attributes. Finally, all of these factors were jointly treated as the attributes. Thus, in the first experiment, the number of attributes $n = 3$, in the second one $n = 4$, and in the third experiment $n = 7$. The aim of these experiments is to show the influence of the attributes on the diagnosis result, and in addition to provide more specific information concerning the diagnosis with regard to particular patients. The classes are the degrees of advance of the tumor. The results and conclusions are included in Section 6.

6   Results and Conclusions

The multi-stage classification method, applied to the larynx cancer data of the 25 patients, produces exactly the same diagnosis result as the medical doctor's diagnosis. Each of the three experiments, described in Section 5, requires two stages of the multi-stage method. In the first, second, and third experiment, 17, 16, and 5 data vectors were unclassified ("I do not know" decision), respectively, at the first stage. All these data vectors have been correctly classified at the second stage. However, we can conclude that it is better to use all the factors together, i.e. CEA, SCC, ferritin, global protein, alpha1, alpha2, beta globulins (third experiment). In this case, more data vectors are easier to be classified.

The multi-stage method gives additional, very useful information. With regard to the 5 patients unclassified at the first stage, the system informs that patient no. 6 can be classified to class 1 or 2, patients no. 15, 16, 21 can belong to class 3 or 4, patient no. 20 may be assigned to class 1, 3 or 4. The usefulness of this information was confirmed, knowing that patients no. 15, 16, classified to class 3, were hospitalized later, and patients no. 22, 24 died. This means that the former cases were close to class 4, and the latter were definitely in class 4. Thus, the additional information, produced by the multi-stage classification method, can be very important from the prognostic point of view.

References

1. Duda R.O., Hart P.E.: Pattern Classification and Sciene Analysis. John Wiley & Sons. New York (1973)
2. Cierniak R., Cpałka K., Klimala K.J.: Comparison of neural networks and neuro-fuzzy systems in a medical application. Proc. Fifth Conference: Neural Networks and Soft Computing. Zakopane. Poland (2000) 533-538
3. Klimala K.J.: Usefulness of Chosen Tumor Markers, CEA, SCC, and Ferritin, in Larynx Cancer Patients. Ph.D. Dissertation. Zabrze. Poland (1996); in Polish
4. Klimala K.J.: The role of biochemical tumor markers in the diagnosis and ca-tamnesis of laryngeal cancer. Proc. Third Conference: Neural Networks and Their Applications, Kule-Czestochowa. Poland (1997) 713-721
5. Klimala K.J.: Usefulness of joint CEA, SCC and ferritin determination in laryngeal cancer patients. Proc. Third Conference: Neural Networks and Their Applications, Kule-Czestochowa. Poland (1997) 722-729
6. Kuncheva L.I.: Fuzzy Classifier Design. Physica-Verlag. A Springer-Verlag Company. Heidelberg. New York (2000)
7. Rutkowska D.: Neuro-Fuzzy Architectures and Hybrid Learning. Physica-Verlag. A Springer-Verlag Company. Heidelberg. New York (2002)
8. Rutkowska D.: A perception-based classification system. Proc. CIMCA 2003 Conference. Vienna. Austria (2003) 52-61
9. Rutkowska D.: Perception-based systems for medical diagnosis. Proc. Third EUS-FLAT 2003. Zittau. Germany (2003) 741-746
10. Zadeh L.A.: A new direction in AI: Toward a computational theory of perceptions. AI Magazine. **22**. 1 (2001) 73-84
11. Żurada J.M.: Introduction to Artificial Neural Systems. West Publishing Company (1992)

Multi-neural Network Approach for Classification of Brainstem Evoked Response Auditory

Mariusz Rybnik, Saliou Diouf, Abdennasser Chebira,
Veronique Amarger, and Kurosh Madani

Intelligence in Instrumentation and Systems Lab. (I²S / JE 2353)
– SENART Institute of Technology - University PARIS XII, Avenue Pierre
POINT, F-77127 Lieusaint, France
{chebira,amarger,madani}@univ-paris12.fr
http://li2S.free.fr

Abstract. Dealing with expert (human) knowledge consideration, the computer aided medical diagnosis dilemma is one of most interesting, but also one of the most difficult problems. Among difficulties contributing to the challenging nature of this problem, one can mention the need of fine classification. In this paper, we present a new classification approach founded on a tree like neural network based multiple-models structure, able to split a complex problem to a set of simpler sub-problems. This new concept has been used to design a Computer aided medical diagnostic tool that asserts auditory pathologies based on Brain-stem Evoked Response Auditory based biomedical test, which provides an ef-fective measure of the integrity of the auditory pathway.

1 Introduction

Computer aided medical diagnostic (CAMD) is an attractive area leading to future promising applications in biomedical domain. However, dealing with expert (human) knowledge consideration, the computer aided medical diagnosis dilemma is one of most interesting, but also one of the most difficult problems. Among difficulties con-tributing to challenging nature of this problem, one can mention the need of fine clas-sification.

Over the past decades, Artificial Neural Networks and related techniques show many attractive features in solution of a wide class of problems [1], among which classification, expert knowledge modeling and decision-making [2][3][4]. In this pa-per, we present a new classification approach based on a tree like neural network based multiple-models structure, able to split a complex problem into a set of simpler sub-problems. The main idea of the T-DTS is based on the notion "Divide et impera" [1] (Julius Caesar) [5]. This new concept has been used to design a CAMD tool, which asserts auditory pathologies based on Brainstem

---

[1] "divide and rule".

L. Rutkowski et al. (Eds.): ICAISC 2004, LNAI 3070, pp. 1043–1049, 2004.
© Springer-Verlag Berlin Heidelberg 2004

Evoked Response Auditory (BERA) based biomedical test, which provides an effective measure of the whole the auditory pathway.

In the next section, we present the BERA signals. Then we expose the approach based on tree neural network's structure. In section 4, we present the classification re-sults we obtained by using a database of 213 BERA waveforms. A comparison study with conventional neural network techniques has been performed. Finally, we con-clude and give the prospects that follow from our work.

2   Brainstem Evoked Response Auditory (BERA)

Brainstem Evoked Response Auditory based clinical test provides an effective measure of the whole the auditory pathway up to the upper brainstem level. It is based on "Evoked Potentials" analysis, which are electrical response caused by a brief stimulation of a sensing system. In fact, the stimulus triggers a number of neurophysi-ologic responses along the auditory pathway. An action potential is conducted along the eight nerve, the brainstem and finally to the brain. A few times after the initial stimulation, the signal evokes a response in the area of brain where sounds are inter-preted. The right picture of figure 1 (extracted from [6]) represents two critical cases of such BERA: the first one corresponds to a healthy patient and the other one to a an auditory disorder pathology. Usually, the experts diagnose the pathology using a sur-face of 50 estimations called "Temporal Dynamic of the Cerebral" trunk (TDC).

In general, for a patient who has a normal audition, the result of the TDC test is a regular surface. However, results of the TDC test for diseased patients are close to those corresponding to healthy ones. Moreover, results can vary for different test ses-sions for the same patient, because they depend on the person's relaxation, the test's conditions, the signal-to-noise ratio, etc. The diagnosis difficulty leads to use a tech-nique taking advantage of expert's knowledge. That's why a neural network based ap-proach has been considered.

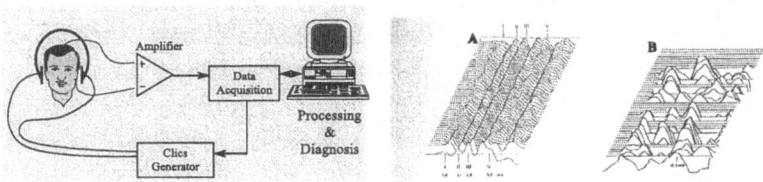

Fig. 1. BERA based clinical test chain (left) and examples of obtained TDC Surfaces showing a healthy (A) and an auditory disorder (B) cases respectively (right).

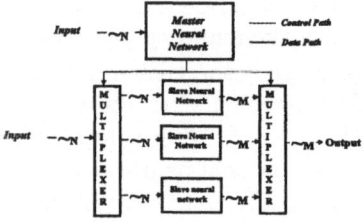

Fig. 2. T-DTS neural architecture.

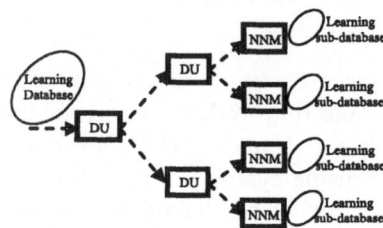

Fig. 3. Learning database decomposition.

3   T-DTS Based Approach

T-DTS (Treelike Divide To Simplify) is a data driven neural networks based Multiple Processing (multiple model) structure. It is able to reduce complexity on both data and processing chain levels. T-DTS construct a treelike evolutionary neural architecture automatically, where nodes are *Decision Units (DU)* and leafs correspond to processing units called *Neural Network Models (NNM)*[5], as presented in figure 2. The structure decomposes complex task into several simpler ones to ease the processing. Each NN model covers a small distinct area of feature space. All together, they cover the whole feature space.

T-DTS operating modes: The T-DTS operates according to two main operational modes. The first one, called "learning phase", concerns the T-DTS training and structuring. The second one, called "generalization phase", involves with unlearned data processing.

Learning phase is an important phase during which T-DTS builds decomposition structure and trains NNM models. In the learning phase, T-DTS algorithm constructs a neural tree structure dynamically and without operator's intervention. A given learning dataset is decomposed in a recursive way using Decomposition Units (i.e. unsupervised Neural Networks). To obtain decomposition decision many techniques can be used, including *classification complexity estimation* [7]. In this case, the decomposition decisions (*to-split-or-not*) are based on the splitting threshold, which is a parameter representing required degree of decomposition. We have used a data dispersion rule founded on a standard deviation based indicator (MaxStd), representing maximum tolerated data dispersion in a given subset.

After decomposition tree was built, learning database is decomposed into set of learning sub-databases (see figure 3). A **prototype** (representation of most typical in-put vector) is assigned to each learning sub-database to represent the most common features of vectors in the sub-database.

The sub-databases are used to train a corresponding set of NN Models. Each NN model covers a small area of feature space. Ensemble of Neural Network Models cov-ers (model) the system behavior region-by-region in the problem's feature space. In this way, a complex problem is decomposed recursively into a set of simpler sub-problems: the initial feature space is divided into M sub-spaces.

In generalization phase, each incoming data pattern is assigned to a process by the most appropriate NN model. It can be done by interacting with decomposition tree structure or by evaluating the similarity with sub-databases prototypes (to find the most similar cases). Then, the most appropriated NN Model is authorized (activated) to process that pattern. The output is gathered from individual NN models to create output matrix for the whole generalization database. Let: $\Psi(t)$ be the input ($\Psi(t) \in \Re^{n_\Psi}$), a n_Ψ-Dimensional vector and $Y_k(t) \in \Re^{n_Y}$ be the k-th ($k \in \{1, \cdots, M\}$) model's output vector of dimension n_y; $F_k(.) : \Re^{n_\Psi} \to \Re^{n_Y}$ be the k-th NNM's transfer function; then the DU output $S(\Psi(t), p, \xi) \in B^M$ (with $B = \{0,1\}$) could be expressed by relation (1).

$$S(\Psi(t), p, \xi) = (s_1 ... s_k ... s_M)^T \text{ with } \begin{bmatrix} s_k = 1 \ if \ p = p_k \ and \ \xi = \xi_k \\ s_k = 0 \quad\quad\quad else \end{bmatrix} \quad (1)$$

where p and ξ represent some parameters or conditions. Depending to $S(g\Psi, p, \xi)$ the processing of an unlearned input data will be performed by the selected NNM according to the relation (2).

$$Y(\Psi, t) = Y_k(t) = F_k(\Psi(t)) \quad (2)$$

4   Experimental Results and Validation

In order to test T-DTS performance, we use a database, which contains the BERA signals and the associated pathologies. We choose three categories of patients according to the type of their auditory disorder. These categories are: **normal** corresponding to healthy patients, **endocochlear** corresponding to patients suffering from disorders concerning pre-cochlear structure and **retrocochlear** corresponding to patients suffering from disorders related to the post-cochlear level. In order to build our training database, we choose signals that come from patient whose pathology is given for sure. We have selected 213 signals. 92 belong to the normal class, 83 to the endocochlear class and 38 to the retrocochlear class. All BERA signals come from the same experimental system. The signals corresponding to retrocochlear and endocohlear disorders are associated to the class 1; healthy cases are associated to the class 2.

Table 1. Results: classification ability for RBF, LVQ and T-DTS respectively.

Used Classifier	Diseased (120 patterns)	Normal (93 patterns)	Global (213 patterns)
RBF	64.2%	83.9%	**72.8%**
LVQ	54.2%	82.8%	**66.7%**
T-DTS	84.6%	77.0%	**81.2%**

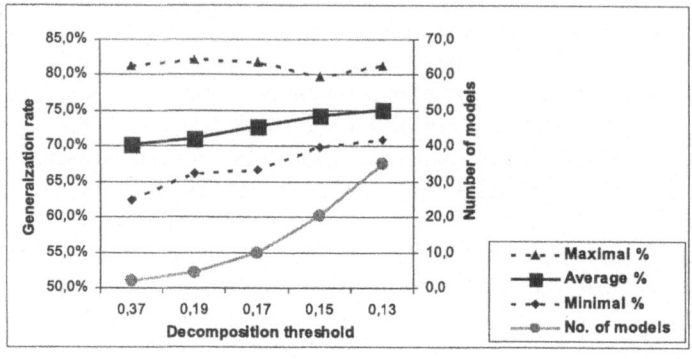

Fig. 4. Generalization rates and number of models versus decomposition threshold.

The aim of our work is to classify these signals using the tree neural network based structure. In our case, the components of input vectors are the samples of the BERA average signals and the output vectors correspond to different possible classes. We have compared the proposed structure to two conventional Artificial Neural Networks. One of them is Radial Basis Function (RBF) ANN and the other is the Learning Vector Quantization (LVQ) ANN [8] [9]. The structures of the RBF and LVQ ANNs are composed as follows. The number of input neurons, which is the same for RBF and LVQ ANNs, corresponds to the number of components of the input vectors: each input signal compounds of 89 values representing the average BERA values. The output layer of RBF as well as for the LVQ ANN contains 2 neurons, corresponding to the 2 classes (healthy and unhealthy). For RBF ANN, the number of neurons of the hidden layer (in this case, 98 neurons) has been determined by learning. Concerning the case of LVQ ANN, the number of hidden neurons has been set to 30 neurons after an empirical optimization. In both cases, the learning database contains 100 signals, 50 of them are diseased, 50 normal. For the generalization phase, we have used the full database, including also the learning database. The results we obtain are given in table 1. In both cases, the learning database has been learnt with 100% classification rate. The RBF network classifies correctly about **73%** of the full database (including the learnt vectors). The LVQ network classifies correctly about **67%** of the full database (including the learnt vectors). In the used T-DTS structure, DU are *Competitive Networks* with *two neurons*, resulting in a binary decomposition tree. The processing leaves are single hidden layer *Multi-Layer Perceptrons* (MLP) with 2

Log-Sigmoid neurons. For decomposition decision, we have used MaxStd decomposition indicator, which should give regular set decomposition. The learning database contains 106 signals, with 53 of them corresponding to diseased patients and 53 to healthy (normal) patients. For the generalization, we have used the whole database containing 213 signals, including 120 diseased and 93 normal.

Figure 4 represents minimal, average and maximal values of generalization rates and numbers of leaf-level models for different T-DTS architectures. One can notice examining the figure that as the decomposition threshold value decreases so increases the amount of decomposition, represented here by number of leaf-level models (low line, right axis). This leads to improvement in generalization correct classification ratios, represented by upper line on left axis. Decomposition thus eases the modeling task and allows achieving better performance in term of correct classification rates. One of the best results, obtained for standard deviation threshold value stated at 0.13, leaded to 37 subsets. The learning database has been trained with 97.2% classification rate. The T-DTS has classified correctly **81.2%** of the generalization database (including the learnt vectors). The results obtained by T-DTS are better than those performed by conventional ANNs: a classification rate improvement of about 15% is achieved. One can also remark that contrary to the results obtained from conventional ANN based techniques (RBF and LVQ), the classification rates for the two considered classes (healthy and unhealthy) are well-balanced in the case of the proposed solution.

5   Conclusion

The results obtained from T-DTS are better than those of conventional ANNs in term of generalization accuracy. That shows that intelligent decomposition ability improves the classification performances. This encouraging results show also the feasibility of neural networks based Computer Aided Medical Diagnostic (CAMD) tool. We are actually working on T-DTS splitting decision rule enhancement as well as on its processing leaves structure improvement.

References

1. Widrow B., Lehr M.A.: "30 years of adaptative Neural Networks: Perceptron, Madaline, and Backpropagation", Proceeding of the IEEE, Vol.78, pp. 1415-1441, 1990.
2. Bazoon M., A. Stacey D., Cui C.: " A Hierarchical Artificial Neural Network System for the Classification of Cervical Cells", IEEE Int. Conf. on Neural Networks, Orlando, July, 1994.
3. Jordan M. I. and Xu L., "Convergence Results for the EM Approach to Mixture of Experts Architectures", Neural Networks, Vol. 8, N° 9, pp 1409-1431, Pergamon, Elsevier, 1995.
4. Goonatilake S. and Khebbal S.: Issues, Classification and Future Directions. In Intelligent Hybrid Systems. John Wiley & Sons, pp 1-20, ISBN 0 471 94242 1.
5. Madani K., Chebira A., Rybnik M.: Data Driven Multiple Neural Network Models Generator Based on a Tree-like Scheduler, LNCS: "Computational Methods in Neural Modeling", Ed. Jose Mira, Jose R. Alvarez - Springer Verlag 2003, ISBN 3-540-40210-1, pp. 382-389.

6. Motsch J-F: "La dynamique temporelle du tronc cérébral: Recueil, extraction et analyse optimale des potentiels évoqués auditifs du tronc cérébral", PhD thesis report (thèse d'état), University of Créteil-Paris XII, 1987.
7. T. Kohonen, "Self-Organization and Associative Memory", Second Edition, Springer-Verlag, New York, 1988.
8. M.A. Arbib (ed.), "Handbook of Brain Theory and Neural Networks" 2ed. M.I.T. Press. 2003.
9. Ho T. K., Data complexity analysis for classifier combination, Proc. Of the 2nd Int. Workshop on multiple classifier systems, Cambridge UK, July 2-4, 2001, pp. 53-67.

The Study of Hierarchy Importance of Descriptive Attributes in Computer Assisted Classification of Melanocytic Skin Lesions

Aleksander Sokołowski[1] and Alicja Dereń[2]

[1] Rzeszow University of Technology,
ul. W. Pola 2, 35-959 Rzeszów, Poland,
alex5@prz.rzeszow.pl
[2] University of Information Technology and Management,
ul. Sucharskiego 2, 35-225 Rzeszów, Poland,
aderen@wenus.wsiz.rzeszow.pl

Abstract. In the paper the results of application of the neural network algorithm to identify the melanocytic spots are described. The algorithm was used to create, learning and making diagnoses on the ground of three bases containing the cases described in terms of fourteen attributes. The SNN (Statistica Neural Networks) was used to create the best neural networks and to find out of the hierarchy importance of descriptive attributes in computer assisted classification of melanocytic skin lessons.

1 Introduction

The aim of our work is to investigate the usefulness of neural network employed in process of making medical diagnosis. The databases mentioned in Tab. 1 have been collected at the Regional Dermatology Center in Rzeszow [1], and are the subjects of research on making medical diagnosis. Recently melanoma is routinely diagnosed with help of so-called **ABCD** formula (**A** indicates Asymmetry, **B** - Borders, **C** - Color, and **D** - Diversity of structure) [2,3]. The databases are used in research on optimization of the above formula, using the data mining system LERS (Learning from Examples using Rough Sets) [4,5]. The results were reported in [6–9]. The medical diagnosis problems can be investigated with help of classical expert systems, but not only. It seems that the neural network method [10] can be a satisfactory tool to explore the above area. This method is successfully used in making medical diagnosis processes [11]. In this connection we set our mind on exploring the bases mentioned in Table 1 with help of simulated neural nets.

The above bases include the attributes that are divided into five categories: ⟨*Asymmetry*⟩, ⟨*Border*⟩, ⟨*Color*⟩, ⟨*Diversity* ⟩, and ⟨*TDS*⟩ (Total Dermatos-copy Score). The domain of ⟨*Asymmetry*⟩ encloses three different values: *symmetric spot, single axial symmetry, double axial symmetry*. ⟨*Border*⟩ is the numerical attribute, with value changing from 0 to 8 (integer values). The

L. Rutkowski et al. (Eds.): ICAISC 2004, LNAI 3070, pp. 1050–1055, 2004.
© Springer-Verlag Berlin Heidelberg 2004

Table 1. Numbers of cases included in several databases used in our research.

No.	Database	Number of cases
1	E200144	134
2	E250144	250
3	E300144	138

attributes ⟨*Asymmetry*⟩ and ⟨*Border*⟩ are the functions of single variable. The attributes ⟨*Color*⟩ and ⟨*Diversity*⟩ are the functions of several variables. ⟨*Color*⟩ is the function of six variables: *black, blue, dark brown, light brown, red,* and *white* [3]. Similarly, ⟨*Diversity*⟩ is the function of five variables: *pigment dots, pigment globules, pigment network, structureless areas,* and *branched stricks.* Then every medical case is characterized by the values of the above variables. The value of ⟨*TDS*⟩ attribute is calculated on the ground of the above variables as follows:

$$TDS = 1.3*Asymmetry + 0.1*Border + 0.5*\sum Colors + 0.5*\sum Diversities, \quad (1)$$

where for the ⟨*Asymmetry*⟩ attribute the value of *symmetric spot* counts as 0, *single axial symmetry* counts as 1, and *double axial symmetry* counts as 2. The symbol $\sum Colors$ represents the sum of all six variable values of color attribute, and $\sum Diversities$ represents the sum of all five variable values of diversity attribute. The variables of the color and diversity attributes take the value 0, when there isn't suitable feature and the value 1, when there is suitable feature.

Every case in the databases is described by means of 14 attribute variables, which help to make diagnosis to classify every case into one of the four nevus category: benign-nevus, blue-nevus, suspicious-nevus, and malignant-nevus.

2   The Research Tools

The estimation of attribute importance hierarchy has been made with use of the neural nets creating **SNN (Statistica Neural Networks)** package, and with use of the **IPS (Intelligent Problem Solver)**, which one allows us to create simulated neural nets basing on the data sets included in the above mentioned databases. The possibility of extracting the most important attributes as the components of the input neural layer is the one of many advantages of the package. The created neural nets have input layer, output layer, and one fold hide layer. Our study can be divided into two parts.

In first the generation of optimum topology of neural nets has been performed with use of ten-folded cross validation process. The process has been applied to all data-bases mentioned above. Ten pairs of the files have been separated from each database with help of our program ScoreSEEKER. One file was used to creation and learning of neural nets, and second one was used to testing of neural nets for each pair of files.

In second part one database was used to creation and learning of neural nets and the remaining two was used as tested bases. Each base from Tab. 1 in succession was used as learning base giving three sets of results as it can see in Tab. 3.

3 Experiments with Use of Ten-Fold Cross Validation Process

The results of this experiment are presented in Tab. 2.

Comparing the three tables in Tab. 2 to each other it can be seen, that the way of extracting ten pairs of files from the base can have the influence on the quality of results. The analysis of tables (b) and (c) suggests the importance of all 14 attributes regardless of the number of cases in the database. However the number of cases in database has the influence on the quality of tests. As the number of cases is greater, the value of mean error of tests is less.

Table 2. Results of learning and testing simulated neural nets for databases mentioned in Tab. 1.

Table (a) includes results for base E200144,
Table (b) includes results for base E300144,
and Table (c) includes results for base
E250144. Fourth column in each Table includes the attributes chosen by SNN package.
[1] without the *structureless areas* attribute of **Diversity**
[2] without the *black* attribute of **Color**
[3] without the *dark brown* attribute of **Color**
[4] without the *white* attribute of **Color**
[5] without the *light brown* attribute of **Color**
[6] without the **TDS** attribute

Pair of files	Error rate in learning [%]	in testing [%]	Number of attributes
1	4.6	19.7	13[1]
2	0.4	26.5	14
3	4.5	23.1	13[1]
4	4.6	34.2	13[1]
5	4.6	25.6	13[1]
6	0.4	19.4	14
7	4.6	19.6	13[1]
8	0.1	24.8	14
9	4.6	14.4	13[1]
10	4.6	27.5	13[1]

(a)

Pair of files	Error rate in learning [%]	in testing [%]	Number of attributes	Pair of files	Error rate in learning [%]	in testing [%]	Number of attributes
1	0.2	0.1	14	1	0.1	4.1	14
2	0.2	37.6	11[2,3,4]	2	0.1	18.8	14
3	0.2	31.9	12[3,5]	3	0.2	14.1	14
4	0.2	16.9	14	4	0.1	27.5	13[5]
5	0.1	32.0	13[3]	5	0.2	19.8	14
6	0.1	1.7	14	6	0.1	1.7	13[6]
7	0.1	22.7	13[5]	7	0.2	15.4	14
8	0.2	22.6	14	8	0.1	13.0	14
9	0.2	34.7	14	9	0.1	24.5	13[5]
10	0.1	31.9	14	10	0.2	14.2	13[5]

(b)   (c)

4   The Experiments with Use of Three Bases

The results of this experiment are presented in Tab. 3. There are shown three cases. The first one (a) represents the instance, where E200144 is learning base, while E250144 and E300144 are tested bases. The second one (b) is the case, where E250144 is learning base, while E200144 and E300144 are tested bases. The third one (c) is the case, where E300144 is learning base, and the remaining two are tested bases. The columns from *benign* to *blue* represent the types of diagnosis: *benign* as *benign nevus*, *malign* as *melanoma malignant*, *susp* as *suspicious nevus*, and *blue* as *blue nevus*. The second row in each table (all cases) summarizes all cases for each type of diagnosis. The third row (correct recognized) summarizes all correct recognized cases for each type of diagnosis. The remaining rows describe the wrong diagnosis in detail. For example, the cell of intersection of column *benign* and row *malign* in Tab. 3.(a) includes the value of 4.

This means that *benign nevus* has been incorrectly recognized as *melanoma malignant* in four cases. The incorrect decisions are here of two kinds. The first one called here as *false positive diagnosis* means alert for patient, because the recognition suggest false danger. The second one called *false negative diagnosis* means dangerous calm for patient, because recognition doesn't suggest true danger. When E200144 is the learning base, the number of incorrect diagnosis is equal to 73 (18.8% of all cases). This includes 45 cases of false positive diagnoses (11.6%) and 28 cases of false negative diagnoses (7.2%). For E250144 as learning base the number of incorrect decision is equal to 52 (19.1%). This includes 46 cases of false positive diagnoses (16.5%) and 6 cases of false negative diagnoses (2.2%). For E300144 as learning base, the number of incorrect decisions is equal to 148 (38.5%). This includes 83 cases of false positive diagnoses (21.6%) and 65 cases of false negative diagnoses (16.9%). The last results are poor with respect to the previous two. The cause of it is fact that the base E300144 doesn't include any *blue nevus* case. If the learning base doesn't include some type of cases, the system isn't able to learn to recognize such a type.

5   Conclusions

The results included in Tab. 2 suggest that the best neural nets created for all three bases use all 14 attributes in making decision process. The mean error of test for the bases: 23.5% for E200144, 23.1% for E300144, and 15.3% for E250144 shows the tendency to decrease its value when the number of cases in the base grows up. This is comprehensible tendency. The more cases help the system to learn the better decision system takes. Unfortunately this inclination appears to be asymptotic, i.e. some part of decision will be always incorrect. It can be arise from that, the simulated neural nets work in rough approximation like a human brain, but incorrect decisions happen to people irrespective of how old are they.

The results included in Tab. 3 show the incorrect diagnosis in more details. The number of all *false positive diagnoses* is equal to 174 and the number

Table 3. The results of learning and testing neural nets, where (a) E200144 is the learning base, and remaining two are the tested bases; (b) - E250144 is the learning base; (c) E300144 is the learning base.

Tested base	cases	benign	malign	susp	blue
E250144	all cases	62	62	62	64
	correct recognized cases	50	56	35	48
	benign			5	15
	malign	4		22	
	susp	8	6		1
E300144	all cases	102	18	18	0
	correct recognized cases	98	16	12	0
	malign			6	
	susp	4	1		
	blue		1		

(a)

Tested base	cases	benign	malign	susp	blue
E200144	all cases	78	27	22	7
	correct recognized cases	59	27	14	7
	malign	3		7	
	susp	2			
	blue	14		1	
E300144	all cases	102	18	18	0
	correct recognized cases	86	17	10	0
	benign			1	
	malign	1		4	
	susp	5	1		
	blue	10		3	

(b)

Tested base	cases	benign	malign	susp	blue
E200144	all cases	78	27	22	7
	correct recognized cases	77	21	14	0
	benign		1	2	7
	malign	1		6	
	susp		5		
E250144	all cases	62	62	62	64
	correct recognized cases	59	43	22	0
	benign		4	28	61
	malign	1		12	
	susp	2	15		3

(c)

of *false negative diagnoses* is equal to 99. It means that for all incorrect diagnoses, more of them are advantageous to patients. Is it permanent tendency? To answer this question it should be greater and more bases explored.

Acknowledgments. The authors would like to thank Prof. Z. S. Hippe for his help and discussions in preparing this paper.

References

1. Z. S. Hippe, Computer database NEVI on endargement by melanoma, Task Quarterly 4 (1999) 483-488.
2. R. J. Friedman, D. S. Rigel, A. W. Kopf, Early detection of malignant melanoma: the role of physician examination and self-examination of the skin, CA Cancer J. Clin., 35 (1985) 130-151.
3. JW. Stolz, O. Braun-Falco, P. Bilek, A. B. Landthaler, A. B. Cogneta, Color Atlas of Derma-tology, Blackwell Science Inc., Cambridge, MA (1993).
4. J. W. Grzymala-Busse, LERS - A system for learning from examples based on rough sets, in Intelligent Decision Support. Handbook of Application and Advances of the Rough Sets Theory. R. Slowinski (ed.), Kluwer Academic Publishers, Dordrecht, Boston, London (1992) 3-18.
5. J. W. Grzymala-Busse, A new version of the rule induction system LERS, Fundamenta Informaticae 31 (1997) 27-39.
6. A. Alvarez, F. M. Brown, J. W. Grzymala-Busse, and Z. S. Hippe, Optimization of the ABCD formula used for melanoma diagnosis, Proc. of the II PWM'2003, Int. Conf. On Intelligent Information Processing and WEB Mining Systems, Zakopane, Poland, June 2-5 (2003) 233-240.
7. J. P. Grzymala-Busse, J. W. Grzymala-Busse, and Z. S. Hippe, Melanoma prediction using data mining system LERS, Proceedings of the 25th Anniversary Annual International Computer Software and Applications Conference COMPSAC 2001, Chicago, IL, October 8-12 (2001) 615-620.
8. J. W. Grzymala-Busse, and Z. S. Hippe, Postprocessing of rule sets induced from a melanoma data sets, Proc. of the COMPSAC 2002, 26th Annual International Conference on Computer Software and Applications, Oxford, England, August 26-29 (2002) 1146-1151.
9. J. W. Grzymala-Busse, and Z. S. Hippe, A search for the best data mining method to predict melanoma, Proceedings of the RSCTC 2002, Third International Conference on Rough Sets and Current Trends In Computing, Malvern, PA, October 14-16 (2002) Springer-Verlag, 538-545.
10. W. McCulloch, and W. Pitts, A Logical Calculus of Ideas Immanent in Nervous Activity, Bulletin of Mathematical Biophysics 5 (1943) 115-133.
11. A. F. G. Taktak, A. C. Fisher, and B. E. Damato, Modelling survival after treatment of intraocular melanoma using artificial neural networks and Bayes theorem, Phys. Med. Biol., 49 (2004) 87-98.

Medical Knowledge Representation in Terms of IF-THEN Rules and the Dempster-Shafer Theory

Ewa Straszecka

Institute of Electronics
Silesian University of Technology
Akademicka 16, 44-100 Gliwice, Poland
ewa@boss.iele.polsl.gliwice.pl

Abstract. The paper proposes a method of knowledge and certainty representation that is an alternative to fuzzy reasoning and classical probability based techniques. It makes possible to represent symptoms of different nature and is acceptable for physicians. The proposed solutions are based on the Dempster-Shafer theory of evidence, still, different definition for focal elements is proposed and specific method of basic probability assignment calculation for symptoms is suggested. It has been shown on examples of thyroid gland diseases diagnosis support that the method is efficient and numerically easy.

1 Introduction

So far medical expert systems have not been widely used as tools of diagnostic decision support. Still, nowadays the number of freeware expert systems provided by the Internet increases. This will probably result in wider use of professional systems composed with the contribution of specialists in medicine. The standard ways of knowledge description in the systems are IF-THEN rules. Instead, diversity of methods of conclusion certainty estimation is used. Professional and research systems (e.g. CADIAG [1], Iliad [3]) use fuzzy sets or probability measures. Certainty factors should make it possible to express: i) experts opinion about possibility of conclusion given conditions; ii) interpretation of frequency dependencies observed in patients databases; iii) possibility of a disease given patients symptoms; iv) differentiation among several possible diseases of a patient. Certainty factors must change monotonously, i.e. certainty of a disease must not diminish while adding symptoms, though the possibility of the opposing disease increases. Calculation of the factors should be numerically easy. The paper proposes an alternative to fuzzy reasoning that maintain generally accepted method of knowledge description by IF-THEN rules, ensuring the above mentioned features of reliable reasoning. It makes possible to represent symptoms of various nature and is acceptable for physicians. It has been shown both during simulation as well as on an example of classification of an Internet database that the proposed method is efficient in diagnosis support. The examples concern thyroid

L. Rutkowski et al. (Eds.): ICAISC 2004, LNAI 3070, pp. 1056–1061, 2004.
© Springer-Verlag Berlin Heidelberg 2004

gland diseases. The proposed solutions are based on the Dempster-Shafer theory of evidence. Still, different definition for focal elements is proposed and specific method of basic probability assignment calculation for symptoms is suggested. Belief measure is used to state certainty of a disease while plausibility measure informs about a quality of a diagnosis.

2   IF-THEN Rule Representation

The most convenient way of experts knowledge description are if-then rules. In medical expert systems knowledge is represented using rules $IF \ s_1^d \ and \cdots$ and $s_n^d \ THEN \ d$, where s_i^d is the i-th symptom of the d diagnosis. The symptom is defined as: $s_i^d \equiv (parameter_i = value)$ is true (for instance: *undergone operations = thyroid gland operation*, or: *state=pregnancy)*; as well as: $s_j^d \equiv (parameter_j > value)$ is true, or $s_j^d \equiv (parameter_j < value)$ is true, or $s_k^d \equiv (parameter_k \in [value_1, value_2])$ is true (for instance: *result of the laboratory test is above the norm limit*, or: *result of the laboratory test is inside the norm interval)*, which can be easily unified using the pattern:

$$s_i^d \equiv (parameter_i < relation > value) \ \text{is true.} \qquad (1)$$

If a fuzzy set represents a symptom "result of the laboratory test is little above the norm limit", the truth of the symptom is described by the interval $[0, 1]$. The actual value of truth measure is found when the symptom formulated in a knowledge base is compared with the parameter value of a patient. For instance, if the test result is t_p, then the truth measure is equal:

$$\eta_i^d = \max_t \min(\mu_{s_i^d}(t), \mu_{s_i^d}^*(t_p)) = \max_t \min(\mu_{s_i^d}(t), \delta_{t,t_p}) = \mu_{s_i^d}(t_p) \qquad (2)$$

where $\mu_{s_i^d}$ denotes membership function assigned to the symptom s_i^d, $\mu_{s_i^d}^*$ – membership function of the observation, and δ_{t,t_p} the singleton of t_p observation. From (2) it results that not only exact values, but also fuzzy observations can be analyzed by matching the formulated symptom with the observed value. Symptoms can be analyzed individually or in collections. In the latter case they can be considered as a complex symptom referring to two or more parameters. Thus, a rule can be written as:

$$IF \ s_r^d \ THEN \ d, \qquad (3)$$

where r is the number of the rule. The unification of symptom representation is helpful while creating collections of symptoms S_l resembling diagnosis d_l, e.g. $S_l = \{s_1^l, \cdots, s_r^l, \cdots, s_{n_l}^l\}$, $l = 1, 2, 3$ in case of considering three thyroid gland states: euthyroidism (health), hyperthyroidism, and hypothyroidism. It must be stressed that in (3) "THEN" does not denote an implication (as it appears in fuzzy rules) but assigning diagnosis to symptoms. The choice of a diagnosis involves S_l selection. This allows considering symptoms as focal elements in the Dempster-Shafer theory of evidence (DST). Focal elements are predicates that we have information about. The predicates consist in formulation of symptoms, while information consists in our knowledge how often the symptom is present with the chosen diagnosis. True predicates support the d_l diagnostic conclusion with strength expressed by the basic probability assignment (BPA). The symptom is true when its truth measure η_r^l is greater than a threshold. The threshold can be changed according to our wishes: if we want to base on the surest symptoms it should be high, if we lower it, we permit less precise information to be used in a diagnostic process. The threshold does not need to keep the same value during rules formulation and rules firing. Lets denote the threshold during knowledge base preparation as η_{BPA}. Then BPA is defined as [2], [4]:

$$m_l(f) = 0, \quad \sum_{\substack{\eta_r^l \geq \eta_{BPA}, \\ r=1,\cdots,n_l}} m_l(s_r^l) = 1, \tag{4}$$

where f denotes a false predicate (none of the symptoms is true) and $s_r^l = \{s_{ri}^l\}, i \geq 1$. In case of a complex symptom its truth is interpreted as minimum of truth measures of composing symptoms: $\eta_r^l = \min_i \eta_{ri}^l \, i = 1, \cdots, n_r$, where n_r is the number of single symptoms in the r-th rule. BPA can be determined as a normalized frequency of occurrence of s_r^l found for a database of patients with d_l diagnosis. The most important advantage of (4) in comparison to classical probability based methods is that symptoms dependence is neglected. The proposed symptom formulation (1) makes also simultaneous and intuitively consistent considering of all numerical and non-numerical parameters possible. Once rules and the BPA are determined the knowledge base is ready and we can start consultation.

Let us consider a patient that needs a diagnosis. We observe his s_i^{l*} symptoms. A symptom of d_l can be true (then $s_i^{l*} \cap S_l = s_r^l$), partly true ($s_i^{l*} \cap S_l = \tilde{s}_r^l \neq \varnothing$, $\tilde{s}_r^l \subseteq s_r^l$), or false ($s_i^{l*} \cap S_l = \varnothing$). Taking into account the concept of truth measure and following [2],[4], we calculate the belief in a diagnosis as:

$$Bel(d_l) = \sum_{\substack{\eta_r^l \geq \eta_T \\ r=1,\cdots,n_l}} m_l(s_r^l), \tag{5}$$

where η_T denotes the threshold value of truth measure for reasoning. The belief measure rarely reaches the maximal value of 1, and it depends on the number of known symptoms. Usually in medical diagnostics among many symptoms described in the literature, only few are examined with a patient, because of high cost of tests and invasive propensity. This causes difficulty in reasoning with certainty factors that use algebraic sum (e.g. score tests). On the other hand, the diagnosis can hardly relay on one, even the most certain symptom, as fuzzy-rules systems tend to perform. We suggest taking the final decision after comparing beliefs in several competing diagnoses (at least two: a disease and health). The diagnosis with the greatest belief wins. In case of two opposing diagnoses with the same belief, a conclusion cannot be stated. In DST a dual measure for Bel, i.e. the plausibility is determined, which following [4] can be defined for medical diagnosis as:

$$Pl(d_l) = \sum_{s_i^{l*} \cap s_r^l \neq \oslash} m_l(s_r^l). \tag{6}$$

The plausibility describes total influence of true and partly true symptoms on a diagnosis. In analogy to plausibility definition in DST [2], we should sum up BPA values for observations that have something in common with s_r^l. It means that unlike of m and Bel calculations, a complex symptom is considered as plausible when:

$$\eta_r^l > 0; \eta_r^l = \min_i \eta_{ri}^l, i = 1, \cdots n_r, \text{or} \tag{7}$$

$$\eta_r^l > \eta_T; \eta_{ORr}^l = \max_i \eta_{ri}^l, i = 1, \cdots n_r. \tag{8}$$

Formula (7) assumes maximal threshold lowering (in comparison to Bel) during Pl calculation. In (8) the definition of the truth measure is changed for concordant with that used in fuzzy rules. It cannot be decided without trials which interpretation is better. For independent and single symptoms $Bel(d_l) = Pl(d_l) = P(d_l)$. Generally, correlation can be found among symptoms as well as some symptoms are naturally considered in couples (e.g. systolic and diastolic blood pressure), hence certainty of the d_l diagnosis is given by the $[Bel(d_l), Pl(d_l)]$ interval. Belief must be preferred while decision making, as medical conclusions should be drawn very cautiously. Plausibility describes what is known about the patient and $1 - Pl(d_l)$ value inform what is the worth of symptoms that are either unknown or deny the diagnosis. If both $Bel(d_l)$ and $Pl(d_l)$ are small it means that the diagnosis considers few symptoms (is of low quality). That is why both measures are informative during a consultation session.

3   Results

The proposed interpretation of the diagnostic rules was checked for the database ftp.ics.uci.edu/pub/machine-learning-databases/thyroid-disease, files new-thyr.*, regarding thyroid gland diseases, found in the Internet. The database included values of five medical parameter variables for which diagnosis about a thyroid gland disease was stated. Global error, i.e. the percentage of wrong or not stated diagnoses was calculated. To this end, the data were divided for learning/test sets in three categories: d_1 - euthyroidismn (health) - 75/75; d_2 - hyperthyroidism 15/20; and d_3 - hypothyroidism 15/15. The final decision was based on comparing $Bel(d_i)$ values, $i = 1, 2, 3$. The percentage of wrong classifications was determined separately for each diagnosis, (i.e. if all classifications were wrong, maximum global error would be 300%). As the data were not numerous, the calculations were repeated for generated data of the same normal distributions and correlation among variables as in the Internet files. The simulated data composed 3 learning/test data sets of 100/100 cases. Learning and

Table 1. Threshold intervals for minimal values of the global error

	Internet data $error = 2.67\%$	generated data $error = 8\%$	Internet data $error < 10\%$	generated data $error < 10\%$
η_{BPA}	$[0.09, 0.4]$	$[0.69, 0.86]$	$[0.09, 0.4]$	$[0.2, 0.23]$ $[0.53, 0.76]$
η_T	$[0.17, 0.23]$ $[0.86, 0.9]$	$[0.85, 0.91]$	$[0.12, 0.42]$ $[0.86, 0.94]$	$[0.29, 0.44]$ $[0.8, 0.94]$

data cases were independently generated. Minimum of the global error for the Internet and generated data was searched by η_{BPA} and η_T change with 0.01 step.

Global error values found for belief comparison are presented in Tab. 1. The minimal values of the global error were 2.67% and 8% for the Internet and generated data, respectively. Threshold values η_T are similar for the both kinds of data, but η_{BPA} considerably differ. It seems that dealing with the Internet data we must use every possible information to minimize error, while having sufficient number and well-covered domain by the generated data, we should use the most sure information. Indeed, thanks to a special construction of membership functions [5], rules built with the both threshold values are coherent. If we allow an interval for the admissible global error (e.g. assume that the error is smaller than 10%) we observe that areas of error minimum determined by η_T and η_{BPA} overlap, so the result are coherent. It is noticeable that two areas of small error are found, both for the small inference threshold. Apparently, all patients symptoms, even if they are not very sure are valuable for consultation. The BPA threshold is not so high as it could be expected. It can be concluded that even during knowledge base constructing it is better to allow some imprecision instead of defining rules that are always true. Thresholds around 0.5 cause big error. The results of the proposed method for the Internet data were far better than that obtained for fuzzy reasoning. The error in the latter case was about 50% [5]. Minimal error regions can be found using a function relation between η_{BPA} and η_T, which will speed up numerical calculation. The most interesting result of the numerical investigation was that the best classification was obtained when Bel and Pl measures were simultaneously calculated and next beliefs for the maximum Pl were compared. No differences for definitions (7) and (8) were noticed. Thus, a well-determined algorithm could describe the process of finding minimal error of a diagnosis.

4   Conclusions

The paper proposes an interpretation of IF-THEN rules that is an alternative to that hitherto used in expert systems. On one hand the rule premise is interpreted in fuzzy terms, on the other hand the conclusion is estimated similarly as in probability-based systems. Uncertainty representation is universal for two-valued as well as measurable and linguistic symptoms. Symptoms can be modelled with fuzzy sets and entire or partial matching between an observation and a symptom can be estimated. A knowledge base, though formulated as IF-THEN rules, is a collection of symptoms assigned to diagnoses. After constructing rules, imprecision of their fuzzy predicates is found by defining their membership functions, and certainty of the rules is detected by determining the basic probability assignment. Thus, that a learning process that tunes general knowledge to the particular circumstances succeeds rules formulation. This allows improving capability of advice. A system using the proposed method can flexibly adapt to individual patients data by considering all disease categories with their maximum plausibility. For the maximal plausibility values beliefs in diagnoses can be compared. The diagnosis with the greatest belief wins. The plausibility values inform about diagnosis quality. The minimal classification error for diagnosis support can be found assuming a relation between BPA and inference thresholds. The proposed method offers considerable simplified computations in comparison to the classical probability calculus. Results of the exemplary medical data confirm that the method can successfully solve difficult problems of medical diagnosis, lowering the global error of three diagnostic categories for thyroid gland diseases to the value of 2.67%. The proposed method of diagnosis support allows for compact, clear and efficient interpretation of numerous symptoms of various natures.

References

1. Adlassnig K.-P. (1986) Fuzzy Modelling and Reasoning in a Medical Diagnostic Expert System, EDV in Medizin und Biologie 1/2, 12- 20.
2. Gordon J, Shortliffe E. H. (1984) - The Dempster-Shafer Theory of Evidence,. In: Rule -Based Expert Systems Buchanan B.G., Shortliffe E.H. Eds, Addison Wesley, 272-292.
3. Iliad, Windows-Based Diagnostic Decision Support Tools for Internal Medicine - User Manual, Applied Medical Informatics, (1994).
4. Kacprzyk J., Fedrizzi M. Eds,(1994) Advances in Dempster-Shafer Theory of Evidence. J. Wiley, New York.
5. Straszecka E.,(2000) An interpretation of focal elements as fuzzy sets. Int. J. of Intelligent Systems, vol. 18, 821-835.

Online Neural Network Training for Automatic Ischemia Episode Detection

D.K. Tasoulis[1,*], L. Vladutu[2], V.P. Plagianakos[3,*],
A. Bezerianos[2], and M.N. Vrahatis[1,*]

[1] Department of Mathematics and University of Patras Artificial Intelligence
Research Center (UPAIRC), University of Patras, GR-26110 Patras, Greece,
{dtas,vrahatis}@math.upatras.gr
[2] Department of Medical Physics, University of Patras, GR-26500 Patras, Greece,
bezer@patreas.upatras.gr, LiviuVladutu@ieee.org
[3] Department of Information and Communication Systems Engineering,
University of the Aegean, GR-83200 Samos, Greece, vpp@aegean.gr

Abstract. Myocardial ischemia is caused by a lack of oxygen and
nutrients to the contractile cells and may lead to myocardial infarction
with its severe consequence of heart failure and arrhythmia. An
electrocardiogram (ECG) represents a recording of changes occurring
in the electrical potentials between different sites on the skin as a
result of the cardiac activity. Since the ECG is recorded easily and
non–invasively, it becomes very important to provide means of reliable
ischemia detection. Ischemic changes of the ECG frequently affect
the entire repolarization wave shape. In this paper we propose a new
classification methodology that draws from the disciplines of clustering
and artificial neural networks, and apply it to the problem of myocardial
ischemia detection. The results obtained are promising.

Keywords: Online training, ischemia episode detection.

1 Introduction

Myocardial ischemia is the most common cause of death in the industrialized
countries and, as a consequence, its early diagnosis and treatment is of great
importance. Myocardial ischemia diagnosis using long–duration electrocardio-
graphic recordings is a simple and non–invasive method that needs further development before being used in everyday medical practice. The capability of
accurate and early detection of an acute ischemic event is critical for the per-
suadation of the proper treatment. The Electrocardiogram (ECG) represents a
recording of the changes occurring in the electrical potentials between different
sites on the skin as a result of the cardiac activity. Since the ECG is recorded

---

* This work was supported in part by the "Karatheodoris" research grant awarded by
the Research Committee of the University of Patras, and the "Pythagoras" research
grant awarded by the Greek Ministry of Education and the European Union.

L. Rutkowski et al. (Eds.): ICAISC 2004, LNAI 3070, pp. 1062–1068, 2004.
© Springer-Verlag Berlin Heidelberg 2004

easily and noninvasively, it becomes very important to provide means for reliable ischemia detection from ECG analysis.

There are a few mandatory steps for automated detection of ischemic episodes. After the initial removal of noise it follows the second stage, when all the important ECG features (J point, isoelectric line, and T wave peak) are extracted. Using the above features, in the third stage each cardiac beat is classified as normal or ischemic. In the final stage, sequential ischemic beats are grouped properly and the ischemic episodes can be identified.

The ST–T Complex of the ECG represents the time period from the end of the ventricular depolarization to the end of the corresponding repolarization in the electrical cardiac cycle. Ischemic changes of the ECG frequently affect the entire repolarization wave shape and thus are inadequately described by isolated features, even if these are obtained as an average of several signal samples [1]. Additionally, in many cases the ST segment is sloped or is influenced by noise. The approach proposed at the current work avoids the utilization of local, isolated features by designing upon the Principal Component Analysis (PCA) technique for extracting PCA coefficients (features) that describe the global content of the ST–T Complex.

2 Preprocessing

A description of the European ST-T Database is provided in [2], explaining the rules for the localization of the ST and T episodes. The main aim of the ECG signal preprocessing is to prepare a compact description of the ST–T complex, composed from the ST Segment and the T–wave, for input to the classification methodology with the minimum loss of information. From the samples composing each beat, a window of 400 msec is selected (100 samples at the 250 Hz sampling frequency). This signal component will form the input to the PCA to describe most of its content within a few (i.e. five) coefficients. To have a reference for the extraction of the relevant segment, the position of the R–peak should be detected. The start of the ST–T Segment was selected at approximately 60 msec after the detected R peak. However, in the database, there are both patients with bradycardia and tachycardia. Therefore, a more flexible approach that accounts for heart rate variations is required. The selection of the distance between the S point and the previously detected R–peak is correlated with the heart rhythm of the patient. The distance between the R–peak and the J point is in the range of 45–80 msec. Due to the fact that the correction of the ST–T length using the Bazett's formula, yields to a similar PCA basis function set, an analysis approach is selected with a fixed time window of 400 msec. This assumption is valid for the set of first 5 Principal Components (PCs) we used for representation. During the ST–T segment extraction, we rejected a small number (less than 1%) of ST–T segments, considered as particularly noisy.

The PCA method transforms a set of correlated random variables of dimensionality m, to a set of $d \leqslant m$ uncorrelated (in terms of their second order statistics) variables according to the direction of maximum variance reduction in the training set. The uncorrelated variables correspond to the subspace decomposition based on the first principal components of the input data. This decomposition is in terms of second order statistics optimum, in the sense that it permits an optimal reconstruction of the original data in the mean–square error sense. In our case, PCA has performed well for the extraction of representative vectors with only five coefficients. Thus, at the particular dimensionality reduction problem there is not sufficient evidence that the successive samples of the ECG signal are correlated in complex nonlinear ways. The ST–T Segment can be reconstructed effectively with the first five PCA projections that represent about 98.1% of the total signal energy. The PCA projection coefficients are then fed to the Feedforward Neural Network (FNN) to perform the classification decision about the category pertaining to each analysis case (i.e. normal, abnormal, artifact). The first PC and the second one (but to a less extent) represent the dominant low frequency component of the ST–T segment; the third, fourth and fifth contain more high frequency energy.

Following the extraction of principal components a noise reduction approach is used to improve these coefficients. The utilization of an advanced wavelet denoising technique has improved the classification results. The selected noise reduction approach was based on soft thresholding [3]. We have chosen five levels of wavelet decomposition and Daubechies–type wavelets.

3   The Classification Methodology

In this paper instead of constructing a global model for the pattern classification, we construct several local models, for neighborhoods of the state space. For this task, we use the novel k-windows clustering algorithm [4], to automatically detect neighborhoods in the state space. This algorithm, with a slight modification (unsupervised k-windows algorithm) has the ability to endogenously determine the number of clusters present in the dataset during the clustering process. Once the clustering process is complete, a trained FNN acts as the local predictor for each cluster. In synopsis, the proposed methodology consists of the following four steps:

1. Identify the clusters present in the training set.
2. For each cluster, train a different FNN using for training patterns, patterns from this cluster solely.
3. Assign the patterns of the test set to the clusters according to their distance from the center of the cluster.
4. Use the trained FNNs to obtain the classification scores on the test set.

The unsupervised k-windows algorithm generalizes the original algorithm [4]. Intuitively, the k-windows algorithm tries to place a d-dimensional window (box) containing all patterns that belong to a single cluster; for all clusters present in the dataset. At first, k points are selected (possibly in a random manner). The k initial d-ranges (windows), of size a, have as centers these points. Subsequently, the patterns that lie within each d-range are identified. Next, the mean of the

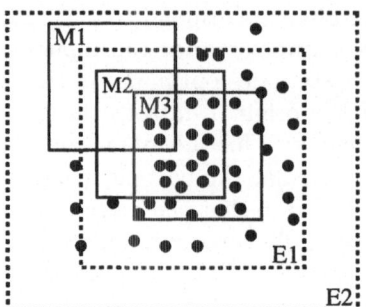 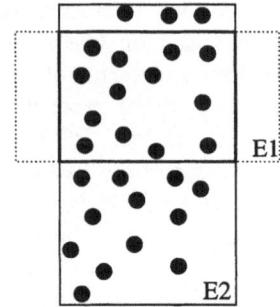

Fig. 1. Left: Movements (solid lines) and enlargements (dashed lines). Right: The enlargement process

patterns that lie within each d-range is calculated. The new position of the d-range is such that its center coincides with the previously computed mean value. The last two steps are repeatedly executed as long as the increase in the number of patterns included in the d-range that results from this motion satisfies a stopping criterion. The stopping criterion is determined by a variability threshold θ_v that corresponds to the least change in the center of a d-range that is acceptable to recenter the d-range (Figure 1, left).

Once movement is terminated, the d-ranges are enlarged in order to capture as many patterns as possible from the cluster. Enlargement takes place at each dimension separately. The d-ranges are enlarged by θ_e/l percent at each dimension, where θ_e is user defined, and l stands for the number of previous successful enlargements. After the enlargement in one dimension is performed, the window is moved, as described above. Once movement terminates, the proportional increase in the number of patterns included in the window is calculated. If this proportion does not exceed the user–defined coverage threshold, θ_c, the enlargement and movement steps are rejected and the position and size of the d-range are reverted to their prior to enlargement values. Otherwise, the new size and position are accepted. If enlargement is accepted for dimension $d' \geqslant 2$, then for all dimensions d'', such that $d'' < d'$, the enlargement process is performed again assuming as initial position the current position of the window.

This process terminates if enlargement in any dimension does not result in a proportional increase in the number of patterns included in the window beyond the threshold θ_c (Figure 1, right). In the figure the window is initially enlarged horizontally ($E1$). This enlargement is rejected since it does not produce an increase in the number of patterns included. Next the window is enlarged vertically, this enlargement is accepted, and the result of the subsequent movements and enlargements is the initial window to become $E2$. The key idea to automatically determine the number of clusters, is to apply the k-windows algorithm using a sufficiently large number of initial windows. The windowing technique of the k-windows algorithm allows for a large number of initial windows to be examined, without any significant overhead in time complexity. Once all the processes of movement and enlargement for all windows terminate, all overlapping windows are considered for merging. The merge operation is

Table 1. Percentages of correct classification on the test sets over 100 iterations

	FNN Classification Performance					
Test set	E103	E104	E106	E107	E108	E111
			RPROP			
mean	75.60	86.63	**59.78**	79.07	73.95	92.19
std	0.39	0.96	2.20	2.48	1.13	2.28
max	76.21	88.87	66.04	85.76	75.85	94.55
min	74.76	84.34	57.58	73.67	71.57	87.51
			iRPROP			
mean	75.64	87.07	59.87	**78.48**	73.91	**91.84**
std	0.54	0.73	2.88	1.62	1.10	4.00
max	76.53	88.29	69.17	81.71	75.75	94.92
min	74.36	84.57	57.48	75.24	71.97	80.41
			SCG			
mean	77.46	85.77	62.51	79.07	73.57	92.45
std	0.77	0.80	4.74	2.13	1.61	1.49
max	79.05	87.09	71.15	84.38	76.16	94.77
min	75.76	83.64	58.54	72.61	69.62	89.82
			BPVS			
mean	**72.50**	84.29	67.94	83.28	70.00	93.91
std	0.02	0.45	0.17	0.07	0.007	0.03
max	72.57	85.27	68.08	83.34	70.01	93.99
min	72.49	84.06	67.72	83.17	69.99	93.86
			AOBP			
mean	73.69	**83.83**	71.68	83.10	**69.67**	93.21
std	0.59	0.09	0.00	0.01	0.005	0.30
max	73.88	83.91	71.68	83.14	69.67	93.86
min	71.93	83.72	71.68	83.10	69.64	93.05

guided by a merge threshold θ_m. Having identified two overlapping windows, the number of patterns that lie in their intersection is calculated. Next the proportion of this number to the total patterns included in each window is calculated. If the mean of these two proportions exceeds θ_m, then the windows are considered to belong to a single cluster and are merged.

4 Numerical Results

Numerical experiments were performed using a Clustering, and a Neural Network, C++ Interface built under the Red Hat Linux 7.3 operating system using the GNU compiler collection (gcc) version 3.2. The efficient supervised training of FNNs is a subject of considerable ongoing research and numerous algorithms have been proposed to this end. In this work, we consider the following neural network training methods:

- Resilient Back Propagation (RPROP),
- Improved Resilient Back Propagation (iRPROP) [5],
- Scaled Conjugate Gradient (SCG),
- Adaptive On–Line Back Propagation (AOBP) [6],
- Back Propagation with Variable Stepsize(BPVS) [7],

After extensive experimentation the network architecture selected consisted of 8 nodes in the first hidden layer, 7 nodes in the second hidden layer, and two output nodes (5–8–7–2). All FNNs were trained for 300 epochs on the patterns of the training set and subsequently their performance was evaluated on the test sets. This process was repeated 100 times for all the training algorithms considered. The classification capability of the trained FNNs with respect to the accurate pattern classification in the test sets are reported in Table 1.

In the datasets E103, E104, and E108, FNNs trained with RPROP and iR-PROP outperformed all other methods. The drawback of these two methods is the relatively high standard deviation. SCG also suffers from the same drawback. The performance of RPROP and iRPROP on dataset E106 is discouraging. For the remaining datasets FNNs trained with BPVS and AOBP, produced the best results. A significant advantage of AOBP, and to an extent BPVS, is the fact that the standard deviation of their performance is negligible. Overall, for the datasets E104, E107 and E111, the classification ability of the proposed methodology is very good.

5   Conclusions

This paper presents a methodology for automatic recognition of ischemic episodes, which draws from the disciplines of clustering and artificial neural networks. The methodology consists of four stages. To effectively partition the state space, the training patterns are subjected to clustering through the unsupervised k-windows algorithm. Subsequently, a different FNN is trained on each cluster. At the third stage, the patterns in the test set are assigned to the clusters identified in the training set. Finally, the trained FNNs are used to classify each test pattern. This methodology was applied to classify several test cases of the European ST–T database and the obtained results were promising.

References

1. Maglaveras, N., Stamkopoulos, T., Pappas, C., Strintzis, M.: An adaptive backpropagation neural network for real-time ischemia episodes detection. IEEE Transactions on Biomedical Engineering **45** (1998) 805–813
2. Vladutu, L., Bezerianos, A., Papadimitriou, S.: Hierarchical state space partitioning with a network self-organizing map for the recognition of $st - t$ segment changes. Medical & Biological Engineering & Computing **38** (2000) 406–415
3. Donoho, D., Johnstone, I.: Ideal spatial adaptation by wavelet shrinkage. Biometrika **81** (1994) 425–455
4. Vrahatis, M., Boutsinas, B., Alevizos, P., Pavlides, G.: The new k-windows algorithm for improving the k-means clustering algorithm. Journal of Complexity **18** (2002) 375–391
5. Igel, C., Hüsken, M.: Improving the Rprop learning algorithm. In Bothe, H., Rojas, R., eds.: Proceedings of the Second International ICSC Symposium on Neural Computation (NC 2000), ICSC Academic Press (2000) 115–121

6. Magoulas, G., Plagianakos, V., Vrahatis, M.: Adaptive stepsize algorithms for on-line training of neural networks. Nonlinear Analysis, T.M.A. **47** (2001) 3425–3430
7. Magoulas, G., Vrahatis, M., Androulakis, G.: Effective backpropagation training with variable stepsize. Neural Networks **10** (1997) 69–82

Sequential and Distributed Evolutionary Computations in Structural Optimization

Tadeusz Burczyński[1,2], Wacław Kuś[1], Adam Długosz[1], Arkadiusz Poteralski[1], and Mirosław Szczepanik[1]

[1] Department for Strength of Materials and Computational Mechanics,
Silesian University of Technology, Konarskiego 18a, 44-100 Glwice, Poland
`Tadeusz.Burczynski@polsl.pl`,
[2] Institute of Computer Modelling, Cracow University of Technology
Cracow, Poland

Abstract. The aim of the paper is to present the application of the sequential and distributed evolutionary algorithms to selected structural optimization problems. The coupling of evolutionary algorithms with the finite element method and the boundary element method creates a computational intelligence technique that is very suitable in computer aided optimal design. Several numerical examples for shape, topology and material optimization are presented.

1 Introduction

Evolutionary methods have found various applications in mechanics, especially in structural optimization [2], [5]. The main feature of such applications is the fact that design process of artificial systems like structural or mechanical components is simulated by biological processes based on heredity principles (genetics) and the natural selection (the theory of evolution). The paper is devoted to structural optimization using sequential and distributed evolutionary algorithms. Solutions of optimization problems are very time consuming when sequential evolutionary algorithms are applied. The long time of computations is due to the fitness function evaluation which requires solution of direct (boundary-value or initial boundary-value) problems. The fitness function is computed with the use of the boundary element method (BEM) or the finite method (FEM) [8]. In order to speed up evolutionary optimization the distributed evolutionary algorithms can be proposed instead of the sequential evolutionary algorithms [4]. This paper is extension of previous papers devoted to optimization using sequential and distributed evolutionary algorithms in thermoelastic problems [3],[7], shape and topology optimization of 2D and 3D structures [6],[10].

2 Formulation of the Evolutionary Design

A body, which occupies a domain Ω bounded by a boundary Γ, is considered. Boundary conditions in the form of the displacement and traction fields are prescribed. In the case of dynamical problems initial conditions are also prescribed.

L. Rutkowski et al. (Eds.): ICAISC 2004, LNAI 3070, pp. 1069–1074, 2004.
© Springer-Verlag Berlin Heidelberg 2004

One should find optimal shape or topology of the structure by minimizing an objective functional:

$$\min_{\mathbf{Ch}} J_o(\mathbf{Ch}) \tag{1}$$

with imposed constraints:

$$J_\alpha(\mathbf{Ch}) = 0, \alpha = 1, 2, .., A; J_\beta \leq 0, \beta = 1, 2, .., B \tag{2}$$

Ch is a vector of design parameters which is represented by a chromosome with floating point representation

$$\mathbf{Ch} = [g_1, g_2, .., g_i, .., g_N] \tag{3}$$

where restrictions on genes are imposed in the form

$$g_{iL} \leq g_i \leq g_{iR}, i = 1, 2, .., N \tag{4}$$

Genes are responsible for shape, topology and material parameters of the structures. General form of the objective functional J_o and performance functional J_α and J_β can be expressed in structural optimization as follows

$$J = \int_\Omega \Psi(\sigma, \varepsilon, u, T) \, d\Omega + \int_\Gamma \varphi(u, p, T, q) d\Gamma \tag{5}$$

where Ψ is an arbitrary function of stress σ, strain ε, displacement u and temperature T fields in the domain Ω, respectively, φ is an arbitrary function of displacement u, traction p, temperature T and heat flux q fields on the boundary Γ, respectively.

Using the penalty function method the optimization problem (1) and (2) is transformed into non-constrained problem and the fitness function consists of functionals J_o, J_α and J_β. In order to evaluate the fitness function one should solve the boundary-value problem using FEM or BEM.

3   Shape, Topology, and Material Parametrization by Genes

The geometry of the structure is specified by NURBS - Non Uniform Rational B-Spline. Co-ordinates of control points of the NURBS play the role of genes. The distribution of material properties as Young's modulus $E(\mathbf{x})$, $\mathbf{x} \in \Omega$ in the structure is describing by a surface $W(\mathbf{x})$, $\mathbf{x} \in H^2$ (for 2-D) or a hyper surface $W(\mathbf{x})$, $\mathbf{x} \in H^3$ (for 3-D). $W(\mathbf{x})$ is stretched under $H^d \subset E^d$, $(d = 2, 3)$ and the domain Ω is included in H^d, i.e. $(\Omega \subseteq H^d)$. The shape of the surface (hyper surface)$W(\mathbf{x})$ is controlled by genes g_i, $i = 1, 2, .., N$, which create the chromosome (3). Genes take values of the function $W(\mathbf{x})$ in interpolation nodes $\mathbf{x_j}$, i.e. $g_j = W(\mathbf{x_j})$, $j = 1, 2, ..., N$. If the structure is discretized by FEM the assignation of Young's moduli to each finite element is performed by the mapping [6]:

$$E_e = W(\mathbf{x_e}), \ \mathbf{x_e} \in \Omega_e, \ e = 1, 2, ..., R \tag{6}$$

It means that each finite element contains different material. When the value of Young's modulus E for the e-th finite element is included in the interval $0 \le E_e < E_{min}$, the finite element is eliminated. Otherwise the finite element remains having the value of the Young's modulus from this material.

4 Distributed Evolutionary Algorithms

Distributed evolutionary algorithms [1],[4],[11] are based on the theory of co-evolutionary algorithms. The process of evolution is faster, if isolated subpopulations of small number of interchangeable individuals evolve. In this algorithm a population of individuals is divided into several subpopulations. Each of the subpopulations evolves separately, and from time to time only a migration phase occurs, during which a part of individuals is interchanged between the subpopulations. The distributed evolutionary algorithm works as a few isolated sequential evolutionary algorithms [9] communicating between each other during migration phases. The evolutionary optimization is performed in a few steps (Figure 1).

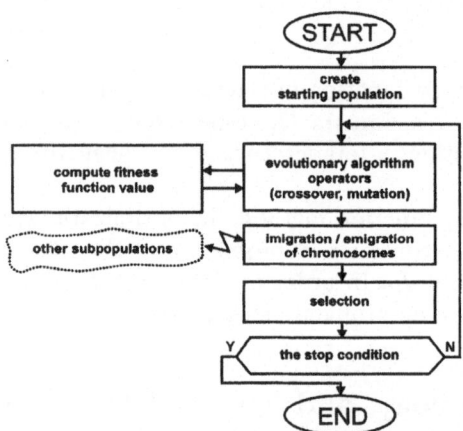

Fig. 1. The distributed evolutionary algorithm (one subpopulation)

At the beginning the starting population of chromosomes is generated randomly. The floating point representation is used. The population is divided into M subpopulations. Then the fitness function values for every chromosome are computed. The evolutionary algorithm operators as the crossover (simple, arithmetical and heuristic) and the mutation (uniform, boundary, non-uniform and Gaussian) are applied next. When the migration phase occurs, some chromosomes from subpopulations migrate to other subpopulations. The topology of the migration decides between which subpopulations the migration occurs. The elementary parameters defining the migration are: the migration frequency, the number of migrating individuals, the cloning or the eliminating an emigrating individual from a subpopulation, the selection of emigrating individuals, the way of introducing immigrating individuals to a subpopulation, the topology of the connections among subpopulations. The migration frequency defines the number of generations after which an individual emigrates. When the migration is too frequent, other subpopulations may be dominated by the solutions achieved in the current subpopulation. If it is too rare, in an extreme situation subpopulations will be isolated and they will evolve independently. The number of migrating individuals defines which part of a population will emigrate. If this number is too big, the algorithm starts to behave like a sequential algorithm with a single population. The ranking selection creates the offspring subpopulation based on the parent subpopulation modified by evolutionary operators. When selection is performed immigrated chromosomes from other subpopulations are also considered. The next iteration is performed if the stop condition is not fulfilled. The end computing condition can be expressed as the maximum number of iterations or the best chromosome fitness function value. The speedup, which is a measure of increasing of distributed computations, is defined as: $k_o = \frac{t_n}{t_1}$ where t_n means the time of performing the computation when n processing units (usually processors) are used, and t_1 - the computation time on a single unit.

5   Numerical Examples of Evolutionary Design

5.1   Shape and Topology Evolutionary Design of Thermomechanical Structures

A square plate with a circular void is considered (Figure 2a). For the sake of the symmetry only a quarter of the structure is taken into consideration. The considered quarter of the structure contains a gap bounded by an unknown internal boundary shown in the Figure 2b. The values of the boundary conditions are: $T_1^0 = 300^0C$, $T_2^0 = 20^0C$, $q_0 = 0$, $p_0 = 100kN/m$, $\alpha_1 = 1000W/m^2K$, $\alpha 2 = 20W/m^2K$, $u_0 = 0$. The model consists of 90 boundary elements. The optimization problem consists in searching an optimal: a) shape of the internal boundary, b) width of the gap, c) distribution of the temperature T^0* on the internal boundary for minimization of the radial displacements given by the functional (5) with $\Psi = 0$ and $\varphi = (u/u_o)^{2n}$, where u is a field of boundary displacements where tractions p_0 are prescribed, u_0 is a reference displacement, n is natural number. Shape of the internal boundary was modeled using NURBS curve which consists of 7 control points, whereas width of the gap and temperature T^0* using NURBS curve consist of 6 control points (Figure 2c). For the sake of the symmetry along line AB (Figure 2c) the total number of design parameters was equal to 13. The range of the variability of each control point for the width of the gap is between 0.2 and 0.8, whereas for the temperature is between 5^0C and 80^0C. The number of subpopulations was 2 and the number of chromosomes in each subpopulation was 10. Figure 2d shows results of the optimization.

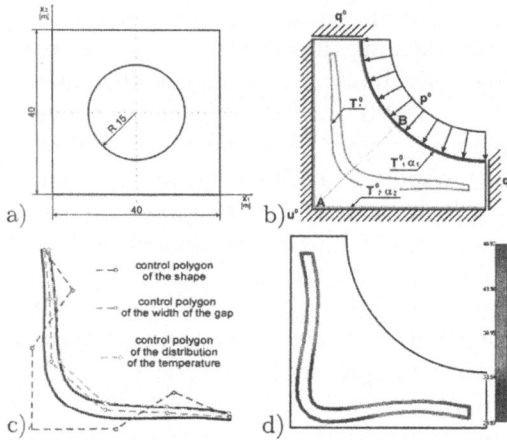

Fig. 2. Square plate with circular void: a) geometry, b) boundary conditions, c) NURBS curves, d) best result

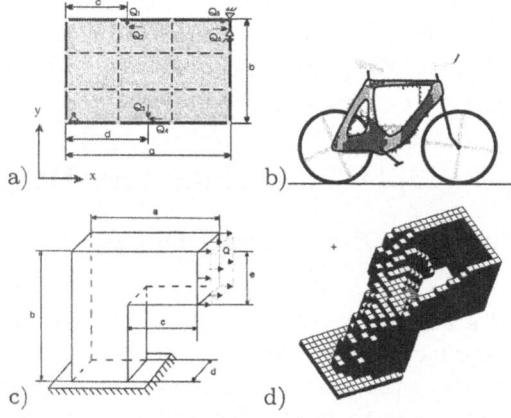

Fig. 3. Evolutionary design of a bicycle frame: a) plate and boundary conditions, best result, b) proposed frame; Evolutionary design of 3D structure: c) geometry, d) best result

5.2   Shape, Topology, and Material Evolutionary Optimization

Two numerical examples are considered for this kind of evolutionary design. The first example (Figure 3a,b) refers to evolutionary design of 2-D structures: (a bicycle frame - plain stress). The structures is discretized by triangular finite elements and subjected to the volume constraints. The second example (Figure 3c,d) is the 3-D problem where the body is discretized by hexahedral finite elements and subjected to the stress constraint. Using proposed method, material properties of finite elements are changing evolutionally and some of them are eliminated. As a result the optimal shape, topology and material or thickness of the structures are obtained.

6 Conclusions

An effective tool of evolutionary design of structures has been presented. Using this approach the evolutionary process of creating the shape, topology and material is performed simultaneously. The important feature of this approach is its great flexibility for 2-D and 3-D problems and the strong probability of finding the global optimal solutions.

Acknowledgements. This research was carried out in the framework of the KBN grant no. 4T11F00822.

References

1. Aleander J.T., An Indexed Bibliography of Distributed Genetic Algorithms, University of Vaasa, Report 94-1-PARA, Vaasa, Finland, (2000).
2. Burczyński T., Beluch W., Długosz A., Kuś W., Nowakowski M. and Orantek P.: Evolutionary computation in optimization and identification. Computer Assisted Mechanics and Engineering Sciences, Vol.9, No. 1 2002, pp. 3-20.
3. Burczyński, T., Długosz, A., Evolutionary optimization in thermoelastic problems using the boundary element method. Computational Mechanics, Vol. 28, No. 3-4, Springer 2002.
4. Burczyński, T., Kuś, W., Distributed evolutionary algorithms in optimization of nonlinear solids. In: Evolutionary Methods in Mechanics (eds. T. Burczyński and A. Osyczka). Kluwer, 2004.
5. Burczyński T., Osyczka A. (eds): Evolutionary Methods in Mechanics, Kluwer, Dordrecht 2004.
6. Burczyński T., Poteralski A., Szczepanik M., Genetic generation of 2D and 3D structures. Computational Fluid and Solid Mechanics (ed. K.J. Bathe), Elsevier, Amsterdam 2003, pp. 2221-2225.
7. Długosz, A., Evolutionary computation in thermoelastic problems. In: Evolutionary Methods in Mechanics (eds. Burczynski, T. and Osyczka, A.), Kluwer, 2003.
8. Kleiber, M., (ed.), Handbook of Computational Solid Mechanics, Springer, Berlin, 1998.
9. Michalewicz Z.: Genetic Algorithms + Data Structures = Evolutionary Algorithms, Springer-Verlag, Berlin 1996.
10. Poteralski A., Burczyński T., Szczepanik M., Evolutionary optimisation of 3-D structures. Proc. CMM 2003 15th International Conference on Computer Methods in Mechanics, Wisła, 2003.
11. Tanese R.: Distributed Genetic Algorithms. Proc. 3rd ICGA, pp.434-439, Ed. J.D. Schaffer. San Mateo, USA, (1989).

Neural Analysis of Concrete Fatigue Durability by the Neuro-Fuzzy FWNN

Magdalena Jakubek and Zenon Waszczyszyn

Institute of Computer Methods in Civil Engineering, Cracow University of Technology, ul. Warszawska 24, 31-155 Kraków, Poland
mj,zenwa@twins.pk.edu.pl

Abstract. Two problems related to the concrete fatigue durability analysis, originated in papers [2,3] and based on the data banks taken from [1], are developed. The first problem deals with the neural simulation of the durability of concrete, defined as a number of cycles of compressive stresses N. The second problem corresponds to the identification of concrete strength associated with N. In the paper a neuro-fuzzy network FWNN (Fuzzy Weight NN), formulated in [4], was used to obtain better results than approximations by the standard (crisp) Back-Propagation NNs.

1 Introduction

Fatigue durability is defined as a number of load cycles N causing fatigue damage of plain concrete specimens. In paper by Furtak [1] there was collected evidence corresponding to more than 400 cubic or cylindrical specimens, tested in many laboratories in years 1934 – 80, cf. Table 1. All the specimens were subjected to compressive loads within cycles at fixed frequencies.

In [1] fatigue durability N was related to mechanical properties of concrete and to the characteristics of the load cycle. A relationship between N and four input parameters x_j was derived in the same paper as an empirical formula $F(N, x_j) = 0$.

The neurocomputing used in [2] gave much better approximation than the empirical formula. A feed-forward multilayer neural network, called in [2] the Back-Propagation Neural Network (BPNN), was applied to predict (simulate) N for the same input variables as those used in the empirical formula. Additionally, in [2] the identification of concrete strength f_c was performed for those tests, listed in Table 1, for which only intervals $[f_{c\ min}, f_{c\ max}]$ were evaluated.

Following paper [3] a neuro-fuzzy modification of BPNN, called in [4] FWNN (Fuzzy Weight Neural Network), is explored in the present paper. The application of FWNN is discussed with respect to neural simulation of concrete durability and the identification of concrete strength.

L. Rutkowski et al. (Eds.): ICAISC 2004, LNAI 3070, pp. 1075–1080, 2004.
© Springer-Verlag Berlin Heidelberg 2004

Table 1. Experimental evidence collected in [1]

Nos	Nos of figures in [1]	Referen- ces in [1]	$R=$ $\sigma_{min}/\sigma_{max}$	f [Hz]	f_c [MN/m²]	Dimensions of specimens [cm]
1	2	3	4	5	6	7
1	7	37	0.025	16.7	28.0	ϕ 7.6×15.2
2	8	38	0.15, 0.38, 0.60, 0.88	150.0	41.0	ϕ 5.1×10.2
3	9	39	0.44	0.025	28.0	10.2×10.2×30.5
4	10	40	0	5.0	[20.0, 30.0]	7.0×7.0×21.0
5	11	41	0.14, 0.75	7.5	[14.8, 32.7]	13.0×13.0×40.0
6	12	42	0	20.0	[20.0, 45.0]	10.2×10.2×50.8
7	13	43	0	20.0	[33.1, 44.8]	10.2×10.2×50.8
8	14	19,20	0.044, 0.75	7.5	[14.8, 32.7]	13.0×13.0×40.0
9	15	44	0.05	16.7	25.5, 42.7	ϕ 7.6×15.2
10	16	45	0.05	1.167	24.8, 33.1	15.2×15.2×162.6
11	17	21	0	[5.0,16.7]	[20.0, 30.0]	Different
12	18	46	0.074, 0.253	10.0	45.2	ϕ 5.0×10.0
13	19	47	0	0.25	20.7	10.2×13.0×82.7
14	20	-	0	6.67,15.0	26.2	15.0×15.0×15.0

2   Tests on Laboratory Specimens and Empirical Formula

In Table 1 there are listed tests performed in 14 laboratories on more than 400 cubic or cylindrical specimens. The numbers of figures and references to corresponding data bases, listed in [1], are written in Columns 3 and 4 of Table 1. The tests corresponding to data bases can be split into two groups. Group I corresponded to 8 data bases with crisp values of concrete strength f_c (Nos 1, 2, 3, 9, 12, 13, 14 in Table 1). Group II was associated with fuzzy values of the strength related to interval $f_c \in [f_{c\,min}, f_{c\,max}]$ – (Nos 4, 5, 6, 7, 8, 11 in Table 1). The data base No.11 was eliminated from the analysis since in the evidence there were some uncertainties of both strength f_c and frequency f.

Basing on the results of laboratory tests listed in Table 1 the following empirical formula was derived in [1]:

$$\log N = \frac{1}{A}[\log(CC_f/\chi + \log(1 + BR\log N)], \tag{1}$$

where the following basic variables were used: N - number of cycles associated with the fatigue damage, f_c - ultimate strength of concrete in compression, $\chi = f_{cN}/f_c$ - ratio of strengths corresponding to fatigue strength of concrete f_{cN} and strength f_c, $R = \sigma_{min}/\sigma_{max}$ - ratio of minimal and maximal stesses in a loading cycle, f[Hz] - cycle frequency. Additional functions A, B, C_f depending on basic variables and parameter C are defined in [1].

Table 2. Errors and statistical parameters of neural approximation for concrete durability

Approximators and references	$RMSE(V)$		avr$ep(V)$ [%]		r_P	St eP
	L	T	L	T		
Formula (1)	0.156		36.0		0.638	1.12
BPNN: 4-5-4-1 [2]	0.077	0.077	12.3	13.3	0.854	0.76
FWNN: 4-5-4-1, α=1.0 [3]	0.070	0.078	10.7	13.8	0.863	0.73

3 Neural Simulation of Concrete Durability

The standard (crisp) neural network BPNN and neuro-fuzzy networks FWNN were used for modelling of the relationship $F(N, x_j) = 0$, where N number of fatigue cycles, x_j - basic variabes of formula (1). The problem of fatigue durability prediction was formulated as the following mapping:

$$\mathbf{x}_{4\times1} = \{f_c, \chi, R, f\} \quad \rightarrow \quad y = \log N. \tag{2}$$

$P = 218$ patterns corresponding to Group I of tested specimens were randomly split into $L = 118$ learning patterns and $T = 100$ training patterns. BPNNs were trained in [2] using the simulator MATLAB NN Toolbox and BP plus Momentum term learning method [5]. After the cross-validation the network BPNN: 4-5-4-1 was designed. In Table 2 there are written $RMSE(V)$ and average relative errors:

$$RMSE(V) = \sqrt{\frac{1}{V}\sum_{p=1}^{V}(t_p - y_p)^2}, \quad \text{avr } ep(V) = \frac{1}{V}\sum_{p=1}^{V}|1 - y_p/t_p| \cdot 100\%, \tag{3}$$

where: $V = L, T, P$ - training, testing and total number of patterns, respectively, t_p, y_p - target and neurally computed output values for pth pattern. In Table 2 also statistical parameters r_P and SteP are listed. Comparing the results listed in Table 2 a great difference of accuracy obtained by empirical formula (1) and by different neural networks is visible. It was stated in [2] that 85 % of correctly predicted patterns was located in the area of 20 % of relative error ep.

In Fig. 1 the results of neural predictions and by empirical formula (1) are shown for data banks listed in Table 1 as Nos 3 and 9b. It is visible that the neural predictions by BPNN (shown as solid curves) fit much better nonlinear relations $\chi(\log N)$ than formula (1). This concerns especially data bank No. 9b.

Computations by FWNN were carried out according to the algorithm formulated in [4] using the triangular membership functions for the NN weights. The simulator MATLAB NN Toolbox and the Levenberg - Marquardt method were applied [5]. The results shown in Fig. 1 correspond to intervals $[\log N_{com}^L, \log N_{com}^R]_\alpha$ for cuts $\alpha = 0.75, 0.9, 1.0$. The results listed in Table 2 for the cut $\alpha = 1.0$ are slightly different from those computed by means of the standard (crisp) network BPNN: 4-5-4-1. The interval prediction, obtained in [3], enables us to 'cover' partially results of tests on concrete specimens, called for short patterns. In case

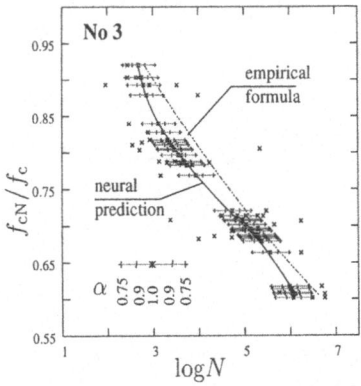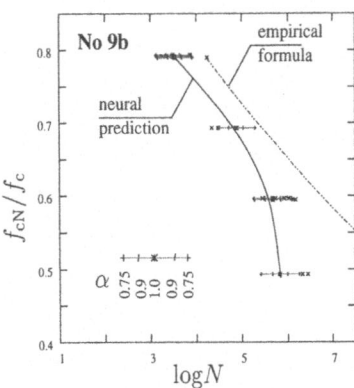

Fig. 1. Neural crisp and interval predictions of relation $\chi = f_{cN}/f_c - \log N$ for patterns taken from data banks Nos 3 and 9b

of data bank No. 3 ca. 45 % of patterns are placed within of computed intervals for $\alpha = 075\%$. For data bank No. 9b ca. 20 and 60 % of patterns are placed within intervals corresponding to $\alpha = 0.9$ and 0.75%, respectively.

4   Neural Identification of Concrete Strength

The problem of identification of ultimate concrete strength in compression f_c is associated with Group II data, Section 2. The network of BPNN: 4-5-4-1 with the following input and output vectors:

$$\mathbf{x}_{4\times 1} = \{\log N, \chi, R, f\}, \qquad y = f_c \tag{4}$$

was lernt by means of the same $L = 118$ patterns from Group I, which was discussed in Section 3 and used for the prediction of fatigue cycles N. After $S = 2000$ epochs the learning error was $MSEL = 0.090$.

Then data banks of Group II were used for computing the concrete strength f_c of specimens from the data bases Nos 4 - 8 listed in Table 1. From among the results presented in [2] there are shown in Figs 2 only two predictions corresponding to data banks listed in Table 1 as Nos 6 and 4. It is clear that identification of concrete strength f_c shown in Fig. 2a, related to data bank No.6 is correct since all the identified patterns are placed within the range $[f_{c\ max}, f_{c\ min}] = [20, 45]$ MPa given in Table. I. In case of data bank No.4 the BPNN prediction is false since all the patterns are out of the interval $f_c \in [20, 30]$ MPa, cf. Table 1 and Fig. 2b.

The identification of concrete strength was repeated by means of FWNN for the above discussed data banks Nos 6 and 4. The interval values of concrete strength $[f_{c\ min}, f_{c\ max}]_{\alpha=1}$ were introduced instead of the crisp input f_c. The computations were carried out for the cut $\alpha = 1$ by FWNN, trained on $L=118$ patterns for the simulation problem discussed in Section 2.

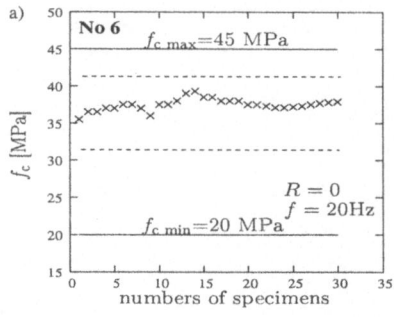
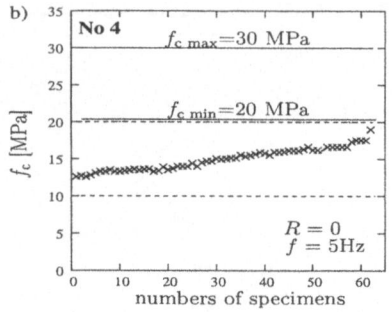

Fig. 2. Neural identification of concrete strength f_c with respect to tests by: a) Graff and Brenner, 1934, cf.[19,20] in [1], b) Beychenyeva, 1961, cf. ref. [40] in [1]

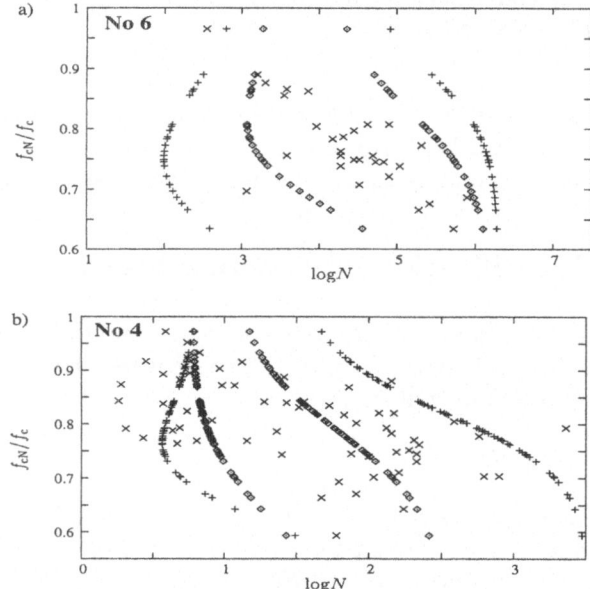

Fig. 3. FWNN interval prediction of relation f_{cN}/f_c – $\log N$ for: a) data bank No.6 (+ limits for $f_c \in [20,45]$ MPa, $\diamond$ -limits for $f_c \in [32,42]$ MPa), b) data bank No.4 (+ limits for $f_c \in [20,35]$ MPa, $\diamond$ -limits for $f_c \in [10,20]$ MPa)

In Fig. 3 there are shown interval approximations of $[\log N^L, \log N^R]_{\alpha=1}$ for all the patterns of data banks Nos 6 and 4. In case of data bank No.6 the interval $f_c \in [20,45]$ MPa gives covering ca. 97 % of patterns. This result fully corresponds to the prediction obtained by the crisp network BPNN, cf. Fig. 2a. In this case quite an accurate prediction was obtained by FWNN for the narrow interval $f_c = [32,42]$ MPa, which enables as to cover 93 % of patterns.

A similar approximation was also obtained for data bank No.4. The prediction from the Table 1 was much better confirmed by the results obtained by

FWNN than by BPNN. In Fig. 3b there are shown evaluations for two intervals. The first interval, corresponding to $f_c \in [10,20]$MPa, covers all the patterns shown in Fig.2a but only 50 % of patterns predicted by FWNN. In case of the second interval $f_c \in [20, 35]$ MPa the prediction by FWNN covers ca. 82 % of patterns.

5   Conclusions

1. The standard (crisp) networks BPNN and neuro-fuzzy network FWNN give comparable average results for the simulation problem of concrete fatigue durability prediction.
2. FWNN enables us to 'cover' a great number of experimental results by interval predictions.
3. FWNN gives better identification of concrete strength than BPNN.

Acknowledgment. Financial support by the Foundation for the Polish Science, Subsidy No. 13/2001 "Application of Artificial Neural Networks to the Analysis of Civil Engineering Problems" is gratefully acknowledged.

References

1. Furtak, K.: Strength of concrete subjected to multiple repeated loadings (in Polish). Arch. of Civ. Eng. **30** (1984) 677–698
2. Kaliszuk, J., Urbańska, A., Waszczyszyn, Z.: Neural analysis of concrete fatigue durability on the basis of experimental evidence. Arch. of Civ. Eng. **47** (2001) 327–339
3. Jakubek, M., Urbańska, A., Waszczyszyn, Z.: Application of FWNN to the analysis of experimental mechanics problems. Numerical Methods in Continuum Mechanics - Proceedings of the 9th Conference NMCM2003, Žilina, Slovak Republic, September 9-12, 2003. CD-ROM, 12pp
4. Pabisek, E., Jakubek, M., Waszczyszyn, Z.: A fuzzy network for the analysis of experimental structural engineering problems. In L. Rutkowski, J. Kacprzyk, Eds. Neural Networks and Soft Computing. Physica-Verlag, Springer, Heidelberg (2003) 772–777
5. Neural network toolbox for use with MATLAB. User's Guide. Version 3. The Math Works, Inc. Natick, MA (1998)

Neural and Finite Element Analysis of a Plane Steel Frame Reliability by the Classical Monte Carlo Method

Ewa Pabisek[1], Joanna Kaliszuk[2], and Zenon Waszczyszyn[1]

[1] Cracow University of Techology, ul. Warszawska 24, 31-155 Kraków, Poland
{e.pabisek,zenwa}@twins.pk.edu.pl
[2] University of Zielona Góra, ul. Prof. Z. Szafrana 2, 65-516 Zielona Góra, Poland
j.kaliszuk@uz.zgora.pl

Abstract. The paper is a continuation of [4], where a feed-forward neural network was used for generating samples in the Monte Carlo methods. The patterns for network training and testing were computed by an FEM program. A high numerical efficiency of neural generating MC samples does not correspond to the much more time consuming FEM computation of patterns. This question and an evaluation of the number of random inputs is discussed in the presented paper on an example of plane steel frame, called in [5] a calibrating frame.

1   Introduction

The probabilistic analysis has to be applied to the assessment of structural reliability [1]. Complexity of analysis can be overcome by computer simulations and especially by simulations associated with Monte Carlo methods [2]. Neurocomputing can be efficiently used for generating samples in these methods [3, 4]. It was proved in [4] that the trained simple neural networks (in [4] they are called Back - Propagation NNs - BPNNs) are numerically so efficient that we can base on the simplest, classical (crude) Monte Carlo method (CMC) for generating samples.

In structural engineering the samples are usually computed by the Finite Element Method (FEM) programs [2,3,4]. A great number of samples is needed in the MC simulation so the application of FEM program is numerically inefficient for large scale problems because of high computational time. That is why in [3,4] neural networks were explored for generating MC samples. Patterns (quasi experimental data) for the network training and testing are computed by FEM. A number of patterns for the network training and testing is a crucial question in such an hybrid approach. This is related to both the complexity of considered structure and the number and nature of random inputs (independent random actions).

In [4] a very simple plane frame, taken from [2], was analyzed assuming two material random variables. That is why in the presented paper a more realistic plane frame is analyzed, called in [5] a calibrating frame. Besides two material

L. Rutkowski et al. (Eds.): ICAISC 2004, LNAI 3070, pp. 1081–1086, 2004.
© Springer-Verlag Berlin Heidelberg 2004

variables (yield points of frame columns and beams) the third structural random variable is introduced (initial global inclination of frame columns). Reliability curves for the analyzed frame are used, cf. [4], as a base for deducing engineering type conclusions about the numerical efficiency of the proposed hybrid approach.

2   Structural Reliability and Monte Carlo Simulation

Stationary type structural problems are analyzed and the probability of reliability for a fixed time is defined by the following relationship:

$$p_r = \text{Prob}\, \{G(R, S) > 0\} \equiv \text{Prob}\, \{R > S\} = \int_{G(\mathbf{X})>0} f(\mathbf{X})\, d\mathbf{X}\,, \qquad (1)$$

where: p_r - probability of reliability, R - resistance of structure, S - actions (loads) applied to structure, $\mathbf{X} = [\mathbf{X}^R, \mathbf{X}^S]$ - vector of random variables. The complement of p_r is the probability of failure $p_f = 1 - p_r$ that the structure will fail.

The Monte Carlo simulation corresponds to computation of integral in (1). Following the law of large numbers the Classical Monte Carlo (CMC) estimator of the probability of failure is:

$$\bar{p}_r = \frac{1}{NMC} \sum_{i=1}^{NMC} I(\mathbf{X}_i)\,, \qquad (2)$$

3   Ultimate Load and Training Patterns

An FEM program is frequently used for generating patterns for the training and testing off line a feed-forward NN. In the considered problem the input and output vectors are assumed to be:

$$\mathbf{x}_{N \times 1} = \{x_1, \dots, x_N\}\,, \qquad \mathbf{y} = \lambda_{\text{ult}}\,, \qquad (3)$$

where: x_i - random variables corresponding to structural or material parameters, λ_{ult} - ultimate load parameter. In what follows only single parameter loads are analyzed $\mathbf{P} = \lambda \mathbf{P}^\star$, where: $\mathbf{P}^\star \in \mathcal{R}^F$ - load reference vector. The ultimate load parameter λ_{ult} corresponds to the global buckling of the considered frame [6].

4   Reliability Analysis of a Plane Elastoplastic Frame

4.1   Data for FRAME I

The computation was carried out for the so-called calibrating FRAME I, cf. [5], shown in Fig. 1a. It was assumed that the frame members were made of steel with the mean value of yield point $\sigma_0 = \bar{R}$. In Fig. 1b the frame cross-section is shown with the Simpson points of numerical integration j. Elastic perfect plastic material was assumed with the elastic and tangent stiffnesses $E = 205\text{GPa}$, $E_p = 0$.

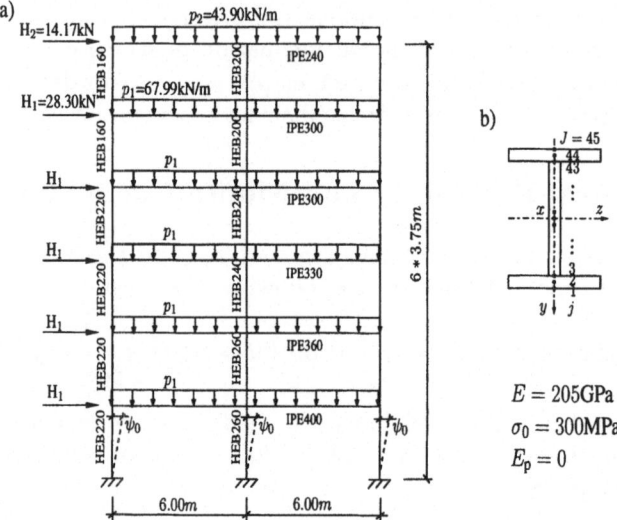

Fig. 1. a) Scheme of FRAME I, b) Simpson points $j = 1, \ldots, 45$ and mechanical data for I cross-section

4.2   Generation of Training and Testing Sets of Patterns

Computations were carried out by the ELPLAFv1 program [6] assuming that the random yield point R of frame members is a random variable of normal PDF and parameters: corresponding to the mean value $\bar{R} = 300$MPa and variance $\sigma_R = 30$MPa. For computations the range of yield point values was assumed:

$$R \in [\bar{R} - 4\sigma_R, \bar{R} + 4\sigma_R] = [180, 420]\text{MPa} , \qquad (4)$$

The global sway of columns ψ_0 was also assumed as a random variable of normal PDF and variance σ_ψ defined by formula taken from [7]:

$$\psi_0 \in [-2\sigma_\psi, 2\sigma_\psi] \quad \text{for} \quad \sigma_p si = \frac{1}{200} \frac{1}{2} \left(1 + \frac{1}{\sqrt{3}} \right) \approx \frac{1}{254} = 0.00394 . \qquad (5)$$

Two numerical examples were considered with the following input vectors:

$$1) N = 2 : \mathbf{x} = \{R_b, R_c\}, \qquad 2) N = 3 : \mathbf{x} = \{R_b, R_c, \psi_0\} , \qquad (6)$$

where: R_b, R_c - yield points of frame beams and columns, respectively, ψ_0 - initial sway of columns, cf. Fig.1a. In the first case $N = 2$ the fixed value of sway $\psi_0 = 1/450$ was adopted, cf. [5].

The number of training patterns L was computed by formula $L = (n + 1)^N$, where: N - dimension of input space, n - number of equal parts at uniform division of the N-cube side. The numbers L are listed in Table 1. The testing set was composed of $T = 2000$ patterns randomly selected assuming two or three random variables according to formulae (6).

The computations were performed on PC computer Intel Pentium IV of clock frequency 2.0 GHz. The CPU time needed for randomly selected 1000 patterns by means of the program ELPLAFv.1 was 26724 sec. That gives the average time ca. 26.7 sec. for one pattern.

4.3   Training, Testing, and Design of BPNNs

Two families of BPNNs (Back-Propagation Neural Networks) were assumed, corresponding to one or two hidden layers of structures N-H-1 and N-H1-H2-1, respectively. Sigmoid binary activation functions were used in the hidden layers and identity function in the output neuron.

An extensive design procedure was performed assuming the multifold cross-validation procedure and taking the number of hidden neurons $H \in [2, 30]$ for $N = 2$ and $H1 \in [3, 11]$, $H2 \in [1, 9]$ for $N = 3$. MATLAB Neural Network Toolbox and the Levenberg-Marquardt learning method were used [8]. After introductory computations the stopping criteria were assumed as corresponding to the number of epochs $S \leq 1000$ or training error $MSEL(s) = (RMSEL(s))^2 \leq 1 \star 10^{-5}$.

In Table 1 there are listed selected results corresponding to the following errors:

$$\text{avr } ep(V) = \frac{1}{V} \sum_{p=1}^{V} ep, \quad \max ep(V) = \max_{p} ep, \quad \text{for} \quad ep = |1 - y_p/t_p| \, 100\% .$$

$$RMSE(V) = \sqrt{\frac{1}{V} \sum_{p=1}^{V} (t_p - y_p)^2} , \tag{7}$$

where: $V = L$, T - number of patterns for the network training and testing, respectively, t_p, y_p - output values for known and neurally computed output for the p-th pattern.

Table 1. Errors of neural approximation

N	n	L	$BPNN$	$RMSE \star 10^2$		avr $ep[\%]$		max $ep[\%]$	
				L	T	L	T	X	T
	2	9	2-2-1	2.70	7.14	2.44	3.89	7.12	23.9
	4	25	2-5-1	1.39	1.73	1.39	1.39	3.36	8.60
	8	81	2-6-1	0.60	0.87	0.52	0.59	2.57	9.26
2	16	289	2-5-5-1	1.04	0.72	0.56	0.41	5.17	10 .07
	32	1089	2-5-4-1	1.71	0.69	1.26	0.41	9.39	8.90
	2	27	3-2-1	1.93	2.24	1.92	2.04	5.77	6.28
	4	125	3-8-1	0.98	0.90	0.78	0.69	5.31	4.37
3	8	729	3-5-4-1	1.21	0.74	0.67	0.52	10.13	5.03
	16	4913	3-20-6-1	0.71	0.70	0.38	0.38	7.43	6.07

4.4   Neural CMC Simulations and Reliability Curves

The trained BPNN can be efficiently used in the operational phase of CMC (Crude Monte Carlo) method for computing indicators $I(\mathbf{x}_i)$ in formula (2). The MC indicator can be directly related to the reliability of elastoplastic frame, i.e. if $\lambda_i > 1$ then $I(\mathbf{x}_i) = 1$ else $I(\mathbf{x}_i) = 0$.

Basing on formula (2) a reliability curve $\bar{p}_r(\lambda)$ can be computed for a sequence of fixed load parameters λ_i, assuming a step $\Delta\lambda$. The computation can be significantly sped up if the random selection of variables $\mathbf{x}_i$ is performed only once and the neural simulation of $\lambda_{\mathrm{ult}}(\mathbf{x}_i) = \lambda_{\mathrm{BPNN}}(\mathbf{x}_i)$ is applied. In order to have a statistically representative set a great number of randomly selected samples is generated. In what follows the number of samples is $NMC = 1 \star 10^5$.

Using the designed networks listed in Table 1 reliability curves were computed for $\lambda \in [0.6, 1.3]$ with the step $\Delta\lambda = 0.0125$, which gives 57 points at the curve $\bar{p}_r(\lambda)$. At the beginning the computations were carried out for the networks of great prediction accuracy, i.e. for BPNN: 2-5-4-1 and BPNN: 3-20-6-1. In Fig.2a there are depicted the corresponding reliability curves $\bar{p}_r(\lambda)$. There are also shown values of the load parameter corresponding to the assumed probability of the frame reliability. If we consider the case $N = 2$, and for instance, probability $\bar{p}_r(\lambda) = 0.99$, then the frame will be reliable for $\lambda \leq 0.78802$ and for $\lambda \leq 0.8413$ if $\bar{p}_r = 0.95$. Introduction of the third random variable ψ_0 does not change significantly these figures.

In Fig.2b reliability curves are shown, obtained for three networks and two random variables, i.e. for case $N = 2$.

The curve computed by the network BPNN: 2-5-4-1, trained by means of $L = 1089$ patterns, is very close to the curve computed by BPNN: 2-6-1 trained by only 81 patterns.

a)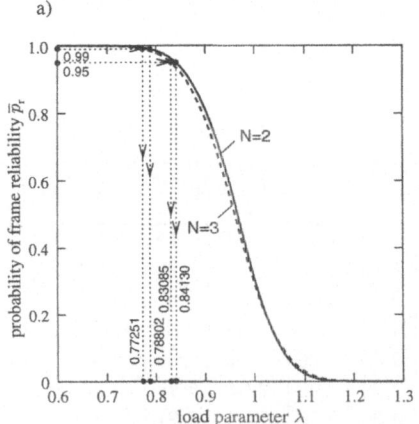   b)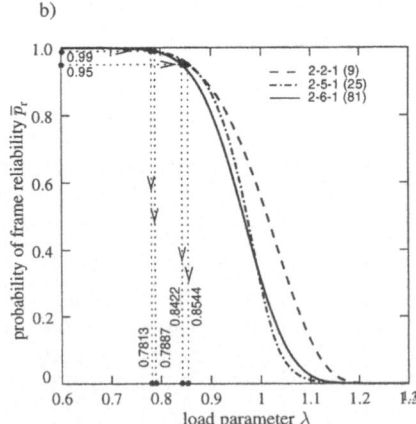

Fig. 2. Reliability curves $\bar{p}_r(\lambda)$ corresponding to simulation by network: a) BPNN: 2-5-4-1(1089) trained by means of $L = 1089$ patterns, BPNN: 3-20-6-1(4913), b) BPNN: 2-2-1(9), BPNN: 2-5-1(25), BPNN: 2-6-1(81)

4.5   Execution Times

In order to check the numerical efficiency of neural simulation the computations by a trained network were performed for $NMC = 100000$ samples for the network BPNN: 2-5-4-1 of the number of network parameters $NNP = 44$ and BPNN: 3-20-6-1 with $NNP = 213$. In case $N = 2$ the time of random search and computing of 57 points at the reliability curve was ca. 34 sec. for BPNN: 2-5-4-1 and ca. 58 sec. for BPNN: 3-20-6-1.

In case of computing by the FE program ELPLAFv1 the time of generating one pattern was pointed out in Point 4.2 as ca. 27 sec. Thus if we assume hypothetically that $P = 100000$ samples are generated by ELPLAF then the CPU execution time would be ca. $27 \star 10^5 = 2.7 \star 10^6$ sec., that is ca. 10^5 times higher than the neural simulation time. Of course in the time balance of neural simulation we should take into account the time of BPNNs formulation and generating of training and testing patterns.

5   Final Conclusions

1. Application of BPPNs can significantly decrease the time of samples simulations in the classical Monte Carlo Method.
2. The total CPU time strongly depends on the number of training and testing patterns computed by an FEM program. That is why the number of patterns should be carefully evaluated on the base of reliability curves computed by trained BPNNs.

References

1. Nowak, A., Collins, K.: Reliability of Structures. Mc Graw-Hill, Intern. Edition/Civil Eng. Series. (2000)
2. Marek, P., Gubrevestar, M., Anagnos, Th.: Probabilistic Assessment of Structures using Monte Carlo Simulation. TeReCo. (2002)
3. Pulido, J.E., Jacobs, T.L., Prates de Lima, E.C.: Structural reliability using Monte Carlo simulation with variance reduction techniques on elastic-plastic structures. Comp. & Struct. **43** (1996) 419–430
4. Papadrakakis, M., Papadopoulos, V., Lagaros, N.D.: Structural reliability analysis of elastic-plastic structures using neural network and Monte Carlo simulation. Comp. Meth. Appl. Mech. Eng. **136** (1996) 145–163
5. Kaliszuk, J., Waszczyszyn, Z.: Reliability analysis of structures by neural network supported Monte Carlo methods. In L. Rutkowski, J. Kacprzyk, Eds. Neural Networks and Soft Computing. Phisica-Verlag, Springer Heidelberg (2003) 754–759
6. Vogel, U.: Calibrating frames. Stahlbau **10** (1985) 295–301
7. Waszczyszyn, Z., Pabisek, E.: Elastoplastic analysis of plane steel frames by a new superelement. Arch. of Civ. Eng. **48** (2002) 159–181
8. Machowski, A.: Ultimate states and reliability of multi-storey steel buildings (in Polish). Cracow Univ. of Technology. Civil Engineering Series. Monograph No. 262
9. Neural network toolbox for use with MATLAB. User's Guide. Version 3. The Math Works, Inc. Natick, MA (1998)

The Solution of an Inverse Problem in Plates by Means of Artificial Neural Networks

Grzegorz Piątkowski and Leonard Ziemiański

Rzeszów University of Technology, Department of Structural Mechanics,
ul. W.Pola 2, 35-959 Rzeszów, Poland
{pgrzes,ziele}@prz.rzeszow.pl

Abstract. The paper presents the application of Artificial Neural Networks (ANNs) for solution of an inverse problem [1]. Based on the dynamic characteristics of a plate, the neural identification of parameters of circular hole and additional mass have been performed. An emphasis was placed on the effective preparation of learning data, which were produced both by the finite element method and by experiment.

1 Introduction

The assessment of the structure's state is a task which requires continuous researches and its development. There are a lot of methods based on a non-destructive testing of the structural elements. Some of these methods utilize dynamics parameters of a monitored structure, such as modal characteristics (resonance frequencies) [2,3]. One of the most important objective of these methods is a detection and localisation of changes, failures and defects in the structural elements.

2 Detection of a Void

The numerical tests have been carried out for rectangular plates with an internal defect in a form of the circular void. The position of the void's centre was defined by two parameters which are OY and OZ coordinates. These coordinates and its diameter D were unknown parameters of the inverse problem.

For each considered location of the void, a Finite Element Method (FEM) model (presented at Fig. 1) of the plate has been calculated by means of the Adina system of the finite element method. Numerical models have been built with 2D solid quadrilateral, eight nodes, plane stress elements [4]. The eigenproblem has been solved with subspace-iteration method of frequency calculation. The number of 10 frequencies have been calculated.

Next, the artificial neural network analysis of the calculated eigenfrequencies has been performed to obtain the hole's centre coordinates and hole's diameter. The multi-layer feed-forward (MLFF) back-propagation neural networks with the Levenberg-Marquardt training function have been applied [5]. Single networks and cascade sets (two- or three-stages) of MLFF back-propagation neural

L. Rutkowski et al. (Eds.): ICAISC 2004, LNAI 3070, pp. 1087–1092, 2004.
© Springer-Verlag Berlin Heidelberg 2004

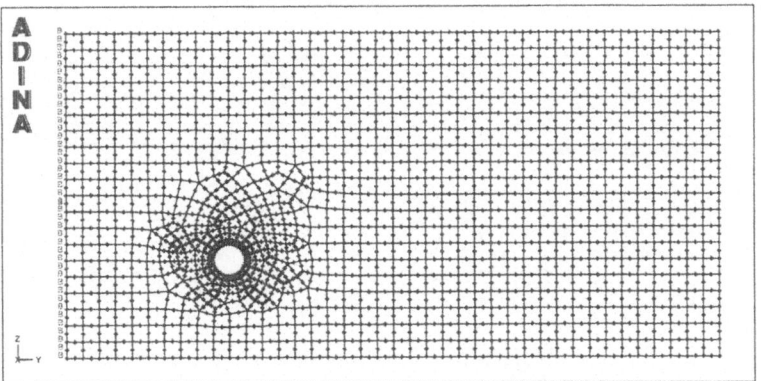

Fig. 1. Example mesh of numerical model of the plate

networks have been used [1,3,6]. The Neural Network Toolbox available within the Matlab has been used in building and training of networks [7].

An identification of two coordinates of centre of void with diameter $D = 0.02m$ on basis of eigenfrequencies was the first neural experiment. The computations, which have been carried out showed that acceptable accuracy could be achieved by input vector with five elements only. These elements were the relative changes of first five eigenfrequencies. Moreover, better results have been obtained from cascade network [6].

On basis of this results, the identification of three parameters of void $\{OY, OZ, D\}$ has been performed. In this task the number of voids' positions have been decreased to the number of 39. Nine diameters of each void have been simulated in range of $0.004 \div 0.02m$. Thus, the total number of patterns were 351. Relied on experiences from previous experiment, the three-stage cascade neural network has been applied. It has been experimentally determined that the best results have been given by the cascade network with parameters' prediction order as follows $D \triangleright OY \triangleright OZ$. The results presented at Fig. 2 include multiple marks ('x'), which relate to different diameters of void at given position. One can see that the vertical coordinate of voids has been predicted with a higher error (a relative error of $\pm 10\%$) than the horizontal one ($\pm 2\%$). The third parameter of void, its diameter, has been identified with a relative error of $\pm 4\%$ with relation to diameters' range $0.004 \div 0.020m$.

3   Detection of an Additional Mass

Two laboratory models have been built as it is shown at Fig. 3. The models have been made of a steel and an aluminium alloy plates, fixed to a massive stand by high-tensile bolts.

An experimental set consisted of eight PCB acceleration sensors. Scadas III analyzer with LMS software, has been applied to measure a response of the struc-

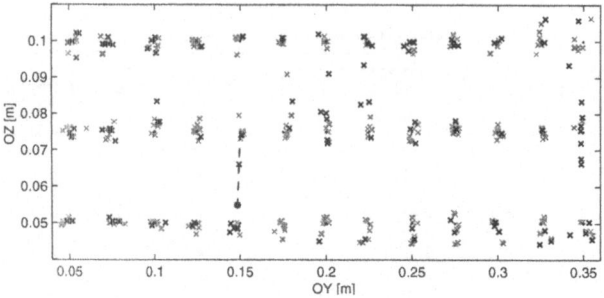

Fig. 2. Results for cascade network of architecture $5 - 7 - 1 \triangleright 6 - 7 - 1 \triangleright 7 - 7 - 1$

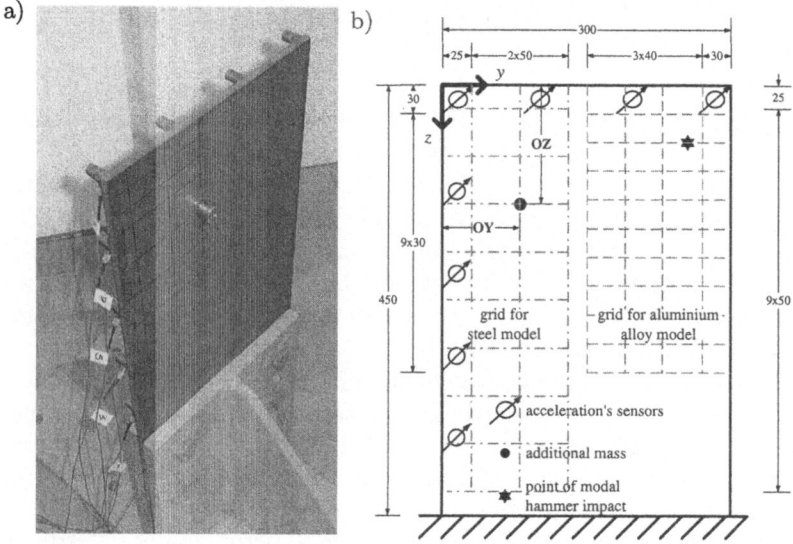

Fig. 3. a) Experimental model of the steel plate, b) Scheme of plates

ture. The locations of sensors and point of impact are shown at Fig. 3. The out-plane vibrations of the plate have been forced with a modal hammer. Therefore, this part of research is not exact continuation of numerical simulations, which were described at item 2 of this paper and concerned in-plane vibrations of plate.

The additional mass, which position has been detected, has had 3% or 8% of plates' masses, respectively for the steel or the aluminium alloy models. The mass has been located in nodes of the measurement grid. The grids for both models are shown at Fig. 3b. The 27 locations of additional mass at steel model have been considered. For aluminium alloy model the grid has been changed. Thus, the vibrations of plate for 40 locations of the additional mass have been measured.

The acceleration signals in time domain have been transformed by means of Fast Fourier Transformation into frequency domain. Obtained frequency cha-

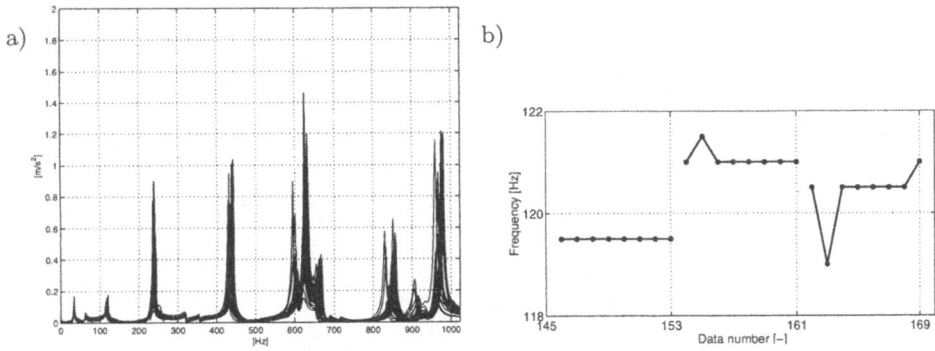

Fig. 4. a) Selected frequency characteristics for the steel plate, b) The fragment of processed band for the steel plate

racteristics have had resolution of $0.25Hz$. Figure 4a) shows selected frequency characteristics for the steel plate.

These characteristics have been analysed in the selected bands. Consequently, within these bands the harmonics with the highest amplitudes have been searched out. Finally, the sets of frequencies of vibration of the plates with additional mass have been obtained.

Then, the inputs vectors for ANN training have been prepared by a process of elimination of measurements with noticeable error. After this, the average frequency in each band for each location of the mass has been calculated. The legitimacy of this process is shown at Fig. 4b), where the frequencies for three consecutive locations of the mass have been grouped together. As one can see, only one or two among eight frequencies (measured by eight sensors) are different. Consequently, for steel plate the [27x7] input data set has been prepared for training of networks used to mass identification.

In case of aluminium alloy plate a number of frequency characteristics has been much higher and has been equal to 1528. The number of 1528 characteristics has been a result of considering of 40 locations of mass, of conducting of measurements with eight sensors and of recording of plate's vibrations for at least three hammer's impacts. These characteristics have been analysed in six selected bands. Finally the [1528x6] set of characteristics has been obtained. In order to prepare input data, averaging of the whole set of frequencies has been performed using neural networks. Six networks of $2 - 10 - 1$ architecture have been built - separately for six bands. These networks have been learnt re-mapping of two coordinates of additional mass to modal frequency within selected band. The examples of measured and averaged frequencies are shown at Fig. 5. Consequently, the [40x6] input data set has been prepared.

Due to a small number of patterns (27 for steel plate and 40 for aluminium alloy plate) it has been decided to calculate additional ones by adding the noise with a normal distribution. The number of patterns have been increased to few hundreds in that way.

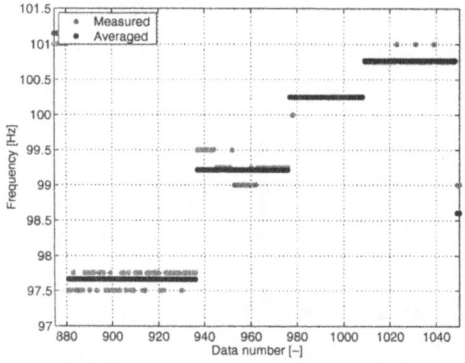

Fig. 5. The fragment of processed band for aluminium alloy plate

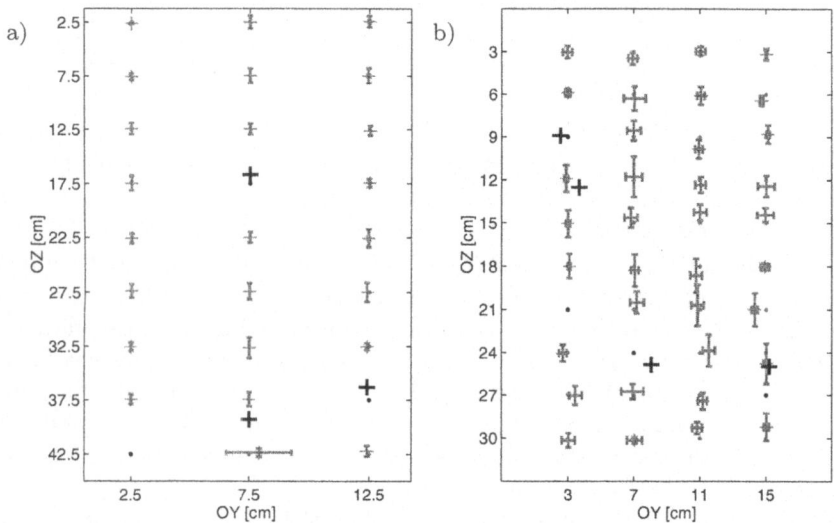

Fig. 6. a) Results of identification of additional mass at steel plate - cascade network $7-5-1 \triangleright 8-5-2$, b) Results of identification of additional mass at aluminium alloy plate - cascade network $6-5-1 \triangleright 6-5-2$

The best accuracy has been obtained from $OY \triangleright OZ$ cascade neural network of architecture $7-5-1 \triangleright 8-5-2$. The results for training (gray coloured marks) and testing sets (black coloured marks) are shown at Fig. 6a). The horizontal and vertical bars are proportional to standard deviation of determination of OY and OZ coordinates, due to noised input vectors.

For aluminium alloy plate, results (Fig. 6b)) have been analogous to this obtained for steel model. Again, the best determination of location of additional mass has been obtained from cascade network.

4   Final Remarks

Some general conclusions can be presented on the basis of the achieved results.

- Neural networks make it possible to use the analysis of the dynamics parameters for detection and assessment of the circular void and additional mass in the cantilever plates
- Application of the cascade networks improves accuracy of neural approximation in all analysed cases.
- The used methods of the preprocessing of time signals and measurement data have proved its usefulness in the preparation of the input vectors for neural networks.

References

1. Waszczyszyn Z., Ziemiański L., Neural Networks in Mechanics of Structures and Materials – New Results and Prospects of Applications in Computers&Structures 79:2261–2276, (2001)
2. Yagawa G., Okuda H., Neural networks in computational mechanics. Archives of Computational Methods in Engineering, (3-4), 435–512, (1996).
3. Piątkowski G., L. Ziemiański. Neural Network Identification of a Circular Hole in the Rectangular Plate, In: L. Rutkowski, J. Kacprzyk, eds., Advances in Soft Computing, Physica–Verlag a Springer–Verlag Company, (2003)
4. Theory and modeling guide, ADINA System Online Manuals, ADINA R&D Inc., Watertown, (2001)
5. Haykin S., Neural Networks: a Comprehensive Foundation, Prentice Hall International, Inc., 2nd ed., (1999)
6. Piątkowski G., Ziemiański L., Identification of Circular Hole in Rectangular Plate Using Neural Networks, Proceedings of AI-Meth Symposium on Methods of Artificial Intelligence, 329–332, (2002)
7. Neural Network Toolbox for Use with Matlab, User's Guide, Version 3.0., The MathWorks, Inc., Natick, MA (1998)

Filtering of Thermomagnetic Data Curve Using Artificial Neural Network and Wavelet Analysis

Łukasz Rauch[1], Jolanta Talar[1], Tomáš Žák[2], and Jan Kusiak[1]

[1] Akademia Górniczo-Hutnicza
Al. Mickiewicza 30, 30-059 Kraków, POLAND
[2] Academy of Science of the Czech Republik
Zizkova 22 CZ-616 62 Brno, CZECH REPUBLIC

Abstract. New methods of filtering of experimental data curves, based on the artificial neural networks and the wavelet analysis are presented in the paper. The thermomagnetic data curves were filtered using these methods. The obtained results were validated using the modified algorithm of the cubic spline approximation.

1 Introduction

Modern magnetic materials are usually produced by a rapid cooling of the alloys characterized by a complex composition. The as-prepared material is usually in an amorphous or microcrystalline form and its optimal properties can be obtained by a specific heat treatment, resulting in irreversible changes of the structure and orientation. Typical example of such materials are nanocrystalline iron- or nickel-based amorphous alloys obtained by various techniques prepared by controlled crystallization. The incorrect technology results not only in inappropriate properties, but also causes the total degradation of the material. The characteristic parameter of magnetic materials which should be optimized is coercivity (the maximum or minimum value is searched) or, in some cases, the saturation of magnetization.

Heat treatment of above-mentioned materials can be characterized by the temperature of the annealing process and by the time for which the elevated temperature is acting. During the treatment process only limited changes in the material structure are admitted. Usually, they include some stress relieve, fine crystalline structure building or precipitation. Localization of critical temperatures and classification of these processes can be done through the analysis of the thermomagnetic curve, which is a graphic representation of a relationship between the magnetic moment and temperature. Such curve can be of complex, usually not smooth shape. At least one steep peak connected with the Curie temperature phenomenon of the material is always present and the sample is no more magnetic above that temperature. This (or these) peaks are the most important in the analysis of a whole thermomagnetic curve. The other minor

L. Rutkowski et al. (Eds.): ICAISC 2004, LNAI 3070, pp. 1093–1098, 2004.
© Springer-Verlag Berlin Heidelberg 2004

peaks, which are often caused by the measurement noise, can be neglected. Therefore, the filtering process of experimental data must be very sensitive. The minor peaks must be eliminated, while the major peaks must be conserved. The common method of the filtering of these data is the analysis of derivatives of the data curve. This can ease the extraction of the important information from the measured data. The differentiation of the curve causes changes of the slopes into evident peaks. The peak position is connected with the critical temperature of the given process and the character of the process can be predicted from the peak width. The secondary effect of the differentiation process is amplification of a noise which is always present in the experimental data. Therefore, before any further processing of a curve, the first step is preprocessing of the data curve, e.i. smoothing (filtering) of data.

The aim of this work is to compare smoothing procedures of the thermomagnetic curves.

2   Artificial Neural Network Approach

The first proposed filtering method is based on the Generalized Regression Neural Network (GRNN) approach. The GRNN method [4] is often used for the approximation of the unknown function. The advantage of the GRNN approach is a simplicity and short training time. Drawback of this technique is a large size of a network and rather high computational costs. The GRNN is based on the estimation of a function of probability density of observed samples. It uses a probabilistic model based on the vector of random independent variable X of dimensions D, and a dependent scalar variable Y. Assuming, that x and y are measured values corresponding the variables X and Y, respectively, and $f(X,Y)$ represents the known joint continuous probability density function and assuming that $f(X,Y)$ is also known, the expected value of Y for a given x (the regression of Y on x) can be evaluated by:

$$E[Y|x] = \frac{\int_{-\infty}^{\infty} Y f(x,Y)dY}{\int_{-\infty}^{\infty} f(x,Y)dY} \tag{1}$$

The experimental measurements of the annealing process and results of two different ANN approaches (ANN(1) and ANN(2)) to the filtering of thermomagnetic curves of these materials are presented. The first one (ANN(1)) is simply filtering of the thermomagnetic curve in the whole range of temperatures. The obtained results are not satisfactory. The smoothing procedure of the given data eliminated some important peaks. Therefore, another approach has been used. The temperature range was divided into several subregions corresponding the temperatures at which important peaks were observed, and which have been eliminated during the ANN(1) preprocessing. Another ANN(2) analysis was done inside these sections. The resulting filtered curves are the effect of joining of individual segments of de-noised by the ANN(2) thermomagnetic data curves.

The ANN had one input - the temperature of material, and one output - the magnetic moment. Different thermomagnetic curves of the following three

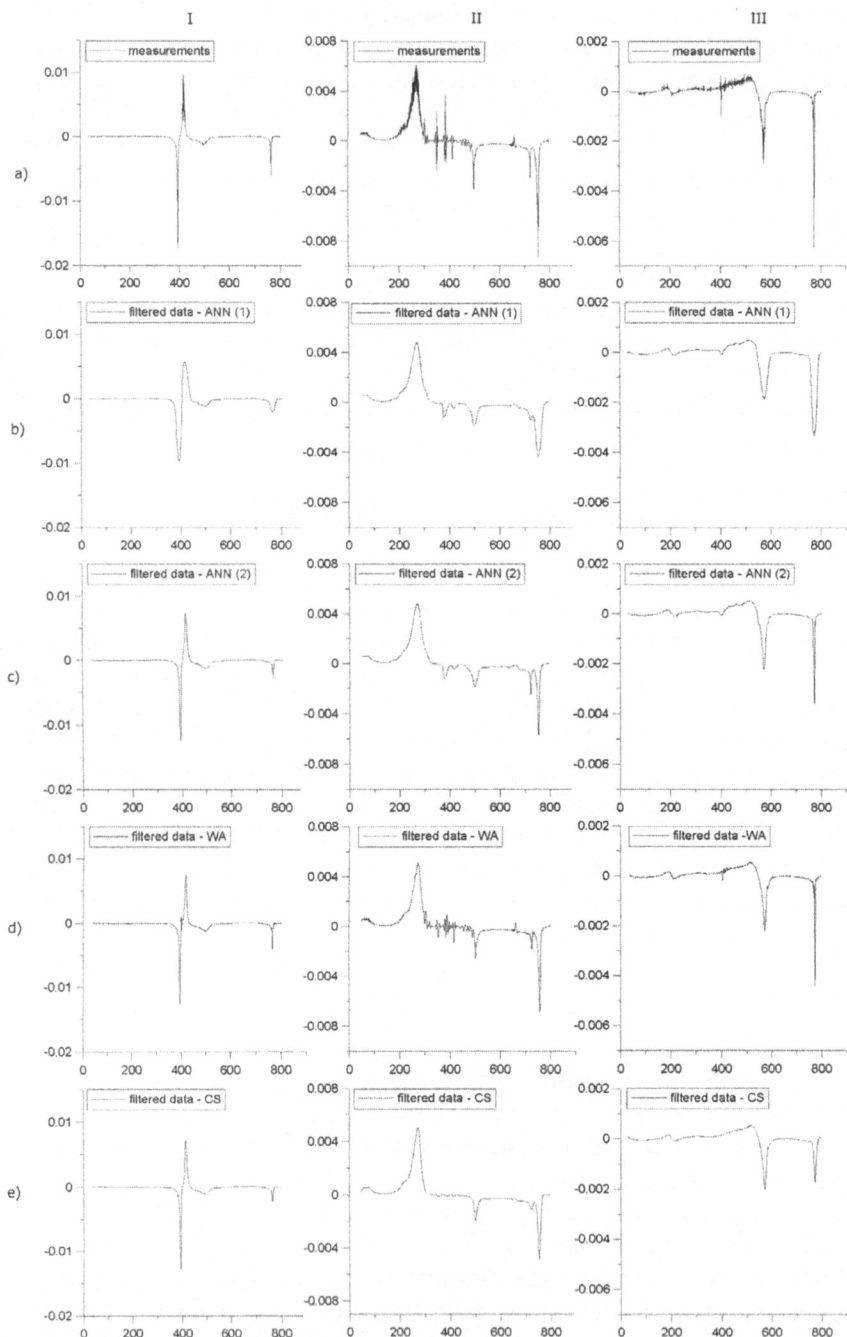

Fig. 1. Filtering of thermomagnetic curves of three different metals (I, II, III). a) - registered data; b),c) - ANN(1) and ANN(2) filtering, respectively; d) - wavelet analysis; e) - filtering by the modified cubic spline approximation

materials were analyzed: tough magnetic material (the Fe-Nd-B base alloy)(I), the $Fe_{80}B_{20}$ alloy (II) and iron with inclusions of carbides and oxides (III). In the ANN(2) approach, the temperature range was divided into 5, 2 and 3 subregions, respectively to analyzed material (I, II or III). The obtained results of both filtering procedures are shown in Figures 1b,c, respectively.

3   Wavelet Analysis

Wavelets are mathematical functions that divide the data into different frequency components and then analyze each component with a resolution matched to its scale. The wavelet analysis is very similar to the traditional Fourier method, but is more effective in analyzing physical situations where the signal contains discontinuities and sharp peaks [5].

It can be distinguished two principal types of wavelet analysis i.e. discrete wavelet transform and continuous wavelet transform. In case of signal de-noising application the approach we are interested in is the discrete wavelet transform (DWT). This solution was developed as an alternative to the short time Fourier transform (STFT). STFT provides uniform time resolution for all frequencies. On the other hand DWT approach provides [6]:

1. high frequency resolution and low time resolution for low frequencies,
2. low frequency resolution and high time resolution for high frequencies.

This is an important feature in the technique used in the performed calculations called *wavelet shrinkage and thresholding method*[7].

The goal of the mentioned above method is to suppress the additive noise $n(t)$ from the signal $s(t)$ to obtain the original de-noised signal $o(t)$, where $s(t) = o(t) + n(t)$. The first stage that should be accomplished is the DWT analysis of $s(t)$. The signal is decomposed into L-level of wavelet transform as follows:

$$s(t) = \sum_{j=1}^{L}\sum_{k} d_j(k)\psi_j(t) + \sum_{k} c_L(k)\varphi_L(t), \tag{2}$$

where $\varphi_L(t)$ is the L-th level scaling function and $\psi_j(t)$ for $j = 1,..,L$ are the wavelet functions for L different levels. The k variable is the domain of the result of these calculations that is the sequence of L wavelet $d_j(k)$ and scaling $c_L(k)$ coefficients. Generally, it is assumed that the lowest level approximation (the highest scale) is the discrete signal at its original resolution ie. $c_0(k) = s(k)$. Following this equation, the relationship between the coefficients at the level j in terms of those at the previous level can be given as:

$$c_{j+1}(k) = \sum_{m} h(m - 2k)c_j(m) \tag{3}$$

$$d_{j+1}(k) = \sum_{m} g(m - 2k)c_j(m) \tag{4}$$

where $g(k)$ and $h(k)$ are highpass and lowpass filters, respectively. For given wavelet system e.g. Haar, Daubechies or Coiflet wavelet families, with known low- and highpass filters. It is a possible to calculate recursively the wavelet coefficients at all given levels. However, the idea of thresholding is to set the proper values of thresholds at each level. Then the coefficients, that are lower than the particular values, are set to zero. New coefficients are used during the inverse wavelet transformation to reconstruct the input signal. The output of the process is de-noised signal that still contains important peaks. The wavelet method was applied to the filtering process of considered three thermomagnetic curves.

Wavelet analysis of thermomagnetic curve was applied using several wavelet families. However, the best results gives the Coiflet family approach, which can be used even if the input curves differ significantly from each other.

One dimensional discrete wavelet analysis with five decomposition levels was performed. The chosen wavelet family is Coiflet with the smooth scaling and the mother wavelet function followed by proper highpass and lowpass filters. All calculations were done using the Matlab v6.5 software.

The results of de-noising process using wavelet analysis for three different data sets are presented in Figure 1d.

4   Validation of Filtering Results

The validation of the obtained results of the ANN and wavelet filtering of the thermomagnetic data curves was performed using the modified algorithm of the cubic spline approximation described in [3]. It allows not only the computation of the value of spline, but also its first and second derivatives in a given point.

The applied modified algorithm of the cubic spline approximation of the function $Y = f(X)$ of the vector of independent variable X consists of the following steps:

1. Computation of the arrays of coefficients A, B, C, and D of the spline function $F(X)$. The spline function $F(X)$ has such form that the sum of squares $(F(X_i) - Y_i^2)$ is not greater than a given parameter S, which controls the smoothing effect.
2. For the given point XX in the i-th interval between X_i and X_{i+1} ($X_i < XX < X_{i+1}$), the corresponding value of the analyzed function is evaluated using the elaborated cubic spline approximation:
$F(XX) = ((D_i * H + C_i) * H + B_i) * H + A_i$
3. The first derivative of the function at the XX point is:
$F\prime(XX) = (3D_i * H + 2C_i) * H + B_i$
where $H = XX - X_I$

The results of the filtering of thermomagnetic data curve using the described modified cubic spline algorithm are presented in Figure 1e. They show the good agreement with results obtained by the ANN and wavelet filtering.

The advantage of the presented algorithm is possibility of direct computation of smoothed derivative of the measured curve. Changing the parameter S allows the control of the smoothing efficiency, which is very important in case of the analysis of such complex curves as the thermomagnetic one, where many narrow peaks of various amplitudes are observed.

5   Conclusions and Remarks

Presented methods of the filtering of experimental data, based on artificial neural networks and the wavelet analysis, appear very efficient in the de-noising problem of the thermomagnetic data curves. It can be seen that obtained filtered signals are very close to their original shapes and the width of the most important peaks seems to be unchanged. Less important parts of the curves were removed during the de-noising procedure. This valuable feature allows the further analysis of the annealing process based on the data smoothed by presented methods.

The filtered curves were validated using the modified cubic spline approximation and obtained results show good agreement of these three techniques. It confirms the usefulness of the two proposed methods (ANN and wavelet techniques) in the field of the de-noising of experimental data. Moreover, the artificial neural network approach and the wavelet analysis can be more precise in complex shapes of the filtered data curves.

The further research will focus on the automatization of the filtering process. The choice of the filtering method should be automatic, depending of the character of registered measurement data.

Acknowledgments. The research were financially supported by the APOMAT, COST526 action.

References

1. Žák, T., Jirásková, Y., Schneeweiss, O., Sólyom, A., Marko, P.: High temperature magnetization of 3.5% Si steel. J. Magn. Magn. Mater. 157/158 (1996) 453–454
2. Žák, T., Havlíček, S., Schneeweiss, O., Vondráček, M.: Mössbauer and magnetic study of mechanical alloying of Fe_3Si. Czech. J. Phys. 47 (1997) 585–588
3. Reinsch, C.H.: NUMER.MAT. 10 (1967), 177-183
4. Specht, D.F.: A General Regression Neural Network, IEEE Transaction on Neural Network, 2, 6, (1997), 568-576.
5. Bialasiewicz, J. T.: Falki i aproksymacje, WNT, Warszawa (2000)
6. He , T. X.: Short Time Fourier Transform, Integral Wavelet Transform, and Wavelet Functions Associated with Splines, Journal of Mathematical Analysis and Applications, 224 (1998) 182–200
7. Chen, Z., Karim, M. A.: Frequency-refined multiresolution decomposition using wavelet splitting, Optics Communications, 173 (2000) 81–94

Evolutionary Negotiation Strategies in Emerging Electricity Markets

Salem Al-Agtash

Yarmouk University, Irbid 21163, Jordan
alagtash@yu.edu.jo

Abstract. This paper presents an evolutionary negotiating agent to conduct negotiation tasks between power generating and consuming companies in electricity markets. The agent select the best negotiation strategy that meets the underlying company objectives and interests. It generates a sequence of improving strategy population as the outcome of a search modeled by the selection, crossover, and mutation genetic operators. Agents use a content specification language based on an extended object model to specify the requirements, constraints, and negotiation strategic rules, which are used by the negotiation server to conduct a negotiation. A design architecture for negotiation is presented with KQML communication primitives. Various software technologies have been used for implementation and tested in a C++ environment.

1   Introduction

Restructuring the electricity industry into an open market has created demands for new software tools to meet future challenges and expanding requirements of competitive power systems. Electricity markets have evolved over the past decade to substitute ever-existing regulated monopolies in the electric utility industry. The basic markets are: the power pool, power exchange auction, and multilateral contracts. The power pool balances power supply and demand based on the supply bids of power generating companies and the forecasted system demand. The power exchange auction solicits bids from power generating and consuming companies, then determines winning bids and market-clearing prices. The multilateral contracts define direct negotiated agreements between supply and demand companies to exchange power at a certain price. A combination of these approaches has generally been implemented to shape different electricity markets. A considerable amount of effort has been devoted to develop optimized bidding strategies in electricity power exchange and power pool markets. The theory of oligopoly in economics has established a basis for shaping these strategies,[5,8,11]. By contrast, very little effort has been made to develop optimized negotiation strategies in the multilateral contract market. Negotiation involves issuing proposal and counterproposal between negotiating parties until a mutual agreement or disagreement is reached. The design of optimized negotiation processes have been based on game theory, genetic algorithms and business negotiation technologies, [9]. In this paper, evolutionary negotiation strategies

L. Rutkowski et al. (Eds.): ICAISC 2004, LNAI 3070, pp. 1099–1104, 2004.
© Springer-Verlag Berlin Heidelberg 2004

are developed within an agent-based electricity market. The negotiating agent generates a sequence of improving strategy population as the outcome of a search modeled by the selection, crossover, and mutation genetic operators. The agent adopts a strategy that maximizes its utility while meeting constraints. Various software technologies were employed to implement the negotiating agents within Visual C++ environment. Implementation work is in progress to build a negotiating agent within a working agent environment.

2 Electricity Negotiation

Negotiation is defined as a process by which a joint decision is made by two or more parties. The parties first verbalize contradictory demands and then move towards agreements,[7]. In electricity markets, the negotiating commodity is electric energy. The negotiating parties are power generating and power-consuming companies (denoted respectively as GenCo and ConCo) and/or energy brokers. The parties communicate through the Internet by utilizing agents to automate the negotiation process, facilitate computational overhead, be able to analyze instantaneously larger stacks of data, and reduce human intervention. An agent is an autonomous software entity, which decides for its underlying negotiating party. It communicates with its peer negotiating agents using a common architecture. Furthermore, negotiating agents are adaptive, responsive to market changes, and apt to learning-by-doing. The architecture of a negotiating agent is shown in Fig. 1. The agent server represents the negotiation activity functions [2,10]: management, directory service, and ACC (Agent Communication Channel). A management component keeps track of connected agents. A directory service keeps record of agents connected to the platform. Finally, ACC implements communication with other agents using knowledge query manipulation language (KQML) standards. The negotiation process is initiated by submitting an initial KQML-wrapped offer to a preference list of peer negotiating agents. The peer agents are identified by the Internet Protocol (IP) addresses of their servers. A server carries out the negotiation process by checking the offer parameters against its user-registered information. The server then consults with the user for decision-making, generates a counter-proposal to be returned to the opponent or sends a KQML-wrapped reply.

3 Negotiation Process

The basic approaches to negotiation are: Game theoretic models, heuristic approaches, and argumentation-based approaches, [4]. Game theoretic models assume that agents are allowed to select the best strategy among all possible strategies, by considering all possible interactions. Heuristic approaches associate with each computation or strategy decision a cost (heuristic value) and thus seeks the negotiation space in a non-exhaustive fashion. The generated strategy involves a linear combination of tactics or deliberative mechanisms. Tactics evaluate the overall utility of the strategy while deliberatives evaluate a trade off value.

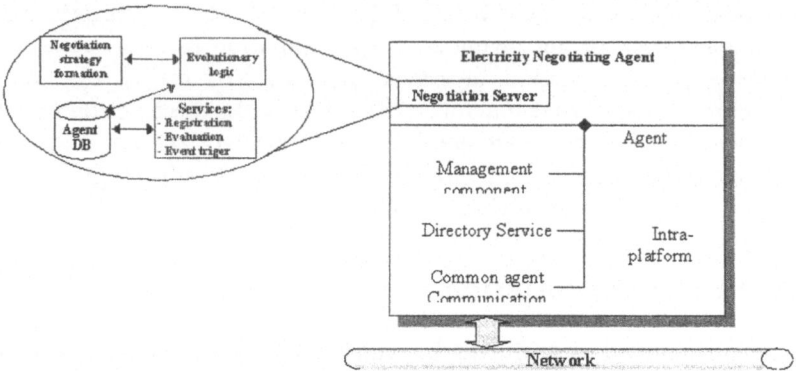

Fig. 1. Negotiating Agent Architecture

Argumentation-based negotiation allows additional information "arguments" to be exchanged over a negotiation strategy. The arguments express the opinion of the agent making the argument being accompanied to the negotiating proposal.

3.1   Tactics and Strategies

Tactics are the set of functions that determine how to compute the value of an issue (price, volume, duration, etc.) with respect to a given criterion. The criterion can be time, or resource. Agents may consider more than one criterion to compute the value of an issue. A weighted combination of the values for different issues and for different criteria will constitute a set of negotiating proposals. Varieties of tactics have been proposed to account for opponent behavior. These include, time-dependent, behavior-dependent and resource dependent, [4]. The aim of the agent negotiation strategy is to determine the best course of action on X that maximizes its scoring function V that defines a profit for GenCo and a benefit for ConCo. An agent receives an offer from an agent opponent. If the offer is unsatisfactory, the agent generates a counter offer. Different combinations of tactics can be used to generate a counter offer. A weighted counter offer $X_{a \to b}^{t+1}[j]$ would then be a linear combination of the tactics given in a matrix $\Gamma_{a \to b}^{t}$ that defines a state of an agent MS containing information about the agent knowledge, resource, attitude, goals, obligations and intentions. The agent counter strategy is then

$$X_{a \to b}^{t_n+1}[j] = (\Gamma_{a \to b}^{t_n+1} * T^a(MS_a^{t_n+1}))[i,j] \tag{1}$$

with $T^a(MS_a^{t_n+1}))[i,j] = (\tau(MS_a^{t_n+1}))[j], \gamma_{ij} \in [0,1]$ and for all issues j $\sum_{i=1}^{m} \gamma_{ji} = 1$ and

$$\Gamma_{a \to b}^{t_n+1} = f(\Gamma_{a \to b}^{t_n}, MS_a^{t_n}) \tag{2}$$

The negotiation model presented in this paper relies on strategies and tactics presented in [6]. A negotiation price issue is considered with a value $X_j \in D_j^a =$

$[\min_j^a, \max_j^a]$. The value of this issue is generated using a tactic based upon a single criterion: time remaining, resource remaining, or the opponent behavior. It is assumed that all ConCos employ the time dependent tactic, while all GenCos employ the behavior dependent tactics.

3.2 Evolutionary Negotiation

A negotiation strategy is encoded as a chromosome with a number of genes. The genes represent the strategy parameters related to the issues and tactics of the strategy. The strategy optimization is based on modeling the process of natural evolution. The problem domain is represented by a set of chromosomes of population N. Each chromosome has a fitness value based on which selection will occur. By applying genetic operators: selection, crossover and mutations, a new population of chromosomes will be generated. Each chromosome (individual) is a string of bits (0 or 1). The individuals of the population are negotiating agent strategies, and their genetic material is defined by the parameters of the negotiating issues and tactics. The bits of the string (the genes) represent the parameters of the agent's negotiation strategy that involves: t_{max}^a: maximum time of negotiation; $D_j^a = [\min_j^a, \max_j^a]$: range of acceptable values. The fitness determines the agent's strategy chance of survival. The greater the fitness, the more likely the strategy is to reproduce. The GenCos and ConCos strategy evaluation is defined by a fitness function $V : X[.] \rightarrow V(X[.])$ such that V defines a profit function for GenCos and a Benefit function for ConCos. Genetic operators include selection, crossover and mutation operators. In the selection process, K individuals are randomly chosen from the population. The individual with the highest fitness among the selected K individuals is placed in the mating pool. This process is repeated m times, where m is the size of the population. During crossover, exchange of genes is implemented. One crossover point within a chromosome is selected randomly, and binary strings are exchanged. Finally, during Mutation, a flip bit mutation operator is chosen. Mutation probability is very low and is usually in a range of 0.02. The algorithm repeats the above genetic operators for each population until convergence is observed or the number of iterations has exceeded a preset number.

4 Implementation

Power GenCo and ConCo implement their negotiation processes within agents. The agents select a negotiation strategy using genetic evolutions. The agents use KQML as a standard for communication, [3]. KQML provides agents with a means of exchanging information and knowledge over the network using a lower-level TCP/IP protocol. KQML is message-oriented and content independent. The main focus of KQML is on an expandable set of performatives that define the permissible operations that the agent may attempt on each other's knowledge and goal shares. The basic sets include: Informative: Tell, Deny, Untell - Database: Insert, Delete, delete-one, Delete-all - Responses: Error, Sorry - Query: Evaluate, Reply, Ask-if, Ask-about, ask-one, ask-all, sorry - Multi-response query:

Stream-about, Stream-all, eos (end of stream) - Effector: Achieve, Unachieve - Generator: Stand-by, ready, next, Rest, Discard - Capability-definition: Advertise - Notification: Subscribe, Monitor - Networking: Register, Unregister, Forward, Broadcast, Pipe, Break, Transport-address - Facilitation: Broker-one, Broker-all, Recommend-one, Recommend-all. Various software technologies were employed to implement the negotiating agents within the Visual C++ environment. These include remote database access via ActiveX Data Objects (ADO), the Winsock library for network communications, the component object model (COM), Win32 multithreading interface. The negotiation module is a component of this agent. Its main task is to negotiate, strategically, on behalf of its respective agent. Negotiation is achieved through inter-process communication. A shared-memory segment is used to exchange control and operational information between the negotiation module and the agent's other modules. Access synchronization for this internal data sharing is implemented using semaphores in order to avoid race conditions, and hence, avoid deadlocks. The negotiation server sleeps on negotiation signals during idle negotiation intervals. The agent sends a wakeup signal to awaken its respective server before sending any request. Synchronized access to the database by multiple instances of the negotiation server is achieved by native database locks, which guarantee consistency and deadlock free operation.

5   Preliminary Numerical Testing

A generic 2-GenCo and 1-ConCo connected by a 3-bus system is used for illustration, [1]. A negotiation process is simulated for one time shot. GenCo 1 has a marginal cost function equal to $35+0.2g1$ \$/MWh and 5-100 MW min-max values. GenCo 2 has a marginal cost function equal to $10+0.1g2$ \$/MWh and 25-500 MW min-max values. ConCo has demand curve equal to160-0.4d \$/MWh and 150-350 MW min-max values. ConCo is assumed to negotiate a contract of fixed 50 MW for 6-month time period. Each GenCo and ConCo has been assigned a negotiating agent. The agent system has been simulated on a Quad-Pentium HP NetServer 6000. GenCos implement behavior dependent tactics and ConCo implements a time dependent tactic. A fitness function of ConCo and GenCo is used as $V(x) = Q * X - A$, $V(X) = Q * X + A$; where Q and A define quantity and cost. Negotiation is assumed on the price issue. GenCos receive a request for negotiation from ConCo. ConCo receives a reply and initiates two threads each handling a separate negotiation process with each GenCo. The agents implement an evolutionary negotiation process as presented above. Selection, mating, crossover, mutation and reproduction operators collectively generate new population of strategies and the process continues until convergence is observed. This is repeated for each negotiation round and on each negotiating agent. The value of the price issue is computed and associated fitness is evaluated. GenCo agents search for strategies that give the maximum fitness, i.e. profit, while ConCo search for strategies that give the maximum benefit value. The negotiation framework is set time bounded to 5 rounds. The ConCo reached price is 50 \$/MWh, while

GenCo 1 reached price is 66.0 \$/MWh and GenCo 2 reached price is 50.6 \$MWh. ConCo terminated the negotiation with GenCo after 2 rounds.

6   Conclusion

An evolutionary negotiation strategy for electricity has been presented within the context of an agent-based electricity market. The agent generates a sequence of improving strategy population as the outcome of a search method modeled by the selection, crossover, and mutation genetic operators. The agent adopts a strategy that maximizes its utility while meeting contract constraints. In such a market environment there are a number of challenges to developing a working agent based electricity system. These include real-time limitations, power availability, fault tolerance, and operational safety.

References

1. S. Al-Agtash, N. Al-Fayoumi, "A Software Architecture for Modeling Competitive Power Systems", Proceedings of the IEEE PES Winter Meeting, **3**(2000) 1674–1679.
2. K. Barber, T. Liu, D. Han, "Agent-Oriented Design", Multi-Agent System Engineering: Proceeding of the 9th European Workshop on Modeling Autonomous Agents in a Multi-Agent World, Valencia, Spain; Lecture Notes in Artificial Intelligence, Garijo &Boman, Springer, (1999) 28–40.
3. T. Finin, Y. Labrou, J. Mayfield, "KQML as an Agent Communication Language," Software Agents, J.M. Bradshaw, ed., MIT Press, (1997) 291–316.
4. N. Jennings, P. Faratin, A. Lomuscio, S. Parsons, C. Sierra, and M. Wooldridge, "Automated Negotiation: Prospects, Methods and Challenges", To appear in the International Journal of Group Decision and Negotiation, (2003).
5. J. Lamont, S. Rajan, "Strategic Bidding in an Energy Brokerage", IEEE Trans. on Power Systems, **12** (1997) 1729–1733.
6. N. Matos, C. Sierra, N. Jennings, "Determining Successful Negotiation Strategies: An Evolutionary Approach", To appear in the International Journal of Group Decision and Negotiation, (2003).
7. D. G. Pruitt, Negotiation Behavior, Academic Press, (1981).
8. C. Richter, G. Sheble, D. Ashlock, "Comprehensive Bidding Strategies with Genetic Programming/ Finite State Automata", IEEE Trans. On Power Systems, **14** (1999), 1207–1212.
9. J. Oliver, "A Machine Learning Approach to Automated Negotiation and Prospects for Electronic Commerce", Journal of Management Information Systems, **13** 83–112; [online]: Available:http://opim.wharton.upenn.edu/ oliver27/papers/jmis.ps
10. Y. Tahara, A. Ohsuga, S. Honiden, "Agent System Development Patterns", In the International Conference on Software Engineering, (ACM 1999) 356–367,.
11. C. Yeung, A. Poon, F. Wu, "Game Theoretical Multi-Agent Modeling of Coalition Formation for Multilateral Trades", IEEE Trans. on Power Systems, **14** (1999) 929–934.

Evolutionary Algorithm for Scheduling of CHP Plant with Urban Heat Distribution Network

Krzysztof Dziedzicki[1], Andrzej Augusiak[2], and Roman Śmierzchalski[1]

[1] Gdynia Maritime University, Faculty of Marine Electrical Engineering,
Morska 83, 81 - 225 Gdynia, Poland,
[2] Gdansk University of Technology, Faculty of Electrical and Control Engineering,
Gabriela Narutowicza 11/12, 80 - 952 Gdańsk, Poland

Abstract. The article discusses a problem of time scheduling by evolutionary algorithm of combined heat and electric power production (CHP - Combined Heat and Power)in urban heat distribution network, aimed at securing maximum profit during a given time period. The developed time schedule takes into account the dynamics of the power station. The formulated model allows simulations of power plant's co-operation with the heat distribution network and the heat collection tank.

1 A Concept of the Combined Power and Heat Generating Plant Model

In formulating the model of the electric power station a structure commonly used in the literature was applied [2, 3, 4, 6]. The effect of an urban heat distribution (DH) network was taken into account. The adopted model takes also into account the dynamical nature of the objects. A block diagram of the model is given in figure 1 below.

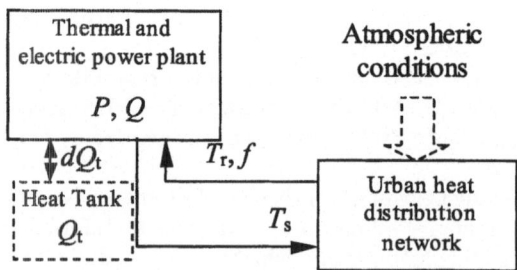

Fig. 1. Block diagram of thermal and electric power station co-operating with urban heat distribution network

The attempted goal is to arrive at a time schedule of production of the electric power $P_{wy}(t)$ and heat $Q_{wy}(t)$ securing maximum profit.

L. Rutkowski et al. (Eds.): ICAISC 2004, LNAI 3070, pp. 1105–1110, 2004.
© Springer-Verlag Berlin Heidelberg 2004

The modelled thermal and electric power station consists of one mixed extraction and counter-pressure turbine unit. Zero steam flux from turbine extraction points was assumed. The modelled unit allows additional steam condensing work. Basic equations of the model make it possible to determine fuel consumption and self load at each time step (DT) of the developed time schedule. The dynamics of the thermal and electric power generating plant is described by equations limiting production change at a time-step. The modelled electric power station can work within the region limited by the equations:

$$
\begin{aligned}
Q(t) &\geq Q_{min} \\
P(t) &\leq c_0 + c_1 \cdot Q(t) \\
P(t) - P_{doc} &= d_0 + d_1 \cdot Q(t) \\
P_{doc} &= (P(t) - (d_0 + d_1 \cdot Q(t))) \cdot X(t)
\end{aligned}
\tag{1}
$$

where: Q_{min} minimum heat production, $c_0..c_1$ coefficients in a relation determining maximum boiler output capacity, $d_0..d_1$ parameters in an equation modelling the work in cogeneration. The sum of the heat produced and taken from the tank makes the output heat:

$$
Q_{wy}(t) = Q(t) + dQ_T(t) \cdot \Delta T
\tag{2}
$$

where: $dQT(t) < 0$ means the heat collected in the tank while $dQT(t) > 0$ the heat taken from the tank. Modular structure of district network system model was used.

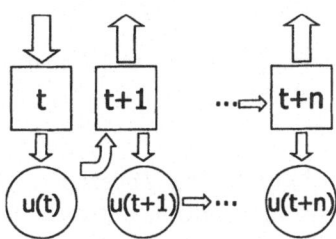

Fig. 2. Modular structure of district heating system model

One time step prognosis is worked out using statistic Box-Jenkins structure described below:

$$
A\left(q^{-1}\right) \cdot y[t] = B\left(q^{-1}\right) \cdot u[t]
\tag{3}
$$

The adopted structure takes into account the dynamics of the heat distribution network. Model can simulate the response (T_r, f) of DH network for known input function (T_s). Mutual relations between the producer and MSC are ruled by the equation:

$$
P_{rz}(t) = k_r(t) \cdot P(t) = (g_0 \cdot f + g_1 \cdot T_r'(t) + g_2) \cdot P(t)
\tag{4}
$$

where: $T'_r(t)$ average temperature of the return water at the examined optimization step, $P_{rz}(t)$ power produced by the thermal and electric power station after taking into account the effects of changing flow rate and temperature of the return water. Finally, the target function has taken a form:

$$max \sum_T \Big(Q_{wy}(t) \cdot c_q(t) + (P_{rz}(t) - P_w(t)) \cdot c_e(t) - B(t) \cdot c_b(t) \Big) \qquad (5)$$

The formulated model also included constraints connected with the work of the urban heat distribution network, such as minimum and maximum supply water temperatures, etc. Supply water temperature at begin and end of given time horizon has to be at similar level. Heat which is collected in the tank after optimization horizon must have positive value.

2   A Concept of the Solution to the Optimization Problem

A detailed description of the presented model of the urban heat distribution network and performed tests is given in [12]. The obtained results seem to stress the necessity of complementing the applied model by water flow prognoses. This requires the use of weather forecasts [5]. For this purpose a co-operation was developed with the Interdisciplinary Centre of Mathematical and Computer Modelling in Warsaw, from which numerical weather forecasts were obtained. The forecast network includes 25 points within the territory of Gdańsk and its surroundings. The forecast is prepared at midnight of each day for the next 48 hours with a one-hour step. At each point the following weather parameters are forecasted:

- temperatures at the ground level and at 1.5 meter above ground,
- strength and direction of wind,
- cloudiness at 4 levels.

This gives a huge volume of input data. Together with the variables describing the state of the urban heat distribution network, the number of parameters exceeds two hundred. In this context, of great importance is proper selection of parameters for the model. Genetic algorithms can turn out useful in this case.

The formulated mathematical model describing the co-operation of the electric power plant with the urban heat distribution network is of an integer-number (the task of production distribution into particular units) and non-linear nature (the model of an individual production unit). A specialised evolutionary algorithm may turn out a useful tool for solving the problem. Since the formulated problem includes numerous constraints, and, what is more, the constraints for permissible level of electric power production are connected with the level of heat production, a special generator of the initial population had to be prepared. A sample graphic schedule drawn with its aid is shown in Fig. 3a, while Fig. 3b presents constraints imposed on particular variables describing the individual; from Fig. 3a. When drawing a population, constraints resulting from the co-operation with the urban heat distribution network are not checked.

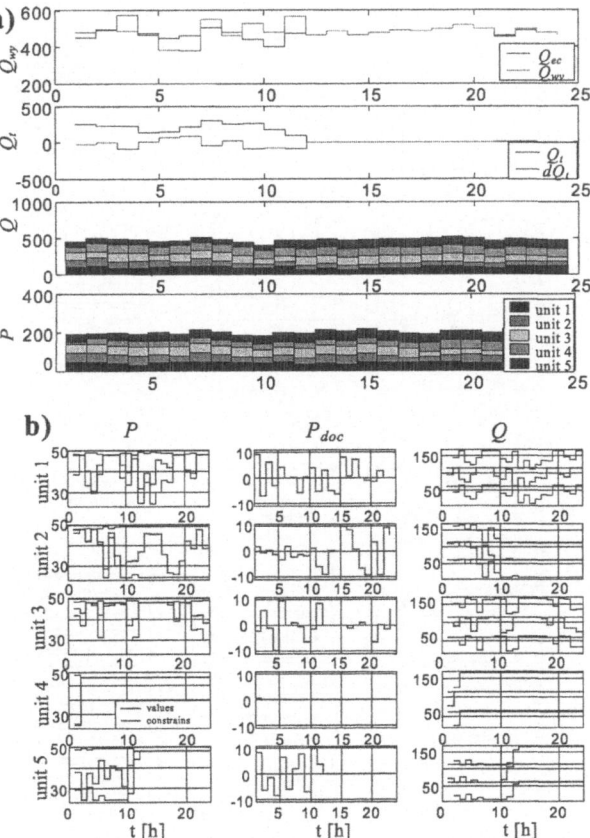

Fig. 3. A sample production schedule drawn by the initial population generator a) heat flow in the tank, and thermal and electric power production, in distribution into particular units; b) technological and dynamical constraints of the electric power plant

The use of standard genetic operators seems aimless for the same reasons for which a specialised generator of initial population had to be developed. Considered is the use of a series of specialised operators adapted to the specific character of the examined problem.

Crossing can be executed as the exchange of the entire (or parts of) schedules of operation of particular production units and the heat collection tank. Four mutation operators are planned to change particular parameters of the schedule under development. The first operator changes the state of the unit: operation/stop. Switching is executed in a number of steps with some probability of finalisation (figure 4a).

In case the production unit is started its production level is drawn. The second operator executes random change of the heat production level, and corresponding electric power production level (figure 4b).

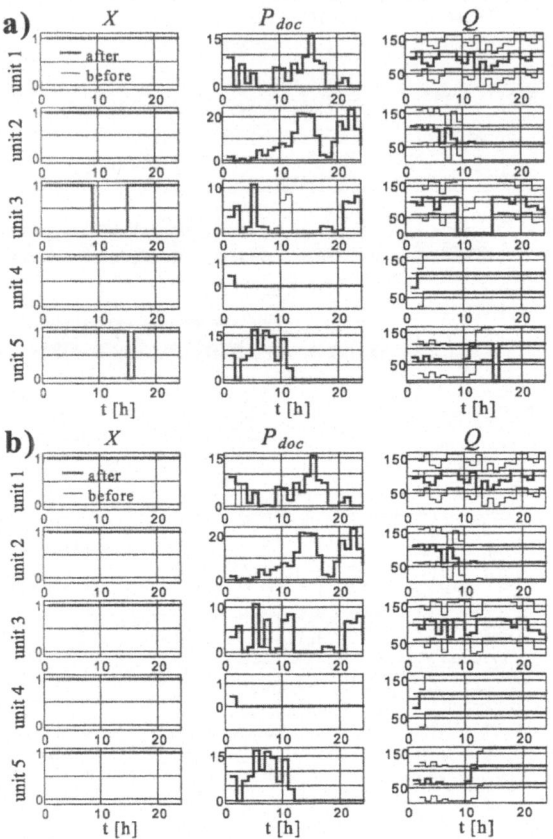

Fig. 4. Effect of action of the proposed mutation operators : a) changing state: operation/stop; b) changing production level

The next operator changes power production level in a pseudo-condenser load, while the last of the proposed operators would cause change of flows in the heat collection tank. Because of their optional nature, any operators changing the production schedule of the heat collection tank should be formulated as separate functions. Procedures which select cutting points of the exchanged sub-sequences of the production schedules during crossing should be constructed in such a way that the action of the operator does not result in breaking constraints of operation of the thermal and electric power plant. The same requirements are formulated for drawing procedures in the proposed mutation operators.

Securing fulfilment of the constraints imposed onto the state of the urban heat distribution network at the level of genetic operators seems pointless due to high cost connected with this action. In this context, the target function formula was complemented by an exponential penalty function, depending on a "distance" from the constraint.

3   Conclusions

he performed tests seem to indicate that the global approach, including the co-operation of the thermal and electric power plant with the urban heat distribution network may be profitable. Taking into account the dynamics of the urban heat distribution network is likely to allow to gain additional profits. It is also advisable to take into account postulates of minimisation of switches between particular units as well as the minimisation of production level fluctuations in an individual production units. Thus the problem is becoming a multi-criterion optimisation task.

References

1. Kardaś D.: Measurements and thermodynamic analysis in unit 5 of CHP plant Gdańsk (in polish). manuscript
2. Dotzauer E.: Algorithm for Short-Term Production-Planning of Cogeneration Plants. manuscript
3. Fu Lin a, Jiang Yi: Optimal operation of a CHP plant for space heating as a peak load regulating plant Energy 25 (2000)
4. Zhao H., Holst J., Arvastson L.: Optimal operation of coproduction with storage. Energy. 10 (1998)
5. Dziedzicki K.: Simulating models of district heating systems for CHP optimisation (in polish). manuscript
6. Dotzauer E.: An Introduction to Short-Term Scheduling of Power and Cogeneration Systems. manuscript.
7. Few P.C., Smitch M.A., Twidell J.W.: Modelling of a combined heat and power (CHP) plant incorporating a heat pump for domestic use. Energy. 7 (1997) Vol. 22 651–659
8. Larsen H.V., Pálsson H., Ravn H.F.: Probabilistic production simulation including combined heat and power plants. Electric Power Systems Research. 48 (1998) 45–56
9. Kodogiannis K.V., Anagnostakis E.M.: A study of advanced learning algorithms for short-term load forecasting. Engineering Applications of Artificial Intelligence. 12 (1999) 159–173
10. Ho S.L., Xie M., Goh T.N.: A comparative study of neural network and Box-Jenkins ARIMA modeling in time series prediction. Computers & Industrial Engineering, 42 (2002) 371–375.
11. Dziedzicki K, Augusiak A., Śmierzchalski R.: A model of combined heat and power generating plant with urban heat distribution network for production scheduling. 9th International Conference MMAR; Międzyzdroje (2003)
12. Michalewicz Z.: Michalewicz, Genetic algorithms+data structures=evolution programs, Warszawa WNT 1996.

Semi-mechanistic Models for State-Estimation – Soft Sensor for Polymer Melt Index Prediction

Balazs Feil[1], Janos Abonyi[1], Peter Pach[1], Sandor Nemeth[1], Peter Arva[1], Miklos Nemeth[2], and Gabor Nagy[2]

[1] University of Veszprem, Department of Process Engineering,
P.O. Box 158, H-8201, Hungary
http://www.fmt.vein.hu/softcomp, abonyij@fmt.vein.hu
[2] Tiszai Vegyi Kombinát Ltd. Tiszaujvaros, P.O. Box 20, H-3581, Hungary

Abstract. Nonlinear state estimation is a useful approach to the monitoring of industrial (polymerization) processes. This paper investigates how this approach can be followed to the development of a soft sensor of the product quality (melt index). The bottleneck of the successful application of advanced state estimation algorithms is the identification of models that can accurately describe the process. This paper presents a semi-mechanistic modeling approach where neural networks describe the unknown phenomena of the system that cannot be formulated by prior knowledge based differential equations. Since in the presented semi-mechanistic model structure the neural network is a part of a nonlinear algebraic-differential equation set, there are no available direct input-output data to train the weights of the network. To handle this problem in this paper a simple, yet practically useful spline-smoothing based technique has been used. The results show that the developed semi-mechanistic model can be efficiently used for on-line state estimation.

1 Introduction

Process monitoring based on multivariate statistical analysis, neural networks and advanced state-estimation tools has recently been investigated by a number of researchers, and widely applied in polymer industry. This is not surprising. Formulated products (plastics, polymer composites) are generally produced from many ingredients, and large number of the interactions between the components and the processing conditions all have the effect on the final product quality. If these effects are detected, significant economic benefits can be realized. The major aims of monitoring plant performance are the reduction of off-specification production, the identification of important process disturbances and the early warning of process malfunctions or plant faults. Furthermore, when a reliable model is available that is able **to estimate the quality of the product**, it can be inverted to obtain the suitable operating conditions required for achieving the target product quality. The above considerations lead the foundation of the "Optimization of Operating Processes" project of the VIKKK Research Center at the University of Veszprem supported by the largest Hungarian polymer production company (TVK Ltd.). The aim of the this paper is to present how neural-networks can be used as soft sensor, and how the neural-network part of the developed semi-mechanistic model can be identified based on a spline-smoothing approach.

L. Rutkowski et al. (Eds.): ICAISC 2004, LNAI 3070, pp. 1111–1117, 2004.
© Springer-Verlag Berlin Heidelberg 2004

Advanced process control and monitoring algorithms are based on state variables which are not always measurable or they are measured off-line. Hence, for the effective application of these tools there is a need for state estimation algorithms that are based on the model of the monitored and/or controlled process. In the presence of additive white Gaussian noise Kalman filter provides optimal (in the sense of maximum likelihood) estimates of the states of a linear dynamical system. For nonlinear processes Extended Kalman Filtering (EKF) should be used. The model of EKF can be a *first-principle model* formulated by a set of nonlinear differential equations or *black-box model*, e.g. a neural network (NN).

Sometimes it is advantageous to combine these modeling approaches. E.g. Psichogios et. al. [2] applied so-called hybrid models that combines a first-principle model with a NN model which serves as an estimator of unmeasured process parameters that are difficult to model from first-principles. Since this seminar paper, many industrial applications of these semi-mechanistic models have been reported, and it has been proofed that this kind of models has better properties than stand-alone NN applications, e.g. in the pyrolysis of ethane [3], in industrial polymerization [4], and or bioprocess optimization [5]. The aim of this paper is the examination of the applicability of semi-mechanistic models in industrial environment, namely how this model structure can be identified and applied for state estimation.

2   Problem Description

The proposed approach is applied to the modeling and monitoring of a medium- and high-density polyethylene plant. The polymerization unit is controlled by a Honeywell Distributed Control System. Measurements are available in every 15 seconds on process variables which consist of input and output variables: $u_{k,(1,...,8)}$ the comonomer, the monomer, the solvent and the chain transfer agent inlet flowrate and temperature, $u_{k,9}$ polymer production rate, $u_{k,10}$ the flowrate of the catalyzator, $u_{k,(11,...,13)}$ cooling water flowrate, inlet and outlet temperature. The product quality y_k is determined by off-line laboratory analysis after drying the polymer that causes one hour time-delay. The interval between the product samples is between half and five hours. Since, it would be useful to know if the product is good before testing it, the monitoring of the process would help in the early detection of poor-quality product. This paper focuses on the melt index prediction. MI depends on the state variables which describe the behavior of the dynamic system, so for the development of a soft-sensor it is necessary to estimate these variables.

The state variables are $x_{k,(1,2)}$ the mass of the fluid and the polymer in the reactor, $x_{k,(3,...,6)}$ the chain transfer agent, monomer, comonomer and catalyst concentration in the loop reactor and $x_{k,7}$ reactor temperature. Measurements are available on the chain transfer agent, monomer and comonomer concentration, reactor temperature and the density of the slurry in the reactor (which is connected with the mass of the fluid and the polymer in the reactor). There are additional state variables which must be identified: $x_{k,(8,...,10)}$ the reaction rate coefficients, because they are not known precisely. The concentration of the comonomer in the instantly formulated polyethylene is $x_{k,11}$, and the melt index is also can be seen as a state variable $x_{k,12}$.

3   Semi-mechanistic Model of the Polimerization Unit

Generally, models used in the state estimation of process systems are formulated by macroscopic balance equations, for instance, mass or energy balances. In general, not all of the terms in these equation are exactly or even partially known. In semi-mechanistic modeling black-box models, like neural networks are used to represent the otherwise difficult-to-obtain parts of the model. Usually, in the modeling phase it turns out which parts of the first principles model are easier and which are more laborious to obtain and often we can get the following hybrid model structure:

$$\mathbf{x}_{k+1} = f(\mathbf{x}_k, \mathbf{u}_k, \mathbf{v}_k, \mathbf{f}_{NN}(\mathbf{x}_k, \mathbf{u}_k), \theta), \quad \mathbf{y}_k = g(\mathbf{x}_k, \mathbf{w}_k), \tag{1}$$

where $\mathbf{x}_k, \mathbf{y}_k$ and $\mathbf{u}_k$ represents the states, the outputs and the inputs of the system, $\mathbf{v}_k$ and $\mathbf{w}_k$ are noise variables. The $\mathbf{f}_{NN} = [f_{NN,1}, \ldots, f_{NN,n}]^T$ represents the black-box elements of the model (neural networks) and θ the parameter set of $\mathbf{f}_{NN}$ represented by feedforward multi-input single-output neural networks with one hidden layer and one output neuron: $f_{NN,i}(\mathbf{z}, \theta) = \mathbf{w}_2 \tanh(\mathbf{W}_1 \mathbf{z} + \mathbf{b}_1) + b_2$ where nn represents the number of hidden neurons, $\mathbf{z} = [z_1, \ldots, z_{ni}]^T$ is the input of network $(ni \times 1)$, $\mathbf{W}_1$ is the weight of hidden layer $(nn \times ni)$, $\mathbf{b}_1$ is the bias of hidden layer $(nn \times 1)$, $\mathbf{w}_2$ is the weight of output layer $(1 \times nn)$, b_2 is the bias of output layer (1×1), so the θ denotes the set of parameters: $\theta = \{\mathbf{W}_1, \mathbf{w}_2, \mathbf{b}_1, b_2\}$.

The melt index of the instantly produced polyethylene is mainly depend on the current ethylene concentration in the loop reactor (x_4), the reactor temperature (x_7) and the concentration of the hexene in the instantly formulated polyethylene (x_{11}). These three variables and the other state variables can be calculated by a nonlinear state estimation algorithm based on the first-principle model of the system (see *FP1* in Figure 1). The *BB1* box contains a black-box in which a neural network calculates the melt index of the instantaneously produced polyethylene $(\mathbf{f}_{NN})$. Since the produced polyethylene which leaves the reactor is the mixture of the previously produced products, the evolving MI can be calculated by the first-principle model of the mixing (see *FP2* in Figure 1):

$$\frac{dx_{12}^\xi}{dt} = \frac{1}{x_2} \left(R f_{NN}^\xi (x_4, x_7, x_{11}) - F_{out} \, x_{12}^\xi - x_{12}^\xi \frac{dx_2}{dt} \right) \tag{2}$$

where $R = (x_8 x_3 x_1 x_6 x_2 + x_9 x_4 x_1 x_6 x_2 + x_{10} x_5 x_1 x_6 x_2)$ represents the instantaneously produced mass of the polyethylene, F_{out} is the polymer mass leaving the reactor, and $\xi = -0.294$ is an empirical coefficient.

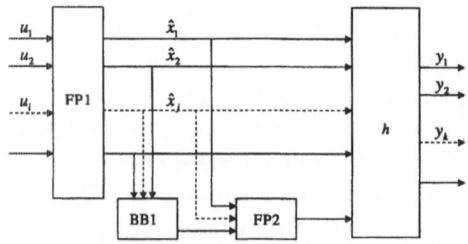

Fig. 1. The semi-mechanistic model of the system

4   Spline-Smoothing Based Identification of Neural Networks

To train the NN parts of the previously presented semi-mechanistic process model, pairs of input/output data should be used to determine the θ parameter set (weights of the NN) in such way that the sum of the squared deviations, $\mathbf{V}_N = \frac{1}{2N} \sum_{k=1}^{N} (y_k - \widetilde{y}_k)^2$ between the predicted output of network and the corresponding training data becomes minimal. The usual way to minimize $\mathbf{V}_N$ is to use gradient procedures, like Gauss-Newton algorithm. Weights in the i-th step of this iterative process are changed in the direction of gradient.

$$\theta^{i+1} = \theta^i - \mu \mathbf{R}_i^{-1} \mathbf{V}_N' \tag{3}$$

where $\mathbf{R}_i = \frac{1}{N} \sum_{k=1}^{N} \mathbf{j}_{k,\theta} \mathbf{j}_{k,\theta}^T$, $\mathbf{V}_N' = -\frac{1}{N} \sum_{k=1}^{N} (\mathbf{y}_k - \widetilde{\mathbf{y}}_k) \mathbf{j}_{k,\theta}, \mathbf{j}_{k,\theta} = \frac{\partial y_{k,\theta}}{\partial \theta} = \frac{\partial g_k}{\partial \mathbf{x}} \frac{\partial \mathbf{x}_{k,\theta}}{\partial \theta}$.

The key problem of the application of this approach is the determination of $\partial \mathbf{x}/\partial \theta$, because in semi-mechanistic models the NN's output does not appear explicitly in the above expression as it is part of the differential equation system. In this case NN can be trained by the integration of the sensitivity equations, using a Nonlinear Programming Technique, using Extended Kalman Filter for state and parameter estimation, or by using a spline-smoothing approach [5].

In this paper the Hermite spine-smoothing method (presented in the appendix) has been applied to interpolate between the measured data (shown in Figure 2) and estimate the corresponding derivatives in the rearranged (2) to obtain the desired outputs of the neural network:

$$\mathbf{f}_{NN}(x_4, x_7, x_{11}) = \left(\frac{1}{R} \left(x_2 \frac{dx_{12}^{\xi}}{dt} + F_{out}\, x_{12}^{\xi} + x_{12}^{\xi} \frac{dx_2}{dt} \right) \right)^{1/\xi} \tag{4}$$

In the applied cubic splines, which are piecewise third-order polynomials, the polynomials are defined such that their values and first derivatives are continuous at so-called knots where the individual polynomials are interconnected. When such splines are iden-

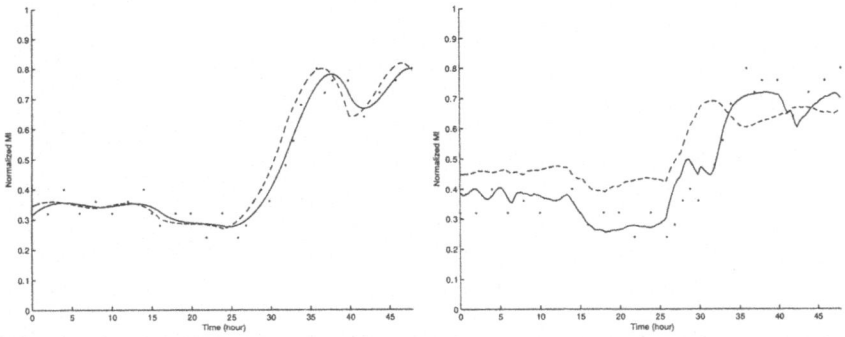

Fig. 2. (left) Spline-interpolation of MI (solid line) and current MI (dashed line), (right) Comparison the NN (solid line) and linear model (dashed line)

tified, a continuous function is fitted to the available measured data, $\mathbf{x} = [x_1, \ldots, x_n]^T$ given at time instants $\mathbf{t} = [t_1, \ldots, t_n]^T$ (see Figure 2).

5 Application in Real-Time State-Estimation

For the identification of the neural network four data set that include the same product transition has been used. Each data set contains 80 hours of operation in which the product change starts around the 50th hour. Among the four data sets three were used for the training of the semi-mechanistic model and the other one for the validation. The Levenberg-Marquardt algorithm was used for training the NN. The number of the hidden neurons, $nn = 4$, was estimated by applying the four cross-validation method. The results were compared with the results of a linear model identified based on the same datasets. The difference between the simple estimation performances of the linear and neural models can be seen on the right side of Figure 2.

The identified hybrid model was used in nonlinear state estimation. The Extended Kalman Filter is based on Taylor linearization of the state transition and output model equations. Instead of this solution, a more advanced state-estimation tool, the DD1 filter, has been used that is based on approximations of the model equations with a multivariable extension of Stirling's interpolation formula. This filter is simple to implement as no derivatives of the model equations are needed, yet it provides excellent accuracy [8]. For the feedback of the filter the $\mathbf{y}_k$ outputs of the system were chosen variables that are measured connected to the reactor and the product. Measurements are available on $y_{k,1}$ chain transfer agent, $y_{k,2}$ monomer and $y_{k,3}$ comonomer concentration in every 8 minutes, $y_{k,4}$ reactor temperature and $y_{k,5}$ density of the slurry in the reactor (which is connected with the mass of the fluid and the polymer in the reactor) in every 15 seconds. Measurements of $y_{k,6}$ melt index was mentioned above. As Figure 3 shows, the resulted soft-sensor gives an excellent performance.

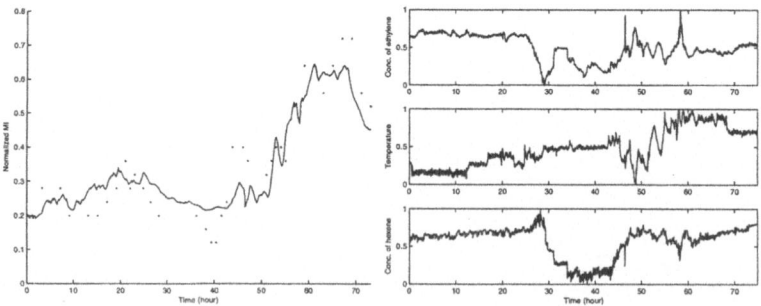

Fig. 3. (left) Estimated MI given by the DD1 algorithm, (right) Estimated state variables used by the $\mathbf{f}_{NN}$ model.

6 Conclusions

Neural networks are widely applied for the design of soft-sensors, e.g. successful applications to bioreactor state estimation and lysine production can be found in [6,7]. In this paper a new method based on semi-mechanistic modeling and nonlinear-state estimation was proposed to estimate the product quality of a polyethylene plant.

For the identification of a neural network a spline-smoothing approach has been followed, where splines have been used to extract the desired outputs of the neural network from infrequent and noisy measurements. The results showed that the proposed method is an efficient and useful tool for state and product quality estimation.

References

1. M. L. Thompson, M. A. Kramer, Modeling Chemical Processes using Prior Knowledge and Neural Networks, AIChE Journal (1994), Vol. 40, No. 8., 1328–1340.
2. D. C. Psichogios, L. H. Ungar, A Hybrid Neural Network-First Principles Approach to Process Modeling, AIChE Journal (1992), Vol. 38, No. 10., 1498–1511.
3. H.-J. Zander, R. Dittmeyer, J. Wagenhuber, Dynamic Modeling of Chemical Reaction Systems with Neural Networks and Hybrid Models, Chemical Engineering Technology (1999), Vol. 7., 571–574.
4. C. A. O. Nascimento, R. Giudici, N. Scherbakoff, Modeling of Industrial Nylon-6,6 Polymerization Process in a Twin-Screw Extruder Reactor. II. Neural Networks and Hybrid Models, Journal of Applied Polymer Science (1999), Vol. 723., 905–912.
5. J. Schubert, R. Simutis, M. Dors, I. Havlik, A. Lübbert, Bioprocess Optimization and Control: Application of Hybrid Modeling, Journal of Biotechnology (1994), Vol. 35., 51–68.
6. A. J. de Assis, R. M. Filho, Soft Sensors Development for On-line Bioreactor State Estimation, Computers and Chemical Engineering (2000), Vol. 24., 1099–1103.
7. S. Linko, J. Luopa, Y.-H. Zhu, Neural Networks ans "Software Sensors" in Enzyme Production, Journal of Biotechnology (1997), Vol. 52., 257–266.
8. M. Norgaard, N. Poulsen, O. Ravn, New Developments in State Estimation for Nonlinear Systems, Automatica (2000), Vol. 36., 1627–1638.
9. J. Madar, J. Abonyi, H. Roubos, F. Szeifert, Incorporating Prior Knowledge in a Cubic Spline Approximation - Application to the Identification of Reaction Kinetic Models, Industrial and Engineering Chemistry Research (2003), Vol. 42., 4043–4049.

Appendix

To formulate the spline smoothing algorithm (see for more details [9]), let us define a cubic spline for a knot sequence: $t_1 = k_1 < k_2 < \ldots < k_{n-1} < k_n = t_N$. The cubic spline is a sequence of cubic polynomials defined for each interval, $[k_1, k_2], [k_2, k_3], \ldots, [k_{n-1}, k_n]$, by the combination of the function-values and the first-order derivatives at the knots $S(t) = s_i' a_i(t) + s_{i+1}' b_i(t) + s_i c_i(t) + s_{i+1} d_i(t)$ for $k_i \leq t < k_{i+1}$, where $s_i = S(k_i)$, $s_i' = \frac{dS(t)}{dt}|_{t=k_i}$, $a_i(t) = \left((k_{i+1} - t)^2 (t - k_i) \right) / h_i^2$, $b_i(t) = -\left((k_{i+1} - t)(t - k_i)^2 \right) / h_i^2$, $c_i(t) = \left((k_{i+1} - t)^2 (2(t - k_i) + h_i) \right) / h_i^3$, $d_i(t) = \left((t - k_i)^2 (2(k_{i+1} - t) + h_i) \right) / h_i^3$, where $h_i = k_{i+1} - k_i$.

As can be seen, the spline is linear in the parameters $\phi = [s_1, s_1', s_2, s_2', \ldots, s_n, s_n']^T$. Hence, the ϕ parameter vector can be determined by minimizing the following quadratic cost function: $\min_\phi Q(\phi)$, where $Q(\phi) = \frac{1}{N} \sum_{i=1}^{N} (x_i - S(t_i))^2$. This optimization problem can be solved analytically by the ordinary linear least squares (LS) method. The advantage of the utilized cubic spline is that the integral and derivative of the spline is also linear in the parameters of the spline, e.g. $\frac{dS(t)}{dt} = s_i' a_i'(t) + s_{i+1}' b_i'(t) + s_i c_i'(t) + s_{i+1} d_i'(t)$, where the $'$ means the derivative on time.

Neural Approach to Time-Frequency Signal Decomposition

Dariusz Grabowski and Janusz Walczak

Silesian University of Technology, Electrical Engineering Faculty,
ul.Akademicka 10, 44-100 Gliwice, Poland
{dgrabows,jwalczak}@polsl.gliwice.pl

Abstract. The problem of time-frequency decomposition of signals by means of neural networks has been investigated. The paper contains formalization of the problem as an optimization task followed by a proposition of recurrent neural network that can be used to solve it. Depending on the applied base functions, the neural network can be used for calculation of several standard time-frequency signal representations including Gabor. However, it can be especially useful in research on new signal decompositions with non-orthogonal bases as well as a part of feature extraction blocks in neural classification systems. The theoretic considerations have been illustrated by an example of analysis of a signal with time-varying parameters.

1   Introduction

Time-frequency decompositions, including short-time Fourier transform (STFT) and Gabor decomposition, are basic tools for analysis of non-stationary signals. The other approach, including Page as well as Wigner-Ville decompositions, consists not in direct decomposition of signals but rather their energy [7]. Completely alternative methodology is based on calculation of signal instantaneous frequency [6]. All these approaches have their own advantages and disadvantages. The decision which one to use should be derived from the given aim of investigation.

Time-frequency decompositions are examples of signal representations that enable solution to difficult engineering problems [3], [7]. More generally they can be interpreted as decompositions of original signals into components called atoms, e.g. in the case of STFT these atoms are defined as:

$$h_{\tau\omega}(t) = h(t - \tau)e^{j\omega t}, \tag{1}$$

where $h(\cdot)$ denotes a window function. The equation which shows how original signal is composed of windowed Fourier atoms (1) is shown below:

$$x(t) = \frac{1}{2\pi} \int\limits_{-\infty}^{\infty} \int\limits_{-\infty}^{\infty} X_h(\tau, \omega) h_{\tau\omega}(t) d\omega d\tau, \tag{2}$$

where X_h is the STFT of $x(t)$ calculated using window h.

L. Rutkowski et al. (Eds.): ICAISC 2004, LNAI 3070, pp. 1118–1123, 2004.
© Springer-Verlag Berlin Heidelberg 2004

Fixed length of window function h, which is translated by parameter τ along time axis, is a distinctive feature of STFT. In opposite to that, Gabor introduced transformation based on windows translated simultaneously along time as well as frequency axes [4]. It is defined as follows:

$$x(t) = \sum_{m=-\infty}^{\infty} \sum_{n=-\infty}^{\infty} a_{mn} h_{mn}(t), \tag{3}$$

where:

$$h_{mn}(t) = h(t - mT) e^{j\frac{2\pi nt}{T}}. \tag{4}$$

Linear combination of atom functions $h_{mn}(t)$ and weight coefficients a_{mn} is called Gabor representation of a signal $x(t)$. Gabor lattice is defined as a set of points with coordinates $(mT, n/T)$ on a time-frequency plane. Gabor coefficient a_{mn} contains information about the signal around the node $(mT, n/T)$ of the lattice.

For discrete-time signals, Gabor representation is expressed as:

$$x_i = \sum_{m=-\infty}^{\infty} \sum_{n=-\infty}^{\infty} a_{mn} h_{mni}, \tag{5}$$

where:

$$h_{mni} = h(iT_0 - mT) e^{j\frac{2\pi niT_0}{T}}, \tag{6}$$

where T and T_0 denote length of a segment of analyzed signal and sampling time, respectively.

Determination of time-frequency signal representations can be carried out using the best approximation approach [9] and in particular optimization neural networks [1], [2]. If the signal $x(t)$ belongs to Hilbert space H with defined norm $\| \cdot \|_H$ this approach in the case of Gabor representation leads to the following optimization problem:

$$\min_{\{a_{mn}\}} \left\| x(t) - \sum_{m=-\infty}^{\infty} \sum_{n=-\infty}^{\infty} a_{mn} h_{mn}(t) \right\|_H. \tag{7}$$

According to (7) the series (3) is convergent to the signal $x(t)$ in the sense of the norm $\| \cdot \|_H$.

This work is a continuation of research devoted to application of neural networks to calculation of frequency representations [5]. In the case of time-frequency representations the direct extension of solution proposed in [5] can be applied only if base functions are defined on different supports. This extension consists in using k neural networks proposed in [5] connected in parallel, Fig. 1. Thus, the time-frequency analyzer is built of a layer of k time-window blocks TW responsible for selecting portions and weighting of an input signal $x(t)$ as well as a layer of recurrent neural networks NN. The system shown in Fig. 1 can be used for example to calculate STFT.

However, application of optimization approach to calculate Gabor representation of a signal requires the other configuration of the neural network. It has been described in details in the following sections.

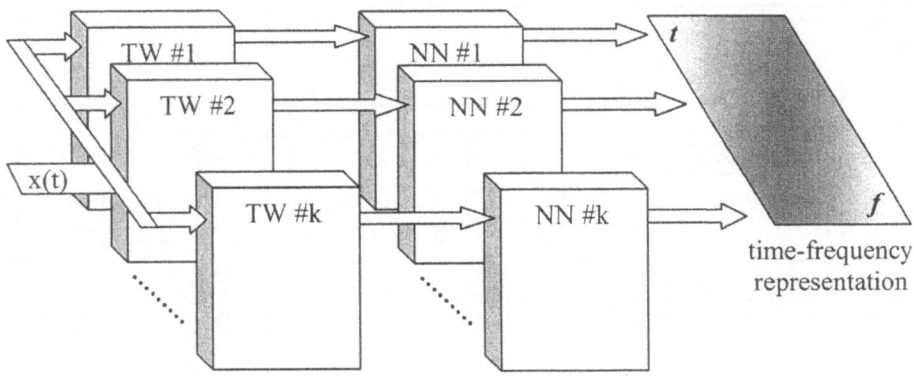

Fig. 1. Architecture of a simple neural system for time-frequency decomposition

2   Formalization of the Problem

Assuming that $(M+1)$ samples x_i of an analyzed signal as well as base functions - atoms h_{mni} are given, the problem of time-frequency decomposition consists in determination of a matrix $\mathbf{A}$ defining coefficients a_{mn} for the finite number $(L+1) \times (K+1)$ of atoms. For M, L and K large enough it can be done using best approximation approach [9] which in the case of RMS norm leads to minimization of the following function:

$$J(\mathbf{A}) = \frac{1}{2} \sum_{i=0}^{M} \left(\sum_{m=0}^{L} \sum_{n=0}^{K} a_{mn} h_{mni} - x_i \right)^2, \tag{8}$$

where:

$$\mathbf{A} = [a_{mn}], \mathbf{H} = [h_{mni}], \mathbf{x} = [x_i]. \tag{9}$$

3   Neural Network Architecture

Recurrent neural networks have been chosen to solve the problem formalized in section 2 as they can be associated with an energy function which is minimized in natural way during learning process [2], [8]. Assuming that the energy function is defined by (8) the dynamic of the network can be expressed by the following system of differential equations $(j = 0, 1, \ldots, L, \quad l = 0, 1, \ldots, K)$:

$$\frac{da_{jl}}{dt} = -\mu_{jl} \sum_{i=0}^{M} h_{jli} \left(\sum_{m=0}^{L} \sum_{n=0}^{K} a_{mn} h_{mni} - x_i \right), \tag{10}$$

where:

μ_{jl} – a learning rate.

The input data for the recurrent network consists of samples x_i of analyzed signal as well as samples of time-frequency atoms h_{mni} taken into account. The

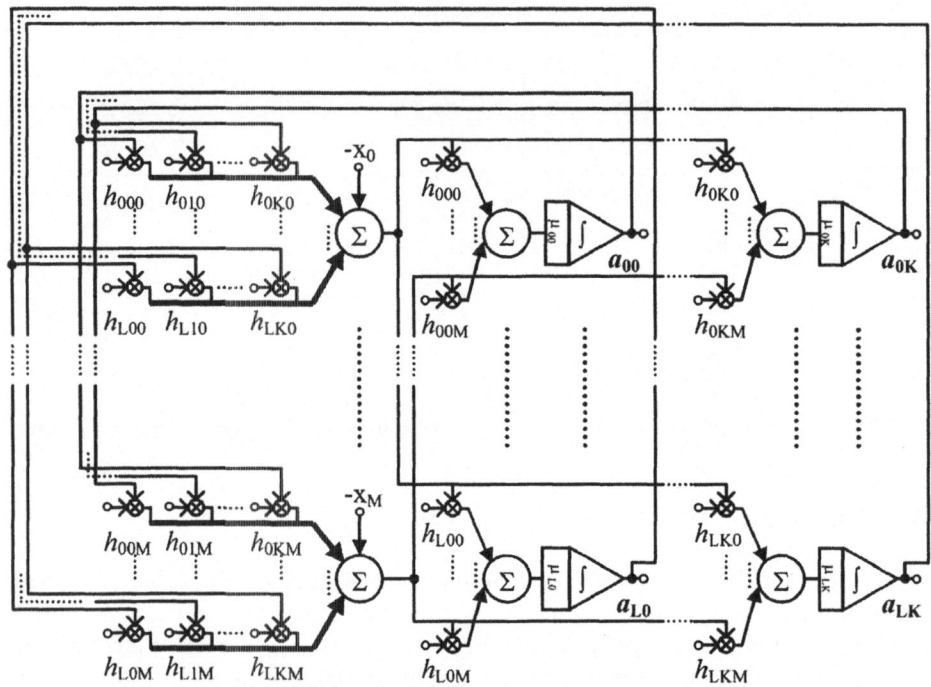

Fig. 2. The block diagram of recurrent neural network for time-frequency analysis

output of the network changes to ensure the best approximation of the analyzed signal and converges to searched set of coefficients a_{mn}. The stability of the learning process depends on the value of learning rates. In general, the vector of learning rates should be positively defined [1].

The block diagram of the recurrent neural network has been shown in Fig. 2. It has the structure which is an extension of the network proposed in [5] for frequency analysis. As a result the neural network shown in Fig. 2 can be considered as its generalization which enables joint time-frequency analysis.

4 Example

The recurrent neural network proposed in the paper (Fig. 2) has been applied to time-frequency decomposition of the following signal:

$$x(t) = \begin{cases} \sin(\omega_x t) & for \ \ t \in [0; 6T_x) \\ \sin(2\omega_x t) & for \ \ t \in [6T_x; 12T_x] \\ 0 & for \ \ t \notin [0; 12T_x] \end{cases} . \tag{11}$$

The time waveform of the signal (11) for $T_x = 20 \ ms$ ($\omega_x = 314 \ rad/s$) has been shown in Fig. 3. The simulation has been performed assuming Gaussian window, number of samples equal to 240 and sampling frequency 1 kHz. Fig. 4

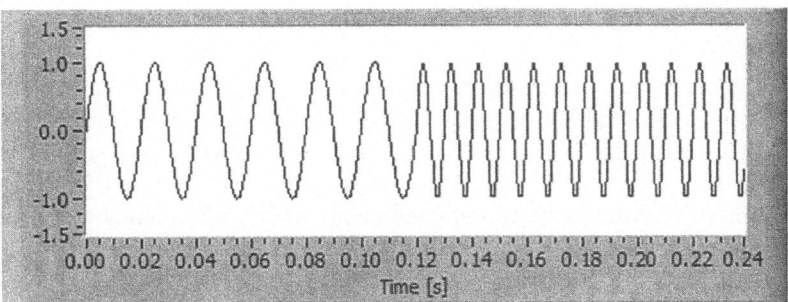

Fig. 3. Time waveform of analyzed signal $x(t)$

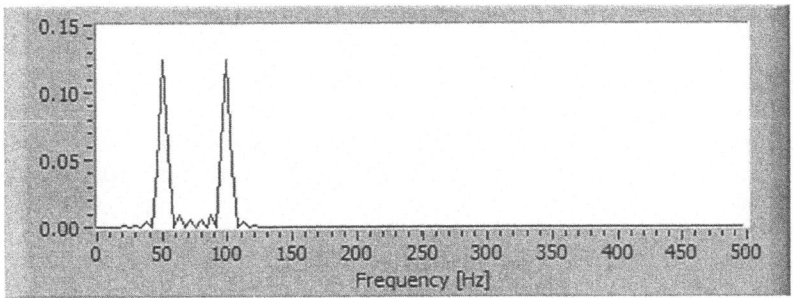

Fig. 4. Power spectrum of analyzed signal $x(t)$

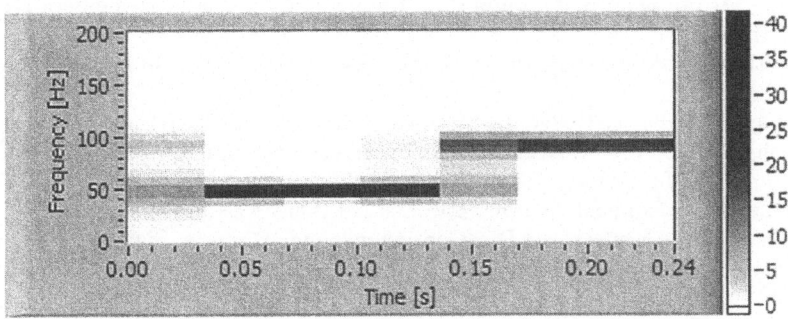

Fig. 5. Gabor representation of analyzed signal $x(t)$

shows that classical frequency analysis gives in that case confusing results – there is no information that two components do not exist at the same time. Results of time-frequency analysis have been presented in Fig. 5. At this instant the time range in which each component exists can be easily found.

5   Conclusions

The paper contains a proposition of neural network that can be used for joint time-frequency analysis of signals. The time-frequency representation is calculated using optimization approach by means of recurrent neural network. It is especially important in the case of non-orthogonal base function for which there are no simple formulae expressing coefficients of time-frequency representation. One of the potential application of the proposed neural network consists in research devoted to search of new base functions – atoms which have good characteristic from the point of view of new applications emerging all the time in the field of data mining.

References

1. Cichocki, A., Unbehauen, R.: Neural Networks for Optimization and Signal Processing. J.Wiley, New York (1993)
2. Daugman, J.G.: Relaxation Neural Network for Nonorthogonal Image Transforms. Proceedings of IEEE International Conference on Neural Networks, vol. 1, (1988) 547–560
3. Feichtinger, H.G., Strohmer, T. (eds.): Gabor Analysis and Algorithms: Theory and Applications. Applied and Numerical Harmonic Analysis. Birkhauser (1998)
4. Gabor, D.: Theory of Communication. J. IEE, vol. 93, part III, no. 26, (1946) 429–457
5. Grabowski, D., Walczak, J.: Generalized Spectrum Analysis by Means of Neural Network. In: Rutkowski, L., Kacprzyk, J. (eds.): Neural Networks and Soft Computing. Advances in Soft Computing. Physica-Verlag, Berlin Heidelberg New York (2003) 704–709
6. Kwiatkowski, W.: Introduction to Digital Signal Processing. (In Polish), IAiR, Warsaw (2003)
7. Lobos, T.: Advanced Signal Processing Methods in Electrical Engineering. (In Polish) Proceedings of International Conference on Fundamentals of Electrotechnics and Circuit Theory, Ustroń (2001) 7–17
8. Mańdziuk, J.: Hopfield Neural Networks. (In Polish) Exit, Warsaw (2000)
9. Soliman, S.S., Srinath, M.D.: Continuous and Discrete Signals and Systems. Prentice-Hall, Upper Saddle River, New Jersey (1998)

ANN Based Modelling and Correction in Dynamic Temperature Measurements

Lidia Jackowska-Strumiłło

Computer Engineering Department, Technical University of Lodz,
Al. Politechniki 11, 90-924 Lodz, Poland
lidia js@kis.p.lodz.pl

Abstract. The paper presents a new method for modelling of non-linear temperature sensor and correction of its dynamic errors by means of Artificial Neural Networks (ANNs). Feedforward multilayer ANNs with a moving window method and recurrent ANNs were applied. In the proposed correction technique an inverse dynamic model of the sensor is implemented by means of a neural corrector. ANN based modelling and correction technique has been evaluated experimentally for small platinum RTD immersed in oil. Recurrent ANN was used as a simulator for modelling sensor's non-linear dynamics and to validate the correction technique.

1 Introduction

Modelling of temperature sensor dynamics plays an essential role in designing temperature measuring and control systems. Resistance Temperature Detectors (RTD) are widely used in many industrial devices. Dynamical behaviour of all temperature sensors depend strongly on their construction and working conditions that may vary in time during the process.

Sensor dynamics can be modelled using the laws of thermokinetics. In particu-lar the Fourier-Kirchoff equation (1) and boundary conditions of IIIrd kind (2) are the fundamental laws, that can be used for describing dynamic behaviour of the sensor situated in a gas or in a fluid [2]:

$$c_k \rho_k \frac{\partial T_k}{\partial t} = \nabla \left(\lambda_k \nabla T_k \right) + q_{vk} \tag{1}$$

$$\frac{\partial T_m}{\partial n} = -\frac{\alpha}{\lambda_m} \left(T_m - T_o \right) \tag{2}$$

where: index k - refers generally to layer k of the sensor, index m - refers to the boundary layer of the sensor, index o - refers to the medium surrounding the sen-sor, T - temperature, t - time, λ - thermal conductivity, c - specific heat, r - den-sity, q_v - internal heat flux intensity in volume v, α - the heat transfer coefficient of the boundary, n - direction normal to the sensor surface.

For a wide class of multilayer temperature sensors in a cylindrical sheath, with negligible heat capacity between the sensing element and its central line

L. Rutkowski et al. (Eds.): ICAISC 2004, LNAI 3070, pp. 1124–1129, 2004.
© Springer-Verlag Berlin Heidelberg 2004

and long enough to assume, that heat flow has only one, radial direction, a transfer function of the thermal conversion stage is given by [6]:

$$G_T(s) = \frac{\Theta_T(s)}{\Theta_O(s)} = \frac{1}{\prod_{i=1}^{n}(1 + sN_i)} \tag{3}$$

where: $\Theta_O(s)$,$\Theta_T(s)$ - are the Laplace transforms of temperature changes correspondingly in the medium surrounding the sensor and in the sensing element evoked by the change of the temperature Θ_O, N_i - thermal time constants.

Theoretical mathematical model given in (1) and (2) is complex and the simpli-fied linear model given in (3) is limited to small temperature ranges and there is a wide class of industrial sensors and applications, for which this model is not cor-rect. Both models need usually to be completed in experimental way. Correction of temperature sensors dynamical errors is also an important and a complex prob-lem. Therefore, in such cases application of Artificial Neural Networks (ANN) presented in the paper is a good alternative solution.

2 ANN Based Identification and Modelling of RTD Dynamics

ANN-based dynamic model of the sensor is constructed on the basis of the relations between sensor's input and output. As it is known from the identification theory, a general discrete-time model for industrial temperature sensor, based on relations between sensors input vector $\mathbf{U}$ and its output vector $\mathbf{Y}$, can be described by the following nonlinear difference equation [5]:

$$y(k+1) = f[y(k), y(k-1), y(k-n+1), u(k), u(k-1), u(k-m+1)] \tag{4}$$

There are two main classes of neural networks, which may be used for modelling temperature sensors dynamics:

1. *multilayer feedforward networks* - which from a systems theoretic view-point perform a static non-linear mapping function; in order to capture the dynamics of the modelled system within a static network structure a so called *moving window* method is usually used in which the network is exposed to current and a number of past samples of system states [1,5].
2. *recurrent neural networks* - in which at least one feedback connection between neurones exists; such a network may be regarded as a non-linear dynamic system and its dynamics may be described by difference equa-tions [1].

The idea of sensors identification and modelling by the use of ANN is shown schematically in Fig. 1.

Firstly, a series-parallel method based on feedforward networks (FFN) was used for sensor identification. Backpropagation training algorithm and Levenberg-Marquardt method were applied to minimise the mean-square error cost function. Next, recurrent networks (RecN) obtained by closing a feedback

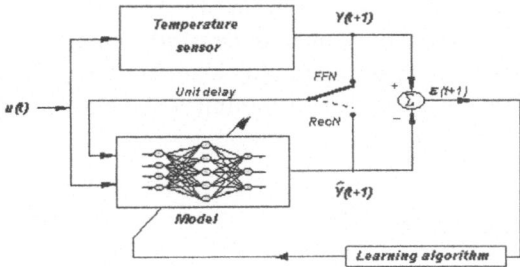

Fig. 1. A schematic diagram of ANN based sensor's identification.

connections were used for the sensor modelling. Finally, an iterative algorithm was applied to choose the best recurrent network to model sensor dynamics. A criterion of mini-mum sum absolute error between the sensor's output and the network output was used.

3   Correction of Dynamic Errors

Generally, correction of dynamic errors may be implemented by means of se-ries, parallel, series-parallel or closed loop schemes [6]. In a series correction method, which is considered in the paper, the corrector module is connected to the output of the sensor. In ANN-based correction method, artificial neural network plays the role of the corrector. Dynamic model of the corrector, implementing an inverse model of the sensor, is constructed by observing interdependence between sensor's input and output signals. A general discrete-time model of the corrector can be described by a non-linear difference equation [4]:

$$y_k(k+1) = f[y(k), y(k-1), \ldots, y(k-n+1)] \tag{5}$$

The method of determination of the corrector's model is shown in Fig.2.

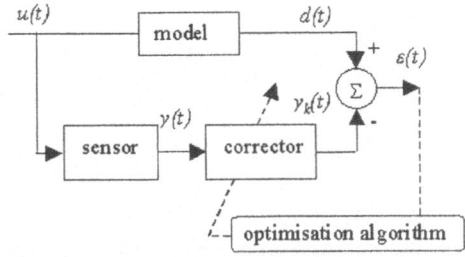

Fig. 2. Training scheme for identifying optimum corrector parameters [4].

Corrector structure defined in equation (5) was implemented by different multilayer perceptron networks and the moving window method [1]. For the considered problem the backpropagation training algorithm with Levenberg-Marquardt opti-misation algorithm was used to minimise the sum square error cost function [1].

4   Experimental Results

A series of identification experiments were performed for a small industrial, resistance temperature sensor, Pt100, in a steel sheath with the diameter of 4 mm. Step response method and different step magnitudes were used. The sensor, was cooled in water and ice to $0°C$ and was plugged into a thermostat filled with a well stirred silicon oil of higher temperature. Sensor output signal was register by a computerised measuring system [3]. Because the oil viscosity depends strongly on temperature, the heat transfer coefficient of the sensor's boundary, a, is also depends on oil temperature. Consequently, equation (2) is non-linear. For each single interrogation step, the oil temperature is constant and the sensor dynamics may be approximated by the simplified linear model given in (3). Sec-ond order model ensured high approximation accuracy. For each step response, sensor's equivalent time constants N_1, N_2 were computed. Dependence of sensor time constants on oil temperature was approximated by a small MLP networks: with the structure (1-6-1), i.e., one input, 6 neurons with sigmoidal activation function in the hidden layer and one output, for modelling N_1 time constant and (1-3-1) network for modelling N_2 (Fig.3a).

The trained networks were employed to compute 15 step responses of RTD (in Fig.3b). In ANN based approach from the fifteen step responses, thirteen were used as the data for the networks training and two were used for network testing.

Different feedforward two-layer perceptron networks were tested as the cor-rectors. The main criteria considered by choosing the best network structure was minimum of the sum square error (SSE), computed for the testing data. Also maximum absolute error and SSE for the training data were taken under consid-eration. The best results were obtained for the (6-16-1) MLP network

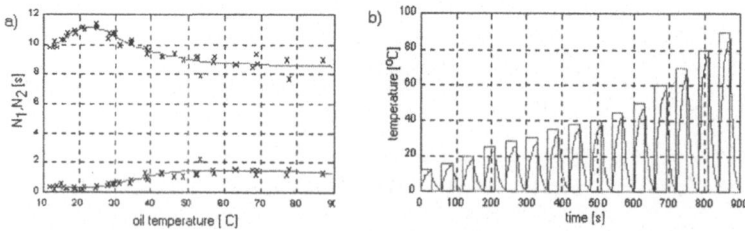

Fig. 3. a) Sensor's equivalent time constants N_1, N_2 versus oil temperature, b) experimental data for networks training and testing: temperature step interrogation - dashed line, sensor's output - solid line.

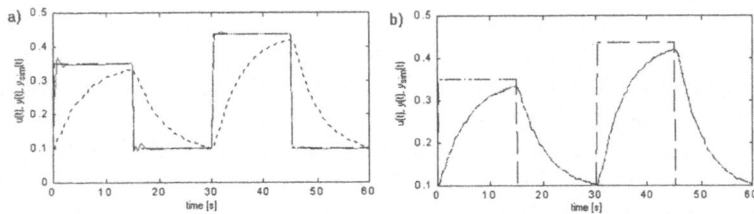

Fig. 4. a) Result of neural correction obtained by means of FFN (6-16-1); b) RTD modelling by means of FFN (5-20-1); interrogating signal - dashed line; sensor's output - dotted line; neural correction and modelling - solid line.

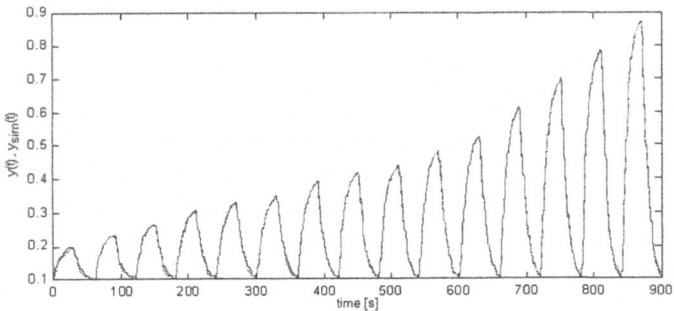

Fig. 5. Result of neural modelling obtained by means of recurrent network (5-20-1) with three feedback connections: sensor's output - solid line; neural modelling - dashed line.

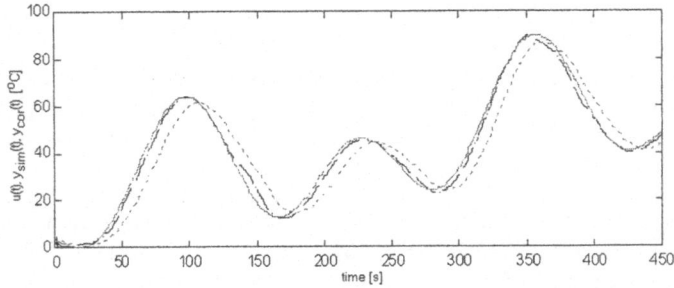

Fig. 6. Result of neural correction and modelling by means of RecN: interrogating signal $u(t) = 0.01t + 2\sin(wt) + 2\sin(3wt) - 2\sin(7wt)$ - solid line; sensor's output computed by RecN - dotted line; neural correction - dashed line.

The net-work's input vector consists of current value of the signal from the sensor's output $y(k)$ and five consecutive signal samples from the past. The corrected temperature value $y_K(k+1)$ is computed at the network output. Results of the correction proce-dure for the testing data confirmed the validity of the method for step responses (Fig.4a). The method should also be proved for other, analogue interrogating sig-nals, but their generation in experimental way is difficult for technical reasons. Therefore, a non-linear neural simulator of RTD dynamics was implemented.

Sensor's response was computed by recurrent (5-20-1) MLP network obtained from the corresponding FFN (5-20-1). The network's input vector consists of current value of the interrogating signal $u(k)$ and one past sample $u(k-1)$, current sig-nal from the sensor's output $y(k)$ and two consecutive signal samples from the past $y(k-1)$, $y(k-2)$, thus the network features three feedback connections. The predicted temperature value $y(k+1)$ is computed at the network output. Results of this mod-eling procedure are shown in Fig.5 and correction results are shown in Fig.6.

5   Conclusions

Temperature sensors immersed in oil exhibit non-linear dynamic behaviour. Application of the presented ANN based modelling and correction methods create a new possibility to increase the accuracy in dynamic temperature measurements.

References

[1] Haykin S.: Neural Networks: a comprehensive foundation – 2nd ed. Prentice Hall, 1999

[2] Jackowska-Strumiłło L., Sankowski D., McGhee J., Henderson I.A.: Modelling and MBS experimentation for temperature sensors. Meas., Vol.20, No.1, pp.49-60, 1997.

[3] Jackowska-Strumiłło L.: Computerised System for RTD Dynamics Identification. Int. IMEKO Seminar on Low Temperature Thermometry and Dynamic Temperature Measurement. Wrocław, (1997), pp. D-(25-30).

[4] Jackowska-Strumiłło L.: Correction of non-linear dynamic properties of temperature sensors by the use of ANN, in L.Rutkowski, J.Kacprzyk (Ed.): Advances in Soft Computing - Neural Networks and Soft Computing, Physica-Verlag, Heidelberg 2003, pp. 837-842.

[5] Jackowska-Strumiłło L.: Application of artificial neural networks for modelling of RTD dynamics. Third Int. Symp. on Methods and Models in Automation and Robotics. MMAR'96. Międzyzdroje, 1996, Proc., Vol. 3, pp.1185-1188.

[6] Michalski L., Eckersdorf K., McGhee J.: Temperature Measurement. John Wiley and Sons Ltd., Chichester, 1991.

One Day Prediction of NIKKEI Index Considering Information from Other Stock Markets

Marcin Jaruszewicz and Jacek Mańdziuk

Faculty of Mathematics and Information Science, Warsaw University of Technology,
Plac Politechniki 1, 00-661 Warsaw, POLAND
jaruszewicz@data.pl, mandziuk@mini.pw.edu.pl

Abstract. A task of a stock index prediction is presented in this paper. Several issues are considered. The data is gathered at the concerned stock market (NIKKEI) and two other markets (NASDAQ and DAX). The data contains not only original numerical values from the markets but also indicators pre-processed in terms of technical analysis, i.e. the oscillators are calculated and the structures of a value chart are extracted. Selected data is input to a neural network that is functionally divided into separate modules. The prediction goal was next day opening value of Japanese stock market index NIKKEI with consideration of German and USA stock markets' indexes. The average prediction error on the test set equals 43 points and the average percentage prediction error is equal to 0.27% while the average index volatility equals 0.96%.

1   Introduction

Prediction of a stock market index is a very complex task due to the lack of the autocorrelation of an index value changes even in a period of one day [1]. Despite there is only one variable to be traced, many derived variables are considered. Also not measurable incidents like economic or political situation, catastrophe or war may cause the change of a stock market index [1]. Except for the above variables there is also some information provided by technical analysis [2], which should be considered. Prediction system presented in the paper uses all the above different types of information. The most important stage of a prediction process is a complex data analysis and pre-processing. In the next parts the data pre-processing and neural network are described in detail. In our experiment the first task was prediction based solely on historical data from one stock market only. In the next step the data from two other stock markets was added [3] and the most important input variables were selected [4]. Finally, based on the above two steps the network with separated regions (by incomplete weights) was created [5,6].

2   Data Pre-processing

The data was collected on a daily basis. For each day the sample was composed of the date, the opening, closing, highest and lowest values.

L. Rutkowski et al. (Eds.): ICAISC 2004, LNAI 3070, pp. 1130–1135, 2004.
© Springer-Verlag Berlin Heidelberg 2004

Having values of a stock market index statistical variables were calculated. First of all, percentage changes in the period of 1, 5, 10 and 20 days in the past, resp. were evaluated. Weighted moving averages for the last 5, 10 and 20 days, resp. were also calculated:

$$mov(v,k) = \frac{\sum_{i=0}^{k-1}(k-i)v_{t-i}}{\sum_{i=0}^{k-1}(k-i)} \tag{1}$$

where v_t is an index value in time t, k is the length of a period. Finally technical analysis data was evaluated. Three different oscillators were calculated [7]. Proper definitions are described below.

$$MACD = mov(C,10) - mov(C,20), \qquad MACD_{SIGNAL} = mov(MACD,5) \tag{2}$$

where C is the index closing value. Signals are generated in the intersections of $MACD$ and $MACD_{SIGNAL}$.

$$WILLIAMS(n) = \frac{\max(H,n) - C}{\max(H,n) - \min(L,n)}(-100) \tag{3}$$

where n is a period of time (set to 10 days in the paper), $\max(H,n)$ is the highest index value in this period, C is index closing value. The final oscillator called "Two averages":

$$2AVG = mov(C,5) - mov(C,20) \tag{4}$$

generates signals according to its sign changes.

Signals generated by the above oscillators were added to the learning data. Also structures known in technical analysis [7] were extracted. An extraction is based on an analysis of the shape of the chart of the index value. These structures forecast change or continuation of a trend. Information of structures and signals of trend changes generated according to them were also included in the learning data. All "buy" signals were coded as 0.8 value and all "sell" signals as −0.8. Information about signal was copied into samples through the next 5 days with values linearly decreasing in time. It was done to prevent the existence of too many samples with no signal value. Anyway, in practice, the signal is usually correct during the next few days after its appearance. Signals cumulate when appear more than once for a single record. All above data was generated for three aforementioned stock markets. After all the above calculations 4 399 records were created covering dates 1985/10/30 − 2003/06/02. 400 records out of the above number were randomly selected as the testing set. This data was not used in the training phase. Since the stopping condition depended only on the number of training epochs (there were 4, 000 epochs for single, preliminary networks and 10, 000 ones for final one), no validation set was used in the experiment.

3   System Architecture

In the past, different predictors were considered with a prediction of stock markets [8,9]. In this paper we focus on data strucures, so the prediction system was

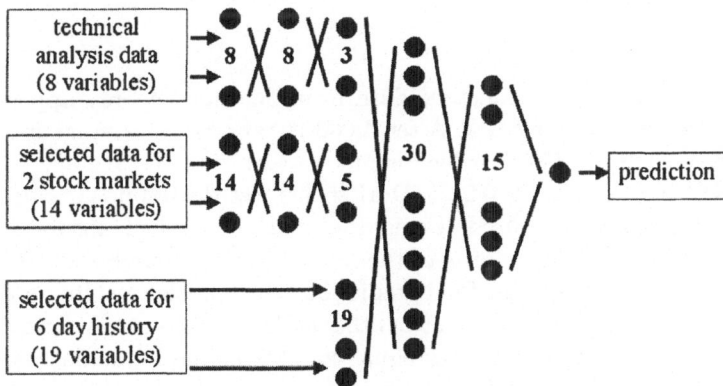

Fig. 1. Structure of the final network with separated regions for different input data types. Values in parentheses denote the sizes of subsequent layers - from the input layer (the left value) to the output one (the right value).

based on a simple multilayer perceptron network. In the first half of training iterations a backpropagation method with momentum was used, and for the rest of iterations the standard backpropagation method was applied. The input data was normalized and scaled to the range (-1, 1). In all neurons sigmoidal activation function was used.

Initially, all weights in the network were randomly chosen from the range (-0.01, 0.01). Due to a large number of potential input variables, before the final prediction some tests of variables importance were made. First of all prediction using only one considered stock market and its past 6 days history was done by neural network of size 108 x 50 x 1 with one hidden layer. In the input layer 108 values representing the data from the target stock market were presented. In the output layer the next day's opening value was predicted.

In the next test the data from three stock markets was considered. Together there were 55 variables describing situation on these markets during one day of prediction. The size of a hidden layer was equal to 30 and the output layer was composed of one neuron. Both tests aimed at selection of the most relevant inputs for the final prediction system.

The final prediction was made by a network with separate regions for each input data type. The first region processed the most relevant data (selected in preliminary stage) from two stock markets other than the market concerned in prediction. The second region processed the most important technical analysis data from target stock market. The most relevant data from 6 day history was given to the network without any further preprocessing. A structure of the final neural network is presented in Fig. 1.

4   Results

Prediction based on 6 day history data from one market only appeared to be
a difficult task for the network. After 4 000 iterations the average error on test
samples was equal to 4.85%, which is much more than the average volatility of
the NIKKEI index, which is 0.96%. During this test the importance of particular
input variables was measured. Using the chart of sum of absolute values of
outgoing weights for each neuron of the input layer, the number of 19 out of 108
variables were selected for the final prediction. Much better results were obtained
after adding the information from two other stock markets except historical data.
The average percentage error was equal to 1.96%. The input data was from a
single day for three stock markets (target and two additional) in the number
of 55. After the learning process 14 variables from two non-target markets were
selected for the final experiment.

In the final experiment, except for the historical data and the data from
two other markets also a technical analysis data was used. Therefore the final
selection of input variables was the following (cf. Fig. 1). In the **historical data**
19 inputs, i.e. opening, closing, lowest values and moving average for 20 days
for **day t**; closing , lowest values and moving averages for 20 days for **days t-1,
t-2, t-3** and **t-4**; lowest value as well as moving averages for 20 and 5 days
for **day t-5**. Among **other markets' data** 14 inputs, i.e. the opening, closing,
highest and lowest values as well as moving averages for 5, 10 and 20 days for
two non-target stock markets. And in **technical analysis data**, (8 inputs):
closing value, structure type, MACD line, MACD signal line, Williams as well
as 3 signals generated by oscillators: MACD, Williams, Two Averages.

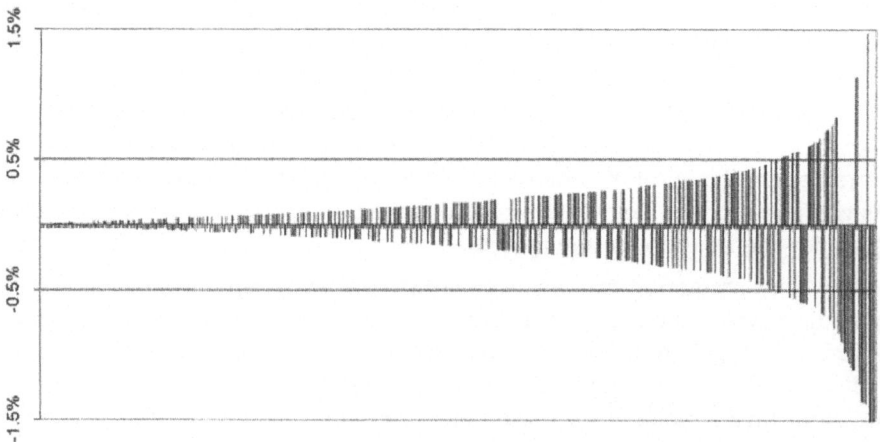

Fig. 2. A structure of a percentage prediction error (Y-axe) on test samples (X-axe)
in the final experiment. Samples are ordered from the least to the highest module of a
value of a percentage error.

After 10 000 iterations the average percentage error was equal to 0.27%. Prediction error accomplished in the final experiment is more than three times lower than the average volatility of NIKKEI index, i.e. 0.96% (with maximum equal to 13.23%).

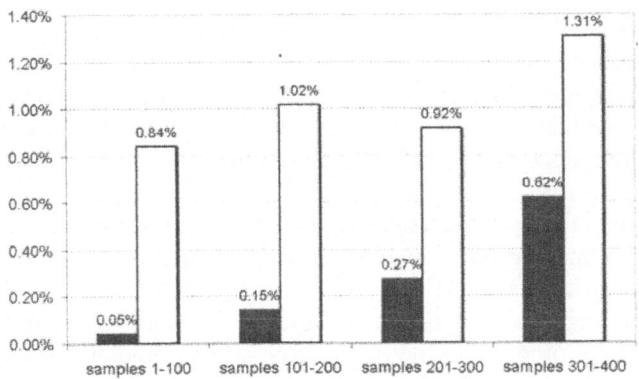

Fig. 3. A cumulated prediction error in the final experiment - average percentage values (Y-axe) of an error (black boxes) and index volatility (white boxes) for the sets of samples (X-axe). The size of each set is equal to 100.

The structure of the error is presented in Fig. 2. Samples are sorted by increasing value of module of a value of a percentage error. The manifest observation is that the value of an error doesn't grow linearly.

In Fig. 3. the average values of an error are shown for different set of test samples together with the average real volatility of an index value. Each set consist of 100 samples. The first 100 test samples (with the lowest error) have the average error of 0.05%. Results for the next sets of samples are 0.15% and 0.27%, respectively. An error value for the last 100 samples (with the highest error) equals 0.62%. The volatility of an index value changes from 0.84% to 1.31%. Despite there is no strong correlation between an error value and volatility of an index, the error value grows together with the volatility value. Samples with a rapid index change during a day are a little more difficult for prediction than samples with the low volatility.

Similarly to preliminary experiments the relative importance of particular inputs was measured based on the sum of modules of all outgoing weights divided by the number of these weights. It appeared that the most important was the data from two other (non-target) stock markets with the average value of 0.33. Values for historical and technical analysis data were equal to 0.22 and 0.01, respectively.

After removing the entire region devoted to technical analysis data (see Fig. 1) the average percentage error increased to 0.37%.

5   Conclusions

A way from a simple neural network to a network based on separate regions producing better forecast was presented. Promising test results were obtained. The percentage error equal to 0.27% is a good starting point for further investigation, especially in comparison with an average volatility of the index value being at the level of 0.96%.

Further research will focus on usefulness of technical analysis data. The main point is the observation that oscillators have very unstable impact on proper buy/sell signal generation. Each oscillator is useful only in a short period of time. In that case weights between 'technical analysis' region and the main network should change respectively. Probably the same observation is correct for other variables.

Another field of experiments is research on a structure of the network. Simple model-based input variables selection described in this paper will be extended by model-free methods [10,11].

A far-reaching goal is a buy/sell signal prediction, which is more complex task than a value prediction due to the necessity to predict a trend in a horizon longer than one day.

References

1. Mantegna, R., Stanley, E.: An introduction to econophysics. Correlations and complexity in finance. Cambridge University Press (2000)
2. Dempster, T.P., et al.: Computational learning techniques for intraday fx trading using popular technical indicators. IEEE Transactions on Neural Networks **12** (2001) 744–754
3. Podding, T., Rehkegler, H.: A "world" model of integrated financial markets using artificial neural networks. Neurocomputing **10** (1996) 251–273
4. Chenoweth, T., Obradović, Z.: A multi-component nonlinear prediction system for the s&p 500 index. Neurocomputing **10** (1996) 275–290
5. Fu, H.C., Lee, Y.P., et al.: Divide-and-conquer learning and modular perceptron networks. IEEE Transactions on Neural Networks **12** (2001) 250–263
6. Khotanzad, A., Elragal, H., et al.: Combination of artificial neural-network forecasters for prediction of natural gas consumption. IEEE Transactions on Neural Networks **11** (2000) 464–473
7. Murphy, J.: Technical analysis of the financial markets. New York Institiute of Finance (1999)
8. Tony Gestel, J.S., et al.: Financial time series prediction using least squares support vector machnies within the evidence framework. IEEE Transactions on Neural Networks **12** (2001) 809–820
9. Peter Tino, C.S., et al.: Financial volatility trading using recurent neural networks. IEEE Transactions on Neural Networks **12** (2001) 865–874
10. Back, A., Trappenberg, T.: Selecting inputs for modeling using normalized higher order statistics and independent component analysis. IEEE Transactions on Neural Networks **12** (2001) 612–617
11. Refenes, A., Holt, W.: Forecasting volatility with neural regression: A contribution to model adequacy. IEEE Transactions on Neural Networks **12** (2001) 850–864

Application of Neural Network Topologies in the Intelligent Heat Use Prediction System

Leszek Kiełtyka, Robert Kucęba, and Adam Sokołowski

Department of Management Information Systems
Częstochowa University of Technology - Faculty of Management
Al. Armii Krajowej 19, paw.B, 42-200 Częstochowa, Poland
{lekiel,robertk,adams}@zim.pcz.czest.pl
http://zim.pcz.czest.pl/KISZ

Abstract. The authors describe the structure of an Intelligent Prediction System (IPS) basing on neural networks simulated in the STATISTICA Neural Networks artificial intelligence package. The system has been adopted in the process of predicting regional heat use. The authors focus on the methods applied to select optimum neural networks in the prediction mode of the analysed phenomenon and present prediction results for the best networks.

1 Introduction

The problem of decreasing energy use due to environmental and economic reasons has been one of the major concerns of the contemporary world for the past few years. The economic reasons comprise two basic issues: necessity of lowering charges for heat paid by end users and adaptation of heat prices to the requirements of market economy. It is thus necessary to work out methods supporting management of heat carrier selection. In the paper we describe a method of predicting heat use basing on an Intelligent Prediction System.

The Intelligent Prediction System (IPS) has been applied in the process of predicting heat use in voivodships demarcated according to the former administrative division of Poland. The IPS structure was based on selected topologies of artificial neural networks. Due to the fact that one cannot relate mathematically the input variables influencing regional heat use and that they exert influence on the output variable, artificial neural networks were applied to trace relations between variables that were not mathematically related [1]. It was assumed in the research that prediction accuracy depends on regional parameters, taking into account special characteristics of a particular voivodship. As heat demand was similar in some regions, voivodships were divided into groups characterised by similar heat market features. A professional package of artificial intelligence - Statistica Neural Networks was applied in the research [2]. The software choice was not accidental as STATISTICA Neural Networks package enables its users to construct the major neural network topologies [3].

L. Rutkowski et al. (Eds.): ICAISC 2004, LNAI 3070, pp. 1136–1141, 2004.
© Springer-Verlag Berlin Heidelberg 2004

2   Structure of the Intelligent Heat Prediction System

There are several different modes in the studied Intelligent Prediction System. One may activate and deactivate particular modes, depending on the preferences and analysis in question [4]. The following main modes have been defined in the suggested intelligent system (Fig. 1): data mining mode, input mode, preprocessing mode included in the prediction mode, prediction (executive) mode, verification mode.

Data updating and aggregating mechanisms have been defined in the **data mining mode**. This data describes the phenomenon analysed - regional network heat use. The data was analysed in external data sets, created with the application of MS Excel. The key input variables in these sets are the following: capacity of the heated buildings in thousands of cubic meters, total area of the centrally heated apartments in thousands of square meters, time of power utilisation h/a, heat production TJ, extreme temperature ^0C, length of heating seasons - in months.

The **input mode** includes information being an important element in neural network processing. Input set variables were created on the basis of formulae whose definition was stored in a separate set. The formulae were created on the basis of an economic analysis of the regional heat market. They were later applied as input variables in the executive mode of the intelligent prediction system.

The input set was defined in the input mode and preliminarily processed by preprocessing procedures. It was a prototype for the training, testing and validating sets. This data was separated from each other and constituted independent subsets created from the input set [5]. The training set was applied in the process of training the neural network and testing and validating sets supported the process of verifying the operation of the suboptimal network architecture. The structure of the databases in which variables were gathered was also defined within the input mode of the intelligent prediction system.

In the IPS **preprocessing mode** the executive (prediction) mode input data was scaled and standardized. This mode was included in the functional structure of the executive mode. The commonly accepted assumptions concerning neural networks were applied to define preprocessing procedures. In this stage it was also of key importance to properly define the criteria applied when dividing the input set into the training, testing and validating subsets. Summing up, one may say that preprocessing procedures were aimed at preliminary optimisation of the data processed by the neural network [6]. **The prediction mode** was the executive mode of the IPS. Here, the optimum architectures of neural networks were defined [5]. The neural network set was also defined (preserving the structural diversity of the networks).

The following networks have been analysed and defined in the prediction process: RBF (Radial Basis Function Networks, GRNN (Generalized Regression Neural Network), MLP (Multilayer Perceptrons) and Linear Networks. The choice of these networks was not accidental as they are all applied in the prediction processes [7]. Kohonen Self-Organizing Feature Maps and PNN (Proba-

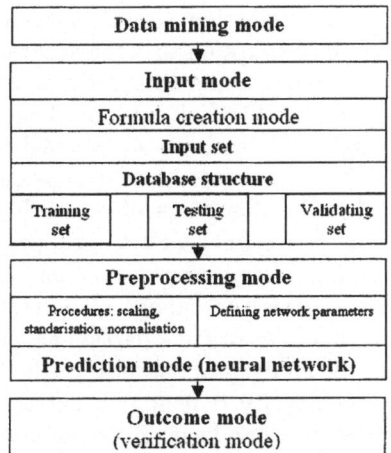

Fig. 1. An outline of the intelligent prediction system

bilistic Neural Networks) were not analysed as they are applied in classification processes where a symbolic variable is generated on the output.

In order to check the reliability of the generated prediction results and to define the set of optimum neural networks, universal prediction standards were applied in the verification mode. These standards include for example ex post errors, prediction accuracy ratio, average square error [2]. In the analysis in question, the prediction quality was verified on an experimental prediction series. Time series elements were defined in the training and validating sets as training example constituents.

3   Analysis of Heat Use Prediction Obtained in the Intelligent Prediction Mode

There were two stages of the research on heat use prediction. The first stage was devoted to the prediction of heat use in particular voivodships. However, the defined training set did not cover the regional perspective. In this stage of research all input parameters, characteristic to each region were cumulated into one training set. The results of this stage were to answer the question of whether it was enough to create one neural network model common to all voivodships or should there be regional training sets? Input variables for all voivodships were introduced in the input layer of the network [8].

In the second stage of the research, heat use in particular voivodships was predicted. In this stage, training sets division criteria were defined, taking into account the regional factors (preprocessing mode). Heat use prediction for both stages was conducted in two phases. In the former one, input database was defined. The second phase consisted in defining the training, testing and validating sets on the basis of the input set. Time range of four years in a yearly time series was applied in the process of training the network to predict heat use in the following year.

The analysis of heat use prediction results obtained in the first stage of research confirmed the initial assumption that the accuracy of heat use prediction depends on regional parameters, taking into account characteristic features of a particular voivodship. Due to this fact, regional heat use prediction was the objective of the second stage of research [9]. As the real heat demand was similar in some regions, voivodships were divided into groups characterised by common features of the heat market. In this stage of research (second stage) training sets were divided according to regional factors, grouping voivodships of similar heat production and use. The initial assumption was that the main definition predicate for the training set was the cubage of centrally heated apartments - being the value influencing heat density of a particular region. This condition was introduced on the basis of the analysis of heat use prediction, by cumulated input variables (first stage). Heat density depends on cubage, usable area of heated apartments and real use of network heat. By cumulated input variables, heat density influenced directly the prediction accuracy.

In the subsequent part of the research, aggregated set of suboptimum neural networks was defined. Quality was accepted as the selection criterion for best networks of diversified architecture. It was defined by the following relation [3]:

$$J = \frac{\sigma(\delta_i)}{\sigma(x_i)}. \tag{1}$$

where:

$\sigma(\delta_i)$ − standard deviation of the validating error,

$\sigma(x_i)$ − standard deviation of input variables.

Training, testing and validation errors were also taken into account in the process of optimising neural networks [10]. Due to their architecture, neural networks were trained on the basis of appropriately compiled training algorithms. In case of Multilayer Perceptrons the following algorithms were applied in the training process: back propagation algorithm, conjugated gradients algorithm.

The version of back propagation algorithm supporting the training process of multilayer networks applied in the STATISTICA Neural Networks programme is characterised by the following qualities: time-varying learning rate, time-varying inertia rate, random sequence of training cases, independent testing conducted by the validation set, optional error functions.

In case of the Radial Basis Function Networks defined in the aggregated set of suboptimum solutions the following algorithms (defining the full training cycle) were suggested: K-means, centre assignment, K-nearest neighbours, deviation assignment, pseudo-inverse, linear optimisation of least squares.

Generalized Regression Neural Network (GRNN) implementing the probabilistic (Bayesian) technique of estimating the value of output variable with the use of input values was applied on the basis of the following formula:

$$E(z|\bar{x}) = \frac{\int_{-\infty}^{+\infty} z f(\bar{x}, z) dz}{\int_{-\infty}^{+\infty} f(\bar{x}, z) dz}. \tag{2}$$

z - is the output variable Z,

x - is the input case (for which the value of the output variable Z is estimated),

f - is a density probability function of the input values x and the output value z.

Neural networks were preliminarily trained taking into account their diversity. Corresponding freedom parameters (weight values) were also defined [5]. A suboptimum set of neural networks was thus created. The initially selected neural networks were then further trained in order to improve their quality. The final verification criterion for the networks defined were universal EX POST errors: relative error, absolute error, mean absolute error.

Table 1 presents the IPS prediction results for optimum neural networks (with regional diversity taken into account). Table 1 presents network topologies and corresponding architectures that produced best results in the process of predicting regional heat use.

On the basis of the above table it was stated that the Multilayer Perceptron Network prediction was most accurate (99,99[%]). The network structure had two hidden layers in the framework of which twenty and thirteen hidden neurons were defined respectively. In case of the remaining voivodships mean accuracy of the IPS prediction produced by the Multilayer Perceptron Network was 98,97[%]. The table presents the neural networks implemented in the Intelligent Prediction System whose predictions were most accurate (their structural diversity taken into account).

Table 1. Neural network topologies implemented in the process of network heat use prediction

Network type	Number of neurons in the hidden layer (1)	Number of neurons in the hidden layer (2)	Set value	Predicted value	Absolute error	Relative error[%]	Network quality	Prediction quality
RBF	79	-	56432	53980,320	2451,680	4,344	0,778	95,656
RBF	52	-	56432	54759,540	1672,460	2,964	0,724	97,036
RBF	46	-	56432	55433,970	998,030	1,769	0,723	98,231
MLP	20	13	56432	56434,700	-2,700	-0,005	0,658	99,995
MLP	17	-	56432	54682,160	1749,840	3,101	0,692	96,899
MLP	31	-	56432	58496,020	-2064,020	-3,658	0,729	96,342
GRNN	153	2	56432	53099,910	3332,090	5,905	0,827	94,095
Linear	-	-	56432	48891,820	7540,180	13,362	2,496	86,638

4   Summary

Summing up, one may state that the suggested Intelligent Prediction System applying artificial intelligence methods is a new approach to the process of planning network heat use. The obtained results not only confirm the correct design of the Intelligent Prediction System but also prove the practical applicability of neural networks in prediction and optimisation processes [11].

During the research in question it was stated that the implementation of neural network prediction is not only an attempt at solving a particular problem but it also verifies and updates the data gathered. A spectacular characteristic of the Intelligent Prediction System in question is self-adaptation, that is the ability to constantly change and develop. The possibility of constant training and the special structure of the model (comprising a neural network of parallel architecture) make the suggested system an efficient tool supporting the process of predicting regional network heat use.

References

1. Kiełtyka, L., and Kucęba, R.: The Application of Artifical Neural Networks for Heat Energy Use Prediction. Proceedings of the Fourth International Conference on Enterprise Information Systems ICEIS 2002.Vol.1. Ciudad Real, Spain (2002)
2. Duch, W., Korbicz, J., Rutkowski, L., Tadusiewicz, R.: Biocybernetics and Biomedical Engineering. Neural Networks. Volume 6", ed. by Maciej Nałęcz, Exit Academic Publishing House, Warsaw (2000) (in Polish)
3. STATISTICA Neural Networks^{TM} User Manual, StatSoft Poland Ltd., Cracov (2001) (in Polish)
4. Kiełtyka, L., Dubicki, J., Kucęba, R., Sokołowski, A.: Algorithms Monitoring and Evaluating Marketing Phenomena, Report from a research project for the State Committee for Scientific Research No 1 H02D 035 15, Częstochowa (1999) (in Polish)
5. Kiełtyka, L., Dubicki, J., Kucęba, R., Sokołowski, A.: Intelligent Prediction System. ed. by Leszek Kiełtyka. Publishing House of the Technical University of Częstochowa. Częstochowa (2000) (in Polish)
6. Sokołowski A.: Information Processing and Preprocessing in an Intelligent Prediction System. Information Technologies. ed. by Leszek Kiełtyka. Publishing House of the Faculty of Management of the Technical University of Częstochowa, Częstochowa (2001), pp. 48-59 (in Polish)
7. Tadeusiewicz R.: "Neural Networks", WNT, Warsaw (1993) (in Polish)
8. Kiełtyka, L., Kucęba R.: The Use of Neural Networks through the Optimisation of Production Capacity Based on the Example of Local Heating Plants. Proceedings of the International Conference TRANSFER 2001, Trencin (2001)
9. Kucęba, R.: A Virtual Power Plant Basing on Dispersed and Distributed Generation. Proceedings of the International Association for Development of the Information Society International Conference e-Society 2003. Volume I. Lisbon, Portugal (2003), pp. 381-386.
10. Tadeusiewicz R.: Introduction to Neural Networks, PLJ Academic Publishing House, Warsaw (1998) (in Polish)
11. Kiełtyka, L., Sokołowski, S.: Optimisation of Selected Industrial Processes on the Basis of Intelligent Systems. Proceedings of the International Conference TRANSFER 2001, Trencin (2001), pp.243-248

Genetic Algorithm for Database Indexing

Marcin Korytkowski[1], Marcin Gabryel[1], Robert Nowicki[1,2], and
Rafał Scherer[1,2]

[1] Department of Computer Engineering, Częstochowa University of Technology
Al. Armii Krajowej 36, 42-200 Częstochowa, Poland
{marcink, marcing, rnowicki}@kik.pcz.czest.pl, rafal@ieee.org
http://kik.pcz.pl
[2] Department of Artificial Intelligence, WSHE University in Łódź
ul. Rewolucji 1905 nr 64, Łódź, Poland
http://www.wshe.lodz.pl

Abstract. In this paper we propose a new method for improving efficiency of database systems, using genetic algorithms. We show how table
indexes can be coded in chromosomes, and a way to automatically find
the best set of indexes for databases.

1 Introduction

Nowadays it is hard to imagine a corporation which can operate without databases. Usually, databases are relational database systems. They are based on
tables, which store structured information of a given type. Yet, database systems consist not only of tables and information collected in them. Databases
enable to browse, modify, add and delete data by many users at once. Programmers creating a database can utilize plenty of tools: stored procedures, view,
generators, triggers etc. Database administrator can secure data integrity using
primary keys or secondary keys. He or she can restrict the user rights to secure
the data against unauthorized access by granting or revoking rights or roles.

Development of these systems led to creating three languages for databases:

- DDL - data definition language,
- DML - data manipulation language,
- DCL - data control language.

The most known database systems are Oracle, DB2, Interbase, Paradox, MySQL.
Artificial intelligence techniques are used usually to data mining, or searching
for dependencies in data, for example in banking to find dependency between
customer age and number of accounts they open. In our approach we would like
to show the possibility of using genetic algorithms to improve performance of
databases. As aforementioned, a database system can be operated by enormous
number of users at the same time, all of whom want to have quick access to data.
Internal searching mechanisms of database systems and good design of tables
and relations between them are very important in assuring suitable efficiency.
Indexes have big impact on searching speed. In this paper we propose a new
method which utilize genetic algorithms to search for optimal set of indexes in
a database system.

L. Rutkowski et al. (Eds.): ICAISC 2004, LNAI 3070, pp. 1142–1147, 2004.
© Springer-Verlag Berlin Heidelberg 2004

2   Algorithm Description

As we said before, tables store information in columns with data of the same type in each row. We can see an example in Table 1 where in LastName and FirstName columns we have *char* type data and in Age column we have *integer* type data. To find, say, client data ordered by name, with age of above 33 years, a database user can define the following query

```
select * from employees where age > 33 order by LastName
```

The database system must search through all records to return right answer what can be very time-consuming, depending on the database size. To decrease searching time we can create indexes. The optimal index can reduce searching time from several hours to a few seconds. An index as a database object does not have any direct impact on data and it is physically separated from tables with data. It can be placed in the same file as the data or in another file (it depends on a database server type). Thanks to this, it can be modified or deleted, and these changes do not cause data loss or damage. Indexes are created using the following comand:

```
Create index index_name on table_name (1st_kolumn_name,
                          2nd_column_name etc)
```

We can see in above command that an index is created for given columns in a given table.

Table 1. Exemplary database table

ID	LastName	FirstName	Age
1	Kowalsky	John	33
2	Smith	Arnold	43
3	Damca	Sylvester	56

Usually indexes take form of so called trees. These are certain number of pages in memory, consisting of index key, pointer to pages located below, and so called ROWID - table row identifier. Exemplary form of the index tree in an Oracle system for a column with names can look like:

```
Johnson; Williams; Adams; Skubis; Kowalsky; Schmidt; Cook; Bende;
MacDonald; Montgomery; Furmans; Jorge; Ammer; Tai
```

Thus, searching for data takes less time than looking up whole table with data. Of course, the database system chooses which index has to be taken into account during searching, although the user can use other index than proposed by the server. It could be tempting to create indexes for all data in our database, but during data modification or insertion, the system has to modify the corresponding index. This operation of index rebuilding is again time-consuming.

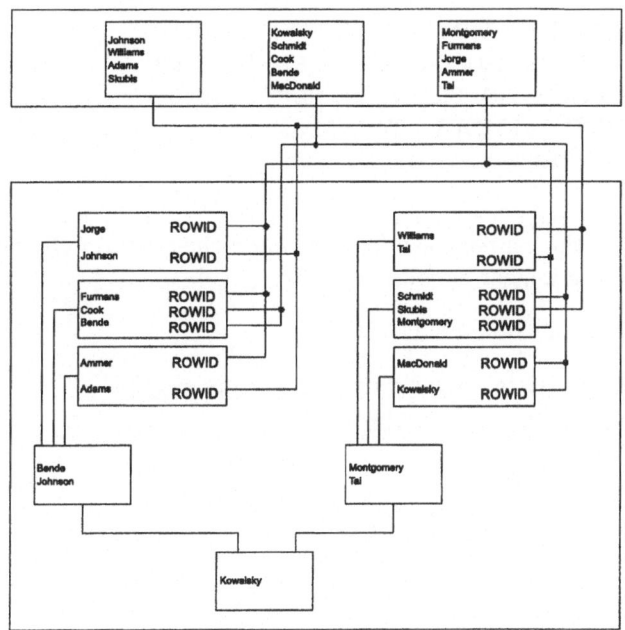

Fig. 1. The example of tree index structure.

Moreover, the size of database files grows with the number of indexes. Therefore, database system designer has to find trade-off between search speed and the size of the database. Creating an index on a column with repetitive data, e.g. a column with sex information, or on a table with little information, is pointless, because of it will not speed up the searching process. Database programmes do not know what information are going to be inserted into the table (if the information will be repetitive), what tables and columns will be searched most often, and to which of them information will be inserted. Without this information, we cannot create the optimal index set. We propose creating a database without indexes and letting it to operate for normal, daily use. Then a special application is launched periodically for acquiring operations executed by the database users.

Having the information about usage statistics we can index the database by a genetic algorithm. We used Borland InterBase 6.0 system for our simulations. We created two tables: Employees and Departments. The Employees table was created as follows:

```
CREATE TABLE "EMPLOYEES"
(
 "ID" INTEGER NOT NULL,
 "NAME" VARCHAR(50) CHARACTER SET WIN1250 NOT NULL,
 "FIRSTNAME" VARCHAR(30) CHARACTER SET WIN1250 NOT NULL,
 "AGE"   INTEGER,
 "SALARY" DOUBLE PRECISION DEFAULT 0,
```

```
"CITY" VARCHAR(50) CHARACTER SET WIN1250,
"ADDRESS" VARCHAR(30) CHARACTER SET WIN1250,
"NUMBER" VARCHAR(20) CHARACTER SET WIN1250,
"ID_DEPARTMENT" INTEGER NOT NULL,
PRIMARY KEY ("ID")
);
```

To be sure that the primary key is unique and there is no null value we created a generator and a trigger as follows

```
CREATE GENERATOR "GEN_EMPLOYEES";

CREATE TRIGGER "TRIG_EMPLOYEES" FOR "EMPLOYEES"
ACTIVE BEFORE INSERT POSITION 0
AS
BEGIN
 NEW.ID=GEN_ID(GEN_EMPLOYEES,1);
END ^

COMMIT WORK ^

CREATE TABLE "DEPARTMENT"
(
 "ID" INTEGER NOT NULL,
 "IDDEPARTMENT" INTEGER NOT NULL,
 "NAME" VARCHAR(50) CHARACTER SET WIN1250 NOT NULL,
 PRIMARY KEY ("ID")
);

CREATE GENERATOR "GEN_DEPARTMENT";

CREATE TRIGGER "TRIG_DEPARTMENT" FOR " DEPARTMENT"
ACTIVE BEFORE INSERT POSITION 0
AS
BEGIN
 NEW.ID=GEN_ID(GEN_DEPARTMENT,1);
END ^

COMMIT WORK ^
```

The first stage was importing names of tables and fields into our application from the database. On that basis, we could create the genotype structure. In our case, a single chromosome corresponds with indexes created on a single table. The genotype consists of as many chromosomes as the number of tables in a database system.

Now we present the coding scheme used in our approach. The gene number in a chromosome, after converting to binary format, means the number of columns in a table to create index on. For example, the first gene means that index has to be created only on the first column, the fifth gene $5_{10} = [101]_2$ means that index has to be created on the first and thrid column. The value of genes (1 or 0) tells us if an index has to be created or not. The genotype consists of as many chromosoms as tables in our database.

Example
Let we have two tables, one with three columns and the second with four columns. We decreased the number of columns in the example, to ease analyze. The length of the chromosome for the first table is $2^{number\_of\_columns}$, thus $2^3 = 8$, and accordingly for the second table $2^4 = 16$. The length of the genotype is 24. Let the gene values chosen randomly are in Fig. 2.

1	2	3	4	5	6	7	8	9	10	11	12	13	14	15	16	17	18	19	20	21	22	23	24
0	0	0	1	1	0	0	0	0	0	1	0	0	0	0	0	0	0	0	0	0	0	0	0
Chromosom 1								Chromosom 2															

Fig. 2. The example of genotype.

In this case we have to create the following indexes:

```
Create index ind1 on table1 (col3)
Create index ind2 on table1 (col1, col3)
Create index ind3 on table2 (col1, col2)
```

Important thing is, that the number of indexes for a table is limited by a database system, so we have to handle this exception, and delete indexes.

The value of the fitness function was computed as follows. After creating index set for a given genotype, we computed overall time of all **INSERT** executions multiplied by frequency of queries from users and overall time of queries multiplied by frequency. Then, the sum of these time inverses gave us the final fitness function value (1). Of course, we tend to the situation when the computed value is biggest. During the experiments we tried to optimize our database, e.g. for queries - then again the activation function value consisted of sum of queries and insertions time inverse, but this time the queries time was multiplied by a certain positive number. Accordingly, we can optimize the database engine with respect to several chosen queries. After computing fitness function values for all genotypes we attempted to perform mutation and crossover operations. Before the fitness function values computation, the database has to be clean, i.e. indexes from the previous generation have to be removed. The fittnes fuction is computed by

$$f = \frac{1}{\sum_{i=1}^{N_i} t_{Ins}\mu_i} + \frac{1}{\sum_{i=1}^{N_q} t_{quer}\eta_i} , \tag{1}$$

where
t_{ins} – execution time of Insert command
t_{quer} – execution time of Select command
μ_i, η_i – how many times users executed Insert and Select command, respectively
N_i – number of Insert commands
N_q – number of Select commands

3   Numerical Simulations

In our simulations, we tried to find the optimal index for the employees table. The database was filled with artificial data. In the LastName column there were unique names created from random letters. The size of the database was 200MB. The optimized query had the form

```
Select name, firstname, city from employees
order by name, firstname, city
```

The execution frequency was 80. In the experiment we also inserted data into every column with 60 frequency. The time before the indexing was 15 seconds. Our genetic algorithm found the optimal answer 7 times out of 10 runs. The right index here was the index created on the fields name, first name, city. The drawback of this approach was a long time of optimal solution searching, but this is a common characteristic of genetic algorithms.

4   Conclusions

In the paper we developed a new way to find the best set of indexes in large databases. The proposed approach is based on a genetic algorithm with a fitness function depending on the execution time of query and insert operations. Simulation results confirmed that the algorithm is able to find the best set of indexes resulting in improved efficiency of the database system.

References

1. Arabas J., *Lectures of evolutionary algorithms* (in Polish), WNT, Warsaw, 2001
2. Babuska R., *Fuzzy Modeling For Control*, Kluwer Academic Press, Boston, 998.
3. Gnybek Jadwiga, *Oracle latwiejszy niz przypuszczasz* (in Polish), Helion, 2000
4. Goldberg David, *Genetic Algorithms in Search, Optimization, and Machine Learning* (in Polish), WNT, Warsaw, 1998
5. Gutta Rayendra, *Oracle DBA Automation Scripts*,SAMS Publishing 2002
6. Honour Edward, Dalberth Paul, Kaplan Ari, Mehta Atul , *Oracle 8 How-To*, Sams Corporation
7. Jakubowski Arkadiusz, *SQL in Interbase* (in Polish), Helion, 2001
8. Rutkowska Danuta, Pilinski Maciej, Rutkowski Leszek, *Neural Networks, Genetic Algorithms and Fuzzy Systems* (in Polish), PWN, 1997
9. Urman Scott, *Oracle 9i PL/SQL Programming*,The McGraw-Hill/Osborne 2002

Application of Neural Networks and Two Representations of Color Components for Recognition of Wheat Grains Infected by *Fusarium Culmorum* Fungi*

Aleksander Kubiak[1] and Zbigniew Mikrut[2]

[1] University of Warmia and Mazury, Faculty of Food Sciences,
Institute of Process Engineering and Equipment, ul.Oczapowskiego 7,
10-725 Olsztyn, Poland
Aleksander.Kubiak@uwm.edu.pl
[2] AGH University of Science and Technology, Institute of Automatics,
Biocybernetic Laboratory, al.Mickiewicza 30
30-059 Kraków, Poland
zibi@agh.edu.pl

Abstract. The paper presents a study of utility of two representation types: the log-polar representation and histograms of individual color components of grain surface images for recognition of wheat infected by the *Fusarium* genus fungi. The representations have been used as input data for a *backpropagation* type neural networks of various sizes of the hidden layer and - as a reference - for a Nearest Neighbor classifier. The best individual recognition rate has been obtained for the log-polar representation of Blue color component (98.8%). Quality assessment has been also done (in the sense of robustness of results obtained from neural networks of various structures).

1 Introduction

The recently observed increase in the occurrence of symptoms of wheat grain infection by *Fusarium* genus fungi presents one of the primary problems in the area of consumable products safety. The wheat grains infected by *Fusarium* are easily recognized by the slightly chalky or pink shade of their surface. Frequently they are also smaller and their surface is wrinkled but these features cannot be used as criteria for *Fusarium* infection, because the presence of size and shape variety for seeds in one ear is a natural situation. The standard methods of evaluation of the grain infection level are based on time-consuming microbiological analyses or visual evaluation of the seed sample by a team of experts. Such evaluation is laborious, subjective and dependent on the professional training level of the experts. The evaluation of the level of wheat grain infection by *Fusarium* by application of computer image analysis has been the subject of [5], however the study has

---

* This work was partially supported by the AGH UST grant No 10.10.120.39.

L. Rutkowski et al. (Eds.): ICAISC 2004, LNAI 3070, pp. 1148–1153, 2004.
© Springer-Verlag Berlin Heidelberg 2004

been focused on changes in color of the whole layer of grains. The objective of the present work is the evaluation of two representations used for six basic color components: the histogram and log-polar representations for identification of **individual** wheat grains infected by the *Fusarium* genus fungi. The representations have been used as input data for neural networks and k-NN classifiers.

2   Research Material

The research material used was the Torka wheat variety, the ears of which have been intentionally infected by the *Fusarium Culmorum* fungi spores. Taking into account the fact that not all seed in the infected ears have to exhibit microbiological infection [3] the following sample of the material has been taken for the analysis: 200 seeds with visible *Fusarium* infection symptoms and 200 seeds used as a reference (uninfected) sample. Such a procedure conforms to the standard method used for evaluation of wheat seed infection by fungi and is usually carried out by a team of professionally trained experts.

3   Generation of Object Representations

The images of grains in the "crease down" position have been registered in a research setup for computer image analysis in scattered light. The setup consisted of the following elements:

- half-cylinder shaped screen with 150mm x 150mm basis dimensions and 75mm height, covered with white, mat paint layer,
- directional light with halogen lamp and two extra bunches of optical fibres enabling the proper lighting of the screen,
- standard color CCD camera,
- Matrox Magic image analysis video card with Lucia 4.61 software.

The color images of grains have been decomposed into color components in the two most popular systems of color coding: RGB and HSI. For all of the six components two types of representations have been determined: the histogram and log-polar representations. The histogram representation has been determined for the whole area of the isolated object (without the background). After binarizing the image the mask of the object has been superimposed on the individual color component maps and 128 point histograms have been produced.

For construction of the second representation the log-polar transform [6,7, 8] has been used. The Cartesian space of the digital image is transformed by projecting over it a set of fields (sectors) contained between concentric circles of exponentially growing radii and radial lines uniformly distributed on the circumference of the circles (see Fig.1a). Pixels contained within each field are summed and averaged.

The log-polar transform exhibits several valuable advantages. They include: large information reduction and convenience of performing such operations like

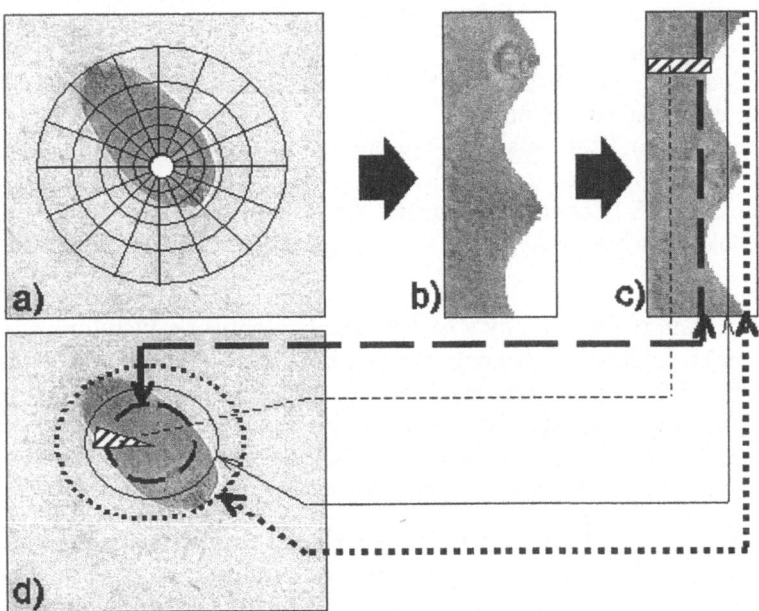

Fig. 1. Generation of the log-polar representation: a) the source image (the B color component), b) log-polar representation after centering, c) after angular normalization and division into appropriate areas, d) the same as c) but in Cartesian space. The log-polar image has been magnified in vertical direction about 5 times

object centering and its angular normalization. In the present work the applied log-polar transform covered 144x50 fields (angles x circles). The process of generation of the respective log-polar transform has been schematically shown in Fig.1. The object (grain) is iteratively centered in the log-polar space, and then undergoes the angular normalization (see Fig.1a,b,c).

The details of that procedure have been described in previous papers [2,4], therefore in the present paper only the last stage of calculations is described. In the log-polar image of the grain two lines are determined, adjacent respectively to the most outer and most inner points in the grain's edge. These lines can be attributed respectively to the circumscribed and inscribed circles on the grain's outline (see Fig.1d). In the middle of the distance between the lines third line is drawn, which marks the area for calculation of averaged object's pixel values for each of the 144 sectors. The averaging is carried out along radial coordinate, what is equivalent to averaging pixel values along the horizontal coordinate in the log-polar space. This is done for pixels which belong to the object and at the same time lie below the demarcation line formed by the middle circle. An exemplary averaging area has been schematically shown in Fig.1c, as a hatched rectangle and in Fig.1d as the respective circular section in the Cartesian space. The limitation of the analysis area in the log-polar representation results in taking into account the most important changes in the seed's color: it discards the most outer area of the seed like the germ and brush, which in the experts' opinions, contribute little information about the level of *Fusarium* infection. The color component representation of the wheat grains in the log-polar space after averaging consisted of 144 points.

The learning and test sets both consisted of 200 grains: 100 uninfected grains (class 1) and 100 infected grains (class 2). The data sets have been collected for all six (R,G,B,H,S,I) color components. The calculation have been done using the PRTools software package [1], from which the following options have been applied:

- learning and recognition by a *backpropagation* network, including one hidden layer with number of elements varying between 3 and 30. The experiments with the BP network have been repeated three times,
- learning and recognition by the k-NN (Nearest Neighbor) method for both representations, using k=1 and "optimal" k. The latter has been optimized over the learning set using a leave-one-out error estimation [1].

All calculations have been carried out for all color components for both representations: log-polar and histograms. Such an approach required carrying out: 6 x 28(layers) x 2(representations) x 3(times) = 1008 experiments with neural networks and 6 x 2(representations) x 2(one neighbor and "optimal" number of neighbors) = 24 experiments with the k-NN method.

4   Results

The list of the best recognition rates (test set) for individual color components and various network configurations is shown in Table 1.

Table 1. The recognition results for the test sets for individual color components (* - average value of 3 repetitions, ** - "optimal" k=2)

Color components	Recognition rate BP* 144-12-2 log-polar	Recognition rate BP* 128-18-2 histograms	Recognition rate k-NN (k=1) log-polar	Recognition rate k-NN (k=1) histograms
R	92.8%	96.2%	89.0%	93.5%**
G	95.3%	96.3%	94.5%	97.5%
B	**98.8%**	96.3%	**97.5%**	97.0%
H	87.2%	93.5%	85.0%	92.0%
S	98.0%	96.8%	95.0%	98.0%
I	96.3%	**98.0%**	95.0%	**98.0%****

For all the color components (R,G,B,H,S,I) used an additional parameter, called "result stability", has been determined as average value of the recognition rates and theirs respective standard deviations as a function of number of elements in the hidden layer (see Table 2).

Table 2. The "result stability" values for log-polar and histogram representations

Color	Log-polar representation		Histogram representation	
components	Average value	Standard deviation	Average value	Standard deviation
R	92.82%	0.86%	95.50%	1.18%
G	95.80%	0.80%	95.83%	0.97%
B	**98.32%**	**0.38%**	96.78%	0.76%
H	87.26%	1.22%	93.26%	1.22%
S	97.32%	0.78%	96.83%	1.04%
I	96.62%	0.63%	**98.07%**	**0.22%**

5   Discussion and Conclusions

Among the log-polar representations the **B**lue component representation turned out to be the best, with average recognition rate 98.8% for a neural network with 12 neurons in the hidden layer (see Table 1). For the same color component and the same representation the recognition rate obtained by Nearest Neighbor (k-NN) method was 97.5%. For the histogram representations the best result (98%) has been obtained for the **I**ntensity component. However the best result has been obtained for greater number of neurons in the hidden layer (18), than for the log-polar representation. For the same color component and the same representation the recognition rate by the Nearest Neighbor (k-NN) methods was also equal to 98.0%.

In the course of analysis of the recognition results of log-polar representation for the other 4 color components: **R**ed and **G**reen as well as **H**ue and **S**aturation it has been found, that for all the cases examined the recognition rate was higher for the neural network method than for the Nearest Neighbor. The recognition rate by the neural network for the log-polar representations of these components (R,G,H,S) has been found to lie between 87.2% for **H** and 98.0% for **S**. For the k-NN classifier the respective values were between 85.0% for **H** and 95% for **S**. The recognition rate for the histogram representations varied between 93.5% for **H** and 96.8% for **S** components when neural network recognition was used and between 92% for **H** and 98% for **S** when recognized by the Nearest Neighbor method.

One of the objectives of the present research was to find out which representation and which color component is the best in correct recognition of *Fusarium* infected grains. For the results, obtained for specific architectures of the neural networks, the concepts of so called "recognition reliability" and the related rejection rate can be applied [2]. If results of a sufficiently wide research program were available it would be possible to carry out a simple statistical analysis of individual experiment series, in which the number of neurons in the hidden layer of the *backpropagation* neural network could be changed for a specific combination of representation and color component (see Table 2).

The motivation for carrying out such an analysis can be as follows. Both representations are somewhat similar in their nature: histograms are statistical distributions for pixels of a specific color, while the log-polar representation also presents some spatially distributed statistical dependencies (averaging over specific areas). Therefore the recognition should comprise the detection of proper intensities of color components in some (separate) areas of the input vector. It seems that for such a case the very precise adjustment of the neural network to the input vectors is not required (contrary to the case of object outline analysis, when it is necessary for detection of minute differences). For the cases of "appropriate" representation the recognition results obtained for networks with various hidden layers should be similar (at least within some range of the changes). As a result of the analysis of "result stability", understood as the comparison of average values and standard deviations of respective recognition rates for various number of elements in the hidden layer it was found that for the log-polar representation the best color component was the Blue one, for which the average recognition rate was 98.32%, with a standard deviation of 0.38%. For the histogram representation the best was Intensity component (98.07% and 0.22% respectively). The results indicate the relevance of both representations for such application, however the recognition rate for the application of neural networks and log-polar representation seems to give the best results.

References

1. Duin, R.P.W.: PRTools Version 3.0 - a Matlab Toolbox for Pattern Recognition. Delft University of Technology, http://www.ph.tn.tudelft.nl/prtools (2000)
2. Kubiak, A., Mikrut, Z.: Method for Detection of Grain Damage with Application of Neural Networks. In: Rutkowski, J., Kacprzyk, J., Eds: Proc. of the 6th Int. Conf. on Neural Networks and Soft Computing, Zakopane, Poland, Advances in Soft Computing, Physica-Verlag, Heidelberg New York (2003)
3. McMullen, M.P., Stack, R.W.: Fusarium Head Blight (Scab) of small grains. North Dakota State University Extension Service, PP-804 (1999) 1–5
   http://www.extnodak.edu/extpubs/smgrains/pp804w.htm
4. Mikrut, Z.: Recognition of objects normalized in Log-polar space using Kohonen networks. Proc. of the 2nd Int. Symp. on Image and Signal Processing and Analysis, Pula, Croatia (2001)
5. Ruan, R., Ning, S., Song, A., Ning, A., Jones, R., Chen, P.L.: Estimation of Fusarium scab in wheat using machine vision and neural network. Cereal Chemistry 75 (1997) 455–459
6. Schwartz, E.L.: Spatial mapping in the primate sensory projection: analytic structure and the relevance to perception. Biological Cybernetics, 25 (1977) 181–194
7. Tadeusiewicz R., Mikrut Z.: Neural-Based Object Recognition Support: from Classical Preprocessing to Space-Variant Sensing. Proc. of the ICSC/IFAC Symposium on Neural Computation '98, Vienna, Austria (1998) 463–468
8. Weiman, C.F.R.: Polar exponential sensor arrays unify iconic and Hough space representation. SPIE vol.1192: Intelligent robots and computer vision VIII (1989)

Hybrid Neural Model of the Sea Bottom Surface

Jacek Lubczonek

Maritime Academy, Waly Chrobrego 1/2, 70-500 Szczecin, Poland,
jaclub@wsm.szczecin.pl

Abstract. Paper presents method of construction neural model of the
sea bottom. Constructed model consisted of set of smaller models (local
approximators). For model approximation was used set of *RBF* networks
with various kernels, what enabled approximation of the entire model by
networks with different structure. Experimental results show that in this
way we can obtain better results than applying neural model based on
local approximators with the same structure.

1 Introduction

A faithful shape of the real surface of the sea bottom requires maximum accuracy, as it is needed in the marine navigation in calculating the depth of an area.
Now the bottom surface in electronic chart is presented in the form of points
and contour lines. In more advanced chart there are applied digital terrain models, which can be created by applying different surface modelling method. In
this case, the accuracy of surface representation depends on the number and distribution of measurement points and on the applied surface modelling method,
which sometimes features several options [9]. The shape of a modelled surface is
also important as it may sometimes have regular or irregular forms. The proper
interpretation and choice of these factors affect the quality of the digital model
of the seabed. Covering all of these factors is very difficult, especially during
large and irregular surfaces modelling. Good alternatives to traditional methods
of surface modelling are neural networks[5][6], because during network training
we can cover all above factors. Moreover, having trained network it is possible
to calculate unknown depth value at any points without application of additional algorithms, what simplifies data processing. This paper presents hybrid
neural model, which enables surface modelling based on smaller and optimized
local approximators. Presented hybrid neural model has solved problem of model building from a larger dataset. Experimental results show also that it can
improve accuracy of surface approximation.

2 Structure of Neural Model

Concept of building the sea bottom model was presented in [1]. That model
consisted of the set of smaller models (local approximators), which enabled approximation of modelled phenomenon. In the proposed solution model had two

L. Rutkowski et al. (Eds.): ICAISC 2004, LNAI 3070, pp. 1154–1160, 2004.
© Springer-Verlag Berlin Heidelberg 2004

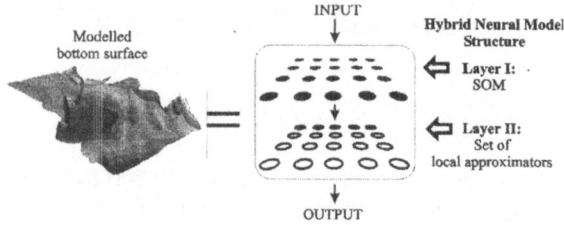

Fig. 1. Structure of neural model and modelled bottom surface

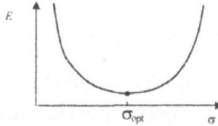

Fig. 2. Minimum of error curve corresponds to optimal value of RBF radius

layers. The first layer consisted of the self-organising network. In the second layer was situated a set of networks, which locally approximated the surface. Structure of neural model of bottom surface was illustrated in figure 1. Those local approximators were situated in 2D space by self-organized network, which enabled the model construction and further data processing. Applying such structure there were solved such problems like surface approximation from bigger data sets, training sets' creation and automated data processing. During depth computation self-organized network classified an input vector to the neuron with biggest activation, which indicated proper trained network in the second layer. To obtain digital model of bottom there was presented on model input set of *GRID* knots (x, y), what allows creating set of trios (x, y, z), used further for surface visualization.

3   Optimisation of Local Approximators

The second layer of model consisted of the set of radial networks. Radial networks in contrast to mutilayer perceptron are easier in optimalisation - they have constant number of layers. We can also choose between exact solution (interpolation) and approximation, by reducing or not data set. The main reason of applying them was their local character of approximation, what enables preserving irregular forms of nautical bottom and some features of transfer functions with adjustable radius. By changing RBF radius, the surface being approximated could be fitted to the set of data points with required accuracy. This feature also allows controlling and determining error of surface approximation by optimalisation of the one parameter. It causes that the RBF radius (σ) plays the role of the shape parameter and its optimal value (σ_{opt}) minimize the error of surface approximation E [7], what was illustrated in figure 2.

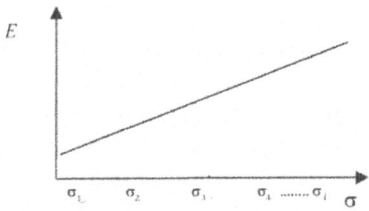

Fig. 3. Approximate graph of error curve for unfavourable spatial distribution of data

During surface reconstruction from track data we rather should apply exact solution – interpolation. Such way of reconstruction preserves all data values, what is important in the case of occurring underwater dangers (they induce often rapid changes of surface shape). In that case, the problem of surface reconstruction seems to be easy - to minimize an approximation error there should be find the optimal σ value. However, some experiments proved that some unfavourable spatial layout of data had significant influence on RBF radius optimalisation. The problem of optimalisation concerned *multiquadric* function (1), widely applied in geographical surface modelling.

$$\varphi_i(x) = \left[\|x - t_i\|^2 + \sigma^2\right]^{1/2} \tag{1}$$

where: φ – radial basis function, x – input vector, t – centre of radial basis function, σ – *RBF* radius (exactly some positive parameter).

In some cases, better results were obtained by applying very small σ parameter, which during optimalisation converged to zero [8]. Similar results were obtained during own experiments, where studied error of surface approximation was still increased like in figure 3.

Thus, the next step was the experiment with $\sigma = 0$, what also has changed type of transfer function - from *multiquadric* to *linear* (2).

$$\varphi_i(x) = \|x - t_i\| \tag{2}$$

By applying kernels with linear function there have been achieved better results for some cases than by applying *MQ* function with very little σ. In structure of neural model of the sea bottom it means, that the second layer can consist of radial networks with different kernels - multiquadric or linear.

4   Algorithm of Kernel Choosing

Neural models of the bottom surface may have many local approximators with different kernels. For automation of kernel choosing there was modified an algorithm of radius optimalisation, which was presented in previous work [2]. The main aim of that research was to work out the method of determination the optimal value of σ, which covered all factors having influence on the surface shape.

It consisted of two stages. At the first stage there was selected subset of testing points from dataset. It was used to calculate *RMS* error for various values of the shape parameter (σ) by applying *cross-validation* method. The sought value of the shape parameter has corresponded to the minimum of error curve; analogue like in figure 2. In this way, there could be found approximate solution (σ^*), because independent subset does not always guarantee the convergence to the optimal solution; there is known problem of optimal division data set into the training and testing subset [4]. Thus, at the second stage the optimal value of the shape parameter (σ_{opt}) was calculated by applying *leave-one-out* method, which is based on one-element testing set. However, this efficient method for estimating model quality is very time-consuming. On the one hand, by applying it we can create accurate neural model of phenomenon, but on the other it is rather not applicable in the case of big number of data sets. Thus, searching the optimal value of the shape parameter was started from approximate solution (σ^*). In this way we can efficiently shorten time of calculation and conduct optimalisation for the set of local approximators in the second layer of neural model. That algorithm was modified in aspect of choosing proper type of transfer function. Below are described the algorithm steps:

1) Create the set of testing data points (15% of data number);

2) Perform data pre-processing by applying *minimax* function [4];

3) Calculate approximate value of σ (σ^*). Firstly calculate surface approximation errors (RMS_i) by using testing set for successive values of σ_i, where $\sigma_{i+1} - \sigma_i = c$ (c denotes little constant interval, e.g. $c = 0.2$). Calculation should start from $\sigma_1 = 0$, and stop when $\sigma > 2 * \sigma_e$ (σ_e denotes value of kernel radius calculated by empirical method, e.g. presented in [7]). Then, having RMS errors' values, approximate error curve and find its minimum, which corresponds to approximate kernel radius (σ^*).

4) Calculation of optimal value (σ_{opt}) and kernel choosing. Start calculations for $\sigma_i = \sigma^*$. Calculate mean approximation errors (e_{i-1}, e_i, e_{i+1}) for σ_{i-1}, σ_i, σ_{i+1} for testing points by using *leave-one-out* method (interval between σ's equals certain little value b, e.g. $b = 0.1$). Continue calculation to find error minimum; if $e_i < e_{i+1}$ and $e_i < e_{i-1}$ then $\sigma_{opt} = \sigma_i$. If the minimal error was achieved for $\sigma = 0$ then the linear transfer function was chosen. While approximation error was decreasing, there was possibility to calculate minimum of error curve and σ_{opt} corresponded to that minimum.

5) Stop and start calculation for the next neural network.

5   Experimental Results

Surface modelling was conducted on 1314 real data. Data were recorded during hydrographical survey in port of Gdansk by using singlebeam echo-sounder. That surface had irregular shape and domain. Constructed hybrid neural model consisted of 26 neurons, what automatically gave the same number of local approximators (*RBF* networks). In each training subset were about 137 trai-

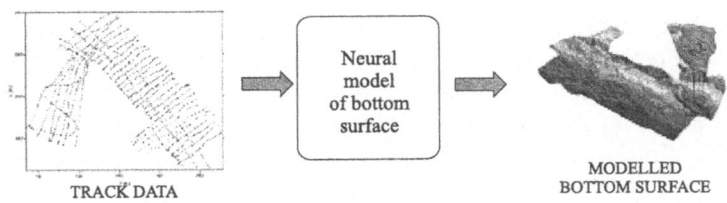

Fig. 4. Modelling surface from track data by application of hybrid neural model

ning data. Spatial layout of data points, modelled shape of bottom surface and general idea of reconstruction was presented in figure 4.

Modelling was performed for three various structures of hybrid neural model (HNM): *Case 1* - interpolation, without neurons' reduction (HNM1); *Case 2* - approximation, with constant number of 30 neurons in hidden layer (HNM2); *Case 3* - approximation, with various numbers of neurons, where error of surface approximation has not exceeded 0.42 m (HNM3). Numbers of approximators with various transfers function for each case were different. In the first case, there was more networks with linear transfer functions, in the second and third - more multiquadric functions (tab.1).

Table 1. Number of approximators with *MQ* and linear kernels

Type of kernel	Case 1	Case 2	Case 3
MQ	4	22	25
Linear	22	4	1

There were also calculated errors of surface approximation on independent testing subset (5% of data number). For comparison, modelling was performed by applying neural models with different structure. In the second layers were used radial networks with MQ function (HNM MQ) and multilayer perceptrons with 30 neurons in hidden layer, trained by Levenberg - Marquardt algorithm (MLP). Neural methods were also compared to traditional methods like: *kriging* (settings: linear semivariogram, interpolation from 24 nearest samples, four-sector sample search); *Minimum Curvature Method* (settings: internal tension = 0, boundary tension = 0.5, maximum iteration number = 8000, maximum residual = 0.008); *Natural Neighbor Method*; *Inverse Distance to a Power* (settings: power = 2, interpolation from 24 nearest samples, four-sector sample search); *Triangulation*. Results are given in Tab.2.

Table 2. Comparison of neural and traditional methods

Method	MNM1	Krig.	MCM	NNM	MLP	HNM2	Triang.	IDM	HNM MQ	HNM3
RMS[m]	0.16	0.19	0.20	0.21	0.21	0.22	0.25	0.26	0.28	to 0.42

As we can note, the best result was obtained by using neural model with mixed neural networks (HNM 1). That value was equalled 0.16 m. Worse results were obtained for the second case (HNM 2) and for MLP networks - 0.22 m and 0.21 m. For RBF approximators with MQ kernel error value was higher - 0.28 m (HNM MQ). In the third case (HNM 3), error has reached constant threshold - 0.42 m. Better results had traditional methods like kriging (0.19 m), minimum curvature (0.20 m) or natural neighbour (0.21 m).

6   Conclusion

Paper has presented method of surface modelling based on hybrid neural model. That model consisted of set of local approximators. Construction of that model was done by self-organized network, which enabled to create smaller training subsets and distribute local approximators within model space. For better model approximation there was used mixed set of approximators - RBF networks with linear or MQ kernels. Proper kernels can be chosen by presented algorithm based on optimalisation of RBF radius. Such structure of bottom neural model allows building bottom model, which covers all factors influenced on accuracy of bottom approximation. During surface reconstruction there is no need of parameter optimalisation, what is essential and sometimes complicated while application of traditional methods. For the studied case, application of RBF networks with different kernels has given the best results, what enabled obtaining more accurate bathymetric data.

References

[1] Łubczonek J., Stateczny A. Concept of Neural Model of the Sea Bottom Surface. Advances in Soft Computing, Proceedings of the Sixth International, Conference on Neural Network and Soft Computing, Zakopane, Poland, June, 11-15, 2002, Rutkowski, Kacprzyk, Eds., Physica-Verlag (2002), pp. 861-866.

[2] Stateczny A., Łubczonek J. The construction of digital terrain model by using neural networks with optimized radial basis functions, Reports on Geodesy (2003), pp. 185-195.

[3] Stateczny A., Łubczonek J. Spatial sea chart – new possibilities of presenting navigational information. Ist International Congress of Seas and Oceans (vol 1), Miedzyzdroje (2001), pp. 523-528.

[4] Duch W., Korbicz J., Rutkowski L., Tadeusiewicz R. Biocybernetic and biomedical engineering 2000 (vol 6 Neural networks). Academic Publishing House, Warsaw (2000), (in Polish), pp. 67-69.

[5] Balicki J., Kitowski Z., Stateczny A. Artificial neural networks for modelling of spatial shape of sea bottom. IV Conference of Neural Networks and Their Applications, Zakopane (1999), pp. 637-643.

[6] Stateczny A., The Neural Method of Sea Bottom Shape Modelling for Spatial Maritime Information System. Marine Engineering and Ports II. Editors C.A. Brebbia & J. Olivella. WIT Press Southampton, Boston (2000).

[7] Tarwater A. E., A Parameter Study of Hardy's Multiquadric Method for Scattered Data Interpolation. Technical Report UCRL-53670. Lawrence Livermore National Laboratory, California (1985).

[8] Carlson R. E., Foley T.A. Radial Basis Interpolation Methods on Track Data. Technical Report UCLR-JC-1074238. Lawrence Livermore National Laboratory, California (1991).

[9] Lubczonek J., A Comparison of Selected Method of Surface Modelling: an Example of Seabed Surface, Scientific Bulletin No. 59, Maritime Academy, Szczecin 2000.

Fuzzy Economic Analysis of Simulated Discrete Transport System

Jacek Mazurkiewicz and Tomasz Walkowiak

Institute of Engineering Cybernetics, Wroclaw University of Technology,
ul. Janiszewskiego 11/17, 50-372 Wroclaw, Poland
{jmazur,twalkow}@ict.pwr.wroc.pl

Abstract. The paper presents fuzzy economic analysis of discrete transport systems in a function of system element reliability. Such approach can be used for a description of different problems related to transport logistics. No restriction on the system structure and on a kind of distribution is the main advantage of the proposed solution. Additionally the results of reliability and functional analysis can be used as a basis for economic aspects discussion related to discrete transport system. Fuzzy approach allows to reduce the problem of assumptions of reliability distributions.

1 Introduction

Modern transportation systems often have a complex network of connections. From the reliability point of view [1] the systems are characterized by a very complex structure. The classical models used for reliability analysis are mainly based on Markov or Semi-Markov processes [1] which are idealized and it is hard to reconcile them with practice. The typical structures with reliability focused analysis are not complicated and use very strict assumptions related to the life or repair time and random variables distributions of the analyzed system elements. There is a possibility to use a time event simulation with Monte Carlo analysis [2] instead of classic reliability analysis. It allows to calculate any point wise parameters. We can also estimate different distributions of time being in a state or in a set of states. Modern trucks are characterized by very screwed up reliability parameters and there are quite serious problems with assumptions related to the reliability distributions. Therefore, the reliability parameters are fixed based on experts' experience. This fact is the reason why fuzzy approach to reliability parameters description is justifiable [7].

2 Discrete Transport System (DTS)

2.1 System Overview

Basic elements of system are as follow: store-houses of tradesperson, roads, vehicles, trans-shipping points, store-houses of addressee and transported media

L. Rutkowski et al. (Eds.): ICAISC 2004, LNAI 3070, pp. 1161–1167, 2004.
© Springer-Verlag Berlin Heidelberg 2004

(commodities). The commodities are taken from store-houses of tradesperson and transported by vehicles to trans-shipping points. Other vehicles transport commodities from trans-shipping points to next trans-shipping points or to final store-houses of addressees. Moreover, in time of transportation vehicles dedicated to commodities could failed and then they are repaired (Fig. 1) [3], [4].

Different *commodities* are characterized by common attribute which can be used for their mutual comparison: capacity of commodities. The following assumptions related to the commodities are taken: it is possible to transport n different kinds of commodity in the system and each kind of commodity is measured by its capacity.

Road is an ordered double of system elements. The first element must be a store-house of tradesperson or trans-shipping point, the second element must be a trans-shipping point or store-house of addressee. Moreover, the road is described by following parameters: length, number of maintain crews, number of vehicles moving on the road. The road is assumed to have no damages.

A single *vehicle* transports commodities from start to end point of a single road, return journey realizes in an empty status and the whole cycle is repeated. The assumptions are as follow: a single kind of commodity is transported at the moment, vehicles are universal. Moreover, the vehicle is described by following parameters - capacity, mean speed of journey and - described by distribution: journey time, time to vehicle failure, time of vehicle maintenance. The distributions of mentioned random variables can be unrestricted.

The *store-house of tradesperson* is an infinity source of single kind of commodity. *Trans-shipping points* are a transition part of the system which are able to store the commodities. The trans-shipping point is described by following parameters: global capacity, initial state described by capacity vector of commodities stored when the system observation begins, delivery matrix. This matrix defines which road is chosen when each kind of commodity leaves the shipping point. The commodity could be routed to more then one direction. Only one vehicle can be unloaded at the moment. If the vehicle can be unloaded, the commodity is stored in the trans-shipping point. If not, the vehicle is waiting in the only one input queue serviced by FIFO algorithm. Only one vehicle can be loaded at the moment. If the vehicle can be loaded (i.e. the proper commodity is presented and it could be routed a given road) the state of trans-shipping is reduced. If not, the vehicle is waiting in the each output road FIFO queue.

The main task of the *store-houses of addressee* is to store the commodity as long as the medium is spent by the recipient. The store-house of addressee is described by following parameters: global capacity, initial state described as for the trans-shipping point, function or rule which describes how each kind of commodity is spent by recipients. Input algorithm is exactly the same as for trans-shipping point. Output algorithm can be described as: stochastic process, continuous deterministic or discrete deterministic one. Moreover, the following assumptions are taken: the capacity of the commodity can't be less than zero, "no commodity state" - is generated when there is a lack of required kind of commodity.

2.2   Programming Simulation

The DTS model could be analyzed be means of computer simulation. A software package for simulation of the discrete transport system has been developed. The DTS is described by input file (with syntax similar to XML). The main task of the software package (written in C++) is the Monte-Carlo simulation [2]. The simulation algorithm is based on tracking all states of system elements. The state is a base for a definition of an event, which is understood as a triple: time of being happened, object identifier and state. Based on each event and states of all system elements rules for making a new event has been encoded in the simulation program. The random number generator was used to deal with random events, i.e. failures.

2.3   Economic Analysis

The economic analysis is realized from vehicle owner's view-point [4]. The revenue is proportional to number of store-houses of addressee, number of deliveries realized to single store-house of addressee and gain for single delivery to single store-house of addressee. Following costs are taken into account: penalty costs - paid by a transportation firm when there is a lack of commodity in the store-house of addressee, repair costs - proportional to a unit of repair time, vehicle usage costs - in a function of time (salary of drivers) and in a function of distance (i.e. costs of petrol). The economic quality of discrete transport system is described by overall gain function $G(T)$ estimated in given time-period T as difference between the revenue and costs. We have to remember that the overall gain $G(T)$ is a random variable.

3   Fuzzy Analysis

3.1   Case Study

To show the possibilities of the proposed model we have analyzed an exemplar transport network presented in Fig. 1. It consists of two different commodities transported over network (marked as A and B) from two producers through two trans-shipping points to two consumers. Each commodity is spent by a given recipient. The process is continuous deterministic. Roads lengths and the number of vehicles are presented in Fig. 1. All vehicles have the same parameters (see section 2.1). To each road one maintains crew is assigned. Number of vehicles assigned to each road was calculated on a basis on required amount of commodities spent by each recipient taking into account some redundancy due to the fact of vehicle failures [5].

3.2   Fuzzy Reliability Parameters

We want to analyze the overall system gain $G(T)$ in a function of fuzzy representation of truck reliability parameter: mean time of failures. We are not analyzing

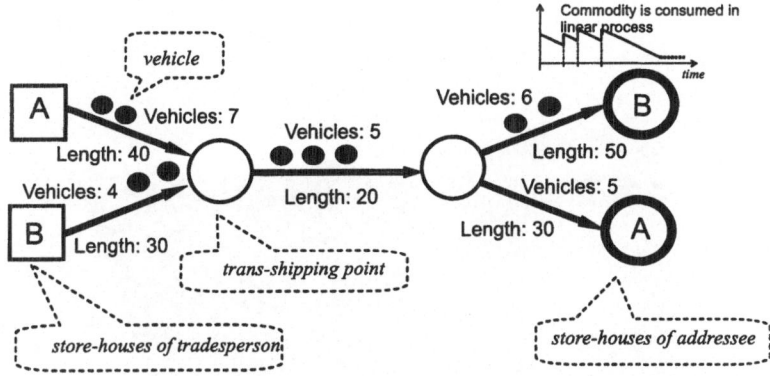

Fig. 1. Discrete transport system - case study example

the classical reliability values: intensities of failures by its inverse of intensities since we think that it is much easer for expert to express the failure parameter in time units [7].

For case study exemplar we assumed trapezoidal membership function for fuzzy representation of mean time of failure (let denotate is as: $\mu_{M_\mu}(m)$). The four trapezoidal parameters has been set to (500,1000,2000,3000) hours. Assumption of the fuzzy membership function shape does not bound following analysis. One could use any other membership function and apply presented here methodology. Such system could be understood as a simple single input and single output fuzzy system. Applying fuzzy operator like max one could have achieved results. However, as it is stated in section 2.3, the overall gain is a random value. Therefore for a given system parameters (i.e. a given mean time repair time) we got a set of overall gain values.

3.3   Fuzzy Gain Representation

A classical way of presentation of random values is a mean value. In our case mean value of the overall gain [4]. However, such method looses a very important information from simulation results. Therefore, we propose to represent the gain $G(T)$ as a fuzzy number. It could be done using for example the trapezoidal membership function. It's four parameters has been set based on mean value m and standard deviation std of achieved gain as $(m - 3std, m - std, m + std, m + 3std)$. The results of fuzzy gain $\mu_G(g, m)$ (g spans possible values of gain, m spans possible values of mean time to failure) for case study system is presented in Fig 2. However, the results are not taking into consideration the assumptions of fuzzy representation of mean time to failures (section 3.2).

3.4   Fuzzy Gain in Function of Fuzzy Reliability

Having the fuzzy gain representation $\mu_G(g, m)$ for each crisp value of the fuzzy reliability parameter $\mu_{M_\mu}(m)$, presented in Fig 2, we need to combine these

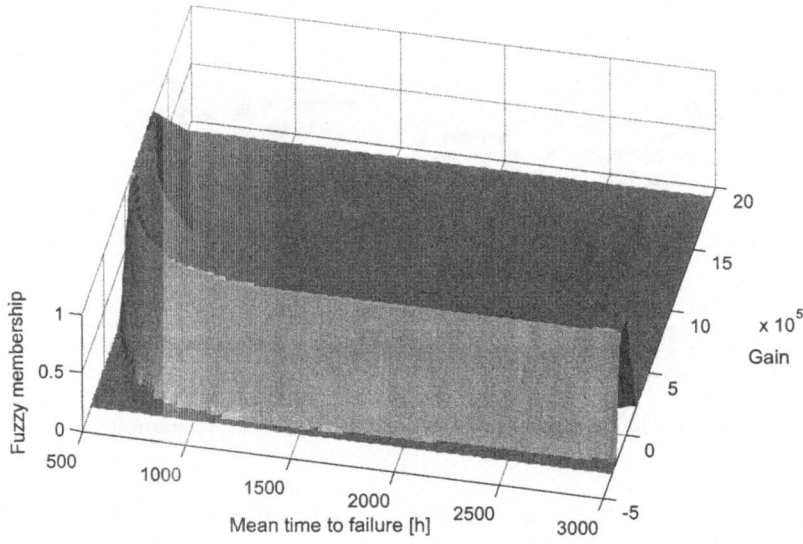

Fig. 2. Fuzzy representation of overall gain in function of mean time to failure

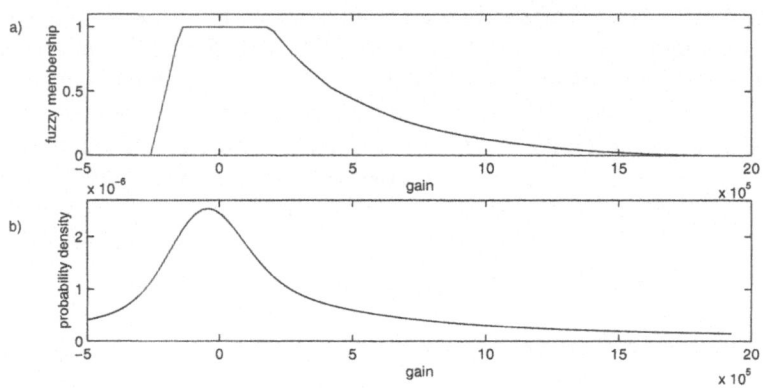

Fig. 3. Results: the overall gain presentation by a) fuzzy method and b) probability density method

two measures to achieve an overall fuzzy gain. We propose to apply max and multiply operator to solve this problem (results are presented on Fig. 3a). It gives the following equation for the fuzzy gain membership function:

$$\mu_G(g) = \underset{m}{MAX}\left\{\mu_G(g,m) \cdot \mu_{M_\mu}(m)\right\} \tag{1}$$

where: m - mean time to failure, g - gain value.

3.5   Probability Density Method

We propose also other way of final results presentation, based on probability density function estimation. Assuming that the fuzzy representation of mean time to failure (section 3.2) is a way of stating the probability of vehicle mean time to failure, we could calculate the overall gain probability density function using slightly modified kernel method (with Gaussian kernels). The modification is done by multiplication each kernel by the weighted fuzzy trapezoidal function. Based on N results of overall gain g_i from computer simulation, calculated for given values of meant time to failure m_i, the density function $f(g)$ is given by:

$$f(g) = \frac{1}{h \sum\limits_{j=1}^{N} \mu_{M_\mu}(m_j)} \sum_{i=1}^{N} \frac{1}{\sqrt{2\pi}} \exp\left(-\frac{1}{2}\left(\frac{g_i - g}{h}\right)^2\right) \cdot \mu_{M_\mu}(m_i) \qquad (2)$$

where h is a bandwidth parameter. It is set to optimal value based on maximal smoothing principle: AMISE - the asymptotic mean square error. Results for the case study DTS is presented in Fig. 3b.

4   Conclusion

Summarizing, we proposed a new method of fuzzy economic analysis. It is based on fuzzy reliability representation which allows to soften the typical assumptions related to the system structure and to reliability parameters of discrete transport system elements. The presented approach could be used as a foundation for a new methodology of the reliability and economic analysis, which is much closer to the practice experience.

Acknowledgment. Work reported in this paper was sponsored by a grant No. 5 T12C 021 25, (years: 2003-2006) from the Polish Committee for Scientific Research (KBN).

References

1. Barlow, R., Proschan, F.: Mathematical Theory of Reliability. Society for Industrial and Applied Mathematics, Philadelphia (1996)
2. Fishman, G.: Monte Carlo: Concepts, Algorithms, and Applications. Springer-Verlag, New York (1996)
3. Jarnicki, J., Mazurkiewicz, J., Zamojski, W.: Model of Discrete Transport System (In Polish). XXX Winter School of Reliability, Poland, Szczyrk (2002) 149–157
4. Kaplon, K., Mazurkiewicz, J., Walkowiak, T.: Economic Analysis of Discrete Transport Systems. Risk Decision and Policy **8** (2003) 179–190
5. Kaplon, K., Walkowiak, T.: Economic Aspects of Redundancy in Discrete Transport Systems (In Polish). XXXII Winter School of Reliability, Poland, Szczyrk (2004) 142–153

6. Mazurkiewicz J., Walkowiak T.: Simulation of Discrete Transport System. 36th International Conference Modeling and Simulation of Systems: MOSIS'2002, Czech Republic, Roznov pod Radhostem 1 (2002) 191–198
7. Mazurkiewicz J., Walkowiak T.: Fuzzy Reliability Analysis. ICNNSC'2002 – 6th International Conference Neural Networks and Soft Computing, Poland, Zakopane. Advances in Soft Computing, Physica-Verlag (2003) 298–303

A Survey on US Economic Sanction Effects on Iranian High Tech Industries: Fuzzy Logic Approach

Mohammad R. Mehregan[1,2], Hossein Safari[1,2], Parviz Naseri[1],
Farshid Hosseini[2], and Kumars Sharifi[2]

[1] Sanaray Software Export Research and Development Co., Tehran, Iran
[2] Department of Management, University of Tehran, Iran
h_safari@sanaray.com, pn@neda.net

Abstract. Economic sanctions have been a prominent part of American statecraft since World War II, and increasingly so since the end of the Cold War. Sanction usually consists of a ban on the sale and shipment of products to a country and on the purchase of its exports. Our objective is to conduct a comprehensive empirical analysis of US economic sanctions on Iranain high tech industries by means of fuzzy logic approach. We will measure US sanction effects on Iranian high tech industries and rank high Iranian tech industries based on their vulnerability from US sanction. Our methodology is based on these steps: determining attributes of US sanction affected on Iranain high techs', filtering selected attributes through fuzzy hypothesis test, and ranking of alternatives through Fuzzy Analytic Hierarchical Process (FAHP).

1 Introduction

The conventional understanding of economic sanctions is that they are an instrument of coercive diplomacy used by one state in an attempt to influence another state to change its policy or behavior. [4, 10] Economic sanctions seek to asphyxiate a nation by reducing or eliminating its access to foreign goods, capital, and/or markets. [8] There are two basic kinds of economic sanctions: trade sanctions and financial sanctions. Trade sanctions restrict imports and exports to and from the target country. Financial sanctions include blocking government assets held abroad, limiting access to financial markets and restricting loans and credits, restricting international transfer payments and restricting the sale and trade of property abroad. [9]The United States has maintained broad economic sanctions against Iran since 1984 and a near-total ban on United States imports from Iran since late 1987. [9]

In literature review, we can see more case studies than econometric analysis. Hufbauer et al [5] is among the few empirical studies of US unilateral economic sanctions using comprehensive economic (trade) data to quantify the impact of economic sanctions. There are other authors in this field like as Miyagawa [11], Kaempfer & Lowenberg [6], Peter Wallensteen [13], Parsi [12] and Askari et al [2].

L. Rutkowski et al. (Eds.): ICAISC 2004, LNAI 3070, pp. 1168–1174, 2004.
© Springer-Verlag Berlin Heidelberg 2004

The rest of the paper is organized as follows. In Section 2, we provide a description of the proposed methodology. In Section 3, we utilize our method for measuring vulnerability of high tech industries through fuzzy approach. Section 4 concludes the paper.

2   Methodology

This paper introduces a heuristic method applied for determining US sanction effects on Iranian high tech. This method includes four steps. (Fig. 1)

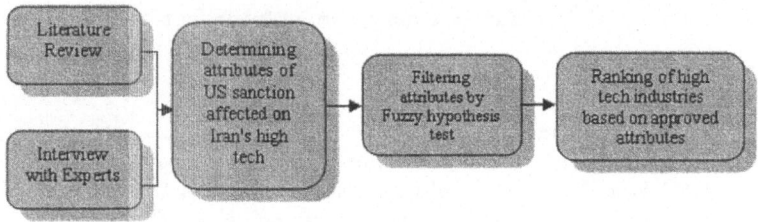

Fig. 1. Methodology of research

2.1   Determining Attributes of US Sanction

Two basic research methods have been employed: literature review and interview with experts. These works led us to find main vulnerable points of high tech by sanction.

2.2   Filtering Initial Attributes

In this section, intervening or not intervening of initial attributes (main vulnerable points) on Iranian high tech industries will be tested via fuzzy hypothesis test approach. Fuzzy hypothesis test includes four steps: [1]

Step1. *Hypotheses Formulation:* In this paper, seven based spectrum is used for formulating hypothesizes. Then for each attribute, we have:

H0: Importance of the i th attribute in US's sanction is "very much".
... and
H6: importance of the i th attribute in US's sanction is "very little"

Step2. Sampling: Sampling can be defined thorough researcher.

Step3. Testing: In this step, Larson requirement is used as formula (1); semantic variables of each hypothesis (e.g. very much) should be multiplied.

$$R(u_1 \otimes ... \otimes u_k \otimes v) = \mu_{\tilde{A}1}(u_1) \otimes \mu_{\tilde{A}2}(u_2) \otimes ... \otimes \mu_{\tilde{A}k}(u_k) \otimes \mu_B(v). \quad (1)$$

Finally, Average of $R(u_1 \otimes ... \otimes u_k \otimes v)$ in all of questionnaires is calculated.

$$M_L(D) = \frac{\sum_i M_L(x_i)}{\sigma}. \quad L = 0, 1, ..., r \ , \ \sigma = Quantity\,of\,Questionnaire \quad (2)$$

Step4. Decision Making: We have following conditions to test every attribute.

$$\begin{cases} \mu_0 + \mu_1 + \mu_2 + \mu_3 \geq 0.6 & \text{i th variable will be accept} \\ on\ the\ other\ case & \text{i th variable will not be accept} \end{cases} \tag{3}$$

2.3   Ranking of Iranain High Tech Industries Using FAHP

Based on this technique, decision makers can select the most optimal choice among several alternatives. [7] In 1983, two Dutch researchers, Wan Laurhaven & Pedrycg, proposed an approach for FAHP based on logarithmic least square and use fuzzy triangular numbers. After that a Chinese researcher, Dayong [3], introduced another method known as Extend Analysis (EA). [15] Also in our study, FAHP is used with Extend Analysis method. Executive steps of FAHP are sequentially: [14]

First step- Drawing decision hierarchy tree

Second step- Pairwise comparison

Third step- Calculations: Following formulas are used for analysis of collected data.

$$S_i = \sum_{j=1}^{n} M_{gi}^{\otimes} [\sum_{j=1}^{n} \sum_{j=1}^{m} M_{gi}^j]^{-1} . \tag{4}$$

$$V(S_i \geq S_j) = \begin{cases} 1 & m_i \geq m_j \\ hgt(S_j \cap S_i) = \frac{l_i - u_i}{(m_j - u_j) - (m_i - l_i)} & otherwise \end{cases} \tag{5}$$

$$W'(A_i) = Min[Si \geq S_1, S_2, ..., S_k] . \tag{6}$$

$$W_i = \frac{W_i'}{\sum W_i'} . \tag{7}$$

Forth step- Ranking the alternatives: By formula (8), alternatives will be rank.

$$W_i^* = P^T \times W_i \tag{8}$$

Where P^T is the transposed vector of weighted attributes and W_i is the matrix of sequencing of attributes and each alternatives.

3   Measuring Vulnerability of Iranain High Tech Industries

Iranian High Tech Center has eight committees. These committees are micro-electronic, biotechnology, aerospace, nanotechnology, software, new materials, laser and optic, and technology management. But in our study six committees surveyed.

Table 1. List of accepted attributes

Attributes No	Attributes Description	Membership Function
A_1	Imports	0.73
A_2	Buying professional software	0.71
A_3	Production Technology	0.70
A_4	Support Services	0.70
A_5	Knowledge Transition	0.62
A_6	Transactions between internal and external companies	0.67
A_7	Foreign Investment	0.72
A_8	Intermediation Channels	0.73
A_9	Copy of foreign software	0.67

3.1 Determining Attributes of US Sanction Effected on Iranian High Tech

Whereas we use multi attribute decision making in our analysis, there is a need to find some attributes for study of US sanction effects. Then we extracted 19 attributes from literature review that classified in eight categories and 54 attributes from 40 interviews with experts that classified in seven categories. Finally we combined two groups of attributes and quantity of attributes became to 62.

3.2 Filtering Selected Attributes through Fuzzy Hypothesis Test

In this step, a questionnaire based on above 62 attributes is designed. Then 60 people of experts are selected and questionnaire sent to them. From all of distributed questionnaires, 32 questionnaires were answered and returned. Analysis results of questionnaires, accepted attributes, are summarized in table 1.

3.3 Ranking of Alternatives through Fuzzy Analytic Hierarchical Process (FAHP)

In this step, at first, decision hierarchy tree as figure 2 is drawn. (In this figure, A_i is ith attribute and B_i is ith alternatives) Then, required data was collected via questionnaire. Table 2 shows pairwise data collected for attribute 5, knowledge transition, as a sample. Totally 65 questionnaires were distributed that 26 questionnaires came back.

From the formulae (4), for table 2, we get:

S1= (0.02, 0.13, 0.56), S2= (0.02, 0.10, 0.35), S3= (0.06, 0.22, 0.91),
S4= (0.04, 0.17, 0.74), S5= (0.04, 0.16, 0.71), S6= (0.05, 0.21, 0.86)

According to the formula (5) and (6), the simple sequencing of the six evaluation alternatives was derived: $W^T(A_i) = (0.84, 0.71, 1.00, 0.93, 0.91, 0.98)^T$.

And with respect to formula (7), we have: W_i= (0.16, 0.13, 0.19, 0.17, 0.17, 0.18).

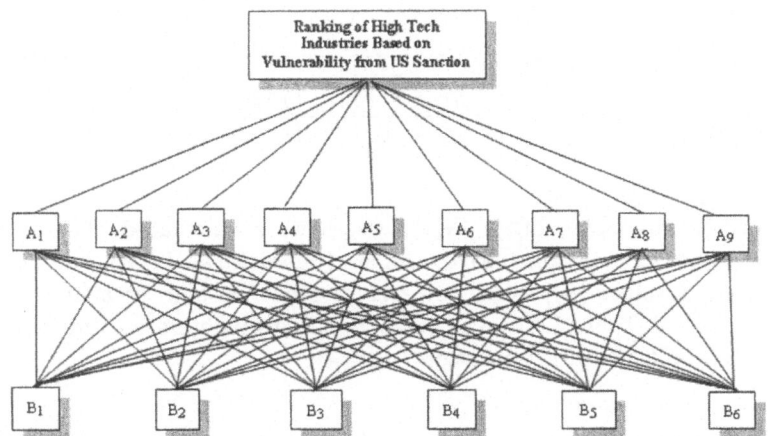

Fig. 2. Decision hierarchy tree

Table 2. Data of expert evaluation for Industries comparison based on Knowledge Transition

	B₁	B₂	B₃	B₄	B₅	B₆
B₁	(1, 1, 1)	(0.6, 1.3, 2.8)	(0, 0.6, 0.9)	(0, 0.8, 1.3)	(0, 0.8, 1.4)	(0, 0.6, 1)
B₂	(0.4, 0.8, 1)	(1, 1, 1)	(0, 0.5, 0.8)	(0, 0.6, 1.2)	(0, 0.6, 1.4)	(0, 0.5, 0.9)
B₃	(1.1, 1.7, 2.9)	(1.2, 2.2, 4.3)	(1, 1, 1)	(0.2, 1.3, 1.9)	(0.2, 1.4, 2.2)	(0, 1.1, 1.5)
B₄	(0.8, 1.3, 2.4)	(0.8, 1.7, 3.6)	(0, 0.8, 1.1)	(1, 1, 1)	(0, 1.1, 1.8)	(0, 0.8, 1.2)
B₅	(0.7, 1.2, 2.3)	(0.7, 1.6, 3.5)	(0, 0.7, 1.1)	(0, 0.9, 1.6)	(1, 1, 1)	(0, 0.8, 1.2)
B₆	(1, 1.6, 2.7)	(1.1, 2.1, 4.1)	(0, 0.9, 1.3)	(0, 1.2, 1.8)	(0, 1.3, 2)	(1, 1, 1)

Table 3. Simple sequencing of the nine attributes

A₁	A₂	A₃	A₄	A₅	A₆	A₇	A₈	A₉
0.105	0.131	0.120	0.127	0.112	0.120	0.096	0.074	0.116

Table 4. Simple sequencing of attributes and the sequencing weight for each alternatives

	A₁	A₂	A₃	A₄	A₅	A₆	A₇	A₈	A₉
B₁	0.000	0.170	0.148	0.157	0.109	0.144	0.143	0.140	0.109
B₂	0.000	0.120	0.141	0.131	0.113	0.131	0.137	0.155	0.180
B₃	0.317	0.190	0.194	0.186	0.195	0.197	0.161	0.154	0.353
B₄	0.000	0.18	0.157	0.173	0.176	0.162	0.154	0.172	0.139
B₅	0.000	0.170	0.163	0.170	0.149	0.149	0.168	0.178	0.124
B₆	0.683	0.180	0.197	0.183	0.357	0.217	0.237	0.201	0.267

Table 5. Final weights of six Iranian high industries

Alternative	B_6	B_3	B_4	B_5	B_1	B_2
Weight	0.266	0.207	0.147	0.142	0.126	0.115
Rank	1	2	3	4	5	6

According to above, other Wi matrices were calculated. The sequencing weighted vector of each alternatives and attributes are as Tables 3 and 4. Finally, according to formula (8), weight of each alternative, high tech industries, and their rank are as Table 5. In a Meanwhile, these weights are equal to degree of their vulnerability from US sanction.

4   Conclusion

In this paper, we investigated the affects of US economics sanction on Iranain high tech industries. To this end, a three-step method based on fuzzy logic architecture was proposed. These steps are: determining attributes of US sanction affected on Iranain high tech, filtering selected attributes using fuzzy hypothesis test, and ranking of high tech industries using fuzzy analytic hierarchical process. At end, Iranian high tech industries ranked.

References

1. Azar Adel, Faraji Hojjat.: Fuzzy Management Science, Iran, Tehran, Egtemae Distribution (2002)
2. Askari Hossein, Forrer John, Teegen Hildy, Yang Jiawen.: U.S. Economic Sanctions: An Empirical Study, School of Business and Public Management, The George Washington University (2003)
3. Chan Da-Yong.: Applications of the Extent Analysis Method on Fuzzy AHP, European Journal of operational Research, Vol. 116 (1996) 649-655.
4. David A. Baldwin.: Economic Statecraft, Princeton, New Jersey: Princeton University Press, (1985) 36-38.
5. Hufbauer, Gary Clyde, Kimberly Ann Elliott, Tess Cyrus, and Elizabeth Winston.: U.S. Economic Sanctions: Their Impact on Trade, Jobs and Wages, Washington, D.C., Institute for International Economics (1997)
6. Kaempfer, William H., Anton D. Lowenberg.: The Theory of International Economic Sanctions: A Public Choice Approach, American Economic Review, Vol. 78 (1988) 786-793.
7. Korvin A. de & Kleyle R.: Fuzzy Analytical Hierarchical Processes, Journal of Intelligent and Fuzzy Systems, Vol. 7 (1999) 387-400
8. Levin, Franklin L.: Asphyxiation or oxygen? the sanctions dilemma, Foreign Policy (1996)
9. Marc Bossuyt.: The adverse consequences of economic sanctions on the enjoyment of human rights, Economic and Social Council UN (2000)
10. Michel Rossignol.: Sanctions: the economic weapon in the new world order, Political and social affairs division, library of parliament (2000)

11. Miyagawa, M. Do Economic Sanctions Work?, Macmillan Press, Houndmills (1992)
12. Parsi Trita: Economic Sanctions: Explaining Their Proliferation -A case study of Iran, Stockholm School of Economics, Department of International Economics (2000)
13. Wallensteen P.: Economic Sanctions: Ten Modern Cases and Three Important Lessons, Dilemmas of Economic Coercion: Sanctions in World Politics, ed. Miroslav Nincic and Peter Wallensteen, New York: Praeger Publishers, (1983) 87-129
14. Weck M. & Klocke F. & Schell H. & Ruenauver E.: Evaluating Alternative Production Cycles Using the Extended Fuzzy AHP Method, European Journal of Operational Research, Vol. 100 (1997) 351-366
15. Zhu ke-Jun & Jing Yu & Chang Da-Yong.: A Discussion on Extent Analysis Method and Applications of Fuzzy AHP, European Journal of Operational Research, Vol. 95 (1998) 450-456

Modeling of Optoelectronic Devices through Neuro-Fuzzy Architectures

Antonio Vanderlei Ortega and Ivan Nunes da Silva

São Paulo State University - UNESP/FE/DEE
School of Engineering, Department of Electrical Engineering
CP 473, CEP 17033.360, Bauru-SP, Brazil

Abstract. The advantages offered by the electronic component LED (Light Emitting Diode) have caused a quick and wide application of this device in replacement of incandescent lights. However, in its combined application, the relationship between the design variables and the desired effect or result is very complex and it becomes difficult to model by conventional techniques. This work consists of the development of a technique, through comparative analysis of neuro-fuzzy architectures, to make possible to obtain the luminous intensity values of brake lights using LEDs from design data.

1   Introduction

The LED device is an electronic semiconductor component that emits light. At present time, it has been used in replacement of incandescent lights because of its advantages, such as longer useful life (around 100,000 hours), larger mechanic resistance to vibrations, lesser heating, lower electric current consumption and high fidelity of the emitted light color [1].

In automobile industry, incandescent lights have been replaced by LEDs in the brake lights, which are a third light of brakes [2]. The approval of brake lights prototypes is made through measurements of luminous intensity in different angles, and the minimum value of luminous intensity for each angle is defined according to the application [3].

The main difficulty found in the development of brake lights is in finding the existent relationship between the following parameters: luminous intensity (I_V) of the LED, distance between LEDs (d) and number of LEDs (n), with the desired effect or result, that is, there is a complexity in making a model by conventional techniques of modeling, which are capable to identify properly the relationship between such variables. The prototype designs of brake lights have been made through trials and errors, causing increasing costs of implementation due to time spent in this stage.

2   LEDs Applied in Brake Lights

LED is an electronic device composed by a chip of semiconductor junction that when traversed by an electric current provides a recombination of electrons and holes. Figure 1 shows the representation of a junction being polarized.

L. Rutkowski et al. (Eds.): ICAISC 2004, LNAI 3070, pp. 1175–1180, 2004.
© Springer-Verlag Berlin Heidelberg 2004

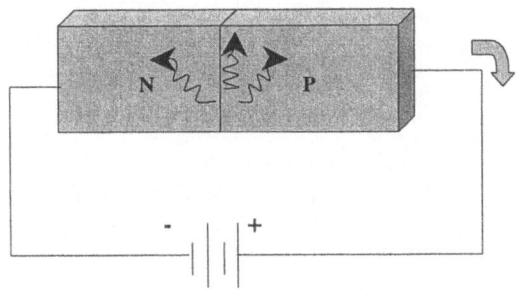

Fig. 1. Junction PN being polarized.

However, this recombination demands that the energy produced by free electrons can be transferred to another state. In semiconductor junctions, this energy is released in form of heat and by emission of photons, that is, light emission [4]. In silicon and germanium the largest energy emission occurs in form of heat, with insignificant light emission. However, in other materials, such as GaAsP or GaP, the number of light photons emitted is sufficient to build a source of quite visible light [5].

In brake lights the LEDs are applied in set and generally organized in a straight line on a printed circuit board (PCB). In this PCB, besides the LEDs, there are electronic components, basically resistors, which are responsible for the limitation of electric current that circulates through the LEDs [6].

The main parameters used in brake lights designs are given by: LED luminous intensity (I_V), distance between LEDs (d) and number of LEDs (n). In Figure 2 is illustrated a basic representation of a brake light.

The process for the prototype validation is made by measuring the luminous intensity of the brake light in eighteen positions or different angles (Figure 3). After this process, the values obtained in each angle are compared with those values established by governmental rules. The minimum value of luminous intensity (I_{VBL}) in each angle varies according to the application. In Figure 3 is shown a representation of a generic distribution diagram of brake light luminous intensity (I_{VBL}) in relation to angle. The mean horizontal position is indicated by 0°H and the mean vertical position is indicated by 0°V. Thus, the position defined by the pair of angles (0°V, 5°L) is represented by the shaded position shown in Figure 3.

3   Basic Concepts of Neural Networks and Fuzzy Logic

The artificial neural networks are computational models inspired in the human brain, structured by a set of interlinked processor units (neurons). The artificial neural network stands out for its capability to learn from its environment and to generalize solutions. Each neuron of the network can be modeled as shown in Figure 4.

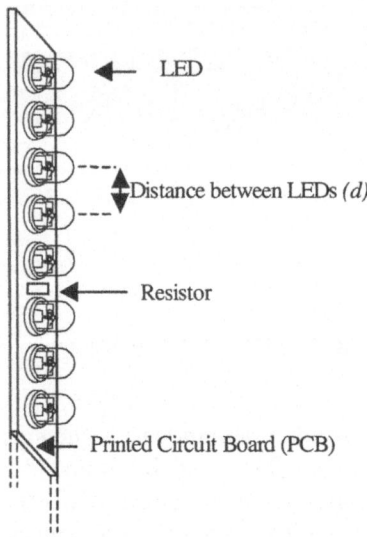

Fig. 2. Representation of a brake light.

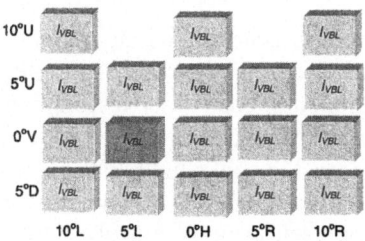

Fig. 3. Generic diagram of luminous intensity (I_{VBL}) in relation to angle.

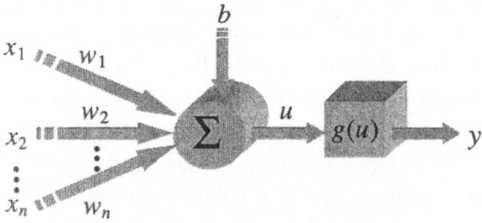

Fig. 4. Scheme of the artificial neuron.

Where:

n is the number of inputs of the neuron.

x_i is the i-th input of the neuron.

w_i is the weight associated with the i-th input.

b is the threshold associated with the neuron.

$g(.)$ is the activation function of the neuron.

y is the output of the neuron.

Fuzzy logic systems provide a powerful framework for manipulating uncertain information. In fuzzy logic, a system can represent imprecise concepts, not only by linguistic variables such as fast, low and small, but also through mathematical principles. Moreover, it can use these concepts to make deductions about the system.

In fuzzy logic an information element can reside in more than one set of different degrees of similarity. Fuzzy relations represent a degree of presence or absence of association, interaction or interconnectedness between the information elements of two or more fuzzy sets.

4   Materials and Methods

For this work, it has been built 45 samples of break lights with the following parameter variations:

- Distance between LEDs (d): 7.0 mm , 8.5 mm and 10.0 mm.
- Number of LEDs (n): 20, 25 and 30.
- Luminous intensity of LED (I_V): 200 mcd, 400 mcd, 600 mcd, 1000 mcd and 1500 mcd.

This combination of parameters referent to each sample can be seen in Table 1.

The equipment used to measure the luminous intensity of the samples was the LMT - System Photometer, model S 1000, where is coupled a device that allows angle variation in vertical and horizontal, this way it is possible to obtain the luminous intensity value in 18 different angles.

Initially, the first sample is placed on the measurement device. The first angle is positioned, the measurement of the luminous intensity is made and the value is registered. This procedure is repeated until registering the luminous intensity value referent to last angle of the sample.

The sample is removed the device and a new sample is placed on it to measure the luminous intensity, and is repeated all procedure until registering the last value referent to the last angle of the last sample.

5   Results and Discussion

After the training process, the neural model using a perceptron network [7] and the fuzzy system were used to obtain luminous intensity values of brake lights. Figure 5 illustrates a comparison between luminous intensity values (I_{VBL}) obtained by experimental tests (ET), estimated by the fuzzy system (FS) and those estimated by the artificial neural network (ANN). In this configuration the used sample presents the distance (d) between LEDs equal to 7.0 mm, the number of LEDs (n) is equal to 20 and the luminous intensity of each LED (I_V) has a value equal to 400 mcd.

The results of I_{VBL} provided by the network are close to those provided by experimental tests, being the mean relative error around 3.90%. The mean

Table 1. Combination of parameters in each sample.

Sample	d (mm)	n (unit)	I_V (mcd)	Sample	d (mm)	n (unit)	I_V (mcd)
01	7.0	20	200	24	8.5	25	1000
02	7.0	20	400	25	8.5	25	1500
03	7.0	20	600	26	8.5	30	200
04	7.0	20	1000	27	8.5	30	400
05	7.0	20	1500	28	8.5	30	600
06	7.0	25	200	29	8.5	30	1000
07	7.0	25	400	30	8.5	30	1500
08	7.0	25	600	31	10.0	20	200
09	7.0	25	1000	32	10.0	20	400
10	7.0	25	1500	33	10.0	20	600
11	7.0	30	200	34	10.0	20	1000
12	7.0	30	400	35	10.0	20	1500
13	7.0	30	600	36	10.0	25	200
14	7.0	30	1000	37	10.0	25	400
15	7.0	30	1500	38	10.0	25	600
16	8.5	20	200	39	10.0	25	1000
17	8.5	20	400	40	10.0	25	1500
18	8.5	20	600	41	10.0	30	200
19	8.5	20	1000	42	10.0	30	400
20	8.5	20	1500	43	10.0	30	600
21	8.5	25	200	44	10.0	30	1000
22	8.5	25	400	45	10.0	30	1500
23	8.5	25	600				

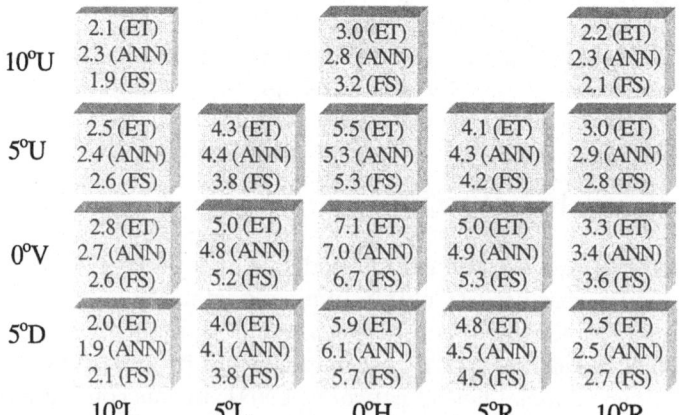

Fig. 5. Comparative Illustration.

relative errors calculated was around 6.00% for comparison between luminous intensity values (I_{VBL}) obtained by experimental tests (ET) and those estimated by the fuzzy system (FS). In the selection process of the best neural architecture used in simulations was adopted the technique cross-validation [7].

6   Conclusion

This work presents a technique based on use of artificial neural networks and fuzzy system for determination of luminous intensity values for brake lights (I_{VBL}), in which are considered the main design characteristics.

The developed methodology can also be generalized and used in other applications that use groups of LEDs, such as in traffic lights and electronic panels of messages.

This developed tool has significantly contributed for reduction of costs in relation to implementation stage of brake lights, that is, it minimizes spent time in prototype designs. The tool has also allowed simulating many options for configurations of brake lights, providing the choice of a sample that offers an appropriate relationship between cost and benefit.

References

1. Peralta, S. B., Ruda, H. E.: Applications for Advanced Solid-State Lamps. IEEE Industry Applications Magazine. (1998) 31–42
2. Werner, K.: Higher Visibility for LEDs. IEEE Spectrum. **39** (1994) 30–34
3. Young, W. R., Wilson, W.: Efficient Electric Vehicle Lighting Using LEDs. Proc. of Southcon. (1996) 276–280
4. Streetman, B. G.: Solid State Electronic Devices. Prentice Hall. (1990)
5. Craford, M. G.: LEDs Challenge the Incandescents. IEEE Circuits and Devices. (1992) 24–29
6. Griffiths, P., Langer, D., Misener, J. A., Siegel, M., Thorpe, C.: Sensor-Friendly Vehicle and Roadway Systems. IEEE Instrumentation and Measurement. (2001) 1036–1040
7. Haykin, S.: Neural Networks. 2nd Edition, Prentice-Hall. (1999)

Neural Network Based Simulation of the Sieve Plate Absorption Column in Nitric Acid Industry

Edward Rój and Marcin Wilk

Fertilizers Research Institute (Instytut Nawozów Sztucznych - INS)
ul. Aleja 1000-Lecia PP 13A, 24-110 Puławy, Poland
{eroj,mwilk}@atena.ins.pulawy.pl

Abstract. Modeling of an absorption column performance using feed-forward type of neural network has been presented. The input and output data for training of the neural network are obtained from a rigorous model of the absorption column. The results obtained from the neural network models are then compared with the results obtained mainly from the simulation calculations. The results show that relatively simple neural network models can be used to model the steady state behavior of the column.

1 Introduction

Absorption column is one of the most important and expensive apparatus in nitric acid plant. Modern industrial nitric acid plants use mainly sieve plate absorption columns with weirs. Absorption columns built about presently are over 6 m in diameter and heights over 80 m. From the point of view of high capital costs and environmental protection regulation requirements the exact mathematical model of processes taking place in the column is very important. Ability of prediction of result of mass flow rate changes as well as temperature and pressure variations is useful for operational conditions of any absorption column. In initial period of development of nitric acid technology, the absorption columns were designed using experimental data collected from commercial plants. During growth of knowledge of basic theory of the process some calculations were made using graphic methods. Application of computers allowed to develop more precise mathematical models of the absorption process and to perform fast and exact calculations of the columns. Problem of mathematical modeling of absorption columns was object of interest of many researchers and practitioners. INS Puławy has developed a model of sieve plate absorption column which is a result of a long time experience. The model is based on plate efficiency strategy. Comparing another models, the developed model is significantly complex. Using the model a simulation calculations of heat and mass transfer can be done for each plate of the column. Of course, the model can be applied to any sieve plate column. The model has been tested using data collected from different nitric acid industrial plants. Positive results allowed us to use the model to design a column for a new commercial plants [1,2]. Furthermore, simulation results obtained with the model allowed designing a new type of absorption column. To speed up calculations and to make the calculations easier, particularly for process operators, a neural model approach has been applied. The new approach will be able to assure an application the model for optimization of a nitric acid plant performance. The neural network based model can be easily incorporated into the existing environment using available data collected from the computer based data acquisition systems.

2   Mathematical Model

In the nitric acid plant the mixture of ammonia and air is passed over catalyst gauze. Among many reactions the is major one:

$$4NH_2 + 2O_2 = 4NO + 6H_2O \tag{1}$$

The gas stream leaving the ammonia oxidation reactor is cooled in a heat exchanger. If its temperature is below a determined limit, than NO is transformed into NO_2, and N_2O_4, and a condensate appears as well. Some part of nitric oxides reacts with condensing water forming a solution of weak nitric acid which concentration depends on time of contact and amount of the condensed water. The condensate is then fed with a pump to a proper plate of the absorption column. In the absorption column the different reactions can occur in gas and liquid phase from which the most important are:

– Oxidizing of nitric oxide to nitric dioxide and dimerization to N_2O_4

$$2NO + O_2 \rightarrow 2NO_2 \tag{2}$$

$$2NO_2 \leftrightarrow N_2O_4 \tag{3}$$

– Reaction of dioxide and tetroxide with water

$$2NO_2 + H_2O \rightarrow HNO_2 + HNO_3 \tag{4}$$

$$N_2O_4 + H_2O \rightarrow HNO_2 + HNO_3 \tag{5}$$

$$HNO_2 \rightarrow HNO_3 + 2NO + H_2O \tag{6}$$

– Besides, gas is bubbled through a pool of liquid where water vapor con-denses. The cool gas stream consisting of NO, NO_2, N_2O_4, O_2, H_2O and small amount of N_2O, CO_2 and Ar is introduced at the bottom of the column. Besides, one of the sieve plate is supplied with acid condensate formed in the condenser. The last plate is fed with water producing a stream of nitric acid of desired concentration. Heat transfer coils filled with water are placed in the pool of liquid over the plates. They are designed to remove the heat liberated during oxidation of NO and formation of NO_2, N_2O_4 and HNO_3.

Detailed mass and heat balance based models are presented in [3,4]. Using the models, a software for nitric acid column simulation has been developed. The software was tested in a wide range of industrial plant performance conditions. Quite good results have been obtained comparing the theoretical and experimental results, Fig. 1. For simulation and control purposes it is sometimes useful to make quick calculations or simulations by non-experienced process operators. To meet the needs a neural approach has been applied.

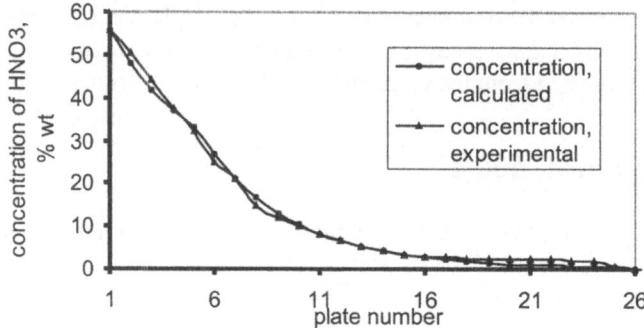

Fig. 1. Simulation of a commercial nitric acid column - concentration of HNO_3 vs. plate number

3 Neural Networks

Neural network (NN) approaches have been proposed as useful and powerful tools for process modeling and simulation by a number of researchers [5]. One of the main features of the neural networks is the potential to perform nonlinear system identification on the basis of historical or currently collected data. After being trained on a number of examples of relationship, they can often induce a complete relationship that interpolates from the examples in a sensible manner. Neural networks with feed-forward architecture can approximate with arbitrary precision, static nonlinear functions.

3.1 Feed-Forward Neural Networks

Neural networks are parallel structures of activation elements often of the same type [6, 7]. Signals are propagated from the input nodes to the hidden nodes via weighted connections. The signals from the hidden nodes feed forward to the output nodes. Computation via a transfer function occurs only in the hidden and output nodes. The weights of a network contain representational information and are the decision variables adjusted during training. Feed-forward networks have been usually trained using a back-propagation algorithm. The back-propagation algorithm is a first order gradient descent based method (an optimization technique) that can adjust the network weights minimizing the mean squared error between the network outputs and target outputs for a set of training data. The feed forward networks perform a static nonlinear mapping of the input to output space.

3.2 Modeling of a Sieve Plate Column Using a Neural Networks

The developed model of the sieve plate absorption column has been used as a reference model providing data for training the feed-forward neural network. Some input and output data for neural network training are listed below. Input variables cover gas stream G consisting of nitrous gas components (NO, NO_2, N_2O_4, O_2, H_2O, N_2), condensate stream g_k at concentration c_k and temperature t_k, process water w_{hg} at temperature t_w and cooling water temperature, t_{wc}. Output variables cover tail gas stream G_{out}

consisting of the following components: NO_x, O_2, H_2O, N_2 (where $NO_x = NO + NO_2$), nitric acid stream G_{HNO_3} at concentration c_{HNO_3}. Another parameters as nitric acid temperature and cooling water temperature are not included. For practical purposes the most interesting absorption column output is nitric acid production G_{HNO_3} and its concentration c_{HNO_3} as well as NO_x emission. These components are strongly dependent on gas load G and its parameters T and P and process water flow rate w_{hg} as well as condensate flow rate g_k and its concentration c_k.

3.3   Determination of Architecture of the Neural Network

This task in system modeling corresponds to the determination of the architecture of the multi-layered perceptron (MLP) type network, that is, the number of input variables, which gives the number of input layer nodes, the number of hidden layers, and the number of nodes in each of the hidden layers. The final step is the determination of the output layer nodes corresponding to the number of output variables. There are no definitive methods for deciding a priori the number of layers and units in the hidden layers. The one hidden layer is usually sufficient to model any continuous function. The number of nodes is related to the complexity of the nonlinear function, which can be generated by the neural network. One approach to selecting the number of hidden layer nodes involves randomly splitting the data into two subsets, using one of the sets for training and the other for testing the output results. If the average error on the training subset is significantly less than the testing subset, over-fitting is indicated and the number of nodes should be reduced. One of the possible procedure is to start with a small number of nodes and increasing the number of nodes until there is no significant increase in modeling accuracy gained by increasing the number of nodes. The weights of the neural connections are determined by using a back-propagation algorithm.

3.4   Model Validation

Model validation is usually a final step of any identification procedure. If the system under test is nonlinear then well known covariance tests covering autocorrelation or cross-correlation tests, developed for linear systems, provide incorrect information. So that extended tests can be applied to validate the neural network models. If the modeling data are noise-free, the neural network test can be performed using noise corrupted input signals. A standard error of estimates defined as:

$$\epsilon = \sqrt{\frac{\sum_{k=1}^{N}(y_{mk} - y_{sk})^2}{\sum_{k=1}^{N} y_{sk}^2}} \tag{7}$$

ϵ is a measure of quality of any developed model.

4   Results

A set of about 4000 data values have been obtained as a result of simulations carried out using the developed absorption column model. The data were divided into two equal

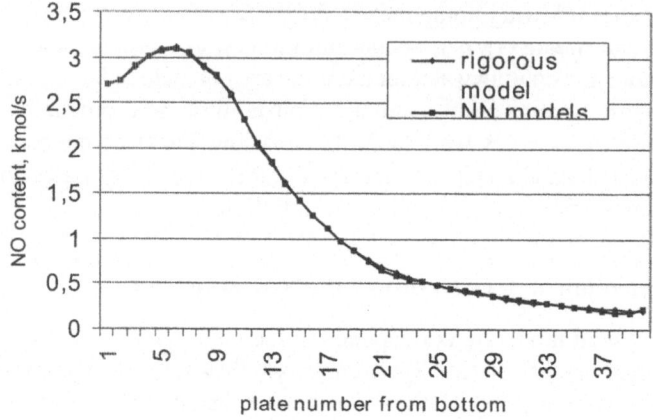

Fig. 2. Nitric oxide content distribution along the column, NO concentration vs. plate number

subsets. One of the subset was used as the training data set and on other one as the testing set. Using the incremental procedure mentioned above the number of nodes in the hidden layer was obtained. The number of nodes in the hidden layer required to model the system adequately is determined as 14. This results in all overall network with 8 nodes in the input layer, 14 nodes in the hidden layer and 3 nodes in the output layer. This results in a total 168 weights including bias connections. The activation function is of sigmoid type as:

$$f(x) = \frac{1}{1 + \exp(-x)} \tag{8}$$

The obtained results have proved that neural networks can approximate exactly the desired output variables, Fig. 2, particularly for steady state conditions. The accuracy of the neural network models is sufficient for modeling of the industrial absorption column performance.

5   Conclusions

The work demonstrates that the nonlinear absorption column model can be approximated using feed-forward neural networks. The comparison of the responses of the nonlinear simulations with the responses of the identified models indicates very good agreement. The identified model can be used for simulation and optimization purposes.

References

1. Wilk M., Kozłowski K., and Nieścioruk J. New Projects of Nitric Acid Industry (in Polish). *Przemysł Chemiczny*, 67(10):464–465, 1988.
2. Kozłowski K., Nieścioruk J., Kowalik J., and Ochał A. A New Nitric Acid Plant 5.4/12.4 bar, 600 t HNO3/d in Zakłady Azotowe "Kedzierzyn" S.A. (in Polish). *Pr. Nauk. Inst. Techn. Nieorg. i Naw. Min. Pol. Wroc.*, 43(25):70–76, 1995.

3. Rój E. and Wilk M. Simulation of an Absorption Column Performance Using Feed-forward Neural Networks in Nitric Acid Production. *Computers Chem. Engng.*, 22:909–912, 1998.

4. Rój E. and Wilk M. Simulation of the sieve plate absorption column for nitric acid absorption process using neural networks. In *International Conference on Distillation and Absorption*, Baden-Baden, Germany, 2002.

5. Bhat N. and McAvoy J. Use of Neural Nets for Dynamic Modeling and Control of Chemical Process Systems. *Computers Chem. Engng.*, 14(4/5):573–583, 1990.

6. Leonard J. and Kramer M. A. Improvement of the Backpropagation Algorithm for Training Neural Networks. *Comput. Chem. Eng.*, 14(3):337–341, 1990.

7. Rummelhart D.E. and McClelland J.L. Parallel Distributed Processing. pages 319–330. The MIT Press, Cambridge, Massachusetts, London, 1988.

Artificial Neural Networks for Comparative Navigation

Andrzej Stateczny

Maritime University, Waly Chrobrego 1/2, 70-500 Szczecin, Poland

Abstract. The article presents methods of computer ship's position plotting by means of comparative methods. A new approach in comparative navigation is the use of artificial neural networks for plotting the ship's position. Two main problems should be solved during ship's positioning process: compressing (coding) image and recognition (interpolation) ship's position.

1 Introduction

Satellite and radar systems have been the main information sources in marine navigation in recent years. Apart from commonly known anti-collision functions, the marine navigational radar constitutes the basis for a future comparative system of ship positioning. The sonar is an additional source of image information in the system. In this way, the data are derived from observing the surroundings of the ship's total measuring area. The system of comparative navigation is an attractive alternative to satellite navigation due to its autonomy and independence from external appliances.

Plotting the ship's position by comparative methods can be performed by three basic methods:

• Determining the point of best match of the image with the pattern. The logical product algorithm is used in this method which makes it possible to find the point of best matching of images recorded in the form of digital matrix.

• Using the previously registered real images associated with the position of their registration. This method uses the artificial neural network taught by a sequence created from vectors representing the compressed images and the corresponding position of the ship.

• Using the generated map of patterns. The artificial neural network is taught by a representation of selected images corresponding to the potential positions of the ship. The patterns are generated on the basis of a numerical terrain model, knowledge of the hydrometeorological conditions effect and the observation specificity of the selected device.

During using artificial neural networks for plotting the ship's position there is the problem of selecting the teaching sequence designed to teach the network. The images must be subjected to treatment for the purpose of data reduction and compression. The advantage of this method is that once thought neural network

L. Rutkowski et al. (Eds.): ICAISC 2004, LNAI 3070, pp. 1187–1192, 2004.
© Springer-Verlag Berlin Heidelberg 2004

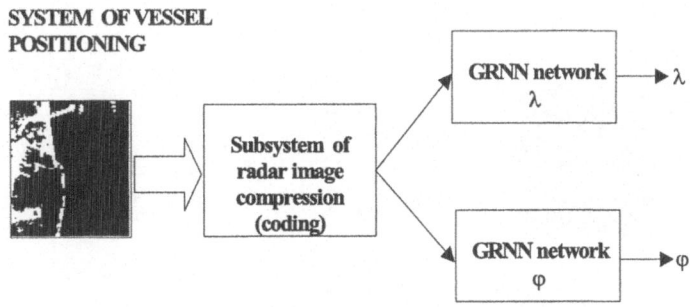

Fig. 1. Diagram of a ship positioning system.

(neural processor) can be use many times and new measurements might be added to increase the accuracy and reliability of system.

After initial treatment of the analyzed image a teaching sequence of the artificial neural network is prepared. In the process of teaching the network it is the task of the network to work out a mapping function associating the analyzed image with the geographical position. Numerous experiments have shown a decided advantage of the GRNN network over other solutions.

2   Kohonen Network

Kohonen network changes the image given at its input (image segment) into the index of one of its neurons. The return number obtained corresponds to the neuron which is closest to the input image according to selected metric. And so, if image segments are given successively at the input of Kohonen network, an index vector of Kohonen network will be obtained at the output. The size of the vector will be equal to the number of segments.

The accuracy of the mapping obtained in this way depends on the number of neurons in Kohonen network in relation to the number of various possible pixel combinations in the input picture. For example, for black-and-white images with size NxM (N – image width in pixels, M – image height in pixels) the maximum number of various images possible to obtain equals 2NxM. With a large number of network neurons – closest to the maximum value – compression will be very accurate and each image will have its unique compressed counterpart. A network poorer in neurons will make larger generalizations which will bring about a situation with similar images having the same counterpart on the compressed side.

A more accurate mapping of image concentration during their compression can also be obtained by proper selection of indexes for the neurons of Kohonen network. Their ordering should represent in the best degree the distribution of images associated with each neuron in the image space. Neurons similar to each other should have close indexes. Neurons differing strongly by weight should be characterized by distant indexes. This effect can be obtained by using Sammon mapping; it allows to project multi-dimensional vectors into spaces of smaller

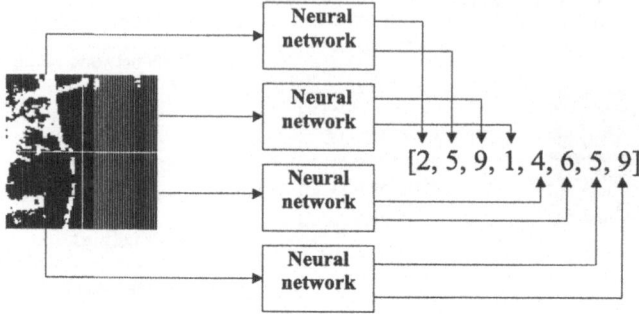

Fig. 2. Increasing compression accuracy – two-output network [17]

dimensions. Thanks to this mapping of vectors we are able to assign a real number to each image (image segment). This will make possible to bind every neuron of Kohonen network with the value corresponding to it. In this way, during compression the network will not return to us the neuron number selected at random, but the real number associated with it corresponding to the location of this neuron (image associated with the neuron) in the image space.

3   GRNN Network

Kohonen network has a limited number of values which it is able to return to us. It is the set of indexes or numerical values associated with each neuron. In the case when the image appears at the network output, the network will return to us the value bound with the neuron most similar to this image. The more neurons there are in the network the smaller the degree of generalization made by it, and the compressed image will be more similar to the original after decompression. GRNN network, on the other hand, instead of the value associated with the most similar neuron will return to us the value adequate to the degree of similarity of the input image to particular network neurons.

The compressing GRNN network can be constructed based on information included in Kohonen network. Pairs (x,y) of the GRNN-network teaching sequence will in this case contain neurons of Kohonen network as images x and the values associated with each neuron of this network (neuron index or value determined by means of Sammon mapping) as parameters y.

The construction of GRNN network can also be based directly on images (image segments) placed in the teaching sequence, completely omitting the stage of constructing Kohonen network. For this purpose every teaching image should be assigned by Sammon mapping a number value or a 2- 3-dimensional vector, and then GRNN network should be constructed on the basis of teaching pairs (x,y) thus obtained.

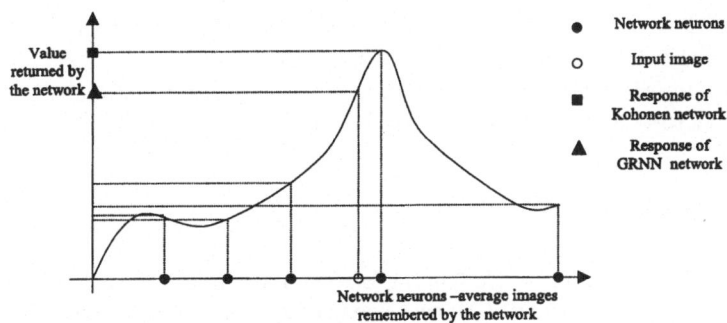

Fig. 3. Functioning principle of GRNN network in image compression. [17]

4   Numerical Experiments

Original radar images reduced to the size 100*100 pixels were used for the research. All images were subjected to the process of segmentation. Each of them was divided into 100 equal-sized segments of 10*10 pixel dimensions.

Comparing the effect of neuron number on the described methods it should be stated that the small number of neurons in each case causes the approximating system to generate very inaccurate positions. The classical Kohonen network of small size makes it possible to plot a more accurate position than other compression methods, but in spite of this the system's accuracy in this case continues to be extremely insufficient. With a larger number of neurons for each method it could be obtained more and more accurate positions. For 2-output networks the effect of each method on the approximating system and the generated results is similar. The differences are perceptible with 3-output networks. In this case it could be observed a better functioning of the positioning system when compressing the radar image by GRNN network and Kohonen network with ordered structure than for the classical Kohonen network. The application of GRNN network and Kohonen network with ordered structure makes it possible to obtain equally accurate positions as in the case of the classical Kohonen network, but with a smaller size of each. It should be remembered that a result like this is obtained using 3-output networks which causes the amount of information flowing into the approximation system to be larger than in the case of 2-output and 3-output networks (smaller degree of compression – longer functioning time of the position approximating subsystem). In this case, however, due to the smaller number of processing elements at the stage of compression the time of performing it will be shorter, which can compensate for the longer time of calculations made in the position approximating subsystem.

5   Sum-Up

It is a merit of comparative navigation that the knowledge about the ship's nearest surroundings, i.e. the coastline and the sea bottom, is used for plotting the ship's position. The direct control of potential navigational obstacles decisively increases the safety of the navigational process.

Many numeric experiments have shown considerable resistance of the presented method to disturbances of registered images.

References

[1]   Austin G. L., Bellon A., Ballantyne E., Sea Trials of a Navigation System Based on Computer Processing of Marine Radar Images. The Journal of Navigation 1987 Vol. 40.

[2]   Austin G. L., Bellon A., Riley M., Ballantyne E., Navigation by Computer Processing of Marine Radar Images. The Journal of Navigation 1985 No 3.

[3]   Bell J.M., Application of optical ray tracing techniques to the simulation of sonar images, Optical Engineering, 36(6), June 1997

[4]   Bell J.M., Chantler M.J., Wittig T., Sidescan Sonar: a directional filter of seabed texture?, IEEE Proceedings. - Radar, Sonar and Navigation. 146(1), 1999.

[5]   Bell J.M., Linnett L.M. Simulation and Analysis of Synthetic Sidescan Sonar Images, IEEE Proceedings - Radar, Sonar and Navigation, 144(4), 1997.

[6]   Cohen P., Bathymetric Navigation and Charting, Ayaderr Co Pub, 1980.

[7]   Giro J., Amat J., Grassia A.: Automatic ship's position fixing by matching chart and radar images. Genova ISSOA 1982.

[8]   Hayashi S., Kuwajima S., Sotooka K., Yamazaki H., Murase H., A Stranding Avoidance System Using Radar Image Matching - Development and Experiment. The Journal of Navigation May 1991 Vol. 44 No 2.

[9]   Łubczonek J., Stateczny A Concept of neural model of the sea bottom surface. Advances in Soft Computing, Proceedings of the Sixth International Conference on Neural Network and Soft Computing, Zakopane, Poland, June 11-15, 2002, Advances in Soft Computing Rutkowski, Kacprzyk, Eds., Physica-Verlag, A Springer-Verlag Company 2003.

[10] Stateczny A. (editor): Methods of Comparative Navigation. Gdansk Science Society, Gdańsk 2003.

[11] Stateczny A., A comparative system concept of plotting the ship's position. Proceedings of International Conference on Marine Navigation and Technology "ME-LAHA 2002" organized by Arab Institute of Navigation Alexandria Egypt 2002. (CD-ROM).

[12] Stateczny A., Comparative Navigation as an Alternative Positioning System. Proceedings of the 11th IAIN World Congress "Smart navigation – Systems and Services", Berlin 2003.

[13] Stateczny A., Comparative Navigation. Gdansk Science Society, Gdańsk 2001.

[14] Stateczny A., Comparative positioning of ships on the basis of neural processing of digital images. Proceedings of the European Geophysical Society Symposium G9 "Geodetic and Geodynamic Programmes of the CEI (Central European Initiative)" Nice 2003. Reports on Geodesy No. 1(64), 2003.

[15] Stateczny A., Methods of comparative plotting of the ship's position. Marine Engineering and Ports III. Editors C.A. Brebbia & J. Olivella. WIT Press Southampton, Boston 2002.

[16] Stateczny A., Praczyk T., Artificial Neural Networks in Radar Image Compression. Proceedings of the International Radar Symposium, Dresden 2003.

[17] Stateczny A., Praczyk T.: Artificial Neural Networks in Maritime Objects Recognition. Gdansk Science Society, Gdańsk 2002.

[18] Stateczny A., Problems of comparative plotting of the ship's position. Proceedings of the European Geophysical Society Symposium G9 "Geodetic and Geodynamic Programmes of the CEI (Central European Initiative)" Nice 2002. Reports on Geodesy No. 1 (61), 2002.

[19] Stateczny A., Problems of Computer Ship Position Plotting by Comparative Methods. Science works of Naval Academy 107A/1990, Gdynia 1990.

[20] Stateczny A., Szulc D., Dynamic Ships Positioning Based on Hydroacoustic Systems. Hydroacoustic 2003 vol. 5/6 Annual Journal.

[21] Stateczny A., Wąż M., Szulc D., The aspects of the simulation of the sea bottom sonar image obtained as a result of mathematical modeling of the sounding profiles. Science works of Maritime University Szczecin No 65, 2002.

Predicting Women's Apparel Sales by Soft Computing

Les M. Sztandera, Celia Frank, and Balaji Vemulapali

Philadelphia University, Philadelphia, PA 19144, USA
SztanderaL@PhilaU.edu

Abstract. In this research, forecasting models were built based on both univariate and multivariate analysis. Models built on multivariate fuzzy logic analysis were better in comparison to those built on other models. The performance of the models was tested by comparing one of the goodness-of-fit statistics, R^2, and also by comparing actual sales with the forecasted sales of different types of garments. Five months sales data (August-December 2001) was used as back cast data in our models and a forecast was made for one month of the year 2002. The performance of the models was tested by comparing one of the goodness-of-fit statistics, R^2, and also by comparing actual sales with the forecasted sales. An R^2 of 0.93 was obtained for multivariate analysis (0.75 for univariate analysis), which is significantly higher than those of 0.90 and 0.75 found for Single Seasonal Exponential Smoothing and Winters' three parameter model, respectively. Yet another model, based on artificial neural network approach, gave an R^2 averaging 0.82 for multivariate analysis and 0.92 for univariate analysis.

1 Introduction

Sales Forecasting is an integral part of apparel supply chain management and very important in order to sustain profitability. Apparel managers require a sophisticated forecasting tool, which can take both exogenous factors like size, price, color, and climatic data, price changes, marketing strategies and endogenous factors like time into consideration. Although models built on conventional statistical forecasting tools are very popular they model sales only on historic data and tend to be linear in nature. Unconventional artificial intelligence tools like fuzzy logic and ANN can efficiently model sales taking into account both exogenous and endogenous factors and allow arbitrary non-linear approximation functions derived (learned) directly from the data.

A multivariate fuzzy model has been built based on important product variables of color, time and size. This model is being extended to include other variables like climate, economic conditions etc., which would be used in building a comprehensive forecasting software package.

L. Rutkowski et al. (Eds.): ICAISC 2004, LNAI 3070, pp. 1193–1198, 2004.
© Springer-Verlag Berlin Heidelberg 2004

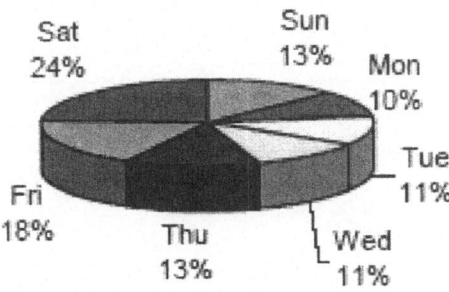

Fig. 1. Fraction of Weekly Sales Distributed Among 7 Days

2   Methodology and Results

Since our present research is based on multivariate analysis, a sales data containing multiple independent variables is being used in a multivariable fuzzy logic and ANN models. Two product variables color, time and size, which significantly affect apparel sales, were chosen to model sales. The converted data were grouped based on different class-size combinations, trained and then sales were forecasted for each grouping using ANN and fuzzy logic modeling.

The daily sales were calculated from grouped sales using two different methods: fractional contribution method and Winters' three parameter model. The forecasted daily sales were then compared with actual sales by using goodness-of-fit statistics, R^2. Fuzzy logic model was applied to grouped data and sales values were calculated for each size-class combination. Total sales value for the whole period was calculated by summing up the sales values of all the grouped items. In order to calculate daily sales, two different methods were used:

Fractional contribution method. It was observed that the fraction contribution of each weekday towards total week sales was constant (Frank et. al., 2002). Figure 1 depicts the average fractional contribution of a weekday towards total sales of a week, which can be used to forecast the daily sales from the forecasted weekly sales. The daily sales were calculated as a fraction of total sales. The R^2 of the model was 0.93 and the correlation coefficient R between actual and forecasted daily sales for October 2002 was 0.96. Figure 2 shows the actual versus forecasted sales values for October-2002 month.

Winters' Three Parameter Exponential Smoothing Model. Winters' smoothing model assumes that:

$$Y_{t+m} = (S_t + b_t)I_{t-L+m} \qquad (1)$$

where: S_t = smoothed nonseasonal level of the series at end of t, b_t = smoothed trend in period t, m = horizon length of the forecasts of Y_{t+m}, I_{t-L+m} = smoothed seasonal index for period $t + m$ That is, Y_{t+m} the actual value of a series

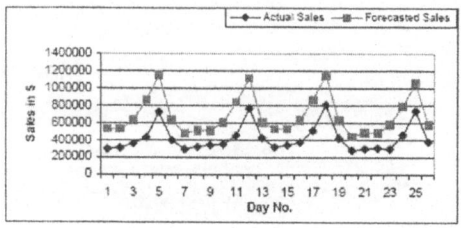

Fig. 2. Actual vs. forecasted sales for October 2002 using fuzzy model

equals a smoothed level value S_t plus an estimate of trend b_t times a seasonal index I_{t-L+m}. These three components of demand are each exponentially smoothed values available at the end of period t (DeLurigo, 1998). The smoothed values were estimated as follows:

$$S_t = \alpha(\frac{Y_t}{I_{t-L}}) + (1 - \alpha)(S_{t-1} + b_{t-1}) \tag{2}$$

$$b_t = \beta(S_t - S_{t-1}) + (1 - \beta)b_{t-1} \tag{3}$$

$$I_t = \gamma(\frac{Y_t}{S_t}) + (1 - \gamma)I_{t-L+m} \tag{4}$$

$$Y_{t+m} = (S_t + b_t m)I_{t-1+m} \tag{5}$$

where: Y_t = value of actual demand at end of period t, α = smoothing constant used for S_t, S_t = smoothed value at end of t after adjusting for seasonality, β = smoothing constant used to calculate the trend (bt), b_t = smoothed value of trend through period t, I_{t-L} = smoothed seasonal index L periods ago, L = length of the seasonal cycle (e.g., 5 months), γ = smoothing constant, gamma for calculating the seasonal index in period t I_t = smoothed seasonal index at end of period t, m = horizon length of the forecasts of Y_{t+m}.Equation 2 is required to calculate the overall level of the series. S_t in equation 3 is the trend-adjusted, deseasonalized level at the end of period t. S_t is used in equation 5 to generate forecasts, Y_{t+m}. Equation 3 estimates the trend by smoothing the difference between the smoothed values S_t and $S_t - 1$. This estimates the period-to-period change (trend) in the level of Y_t. Equation 4 illustrates the calculation of the smoothed seasonal index, I_t. This seasonal factor is calculated for the next cycle of forecasting and used to forecast values for one or more seasonal cycles ahead. Alpha, beta, and gamma values were chosen using minimum mean squared error (MSE) as the criterion. Applying a forecast model built on five months sales data, a daily forecast of sales ratio was done for October of 2002. Figure 3 shows the actual versus forecasted sales values for October-2002 month. The parameters used were: α=0.6, β=0.01, γ=1, and R^2=0.97, R=0.98.

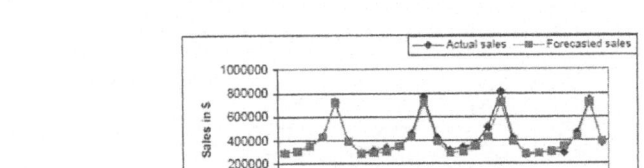

Fig. 3. Actual vs. forecasted for fuzzy approach with Winters three par. model

Neural Network Model. In our research, a feed forward neural network, with back propagation, was implemented with 10 neurons in the input layer, 30 neurons in the hidden layer and 1 neuron in the output layer. Grouped sales data over a period of 10 months was used, out of which the first 32 rows were used as training set, next 34 rows were used in test set and the last 234 rows were used in production set.

Fractional contribution method. The fractional contribution method described under fuzzy logic section was implemented for NN model. R^2 of the model was 0.82, and the correlation coefficient R between actual and forecasted daily sales for October 2002 was 0.93. Figure 4 shows the actual versus forecasted sales values for October-2002 month.

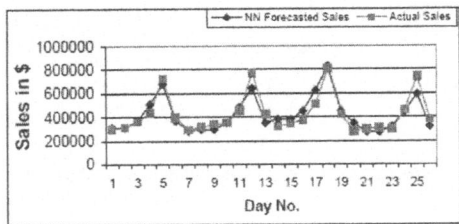

Fig. 4. Actual vs. forecasted sales by using ANN

Winters' three parameter model. The winters' three parameter model method described under fuzzy logic section was implemented for NN model. The following parameters were used: α=0.6, β=0.01, γ=1, and $R^2 = 0.44$, R = 0.67 were obtained. Figure 5 shows the actual versus forecasted sales values for October-2002 month.

Univariate Forecasting Models. Forecasting models were built on univariate analysis using both conventional statistical models as well as unconventional soft-computing methods. Among all the models, the ANN model performed the best.

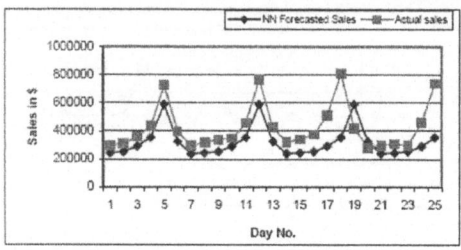

Fig. 5. Actual vs. forecasted sales using ANN

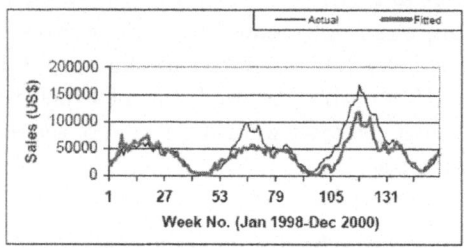

Fig. 6. Actual vs. forecasted sales for SES model ($R^2 = 0.90$)

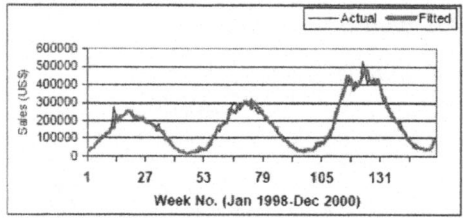

Fig. 7. Actual vs. forecasted sales for Winters' three parameter model ($R^2 = 0.75$)

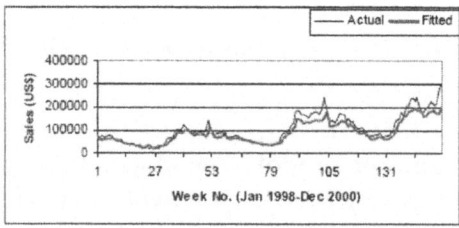

Fig. 8. Actual vs. forecasted sales for ANN model ($R^2 = 0.92$)

However all the models could not forecast with precision because they were built using a single variable time. A plot of actual versus forecasted sales for various models done using univariate analysis are shown in Figures 6, 7 and 8.

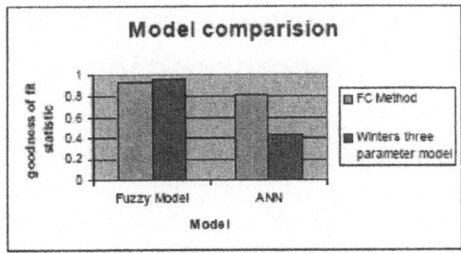

Fig. 9. Goodness of fit statistic for models based on multivariate analysis

3   Conclusions

Multivariable fuzzy logic model can be an effective sales forecasting tool as demonstrated by our results. A correlation of 0.93 was obtained, better than that obtained by using the NN model, which showed a correlation of 0.82 (for the fractional contribution method). The values for the three parameter model were: 0.97 and 0.44, respectively. The poor correlation in the case of the NN model can be attributed to the noise in the sales data. The fuzzy model performed best because of its ability to identify nonlinear relationships in the input data. However, the correlation was better for short-term forecasts and not as good for longer time periods. However the multivariate fuzzy logic model performed better in comparison to those based on univariate analysis, which goes on to prove that multivariate analysis is better compared to that of univariate analysis. A much more comprehensive model can be built by taking into account other factors like climate, % price change, marketing strategies etc.

References

C. Frank, A. Garg, A. Raheja, L. Sztandera (2002), Forecasting Women's Apparel Sales Using Mathematical Modeling, International Journal of Clothing Science and Technology 15(2), 107–125.

Model Improvement by the Statistical Decomposition

Ryszard Szupiluk[1,2], Piotr Wojewnik[1,2], and Tomasz Zabkowski[1]

[1] Polska Telefonia Cyfrowa Ltd., Al. Jerozolimskie 181, 02-222 Warsaw, Poland
[2] Warsaw School of Economics, Al. Niepodleglosci 162, 02-554 Warsaw, Poland
{rszupiluk,pwojewnik,tzabkowski}@era.pl

Abstract. In this paper we propose applying multidimensional decompositions for modeling improvement. Results generated by different models usually include both wanted and destructive components. Many of the components are common to all the models. Our aim is to find the basis variables with the positive and the negative influence on the modeling task. It will be perofrmed with multidimensional transforamtions such as ICA and PCA.

1 Introduction

A frequent problem encountered in such disciplines as statistics, data analysis, signal processing and data mining is finding a suitable model or system to explore existing dependencies [11],[12],[13]. It is quite typical that several models can be proposed to describe the investigated task and we need to decide which model is best able to meet defined goals. This leads us to the model selection task [1],[2],[14]. But often we have problem that according to various criteria different models appear as the best solution. Therefore, it seems natural to integrate or to utilize the information generated by many models. Usually solutions propose the combination of a few models by mixing their results or parameters [3],[9],[15]. In this paper we propose an alternative conception of model results improvement based on multidimensional decompositions when many models are tested.

If different models give relatively good results it means that all of them are located close to the target and the results of every model possess the wanted components as well as destructive components and noises. We can assume that there exist the elements common to all the models. The common wanted components are associated with the true unknown value, of course. On the second hand the negative components can be present due to the many reasons as: missing data, not precise parameter estimation and distribution assumptions. Our aim is to identify destructive elements and to eliminate them for modeling improvement. To obtain interesting components we propose a multidimensional transformation of the model's results. From many adequate transformations with different properties and characteristics we concentrate on linear transformations due to its computational and conceptual simplicity that facilitates the interpretation of the results. We focus on prediction models but described analysis can be easy applied for other task.

L. Rutkowski et al. (Eds.): ICAISC 2004, LNAI 3070, pp. 1199–1204, 2004.
© Springer-Verlag Berlin Heidelberg 2004

2   Data Model

Let's assume we test m prediction systems. To analyze their results we need some model for the outcomes. If the predictive model is chosen and estimated properly then it is close to the target so we can expect its results involve elements of the trend variable. But next to the target component there are also residuals. They can be both stochastic and deterministic and their character can be individual or common to all the models. We express the results of each predictive system by the linear combination of the elements described above. Therefore the model of i-th system outcome can be formulated as:

$$x_i = \alpha_i t + \beta_i r + e_i ,$$ (1)

where x_i means i-th system result, t – trend value, r – residual common to all the systems, e_i – individual noise and α_i, β_i – scalling coefficients.

The deeper analysis can utilize the fact, that there exist some bases $\{s_1, \ldots, s_j\}$ for target t and $\{s_{j+1}, \ldots, s_n\}$ for common residuals r. Therefore the model of i-th system outcome can be written as:

$$x_i = \overbrace{\alpha_{i1}s_1 + \alpha_{i2}s_2 + \ldots + \alpha_{ij}s_j}^{TREND\ \alpha_i t} + \overbrace{\alpha_{ij+1}s_{j+1} + \ldots + \alpha_{in}s_n}^{RESIDUALS\ \beta_i r} + e_i .$$ (2)

The full model of m systems results with N observations can be written in a short form:

$$\mathbf{x}(k) = \mathbf{A}\mathbf{s}(k) + \mathbf{e}(k), k = 1, 2, \ldots, N ,$$ (3)

where $\mathbf{x}(k) = [x_1\ x_2 \ldots x_m]^T$ is a $m \times 1$ vector of models' results, $\mathbf{A} = [a_{ij}]_{m \times n}$ is a $m \times n$ matrix of mixing coefficients, $\mathbf{s} = [s_1\ s_2 \ldots s_n]^T$ is a $n \times 1$ vector of basis components and $\mathbf{e} = [e_1\ e_2 \ldots e_m]^T$ is a $m \times 1$ vector of individual models' residuals.

In such data relation $\mathbf{s}$ can be treated as a set of basis components that are related to wanted variables as well as unwanted residuals. If we obtain the knowledge about $\mathbf{s}$ and $\mathbf{A}$ we can utilize it to improve modeling results. Therefore our aim is to identify basis variables $\mathbf{s}$ from models' results $\mathbf{x}$. There are many different sets of $\mathbf{s}$ variables, which can be obtained by adequate transformations or decompositions. It is our decision which properties and characteristics are analyzed. In this paper we explore statistical structure of the observed variables $\mathbf{x}$ and dependencies between them, so ICA and PCA methods are used. In many situations it can be convenient to arrange set of observations' vectors into the matrix $\mathbf{X} = [\mathbf{x}(1), \mathbf{x}(2), \ldots, \mathbf{x}(N)]$, thus the vector form (3) can be aggregated to the compact matrix equation:

$$\mathbf{X} = \mathbf{A}\mathbf{S} + \mathbf{E} ,$$ (4)

where $\mathbf{S} \in R^{n \times N}$ contains all hidden components, $\mathbf{X} \in R^{m \times N}$ is a matrix of observation results, $\mathbf{E} \in R^{m \times N}$ is a matrix representing individual residuals and noises. From algebraic point of view our analysis can be considered as a pro-blem of $\mathbf{X}$ matrix factorization. Since we focus on $\mathbf{s}$ estimation one of the main problems is associated with the presence of an additive component $\mathbf{e}$ in (3). If $\mathbf{e}$ is not large and can be neglected then the data model is reduced to $\mathbf{x}=\mathbf{As}$, what makes estimation and interpretation of $\mathbf{s}$ much more simple. In opposite case when an additive component is essential some special transformations with robust to noise properties should be used [19],[20].

After $\mathbf{s}$ variable is estimated the next step is to check the influence of each basis component on the models' predictions and to eliminate the ones with the negative impact. If we assume that the components $s_1, \ldots, s_j$ have the positive and the components $s_{j+1}, \ldots, s_n$ the negative influence on the models' performance, we postulate the last ones should be eliminated (replaced with zeros) $\hat{\mathbf{s}} = [s_1, \ldots, s_j, 0, \ldots, 0]^T$. The last stage is to turn back from cleared signal $\hat{\mathbf{s}}$ to model results by the following transformation:

$$\hat{\mathbf{x}} = \mathbf{A}\hat{\mathbf{s}} . \tag{5}$$

We expect that $\hat{x}$ will be the improved version of models' results $\mathbf{x}$ due to elimination of the destructive components.

3   Data Transformation

There are many methods of linear data decomposition and representation. Principal Component Analysis (PCA) [17], Factor Analysis (FA) [18], Sparse Component Analysis (SCA) [16], Smooth Component Analysis (SmoCA) [5] or Independent Component Analysis (ICA) [4],[5],[10] utilize different features and properties of data, but most of those techniques can be described as looking for such matrix $\mathbf{W} \in R^{n \times m}$ that for observed data $\mathbf{x}$ we have:

$$\mathbf{y} = \mathbf{Wx} , \tag{6}$$

where $\mathbf{y}=[y_1, y_2, \ldots, y_n]^T$ satisfies specific criteria. In this work $\mathbf{y}$ is related to $\mathbf{s}$, and if $\mathbf{e}=\mathbf{0}$ we have $\mathbf{y}=\mathbf{s}$. For our purpose we explore statistical characteristics of data especially we inspect second or higher order statistical dependencies what can be performed by PCA and ICA methods.

Principal Component Analysis - is one of the most popular second order statistics based methods. For multidimensional variable $\mathbf{x} = [x_1, x_2, \ldots, x_m]^T$, with matrix correlation $\mathbf{R}_{xx}$, after PCA we have orthogonal variables ordered by decreasing variance. The transformation matrix can be obtained from EVD decomposition as

$$\mathbf{W} = \mathbf{U}^T , \tag{7}$$

where $\mathbf{U} = [\mathbf{u}_1, \mathbf{u}_2, \ldots, \mathbf{u}_m]$ - is orthogonal matrix of eigenvectors related to eigenvalues ordered by decreasing value.

Independent Component Analysis – it is a higher order statistics based method aiming at extracting independent components from observed data [7]. Variables after ICA should satisfy the following equation

$$p_1(y_1)p_2(y_2) \ldots p_n(y_n) = p_{1 \ldots n}(y_1, y_2, \ldots, y_n) . \tag{8}$$

Transformation matrix $\mathbf{W}$ can be estimated by adaptive rule of the form

$$\Delta \mathbf{W}(k) = \mu(k)[\mathbf{I} - \mathbf{f}(\mathbf{y}(k))\mathbf{y}^T(k)]\mathbf{W}(k) , \qquad (9)$$

where

$$\mathbf{f}(\mathbf{y}) = [f_1(y_1), \ldots, f_n(y_n)]^T, \qquad (10)$$

with

$$f_i(y_i) = \frac{\partial \log(p_i(y_i))}{\partial y_i} = \frac{1}{p_i(y_i)} \frac{\partial p_i(y_i)}{\partial y_i} . \qquad (11)$$

Theoretically only one result variable x_i can be Gaussian and the overall amount of the observed signals is at least equal to the number of sources $m \geq n$. In practice these limitations can be relaxed. Details about data preprocesing, assumptions and numerical aspects of the algorithm (9) are given in [5], [10].

4   Modeling Process and Multidimensional Filtration

The methodology described above with the multidimensional transformations can be treated as a special case of multidimensional filtration. The process involves identification and elimination of the negative components that were estimated from data. In contradistinction to classical filtration we use the information given simultaneously by many variables. One of the main questions is which transformation should be used to obtain optimal performance. The ones given by the authors are only the examples from the set of possibilities and it is up to the problem or resources what will be applied to solve the problem (Fig.1).

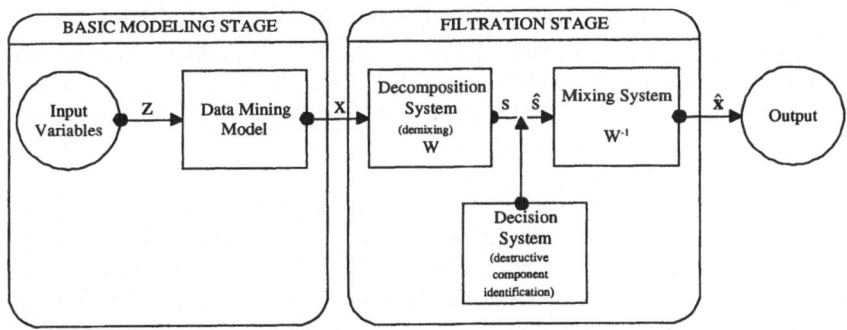

Fig. 1. Data Mining with multidimensional filtration

Methods from paragraph 3 can be sensitive to additive individual residuals e. To reduce their influence we can apply related robust techniques as noisy ICA algorithms or robust whitening [5], [20], [21]. But choice of the method should be preceded by analysis of the e residual nature. Presented in this paper ICA and PCA methods are based on spatial statistical characteristic of data [4]. Methods like robust whitening assume that additive variable is white noise and has spatio-temporal structure what can be inadequate for many tasks.

5   Practical Experiment

To check the capabilities of the presented approach we applied PCA and ICA in invoice amount prediction task. Eight different models of type MLP, RBF and Generalized Regression Neural Netwroks were estimated and their performance was measured by: $\text{MSE}=\frac{1}{N}\cdot\sum_{i=1}^{N}\epsilon_i^2$, $\text{MAD}=\frac{1}{N}\cdot\sum_{i=1}^{N}|\epsilon_i|$ and $\text{LAD}=\max_{i\in N}|\epsilon_i|$; where N means the number of instances and ϵ_i – the i-th instance residual [8].

Table 1. MSE of the basis models and their improved versions

MSE[×1000]	MLP-1	MLP-2	RBF-1	RBF-2	RBF-3	GRN-1	GRN-2	GRN-3
Basis models	3,069	5,843	5,799	6,307	6,009	5,129	3,015	3,069
PCA improved	2,735	4,258	4,294	4,613	4,382	3,581	3,011	2,735
ICA improved	3,250	5,568	5,533	6,203	5,743	5,136	3,006	3,250

Table 2. MAD of the basis models and their improved versions

MAD	MLP-1	MLP-2	RBF-1	RBF-2	RBF-3	GRN-1	GRN-2	GRN-3
Basis models	25,06	51,54	51,30	50,70	45,77	39,04	25,97	25,06
PCA improved	23,36	43,58	43,73	44,45	39,61	33,94	25,97	23,36
ICA improved	29,09	49,88	49,73	50,21	44,21	39,08	25,96	29,09

Table 3. LAD of the basis models and their improved versions

LAD[×1000]	MLP-1	MLP-2	RBF-1	RBF-2	RBF-3	GRN-1	GRN-2	GRN-3
Basis models	0,496	1,221	1,229	1,456	1,427	1,428	1,473	0,496
PCA improved	0,399	0,646	0,676	0,832	0,821	0,868	0,933	0,399
ICA improved	0,488	1,207	1,222	1,451	1,422	1,421	1,466	0,488

Next the outcomes of these models were decomposed and one of the components was rejected. The performances of the models shown in Tables 1-3 are received after rejection of the component optimal for each model. Almost in all cases using ICA or PCA transformation leads to improvement of the model quality. Nevertheless there is still open question of choosing the signal that should be rejected and deeper research is needed.

Conclusions. This paper presents the methods for model improvement based on the results from several models that were tested. In order to identify the negative components the multidimensional ICA and PCA transformations were proposed. The results reveal that in many cases the application of our approach can improve the quality of the models. There are many questions for further research like how to determine the role of every component. In this case a simple heuristic approach was used which was to check the influence of all decomposed signals. Another issue is to choose the transformation itself and the method for estimating the transformation parameters. As far as we use PCA transformation the deployment seems to be quite easy from the computational point of the view, but with ICA method the final result mainly depends on the algorithms for estimating the components. Despite these disadvantages the presented methodology seems to be effective and meets expectations for integrating the information from different models. Additionally the risk of choosing non-optimal solution is minimized due to the fact that we use the information about the target from a set of the models.

References

1. Akaike, H.: A new look at the statistical model identification. IEEE Transactions on Automatic Control 19(6), (1974) 716-723
2. Armstrong, J.S., Collopy, F.: Error Measures For Generalizing About Forecasting Methods: Empirical Comparisons. International Journal of Forecasting 8 (1992)
3. Breiman, L.: Bagging predictors. Machine Learning 24 (1996) 123-140.
4. Cardoso, J.F.: High-order contrasts for independent component analysis. Neural Computation 11 (1), (1999) 157-192
5. Cichocki, A., Amari, S.: Adaptive Blind Signal and Image Processing. John Wiley, Chichester (2002)
6. Cichocki, A., Sabala, I., Choi, S., Orsier, B., Szupiluk, R.: Self adaptive independent component analysis for sub-Gaussian and super-Gaussian mixtures with unknown number of sources and additive noise (NOLTA-97) 2 Hawaii USA (1997) 731-734
7. Comon P.: Independent component analysis, a new concept? Signal Processing, Elsevier 36(3), (1994) 287-314
8. Greene, W.H.: Econometric analysis. NJ Prentice Hall (2000)
9. Hoeting, J., Madigan, D., Raftery, A., Volinsky, C.: Bayesian model averaging: a tutorial. Statistical Science 14 (1999) 382-417
10. Hyvärinen, A., Karhunen, J., Oja, E.: Independent Component Analysis. John Wiley (2001)
11. Kennedy, R.L.(ed.), Lee, Y., Van Roy, B., Reed, C., Lippman, R.P.: Solving Data Mining Problems with Pattern Recognition, Prentice Hall (1997)
12. Mitchell, T.: Machine Learning. McGraw-Hill (1997) Boston
13. Mitra, S., Pal, S.K., Mitra, P.: Data Mining in Soft Computing Framework: A Survey. IEEE Transactions on Neural Networks 13(1) (2002)
14. Schwarz, G.: Estimating the dimension of a model. Ann. Statistics 6 (1978) 461-464
15. Yang, Y.: Adaptive regression by mixing. Journal of American Statistical Association 96 (2001) 574-588
16. Chen, S., Donoho, D., Saunders, M.A.: Atomic Decomposition by Basis Pursuit SIAM Journal on Scientific Computing (1996)
17. Jolliffe, I.T.: Principal Component Analysis, Springer-Verlag (1986)
18. Kendall, M.: Multivariate Analysis, Charles Griffin&Co (1975)
19. Cruces, S., Castedo, L., Cichocki, A.: Robust blind Source Separation Algorithms using Cumulants. Neurocomputing 49 (2002)
20. Choi, S., Cichocki, A.: A Robust Whitening Procedure In Blind Separation Context. Electronics Letters 36 (2002)

Author Index

Abonyi, Janos 1111
Ahn, Byung-Ha 480
Al-Agtash, Salem 1099
Alçı, Mustafa 670
Ali, Jafar M. 1002
Alp, Murat 166
Amarger, Veronique 1043
Araabi, B.N. 532
Arana-Daniel, Nancy 9
Ardagna, Danilo 1
Arinton, Eugen 145
Arva, Peter 1111
Augusiak, Andrzej 1105

Babczyński, Tomasz 810
Bałamut, Jerzy 823
Balicki, Jerzy 394
Ban, Sang-Woo 730
Bayro-Corrochano, Eduardo 9
Beşdok, Erkan 670
Bezerianos, A. 1062
Bhattacharyya, Sudeepa 486
Białko, Michał 468, 474
Bielecki, Andrzej 816
Bilski, Jarosław 151, 158
Bobrowski, Leon 544, 1008
Boguś, Piotr 550
Boratyn, Grzegorz M. 486
Borgosz, Jan 712
Bożejko, Wojciech 400, 853
Bubnicki, Zdzislaw 17
Burczyński, Tadeusz 1069
Butkiewicz, Bohdan 278
Byrski, Aleksander 823

Cader, Andrzej 942
Capizzi, Giacomo 676
Chebira, Abdennasser 1043
Chenoweth, Darrel L. 538
Cho, Young Im 829
Choi, Sang-Bok 730
Cholewa, Wojciech 948
Choraś, Michał 688
Choraś, Ryszard S. 682
Chua, Joselíto J. 694

Chung, Min Gyo 700
Cichocki, Andrzej 30
Cierniak, Robert 706
Cigizoglu, H. Kerem 166
Citko, Wieslaw 266
Çivicioğlu, Pınar 670
Coco, Salvatore 676
Cpalka, Krzysztof 284
Cruz-Chavez, Marco Antonio 860
Cyganek, Boguslaw 712, 718
Czarnowski, Ireneusz 172

Dereń, Alicja 1050
Diouf, Saliou 1043
Długosz, Adam 1069
Dong, Jiyoun 700
Drzymala, Pawel 942
Duch, Włodzisław 38, 44, 217
Dudek-Dyduch, Ewa 406
Duru, Nevcihan 290
Duru, Tarik 290
Dyduch, Tadeusz 414
Dzemyda, Gintautas 178
Dziedzicki, Krzysztof 1105

Falsafian, Kambiz 960
Fashandi, H. 724
Feil, Balazs 1111
Fernández-Redondo, Mercedes 184, 197
Francalanci, Chiara 1
Frank, Celia 1193
Frausto-Solis, Juan 860
Fujarewicz, Krzysztof 190

Gabryel, Marcin 1142
Gad, Stanisław 296
Galuszka, Adam 190, 768
Gaweda, Adam E. 302
Gorzałczany, Marian B. 556, 562
Grąbczewski, Krzysztof 574
Grabowski, Dariusz 1118
Grabowski, Szymon 568
Greco, Salvatore 118
Grochowski, Marek 580, 598
Groumpos, P.P. 344, 1031
Grudziński, Karol 586

Grzenda, Maciej   866
Grzymala-Busse, Jerzy W.   50, 996

Hajduk, Zbigniew   314
Hajto, Paweł   816
Hamilton, Jay   996
Hammer, Barbara   592
Hassanien, Aboul Ella   1002
Hendzel, Zenon   774
Hernández-Espinosa, Carlos   184, 197
Hippe, Zdzisław S.   996
Hirsbrunner, Béat   835
Homenda, Wladyslaw   872
Hong, J.H.   972
Hosseini, Farshid   1168

Jackowska-Strumiłło, Lidia   1124
Jakóbczak, Dariusz   266
Jakubek, Magdalena   1075
Jalili-Kharaajoo, Mahdi   308, 960
Jamroga, Wojciech   879
Jankowski, Norbert   580, 598
Jarczyk, Dominik   406
Jaruszewicz, Marcin   1130
Jędrzejowicz, Piotr   172
Jelonek, Jacek   492
Jelonkiewicz, Jerzy   966
Jia, Jiong   203
Juillerat, Nicolas   835
Jung, Bum-Soo   730
Jurek, Janusz   604

Kacalak, Wojciech   610
Kacprzyk, Janusz   388
Kaczorek, Tadeusz   56
Kaliszuk, Joanna   1081
Kaminski, K.   616
Kaminski, W.   616
Kannan, A.   847
Karcz-Dulęba, Iwona   420
Karras, D.A.   622, 628
Kazimierczak, Jan   780
Kerre, Etienne E.   526
Kiełtyka, Leszek   1136
Kisiel-Dorohinicki, Marek   841
Kléma, Jiří   897
Klimala, Jacek K.   1037
Kłopotek, Mieczysław Alojzy   885
Kluska, Jacek   314
Koleśnik, Roman   320

Komanski, Rafal   736
Kompanets, Leonid   742
Korbicz, Józef   145, 210
Kordos, Mirosław   217
Korytkowski, Marcin   1142
Korzeń, Marcin   426
Kosiński, Witold   320, 326
Koszlaga, Jan   223
Kratica, Jozef   462
Krętowska, Małgorzata   1008
Krętowski, Marek   432
Kruczkiewicz, Zofia   810
Kruś, Lech   891
Kryger, P.   504
Krzyżak, Adam   229
Kubalík, Jiří   897
Kubanek, Mariusz   742
Kubia, Aleksander   1148
Kucęba, Robert   1136
Kulich, Miroslav   897
Kulikowski, Roman   64
Kurasova, Olga   178
Kurek, J.E.   792
Kurzynski, Marek   1014
Kuś, Wacław   1069
Kusiak, Jan   1093
Kusy, Maciej   1020
Kusztelak, Grzegorz   438
Kwak, K.   972
Kwaśnicka, Halina   444
Kwolek, Bogdan   786

Łaskawski, Mariusz   296
Laudani, Antonio   676
Lee, Minho   730
Lee, Soo-Young   73
Leski, Jacek   640
Lewandowska, Katarzyna D.   550
Li, Xiao-Mei   928
Liang, Jiuzhen   203, 634
Ligęza, Antoni   903
Lis, B.   760
Litwiński, Sławomir   158
Lubczonek, Jacek   1154
Łukasik, Ewa   492
Lukaszuk, Tomasz   544

Macukow, Bohdan   736
Madani, Kurosh   79, 1043
Magott, Jan   810

Majewski, Maciej   610
Mańdziuk, Jacek   909, 915, 1130
Markowska-Kaczmar, Urszula   450
Matykiewicz, Paweł   235
Mazurkiewicz, Jacek   1161
Mehregan, Mohammad R.   1168
Melis, Erica   91
Metenidis, Mihai F.   210
Midić, Uroš   462
Mieszkowicz-Rolka, Alicja   498
Mikrut, Zbigniew   1148
Milanova, Mariofanna   486
Moin, M.S.   724
Montseny, Eduard   754
Morajda, Janusz   646
Moshiri, Behzad   984
Mossakowski, Krzysztof   915
Możaryn, J.   792
Mrugalski, Marcin   210

Na, Jae Hyung   748
Naganowski, Aleksander   492
Nagy, Gabor   1111
Naseri, Parviz   1168
Nemeth, Miklos   1111
Nemeth, Sandor   1111
Niemczak, Marcin   866
Niewiadomski, A.   504
Nikiforidis, G.C.   1031
Nikodem, Piotr   456
Nobuhara, Hajime   1002
Nowicki, Robert   332, 510, 518, 1142
Nunes da Silva, Ivan   954
Nunes de Souza, Andre   954

Obuchowicz, Andrzej   350
Özyılmaz, Lale   1026
Ogiela, Marek R.   133
Ognjanović, Zoran   462
Oh, Hae Seok   748
Ortega, Antonio Vanderlei   1175
Ortiz-Gómez, Mamen   184
Osman, Daniel   909
Owczarek, Aleksander   640

Pabarskaite, Zidrina   260
Pabisek, Ewa   1081
Pach, Peter   1111
Pacut, Andrzej   934
Pal, Asim K.   664

Pankowska, Anna   338
Papageorgiou, E.I.   344, 1031
Pappalardo, Giuseppe   676
Paradowski, Mariusz   444
Park, J.   972
Park, Jisook   700
Park, Y.   972
Parsopoulos, K.E.   344
Pawlak, M.   253
Pawlak, Zdzisław   102
Petalas, Y.G.   241
Piątkowski, Grzegorz   1087
Pieczyński, Andrzej   350, 370
Piegat, Andrzej   356
Piękniewski, Filip   247
Pietrzykowski, Zbigniew   364
Piuri, Vincenzo   1
Plagianakos, V.P.   1062
Pokropińska, Agata   332
Poteralski, Arkadiusz   1069
Prokopowicz, Piotr   320
Przybył, Andrzej   966

Radzikowska, Anna Maria   526
Rafajłowicz, E.   253
Rafimanzelat, M.R.   532
Ramasubramanian, P.   847
Rashidi, Farzan   978, 984
Rashidi, Mehran   978
Rauch, Łukasz   1093
Raudys, Sarunas   260
Raudys, Šarūnas   109
Ravazoula, P.   1031
Rejer, Izabela   652
Robak, Silva   370
Rój, Edward   1181
Rolka, Leszek   498
Rudnicki, Marek   438
Rudziński, Filip   556, 562
Rutkowska, Danuta   1037
Rutkowski, Leszek   284, 376
Rybicki, Leszek   247
Rybnik, Mariusz   1043
Rydzek, Szymon   742

Saeed, Khalid   658
Safari, Hossein   1168
Scherer, Rafał   302, 376, 1142
Scotti, Fabio   1
Sharifi, Kumars   1168

Siekmann, Jörg   91
Sienko, Wieslaw   266
Silva, Ivan Nunes da   1175
Skrzypczyk, Krzysztof   798
Skubalska-Rafajłowicz, Ewa   229, 272
Słoń, Grzegorz   296
Słowik, Adam   468, 474
Slowinski, Roman   118, 492
Śmierzchalski, Roman   1105
Smoląg, Jacek   158
Smolinski, Tomasz G.   486, 538
Soak, Sang-Moon   480
Sobrevilla, Pilar   754
Sokolowski, Adam   1136
Sokolowski, Aleksander   1050
Spyridonos, P.P.   1031
Starczewski, Janusz T.   381
Stateczny, Andrzej   1187
Straszecka, Ewa   1056
Strickert, Marc   592
Strug, Barbara   456
Strumillo, Pawel   223, 616
Stylios, C.D.   1031
Sundararajan, Ramasubramanian   664
Suva, Larry J.   486
Swiatek, Jerzy   990
Swierniak, Andrzej   768
Szczepaniak, P.S.   504, 760
Szczepanik, Mirosław   1069
Szmidt, Eulalia   388
Szpyrka, Marcin   903
Sztandera, Les M.   1193
Szupiluk, Ryszard   1199

Tabedzki, Marek   658
Tadeusiewicz, Ryszard   133
Talar, Jolanta   1093
Tasoulis, D.K.   241, 1062

Temurtas, Fevzullah   804
Temurtas, Hasan   804
Tischer, Peter E.   694
Tomczyk, A.   760
Torres-Sospedra, Joaquín   184, 197

Ulson, Jose Alfredo C.   954

Vallejo-Gutiérres, J. Refugio   9
Vemulapali, Balaji   1193
Villmann, Thomas   592
Vladutu, L.   1062
Vrahatis, M.N.   241, 344, 1062

Walczak, Janusz   1118
Walkowiak, Krzysztof   922
Walkowiak, Tomasz   1161
Wang, Yong-Xian   928
Wang, Zheng-Hua   928
Waszczyszyn, Zenon   1075, 1081
Wawrzynski, Pawel   934
Welfle, Henryk   942
Wiak, Slawomir   438, 942
Wilk, Marcin   1181
Witczak, Marcin   210
Wnuk-Lipiński, Paweł   450
Wodecki, Mieczysław   400, 853
Wojewnik, Piotr   1199
Wygralak, Maciej   338

Yastrebov, Alexander   296
Yıldırım, Tülay   1026
Yumusak, Nejat   804

Zabkowski, Tomasz   1199
Žák, Tomáš   1093
Zawadzki, Andrzej   296
Ziemiański, Leonard   1087
Zurada, Jacek M.   30, 486, 538

Lecture Notes in Artificial Intelligence (LNAI)

Vol. 3070: L. Rutkowski, J. Siekmann, R. Tadeusiewicz, L.A. Zadeh (Eds.), Artificial Intelligence and Soft Computing - ICAISC 2004. XXV, 1208 pages. 2004.

Vol. 3066: S. Tsumoto, R. Słowiński, J. Komorowski, J.W. Grzymala-Busse (Eds.), Rough Sets and Current Trends in Computing. XX, 853 pages. 2004.

Vol. 3065: A. Lomuscio, D. Nute (Eds.), Deontic Logic. X, 275 pages. 2004.

Vol. 3060: A.Y. Tawfik, S.D. Goodwin (Eds.), Advances in Artificial Intelligence. XIII, 582 pages. 2004.

Vol. 3056: H. Dai, R. Srikant, C. Zhang (Eds.), Advances in Knowledge Discovery and Data Mining. XIX, 713 pages. 2004.

Vol. 3035: M.A. Wimmer (Ed.), Knowledge Management in Electronic Government. XII, 326 pages. 2004.

Vol. 3034: J. Favela, E. Menasalvas, E. Chávez (Eds.), Advances in Web Intelligence. XIII, 227 pages. 2004.

Vol. 3030: P. Giorgini, B. Henderson-Sellers, M. Winikoff (Eds.), Agent-Oriented Information Systems. XIV, 207 pages. 2004.

Vol. 3029: B. Orchard, C. Yang, M. Ali (Eds.), Innovations in Applied Artificial Intelligence. XXI, 1272 pages. 2004.

Vol. 3025: G.A. Vouros, T. Panayiotopoulos (Eds.), Methods and Applications of Artificial Intelligence. XV, 546 pages. 2004.

Vol. 3012: K. Kurumatani, S.-H. Chen, A. Ohuchi (Eds.), Multi-Agnets for Mass User Support. X, 217 pages. 2004.

Vol. 3010: K.R. Apt, F. Fages, F. Rossi, P. Szeredi, J. Váncza (Eds.), Recent Advances in Constraints. VIII, 285 pages. 2004.

Vol. 2990: J. Leite, A. Omicini, L. Sterling, P. Torroni (Eds.), Declarative Agent Languages and Techniques. XII, 281 pages. 2004.

Vol. 2980: A. Blackwell, K. Marriott, A. Shimojima (Eds.), Diagrammatic Representation and Inference. XV, 448 pages. 2004.

Vol. 2977: G. Di Marzo Serugendo, A. Karageorgos, O.F. Rana, F. Zambonelli (Eds.), Engineering Self-Organising Systems. X, 299 pages. 2004.

Vol. 2972: R. Monroy, G. Arroyo-Figueroa, L.E. Sucar, H. Sossa (Eds.), MICAI 2004: Advances in Artificial Intelligence. XVII, 923 pages. 2004.

Vol. 2961: P. Eklund (Ed.), Concept Lattices. IX, 411 pages. 2004.

Vol. 2953: K. Konrad, Model Generation for Natural Language Interpretation and Analysis. XIII, 166 pages. 2004.

Vol. 2934: G. Lindemann, D. Moldt, M. Paolucci (Eds.), Regulated Agent-Based Social Systems. X, 301 pages. 2004.

Vol. 2930: F. Winkler (Ed.), Automated Deduction in Geometry. VII, 231 pages. 2004.

Vol. 2926: L. van Elst, V. Dignum, A. Abecker (Eds.), Agent-Mediated Knowledge Management. XI, 428 pages. 2004.

Vol. 2923: V. Lifschitz, I. Niemelä (Eds.), Logic Programming and Nonmonotonic Reasoning. IX, 365 pages. 2004.

Vol. 2915: A. Camurri, G. Volpe (Eds.), Gesture-Based Communication in Human-Computer Interaction. XIII, 558 pages. 2004.

Vol. 2913: T.M. Pinkston, V.K. Prasanna (Eds.), High Performance Computing - HiPC 2003. XX, 512 pages. 2003.

Vol. 2903: T.D. Gedeon, L.C.C. Fung (Eds.), AI 2003: Advances in Artificial Intelligence. XVI, 1075 pages. 2003.

Vol. 2902: F.M. Pires, S.P. Abreu (Eds.), Progress in Artificial Intelligence. XV, 504 pages. 2003.

Vol. 2892: F. Dau, The Logic System of Concept Graphs with Negation. XI, 213 pages. 2003.

Vol. 2891: J. Lee, M. Barley (Eds.), Intelligent Agents and Multi-Agent Systems. X, 215 pages. 2003.

Vol. 2882: D. Veit, Matchmaking in Electronic Markets. XV, 180 pages. 2003.

Vol. 2871: N. Zhong, Z.W. Raś, S. Tsumoto, E. Suzuki (Eds.), Foundations of Intelligent Systems. XV, 697 pages. 2003.

Vol. 2854: J. Hoffmann, Utilizing Problem Structure in Planing. XIII, 251 pages. 2003.

Vol. 2843: G. Grieser, Y. Tanaka, A. Yamamoto (Eds.), Discovery Science. XII, 504 pages. 2003.

Vol. 2842: R. Gavaldá, K.P. Jantke, E. Takimoto (Eds.), Algorithmic Learning Theory. XI, 313 pages. 2003.

Vol. 2838: N. Lavrač, D. Gamberger, L. Todorovski, H. Blockeel (Eds.), Knowledge Discovery in Databases: PKDD 2003. XVI, 508 pages. 2003.

Vol. 2837: N. Lavrač, D. Gamberger, L. Todorovski, H. Blockeel (Eds.), Machine Learning: ECML 2003. XVI, 504 pages. 2003.

Vol. 2835: T. Horváth, A. Yamamoto (Eds.), Inductive Logic Programming. X, 401 pages. 2003.

Vol. 2821: A. Günter, R. Kruse, B. Neumann (Eds.), KI 2003: Advances in Artificial Intelligence. XII, 662 pages. 2003.

Vol. 2807: V. Matoušek, P. Mautner (Eds.), Text, Speech and Dialogue. XIII, 426 pages. 2003.

Vol. 2801: W. Banzhaf, J. Ziegler, T. Christaller, P. Dittrich, J.T. Kim (Eds.), Advances in Artificial Life. XVI, 905 pages. 2003.

Vol. 2797: O.R. Zaïane, S.J. Simoff, C. Djeraba (Eds.), Mining Multimedia and Complex Data. XII, 281 pages. 2003.

Vol. 2792: T. Rist, R.S. Aylett, D. Ballin, J. Rickel (Eds.), Intelligent Virtual Agents. XV, 364 pages. 2003.

Vol. 2782: M. Klusch, A. Omicini, S. Ossowski, H. Laamanen (Eds.), Cooperative Information Agents VII. XI, 345 pages. 2003.

Vol. 2780: M. Dojat, E. Keravnou, P. Barahona (Eds.), Artificial Intelligence in Medicine. XIII, 388 pages. 2003.

Vol. 2777: B. Schölkopf, M.K. Warmuth (Eds.), Learning Theory and Kernel Machines. XIV, 746 pages. 2003.

Vol. 2752: G.A. Kaminka, P.U. Lima, R. Rojas (Eds.), RoboCup 2002: Robot Soccer World Cup VI. XVI, 498 pages. 2003.

Vol. 2741: F. Baader (Ed.), Automated Deduction – CADE-19. XII, 503 pages. 2003.

Vol. 2705: S. Renals, G. Grefenstette (Eds.), Text- and Speech-Triggered Information Access. VII, 197 pages. 2003.

Vol. 2703: O.R. Zaïane, J. Srivastava, M. Spiliopoulou, B. Masand (Eds.), WEBKDD 2002 - MiningWeb Data for Discovering Usage Patterns and Profiles. IX, 181 pages. 2003.

Vol. 2700: M.T. Pazienza (Ed.), Extraction in the Web Era. XIII, 163 pages. 2003.

Vol. 2699: M.G. Hinchey, J.L. Rash, W.F. Truszkowski, C.A. Rouff, D.F. Gordon-Spears (Eds.), Formal Approaches to Agent-Based Systems. IX, 297 pages. 2002.

Vol. 2691: V. Mařík, J.P. Müller, M. Pechoucek (Eds.), Multi-Agent Systems and Applications III. XIV, 660 pages. 2003.

Vol. 2684: M.V. Butz, O. Sigaud, P. Gérard (Eds.), Anticipatory Behavior in Adaptive Learning Systems. X, 303 pages. 2003.

Vol. 2671: Y. Xiang, B. Chaib-draa (Eds.), Advances in Artificial Intelligence. XIV, 642 pages. 2003.

Vol. 2663: E. Menasalvas, J. Segovia, P.S. Szczepaniak (Eds.), Advances in Web Intelligence. XII, 350 pages. 2003.

Vol. 2661: P.L. Lanzi, W. Stolzmann, S.W. Wilson (Eds.), Learning Classifier Systems. VII, 231 pages. 2003.

Vol. 2654: U. Schmid, Inductive Synthesis of Functional Programs. XXII, 398 pages. 2003.

Vol. 2650: M.-P. Huget (Ed.), Communications in Multiagent Systems. VIII, 323 pages. 2003.

Vol. 2645: M.A. Wimmer (Ed.), Knowledge Management in Electronic Government. XI, 320 pages. 2003.

Vol. 2639: G. Wang, Q. Liu, Y. Yao, A. Skowron (Eds.), Rough Sets, Fuzzy Sets, Data Mining, and Granular Computing. XVII, 741 pages. 2003.

Vol. 2637: K.-Y. Whang, J. Jeon, K. Shim, J. Srivastava, Advances in Knowledge Discovery and Data Mining. XVIII, 610 pages. 2003.

Vol. 2636: E. Alonso, D. Kudenko, D. Kazakov (Eds.), Adaptive Agents and Multi-Agent Systems. XIV, 323 pages. 2003.

Vol. 2627: B. O'Sullivan (Ed.), Recent Advances in Constraints. X, 201 pages. 2003.

Vol. 2600: S. Mendelson, A.J. Smola (Eds.), Advanced Lectures on Machine Learning. IX, 259 pages. 2003.

Vol. 2592: R. Kowalczyk, J.P. Müller, H. Tianfield, R. Unland (Eds.), Agent Technologies, Infrastructures, Tools, and Applications for E-Services. XVII, 371 pages. 2003.

Vol. 2586: M. Klusch, S. Bergamaschi, P. Edwards, P. Petta (Eds.), Intelligent Information Agents. VI, 275 pages. 2003.

Vol. 2583: S. Matwin, C. Sammut (Eds.), Inductive Logic Programming. X, 351 pages. 2003.

Vol. 2581: J.S. Sichman, F. Bousquet, P. Davidsson (Eds.), Multi-Agent-Based Simulation. X, 195 pages. 2003.

Vol. 2577: P. Petta, R. Tolksdorf, F. Zambonelli (Eds.), Engineering Societies in the Agents World III. X, 285 pages. 2003.

Vol. 2569: D. Karagiannis, U. Reimer (Eds.), Practical Aspects of Knowledge Management. XIII, 648 pages. 2002.

Vol. 2560: S. Goronzy, Robust Adaptation to Non-Native Accents in Automatic Speech Recognition. XI, 144 pages. 2002.

Vol. 2557: B. McKay, J. Slaney (Eds.), AI 2002: Advances in Artificial Intelligence. XV, 730 pages. 2002.

Vol. 2554: M. Beetz, Plan-Based Control of Robotic Agents. XI, 191 pages. 2002.

Vol. 2543: O. Bartenstein, U. Geske, M. Hannebauer, O. Yoshie (Eds.), Web Knowledge Management and Decision Support. X, 307 pages. 2003.

Vol. 2541: T. Barkowsky, Mental Representation and Processing of Geographic Knowledge. X, 174 pages. 2002.

Vol. 2533: N. Cesa-Bianchi, M. Numao, R. Reischuk (Eds.), Algorithmic Learning Theory. XI, 415 pages. 2002.

Vol. 2531: J. Padget, O. Shehory, D. Parkes, N.M. Sadeh, W.E. Walsh (Eds.), Agent-Mediated Electronic Commerce IV. Designing Mechanisms and Systems. XVII, 341 pages. 2002.

Vol. 2527: F.J. Garijo, J.-C. Riquelme, M. Toro (Eds.), Advances in Artificial Intelligence - IBERAMIA 2002. XVIII, 955 pages. 2002.

Vol. 2522: T. Andreasen, A. Motro, H. Christiansen, H.L. Larsen (Eds.), Flexible Query Answering Systems. X, 383 pages. 2002.

Vol. 2514: M. Baaz, A. Voronkov (Eds.), Logic for Programming, Artificial Intelligence, and Reasoning. XIII, 465 pages. 2002.

Vol. 2507: G. Bittencourt, G.L. Ramalho (Eds.), Advances in Artificial Intelligence. XIII, 417 pages. 2002.

Vol. 2504: M.T. Escrig, F. Toledo, E. Golobardes (Eds.), Topics in Artificial Intelligence. XI, 427 pages. 2002.

Vol. 2499: S.D. Richardson (Ed.), Machine Translation: From Research to Real Users. XXI, 254 pages. 2002.

Vol. 2484: P. Adriaans, H. Fernau, M. van Zaanen (Eds.), Grammatical Inference: Algorithms and Applications. IX, 315 pages. 2002.

Vol. 2479: M. Jarke, J. Koehler, G. Lakemeyer (Eds.), KI 2002: Advances in Artificial Intelligence. XIII, 327 pages. 2002.

Vol. 2475: J.J. Alpigini, J.F. Peters, A. Skowron, N. Zhong (Eds.), Rough Sets and Current Trends in Computing. XV, 640 pages. 2002.